Core Reference

Microsoft®

XML PROGRAMMING

R. Allen Wyke
Sultan Rehman
Brad Leupen

PUBLISHED BY
Microsoft Press
A Division of Microsoft Corporation
One Microsoft Way
Redmond, Washington 98052-6399

Library of Congress Cataloging-in-Publication Data
Wyke, R. Allen.
XML Programming (Core Reference) / R. Allen Wyke, Sultan Rehman, Brad Leupen.
p. cm.
Includes index.
ISBN 0-7356-1185-8
1. XML (Document markup language) 2. Computer programming. I. Rehman, Sultan. II. Leupen, Bradley. III. Title.

QA76.76.H94 W78 2001
005.7'2--dc21 2001135476

Printed and bound in the United States of America.

1 2 3 4 5 6 7 8 9 QWT 7 6 5 4 3 2

Distributed in Canada by Penguin Books Canada Limited.

A CIP catalogue record for this book is available from the British Library.

Microsoft Press books are available through booksellers and distributors worldwide. For further information about international editions, contact your local Microsoft Corporation office or contact Microsoft Press International directly at fax (425) 936-7329. Visit our Web site at www.microsoft.com/mspress. Send comments to *mspinput@microsoft.com.*

Acquisitions Editor: David Clark
Project Editor: Barbara Moreland

Body Part No. X08-05017

This book is definitely for my girl—J. She has helped me through some very tough times and situations, and through it all maintained the love and wonderful smile that makes every day worth living.

—R. Allen Wyke

This book is dedicated to my friends, family, and loved ones. C., I could not have done it without your support and encouragement.

—Brad Leupen

To Meeasap—I wish you could have seen this.

—Sultan Rehman

Contents at a Glance

Table of Contents

Part V Appendices

Acknowledgements

R. Allen Wyke

On the publishing side I would like to thank Bob Kern of TIPS Publishing and my coauthors, Sultan and Brad, for their professionalism, hard work, and overall support in proposing and the writing of this book. I would also like to thank all the people at Microsoft Press who worked on the book and helped make sure it was the best it could be.

Finally I would like to thank Phil and Donald for our weekly ATV trips. Often battered and bruised, these rides reduced more stress than a person could imagine.

Brad Leupen

I would also like to thank Bob Kern of TIPS Publishing and my coauthors for their hard work and dedication, including Alan Houser for his excellent work. Writing a book of this scope is a team effort. Their help has been invaluable. I would also like to thank the folks at Microsoft Press for making this project a reality.

Last, but not least, I would like to thank Chris Reeves for his help in building the example application. His hard work and perseverance are much appreciated.

Sultan Rehman

I would like to thank the many people who have helped to bring this book to fruition. I especially owe a great debt of gratitude to my coauthor, colleague and friend, Allen Wyke. Without your support and comments my chapters would have needed a considerable amount of editing.

Thanks to my wife, Candy, for your unending love and for streamlining my life so that I could concentrate on my work.

Last, but definitely not least, I would like to thank my brother, Sam, for your companionship and for showing me that struggling is a gift in life.

Introduction

Forty-five years. That's about how long computers, as we know them, have been around. When you consider that the Great Pyramids of Egypt have been around for over 3000 years, 45 years seems insignificant. Yet no other technology has so profoundly changed the lives of so many in such a short time. When you add the explosion of information available through the Internet, computers have irrevocably changed what the future will be like.

You can't move around today without running into a computer in some form or another—in grocery stores, department stores, gas stations, and coffee shops. How did we get to this point? What has happened in the world of computers that has caused them to be so widely implemented? How is it that computers have been so quickly deployed?

Computing Advances and Networking

Computing advances are the result of two major factors: the drive to make computers smaller, faster, and less expensive, and more recently, the explosion of the Internet. These two items alone have

- provided a means to capture the entire abilities of a computer within a very small device.
- allowed us to network these computers and devices together, not only within a given wired network, but also wirelessly and across the world.

There appear to be no boundaries to the possibilities computing offers, but the hardware and network only represent part of the equation. The other part is the content, the data itself, that is transmitted, exchanged, and passed between machines. Enter XML!

XML for Data Description

Extensible Markup Language (XML) has taken off over the last few years. The ability to use and leverage XML to its fullest potential is no longer a dream—it is becoming a reality. With the most recent releases of server and client software products from popular suppliers, using XML in the real world is not only possible, but is often the preferred method for exchanging data and interconnecting applications.

While XML does present challenges of its own, the ease of integration and the flexibility present within a good XML architecture is hard to ignore when creating innovative solutions. XML provides an inexpensive means to markup and describe your data, and with the wealth of tools and applications which support it today, you can bet on easy integration.

While we could ramble on about how great XML is, we are well aware that developers want to skip the fluff and get right into the details. For that reason, we're going to quickly roadmap where you can expect to go within the pages of this book, and then turn you loose.

About the Book

This book is divided into five parts. Part I, "Getting Started", accomplishes a few educational and informational tasks. Chapter 1 provides information about the challenges historically associated with building client/server applications and solutions. It then introduces you to XML and describes it's possibilities—all before touching on how Microsoft, with its .NET initiative, has created tools and servers to support the next generation of server-to-server communications and collaborations.

Chapters 2 and 3 take you through XML basics and the details of XML parsers. You can expect to cover briefly everything from language semantics and syntax to the differences between DOM (Document Object Model) and SAX (Simple API for XML) parsing of XML documents.

In Part II, "Application Development", you dive deeper by creating real-world XML solutions and .NET applications. Chapters 4 through 7 will maneuver you through creating database, Web, user-interface, and messaging applications while exposing you to standards like SOAP (Simple Object Access Protocol) and XSLT (Extensible Stylesheet Language Transformations). You will then dive into the world of metadata in Chapter 8. Chapters 9 and 10 will walk you through building both a server and client application based on .NET and its supporting technologies. XML, of course is at the heart of these chapters.

Part III, "Interoperability", gives you a slight break from coding. Chapters 11 through 13 will discuss and cover topics on creating multiplatform solutions, integrating with legacy systems, and building solutions that can be accessed, and therefore easily deployed, on devices like handhelds and cell phones.

We will focus on XML and Microsoft .NET in Part IV. While we will have touched on items like SOAP and BizTalk in previous chapters, Chapters 14 and 15 will cover them in detail. Chapter 16 will pull together all the information you have learned about XML and .NET to discuss how .NET works and what can be achieved with it (beyond what our examples have demonstrated).

Finally we have Part V, the appendices. While most appendices in books offer rather useless resource information, Appendix A and Appendix B are full chapters. In designing the structure of the book we felt it was important not only to discuss some of the related standards, like XSD (XML) Schema, but also the tools that are available to work with these XML-based efforts. Don't pass these up; you will find some useful information and examples there.

About the CD

The source code for the programs discussed in this book is included on the companion CD and is arranged by chapter. Use the Setup porgram included on the CD to copy the samples to your hard disk. They require about 3 MB of hard disk space. If your computer's operating system is Microsoft Windows NT 4.0, Microsoft Windows 2000, or Microsoft Windows XP, you will need administrative privileges to install the sample files. To uninstall the sample files, make the appropriate selection from Add/Remove Programs in the Control Panel. Many examples require the Microsoft XML Core Services 4.0 Parser (also included on the CD) to be installed on your computer. For more information, refer to the Readme.txt file in the root folder of the companion CD.

The examples in Chapters 5, 6, and 10 require Internet Information Server (IIS) or Microsoft Personal Web Server to be running on your computer. The folders containing these examples (ch05 code, ch06 code, and ch10 code) should be shared on your Web server. To do so, right-click the folder in Windows Explorer and click Sharing in the Context menu. Click the Web Sharing tab and specify the share name.

In order to run the examples in Chapters 8, 9, 10, 13, 14, and 16 you will need the .NET Framework. These examples can also be run under Visual Studio .NET, although this software is NOT required to run the examples.

Conventions

Once you dive into the book and code examples, you will come across instances where lines of code are longer than the width of a single line on the page. In these instances we've wrapped the code back to the first position on the page, which indicates that this code is from the previous line. As there are no end-of-line markers in XML, we've tried to break long lines of code in such a way that you can easily see what's going on. Hyphens at the end of lines of code that wrap are part of the actual code. If you are ever in doubt about code structure, refer to the source code on the CD that contains the proper structure.

Diving In

We have included some interesting and detailed examples within the book, and we have covered a lot of topics, standards, and theories about the deployment of XML-based solutions. We hope you enjoy the book!

R. Allen Wyke
Brad Leupen
Sultan Rehman

Part I

Getting Started

1

An Architectural Overview of XML

When first exposed to the Extensible Markup Language (XML), you might ask yourself how it fits in the overall picture of Web-related items. This is the same question developers, managers, and presidents ask, not only of their peers, but of themselves as well. Ironically, this is the same question people in those roles asked themselves years ago with other computer-based equipment such as personal computers, databases, and even Microsoft Windows.

In determining how a particular technology fills a void and solves a problem, one must first know what the problem is and why it is present. Without this basic information, trying to create the right solution is a gamble. We've all seen, and most likely worked for, companies that build a product and service just because "it's cool" or "great" without knowing and understanding the problem it was supposed to solve.

In this chapter, we will go over how XML fits into the big picture and how it can help solve problems you might be facing. We touch on how XML is able to accomplish these tasks and point you in the right direction for the next steps. This chapter will also describe the landscape for the rest of the book so that the information and examples that follow are understandable, not only from a technical perspective, but from a problem-solving one as well. Exactly how these developments affect software development will be examined. We'll also discuss how a new programming model is required to address the needs of today's computer users and how Microsoft answers those needs with the Microsoft .NET Framework.

How Computing Started and Has Evolved

The world of computing was dominated by the mainframe just over 20 years ago. Few people had access to computers, and then only via the nearest IT department. The Personal Computer (PC) and the Graphical User Interface (GUI) changed that, opening the doors to computing for tens of millions of people and transforming the computer into a mass-market product. Corporations realized that networks of PCs and PC-based servers could change the way they did business.

When the Internet arrived, it revolutionized communications, created a rich source of information and entertainment, and added an "e" to business. Now close to 300 million people use the World Wide Web. According to International Data Corporation, more than a quarter of a trillion dollars in business will be transacted over the Internet this year alone.

System Design Issues

Computers and the Internet developed in parallel for some time and in some sense drive each other. However, they did not previously support each other as much as they could have. For example, some Internet and Web technologies—initially developed in the late 1960s and early 1970s and enhanced and refined in the early 1990s—are constrained by design to the least common denominator of computing devices connected to the Internet. They do not even take advantage of the enormous capabilities of today's least expensive PCs.

At the same time, most application software designed for PCs does not yet fully exploit the capabilities of internal corporate networks, let alone the power of a global network capable of supplying electronic applications on demand. The client/server development model that dominated the past decade tried to harness some of this power.

Client/Server Development

Client/server development breaks an application down into two or more layers, usually these three: the presentation layer, which encapsulates interacting with the user; the application layer, which encapsulates business rules and object persistence; and the data layer, which encapsulates access to database management systems. Objects in each of these layers perform small, discreet functions.

Because an application could be broken into multiple components, developers gained the ability to distribute components between multiple PCs within a corporate network, thereby harnessing some of the lost processing power by using a single machine for each component. To distribute these objects, however, they had to contain information on how and where another object could be found. The objects, therefore, became tightly coupled.

This coupling required a homogeneous computing environment so the system could run at peak efficiency. While corporations were able to control their own computing environment (at least to some extent), as soon as these applications crossed a firewall to the Internet, the computing environment changed drastically from one Web site to the next.

Needs of These Systems

Today's Internet combines the old mainframe model and the current client/server model. Despite the availability of bandwidth, information is still locked up in centralized databases, with gatekeepers (Web servers) controlling access. Users rely on these servers to perform most operations, just like the mainframe timesharing model. The Web server, in turn, invokes objects on other servers to perform several tasks simultaneously. Still, even with this interaction between Web servers, application servers, and database servers, Web sites are isolated islands of information and functionality.

In this environment the user must adapt to the technology instead of vice versa. Corporate administrators and planners face additional challenges. While the introduction of server farms has made the overall computing experience more reliable, it has also made system management more complex. Performance measurement, capacity planning, and operations management are more challenging in today's multitier, multifunction Web sites.

What we need is a model for developing software that will allow developers to exploit both the power of the PC and the global network, which will make truly distributed computing possible. Furthermore, this framework must facilitate the separation of data from the way in which the data is presented—it must be a true peer-to-peer network that will allow information to flow freely between devices.

Introducing XML

The Web gives you unlimited amounts of information—or does it? You can buy a ticket for a flight from New York to Miami over the Internet, but can you search for the cheapest fare? Can you price a different route when disconnected from the Web? Can you load the fare into your expense report? The answers is always no. The Web and the Hypertext Markup Language (HTML) give you access to information, but they do not enable you to leverage it.

For example, say you want to purchase a ticket. You go to *http://www.myfavoriteairlines.com* and download the Extensible Hypertext Markup Language (XHTML) page, mfa-index.html, shown in Listing 1-1.

Listing 1-1 mfa-index.html: An airline ticket purchase page.

```
<!DOCTYPE html PUBLIC "-//W3C//DTD XHTML 1.0 Transitional//EN"
          "http://www.w3.org/TR/xhtml1/DTD/xhtml1-transitional.dtd">
<html xmlns="http://www.w3.org/1999/xhtml" lang="en" xml:lang="en">
  <head>
    <title>Welcome to My Favorite Airlines</title>
  </head>
  <body>
    <h1>Connecting flights to Miami</h1>
    <p>
     Buy Direct from us and Save $$$! New York - Orlando - Miami..$95
    </p>
    <h1> Direct flights to Miami</h1>
    <p>
     Buy Direct from us and Save $$$!  New York - Miami..$195
    </p>
    <h1> Your Selection</h1>
    <p>
     Your flight with tax and headphones: $210
    </p>
 </body>
</html>
```

This page, shown in Figure 1-1, displays information about flights to Miami, but you can't use it for much more. If you wanted to search for the fare itself, a simple search engine might look for a dollar sign, but in this example you would erroneously get a hit on "Save $$$." If you wanted to list only direct flights, a filter could try to interpret the text by looking for the word "Direct." Screen-scraping algorithms, however, are limited by how cleverly they can interpret the author's use of language. So, XML to the rescue!

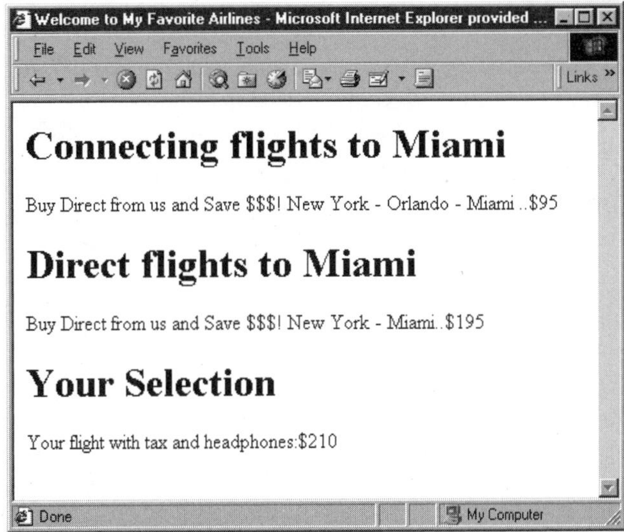

Figure 1-1 Viewing our simple XHTML document in a browser.

XML Compared to XTML

XML is a Recommendation from the World Wide Web Consortium, commonly referred to as the W3C *(http://www.w3.org)*, the multicompany group that defined XHTML and its predecessor, HTML. XML is a vehicle for information that brings usable data to the desktop and is a universal data format that does for data what HTML does for Web content—it provides the necessary markup. Because the source code of languages defined in XML looks like HTML, it's useful to compare the two.

XML consists of hierarchically nested fields like HTML, it is just as easy to read, and it is portable. However, where HTML contains titles, headings, and italics, XML can contain customers, order numbers, prices, or any data element you need. XML is fully extensible so you can add new tags and new elements to support your application.

The Core of XML

Structured information contains both content (words, pictures, and so forth) and a suggestion of what function that content plays. For example, content in a section heading has a different meaning from content in a footnote, which is different from content in a figure caption or a database table. The XML specification defines a standard way to structure the markup of documents.

Why XML?

Programmers created XML so that richly structured documents could be used over the Web. The only viable alternatives, HTML and the Standard Generalized Markup Language (SGML), are not practical for this purpose. HTML comes bound with a set of semantics and does not provide arbitrary structure. SGML provides arbitrary structure, but implementing SGML is too difficult for a Web browser to do on its own. XML specifies neither semantics nor a tag set. It is a metalanguage for describing markup languages and provides a facility for defining tags and the structural relationships between them. Because there's no predefined tag set, there aren't any preconceived semantics. The semantics of an XML document will either be defined by the applications that process them or by style sheets.

XML Documents

If you use HTML or SGML, XML documents will look familiar. Let's revisit the airline example. If the Web page included XML data as in Listing 1-2, the information in mfa-sample.xml could be sent with the page.

Listing 1-2 mfa-sample.xml: An XML version of our airline ticket information.

```
<?xml version="1.0"?>
<flightdata>
    <ny_mia_flights>
      <direct>
        <cost>195</cost>
      </direct>
      <connecting>
        <layover duration="90" durationtype="minutes">Orlando</layover>
        <cost>95</cost>
      </connecting>
    </ny_mia_flights>
</flightdata>
```

The document, which is displayed in Figure 1-2, begins with an XML declaration: *<?xml ...?>*. While not required, its presence unequivocally identifies the document as an XML document and indicates the version of XML to which it was authored.

Elements are the most common form of markup. Delimited by angle brackets, most elements identify the nature of the content they surround. Some elements might be empty, in which case they have no content. If an element is not empty it begins with a start-tag, *<element>* and ends with an end-tag, *</element>*.

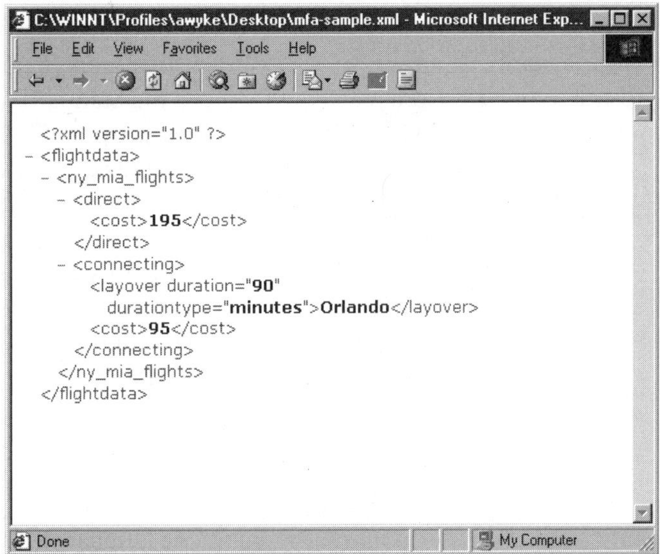

Figure 1-2 Loading our sample XML document in Microsoft Internet Explorer.

Attributes are name-value pairs that occur inside start-tags after the element name. For example, *<layover duration="90" durationtype="minutes">* is a *<layover>* element where the attributes duration and duration type have the values "90" and "minutes". All attribute values must be quoted. Either single or double quotes can be used in pairs.

If the HTML page described earlier included this data, you could easily identify the price of a flight because it is delimited with *<cost>* tags. Identifying which flights are direct is also simple because the *<direct>* element is nested within *<ny_mia_flights>*.

Usable data is shipped with the Web page, so you can calculate how much more a direct flight would have cost while you're stranded on the runway at Orlando on your connecting flight in the middle of a hurricane. XML is great for customers and it makes Web sites easier to build and maintain. If My Favorite Airlines used XML for its data-driven Web site, the company could use the same applet to calculate the total fare on every page. And should the tax rate change, when using appropriately structured XML you need only update the database, not every HTML page. XML is also extensible, so My Favorite Airlines can add a new element for meal preference (for example, *<meal>Vegetarian</meal>*) without disrupting the rest of the site.

Document Type Declarations

For any given application, however, elements occurring in a completely arbitrary order are meaningless. Consider the flight data example in Listing 1-3. Would the contents of the following mfa-bad.xml be meaningful?

Listing 1-3 mfa-bad.xml: A bad example of using XML.

```
<flightdata>
  <meal>
    <layover>
      orlando
      vegetarian
    </layover>
  </meal>
  <cost>
    <direct>
      195
    </direct>
  </cost>
</flightdata>
```

This example document is so far outside the bounds of what we expect that it's absurd. It doesn't mean anything, as you can see in Figure 1-3. From a

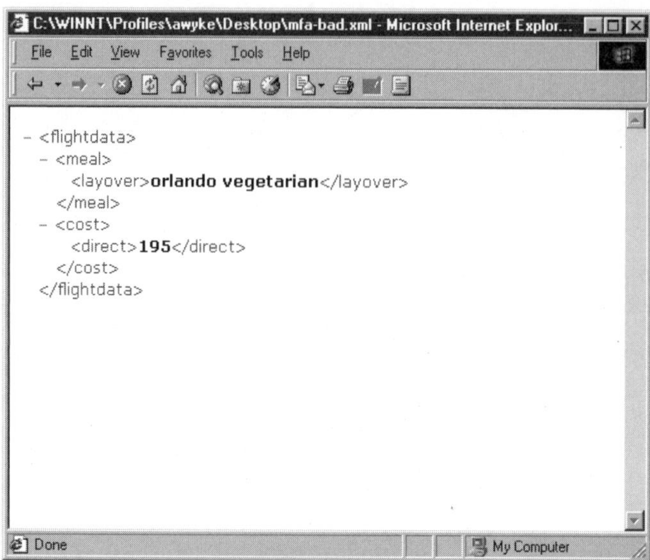

Figure 1-3 Meaninglessly defining our content in a semi-XML format.

strictly syntactic point of view, however, there's nothing wrong with this document. Therefore, if the document is to have meaning, and certainly if you need an application to process it, there must be some constraint on the sequence and nesting of tags. These constraints can be expressed in a Document Type Definition (DTD) or the newer XML Schemas (XSD).

XML 1.0 and XML Schema

The W3C released the XML 1.0 Recommendation in February 1998. The full text can be accessed at *http://www.w3.org/TR/1998/REC-xml-19980210*. The WC3 issued an update, with minor corrections, in October 2000, which is located at *http://www.w3.org/TR/2000/REC-xml-20001006*.

The XML Schema specification reached full W3C Recommendation status in May 2001. It has two normative parts. Part 1 (Structures) is at *http://www.w3.org/TR/xmlschema-1/*. Part 2 (Datatypes) is at *http://www.w3.org/TR/xmlschema-2/*. In addition to the two normative documents, the W3C has provided a useful non-normative Primer to XML Schema, Part 0, at *http://www.w3.org/TR/xmlschema-0/*.

Generally, DTDs and XML Schemas allow a document to communicate metadata to the parser about its content. Meta-information includes the allowed sequence and nesting of tags, attribute values and their types and defaults, the names of external files that might be referenced and whether or not they contain XML, the formats of some external (non-XML) data that might be referenced, and the entities that might be encountered.

Well-Formed and Valid Documents

The are two categories of XML documents. A document is either "well-formed" or "valid". A document can be well-formed only if it obeys the syntax of XML. A document that includes sequences of markup characters that cannot be parsed or are invalid cannot be well-formed. In addition, the document must meet all of the following conditions:

- There can be one, and only one, root element.
- All tags that are opened must be closed.
- Tag names are case-sensitive.

Additional, less critical rules include

- No attribute can appear more than once on the same start-tag.
- Non-empty tags must be properly nested.
- Parameter entities must be declared before they are used. If a document is not well-formed, it is not XML. This means that all XML documents are well-formed, and XML processors are not required to do anything with documents that are not.

A well-formed document is valid only if it contains or refers to a proper DTD or XML Schema and if the XML document obeys the constraints of that DTD or XML Schema (that element sequence and nesting is valid, required attributes are provided, attribute values are of the correct type, and so forth). We will talk more about validity in Chapter 2.

How Is XML Relevant?

Although the idea of using "metadata" to describe data only recently came to the fore, the concept has been around for a long time. Databases, for instance, are made up of tables, columns, views, and such, which are nothing more than metadata about the actual data contained in other tables. These items help describe the data without knowing what is contained in it. However, simply using names, perhaps combined with data types, does not solve all the problems present when trying to describe and ultimately understand data.

XML becomes the glue that binds what a piece of data actually is to what it is supposed to accomplish. It's used to describe all aspects of the data, ranging from near-physical properties to usage instructions, and its relationship to other data. This information can be used for human and machine-readable purposes, one of the true advantages of XML.

What Problem Does XML Solve?

Before the release and widespread adoption of XML, there were relatively few methods that could solve the problem of describing data in a standardized method so that anyone, including machines, could understand what the data meant. Work, on SGML and other electronic data such as the Electronic Data Interchange (EDI) for example, was done in the publishing world that demonstrated the potential of standardized systems, descriptions, and methods. However, SGML and EDI were expensive, either because of the software needed to handle the data or the training necessary to teach these complex markup languages.

Research helped create XML (a subset of SGML), which is able to describe data in a standardized way but is easier to understand and implement. Another reason this is useful is because today most everyone uses computers, so even the "nontechnical" people might need to be able to describe the data they have so others can understand it. A simple example is meeting.xml, shown in Listing 1-4.

Listing 1-4 meeting.xml: A quick XML example that can be used for nontechnical purposes.

```
<?xml version="1.0"?>
<meeting date="2001-07-29" time="14:30:00">
  <actionItem who="fred">Send out minutes after meeting</actionItem>
  <actionItem who="sally">Set up presentation for Thursday</actionItem>
  <actionItem who="dan">Present product roadmap</actionItem>
  <actionItem who="tom">Send out agenda for next meeting</actionItem>
</meeting>
```

Even though we didn't describe what this code listing is, do you have any doubt as to what it represents? It represents action items from a meeting on July 29, 2001 at 14:30:00 (2:30 P.M.).

Another example is map.xml, shown in Listing 1-5, which defines directions from one location to another. These examples demonstrate how you can use XML to describe data that can be understood by a human, machine, or software.

Listing 1-5 map.xml: Using XML to describe directions to a particular location.

```
<?xml version="1.0"?>
<map>
  <start>
    <addr1>100 West Morgan St</addr1>
    <city>Raleigh</city>
    <state>NC</state>
    <zip>27603</zip>
  </start>
  <directions>
    <left distance="0.11 miles">W MORGAN ST</left>
    <left distance="0.11 miles">S WILMINGTON ST</left>
    <left distance="0.44 miles">E EDENTON ST</left>
    <right distance="0.09 miles">N WEST ST</right>
    <left distance="0.02 miles">W JONES ST</left>
  </directions>
  <destination>
    <addr1>508 W Jones St</addr1>
    <city>Raleigh</city>
    <state>NC</state>
    <zip>27603</zip>
  </destination>
</map>
```

We specifically used these nontechnical examples to show that XML can solve many of the difficulties of exchanging or communicating data between two parties, human or machine. Although XML is often considered good only for moving data from A to B (in a manner where B understands what the data is), it can also be used for a variety of tasks, as the following examples demonstrate.

Why Is XML a Good Choice?

If you asked a few years ago whether XML was a good choice for defining your data, you would have received mixed responses. While most people would have agreed that XML would soon evolve as the de facto standard, they would have hedged their bets by saying that it might be wise to wait to ensure wide spread adoption. The flexibility and extensibility of using it as a means to describe data, on the other hand, positioned it for certain success. Today, when Microsoft Windows XP, Microsoft Office XP, and the .NET line of server products are on the shelves, XML is likely a requirement.

Let's take a simple example and demonstrate XML's flexibility by using it to define the dimensions of a door. We can use it not only to describe the data, but also to apply an Extensible Stylesheet Language Transformation (XSLT) to transform it into XHTML.

If we load the example in Listing 1-6 in an XML-supporting version of Internet Explorer, we should see something like Figure 1-4. This is a display of the text, with a default style sheet applied, after it is verified as well-formed. If something is mistyped, like the name of an element, an error will be generated.

Listing 1-6 door.xml: A document describing the dimensions of a wooden door.

```
<?xml version="1.0"?>
<door>
  <height type="inches">80</height>
  <width type="inches">36</width>
  <material type="wood"/>
</door>
```

We could send this information to a supplier to see if they had any wooden doors that measure 36 by 80 inches, but that is not the limit of what we can do with this data. Suppose we wanted to display this information on a Web site, which would require us to format the information in HTML/XHTML. We can do this by including the following line in the document:

```
<?xml-stylesheet type="text/xsl" href="transform.xsl"?>
```

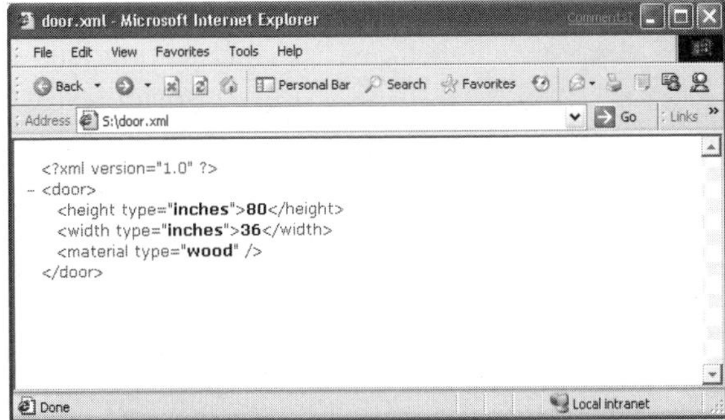

Figure 1-4 Loading a simple XML document into Internet Explorer 5.

Adding this line, by itself, does not perform the necessary transformation from XML into XHTML; it only tells the parser that a corresponding style sheet for the document exists. We must now create a transform.xsl document to define the transformation, which would look like Listing 1-7.

Listing 1-7 transform.xsl: An XSLT style sheet responsible for transforming our XML document into XHTML.

```
<?xml version="1.0"?>
<xsl:stylesheet
     xmlns:xsl="http://www.w3.org/1999/XSL/Transform"
     version="1.0">
<xsl:output method="html"/>
<xsl:template match="/">
<html xmlns="http://www.w3.org/1999/xhtml" lang="en"
      xml:lang="en">
<head>
  <title>Door Information</title>
</head>
<body>
  <h1>Door Information</h1>
  <p>
    <strong>
      Material:
    </strong>
    <xsl:value-of select="//door/material/@type"/>
    <br/>
    <strong>
      Height:
    </strong>
    <xsl:value-of select="//door/height"/>
    (measured in <xsl:value-of select="//door/height/@type"/>)
    <br/>
```

(continued)

Listing 1-7 *continued*

```
    <strong>
      Width:
    </strong>
    <xsl:value-of select="//door/width"/>
    (measured in <xsl:value-of select="//door/width/@type"/>)
  </p>
</body>
</html>
</xsl:template>
</xsl:stylesheet>
```

> **Note** The Microsoft XML 3 parser (MSXML) introduced XSLT support into Microsoft's XML-supporting line of products. This parser, which was first available for Internet Explorer 4.01 Service Pack 1 as a separate download, had limited XSLT support. If you want to see this example work in Internet Explorer 5 or greater, you will need MSXML 4, which you can download from *http://msdn.microsoft.com.*

If we load door.xml in Internet Explorer the browser will apply the style sheet, transforming it from XML into XHTML, and you will see something like Figure 1-5.

This example illustrates why XML is a good choice for describing data. Data can be exchanged with partners, affiliates, and internal applications, and it can be used to describe your own internal content. With a little imagination you can see just how useful XML can be.

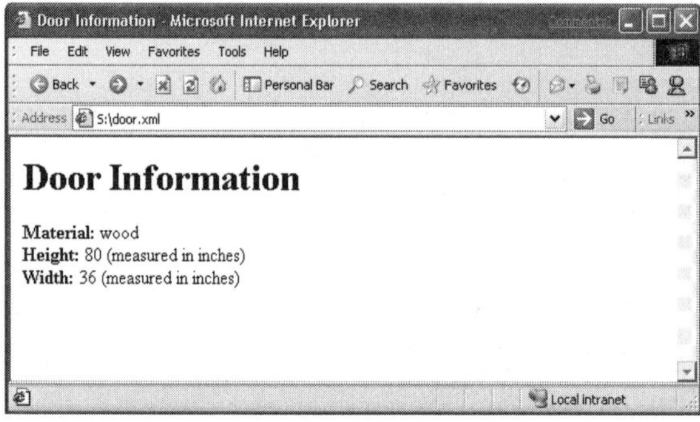

Figure 1-5 Transforming our door.xml document into XHTML.

What Can It Help?

We've heard how great XML is, how it helps with certain issues, and seen a few examples, but what does this mean? What types of difficulties does it solve, how does it solve them, and why is XML the solution for these issues? These are questions that we need to ask ourselves before choosing XML as our solution-providing method. We need to be sure it is the right means to provide integration points with our applications, or descriptions and structure to our content.

In this section we will talk about specific uses of XML and how they work. Because most of these concepts will be applied in greater detail later in the book, these example cases will not cover every detail of the code involved. What is important to understand after completing this section is that XML can be used in the creation of objects, application messaging, and process modeling.

Working with Objects

Those of you familiar with the principles and practices of object-oriented programming will have added respect, and probably motivation, for creating items in an object-oriented manner. Doing so allows for a degree of flexibility and potential component reuse that is not possible when operating in a non-object environment. XML is no different and has its own object-like implementations and uses. We will cover these in the following sections.

Modeling

Soon after XML 1.0 was released, gaps in the language were filled with complementary standards. One such limitation of XML was the inability to present data in an object-oriented manner. To help fill this void, a Note at the W3C was published titled "Schema for Object-Oriented XML (SOX)". This Note, which became an important part of the foundation that was used to build XSD, extended XML 1.0 by supporting the following six items. (Because we cover XSD in Appendix A, we use SOX in this example.)

- An extensive and extensible set of datatypes
- Inheritance among element types
- Namespaces
- Polymorphic content
- Embedded documentation
- Features that enable robust distributed schema management

SOX makes it possible, for example, to create a *home computer* object that contains a monitor, housing (CPU, RAM, hard disk, and so forth), speakers, a keyboard, and a mouse. The definition of this schema shown, in Listing 1-8, home_computer.sox, gives you the ability to create documents describing various home computers but does not allow you to describe another type of computer that might have more options.

> **Note** Because SOX enforces a valid Uniform Resource Identifier (URI), we must include the file:// portion of the URL in the *<schema>* element. For this example we have placed the schema on the S: drive of a Windows machine, so please adjust this attribute value for your system.

Listing 1-8 home_computer.sox: A schema describing our home computer.

```
<?xml version = "1.0" encoding = "UTF-8"?>
<!DOCTYPE schema SYSTEM
  "urn:x-commerceone:document:com:commerceone:xdk:xml:schema.dtd$1.0">
<schema uri = "file:///S:/home_computer.sox" soxlang-version = "V0.2.2">
   <elementtype name = "home_computer">
       <model>
           <sequence>
               <element type = "monitor"/>
               <element type = "housing"/>
               <element type = "speakers"/>
               <element type = "keyboard"/>
               <element type = "mouse"/>
           </sequence>
       </model>
   </elementtype>
   <elementtype name = "monitor">
       <model>
           <string/>
       </model>
   </elementtype>
   <elementtype name = "housing">
       <model>
           <sequence>
               <element type = "cpu"/>
               <element type = "ram"/>
               <element type = "disk_space"/>
```

```
                <element type = "modem"/>
            </sequence>
        </model>
    </elementtype>
    <elementtype name = "speakers">
        <model>
            <string/>
        </model>
    </elementtype>
    <elementtype name = "keyboard">
        <model>
            <string/>
        </model>
    </elementtype>
    <elementtype name = "mouse">
        <model>
            <string/>
        </model>
    </elementtype>
    <elementtype name = "cpu">
        <model>
            <string/>
        </model>
    </elementtype>
    <elementtype name = "ram">
        <model>
            <string/>
        </model>
    </elementtype>
    <elementtype name = "disk_space">
        <model>
            <string/>
        </model>
    </elementtype>
    <elementtype name = "modem">
        <model>
            <string/>
        </model>
    </elementtype>
</schema>
```

Figure 1-6 is a visual representation of this schema.

This data model is fine if we only define home computers, but what happens if we want to define a work computer? Using SOX we can build such an object by extending our base *<home_computer>* element as shown in Listing 1-9. If we link in our home_computer.sox schema, define a new element called *<work_computer>*, and say it extends *<home_computer>*, we are able to add items like a printer, scanner, and zip drive. This new schema, work_computer.sox,

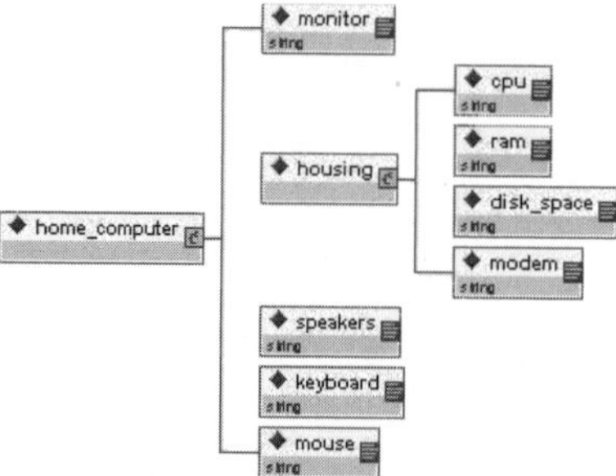

Figure 1-6 A visual representation of our home computer data model.

now inherits all the elements in the original schema and requires only that we define the additions.

Listing 1-9 work_computer.sox: A new schema extending our home_computer.sox schema.

```
<?xml version = "1.0" encoding = "UTF-8"?>
<!DOCTYPE schema SYSTEM
  "urn:x-commerceone:document:com:commerceone:xdk:xml:schema.dtd$1.0">
<schema uri = "file:///S:/home_computer.sox" soxlang-version = "V0.2.2">
   <join system = "file:///S:/home_computer.sox"/>
   <elementtype name = "work_computer">
       <extends type = "home_computer">
           <append>
               <sequence>
                   <element type = "scanner"/>
                   <element type = "zip_drive"/>
                   <element type = "printer"/>
               </sequence>
           </append>
       </extends>
   </elementtype>
   <elementtype name = "scanner">
       <model>
           <string/>
       </model>
   </elementtype>
   <elementtype name = "zip_drive">
       <model>
           <string/>
       </model>
   </elementtype>
   <elementtype name = "printer">
       <model>
           <string/>
```

```
        </model>
    </elementtype>
</schema>
```

Figure 1-7 provides a representation of this new schema so you can compare it to the home_computer.sox schema.

Now that the work computer schema is defined, we can create an instance document of this schema. Because SOX-compliant parsers will pull in the necessary parent schemas, we only need to reference the work_computer.sox schema in our example shown in Listing 1-10.

Listing 1-10 first_work_computer.xml: An instance of our work_computer.sox schema

```
<?xml version = "1.0" encoding = "UTF-8"?>
<?soxtype file:///S:/work_computer.sox?>
<work_computer>
    <monitor>15 inch</monitor>
    <housing>
        <cpu>1 GHz</cpu>
        <ram>256 MB</ram>
        <disk_space>60 GB</disk_space>
        <modem>56k</modem>
    </housing>
    <speakers>JBL</speakers>
    <keyboard>Microsoft</keyboard>
    <mouse>Microsoft</mouse>
    <scanner>Microtek</scanner>
    <zip_drive>100 MB</zip_drive>
    <printer>HP</printer>
</work_computer>
```

Object modeling allows you to reuse components of XML schema dialects, like SOX or XSD, which can lead to increased productivity within your development environment by cutting down on redundant work.

Procedure Invocation

Invoking new derivative classes of XML objects is not the only way you can use XML in an object-oriented manner. The ability to invoke a procedure on a different system using XML is also possible with several standards, such as Simple Object Access Protocol (SOAP), which we cover in Chapter 14, and XML-Remote Procedure Call (XML-RPC). Both standards represent a way you can pass information to an object (an application in many cases), process the information, and return the results.

RPC allows you to tap another machine, application, or device for its functionality, creating a virtual application to perform a given task. RPC is not a new

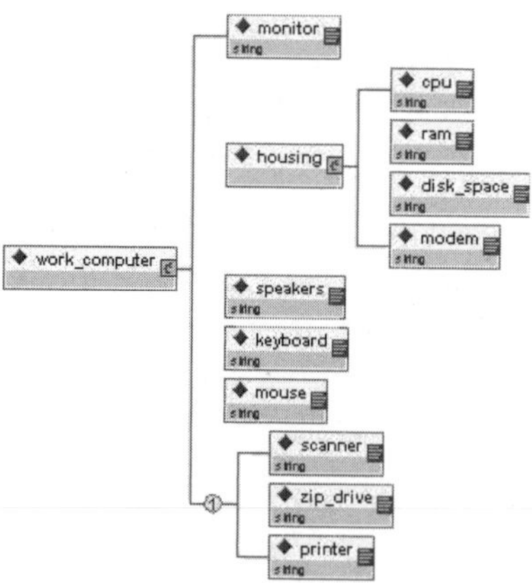

Figure 1-7 A visual representation of our new schema base on our home computer schema.

concept, so many of you might have some experience working with it. XML-RPC, however, is relatively new.

XML-RPC is a simple specification that uses a Hypertext Transfer Protocol (HTTP) POST request to pass a set of commands, parameters, and so forth to a remote object. This request, which is broken into a header and payload, is then processed by the remote application. A response is returned once complete, which could contain either the results of the processing or an appropriate error. Let's walk through an example to help describe the requirements of XML-RPC.

While the request is a standard HTTP POST, XML-RPC dictates that the following items must be contained in the head of the request. Note that the traditional first line of an HTTP request, which contains the method (POST), requested URI (such as /scripts/xml-rpc-processor.exe) and protocol version (such as HTTP/1.1), is implied in this list, so we will not list these requirements separately. A sample is included after the list.

- User-Agent: user agent making the request
- Host: hostname of the application making the request
- Content-Type: should state text/xml to define that the request contains XML information
- Content-Length: the size of the document being passed

```
User-Agent: SomeApp/1.1 (Windows XP)
Host: database.example.com
Content-Type: text/xml
Content-length: 361
```

The body of the request contains the elements necessary to identify the procedure as well as pass in any arguments. In rpc-request.xml shown in Listing 1-11, we will use an application called validateUser.exe and we will pass it a first name and age parameter. Although this is a fictitious application, it could represent an application that validated a user's access, by name and age, against certain information. Note that the server processing the XML-RPC request would need to know what validateUser.exe was or where it was located; it would need to be able to launch the application.

Listing 1-11 rpc-request.xml: An XML-RPC request document.

```
<?xml version="1.0"?>
<methodCall>
  <methodName>validateUser.exe</methodName>
  <params>
    <param>
      <value>
        <struct>
          <member>
            <name>FirstName</name>
            <value>
              <string>John</string>
            </value>
          </member>
          <member>
            <name>Age</name>
            <value>
              <i4>28</i4>
            </value>
          </member>
        </struct>
      </value>
    </param>
  </params>
</methodCall>
```

> **Note** More information on these values and what they mean in HTTP terms can be found at *http://www.w3.org/Protocols/rfc2616/rfc2616.txt.*

The document begins with the *<methodCall>* element followed by the *<methodName>* and a list of *<params>*. For more information on the various types of information you can pass, visit *http://www.xmlrpc.com/spec*.

The response, like the request, will use the HTTP protocol. To be validated, at a minimum it must return the following information in the header:

- Response Code: see HTTP specification for more information on the various response codes
- Content-Length: the size of the document being passed
- Content-Type: should state text/xml to define that the request contains XML information

An example would look like this:

```
HTTP/1.1 200 OK
Content-Length: 219
Content-Type: text/xml
```

As before, you can visit *http://www.w3.org/Protocols/rfc2616/rfc2616.txt* for more information on HTTP responses.

The body of the response contains markup outlining the procedure returned from its processing. This information is stored in a *<methodResponse>* element, which can contain a single *<params>* or *<fault>* element depending on the successfulness of the processing. For example, if no error occurred, you might see a result like the one in rpc-response-success.xml in Listing 1-12, which states that the user was accepted.

Listing 1-12 rpc-response-success.xml: A successful response from our procedure call.

```
<?xml version="1.0"?>
<methodResponse>
  <params>
    <param>
      <value>
        <string>Accepted</string>
      </value>
    </param>
  </params>
</methodResponse>
```

If an error occurred in the processing you might see something like rpc-response-error.xml shown in Listing 1-13, where the application validateUser.exe was not found.

Listing 1-13 rpc-response-error.xml: An error stating the application was not found on the system.

```
<?xml version="1.0"?>
<methodResponse>
  <fault>
    <value>
      <struct>
        <member>
          <name>ErrorCode</name>
          <value>
            <int>1</int>
          </value>
        </member>
        <member>
          <name>ErrorMessage</name>
          <value>
            <string>Application not found.</string>
          </value>
        </member>
      </struct>
    </value>
  </fault>
</methodResponse>
```

Invoking procedures, applications, and processes on remote systems offers a compelling reason to look into and potentially use XML-RPC. Remember that we will discuss SOAP later in this book, so before you make any decisions, be sure to understand the benefits and issues of both of these standards.

Application Messaging

The term "messaging" is often thought of as messaging between friends and family, such as with Microsoft Network Messenger, and not between full blown enterprise-level applications, which could in turn connect your data repositories to those of your partners and affiliates. XML changed all that, and with the help of standards like SOAP, application messaging is now a reality.

XML is used to describe the Application Programming Interface (API) to a Web Service, which allows applications to partially automate the process by which they communicate. The requesting application can understand the capabilities of the responding server and determine if it is compatible with its own data structure and type.

What Is Messaging?

The purpose of application messaging is for software applications, potentially in geographically different locations, to communicate in a near-automated fashion. Communicating usually involves receiving a request, processing that request, and a returning a result to the requesting application. XML emerges as the language of choice for describing not only the request, but also the response. This description might contain the path or route of the request, the type of information requested, and the actual data returned (marked up in XML, of course), but this is only part of the solution.

With the shift to Web Services as the next generation of Application Service Providers, XML is used not only for application-to-application messaging, but also for describing the services themselves. This description could contain anything from the type of data that can be requested to outlining the result options. Following this model, applications can query other applications to understand their capabilities before making a request.

A Simple Example of Messaging

News Feed, Inc. builds a system that returns the daily news to a requesting application. The system has everything from sports, financial news, and local news, to world, weather, and travel news. The application has the ability to be queried and pass a date to see if it has any relevant news for a given day. This query also contains the type of information you're looking for, what you want returned (count, headers, all data), and how many results are returned. The XML schema used to describe this query is located in Listing 1-14. In Chapter 7 you will see that standards exist that provide an entire framework for this type of communication, so treat this as a simple example of how you might implement a messaging system.

Listing 1-14 NFQuery.dtd: An XML schema for querying the News Feed system.

```
<?xml version='1.0' encoding='UTF-8' ?>
<!ELEMENT query (news)>
<!ELEMENT news EMPTY>
<!ATTLIST news  date  CDATA  #REQUIRED
          type   (global | local | financial |
                  sports | travel | weather )  #REQUIRED
          what   (count | headers | all )  #REQUIRED
         limit CDATA  #IMPLIED >
```

Joe's Sports Tips, a local newspaper that uses News Feed's data, only wants to retrieve sports news. Because of this, Joe's first sends a query to the News Feed system to see how many sports headlines it has for a given date. The query, contained in Listing 1-15, requests the number of sport headlines for October 10, 2001.

Listing 1-15 2001-10-10_sports_query.xml: The Joe's Sports Tips query of the News Feed system.

```
<?xml version = "1.0" encoding = "UTF-8"?>
<!DOCTYPE query SYSTEM "NFQuery.dtd">
<query>
   <news date = "2001-10-10" type = "sports" what = "count"/>
</query>
```

The next part of the process is for News Feed to return a response to Joe's. The format of the response is governed by the NFResponse.dtd schema in Listing 1-16. The response, shown in Listing 1-17, shows 53 items in sports news on October 10.

Listing 1-16 NFResponse.dtd: A schema for News Feed's response.

```
<?xml version='1.0' encoding='UTF-8' ?>
<!ELEMENT results (count | headers | all)>
<!ATTLIST results  date CDATA  #REQUIRED
          type  (global | local | financial |
                sports | travel | weather )  #REQUIRED >
<!ELEMENT count (#PCDATA)>
<!ELEMENT headers (#PCDATA)>
<!ELEMENT all (headline+)>
<!ELEMENT headline (#PCDATA)>
```

Listing 1-17 2001-10-10_sports_query_response.xml: The response from News Feed.

```
<?xml version = "1.0" encoding = "UTF-8"?>
<!DOCTYPE results SYSTEM "NFResponse.dtd">
<results date = "2001-10-10" type = "sports">
   <count>53</count>
</results>
```

Now that Joe's knows how many items it can access, the system decides to request the first 10 articles. Again using the NFQuery.dtd data model, it changes the initial query to reflect that it wants 10 items and the entire article for these items.

Listing 1-18 2001-10-10_get_sports.xml: A request for the first 10 sport news stories.

```
<?xml version = "1.0" encoding = "UTF-8"?>
<!DOCTYPE query SYSTEM "NFQuery.dtd">
<query>
   <news date="2001-10-10"
         type="sports" what="all" limit="10"/>
</query>
```

Several sections in this book discuss this type of application-to-application messaging and communication. Chapter 4 and Chapter 15 are dedicated to messaging and Microsoft's BizTalk Server, which provides all the components necessary to get you up and running, including Microsoft BizTalk Messaging Manager.

Process Modeling

A relatively new use of XML is to model processes and workflow. Remember the map.xml document earlier in this chapter? That document was a good example of steps, or a process, that needed to occur in a specific order. Not following this order, or the directions in our example, will result in someone getting lost.

Representing UML

Those of you familiar with the Unified Modeling Language (UML) know that it can be used for process modeling by outlining the flow from one step to another. Using the UML is a way you can describe a model in a language-agnostic way. The model could be an application, or maybe how a waiter takes your order at a restaurant. These models are made up of properties and behaviors. The important part of this approach is not that Step #2 comes after Step #1, but the relative relationship between these steps. Knowing that Step #1 is before Step #2 and is two steps away from #3 is just as important.

Because UML is quickly evolving as a standard way to represent models, and because XML is a standard used to describe them, many UML applications now support XML as an exportable format.

Using XML to model processes is not just a means by which you can describe how something works. Because it was implemented in XML, it inherits all the abilities of the XML language, such as validation. This provides a second level of verification when it comes to ensuring that processes are defined according to the rules and objectives set forth.

Microsoft .NET

Microsoft took the lead in developing a framework that allows for developing a new generation of software. This framework melds computing and communications in an innovative way, offering developers the tools they need to transform the Web and every other aspect of the computing experience. Microsoft dubbed this framework, which relies and is built heavily on the use of the XML, .NET (dot Net) framework.

For the first time a framework exists that allows developers, businesses, and consumers to harness technology on their terms. The creation of truly distributed Web Services that will integrate and collaborate with a range of complementary services to serve customers in ways that today's dotcoms can only dream of is one of the foundations of .NET. Applications based on the .NET Framework can make information available at any time, in any place, and on any device.

Microsoft's innovative work with .NET resulted in a powerful message and platform for application development and deployment. We will go over many aspects of .NET within this book, so we will introduce you to its concepts here.

Back to Fundamentals

The fundamental idea behind the .NET Framework is that the focus is shifting from individual Web sites or devices connected to the Internet to constellations of computers, devices, and services that work together to deliver richer, broader solutions. People will control what, when, and how information is delivered to them. Computers, devices, and services will collaborate with each other to provide rich services instead of being isolated islands where the user provides the only integration. Businesses will offer their products and services in a way that lets customers seamlessly embed them in their own electronic fabric.

The .NET Framework will help drive a transformation in the Internet that will see HTML-based presentation augmented by programmable XML-based information.

The Software as a Service Approach

Programming models previously focused on a single system. Current object models like the Component Object Model (COM) and the Common Object Request Broker Architecture (CORBA) rely heavily on model-specific protocols such as Distributed COM (DCOM), Remote Method Invocation (RMI), or Internet Inter-Orb Protocol (IIOP) residing in a homogenous infrastructure. On the other hand, the .NET Framework is explicitly designed to allow the integration of any group of resources on the Internet into a single solution. Currently this type of integration is extremely complex and costly. The .NET Framework will make the integration and assembly of software services intrinsic to all software development projects.

The loosely coupled XML-based .NET programming model introduces the concept of creating XML-based Web Services. Whereas today's Web sites are handcrafted and don't work with other sites without significant additional development, the .NET programming model provides a built-in mechanism to build any Web site or service so that it will coalesce and collaborate seamlessly with others. Just as the introduction of interchangeable components accelerated the industrial revolution, the .NET Framework promises to hasten the development of software as a service.

Web Services

Broadly speaking, a Web Service is simply an application that can be integrated with other Web Services using Internet standards. In other words, it's a URL-addressable resource that programmatically returns information to clients who want to use it. One important feature of Web Services is that clients don't need to know how a service is implemented. The ability, or methods from a programming standpoint, are exposed and can be discovered using a specific process, which allows applications to be more dynamic and therefore require less attention as time goes on.

Like components, Web Services represent black-box functionality that can be reused without worrying about how the service is implemented. Web Services provide well-defined interfaces, called contracts, which describe the services provided. Developers can assemble applications using a combination of remote services, local services, and custom code. For example, a company might assemble an online store using the Microsoft Passport service to authenticate users, a third-party personalization service to adapt Web pages to each user's preferences, and a credit card processing service.

Unlike current component technologies, however, Web Services do not use object model-specific protocols such as DCOM, RMI, or IIOP as the set of participants in an integrated business process, and as technology changes over time, it becomes difficult to guarantee a single, unified infrastructure among all participants. Web Services take a different approach: they communicate using ubiquitous Web protocols and data formats such as HTTP and XML. Any system supporting these Web standards will be able to support Web Services.

Using XML within .NET

XML is the obvious choice for defining a standard yet extensible language to represent commands and typed data, and it's only appropriate that Windows .NET has adopted its use widely within its framework. While rules for representing commands and typed data using other techniques (such as encoding this information in a query string) could be defined, XML is specifically designed as a standard metalanguage for describing data. SOAP is an industry standard for using XML to represent data and commands in an extensible way. SOAP is being further developed at W3C under the name of XML Protocol (*XMLP*).

XML is the enabling technology for the Web Service contracts. The Service Contract Language *(SCL)* is an XML grammar for documenting Web Service contracts. Because SCL is XML-based, contracts are easy for both developers and developer tools to create and interpret. Microsoft is also a contributor to the Web Services Description Language (WSDL), recently submitted to W3C for further development (see *http://www.w3.org/TR/2001/NOTE-wsdl-20010315*). Standards like SOAP, SCL, and Discovery Protocol (DISCO), an XML-based format for Web Service discovery, help developers because they do not need to understand and implement different ways to access each Web Service they use.

Obviously, the advantages of the model are many. Companies can not only more easily integrate internal applications, but they can also access services offered by other businesses. By combining Web Services on the Internet, companies can create a wide variety of value-added applications.

What Are the Next Steps?

Before you can really dive into XML you need to understand XML-based languages and know what software to use and where to get help. If you have previous experience with deploying XML solutions, the following parts will be a refresher. If you have experience with XML but have not developed any large-scale applications and systems using it, the items in this section should help you on your way. You will be reminded of important exposure you should have and about the kinds of applications you should consider using. Additionally, we have included places where you can get help if you need it.

Necessary Knowledge

Few people learn XML as their first markup-based language; most have had previous experience with SGML or HTML/XHTML. Even if you have no prior experience, XML is an easy language to learn conceptually. It is simply metadata used to describe a markup language. But conceptual understanding is not the biggest problem in knowing and using XML.

XML 1.0 is a means used to create the markup language. Saying that you know XML states that you can understand the constructs of a given XML-based language, but does not necessarily mean that you understand the purpose and usage of that language. While learning XML you should take the time to learn XML-based languages created with it. For instance, you should explore other standards such as Namespaces in XML, XPath, or SOAP. Your usage of XML will surely go beyond just the details of the language itself and will involve many of the other XML-based implementations.

Because understanding some of the more important XML-based languages is so important, we cover several in Appendix A. As you create your solution you will come across an instance where you will say, "Gee, I really need X," where X is a type of functionality not inherent in XML or your deployment environment. With research and exposure to other standards, you are sure to find something that performs at least 85 percent of what you are looking for, if not more.

> **Note** The Universal Description, Discovery, and Integration (UDDI) was recently launched to host Yellow Pages-like entries for Web Services that are available via their defined protocol. For instance, if you want to find a company that could perform credit card validation by passing them an XML document, you should first check *http://www.uddi.com* to see who is currently offering this type of service.

XML Software

Using XML for personal or professional uses requires software. How much software you require is completely dependent on what you, from knowledge and programming standpoints, are comfortable with providing. You may opt to use a text editor, like Notepad, in writing your schemas and instance documents instead of performing these tasks in some kind of Integrated Development Environment (IDE).

You may also, in accordance with the published standards, opt to write your own parser for validating instance documents. Although this is unlikely, the application you build will be larger if a prebuilt parser is included. This could be anything from a type of user agent to a server that processes XML documents for insertion into a database.

We cover parsers in detail in Chapter 3 and touch on several popular XML software offerings in Appendix B. To give you a leg up until then, we listed several tools you might want to consider in Table 1-1.

Table 1-1 Tools of the XML Trade

Tool Function	Description
Schema and DTD	Tools used to create XML DTDs and schemas to describe data models. These tools usually follow the XML 1.0 or XML Schema Recommendations from the W3C *(http://www.w3.org)*, or some other standard based on these.
Document instance	Tools that will create an XML document. These documents might only be well-formed, or they might also be validated against a DTD or schema.
Parsers	Applications responsible for parsing an instance document, potentially validating it against a DTD or schema, and then exposing the various aspects of the data in a programmatic view (that is, as an object or some other API). It will also check to make sure that the document conforms to the XML standard.
Application	Application that takes the document after parsing and performs a given task with the data. For instance, this could be a database that inserts the data in the instance document into the appropriate tables.

After you finish Chapter 2 and 3 and glance at Appendix B, you will not only be ready to move into the real meat of the book where you will build applications using XML, but you will also have a good idea as to what, if any, extra software you might want to use in your projects.

Where to Get Help

Obtaining help is one of the most overlooked and untapped benefits of today's computer world. Not only have complex applications provided detailed help files that are searchable like a mini-database (using the Help system in Windows is one great example), but the ability to use the Internet to search for similar or related problems makes it easy to find a solution. The combination of these resources alone gives developers a leg up on difficulties they might come across.

Several places on the Web offer you help, and several methods can help you get it. In Table 1-2, for instance, we included the URLs to the standards bodies that you should come to know and understand. While everyone is free to monitor and participate, they all provide a large number of resources, standards, and other information that you will find useful.

Table 1-2 Standards-Based Sites

URL	Description
http://www.w3.org	The World Wide Web Consortium is where many of the XML standards are housed, including the XML 1.0 Recommendation and the newly adopted XML Schema Recommendation.
http://www.oasis-open.org	The Organization for the Advancement of Structured Information Standards (OASIS) is like the W3C in many ways. It hosts standards and provides the framework to propose and produce a standard for paying members.
http://www.ietf.org	The Internet Engineering Task Force (IETF) is by no means focused on XML, but they do work that uses XML heavily. One particular item is their WWW Distributed Authoring and Versioning (WebDAV) group. Microsoft included support for WebDAV in applications such as BizTalk Server, so we recommend you stay alert on the IETF efforts.

If you are serious about following up on XML after reading this book, we suggest you try the sites listed in Table 1-3. You will probably find what you're looking for, or at least a pointer to it. For those of you using Microsoft servers and products for your implementation, the Microsoft Developer Network Online link (MSDN Online) should be of special interest because many questions can be answered there.

Finding help is not always easy, so if all else fails you can fall back on your favorite search engine and a few keywords to see if any additional sites cove your topic of interest. If you do take this approach, remember that you should use specific keywords to narrow your search to items that are likely to represent what you are actually seeking.

Table 1-3 Useful XML Sites

URL	Description
http://msdn.microsoft.com/workshop/xml/index.asp	A nicely done and thorough section of the MSDN Online site. It contains generic information on XML and related standards and specific information on XML support within their applications.
http://www.xml.com	XML.com, which is an O'Reilly supported site, offers free content in the form of articles, examples, and other resources for the new and seasoned XML programmer.
http://www.ibm.com/developerworks/xml	The developerWorks site provides tools, code, and examples on many open standards, one of which is XML. It provides basic self-help information and descriptions of tools and other helpful items available to those implementing XML.
http://www.xml.org	The XML.org site, which is hosted by OASIS, is an open forum for the discussion and exchange of information on XML. Its purpose is to distribute information they have assembled and collected about XML, tools, and communities that use it.

Where Do You Want to Go?

Developers historically built applications by integrating local system services. This model gave developers access to a rich set of development resources and precise control over how the application behaves. Developers moved beyond this model by building complex n-tier systems that integrate entire applications from all over their networks and add unique value on top. More is needed, however, and the flexibility of XML and the Internet creates the perfect platform to accomplish these goals.

In this chapter we have laid the foundation for using XML in many aspects of enterprise-level solutions. We have introduced you to the specifics that will be covered and carried throughout the book and into the examples. We have also seen a mix of technology and business in the application of these ideas and methods. We know that technology is the main focus for many of the readers, but at the same time, by providing this added insight into the business-side of the equation, we have prepared you to have an understanding beyond just the code you write. We attempted to answer that famous question "But, why?" that so many of us ask day to day.

Chapter 2 begins a section dedicated to discussing the details of XML and implementing it. This includes a refresher on the XML language and exposure to related standards based on XML, as well as applications you might want to consider within your implementations.

2

XML Basics

Although Chapter 1 is important for building the foundation you'll need for deploying XML solutions, in this chapter we begin our headfirst dive into the XML language. Because the main focus of this book is using XML and not the semantics, this chapter will be short and to the point. Our objective is simple: to provide you with a refresher course on the syntax and semantics of XML to carry you through the rest of the book.

As you know, the importance of XML in today's interconnected world demands that we fully understand our tasks, objectives, and milestones for projects. In the chapters that follow we will walk you through real-world examples of building applications and solving problems. First, however, we will fine-tune your knowledge of the language.

The Goals of XML

Before you can fully understand and appreciate what XML introduces into the application integration equations, we must take a moment to talk about the initial goals behind creating the language. The original XML Working Group at the W3C was formed out of the SGML Editorial Review Board, and it made 10 design goals while creating the XML language. According to the XML 1.0 Recommendation (*http://www.w3.org/TR/2000/REC-xml-20001006#sec-origin-goals*), these were as follows:

1. XML shall be straightforwardly usable over the Internet.
2. XML shall support a wide variety of applications.
3. XML shall be compatible with SGML.
4. It shall be easy to write programs which process XML documents.
5. The number of optional features in XML is to be kept to the absolute minimum, ideally zero.
6. XML documents should be human-legible and reasonably clear.
7. The XML design should be prepared quickly.
8. The design of XML shall be formal and concise.
9. XML documents shall be easy to create.
10. Terseness in XML markup is of minimal importance.

You should be exposed to these items because they lay the foundation for the design and objectives of the language. If you plan on using XML, you should make sure your objectives are in line with these design goals. Failure to do so could result in using XML for a purpose outside the bounds of the language, and therefore create a limiting implementation.

> **Note** SGML was the parent standard for HTML. You can find more information on SGML at *http://www.w3.org/MarkUp/SGML.*

The XML Language

XML is a subset, or a pared down version, of SGML. If you are familiar with SGML you will notice the similarities. Unlike SGML, the XML syntax is simple, which is one reason why it has seen much success, especially over the last year. In this section we go over some basic language semantics and syntax that you need to understand, such as elements, entities, comments, and processing instructions.

> **Note** In various parts of this chapter we will refer to the term "schema." We are not speaking of XSD, but of a simple data schema. Specific references to XSD are made using a capitalized S, such as in "Schema," or the abbreviation XSD.

Elements

Elements represent the tags, or language, that you create with XML. To define an element in a DTD you use the following syntax.

```
<!ELEMENT name type>
```

The *name* is the element name you want to define and the *type* is the type of content the element contains. This could be text, other elements, or a combination of the two. Here's an example to give you a better idea of what this means.

Suppose you want to create a customer schema that includes their name and contact information. To provide another level of granularity we break the name into first, last, and middle names, and contact into address and phone. Taking it one more step, we will break address into street, city, state, and zip, while we break phone into home, work, and mobile. Figure 2-1 is a visual representation of this data model.

Because declaration within XML DTDs must appear in a specific order, we first define our customer element. This element contains two child elements as its content, so the DTD representation of this XML element takes the following form:

```
<!ELEMENT customer (name , contact)>
```

In this definition, for the document to be valid (more on what valid is later in the chapter), it *must* contain a single instance of the *<name>* element followed by a single instance of the *<contact>* element. You can impose some rules on this, such as having name OR contact or making one or both optional, but we will discuss those later.

Defining *<name>* and *<contact>* is similar because they are parent elements of child elements. So are *<address>* and *<phone>*. The definition for these can be represented as follows:

```
<!ELEMENT name (first , middle , last)>
<!ELEMENT contact (address , phone)>
<!ELEMENT address (street , city , state , zip)>
<!ELEMENT phone (home , work , mobile)>
```

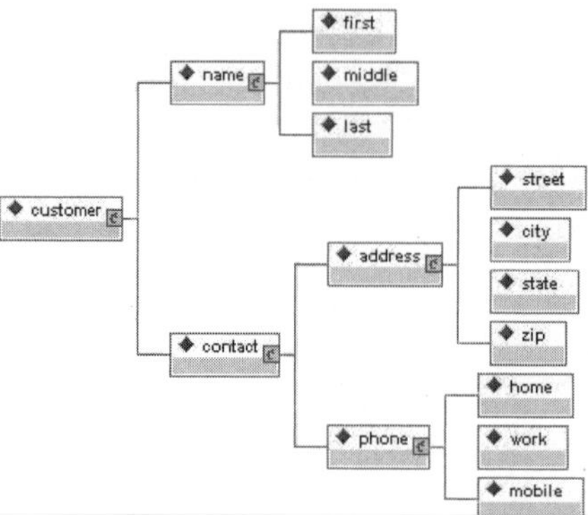

Figure 2-1 A visual representation of our customer data model.

The final step is to define the elements that actually hold the instance data. These include the child elements first, middle, last, street, city, state, zip, home, work, and mobile. We want these elements to hold only regular text, which is referred to as *parsed character data*, so we will define them as having #PCDATA. These definitions look like:

```
<!ELEMENT first (#PCDATA)>
<!ELEMENT middle (#PCDATA)>
<!ELEMENT last (#PCDATA)>
<!ELEMENT street (#PCDATA)>
<!ELEMENT city (#PCDATA)>
<!ELEMENT state (#PCDATA)>
<!ELEMENT zip (#PCDATA)>
<!ELEMENT home (#PCDATA)>
<!ELEMENT work (#PCDATA)>
<!ELEMENT mobile (#PCDATA)>
```

The last piece we need, which is actually the first item in our schema definition, is the *<?xml>* declaration. This is nothing more than

```
<?xml version='1.0' encoding='UTF-8' ?>
```

Our completed schema shown in Listing 2-1, customer.dtd, can now be referenced and used in instance documents such as johndoe.xml in Listing 2-2, which is displayed in Microsoft Internet Explorer in Figure 2-2. We added comments in the johndoe.xml file to help you understand what information is included.

Listing 2-1 customer.dtd: The XML definition of the customer data model.

```
<?xml version='1.0' encoding='UTF-8' ?>
<!ELEMENT customer (name , contact)>
<!ELEMENT name (first , middle , last)>
```

```
<!ELEMENT contact (address , phone)>
<!ELEMENT address (street , city , state , zip)>
<!ELEMENT phone (home , work , mobile)>
<!ELEMENT first (#PCDATA)>
<!ELEMENT middle (#PCDATA)>
<!ELEMENT last (#PCDATA)>
<!ELEMENT street (#PCDATA)>
<!ELEMENT city (#PCDATA)>
<!ELEMENT state (#PCDATA)>
<!ELEMENT zip (#PCDATA)>
<!ELEMENT home (#PCDATA)>
<!ELEMENT work (#PCDATA)>
<!ELEMENT mobile (#PCDATA)>
```

Listing 2-2 johndoe.xml: An instance of the customer.dtd document.

```
<?xml version = "1.0"?>
<!DOCTYPE customer SYSTEM "customer.dtd">
<customer>
  <!--(name , contact)-->
  <name>
    <!--(first , middle , last)-->
    <first>John</first>
    <middle>Smithy</middle>
    <last>Doe</last>
  </name>
  <contact>
    <!--(address , phone)-->
    <address>
      <!--(street , city , state , zip)-->
      <street>123 Some Street</street>
      <city>Anytown</city>
      <state>NC</state>
      <zip>25555</zip>
    </address>
    <phone>
      <!--(home , work , mobile)-->
      <home>919.555.1212</home>
      <work>919.555.1213</work>
      <mobile>919.555.1214</mobile>
    </phone>
  </contact>
</customer>
```

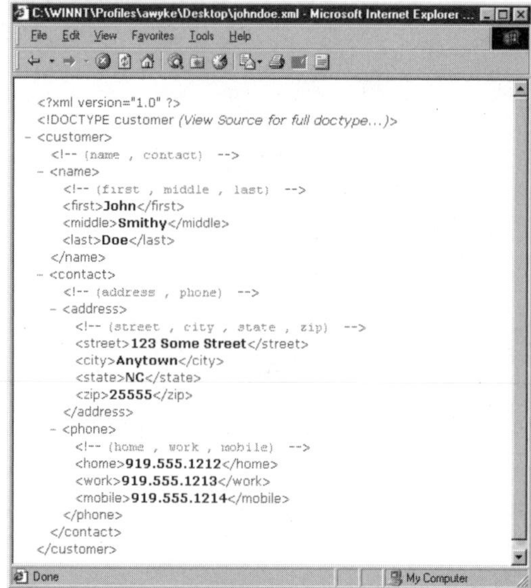

Figure 2-2 Loading our johndoe.xml document in Microsoft Internet Explorer.

Element Attributes

Sometimes an element needs to be annotated by adding additional information. This step is called "adding attributes." This information can be used for a variety of purposes, but most commonly falls within one of the following categories:

- As a distinguishing factor on the type of element
- Additive descriptive information
- Information to be used by the application in processing the data

Attributes are fairly easy to add to schemas and are often shared across elements. The basic syntax for adding attributes is:

```
<!ATTLIST element  name datatype #use >
```

The *element* refers to the element that the attribute should be associated with, while the *name* is the name you give the attribute. In your document instances you will use a *name="value"* pair to assign attribute values.

The *datatype* can be one of three types. It can either be a string (CDATA), a set of tokenized types (ID, IDREF, IDREFS, ENTITY, ENTITIES, NMTOKEN, or NMTOKENS), or enumerated types. The string type can take any literal string, while the tokenized types have varying lexical and semantic constraints. Enumerated types can take one of a list of possible values. If you need a refresher on what the tokenized data types mean, go to *http://www.w3.org/TR/2000/REC-xml-20001006#sec-attribute-types.*

Finally the *#use* is a requirement for specifying if the attribute is required or not. If it is required, this will contain #REQUIRED, and if not, #IMPLIED. Because an element can have more than one attribute, you are able to repeat the name, datatype, and *#use* combination within the same *<!ATTLIST>* instance. To help you understand this, let's create a new version of our customer.dtd schema, called customer_v2.dtd, and add attributes. This new schema will then be used to create instance documents such as johndoe_v2.xml in Listing 2-3

We add a type attribute to our *<customer>* element and define it as an enumerated data type with the option of being either "current" or "past", which will require this attribute to be set. We also add a type attribute to our *<mobile>* element and define it as a string. This will point out how more than one element can have the same attribute name but with a different meaning. Finally we define a tokenized ID type for *<customer>*, which will allow us to identify this element by a character ID, though the attribute is not required.

To create these attributes we need to add the following lines to our schema.

```
<!ATTLIST customer  type  (current | past )  #REQUIRED
                    id   ID  #IMPLIED >
<!ATTLIST mobile  type CDATA  #IMPLIED >
```

As you can see, this is a simple task. You see the names of the elements we created attributes for, the type of attributes they are, and whether they are required or not. You should also notice how our enumeration type attribute for *<customer>* is specified within the parentheses. The | character is a choice, or an OR condition, between the possible values of type.

Listing 2-3 johndoe_v2.xml: An updated document instance supporting our new attributes.

```
<?xml version = "1.0"?>
<!DOCTYPE customer SYSTEM "customer_v2.dtd">
<customer type = "current" id = "abc">
  <name>
    <first>John</first>
    <middle>Smithy</middle>
    <last>Doe</last>
  </name>
  <contact>
    <address>
      <street>123 Some Street</street>
      <city>Anytown</city>
      <state>NC</state>
      <zip>25555</zip>
    </address>
```

(continued)

Listing 2-2 *continued*

```
    <phone>
      <home>919.555.1212</home>
      <work>919.555.1213</work>
      <mobile type = "phone">919.555.1214</mobile>
    </phone>
  </contact>
</customer>
```

Extra Flexibility

As we saw in the previous attribute example, conditions can be imposed on attributes. This functionality is also available in defining elements. You can represent OR statements and specify whether elements are optional or repeatable. Additionally, you can nest items within parentheses to add more flexibility. The lists below contain a list of the characters you should use to define these statements.

Character	Description
?	Optional
+	Repeatable
*	Optional and Repeatable
|	OR

For example, let's create a customer_v3.dtd, building on our second version, which does the following:

- <*middle*> element optional and repeatable
- <*home*> element optional
- <*mobile*> element optional

To create this variation we need to change two lines of code to the following:

```
<!ELEMENT name (first , middle* , last)>
<!ELEMENT phone (home? , work , mobile?)>
```

Now we can create johndoe_v3.xml as shown in Listing 2-4 with two middle names and no home or mobile number, and the document will be valid.

Listing 2-4 johndoe_v3.xml: Changing our example document instance to include two middle names and no home or work number.

```
<?xml version = "1.0" encoding = "UTF-8"?>
<!DOCTYPE customer SYSTEM "customer_v3.dtd">
<customer type = "current" id = "abc">
  <name>
    <first>John</first>
    <middle>Smithy</middle>
    <middle>Anderson</middle>
    <last>Doe</last>
  </name>
  <contact>
    <address>
      <street>123 Some Street</street>
      <city>Anytown</city>
      <state>NC</state>
      <zip>25555</zip>
    </address>
    <phone>
      <work>919.555.1213</work>
    </phone>
  </contact>
</customer>
```

Entities

XML is made of *entities* and parsed or unparsed data. Entities are a single character construct or a collection of named constructs that are referenced in the document. Parsed data is made up of character data or markup and is processed by an XML processor. Unparsed data, on the other hand, is raw text not processed as XML. In this part we look at internal and external entity declarations and how they're referenced in instance documents.

Internal Entities

Internal entities are entities whose content is defined within the current schema. We focus on the definition first and then show you how to reference them.

Suppose you want to define an entity to hold the name of the author of the DTD so that it can be referenced in instance documents without explicitly typing it. The following code would construct this entity. By defining this entity, all an instance document author needs to do is place &dtd-author in the document to reference “R. Allen Wyke”.

Processors and Parsers

We need to clarify the difference between a *processor* and a *parser* (which we will talk about in Chapter 3). A processor is a software module that reads an XML instance document and provides access to its content and structure. The parser is the part of the processor that analyzes the markup and determines the structure of the document data. If it is a validating parser it can also perform a validation of the structure against a DTD.

```
<!ENTITY dtd-author "R. Allen Wyke">
```

This entity instance is not the only type of entity that can be created within a schema and used in an instance document. It is also possible to define a list of elements or attributes as an entity so they can all inherit the same list. The syntax for defining groups of elements under a single name is

```
<!ENTITY % name "elements">
```

Just like in a content model for an element, you can have one or more elements defined in *elements*, and you can impose conditions using the characters listed on page 8. Defining reusable attribute entities, however, is slightly different. For these you must include whole attribute definition, which is accomplished using the *<!ATTLIST>* declaration, like in customer_v2.dtd.

```
<!ATTLIST % name  attrname datatype #use >
                  attrname datatype #use >
```

These attribute-lists entities also differ from attribute lists because they are referenced in the schema, not the instance document. This is accomplished by placing a % in front of the entity name.

To make sure we're all on the same page, let's build customer_v4.dtd on our version 3 schema and define some internal entities. We are going to

- Define a dtd-author entity
- Create an element entity called cus-basic that contains *<name>* and *<contact>*
- Define *<author>*, *<internal>*, and *<external>* elements and define the content model of *<internal>* and *<external>* with %cus-basic
- Replace the current content module of *<customer>* with a choice of *<internal>* or *<external>* AND include an *<author>* element instance

- Define an attribute entity called attr-basic that contains ID and type
- Include %attr-basic list as attributes for *<customer>*, *<internal>*, and *<external>*

The first step is to create the dtd-author entity, which we showed you how to do earlier. Next we need to add an element entity named cus-basic that contains *<name>* and *<contact>* and define three new elements. The content model for *<internal>* and *<external>* should include our newly defined cus-basic. These three steps will require the following additions to our schema.

```
<!ENTITY dtd-author "R. Allen Wyke">
<!ENTITY % cus-basic "name , contact">
<!ELEMENT internal (%cus-basic;)>
<!ELEMENT external (%cus-basic;)>
<!ELEMENT author (#PCDATA)>
```

Next we want to redefine the *<customer>* content model to include a choice of *<internal>* or *<external>* and an *<author>* instance. Following this step we will define an attribute entity list called attr-basic, which contains ID and type, and use it as the only attributes for *<customer>*, *<internal>*, and *<external>*.

```
<!ELEMENT customer ((internal | external) , author)>
<!ENTITY % attr-basic " type CDATA  #IMPLIED
                        id   CDATA  #IMPLIED">
<!ATTLIST customer  %attr-basic; >
<!ATTLIST internal  %attr-basic; >
<!ATTLIST external  %attr-basic; >
```

Figure 2-3 is a visual representation of our completed schema, and the DTD is shown in customer_v4.dtd.

Here is what customer_v4.dtd contains:

```
<?xml version='1.0' encoding='UTF-8' ?>
<!ENTITY % attr-basic " type CDATA  #REQUIRED
                        id   CDATA  #IMPLIED">
<!ENTITY % cus-basic "name , contact">
<!ELEMENT customer ((internal | external) , author)>
<!ATTLIST customer  %attr-basic; >
<!ELEMENT name (first , middle* , last)>
<!ELEMENT contact (address , phone)>
<!ELEMENT address (street , city , state , zip)>
<!ELEMENT phone (home? , work , mobile?)>
<!ELEMENT first (#PCDATA)>
<!ELEMENT middle (#PCDATA)>
<!ELEMENT last (#PCDATA)>
<!ELEMENT street (#PCDATA)>
<!ELEMENT city (#PCDATA)>
<!ELEMENT state (#PCDATA)>
```

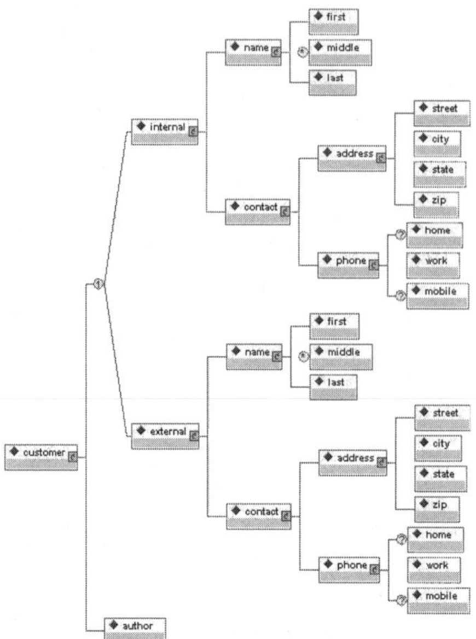

Figure 2-3 A visual representation of our revised schema.

```
<!ELEMENT zip (#PCDATA)>
<!ELEMENT home (#PCDATA)>
<!ELEMENT work (#PCDATA)>
<!ELEMENT mobile (#PCDATA)>
<!ATTLIST mobile  type CDATA  #IMPLIED >
<!ENTITY dtd-author "R. Allen Wyke">
<!ELEMENT internal (%cus-basic;)>
<!ATTLIST internal  %attr-basic; >
<!ELEMENT external (%cus-basic;)>
<!ATTLIST external  %attr-basic; >
<!ELEMENT author (#PCDATA)>
```

Listing 2-5 johndoe_v4.xml: A sample document using the new schema.

```
<?xml version = "1.0"?>
<!DOCTYPE customer SYSTEM "customer_v4.dtd">
<customer type = "current" id = "xyz">
  <internal type = "current" id = "xyz">
    <name>
      <first>John</first>
      <middle>Smithy</middle>
      <middle>Smithy</middle>
      <last>Doe</last>
    </name>
    <contact>
```

```
      <address>
        <street>123 Some Street</street>
        <city>Anytown</city>
        <state>NC</state>
        <zip>25555</zip>
      </address>
      <phone>
        <work>919.555.1213</work>
      </phone>
    </contact>
  </internal>
  <author>&dtd-author;</author>
</customer>
```

Figure 2-4 shows a sample document, johndoe_v4.xml, loaded into Microsoft Internet Explorer. Notice how the parser replaced the entity reference to dtd-author with the string "R. Allen Wyke".

Figure 2-4 The dtd-author entity reference replaced.

External Entities

External entities are what the name implies: entities defined in external files. This file is "imported" using the *<!ENTITY>* declaration and includes a *name*, *identifier* (SYSTEM or PUBLIC), and a *literal* (URI or path), in the form:

```
<!ENTITY name identifier "literal">
```

Although we will not go into much detail about external entities in this chapter, the detail you should note is that this is the method you use to include other elements, like images, schemas, and the like, into your schema.

A good example of how this might be used is if you want to build your schema in modules. If you wanted to include customer_v4.dtd as part of another schema so that it would inherit the data model, you could include the following:

```
<!ENTITY % customer_v4.dtd SYSTEM "customer_v4.dtd">
```

If customer_v4.dtd is not in the current working directory, you need to be sure to include a path to the file. Additionally, if you have stored your schema on a server accessible to your customers or partners, you could replace SYSTEM with PUBLIC and include the URI in the schema.

```
<!ENTITY % customer_v4.dtd PUBLIC
    "http://www.microsoft.com/dtds/customer_v4.dtd">
```

Comments

Comments within your XML schemas and documents are useful and important, as they are in any type of language. Although the ability to create human-readable markup is one of the objectives of XML, sections, elements, attributes, or other items might need more description.

XML follows the syntax HTML uses for comments. They begin with <!-- and end with -->. A few examples follow. In the second example we show how these comments can span multiple lines.

```
<!-- here is a one line comment -->
<!-- here is a comment
     that spans more than one line
-->
```

> **Note** The XML grammar does not allow your comment to end with ---> (three hyphens). This violates the document's requirement to be well-formed, which we discuss at the end of the chapter.

Processing Instructions

Another function of XML is to pass processing instructions within the document. The thought behind this functionality is the ability to remove, as much as possible, any software-specific markup that your schema might require. This prevents any need to include elements and attributes in your schema that do not increase the description of the data, keeping only what it should be used for by the application.

As an example, say you're passing an instance of the customer_v4.dtd schema to an application that will transform the schema into another XML dialect, like a Microsoft BizTalk compatible. Say this application is a Web Service and is accessible through a URL. To include this reference in your schema you could have something like the following, where *dtd2biztalk* is the target name and *href="http://www.microsoft.com/scripts/dtd2biztalk.exe"* is the instruction your application would understand:

```
<?dtd2biztalk
    href="http://www.microsoft.com/scripts/dtd2biztalk.exe?>
```

Document Instances

The XML 1.0 Recommendation states that XML documents can come in two forms: *well-formed* and *valid*. A well-formed document is generally more flexible, or less strict, than a valid one. As we will discuss in the next section, this type of document needs only to have the proper beginning and ending tags as well as proper nesting to be considered an XML document. Valid documents, on the other hand, must conform in accordance to the referenced DTD. You should understand both types because both are acceptable in XML.

Well-Formed Documents

Well-formed XML conforms to the Recommendation by fulfilling several requirements:

- There can be only one root element.
- All open elements must be properly closed (that is, if a start tag is present, there should be an end tag, or if the element is empty, it should be appropriately tagged as such).
- Any nested elements should be ended in correct order.

The first requirement is a simple one: there can be only one root element. For instance, if the two-roots.xml document in Listing 2-6 was building off the customer_v4.dtd schema, it would not be well formed.

Listing 2-6 two-roots.xml: A well-formed XML document with only one root element.

```
<?xml version = "1.0"?>
<!DOCTYPE customer SYSTEM "customer_v4.dtd">
<!-- being the root element -->
<customer type = "current" id = "xyz">
  <internal type = "current" id = "xyz">
    <name>
      <first>John</first>
      <middle>Smithy</middle>
      <middle>Smithy</middle>
      <last>Doe</last>
    </name>
    <contact>
      <address>
        <street>123 Some Street</street>
        <city>Anytown</city>
        <state>NC</state>
        <zip>25555</zip>
      </address>
      <phone>
        <work>919.555.1213</work>
      </phone>
    </contact>
  </internal>
  <author>&dtd-author;</author>
</customer>
<customer type = "past" id = "xyz">
  <external type = "past" id = "xyz">
    <name>
      <first>Jane</first>
      <last>Doe</last>
    </name>
    <contact>
      <address>
        <street>123 Some Street</street>
        <city>Anytown</city>
        <state>NC</state>
        <zip>25555</zip>
      </address>
      <phone>
        <work>919.555.1220</work>
      </phone>
    </contact>
  </external>
  <author>&dtd-author;</author>
</customer>
```

Figure 2-5 shows the error reported by Internet Explorer 5.5, which contains an XML parser that will check for a well-formed (but not valid) document. As you can see, this document is not well formed because it has two instances of the *<customer>* element and no single governing root element.

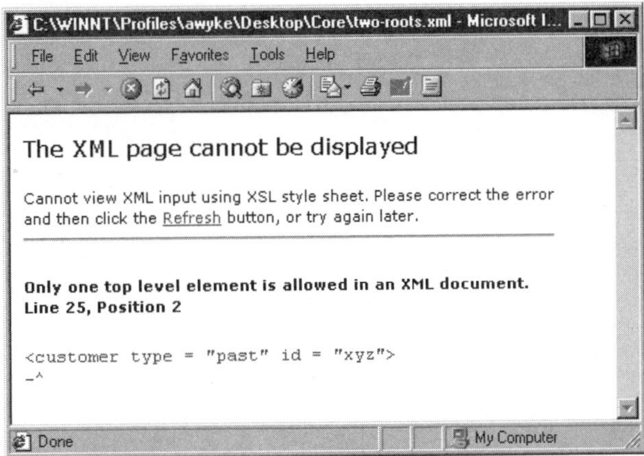

Figure 2-5 The error reported by Internet Explorer 5.5 because the document has multiple root elements.

The second requirement is that all open elements should be properly closed. If we build on the same example but remove the second instance of *<customer>* and leave off our ending *</customer>* element, we again violate the rules for a well-formed document. To demonstrate, we will load the example in Listing 2-7, missing-closing.xml, into Internet Explorer 5.5.

Listing 2-7 missing-closing.xml: Missing the closing *</customer>* tag and therefore not well formed.

```
<?xml version = "1.0"?>
<!DOCTYPE customer SYSTEM "customer_v4.dtd">
<customer type = "current" id = "xyz">
  <internal type = "current" id = "xyz">
    <name>
      <first>John</first>
      <middle>Smithy</middle>
      <last>Doe</last>
    </name>
    <contact>
      <address>
        <street>123 Some Street</street>
```

(continued)

Listing 2-7 *continued*

```
        <city>Anytown</city>
        <state>NC</state>
        <zip>25555</zip>
      </address>
      <phone>
        <work>919.555.1213</work>
      </phone>
    </contact>
  </internal>
  <author>&dtd-author;</author>
```

Because Internet Explorer 5.5 contains a parser that validates whether documents are well formed, loading the previous document results in the error shown in Figure 2-6. Do not worry about parsers at this point. They will be covered in detail in Chapter 3.

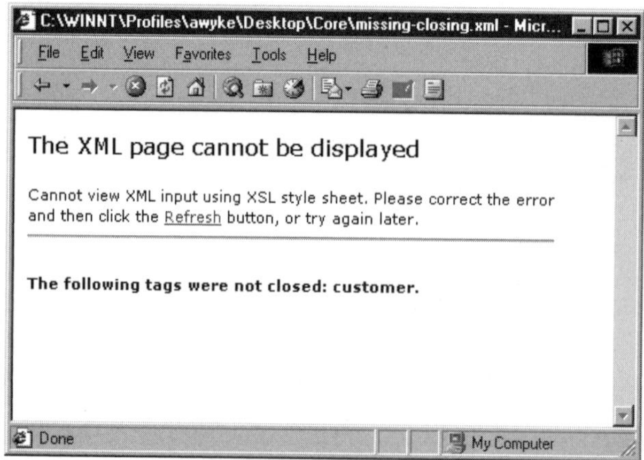

Figure 2-6 Internet Explorer generating an error because an ending tag is missing.

The last requirement of a well-formed document is that any nesting of elements must occur in the proper format. For this example we will use XHTML because improper nesting of HTML elements was commonly accepted until the release of XHTML. In nested-error.html, shown in Listing 2-8, the <*strong*> element improperly ends before the <*em*> element.

Well-formed documents have few requirements for conforming to XML 1.0, but they can be useful and helpful in your projects. However, because much of your work will also demand a specific element structure, as well as any required attributes or elements, you might need documents that are not only well formed, but valid as well.

Listing 2-8 nested-error.html: Incorrectly ending the *<strong>* element before the nested *<em>* element.

```
<!DOCTYPE html PUBLIC "-//W3C//DTD XHTML 1.0 Transitional//EN"
  "http://www.w3.org/TR/xhtml1/DTD/xhtml1-transitional.dtd">
<html xmlns="http://www.w3.org/1999/xhtml" lang="en"
      xml:lang="en">
<head>
  <title>Core XML</title>
</head>
<body>
<p>
  Sometimes you <strong>really <em>need</strong></em>
  to make sure you do the right thing.
</p>
</body>
</html>
```

Valid and Non-Valid Documents

The second way to verify XML documents is to compare their structure to a governing DTD or schema. A DTD or schema can define everything from the structure of the document to the data types, required attributes, and other requirements for how elements and attributes can be included in the document.

If any part of the document does not conform to the referenced DTD, it is not a valid document. This method of verifying documents is most often used in industry standards or application-to-application communication. These types of environments demand that the documents they exchange conform to a specific model, because without such a requirement the risk of processing invalid data is high and could adversely affect the entire system.

Using the customer_v4.dtd schema, we impose the requirement that the *<customer>* element should contain a type attribute value of either current or previous. If we exclude this value, as we did in johndoe_v5.xml, and run the document through a parser, checking only to see if the document is well formed, the document will be processed without any warning or error.

```
<?xml version = "1.0" encoding = "UTF-8"?>
<!DOCTYPE customer SYSTEM "customer.dtd">
<customer id="xyz">
    <name>
        <first>John</first>
            <middle>Smithy</middle>
        <last>Doe</last>
    </name>
    <address>
```

```
            <line1>123 Some Street</line1>
            <line2>P.O. Box 555</line2>
            <city>Anytown</city>
            <state>NC</state>
            <zip>55555</zip>
        </address>
        <phone>
            <home>5551212</home>
            <work>5551213</work>
        </phone>
        <online>
            <email>john@doe.com</email>
            <url>http://www.doe.com</url>
        </online>
    </customer>
```

However, if we ran the same example through a parser checking for validity, such as Xerces from the Apache group (*http://xml.apache.org*), we get an error complaining that the required type attribute is not included.

Moving Forward

Although this book focuses on the overall use of XML and not XML syntax, we've covered many important details in this chapter. We have essentially gone through a crash course on the XML language, and we have pointed out some of the details we will be using in later chapters. Our overall objective here was to refresh the memory of you experienced XML developers, while at the same time providing a baseline for those of you new to the language.

At this point we are ready to jump into implementing XML within a large enterprise environment. The first step in this process is to determine the parser you want to use, and therefore the parsing method, which will be covered in Chapter 3.

3

Parsing XML Documents

Using XML to solve integration and implementation problems is not as easy as defining a data model and creating instance documents. What will you do with these documents after you create them? How will you read them into your application or database for processing? Part of using XML as a solution involves an XML processor, which is the application responsible for processing these documents. One function of this processor, and the focus of this chapter, is parsing documents. The parser is responsible for parsing the XML document and verifying it by checking for well-formedness or by validating it against a schema. If these tasks are performed successfully, the data contained within the document is exposed in a method that makes it available for other manipulations.

Parsing is not always as simple as just reading through an XML document and verifying it for ASCII text. The structure and rules of your governing DTD can be verified when processing these instance documents if yours is a validating parser. You need this parsing application to evaluate the instance document and determine if it's valid and then make it available for secondary applications to utilize the data contained therein.

In this chapter we'll review what an XML parser does, examine the different models used to process XML documents, and introduce how XML can be manipulated using objects within the .NET Framework. By the end of the chapter you should have a good understanding of when to use which processing model, as well as which parser will best fit your needs.

So, what is *parsing*? According to *http://www.dictionary.com,* it's defined as follows:

1. To break (a sentence) down into its component parts of speech with an explanation of the form, function, and syntactical relationship of each part
2. To describe (a word) by stating its part of speech, form, and syntactical relationships in a sentence
3. To examine closely or subject to detailed analysis, especially by breaking up into components: "What are we missing by parsing the behavior of chimpanzees into the conventional categories recognized largely from our own behavior?" (Stephen Jay Gould)
4. To make sense of; comprehend: I simply couldn't parse what you just said
5. Computer Science. To analyze or separate (input, for example) into more easily processed components

Parsing is an essential task for any application that uses language-based data or code as input. XML processors, which rely heavily on parsers, provide a standard mechanism for navigating and manipulating XML documents. If you have an XML document and need to get data out of it, change the data, or modify the XML document structure, you don't need to write code to load the XML file, validate it for specific characters and elements, and process this information accordingly. You can use an XML parser instead, which will load the document and give you access to its contents in the form of objects.

What Does an XML Parser Do?

Parsing a language refers to the process of taking a piece of code or data written in that language and breaking it into component parts as defined by the rules of that language. XML parsers are classified along two independent dimensions: validating vs. nonvalidating and stream based vs. tree based.

Validating and Non-Validating Parsers

A *validating* parser can use a DTD or schema to verify that a document is properly constructed according to the rules for the XML application it's an instance of, and it is supposed to complain loudly if the rules aren't followed. A DTD can also specify default values for the attributes of various elements, and a validating parser can fill them in when it encounters elements with no attributes listed. This capabililty can be important when you're processing XML documents you've received from the outside world. For example, if vendors send XML-marked invoices to your company, you'll want to ensure that they contain the right elements in the right order.

A *non-validating* parser only requires that the document be well-formed. Because of the design of XML, it's possible to parse well-formed documents without referring to a DTD or XSD schema. Additional information for being well-formed, which was discussed in Chapter 2, can be found in the XML 1.0 Recommendation *(http://www.w3.org/TR/2000/REC-xml-20001006)*.

Non-validating parsers are simpler, and many of the free parsers available over the Web are non-validating. They are usually adequate for processing XML documents generated within the same organization or documents whose validity constraints are so complex that they can't be expressed by a DTD and need to be verified by application logic instead.

Stream-Based and Tree-Based Parsers

A parser can make the components of an XML document known to an application in two ways. It can read through the document and signal the application every time a new component appears, or it can read the entire document and give the application a tree structure corresponding to the element structure of the document. Parsers that use the first method are called *stream-based* or *event-driven* parsers. Parsers that use the second method are *tree-based* parsers. Both methods will be discussed in greater detail later.

You'll hear two common terms regarding these methods: Simple API for XML (SAX) and the Document Object Model (DOM). SAX is a standard developed informally by members of the xml-dev mailing list for how a stream-based parser should "talk" to an application (see *http://www.megginson.com/SAX/index.html*). The DOM is a formal Recommendation of the W3C on how an application can access and manipulate the tree structure of a document (for an example see *http://www.w3.org/TR/1998/REC-DOM-Level-1-19981001* where the first edition is referred to as Level 1).

Tree-Based Parsing with the DOM

The DOM API defines a minimal set of language and platform-independent interfaces for accessing and manipulating the content and structure of information stored in XML documents. In this section we will cover DOM's major interfaces and briefly touch on the minor ones.

In tree-based parsing with the DOM the document is checked to see if it is well-formed and valid, depending on the type of parser. The parser then converts the document's information into a tree of nodes. The entire document, no matter how simple or complex, is converted into a tree that starts from one root node, which, in DOM terms, is called a *document* object instance (hence *Document* Object Model). Once a document object tree is created, access to the elements allows you to modify, delete, and create leaves and branches by using the interfaces in the API.

We are using Titles.xml as the example XML file during this discussion. This file, shown in Listing 3-1, presents a collection of books based on the sample pubs database that comes with Microsoft SQL Server.

Listing 3-1 Titles.xml: A sample XML document.

```
<?xml version="1.0" encoding="UTF-8"?>
<BookList>
    <Book>
      <book_id>BU1111</book_id>
      <title>Cooking with Computers: Surreptitious Balance Sheets</title>
      <type>business</type>
      <pub_id>1389</pub_id>
      <price>11.95</price>
      <advance>5000</advance>
      <royalty>10</royalty>
      <ytd_sales>3876</ytd_sales>
      <notes>Helpful hints on how to use your electronic...</notes>
      <pubdate>1991-06-09T05:00:00</pubdate>
    </Book>
    <Book>
      <book_id>BU7832</book_id>
      <title>Straight Talk About Computers</title>
      <type>business</type>
      <pub_id>1389</pub_id>
      <price>19.99</price>
      <advance>5000</advance>
      <royalty>10</royalty>
      <ytd_sales>4095</ytd_sales>
      <notes>Annotated analysis of what computers can do for you</notes>
      <pubdate>1991-06-22T05:00:00</pubdate>
    </Book>
</BookList>
```

Figure 3-1 is a visual representation of how Titles.xml can be represented as a tree of nodes.

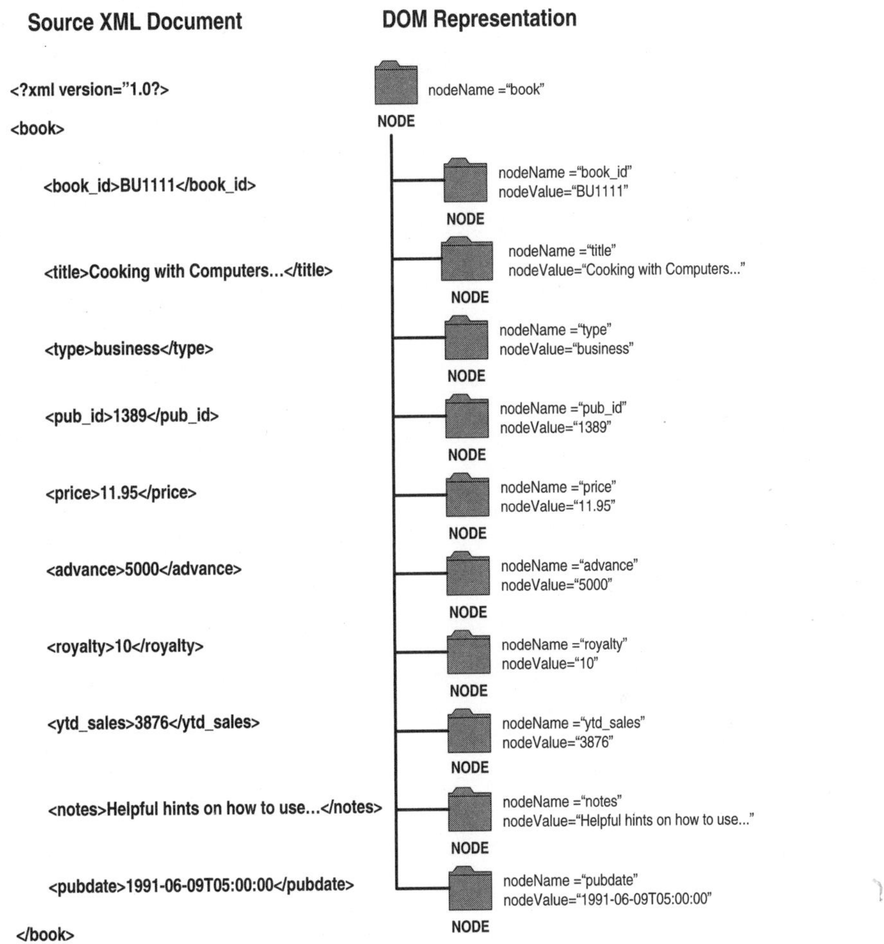

Figure 3-1 A DOM hierarchy representation of Titles.xml.

Everything is a node in the *Document* object tree. These nodes might have child nodes or hold information like its tag name (*nodeName*) and value (*nodeValue*). This hierarchical organization of information is similar to a file system, where folders might contain files or other folders, except everything descends from one root folder.

Important Interfaces in the DOM

The DOM provides interfaces in its hierarchy of *Node* objects. The interfaces either have child nodes that contain other nodes or are leaf nodes that do not contain anything after them in the document structure. Some types of child or leaf nodes are *Node*, *Element*, and *NodeList*, all of which are interfaces in the DOM.

Node

An XML *Document* object created after a DOM parser reads an XML file often contains a tree-like representation of *Node* objects instances, while other interfaces are provided to create a more object-oriented environment. You can manipulate all the information in the DOM by using the *Node* interface. Even though the DOM Recommendation specifically states that it isn't necessarily a tree, for the purposes of the discussions in this chapter and the examples therein we will focus on the tree-like representations. Figure 3-2 shows the inheritance relationships between some of the important interfaces.

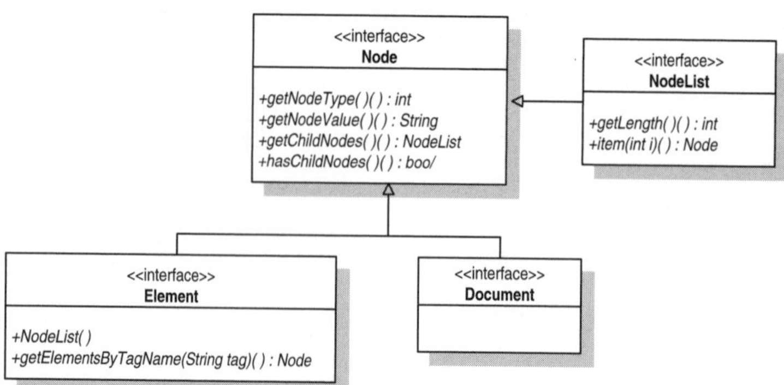

Figure 3-2 DOM interfaces and inheritance relationships.

Because the *Document* object is a subclass of *Node*, the root *Node* object of the tree is also a *Document* object. Every DOM object must have a root. Figure 3-3 illustrates a sample XML *Document* object tree and describes some of the *Node* objects that it contains.

You can find out if a *Node* has children by using the *hasChildNodes()* method. This method, which takes no parameters, returns a Boolean true if the node has children and false if not.

The *getNodeType()* method, which is part of the Java bindings defined by DOM, is another important method of *Node*. It returns the type of a particular *Node*. The type is a constant integer used to identify different types of *Nodes*.

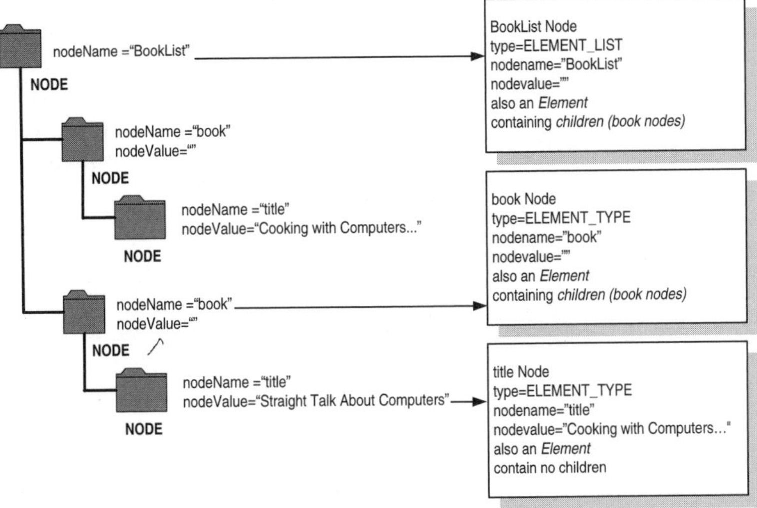

Figure 3-3 A *Document* object, where everything in the DOM is a *Node*.

For example, the *Node.ELEMENT_NODE* type identifies a *Node* to be an element. Table 3-1 contains a list of the other methods available for the *Node* object as well.

Table 3-1 Other Methods of the *Node* Object

Method	Description
appendChild()	Adds a new child object, which is passed to the method, to the current *Node*.
cloneNode()	Returns a duplicate of the *Node*.
hasAttributes()	Returns a Boolean true if the *Node* has any attributes. This method was added in DOM Level 2.
insertBefore()	Takes a new child *Node* and a reference child *Node* and inserts the new child *Node* before the reference *Node*.
isSupported()	Tests whether or not this implementation of the DOM supports a specific feature. This method was added in DOM Level 2 and takes a version number and a feature as parameters.

(continued)

Table 3-1 Other Methods of the *Node* Object *(continued)*

Method	Description
normalize()	Puts all text nodes in the full depth of the sub-tree underneath this *Node*.
removeChild()	Removes the specified child.
replaceChild()	Replaces the specified child with the new child passed.

Element

The *Element* interface, which is a subclass of *Node*, is another important interface. It can be used to access the elements in a DOM *Document* object tree, which allows you to read in attributes and their values, as well as change, delete, or add to them. Table 3-2 contains the list of methods of the *Element* object.

Table 3-2 Methods of the *Element* Object

Method	Description
getAttribute()	Retrieves the specified attribute.
getAttributeNS()	Retrieves the specified attribute by local name and namespace. This method was added in Level 2.
getAttributeNode()	Retrieves an *Attr* node by name.
getAttributeNodeNS()	Retrieves an *Attr* node by local name and namespace. This method was added in Level 2.
getElementsByTagName()	Returns a *NodeList* of all child elements of a given tag name in the order in which they are encountered.
getElementsByTagNameNS()	Returns a *NodeList* of all child elements of a given tag by local name and namespace in the order in which they are encountered. This method was added in Level 2.
hasAttribute()	Returns a Boolean true if the specified attribute is present. Returns Boolean false otherwise.
hasAttributeNS()	Returns a Boolean true if the specified attribute, by local name and namespace, is present. Returns Boolean false otherwise. This method was added in Level 2.

Table 3-2 Methods of the *Element* Object *(continued)*

Method	Description
removeAttribute()	Removes the specified attribute.
removeAttributeNS()	Removes the attribute specified by local name and namespace. This method was added in Level 2.
removeAttributeNode()	Removes the specified *Attr* node.
setAttribute()	Adds a new attribute. If an attribute of the same name exists, its value is changed to the specified value.
setAttributeNS()	Adds a new attribute. If an attribute of the same local name and namespace exists, its value is changed to the specified value. This method was added in Level 2.
setAttributeNode()	Adds a new *Attr* node. If an *Attr* node of the same name exists, its value is changed to the specified value.
setAttributeNodeNS()	Adds a new *Attr* node. If an *Attr* node of the same local name and namespace exists, its value is changed to the specified value. This method was added in Level 2.

NodeList

Some methods of the *Node* interface allow traversal of a *Node* tree. The *getChildNodes()* method is useful for gathering all the elements inside a *Node*. This method returns all *Node*s, if they exist, in a container for *Node* objects. *NodeList* is an iterator for a list of *Node*s. Figure 3-4 illustrates a *NodeList*.

Unlike *Node* and *Element*, *NodeList* has only a single method, *item()*. This method returns the *Node* located at the indexed position passed to the method. For instance, if you want to retrieve the first *Node*, you call the method using *item(0)*.

Other DOM Interfaces

Node, *Element*, and *NodeList* are not the only interfaces specified by the DOM. Because we do not cover all of them, we've included a list in Table 3-3 along with any children interfaces they have and a brief description. This table contains only those interfaces found in the DOM Level 1 and 2 Core and does not contain the HTML bindings.

Table 3-3 DOM Interfaces

Interface	Children	Description
Attr	Text, EntityReference	Represents an attribute of an *Element* object.
CDATASection	Contains no children	Used to escape characters of text that would otherwise be considered markup.
Comment	Contains no children	Stores the content of an XML or HTML comment.
Document	*Element* (max. of one), *ProcessingInstruction, Comment, DocumentType* (max. of one)	Represents the entire XML or HTML document.
DocumentFrag-ment	Element, ProcessingIn-struction, Comment, Text, CDATASection, EntityReference	A minimal *Document* object instance.
DocumentType	Contains no children	Represents the document type stored in the *doctype* attribute of the *Docu-ment* object instance.
Element	Element, Text, Comment, ProcessingInstruction, CDATASection, EntityReference	Represents an element in an XML or HTML document.
Entity	Element, ProcessingIn-struction, Comment, Text, CDATASection, EntityReference	Represents an entity, whether it's parsed or unparsed.
EntityReference	Element, ProcessingIn-struction, Comment, Text, CDATASection, EntityReference	Can be inserted into a structured model when an the entity reference is in the source document or when you want to insert a reference.
Notation	Contains no children	Represents a notation declared in a DTD.
ProcessingIn-struction	Contains no children	Used to represent a "processing instruction."
Text	Contains no children	Contains textual content (character data).

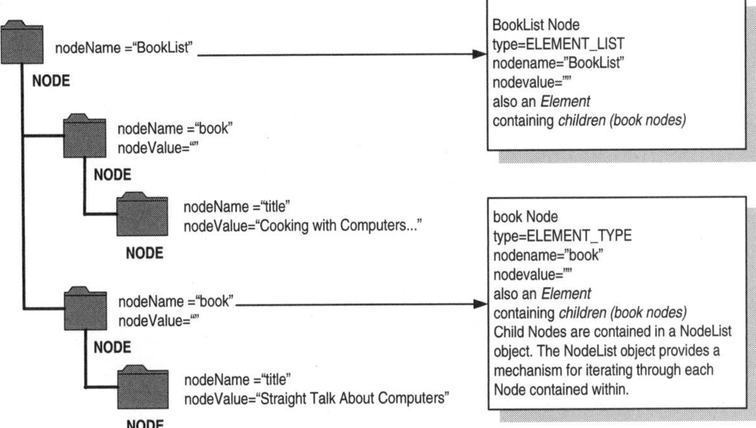

Figure 3-4 A DOM NodeList Object.

Stream-Based Parsing with SAX

One of the major disadvantages of the DOM is how it processes large files. Because the DOM requires the entire file to be read in by the parser, memory can constrain the performance of your applications, if not render them useless. SAX parsers solve this problem by streaming in the document according to specific events. In this section we cover the behavior of a SAX parser and how to use one.

The Behavior of a SAX Parser

Unlike the DOM, which creates a tree-based representation, SAX doesn't have a default object model. When you use a SAX parser and read in a document, you will not be given a default object model. These parsers only read in your XML document and fire events based on the following:

- Open or start of elements
- Closing or end of elements
- *#PCDATA* and *CDATA* sections
- Processing instructions, comments, and entity declarations

Three Steps to Using SAX

The three steps to using SAX in your applications are

1. Creating a custom object model, like a Book class
2. Creating a SAX parser
3. Creating a document handler to turn your document into instances of your custom object model

Because SAX does not come with a default object model representation for the data in your XML document, you need to create your own the first time you use this method. The model could be something as simple as creating a *Book* class if your XML document is an address book.

After your custom model is created to hold your data in your application, the next step is creating a "document handler" to initialize instances of your object models from the document. This document handler is a listener for the various events we listed that are fired by the SAX parser. Most of the work involved in using SAX is in creating these document handlers.

As the SAX parser reads a document, events are fired based on all the "registered" document event listeners and translated into method calls on your document handler implementation. The document handler must then do something useful with these method calls.

Figure 3-5 shows the sequence of method calls the SAX parser makes on your document handler implementation. You can see from this picture how the SAX parser exposes the document as a series of events that are translated into method calls in your document handler implementation.

Choosing a Parsing Method

You should choose your parser depending on the nature of the processing and the size of the XML documents. A tree-based parser usually needs to load the entire document into memory, so it can be impractical because of physical constraints on memory when processing documents like dictionaries or large databases. With a stream-based parser you can skip over elements that you aren't interested in (for example, when looking up a particular word in a dictionary). If your application needs to process certain elements in relation to other elements, however, a tree-based parser is much easier to work with. It's worth noting that a tree-based parser can be built on top of a stream-based parser and that the output of a tree-based parser can be "walked" to provide a stream-based interface to an application. In this section we cover the DOM and

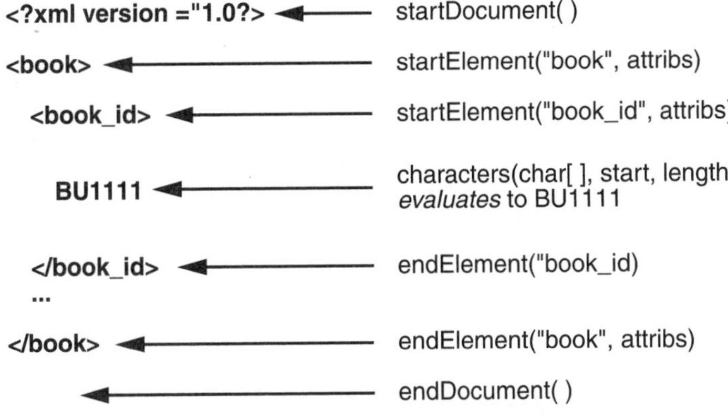

Figure 3-5 A SAX Event Order.

SAX parsing methods and provide example scenarios in which you can decide which method is appropriate for a given task.

> **Note** The term "walked" refers to taking pieces of the document and sending them out in parts. You are traversing, or walking, the document objective model.

The DOM Method

DOM implementations are currently biased toward in-memory storage of the document, but this may change as Persistent DOM (PDOM) implementations become more popular. Even with memory limitations, however, DOM certainly has a place because of features that help it access and manipulate documents. The following are DOM benefits you should focus on:

- It allows random access to the document.
- Complex searches can be easily implemented.
- The DTD or schema is available.
- The DOM is read/write.

The first two benefits are the ability to randomly access the document and create complex searches. These provide a means for searching for elements and retrieving information, such as data and attributes, on these elements. The DOM can also be bound to an XML DTD or schema, which means it can be checked to make sure the data contained in the document is valid according to the rules of the DTD or schema. Finally it provides the ability to read data out of a document and write data to it.

The DOM's simplicity, powerful access to the document, and a well-defined specification make it a popular parser method. It also pairs well with XSLT and other document-transformation solutions you might require. Therefore, if your project is small and you need to complete it quickly, using a DOM-based method is a great choice. However, if you are going to process large files and have the time to write a more robust application, you should look into a SAX-based implementation.

The SAX Method

If you need to parse and process huge XML documents, SAX implementations offer some benefits over DOM-based ones. You should first ask yourself, however, if an improved design would remove the need for large documents. For example, prefiltering in a database that can stream XML might suit your needs. By going with SAX, however, you can enforce options for document manipulation by using XSLT and requiring your team to write code to internally manage, store, and rewrite the document.

Like the DOM, SAX has a particular set of benefits. The following list contains some of the most useful:

1. It can parse files of any size.
2. You can build your own data structure.
3. You can access only a small subset of the information if you desire.
4. It is fast.

The biggest advantage of SAX is, arguably, its ability to process files of any size. The way the parser streams data in and out (exposes data) allows it to handle files of any size. SAX is also useful when you want to build your own data structure and allows you to grab only subsets of the information in a given document. Finally it can be a fast method of processing documents, especially when parsing large files.

SAX is best suited to sequential-scan applications when you want to go through the XML document quickly from start to finish. Also, sometimes you won't need the overhead of the full-blown DOM, so a SAX parser will be sufficient for creating a lightweight and compact internal data structure.

Example Scenarios

To help you choose a method we included a few example scenarios. While processing and using XML documents is more widely adopted every day, many lessons have gone unnoticed because of lack of experience. These scenarios should help by allowing you to walk down a decision path and choose the right approach. With these benefits in mind, review the following scenarios and determine which parser is appropriate for each one.

Scenario 1

Company XYZ currently has 20,000 employees. The Human Resources data file is currently stored in XML format, and you are to write an application that returns the average annual salary of all employees.

If you use the DOM interface your application will need to load the entire employee database into memory and retrieve the *document.employee[i].annual_salary[0]* value for each employee, and then average the values.

Using the SAX approach you could write an event handler that looks for only the *<annual_salary>* element and ignores everything else. You could parse through the file systematically and efficiently. The solution in this scenario is clear: SAX makes one pass through a large file and looks for specific data.

Scenario 2

Company ABC has 375 employees. The Human Resources data file is stored in XML format, and you are to write an application that allows users to scroll through the list of employees and find detailed information on an employee.

If you tried this with the SAX approach you would either have to parse through the XML document every time you wanted to display information to the user, which is inefficient, or you would have to build your own memory structure so that you could parse it once and then access it multiple times. You'd need to keep track of all the information yourself and develop and maintain the code required to support this data storage scheme.

By using the DOM you have access to the entire employee database as nodes in a tree. The data storage mechanism and the code that supports it is essentially provided by the parser. This is a much easier solution!

Scenario 3

If we return to the first scenario, let's say you're asked to modify your application to give 7 percent raises to those employees below the company average and 4 percent to those above it.

Your application would need to be parsed with the DOM. SAX does not support modification of data. Even if it did, as an event-based parser it would be difficult to write two sets of event handlers: one to calculate the average and one to update the data as it's parsed for the second time.

Available Parsers

Now that you've seen the two main parsing methods, let's talk about a few of the parsers you can use for processing, in particular Microsoft's MSXML, the Apache Group's Xerces, and a few others. Each of these comes as a library that can be added to applications, such as a server that can accept XML documents via HTTP posts, or is part of existing applications.

MSXML

The first parser, which can perform both SAX and DOM-based parsing, is Microsoft's MSXML. This parser, which is currently at version 3.0, supports several standards and can handle most of your parsing needs. Some of the supported standards include

- XSLT
- XML Path Language (XPath)
- SAX2

MSXML is available as a Microsoft Windows library file (DLL) that can be embedded into applications for processing. The first version of this parser appeared in Microsoft Internet Explorer 4 and late versions of Windows 95. You should know what version of the parser you are using because different versions support different standards. For this reason, we included Table 3-4, which contains the parser version, filename, and file version.

In addition to these library files, Microsoft also embedded its parser in several of its applications. Table 3-5 provides a list of these applications, their corresponding Internet Explorer versions, if applicable, and the MSXML version.

Beginning with the beta release of MSXML 3.0, the installation of the msxml3 DLL was performed in a "side-by-side" mode—the original, older version was left intact. Additionally, Microsoft Internet Explorer and Microsoft Windows 95 and later versions would continue using the older parser library.

To upgrade your system to utilize the version 3.0 library, it's necessary to run the xmlinst.exe application that can be downloaded from the Microsoft Download Center *(http://msdn.microsoft.com/downloads/default.asp?URL=/code/sample.asp?url=/msdn-files/027/001/469/msdncompositedoc.xml)*. The application, when passed the appropriate arguments, will remove the registry entries for the older parser and replace them with the version 3.0 entries, thereby updating the system.

Table 3-4 MSXML Versions

Parser Version	File Name	File Version
1.0	msxml DLL	4.71.1712.5
1.0a	msxml DLL	4.72.2106.4
1.0 Service Pack 1 (SP1)	msxml DLL	4.72.3110.0
2.0	msxml DLL	5.0.2014.0206
2.0a	msxml DLL	5.0.2314.1000
2.0b	msxml DLL	5.0.2614.3500
2.5 Beta 2	msxml DLL	5.0.2919.38
2.5a	msxml DLL	5.0.2919.6303
2.5	msxml DLL	5.0.2920.0
2.5 Service Pack 1 (SP1)	msxml DLL	8.0.5226
2.6 January 2000 Web Release	msxml2 DLL (January Web Release)	7.50.4920.0
2.6 Beta 2	msxml2 DLL	8.0.5207.3
2.6	msxml2 DLL	8.0.6518.1
3.0 March 2000 Web Release	msxml3 DLL (March Web Release)	7.50.5108.0
3.0 May 2000 Web Release	msxml3 DLL (May Web Release)	8.0.7309.3
3.0 July 2000 Web Release	msxml3 DLL (July Web Release)	8.0.7520.1
3.0 September 2000 Web Release	msxml3 DLL (September Web Release)	8.0.7728.0
3.0 Release	msxml3 DLL	8.0.7820.0

Table 3-5 XML Versions Shipped with Microsoft Products

Application	Internet Explorer	MSXML Version
Not applicable	Internet Explorer 4.0	1.0
Windows 95, OEM Service Release 2.5	Internet Explorer 4.0a	1.0a
Not applicable	Internet Explorer 4.01, Service Pack 1 (SP1), or Internet Explorer 5.0	2.0
Microsoft Office 2000	Internet Explorer 5.0a	2.0a
Windows 98, Second Edition	Internet Explorer 5.0b	2.0b
Windows 95, Windows 98, or Windows NT 4.0	Internet Explorer 5.01	2.5a
Windows 2000	Internet Explorer 5.01	2.5
Windows 2000	Internet Explorer 5.01, Service Pack 1 (SP1)	2.5 Service Pack 1 (SP1)
Windows 95, Windows 98, Windows NT 4, Windows 2000, or Windows 2000 Service Pack 1 (SP1)	Internet Explorer 5.5	2.5 Service Pack 1 (SP1)
Microsoft SQL Server 2000, Beta 2		2.6 Beta 2
SQL Server 2000		2.6
Microsoft BizTalk Server (technology preview and beta)		2.6

Embedding MSXML in Your Applications

After getting MSXML installed you'll want to start using it in your applications. This section covers how to use MSXML from Microsoft Visual Basic, starting with DOM and then SAX2. The DOM example code will build the tree in memory and will then access nodes in the memory structure. The SAX2 example responds to events while the XML document is parsed.

Using DOM

By choosing DOM you assume that you won't have any problem storing the entire XML tree in memory. You will also be able to make changes to the XML and save those as a file. In this example you will create a simple DOM object that catalogs the salaries of all the employees and gives everyone a 4 percent raise. The XML code is as follows:

```
<payroll>
<employee>
<last_name>Smith</last_name>
<first_name>John</first_name>
<salary>60000</salary>
<performance>Excellent</performance>
<title>Accounts Payable Manager</title>
   </employee>
</payroll>
```

First you'll need to instantiate the DOM Document object.

```
Dim xmlDoc As DOMDocument
Set xmldoc = New DOMDocument
xmldoc.validateOnParse = True
xmldoc.async = False
```

The first two statements probably look straightforward. The third statement asks the parser to validate the document when it's parsed. The last statement declares that the document shouldn't be loaded asynchronously. This means that you don't have to worry about whether the XML is fully loaded before you attempt to read and manipulate the code.

Now that you've created the object, load the XML. You can do this by loading a URL, a local file, or the XML text itself. This *load()* method will take either a URL or a path as its argument. This code snippet loads the XML from the intranet.

```
xmldoc.load("http://my.intra.net/salary.xml")
```

To load the XML directly you use the *xmldoc.loadXML()* method.

```
xmldoc.loadXML("<payroll><employee><last_name>Smith
</last_name><first_name>John</first_name><salary>60000</salary>
<performance>Excellent</performance><title>Accounts Payable Manager
</title></employee></payroll>")
```

For our example it doesn't make any sense to use the *loadXML()* method because we can access the data URL. However, remember that XML makes a good data structure for your internal programming needs. If another part of your application system needs to store some data in a tree structure, it might be efficient for it to generate XML and pass it to you as a string. Afterward you would load it into your *DOMDocument* using *loadXML*.

Now that you have the *DOMDocument* created and loaded with real data, you can start giving people raises. The first step is to set up a loop to iterate through all the nodes. In this example you need to locate the salary nodes and increase the value by 4 percent.

```
Set ElemList = xmldoc.getElementsByTagName("SALARY")
  For i=0 To (ElemList.length -1)
ElemList.item(1).text=Str$(Val(ElemList.item(1).text)*1.04)
  Next
```

With the salary increases in place, the next step is to write the new XML out to disk by using the following code:

```
xmldoc.save("NewSalary.xml")
```

You may not want to give everyone the same raise. In the following example, employees who perform at an "Excellent" level are the only ones who will get raises. The *getNodes()* method takes advantage of Extensible Stylesheet Language (XSL) patterns, which are covered in more detail later in the book.

```
Set ElemList = xmldoc.getNodes("PAYROLL/EMPLOYEE[PERFORMANCE=
'EXCELLENT']")
  For i=0 To (ElemList.length -1)
ElemList.item(1).text=Str$(Val(ElemList.item(1).text)*1.04)
  Next
```

Using SAX

In the previous example you were able to read all of your data in memory and you were also able to manipulate the data and save a new XML file. If you're using SAX, you probably aren't able to store all of the data in memory and you loose the ability to save the data. This section covers how to use the SAX interface of MSXML by writing a content handler. The content handler will be fired when a particular node is encountered.

For this example you'll use the same XML file as before. Instead of giving people raises, your code will calculate the total payroll for your company. The first step is creating a class that implements the *IVBSAXContentHandler* interface. This can be done with Microsoft Visual Basic 6 as follows:

1. Download and install MSXML if it isn't already installed.
2. Create a new project (for these examples, create a standard .EXE).
3. In the "Available Resources" list, select Microsoft XML version 3.
4. Create a new class and select *IVBSAXContentHandler* from the interface's drop-down list.

This example implements two methods: *startElement()* and *characters()*. When the opening salary tag is encountered, a Boolean is set so that when the next characters call is made, the salary value is grabbed and added to the total.

```
Option Explicit

Implements IVBSAXContentHandler

Dim total As Integer
Dim salaryTag As Boolean
Total = 0
SalaryTag=False
Private Sub IVBSAXContentHandler_startElement(strNamespaceURI As_
  String,_strLocalName As String, strQName As String, ByVal attributes
As_
  MSXML2.IVBSAXAttributes)
    If strLocalName = "SALARY"then
        SalaryTag= True
    End if
End Sub

Private Sub IVBSAXContentHandler_characters(text As String)
    TotalPayroll=totalPayroll+Val(text)
    SalaryTag=False
End Sub
```

Xerces

Another popular parser is available from the Apache Group, an open source movement that made its name with a Web server, and it can be downloaded from *http://xml.apache.org*. The Xerces implementation, like MSXML, comes as a library, but it is available in three languages. These are a C++ library, a set of Java classes, and a COM and Perl binding/wrapper for the C++ implementation.

Xerces supports DOM Level 1 and 2 and SAX2. While it does not support some of the additional standards that MSXML does, if you need a common parser across various platforms and environments, Xerces might be the choice for you.

Developing applications with Xerces is similar to developing applications with any open source package: you download, follow the instructions for installation, write a sample to make sure everything is set up correctly, and then consult online documentation and news groups for information about how to build your particular application. In this example you'll learn how to get started with the Java implementation of Xerces.

> **Note** You might find some minor differences between the C++ and Java implementations, so be aware of this during testing.

The first step is to download the Xerces distribution and make sure that xerces.jar is registered on your class path. While you are at the *http://xml.apache.org* site you might want to browse the API documentation and FAQs at *http://xml.apache.org/xerces-j/api.html* and *http://xml.apache.org/xerces-j/faqs.html*. To test your installation you can try writing a very simple application.

```
import org.apache.xerces.parsers.DOMParser;
import org.w3c.dom.Document;
import org.w3c.dom.Node;
import org.w3c.dom.Element;
import org.w3c.dom.NodeList;
import org.xml.sax.SAXException;
import java.io.IOException;

public static void main(String args[]) {
    DOMParser parser = new DOMParser();
    try {
         parser.parse(args[0]);
         Document document = parser.getDocument();
        NodeList salaries = document.getElementsByTagName("SALARY");
        for (int i=0;i++;i<salaries.getLength()) {
            Node salary=salaries.item(i);
            String orgSalary=salary.getNodeValue();
            int newSalary=1.04*Integer.parseInt(orgSalary);
            salary.setNodeValue(""+newSalary);
            }
          } catch (SAXException e) {
         System.err.println (e);
           } catch (IOException e) {
         System.err.println (e);
          }
    System.out.println("Parsing done!");
    System.out.println(document.toString());
}
}
```

This application will parse the document and print *Parsing done!* and the new XML, or it will print an error. If you are able to compile and run this example, your installation succeeded. You've also taken your first steps in using the DOM functionality of Xerces. The next example uses SAX to total the salaries of all employees. As with the Visual Basic example, you need to implement a content handler to receive the incoming events:

```
import org.apache.xerces.parsers.SAXParser;
import org.xml.sax.Attributes;
import org.xml.sax.helpers.DefaultHandler;
import org.xml.sax.SAXParseException;
import org.xml.sax.SAXException;
import java.io.IOException;

public class PayrollCalculator implements DefaultHandler {
private int totalPayroll=0;
private boolean inSalaryElement=false;
public PayrollCalculator(String input) {
    SAXParser parser=new SAXParser();
    Parser.setContentHandler(this);
    Try {
        Parser.parse(input);
          } catch (SAXException e) {
        System.out.println(e);
          } catch (IOException e) {
        System.out.println(e);
         }
    }
public void startElement(String uri, String local, String qName,
Attributes atts) {
    if (local.equals("SALARY")) {
        inSalaryElement=true;
        }

public void characters (String text) {
    if (inSalaryElement) {
        totalPayroll=totalPayroll+Integer.parseInt(text);
        inSalaryElement=false;
        }
    }
public int getTotalPayroll() {
    return totalPayroll;}
}
public void static main(String args[]) {
    PayrollCalculator calc=new PayrollCalculator(args[0]);
    System.out.println("Total payroll == "+calc.getTotalPayroll());
    }
}
```

Other Parsers

MSXML and Xerces are not the only parsers available. Within the Java community alone, programmers have a multitude of choices. Because DOM Level 1 and SAX2 are the heavyweights, you should ensure that your parser supports these methods. Table 3-6 contains a list of parsers written in Java and tells whether they are validating or not and what standards they support.

Table 3-6 Other DOM and SAX Parsers Written in Java

Parser	URL	Validating	Standards Supported
IBM's XML for Java	*http://www.alphaworks.ibm.com/formula/xml*	Yes	DOM Level 1, DOM Level 2, SAX 1, SAX 2, and Namespaces
Microstar's lfred	*http://home.pacbell.net/david-b/xml/*	Namespace validation only	DOM Level 1, DOM Level 2, SAX 1, and SAX 2
Sun's Java API for XML	*http://java.sun.com/products/xml*	Yes	DOM Level 1, SAX 1, and Namespaces
Oracle's XML Parser for Java	*http://technet.oracle.com/*	Yes	DOM Level 1, SAX 1, and Namespaces

Parsing XML Within the .NET Framework

The Microsoft .NET Framework and ADO.NET provide a unified programming model to access data represented as both *XML data* (text delimited by tags that structure the data) and *relational data* (tables consisting of rows and columns). This framework reads XML data from any data stream into DOM node trees, where data can be accessed programmatically, while ADO.NET provides the means to access and manipulate relational data within a *DataSet* object. Here we look at the three key components for data access in ADO.NET and the .NET Framework, as defined in Table 3-7.

Within this table *XmlDataDocument* is a subclass of the *XmlDocument*. A .NET application can use the *XmlDataDocument* to load either relational or XML data and manipulate the data using the DOM. When the *XmlDataDocu-*

Table 3-7 Key Components for Data Access

Component	Description
DataSet	Represents a relational data source in ADO.NET.
XmlDocument	Implements the DOM in the .NET Framework.
XmlDataDocument	Unifies ADO.NET and the .NET Framework by representing relational data from a *DataSet* and synchronizing it with the XML document model.

ment loads relational data, it synchronizes data between the *DataSet* and the DOM. After an *XmlDataDocument* loads relational data, an application can access the data programmatically using the .NET Framework.

The classes that comprise the .NET Framework and ADO.NET enable three broad scenarios. In Table 3-8 we cover these scenarios.

Table 3-8 Scenarios Enabled by the Classes

Scenario	Description
Accessing relational data with ADO.NET	Create and use a *DataSet* to access relational data without using XML. Read and write XML data to or from a *DataSet* without using an *XmlDataDocument*. (Any XML information not relevant to the relational presentation is lost.)
Accessing XML documents	Create and use an *XmlDocument* to access XML data streams. Use structured data in an *XmlDataDocument* without tables, rows, columns, relationships, and other relational elements. This makes it identical to the *XmlDocument*.
Accessing Relational Data in XML Documents (XML and ADO.NET)	Structure relational data in an *XmlDataDocument* with a *DataSet*. Obtain a *DataSet* from an *XmlDataDocument* to relationally view and query the structured content of an XML document. Work with the XML view of relational data in a *DataSet*. Provide relational and XML-based components for a data application. For example, you can edit and expose relational data without affecting the fidelity of an XML document and apply XSLT to relational data. Performs XPath queries over relational data.

Conclusion

We covered a lot of information on parsers in this chapter. We looked at the parser's responsibility, different parsing methods, and different parsers. Although you might not be writing a parser as part of your efforts, understanding how they work and how to choose one is important. You will require a parser to properly—and by a true implementation definition, "absolutely"—implement XML solutions. The function of parsing documents, be it for making sure a document is well-formed or for schema validation, is a task you want to leave to another application. Additionally, being able to specify the method by which you have access to the document's data is an advantage and a huge step toward completing your task.

In this chapter we touched on both the DOM and SAX standards, and we will dedicate Chapter 4 to other, related standards. Many groups use XML as a means to accomplish a variety of tasks. These projects are often the same tasks you are attempting to overcome, so take the time to go over a few of them.

Part II

Application Development

4

Database Integration

So far we've covered the basics of XML and parsing XML documents. While these topics lay the foundation for using XML, they do not show you how to really apply XML. This chapter begins our exploration of using XML for solving real-world problems by focusing on a usage currently in the spotlight: using XML with databases.

We will begin this chapter with a short introduction to some important database-related history and concepts. We will also look at why XML is used with databases and discover some of the issues that can arise through the use of XML with databases. We will then take a closer look at using XML with one particular type of database, namely the relational database, where you will learn some of the common techniques used for exposing and persisting XML documents with databases. Finally, we will explore the features and capabilities provided by Microsoft SQL Server 2000 and Oracle 9i for supporting XML.

Databases and XML

One of the computer's most powerful applications is the ability to store, organize, and retrieve large quantities of data. An organized collection of data is referred to as a database, and the programs designed to manage databases are known as Database Management Systems (DBMSs).

In this era of information explosion, DBMS has evolved into the foundation of virtually all of an organization's information management. Performing a substantial information search without using a DBMS is rare indeed.

In this section we will take a quick look at some popular DBMSs. We will also briefly introduce some of the issues in using XML with databases.

Types of DBMS

A number of different types of DBMS have emerged over the years. The most significant difference between them is the model used to store, manage, and query databases. Besides affecting what software you need to acquire, the model used affects the way you will think about data and can be surprisingly difficult to change later. Let's take a quick look at some of the more popular DBMSs, their designs, their advantages, and their disadvantages.

Hierarchical DBMS

Widely used during the mainframe era, a Hierarchical DBMS (HDBMS) links records, also called *nodes,* together like a family tree such that each record type has only one owner. For example, an order is owned by only one customer. Figure 4-1 shows a sample hierarchical database containing customers and the orders they've placed.

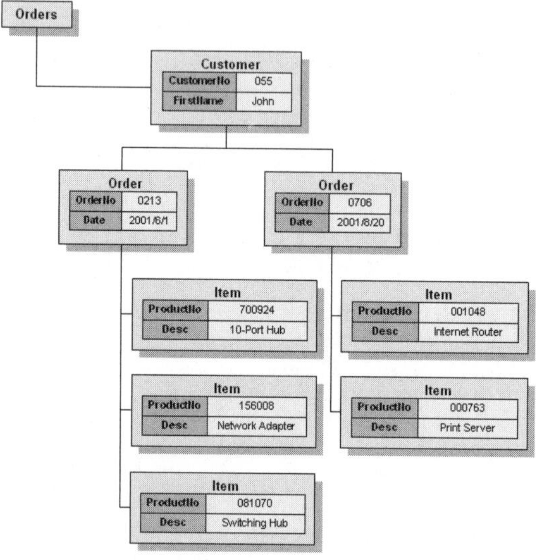

Figure 4-1 An HDBMS example.

The Orders hierarchical database shown in Figure 4-1 has six nodes of type Customer and six of type Order. These nodes are linked together by *pointers* that the user must explicitly specify. For example, Order (0706) is linked to Customer (055). All the nodes linked together form a strictly defined tree structure.

The major disadvantage of a hierarchical database is that it can be hard to query flexibly in ways that go against the tight coupling of the data hierarchies. For example, a query to retrieve the Item node of Item No 000763 in the Orders database in Figure 4-1 might look like the following:

```
055/0706/000763
```

Note that this query follows a precise path to the required node. (The acute reader will notice that this is very similar to how one would use XPath to traverse to a node in XML). However, if you wanted to know all the Orders that also used the Item of this ItemNo, the only way to discover this would be through an extremely costly search of every Order node.

Relational DBMS

The relation database model was first proposed by Dr. E. F. Codd of IBM in his seminal paper titled "A Relational Model of Data for Large Shared Data Banks" in 1970. A Relational DBMS (RDBMS) models data as a set of tables where each table consists of a fixed collection of columns, or fields. An indefinite number of rows, or records, can occur within each table. Compared to the hierarchical model, the relational model is complicated. However, the relational model provides a much more flexible framework for data access and manipulation. You can ask any question you want of an RDBMS, but for an HDBMS you can ask only the questions programmed into the system.

Figure 4-2 shows the relational database structure of three example tables: Customer, Order, and Item.

Unlike hierarchical databases, relationships between the tables in a relational database are built at runtime by linking *key* columns from one table to another. The database uses two types of key columns. The first one, called a *primary key*, is mandatory for every table in a relational database and is used to uniquely identify rows in a table. The second type, called a *foreign key*, corresponds with the primary key of other tables to form a *parent-child* relationship. For example, in Figure 4-2, CustomerNo is the primary key column of the Customer table, while OrderNo is the primary key column of the Order table. The Order table also has a foreign key column, CustomerNo, which links to the CustomerNo column of the Customer table. Therefore, in this case the Customer table is said to be the parent and Order the child.

The process of linking tables together at runtime using key fields is called *joining the tables*. One of the key features of relational databases is that they

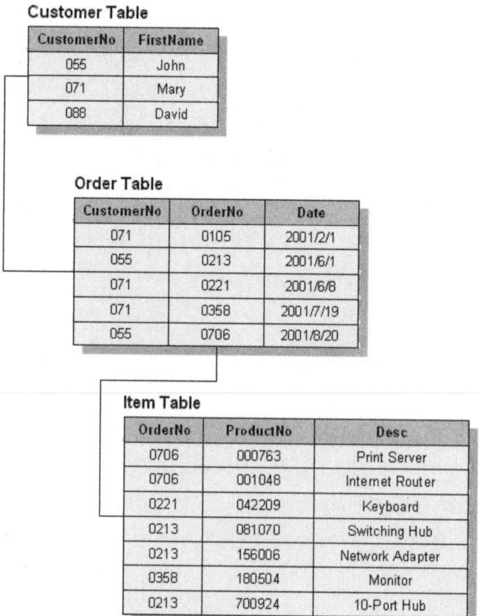
Customer Table

CustomerNo	FirstName
055	John
071	Mary
088	David

Order Table

CustomerNo	OrderNo	Date
071	0105	2001/2/1
055	0213	2001/6/1
071	0221	2001/6/8
071	0358	2001/7/19
055	0706	2001/8/20

Item Table

OrderNo	ProductNo	Desc
0706	000763	Print Server
0706	001048	Internet Router
0221	042209	Keyboard
0213	081070	Switching Hub
0213	156006	Network Adapter
0358	180504	Monitor
0213	700924	10-Port Hub

Figure 4-2 An RDBMS example.

require few assumptions about how tables can be joined and data extracted. This flexibility allows the same database to be viewed and used in different ways.

In addition, because a single relational database can be spread across several tables, the database can be designed so that data redundancy is minimized. This is known as *normalization,* and the objective is to isolate data so that additions, deletions, and modifications can be made in just one table and propagated throughout the rest of the database based on the defined relationships.

Finally, true RDBMSs use Structured Query Language (SQL) to query, extract, and update data stored in databases and conform the data as closely as possible to the theoretical relational rules of normalization. For example, to find all Items ordered by Customer John, you can use the following SQL query:

```
SELECT ProductNo, Desc
  FROM Customer, Order, Item
  WHERE Customer.CustomerNo = Order.CustomerNo
  AND Order.ItemNo = Item.ItemNo
  AND Customer.FirstName = 'John'
```

Object-Oriented DBMS

Object orientation for a database means the capability of storing and retrieving *objects* in addition to mere data. Objects are bundles of data and behaviors. Because the data in an object can be just another object or collection of objects,

objects are similar to the nodes of an HDBMS, which likewise contains a collection of child nodes.

The ability to query objects is often provided through a set of methods inherited from a parent object provided by the Object-Oriented DBMS (OODBMS) framework. Each object can implement these methods in a manner appropriate for its purposes. A SQL, called OQL, that allows for the querying of these systems in a standardized way, has been proposed by the Object Database Management Group (ODMG) *(http://www.odmg.org)*.

One of the biggest advantages of OODBMSs is their direct integration with object-oriented programming languages. Another important advantage is that the amount of data that can be modeled by an OODBMS is increased, and modeling this information is easier.

Why XML?

Over the past five years there has been an explosion in demand for access over the Internet to the data stored in enterprise databases and for the ability to use the databases to support electronic business operations. These include transactions between systems within an enterprise ("enterprise integration"), between businesses in a supply chain ("B2B e-commerce"), and directly to customers ("B2C e-commerce"). Because so many types and brands of DBMSs exist, two parties involved in the business transactional exchanges will likely be using incompatible DBMSs. On the other hand, even if they are using the same DBMS, their schemas might be so different that offering systems direct access to the other database can turn out to be complicated at best and disastrous at worst. If, miraculously, the two parties are using the same schemas, the protocols used by the DBMSs might not be accessible or even secured over a public network like the Internet.

Therefore, what many organizations are striving for is universal access to data in a fashion that is easy to manage and in a format that is self-describing and standards compliant. To help facilitate this goal, several industry vendors are turning to XML.

The Challenges of Using XML with a DBMS

Even though XML offers many advantages as a universal data-exchange format, using it with a DBMS can be problematic. For example, the way XML data is structured (that is, data modeling) can be radically different from the structure in many databases. This means that some sort of data model mapping must be used before XML can be retrieved from or stored in databases. In this section we will take a brief look at some of the issues that can arise through the use of XML with a DBMS.

Data Modeling

A data model is a conceptual representation of data structures. The data structures include the data objects, the relationships between the objects, and the rules that govern which operations can be performed on the objects.

Before we explore the problem with data modeling, you should realize that XML documents can be categorized into two major types: *data-centric* and *document-centric*. This categorization is important because it will often govern what's possible and what isn't when using XML with a DBMS.

Data-Centric XML Documents

The main characteristics of a data-centric XML document are a more organized and regular structure and a lack of (or very little) mixed content. Data-centric XML documents are designed for application consumption and application-to-application data exchange. Common examples include invoices, stock quotes, product catalogs, and application configuration files.

Listing 4-1 is an example of a data-centric XML document used to hold contact information for a personal phonebook. Notice that every information item, such as the full name, and the zip or postal code, is represented by an element, and there is no mixed content.

Listing 4-1 data_centric.xml: A sample data-centric XML document.

```
<?xml version="1.0"?>
<Contacts>
  <Contact ContactNumber="197459531">
    <FullName>Abercrombie, Kim</FullName>
    <CompanyName>Tailspin Toys</CompanyName>
    <EMail>akim@tailspintoys.com</EMail>
    <PhoneNo type="business">1-415-123-1234</PhoneNo>
    <Address>
      <Street>123 Main St.</Street>
      <City>San Francisco</City>
      <State>CA</State>
      <PostalCode>94116</PostalCode>
      <CountryCode>US</CountryCode>
    </Address>
  </Contact>
  <Contact ContactNumber="250021025">
    <FullName>Chen, John Y.</FullName>
    <CompanyName>Contoso, Ltd</CompanyName>
<EMail>johny.chen@contoso.com</EMail>
    <PhoneNo>852-1234-5678</PhoneNo>
    <Address>
      <Street>99 Dry St.</Street>
```

```
      <City>Cardiff</City>
      <PostalCode>CF17XX</PostalCode>
      <CountryCode>UK</CountryCode>
    </Address>
  </Contact>
</Contacts>
```

Document-Centric XML Documents

Document-centric design represents a more liberal use of free-form text that is "marked-up" with elements. Document-centric XML documents are usually meant for human consumption and are characterized by a less regular structure with plenty of mixed content. Examples are books, letters, e-mails, and HTML/XHTML documents. Listing 4-2 is an example of a document-centric XML document. Notice that while some parts of the document may look well-structured (*<number>*, *<author>*, and so forth), mixed content is present within the *<bullet>* and *<para>* elements.

Listing 4-2 document_centric.xml: A sample document-centric XML document.

```
<?xml version="1.0"?>
<chapter>
  <number>4</number>
  <title>Sample Chapter</title>
  <author email="john.kelly@thephone-company.com">Kelly, John
</author>
  <contents>
    <header level="1">
      <para>This is a sample paragraph.</para>
      <list>
        <bullet>This is <ref link="#12">item 1</ref></bullet>
        <bullet>This is <ref link="#13">item 2</ref></bullet>
      </list>
      <header level="2">
        <para>This is paragraph with embedded <bold>formatting
</bold>.</para>
      </header>
    </header>
  </contents>
</chapter>
```

Modeling Issues

On the surface XML appears to fit in the hierarchical modeling category. In practice, XML is a hybrid. XML is probably most similar to object modeling because it can be regarded as consisting of nodes, and nodes can contain heterogeneous data. On the other hand, document-oriented XML documents can have a high degree of heterogeneity of nodes (almost any element can appear almost anywhere) that few database models are able to replicate in terms of flexibility. In fact, it can be argued that the verbosity and formatting looseness of XML is the opposite of the strategies most DBMSs use to maximize performance and reliability.

Because of all these issues, most DBMS vendors provide indirect support for XML. Support for retrieving data-centric XML documents is usually generated dynamically from the underlying data models using predefined mapping rules. Some vendors support persisting the data-centric XML documents, and they use similar mapping rules to translate XML into data models supported by the DBMS. The biggest problem with this approach is that perfect *round-tripping* of a document (that is, storing the data from a document in the database and then reconstructing the document from the data) might not be possible because of the difference in data representation.

The complexity of providing a modeling framework that can handle the sheer flexibility involved means that most DBMSs do not provide any special built-in support for storage and retrieval of document-centric XML documents. Some DBMSs allow the user to store XML documents as *Binary Large Object* (BLOB) columns designed for storing unstructured or binary data. This approach gives you the usual advantages provided by databases, such as transactional control, security and centralized access. More sophisticated DBMSs have XML-aware tools with full-text query capabilities (such as proximity, synonym, and fuzzy searches) for the XML documents stored in the databases.

Data Types

Strictly speaking, text is the only data type supported by an XML Document Type Definition (DTD). Most databases, however, have strong data type support. Therefore, RDBMSs will need to convert data from text in the XML document to their native types in the databases and vice versa. The biggest problem with this is that no universal standard exists for textual representation of the different types of data. Dates are especially problematic because the range of possible formats is enormous.

Fortunately, W3C XSD provides a richer set of data types than DTDs, including number and date, and allows users to derive their own data types. RDBMSs that support XSD can therefore provide a more accurate representation of a database table schema using XML.

Binary Data

Because everything in XML is textual, binary data must be encoded before they can be included in an XML document. The two most common ways of encoding binary data in XML are unparsed entities and Base64 encoding. Unfortunately, if you're using a DTD, no standard XML notation exists for indicating that an element contains Base64-encoded data, so software might not recognize that the data is binary-encoded. With RDBMSs that support XSD, however, users can use the base64Binary data type to indicate that a certain data unit contains encoded binary data.

Null Values

Data with null values has a special meaning in the database world. They're used to represent such factors as uninitialized columns, invalid values, or data that simply isn't there. Note that this is different from a value of *0* for numbers or zero length strings. For example, two columns of null values are not considered equal, while two zero length strings are.

In XML optional elements and attributes can be used to represent null values. If a database value is null, it is simply not included in the corresponding XML element or attribute. Note that, just as with databases, empty values (such as zero length string) are represented by elements or attributes without any content (for example, *<element />* or *attribute=""*).

Instead of leaving out optional elements and attributes, some RDBMSs allow the user to define what constitutes null in an XML document, including supporting the XSD *xsi:null* type attribute.

Charsets

A charset is a byte-sequence-to-character mapping method and its associated data structures. For most Western European languages the charset, specified by the ISO-8859-1 standard (also called Latin-1), is simply a one-to-one byte-to-character mapping table. For other languages a different charset might be required. For example, for the Hebrew alphabet the ISO-8859-8 charset can be used. Some languages, though, might require more complex mapping structures and rules. For example, for some Asian languages that contain thousands of characters, including Chinese, Korean, and Japanese, a charset that uses multibyte characters is required. The EUC-KR charset is used for Korean, and the Shift_JIS charset is used for Japanese. Finally, the Unicode standard provides a single 16-bit charset that can be used to represent practically all the common languages used in the world today.

> **Note** A charset is not the same as a character set. For a full explanation of the difference, check out RFC 2278 at *http://www.ietf.org/rfc/rfc2278.txt.*

Being text, XML is designed to support different charsets, including Unicode. Databases, on the other hand, often offer limited support at best for charsets. Most RDBMSs can support only one charset for the entire table or even the entire database. Therefore, retrieving and storing XML documents with databases might sometimes require an intermediate charset conversion step.

Using XML with Relational Database Management Systems

RDBMSs have emerged as the predominant DBMS available today. Corporations large and small depend on extremely reliable and scalable RDBMSs to manage the data required by applications for automating their business processes. Because of their popularity in the business world, most XML database integration projects are implemented with RDBMSs. In this section we will explore the different ways that RDBMSs have evolved to adopt support for XML.

Retrieving and Storing Data-Centric XML Documents

To retrieve and store data-centric XML documents, most RDBMSs provide a mapping mechanism to allow the transformation of relational data to and from XML data. Broadly speaking, the different mapping mechanisms provided can be categorized as two types: *resultset-based* mapping and *schema-based* mapping. These two mapping methods allow you to dynamically discover and represent your database structures from and into XML documents.

Resultset-Based Mapping

Resultset-based mapping models XML documents based on the tabular nature of the resultset generated by SQL queries. The columns and rows in a resultset are usually mapped as either XML elements or attributes or a combination of both. Consider Listing 4-3, a simple SQL query that returns records from the Employee table.

Listing 4-3 sample_query1.sql: A simple SQL query that returns a list of employee records.

```
SELECT Employee_ID, First_Name, Last_Name, Dept_No
  FROM Employee
```

This query will generate a resultset that might look like that shown in Figure 4-3.

To transform this into an XML document, we can decide to map the rows as elements of the XML document and the columns as attributes of these elements. An example of such an XML document is shown in Listing 4-4.

Employee_ID	First_Name	Last_Name	Dept_No
1	Adam	Barr	3
2	Katie	Jordan	2
3	Scott	MacDonald	1
4	Tim	O'Brien	2
5	Sunil	Koduri	3
6	Laura	Norman	2

Figure 4-3 A sample resultset returned from the SQL query shown in Listing 4-3.

Listing 4-4 sample_query1.xml: A sample XML representation of the Employee table shown in Figure 4-3.

```
<?xml version="1.0"?>
<ROOT>
  <row Employee_ID="1" First_Name="Adam" Last_Name="Barr"
Dept_No="3"/>
  <row Employee_ID="2" First_Name="Katie" Last_Name="Jordan"
Dept_No="2"/>
  <row Employee_ID="3" First_Name="Scott" Last_Name="MacDonald"
Dept_No="1"/>
  <row Employee_ID="4" First_Name="Tim" Last_Name="O'Brien"
Dept_No="2"/>
  <row Employee_ID="5" First_Name="Sunil" Last_Name="Koduri"
Dept_No="3"/>
  <row Employee_ID="6" First_Name="Laura" Last_Name="Norman"
Dept_No="2"/>
</ROOT>
```

> **Note** To ensure that the XML document is well-formed, we have included a root element that we call *<ROOT>*. One alternative naming convention is to use the name of the table, Employee in this case, as the root element name.

For each row in the resultset, we generated a *<row>* element in the XML document. The columns are then mapped to attributes of these *<row>* elements. Another way to map columns is to generate the child elements of the *<row>* elements, as shown in Listing 4-5.

Listing 4-5 sample_query2.xml: Same as Sample_Query1.xml, but using elements instead of attribute values to represent records.

```
<?xml version="1.0"?>
<ROOT>
  <row>
<Employee_ID>1</Employee_ID>
<First_Name>Adam</First_Name>
<Last_Name>Barr</Last_Name>
<Dept_No>3</Dept_No>
  </row>
  <row>
<Employee_ID>2</Employee_ID>
<First_Name>Katie</First_Name>
<Last_Name>Jordan</Last_Name>
<Dept_No>2</Dept_No>
  </row>
  <row>
<Employee_ID>3</Employee_ID>
<First_Name>Scott</First_Name>
<Last_Name>MacDonald</Last_Name>
<Dept_No>1</Dept_No>
  </row>
  <row>
<Employee_ID>4</Employee_ID>
<First_Name>Tim</First_Name>
<Last_Name>O'Brien</Last_Name>
<Dept_No>2</Dept_No>
  </row>
  <row>
<Employee_ID>5</Employee_ID>
<First_Name>Sunil</First_Name>
<Last_Name>Koduri</Last_Name>
<Dept_No>3</Dept_No>
  </row>
  <row>
<Employee_ID>6</Employee_ID>
<First_Name>Laura</First_Name>
<Last_Name>Norman</Last_Name>
<Dept_No>2</Dept_No>
  </row>
</ROOT>
```

One advantage of resultset-based mapping is that the generated XML document automatically reflects the live data and schema information present in the resultset from which the XML document is generated. This means that, by controlling the number of columns and rows in a resultset using standard SQL constructs, you automatically restrict the amount of data that will be included in the resultant XML document. In addition, aliased and computed columns will also be reflected in the XML document. For example, the following SQL query will generate a resultset that can be transformed into an XML document:

```
SELECT CONCATENATE( LastName, ' ', FirstName ) AS FullName
  FROM Employee
WHERE LastName = 'Jordan'
```

The document would then look like Listing 4-6.

Listing 4-6 sample_query3.xml: XML representation of a resultset with computed columns.

```
<?xml version="1.0">
<ROOT>
  <row Employee_ID="2" FullName="Jordan, Katie"/>
</ROOT>
```

> **Note** Only the row matching the condition specified in the WHERE clause is included in the XML document. Also, we've automatically picked up the *FullName* alias from the resultset and used it in the XML document.

Resultset mapping will function just as effectively for a resultset that consists of rows originating from more than one table. Consider the following multijoin SQL query as an example:

```
SELECT Dept.Dept_ID,
       Dept.Dept_Name,
       Employee.Employee_ID,
       CONCATENATE( Employee.Last_Name, ' ', Employee.First_Name ) AS
Employee_Name
  FROM Dept, Employee
  WHERE Dept.Dept_ID = Employee.Dept_ID
  ORDER BY Dept.Dept_ID, Employee.Employee_ID
```

This query will generate a resultset that looks like that shown in Figure 4-4. We can easily transform this resultset into the XML document in Listing 4-7.

Dept_ID	Dept_Name	Employee_ID	Employee_Names
1	IT	3	McDonald, Scott
2	HR	2	Jordan, Katie
2	HR	4	O'Brien, Tim
3	HR	6	Norman, Laura
3	Operations	1	Barr, Adam
4	Operations	5	Koduri, Sunil

Figure 4-4 A multitable resultset.

Listing 4-7 sample_query4.xml: XML generated from the resultset in Figure 4-4.

```
<?xml version="1.0"?>
<ROOT>
  <row Dept_ID="1" Dept_Name="IT" Employee_ID="3"
Employee_Name="MacDonald, Scott"/>
  <row Dept_ID="2" Dept_Name="HR" Employee_ID="2"
Employee_Name="Jordan, Katie"/>
  <row Dept_ID="2" Dept_Name="HR" Employee_ID="4"
Employee_Name="O'Brien, Tim"/>
  <row Dept_ID="2" Dept_Name="HR" Employee_ID="6"
Employee_Name="Norman, Laura"/>
  <row Dept_ID="3" Dept_Name="Operations" Employee_ID="1"
Employee_Name="Barr, Adam"/>
  <row Dept_ID="3" Dept_Name="HR" Employee_ID="5"
Employee_Name="Koduri, Sunil"/>
  </row>
</ROOT>
```

Our multitable XML document has one significant weakness. It doesn't represent the true hierarchical nature of the resultset. Ideally, what we might want is to group Employee rows that have the same *Dept_ID* under the same container element. Listing 4-8 is an example.

Listing 4-8 sample_query5.xml: Using nested elements to represent a multitable resultset.

```
<?xml version="1.0"?>
<ROOT>
  <Dept Dept_ID="1" Dept_Name="IT">
```

```
    <Employee Employee_ID="3" Employee_Name="MacDonald, Scott"/>
  </Dept>
  <Dept Dept_ID="2" Dept_Name="HR">
    <Employee Employee_ID="2" Employee_Name="Jordan, Katie"/>
    <Employee Employee_ID="4" Employee_Name="O'Brien, Tim"/>
    <Employee Employee_ID="6" Employee_Name="Norman, Laura"/>
  </Dept>
  <Dept Dept_ID="3" Dept_Name="Operations">
    <Employee Employee_ID="1" Employee_Name="Barr, Adam"/>
    <Employee Employee_ID="5" Employee_Name="Koduri, Sunil"/>
  </Dept>
</ROOT>
```

Notice that we needed a new container element to hold data that is specific to a department (Dept). Instead of just using *<row>*, we decided to name this element according to the name of the table itself, *<Dept>*. Similarly, we've named the element used to hold data from each row of the Employee table as *<Employee>*.

To transform the resultset in Figure 4-4 into a nested XML document that looks like that shown in Listing 4-8, an RDBMS needs to navigate the rows in the resultset in a forward-only fashion and the columns in a left-to-right fashion. By comparing the column values of the current row with those of the previous rows, an RDBMS can infer the necessary hierarchical structure of the resultset. The nesting order is determined by the order in which the columns will appear in the resultset.

To better illustrate what's really involved, let's step through the process with the resultset shown in Figure 4-4. Before we begin using XML to mark up the data, we will first need to generate the header and root element, like the following:

```
<?xml version="1.0"?>
<ROOTSET>
```

Now let's start from the top of the resultset in Figure 4-4. Because this is the first row, however, we only need to "remember" the values here. We don't generate any XML at this point. We can move on to the second row.

Comparing the second row with the first row, we immediately find that the data has changed, so we need to generate elements in the XML. Because we see two groups of columns belonging to two different tables in these rows—Dept_ID and Dept_Name of the Dept table and Employee_ID and Employee_Name of the Employee table—we know we will need two separate elements to hold the column values. Furthermore, because the columns of the Dept table precede those of the Employee table, we will nest the element corresponding to the rows of the Employee table within those of the Dept table. The following XML fragment shows the result of this process:

```
  <Dept Dept_ID="1" Dept_Name="IT">
    <Employee Employee_ID="3" Employee_Name="MacDonald, Scott"/>
```

Here we have generated the elements and attributes for the previous row (row one) and not for the current row. This occurs because at this point we know only that the previous row is different from the current row. We don't yet know whether the current one will be different from the next row. Therefore, we need to generate the XML data for the previous row and remember the data in the current row. This is the general pattern we're going to follow until we reach the end of the resultset.

After moving on to the third row and comparing it with the previous row (row two), we find that both Dept_ID and Dept_Name stayed the same, but Employee_ID and Employee_Name have changed. This change means we need to add another *<Employee>* element to represent the Employee data in the previous row.

There is one slight complication. Because the column values of the row we're about to generate for both the Dept table and Employee table (that is, those of the second row) are different from those we have just generated (that is, those of the first row), we know we need to generate a new *<Dept>* element. However, because *<Dept>* is rendered as a container element, we also need to close the previous *<Dept>* element, as shown in the following code:

```
</Dept>
  <Dept Dept_ID="2" Dept_Name="HR">
    <Employee Employee_ID="2" Employee_Name="Jordan, Katie"/>
```

Now we will move on to the fourth row, where we find that, compared to the previous row, the column values of the Employee table have changed, which means we need to generate a new *<Employee>* element. The resulting XML that will be added looks like the following:

```
<Employee Employee_ID="4" Employee_Name="O'Brien, Tim"/>
```

Once we have this element, we move on to the fifth row where we encounter a situation similar to the second row. Therefore, we use the same solution and generate the necessary elements.

The XML result that we add to our growing document as follows here:

```
<Employee Employee_ID="6" Employee_Name="Norman, Laura"/>
  </Dept>
  <Dept Dept_ID="3" Dept_Name="Operations">
```

Now we hit the sixth row. First we find that the Employee column values have changed, so we generate a new *<Employee>* element, as shown here:

```
    <Employee Employee_ID="1" Employee_Name="Barr, Adam"/>
```

Finally we find that we've hit the end of the resultset. Therefore, the only task left is to spit out the elements for the last row and properly end our XML elements. We also know that we have a *<Dept>* element open, so we need to close it. Lastly we add a *</ROOT>* end tag to get our remaining elements. These steps are shown below:

```
    <Employee Employee_ID="5" Employee_Name="Koduri, Sunil"/>
  </Dept>
</ROOT>
```

You can see that the process is not that complicated and can easily be automated with some simple software.

Schema-Based Mapping

In this section we will show you how to generate database schemas to and from XSDs. Before we begin, however, you should realize that, because you can model an XSD in more than one way, the mapping method we are about to explore with you is not the only legitimate means of mapping XSD with database schemas. As you will learn soon, a few constructs in a database schema have no direct correspondence in XSD, and the solution we will use to solve this problem might be different from other people's similar attempts.

In a relational database the hierarchical relationship between tables can be modeled by using foreign keys. Therefore, in principle, we can model an XML representation of databases based on information found in the database schema. Take note, however, that this mapping method is most often used at design time to generate only an XML DTD or XSD schema. The reason for this is that, because most applications work with a known database schema, this method is not suitable for storing random XML documents in databases. That would require altering database schemas from XML at runtime.

> **Note** This section makes heavy use of XSD. For a quick introduction to XSD, please read Appendix A. A more detailed coverage of the subject, "XML Schema Primer 0," can be found at *http://www.w3.org/TR/xmlschema-0/.*

Generating XSD from a Database Schema

The exercise in this section is to generate an XSD schema that can correctly model both the database schemas shown in Listing 4-9. Note that *Employee* and

Dept have a parent-child relationship because of the presence of the foreign key reference in the Employee table.

Listing 4-9 db_schema1.sql: Database schema for sample Dept and Employee tables.

```
CREATE TABLE Dept
(
  DeptID INT PRIMARY KEY NOT NULL,
  DeptName VARCHAR( 20 ) NOT NULL
)
CREATE TABLE Employee
(
  EmployeeID INT PRIMARY KEY NOT NULL,
  FirstName VARCHAR( 20 ),
  LastName VARCHAR( 20 ) NOT NULL,
  DeptID NUMBER REFERENCES Dept( Dept_ID ) NOT NULL
)
```

First we need to pick one of the two tables to generate an XSD model for it. Let's start with the Employee table. Now for each data column in the Employee table, namely *FirstName* and *LastName*, we need to generate a corresponding element in the XSD. Before we can do this, however, we need to define a new data type to model the *VARCHAR(20)* data type definition that is used by both *FirstName* and *LastName* in our database schema. We can do this by extending the *xsd:string* data type to include this 20-character limit:

```
<xsd:simpleType name="varchar20">
  <xsd:restriction base="xsd:string">
<xsd:maxLength value="20"/>
  </xsd:restriction>
</xsd:simpleType>
```

We can now define the elements for *FirstName* and *LastName* as *varchar20*.

```
<xsd:element name="FirstName" type="varchar20"/>
<xsd:element name="LastName" use="required" type="varchar20"/>
```

Notice that, in addition to using our new *varchar20* data type, we have also specified *LastName* as *required* because it is defined as not nullable in the database schema.

Next we tackle the primary key field of the Employee table, namely *EmployeeID*. First we model it as a unique and required element.

```
<xsd:element name="EmployeeID" use="required" type="xsd:int">
  <xsd:unique name="EmployeeUnique">
    <xsd:selector xpath="my:Employee"/>
```

```
    <xsd:field xpath="EmployeeID"/>
   </xsd:unique>
</xsd:element>
```

Notice that the uniqueness of the *EmployeeID* element is defined using the *<xsd:unique>* element. The *<xsd:selector>* element specifies that any value of *EmployeeID* must be unique within the *<Employee>* element. (We will include the definition for the *my* namespace URI used here when we get to the final steps of completing our XSD.) The *<xsd:field>* element associates this *<xsd:unique>* definition with the *EmployeeID* element.

Our model for the *EmployeeID* field has a problem, though. In a database schema a column can be defined as not primary key but still unique. Just saying that our *EmployeeID* is required is not enough; we need to be able to specify that *EmployeeID* is also a primary key.

It turns out that XSD has no direct notation to represent the concept of a primary key. One possible way to embed this extra information in our XSD is by using an *<appinfo><annotation>*. An *<appinfo><annotation>* is analogous to processing instructions in XML 1 because it is intended to be used for passing information to a processing application. Therefore, let's add our custom *primary-key <appinfo><annotation>* to our XSD.

```
<xsd:element name="EmployeeID" use="required" type="xsd:int">
  <xsd:unique name="EmployeeUnique">
 <xsd:selector xpath="my:Employee"/>
    <xsd:field xpath="EmployeeID"/>
      <xsd:annotation>
        <xsd:appinfo>
          primary-key
        </xsd:appinfo>
      </xsd:annotation>
    </xsd:unique>
  </xsd:element>
```

Here we have included the *<annotation>* element within the *<unique>* element so that a processor can easily associate this *primary-key* property with the correct element.

Note Besides primary key, many other attributes and metadata of databases cannot easily be modeled directly using the existing XSD constructs. One important example is all the information related to the definition of indexes. Of course, you can use the same *<appinfo>* *<annotation>* technique shown here for these purposes.

The only column left to model now is *DeptID*. In the Dept table, *DeptID* is defined as a foreign key. How do we represent this in our XSD? The XSD language has constructs that are perfect for this purpose, the *<key>* and *<keyref>* elements. Here *<keyref>* acts as a foreign key while *<key>* acts as a primary key. We can now model the *DeptID* field as follows:

```
<xsd:element name="DeptID" use="required" type="xsd:int">
  <xsd:keyref name="DeptKeyRef" refer="DeptKey">
    <xsd:selector xpath="my:Employee"/>
    <xsd:field xpath="DeptID"/>
  </xsd:keyref>
</xsd:element>
```

As you will notice, the syntax of *<keyref>* is very similar to *<unique>*, in that we use *<selector>* and *<field>* child elements to specify where we want the key relationship to be placed, and in what range it must be unique. The *refer* attribute is used to specify the name of the *<key>* element that we want to refer back to. When we model the *DeptID* field of the Dept table, we will name the associated *<key>* element as *DeptKey*.

Now that our XSD model for the Employee table is complete, we can move on to the Dept table. Modeling the *DeptName* field is easy because it is the same as the *FirstName* field of the Employee table:

```
<xsd:element name="DeptName" type="varchar20"/>
```

The *DeptID* field is defined as a primary key in the Dept table. We already know how to model a primary key from when we tackled the *<EmployeeID>* element, so we can quickly jump to the following definition of the *<DeptID>* element:

```
<xsd:element name="DeptID" use="required" type="xsd:int"/>
  <xsd:unique name="DeptUnique">
  <xsd:selector xpath="my:Dept"/>
  <xsd:field xpath="DeptID"/>
  <xsd:annotation>
    <xsd:appinfo>
      primary-key
    </xsd:appinfo>
  </xsd:annotation>
</xsd:unique>
```

However, one piece of information is still missing. We need to include a *<key>* element here so that our earlier *<keyref>* definition in the *<DeptID>* child element of the *<Employee>* element is complete. The final definition for the *<DeptID>* element is as follows:

```
<xsd:element name="DeptID" use="required" type="xsd:int"/>
  <xsd:unique name="DeptUnique">
    <xsd:selector xpath="my:Dept"/>
    <xsd:field xpath="DeptID"/>
    <xsd:annotation>
      <xsd:appinfo>
        primary-key
      </xsd:appinfo>
    </xsd:annotation>
  </xsd:unique>
  <xsd:key name="DeptKey">
    <xsd:selector xpath="my:Dept"/>
    <xsd:field xpath="DeptID"/>
  </xsd:key>
</xsd:element>
```

Now that we have all the pieces, we can tie them together into a complete XSD schema document. Our final completed XSD schema, including the XML header and definition for a root element, is shown in Listing 4-10.

Listing 4-10 employee_dept.xsd: XSD generated from the Employee and Dept schemas.

```
<?xml version="1.0"?>
<xsd:schema xmlns:xsd="http://www.w3c.org/2001/XMLSchema"
            targetNamespace="http://mspress.microsoft.com/corexml/"
            xmlns:my="http://mspress.microsoft.com/corexml/">
  <xsd:element name="ROOT">
    <xsd:complexType>
      <xsd:sequence>
        <xsd:element ref="Employee" minOccurs="0"
maxOccurs="unbounded"/>
       <xsd:element ref="Dept" minOccurs="0" maxOccurs="unbounded"/>
      </xsd:sequence>
    </xsd:complexType>
  </xsd:element>
  <xsd:simpleType name="varchar20">
    <xsd:restriction base="xsd:string">
  <xsd:maxLength value="20"/>
  </xsd:restriction>
  </xsd:simpleType>
  <xsd:element name="Employee">
    <xsd:complexType>
      <xsd:sequence>
       <xsd:element name="EmployeeID" use="required" type="xsd:int">
          <xsd:unique name="EmployeeUnique">
            <xsd:selector xpath="my:Employee"/>
            <xsd:field xpath="EmployeeID"/>
            <xsd:annotation>
```

(continued)

Listing 4-10 *continued*

```
            <xsd:appinfo>
              primary-key
            </xsd:appinfo>
          </xsd:annotation>
        </xsd:unique>
      </xsd:element>
      <xsd:element name="FirstName" type="varchar20"/>
      <xsd:element name="LastName" use="required" type="varchar20"/>
      <xsd:element name="DeptID" use="required" type="xsd:int">
        <xsd:keyref name="DeptKeyRef" refer="DeptKey">
         <xsd:selector xpath="my:Employee"/>
          <xsd:field xpath="DeptID"/>
        </xsd:unique>
      </xsd:element>
    </xsd:sequence>
  </xsd:complexType>
</xsd:element>
<xsd:element name="Dept">
  <xsd:complexType>
    <xsd:sequence>
      <xsd:element name="DeptID" use="required" type="xsd:int"/>
        <xsd:unique name="DeptUnique">
          <xsd:selector xpath="my:Dept"/>
          <xsd:field xpath="DeptID"/>
          <xsd:annotation>
            <xsd:appinfo>
              primary-key
            </xsd:appinfo>
          </xsd:annotation>
        </xsd:unique>
        <xsd:key name="DeptKey">
          <xsd:selector xpath="my:Dept"/>
          <xsd:field xpath="DeptID"/>
        </xsd:key>
      </xsd:element>
      <xsd:element name="DeptName" type="varchar20"/>
    </xsd:sequence>
  </xsd:complexType>
</xsd:element>
</xsd:schema>
```

As you can see, the XSD language provides many features, such as the unique and key elements we showed you here, to enable accurate mapping to and from database schemas. For the actions that cannot be easily implemented directly in XSD, such as the *primary-key* property, we can use methods such as annotation to achieve a workable solution at least.

Generating a Database Schema from an XSD

In this section we will show you how to generate a database schema based on an XSD. For the examples here we will use the XSD schema in Listing 4-10 that we generated in the previous section. To better illustrate the mapping process, our database schema will be represented by an SQL creation script.

The first detail we need to decide on is what tables we're going to be mapping. For our case this is easy, because in Listing 4-10 we know that all these tables will be listed under the *<ROOT>* element. For each of the tables listed we generate a *CREATE TABLE* statement block for it in our SQL script.

```
CREATE TABLE Employee
(
)
CREATE TABLE Dept
(
)
```

Now we need to work through each of these tables to model their structures as XSD. Let's start with the Employee table because it's the first table listed in *<ROOT>*. In Listing 4-10 we know that every table is modeled as a *<complexType>* and that each column in a specific table is modeled as a child element. Armed with this knowledge, we find that the Employee table needs four columns.

Each of the columns in this table will have a corresponding child element defined under the *<Employee><complexType>*. In addition to their names, we also find other important information about these columns, such as whether they are required, unique, or both. We will need to generate the appropriate column definitions for each of these columns in our SQL script. Notice that the required attribute of the elements is represented in our SQL scripts using the *NOT NULL* standard SQL modifiers.

```
CREATE TABLE Employee
(
  EmployeeID INT NOT NULL,
  FirstName VARCHAR( 20 ),
  LastName VARCHAR( 20 ) NOT NULL,
  DeptID INT NOT NULL
)
```

Going back to our XSD in Employee_Dept.xsd, we find that *EmployeeID* has an associated unique element and a *primary-key <appinfo><annotation>*. As we've seen, the use of these two pieces of information represent our way of saying this element is a primary key column. Let's add this information to our SQL script:

```
  EmployeeID INT PRIMARY KEY NOT NULL,
```

Now comes the fun part: modeling the foreign key. We find from the definition of *DeptID* in the *<Employee>* element that it has a *<keyref>* to a *<key>* called *DeptKey*. Searching through Listing 4-10, we find that this *DeptKey <keyref>* is associated with the *DeptID* element within the *<Dept><complexType>* element. Now we have the information we need to model this foreign key relationship in our database schema.

```
  DeptID INT REFERENCES Dept( DeptID ) NOT NULL
```

This step completes our modeling for the Employee table, so now let's turn to the Dept table.

As before, first we add a column to our database schema for each element defined within the *<Dept><complexType>*.

```
CREATE TABLE Dept
(
  DeptID INT NOT NULL,
  Name VARCHAR( 20 ) NOT NULL
)
```

Now we find out that *DeptID* should be defined as a primary key because of the presence of the *primary-key <appinfo><annotation>*. Here we make the final change to our database schema, which yields Listing 4-11.

Listing 4-11 generated_db_schema.sql: DB Schema generated from the Employee_Dept.xsd XML document.

```
CREATE TABLE Employee
(
  EmployeeID INT PRIMARY KEY NOT NULL,
  FirstName VARCHAR( 20 ),
  LastName VARCHAR( 20 ) NOT NULL,
  DeptID INTEGER REFERENCES Dept(DeptID) NOT NULL
)
CREATE TABLE Dept
(
  DeptID INT PRIMARY KEY NOT NULL,
  Name VARCHAR( 20 ) NOT NULL
)
```

Storing and Retrieving Document-Centric XML Documents

Support for document-centric XML documents in most RDBMS products is usually minimal, if not totally missing. This absence results from the freeform and less organized nature of document-centric XML documents that makes them difficult to fit into the framework of a relational model. To illustrate this difficulty, consider Listing 4-12.

Listing 4-12 sample_html.html: An sample document-centric HTML document.

```
<html>
  <head>
    <title>Sample HTML</title>
  </head>
  <body>
    <h1>This is a header</h1>
    Some other text
    <p>This is a paragraph.</p>
    <p>This is <b>another</b> paragraph.</p>
  </body>
</html>
```

Note that although some elements look well structured, such as the *<title>* element, some mixed content is in the document, such as the *<b>* element within the *<p>* element. The presence of mixed content and deeply nested elements in the document makes it difficult to model properly using a relational model. For example, which elements do you model as tables and which as rows/columns? Also, is there a point to decomposing this document to fit into a relational model? What will you gain by doing that?

Most RDBMS products recommend that you store document-centric XML documents as Character Large Object (CLOB) or BLOB columns in a relational database. Doing so allows XML documents of arbitrary size to be easily stored in and retrieved from databases.

This concludes our discussion of using XML with RDBMS in general. In the following sections, we will explore the XML features provided by some commercial RDBMS products.

XML Support in Commercial Relational Database Management Systems

In the race to provide the "best" XML support, RDBMS vendors have developed tools to XML-enable their products. The level of support can vary greatly, though. Most RDBMSs support XML as an output format by using dynamic resultset-based mapping. Only a few RDBMS products, however, have built-in support for updating databases using XML. In this section we will explore the XML capabilities of two of the more popular RDBMSs in the market: Microsoft SQL Server 2000 and Oracle 9i.

Microsoft SQL Server 2000

SQL Server 2000 provides a host of built-in features for delivering XML support. Most of these concentrate on enabling the user to translate relational data into XML documents. In addition, SQL Server 2000 has a mechanism for updating databases using XML.

Using *SELECT FOR XML* to Expose Relational Data as XML

SQL Server 2000 features a new clause of the *SELECT* statement that can be used to expose existing relational data as XML instead of as standard resultsets. This capability makes it trivial to expose resultsets generated by any SQL queries as XML documents. It also eliminates the need for you to write any custom code to manually do the transformation from resultsets to XML.

The new *FOR XML* clause supports three modes—*RAW*, *AUTO*, and *EXPLICIT*—for controlling the shape of the resulting XML.

The *RAW* Mode

The *RAW* mode is the simplest of the three modes. Unfortunately, it is also the most limited. The *RAW* mode provides a simple one-to-one row mapping to XML.

Let's start with a simple example. The following query will return all rows in the Employees table:

```
SELECT EmployeeID, FirstName, LastName
  FROM Employees
```

> **Note** The Employees table, all other tables, and their data mentioned in this section can be found in the *Northwind* sample database that is installed by default with SQL Server 2000.

The resultant resultset is shown in Figure 4-5.

To return an XML you can add the *FOR XML RAW* clause to the *SELECT* query in Listing 4-13.

Listing 4-13 raw.sql: An XML-generating simple query.

```
SELECT EmployeeID, FirstName, LastName
  FROM Employees
  FOR XML RAW
```

EmployeeID	FirstName	LastName
1	Nancy	Davolio
2	Andrew	Fuller
3	Janet	Leverling
4	Margaret	Peacock
5	Steven	Buchanan
6	Michael	Suyama
7	Robert	King
8	Laura	Callanan
9	Annee	Dodsworth

Figure 4-5 The Employees resultset.

With this addition, Listing 4-14 will be returned.

Listing 4-14 raw.xml: XML generated by the query in Listing 4-13.

```
<row EmployeeID="1" FirstName="Nancy" LastName="Davolio"/>
<row EmployeeID="2" FirstName="Andrew" LastName="Fuller"/>
<row EmployeeID="3" FirstName="Janet" LastName="Leverling"/>
<row EmployeeID="4" FirstName="Margaret" LastName="Peacock"/>
<row EmployeeID="5" FirstName="Steven" LastName="Buchanan"/>
<row EmployeeID="6" FirstName="Michael" LastName="Suyama"/>
<row EmployeeID="7" FirstName="Robert" LastName="King"/>
<row EmployeeID="8" FirstName="Laura" LastName="Callanan"/>
<row EmployeeID="9" FirstName="Annee" LastName="Dodsworth"/>
```

As shown in Listing 4-14, any XML document returned by *FOR XML* does not automatically include any prolog, such as *<?xml version="1"?>*, and a root element. We will show you one way to deal with this issue in a later section where we discuss the XML Templates feature of SQL Server 2000.

The *RAW* mode of querying transforms each row in the resultset generated by the query into an XML *<row>* element. Each column is rendered as an attribute of the same name. One of the biggest limitations of the *RAW* mode is that it cannot be used to generate a hierarchical XML document from a multitable resultset. To illustrate this limitation, let's use the multitable query shown in Listing 4-15 to generate a *resultset.*

Listing 4-15 multitable.sql: A multitable query.

```
SELECT Customers.CustomerID, Customers.CompanyName,
       Orders.OrderID, Orders.OrderDate,
```

(continued)

Listing 4-15 *continued*

```
       [Order Details].ProductID, [Order Details].Quantity,
  [Order Details].UnitPrice
   FROM Customers, Orders, [Order Details]
   WHERE Customers.CustomerID = Orders.CustomerID
     AND Orders.OrderID = [Order Details].OrderID
 AND Customers.CustomerID = 'BOLID'
   ORDER BY Customers.CustomerID, Orders.OrderID
```

The resultant resultset of this query is shown in Figure 4-6.

CustomerID	CompanyName	OrderID	OrderDate	ProductID	Quantity	UnitPrice
BOLID	Bolido Comidas preparadas	10326	1996-10-10T00:00:00	4	24	17.6
BOLID	Bolido Comidas preparadas	10326	1996-10-10T00:00:00	57	16	15.6
BOLID	Bolido Comidas preparadas	10326	1996-10-10T00:00:00	75	50	6.2
BOLID	Bolido Comidas preparadas	10801	1997-12-26T12:00:00	17	40	39
BOLID	Bolido Comidas preparadas	10801	1997-12-26T12:00:00	29	20	123.79
BOLID	Bolido Comidas preparadas	10970	1998-03-24T00:00	52	40	7

Figure 4-6 The resultset generated by Listing 4-15.

Again, to generate XML, we add the *FOR XML RAW* to our query. The result is shown in Listing 4-16.

Listing 4-16 raw2. xml: XML generated by the *RAW* mode query in Listing 4-15.

```
<row CustomerID="BOLID" CompanyName="Bolido Comidas preparadas"
OrderID="10326" OrderDate="1996-10-10T00:00:00" ProductID="4"
Quantity="24" UnitPrice="17.6"/>
<row CustomerID="BOLID" CompanyName="Bolido Comidas preparadas"
OrderID="10326" OrderDate="1996-10-10T00:00:00" ProductID="57"
Quantity="16" UnitPrice="15.6"/>
<row CustomerID="BOLID" CompanyName="Bolido Comidas preparadas"
OrderID="10326" OrderDate="1996-10-10T00:00:00" ProductID="75"
Quantity="50" UnitPrice="6.2"/>
<row CustomerID="BOLID" CompanyName="Bolido Comidas preparadas"
OrderID="10801" OrderDate="1997-12-26T12:00:00" ProductID="17"
Quantity="40" UnitPrice="39"/>
<row CustomerID="BOLID" CompanyName="Bolido Comidas preparadas"
OrderID="10801" OrderDate="1997-12-26T12:00:00" ProductID="29"
Quantity="20" UnitPrice="123.79"/>
<row CustomerID="BOLID" CompanyName="Bolido Comidas preparadas"
OrderID="10970" OrderDate="1998-03-24T00:00:00" ProductID="52"
Quantity="40" UnitPrice="7"/>
```

As you can see, this does not reflect the hierarchy of our resultset Order Details under Orders under Customer. Luckily, the next mode we're going to discuss, the *AUTO* mode, is just as convenient to use but can also handle hierarchical data automatically.

The *AUTO* Mode

For a more configurable and powerful way to expose a resultset that is just as simple to use as the *RAW* mode, SQL Server 2000 provides the *AUTO* mode. The biggest improvement over the *RAW* mode is that the *AUTO* mode can be used to expose a multitable resultset as a hierarchical XML document. The query in Listing 4-17 is the same query shown in Listing 4-15 except that it now uses the *AUTO* mode.

Listing 4-17 auto.sql: SQL query to illustrate the *AUTO* mode.

```
SELECT Customers.CustomerID, Customers.CompanyName,
       Orders.OrderID, Orders.OrderDate,
       [Order Details].ProductID, [Order Details].Quantity,
 [Order Details].UnitPrice
  FROM Customers, Orders, [Order Details]
  WHERE Customers.CustomerID = Orders.CustomerID
    AND Orders.OrderID = [Order Details].OrderID
AND Customers.CustomerID = 'BOLID'
  ORDER BY Customers.CustomerID, Orders.OrderID
  FOR XML AUTO
```

The resultant XML is shown in Listing 4-18. As you will see, the *AUTO* mode has correctly rendered the hierarchical structure of our data in this XML.

Listing 4-18 auto.xml: XML generated using the query in AUTO.sql.

```
<Customers CustomerID="BOLID" CompanyName="Bolido Comidas preparadas">
  <Orders OrderID="10326" OrderDate="1996-10-10T00:00">
    <Order_Details ProductID="4" Quantity="24" UnitPrice="17.6"/>
    <Order_Details ProductID="57" Quantity="16" UnitPrice="15.6"/>
    <Order_Details ProductID="75" Quantity="50" UnitPrice="6.2"/>
  </Orders>
  <Orders OrderID="10801" OrderDate="1997-12-26T00:00">
    <Order_Details ProductID="17" Quantity="40" UnitPrice="39"/>
    <Order_Details ProductID="29" Quantity="20" UnitPrice="123.79"/>
  </Orders>
  <Orders OrderID="10801" OrderDate="1997-12-26T00:00">
    <Order_Details ProductID="52" Quantity="40" UnitPrice="7"/>
  </Orders>
</Customers>
```

In *AUTO* mode each table in the *FROM* clause is represented by a corresponding XML element. The columns listed in the query are mapped to the appropriate attribute of the element. The order in which column names are specified in the *SELECT* query is significant because it's used to control the hierarchy of the resultant XML. Therefore, in Listing 4-18, *<Customers>* contains the *<Orders>* elements which in turn contain the *<Order_Details>* elements because this is the order in which the corresponding tables are listed in the *FROM* clause.

The *EXPLICIT* Mode

The *EXPLICIT* mode of the *FOR XML* clause is designed to enable the user to control the shape of the XML explicitly. Using this mode, however, requires a steep learning curve. The query must be written so that the additional information about the expected nesting is explicitly specified as part of the query. SQL Server 2000 directives can be used to specify additional configurations information at the column level. For example, the user can specify whether a particular column should be represented as an element or attribute in the XML.

The *EXPLICIT* mode expects the resultset resulting from an SQL query to follow a specific format. This resultset, called the Universal Table, should contain not just the data represented within the XML, but also metadata describing how the XML should be structured. This information is obtained by requiring the SQL query author to include two extract columns in the Universal Table and to name the columns according to a special encoding convention.

The two extra columns required by the *EXPLICIT* mode must be named *Tag* and *Parent.*

- Tag must be specified as the first column in the Universal Table and is used to indicate the tag number of the current element. Tag is an integer and is numbered starting at 1.
- The second column in the Universal Table must be called Parent. It's used to specify the tag number of the parent element. Parent is also an integer. To specify that an element has no parent (that is, it's at the top level of the tree), use a value of 0 or NULL.

These two elements determine the parent-child hierarchy in the resultant XML tree. For example, the elements in Listing 4-19 will have the Tag and Parent values in Table 4-1.

Listing 4-19 skeletal1.xml: Skeletal XML used to illustrate the Tag and Parent values used in the EXPLICIT mode.

```
<Customers ...>
  ...
  <Orders ...>
    ...
<Details ...>
  ...
</Details>
...
  </Orders>
  ...
</Customers>
```

Table 4-1 Tag and Parents Values of the Elements in Skeletal1.xml

Element	Tag	Parent
Customers	1	0
Orders	2	1
Details	3	2

After the Tag and Parent columns you will need to include one column for each of the data items in the XML. For example, the following XML fragment will need four columns because it has four data items: *CustomerID*, *ContactName*, *OrderID*, and *OrderDate*.

```
<Customers CustomerID="..." ContactName="...">
  ...
  <Orders OrderID="..." OrderDate="..."/>
  ...
</Customers>
```

These columns in the Universal Table must be named according to a specific convention. This encoding convention is used to specify metadata about the element or attribute that will represent the column. Every column must be named using the following convention:

```
ElementName!TagNumber!AttributeName![Directive]
```

- *ElementName* represents the element name that the column belongs to.
- *TagNumber* specifies the tag number of the element.
- *AttributeName* specifies the attribute or element name within the XML.
- *Directive* is optional and is used to specify how a column should be rendered in the XML. For example, a column is generated as an attribute in the XML by default. By specifying the "element" *Directive*, the column will be rendered as a contained element instead. *Directive* supports many other options, and we will see some of them later in this section.

For example, the two data items, *CustomerID* and *ContactName*, in the following XML fragment can be described by the column names, Customers!1!CustomerID and Customers!1!ContactName.

```
<Customers CustomerID="..." ContactName="...">
...
```

Each row in the Universal Table identifies an occurrence of an element in the resultant XML. Therefore, there will be as many rows in the Universal Table as the number of elements in the resultant XML. Now that you've learned the theory, it's time for some real actions! Let's build the Universal Table for the XML first shown in Listing 4-18.

We know of 10 element occurrences (one occurrence of *<Customers>* plus three occurrences of *<Orders>* plus six occurrences of *<Order_Details>*), so we will need 10 rows in the Universal Table. Looking at the XML, it should be easy to fill in the Tag and Parent values. These values are shown in Table 4-2.

Table 4-2 Tag and Parent Values

Tag	Parent
1	0
2	1
3	2
3	2
2	1
3	2
2	1

Table 4-2 Tag and Parent Values *(continued)*

Tag	Parent
3	2
3	2
3	2

Next we define the other columns. From the XML we find seven data items (*CustomerID*, *CompanyName*, *OrderID*, *OrderDate*, *ProductID*, *Quantity*, and *UnitPrice*), so we need seven extra columns in the Universal Table to describe these items. This is shown in Table 4-3.

Table 4-3 Data Columns of the Universal Table for Generating AUTO.xml

Containing Element Name	Containing Element Tag Number	Item Name	Universal Table's Column Name
<Customers>	1	*CustomerID*	Customers!1!CustomerID
<Customersk>	1	*ContactName*	Customers!1!CompanyName
<Orders>	2	*OrderID*	Orders!2!OrderID
<Orders>	2	*OrderDate*	Orders!2!OrderDate
<Order_Details>	3	*ProductID*	Order_Details!3!ProductID
<Order_Details>	3	*Quantity*	Order_Details!3!Quantity
<Order_Details>	3	*UnitPrice*	Order_Details!3!UnitPrice

We now have the complete columns definition for our Universal Table. We also know how many rows we will have and their corresponding Tag and Parent values. What's left now is to put in the actual data, which you can see in Figure 4-7.

The first row corresponds to the first occurrence of the *<Customers>* element, and we need to store the values found in its *CustomerID* and *ContactName* attributes in the Customers!1!CustomerID and Customers!1!CompanyName columns, respectively. Note that we leave the rest of the columns blank (with a NULL value) because they don't have any values in the current element.

Tag	Parent	Customers!1!CustomerID	Customers!1!CompanyName	Orders!2!OrderID	Orders!2!OrderDate	Order_Details!3!ProductID	Order_Details!3!Quantity	Order_Details!3!UnitPrice
1	0	BOLID	Bolido Comidas preparadas	NULL	NULL	NULL	NULL	NULL
2	1	BOLID	NUL	10326	1996-10-10T00:00	NULL	NULL	NULL
3	2	BOLID	NULL	10326	NULL	4	24	17.6
3	2	BOLID	NULL	10326	NULL	57	16	15.6
3	2	BOLID	NULL	10326	NULL	75	50	6.2
2	1	BOLID	NULL	10801	1997-12-26T12:00	NULL	NULL	NULL
3	2	BOLID	NULL	10801	NULL	17	40	39
3	2	BOLID	NULL	10801	NULL	29	20	123.79
2	1	BOLID	NULL	10970	1997-03-24T00:00	NULL	NULL	NULL
3	2	BOLID	NULL	10970	NULL	52	40	7

Figure 4-7 The completed Universal Table for generating the XML shown in Listing 4-18.

The second row corresponds to the first occurrence of the *<Orders>* element in the XML. This time we put the values stored in its *OrderID* and *OrderDate* attributes into the corresponding Orders!2!OrderID and Orders!2!OrderDate columns. We can leave the rest of the columns blank. Notice we have repeated the value for the CustomerID column from the previous row but left the CompanyName column blank. The reason for doing this will become clearer when we examine the SQL query needed to generate this Universal Table.

In the third row, we hit the first occurrence of the *<Order_Details>* element. Following the same rules described earlier, we fill this row out. Notice that this time we've copied the values for both the CustomerID and OrderID columns from the previous row while leaving the CompanyName and OrderDate blank. As promised, the reasons for this will be explained later in this section.

The fourth row is the same as the third row in terms of which columns it needs to complete; we just need to fill in the different column values. The fifth row is also similar to the third and fourth.

Now we have completed the first occurrence of *<Order>* and hit the second occurrence. We will use the same rules we employed in building the previous five rows in completing the second occurence here.

The Universal Table we will need for SQL Server 2000 to generate the appropriate XML in Listing 4-18 is now complete. However, given the table's relationship in Listing 4-16, we must use the proper SQL to generate a resultset like that shown in Figure 4-7. The *UNION ALL* statement is a perfect fit for achieving this effect. Listing 4-20 shows the SQL query required to generate the XML shown in Listing 4-18.

If we take a closer look at Listing 4-20, the first detail we notice is the three separate SQL queries joined by two *UNION ALL* statements. This corresponds to the number of distinct element types we have in AUTO.xml, namely *<Customers>*, *<Orders>*, and *<Order-Details>*.

Listing 4-20 explicit.sql: The *EXPLICIT* mode SQL query that can be used to generate the Universal Table shown in Figure 4-7.

```
SELECT 1 AS Tag,
       0 AS Parent,
       CustomerID AS [Customers!1!CustomerID],
       CompanyName AS [Customers!1!ContactName],
       NULL AS [Orders!2!OrderID],
       NULL AS [Orders!2!OrderDate],
       NULL AS [Order_Details!3!ProductID],
       NULL AS [Order_Details!3!Quantity],
       NULL AS [Order_Details!3!UnitPrice]
  FROM Customers
  WHERE CustomerID = 'BOLID'
UNION ALL
SELECT 2,
       1,
       CustomerID,
       NULL,
       Orders.OrderID,
       Orders.OrderDate,
       NULL,
       NULL,
       NULL
  FROM Orders, Customers
  WHERE Orders.CustomerID = Customers.CustomerID
    AND Customers.CustomerID = 'BOLID'
UNION ALL
  SELECT 3,
         2,
         CustomerID,
         NULL,
         OrderID,
         NULL,
         [Order Details].ProductID,
         [Order Details].Quantity,
         [Order Details].UnitPrice,
  FROM Orders, Customers, [Order Details]
  WHERE Orders.CustomerID =  Customers.CustomerID
    AND [Order Details].OrderID = Orders.OrderID
AND Customers.CustomerID = 'BOLID'
  ORDER BY Customers.CustomerID, Orders.OrderID
  FOR XML EXPLICIT
```

In the first query all the attribute values for the *<Customers>* element are obtained. We have given aliases to the columns according to the naming conventions required by the Universal Table. Notice that values for all the columns not related to the *<Customers>* element are set to *NULL*. Finally the values for the Tag and Parent columns are set to required values, in this case *1* and *0*.

In the second query all the attribute values for the *<Orders>* element are retrieved. Notice that we've joined the Orders table to the Customers table, and we used the same criteria for selection of the Customers row as we used in the first query. This step ensures that the Customers we found in this query match those found in the first query. Also note that, except for CustomerID, all the columns not related to the *<Orders>* element are set to *NULL*. We've also assigned the values of *2* and *1* to the Tag and Parent columns.

In the final query we obtain all the attribute values for the *<Order_Details>* element. Notice that this time we have retained both the CustomerID and OrderID columns and left the other columns not related to the *<Order_Details>* element as *NULL*. We've also set up the same relationship between the Customers and Orders tables as the previous query to ensure that the rows returned in this query are consistent with those returned in the previous two queries.

In the *EXPLICIT* mode the resultset representing the Universal Table is scanned one row at a time in a forward-only manner, producing the resultant XML tree. To yield the proper XML hierarchy, use an *ORDER BY* clause in the query to ensure the correct order of the rows in the resultset.

The need for this *ORDER BY* clause also explains why we've repeated certain column values in the Universal Table but left others *NULL*. The proper order required by the *EXPLICIT* mode is ensured by having the values of the columns specified in the *ORDER BY* clause present in all the rows in the resultset.

It would be pointless to work through the complexity of using the *EXPLICIT* mode just so you can create XML documents that can be easily generated using the *AUTO* mode. The *EXPLICIT* mode is also designed to do much more. As an example, let's make a few modifications to the XML in Listing 4-18. This new XML is shown in Listing 4-21.

We've made some significant modifications in Listing 4-21. First we renamed all the elements; *<Customers>* became *<Customer>*, *<Orders>* became *<Order>*, and *<Order_Details>* became *<Item>*. Second we changed some of the data items into elements: *CompanyName*, *OrderDate*, *UnitPrice*, and *Quantity*. Generating an XML like this is impossible to achieve using the *AUTO* mode. With the *EXPLICIT* mode, however, it's almost trivial. Listing 4-22 shows the required query.

Listing 4-21 explicit.xml: An XML document based on AUTO.xml and customized with mixed attribute and element data values.

```
<Customer CustomerID="BOLID">
  <CompanyName>Bolido Comidas preparadas</CompanyName>
  <Order OrderID="10326">
    <OrderDate>1996-10-10T00:00</OrderDate>
<Item ProductID="4">
  <Quantity>24</Quantity>
  <UnitPrice>17.6</UnitPrice>
</Item>
<Item ProductID="57">
  <Quantity>16</Quantity>
  <UnitPrice>15.6</UnitPrice>
</Item>
<Item ProductID="75">
  <Quantity>50</Quantity>
  <UnitPrice>6.2</UnitPrice>
</Item>
  </Order>
  <Order OrderID="10801">
    <OrderDate>1997-12-26T00:00</OrderDate>
<Item ProductID="17">
  <Quantity>40</Quantity>
  <UnitPrice>39</UnitPrice>
</Item>
<Item ProductID="29">
  <Quantity>20</Quantity>
  <UnitPrice>123.79</UnitPrice>
</Item>
  </Order>
  <Order OrderID="10970">
    <OrderDate>1998-03-24T00:00</OrderDate>
<Item ProductID="52">
  <Quantity>40</Quantity>
  <UnitPrice>7</UnitPrice>
</Item>
  </Order>
</Customer>
```

Listing 4-22 explicit2.sql: An SQL query that can be used to generate the XML in EXPLICIT.xml.

```
SELECT 1 AS Tag,
       0 AS Parent,
       CustomerID AS [Customer!1!CustomerID],
       ContactName AS [Customer!1!CompanyName!element],
```

(continued)

Listing 4-22 *continued*

```
       NULL AS [Order!2!OrderID],
       NULL AS [Order!2!OrderDate!element],
       NULL AS [Item!3!ProductID],
       NULL AS [Item!3!Quantity!element],
       NULL AS [Item!3!UnitPrice!element]
   FROM Customers
   WHERE CustomerID = 'BOLID'
  UNION ALL
 SELECT 2,
       1,
       CustomerID,
       NULL,
       Orders.OrderID,
       Orders.OrderDate,
       NULL,
       NULL,
       NULL
   FROM Orders, Customers
   WHERE Orders.CustomerID = Customers.CustomerID
     AND Customers.CustomerID = 'BOLID'
 UNION ALL
   SELECT 3,
         2,
         CustomerID,
         NULL,
         OrderID,
         NULL,
         [Order Details].ProductID,
         [Order Details].Quantity,
         [Order Details].UnitPrice,
   FROM Orders, Customers, [Order Details]
   WHERE Orders.CustomerID =  Customers.CustomerID
     AND [Order Details].OrderID = Orders.OrderID
 AND Customers.CustomerID = 'BOLID'
   ORDER BY Customers.CustomerID, Orders.OrderID
   FOR XML EXPLICIT
```

Notice that all the changes required are isolated to the first query, and all we had to do was specify different aliases for the columns affected. Specifically, all the elements were renamed accordingly (*Customer*, *Order*, and *Item*). In addition, we included the *element* directive for those columns that we wanted to render as elements instead of attributes.

Many other options are available to tweak the behavior of the *EXPLICIT* mode. We have shown you the basics in this section, and if you're interested we encourage you to consult your SQL Server 2000 documentation for further details.

XML Templates

SQL Server 2000 provides a new feature, called XML Templates, that can be used to wrap multiple *FOR XML* queries or stored procedures into a valid XML document. XML Templates also support advanced features such as runtime parameter substitution and support for XSLT of the resulting XML document.

An XML Template is an XML document that contains the query strings or stored procedures to execute. Listing 4-23 shows how you can wrap a *RAW* mode query that returns all rows from the Employees table within an XML Template.

Listing 4-23 xml_template.xml: A simple XML Template.

```
<?xml version="1.0"?>
<ROOT xmlns:sql="urn:schemas-microsoft-com:xml-sql">
  <sql:query>
    SELECT EmployeeID, FirstName, LastName
      FROM Employees
      FOR XML RAW
  </sql:query>
</ROOT>
```

In Listing 4-23 the *<ROOT>* element specifies the root element of the resulting XML document. You can, of course, call it anything you want, such as *<Customers>*. This root element serves to make the resulting XML document valid. Notice that we've also included the XML Template namespace definition in the *<ROOT>* element. The SQL Server 2000 XML Template XSD is identified by a URI of *urn:schemas-microsoft-com:xml-sql*.

As shown in Listing 4-23, you use the *<query>* element to specify a query or stored procedure to execute. You can have as many *<query>* elements as you like, and the results of all the queries are included together in the final XML document.

Now we need to actually execute our XML Template to retrieve the resulting XML document. One of the methods SQL Server 2000 provides for achieving this is using an HTTP URL. This feature requires you to set up a *virtual directory* and a *virtual name* of *template* type in Microsoft Internet Information Server (IIS) by using the IIS utility, Virtual Directory Management for SQL Server 2000. For instructions on configuring IIS this way, please consult your SQL Server 2000 documentation. Once IIS is configured properly, you can execute our XML Template using a URL similar to the following:

```
http://localhost/nwind/templates/XML_Template1.xml
```

In the above URL *nwind* and *templates* are examples of the virtual directory and virtual name, respectively. Listing 4-24 shows the resulting XML document when this URL is opened in a browser.

Listing 4-24 xml_template_result.xml: XML document generated from an XML Template.

```
<?xml version="1.0"?>
<ROOT xmlns:sql="urn:schemas-microsoft-com:xml-sql">
  <row EmployeeID="1" FirstName="Nancy" LastName="Davolio"/>
  <row EmployeeID="2" FirstName="Andrew" LastName="Fuller"/>
  <row EmployeeID="3" FirstName="Janet" LastName="Leverling"/>
  <row EmployeeID="4" FirstName="Margaret" LastName="Peacock"/>
  <row EmployeeID="5" FirstName="Steven" LastName="Buchanan"/>
  <row EmployeeID="6" FirstName="Michael" LastName="Suyama"/>
  <row EmployeeID="7" FirstName="Robert" LastName="King"/>
  <row EmployeeID="8" FirstName="Laura" LastName="Callanan"/>
  <row EmployeeID="9" FirstName="Annee" LastName="Dodsworth"/>
</ROOT>
```

As shown, SQL Server 2000 executed our *RAW* mode query and inserted the result within the *<ROOT>* element.

XML View

For users who need to be able to shape the XML extensively but find using the *EXPLICIT* mode too difficult, SQL Server 2000 provides a new feature referred to as XML View. XML View is basically an XML-to-relational database mapping mechanism that allows the user to fine-tune the shape of the XML. In addition, queries against XML Views are made by using a subset of the XPath language. This approach is similar to creating SQL views using *CREATE VIEW* statements and then querying against these views using *SELECT* statements.

In XML, View XML-to-relational database mapping is specified through a number of Microsoft-defined annotations to the XSD schema language. These annotations allow the user to specify the mapping between elements and attributes in the XSD schema to tables and columns in the databases. They are also used to specify the hierarchical relationships in the XML. For example, suppose we want to use the same tables and relationships as those used in generating the XML shown in Listing 4-18, but want a resultant XML that looks like that shown in Listing 4-25.

Listing 4-25 xml_view.xml: Another customized version of Listing 4-18 used to illustrate the capability of the XML View feature.

```
<Customer CustomerID="BOLID">
  <Name>Bolido Comidas preparadas</Name>
  <Order OrderID="10326">
    <Date>1996-10-10T00:00</Date>
<Item>
  <ProductID>4</ProductID>
  <Quantity>24</Quantity>
  <Price>17.6</Price>
</Item>
<Item>
  <ProductID>57</ProductID>
  <Quantity>16</Quantity>
  <Price>15.6</Price>
</Item>
<Item>
  <ProductID>75</ProductID>
  <Quantity>50</Quantity>
  <Price>6.2</Price>
</Item>
  </Order>
  <Order OrderID="10801">
    <Date>1997-12-26T00:00</Date>
<Item>
  <ProductID>17</ProductID>
  <Quantity>40</Quantity>
  <Price>39</Price>
</Item>
<Item>
  <ProductID>29</ProductID>
  <Quantity>20</Quantity>
  <Price>123.79</Price>
</Item>
  </Order>
  <Order OrderID="10970">
    <Date>1998-03-24T00:00</Date>
<Item>
  <ProductID>52</ProductID>
  <Quantity>40</Quantity>
  <Price>7</Price>
</Item>
  </Order>
</Customer>
```

To be able to generate an XML document like this, SQL Server 2000 requires that we specify an XSD with the appropriate mapping annotations. This special

XSD is known as a *mapping schema*. The annotations are used to specify which XML elements correspond to which columns in a database table. They also specify the parent-child relationships between the tables.

The XSD schema for our example is shown here in Listing 4-26. Notice that all annotations defined in a mapping schema belong to the SQL Server 2000 XML View namespace, namely *urn:schemas-microsoft-com:mapping-schema*. In Listing 4-24 this namespace is mapped to the *sql* prefix.

Listing 4-26 xml_view.xsd: Mapping schema for the XML in Listing 4-25.

```
<xsd:schema xmlns:xsd="http://www.w3.org/2001/XMLSchema"
            xmlns:sql="urn:schemas-microsoft-com:mapping-schema">
  <xsd:element name="Customer" sql:relation="Customers">
    <xsd:complexType>
      <xsd:sequence>
        <xsd:element name="Name" sql:field="CompanyName"
type="xsd:string" />
        <xsd:element ref="Orders" sql:relationship="relOrders"/>
      </xsd:sequence>
      <xsd:attribute name="CustomerID" sql:field="CustomerID"
type="xsd:string"/>
    </xsd:complexType>
  </xsd:element>
  <xsd:element name="Order" sql:relation="Orders">
    <xsd:complexType>
      <xsd:sequence>
        <xsd:element name="Date" sql:field="OrderDate"
type="xsd:dateTime"/>
        <xsd:element ref="Item" sql:relationship="relItems"/>
      </xsd:sequence>
      <xsd:attribute name="OrderID" type="xsd:int"/>
    </xsd:complexType>
  </xsd:element>
  <xsd:element name="Item" sql:relation="Order Details">
    <xsd:complexType>
      <xsd:element name="ProductID" sql:field="ProductID"
type="xsd:string"/>
      <xsd:element name="Price" sql:field="UnitPrice" type="xsd:int"/>
      <xsd:element name="Quantity" sql:field="Quantity"
type="xsd:int"/>
    </xsd:complexType>
  </xsd:element>
  <xsd:annotation>
    <xsd:appinfo>
      <sql:relationship name="relOrders"
                        parent="Customers"
                        parent-key="CustomerID"
                        child="Orders"
```

```
                            child-key="CustomerID"/>
      <sql:relationship name="relDetails"
                            parent="Orders"
                            parent-key="OrderID"
                            child="Order Details"
                            child-key="OrderID"/>
    </xsd:appinfo>
  </xsd:annotation>
</xsd:schema>
```

To specify the mapping between elements in the XML and columns in a database table, you use the *sql:field* attribute. The table where these columns can be found is specified using the *sql:relation* attribute. For example, the following fragment from Listing 4-26 defines the complex element *<Item>* as having subelements *<ProductID>*, *<Price>*, and *<Quantity>* mapped to the ProductID, UnitPrice, and the Quantity fields of the Details table respectively:

```
<xsd:element name="Item" sql:relation="Order Details">
  <xsd:complexType>
    <xsd:element name="ProductID" sql:field="ProductID"
type="xsd:string"/>
    <xsd:element name="Price" sql:field="UnitPrice" type="xsd:int"/>
    <xsd:element name="Quantity" sql:field="Quantity"
type="xsd:int"/>
  </xsd:complexType>
</xsd:element>
```

In addition to the column and table mapping specifications, we said earlier that XML View also allows you to specify the hierarchical shape of the XML. This is specified using the *<sql:relationship>* element. You need to use this annotation in two places.

First you need to specify how tables/views are to be joined. These join relationships are defined inside an annotation section using the first form of *<sql:relationship>*. The following fragment shows one of the join relationships we have defined in Listing 4-26:

```
<sql:relationship name="relOrders"
                  parent="Customers"
                  parent-key="CustomerID"
                  child="Orders"
                  child-key="CustomerID"/>
```

Each join relationship, or table join, is defined by an *<sql:relationship>* element. A *name* attribute is used to uniquely identify this relationship so that it can be referenced elsewhere in the XSD. Which tables and columns are involved in the join are defined by the four self-explanatory attributes *parent*, *parent-key*, *child*, and *child-key*. The previous fragment means that we are joining the Orders table to the Customers table using the CustomerID column of each of these tables as the keys. This is functionally equivalent to the following *WHERE* clause:

```
WHERE Customers.CustomerID = Orders.CustomerID
```

Now that you have the join relationships defined, you can use them to specify corresponding elements to be included in the resultant XML by defining an element that references one of these join relationships. Here the *sql:relationship* attribute is used to specify the name of the join relationship defined in the annotation section:

```
  <xsd:element ref="Item" sql:relationship="relItems"/>
```

Now that we have completed the design of our schema, how do we ask SQL Server 2000 to create an XML document using this schema? The answer is that SQL Server 2000 features a subset of the XPath language for querying against XML Views. For example, to perform the equivalent of the *SELECT WHERE Customers.CustomerID = 'BOLID'* that we've used in our earlier examples, we can use the following XPath, which will return an XML like that shown in XML_view.xml:

```
/Customer[@CustomerID='BOLID']
```

You don't have to stop there. You can restrict the XML document to return only the list of the *<Item>* elements without the *<Customer>* and *<Order>* elements. Here is the XPath to achieve this:

```
/Customer[@CustomerID='BOLID'/Order/Item]
```

Using this string will return an XML fragment similar to the following:

```
<Item>
  <ProductID>918234</ProductID>
  <Price>12.00</Price>
  <Quantity>4</Quantity>
</Item>
<Item>
  <ProductID>170018</ProductID>
  <Price>20.00</Price>
  <Quantity>2</Quantity>
</Item>
<Item>
  <ProductID>100144</ProductID>
  <UnitPrice>49.95</UnitPrice>
  <Quantity>10</Quantity>
</Item>
<Item>
  <ProductID>710050</ProductID>
```

```
  <UnitPrice>199.95</UnitPrice>
  <Quantity>1</Quantity>
</Item>
<Item>
  <ProductID>918234</ProductID>
  <UnitPrice>12.00</UnitPrice>
  <Quantity>10</Quantity>
</Item>
<Item>
  <ProductID>001460</ProductID>
  <UnitPrice>299.95</UnitPrice>
  <Quantity>1</Quantity>
</Item>
```

Persisting XML Data Using OPENXML

SQL Server 2000 also features a resultset provider, called OPENXML, that provides a resultset view over an XML document. This feature can be useful when you want to send an XML document as a parameter to an SQL statement or stored procedure and then insert the data found in the document into the appropriate relational tables.

Functionally, OPENXML is similar to other resultset providers such as OPENQUERY and OPENROWSET. The major difference is that, with OPENXML, you need to use a special stored procedure to prepare your XML document and clear it from memory with another stored procedure after you're done.

To prepare your XML document, you call the *sp_xml_prepareDocument* stored procedure. This loads the XML document, passed in through the string parameter, into memory, preparses it for optimal query performance, and turns it into a resultset. The procedure, *sp_xml_prepareDocument*, returns an *INT* value, which represents a handle to the XML resultset in memory. You use this handle when you want to use the associated XML resultset. When you're done using this resultset, pass the handle to the *sp_xml_removeDocument* stored procedure to clear up the used memory.

The SQL script in Listing 4-27 shows how you can use OPENXML to insert data defined in a specific XML document into the Employees table.

You can see that the *sp_xml_prepareDocument* stored procedure takes two parameters. The first is an output parameter and is the returned handle value. The second is the XML document represented as a string. Depending on the size of the XML string, this input parameter can be *CHAR*, *TEXT*, or *VARCHAR*. You can also use the Unicode-ready version of these data types (*NCHAR*, *NTEXT*, and *NVARCHAR*).

Listing 4-27 openxml.sql: Inserting records using OPENXML.

```
DECLARE @xmlHnd INT
DECLARE @xmlDoc VARCHAR( 1000 )
-- prepare the XML document
SET @xmlDoc =
'<ROOT>
  <Employees EmployeeID="2" FirstName="Albert" LastName="Adams"/>
  <Employees EmployeeID="4" FirstName="Ed" LastName="Davis"/>
  <Employees EmployeeID="10" FirstName="Joe" LastName="Young"/>
</ROOT>'
-- Load and parse the XML document
EXEC sp_xml_prepareDocument @xmlHnd OUTPUT, @xmlDoc
-- Insert the three Employees record specified in the XML INSERT
Employees
  SELECT *
    FROM OPENXML( @xmlHnd, '/ROOT/Employees', 0 )
           WITH ( EmployeeID INT, FirstName VARCHAR( 20 ), LastName
VARCHAR( 20 ) )
-- release reference to the XML document
EXEC sp_xml_removeDocument @hXmlDoc
```

To turn the XML document identified by the handle that is returned by *sp_xml_prepareDocument* into a resultset, you use the OPENXML resultset function. OPENXML has the following syntax:

```
OPENXML( Handle, XPath[, Attributes] ) WITH SchemaDeclaration
```

- *Handle* is the handle value returned by the *sp_xml_prepareDocument* stored procedure.
- *XPath* is an XPath expression used to identify the nodes in the XML document that should be included in the resultset. Each node identified by the XPath expression corresponds to a single row in the resultset generated by OPENXML.
- *Attributes* are optional and are used to specify the type of mapping (attribute-centric or element-centric) between the resultset columns and the XML nodes identified by the XPath expression. *Attributes* are integer values and the default value of 0 uses an attribute-centric mapping. A value of 2 identifies element-centric mapping.
- *SchemaDeclaration* identifies the database schema declaration that OPENXML uses to generate the resultset. *SchemaDeclaration* uses a syntax similar to that used by the *CREATE TABLE* statement, namely ColumnName1 ColumnType1, ColumnName2, ColumnType2, and so

forth. Alternatively, you can specify the name of a table for *Schema-Declarations* if this table already exists with the desired schema.

In our previous openxml.sql example our OPENXML call looks like the following:

```
OPENXML( @xmlHnd, '/ROOT/Employees', 0 ) WITH Employees
```

This code specifies that our XML document, identified by the *xmlHnd* handle, is attribute-centric by passing a value of *0* to the *Attributes* parameter (the third parameter). Next the *XPath* identifies that we intend to use the nodes found under the */ROOT/Employees* element to generate the rows in the OPENXML resultset. Finally the *WITH* clause specifies the schema that will be used to construct the resultset.

Oracle 9i

SQL Server 2000 is not the only database that supports a wealth of XML integration. Oracle 9i also provides a number of powerful tools for building XML applications. However, compared to SQL Server 2000, these features are more complicated and usually require more programming.

Most of the XML features provided by Oracle 9i can be found in the Oracle XML Development Kits (XDK). Oracle makes XDKs for Java, C/C++, and PL/SQL. Components supplied in these XDKs include XML parsers, XLST processors, and other tools. One of these tools is the XML SQL Utility (XSU), which is used to generate XML documents from SQL queries.

Oracle 9i also provides a new data type, called XMLType, that can be used to natively persist both data-centric and document-centric XML documents in the database. This feature simplifies the task of using the database as an XML repository. Oracle 9i supports indexing the XML documents stored using XMLType through the Oracle Text package. Once indexed, these XML documents can be searched as text or as document sections.

In the code examples in the rest of this section we will use the tables and objects created and populated using the oracle_script.sql SQL script and displayed in Listing 4-28. If you are running these examples, use this script to create and populate your tables.

Listing 4-28 oracle_script.sql: A creation script for sample tables.

```
-- create and populate the Dept table
CREATE TABLE Dept
(
  Dept_No NUMBER PRIMARY KEY
  Dept_Name VARCHAR2( 20 ) NOT NULL
```

(continued)

Listing 4-28 *continued*

```
);
/
INSERT INTO Dept VALUES ( 1, 'IT' );
/
INSERT INTO Dept VALUES ( 2, 'Marketing' );
/
INSERT INTO Dept VALUES ( 3, 'HR' );
/
INSERT INTO Dept VALUES ( 4, 'Accounting' );
/
INSERT INTO Dept VALUES ( 5, 'Operations' );
/
-- create and populate the Employee table
CREATE TABLE Employee
(
  Employee_No NUMBER PRIMARY KEY,
  First_Name VARCHAR2( 20 ),
  Last_Name VARCHAR2( 20 ) NOT NULL,
  Dept_No NUMBER REFERENCES Dept( Dept_No )
);
/
INSERT INTO Employee VALUES ( 1, 'Sean', 'Chai', 1 )
/
INSERT INTO Employee VALUES ( 2, 'Aaron', 'Con', 1 )
/
INSERT INTO Employee VALUES ( 3, 'Andrew', 'Dixon', 2 )
/
INSERT INTO Employee VALUES ( 4, 'Ted', 'Bremer', 3 )
/
INSERT INTO Employee VALUES ( 5, 'Randall', 'Boseman', 4 )
/
INSERT INTO Employee VALUES ( 6, 'Jane', 'Clayton', 1 )
/
INSERT INTO Employee VALUES ( 7, 'Peter', 'Connelly', 2 )
/
INSERT INTO Employee VALUES ( 8, 'Eva', 'Corets', 3 )
/
INSERT INTO Employee VALUES ( 9, 'Nate', 'Sun', 5 )
/
```

The XML SQL Utility

XSU is supplied as part of the Oracle XDK and is designed to enable the user to perform the following three tasks:

- Generate an XML document from any SQL queries or Java JDBC Resultset objects.
- Extract the data from an XML document and insert the data into the appropriate columns/attributes of a table or view.
- Extract the data from an XML document and use this data to update or delete values of the appropriate columns/attributes or both.

The various XSU functionalities are accessible through a Java API, a PL/SQL API, or a command-line utility. For the examples in this section we will be using the Java API to illustrate using XSU. XSU uses a set of customizable resultset-based mapping rules, called SQL-XML mapping, to go from SQL to XML and vice versa. Let's take a look at what the default mapping does. Submit the following SQL query to XSU:

```
SELECT Employee_ID, First_Name, Last_Name
  FROM Employee
  ORDER BY Employee_ID
```

This simple SQL query generates Listing 4-29.

Listing 4-29 xsu_generated_xml1.xml: XML generated by XSU using default mapping.

```
<?xml version="1.0"?>
<ROWSET>
  <ROW num="1">
    <EMPLOYEE_ID>1</EMPLOYEE_ID>
    <FIRST_NAME>Sean</FIRST_NAME>
    <LAST_NAME>Chai</LAST_NAME>
  </ROW>
  <ROW num="2">
    <EMPLOYEE_ID>2</EMPLOYEE_ID>
    <FIRST_NAME>Aaron</FIRST_NAME>
    <LAST_NAME>Con</LAST_NAME>
  </ROW>
  <ROW num="3">
    <EMPLOYEE_ID>3</EMPLOYEE_ID>
    <FIRST_NAME>Andrew</FIRST_NAME>
    <LAST_NAME>Dixon</LAST_NAME>
  </ROW>
  <ROW num="4">
    <EMPLOYEE_ID>4</EMPLOYEE_ID>
    <FIRST_NAME>Ted</FIRST_NAME>
    <LAST_NAME>Bremer</LAST_NAME>
  </ROW>
  <ROW num="5">
    <EMPLOYEE_ID>5</EMPLOYEE_ID>
```

(continued)

Listing 4-29 *continued*

```
    <FIRST_NAME>Randall</FIRST_NAME>
    <LAST_NAME>Boseman</LAST_NAME>
  </ROW>
  <ROW num="6">
    <EMPLOYEE_ID>6</EMPLOYEE_ID>
    <FIRST_NAME>Jane</FIRST_NAME>
    <LAST_NAME>Clayton</LAST_NAME>
  </ROW>
  <ROW num="7">
    <EMPLOYEE_ID>7</EMPLOYEE_ID>
    <FIRST_NAME>Peter</FIRST_NAME>
    <LAST_NAME>Connelly</LAST_NAME>
  </ROW>
  <ROW num="8">
    <EMPLOYEE_ID>8</EMPLOYEE_ID>
    <FIRST_NAME>Eva</FIRST_NAME>
    <LAST_NAME>Cosets</LAST_NAME>
  </ROW>
  <ROW num="9">
    <EMPLOYEE_ID>9</EMPLOYEE_ID>
    <FIRST_NAME>Nate</FIRST_NAME>
    <LAST_NAME>Sun</LAST_NAME>
  </ROW>
</ROWSET>
```

With the default mapping, the root element is called *<ROWSET>*. *<ROWSET>* contains one or more *<ROW>* child elements, each of which is used to represent a row in the resultset. *<ROW>* has a single attribute, called *num* and is used to indicated the *logical* row number for the associated row. Finally each *<ROW>* element contains one or more child elements whose names and contents represent the columns in the resultset.

Generating XML Documents

To generate XML documents from resultsets you will need to write some Java code. All the functionality related to generating XML documents is provided by the *oracle.xml.sql.query.OracleXMLQuery* Java class. The general steps required to generate an XML document using XSU are

1. Get a connection to the required Oracle database by using the Oracle JDBC Driver. You can use any Oracle-supported JDBC Driver such as the OCI8, Thin, or the server-side internal JDBC Driver.
2. Create an instance of the *OracleXMLQuery* class and passing the constructor the SQL query in the form of a java.lang.String, a java.sql.ResultSet, or an *oracle.xml.sql.dataset.OracleXMLDataSet*.

3. Specify optional features such as a different resultset, row name or both, defining the format for dates, or even specifying a style sheet header.

4. Retrieve the generated XML document. You can get a string or DOM representation of this XML document by calling the *getDOM ()* or *getXML()* method, respectively.

5. Release resources held by the *OracleXMLQuery* by calling its *close()* method.

Listing 4-30 shows a simple example of a Java console application that uses XSU to generate an XML document from a query.

Listing 4-30 xsu_select.java: Using XSU to generate an XML document from an SQL query.

```
import java.sql.*;
import oracle.jdbc.driver.*;
import oracle.xml.sql.query.*;
/* class to test the String generation! */
public class XSU_Select
{
  public static void main( String argv[] ) throws Exception
  {
    /* connect to Oracle */
    DriverManager.registerDriver( new oracle.jdbc.driver.
OracleDriver() );
    Connection conn = DriverManager.getConnection(
"jdbc:oracle:oci8:@", "scott", "tiger" );
    /* setup the SQL string */
    String sqlStr = "SELECT Last_Name || ', ' || First_Name
Employee_Name, Dept_Name" +
                    "  FROM Employee, Dept" +
                    "  WHERE Employee.Dept_No = Dept.Dept_No" +
                    "  ORDER BY Employee_ID";
    /* initiate an OracleXMLQuery with our SQL string */
    OracleXMLQuery qry = new OracleXMLQuery( conn, sqlStr );
    /* get the generated XML string */
    String xmlStr = qry.getXMLString();
    /* output the XML string to the console */
    System.out.println( xmlStr );
    /* always remember to close the OracleXMLQuery object after use
*/
    qry.close();
  }
}
```

Listing 4-30 first sets up a JDBC Connection to Oracle using the Oracle OCI8 JDBC driver (*oracle.jdbc.driver.OracleDriver*).

> **Note** Listing 4-30 connects to the default database (identified by the ORA_SID environment variable) as user *scott*. To test this program in your environment, be certain that you make the necessary modifications to properly log in first.

Next an instance of the *OracleXMLQuery* class is created, passing it the JDBC Connection object and the SQL query string. Then xsu_select.java then calls the *getXMLString()* method of *OracleXMLQuery* to generate and return the XML document as a java.lang.String. This XML document is then displayed on the console. Finally Listing 4-30 releases the memory occupied by the instance of *OracleXMLQuery*.

> **Note** To compile, first make sure you have the necessary CLASSPATH specified. Execute the command *javac xsu_select.java*. Once it is successfully compiled, execute *XSU_select* by entering *java xsu_select*.

Listing 4-31 is an example of the output that will be generated.

Listing 4-31 xsu_select.xml: XML generated by Listing 4-30.

```
<?xml version="1.0"?>
<ROWSET>
  <ROW num="1">
    <EMPLOYEE_ID>1</EMPLOYEE_ID>
    <EMPLOYEE_NAME>Chai, Sean</EMPLOYEE_NAME>
    <DEPT_NAME>IT</DEPT_NAME>
  </ROW>
  <ROW num="2">
    <EMPLOYEE_ID>2</EMPLOYEE_ID>
    <EMPLOYEE_NAME>Con, Aaron</EMPLOYEE_NAME>
    <DEPT_NAME>IT</DEPT_NAME>
  </ROW>
  <ROW num="3">
```

```
    <EMPLOYEE_ID>3</EMPLOYEE_ID>
    <EMPLOYEE_NAME>Dixon, Andrew</EMPLOYEE_NAME>
    <DEPT_NAME>Marketing</DEPT_NAME>
  </ROW>
  <ROW num="4">
    <EMPLOYEE_ID>4</EMPLOYEE_ID>
    <EMPLOYEE_NAME>Bremer, Ted</EMPLOYEE_NAME>
    <DEPT_NAME>HR</DEPT_NAME>
  </ROW>
  <ROW num="5">
    <EMPLOYEE_ID>5</EMPLOYEE_ID>
    <EMPLOYEE_NAME>Boseman, Randall</EMPLOYEE_NAME>
    <DEPT_NAME>Accounting</DEPT_NAME>
  </ROW>
  <ROW num="6">
    <EMPLOYEE_ID>6</EMPLOYEE_ID>
    <EMPLOYEE_NAME>Clayton, Jane</EMPLOYEE_NAME>
    <DEPT_NAME>IT</DEPT_NAME>
  </ROW>
  <ROW num="7">
    <EMPLOYEE_ID>7</EMPLOYEE_ID>
    <EMPLOYEE_NAME>Connelly, Peter</EMPLOYEE_NAME>
    <DEPT_NAME>Marketing</DEPT_NAME>
  </ROW>
  <ROW num="8">
    <EMPLOYEE_ID>8</EMPLOYEE_ID>
    <EMPLOYEE_NAME>Corets, Eva</EMPLOYEE_NAME>
    <DEPT_NAME>HR</DEPT_NAME>
  </ROW>
  <ROW num="9">
    <EMPLOYEE_ID>9</EMPLOYEE_ID>
    <EMPLOYEE_NAME>Sun, Nate</EMPLOYEE_NAME>
    <DEPT_NAME>Operations</DEPT_NAME>
  </ROW>
</ROWSET>
```

Storing XML Data

In addition to transforming a resultset into XML, XSU can also be used to insert XML data into tables, update existing tables with the data extracted from XML documents, and delete rows from tables based on element values stored in the XML documents. These are all provided by methods found in the *oracle.xml.sql.dml.OracleXMLSave* class. Using *OracleXMLSave* generally involves following these basic steps:

- Get a connection to the required Oracle database by using the Oracle JDBC Driver. You can use any Oracle-supported JDBC Driver, such as the OCI8, Thin, or the server-side internal JDBC Driver.
- Create an instance of the *OracleXMLSave* class and passing the constructor the name of the table or view on which insertions, updating, or deletions need to be done.
- For insertion you have the option to specify a list of column names that you want the insert to work on. To do this you construct an array of java.lang.String containing the column names and then pass it to the *setUpdateColumnList()* method.
- For updating you need to specify the list of key column names that will be used to select the rows for updating. You do this by building an array of java.lang.String containing the key column names and passing it to the *setKeyColumnList()* method. You can also specify the specific columns that you want to update instead of updating all the columns. To do this you construct an array of java.lang.String containing the column names and then pass it to the *setUpdateColumnList()* method.
- For deletion you can specify the list of key column names that will be used to select the rows for deletion. You do this by building an array of java.lang.String containing the key column names and passing it to the *setKeyColumnList()* method.
- Construct an XML document as a java.lang.String, java.io.InputStream, java.io.Reader, or as a DOM object.
- For insertion invoke the *insertXML()* method and pass it the XML document constructed in the previous step.
- For updating invoke the *updateXML()* method and pass it the XML document constructed in the previous step.
- For deletion invoke the *deleteXML()* method and pass it the XML document constructed in the previous step.
- Release resources held by the *OracleXMLSave* by calling its *close()* method.

Listing 4-32 is an example Java program that illustrates the insertion process.

Listing 4-32 xsu_insert.java: Inserting XML data into a table.

```
import java.sql.*;
import oracle.jdbc.driver.*;
import oracle.xml.sql.dml.*;
public class XSU_Insert
{
  public static void main( String argv[] ) throws Exception
  {
    /* connect to Oracle */
    DriverManager.registerDriver( new oracle.jdbc.driver.
OracleDriver() );
    Connection conn = DriverManager.getConnection( "jdbc:
oracle:oci8:@", "scott", "tiger" );
    /* instantiate the OracleXMLSave object and specify that
       we will be inserting into the Employee table */
    OracleXMLSave sav = new OracleXMLSave( conn, "Employee" );
    /* setup the XML string */
    String xmlStr = "<?xml version=\"1.0\"?>" +
                    "<ROWSET>" +
                    "  <ROW num=\"1\">" +
                    "    <EMPLOYEE_NO>10</EMPLOYEE_NO>" +
                    "    <FIRST_NAME>Joshua</FIRST_NAME>" +
                    "    <LAST_NAME>Lehman</LAST_NAME>" +
                    "    <DEPT_NO>5</DEPT_NO>" +
                    "  </ROW>" +
                    "</ROWSET>";
    /* insert the row */
    sav.insertXML( xmlStr );
    /* always remember to close the OracleXMLSave object after use */
    sav.close();
  }
}
```

Like the last example, Listing 4-32 sets up a JDBC Connection to Oracle using the Oracle OCI8 JDBC driver. Doing so creates an instance of the *OracleXMLSave* class, passing the JDBC Connection object and also the name of the table (in this case Employee). Listing 4-32 then sets up the string used to hold the XML document containing the specification for the row to be inserted into the Employee table.

Listing 4-32 then calls the *insertXML()* method of the *OracleXMLSave()* class to insert the row represented by the XML document specified in *xmlStr* into the Employee table. Finally Listing 4-32 releases the memory occupied by the instance of OracleXMLSave.

> **Note** Compiling and running this example has the same requirements as the previous example.

Once it has finished executing you might want to verify for yourself that the row has been inserted into the table. To do this fire up SQL*PLUS and execute the following query:

```
SQL>SELECT * FROM Employee ORDER BY Employee_ID;
```

Here is the response you can expect back if Listing 4-32 executed correctly:

```
EMPLOYEE_NO FIRST_NAME LAST_NAME DEPT_NO
----------- ---------- --------- -------
          1 Sean       Chai            1
          2 Aaron      Con             1
          3 Andrew     Dixon           2
          4 Ted        Bremer          3
          5 Randall    Boseman         4
          6 Jane       Clayton         1
          7 Peter      Connelly        2
          8 Eva        Corets          3
          9 Nate       Sun             5
```

XMLType

Oracle 9i features a new system-defined object type, XMLType, for storing XML documents. The method, exposed by XMLType, provides mechanisms for creating, extracting, and indexing XML data. XMLType can be used as columns in tables and views. It can also be used in PL/SQL and Java code as parameters, return values, and variables. XMLType has a number of uses, including the four we will discuss in the following sections.

Creating XMLType Columns

As mentioned previously, XMLType can be used as table/view columns. The following example creates a product information table that, among other normal columns, has an XMLType column used to store a product description.

```
CREATE TABLE Product_Info
(
  Product_Number INTEGER PRIMARY KEY,
  Product_Name VARCHAR2( 20 ) NOT NULL,
  Comments SYS.XMLType NOT NULL
)
```

Notice that, just like a normal column, you can use the *NOT NULL* constraint on an XMLType column. However, you cannot currently use default values and check constraints with XMLType columns.

Inserting and Updating XMLType Columns

You can use an *INSERT* statement to insert an XML document into an XMLType column. If your XML data is stored as a string or CLOB, you first need to convert it to the XMLType before you can insert into an XMLType column. In both cases you use the built-in *createXML()* method that creates and returns an instance of XMLType. You can pass *createXML()* in its argument the XML document as either a string or CLOB argument.

> **Note** At the time of writing, Oracle only supports insertion of well-formed and complete XML documents. You cannot store fragments or other non-well-formed XML into XMLType columns.

The following example inserts two rows into the Product_Info table using SQL*Plus:

```
SQL>INSERT INTO Product_Info
      VALUES ( 10, 'VideoMan LPV-240', SYS.XMLType.createXML( '<?xml
version="1.0"?><Comments><Comment user=\"tjane\">Nice value but not
enough features</Comment><Comment user=\"rjlehman\">User interface too
complicated</Comment></Comments>' ) );
1 row created.
SQL>INSERT INTO Product_Info
      VALUES ( 12, 'Ultra DVD210', SYS.XMLType.createXML( '<?xml
version="1.0"?><Comments><Comment user=\"rhackman\">Positively
Amazing! Best output quality I have seen!</Comment><Comment
user=\"qiwong\">Great video quality. Bad VCD support</Comment>
</Comments>' ) );
1 row created.
SQL>
```

Here the two XML documents, represented as strings, are first converted to an XMLType by using the *createXML()* method before they are inserted into the Product_Info table. To replace the XML stored in an XMLType column with another, you can simply use the *UPDATE* statement. As in the case of insertion, unless your new XML is an XMLType, you will have to use the *createXML()* method to convert your XML into an XMLType first.

Here is a simple example of using the *UPDATE* statement to update one of the rows inserted in the preceding *INSERT* example:

```
UPDATE Product_Info
  SET Comments = SYS.XMLType.createXML( '<?xml version="1.0"?>
<Comments><Comment user=\"tjane\">Nice value but not enough features
</Comment><Comment user=\"rjlehman\">User interface too complicated
</Comments><Comment user=\"mgoodman\"> For an off brand this one seems
to be one of the better ones</Comment></Comments>' )
  WHERE Product_No = 10
```

Using XMLType Columns in *SELECT* Statements

XMLType can also be used in *SELECT* statements. In PL/SQL or Java you can use *SELECT* to transfer XMLType column values to and from XMLType-typed variables. You can also use the built-in *getClobValue()*, *getStringVal()*, or *getNumberVal()* methods to get the value of an XMLType as a CLOB, varchar, or a number respectively.

For instance, the following *SELECT* statement displays the XML document stored in the Comments field of Product_Info table:

```
SQL>SELECT Product_No, Product_Name, Comments.getStringVal() AS
Users_Comments
      FROM Product_Info;
PRODUCT_NO PRODUCT_NAME     USERS_COMMENTS
        10 VideoMan LPV-240 <?xml version="1.0"?><Comments><Comment
user=\"tjane\">Nice value but not enough features</Comment><Comment
user=\"rjlehman\">User interface too complicated</Comments><Comment
user=\"mgoodman\"> For an off brand this one seems to be one of the
better ones</Comment></Comments>
        20 Ultra DVD210     <?xml version="1.0"?><Comments><Comment
user=\"rhackman\">Positively Amazing! Best output quality I have
seen!</Comment><Comment user=\"qiwong\">Great video quality. Bad VCD
support</Comment></Comments>
SQL>
```

Using XPath to Query XML Data

One of the most powerful features of XMLType is the built-in support for advanced XPath XML querying capabilities. XPath support is provided through the *ExistsNode()* and *Extract()* built-in methods. The *ExistsNode()* method is used to check if an XPath expression passed to it as an argument evaluates to at least a single XML element or text node. If the check is true, *ExistsNode()* returns *1*. Otherwise, it returns *0*. You can use this method anywhere functions can be used.

In the following example we use *ExistsNode()* in the *WHERE* clause of a *SELECT* statement to look for rows in the Product_Info table that match a specific XPath expression.

```
SQL>SELECT Product_No, Product_Name, Comments.getStringVal() AS
Users_Comments
       FROM Product_Info
      WHERE Comments.ExistsNode( '/Comments/Comment[@user= mgoodman]' ) = 1
PRODUCT_NO PRODUCT_NAME      USERS_COMMENTS
        10 VideoMan LPV-240 <?xml version="1.0"?><Comments><Comment
user=\"tjane\">Nice value but not enough features</Comment><Comment
user=\"rjlehman\">User interface too complicated</Comments><Comment
user=\"mgoodman\"> For an off brand this one seems to be one of the
better ones</Comment></Comments>
SQL>
```

The second method supported by XMLType for XPath querying, *Extract()*, is used to extract nodes from the XML stored in an XMLType. The result returned from applying an XPath is another XMLType. However, this XMLType does not need to be well-formed; it can consist of a set of nodes or simple scalar types. The following example extends the *SELECT* statement in the previous example to extract contents from the node that matches the XPath expression.

```
SQL>SELECT Product_No, Product_Name, Comments.Extract( '/Comments/
Comment[@user=mgoodman]' ).getStringVal() AS USER_COMMENT
       FROM Product_Info
      WHERE Comments.ExistsNode( '/Comments/Comment[@user= mgoodman]' ) = 1
PRODUCT_NO PRODUCT_NAME      USERS_COMMENTS
        10 VideoMan LPV-240 For an off brand this one seems to be one
of the better ones
SQL>
Note: We had to convert the result into a string value by using the
getStringVal() method so that it can be displayed in SQL*Plus.
```

Conclusion

In this chapter we've seen why corporations all over the globe use XML with databases. We discussed the issues and solutions for exposing data stored in databases as XML documents. We also looked at how XML documents can be persisted as database data. Finally we explored the features provided by some commercial RDBMS products for supporting XML.

In Chapter 5 we will look at another major real-world application of XML: Web development.

5

Web Development

Though still in its infancy, XML has significantly affected Web page design and deployment. XML brought about a new approach to Web development by encouraging developers to separate content from presentation. This chapter will dive into the new Web paradigm. We will begin with a discussion of the history of Web programming before moving on to discuss how savvy Web developers can use XML to solve practical problems that plague traditional Web page design. Finally we will use the technologies that we learn in this chapter to build a real-world Web site.

The Web Publishing Process

XML makes the Web publishing process much easier than it was before, when Web site programmers relied solely on HTML. To appreciate how XML helps, we're going to take a brief look at the history of Web publishing and see how dismal the situation was before XML appeared. Afterwards we will introduce the example XML document we will use while solving the Web problems of a fictional company.

When Web sites first began popping up, the designers didn't have many options in the form of Web design languages. Designers created Web pages statically using HTML. Though considered old now, HTML does have a number of attractive features. It consists only of rich, plain text, which makes it easy to transfer, store, and view. Armed with a strong knowledge of Cascading Style Sheets (CSS) and table manipulation, a competent Web page designer could create an impressive-looking document.

HTML's significant shortcoming, however, is that it is static. The Web's explosion into commerce heightened the need for dynamic content. Stock quotes, book prices, and inventory information needed to be displayed with immediacy. With these changes came the Common Gateway Interface (CGI), which allowed developers to write programs and scripts, hosted and run by a Web server, to produce dynamic HTML pages. The programs could now process form data, query databases, and build dynamic output.

CGI paved the way for other technologies, such as Microsoft's Active Server Pages (ASP), Allaire's ColdFusion, and many other server-side scripting engines. These technologies offered significant improvements over CGI, such as performance and scalability, and took a giant leap forward through multithreading, a lightweight alternative to creating a new process with each CGI request. Scripts could now be embedded directly into HTML source code, shortening the learning curve for beginning programmers. These tools also made database access for developers easier. Suddenly huge repositories of information could be accessed and updated online. The ubiquitous Web browser made an ideal distributed client as well.

Ironically, the speed of the Web's growth hindered its maturation. Fueled by the promises of riches through e-commerce, companies raced to stake a claim on the Internet. For the developers of sought-after Web products, time to market became more important than sound application design. A paradigm shift began.

Web content underwent a metamorphosis from scholarly publications to corporate billboards to online shopping markets to full-blown enterprise applications. Business logic, database queries, and service communication logic crept into HTML source code. Web pages increased in complexity and began to resemble computer programs instead of publishing documents. A number of the following problems arose with this phenomenon:

- Scripting languages, while ideal for small amounts of logic, are not robust enough for large-scale applications development. They discourage the use of object-oriented design and do not scale well as an application's complexity grows over time.

- A tight coupling of presentation and content hinders application extensibility. How many developers have solved browser incompatibilities quickly by copying and pasting chunks of similar code? This solution looks easy until you have several versions of one site to maintain! Similarly, how many hours have Web designers spent changing colors, fonts, and page layouts after a company decided to change its corporate logo or image?
- A tight coupling of presentation and content leads to a tight coupling of employee skill sets. Many people can design and code a slick Web site or understand complex business rules and database schemas. Only a precious few can do both. How much time is spent fixing bugs in a design specialist's logic or making a code guru's attempt at page layout passable?

Intuitive Web professionals began to see the need to divide the content of a Web page from the rules that govern its display on browsers or small devices. This distinction is what XML seeks to achieve.

An XML Navigation Example

Navigation has always been an important element to any Web site. The developing field of E-commerce placed an even greater emphasis on effective navigation. If potential customers cannot quickly find what they are looking for, they will spend their money elsewhere.

XML is a useful tool for achieving effective Web site navigation. Expandable and collapsible trees are familiar navigation devices but are tricky to implement because they must work with many browsers. Regardless of implementation, all trees share the same conceptual organization. They consist of a number of nodes (or elements) that are assembled in a hierarchical fashion. Such a tree can easily be modeled in an XML document.

Listing 5-1 is an example of such a document. Each *<navitem>* element contains a description, one or more images, a hyperlink to another document, and an optional list of children.

The data in this example can be modified to represent anything from Web site navigation to a help document's table of contents. In fact, this document is an excerpt from Microsoft's XML 3 Software Development Kit (SDK) documentation. Its generic navigation information can easily be transformed into a browser-specific UI, and Figure 5-1 shows how Microsoft Internet Explorer 5.5 displays this document by using its default transformation.

Figure 5-2 shows the same document transformed into an interface suitable for a user.

Listing 5-1 Navigation.xml: An XML model of a simple navigation tree.

```
<?xml version="1.0"?>
<navigation type="tree">
  <description>XML (Extensible Markup Language)</description>
  <openImage>/xmlbook/images/general/open.gif</openImage>
  <closedImage>/xmlbook/images/general/closed.gif</closedImage>
  <href target="detail">item2.htm</href>
  <navitem>
    <description>What's New</description>
    <image>/xmlbook/images/general/item.gif</image>
    <href target="detail">item2.htm</href>
  </navitem>
  <navitem>
    <description>Copyright and Legal Information</description>
    <image>/xmlbook/images/general/item.gif</image>
    <href target="detail">item2.htm</href>
  </navitem>
  <navitem>
    <description>XML Developer's Guide</description>
    <openImage>/xmlbook/images/general/open.gif</openImage>
    <closedImage>/xmlbook/images/general/closed.gif</closedImage>
    <href target="detail">item1.html</href>
    <children>
      <navitem>
        <description>Introduction to XML</description>
    <openImage>/xmlbook/images/general/open.gif</openImage>
    <closedImage>/xmlbook/images/general/closed.gif</closedImage>
    <href target="detail">item1.htm</href>
    <children>
      <navitem>
        <description>Advantages of the XML Format</description>
        <image>/xmlbook/images/general/item.gif</image>
        <href target="detail">item1.htm</href>
      </navitem>
      <navitem>
        <description>Creating a Simple XML Document</description>
        <image>/xmlbook/images/general/item.gif</image>
        <href target="detail">item1.htm</href>
      </navitem>
      <navitem>
        <description>Displaying the File in Internet xplorer
</description>
             <image>/xmlbook/images/general/item.gif</image>
             <href target="detail">item1.htm</href>
      </navitem>
    </children>
      </navitem>
    </children>
  </navitem>
  . . . .
</navigation>
```

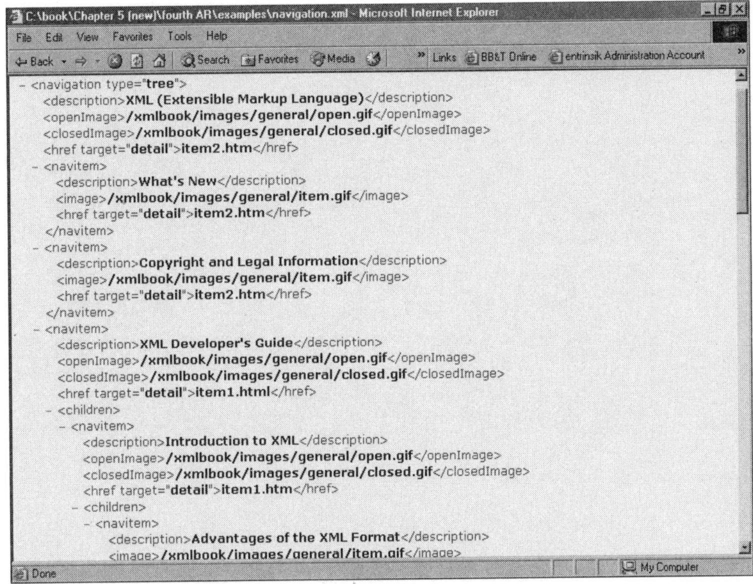

Figure 5-1 Internet Explorer displaying the navigation XML document.

Using a New Publishing Technique with XML

Later in this chapter we will explore a real-world example using XML in the Web publishing process. XML will be used to model the different elements of a fictitious company's Web site. The company, Noverant, sells CDs through its online storefront. Noverant wants to convert its site to XML in an effort to lower ongoing maintenance and development costs. The site will support all major browsers (even those without XML support) and will take advantage of some browser-specific features for a richer user experience.

Although this example is discussed later, it's useful to introduce some of the concepts now so that you can get an early start. The Noverant site will use a design pattern known as *Front Controller*. This pattern prescribes a centralized access point for all page requests in the site.

All user requests will flow through a single ASP that will perform the following duties:

1. The controller will check the user's request arguments and will set any relevant security or device-specific flags.
2. The controller will parse the browser's request string for the requested page.
3. The controller will call a helper ASP to build an XML model of the requested view.

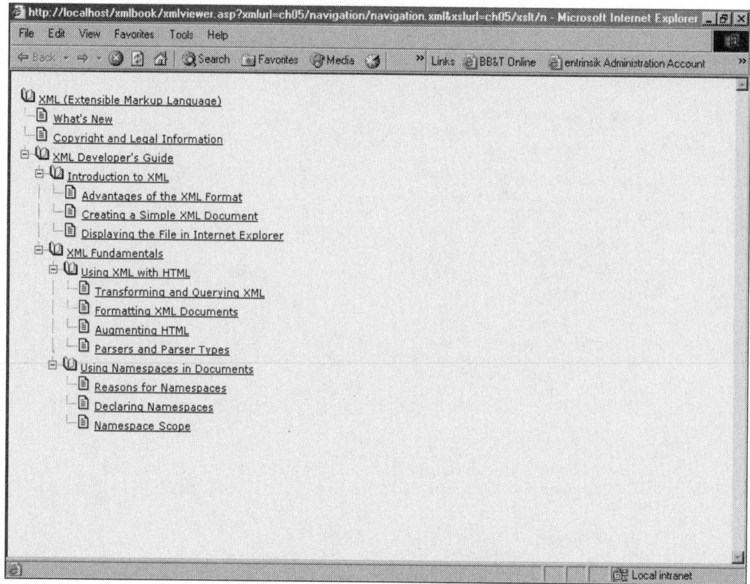

Figure 5-2 A more user-friendly presentation of the navigation XML document.

4. The controller will choose a user-interface "skin" to govern the transformation of the view XML. The skin will contain the majority of the HTML code that will ultimately be shown in the browser.

5. The controller will either produce the final HTML document itself or, depending on browser versions and user settings, will return the XML and XSLT code to the client to be processed locally.

By having a single access point act as a proxy to the Web site, it will be much easier to control the flow of information through the site. Global settings can be applied once rather than copied and pasted into every page on the server.

Cascading Style Sheets

CSS is the most familiar method for transforming XML documents for rendering on the Web. CSS styling for XML works much like it does for HTML. Just as traditional CSS applies specialized formatting to generic HTML, it can also apply limited formatting logic to XML so that it can be displayed in a browser. In this section we will go over when to use CSS and browser-compatibility issues.

When to Use CSS to Style XML

CSS cannot significantly alter pieces of an XML document or perform any conditional logic based on the data contained therein. This limitation restricts the use of CSS to transformations where the structure of the resulting HTML looks almost identical to the structure of the original XML document. The way to get around this is to assign formatting properties to each element within the tree. Elements and their children can be hidden or altered in appearance but cannot easily be otherwise rearranged or manipulated. Therefore, you should use CSS when you want to transform an XML document into a document similar in structure to your original. If all you need to do is apply formatting rules to the source XML document, CSS is most likely your tool of choice.

Consider the Listing 5-1 table of contents document shown earlier. Suppose we want to convert that listing into an indented display formatted for the printer. Because the output will be static and the *<navitem>* elements will be displayed in order, CSS looks like the logical formatting tool. To do this we will start by building a simple style sheet that will create block displays for the elements we want to show.

```
navigation  { display: block; }
navitem    { display: block; }
description  { display: block; }
href         { display: none; }
openImage      { display: none; }
closedImage  { display: none; }
image    { display: none; }
```

We can associate this style sheet to our XML document in Figure 5-1 by inserting the line *<?xml-stylesheet type="text/css" href="navigation_simple.css"?>* just before the *<navigation>* element. Figure 5-3 shows how this document will look if opened in Internet Explorer 5.5.

This does not look attractive, but you can see what the CSS processor did to the document. It created block displays for the *<navigation>*, *<navitem>*, and *<description>* elements in place and omitted the *<href>*, *<openImage>*, *<closedImage>*, and *<image>* elements. Let's jazz it up by altering our style sheet slightly as in Listing 5-2.

This version of the CSS improves the readability of the *<navigation>* and *<navitem>* elements by adding font families, colors, sizes, and weights. More importantly, the new stylization rules include *<padding>* elements. This has the desired effect of incrementally indenting subelements by a fixed amount. The result of this transformation appears in Figure 5-4.

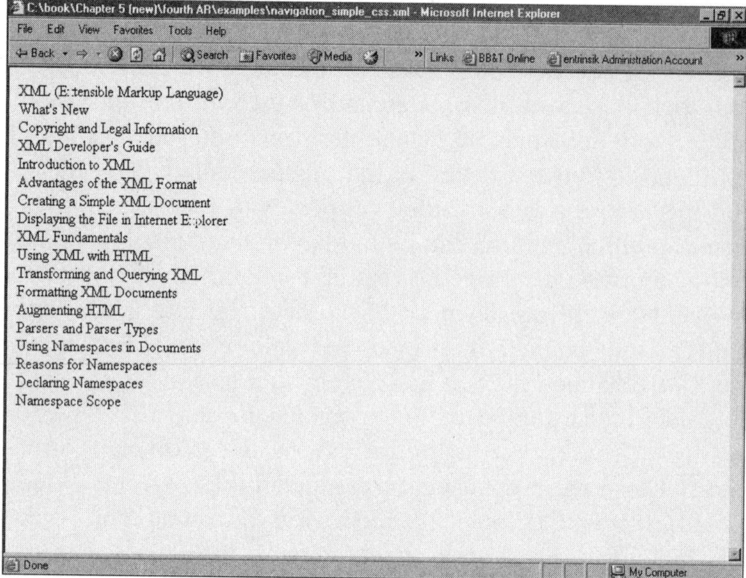

Figure 5-3 The same navigation XML source styled by using CSS.

Listing 5-2 A CSS transformation that produces a better-looking result document.

```
navigation
{
  font-family: verdana;
  color: black;
  font-size: 14;
  font-weight: 800;
  padding: 1em;
  display: block;
}
navitem
{
  font-family: verdana;
  color: black;
  font-size: 11;
  font-weight: 400;
  padding: 1em;
  display: block;
}
description  { display: block; }
href         { display: none; }
openImage      { display: none; }
closedImage  { display: none; }
image    { display: none; }
```

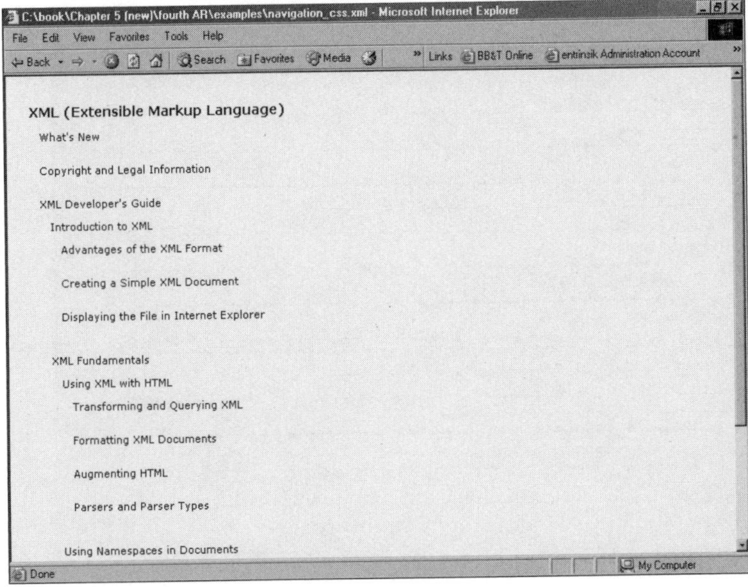

Figure 5-4 The CSS-styled navigation tree showing indentation of the branches.

How does the CSS processor know to indent items at the same depth in the tree by the same amount? It does so by recursively creating block display areas for each *<navitem>* element that contains similar block areas for each of that element's children. This process is best illustrated by adding a one-pixel border to the *<navigation>* and *<navitem>* elements in the style sheet, as shown in Figure 5-5.

When Not to Use CSS

CSS provides a familiar mechanism for preparing XML documents for rendering on a Web browser. Unfortunately, the capabilities of CSS are limited. Elements can only be transformed in place, meaning that they cannot be reordered. New tags, such as lists and images, cannot be dynamically inserted into the resulting document. The source XML document must be changed to include these tags to accommodate such extensions.

Another drawback to CSS is that it cannot perform logical operations such as "if-then" constructs. Furthermore, CSS is useful only for formatting. It cannot, for example, massage an XML document into another, similar XML document. Web developers must look elsewhere if their transformation requirements transcend simple formatting.

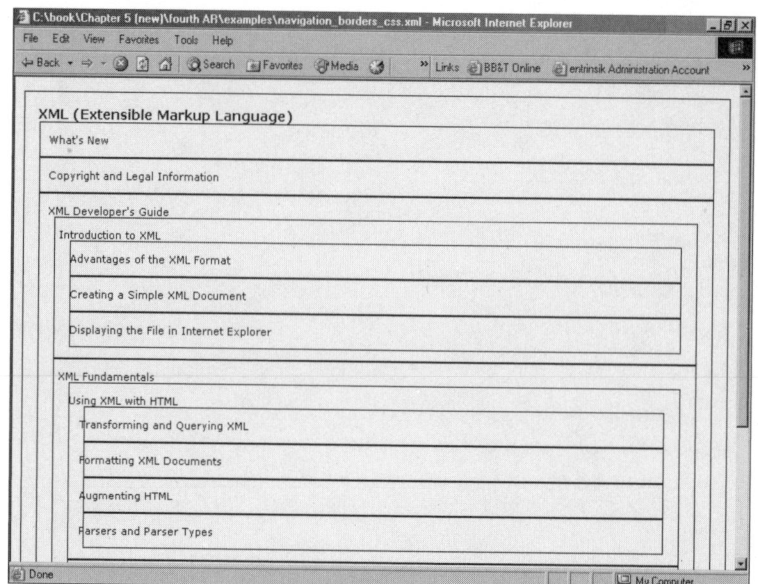

Figure 5-5 The CSS-styled navigation tree with borders to illustrate the padded block elements.

CSS Browser Compliance

One useful feature of CSS is that it is widely supported by popular browsers. Internet Explorer 5.0 and Netscape Navigator 6.0 both support client-side CSS styling of XML documents. Be aware, however, that the major browsers do not currently provide a complete implementation of CSS.

Extensible Stylesheet Language Transformation

The development of CSS leads to the main thrust of this chapter, XSLT, a technology that can perform tighter manipulation of XML than CSS. XSLT is an outgrowth of the XSL developed in 1999 by a W3C committee. The original draft of an XSL specification sought to define how XML documents should be formatted and transformed. This was a large task and the specification attacked each of the requirements separately. In this section we will go over the development of the XSL and XSLT specifications, benefits of their use, and some examples.

XSL Formatting Objects

To accomplish XSL formatting, the XSL specification introduced a new type of XML document that consisted of *Formatting Objects*. Formatting Objects represent how an XML document should be formatted without regard to typesetting specifics (for example, Microsoft Rich Text Format (RTF), Adobe PDF, and other print languages).

Like CSS and HTML together, an XSL Formatting Object tree describes blocks of content, which might contain text, tables, graphics, and other visual elements. This document provides generic information concerning layout, font characteristics, and color. In order for a Formatting Object document to be converted into a format readable by, say, Microsoft Word, typesetting converters must be used. Typesetting converters take a Formatting Object stream and build documents suitable for a particular renderer, in this case the RTF. In this way Web applications can create a single Formatting Object document that can be converted into many different forms of output. The equations here show how it's done.

Figure 5-6 shows how Formatting Objects and converters can be used to transform a single source XML document into many different types of output.

This technology is still young, and few Formatting Object converters exist. One exception is the Apache Group's FOP project, which converts Formatting Object documents into Adobe PDF *(http://xml.apache.org)*. However, preview releases of XSL formatters that can display XSL-FO natively on the Web are available. Information on the Antenna House XSL Formatter is available at *http://www.antennahouse.com/* and the X-Smiles browser is described at *http://www.xsmiles.org/*.

XSL Transformations

The second part of the XSL specification governing XML transformations matured more quickly than its formatting counterpart. The XSLT language owes much of its rapid adoption to Microsoft, which incorporated an early draft of the specification into its widely distributed Internet Explorer 5.0 browser. Although criticized at the time for releasing software based on an unfinished specification, by placing this powerful technology into the hands of eager programmers, Microsoft exposed a large portion of the developer community to the possibilities XML transformations allow.

Partly because of this sudden, wide distribution of XSL transformation technology, the W3C broke out the transformation component of the XSLT specification and created a new XSLT proposal. Although XSL still contains Formatting Object support, it defers to the XSLT specification for rules governing transformations.

Formally speaking, an XSLT is an XML document that describes how to convert one XML document into another. This sounds trivial, but the applications of the idea are far-reaching. Let's return to the navigation tree we looked at earlier.

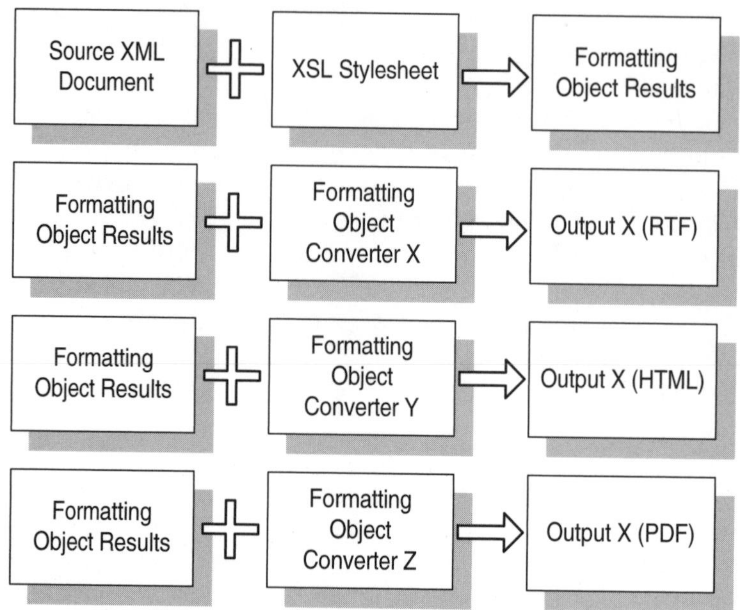

Figure 5-6 XSL styling with Formatting Objects

We can construct an XSLT that converts the XML document into an HTML document for viewing in a Web browser, a Formatting Object XML document for display or conversion into a Word table of contents, or into another XML document all together.

When to Use XSLT

We've seen that CSS can be a useful tool for styling XML when the source document closely resembles the desired display format. Unfortunately, this is rarely the case. The metamorphosis an XML document must often undergo, from generic markup to browser-specific HTML, is significant. Branches must be conditionally selected while HTML elements and script must be inserted into the result document. Sometimes HTML is not even the desired output. This is often the case in e-commerce applications where XML documents must be massaged so they can be exchanged cleanly. In such instances XSLT is the transformation tool of choice.

XSLT Browser Compliance

The downside to XSLT is that it is relatively new and few browsers support it at the time of this writing, which is not surprising when one realizes that not all browsers support CSS 1. So far, Microsoft has pursued the technology aggressively. Version 2.0 of the MSXML parser, which shipped with Internet Explorer

5.0, offered an introduction to XSLT, but was not ready for commercial use. Version 3.0 of the parser offers full support of the XSLT 1.0 specification and includes a multithreaded parser, making it a more viable commercial product. Netscape Navigator does not support XSLT in its version 6.0. Fortunately, developers need not wait for browser support before beginning XML projects. Server-side XSLT transformations provide all of the benefit of XSL processing and none of the worry associated with supporting specific Web browsers.

Using XSL Transformations

Programmers use XSLT to alter XML documents by associating transformation rules with particular nodes in the source tree. Basically, the programmer tells the XSLT engine, "Whenever you encounter this type of node or element, update the result document with this information."

In this example we will create a transformation that converts the tree into an HTML document suitable for rendering on Internet Explorer 5.0 or later. Nodes are selected by using the XPath expression language. XPath is a rich query language designed specifically for filtering the content in an XML document. XPath expressions are always based on a context node and are somewhat similar to directory commands often used in MS-DOS and UNIX shells. Here are some brief examples using the root node of Listing 5-1 as the context node:

1. *navitem* Selects all of the *navitem* nodes directly beneath the root node.
2. *navitem[children]* Selects all the *navitem* nodes that have children elements directly beneath the root node.
3. *//navitem[children]* Selects all of the *navitem* nodes with children elements as children.
4. *navitem[1]* Selects the first *navitem* node.
5. *navitem[last()]* Selects the last *navitem* node which is a child of the context node.
6. *navitem[last()]/description* Selects the *<description>* element children of the last *navitem* node.

Once we've identified the nodes we want to transform, we need to specify what should be done to them. This task is accomplished by using the XSLT *<template>* element. For example, the following code will replace all occurrences of the *<navitem>* element with the content of the *<description>* element before applying further template rules to its children.

```
<xsl:template match="navitem">
  <xsl:value-of select="description">
  <xsl:apply-templates/>
</xsl:template>
```

XSL Transformation Examples

Now we will go over an example of an XSLT and embellish that example by adding interactivity. The first line of our example is the style sheet declaration that must appear at the beginning of all XSLT documents. Notice that the XSLT namespace points to *http://www.w3.org/1999/XSL/Transform*. This address is different from the Internet Explorer 5.0 release of the parser (based on the working draft of the XSL specification) that looked to *http://www.w3.org/TR/WD-xsl*. The version attribute is mandatory. This line looks like

```
<xsl:stylesheet xmlns:xsl="http://www.w3.org/1999/XSL/Transform" version="1.0">
```

The next line contains the *<xsl:output>* element that tells the XSLT processor to produce a particular type of document. Possible values for the method attribute are "text", "html", and "xml".

```
<xsl:output method="html"/>
```

Now we're in the meat of the transformation. Let's start by selecting the root navigation node of the document and initializing the resulting HTML document.

```
  <xsl:template match="navigation[@type='tree']">
   <html>
     <head>
       <style>
         a:visited {background-color:white; color:black;
text-decoration: underline}
        a:link {background-color:white; color:black; text-decoration:
underline}
         a:active {background-color:activecaption; color:captiontext;
text-decoration: underline}
        a:hover {background-color:white; color:black; text-decoration:
underline}
         .clsHeading {font-family: verdana; color: black; font-size:
11; font-weight: 800;}
         .clsEntryText {padding-top: 2px; padding-left: 20px;
font-family: verdana; color: black; font-size: 11; font-weight: 400;
background-color:#FFFFFF;}
         .clsWarningText {font-family: verdana; color: #B80A2D;
font-size: 11; font-weight: 600; width:550;
background-color:#EFE7EA;}
         .clsCopy {font-family: verdana; color: black; font-size: 11;
font-weight: 400;  background-color:#FFFFFF;}
```

```
      </style>
    </head>
```

Now we will create a division to hold the contents of the root element in the tree. The division will be useful later when we extend the transformation to support the dynamic expanding and collapsing of tree branches. Also note the *{generate-id()}* directive to the XSLT processor. Similar to "<% … %>" in ASP, braces ("{.}") found within attributes prompt the XSLT processor to evaluate the expression and include the result in the result document. In this case the *generate-id()* function will return a unique alphanumeric id for the current element in the XML source document.

```
<body>
  <div class="clsHeading" id="open_{generate-id()}">
```

Next we need to test for the existence of *openImage* and *href* elements and display them if they are present.

```
<xsl:if test="openImage">
  <img src="{openImage}"/> 
</xsl:if>
<xsl:if test="href">
  <a href="{href}">
<xsl:if test="href/@target">
  <xsl:attribute name="target">
    <xsl:value-of select="href/@target"/>
  </xsl:attribute>
</xsl:if>
  <xsl:value-of select="description"/>
  </a>
</xsl:if>
<xsl:if test="not(href)"><xsl:value-of select="description"/></xsl:if>
```

Finally we need to select all the child *<navitem>* elements, apply transformation rules to them, and close out the navigation template. The *<xsl:apply-templates>* element will search for *<navitem>* elements below the root node, process them, and insert their transformed values into this location in the result tree.

```
        <xsl:apply-templates select="navitem"/>
      </div>
    </body>
  </html>
</xsl:template>
```

That takes care of the *root navigation* node. Now we need to provide a rule for transforming a generic *<navitem>* element.

```
<xsl:template match="navitem">
```

The icon we use to display a *<navitem>* element will depend on whether or not the *<navitem>* has any children. If the element has children we will display a folder icon.

```
<xsl:choose>
  <xsl:when test="children">
  <div class="clsEntryText" id="open_{generate-id()}">
      <xsl:if test="openImage">
        <img src="{openImage}"/> 
      </xsl:if>
      <xsl:if test="href">
        <a href="{href}">
      <xsl:if test="href/@target">
        <xsl:attribute name="target"><xsl:value-of select=
"href/@target"/></xsl:attribute>
      </xsl:if>
        <xsl:value-of select="description"/></a>
      </xsl:if>
      <xsl:if test="not(href)">
        <xsl:value-of select="description"/>
      </xsl:if>
```

Next we need to select all the children *<navitem>* elements and apply their templates recursively.

```
<xsl:apply-templates select="children"/>
```

Finally we handle the case where a *<navitem>* element has no children.

```
        </div>
      </xsl:when>
      <xsl:otherwise>
        <div class="clsEntryText">
          <xsl:if test="image"><img src="{image}"/> </xsl:if>
          <xsl:if test="href"><a href="{href}">
            <xsl:if test="href/@target"><xsl:attribute name=
"target"><xsl:value-of select="href/@target"/></xsl:attribute></xsl:if>
            <xsl:value-of select="description"/></a>
          </xsl:if>
          <xsl:if test="not(href)">
<xsl:value-of select="description"/></xsl:if>
        </div>
      </xsl:otherwise>
    </xsl:choose>
  </xsl:template>
</xsl:stylesheet>
```

Listing 5-3 shows the complete code listing for this transformation.

Listing 5-3 Navigation.xsl: When applied to Navigation.xml, produces a graphical display of the tree.

```
<xsl:stylesheet xmlns:xsl="http://www.w3.org/1999/XSL/Transform"
version="1.0">
  <xsl:output method="html"/>
  <xsl:template match="navigation[@type='tree']">
    <html>
      <head>
        <style>
          a:visited {background-color:white; color:black;
text-decoration: underline}
          a:link {background-color:white; color:black;
text-decoration: underline}
          a:active {background-color:activecaption; color:
captiontext; text-decoration: underline}
          a:hover {background-color:white; color:black;
text-decoration: underline}
          .clsHeading {font-family: verdana; color: black;
font-size: 11; font-weight: 800;}
          .clsEntryText {padding-top: 2px; padding-left: 20px;
font-family: verdana; color: black; font-size: 11; font-weight: 400;
background-color:#FFFFFF;}
          .clsWarningText {font-family: verdana; color: #B80A2D;
font-size: 11; font-weight: 600; width:550;  background-
color:#EFE7EA;}
          .clsCopy {font-family: verdana; color: black; font-size:
11; font-weight: 400;  background-color:#FFFFFF;}
        </style>
      </head>
      <body>
        <div class="clsHeading" id="open_{generate-id()}">
          <xsl:if test="openImage"><img src="{openImage}"/> 
</xsl:if>
          <xsl:if test="href"><a href="{href}">
            <xsl:if test="href/@target"><xsl:attribute name=
"target"><xsl:value-of select="href/@target"/></xsl:attribute>
</xsl:if>
            <xsl:value-of select="description"/></a>
          </xsl:if>
          <xsl:if test="not(href)">
<xsl:value-of select="description"/></xsl:if>
          <xsl:apply-templates select="navitem"/>
        </div>
      </body>
    </html>
  </xsl:template>
  <xsl:template match="navitem">
```

(continued)

Listing 5-3 *continued*

```
      <xsl:choose>
        <xsl:when test="children">
          <div class="clsEntryText" id="open_{generate-id()}">
            <xsl:if test="openImage"><img src="{openImage}"/> 
</xsl:if>
            <xsl:if test="href"><a href="{href}">
              <xsl:if test="href/@target">
<xsl:attribute name="target"><xsl:value-of select="href/@target"/>
</xsl:attribute></xsl:if>
              <xsl:value-of select="description"/></a>
            </xsl:if>
            <xsl:if test="not(href)">
<xsl:value-of select="description"/></xsl:if>
            <xsl:apply-templates select="children"/>
          </div>
        </xsl:when>
        <xsl:otherwise>
          <div class="clsEntryText">
            <xsl:if test="image"><img src="{image}"/> </xsl:if>
            <xsl:if test="href"><a href="{href}">
              <xsl:if test="href/@target">
<xsl:attribute name="target"><xsl:value-of select="href/@target"/>
</xsl:attribute></xsl:if>
              <xsl:value-of select="description"/></a>
            </xsl:if>
            <xsl:if test="not(href)"><xsl:value-of select=
"description"/></xsl:if>
          </div>
        </xsl:otherwise>
      </xsl:choose>
    </xsl:template>
</xsl:stylesheet>
```

The transformation mentioned in Listing 5-3 will produce a Microsoft Windows Explorer–like tree with all of its branches expanded, which can be seen in Figure 5-7.

This example looks much better than the CSS version. We still might want to add a few more features to the transformation, so it might be useful to allow users to expand and collapse branches of the tree dynamically. To do this requires little extra work on the part of the XSLT and makes the tree navigation tool more interactive for the user.

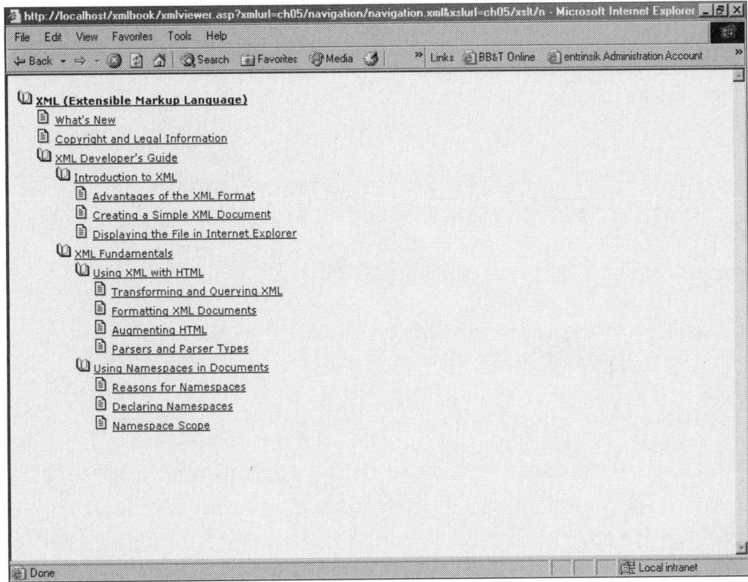

Figure 5-7 The navigation tree transformed into a static HTML document by using XSLT.

> **Note** The *captiontext* color is specific to Internet Explorer and borrows from your Microsoft Windows color settings. Other system colors supported by Internet Explorer include *background*, *scrollbar*, *window*, and *appworkspace*. See *http://msdn.microsoft.com/library/default.asp?url=/workshop/author/dhtml/reference/colors/colors.asp* for a more complete listing.

An expandable and collapsible tree can be implemented by creating two divisions for each parent node in the tree. One division displays the node collapsed and uses an icon to represent the closed state—a closed book, perhaps. The other division displays the node expanded. Only the expanded division will contain divisions for its children (each of which will also have a collapsed and expanded division).

This transformation will be nearly identical to the static version. The first difference will be to write the JavaScript *expand()* and *collapse()* functions. The script itself is simple. Both functions will expect a division ID to uniquely identify a specific division in the page. We will use the XSL function *generate-id()*

to create ID values. The *expand()* and *collapse()* functions will simply toggle the display properties of the open and closed versions of that division.

```
<script language="JavaScript">
  function expand(divid)
  {
     eval("closed_"+divid).style.display = 'none';
     eval("open_"+divid).style.display = '';
  }
  function collapse(divid)
  {
     eval("open_"+divid).style.display = 'none';
     eval("closed_"+divid).style.display = '';
  }
</script>
```

Next we will create two divisions for each parent node, *divid_closed* and *divid_open*. Only one of these divisions will ever be visible at a given time. The first will be the closed division. Notice the *onClick()* event handler attached to the "plus" image. The event handler calls the *expand()* function to toggle the display properties of the open and closed divisions.

```
<xsl:when test="children">
  <div class="clsEntryText" id="closed_{generate-id()}">
    <xsl:for-each select="ancestor::navitem">
      <xsl:choose>
      <xsl:when test="count(following-sibling::navitem) > 0">
          <img src="/xmlbook/images/line.gif"/>
        </xsl:when>
        <xsl:otherwise>
          <img src="/xmlbook/images/nothing.gif"/>
        </xsl:otherwise>
      </xsl:choose>
    </xsl:for-each>
    <img src="/xmlbook/images/folder_plus.gif"
onClick="expand('{generate-id()}')"/>
    <xsl:if test="closedImage">
<img src="{closedImage}"/> 
</xsl:if>
    <xsl:if test="href">
<a href="{href}">
        <xsl:if test="href/@target">
<xsl:attribute name="target"><xsl:value-of select="href/@target"/>
</xsl:attribute>
</xsl:if>
        <xsl:value-of select="description"/>
</a>
    </xsl:if>
    <xsl:if test="not(href)">
```

```
<xsl:value-of select="description"/>
</xsl:if>
  </div>
```

The code for the open division is similar except that its display style property is originally set to "none" and it calls the *<xsl:apply-templates>* XSLT element on its children.

```
<div class="clsEntryText" id="open_{generate-id()}" style="display:none">
  <xsl:for-each select="ancestor::navitem">
    <xsl:choose>
      <xsl:when test="count(following-sibling::navitem) > 0">
        <img src="/xmlbook/images/line.gif"/>
      </xsl:when>
      <xsl:otherwise>
        <img src="/xmlbook/images/nothing.gif"/>
      </xsl:otherwise>
    </xsl:choose>
  </xsl:for-each>
  <img  src="/xmlbook/images/folder_minus.gif" onClick=
"collapse('{generate-id()}')"/>
  <xsl:if test="openImage"><img src="{openImage}"/> </xsl:if>
  <xsl:if test="href"><a href="{href}">
    <xsl:if test="href/@target">
<xsl:attribute name="target"><xsl:value-of select="href/@target"/>
</xsl:attribute>
</xsl:if>
    <xsl:value-of select="description"/></a>
  </xsl:if>
  <xsl:if test="not(href)">
<xsl:value-of select="description"/>
</xsl:if>
  <xsl:apply-templates select="children"/>
</div>
```

Listing 5-4 is a complete listing for the dynamic tree transformation. This transformation will produce an interactive HTML representation of the navigation tree with expandable and collapsible branches.

Figure 5-8 shows the results of this transformation on a navigation tree.

Listing 5-4 navigation_dynamic.xsl

```
<xsl:stylesheet xmlns:xsl="http://www.w3.org/1999/XSL/Transform"
version="1.0"
<xsl:output method="html"/>
  <xsl:template match="navigation[@type='tree']">
    <html>
      <head>
```

(continued)

Listing 5-4 *continued*

```
        <script language="JavaScript">
          function expand(divid)
          {
             eval("closed_"+divid).style.display = 'none';
             eval("open_"+divid).style.display = '';
          }
          function collapse(divid)
          {
             eval("open_"+divid).style.display = 'none';
             eval("closed_"+divid).style.display = '';
          }
        </script>
        <style>
          a:visited {background-color:white; color:black;
 text-decoration: underline}
          a:link {background-color:white; color:black;
 text-decoration: underline}
          a:active {background-color:activecaption;
color:captiontext; text-decoration: underline}
          a:hover {background-color:white; color:black;
text-decoration: underline}
         .clsHeading {font-family: verdana; color: black; font-size:
11; font-weight: 800;}
          .clsEntryText {padding-top: 2px; font-family: verdana;
color: black; font-size: 11; font-weight: 400;
background-color:#FFFFFF;}
          .clsWarningText {font-family: verdana; color: #B80A2D;
font-size: 11; font-weight: 600; width:550;  background-
color:#EFE7EA;}
          .clsCopy {font-family: verdana; color: black; font-size:
11; font-weight: 400;  background-color:#FFFFFF;}
        </style>
      </head>
      <body>
        <div class="clsEntryText" id="open_{generate-id()}">
          <xsl:if test="openImage"><img src="{openImage}"/> 
</xsl:if>
          <xsl:if test="href"><a href="{href}">
            <xsl:if test="href/@target">
<xsl:attribute name="target"><xsl:value-of select="href/@target"/>
</xsl:attribute></xsl:if>
            <xsl:value-of select="description"/></a>
          </xsl:if>
          <xsl:if test="not(href)">
<xsl:value-of select="description"/></xsl:if>
          <xsl:apply-templates select="navitem"/>
        </div>
      </body>
```

```
    </html>
  </xsl:template>
<xsl:template match="navitem">
    <xsl:choose>
      <xsl:when test="children">
        <div class="clsEntryText" id="closed_{generate-id()}">
          <xsl:for-each select="ancestor::navitem">
            <xsl:choose>
             <xsl:when test="count(following-sibling::navitem) > 0">
                <img src="/xmlbook/images/line.gif"/>
              </xsl:when>
              <xsl:otherwise>
                <img src="/xmlbook/images/nothing.gif"/>
              </xsl:otherwise>
            </xsl:choose>
          </xsl:for-each>
          <img src="/xmlbook/images/folder_plus.gif"
onClick="expand('{generate-id()}')"/>
          <xsl:if test="closedImage">
<img src="{closedImage}"/> </xsl:if>
          <xsl:if test="href"><a href="{href}">
            <xsl:if test="href/@target">
<xsl:attribute name="target"><xsl:value-of select="href/@target"/>
</xsl:attribute></xsl:if>
            <xsl:value-of select="description"/></a>
          </xsl:if>
          <xsl:if test="not(href)">
<xsl:value-of select="description"/></xsl:if>
        </div>
        <div class="clsEntryText" id="open_{generate-id()}"
style="display:none">
          <xsl:for-each select="ancestor::navitem">
            <xsl:choose>
             <xsl:when test="count(following-sibling::navitem) > 0">
                <img src="/xmlbook/images/line.gif"/>
              </xsl:when>
              <xsl:otherwise>
                <img src="/xmlbook/images/nothing.gif"/>
              </xsl:otherwise>
            </xsl:choose>
          </xsl:for-each>
          <img  src="/xmlbook/images/folder_minus.gif"
onClick="collapse('{generate-id()}')"/>
          <xsl:if test="openImage"><img src="{openImage}"/> 
</xsl:if>
          <xsl:if test="href"><a href="{href}">
            <xsl:if test="href/@target">
<xsl:attribute name="target">
<xsl:value-of select="href/@target"/>
```

(continued)

Listing 5-4 *continued*

```
</xsl:attribute>
</xsl:if>
            <xsl:value-of select="description"/></a>
          </xsl:if>
          <xsl:if test="not(href)"><xsl:value-of select=
"description"/></xsl:if>
          <xsl:apply-templates select="children"/>
        </div>
      </xsl:when>
      <xsl:otherwise>
        <div class="clsEntryText">
          <xsl:for-each select="ancestor::navitem">
            <xsl:choose>
              <xsl:when test="count(following-sibling::navitem) > 0">
                <img src="/xmlbook/images/line.gif"/>
              </xsl:when>
              <xsl:otherwise>
                <img src="/xmlbook/images/nothing.gif"/>
              </xsl:otherwise>
            </xsl:choose>
          </xsl:for-each>
          <img  src="/xmlbook/images/divider.gif" onClick=
"collapse('{generate-id()}')"/>
          <xsl:if test="image"><img src="{image}"/> </xsl:if>
          <xsl:if test="href"><a href="{href}">
            <xsl:if test="href/@target"><xsl:attribute name=
"target"><xsl:value-of select="href/@target"/></xsl:attribute>
</xsl:if>
            <xsl:value-of select="description"/></a>
          </xsl:if>
          <xsl:if test="not(href)"><xsl:value-of select=
"description"/></xsl:if>
        </div>
      </xsl:otherwise>
    </xsl:choose>
  </xsl:template>
</xsl:stylesheet>
```

An Example Application

Now that we've learned about CSS, XSL, XSLT, and Web publishing in general, let's go through some more difficult examples. In this section we will build a proof-of-concept Web site, based entirely on XML, for a hypothetical company called Noverant.

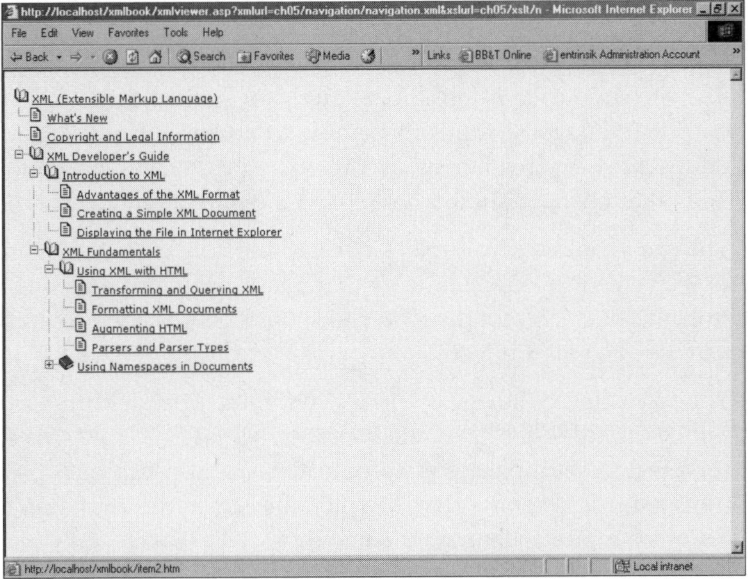

Figure 5-8 A DHTML version of the navigation tree.

The Requirements

Noverant is an online CD reseller. They want to build a Web site that has the following characteristics.

1. Navigation is important. They want buyers to be able to quickly focus in on a particular genre or artist. First and foremost, the site needs a tree-based navigator that will allow users to browse the CD catalog without performing multiple keyword searches. The navigator needs to be dynamic becasue the Noverant CD inventory changes hourly.

2. The site should be easy to maintain. Noverant doesn't have a team of Web developers on staff (that's why they hired you!) that can make complicated changes to HTML. They do, however, have a number of content authors who need to be able to make frequent changes to the listed content listed.

3. Noverant wants to be able to display live news items related to the music industry. They plan to purchase a subscription to a news feed service where they can obtain articles over the Internet. Noverant wants to embed these articles in the site's content.

4. The site should accommodate Internet Explorer 4.0 and later versions and Netscape Navigator 4.71 and later versions. This requirement is

particularly difficult to achieve in light of Noverant's dynamic navigation requirement.

5. The site should be extensible. Should Noverant choose to change its corporate image, it wants to be able to adapt its site using minimal effort. New color schemes, layout strategies, browser technologies, and other changes should not require a complete rebuild of the site.
6. The site should be scaleable. Noverant anticipates a monthly increase of 15 percent in user traffic as they ramp up their marketing efforts over the next six months. The site should be designed to accommodate this increase in load.
7. The site should be inexpensive. Noverant operates under a tight budget and doesn't have much cash to spend on expensive content servers and third-party software. It wants a Web site built using off-the-shelf components that can get the job done and last until it becomes a publically traded company.

Requirement Analysis

Although Noverant's requirements are aggressive, they are not impossible (especially by using XML). Let's break the requirements down one by one and think about how our knowledge of XML and XSLT might give us a head start.

Navigation

We've already learned how to use XML to build a generic navigation tree that can be transformed into a Windows Explorer–like UI. The interface side of this requirement should be easy; in fact, we already have an XSLT to help render the HTML. The difficulty will reside in accommodating Noverant's ever-changing CD catalog. We'll need to design the XML navigation structure so that it can be built dynamically whenever the page is loaded. One solution is to change the static Listing 5-1 document into ASP.

Maintainability

XML can help us enable Noverant's Web authors to change the content of the site without damaging the presentation logic. We can define a document schema for them whereby they create simple XML content documents that adhere to a specific structure that can be transformed by us into formatted content on the site. This is another example of how separating content from presentation can cleanly divide job roles in a company.

News Feeds

The Newspaper Association of America created an XML schema to define a uniform distribution format for news content. The News Industry Text Format (NITF) specification appeared in 1998 and defines how content providers, such as MSNBC, should distribute their information in XML format. The NITF specification makes it easy for sites such as the Noverant project to have a news feed. By implementing a single XSLT that is compatible with NITF, we can support almost any news feed Noverant is likely to purchase.

Cross-Browser Compatibility

The issue of cross-browser compatibility has plagued Web developers for years. How can you take advantage of special features in Browser A and support Browser B without developing two different Web sites? XSLT, that's how! One approach is to develop a "skins" model for rendering content. Under this model each page request will cause two documents to be generated: 1) a generic XML document containing all of the content that can be displayed, and 2) a browser-specific or user-specific XSLT (the skin), or both, that will handle translating the content into appropriate markup for the display device. Different skins can be programmed to convert the same content into Internet Explorer pages, Navigator pages, or WML pages for hand-held devices. The implication of the skins model, however, is the existence of a *controller* page that handles locating XML documents and marrying them with the appropriate skin.

Extensibility

The extensibility XML offers, particularly when using a skins-based browsing model, is obvious. Skins can be modified easily to accommodate new color schemes, layout requirements, content schemas, browser advancements, and so forth. You can even design multiple skins with radically different attitudes for each browser. That way a user could change his or her skin and get a whole new Web site.

Scalability

XML opens up a number of different techniques, in addition to traditional hardware clustering approaches, to help with application scalability. The MSXML 3.0 parser includes a free-threaded model to speed concurrent access to the XML processor. The software also improves server-to-server HTTP communication for quicker exchange of XML, SOAP, or both documents. Web developers can also distribute the load of building and transforming documents across different machines. In Noverant's case the logic that constructs the XML navigation document might be off-loaded to another server. Other strategies include caching documents and compiling XSLTs to speed processing time.

Cost

All of the technologies mentioned in this chapter come free with Microsoft Windows NT and Windows 2000 servers or can be obtained without cost from the Microsoft Web site. No additional software components will be necessary.

The Controller

As mentioned previously, we will need to use a page controller design pattern to pull off the XSLT skin model we want to use. The controller will intercept all Web requests and route information according to our architecture. The flow of control will follow these steps:

1. The client will send an HTTP request to the controller.asp page and will send a URL argument name view (for example, *http://www.noverant.com/controller.asp?view=navigation/navigation_frame*) in addition to any other arguments the page might require.
2. The controller will parse the view argument and will call, via HTTP, a page with the name View.asp (for example, *http://www.noverant.com/navigation/navigation_frame.asp*). The actual location of the ASP page is arbitrary as long as the controller can locate the page based on the view argument alone.
3. The called ASP, or view helper, will be responsible for constructing a well-formed and valid XML document to be processed by a skin. The document must conform to the Noverant document schema we define. The ASP can use function calls, database requests, HTTP requests, or any other means to populate the XML document.
4. The controller will use a heuristic to determine an appropriate skin to apply to the XML returned by the view helper. This controller will certainly consider the browser type (Internet Explorer, Navigator, PDA, and so forth), but might also look at user preferences or other settings before deciding on a skin.
5. Upon choosing a skin, the controller will load the associated XSLT style sheet, process the view XML, and retrieve the transformed document.
6. The controller will return the result document to the client.

Figure 5-9 shows how the Controller interacts with the page content, the XSLT skin, and the client.

A simple implementation of the controller is in *controller.asp*. The first task the controller must perform is to retrieve the view argument from the page

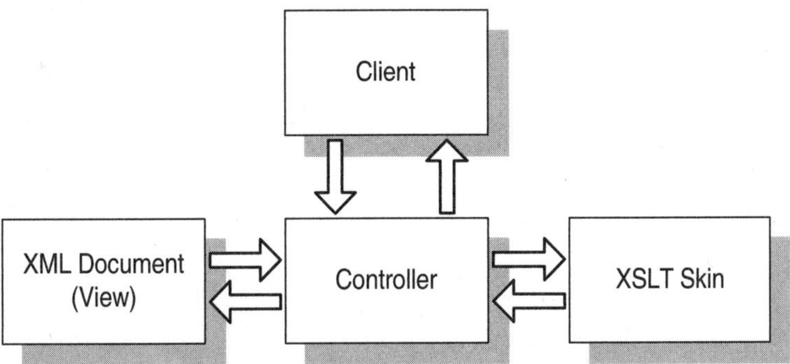

Figure 5-9 A flow-control diagram of the controller architecture.

request and use this argument to complete the URL to the appropriate helper page. The name of the view helper follows the convention of View.asp.

```
  // Get the view argument
  view    = Request.QueryString("view")
  base    = Request.ServerVariables("SERVER_NAME")+
Replace(Request.ServerVariables("URL"),"controller.asp","")
  if Request.ServerVariables("HTTPS") = "ON" Then
    base = "https://"+base
  else
    base = "http://"+base
  end if
  xmlurl = base+view+".asp?"
```

The controller will also need to forward all URL arguments, such as a particular artist, to the helper page. For each item in *Request.QueryString,* the followig applies:

```
    if arguments <> "" then arguments = arguments+"&"
    itemvalue = Request.QueryString(item)
    arguments = arguments+item+"="+itemvalue
  Next
  // Append the argument string to the xmlurl
  xmlurl = xmlurl+arguments
```

Now the controller needs to construct a URL to the XSLT, or skin, responsible for converting the XML data making up the page into the HTML to be returned to the browser. The skin can be chosen based on a variety of factors, including user preference, and browser type. For simplicity's sake the controller will hard-code the skin reference.

```
  // Contstruct a URL to the appropriate skin
  // This implementation uses only the Internet Explorer 5.0 skin
```

```
// Other skins could be used based on the browser type
xslurl = base+"xslt/ie5.xsl"
```

Now that the controller has built URLs to the appropriate helper page and XSLT, it needs to load the source XML and style XSLT into the MSXML2.DOMDocument control. The controller must also check for any parsing errors that might occur along the way.

```
// Load the XML
// A production implementation should use the multi-threaded version
//of the DomDocument.
error = false
Set source = Server.CreateObject("MSXML2.DOMDocument")
source.async = false
source.load(xmlurl)
Set e = source.parseError
if e.errorCode <> 0 then
  Response.write(e.reason)
  if e.line > 0 Then
    Response.write(e.line)
    Response.write(" ")
    Response.write(e.linepos)
    Response.write(" ")
    Response.write(e.srcText)
  end if
  error = true
end if
// Load the XSLT
Set style = Server.CreateObject("MSXML2.DOMDocument")
style.async = false
style.load(xslurl)
Set e = style.parseError
Response.write(e.reason)
if e.errorCode <> 0 Then
  Response.write(e.reason)
  if e.line > 0 Then
    Response.write(e.line)
    Response.write(" ")
    Response.write(e.linepos)
    Response.write(" ")
    Response.write(e.srcText)
  end if
  error = true
end if
```

If no errors are found the controller transforms the XML and sends the result document back to the client.

```
  if error = false Then
    xmlresult = source.transformNode(style)
  end if
  Response.write(xmlresult)
%>
```

Building the Pages

Now that we have a working version of the controller, let's begin building the actual view helper pages. The goal of the view helper pages is to delegate the construction of different XML components to smaller, more specialized ASPs. This strategy promotes code reusability and extensibility and makes the site much easier to maintain over the long haul. We will cover how to build different kinds of helper pages that are tuned for specific tasks and how to incorporate these pages into the controller architecture. Finally we will create specific helper pages for displaying the Noverant CD database.

The CD Database

Noverant's CD catalog will be stored in a large XML "database." The CD descriptions are contained in an XML file in the *db/* directory. An excerpt from this file follows.

```
<cds>
<cd>
<id>152</id>
<title>Tallis/Mass for four voices</title>
<artist>Oxford Camerata cond. Jeremy Summerly</artist>
<genre>classical, choral</genre>
</cd>
<cd>
   <id>1</id>
   <title>Great Organ Works/Bach JS</title>
   <artist>Koopman</artist>
   <genre>classical, organ</genre>
</cd>
...
</cds>
```

All queries against this minidatabase will take the form of XSLT and DOM access. Noverant will likely migrate this information into a more traditional database engine, such as Microsoft's SQL Server, to improve performance as its volume grows. All needs to be changed to accommodate such a transition is an adjustment to the view helper pages to connect to the database, instead of the CD XML document, while constructing the view. Therefore, instead of logic to read and parse the CDs.xml text file, the database-friendly version of the view helper will contain SQL commands to query CD-related tables.

The Noverant Schema

Before we dive into coding the helper pages we will take some time to define the document model that pages in the site will follow by creating an XML schema that describes the site. The significant elements that the site will use are:

1. *<document>* The *<document>* element will form the root node of all content to be shown on the site. You can think of a document node in our document model as serving the same role as the *<html>* tag in HTML documents.

2. *<navigation>* The *<navigation>* element provides a simple mechanism for defining a hierarchical navigation tree. The XML will contain descriptions, images, hyperlink references, and a list of children elements.

3. *<doclet>* A *<doclet>* will form the primary building block for content on the site. Noverant's content developers will be able to create small *<doclets>* to define blocks of content to be transformed and incorporated into a page request. A *<doclet>* will contain a heading, links to one or more images, text, and one or more text excerpts.

4. *<newsitem>* A *<newsitem>* will represent a news story that should appear on the site. The *<newsitems>* can be authored by Noverant content developers or might be pulled from one or more online news content providers.

5. *<list>* The *<list>* element will represent a list of related items. *<list>* elements will provide the data model for tables shown in the site. Although the tables will be simple in the first version of the site, the transformation behind them might eventually be extended to allow sorting, grouping, filtering, and other, more advanced reporting features.

A preliminary version of the schema and a discussion of its elements follows. Note that the schema shown here is an XDR (XML-Data Reduced Language) schema. The MSXML 4.0 parser will support the new XSD (XML Schema Definition) language developed by the W3C. Listing 5-5 shows the schema used for the Noverant Web site.

Listing 5-5 schema.xml: Describes all the elements and attributes that can be included in a valid Noverant Web page.

```
<?xml version="1.0"?>
<Schema name="noverant_dom"
    xmlns="urn:schemas-microsoft-com:xml-data"
    xmlns:dt="urn:schemas-microsoft-com:datatypes">
```

```
  <ElementType name="header" content="textOnly" model="closed"/>
  <ElementType name="image" content="textOnly" model="closed"/>
  <ElementType name="p" content="textOnly" model="closed"/>
  <ElementType name="excerpt" content="textOnly" model="closed"/>
  <ElementType name="id" content="textOnly" model="closed"/>
  <ElementType name="text" content="eltOnly" model="closed">
      <element type="p" minOccurs="0" maxOccurs="*"/>
  </ElementType>
  <ElementType name="doclet" order="many" content="eltOnly"
model="closed">
      <element type="id" minOccurs="0" maxOccurs="1"/>
      <element type="header" minOccurs="0" maxOccurs="1"/>
      <element type="image" minOccurs="0" maxOccurs="*"/>
      <element type="excerpt" minOccurs="0" maxOccurs="*"/>
      <element type="text" minOccurs="1" maxOccurs="1"/>
  </ElementType>
  <ElementType name="title" content="textOnly" model="closed"/>
  <ElementType name="hl1" content="textOnly" model="closed"/>
  <ElementType name="hl2" content="textOnly" model="closed"/>
  <ElementType name="person" content="textOnly" model="closed"/>
  <ElementType name="bytag" content="textOnly" model="closed"/>
  <ElementType name="location" content="textOnly" model="closed"/>
  <ElementType name="story.date" content="textOnly" model="closed"/>
  <ElementType name="head" order="many" content="mixed"
model="open">
      <element type="title" minOccurs="0" maxOccurs="1"/>
  </ElementType>
  <ElementType name="body.end" content="mixed" model="open"/>
  <ElementType name="byline" order="many" content="mixed"
model="open">
      <element type="person" minOccurs="0" maxOccurs="*"/>
      <element type="bytag" minOccurs="0" maxOccurs="*"/>
  </ElementType>
  <ElementType name="dateline" order="many" content="mixed"
model="open">
      <element type="location" minOccurs="0" maxOccurs="*"/>
      <element type="story.date" minOccurs="0" maxOccurs="*"/>
  </ElementType>
  <ElementType name="headline" order="many" content="eltOnly"
model="closed">
      <element type="hl1" minOccurs="1" maxOccurs="1"/>
      <element type="hl2" minOccurs="0" maxOccurs="1"/>
  </ElementType>
  <ElementType name="body.head" order="many" content="eltOnly"
model="closed">
      <element type="headline" minOccurs="1" maxOccurs="1"/>
      <element type="byline" minOccurs="0" maxOccurs="*"/>
      <element type="dateline" minOccurs="0" maxOccurs="1"/>
  </ElementType>
```

(continued)

Listing 5-5 *continued*

```
  <ElementType name="body.content" order="many" content="mixed"
model="open">
      <element type="p" minOccurs="1" maxOccurs="*"/>
  </ElementType>
  <ElementType name="body" order="many" content="eltOnly"
model="closed">
      <element type="body.head" minOccurs="1" maxOccurs="1"/>
      <element type="body.content" minOccurs="1" maxOccurs="1"/>
      <element type="body.end" minOccurs="0" maxOccurs="1"/>
  </ElementType>
  <ElementType name="newsitem" order="many" content="eltOnly"
model="closed">
      <element type="head" minOccurs="1" maxOccurs="1"/>
      <element type="body" minOccurs="1" maxOccurs="1"/>
  </ElementType>
  <ElementType name="column.name" content="textOnly" model="closed"/>
  <ElementType name="column.description" content="textOnly"
model="closed"/>
  <ElementType name="column" order="many" content="eltOnly"
model="closed">
      <element type="column.name" minOccurs="1" maxOccurs="1"/>
      <element type="column.description" minOccurs="1" maxOccurs="1"/>
  </ElementType>
  <ElementType name="columns" order="many" content="eltOnly"
model="closed">
      <element type="column" minOccurs="1" maxOccurs="*"/>
  </ElementType>
  <ElementType name="property.name" content="textOnly"
model="closed"/>
  <ElementType name="property.value" content="textOnly"
model="closed"/>
  <ElementType name="property" order="many" content="eltOnly"
model="closed">
      <element type="property.name" minOccurs="1" maxOccurs="1"/>
      <element type="property.value" minOccurs="1" maxOccurs="1"/>
  </ElementType>
  <ElementType name="item" order="many" content="eltOnly"
model="closed">
      <element type="property" minOccurs="0" maxOccurs="*"/>
  </ElementType>
  <ElementType name="items" order="many" content="eltOnly"
model="closed">
      <element type="item" minOccurs="0" maxOccurs="*"/>
  </ElementType>
  <ElementType name="list" order="many" content="eltOnly"
model="closed">
      <element type="title" minOccurs="1" maxOccurs="1"/>
      <element type="columns" minOccurs="1" maxOccurs="1"/>
```

```
      <element type="items" minOccurs="1" maxOccurs="1"/>
  </ElementType>
  <ElementType name="description" content="textOnly" model="closed"/>
  <ElementType name="openImage" content="textOnly" model="closed"/>
  <ElementType name="closedImage" content="textOnly" model="closed"/>
  <ElementType name="href" order="many" content="textOnly"
model="closed">
      <AttributeType name="target" />
  </ElementType>
  <ElementType name="children" order="many" content="eltOnly"
model="closed">
      <element type="navitem" minOccurs="0" maxOccurs="*"/>
  </ElementType>
  <ElementType name="navitem" order="many" content="eltOnly"
model="closed">
      <element type="description" minOccurs="1" maxOccurs="1"/>
      <element type="image" minOccurs="0" maxOccurs="1"/>
      <element type="openImage" minOccurs="0" maxOccurs="1"/>
      <element type="closedImage" minOccurs="1" maxOccurs="1"/>
      <element type="href" minOccurs="0" maxOccurs="1"/>
      <element type="children" minOccurs="0" maxOccurs="1"/>
  </ElementType>
  <ElementType name="navigation" order="many" content="eltOnly"
model="closed">
      <AttributeType name="type" />
      <element type="description" minOccurs="1" maxOccurs="1"/>
      <element type="image" minOccurs="0" maxOccurs="1"/>
      <element type="openImage" minOccurs="0" maxOccurs="1"/>
      <element type="closedImage" minOccurs="1" maxOccurs="1"/>
      <element type="href" minOccurs="0" maxOccurs="1"/>
      <element type="navitem" minOccurs="0" maxOccurs="*"/>
  </ElementType>
    <ElementType name="document" order="many" content="eltOnly"
model="closed">
        <element type="navigation" minOccurs="0" maxOccurs="*"/>
        <element type="doclet" minOccurs="0" maxOccurs="*"/>
        <element type="newsitem" minOccurs="0" maxOccurs="*"/>
        <element type="list" minOccurs="0" maxOccurs="*"/>
  </ElementType>
</Schema>
```

The first view helper we will write is the navigation view helper. This helper will be responsible for querying the CD database and building a *<navigation>* tree using ASP script. Noverant wants the *<navigation>* tree to organize the CD contents by genre and then by artist. When a user clicks on an artist they should see all albums by that artist on the main page.

We will need to use a combination of XSLT and direct DOM manipulation to construct the tree. XSLT has no easy facility for grouping nodes by a common element, such as genre, and eliminating duplicates. Thus, we will use DOM manipulation to create an unsorted tree of genres and artists and then use XSLT to sort the branches. Listing 5-6 shows the nav_by_genre.asp view helper that is responsible for creating the CD *<navigation>* tree.

Listing 5-6 nav_by_genre.asp: ASP page that creates a *<navigation>* tree out of the genres and artists found in the CD database.

```
<%
  xmlurl = Server.MapPath("../db/CDs.xml")
  Set source = Server.CreateObject("MSXML2.DOMDocument")
  source.async = false
  source.load(xmlurl)
  Set e = source.parseError
  if e.errorCode <> 0 then
  Response.write(e.reason)
  if e.line > 0 Then
     Response.write(e.line)
     Response.write(" ")
     Response.write(e.linepos)
     Response.write(" ")
     Response.write(e.srcText)
  end if
  error = true
  end if
  Set genres = Server.CreateObject("MSXML2.DOMDocument")
  Set children = genres.createElement("children")
  genres.appendChild(children)
  Set cds = source.getElementsByTagName("cd")
  for x = 0 To cds.Length - 1
    Set cd = cds.item(x)
    genre = cd.selectSingleNode("genre").text
  if genre <> "" then
   Set existing = genres.selectNodes("children/navitem[description =
'"+genre+"']")
    if existing.length = 0 then
      Set navelem  = genres.createElement("navitem")
      Set descelem = genres.createElement("description")
      Set desctext = genres.createTextNode(genre)
      Set imgelem  = genres.createElement("image")
      Set imgtext  = genres.createTextNode("images/item.gif")
      Set oielem  = genres.createElement("openImage")
      Set oitext  = genres.createTextNode("images/open.gif")
      Set cielem  = genres.createElement("closedImage")
      Set citext  = genres.createTextNode("images/closed.gif")
      imgelem.appendChild(imgtext)
      oielem.appendChild(oitext)
```

```
      cielem.appendChild(citext)
      descelem.appendChild(desctext)
      navelem.appendChild(imgelem)
      navelem.appendChild(oielem)
      navelem.appendChild(cielem)
      navelem.appendChild(descelem)
      children.appendChild(navelem)
      artist = cd.selectSingleNode("artist").text
      Set artists = genres.createElement("children")
      Set artistnavelem = genres.createElement("navitem")
      Set artistdescelem = genres.createElement("description")
      Set artistdesctext = genres.createTextNode(artist)
      Set artistimgelem = genres.createElement("image")
      Set artistimgtext = genres.createTextNode("images/item.gif")
      artistimgelem.appendChild(artistimgtext)
      artistdescelem.appendChild(artistdesctext)
      artistnavelem.appendChild(artistdescelem)
      artistnavelem.appendChild(artistimgelem)
      artists.appendChild(artistnavelem)
      navelem.appendChild(artists)
    else
      artist = cd.selectSingleNode("artist").text
      Set existingartists = genres.selectNodes("children/
navitem[description = '"+genre+"']/children/navitem[description =
'"+artist+"']")
      if existingartists.length = 0 then
        Set artists = existing.item(0).selectSingleNode("children")
        Set artistnavelem = genres.createElement("navitem")
        Set artistdescelem = genres.createElement("description")
        Set artistdesctext = genres.createTextNode(artist)
        Set artistimgelem = genres.createElement("image")
        Set artistimgtext = genres.createTextNode("images/item.gif")
        artistimgelem.appendChild(artistimgtext)
        artistdescelem.appendChild(artistdesctext)
        artistnavelem.appendChild(artistdescelem)
        artistnavelem.appendChild(artistimgelem)
        artists.appendChild(artistnavelem)
      end if
    end if
  end if
  next
  xslurl = Server.MapPath("nav_by_genre.xsl")
  Set style = Server.CreateObject("MSXML2.DOMDocument")
  style.async = false
  style.load(xslurl)
  Set e = style.parseError
  Response.write(e.reason)
  if e.errorCode <> 0 Then
  Response.write(e.reason)
```

(continued)

Listing 5-6 *continued*

```
  if e.line > 0 Then
     Response.write(e.line)
     Response.write(" ")
     Response.write(e.linepos)
     Response.write(" ")
     Response.write(e.srcText)
  end if
  end if
  xmldata = genres.transformNode(style)
%>
<navigation type="tree">
  <description>Noverant</description>
  <openImage>images/open.gif</openImage>
    <navitem>
      <description>Welcome to Noverant</description>
      <image>images/item.gif</image>
      <href target="main">controller.asp?view=main</href>
    </navitem>
    <navitem>
      <description>CD's by genre</description>
      <openImage>images/open.gif</openImage>
      <closedImage>images/closed.gif</closedImage>
      <image>images/item.gif</image>
      <children>
<%= xmldata %>
      </children>
    </navitem>
</navigation>
```

Listing 5-7 shows the nav_by_genre.xsl transformation. The nav_by_genre.asp script, shown in Listing 5-6, uses this transformation to sort the tree by genre and then by artist.

Listing 5-7 Nav_by_genre.xsl: Sorts a collection of *<navitems>* by their description elements.

```
<xsl:stylesheet xmlns:xsl="http://www.w3.org/1999/XSL/Transform"
version="1.0">
  <xsl:output method="html"/>
  <xsl:template match="/children">
    <children>
      <xsl:apply-templates select="navitem">
        <xsl:sort select="description"/>
      </xsl:apply-templates>
    </children>
  </xsl:template>
```

```
  <xsl:template match="navitem">
    <navitem>
      <description><xsl:value-of select="description"/></description>
      <openImage><xsl:value-of select="openImage"/></openImage>
      <closedImage><xsl:value-of select="closedImage"/></closedImage>
      <image><xsl:value-of select="image"/></image>
      <xsl:if test="children">
        <children>
          <xsl:apply-templates select="children/navitem">
            <xsl:sort select="description"/>
          </xsl:apply-templates>
        </children>
      </xsl:if>
      <xsl:if test="not(children)">
        <href target="main">controller.asp?view=artist/list&amp;
artist=<xsl:value-of select="description"/></href>
      </xsl:if>
    </navitem>
  </xsl:template>
</xsl:stylesheet>
```

Now that we have built a helper to construct a valid *<navigation>* tree, we're almost finished. Recall that, according to our Noverant schema, a *<navigation>* element needs a *<document>* element to contain it before it can be successfully transformed. We will create a front-end helper to wrap the results of the helper we just wrote by using a *<document>* tag. So why not include the *<document>* tag in the original helper? Doing so will preclude us from including *<navigation>* elements in the same document with other elements. The creation of a proxy helper page makes the navigation of the site more extensible. For example, we could later write a "nav_by_artist" helper that is conditionally called by the navigation helper. Listing 5-8 shows the Navigation_frame.asp script, which is responsible for loading the correct navigation scheme.

Listing 5-8 Navigation_frame.asp: A proxy to call the correct navigation helper.

```
<document>
<% Server.execute("nav_by_genre.asp") %>
</document>
```

We're done with the navigation helper! Now we need to write the XSLT to render our tree. Our first skin for the site will be designed specifically for the Internet Explorer 5.0 browser. This skin will pull together all the transformation logic for *<documents>*, *<navigationtrees>*, *<doclets>*, *<lists>*, and *<newsitems>*.

The document template will initialize the result document with the proper HTML header, scripts, and style elements. It also creates a container for all of the Noverant document elements by building a table and calling the *<xsl:apply-templates>* element for all its children. Notice that the document template controls the positioning of the *<navigation>*, *<newsitem>*, *<doclet>*, and *<list>* child elements.

```
<xsl:stylesheet xmlns:xsl="http://www.w3.org/1999/XSL/Transform"
version="1.0">
  <xsl:output method="html"/>
  <xsl:template match="document">
    <html>
      <head>
        <script language="JavaScript">
          function expand(divid)
          {
             eval("closed_"+divid).style.display = 'none';
             eval("open_"+divid).style.display = '';
          }
          function collapse(divid)
          {
             eval("open_"+divid).style.display = 'none';
             eval("closed_"+divid).style.display = '';
          }
        </script>
        <style>
          a:visited {background-color:#C7D2DE; color:black;
text-decoration: underline}
          a:link {background-color:#C7D2DE; color:black;
text-decoration: underline}
         a:active {background-color:activecaption; color:captiontext;
text-decoration: underline}
          a:hover {background-color:#C7D2DE; color:black;
text-decoration: underline}
          .clsHeading {font-family: verdana; color: black; font-size:
11; font-weight: 800;}
        .clsEntryText {padding-top: 2px; font-family: verdana; color:
black; font-size: 11; font-weight: 400; background-color:#C7D2DE;}
          .clsWarningText {font-family: verdana; white-space:pre;
color: #B80A2D; font-size: 11; font-weight: 600; width:550;
background-color:#EFE7EA;}
         .clsCopy {font-family: verdana; color: black; font-size: 11;
font-weight: 400;  background-color:#FFFFFF;}
          .doclet {margin: 5px; padding:8px; display:block;
border:solid 1px; padding-top:2px; font-family:verdana; color:black;
font-size: 13px; font-weight: 400; background-color:white;}
          .docletHeading {padding-top: 2px; font-family: verdana;
color: #003366; font-size: 20; font-weight: 400;}
```

```
        .docletImage {display:inline; padding-top: 2px; font-family:
verdana; color: black; font-size: 11; font-weight: 400;}
        .docletText {display:inline; padding-top: 2px; font-family:
verdana; color: black; font-size: 12; font-weight: 400;}
        .docletExcerpt {display:inline; padding-top: 2px;
font-family: verdana; color: black; font-size: 11; font-weight: 400;}
        .newsItem {margin:5px; vertical-align: top; padding:8px;
display:inline; border:solid 1px; padding-top:2px; font-family:
verdana; color:black; font-size: 13px; font-weight: 400;
background-color:white; width:300px}
        .newsHl1 {padding-top: 2px; font-family: verdana; color:
#003366; font-size: 20; font-weight: 400;}
        .newsHl2 {padding-top: 2px; font-style:italic; font-family:
verdana; color: black; font-size: 14; font-weight: 400;}
        .newsBlPerson {padding: 2px; font-family: verdana; color:
black; font-size: 14; text-decoration:underline; font-weight: 400;
text-align:right;}
       .newsBlTag {padding: 2px; font-family: verdana; color: black;
font-size: 11; font-weight: 600; text-align:right;}
        .newsDlLoc {display:inline; font-family: verdana; color:
black; font-size: 12; font-weight: 600;}
        .newsDlDate {display:inline; font-family: verdana; color:
black; font-size: 12; font-weight: 600;}
       .newsBody {font-family: times; color: black; font-size: 12px;
font-family:verdana; font-weight: 400; text-align:justify;}
        .list {margin:5px; vertical-align: top; padding:8px;
display:inline; border:solid 1px; padding-top:2px; font-family:
verdana; color:black; font-size: 13px; font-weight: 400;
background-color:white; width:600px}
        .listHeading {padding-top: 2px; font-family: verdana; color:
#003366; font-size: 20; font-weight: 400;}
        .listText {display:inline; padding-top: 2px; font-family:
verdana; color: black; font-size: 14; font-weight: 400;}
      </style>
    </head>
    <body style="background-color:#C7D2DE;">
      <table width="100%" cellspacing="5">
        <tr>
          <td nowrap="yes">
            <xsl:apply-templates select="navigation"/>
          </td>
          <td align="left" valign="top">
            <xsl:apply-templates select="doclet"/>
            <xsl:apply-templates select="newsitem"/>
            <xsl:apply-templates select="list"/>
          </td>
          <td>
          </td>
        </tr>
```

```
      </table>
    </body>
  </html>
</xsl:template>
```

The next transformation we define is the *<list>* transformation. The following XSLT will convert a generic list structure into an HTML table.

```
<xsl:template match="list">
  <div class="list" id="list_{generate-id()}">
    <table>
      <tr>
        <td colspan="{count(columns/column)}"><font class=
"docletHeading"><xsl:value-of select="title"/></font></td>
      </tr>
      <tr>
        <xsl:for-each select="columns/column">
          <th align="left"><font class="listText"><b><xsl:value-of
select="description"/></b></font></th>
        </xsl:for-each>
      </tr>
      <xsl:for-each select="items/item">
        <tr>
          <xsl:for-each select="property">
            <td><font class="listText"><xsl:value-of select=
"property.value"/></font></td>
          </xsl:for-each>
        </tr>
      </xsl:for-each>
    </table>
  </div>
</xsl:template>
```

The *<newsitem>* transformation will build a news article format similar to those found on professional news sites. Notice that all of the styling is controlled by embedded CSS code.

```
<xsl:template match="newsitem">
  <div class="newsItem" id="newsitem_{generate-id()}">
    <div class="newsHl1"><xsl:value-of select="body/body.head/
headline/hl1"/></div>
    <div class="newsHl2"><xsl:value-of select="body/body.head/
headline/hl2"/></div>
    <div class="newsBlPerson"><xsl:value-of select="body/body.head/
byline/person"/></div>
    <div class="newsBlTag"><xsl:value-of select="body/body.head/
byline/bytag"/></div>
    <div class="newsDlLoc"><xsl:value-of select="body/body.head/
dateline/location"/>, </div>
```

```
      <div class="newsDlDate"><xsl:value-of select="body/body.head/
dateline/story.date"/></div>
      <div class="newsBody">
        <xsl:for-each select="body/body.content/p"><xsl:value-of
select="."/><p/></xsl:for-each>
      </div>
    </div>
  </xsl:template>
```

The *<doclets>* will take the form of small, self-contained blocks of content. The transformation for this type of element is relatively straightforward.

```
  <xsl:template match="doclet">
    <div id="doclet_{generate-id}" class="doclet">
      <div class="docletHeading"><xsl:value-of select="header"/></div>
      <div class="docletText">
        <xsl:if test="image">
          <img height="100" src="images/{image}" align="left"/>
        </xsl:if>
        <xsl:for-each select="text/p"><xsl:value-of select="."/><p/>
</xsl:for-each>
      </div>
    </div>
  </xsl:template>
</xsl:stylesheet>
```

Finally, we need to include the *<navigation>* transformations into our style sheet. Listing 5-9 shows the IE5 skin in its entirety. The document transformation arranges all the possible components of a Noverant Web page. This transformation is responsible for high-level layout and formatting.

Listing 5-9 IE5.xsl: First skin for the Internet Explorer 5 browser, covering all of the elements found in the Noverant document schema.

```
<xsl:stylesheet xmlns:xsl="http://www.w3.org/1999/XSL/Transform"
version="1.0">
  <xsl:output method="html"/>
  <xsl:template match="document">
    <html>
      <head>
        <script language="JavaScript">
          function expand(divid)
          {
             eval("closed_"+divid).style.display = 'none';
             eval("open_"+divid).style.display = '';
          }
          function collapse(divid)
          {
```

(continued)

Listing 5-9 *continued*

```
                eval("open_"+divid).style.display = 'none';
                eval("closed_"+divid).style.display = '';
            }
        </script>
        <style>
            a:visited {background-color:#C7D2DE; color:black;
text-decoration: underline}
            a:link {background-color:#C7D2DE; color:black;
text-decoration: underline}
            a:active {background-color:activecaption; color:
captiontext; text-decoration: underline}
            a:hover {background-color:#C7D2DE; color:black;
text-decoration: underline}
           .clsHeading {font-family: verdana; color: black; font-size:
11; font-weight: 800;}
            .clsEntryText {padding-top: 2px; font-family: verdana;
color: black; font-size: 11; font-weight: 400;
background-color:#C7D2DE;}
            .clsWarningText {font-family: verdana; white-space:pre;
color: #B80A2D; font-size: 11; font-weight: 600; width:550;
background-color:#EFE7EA;}
            .clsCopy {font-family: verdana; color: black; font-size:
11; font-weight: 400;  background-color:#FFFFFF;}
            .doclet {margin: 5px; padding:8px; display:block;
border:solid 1px; padding-top:2px; font-family:verdana; color:black;
font-size: 13px; font-weight: 400; background-color:white;}
            .docletHeading {padding-top: 2px; font-family: verdana;
color: #003366; font-size: 20; font-weight: 400;}
            .docletImage {display:inline; padding-top: 2px;
font-family: verdana; color: black; font-size: 11; font-weight: 400;}
           .docletText {display:inline; padding-top: 2px; font-family:
verdana; color: black; font-size: 12; font-weight: 400;}
            .docletExcerpt {display:inline; padding-top: 2px;
font-family: verdana; color: black; font-size: 11; font-weight: 400;}
            .newsItem {margin:5px; vertical-align: top; padding:8px;
display:inline; border:solid 1px; padding-top:2px; font-family:
verdana; color:black; font-size: 13px; font-weight: 400;
background-color:white; width:300px}
            .newsHl1 {padding-top: 2px; font-family: verdana; color:
#003366; font-size: 20; font-weight: 400;}
           .newsHl2 {padding-top: 2px; font-style:italic; font-family:
verdana; color: black; font-size: 14; font-weight: 400;}
            .newsBlPerson {padding: 2px; font-family: verdana; color:
black; font-size: 14; text-decoration:underline; font-weight: 400;
text-align:right;}
            .newsBlTag {padding: 2px; font-family: verdana; color:
black; font-size: 11; font-weight: 600; text-align:right;}
            .newsDlLoc {display:inline; font-family: verdana; color:
```

```
black; font-size: 12; font-weight: 600;}
          .newsDlDate {display:inline; font-family: verdana; color:
black; font-size: 12; font-weight: 600;}
          .newsBody {font-family: times; color: black; font-size:
12px; font-family:verdana; font-weight: 400; text-align:justify;}
          .list {margin:5px; vertical-align: top; padding:8px;
display:inline; border:solid 1px; padding-top:2px; font-family:
verdana; color:black; font-size: 13px; font-weight: 400;
background-color:white; width:600px}
          .listHeading {padding-top: 2px; font-family: verdana;
color: #003366; font-size: 20; font-weight: 400;}
          .listText {display:inline; padding-top: 2px; font-family:
verdana; color: black; font-size: 14; font-weight: 400;}
        </style>
      </head>
      <body style="background-color:#C7D2DE;">
        <table width="100%" cellspacing="5">
          <tr>
            <td nowrap="yes">
              <xsl:apply-templates select="navigation"/>
            </td>
            <td align="left" valign="top">
              <xsl:apply-templates select="doclet"/>
              <xsl:apply-templates select="newsitem"/>
              <xsl:apply-templates select="list"/>
            </td>
            <td>
            </td>
          </tr>
        </table>
      </body>
    </html>
  </xsl:template>
  <xsl:template match="list">
    <div class="list" id="list_{generate-id()}">
      <table>
        <tr>
          <td colspan="{count(columns/column)}"><font class=
"docletHeading"><xsl:value-of select="title"/></font></td>
        </tr>
        <tr>
          <xsl:for-each select="columns/column">
            <th align="left"><font class="listText"><b><xsl:value-of
select="description"/></b></font></th>
          </xsl:for-each>
        </tr>
        <xsl:for-each select="items/item">
          <tr>
            <xsl:for-each select="property">
```

(continued)

Listing 5-9 *continued*

```
              <td><font class="listText">
<xsl:value-of select="property.value"/></font></td>
             </xsl:for-each>
           </tr>
         </xsl:for-each>
       </table>
     </div>
   </xsl:template>
   <xsl:template match="newsitem">
     <div class="newsItem" id="newsitem_{generate-id()}">
       <div class="newsHl1"><xsl:value-of select="body/body.head/
headline/hl1"/></div>
       <div class="newsHl2"><xsl:value-of select="body/body.head/
headline/hl2"/></div>
      <div class="newsBlPerson"><xsl:value-of select="body/body.head/
byline/person"/></div>
       <div class="newsBlTag"><xsl:value-of select="body/body.head/
byline/bytag"/></div>
       <div class="newsDlLoc"><xsl:value-of select="body/body.head/
dateline/location"/>, </div>
       <div class="newsDlDate"><xsl:value-of select="body/body.head/
dateline/story.date"/></div>
       <div class="newsBody">
         <xsl:for-each select="body/body.content/p"><xsl:value-of
select="."/><p/></xsl:for-each>
       </div>
     </div>
   </xsl:template>
   <xsl:template match="doclet">
     <div id="doclet_{generate-id}" class="doclet">
       <div class="docletHeading"><xsl:value-of select="header"/></div>
       <div class="docletText">
         <xsl:if test="image">
           <img height="100" src="images/{image}" align="left"/>
         </xsl:if>
         <xsl:for-each select="text/p"><xsl:value-of select="."/>
<p/></xsl:for-each>
       </div>
     </div>
   </xsl:template>
   <xsl:template match="navigation[@type='tree']">
     <div class="clsEntryText" style="padding-left:5px"
id="open_{generate-id()}">
       <xsl:if test="openImage"><img src="{openImage}"/> </xsl:if>
       <xsl:if test="href"><a href="{href}">
         <xsl:if test="href/@target"><xsl:attribute name=
"target"><xsl:value-of select="href/@target"/></xsl:attribute>
<xsl:if>
```

```
        <xsl:value-of select="description"/></a>
      </xsl:if>
      <xsl:if test="not(href)"><xsl:value-of select="description"/>
</xsl:if>
      <xsl:apply-templates select="navitem"/>
    </div>
  </xsl:template>
  <xsl:template match="navitem">
    <xsl:choose>
      <xsl:when test="children">
        <xsl:variable name="childcnt" select="count(.//navitem)"/>
        <div class="clsEntryText" id="closed_{generate-id()}">
          <xsl:for-each select="ancestor::navitem">
            <xsl:choose>
              <xsl:when test="count(following-sibling::navitem) > 0">
                <img src="/xmlbook/images/line.gif"/>
              </xsl:when>
              <xsl:otherwise>
                <img src="/xmlbook/images/nothing.gif"/>
              </xsl:otherwise>
            </xsl:choose>
          </xsl:for-each>
          <img src="/xmlbook/images/folder_plus.gif" style=
"cursor:hand" onClick="expand('{generate-id()}')"/>
          <xsl:if test="closedImage"><img src="{closedImage}"
/> </xsl:if>
          <xsl:if test="href"><a href="{href}">
            <xsl:if test="href/@target"><xsl:attribute name=
"target"><xsl:value-of select="href/@target"/></xsl:attribute>
</xsl:if>
            <xsl:value-of select="description"/></a>
          </xsl:if>
          <xsl:if test="not(href)"><xsl:value-of select=
"description"/></xsl:if>
          (<xsl:value-of select="$childcnt"/> artist<xsl:if
test="$childcnt != 1">s</xsl:if>)
        </div>
        <div class="clsEntryText" id="open_{generate-id()}"
style="display:none">
          <xsl:for-each select="ancestor::navitem">
            <xsl:choose>
              <xsl:when test="count(following-sibling::navitem) > 0">
                <img src="/xmlbook/images/line.gif"/>
              </xsl:when>
              <xsl:otherwise>
                <img src="/xmlbook/images/nothing.gif"/>
              </xsl:otherwise>
            </xsl:choose>
          </xsl:for-each>
```

(continued)

Listing 5-9 *continued*

```
          <img  src="/xmlbook/images/folder_minus.gif" style=
"cursor:hand" onClick="collapse('{generate-id()}')"/>
          <xsl:if test="openImage"><img src="{openImage}"/> 
</xsl:if>
          <xsl:if test="href"><a href="{href}">
            <xsl:if test="href/@target"><xsl:attribute name=
"target"><xsl:value-of select="href/@target"/></xsl:attribute>
</xsl:if>
            <xsl:value-of select="description"/></a>
          </xsl:if>
          <xsl:if test="not(href)"><xsl:value-of select=
"description"/></xsl:if>
           (<xsl:value-of select="$childcnt"/> artist<xsl:if
test="$childcnt != 1">s</xsl:if>)
          <xsl:apply-templates select="children"/>
        </div>
      </xsl:when>
      <xsl:otherwise>
        <div class="clsEntryText">
          <xsl:for-each select="ancestor::navitem">
            <xsl:choose>
              <xsl:when test="count(following-sibling::navitem) > 0">
                <img src="/xmlbook/images/line.gif"/>
              </xsl:when>
              <xsl:otherwise>
                <img src="/xmlbook/images/nothing.gif"/>
              </xsl:otherwise>
            </xsl:choose>
          </xsl:for-each>
          <img  src="/xmlbook/images/divider.gif" onClick=
"collapse('{generate-id()}')"/>
          <xsl:if test="image"><img src="{image}"/> </xsl:if>
          <xsl:if test="href"><a href="{href}">
            <xsl:if test="href/@target"><xsl:attribute name=
"target"><xsl:value-of select="href/@target"/></xsl:attribute>
</xsl:if>
            <xsl:value-of select="description"/></a>
          </xsl:if>
          <xsl:if test="not(href)"><xsl:value-of select=
"description"/></xsl:if>
        </div>
      </xsl:otherwise>
    </xsl:choose>
  </xsl:template>
</xsl:stylesheet>
```

Now let's put the code to the test by calling the controller! Figure 5-10 shows the nav_by_genre view helper.

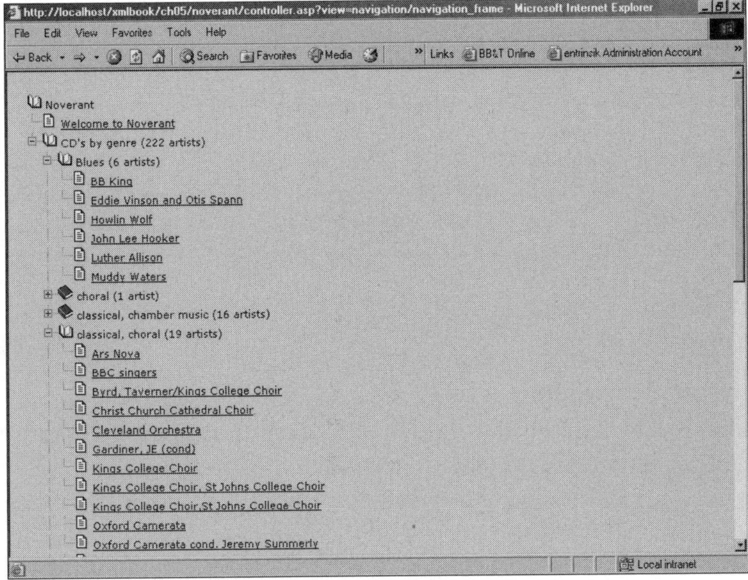

Figure 5-10 A view of the Noverant navigation tree.

The Doclet View Helper

Now we need to write a view helper that will contain the doclet XML. Doclets can be embedded directly in a helper document or can be retrieved dynamically from an external doclet database. For the time being Noverant is willing to write its doclets manually inside a doclet view helper.

This view helper will be (thankfully!) much easier to write than the navigation helper. Noverant's design decision to write doclets manually means the helper can take the form of the doclet code itself. An example follows:

```
<doclet>
  <id>main</id>
  <image>cd.jpg</image>
  <header>Welcome to Noverant</header>
  <excerpt>Do you like tapes or CD's?</excerpt>
  <text>
    <p>
    Headquartered in Raleigh, NC, Noverant.com is revolutionizing the
way you buy music. We buy directly from the world's leading CD
publishers to bring the hottest CDs to your door fast!
    </p>
    <p>
```

```
    Our award-winning e-commerce site, Noverant.com, leverages the
power of XML to help you comb through our vast selection of musical
offerings. Can't find what you're looking for? No sweat! Just drop us a
line and we'll hunt it down for you.
    </p>
    <p>
    Noverant.com guarantees that you will have your purchase in hand
within 24 hours of ordering. If you don't we'll send you another one
for free. Also, make sure to check out our wishlist feature. Don't you
hate it when you can think of a hundred CDs you want at home, only to
draw a blank when you walk in the record store? With our wishlist you
can keep track of the albums you want to buy before you buy them! When
you're ready to spend some cash you'll know exactly what to get!
    </p>
  </text>
</doclet>
```

The News View Helper

The news view helper will, for now, be as easy to write as the doclet view helper. Valid news items can be written directly into the news view helper. Once Noverant signs their contracts with their news content providers, however, the news view helper will need to be extended to handle remote content. If the content provider has SOAP or FTP services configured to distribute news electronically, the handler can connect to the machine dynamically and download the content. Depending on the format of the vendor's news items, the helper might need to massage the data into Noverant's news format through the use of XSLTs.

The Artist View Helper

The artist view helper will be called whenever someone clicks on an artist in the site. The helper can expect to be passed an *artist* argument by the controller. The helper will query the CD database via an XPath expression to extract all the CDs matching the selected artist. Before we can look up any information about the artist, the CDs.xml database must be loaded. This is accomplished by loading the file into the DOMDocument control.

```
<%
  xmlurl = Server.MapPath("../db/CDs.xml")
  Set source = Server.CreateObject("MSXML2.DOMDocument")
  source.async = false
  source.load(xmlurl)
  Set e = source.parseError
  if e.errorCode <> 0 then
  Response.write(e.reason)
  if e.line > 0 Then
     Response.write(e.line)
     Response.write(" ")
```

```
      Response.write(e.linepos)
      Response.write(" ")
      Response.write(e.srcText)
   end if
   error = true
   end if
```

Extracting all of the CDs for a particular artist is a simple matter for the view helper. The DOMDocument control's *selectNodes()* method allows any XPath expression to be run on the source document.

```
   artist = Request.QueryString("artist")
   Set cds = source.selectNodes("cds/cd[artist='"+artist+"']")
  %>
```

Now that the relevant CDs have been extracted from the database, the view helper must prepare the XML list structure to be returned to the controller. An ASP For-loop will be used to iterate over the collection generated by the XPath expression to create each entry in the list document. Listing 5-10 shows the artist helper page responsible for assembling a Noverant XML document for a specific artist.

Listing 5-10 List.asp: Retrieving a musician's CDs and constructing an XML result list with the artist view helper page.

```
<document>
  <doclet>...</doclet>
  <list>
    <title>
      CD Titles by <%= artist %>
    </title>
    <columns>
      <column>
        <column.name>title</column.name>
        <column.description>CD Title</column.description>
      </column>
    </columns>
    <items>
<%
  For x = 0 to cds.length - 1
    Set cd = cds.item(x)
    title = cd.selectSingleNode("title").text
%>
    <item>
      <property>
        <property.name>title</property.name>
        <property.value>
<%= title %>
        </property.value>
```

(continued)

Listing 5-10 *continued*

```
      </property>
    </item>
<% Next %>
    </items>
  </list>
</document>
<%
  xmlurl = Server.MapPath("../db/CDs.xml")
  Set source = Server.CreateObject("MSXML2.DOMDocument")
  source.async = false
  source.load(xmlurl)
  Set e = source.parseError
  if e.errorCode <> 0 then
  Response.write(e.reason)
  if e.line > 0 Then
     Response.write(e.line)
     Response.write(" ")
     Response.write(e.linepos)
     Response.write(" ")
     Response.write(e.srcText)
  end if
  error = true
  end if
  artist = Request.QueryString("artist")
  Set cds = source.selectNodes("cds/cd[artist='"+artist+"']")
 %>
<document>
  <doclet>...</doclet>
  <list>
    <title>
      CD Titles by <%= artist %>
    </title>
    <columns>
      <column>
        <column.name>title</column.name>
        <column.description>CD Title</column.description>
      </column>
    </columns>
    <items>
<%
  For x = 0 to cds.length - 1
    Set cd = cds.item(x)
    title = cd.selectSingleNode("title").text
%>
    <item>
      <property>
        <property.name>title</property.name>
        <property.value>
<%= title %>
        </property.value>
```

```
        </property>
      </item>
<% Next %>
      </items>
    </list>
</document>
```

Bringing it All Together

Next we will build a page to combine our doclets and news items together into a single document to be displayed on the site. This page will be easy to author; all it needs to do is rely on the view helpers that we've already written.

```
<document>
  <% Server.execute("doclet/doclet.asp") %>
  <% Server.execute("news/news.asp") %>
</document>
```

The main page can be tested by issuing an HTTP request directly to the controller and referencing the view in this URL string:

http://localhost/xmlbook/chapter 8/noverant/controller.asp?view=main

Figure 5-11 is the result.

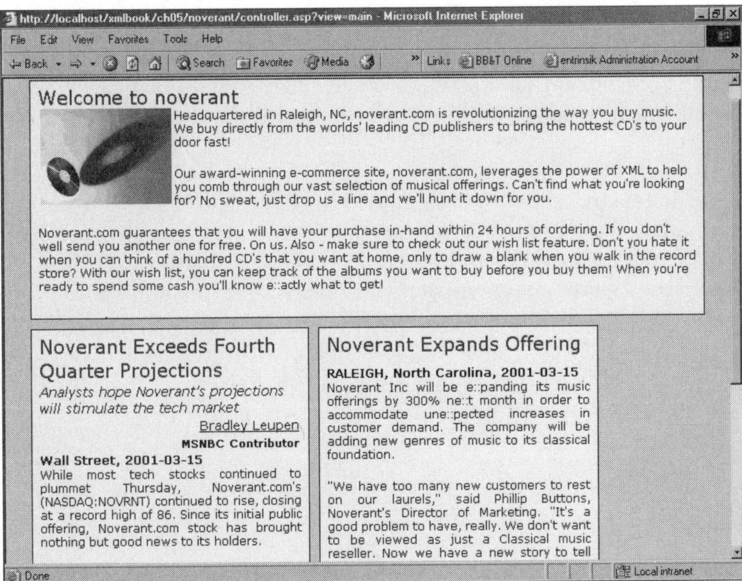

Figure 5-11 The front page for the site, including a *<doclet>* and a *<newsitem>* transformation.

This looks great! All that's left for the front page is to create a logo and put together a frame set, as shown in Listing 5-11 through Listing 5-13.

Listing 5-11 index.htm: This file contains the frame set that organizes the layout of the site.

```
<html>
<title>Noverant Inc</title>
<frameset rows="55,*" frameborder="no" framespacing="0">
  <frame name="masthead" src="masthead.htm" marginwidth="0"
marginheight="0" scrolling="no" frameborder="no" framespacing="0">
  <frame name="body" src="main.htm" marginwidth="0" marginheight="0"
scrolling="no" frameborder="no">
</frameset>
</html>
```

Listing 5-12 masthead.htm: Contains an image to be displayed at the top of all pages in the site.

```
<html>
  <body>
    <img src="images/logo.gif">
  </body>
</html>
```

Listing 5-13 main.htm: Divides frame into two vertical sections, one for global navigation and the other for site content.

```
<html>
<title>Noverant Inc</title>
<frameset cols="20%,*" frameborder="yes" framespacing="0">
  <frame name="nav" src="controller.asp?view=navigation/
navigation_frame" marginwidth="5" marginheight="0" scrolling="auto"
frameborder="no" framespacing="0">
  <frame name="main" src="controller.asp?view=main" marginwidth="0"
marginheight="0" scrolling="auto" frameborder="no">
</frameset>
</html>
```

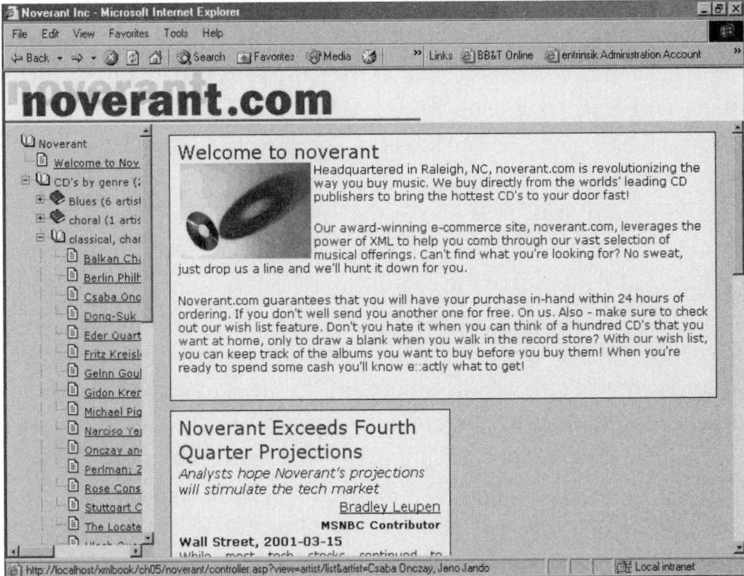

Figure 5-12 The full front page, with separate frames for the masthead, navigation tree, and main body.

Figure 5-12 shows how it looks when we load Listing 5-11 in Internet Explorer. Figure 5-13 shows the artist view helper in action.

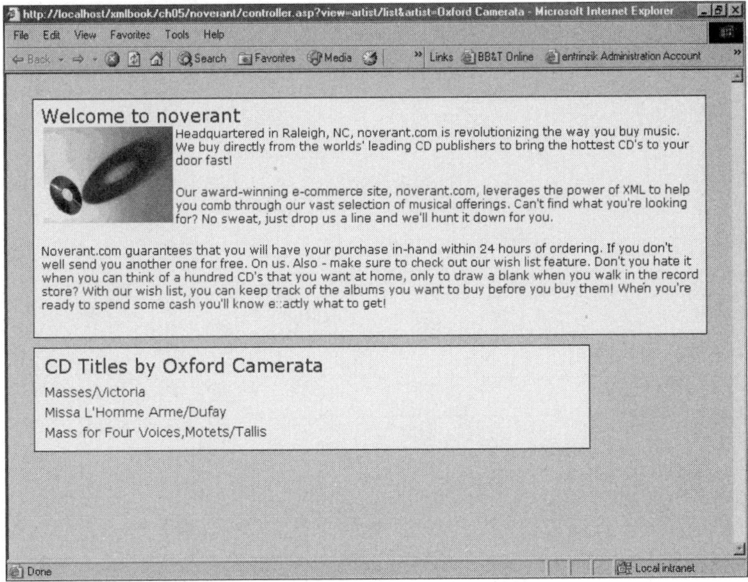

Figure 5-13 A list of CD titles, displayed by clicking on the name by the selected musician.

Final Thoughts

Building Noverant's Web site was a useful project in beginning to explore the capabilities of XML, XSLT, and the XML DOM. As good as this site looks for a proof-of-concept piece, it needs more work before it will be ready for production use.

The document model is somewhat simplistic. The <*doclet*> element in particular needs to be expanded to accommodate different media types, relative priority, and advanced layout requirements. The query page can be enhanced to provide a more flexible query mechanism for a user. More skins need to be written to handle different browsers. The XSLT style sheet(s) should be able to handle more intelligent positioning than is currently possible. The doclet helper should allow for better management of content in the site. Finally the controller should be changed to take advantage of the multithreaded XML parser.

In this chapter we introduced some new XML technologies, such as XSLT, and have seen how they can impact traditional Web application design. The Noverant Web storefront served as a useful example of a Web site designed around XML. Hopefully you have picked up a few ideas that will be of use to you in your Web applications.

By separating presentation from content, XML can help to solve many of the maintenance problems that have plagued traditional Web applications. I recommend that you begin thinking about ways in which you can incorporate XML into new Web projects. In Chapter 6 we will see how XML can be used to develop application user interfaces.

6

Building User Interfaces

Software developers have struggled with creating User Interfaces (UIs) since the birth of the computer, and these interfaces have constantly evolved, even when the tasks they perform have remained the same. A noticeable example can be seen in the progression of Microsoft's operating systems. From MS-DOS to Windows 3 to Windows XP, Microsoft has improved the usability of its most current operating system, so the task of installing, managing, and launching applications are easier than ever.

Similarly, other UIs for desktop and enterprise applications have changed over time. Advances in computing such as faster computers and graphics hardware now enable developers to build graphic-rich applications. The Microsoft Foundation Classes (MFC) armed application developers with a suite of standard, yet powerful UI components. By using these tools, developers can easily include such features as drag-and-drop, cut-and-paste, multimedia, and event-driven logic.

A current interface topic concerns Web browsers. The popularity of the Internet and the Web have made the Web browser ubiquitous. First-generation

Web browsers were meant for viewing content, not building application UIs. The browser, however, was forced to adapt as the Internet grew into a forum for thousands of distributed applications. Developers struggled to create browser-based UIs that were functional at best. Today developers can build browser-based, thin-client applications that are nearly as rich as their thicker cousins.

This chapter will discuss how developers can leverage XML to help them with UI layout, navigation, and input controls. We will explore ways to use XML to create a layer of abstraction on top of traditional UI elements, making them more dynamic and extensible. Finally we will put these ideas to us, in actual code samples.

Modeling a User Interface in XML

The most important trait of an effective UI is consistency because an application with a consistent approach to human interaction is much easier to learn and use. Consistent UIs can also, with practice, be used intuitively. Intuitive use means efficient use; efficient users mean happy users; and happy users mean well-paid developers.

After consistency, the look and feel of an application's UI can be its strongest asset or its worst detractor. Naturally, users see an application's outward appearance first, and from that they draw first impressions. It behooves the software developer to design an interface that is sharp-looking and consistent in its visual presentation. Now you have a new tool for making sure the presentation says what you want it to say.

XML can help enforce visual consistency across the application by wresting the power of making UI design decisions from the hands of content developers and returning it to its original owner, the visual designer. XML can also help incrementally augment a UI's palette of components as new tool sets become available. Thus, the implementation or behavior of a UI component can be modified without altering the underlying model. In addition, separating presentation from content allows visual designers and content developers to work in concert, shortening the project lifecycle.

No matter the nature of the application, all UIs share a number of features, such as layout and navigation. In this section we will identify and describe several of these UI features.

Layout

The layout of an application's UI governs the positioning of its content. Information should be presented so that it is easy to find, manipulate, and analyze. Data should be presented in a clean, uncluttered manner. Closely related information should be tightly grouped and separated from less relevant information. The positioning of material need not be flashy. Simplicity and efficiency are what we want.

Navigation

An intuitive navigation scheme is critical to an application's reception. Users should be able to find the function or item they want quickly and intuitively. Similar functions should be grouped together for easy access. Navigation elements should not relocate themselves. Consistent behavior on the part of the user should be encouraged by the application.

Input Controls and Widgets

Input widgets, or components, are the atomic building blocks out of which all UIs are created. Examples include text fields, text boxes, check boxes, and any other controls that solicit input from the user. Some widgets are interchangeable. For example, combo boxes and radio buttons can often be used interchangeably to ask the user to "choose one of the following options." An application should not alternate between these controls arbitrarily.

User Actions

Actions are used to represent the various ways a user can manipulate data on the screen. Actions can take the form of buttons, pull-down menus, right-click menus, and others. Some actions are global, such as "undo" actions. Other actions are context-specific.

Security

Security in an enterprise application should be flexible enough to accommodate various dynamic roles that accurately reflect the job responsibilities of many different classes of users. An application's security should control the navigation, actions, and data exposed to the user. It should not be intrusive; a restricted user should feel that the application is limited to what they can see.

Extensibility

A well-designed Web UI will take into account changes or variations in browser capabilities. The UI should be able to accommodate more sophisticated browser controls with a minimum of tweaking. Web browsers are dynamic software packages. New features and bug-fixes are constantly being added. Therefore, you should design a UI that is well-suited to change.

Customizability

Flexible UIs should allow some degree of user customization, but interfaces that are too highly customizable create needless complexity. An application should not go overboard by offering the ability to change every label, font, or screen. Ideally, allowing some customization to views, reports, color schemes, and the overall look and feel will make your application more user-friendly.

Color Scheme

Color can be used to improve an application's usability and aesthetic appeal and can have a utilitarian purpose when applied well. For example, colors can be used to separate or associate different content blocks within the UI. All graphical programs within the Windows operating system inherit the environment's color scheme. Additionally, the active window usually has a uniquely colored caption for identification purposes.

XML Benefits

XML can be used in all facets of an application's UI to enforce consistency and offer improved extensibility. By separating content from presentation, XML can help maintain a natural division between the roles of content development and aesthetic design. In this section we will look at various ways in which XML can be incorporated into UI design.

The Controller Pattern Revisited

In Chapter 5 we saw how XML and XSLT can streamline the design, development, and ongoing maintenance of a corporate Web site. At the core of the site was an implementation of the controller design pattern. The idea behind this pattern was to route all requests to the underlying system through a single ASP. This page acted as a proxy for the user, stepping in to render the page before it was returned to the browser.

By architecting a Web application in this way, designers can leverage XML and XSLT to split the process of page construction and presentation into separate tasks. The following sequence describes the chain of events that is initiated whenever a user requests a new page inside the Web application.

1. The user issues a request to the controller, sending in the name of the page they want to see as well as any contextual information (for example, record IDs, user IDs, etc) that page might need to do its job (for example, *see http://www.noverant.com/controller.asp?view=cddetail&cdid=10013*).
2. The controller redirects the request to a page handler that assembles the view the user requested (for example, cddetail1.asp). Like any ASP, the handler might query a database, read a file from the Web server's file system, or even call another URL to gather the data to be shown on the page. Unlike normal ASP pages, however, the handler

does not build an HTML document. Instead, it creates an XML document whose structure is specific to the application and was dictated by the application's UI architect.

3. The page handler returns the page's XML content back to the controller. Now that the controller has an abstract XML version of the page, it must transform the XML version into a form suitable for viewing on the user's browser (for example, HTML). The controller delegates the transformation to an XSLT page built specifically for the job.

4. The XSLT adheres to the same XML document structure that the page handler did when it built the document. The transformation extracts the generic data from the XML document, massages it, applies layout and formatting rules, inserts any necessary script, and delivers the finished product to the controller.

5. The controller delivers the final document to the client.

Listing 6-1 shows an implementation of the controller design pattern using ASPs.

Listing 6-1 controller.asp: a simple implementation of the controller ASP page.

```
<%
   // Get the view argument
   view   = Request.QueryString("view")
   base = Request.ServerVariables("SERVER_NAME")+
Replace(Request.ServerVariables("URL"),"controller.asp","")
   if Request.ServerVariables("HTTPS") = "ON" then
       base = "https://"+base
   else
       base = "http://"+base
   end if
   xmlurl = base+view+".asp?"
   arguments = ""
   // Parse additional arguments
   For Each item in Request.QueryString
       if arguments <> "" then arguments = arguments+"&"
       itemvalue = Request.QueryString(item)
       arguments = arguments+item+"="+itemvalue
   Next
   // Append the argument string to the xmlurl
   xmlurl = xmlurl+arguments
   // Contstruct a URL to the appropriate skin
   // This implementation uses only the Internet Explorer 5.0 skin
   // Other skins could be used based on the browser type
   if Request.QueryString("skin") <> "" then
```

(continued)

Listing 6-1 *continued*

```
        skin = Request.QueryString("skin")
    else
        skin = "ie5"
    end if
    xslurl = base+"xslt/"+skin+".xsl"
    // Load the XML
    // A production implementation should use the multi-threaded
version of the DomDocument.
    error = false
    Set source = Server.CreateObject("MSXML2.DOMDocument")
    source.async = false
    tmp = source.setProperty("ServerHTTPRequest", true)
    source.load(xmlurl)
    Set e = source.parseError
    if e.errorCode <> 0 then
        Response.write(e.reason)
        if e.line > 0 Then
            Response.write(e.line)
            Response.write(" ")
            Response.write(e.linepos)
            Response.write(" ")
            Response.write(e.srcText)
        end if
        error = true
    end if
    // Load the XSLT
    Set style = Server.CreateObject("MSXML2.DOMDocument")
    style.async = false
    tmp = style.setProperty("ServerHTTPRequest", true)
    style.load(xslurl)
    Set e = style.parseError
    if e.errorCode <> 0 Then
        Response.write(e.reason)
        if e.line > 0 Then
            Response.write(e.line)
            Response.write(" ")
            Response.write(e.linepos)
            Response.write(" ")
            Response.write(e.srcText)
        end if
        error = true
    end if
    if error = false Then
        xmlresult = source.transformNode(style)
    end if
    Response.write(xmlresult)
 %>
```

This approach to Web site design can also be applied to UI design for Web applications. It offers a number of benefits. Splitting page rendering into isolated construction and formatting tasks enables parallel development activity and shorter development timelines. Furthermore, these distinct activities can be assigned to specialists. Content authors have greater knowledge of the intricacies of the application's business logic and the various ways used to pull information from the back-end. Layout specialists can focus on the aesthetics of the UI, worrying less about where the information comes from and more about how it should be presented.

This approach is also extensible. The controller can be augmented to decorate or filter XML content based on a user's browser or role within the application. New presentation skins, or transformations, can be plugged into the environment without rewriting every page. This approach also discourages monolithic page design. By promoting the segregation of content from presentation, the controller pattern makes an application easier to maintain over the long run.

The User Interface Schema

Team members need to work together to make a project succeed. In this case content developers and layout designers can communicate in a common, well-defined language by using XML and XSLT to implement a controller-based UI. This language, or schema, defines the documents that flow through the application. The schema acts as a blueprint for content developers when they begin building pages as well as a specification the presentation group uses when constructing their XSLT. The schema is used to validate the documents in the application, and it should address common UI aspects such as layout, navigation, input controls, user actions, and security. Once the schema is finalized, the two groups can begin working independently, so get this out of the way first.

Defining your UI this way forces your team to think abstractly about what they're trying to show in the application. This process yields immediate returns. Presentation specialists will see ways to interpret the UI XML documents in more interesting ways. System architects will uncover newer uses for XML within the program. And once you've defined your project's UI schema, content developers can begin building conformant documents before the presentation rules are even implemented!

Two Approaches to User Interface Schemas

The goal of your UI schema is to define an XML document model that can be easily transformed into UI elements within your application. The nature of this schema depends on many factors. How broad is your application? How many different business entities are involved? What types of clients will be using the system? Will your application need to support a wide range of browsers with different capabilities (such as an Internet application) or just a single browser (an intranet application)?

Generally speaking, your UI schema can follow two broad categories. The schema can be presentation based, in which the elements are associated with UI functions instead of the type of data shown. The XSLTs for this type of schema translate the generic UI controls into browser-specific documents. Conversely, the schema can be business object-based. XML documents under this paradigm model business entities and contexts instead of generic forms. More XSLT work is required in this scenario, as it is responsible for creating the entire UI.

Presentation-Based User Interfaces

Presentation-based UI documents are easiest for traditional HTML developers to understand. Presentation-oriented schemas define generic document structures that all pages in the system must follow. Note that the HTML specification given here is only one example of a presentation-based schema.

Advantages to using a presentation-based UI schema include

- A shorter learning curve. The approach is similar to HTML and is easy for HTML developers to understand.
- A small number of required transformations. This schema requires a transformation template for each piece of the generic content model. New transformations are unnecessary even if the number of pages in the system grows.
- More consistent-looking pages. Associating the schema and transformations with document structure will enforce consistency among the pages in your application.

Disadvantages to this approach include:

- Lost meta-information about the underlying data in the page. The schema does not care what kind of data is being displayed as long as it has a valid document structure.
- Difficulty in defining highly dynamic pages. Some pages in your application will require a lot of client-side scripting to handle user interaction. This can be difficult to achieve without hard coding the scripts directly in the pages.

Therefore, use a presentation-based UI schema if the number of different business entities or the number of pages in your application is large. A presentation-based schema is durable, scaleable, and evenly divides UI responsibilities between content developers and layout designers.

To show you how this type of schema can be useful, Listing 6-2 illustrates what the XML for a specific person might look like under a presentation-based schema.

Listing 6-2 An example of a presentation-based XML document.

```
<document>
  <header>
    <title>Person Detail</title>
    <icon>person.gif</icon>
  <section>
    <header>
      <title>William Jones</title>
    </header>
    <view>
      <properties>
        <property description="First Name">William</property>
           <property description="Last Name">Jones</property>
            <property description="Address">200 Irving Street</property>
           <property description="City">Cambridge</property>
           <property description="State">MA</property>
           <property description="Zip Code">02138</property>
        </properties>
      </view>
    </section>
  </document>
```

This document looks similar to an HTML document, although XML has no hard-coded presentation rules. Instead the layout designer can use a number of clues when rendering this page. Still, not much meta-information describes the nature of the data that the document contains.

Business Object-Based User Interfaces

The second category of UIs is a business object-centric approach to UI XML documents. In this case the underlying XML documents represent business entities instead of document structures. Here XML documents describe the *type* of data being shown (for example, CD, employee, or automobile) on the page and the *context* of the page (for example, detail, edit, or creation). The XSLT developer must create transformations that build unique documents for every type and context combination allowed by the system.

Advantages to using an object-based UI schema include

- More specialized pages. If certain object contexts in your application call for highly dynamic and custom pages, an object-based approach might be the way to go.
- Preserved metadata. XML documents that abide by a business object-oriented schema provide information about what the data is instead of how to display it. Metadata can be useful if your application makes heavy use of it on the client-side.

Some of the disadvantages to an object-based approach are:

- It does not scale well as the number of business entities or their contexts grow. Multiple transformation templates covering a variety of contexts must be implemented whenever a new business entity is introduced.
- Consistency in look and feel is more difficult to achieve. Highly-specialized pages might thwart valiant efforts to install a global look and feel.
- Global changes are more difficult. Presentation rules might be scattered across a number of different object transformation templates. These should be localized if possible.
- This approach places a heavy burden on the XSLT author.

Accounting for the advantages and disadvantages, use an object-based UI schema when your application has few business entities with highly specialized UI requirements. This approach will help you isolate dynamic content into browser-specific XSLTs. Client-side scripts are generated by the XSLTs instead of by the content developers.

The following code details what a business object-based XML document might look like.

```
<person context="detail">
  <firstName>William</firstName>
  <lastName>Jones</lastName>
  <address>200 Irving Street</address>
  <city>Cambridge</city>
  <state>MA</state>
  <zip>02138</zip>
</person>
```

This XML document is noticeably different in structure from the presentation-based document shown previously. The XML elements in this file only relay information about the type of data viewed and the context where it is utilized. The XSLT author is responsible for packaging this information into

UI elements. The XSLT might also need to request additional XML data (such as the person's company information) via a separate HTTP request.

The User Interface Schema in This Chapter

At this point we will adopt a presentation-oriented XML schema for later examples. The examples are not too complex and the time-saving benefits that a presentation-based schema provides outweigh any concerns we might have about dynamic content. For your application, however, you should pick the UI schema approach that works best in your environment. You might even decide to implement a combination of the two approaches, in which specific object-based XML documents are transformed into generic presentation-based XML documents.

Layout Management

One of XML's best features is that it enforces global consistency. This is easily implemented through the use of the controller design pattern. In this section we will use XML to define a unique layout model for designing a simple UI. If you recall the Noverant Web site in Chapter 5, the controller pattern prescribes a single front-end to all page requests in the application. The controller has the following two main jobs:

1. Gather the XML that makes up the content of the requested page. Often, this task is not handled directly by the controller. Doing so would make the controller too complex. Delegating this responsibility to view helpers that are specifically designed for each view is easier.
2. Apply presentation rules to the content by transforming the XML content into a final document to be delivered to the client. The presentation engine is free to produce any type of document suited to a particular context. It might create an HTML document intended for a Web browser, a Wireless Markup Language (WML) document for a wireless device, a PDF or Microsoft Excel document for reporting purposes, an XML document to be processed further by another application, or just plain text.

A Simple Detail View

To begin our examination of the controller, let's look at a simple XML document that will serve as a foundation for our document model. Listing 6-3 is an excerpt from the Noverant back-office application in which a user has requested detailed information about a particular CD.

Listing 6-3 CDDetail1.xml: a generic document describing how a CD should be displayed.

```
<document>
  <header>
    <title>This is our first XML application page</title>
    <icon>document.gif</icon>
  </header>
  <section>
    <header>
      <title>Hello World</title>
      <icon>world.gif</icon>
    </header>
    <view>
      <properties>
        <property description="Property 1">Hello World</property>
      </properties>
    </view>
  </section>
</document>
```

The *<document>* element indicates the beginning and end of the content in this document. Like the *<html>* element in HTML, the *<document>* element is a container for all the information underneath it. The *<document>* element might contain a *<header>* element with a title and an icon.

The *<section>* element represents an area of content on the screen. Zero, one, or more *<section>* elements might appear inside a *<document>* element. The *<section>* element might also have a *<header>* element and one or more *<view>* elements beneath it. A *<view>* element can house many forms of content. The content in a *<view>* might be generic (for example, XML documents that describe property/value pair listings or generic input forms) or it might be a specific entity (for example, an XML document that describes a specific business object).

In this example our document contains a single *<section>* and *<view>* and a small property sheet. Suppose we transform this document into an HTML page suitable for rendering in our application. We will create an XSLT style sheet to perform this transformation. The first lines of the style sheet are used for initialization. The *<xsl:stylesheet>* element signifies the beginning of a transformation, and the *<xsl:output>* element indicates that the result of this transformation will be an HTML document.

```
<xsl:stylesheet xmlns:xsl="http://www.w3.org/1999/XSL/
Transform" version="1.0">
<xsl:output method="html" />
```

First we will match the root *<document>* node and initialize our HTML document. After inserting the *<html>* element the transformation creates a *<head>* element and provides a link to the CSS page that will be used to govern fine-grained formatting in the application. The guts of the transformation affect the body of the document. Inside the *<body>* element, the transformation creates a *<div>* element to house the rest of the information in the page. Notice that this master *<div>* inherits style attributes from the *document* class that appears in our CSS. The final step is to call *<xsl:apply-templates/>* to delegate further transformations to more precise rules.

```
<xsl:template match="document">
  <html>
    <head>
      <link rel="stylesheet" type="text/css" href="css/style.css"/>
    </head>
    <body>
      <div class="document">
        <xsl:apply-templates/>
      </div>
    </body>
  </html>
</xsl:template>
```

The document's header contains information about the page as a whole. The header might contain a title and a link to an icon. This information will be displayed at the top of the screen. The document header template matches on the "document/header" XPath expression to distinguish a *<document>* element's header from a *<section>* element's header.

The first task of this transformation template is to create a division for the header. The division links to the *documentHeader* class in our style sheet. Next the template checks for the existence of an *<icon>* element, transforming it into an *<img>* element if it exists. Notice that the transformation inserts an absolute path to the image directory before inserting the value of the icon. Next the template gets the value of the *<title>* element and inserts it into the result document.

```
<xsl:template match="document/header">
  <div class="documentHeader">
    <xsl:if test="icon">
      <img align="absmiddle" src="images/{icon}"/>
    </xsl:if>
    <xsl:value-of select="title"/>
  </div>
</xsl:template>
```

The section template is similar to the document template. It creates a wrapper division with padding to set it apart from other sections that might appear in the page. It then creates a new division, referring to the *section* CSS class and makes a recursive call to *<xsl:apply-templates>*.

```
<xsl:template match="section">
  <div style="padding:20px;" align="center">
    <div class="section">
      <xsl:apply-templates/>
    </div>
  </div>
</xsl:template>
```

The section header template is, again, similar to the document header template. It creates a new division and inserts the icon and title found in the XML document.

```
<xsl:template match="section/header">
  <div class="sectionHeader">
    <xsl:if test="icon">
      <img align="absmiddle" src="images/{icon}"/>
    </xsl:if>
    <xsl:value-of select="title"/>
  </div>
</xsl:template>
```

In this example the view template does not need to do anything other than look for further templates to apply. This will be extended in later examples.

```
<xsl:template match="view">
  <xsl:apply-templates/>
</xsl:template>
```

We will transform the document's *<properties>* and *<property>* elements into a simple table containing name/value pairs. The properties template sets up the beginning and ending *<table>* elements and defers to the property template to create the individual rows. Properties might also include hyperlinks to other documents. The XSLT tests for the existence of an *href* attribute and creates a hyperlink if one exists.

```
<xsl:template match="properties">
  <table cellpadding="5">
    <xsl:apply-templates/>
  </table>
</xsl:template>
<xsl:template match="property">
  <tr>
    <td bgcolor="a1a1a1">
      <font class="text"><b><xsl:value-of select="@description"/></
```

```
b></font>
    </td>
    <td><font class="text">
      <xsl:choose>
        <xsl:when test="@href"><a href="{@href}"><xsl:value-of
select="."/></a></xsl:when>
        <xsl:otherwise><xsl:value-of select="."/></xsl:otherwise>
      </xsl:choose>
    </font></td>
  </tr>
</xsl:template>
</xsl:stylesheet>
```

> **Note** Try to use *<xsl:apply-templates/>* instead of *<xsl:for-each/>* wherever possible. This syntax will allow you to mix and match components more easily.

The following CSS example, Listing 6-4, contains all the CSS rules for this document.

Listing 6-4 Style.css: a CSS for providing fine-grained element formatting.

```
body {
  background-color: background;
}
.text {
  font-family: Verdana;
  font-size:9pt;
  color: black;
}
.document {
  background-color: background;
  border:0px;
  width: 100%;
}
.documentHeader {
  border:1px solid;
  width: 100%;
  background-color:778899;
  border-bottom:1px solid;
  font-weight: bold;
  color:white;
  font-family: Verdana;
```

(continued)

Listing 6-4 *continued*

```
    font-size:9pt;
}
.section {
    border:0px;
    width: 99%;
    text-align: left;
    background-color:white;
    border: 3px;
    border-style: outset;
    border-color: e0e0e0;
    color:white;
    font-family: Verdana;
    font-size:9pt;
}
.sectionHeader {
    background-color: activeCaption;
    color: captionText;
    align: left;
    border:0px;
    width: 100%;
    border-bottom:1px solid;
    font-family: Verdana;
    font-size:9pt;
}
```

> **Note** Although XSLT is the language of choice for most XML transformations, CSS should still be used to isolate formatting rules for your HTML documents.

What does the XML document look like after the XSL and CSS styling rules are applied? Figure 6-1 shows the results of our transformation.

What have we accomplished here? For starters, we have created a 30-line HTML document out of an 18-line XML document, Although the addition of 12 lines does not sound like much, it amounts to a 60 percent inflation ratio. Therefore, we see that XML can do much of the "dirty work" of page creation for you. A layout specialist needs only to program the XSLT once and the XML engine will create and recreate thousands of lines of fine-tuned HTML code. You don't have to worry about un-closed tags (XSLT requires that all style sheets are well formed, and this feature catches a lot of HTML errors) or plenty of copied-and-pasted formatting logic running rampant in your application.

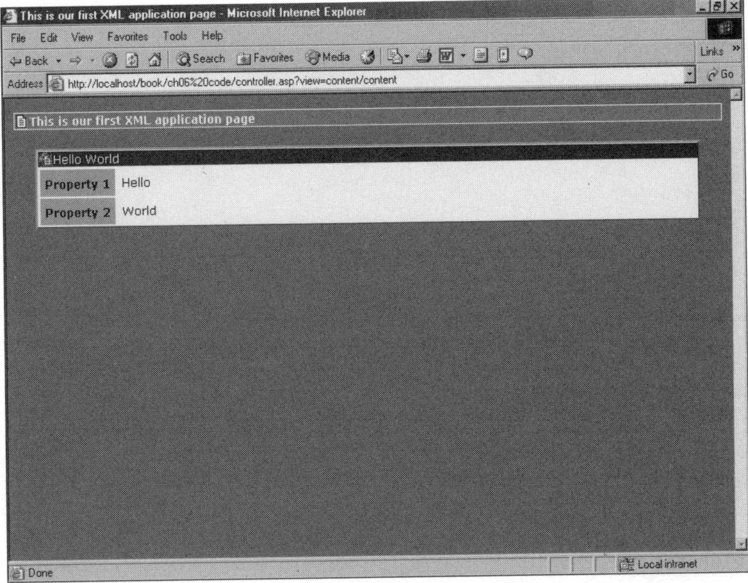

Figure 6-1 Microsoft Internet Explorer displaying a simple application page transformation.

Furthermore, global style changes need to be applied only a single time to a single document to affect every page.

Another detail to notice in this example is that the source XML document is simple. It boils everything down to the essential content to be displayed on the page. This becomes more evident when we look at a more intricate example.

A More Detailed View

Consider the Noverant CD On-Line storefront from the previous example. Presumably, Noverant uses a back-office application to maintain its database of albums and artists. This application allows Noverant employees to browse the inventory, update the database, and easily link to more detailed information. Listing 6-5 is an example of an XML document that contains information about one of the popular albums in the collection.

Listing 6-5 CDDetail2.asp: XML document containing a second *section* element to show the CD's track listing.

```
<document>
  <header>
    <title>The Beatles - Revolver</title>
    <icon>document.gif</icon>
```

(continued)

Listing 6-5 *continued*

```
  </header>
  <section>
    <header>
      <title>General Information</title>
      <icon>world.gif</icon>
    </header>
    <view>
      <properties>
        <property description="Artist">The Beatles</property>
        <property description="Album">Revolver</property>
        <property description="Label">EMI Records Ltd</property>
        <property description="Year Released">1966</property>
        <property description="Price">$13.99</property>
      </properties>
    </view>
  </section>
  <section>
    <header>
      <title>Track Listing</title>
      <icon>world.gif</icon>
    </header>
    <view>
      <properties>
        <property description="Track 1">Taxman [2:39]
(Harrison)</property>
        <property description="Track 2">Eleanor Rigby [2:07]
(Lennon/McCartney)</property>
        <property description="Track 3">I'm Only Sleeping [3:01]
(Lennon/McCartney)</property>
        <property description="Track 4">Love You To [3:01]
(Harrison)</property>
        <property description="Track 5">Here, There, and Everywhere
[2:25] (Lennon/McCartney)</property>
        <property description="Track 6">Yellow Submarine [2:40]
(Lennon/McCartney)</property>
        <property description="Track 7">She Said She Said [2:37]
(Lennon/McCartney)</property>
        <property description="Track 8">Good Day Sunshine [2:09]
(Lennon/McCartney)</property>
       <property description="Track 9">And Your Bird Can Sing [2:01]
(Lennon/McCartney)</property>
        <property description="Track 10">For No One [2:01]
(Lennon/McCartney)</property>
        <property description="Track 11">Doctor Robert [2:15]
(Lennon/McCartney)</property>
        <property description="Track 12">I Want to Tell You [2:29]
(Harrison)</property>
       <property description="Track 13">Got to Get You Into My Life
```

```
[2:30] (Lennon/McCartney)</property>
       <property description="Track 14">Tomorrow Never Knows [2:57]
(Lennon/McCartney)</property>
      </properties>
    </view>
  </section>
</document>
```

This XML document, when transformed with the XSLT listed earlier, produces an HTML page with two content areas. This page is shown in Figure 6-2. Notice that the transformation took care of positioning and styling the information in the result document.

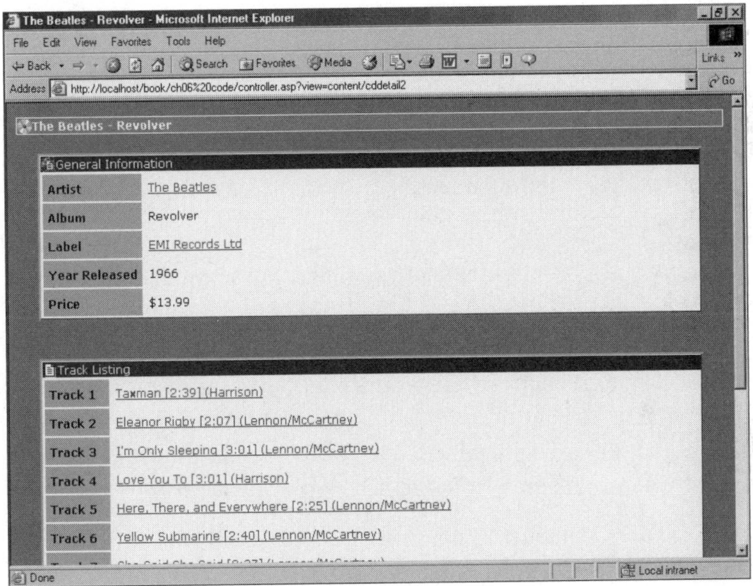

Figure 6-2 A more interesting example of an XSLT–generated application page

These rules can be modified easily by tweaking the XSLT. Suppose that Noverant would like to preserve real estate on its Web pages by adopting a "tab-folder" approach to content layout (instead of stacking content sections on top of one another). This can be achieved by modifying the *section* template of our XSLT.

> **Note** Layout specialists can begin experimenting with different rendering techniques once your XML schema has been defined. Little cost is associated with making global styling changes, as these rules are localized in your XSLT document.

A code listing of the new version of the transformation follows. JavaScript was added to the top of the page to handle tab switching. The *section* template has been augmented to hide all sections except the first one and to display a row of buttons that activate other content sections. Two new classes, *tabButton* and *activeTabButton*, were added to the CSS to control the formatting of the tab buttons.

```
<xsl:stylesheet xmlns:xsl="http://www.w3.org/1999/XSL/Transform"
version="1.0">
<xsl:output method="html" indent="yes" />
<xsl:template match="document">
  <html>
    <head>
      <link rel="stylesheet" type="text/css" href="css/style.css"/>
      <xsl:if test="header/title"><title><xsl:value-of select="header/
title"/></title></xsl:if>
```

The following script implements the "tabbing" action in the screen. The function accepts the ID of a tab, which is brought to the foreground by setting its *display* property. The function then iterates over the other tabs, making them invisible by setting their display style properties to *none*.

```
      <script language="javaScript">
        <![CDATA[
          function showTab(section, scnt) {
            for (i=0; i < scnt; i++) {
              t = document.getElementById("s_"+i);
              if (t) {
                if (i == section) {
                  t.style.display = '';
                } else {
                  t.style.display = 'none';
                }
              }
            }
          }
        ]]>
      </script>
    </head>
```

```
    <body>
      <div class="document">
        <xsl:apply-templates/>
      </div>
    </body>
  </html>
</xsl:template>
<xsl:template match="document/header">
  <div class="documentHeader">
    <xsl:if test="icon">
      <img align="absmiddle" src="images/{icon}"/>
    </xsl:if>
    <xsl:value-of select="title"/>
  </div>
</xsl:template>
```

The *section* transformation template contains the bulk of the changes that are necessary to implement tab folders. The template must now keep track of sibling *<section>* elements to display their tabs at the top. The logic in this template creates darkened tabs for all of the sibling sections and a highlighted tab for the context section. Each of the siblings tabs, or buttons, contains an *onClick()* event handler that calls the *showTab()* JavaScript function to bring that section to the foreground.

```
<xsl:template match="section">
  <xsl:variable name="numsections" select="count(../section)"/>
  <xsl:variable name="precedingsibs"
select="count(preceding-sibling::section)"/>
  <xsl:variable name="sectionid" select="concat('s_',$precedingsibs)"/>
  <div align="center">
    <xsl:if test="$precedingsibs = 0">
      <xsl:attribute name="style">padding-top:20px</xsl:attribute>
    </xsl:if>
    <div id="{$sectionid}" align="center" class="section">
      <xsl:if test="$precedingsibs > 0">
        <xsl:attribute name="style">display:none</xsl:attribute>
      </xsl:if>
      <xsl:apply-templates select="header"/>
      <xsl:if test="$numsections > 1">
        <div align="left">
```

Here the XSLT creates tab buttons for all the previous sections in the document.

```
          <xsl:for-each select="preceding-sibling::section">
            <xsl:choose>
              <xsl:when test="header/shortTitle">
                <button id="button{position}" class="tabButton"
onClick="showTab({position()-1},{$numsections})"><xsl:value-of
select="header/shortTitle"/></button>
```

```
              </xsl:when>
              <xsl:otherwise>
                <button id="button{position}" class="tabButton"
onClick="showTab({position()-1},{$numsections})"><xsl:value-of
select="header/title"/></button>
              </xsl:otherwise>
            </xsl:choose>
          </xsl:for-each>
```

The XSLT now creates a tab for the current *section* node. Notice that the CSS class attached to the button has changed to *activeTabButton* to indicate a selected tab.

```
          <xsl:choose>
            <xsl:when test="header/shortTitle">
              <button id="button{position}" class="activeTabButton"
onClick="showTab({$precedingsibs},{$numsections})"><xsl:value-of
select="header/shortTitle"/></button>
            </xsl:when>
            <xsl:otherwise>
              <button id="button{position}" class="activeTabButton"
onClick="showTab({$precedingsibs},{$numsections})"><xsl:value-of
select="header/title"/></button>
            </xsl:otherwise>
          </xsl:choose>
```

Here the XSLT template iterates over all of the following *<section>* elements. These tabs are also marked as inactive.

```
          <xsl:for-each select="following-sibling::section">
            <xsl:choose>
              <xsl:when test="header/shortTitle">
                <button id="button{position}" class="tabButton"
onClick="showTab({$precedingsibs+position()},{$numsec-
tions})"><xsl:value-of select="header/shortTitle"/></button>
              </xsl:when>
              <xsl:otherwise>
                <button id="button{position}" class="tabButton"
onClick="showTab({$precedingsibs+position()},{$numsec-
tions})"><xsl:value-of select="header/title"/></button>
              </xsl:otherwise>
            </xsl:choose>
          </xsl:for-each>
        </div>
      </xsl:if>
      <xsl:apply-templates select="view"/>
    </div>
  </div>
</xsl:template>
```

The rest of the template remains unchanged.

```
<xsl:template match="section/header">
  <div class="sectionHeader">
    <xsl:if test="icon">
      <img align="absmiddle" src="images/{icon}"/>
    </xsl:if>
    <xsl:value-of select="title"/>
  </div>
</xsl:template>
<xsl:template match="view">
  <xsl:apply-templates/>
</xsl:template>
<xsl:template match="properties">
  <table cellpadding="5">
    <xsl:apply-templates/>
  </table>
</xsl:template>
<xsl:template match="property">
  <tr>
    <td bgcolor="a1a1a1">
      <font class="text"><b><xsl:value-of select="@description"/>
</b></font>
    </td>
    <td><font class="text">
      <xsl:choose>
        <xsl:when test="@href"><a href="{@href}">
<xsl:apply-templates /></a></xsl:when>
        <xsl:otherwise><xsl:apply-templates /></xsl:otherwise>
      </xsl:choose>
    </font></td>
  </tr>
</xsl:template>
</xsl:stylesheet>
```

The effects of applying the new transformation to the same source XML document can be seen in Figure 6-3.

List Views

At this point we've seen how you can use XML and XSLT to create generic content blocks of property listings. This is a familiar approach to displaying related information to a user. Sometimes, however, other layout constructs are more appropriate. For example, the CD Track Listing section might be better shown in a list where each row represents a track with separate columns for the track number, title, length, and author. To accomplish this we need to extend our

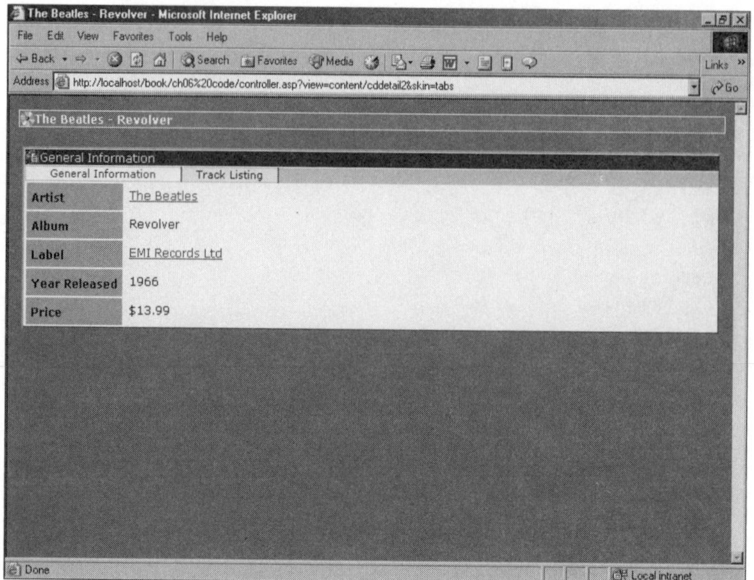

Figure 6-3 A new transformation applied to the Listing 6-5 document to allow tab-based navigation of content sections.

XML schema to support a simple list construct. We will begin by looking at the portion of our XML schema that defines a valid list.

The top level of a list XML document will contain a description and a reference to a default icon that will be displayed on each row. This icon can be overridden by a reference to a row-specific icon.

```
<ElementType name="icon" content="textOnly" model="closed"/>
<ElementType name="list.description" content="textOnly" model="closed"/>
```

The list will also need a collection of columns that define the different types of fields that each row will contain. All columns will have a name, description, and data type. A sorted column will indicate whether or not the data is sorted in ascending or descending order.

```
<ElementType name="list.column.sortdirection" content="textOnly"
model="closed"/>
<ElementType name="list.column.name" content="textOnly"
model="closed"/>
<ElementType name="list.column.description" content="textOnly"
model="closed"/>
<ElementType name="list.column.datatype" content="textOnly"
model="closed"/>
<ElementType name="list.column" order="many" content="eltOnly"
model="closed">
```

```
    <element type="list.column.sortdirection" minOccurs="0"
maxOccurs="1"/>
    <element type="list.column.name" minOccurs="1" maxOccurs="1"/>
    <element type="list.column.description" minOccurs="1"
maxOccurs="1"/>
    <element type="list.column.datatype" minOccurs="1" maxOccurs="1"/>
</ElementType>
```

A list's collection of *column* elements will roll up into a parent *columns* element.

```
<ElementType name="list.columns" order="many" content="eltOnly"
model="closed">
    <element type="list.column" minOccurs="0" maxOccurs="*"/>
</ElementType>
```

All rows in the list will have a collection of properties representing the data to be shown in the row. The *list.property* element contains a *list.property.name* element that matches the value of one of the *list.column.name* elements as well as a corresponding *value* element and an optional *hyperlink* element.

```
<ElementType name="list.property.name" content="textOnly"
model="closed"/>
<ElementType name="list.property.value" content="textOnly"
model="closed"/>
<ElementType name="list.property.href" content="textOnly"
model="closed"/>
<ElementType name="list.property" order="many" content="eltOnly"
model="closed">
    <element type="list.property.name" minOccurs="1" maxOccurs="1"/>
    <element type="list.property.value" minOccurs="1" maxOccurs="1"/>
    <element type="list.property.href" minOccurs="0" maxOccurs="1"/>
</ElementType>
```

No list would be complete without support for grouping rows by a common column value. Summarizing information this way can be an effective means of organizing data. This will be accomplished in our schema by inserting *list.group* elements that indicate the column being grouped, the common value for items in the same group, and a list of children that share that value.

```
<ElementType name="list.group.name" content="textOnly" model="closed"/>
<ElementType name="list.group.description" content="textOnly"
model="closed"/>
<ElementType name="list.group.value" content="textOnly"
model="closed"/>
<ElementType name="list.children" order="many" content="eltOnly"
model="closed">
  <element type="list.item" minOccurs="0" maxOccurs="*"/>
  <element type="list.group" minOccurs="0" maxOccurs="*"/>
</ElementType>
```

```
<ElementType name="list.item" order="many" content="eltOnly"
model="closed">
  <element type="list.property" minOccurs="0" maxOccurs="*"/>
<element type="icon" minOccurs="0" maxOccurs="1"/>
</ElementType>
<ElementType name="list.group" order="many" content="eltOnly"
model="closed">
  <element type="list.group.name" minOccurs="1" maxOccurs="1"/>
  <element type="list.group.description" minOccurs="1" maxOccurs="1"/>
  <element type="list.group.value" minOccurs="1" maxOccurs="1"/>
  <element type="list.children" minOccurs="1" maxOccurs="1"/>
</ElementType>
```

Finally the *list* element type rolls up all its components into a single node.

```
<ElementType name="list" order="many" content="eltOnly"
model="closed">
  <element type="icon" minOccurs="1" maxOccurs="1"/>
  <element type="list.description" minOccurs="1" maxOccurs="1"/>
  <element type="list.columns" minOccurs="1" maxOccurs="1"/>
  <element type="list.children" minOccurs="0" maxOccurs="1"/>
</ElementType>
```

> **Note** Remember to avoid characters such as <, >, and & in your XML data. These characters can creep into your XML pages, particularly when your content is retrieved dynamically from a database, and cause run-time XSLT errors.

Now we replace the bland property-based track listing with one that uses our new list schema. This XML document is much larger than the simpler version we saw before. Generating the code behind such listings can be tedious and error-prone when done by hand. It would be wise to invest time in creating server-side scripts to help automate the process.

```
<document>
  <header>
    <title>The Beatles - Revolver</title>
    <icon>CD.gif</icon>
  </header>
```

The first section of this document stays the same as before.

```
  <section>
    <header>
      <title>General Information</title>
      <icon>world.gif</icon>
```

```
    </header>
    <view>
      <properties>
       <property href="controller.asp?view=artistdetail&amp;id=10001"
description="Artist">The Beatles</property>
        <property description="Album">Revolver</property>
        <property href="controller.asp?view=labeldetail&amp;id=10001"
description="Label">EMI Records Ltd</property>
        <property description="Year Released">1966</property>
        <property description="Price">$13.99</property>
      </properties>
    </view>
  </section>
```

The second section is replaced by an XML list construct. The list view begins with information describing the columns that will appear in the table.

```
  <section>
    <header>
      <title>Track Listing</title>
      <icon>document.gif</icon>
    </header>
    <view>
      <list>
        <icon>CD.gif</icon>
        <list.description>The Beatles / Revolver: Track Listing
</list.description>
        <list.columns>
          <list.column>
            <list.column.sortdirection>asc</list.column.sortdirection>
            <list.column.name>TRACK</list.column.name>
            <list.column.description>Track</list.column.description>
            <list.column.datatype>numeric</list.column.datatype>
          </list.column>
          <list.column>
            <list.column.name>TITLE</list.column.name>
            <list.column.description>Song Title</list.column.description>
            <list.column.datatype>text</list.column.datatype>
          </list.column>
          <list.column>
            <list.column.name>LENGTH</list.column.name>
            <list.column.description>Length</list.column.description>
            <list.column.datatype>text</list.column.datatype>
          </list.column>
          <list.column>
            <list.column.name>WRITER</list.column.name>
           <list.column.description>Song Writer</list.column.description>
            <list.column.datatype>text</list.column.datatype>
```

```
      </list.column>
    </list.columns>
```

We create *<listitem>* elements for each song on the album. Each *listitem*, or row in the table, contains properties for each column defined in the table. The ordering of the properties within the *<listitem>* does not matter; the *columns* collection at the root of the document control the column order.

```
    <list.children>
      <list.item>
        <list.property>
          <list.property.name>TRACK</list.property.name>
          <list.property.value>1</list.property.value>
        </list.property>
        <list.property>
          <list.property.name>TITLE</list.property.name>
          <list.property.value>Taxman</list.property.value>
          <list.property.href>controller.asp?view=
trackdetail&amp;id=10001</list.property.href>
        </list.property>
        <list.property>
          <list.property.name>LENGTH</list.property.name>
          <list.property.value>3:01</list.property.value>
        </list.property>
        <list.property>
          <list.property.name>WRITER</list.property.name>
          <list.property.value>Harrison</list.property.value>
        </list.property>
      </list.item>
      <list.item>
        <list.property>
          <list.property.name>TRACK</list.property.name>
          <list.property.value>2</list.property.value>
        </list.property>
        <list.property>
          <list.property.name>TITLE</list.property.name>
          <list.property.value>Eleanor Rigby</list.property.value>
          <list.property.href>controller.asp?view=
trackdetail&amp;id=10002</list.property.href>
        </list.property>
        <list.property>
          <list.property.name>LENGTH</list.property.name>
          <list.property.value>2:07</list.property.value>
        </list.property>
        <list.property>
          <list.property.name>WRITER</list.property.name>
          <list.property.value>Lennon/McCartney
</list.property.value>
        </list.property>
```

```
          </list.item>
          <list.item>
            <list.property>
              <list.property.name>TRACK</list.property.name>
              <list.property.value>3</list.property.value>
            </list.property>
            <list.property>
              <list.property.name>TITLE</list.property.name>
              <list.property.value>I'm Only Sleeping
</list.property.value>
              <list.property.href>controller.asp?view=
trackdetail&amp;id=10003</list.property.href>
            </list.property>
            <list.property>
              <list.property.name>LENGTH</list.property.name>
              <list.property.value>3:01</list.property.value>
            </list.property>
            <list.property>
              <list.property.name>WRITER</list.property.name>
              <list.property.value>Lennon/McCartney
</list.property.value>
            </list.property>
          </list.item>
          <list.item>
            <list.property>
              <list.property.name>TRACK</list.property.name>
              <list.property.value>4</list.property.value>
            </list.property>
            <list.property>
              <list.property.name>TITLE</list.property.name>
              <list.property.value>Love You To</list.property.value>
              <list.property.href>controller.asp?view=
trackdetail&amp;id=10004</list.property.href>
            </list.property>
            <list.property>
              <list.property.name>LENGTH</list.property.name>
              <list.property.value>3:01</list.property.value>
            </list.property>
            <list.property>
              <list.property.name>WRITER</list.property.name>
              <list.property.value>Harrison</list.property.value>
            </list.property>
          </list.item>
        </list.children>
      </list>
    </view>
  </section>
</document>
```

Finally we need to extend our XSLT so that it understands what it should do with the elements defined in our list schema. The first template will match the *list* element. Its purpose will be to initialize an HTML table that will contain the list.

```
<xsl:template match="list">
  <table class="list" cellspacing="0" cellpadding="0">
    <tr>
      <td valign="top" nowrap="yes">
        <table width="100%" cellpadding="0" cellspacing="1">
```

After inserting the table in the result document, the transformation creates table headers for each of the *<list.column>* elements in the XML document.

```
        <tr bgcolor="a0a0a0" style="padding:2px;spacing-top:0px">
          <td width="1%" class="text" align="center">
            <img src="images/envelope.gif" width="16"/>
          </td>
          <xsl:for-each select="list.columns/list.column">
            <td class="text" align="center" style="color:white;
font-weight:bold">
              <xsl:value-of select="list.column.description"/>
              <xsl:variable name="sort-dir" select=
"list.column.sortdirection"/>
              <xsl:if test="($sort-dir = 'asc')">
                <img src="images/up.gif" hspace="4"/>
              </xsl:if>
              <xsl:if test="($sort-dir = 'desc')">
                <img src="images/down.gif" hspace="4"/>
              </xsl:if>
            </td>
          </xsl:for-each>
        </tr>
```

The transformation then applies further templates to the *list.children* collection to generate the table body. Finally the *list* template appends a footer to the table to provide a summary of the number of lines listed.

```
        <xsl:apply-templates select="list.children"/>
        </table>
      </td>
    </tr>
    <tr bgcolor="e0e0e0">
      <td class="text">
        <xsl:variable name="childrencount" select="count
(.//list.item)"/>
        <xsl:if test="$childrencount=1">
          <xsl:value-of select="$childrencount"/> item
        </xsl:if>
```

```
        <xsl:if test="$childrencount!=1">
          <xsl:value-of select="$childrencount"/> items
        </xsl:if>
      </td>
    </tr>
  </table>
</xsl:template>
```

The job of the *list.item* template is to build a table row for each *<list.item>* element in the document. The template loops over the *list.columns* collection, locates a *list.property* with a matching name, gets its value from the *<list.property.value>* element, and fills in a table cell with that value. The template also includes rules to handle embedded icons and hyperlinks.

```
<xsl:template match="list.item">
  <xsl:variable name="current-item" select="."/>
  <xsl:variable name="current-row" select="position()"/>
  <xsl:variable name="id" select="concat('v',generate-id())"/>
  <tr>
    <xsl:choose>
      <xsl:when test="position() mod 2">
        <xsl:attribute name="style">
          background-color:ffffff
          <xsl:if test="count(ancestor::list.group) > 0">
            ;display:none
          </xsl:if>
        </xsl:attribute>
      </xsl:when>
      <xsl:otherwise>
        <xsl:attribute name="style">
          background-color:f1f1f1
          <xsl:if test="count(ancestor::list.group) > 0">
            ;display:none
          </xsl:if>
        </xsl:attribute>
      </xsl:otherwise>
    </xsl:choose>
    <xsl:attribute name="id"><xsl:value-of select="$id"/>
</xsl:attribute>
    <td class="text" align="center" valign="top">
      <xsl:variable name="iconurl" select="ancestor::list/icon"/>
      <xsl:choose>
        <xsl:when test="icon and icon != ''">
         <img width="16" height="18"><xsl:attribute name="src">images/
<xsl:value-of select="icon"/></xsl:attribute></img>
        </xsl:when>
        <xsl:otherwise>
         <img width="16" height="18"><xsl:attribute name="src">images/
<xsl:value-of select="$iconurl"/></xsl:attribute></img>
```

```
        </xsl:otherwise>
      </xsl:choose>
    </td>
    <xsl:for-each select="ancestor::list/list.columns/list.column">
      <xsl:variable name="current-property" select="list.column.name"/>
      <xsl:variable name="current-datatype" select=
"list.column.datatype"/>
      <xsl:variable name="current-position" select="position()"/>
      <xsl:variable name="last-position" select="last()"/>
      <xsl:variable name="current-description" select=
"list.column.description"/>
      <xsl:for-each select="$current-item/list.property
[list.property.name=$current-property]">
        <td class="text" valign="top">
          <xsl:attribute name="title"><xsl:value-of select=
"$current-description"/>: <xsl:value-of select="list.item.value"/>
</xsl:attribute>
          <xsl:choose>
            <xsl:when test="($current-datatype = 'numeric' or
$current-datatype='monetary' or $current-datatype='date' or
$current-datatype='percentage')">
              <xsl:attribute name="align">right</xsl:attribute>
            </xsl:when>
            <xsl:otherwise>
              <xsl:attribute name="align">left</xsl:attribute>
            </xsl:otherwise>
          </xsl:choose>
          <xsl:if test="list.property.value">
            <xsl:choose>
              <xsl:when test="list.property.href != ''">
                <xsl:element name="a">
                  <xsl:attribute name="href"><xsl:value-of
select="list.property.href"/></xsl:attribute>
                  <xsl:value-of select="list.property.value"
disable-output-escaping="yes"/> 
                </xsl:element>
              </xsl:when>
              <xsl:otherwise>
                <xsl:value-of select="list.property.value"
disable-output-escaping="yes"/> 
              </xsl:otherwise>
            </xsl:choose>
          </xsl:if>
        </td>
      </xsl:for-each>
    </xsl:for-each>
  </tr>
</xsl:template>
```

The *list.group* template is written to handle *n*-levels of groupings within a list. The template assumes that all items in the list have been grouped prior to the transformation. Therefore, a different program must be used to associate the similar line items to be grouped.

```
<xsl:template match="list.group">
```

The following line determines how much space you should use when indenting the group summary lines. The desired stairstep effect can be achieved by multiplying a constant by the number of *list.group* ancestors the node has.

```
  <xsl:variable name="padding" select="20 * count(ancestor::list.group)"/>
  <xsl:variable name="id" select="concat('v',generate-id())"/>
```

The template next creates a row to display the group summary information. The row's display style property is set to *none* if it's a child of another *list.group*. A plus sign is inserted into the row that, when clicked, will expand the group and display all its children. (The JavaScript code to do this will be listed following this transformation.)

```
  <tr>
    <xsl:attribute name="id"><xsl:value-of select="$id"/></xsl:attribute>
    <xsl:if test="ancestor::list.group">
      <xsl:attribute name="style">display:none</xsl:attribute>
    </xsl:if>
    <td>
       <xsl:attribute name="id"><xsl:value-of select="$id"/>_plus
 </xsl:attribute>
      <xsl:attribute name="colspan"><xsl:value-of select="1 +
count(ancestor::list/list.columns/list.column)"/></xsl:attribute>
      <table width="100%" cellpadding="0" cellspacing="0" border="0"
class="listgroup">
      <xsl:attribute name="id"><xsl:value-of select="$id"/>_table
</xsl:attribute>
      <tr>
        <xsl:if test="$padding != 0">
          <td>
            <xsl:attribute name="width">
<xsl:value-of select="round($padding)"/></xsl:attribute>
            <xsl:attribute name="style">background-color:727272
</xsl:attribute>
            <img src="images/spacer.gif" height="1">
              <xsl:attribute name="width">
<xsl:value-of select="round($padding)"/></xsl:attribute>
            </img>
          </td>
        </xsl:if>
        <td width="5" style="cursor:hand">
```

```
        <img src="images/plus.gif" hspace="4" style="border:1px outset">
         <xsl:attribute name="onClick">ExpandCollapse('<xsl:for-each
select="list.children/*[name() = 'list.group' or name() =
'list.item']"><xsl:value-of select="concat('v',generate-id())"
/><xsl:if test="last() > position()">,</xsl:if></xsl:for-
each>','<xsl:value-of select="$id"/><xsl:for-each select=".//*[name()
= 'list.group' or name() =  'list.item']">,<xsl:value-of select=
"concat('v',generate-id())"/></xsl:for-each>')</xsl:attribute>
           <xsl:attribute name="id"><xsl:value-of select="$id"
/>_plus_image</xsl:attribute>
         </img>
       </td>
```

The summary information, including property description, value, and item count, is inserted into the result document. Finally the template makes a call to *<xsl:apply-templates>* to transform child *list.item* and *list.group* nodes.

```
       <td align="left" class="text">
         <xsl:value-of select="list.group.description"
/> : <xsl:value-of select="list.group.value"/>
         <xsl:variable name="childrencount" select="count
(.//list.item)"/>
         <xsl:if test="$childrencount=1">
           (<xsl:value-of select="$childrencount"/> item)
         </xsl:if>
         <xsl:if test="$childrencount>1">
           (<xsl:value-of select="$childrencount"/> items)
         </xsl:if>
       </td>
     </tr>
     </table>
   </td>
  </tr>
  <xsl:apply-templates select="list.children/*"/>
</xsl:template>
```

Note The table-based implementation of the function shown here is much more complicated than its *<div>* element-based cousin. Because *<div>* elements are block displays, their display properties are inherited by all their descendants.

As promised, here is the *expandCollapse()* JavaScript function that opens and closes table groupings. This function is inserted into the document by the XSLT shown previously.

```
function ExpandCollapse(cl,ca) {
  var ca_a    = ca.split(',');
  var cl_a   = cl.split(',');
  cl = document.getElementById(ca_a[1]);
  if (cl.style.display == 'none')
    expand = true;
  else
    expand = false;
  thePlus = ca_a[0]+"_plus_image";
  plus_div = document.getElementById(thePlus);
  if (expand)
  {
    if (plus_div)
      plus_div.src = "images/minus.gif";
    for (i=0; i < cl_a.length; i++)
    {
      theRow = document.getElementById(cl_a[i]);
      theRow.style.display = '';
      plus_div = document.getElementById(cl_a[i]+"_plus_image");
      if (plus_div)
        plus_div.src = "images/plus.gif";
    }
  } else {
    if (plus_div)
      plus_div.src = "images/plus.gif";
    for (i=1; i < ca_a.length; i++)
    {
      theRow = document.getElementById(ca_a[i])
      theRow.style.display = 'none';
    }
  }
}
```

To group the CDs shown on our page, the XML markup must be modified to represent the grouping hierarchy. An excerpt from this document is shown in the following listing.

```
<list.group>
  <list.group.name>WRITER</list.group.name>
  <list.group.description>Song Writer</list.group.description>
  <list.group.value>Harrison</list.group.value>
  <list.children>
    <list.item>
      <list.property>
        <list.property.name>TRACK</list.property.name>
        <list.property.value>1</list.property.value>
      </list.property>
      <list.property>
        <list.property.name>TITLE</list.property.name>
```

```
          <list.property.value>Taxman</list.property.value>
          <list.property.href>controller.asp?view=
trackdetail&amp;id=10001</list.property.href>
        </list.property>
        <list.property>
          <list.property.name>LENGTH</list.property.name>
          <list.property.value>3:01</list.property.value>
        </list.property>
        <list.property>
          <list.property.name>WRITER</list.property.name>
          <list.property.value>Harrison</list.property.value>
        </list.property>
      </list.item>
      <list.item>
        <list.property>
          <list.property.name>TRACK</list.property.name>
          <list.property.value>4</list.property.value>
        </list.property>
        <list.property>
          <list.property.name>TITLE</list.property.name>
          <list.property.value>Love You To</list.property.value>
          <list.property.href>controller.asp?view=
trackdetail&amp;id=10004</list.property.href>
        </list.property>
        <list.property>
          <list.property.name>LENGTH</list.property.name>
          <list.property.value>3:01</list.property.value>
        </list.property>
        <list.property>
          <list.property.name>WRITER</list.property.name>
          <list.property.value>Harrison</list.property.value>
        </list.property>
      </list.item>
      <list.item>
        <list.property>
          <list.property.name>TRACK</list.property.name>
          <list.property.value>12</list.property.value>
        </list.property>
        <list.property>
          <list.property.name>TITLE</list.property.name>
          <list.property.value>I Want to Tell You</list.property.value>
          <list.property.href>controller.asp?view=
trackdetail&amp;id=10012</list.property.href>
        </list.property>
        <list.property>
          <list.property.name>LENGTH</list.property.name>
          <list.property.value>2:29</list.property.value>
        </list.property>
        <list.property>
```

```
        <list.property.name>WRITER</list.property.name>
        <list.property.value>Harrison</list.property.value>
      </list.property>
    </list.item>
  </list.children>
</list.group>
```

As you can tell by the following screen shots, a list-based approach works best for laying out multiple items that share similar properties. Lists can also be extended in your application to support user-defined sorting, grouping, filtration, and export. Figure 6-5 shows how an XML list construct is used to display CD tracks. Figure 6-4 shows the CD tracks grouped by author.

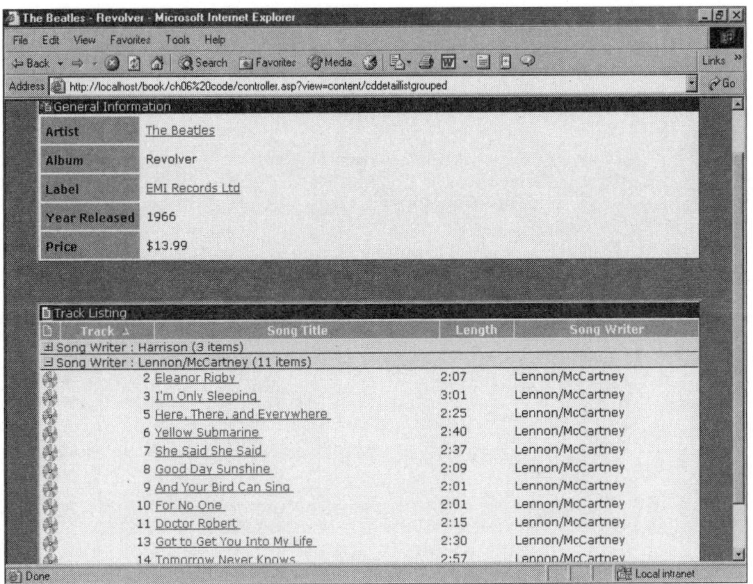

Figure 6-4 CD Tracks again, this time grouped by author.

Navigation

All applications, whether they are large enterprise applications or programs for hand-held devices, have a navigation challenge. There are many questions to consider when designing a navigation system. Should the navigation be function based or data based? Should trees be used? Menus? Menus and trees? Toolbars? Buttonbars? The answer to these questions is (of course),"It depends." The navigation tools your application provides and the way in which it organizes them depends on factors such as the application's purpose, breadth, and user base. The bottom line is that the way users navigate through the system is less important than the speed at which they are able to do it.

Although implementations may vary, most navigation systems have similar abstract characteristics. All navigation systems are merely organized collections of links. They might contain links to forms or links to Web pages. They might be organized by the type of function they perform or by the type of data on which they perform it. Therefore, while XML might not be able to tell you how to solve your program's navigation challenge, using it to model your application's navigation scheme can provide several key benefits.

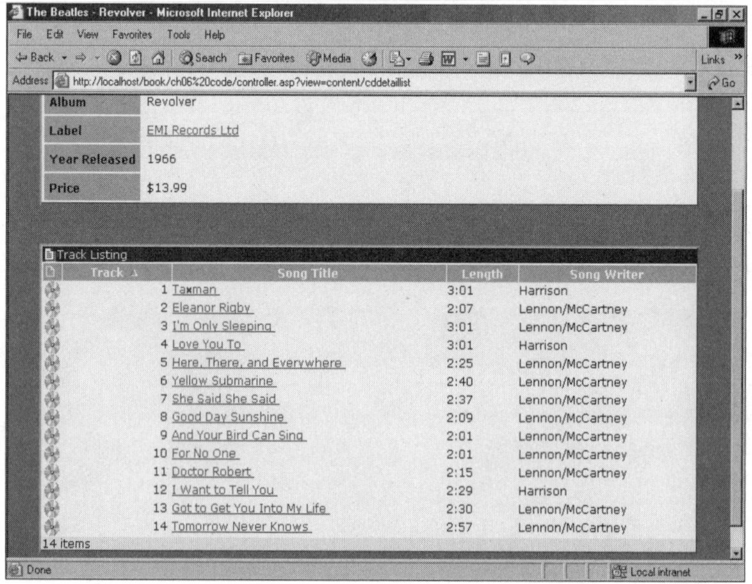

Figure 6-5 Using an XML List construct to display CD Tracks.

- XML helps you think about navigation in more abstract terms. This frees your mind to think outside the box.
- It promotes modularity in your application. The business logic that builds the navigation document should not be cluttered with phrases like If browserType = 'netscape' then . . .
- It makes your UI more extensible. Newer navigation UI schemes can be plugged into the existing navigation structure with no modification to your business logic.

The best way to begin thinking about how XML can help is by looking at a sample navigation schema. In this section we will examine how to model a navigation system useing XML. We will then attempt to transform our navigation model into a format suitable for rendering on a Web browser.

> **Note** Try to think outside the box when incorporating XML into your application. Why not transform an XML navigation tree into a voice-activated UI?

A Simple Navigation Schema

This schema looks similar to the Noverant tree scheme discussed in Chapter 5, and with good reason. A tree is a common navigation component. The heart of the more generic navigation schema is the *<navitem>* element. Each *<navitem>* is a link to a document in a Web-based application. A *<navitem>* contains a description, one or more icons, a hyperlink reference, and a recursive collection of children *navitems*. This schema is simple yet flexible and offers an infinite variety of ways to model a navigation system.

```
<ElementType name="navitem.description" content="textOnly"
model="closed"/>
<ElementType name="navitem.openIcon" content="textOnly"
model="closed"/>
<ElementType name="navitem.closedIcon" content="textOnly"
model="closed"/>
<ElementType name="navitem.icon" content="textOnly" model="closed"/>
<ElementType name="href" order="many" content="textOnly"
model="closed"/>
<ElementType name="navitem.children" order="many" content="eltOnly"
model="closed">
  <element type="navitem" minOccurs="0" maxOccurs="*"/>
</ElementType>
<ElementType name="navitem" order="many" content="eltOnly" model="closed">
  <element type="navitem.description" minOccurs="1" maxOccurs="1"/>
  <element type="navitem.icon" minOccurs="0" maxOccurs="1"/>
  <element type="navitem.openIcon" minOccurs="0" maxOccurs="1"/>
  <element type="navitem.closedIcon" minOccurs="0" maxOccurs="1"/>
  <element type="href" minOccurs="0" maxOccurs="0"/>
  <element type="navitem.children" minOccurs="0" maxOccurs="1"/>
</ElementType>
```

The *<navigation>* element is a special *<navitem>* in that it anchors the navigation hierarchy.

```
<ElementType name="navigation" order="many" content="eltOnly"
model="closed">
  <AttributeType name="type" />
  <element type="navigation.description" minOccurs="1" maxOccurs="1"/>
  <element type="navigation.icon" minOccurs="0" maxOccurs="1"/>
  <element type="navigation.openIcon" minOccurs="0" maxOccurs="1"/>
  <element type="navigation.closedIcon" minOccurs="1" maxOccurs="1"/>
  <element type="href" minOccurs="0" maxOccurs="1"/>
  <element type="navitem.children" minOccurs="0" maxOccurs="1"/>
</ElementType>
```

A Navigation Example

Now let's put the schema from the previous section to use for Noverant. The following navigation XML document is a snippet from Noverant's back-office application. The example includes entries for maintaining the CD, artist, and inventory databases.

```
<navigation>
  <description>Noverant Back-Office Root Menu</description>
  <children>
    <navitem>
      <description>Artists</description>
      <icon>artist.gif</icon>
      <children>
        <navitem>
          <description>Search for an Artist</description>
          <href>controller.asp?view=artistSearch</href>
          <icon>artist.gif</icon>
        </navitem>
        <navitem>
          <description>New Artist</description>
          <href>controller.asp?view=artistAdd</href>
          <icon>newArtist.gif</icon>
        </navitem>
      </children>
    </navitem>
    <navitem>
      <description>CDs</description>
      <icon>cd.gif</icon>
      <children>
        <navitem>
          <description>Search for a CD</description>
          <href>controller.asp?view=cdSearch</href>
          <icon>cd.gif</icon>
        </navitem>
        <navitem>
          <description>New CD</description>
```

```
          <href>controller.asp?view=cdAdd</href>
          <icon>newCD.gif</icon>
        </navitem>
      </children>
    </navitem>
    <navitem>
      <description>Inventory</description>
      <icon>inventory.gif</icon>
      <children>
        <navitem>
          <description>View Current Inventory</description>
          <href>controller.asp?view=inventory</href>
          <icon>inventory.gif</icon>
        </navitem>
        <navitem>
          <description>View Low-Inventory Items</description>
          <href>controller.asp?view=lowinventory</href>
          <icon>lowinventory.gif</icon>
        </navitem>
        <navitem>
          <description>Place Supply Requisition</description>
          <href>controller.asp?view=requisition</href>
          <icon>requisition.gif</icon>
        </navitem>
      </children>
    </navitem>
  </children>
</navigation>
```

Note that not all of the *<navitem>* elements are completely filled out. The code is still valid according to our schema, because only the *<description>* element is required. Why have a *<navitem>* element with no hyperlink? The answer is that not all items that appear in a menu system or table-of-contents tree provide links to documents. Some might serve as placeholders to group children elements.

Think about the preceding XML document and what it represents. More importantly, think about what it does not represent. Nothing in the document indicates how the information should be rendered. The navigation elements can be displayed as a tree, drop-down menu, or tab menu just as easily. Let's explore this example further and create two different XSLT implementations for our navigation document.

Creating a Tab Menu

The first implementation will be a two-tiered tab approach. The presentation rules will assume a two-level navigation document (that is, a list of categories and options) and will build a set of tabs that, when clicked, reveal a list of options from which the user can choose. The following XSLT code will be added to the other template rules we have defined thus far.

```
<xsl:template match="navigation[@type='menu']">
  <html>
    <head>
      <xsl:text disable-output-escaping = "yes">
        <![CDATA[
         <link rel="stylesheet" type="text/css" href="css/style.css"/>
        ]]>
      </xsl:text>
      <style type="text/css">
        body{background-color:C0C0C0}
      </style>
      <script type="text/javascript">
```

The following JavaScript functions handle all user interaction with the tab folders. The *clearFunctions()* function clears out the present set of options whenever a new tab is clicked. The *clearModuleStyles()* deemphasizes the inactive tabs. Finally the *showFunction()* function highlights the chosen tab and builds a new list of options.

```
      <![CDATA[
        function clearFunctions() {
          var i = 1;
          var theFunction = "";
          var isFunction =
          true;
          while (isFunction) {
            theFunction = "function"+i;
            var hideDiv = document.getElementById(theFunction);
            if (hideDiv) {
              hideDiv.style.visibility = "hidden";
              i++;
            } else {
              isFunction = false;
            }
          }
        }
        function clearModuleStyles() {
          var i = 1;
          var theModule = "";
          var isModule = true;
          while (isModule) {
            theModule = "module"+i;
            theModuleLeft = "moduleLeft"+i;
            theModuleRight = "moduleRight"+i;
```

```
        theModuleAnchor = "moduleAnchor"+i;
        cleanStyle = document.getElementById(theModule);
        cleanStyleLeft = document.getElementById(theModuleLeft);
        cleanStyleRight = document.getElementById(theModuleRight);
        cleanStyleAnchor = document.getElementById(theModuleAnchor);
        if (cleanStyle) {
          cleanStyle.style.backgroundColor = 'steelblue';
          cleanStyle.style.borderBottom = '1px solid';
          cleanStyle.style.borderColor = '336699';
          cleanStyleLeft.style.backgroundColor = 'steelblue';
          cleanStyleLeft.style.borderBottom = '1px solid';
          cleanStyleLeft.style.borderColor = '336699';
          cleanStyleRight.style.backgroundColor = 'steelblue';
          cleanStyleRight.style.borderBottom = '1px solid';
          cleanStyleRight.style.borderColor = '336699';
          cleanStyleAnchor.style.color = 'white';
          i++;
        } else {
          isModule = false;
        }
      }
    }
    function showFunction(id) {
      clearFunctions();
      clearModuleStyles();
      theId = "function"+id;
      thisFunction = document.getElementById(theId);
      thisFunction.style.visibility = 'visible';
      theId = "module"+id;
      theLeftId = "moduleLeft"+id;
      theRightId = "moduleRight"+id;
      theAnchorId = "moduleAnchor"+id;
      thisModule = document.getElementById(theId);
      thisModuleRight = document.getElementById(theRightId);
      thisModuleLeft = document.getElementById(theLeftId);
      thisModuleAnchor = document.getElementById(theAnchorId);
      thisModule.style.backgroundColor = 'white';
      thisModule.style.borderBottom = '0';
      thisModuleRight.style.backgroundColor = 'white';
      thisModuleRight.style.borderBottom = '0';
      thisModuleLeft.style.backgroundColor = 'white';
      thisModuleLeft.style.borderBottom = '0';
      thisModuleAnchor.style.color = '336699';
    }
    window.status = "Noverant Back-Office";
  ]]>
  </script>
</head>
```

This transformation assumes that the navigation document will exist in its own frame, as it creates a complete HTML document. The template can easily be modified to share a frame with other UI elements.

In the following section of code the template iterates over the top-level *<navitem>* elements and creates tab folders for each of them. JavaScript methods are attached to *onClick(), onMouseOver(),* and *onMouseOut()* event handlers.

```
  <body marginwidth="0" marginheight="0" leftmargin="0" topmargin="0">
    <div id="nav1" style="display:inline">
      <table cellspacing="0" cellpadding="0" border="0">
      <tr>
        <xsl:for-each select="children/navitem">
          <td height="25" valign="top" id="moduleLeft{position()}">
            <xsl:choose>
              <xsl:when test="position() = 1">
                <xsl:attribute name="style">background-color:white
</xsl:attribute>
              </xsl:when>
              <xsl:otherwise>
                <xsl:attribute name="style">background-color:
steelblue;border-bottom:1px solid;border-color:336699</xsl:attribute>
              </xsl:otherwise>
            </xsl:choose>
            <img src="images/left.gif" width="4" height="4"/>
          </td>
          <td align="center" height="25" id="module{position()}"
nowrap="true">
            <xsl:choose>
              <xsl:when test="position() = 1">
                <xsl:attribute name="style">padding:2px;
background-color:white</xsl:attribute>
              </xsl:when>
              <xsl:otherwise>
                <xsl:attribute name="style">padding:2px;
background-color:steelblue;border-bottom:1pxsolid;
border-color:336699
                </xsl:attribute>
              </xsl:otherwise>
            </xsl:choose>
            <a class="navigation" href="javascript:
showFunction('{position()}');" id="moduleAnchor{position()}">
            <xsl:attribute name="onMouseOver">JavaScript:window.
status='<xsl:value-of select="description"/>'; return true;
</xsl:attribute>
            <xsl:attribute name="onMouseOut">JavaScript:
window.status='Noverant Back-Office'; return true;</xsl:attribute>
            <xsl:if test="position() = 1">
```

```
                <xsl:attribute name="style">color:336699
</xsl:attribute>
              </xsl:if>
              <xsl:value-of select="description"/></a>
            </td>
            <td height="25" valign="top" id="moduleRight{position()}">
              <xsl:choose>
                <xsl:when test="position() = 1">
                  <xsl:attribute name="style">background-color:white
</xsl:attribute>
                </xsl:when>
                <xsl:otherwise>
                  <xsl:attribute name="style">background-color:
steelblue;border-bottom:1px solid;border-color:336699</xsl:attribute>
                </xsl:otherwise>
              </xsl:choose>
              <img src="images/right.gif" width="4" height="4"/>
            </td>
          <td width="1" bgcolor="C0C0C0"><img src="images/spacer.gif"
width="1" height="25"/></td>
          </xsl:for-each>
        </tr>
        </table>
      </div>
```

Note The XSL *generate-id()* function is invaluable for creating unique IDs to attach to elements used in your output document. The *generate-id()* guarantees that it will produce a unique and repeatable ID for every node in the source document.

At this point the template iterates over all of the second-level *<navitem>* elements and creates a list of hyperlinks out of them. These hyperlinks will appear below the tab folders.

```
      <xsl:for-each select="children/navitem">
        <xsl:variable name="i" select="position()"/>
        <div id="function{position()}">
          <xsl:choose>
            <xsl:when test="position() != 1">
              <xsl:attribute name="style">position:absolute;
display:inline;visibility:hidden;width:100%;background-color:white;
border-bottom:1px solid;border-color:steelblue</xsl:attribute>
            </xsl:when>
```

```
            <xsl:otherwise>
              <xsl:attribute name="style">position:absolute;
display:inline;width:100%;background-color:white;border-bottom:1px
solid;border-color:steelblue</xsl:attribute>
            </xsl:otherwise>
          </xsl:choose>
          <table cellspacing="0" cellpadding="0" border="0" style=
"padding:2px">
          <tr>
            <td style="color:336699" class="text">
              <xsl:attribute name="nowrap"/>
              <xsl:for-each select="children/navitem">
                <xsl:variable name="j" select="position()"/>
                <xsl:variable name="functionVar" select=
"concat($i,'_',$j)"/>
                   
                  <a class="subNavigation" name="{generate-id()}"
href="controller.asp?view={href}" target="main">
                    <xsl:attribute name="onMouseOver">JavaScript:
window.status='<xsl:value-of select="description"/>'; return true;
</xsl:attribute>
                    <xsl:attribute name="onMouseOut">JavaScript:
window.status='Noverant Back-Office'; return true;</xsl:attribute>
                    <xsl:value-of select="description"/>
                  </a>
                   
                <xsl:if test="position() != last()"> | 
</xsl:if>
              </xsl:for-each>
            </td>
          </tr>
          </table>
        </div>
      </xsl:for-each>
    </body>
  </html>
</xsl:template>
```

A call to this page from frameset will produce the page in Figure 6-6.

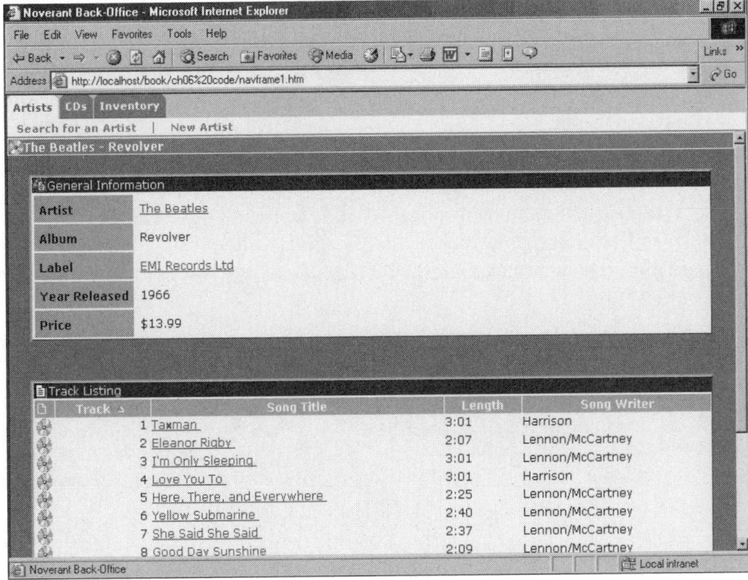

Figure 6-6 A tab-folder approach to navigation.

Creating a Navigation Tree

For the second implementation, the same navigation XML can be used to create a tree-based navigation system. By rewriting the navigation XSLT, a page designer can create a drastically different front-end. This example of an XSLT used to produce a tree demonstrates the flexibility that can be achieved by separating content from presentation.

Like the menu transformation, the tree transformation assumes that the resulting document will reside in its own frame.

```
<xsl:template match="navigation[@type='tree']">
  <html>
    <head>
      <script language="JavaScript">
        function expand(divid)
        {
           eval("closed_"+divid).style.display = 'none';
           eval("open_"+divid).style.display = '';
        }
        function collapse(divid)
        {
           eval("open_"+divid).style.display = 'none';
           eval("closed_"+divid).style.display = '';
        }
      </script>
```

```
        <style>
          a:visited {background-color:#C7D2DE; color:black;
text-decoration: underline}
         a:link {background-color:#C7D2DE; color:black; text-decoration:
underline}
          a:active {background-color:activecaption; color:captiontext;
text-decoration: underline}
          a:hover {background-color:#C7D2DE; color:black;
text-decoration: underline}
         .clsHeading {font-family: verdana; color: black; font-size: 11;
font-weight: 800;}
          .clsEntryText {padding-top: 2px; font-family: verdana; color:
black; font-size: 11; font-weight: 400; background-color:#C7D2DE;}
         .clsWarningText {font-family: verdana; white-space:pre; color:
#B80A2D; font-size: 11; font-weight: 600; width:550;
background-color:#EFE7EA;}
          .clsCopy {font-family: verdana; color: black; font-size: 11;
font-weight: 400;  background-color:#FFFFFF;}
        </style>
      </head>
      <body style="background-color:#C7D2DE;">
        <table width="100%" cellspacing="5">
          <tr>
            <td nowrap="yes">
              <div class="clsEntryText" style="padding-left:5px"
id="open_{generate-id()}">
                <xsl:if test="openIcon"><img src="images/{openIcon}"/>
 </xsl:if>
                <xsl:if test="href"><a href="{href}">
                  <xsl:if test="href/@target"><xsl:attribute name=
"target"><xsl:value-of select="href/@target"/></xsl:attribute>
</xsl:if>
                  <xsl:value-of select="description"/></a>
                </xsl:if>
                <xsl:if test="not(href)"><xsl:value-of select=
"description"/></xsl:if>
                <xsl:apply-templates select="children"/>
              </div>
            </td>
          </tr>
        </table>
      </body>
    </html>
</xsl:template>
```

The recursive nature of the navigation tree schema suits XSLT perfectly. *<navitem>* elements can be transformed in place with little conditional logic.

```
<xsl:template match="navitem">
  <xsl:choose>
    <xsl:when test="children">
      <xsl:variable name="childcnt" select="count(.//navitem)"/>
      <div class="clsEntryText" id="closed_{generate-id()}">
        <xsl:for-each select="ancestor::navitem">
          <xsl:choose>
            <xsl:when test="count(following-sibling::navitem) > 0">
              <img src="/xmlbook/images/line.gif"/>
            </xsl:when>
            <xsl:otherwise>
              <img src="/xmlbook/images/nothing.gif"/>
            </xsl:otherwise>
          </xsl:choose>
        </xsl:for-each>
       <img src="/xmlbook/images/folder_plus.gif" style="cursor:hand"
onClick="expand('{generate-id()}')"/>
        <xsl:choose>
          <xsl:when test="closedIcon"><img src="images/{closedIcon}"
/> </xsl:when>
          <xsl:when test="icon"><img src="images/{icon}"/> 
</xsl:when>
        </xsl:choose>
        <xsl:if test="href"><a href="{href}">
          <xsl:if test="href/@target"><xsl:attribute name=
"target"><xsl:value-of select="href/@target"/></xsl:attribute>
</xsl:if>
          <xsl:value-of select="description"/></a>
        </xsl:if>
        <xsl:if test="not(href)"><xsl:value-of select="description"/>
</xsl:if>
        (<xsl:value-of select="$childcnt"/> artist<xsl:if test=
"$childcnt != 1">s</xsl:if>)
      </div>
      <div class="clsEntryText" id="open_{generate-id()}" style=
  "display:none">
        <xsl:for-each select="ancestor::navitem">
          <xsl:choose>
            <xsl:when test="count(following-sibling::navitem) > 0">
              <img src="/xmlbook/images/line.gif"/>
            </xsl:when>
            <xsl:otherwise>
              <img src="/xmlbook/images/nothing.gif"/>
            </xsl:otherwise>
          </xsl:choose>
        </xsl:for-each>
        <img  src="/xmlbook/images/folder_minus.gif" style=
 "cursor:hand" onClick="collapse('{generate-id()}')"/>
        <xsl:choose>
```

```
          <xsl:when test="openIcon"><img src="images/{openIcon}"
/> </xsl:when>
          <xsl:when test="icon"><img src="images/{icon}"/> 
</xsl:when>
        </xsl:choose>
        <xsl:if test="href"><a href="{href}">
          <xsl:if test="href/@target"><xsl:attribute name=
"target"><xsl:value-of select="href/@target"/></xsl:attribute>
</xsl:if>
          <xsl:value-of select="description"/></a>
        </xsl:if>
        <xsl:if test="not(href)"><xsl:value-of select="description"/>
</xsl:if>
         (<xsl:value-of select="$childcnt"/> artist<xsl:
if test="$childcnt != 1">s</xsl:if>)
        <xsl:apply-templates select="children"/>
      </div>
    </xsl:when>
    <xsl:otherwise>
      <div class="clsEntryText">
        <xsl:for-each select="ancestor::navitem">
          <xsl:choose>
            <xsl:when test="count(following-sibling::navitem) > 0">
              <img src="/xmlbook/images/line.gif"/>
            </xsl:when>
            <xsl:otherwise>
              <img src="/xmlbook/images/nothing.gif"/>
            </xsl:otherwise>
          </xsl:choose>
        </xsl:for-each>
        <img  src="/xmlbook/images/divider.gif" onClick=
"collapse('{generate-id()}')"/>
        <xsl:if test="icon"><img src="images/{icon}"/> </xsl:if>
        <xsl:if test="href"><a href="{href}">
          <xsl:if test="href/@target"><xsl:attribute name=
"target"><xsl:value-of select="href/@target"/></xsl:attribute>
</xsl:if>
          <xsl:value-of select="description"/></a>
        </xsl:if>
        <xsl:if test="not(href)"><xsl:value-of select="description"/>
</xsl:if>
      </div>
    </xsl:otherwise>
  </xsl:choose>
</xsl:template>
```

Figure 6-7 shows what the Noverant back-office application looks like using this transformation.

An XML-based navigation system is inherently extensible. Its presentation rules can be changed in a variety of ways to dramatic effect. Another alternative to the two examples shown here is to develop a transformation that creates drop-down menus. This exercise, however, will be left to the reader.

Input Controls

Input widgets such as buttons, combo boxes, and text fields are essential to UIs. We couldn't do much without them! All development environments provide their own sets of widgets. The HTML specification includes support for many of these controls. Unfortunately, the widget set that HTML provides is not nearly as rich as those found in thick-client applications.

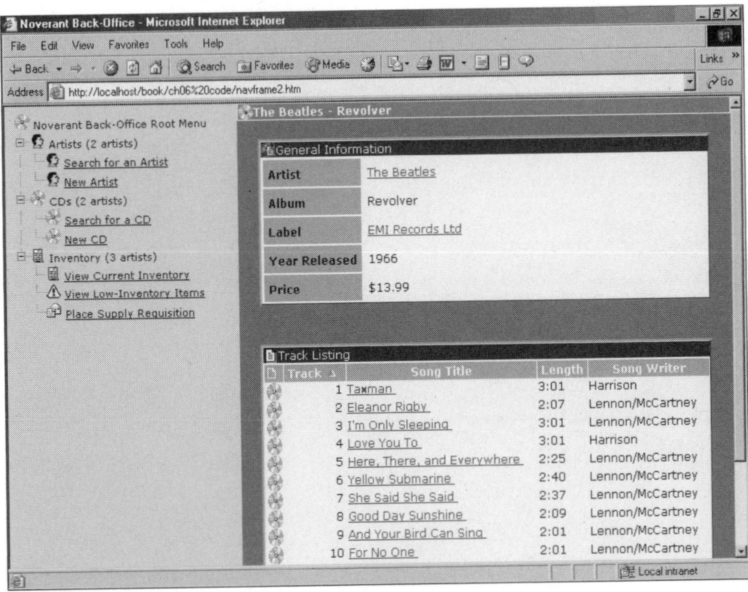

Figure 6-7 A tree-based navigation system.

Fortunately (or unfortunately, as the case may be), browser vendors have ventured beyond the W3C specification in their support for UI controls. Microsoft has added support for drag and drop, "What-You-See-Is-What-You-Get" (WYSIWYG) editing, right-click context menus and a host of other enhancements to its Internet Explorer browser. Netscape has embarked on an XML UI project of its own, called XML User-Interface Language (XUL). XUL was the toolset used to create the Mozilla browser's UI. Hooks to these widgets were added to the browser's API to allow developers to take advantage of them.

While these enhancements certainly allow for a richer browser UI, they can be confusing, if not problematic, to the application developer trying to sort through them. With all these toolsets available, does it make sense to roll your own? Perhaps. This section will explore the benefits of creating your own UI schema and will describe XML models and XSLTs for simple HTML form input controls. We will also learn how to extend these controls to take advantage of some browser-specific features.

Consistency

The internal adoption of your own XML schema to UI control design will enforce visual consistency within your application. For example, select boxes, radio buttons, and check boxes are often used interchangeably. How many times have you seen a Web page that looks like the one in Figure 6-8?

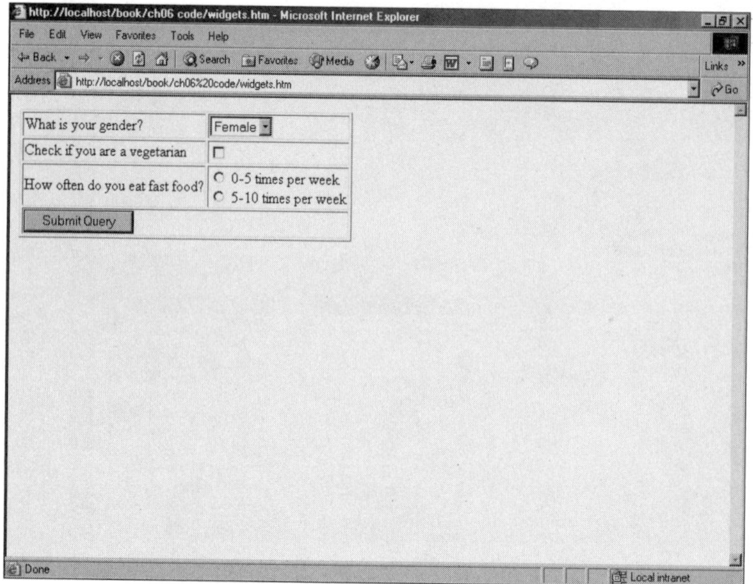

Figure 6-8 Why do these questions need to use different input controls?

All three questions in this page limit the user to binary responses. However, page designers, when left alone, will often mix and match these controls. Sometimes they even do it intentionally! How many times have you thought "I haven't used a check box control in several pages. Why don't I throw one in here"?

XML will rid your application of the "Let's be kind to the check box" syndrome. Imagine programming to a more generic interface when gathering input. For example, the following XML could have been used to clean up the page in Figure 6-8.

```
<property description="What is your gender?">
<choice name="gender" allowmultiple="no">
<option value="F">Female</option>
<option value="M">Male</option>
</choice>
</property>
<property description="Are you a vegetarian?">
<choice name="vegie" allowmultiple="no">
  <option value="Y">Yes</option>
  <option value="N">No</option>
</choice>
</property>
<property description="Which of these vegetables do you like?">
<choice name="favoriteFoods" allowmultiple="yes">
  <option value="turnips">Turnips</option>
  <option value="asparagus">Asparagus</option>
  <option value="carrots">Carrots</option>
  <option value="celery">Celery</option>
</choice>
</property>
```

The XSLT rules will govern what input control to use in a given context. The rule might be "Check boxes for two or more items, select boxes for all others," or it might be "Radio buttons all the time." Regardless, the UI will be consistent. This approach makes everyone's life easier. The page developer needs only remember a single API, and users doesn't need to suffer through three different ways of answering a "Yes/No" question.

You might also note in the previous example that the input fields are encapsulated by a *property* element. As we saw in previous examples, the *property* element makes the page developer's life much easier. Nearly every HTML form you encounter is a table with one column of prompts and another column of input controls. By including the prompt in the XML schema you save the developer from having to build new table rows and table cells for each question. The developer doesn't need to worry about the positioning of attributes or any other layout issues either. These are resolved by the XSLT layout manager.

The *<form>* Element

The first element we need to add to our schema is the *<form>* element, to indicate the presence of an input form. This element will look like the HTML *<form>* element with which you are already familiar. It will have only one essential attribute, the *action* attribute. Here is an example:

```
<form action="controller.asp?view=processresults"/>
```

This element, when transformed, will produce an HTML form that submits its contents to a Web page called controller.asp. Our first attempt to transform this element will be relatively straightforward.

```
<xsl:template match="form">
  <form action="{@action}" method="post">
    <xsl:for-each select="@*[name() != 'action']">
      <xsl:copy><xsl:value-of select="."/></xsl:copy>
    </xsl:for-each>
    <xsl:apply-templates/>
      <input class="text" type="submit"/>
  </form>
</xsl:template>
```

Now that we have a form, we need something to put in it. We will need to define wrapper elements for each of the HTML form controls we will implement.

> **Note** Use the "{*expression*}" shortcut when embedding XPath expressions inside element attributes. This is much less cumbersome than the *<xsl:attribute>* element.

The Text *<input>* Element

The first control we will implement is the standard text input control. This element will also be a subset of the HTML control. The element will be wrapped by a *<property>* element to control layout and formatting. An example of this element follows.

```
<property description="Enter the CD's description">
  <input type="text" size="30" value="Revolver" name="description"/>
</property>
```

The transformation for this element is simple. Notice that this transformation, like the *form* transformation before, iterates over the *<input>* element's attribute list and propagates them through to the output document. This open approach to the schema allows the page developer to pass through other attributes that the XSLT doesn't need to worry about, such as event handlers, to the result document.

```
<xsl:template match="input[@type='text']">
  <input type="text" name="{@name}" value="{@value}" class="text" >
    <xsl:for-each select="@*[name() != 'name' and name() != 'value']">
      <xsl:copy><xsl:value-of select="."/></xsl:copy>
    </xsl:for-each>
  </input>
</xsl:template>
```

The controls we have defined thus far provide enough ammunition to build a simple example. The example will be a CD input page that Noverant employees can use to edit albums in their inventory. The example in Figure 6-9 shows the new form controls.

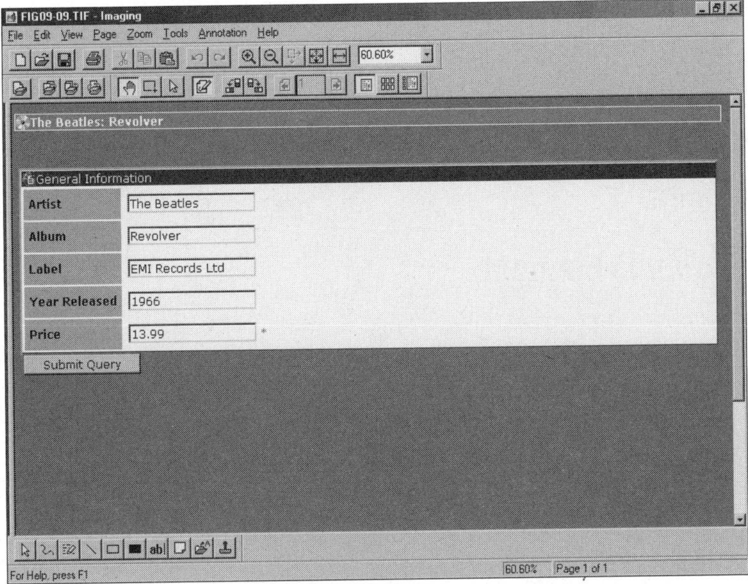

Figure 6-9 A simple CD edit example showing off new form controls.

```
<document>
  <header>
    <title>The Beatles: Revolver</title>
    <icon>CD.gif</icon>
  </header>
  <form action="cdinput.asp">
    <section>
      <header>
        <title>General Information</title>
        <icon>world.gif</icon>
      </header>
      <view>
```

```
            <properties>
              <property description="Artist">
                <input type="text" name="artist" value="The Beatles"/>
              </property>
              <property description="Album">
                <input type="text" name="description" value="Revolver"/>
              </property>
              <property description="Label">
                <input type="text" name="label" value="EMI Records Ltd"/>
              </property>
              <property description="Year Released">
                <input type="text" name="releaseDate" value="1966"/>
              </property>
              <property description="Price">
                <input type="text" name="price" value="13.99"/>
              </property>
            </properties>
          </view>
        </section>
      </form>
    </document>
```

The TextArea *<input>* Element

TextAreas are input controls familiar to Web form developers. They are more cumbersome to use than text input tags but are still necessary to capture longer streams of unstructured data. Our XML implementation will modify this element in three ways.

- It will alter its syntax slightly, making it more consistent with regular text input tags. The HTML 4.01 and XHTML 1.1 specifications defined the textarea syntax to be *<textarea>. . .</textarea>*. This implementation will change the usage to look like *<input type="textarea">. . .</input>* for simplicity's sake. Changing the syntax also helps the content developer remember that he or she is programming to a schema that you have defined.
- It will provide broad height and width defaults so that content developers do not need to worry about them. This will help make the application UI more consistent.
- It will provide support for WYSIWYG editing to those users who have Internet Explorer 5.5 or later. This is a fantastic feature that opens up drag-and-drop and rich-text formatting to Web users.

The syntax for the textarea *<input>* element is exactly like its simple text counterpart, with the exception of a single attribute. Figure 6-10 shows an implementation of the textarea control. Here is an example of its use:

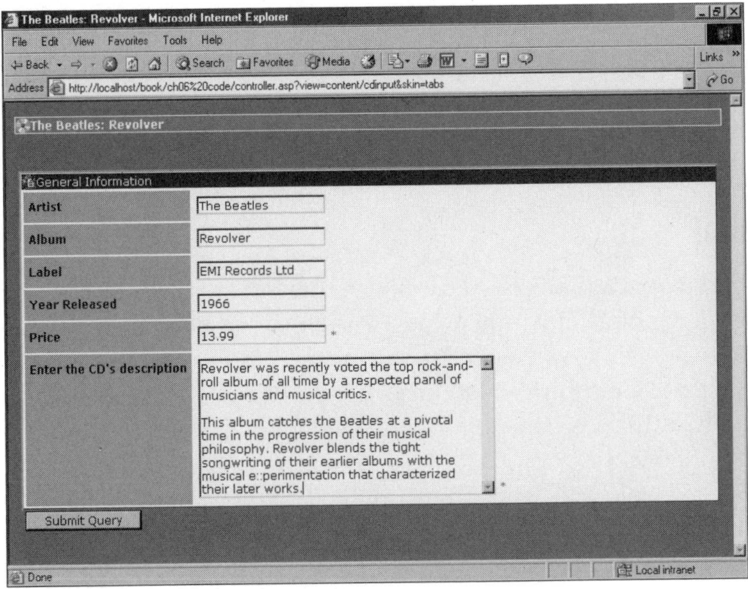

Figure 6-10 An implementation of the textarea control.

```
<property description="Enter the CD's description">
  <input type="textarea" value="" name="notes"/>
</property>
```

The XSLT template to build an HTML textarea is as follows:

```
<xsl:template match="input[@type='textarea']">
  <textarea class="text" wrap="{@word_wrap}" name="{@name}">
    <xsl:choose>
      <xsl:when test="@rows!=''">
        <xsl:attribute name="rows"><xsl:value-of select="@rows"/>
</xsl:attribute>
      </xsl:when>
      <xsl:otherwise>
        <xsl:attribute name="rows">8</xsl:attribute>
      </xsl:otherwise>
    </xsl:choose>
    <xsl:choose>
      <xsl:when test="@cols!=''">
         <xsl:attribute name="cols"><xsl:value-of select="@cols"/>
  </xsl:attribute>
```

```
        </xsl:when>
        <xsl:otherwise>
          <xsl:attribute name="cols">56</xsl:attribute>
        </xsl:otherwise>
      </xsl:choose>
      <xsl:value-of select="@value"/>
    </textarea>
    <xsl:if test="@mandatory = 'yes'">
      <font class="error"> *</font>
    </xsl:if>
  </xsl:template>.
```

Field Validation

Almost all applications need to validate the data that a user has entered before saving it. Some fields might be mandatory, while others, such as numeric fields, expect their values in a certain format. XML can help developers implement client-side form validation with little pain. All that is necessary is to add two new attributes, *mandatory* and *datatype*, to the *<input>* element and to update the XSLT.

For example, the "price" field on the CD edit form example should be mandatory and numeric. The new input field will look like this under the new schema:

```
<property description="Price">
<input type="text" name="price" value="13.99" mandatory="yes"
datatype="numeric"/>
</property>
```

> **Note** The W3C's XForms specification also seeks to solve the client-side data validation problem. See this specification for more interesting ideas on abstract forms. It can be found at *http://www.w3.org/MarkUp/Forms/*.

Nothing more is required of the page developer to indicate restrictions on a particular input field. The bulk of the validation work will be done by the XSLT. It will be modified to include two new functions: *hasValue(obj, obj_type)* and *isOfType(val, data_type)*. These scripts will be placed in a separate .js file that is included by the *document* template. The contents of Listing 6-6 follow.

Listing 6-6 formValidate.js: Contains the functions used for client-side mandatory field checking and datatype validation.

```
function hasValue(obj, obj_type)
{
    if (obj_type == "text" || obj_type == "password")
  {
      if (obj.value.length == 0)
          return false;
      else
          return true;
      }
    else if (obj_type == "select")
  {
        for (i=0; i < obj.length; i++)
        {
    if (obj.options[i].selected)
      return true;
    }
        return false;
  }
    else if (obj_type == "single_radio" || obj_type ==
"single_checkbox")
  {
    if (obj.checked)
      return true;
    else
          return false;
  }
    else if (obj_type == "radio" || obj_type == "checkbox")
  {
        for (i=0; i < obj.length; i++)
        {
    if (obj[i].checked)
      return true;
    }
        return false;
  }
}
function isoftype(the_val, data_type)
{
  if (data_type == "date")
  {
    if (isNaN(Date.parse(the_val)))
    {
      return false;
    } else {
      return true;
```

(continued)

Listing 6-6 *continued*

```
      }
    }
    if (data_type == "time")
    {
      if (isNaN(Date.parse("01/01/1970 "+the_val)))
      {
        return false;
      } else {
        return true;
      }
    }
    if (data_type == "monetary" || data_type == "numeric")
    {
      if (isNaN(the_val))
      {
        return false;
      } else {
        return true;
      }
    }
  }
```

The XSLT must be altered both to include this JavaScript file and to change the form submission process to check for mandatory and restricted fields. First the following line needs to be added to the head of the result document:

```
<script language="javaScript" src="js/formvalidate.js"/>
```

Second the XSLT *form* template must be modified to build a dynamic JavaScript function that validates its contents. This function will be called during the form's *onSubmit()* event.

Because each *validateForm()* function is unique to the contents of a particular form, its name must be unique to prevent collisions with other forms that might exist on the same page. The XSL function *generate-id()* is used for this purpose.

```
<xsl:template match="form">
  <script language="JavaScript">
    function validateForm_<xsl:value-of select="generate-id()"/>
(thisForm)
    {
```

The first part of the function iterates over all input elements in the XML document with the *mandatory* attribute set to "yes". The function then determines, for each mandatory field, the type of input control (for example, *text box*, *textarea*, and so forth), and then makes an appropriate call to the *hasValue()*

function. If *hasValue()* returns false, the *validateForm()* function displays an error message, attempts to set the page focus to the field, and aborts the form submission.

```
<xsl:for-each select="//*[@mandatory='yes']">
  <xsl:choose>
    <xsl:when test="@type = 'text' or @type='textarea'">
      if (!hasValue(thisForm.<xsl:value-of select="@name"/>
,"text"))
      {
        alert("<xsl:value-of select="@name"/> is mandatory.");
        var the_field = thisForm.<xsl:value-of select="@name"/>;
        if(the_field.style.display != "none" &amp;
!the_field.disabled &amp; !the_field.readOnly &amp;
 !the_field.editableDiv)
          the_field.focus();
        return false;
      }
    </xsl:when>
  </xsl:choose>
</xsl:for-each>
```

Next the function needs to check any datatype restrictions mentioned in the XML source. This algorithm is similar to the one used to perform mandatory value checking. The script iterates over all input controls with a *datatype* attribute specified. For each attribute the script makes a call to the *isoftype()* function to match the format of the data entered by the user to the required format. If the *isoftype()* function call returns false, the *validateForm()* script reports the error to the user and aborts the form submission.

```
<xsl:for-each select="//input[@datatype]">
  if (!isoftype(thisForm.<xsl:value-of select="@name"
/>.value,'<xsl:value-of select="@datatype"/>'))
  {
   alert("<xsl:value-of select="@name"/> is not in <xsl:value-of
select="@datatype"/> format");
    return false;
  }
</xsl:for-each>
```

Finally the *validateForm()* function must inspect the form's *onSubmit()* event handler to see if further post processing is required. If the page developer specified an *onSubmit()* function to be called, the *validateForm()* function will call it before completing.

```
<xsl:choose>
  <xsl:when test="@onSubmit">
    var rtnval = <xsl:value-of select="@onSubmit"/>;
```

```
          return rtnval;
        </xsl:when>
        <xsl:otherwise>
          return true;
        </xsl:otherwise>
      </xsl:choose>
    }
  </script>
```

The *<form>* HTML element must now be altered by the template to call the new *formValidate()* function when it is submitted, which is achieved by setting its *onSubmit* attribute.

```
  <form action="{@action}" method="post" onSubmit="return
validateForm_{generate-id()}(this)">
    <xsl:for-each select="@*[name() != 'action']">
      <xsl:copy><xsl:value-of select="."/></xsl:copy>
    </xsl:for-each>
    <xsl:apply-templates/>
      <input class="text" type="submit"/>
  </form>
</xsl:template>
```

WYSIWYG Editing

With the release of Internet Explorer 5.5, Microsoft made the browser's WYSIWYG HTML editing control available for use in Web pages. This control provides many useful options, such as:

- Cut and Paste to and from other Windows applications, such as Microsoft Word
- Embedded images
- Rich-text formatting including bold, italics, underline, left, center, and right justification
- User-defined hyperlinks
- Text range formatting
- Undo/Redo functionality

Developers can use this feature by setting a division's contentEditable attribute. Unfortunately, Internet Explorer does not implement this attribute on standard HTML input controls. For example, *<textarea contentEditable = "true"…/>* will not have the desired effect. Instead, we must accomplish our goal through a bit of trickery. The good news is that the XSLT will handle all of the dirty work for us without any change to our forms XML object model.

This is an excellent illustration of how XML and XSLT facilitate application extensibility.

> **Note** The Microsoft WYSIWYG editing control does a remarkable job of creating well-formed HTML code. Well-formed HTML is much easier to incorporate into XML documents.

The trick to adding WYSIWYG editing to a text box is not to use a text box at all. We will use a combination of divisions and hidden variables to pull this off. To begin, the textarea XSLT template will change to insert a *<div>* element instead of a *<TEXTAREA>* element into the result document. The *<div>* element will have its *contentEditable* attribute set to "true" to enable WYSIWYG editing. You might also note that the template has added support for a new *size* attribute in the textarea *<input>* element. This attribute accepts values of "small", "medium", and "large" so that content developers can control the relative size of the input box without worrying about specifying an exact pixel height and width.

```
<xsl:template match="input[@type='textarea']">
  <div id="d{generate-id()}" contentEditable="true" class="text">
    <xsl:choose>
      <xsl:when test="@size='small'"><xsl:attribute name="style">
display:inline;overflow:scroll;width=350;border:solid;
border-style:ridge;border-width:2;background-color:white;height:150
</xsl:attribute></xsl:when>
      <xsl:when test="@size='medium'"><xsl:attribute name="style">
display:inline;overflow:scroll;width=350;border:solid;
border-style:ridge;border-width:2;background-color:white;height:250
</xsl:attribute></xsl:when>
      <xsl:when test="@size='large'"><xsl:attribute name="style">
display:inline;overflow:scroll;width=350;border:solid;
border-style:ridge;border-width:2;background-color:white;height:350
</xsl:attribute></xsl:when>
      <xsl:otherwise><xsl:attribute name="style">display:inline;
overflow:scroll;width=350;border:solid;border-style:ridge;
border-width:2;background-color:white;height:350</xsl:attribute>
</xsl:otherwise>
    </xsl:choose>
    <xsl:value-of disable-output-escaping="yes" select="value"/>
  </div>
  <input type="hidden" editableDiv="yes" name="{@name}"
value="{@value}"/>
  <xsl:if test="@mandatory = 'yes'">
```

```
    <div style="display:inline"><font class="error"> *</font>
</div>
  </xsl:if>
</xsl:template>
```

This code will insert a WYSIWYG–editable division into the Web page. How do we move the contents of this division into a form variable to be submitted with the form? The answer lies in the form validation function. We need to insert logic into this function that will create hidden form variables with the same names as the textareas to be submitted with the form.

```
function validateForm_<xsl:value-of select="generate-id()"/>(thisForm)
{
  <xsl:for-each select="//input[@type='textarea']">
thisForm.<xsl:value-of select="@name"/>.value =
document.getElementById('d<xsl:value-of select="generate-id()"
/>').innerHTML;
  </xsl:for-each>
  // rest of the validateForm() function goes here
}
```

Now, like magic, users can edit your textareas just as if they were editing a Word document. Figure 6-11 shows the XML document with WYSIWYG editing enabled.

Dynamic XSL Transformations

WYSIWYG editing is fantastic for users with capable browsers, but what about support for older or nonconformant browsers? Our current textarea transformation would produce a division that could not be edited by any browser that does not support WYSIWYG (for example, Internet Explorer 5.0 or later). Certainly, this is a problem.

One solution might be to create a second textarea *<input>* XML element that looked like *<input type="richtextarea" …>*. The ASP page developer could check the user's browser at runtime and use the plain textarea *<input>* element to support older versions. While this scheme might work, it casts the burden of worrying about presentation onto the page developer. This is contrary to XML's philosophy of separating content from presentation and should be avoided if possible.

Another solution might be to create multiple XSLT templates, one for each class of Web browser. The Internet Explorer 5.0 template would use the regular textarea control while the Internet Explorer 5.5 and later templates would take advantage of the rich-text version. The page controller would determine the user's browser and select the correct template for rendering the page results. This approach has merits because it removes the presentation responsibility from the page developer, which is good. The approach is also extensible.

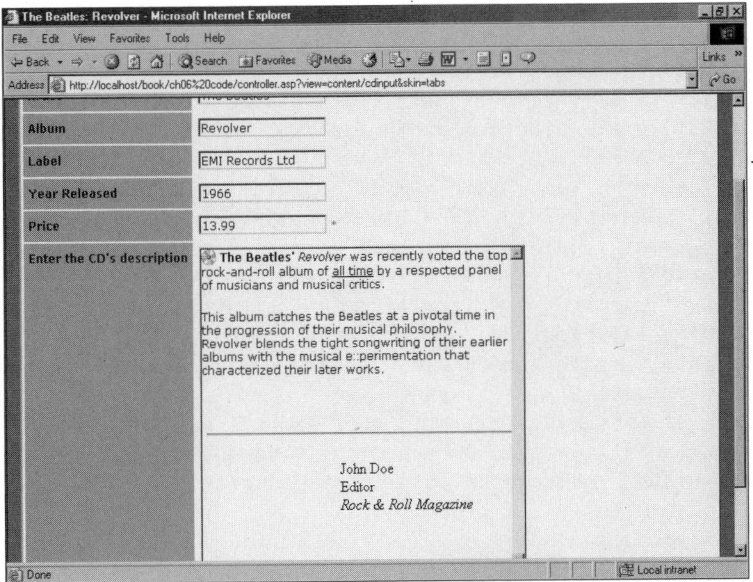

Figure 6-11 Same XML document as in Figure 6-10, with WYSIWYG editing enabled.

Whenever a new browser hits the market, the XSLT designer need only create a new transformation geared to the new software and drop it into the XSLT library.

The downside to this solution is that it yields a proliferation of slightly different skins, all of which must be maintained. This situation becomes particularly problematic when changes are introduced into the application's UI schema. All of the transformations must be updated whenever this happens. While a transformation skin library might be useful for separating wildly different classes of browsers (for example, separating Netscape 4.71 from Internet Explorer 6.0), it behooves the XSLT developer to keep the number of transformations in this library under control.

Instead of creating a new skin for each Web browser, the XSLT developer can make use of another technique, known as "dynamic XSLT," to manage subtle differences between browsers. Dynamic XSLT is simple to explain and understand although its application is limitless (and sometimes mind-bending!). The idea is simple: make your XSLTs ASPs. No rule says XSLT pages need to be static. The plain vs. rich text textarea problem can be solved by a single ASP transformation. The logic in the page might look something like the following:

```
<%
If browser = "MSIE" and broserVersion >= 5.5 Then
%>
<xsl:template match="input[@type='textarea']">
```

```
    <div id="d{generate-id()}" contentEditable="true" class="text">
      <xsl:choose>
        <xsl:when test="@size='small'"><xsl:attribute name="style">
display:inline;overflow:scroll;width=350;border:solid;
border-style:ridge;border-width:2;background-color:white;height:150
</xsl:attribute></xsl:when>
        <xsl:when test="@size='medium'"><xsl:attribute name="style">
display:inline;overflow:scroll;width=350;border:solid;
border-style:ridge;border-width:2;background-color:white;height:250
</xsl:attribute></xsl:when>
        <xsl:when test="@size='large'"><xsl:attribute name="style">
display:inline;overflow:scroll;width=350;border:solid;
border-style:ridge;border-width:2;background-color:white;height:350
</xsl:attribute></xsl:when>
        <xsl:otherwise><xsl:attribute name="style">display:inline;
overflow:scroll;width=350;border:solid;border-style:ridge;
border-width:2;background-color:white;height:350</xsl:attribute>
</xsl:otherwise>
      </xsl:choose>
      <xsl:value-of disable-output-escaping="yes" select="value"/>
    </div>
    <input type="hidden" editableDiv="yes" name="{@name}"
value="{@value}"/>
    <xsl:if test="@mandatory = 'yes'">
      <div style="display:inline"><font class="error"> *</font>
</div>
    </xsl:if>
</xsl:template>
<%
End Else
%>
<xsl:template match="input[@type='textarea']">
    <textarea class="text" wrap="{@word_wrap}" name="{@name}">
      <xsl:choose>
        <xsl:when test="@rows!=''">
          <xsl:attribute name="rows"><xsl:value-of select="@rows"/>
</xsl:attribute>
        </xsl:when>
        <xsl:otherwise>
          <xsl:attribute name="rows">8</xsl:attribute>
        </xsl:otherwise>
      </xsl:choose>
      <xsl:choose>
        <xsl:when test="@cols!=''">
          <xsl:attribute name="cols"><xsl:value-of select="@cols"/>
</xsl:attribute>
        </xsl:when>
        <xsl:otherwise>
          <xsl:attribute name="cols">56</xsl:attribute>
```

```
      </xsl:otherwise>
    </xsl:choose>
    <xsl:value-of select="@value"/>
  </textarea>
  <xsl:if test="@mandatory = 'yes'">
    <font class="error"> *</font>
  </xsl:if>
</xsl:template>
<%
  End
%>
```

> **Note** XSLT documents are well-formed XML and can be transformed by XSLT. Imagine using XSLT to transform another XSLT document to transform a source XML document. Not only is this possible, it is often good design.

Dynamic XSLT offers an ideal solution to tricky differences between otherwise similar browsers. Again, a skin library should be used to isolate presentation rules across different browser classes. However, this technique is very useful, particularly as newer browsers approach the panacea of full W3C specification support.

The *<choice>* Element

The *<choice>* element is used to automate the creation of HTML select boxes, radio buttons, and check boxes. Let's re-examine the example supplied at the beginning of the section.

```
<property description="What is your gender?">
<choice name="gender" allowmultiple="no">
<option value="F">Female</option>
<option value="M">Male</option>
</choice>
</property>
<property description="Are you a vegetarian?">
<choice name="vegie" allowmultiple="no">
  <option value="Y">Yes</option>
  <option value="N">No</option>
</choice>
</property>
<property description="Which of these vegetables do you like?">
<choice name="favoriteFoods" allowmultiple="yes">
```

```
  <option value="turnips">Turnips</option>
  <option value="asparagus">Asparagus</option>
  <option value="carrots">Carrots</option>
  <option value="celery">Celery</option>
</choice>
</property>
```

The XSLT for this control should incorporate presentation rules to determine how the choices should be rendered. The extreme cases are easy to figure out. A choice with two hundred options is probably best displayed inside a *<select>* combo box. At the other end of the spectrum a choice offering two options with the *allowmultiple* attribute turned on is best shown as two check boxes. Our transformation will use five options as an arbitrary cutoff between select boxes and check boxes/radio buttons. Your presentation rules might differ or change over time.

In the transformation you will first notice the test of the option count. If the count is greater than five the template creates a select box, setting its *multiple* and *size* attributes to *yes* and *5*, respectively, if the user is allowed to select more than one option. In the case of small choices, where the option count is at most five, the template creates either a series of check boxes or a series of radio buttons with the same name. Check boxes are used when the *allowmultple* attribute is set to *yes*; radio buttons are used when it is not.

```
<xsl:template match="choice">
  <xsl:choose>
    <xsl:when test="count(option) > 5">
      <select class="text">
        <xsl:for-each select="@*[name() != 'mandatory']">
          <xsl:copy><xsl:value-of select="."/></xsl:copy>
        </xsl:for-each>
        <xsl:if test="@allowmultiple = 'yes'">
          <xsl:attribute name="multiple">yes</xsl:attribute>
          <xsl:attribute name="size">5</xsl:attribute>
        </xsl:if>
        <option value="">Please Choose Below</option>
        <xsl:for-each select="option">
          <option>
            <xsl:attribute name="value"><xsl:value-of select="@value"/>
</xsl:attribute>
            <xsl:if test="@selected='yes'">
              <xsl:attribute name="selected"><xsl:value-of
select="@selected"/></xsl:attribute>
            </xsl:if>
            <xsl:value-of select="."/>
          </option>
        </xsl:for-each>
      </select>
    </xsl:when>
```

```
    <xsl:otherwise>
      <div style="display:inline">
        <xsl:for-each select="option">
          <xsl:choose>
            <xsl:when test="../@allowmultiple = 'yes'">
              <input type="checkbox" name="{../@name}"
value="{@value}"/> <xsl:value-of select="."/><br/>
            </xsl:when>
            <xsl:otherwise>
              <input type="radio" name="{../@name}" value="{@value}"/>
 <xsl:value-of select="."/><br/>
            </xsl:otherwise>
          </xsl:choose>
        </xsl:for-each>
      </div>
    </xsl:otherwise>
  </xsl:choose>
  <xsl:if test="@mandatory = 'yes'">
    <div style="display:inline"><font class="error"> *</font>
</div>
  </xsl:if>
</xsl:template>
```

Figure 6-12 and Figure 6-13 show how the result page differs when the number of select options climbs above five.

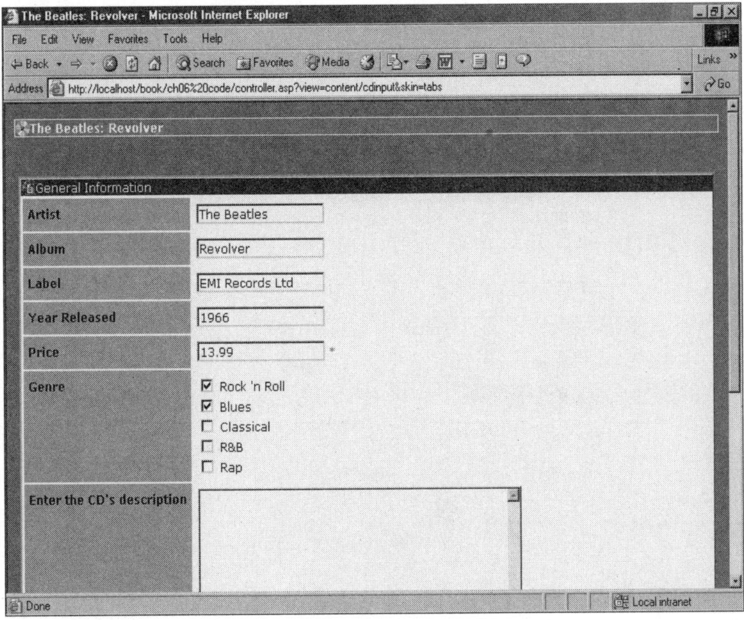

Figure 6-12 Smaller versus larger option sets (smaller set).

That's it for multichoice input controls. The *formValidate()* function will need to be updated to mimic your presentation rules when checking for mandatory fields.

Putting it All Together

XML can affect all aspects of an application's UI design. This chapter touched on a few of those areas: layout, navigation, and user input controls. Your UI, however, need not stop there in its use of XML. From modeling generic user actions to creating drag-and-drop targets, XML can have an impact on your application and development timelines in a variety of ways. Thoughtful use of the technology can cut the time to delivery of a project in half as well as make your application much more maintainable over the long haul.

XML encourages you to think about your UI in a more abstract way, which leads to a more modular and generic design that can be adapted to new situations and requirements. In this chapter we used XML to model various aspects of our UI. In the case of the WYSIWYG text area, we saw how to extend the implementation of that model to provide additional functionality. In Chapter 7 we will examine how to use XML for sending messages between different applications.

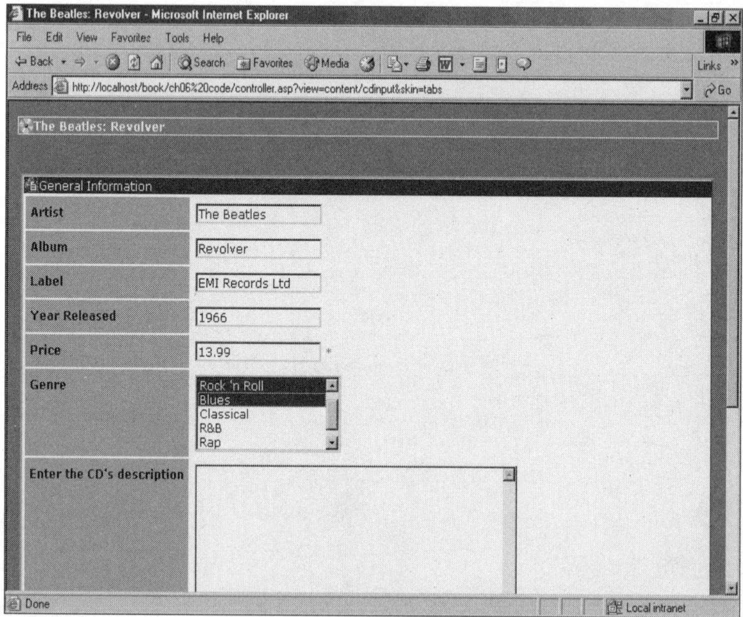

Figure 6-13 Smaller versus larger option sets (larger set).

7

XML-Based Messaging

One recent but rapidly growing application of XML is in communications, especially as applied to messaging. This chapter explores how XML has emerged as the ideal messaging solution for solving some of the most difficult issues of applying the distributed computing paradigm in Web-based environments.

We begin with a discussion about the history and technology of messaging as a distributed computing paradigm and why XML is seen as an evolutionary technology in the field of messaging. We will then take a detailed look at two of the XML-based messaging technologies, SOAP and Web Services, and show you how you can build and deploy Web Services using a variety of tools and languages. Finally we will take a first stab at understanding the Microsoft BizTalk Initiative and find out how XML is being used there to solve application integration problems.

Messaging Overview

Before we can understand "messaging," we must define a "message." Although no generally accepted definition exists, in the context of our XML discussion we can define a message as a self-contained unit of information. A message usually has a *header*, which contains control information about the message. Examples of control information are routing, authentication, and transactional data. A message also has a *body*, which contains the actual content of the message.

Messaging, therefore, is the process of passing messages between applications over a network using a transport protocol to perform a particular function.

The Beginnings of Messaging

Traditionally the term "messaging system" was often used to refer to a type of middleware system known as Message-Oriented Middleware (MOM). Common examples of MOM systems include Microsoft Message Queue Server (MMQS), IBM MQSeries, and Tibco Rendezvous. Among other features, MOM systems allow applications to exchange messages asynchronously so that the caller (the client) doesn't need to wait while the called application (the server) completes the request. Today messaging does not necessarily mean that a MOM system is being used to exchange and manage the messages. It doesn't even have to mean that you're sending messages asynchronously. Instead, messaging can be either synchronous or asynchronous, and MOM systems can be regarded as a special type of transport protocol used to enable messaging. Other common transport protocols used for messaging include HTTP and SMTP.

The Need for Messaging

To better understand the need for messaging, we will compare it to another distributed computing paradigm that has enjoyed widespread adoption: the Remote Procedure Call (RPC) paradigm. RPC today forms the basis for almost all distributed computing platforms, such as DCOM, CORBA, and Java RMI. RPC provides applications with the ability to make function calls across the network. (See the "The RPC Mechanism" sidebar.) By comparing these two paradigms you will get a better idea of the advantages and disadvantages of messaging as a distributed computing paradigm.

Messaging systems usually have little infrastructure because, in contrast to RPC, messaging generally does not support marshaling,unmarshaling and function invocation. Messages are transferred as they are, and messaging software makes no assumption about the structure of these messages. Applications using messaging must parse their own messages and invoke the appropriate functions to handle them. The only contract in a message-oriented system is that the client and server should agree about the format of the messages exchanged. In fact, several messages can be used together to invoke a given function. Messaging systems are, therefore, more loosely coupled than RPC systems because the client is more independent of the server. In addition, messaging systems can often support complex and flexible message formats such as hierarchical and binary data. RPC systems, however, generally support only common programming language data types such as integer, double, string, and sometimes array.

Because the RPC paradigm requires an infrastructure to handle the marshaling,unmarshaling, and function-invocation services, it is usually tied to a specific transport protocol. Messaging, on the other hand, can generally be transport-protocol independent. Still, using RPC is usually easier because it handles all the data packaging and method invocations for you. Messaging is useful when you need every last ounce of performance or your messages cannot be easily represented as method parameters. Table 7-1 summarizes the differences between message-oriented and RPC-oriented systems.

Table 7-1 Message-Oriented vs. RPC-Oriented Systems

Feature	**Messaging**	**RPC**
Coupling between client and server	Loose	Tight
Possible data structures	Complex, including hierarchical	Limited to common programming language data types such as integer and string
Implementation	Relatively difficult	Easy
Programming language	Independent	Tied to a set of programming language
Transport protocol	Can be bound to different transport protocols	Usually bound to a particular protocol

Messaging systems shine in situations where it would be difficult for both the caller and called parties to agree on a common function interface and operating platform. For example, two companies communicating over the Internet might have different business systems and might not want to use the same programming languages. In addition, they might prefer to communicate asynchronously so that neither will depend on the other's application being up and running.

Features of MOM Systems

Most MOM systems support guaranteed delivery of messages using a *store-and-forward* mechanism. Delivery is usually achieved by writing the incoming messages out to persistent queued storage. This mechanism will then deliver all the messages to the recipient when it becomes available. MOM systems usually provide two types of messaging models as well. One is point-to-point queuing and the other is referred to as publish-and-subscribe.

In the point-to-point messaging model messages are sent, through a given queue, from a sender to a single intended recipient or a group of recipients. When the recipient is a group, only one recipient in the group can consume each message. The MOM system ensures that each message is consumed only once by the next available recipient in the group.

In a publish-and-subscribe message model a sender can broadcast a message through a virtual channel to one group of recipients or more. MOM systems usually provide other enterprise-level features such as redundancy, load balancing, and transaction support.

Most mature organizations have legacy and new applications that have been implemented independently and cannot easily interoperate. Integrating these systems is called *Enterprise Application Integration (EAI),* and a MOM system is usually central to achieving integration. MOM systems can be used to help exchange and coordinate the data and events communicated between these systems in the form of messages, while letting the systems remain independent, both physically and architecturally.

MOM systems are also considered central to *Business-to-Business (B2B)* solutions because they allow organizations to cooperate without requiring them to have the same systems or to tightly integrate their systems through proprietary software.

The RPC Mechanism

RPC uses a request-and-reply communication model to allow a client application to invoke functions exposed by a remote server application that is listening for these requests. As far as the programmer is concerned, the remote invocation is similar to invoking an ordinary local function. The RPC Run-time System (RTS) providing the RPC mechanism handles all the underlying communication to make details look simple to the application programmer.

An RPC mechanism has two aspects: definition and execution. The definition, called the *interface definition*, is done before the RPC is actually made. It includes describing the function, its arguments, and the return value, including the associated data types. The format, or grammar, of this definition is called the *Interface Definition Language* (IDL). IDL is used to generate a piece of software called a *stub* or *proxy* that is linked to both the RPC client and server.

The execution starts when the client makes an RPC request. The stub linked to the client intercepts the request and redirects it to the client-side RTS. This RTS packages the arguments in a form suitable for transmission over a network. This process is known as *marshaling*. The client-side RTS then locates and invokes the server-side RTS that, in turn, invokes the appropriate server stub. The server stub performs the operations complementary to those of the client stub: unmarshaling the parameters passed to the function, calling the function, and marshaling the return parameters. This whole process is depicted in Figure 7-1.

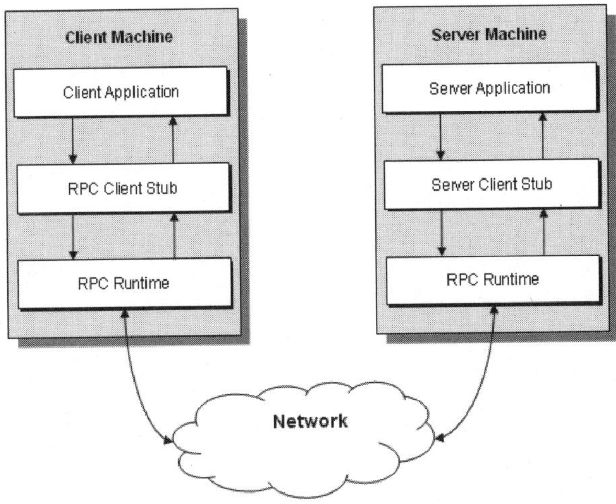

Figure 7-1 Interaction of the RPC components.

XML-Based Messaging

By the 1990s the various distributed computing paradigms were feature-rich and slowly gaining widespread support. Distributed computing technologies such as CORBA and the various enterprise-class MOM systems became well supported by many vendors and several free software projects and were available for different programming languages and operating systems.

The world of distributed computing had, up to that point, consisted of several large factions such as Microsoft DCOM and CORBA, each adhering to its own particular protocols and each with its own preference for operating platforms. Interoperability between different distributed object platforms was difficult to achieve in a cost-effective manner. Most distributed object platforms were also complex and had steep learning curves. Most of them also required substantial development and administrative efforts.

Enterprises originally did not find these issues with the available distributed object computing platforms crippling. They decided to standardize on one particular platform so interoperability wasn't a problem. Technologies like MOM systems and software bridges also helped handle the cases where it was necessary to cross the divides.

The most significant issue with the old distributed computing systems was their sheer complexity. In an attempt to capture the largest market share, all the major players in the distributed computing systems industry apparently fixated on aggressively producing the most technologically advanced solutions, overlooking some of the priorities and compelling needs of the clients. While maybe 10 to 20 percent of the potential users could truly benefit from the broad range of services provided by these systems, most clients would happily trade that wealth of features for an easier technology that could simplify development and deployment.

The second problem was interoperability. With the dawn of the Internet, enterprises found themselves faced with demands for conducting business transactions over the Web. To realize the full vision of E-commerce, seamless B2B integration, and so on, it became clear that the old walls of distributed computing needed to come down.

The goal of XML-based messaging is to eliminate these complexity and interoperability issues with traditional distributed computing platforms. It attempts to do so by following the same model attributes as the other successful Internet standards: simplicity, flexibility, platform neutrality, and open text-based encoding.

The SOAP Messaging Framework

SOAP is an XML-based lightweight protocol designed to work with existing Internet and XML open standards. SOAP was originally designed to support the RPC mechanism over HTTP. Later versions removed these restrictions, and SOAP can now be used for both RPC-oriented and message-oriented operations. SOAP is also transport protocol independent.

The first official SOAP specification (SOAP 1) was announced by Microsoft and DevelopMentor in December 1999. IBM and a number of other key industrial players later joined the SOAP specification working group, and in April 2000 the SOAP 1.1 specification was released. In May 2000 the SOAP 1.1 specification was submitted to the W3C as a Note by Microsoft, IBM, UserLand, and DevelopMentor. SOAP is now under the care of the W3C's XML Protocol Working Group *(http://www.w3.org/2000/xp/)*. In this chapter we will look at the more widely supported version 1.1 specification, which can be found at *http://www.w3.org/TR/SOAP/*. You can find more detailed coverage of the SOAP specifications in Chapter 13.

SOAP rapidly gained widespread industrial acceptance, and today is a core enabler technology for the so-called "Software as Service" revolution in the computer industry. We will have more to say about this revolution, which created what are known as Web Services, later in this chapter.

The SOAP messaging framework consists of three parts: a message structure specification, an encoding standard, and an RPC mechanism. We'll go over each of these parts briefly next.

The Message Structure

A SOAP message is an XML document composed of an outer envelope that can contain a header and a body. This structure is depicted in Figure 7-2.

Listing 7-1 is a skeletal SOAP message with no information in it.

Listing 7-1 soap_skeletal.xml: A skeletal SOAP message.

```
<SOAP-ENV:Envelope xmlns:SOAP-ENV="http://schemas.xmlsoap.org/soap/
envelope/" SOAP-ENV:encodingStyle="http://schemas.xmlsoap.org/soap/
encoding/"/>
  <SOAP-ENV:Header>
  </SOAP-ENV:Header>
  <SOAP-ENV:Body>
  </SOAP-ENV:Body>
</SOAP-ENV:Envelope>
```

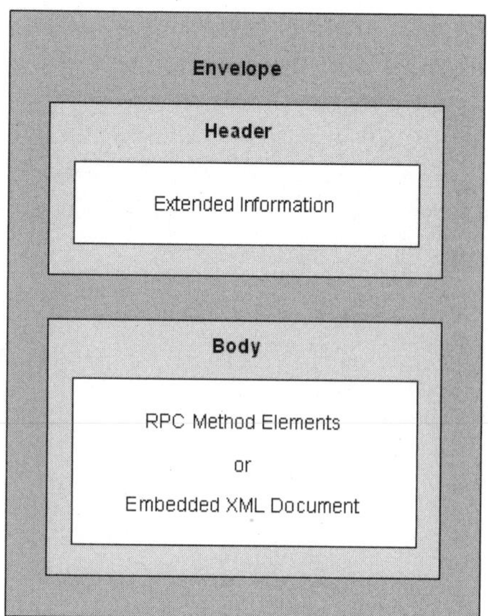

Figure 7-2 The structure of a SOAP Message.

The *<SOAP-ENV:Envelope>* element is the root element of a SOAP message. It is also used to specify options that are global to the whole message, such as the encoding rules of the parameters. *<SOAP-ENV:Header>* is an optional element that provides a mechanism for participants to add extended information about a call. It's typically used to provide contextual information such as that related to security, transaction, payment, and so forth. The *<SOAP-ENV:Body>* element is mandatory and is where the actual contents of a message reside. This is where method parameters are encoded and packaged.

A special type of SOAP message, called a fault, is used to indicate when a request has failed for some particular reason, such as an unrecognizable header field, an authentication error, or some errors that occur while processing the message.

Encoding Rules

SOAP has well-defined (some might even say overly designed) rules for encoding complex data structures such as arrays and structures. For example, the following is an array of string encoding in SOAP:

```
<SOAP-ENC:Array SOAP-ENC:arrayType="xsd:string[4]">
  <SOAP-ENC:string>Item 1</SOAP-ENC:string>
  <SOAP-ENC:string>Item 2</SOAP-ENC:string>
  <SOAP-ENC:string>Item 3</SOAP-ENC:string>
</SOAP-ENC:Array>
```

In addition, SOAP adopts all the types defined in the XML Schema Datatypes specification (*http://www.w3c.org/TR/xmlschema-2/*). Therefore, for simple types, the XML Schema Datatypes can be used directly in the element schemas.

The SOAP RPC Mechanism

SOAP encoding rules also provide the marshaling and unmarshaling mechanism required to provide RPC-oriented operations. SOAP specifies an RPC mechanism that allows applications to invoke functions on the receiving end of a SOAP message. Function arguments are marshaled using the standard encoding rules as part of the SOAP message body. For instance, the following C# method:

```
public int GetValue( int Arg1, int Arg2 );
```

can be marshaled as the following SOAP message:

```
<SOAP-ENV:Envelope xmlns:SOAP-ENV="http://schemas.xmlsoap.org/soap/
envelope/" SOAP-ENV:encodingStyle="http://schemas.xmlsoap.org/soap/
encoding/"
xmlns:xsd="http://www.w3c.org/2001/XMLSchema/"/>
  <SOAP-ENV:Body>
<GetValue>
  <Arg1 xsd:type="xsd:int"></Arg1>
  <Arg2 xsd:type="xsd:int"></Arg2>
</GetValue>
  </SOAP-ENV:Body>
</SOAP-ENV:Envelope>
```

Note that the method name, *GetValue,* is encoded as the immediate child element of the *<SOAP-ENV:Body>* element.

Web Services

The computer technology industry is well known for its mastery of the hype life cycle, but rarely has a concept emerged from obscurity to the "new thing" as quickly as Web Services. Vendors large and small are betting that this emerging technology trend will take hold and enable new possibilities for E-business. But what exactly are Web Services?

The first important fact you should know is that Web Services is not a single technology but a group of closely related, emerging technologies that form a distributed computing architecture based on open and ubiquitous Internet standards.

Although on the surface this might sound like the Application Service Provider model, Web Services are very different. Application Service Providers are entire Web-based applications, while Web Services are reusable software components that provide discrete functionality. Also, while Application Service Provider applications are implemented as a closed "black box," Web Services are designed to be inherently extensible.

For an example, look at the current crop of Web-based auction sites such as eBay or uBid. All these sites offer HTML-based auction services that are meant to be used by people. However, imagine that a company has found a need for auction functionality in its own applications. This company will either need to implement the auction functionality itself or redirect customers to one of the auction sites. If these auction sites have a Web Services interface, this company can remotely invoke the needed functionality to build its own applications.

As we saw earlier, Web Services are not implemented in a monolithic way, but represent a collection of several related technologies. From a developer's point of view, Web Services can be understood as specific implementations of an XML-based messaging system built on the following infrastructure components:

- *Web Service Description* To be able to interact with a Web Service, a client must be made aware of the semantics of its services. The WSDL is an XML document used to describe the interface to a Web Service in a structured and standardized way.
- *Web Service Wire Formats* SOAP is used as the standard wire format for Web Services. Web Services can also use plain HTTP, GET, and HTTP POST, but most are expected to use SOAP and to use HTTP POST as the transport protocol.
- *Web Service Discovery* Web Services make their presence, capabilities, and functionality known throughout the process of discovery. The UDDI specification defines an XML schema and an API that enable clients to dynamically find Web Services.

These technologies together, HTTP + XML + SOAP + WSDL + UDDI, form the core low-level technology stack of Web Services.

Other higher-level technologies are being developed for providing strategic aspects of business processes. One of these technologies is the Web Services Flow Language (WSFL) sponsored by IBM. WSFL aims to define a framework whereby Web Services implementers can describe the business logic required to assemble various services into an end-to-end business process.

Describing Web Services with WSDL

WSDL is the IDL of Web Services. WSDL describes the functionality of a Web Service and how this functionality is made available, and plays a central role in enabling Web Service interoperability. It does so by fully describing the capabilities and use of the service in a platform- and protocol-independent manner. The description is so complete that tools can use WSDL to automate the creation of code such as proxies.

> **Note** WSDL is a W3C-submitted specification and is supported by a number of industry leaders, including Microsoft and IBM. Version 1.1 of the public specification can be found at *http://www.w3.org/TR/wsdl.*

To illustrate the structure of a WSDL document, let's imagine we have a Web Service, called HelloService, which exposes a single method with the following method signature (shown here in C#):

```
String SayHello( String Name )
```

The idea is that the *SayHello()* method, when invoked, will return a string built by concatenating the constant string *Hello* with the *Name* parameter passed in the call. So, for example, SayHello(*Joe*) will return the string *Hello Joe*. Listing 7-2, sayhello_request.xml, is a sample SOAP request.

Listing 7-2 sayhello_request.xml: The SOAP message for the *SayHello* method.

```
<?xml version="1.0" encoding="utf-8"?>
<soap:Envelope xmlns:xsi="http://www.w3.org/2001/XMLSchema-instance"
xmlns:xsd="http://www.w3.org/2001/XMLSchema" xmlns:soap="http://
schemas.xmlsoap.org/soap/envelope/">
  <soap:Body>
    <SayHello xmlns="http://mspress.microsoft.com/corexml/">
      <Name>Joe</Name>
    </SayHello>
  </soap:Body>
</soap:Envelope>
```

As you can see, this is just a standard SOAP message using the RPC encoding rules we saw previously when discussing SOAP. Listing 7-3 is a possible SOAP response for our request.

Listing 7-3 sayhello_response.xml: A response message for sayhello_request.xml.

```
<?xml version="1.0" encoding="utf-8"?>
<soap:Envelope xmlns:xsi="http://www.w3.org/2001/XMLSchema-instance"
xmlns:xsd="http://www.w3.org/2001/XMLSchema" xmlns:soap="http://
schemas.xmlsoap.org/soap/envelope/">
  <soap:Body>
```

(continued)

Listing 7-3 *continued*

```
    <SayHelloResponse xmlns="http://mspress.microsoft.com/corexml/">
      <SayHelloResult>Hello Joe</SayHelloResult>
    </SayHelloResponse>
  </soap:Body>
</soap:Envelope>
```

This response message returns the concatenated string *Hello Joe* to the SOAP client.

Now we need to talk about describing the service that handled this request and returned our response. To do so we must look at the specifics of the syntax as well as its overall semantics, or structure, in terms of XML. Every WSDL document starts off with the *<definitions>* root element, and under this are the following five major sections/elements:

- *<types>* Defines the data types that the Web Service operates on. The *<import>* element can be used in place of the *<types>* element to reference an external schema document.
- *<message>* Describes the format of the individual request and response messages. The types of the parameters can either be referenced from those defined in the *<types>* section or defined directly using the XML Schema default data types.
- *<portType>* Defines the request, response messages, or both (defined in the *<message>* section) that make up the individual methods (called *Web methods*) in a Web Service.
- *<binding>* Specifies the encoding and protocol used by the Web methods defined in the <portType> section.
- *<service>* Used to identify the name and physical location of a Web Service—in other words, the endpoint that services call, as well as any bindings the Web Service uses.

All of this probably sounds foreign to you, but hold tight. After we show you a quick example of describing our sample Web Service in WSDL, we're going to spend a few pages discussing each of these items.

To describe our service we will need a file called helloservice.wsdl (in Listing 7-4). This will be the WSDL document for our imaginary HelloService Web Service.

Now that we have an example under our belt, let's look at each of the WSDL elements in more detail.

Listing 7-4 helloservice.wsdl: A sample WSDL document.

```
<?xml version="1.0" encoding="utf-8"?>
<definitions name="HelloService" xmlns:xsd="http://www.w3.org/2001/
XMLSchema"
            xmlns:soap="http://schemas.xmlsoap.org/wsdl/soap/"
xmlns:tns="http://mspress.microsoft.com/corexml/"
xmlns="http://schemas.xmlsoap.org/wsdl/"
           targetNamespace="http://mspress.microsoft.com/corexml/">
  <types>
  <xsd:schema targetNamespace="http://mspress.microsoft.com/corexml/">
     <xsd:element name="SayHello">
       <xsd:complexType>
         <xsd:sequence>
           <xsd:element name="Name" type="xsd:string"/>
         </xsd:sequence>
       </xsd:complexType>
     </xsd:element>
     <xsd:element name="SayHelloResponse">
       <xsd:complexType>
         <xsd:sequence>
           <xsd:element name="SayHelloResult" type="xsd:string"/>
         </xsd:sequence>
       </xsd:complexType>
     </xsd:element>
    </xsd:schema>
  </types>
  <message name="SayHelloSoapIn">
    <part name="parameters" element="tns:SayHello"/>
  </message>
  <message name="SayHelloSoapOut">
    <part name="parameters" element="tns:SayHelloResponse"/>
  </message>
  <portType name="HelloServiceSoapPortType">
    <operation name="SayHello">
      <input message="tns:SayHelloSoapIn"/>
      <output message="tns:SayHelloSoapOut"/>
    </operation>
  </portType>
  <binding name="HelloServiceSoap" type="tns:HelloServiceSoapPort">
    <soap:binding transport="http://schemas.xmlsoap.org/soap/http"
style="rpc"/>
    <operation name="SayHello">
      <soap:operation soapAction="http://mspress.microsoft.com/
corexml/SayHello"/>
      <input>
        <soap:body use="literal"/>
      </input>
```

(continued)

Listing 7-4 *continued*

```
      <output>
        <soap:body use="literal"/>
      </output>
    </operation>
  </binding>
  <service name="HelloService">
    <port name="HelloServiceSoap" binding="tns:HelloServiceSoap">
      <soap:address location="http://localhost/HelloService.asmx"/>
    </port>
  </service>
</definitions>
```

Types

In WSDL, types are defined using XML Schema. The schema can either be embedded within the *<types>* element, or the *<import>* element can be used to reference an external schema document. In either case the schema itself will be identical.

In helloservice.wsdl we used XML Schema to define the types we need for the request and response SOAP messages. The following is a snippet of code from that file:

```
<types>
  <xsd:schema targetNamespace="http://mspress.microsoft.com/corexml/">
    <xsd:element name="SayHello">
      <xsd:complexType>
        <xsd:sequence>
          <xsd:element name="Name" type="xsd:string"/>
        </xsd:sequence>
      </xsd:complexType>
    </xsd:element>
    <xsd:element name="SayHelloResponse">
      <xsd:complexType>
        <xsd:sequence>
          <xsd:element name="SayHelloResult" type="xsd:string"/>
        </xsd:sequence>
      </xsd:complexType>
    </xsd:element>
  </xsd:schema>
</types>
```

This part of our document is standard XML Schema. For the request message we define that we will accept a single parameter called *Name*, and that it will be an XML Schema *xsd:string* type. For the response message we define the return value in *SayHelloResult*, and it is also of XML Schema *xsd:string* type.

> **Note** The *targetNameSpace*, *http://mspress.microsoft.com/corexml/*, matches the local type namespace (*tns*) declared for the WSDL. This tells the schema processor that the types defined in this schema are part of that namespace, and we can refer to them later using that namespace prefix.

> **Note** The *<types>* element is optional and is meant for defining complex types such as C# structures. For simple types, such as our *Name* parameter, you can omit this section all together and use XML Schema directly when you need to reference the parameter types in the *<message>* section. We will show you how when we discuss the *<message>* section later.

Instead of embedding a schema definition directly in a WSDL document, you can alternatively use the *<import>* element to reference an external schema. The following shows an example use of the *<import>* element:

```
<definitions name="HelloService" xmlns:xsd="http://www.w3.org/2001/
XMLSchema"
             xmlns:soap="http://schemas.xmlsoap.org/wsdl/soap/"
             xmlns:tns="http://mspress.microsoft.com/corexml/"
             xmlns="http://schemas.xmlsoap.org/wsdl/"
             targetNamespace="http://mspress.microsoft.com/corexml/">
  <import location=http://mspress.microsoft.com/corexml/
HelloService.xsd/>
</definitions>
```

In this example you can see we used the location attribute to specify the actual URL that can be used to import the schema.

Message

A *<message>* element corresponds to a single piece of information exchanged between the client and the service. A typical request-response method call has two corresponding messages, one for the request and one for the response.

The name attribute is used to uniquely identify a specific message so it can be referenced in the *<portType>* section later. The subelement *<part>* is used to define the name and type for a single method parameter or return value. For example, in helloservice.wsdl the following message defines that a message called *SayHelloSoapIn* has a single parameter of a complex type, called *SayHello*, which is defined in the *<types>* section:

```
<message name="SayHelloSoapIn">
   <part name="parameters" element="tns:SayHello"/>
</message>
```

The element attribute is used to reference types defined in the *<types>* section. However, if the type of a parameter can be expressed as an XML Schema datatype, you can use the type attribute instead. The following is an example:

```
<message name="SayHelloSoapIn">
   <part name="parameters" type="xsd:string"/>
</message>
```

Here we have declared that our parameter is a simple string type. If all your parameters can be defined using the Schema default data types, you can omit the *<types>* section altogether.

A WSDL document needs to declare *<message>* sections for all the possible ways that the Web methods can be invoked, and all the possible responses. For example, if your Web Services support protocols other than SOAP, such as HTTP GET and HTTP PUT, you will need to include those *<message>* sections as well.

PortType

The *<portType>* section identifies the set of operations and the messages involved with each of the operations that are exposed by a Web Service. A *<portType>* completes the interface definition part of a Web Service.

The *<operation>* section within a *<portType>* represents the definition of a specific Web method. The name attribute specifies the name of this Web method. Within the *<operation>* section we then find the *<input>* and *<output>* elements that reference the message types defined in the *<message>* sections to define the request and response messages, respectively. Depending on the presence and ordering of the *<input>* and *<output>* elements, four types of operations are possible.

- *<input>* A one-way, or write-only, method that accepts a request from a client but does not respond.
- *<input><output>* A request-response method that accepts a request from a client and sends this client a reply.
- *<output><input>* A solicit-response method that sends a message to the client and expects a reply back from the client.

- *<output>* A notification, or read-only, method that sends a message to a client.

For example, in helloservice.wsdl the *SayHello* Web method is defined as a request-response method.

```
<portType name="HelloServiceSoap">
  <operation name="SayHello">
    <input message="tns:SayHelloSoapIn"/>
    <output message="tns:SayHelloSoapOut"/>
  </operation>
</portType>
```

Binding

The *<binding>* section is used to specify the protocol details for the various operations defined in the *<portType>* section and to specify the on-the-wire representation of the messages. The content of the *<binding>* section is mostly specific to the protocol to which the *<portType>* is being bound, but every *<binding>* section will have the following structure:

```
<binding name="..." type="...">
  <!-- binding details for the portType to be bound -->
  <operation name="...">
    <!-- binding details for this operation -->
    <input>
      <!-- binding details for this message -->
    </input>
    <output>
      <!-- binding details for this message -->
    </output>
  </operation>
</binding>
```

Each *<binding>* element has a name attribute that uniquely identifies the binding. It also has a *type* attribute that specifies the *<portType>* element to which this particular binding applies.

First the binding details for the *<portType>* can be specified. Then you specify the binding parameters for each of the operations defined in the *<portType>* section specified in the type attribute. Finally you specify the binding details for each of the input messages, output messages, or both defined (in the same order) in the original *<portType>*. Most Web Services will use SOAP as the wire protocol and, therefore, the SOAP request-response operation is the typical binding type. For example, here is the *<binding>* section for HelloService, which is a SOAP-based Web Service:

```
<binding name="HelloServiceSoap" type="tns:HelloServiceSoapPortType">
    <soap:binding transport="http://schemas.xmlsoap.org/soap/http"
```

```
style="rpc"/>
    <operation name="SayHello">
      <soap:operation soapAction="http://mspress.microsoft.com/
corexml/SayHello"/>
      <input>
        <soap:body use="literal"/>
      </input>
      <output>
        <soap:body use="literal"/>
      </output>
    </operation>
  </binding>
```

The SOAP binding parameters are specified using four basic elements, all of which belong to the *http://schemas.xmlsoap.org/wsdl/soap/namespace*. The *<soap:binding>* element is used to specify details about the transport used. The transport attribute specifies the transport protocol (HTTP, SMTP, FTP, and so forth) used and is specified using a standard URI. The *style* attribute specifies whether the operation specified by this *<portType>* is RPC- or document-oriented. This element must be placed before any *<operation>* elements.

For SOAP-over-HTTP binding the *<soap:operation>* element is used to specify the SOAPAction header of the HTTP request. The *<soap:body>* and the *<soap:header>* elements can be used within both the *<input>* and *<output>* elements and to specify how the messages they represent appear inside the *<Header>* and *<Body>* elements of the SOAP *<Envelope>* element.

Further details of these and other binding elements for other protocols are beyond the scope of this book, but you can refer to the WSDL specifications at *http://msdn.microsoft.com/xml/general/wsdl.asp* if you're interested.

Service

The final section, *<service>*, is used for the collection of bindings that make up a service and also to attach these to physical addresses. This element has a single attribute, *name*, that is used to uniquely identify the Web Service. One or more *<port>* elements within it can be used to specify the different bindings and the associated operations that this Web Service supports. The binding attribute specifies the name of the *<binding>* section to use. Each *<port>* element will contain elements from the binding-specific namespace, for example, *<soap:address>*, that are used to specify the addressing details in the form needed by that particular binding.

In helloservice.wsdl our *<service>* section specifies that we support only one binding, namely HelloServiceSoap, and that the associated operations can be accessed at *http://localhost/HelloService.asmx*.

```
<service name="HelloService">
    <port name="HelloServiceSoap" binding="tns:HelloServiceSoap">
      <soap:address location="http://localhost/HelloService.asmx"/>
    </port>
  </service>
```

> **Note** Although nothing will prevent you from manually writing the WSDL for your Web Services, you should realize that certain tools, such as ASP.NET and the IBM Web Services Toolkit, can help you generate WSDL automatically.

Creating a Web Service

In this section we will show you how you can implement a Web Service and how to invoke methods exposed by the service. We first use the tools provide by the .NET Framework, such as ASP.NET, to implement the service. In later sections, to illustrate the language-independent nature of Web Services, we will show you how you can build consumers, that are not .NET, that can invoke the services provided by the .NET provider.

> **Note** At the time of this writing the Microsoft .NET Framework SDK is still beta software. The examples here were tested on beta 2 of .NET SDK. You can download the .NET SDK and find information on .NET at the Microsoft MSDN site *(http://msdn.microsoft.com/net/).*

Although we have more complex examples in this book, we will use ASP.NET to build a simple Web Services provider and consumer. As you will see, ASP.NET makes creating Web Services almost effortless, which should interest all developers.

Our example provides stock quote information over the Web. Of course, we will not be providing actual real-time stock prices and information in this example, that is clearly beyond the scope of this book, but we will provide some hard-coded stock information.

Creating the Provider

Creating a Web Service provider can be summarized as a four-step process. In the first step we will need to create a new source file for the provider. This file will serve as the entry point to our service. The source file will be a plain text file with an .asmx extension (as opposed to an .aspx extension for an ASP.NET Web application). You need to place this file in an Internet Information Server (IIS) virtual directory that has the executescripts permission turned on.

The first line of this file should contain the special ASP.NET directive:

```
<%@ webservice %>
```

This directive allows you to declare the programming language used to develop this provider and the name of the implementation class. You have the option to include this implementation class in the same file, but that is not a requirement.

Next we will need to instruct our implementation to inherit from the *WebService* class found in the *System.Web.Services* namespace. By inheriting from *WebService*, your provider can gain access to common ASP.NET objects such as *Application*, *Session*, *User*, and *Context*. If you want your provider to be publicly consumed via the Web, you must specify an XML namespace for your Web Service. This task is accomplished by tagging the implementation class with the appropriate namespace attribute. ASP.NET uses the value of this attribute in the WSDL document and the SOAPAction HTTP header field to uniquely identify the Web-callable endpoints. If you don't specify a namespace attribute, ASP.NET uses a default value of *http://tempuri.org/*. Finally any methods you want to be accessible via the Web should be tagged with the *WebMethod* attribute.

The stockservice.asmx file in Listing 7-5 contains the code for our example stock quotes Web Service provider. StockService is designed to return the stock quote information given a stock code. For now, don't worry about how this service can be invoked. We will get to that in a later section when we show you how to implement a consumer for this service.

Listing 7-5 stockservice.asmx: A sample ASP.NET Web Service that returns stock information.

```
<%@ webservice language="C#" class="StockService" %>
using System;
using System.Collections;
using System.Web;
using System.Web.Services;
[WebService(Namespace="http://mspress.microsoft.com/corexml/")]
public class StockService : WebService
{
```

```
  /* Hashtable used to store our sample stocks */
  private static Hashtable Stocks;
  public StockService()
  {
    StockInfo si;
    /* the following code populates our Stocks Hashtable with some
sample stocks */
    Stocks = new Hashtable();
    si = new StockInfo();
    si.Code = "MSFT";
    si.Company = "Microsoft Corporation";
    si.Sector = "Technology";
    si.Industry = "Software and Programming";
    si.Price = 73.00;
    Stocks.Add( si.Code, si );
    si = new StockInfo();
    si.Code = "IBM";
    si.Company = "Int'l Business Machines";
    si.Sector = "Technology";
    si.Industry = "Computer Hardware";
    si.Price = 113.00;
    Stocks.Add( si.Code, si );
    si = new StockInfo();
    si.Code = "GE";
    si.Company = "General Electric Company";
    si.Sector = "Conglomerates";
    si.Industry = "Conglomerates";
    si.Price = 48.00;
    Stocks.Add( si.Code, si );
    si = new StockInfo();
    si.Code = "SONY";
    si.Company = "Sony Corporation";
    si.Sector = "Consumer Cyclical";
    si.Industry = "Audio & Video Equipment";
    si.Price = 65.80;
    Stocks.Add( si.Code, si );
  }
  /* returns StockInfo object for a given stock code */
  [WebMethod(Description="Returns company info and current quote
price for a given stock code",EnableSession=false)]
  public StockInfo GetStockInfo( string Code )
  {
    return ( InternalGetStockInfo( Code ) );
  }
  /* returns the quote price for a given stock code */
  [WebMethod(Description="Returns current quote price for a given
stock code",EnableSession=false)]
  public double GetQuotePrice( string Code )
  {
```

(continued)

Listing 7-5 *continued*

```
    StockInfo si = InternalGetStockInfo( Code );
    if ( si.Code.Equals( Code ) )
    {
      return ( si.Price );
    }
    else
    {
      return ( 0.00 );
    }
  }
  /* Internal method that returns a StockInfo object for a given
stock code. Note that in a real application, you will probably be
calling another service or querying a database here to obtain the
information. */
  private StockInfo InternalGetStockInfo( string Code )
  {
    StockInfo si;
    if ( Stocks.ContainsKey( Code ) )
    {
      si = (StockInfo)Stocks[ Code ];
    }
    else
    {
      si = new StockInfo();
      si.Code = "";
      si.Company = "";
      si.Sector = "";
      si.Industry = "";
      si.Price = 0.00;
    }
    return ( si );
  }
}

/* struct used to hold stock information */
public struct StockInfo
{
  public string Code;
  public string Company;
  public string Sector;
  public string Industry;
  public double Price;
}
```

The first line contains the Web Service ASP.NET directive, where we declare that our provider is written in C# and the implementation class is called *StockService*.

```
<%@ webservice language="C#" class="StockService" %>
```

Next we import the necessary libraries. In our case these are the *System*, *System.Collections*, *System.Web*, and *System.Web.Services* namespaces. The *System.Web* and *System.Web.Services* namespaces reference the ASP.NET and Web Services objects and types. The *System.Collections* namespace contains the *Hashtable* class that we're going to use to store the stock information.

We declare our implementation class, *StockService*, to inherit from the *WebService* class. We have also tagged our Web Service with an XML namespace called *http://mspress.microsoft.com/corexml/*. For your Web Services you should substitute this with your personal or your company's XML namespace.

```
[WebService(Namespace="http://mspress.microsoft.com/corexml/")]
public class StockService : WebService
```

For this example we used a *Hashtable* to store our stock information. The *StockService* constructor initializes this *Hashtable* with a few sample stocks. Note that we've used a C# struct for storing the various pieces of data that constitute our stock information. This struct, called *StockInfo*, is declared at the bottom of the StockService.asmx file.

Methods of an implementation class do not automatically have the ability to be invoked over the Web. These are called Web methods. To define a Web method, apply the *WebMethod* attribute to any public methods that you want exposed as Web methods. Our Web Service has two Web methods, *GetStockInfo()* and *GetQuotePrice()*. *GetStockInfo()* returns a *StockInfo* struct for a given stock code and *GetQuotePrice()* returns the quote price for a given stock code.

Like many other attributes, the *WebMethod* attribute supports several optional properties, as shown in Table 7-2.

That's all you need for a simple Web Service! You don't even have to compile the source file. Simply place the StockService.asmx file in an IIS virtual directory and you can access your Web Service from any Web browser. For our example we use the default/root virtual directory, so our Web Service is accessible through the following URL:

```
http://localhost/StockService.asmx
```

Now that we've built our Web Service provider, let's look at how we can consume it.

Consuming Web Services

One of the many useful features provided automatically for you when you develop Web Services using ASP.NET is a built-in consumer you can use

Table 7-2 *WebMethod* Attributes

Property	Parameter	Description
BufferResponse	Boolean	Specifies whether this Web method's output made through the ASP.NET Response object is buffered.
CacheDuration	int	Specifies the time, in seconds, to keep this method's response. Default is not to cache (zero seconds).
Description	string	Provides a description for this Web method. This will be included in the WSDL.
EnableSession	Boolean	Specifies whether you want to use session state for this Web method. The default is true.
MessageName	string	Lets you specify a name for your Web method that is different from that specified in the implementation class. This is usually used for overloaded methods.
Transaction	enumerated (Disabled, NotSupported, Supported, Required, RequiresNew)	Specifies the Transaction mode for this Web method. Default is Disabled.

interactively from any browser. Before we show you how you can build your own consumer, it is instructive to take a closer look at this default consumer first.

The Built-In ASP.NET Consumer

To see this built-in consumer in action for yourself, fire up your favorite browser and point it to our StockService.asmx URL. Figure 7-3 shows what you will see when you open this link in Microsoft Internet Explorer.

> **Note** This Web page is generated automatically through the use of reflection by ASP.NET with no coding required on your part.

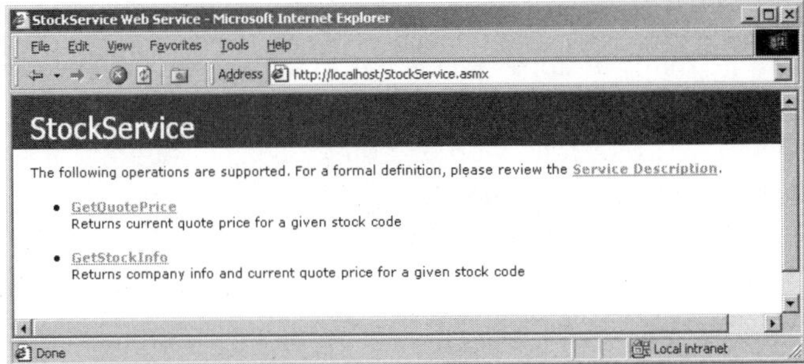

Figure 7-3 Calling StockService.asmx in Internet Explorer.

The first page, shown in Figure 7-3, lists all the Web methods you've defined in your Web Service as clickable links. These links will take you to the autogenerated pages that you can use to invoke these methods. In addition, this page also provides a link that generates the WSDL document for your Web Service. Figure 7-4 shows what you will see when you click on the Service Description link.

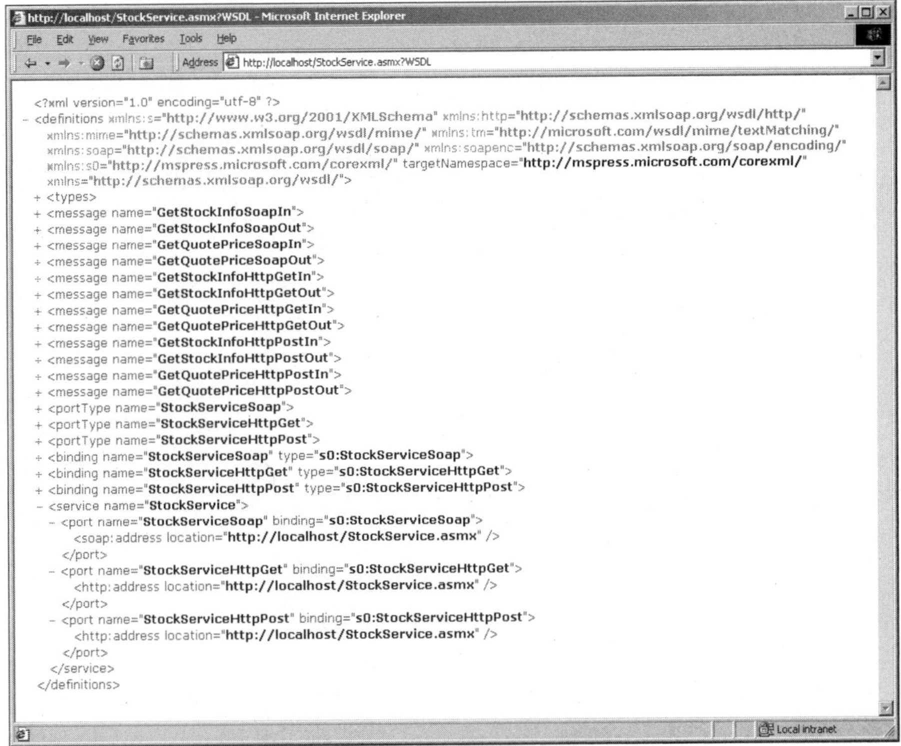

Figure 7-4 The autogenerated WSDL of StockService.

> **Note** Like so many features you've seen so far, this WSDL was generated automatically by ASP.NET. You simply write your Web Service and ASP.NET will use reflection to automatically generate the corresponding WSDL document for you.

If you click on one of the Web methods listed in Figure 7-4 you will see something like Figure 7-5 (which shows the page for the *GetStockInfo()* method).

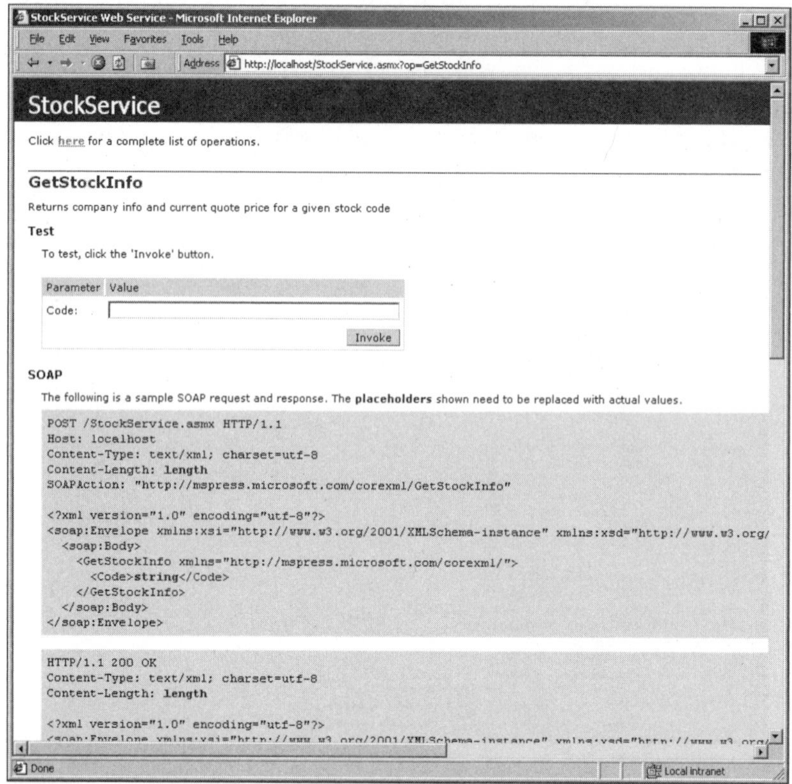

Figure 7-5 Invoking a Web method from Internet Explorer.

You should realize that this page is a true consumer in every right. This consumer, which can be a great tool for testing, uses HTTP GET to communicate with your Web Service provider. It provides an HTML form to let you enter values for the parameters of the Web methods. In the case of our *GetStockInfo()*

Web method you can enter a value for the Code parameter. Figure 7-6 shows the resulting Web page when we enter "MSFT" in the Code input box.

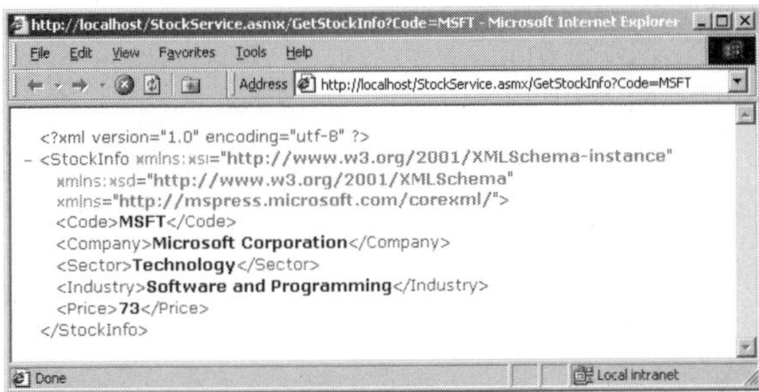

Figure 7-6 The result page generated by invoking the *GetStockInfo*() Web method in Internet Explorer.

> **Note** This is the response when you invoke your Web method using HTTP GET or HTTP POST, which is what this particular consumer uses. A SOAP response will be slightly different.

Going back to the GetStockInfo Web method page shown in Figure 7-5, you see that, in addition to letting you invoke a Web method, you also get useful descriptions of how to access this particular method using SOAP, HTTP GET, and HTTP POST. You also see what their respective responses will look like. For example, this page shows that to invoke the *GetStockInfo()* method via SOAP, you must make the following HTTP transaction:

```
POST /StockService.asmx HTTP/1.1
Host: localhost
Content-Type: text/xml; charset=utf-8
Content-Length: length
 SOAPAction: "http://mspress.microsoft.com/corexml/GetStockInfo"
<?xml version="1.0" encoding="utf-8"?>
<soap:Envelope xmlns:xsi="http://www.w3.org/2001/XMLSchema-instance"
xmlns:xsd="http://www.w3.org/2001/XMLSchema" xmlns:soap=
"http://schemas.xmlsoap.org/soap/envelope/">
  <soap:Body>
    <GetStockInfo xmlns="http://mspress.microsoft.com/corexml/">
      <Code>string</Code>
    </GetStockInfo>
  </soap:Body>
</soap:Envelope>
```

As you can see, the built-in ASP.NET consumer is feature rich. However, it is intended for interactive use, not for programmatic access. To be able to access the StockService Web Service programmatically, we need to create our own consumer.

Writing our own consumer might look like a daunting task on the surface, especially when you consider that a truly useful consumer will need to deal with factors like SOAP and WSDL directly. Luckily, ASP.NET comes to our rescue once again. Now let's learn how we can use the features and tools provided by the .NET Framework.

Creating a .NET Consumer

Implementing a consumer using the .NET Framework is surprisingly simple. The task is greatly simplified through the use of proxy classes, which contain built-in functionality to automatically handle all the gory details of invoking XML Web services, such as making HTTP requests and constructing and parsing SOAP messages. The goal is to invoke services as easily as you would invoke local objects. The great feature in .NET is that you don't have to create these proxy classes for your services. .NET provides several tools to help you generate proxy classes to XML Web services automatically; one of them is wsdl.exe.

The following command line shows how we can use wsdl.exe to generate a proxy class for our StockService Web Service. The wsdl.exe application uses the information found in this WSDL document to build a proxy class tailored to your Web Service specifications.

```
wsdl /language:cs /protocol:soap http://localhost/StockService.asmx?wsdl
```

This command line will generate a proxy class file called StockService.cs. The first parameter, */language:cs*, indicates that we want to generate a proxy class written in C#. The second parameter, */protocol:soap*, specifies that the generated proxy class will use the SOAP protocol to talk to the StockService WebService. Other valid values are *httpget* and *httppost* for the HTTP protocol GET and POST methods. The last parameter specifies the location of the WSDL document for StockService. This can be a URL or a local file specification.

Even though our StockService.cs proxy class is written in C#, by compiling this into a DLL, you can use this proxy from consumers developed in .NET-supported languages. The following command line uses the C# csc.exe compiler to compile the StockService.cs proxy class into a DLL:

```
csc /t:library /r:system.web.services.dll StockService.cs
```

Running this command line will generate a StockService DLL file that you can reference in your consumer projects. Armed with the StockService proxy class, writing a consumer for our StockService Web Service is almost trivial. Listing 7-6, net_consumer.cs, shows an example of such as a consumer.

Listing 7-6 net_consumer.cs: A .NET consumer of the StockService Web Service.

```
using System;
public class TestStockService
{
  public static void Main( string[] Args )
  {
    /* make sure the user has specified a stock code */
    if ( Args.Length < 1 )
    {
      Console.WriteLine( "usage: teststockservice stock_code" );
      return;
    }
    /* sc contains the user specified stock code */
    string sc = Args[ 0 ];
    /* Instantiate the StockService's proxy class */
    StockService ss = new StockService ();
    /* Invoke GetBooks() over SOAP and get the data set. */
    StockInfo si = ss.GetStockInfo( sc );
    /* Display the results */
    Console.Write( "Stock Code: " ); Console.WriteLine( si.Code );
    Console.Write( "Company   : " ); Console.WriteLine( si.Company );
    Console.Write( "Industry  : " ); Console.WriteLine( si.Industry );
    Console.Write( "Sector    : " ); Console.WriteLine( si.Sector );
    Console.Write( "Price     : " ); Console.WriteLine( si.Price );
  }
}
```

NET_Consumer.cs is a simple console application that, given a stock code specified on the command line, will display the respective stock information. See how we access the StockService Web Service by simply using the *new* operator to instantiate an instance of the *StockService* class?

```
StockService ss = new StockService ();
```

The *ss* variable now holds a reference to StockService, which can now be used to access all the Web methods exposed by the StockService Web Service. For example, in NET_Consumer.cs, to invoke the *GetStockInfo()* Web method we simply invoke the corresponding method in the proxy.

```
StockInfo si = ss.GetStockInfo( sc );
```

The rest of NET_Consumer.cs then displays the information returned in the *StockInfo* struct. To compile NET_Consumer.cs, enter the following command line in a console window:

```
csc /r:System.dll /r:StockService.dll NET_Consumer.cs
```

We've included a reference to the StockService DLL file we generated earlier. This instructs the compiler to link in the proxy class with NET_Consumer.cs. Figure 7-7 shows a sample output of compiling and running NET_Consumer.cs so you can see what to expect.

You've now seen how easy it is to create a consumer using ASP.NET. But what if you cannot use .NET because your consumer needs to run in an environment that is not .NET?

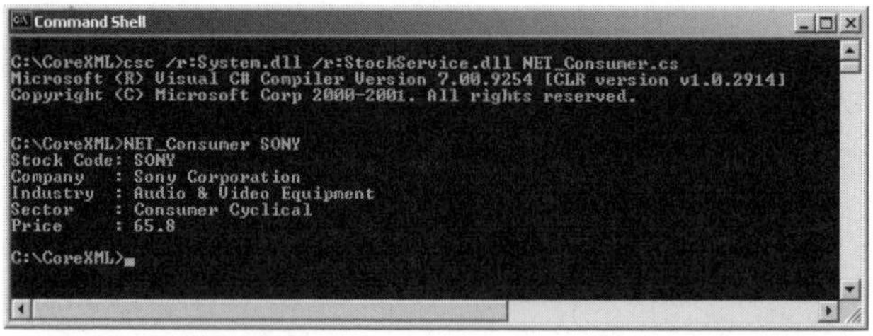

Figure 7-7 An example output of NET_Consumer.exe.

Creating a Non-.NET Consumer

It would be limiting if Web Services developed using the .NET Framework could be accessed only by a .NET-based consumer. Of course, nothing is further from the truth. You can access .NET-based Web Services from any consumer as long as they adhere to the Web Services specifications. In fact, when it comes to support for SOAP and Web Services, you'll find no shortage of available development toolkits from both commercial and non commercial vendors. To give you a leg up on finding some of these tools, Table 7-3 lists some of the currently available toolkits plus their descriptions and Web sites.

In our example we will use the SOAP Toolkit 2 to develop a consumer for our StockService Web Service. We will also use VBScript as the programming language for implementing this consumer. The code for this consumer can be found in Listing 7-7, soap_toolkit_consumer.vbs.

Listing 7-7 soap_toolkit_consumer.vbs: A sample consumer using the SOAP Toolkit.

```
' instantiate MSSOAP object
set SoapClient = CreateObject( "MSSOAP.SoapClient" )
' setup client proxy from the StockService's WSDL
```

```
call SoapClient.MSSoapInit( "http://localhost/
StockService.asmx?wsdl" )
' at this point you can access all the methods exposed by
' StockService through the SoapClient proxy object
' ask user for the stock code
code = InputBox( "Enter Stock Code" )
' invoke the GetQuotePrice method and display the result
WScript.Echo "Price = " & SoapClient.GetQuotePrice( UCase( code ) )
```

Table 7-3 Some SOAP/Web Services Toolkits

Toolkit	Language/Platform	Web Page URL
Microsoft SOAP Toolkit	Can be used by any COM-compatible languages/systems such as Microsoft Visual Basic, Borland Delphi, and so forth	*http://msdn.microsoft.com/library/en-us/soap/htm/soap_overview_3drm.asp*
IBM Web Services Toolkit (WSTK)	Java 2	*http://www.alphaworks.ibm.com/tech/webservicestoolkit*
Apache SOAP	Java 2	*http://xml.apache.org/soap/index.html*
SOAP:Lite	Perl	*http://www.soaplite.com*
Web Services for Python	Python	*http://sourceforge.net/projects/pywebsvcs/*

When soap_toolkit_consumer.vbs is run it will first ask you for the stock code and then display a response. Figure 7-8 shows the message box displayed in a sample response.

Figure 7-8 Running soap_toolkit_consumer.vbs.

As you can see, implementing a basic consumer using the SOAP Toolkit can be extremely easy. You just point it to a WSDL document when you initialize the proxy object through its *MSSoapInit* method. The proxy automatically loads and interprets the WSDL and builds a COM IDispatch interface.

If, for some remote reason, you can't find a toolkit that suits your needs, you can always roll one of your own. After all, it's just HTTP and XML. As an example, the following ASP application in Listing 7-8 uses the XMLHTTP and DOM objects provided by the MSXML version 2 parser to access the StockService Web Service.

Listing 7-8 asp_consumer.asp: An ASP consumer for the StockService Web Service.

```
<%
  ' retrieve submitted Stock Code value
  sCode = "" & Request.Form( "pName" )
%>
<form method="post" action="asp_consumer.asp">
  Enter Stock Code:<br>
  <input name="pName" value="<%= sCode %>"> <input type="submit"
value="Submit">
</form>
<hr>
<br>
<%
  '
  if ( sCode <> "" ) then
    ' we are going to use the MS XMLHTTP object
    set oXmlHttp = Server.CreateObject( "MSXML2.XMLHTTP" )
    ' open a HTTP POST connection to StockService
    oXmlHttp.Open "POST", "http://localhost/StockService.asmx",
False
    ' setup HTTP headers.
    oXmlHttp.SetRequestHeader "Content-Type", "text/xml"
    oXmlHttp.SetRequestHeader "SOAPAction",
               "http://mspress.microsoft.com/corexml/GetStockInfo"
    ' build string to hold the SOAP request message
    sSOAPMsg =
      "<soap:Envelope " & _
      " xmlns:xsi=""http://www.w3.org/2001/XMLSchema-instance""" & _
      " xmlns:xsd=""http://www.w3.org/2001/XMLSchema""" & _
      " xmlns:soap=""http://schemas.xmlsoap.org/soap/envelope/"">" & _
      "  <soap:Body>" & _
      "    <GetStockInfo " &
      "      xmlns=""http://mspress.microsoft.com/corexml/"">" & _
      "      <Code>" & sCode & "</Code>" & _
      "    </GetStockInfo>" & _
```

```
        "  </soap:Body>" & _
        "</soap:Envelope>"
      ' call StockService
      oXMLHTTP.Send sSOAPMsg
      ' retrieve response as a DOM object
      set oResponseDOM = oXmlHttp.ResponseXML
      ' extract the StockInfo node values
      set oNode =
        oResponseDOM.SelectSingleNode( "//GetStockInfoResult/Code" )
      sCode = oNode.Text
      set oNode =
       oResponseDOM.SelectSingleNode( "//GetStockInfoResult/Company" )
      sCompany = oNode.Text
      set oNode =
       oResponseDOM.SelectSingleNode( "//GetStockInfoResult/Industry" )
      sIndustry = oNode.Text
      set oNode =
        oResponseDOM.SelectSingleNode( "//GetStockInfoResult/Sector" )
      sSector = oNode.Text
      set oNode =
        oResponseDOM.SelectSingleNode( "//GetStockInfoResult/Price" )
      sPrice = oNode.Text
    end if
%>
<table border="1">
  <tr>
    <td>
      Code:
    </td>
    <td>
      <%= sCode %>
    </td>
  </tr>
  <tr>
    <td>
      Company:
    </td>
    <td>
      <%= sCompany %>
    </td>
  </tr>
  <tr>
    <td>
      Industry:
    </td>
    <td>
      <%= sIndustry %>
    </td>
  </tr>
```

(continued)

Listing 7-8 *continued*

```
  <tr>
    <td>
      Sector:
    </td>
    <td>
      <%= sSector %>
    </td>
  </tr>
  <tr>
    <td>
      Price:
    </td>
    <td>
      <%= sPrice %>
    </td>
  </tr>
</table>
```

ASP_Consumer.asp features an HTML form to let you enter the stock code you want to query and a table that displays the results of invoking the Stock-Service Web Service. Figure 7-9 shows what ASP_Consumer.asp looks like when loaded in a browser.

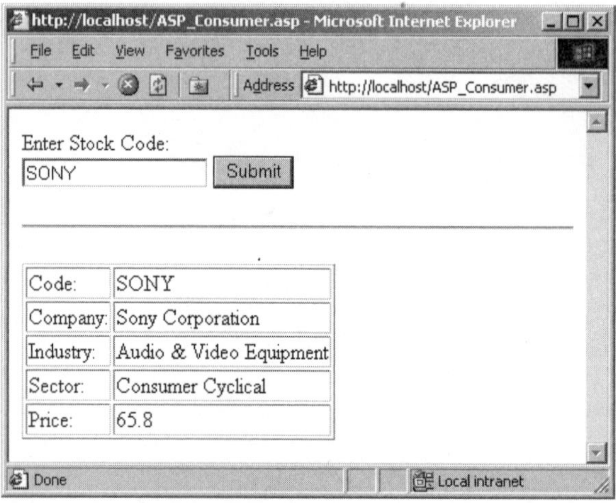

Figure 7-9 Running ASP_Consumer.asp.

In this example we use the *MSXML XMLHTTP* object to handle the HTTP POST transactions we need to make to invoke StockService. This task is accomplished in the following line of code:

```
oXmlHttp.Open "POST", "http://localhost/StockService.asmx", False
```

Next we set up *Content-Type* and *SOAPAction* HTTP header directives as required by the SOAP specifications:

```
    oXmlHttp.SetRequestHeader "Content-Type", "text/xml"
    oXmlHttp.SetRequestHeader "SOAPAction", "http://
mspress.microsoft.com/corexml/GetStockInfo"
```

The only task left to do now to invoke StockService is to build the SOAP *<envelope>* and send the HTTP POST request.

> **Note** *SOAPAction* uses the same XML namespace we specified using the namespace attribute in the StockServer.asmx.

```
sSOAPMsg =
 "<soap:Envelope " & _
 " xmlns:xsi=""http://www.w3.org/2001/XMLSchema-instance""" & _
 " xmlns:xsd=""http://www.w3.org/2001/XMLSchema""" & _
 " xmlns:soap=""http://schemas.xmlsoap.org/soap/envelope/"">" & _
 "  <soap:Body>" & _
 "    <GetStockInfo " &
 "      xmlns=""http://mspress.microsoft.com/corexml/"">" & _
 "      <Code>" & sCode & "</Code>" & _
 "    </GetStockInfo>" & _
 "  </soap:Body>" & _
 "</soap:Envelope>"

 ' call StockService
 oXMLHTTP.Send sSOAPMsg
```

When the call is completed, we retrieve the SOAP response as a DOM object using the XMLHTTP ResponseXML property. Finally we extract the *StockInfo* field values using XPath and display them in an HTML table.

As you can see, invoking Web Services is not overly complicated, even without special tools. However, this approach is only appropriate for accessing simple Web Services because it can quickly become tedious and unmanageable for even slightly more complicated Web Services.

Discovering Web Services with UDDI

So far we've covered how we can describe, implement and deploy Web Services. But our work is only half done. How will clients find these Web Services on the Internet? Just like people use the yellow pages and search engines to locate Web pages, we need a way for applications and people to locate and discover the capabilities of Web Services. This is where UDDI comes in.

The Specification

The UDDI specification was jointly developed by IBM, Microsoft, and Ariba as an open standard for advertising and discovering Web Services. The UDDI specification defines a Web-based registry framework that exposes information about a business and the services it provide. The framework consists of two parts:

- An XML Schema *(http://www.uddi.org/schema/uddi_1.xsd)* that defines data structures that can be used to perform inquiry and publishing functions against any UDDI-compliant registries.
- A set of SOAP-based APIs that provides a programmatic interface for interacting with any UDDI-compliant registries.

A UDDI Business Registry is an implementation of the UDDI registry framework. Additionally, a UDDI Business Registry provides an HTML-based interface to allow businesses to nonprogrammatically describe themselves and the Web Services they provide and for businesses to locate other potential partners. At the time of this writing, three Web sites provide the UDDI Business Registry service:

- The Microsoft UDDI Business Registry at *http://uddi.microsoft.com*
- The IBM UDDI Business Registry at *http://www.ibm.com/services/uddi/*
- The Ariba UDDI Business Registry at *http://uddi.ariba.com*

As you can see, these are also the same three companies that developed the UDDI specification.

> **Note** You can find the specifications and other useful information and resources related to UDDI at *http://www.uddi.org.*

The UDDI Data Model

UDDI organizes the information stored in a UDDI registry into three broad categories. These types of information are represented by three corresponding UDDI data structures. These categories are as follows:

- White Pages contain simple information about a business such as the name, address, contact, and other known identifiers.
- Yellow Pages include industrial categorizations based on standard taxonomies as well as descriptive information about the services provided.
- Green Pages contain the technical information about the services, including references and interfaces to the services.

Figure 7-10 illustrates this data model.

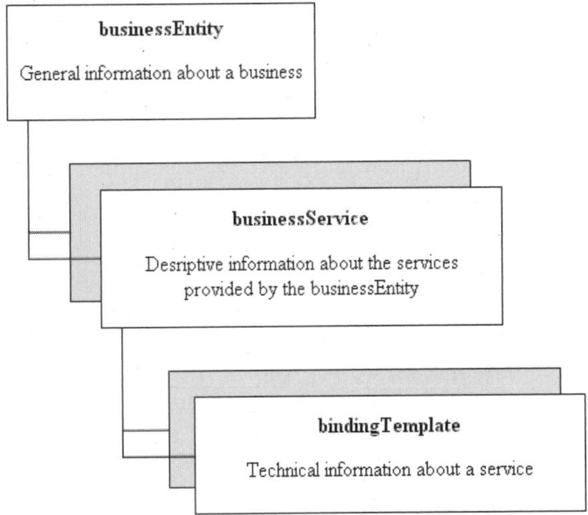

Figure 7-10 UDDI data structures.

These three structures, businessEntities, businessServices, bindingTemplates, represent the complete amount of information provided by the UDDI framework.

The API

The UDDI specification also defines a SOAP-based API that consists of 20 requests and 10 responses, each of which makes use of the data structures outlined previously. The API provides two levels of information. The high-level information returned by the *find* methods consists of general, summary-level data. The low-level information returned by the *get* methods contains specific, detail-level data.

For example, the information returned by the *find_business* UDDI method contains summary information, such as the names and addresses, of businesses that matched the search criteria provided when the method was issued. One of the pieces of information returned is the unique business registration identifier for each of the matching businesses. This identifier can be used with the low-level *get_business* method to get the entire business registration details.

Table 7-4 lists some of the more commonly used API methods and their corresponding response data structures.

Table 7-4 Common UDDI APIs

Method	Purpose	Response Data Structure
find_business	Locates businesses based on category, identity, registered URLs, or name.	businessList
find_service	Locates services based on category or name.	serviceList
find_binding	Locates a particular binding within a specific businessService structure.	bindingDetail
find_tModel	Locates summary information about the registered specifications and namespaces.	tModelList
get_businessDetail	Returns the entire detail of a business registration including all the associated businessServices and bindingTemplates.	bindingDetail
get_serviceDetail	Returns the detailed information of a businessService.	serviceDetail
get_bindingDetail	Returns detailed technical binding information for a registered service.	bindingDetail
get_tModelDetail	Returns complete tModel registration information such as the specifications used to create compatible Web Services.	tModelDetail

Let's say, for instance, that we wanted to find the business registration information of Microsoft. The following uddi_find_business.xml in Listing 7-9 is a UDDI request SOAP message containing a *find_business* method:

Listing 7-9 uddi_find_business.xml: A sample UDDI *find_business* method call.

```
<?xml version="1.0" encoding="UTF-8"?>
<Envelope xmlns="http://schemas.xmlsoap.org/soap/envelope/">
  <Body>
    <find_business generic="1.0" xmlns="urn:uddi-org:api">
      <name>Microsoft</name>
    </find_business>
  </Body>
</Envelope>
```

As you can see, this is just a normal SOAP request message containing a find_business method with a single parameter called *Name*. All UDDI messages belong to the *urn:uddi-org:api* namespace. A sample response of this method is shown in Listing 7-10, uddi_find_business_response.xml.

Listing 7-10 uddi_find_business_response.xml: A sample find_business response.

```
<businessList generic="1.0" operator="Microsoft Corporation"
    truncated="false" xmlns="urn:uddi-org:api">
  <businessInfos>
    <businessInfo businessKey="0076B468-EB27-42E5-AC09-
9955CFF462A3">
      <name>Microsoft Corporation</name>
    <description xml:lang="en">Empowering people through great
software any time, any place and on any device is Microsoft's vision.
As the worldwide leader in software for personal and business
computing, we strive to produce innovative products and services that
meet our customers. </description>
    <serviceInfos>
        <serviceInfo businessKey="0076B468-EB27-42E5-AC09-
9955CFF462A3"
                          serviceKey="1FFE1F71-2AF3-45FB-B788-
09AF7FF151A4">
          <name>Web services for smart searching</name>
        </serviceInfo>
        <serviceInfo businessKey="0076B468-EB27-42E5-AC09-
9955CFF462A3"
                       serviceKey="8BF2F51F-8ED4-43FE-B665-
38D8205D1333">
          <name>Electronic Business Integration Services</name>
        </serviceInfo>
        <serviceInfo businessKey="0076B468-EB27-42E5-AC09-
9955CFF462A3"
                       serviceKey="611C5867-384E-4FFD-B49C-
28F93A7B4F9B">
          <name>Volume Licensing Select Program</name>
        </serviceInfo>
```

(continued)

Listing 7-10 *continued*

```
        <serviceInfo businessKey="0076B468-EB27-42E5-AC09-
9955CFF462A3"
                    serviceKey="5DE3CE59-923E-42D3-B7FB-
34FC3C3CBC16">
          <name>Technet</name>
        </serviceInfo>
        <serviceInfo businessKey="0076B468-EB27-42E5-AC09-
9955CFF462A3"
                    serviceKey="24E553C3-7E3E-484A-8ECA-
80E0D0B4A91F">
          <name>Microsoft Developer Network</name>
        </serviceInfo>
        <serviceInfo businessKey="0076B468-EB27-42E5-AC09-
9955CFF462A3"
                    serviceKey="77DD86E5-CD70-4219-A28C-
37231EAF3901">
          <name>Online Shopping</name>
        </serviceInfo>
        <serviceInfo businessKey="0076B468-EB27-42E5-AC09-
9955CFF462A3"
                    serviceKey="0860E130-D4AF-4BD5-9F5C-
D7F6FA4B1AD8">
          <name>Home Page</name>
        </serviceInfo>
        <serviceInfo businessKey="0076B468-EB27-42E5-AC09-
9955CFF462A3"
                    serviceKey="D2BC296A-723B-4C45-9ED4-
494F9E53F1D1">
          <name>UDDI Web Services</name>
        </serviceInfo>
        <serviceInfo businessKey="0076B468-EB27-42E5-AC09-
9955CFF462A3"
                    serviceKey="A8E4999A-21A3-47FA-802E-
EE50A88B266F">
          <name>UDDI Web Sites</name>
        </serviceInfo>
      </serviceInfos>
    </businessInfo>
  </businessInfos>
</businessList>
```

For clarity, the response is shown without the SOAP *<envelope>*. You can see much summary-level information returned by the *find_business* method, including what services are supported by the matching business entities. Armed with this data, you can now use the *get* methods to obtain detailed information about a particular business entity or service.

You could use, for example, the following *get_serviceDetail* method (Listing 7-11), found in uddi_get_servicedetail.xml, to request detailed information for a specific service identified by a *serviceKey*.

Listing 7-11 uddi_get_servicedetail.xml: A sample get_serviceDetail method call.

```
<get_serviceDetail generic='1.0' xmlns='urn:uddi-org:api'>
  <serviceKey>D2BC296A-723B-4C45-9ED4-494F9E53F1D1</serviceKey>
</get_serviceDetail>
```

Listing 7-12, uddi_get_servicedetail_response.xml, is the corresponding response.

Listing 7-12 uddi_get_servicedetail_response.xml: A sample get_serviceDetail response.

```
<serviceDetail generic="1.0" operator="Microsoft Corporation"
    truncated="false" xmlns="urn:uddi-org:api">
  <businessService businessKey="0076B468-EB27-42E5-AC09-
9955CFF462A3"
    `              serviceKey="D2BC296A-723B-4C45-9ED4-494F9E53F1D1">
    <name>UDDI Web Services</name>
  <description xml:lang="en">UDDI SOAP/XML message-based program-
matic Web
  service interfaces.</description>
  <bindingTemplates>
    <bindingTemplate bindingKey="313C2BF0-021D-405C-8149-
25FD969F7F0B"
                     serviceKey="D2BC296A-723B-4C45-9ED4-
494F9E53F1D1">
      <description xml:lang="en">Production UDDI server,
      Publishing interface</description>
    <accessPoint URLType="https">https://uddi.microsoft.com/
publish</accessPoint>
    <tModelInstanceDetails>
      <tModelInstanceInfo tModelKey="uuid:64C756D1-3374-4E00-AE83-
EE12E38FAE63">
        <description xml:lang="en">UDDI SOAP Publication Interface
</description>
      </tModelInstanceInfo>
      </tModelInstanceDetails>
    </bindingTemplate>
    <bindingTemplate bindingKey="A9CAFBE4-11C6-4BFE-90F5-
595970D3DE24"
        serviceKey="D2BC296A-723B-4C45-9ED4-494F9E53F1D1">
      <description xml:lang="en">Production UDDI server, Inquiry
interface</description>
      <accessPoint URLType="http">http://uddi.microsoft.com/
inquire</accessPoint>
```

(continued)

Listing 7-12 *continued*

```
        <tModelInstanceDetails>
          <tModelInstanceInfo tModelKey="uuid:4CD7E4BC-648B-426D-9936-
443EAAC8AE23">
            <description xml:lang="en">UDDI SOAP Inquiry Interface
</description>
          </tModelInstanceInfo>
          </tModelInstanceDetails>
        </bindingTemplate>
      <bindingTemplate bindingKey="3FE6C834-293E-4341-AF6E-
41DC68949764"
                       serviceKey="D2BC296A-723B-4C45-9ED4-
494F9E53F1D1">
        <description xml:lang="en">Test UDDI server, Publishing
interface</description>
        <accessPoint URLType="https">https://test.uddi.microsoft.com/
publish</accessPoint>
        <tModelInstanceDetails>
          <tModelInstanceInfo tModelKey="uuid:64C756D1-3374-4E00-AE83-
EE12E38FAE63">
            <description xml:lang="en">UDDI SOAP Publication
Interface</description>
          </tModelInstanceInfo>
          <tModelInstanceInfo tModelKey="uuid:F372E009-F372-429C-A09A-
794113A5C5F9">
            <description xml:lang="en">urn:microsoft-com:test
signature-element signifies that this is a testing version of the
service</description>
            </tModelInstanceInfo>
          </tModelInstanceDetails>
        </bindingTemplate>
      <bindingTemplate bindingKey="8ED4AD10-C63B-495E-8969-
B3938F86E937"
                       serviceKey="D2BC296A-723B-4C45-9ED4-
494F9E53F1D1">
        <description xml:lang="en">Test UDDI server, Inquiry
interface</description>
        <accessPoint URLType="http">http://test.uddi.microsoft.com/
inquire</accessPoint>
        <tModelInstanceDetails>
          <tModelInstanceInfo tModelKey="uuid:4CD7E4BC-648B-426D-9936-
443EAAC8AE23">
            <description xml:lang="en">UDDI SOAP Inquiry Interface
</description>
          </tModelInstanceInfo>
          <tModelInstanceInfo tModelKey="uuid:F372E009-F372-429C-A09A-
794113A5C5F9">
            <description xml:lang="en">urn:microsoft-com:test
signature-element signifies that this is a testing version of the
service</description>
```

```
          </tModelInstanceInfo>
        </tModelInstanceDetails>
      </bindingTemplate>
    </bindingTemplates>
  <categoryBag>
    <keyedReference keyName="KEYWORD" keyValue="API"
        tModelKey="uuid:A035A07C-F362-44DD-8F95-E2B134BF43B4">
</keyedReference>
    <keyedReference keyName="KEYWORD" keyValue="SOAP"
        tModelKey="uuid:A035A07C-F362-44DD-8F95-E2B134BF43B4">
</keyedReference>
    <keyedReference keyName="KEYWORD" keyValue="XML"
        tModelKey="uuid:A035A07C-F362-44DD-8F95-E2B134BF43B4">
</keyedReference>
    </categoryBag>
  </businessService>
</serviceDetail>
```

We see a lot of detailed information about the service we requested in these examples. The important information for us, though, is the access points that specify the URLs that can be used to invoke the associated Web Services. Finally you can obtain the associated WSDL documents of these Web Services simply by appending a *?wsdl* character sequence to the end of any of these URLs.

Unfortunately, further details on the UDDI API are beyond the scope of this book. However, the UDDI Web site *(http://www.uddi.org)* is an excellent starting place to learn more about this important technology.

The BizTalk Framework Initiative

Most mature organizations have both legacy and new applications that were implemented independently and cannot easily interoperate directly because of differences in data formats, message structures, and protocols. B2B projects, such as supply chains, face equally daunting problems. Even if both suppliers and buyers shared the same enterprise systems, their data dictionaries, and other customizations probably evolved differently over time. The core problems in both scenarios are the lack of interoperable data definitions and encoding, protocols, and the knowledge of how to process the data across disparate systems.

Microsoft believes it has a solution that spans both a standard framework and a server suite of applications that help businesses describe their data and processes, as well as manage the messaging between integrated servers. This solution to some of the problems we discussed concerning EAI and B2B comes in the form of a set of schemas, guidelines, and software tools collectively called the Microsoft BizTalk Framework Initiative (BFI). Although the BFI was proposed and mostly designed by Microsoft, it is open to everyone.

The BFI consists of three main components:

- BizTalk Framework A set of guidelines and an XML tagging scheme for the construction of readable and reliable messages.
- *BizTalk.org* A community Web site that provides a standard industry schema repository and an information resource center concerning the BFI.
- BizTalk Server A BizTalk Framework compliant software system and suite of applications for providing robust and reliable application integration using XML-based messaging.

The BizTalk Framework

One of the most difficult problems faced by businesses engaged in application integration is the lack of established message schemas for integration purposes. Traditionally businesses used the EDI for integrating applications. However, these systems are generally large and complex and usually expensive to set up and maintain. In addition, businesses might be using different operating systems, communication protocols, and programming languages. All of these factors make application integration between businesses difficult, and until recently, only big organizations have attempted integrating their business processes with trading partners. The BizTalk Framework hopes to solve these issues by providing an open framework that can be used to develop standard message schemas. The core focus of the BizTalk Framework is the definition of the BizTalk document structure.

BizTalk Documents

A BizTalk document is an extension of a SOAP version 1.1 message with BizTalk-specific SOAP header elements (called BizTags) for enhanced message-handling semantics. Instead of an RPC method body, however, a BizTalk document's *<Body>* element contains an application-specific and well-formed XML document containing business data. This embedded XML document is called a business document in the BizTalk Framework specification. Examples include a purchase order, invoice, product catalog, or any other business document.

Listing 7-13 shows sample_biztalk_document.xml, a sample BizTalk document. This document contains a purchase order placement request. This code is essentially a SOAP 1.1 compliant message with a header that contains BizTags and a body that contains an application-specific document.

Listing 7-13 sample_biztalk_document.xml: A sample BizTalk document.

```
<soap:Envelope
   xmlns:soap="http://schemas.xmlsoap.org/soap/envelope/"
   xmlns:xsi="http://www.w3.org/1999/XMLSchema-instance">
  <soap:Header>
   <eps:endpoints soap:mustUnderstand="1"
       xmlns:eps="http://schemas.biztalk.org/btf-2-0/endpoints"
      xmlns:biz="http://schemas.biztalk.org/btf-2-0/address/types">
     <eps:to>
       <eps:address xsi:type="biz:OrganizationName">ACME
</eps:address>
     </eps:to>
     <eps:from>
       <eps:address xsi:type="biz:OrganizationName">CoreXML
</eps:address>
     </eps:from>
   </eps:endpoints>
   <prop:properties soap:mustUnderstand="1"
       xmlns:prop="http://schemas.biztalk.org/btf-2-0/properties">
     <prop:identity>uuid:74b9f5d0-33fb-4a81-b02b-5b760641c1d6
</prop:identity>
     <prop:sentAt>2001-08-21T04:54:00-10:00</prop:sentAt>
     <prop:expiresAt>2001-08-22T04:54:00-10:00</prop:expiresAt>
     <prop:topic>purchase_order</prop:topic>
   </prop:properties>
   </soap:Header>
   <soap:Body>
       <po:PurchaseOrder xmlns:po="http://mspress.microsoft.com/
corexml/">
           <po:ProductID>BX0071801</po:ProductID>
       </po:PurchaseOrder>
   </soap:Body>
</soap:Envelope>
```

Note The current version of the BizTalk Framework uses the *http://www.w3.org/1999/XMLSchema-instance* XML Schema URI instead of the current *http://www.w3c.org/2001/XMLSchema-instance* because the specification was released before XML Schema became a W3C Recommendation.

BizTags

The BizTalk Framework defines four main groups of BizTags. The first group represents the source and destination of the interchange. This is specified by the *<endpoints>* BizTag. This BizTag is mandatory and must appear exactly once, and it consists of *<to>* and *<from>* subelements, each of which, in turn, contains a single *<address>* subelement.

Next the *<properties>* BizTag contains document identify information and other properties that describe the document. This BizTag is also mandatory and must appear exactly once. The *<properties>* element is also used to control the scheduling of a document through its *<sentAt>* and *<expiresAt>* subelements.

Following the *<properties>* element, we have the *<services>* element. The primary purpose of the *<services>* BizTag is to allow applications invoked in message interchange to request receipt acknowledgment from the consumer. The BizTalk Framework supports two kinds of receipts: the delivery receipt and the commitment receipt. Both are BizTalk documents with the addition of a special *<deliveryReceipt>* BizTag for conveying information related to the receipts, such as the identity of the target recipient and the expiration date.

The *<manifest>* BizTag serves to catalog all the contents of a multipart BizTalk message consisting of either multiple business documents or attachments that might not be XML files, such as JPEG images. A multipart BizTalk message must be encoded in a MIME structure the follows the rules of the multipart/related MIME content type.

Finally we have the *<process>* BizTag that provides process-management information that can help the recipient service relate this exchange with an ongoing business process. Together, all these BizTags allow BizTalk documents to be used for reliable and efficient routing message interchange.

BizTalk.org

BizTalk.org is a Web site (*http://www.biztalk.org*) hosted and managed by Microsoft to promote the adoption of BFI. The site has two main purposes. First it serves as an XML schema repository. Second it's a community and resource center for those building and implementing the BizTalk Framework into their services or applications.

The *BizTalk.org* repository aims to facilitate the initial integration efforts of potential partners by providing a fully indexed database of industry-standard and tested XML schemas. Prospective trading partners can use the repository to search for schemas by keywords or industry-standard category identifiers. Upon finding the matching schemas, *BizTalk.org* can help a trading partner determine whether a particular schema is relevant to the partner's need by providing additional documentation that is included with each schema in the repository.

BizTalk.org is also an information and resource center for anything related to BizTalk in particular or application integration in general. In addition, *BizTalk.org* provides community news and forum services. For those of you working with the BizTalk Framework, this site should definitely be a bookmark in your browser.

BizTalk Server

Microsoft's BizTalk Server is an XML-based messaging server that implements the document exchange functionality requirements laid out in the BizTalk Framework specification. Several companies are currently working on software that is BizTalk Framework compliant, but at the time of this writing the only released product is BizTalk Server. You should note that BizTalk Server goes well beyond the call of duty in this implementation, which you will soon see.

BizTalk Server is designed for both users and developers. Being a member of the Microsoft .NET Enterprise Server family of products, it provides a COM-based API for interacting with other BizTalk Servers programmatically. It also provides a rich set of GUI tools to allow users to easily manage the integration of applications. For example, BizTalk Messaging acts as a standard gateway where all low-level messaging is performed for the sending, receiving, and transformation of documents across disparate systems.

BizTalk Server provides two main categories of services: Orchestration Services and Messaging Services. We will also cover document tracking in this section.

Orchestration Services

Application integration is more than just the ability to exchange and process messages exchanged between the participants in the business process, or *workflow*. What must be added to have full integration is the ability to determine the logical order of actions and the corresponding flow of the messages. Traditionally businesses used modeling tools and workflow diagrams to help document the types of relationships and dependencies involved. BizTalk Orchestration Services provide a runtime engine and a design tool to allow users to design and schedule the execution of these workflows.

BizTalk Server provides a Microsoft Visio 2000–based design tool, called BizTalk Orchestration Designer that can be used to describe the business process in terms of a sequence of message exchanges. The user draws a flowchart to describe the relationship between the specific actions performed when messages are exchanged. It is also used to define the flow of data between messages. This flowchart, called a *schedule*, effectively documents how data flows through the business process from message to message. Orchestration

Services store a schedule in an XML document that uses a Microsoft-designed schema called *XLANG* (pronounced "slang").

We will not get into the details of configuring and using Orchestration Services here. You will find that information in Chapter 14.

Messaging Services

BizTalk Messaging Services include receiving incoming documents, parsing and interpreting the embedded processing rules, possibly performing any necessary format transformation, and delivering the documents to their destinations. BizTalk Messaging Services also provide a mechanism for ensuring the integrity, reliability, and security of the document-interchange process. BizTalk Messaging Services are composed of a Messaging Engine and a GUI tool, called BizTalk Messaging Manager, for configuring and administering Messaging Services.

The Messaging Engine places both incoming and outgoing messages in queues. As we have learned, message queuing can greatly improve the reliability and scalability of the whole document interchange process. BizTalk Server is designed to use an external MOM system to handle the actual tasks required for supporting robust message queuing. The default MOM used by BizTalk Server is, unsurprisingly, the MSMQ.

Sending Documents to BizTalk Server

BizTalk Server provides two different methods for submitting documents to the Messaging Engine. First you can configure BizTalk Server to automatically pick up inbound documents found either in a user-specified MSMQ queue or a file-system directory. Alternatively, you can programmatically submit documents to the BizTalk Server through the IInterchange COM interface. Let's take a closer look at these two methods.

Receive Functions

BizTalk Server provides a built-in facility, called *receive functions*, that you can use to get documents into the Messaging Engine without programming. Receive functions are components in BizTalk that can be configured to poll a specific resource for incoming documents. When a document arrives BizTalk will automatically take it off the resource and submit it to the Messaging Engine. Right out of the box, BizTalk supports two types of receive functions: *file receive function* and *MSMQ receive function*.

The file receive function monitors a user-specified file-system folder for incoming files that match a user-specified filename specification. When a matching file is found the file receive function will automatically submit it to the

Messaging Engine. When the file is successfully submitted it will be removed from the folder.

The MSMQ receive function polls a user-specified MSMQ queue for incoming documents. When a document arrives it will be retrieved from the queue and submitted to the Messaging Engine. If the document is successfully submitted, the MSMQ transaction is committed and the document will be removed from the monitored queue. Otherwise, the transaction is rolled back and the document is left untouched in the queue.

The IInterchange COM Interface

In some cases the receive functions might not satisfy your requirements for submitting documents into BizTalk Server. For instance, you might have an ASP.NET application from which you want to submit documents to BizTalk directly. In cases like this, BizTalk offers a COM-based API you can use to submit your documents to BizTalk programmatically. This API is accessible through the IInterchange interface.

The IInterchange interface is simple and contains only a handful of methods. Table 7-5 summarizes the methods exposed by this interface. Note that the IInterchange interface also supports a few methods for interrogating and managing documents found in the suspended queue.

Table 7-5 The IInterchange Interface

Method	Description
Submit	Submits a document to the Messaging Engine for asynchronous processing. The submitted document is placed in a shared queue to await processing by the next available BizTalk Server in the server group. This method accepts only a string variable as the document or interchange. No object, such as COM objects, and other data types are allowed.
SubmitSync	Submits a document to the Messaging Engine and waits for a response. This method accepts only a string variable as the document or interchange. No object, such as COM objects, and other data types are allowed.

(continued)

Table 7-5 The IInterchange Interface *(continued)*

Method	Description
CheckSuspendedQueue	Checks the shared suspended queue and returns a list of handles to documents or interchanges in the queue that match the specified criteria.
GetSuspendedQueueItemDetails	Obtains details of a document in the suspended queue.
DeleteFromSuspendedQueue	Deletes one or more documents from the suspended queue.

Listing 7-14, submit_biztalk.aspx, is an ASP.NET application that submits a document to BizTalk using the *Submit()* method. The application first prompts you for the name of the channel (we will explain what this is in the next section) and document contents. It then submits the specified document string to the specified channel in BizTalk.

Listing 7-14 submit_biztalk.aspx: An ASP.NET application that submits a document to BizTalk.

```
<%@page language="vb"%>
<%
  ' retrieve submitted channel name and document string
  dim sDocument as String = "" & Request.Form( "pDocument" )
  dim sChannel as String  = "" & Request.Form( "pChannel" )
%>
<form method="post" action="submit_biztalk.asp">
  <table borders="0" cellpadding="2" cellspacing="0">
    <tr>
      <td valign="top">Channel</td>
      <td><input name="pChannel" value="<%=sChannel%>"></td>
    </tr>
    <tr>
      <td valign="top">Document</td>
      <td><textarea name="pDocument" cols="50" rows="15">
<%=sDocument%></textarea></td>
    </tr>
    <tr>
      <td></td>
      <td><input type="submit" value="Submit"></td>
    </tr>
  </table>
```

```
</form>
<%
  if ( sDocument <> "" ) then
    dim oInterchange as new Interchange
    dim sHandle as String
    ' submits a document to BizTalk for asynchronous processing
    sHandle = oInterchange.Submit( BIZTALK_OPENNESS_TYPE_NOTOPEN,
sDocument,,,,,, sChannel )
  end if
%>
```

The *BIZTALK_OPENNESS_TYPE_NOTOPEN* enumeration value in the *Submit()* method call shown in Submit_BizTalk.aspx specifies that BizTalk should use a *nonopen messaging port* to receive the specified document. We will explain what a messaging port is in the next section.

We will not go over the details of the syntax of the *Submit* method and its parameters in this chapter. If you're interested you should read the BizTalk manuals or online help for further information.

Figure 7-11 shows a sample screenshot of the Submit_BizTalk.aspx application.

Receiving Documents from BizTalk Server

For applications to receive documents, BizTalk Server provides a set of transport services for delivering documents to their destinations. It offers four types of transport services:

- File
- MSMQ
- Network protocols
- COM-based Application Integration Components (AICs)

The network protocol transport services supported by BizTalk Server are standard Internet protocols including HTTP, HTTPS, and SMTP.

AICs are COM objects that implement the IBTSAppIntegration interface. The IBTSAppIntegration is an extremely simple COM interface that exposes a single method, *ProcessMessage()*. AIC eliminates the need for BizTalk Server to natively understand the myriad of proprietary protocols invented by different application vendors. It also allows the application to be extensible in terms of interfacing with third-party applications. For example, instead of providing native support for SAP (a popular Enterprise Resources Manager System), an SAP AIC can be developed to allow BizTalk Server to send documents to SAP.

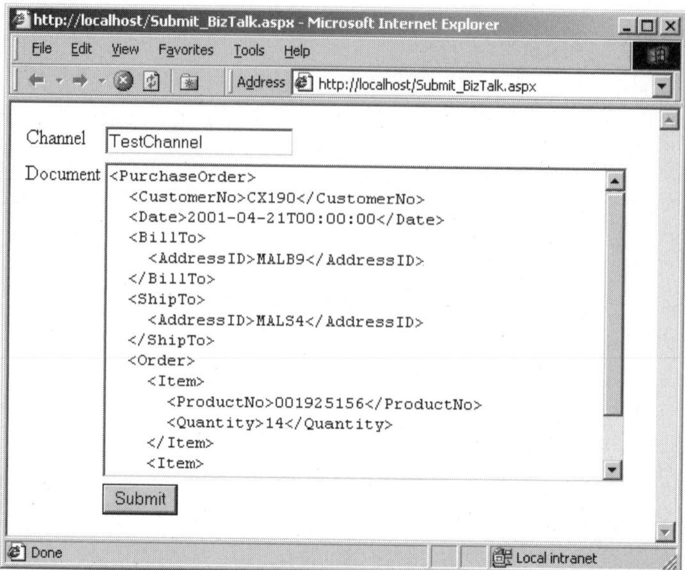

Figure 7-11 Running Submit_BizTalk.aspx.

The Messaging Manager

The BizTalk Messaging Manager, shown in Figure 7-12, is a GUI tool that allows the user to manage the exchange of documents by configuring the various components of Messaging Services.

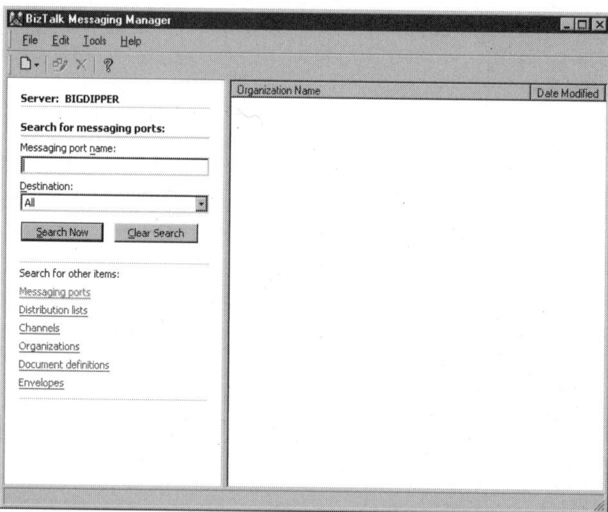

Figure 7-12 The BizTalk Messaging Manager.

The Messaging Manager window is divided into two frames. The left frame provides navigational control to allow the user to select the object type and to search for objects of the selected type to manage. The right frame lists the results of the search depending on the object type. Double clicking on one of these items opens the wizard associated with the object type.

The Messaging Manager has wizards and properties dialogs for creating and configuring the objects that collectively control the operation of Messaging Services. These objects are *organizations*, *document definitions*, *envelopes*, *messaging ports*, and *channels*. Figure 7-13 shows the relationship between some of these objects.

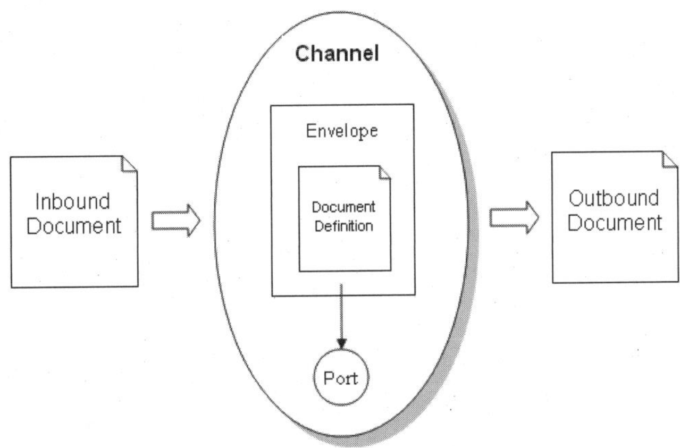

Figure 7-13 BizTalk Messaging Manager objects.

Organizations

Organizations represent the trading partners with which you exchange documents. BizTalk has a special organization type, called *home organization*, that is used to represent your business.

Organizations have *identifiers* that help the Messaging Engine determine the configuration to use for processing documents. Note that BizTalk's only interest in organizations is in organizing configurations. Therefore, you can use organizations to represent departments, workgroups, or any entity that you want to have available for defining messaging configurations.

Figure 7-14 shows the Organization Properties dialog. The General tab is used to specify a name and descriptive comments for an organization. The Identifiers tab lists all the identifiers associated with an organization.

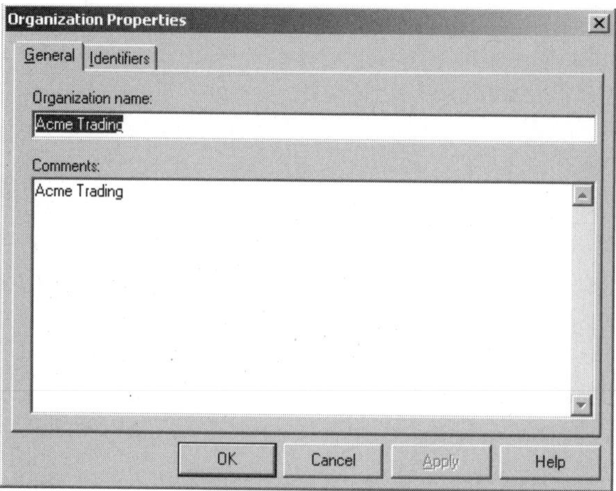

Figure 7-14 The Organization Properties dialog.

Document Definitions

A document definition is used to define a specific type of document that is processed by BizTalk. A document definition provides a pointer to a *specification* that, in turn, is used to define the document structure, type, and version. You will learn more about specifications in Chapter 14.

Figure 7-15 shows the Document Definition Properties dialog. It has three tabs: General, Global Tracking, and Selection Criteria.

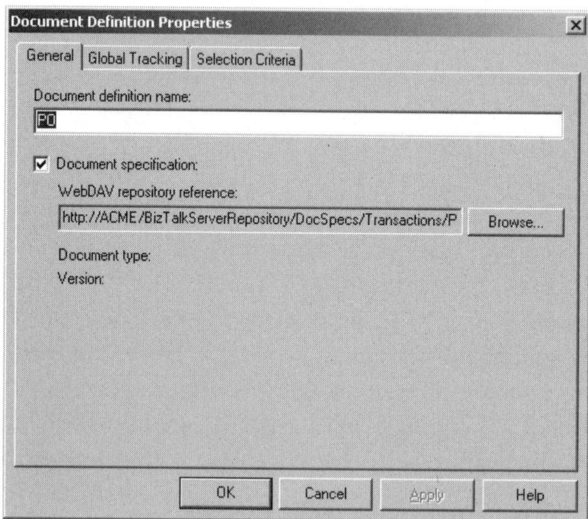

Figure 7-15 The General tab of the Document Definitions properties dialog.

The General tab is used to define the common name and the reference to the associated document specification. For the document specification reference you must specify a WebDAV URL. You can use the Browse button to navigate and locate the appropriate WebDAV repository.

As we will see in a later section, BizTalk provides a messaging tracking capability. By default, BizTalk automatically stores certain basic information, but you can extend this to include other fields specific to your application. The Global Tracking tab, shown in Figure 7-16, lets you define the fields that you want to track.

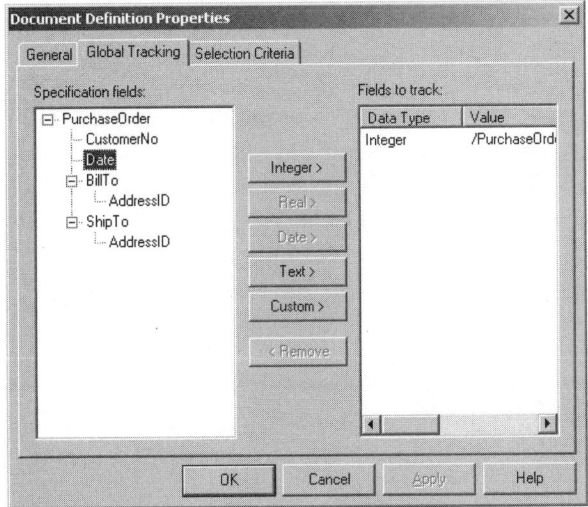

Figure 7-16 The Global Tracking tab of the Document Definitions properties dialog.

The leftmost panel displays a tree-view representation of the fields provided in your document definition. To select a field to track you click on the appropriate button in the middle depending on the data type of the field. Once a field is selected, it will be included in the rightmost panel. This panel lists all the fields to be tracked.

The Selection Criteria tab is used for EDI documents only. It contains a list of name-value pairs that are used by BizTalk to uniquely identify the appropriate document definition for an inbound document. Please refer to the BizTalk Server manuals for further details about EDI documents and the Selection Criteria tab.

Envelopes

Envelopes are used to provide the Messaging Engine with information it needs for processing a document it carries. BizTalk supports the following six types of envelopes:

- XML
- ANSI X12 (an EDI format)
- UN/EDIFACT (an EDI format)
- Flat file (delimited and positional)
- Reliable (BizTalk Framework)
- Custom

Figure 7-17 shows the Envelope Properties dialog. The Envelope name is used to identify this Envelope specification when used in other configuration tasks. The Envelope format drop-down box lists the formats supported by BizTalk. When you select Custom XML, FLATFILE, or CUSTOM, you're required to specify a document specification that describes the structure of the document for which this envelope is intended.

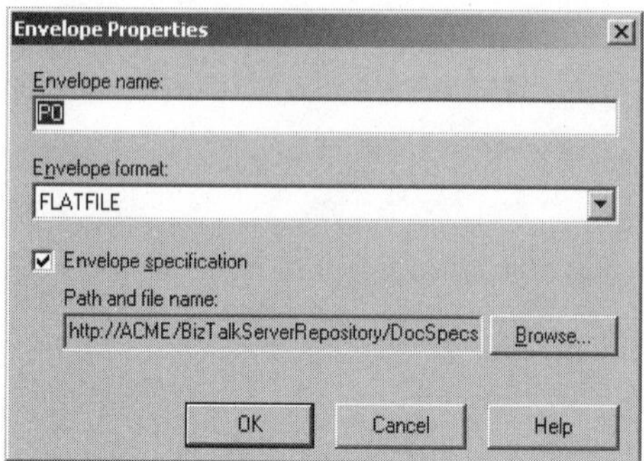

Figure 7-17 The Envelope Properties dialog.

Messaging Ports

A messaging port can be thought of as a set of rules that trading partner organizations accept for exchanging documents. It includes destination, transport type, security, and envelope information.

You create a new messaging port by selecting the New Port menu item from the File menu. The BizTalk Messaging Manager will then display the Messaging Port wizard. The first detail you need to specify is a name and descriptive comments for this new port. When you click the Next button you will be shown a Destination Organization page similar to that shown in Figure 7-18.

You need to specify the destination organization and transport type first. For the destination you can either specify an *open destination* or an explicit organization by selecting from the Organization drop-down list box. An open destination is one where the destination information is determined at runtime based on the information contained in the message itself.

After that, you need to specify the primary transport the Messaging Engine will use to send the processed documents to the specified destination organization. You can use the Browse button to select from a list of available transport protocols such as HTTP, SMTP, and AIC. This option is not available for open destination.

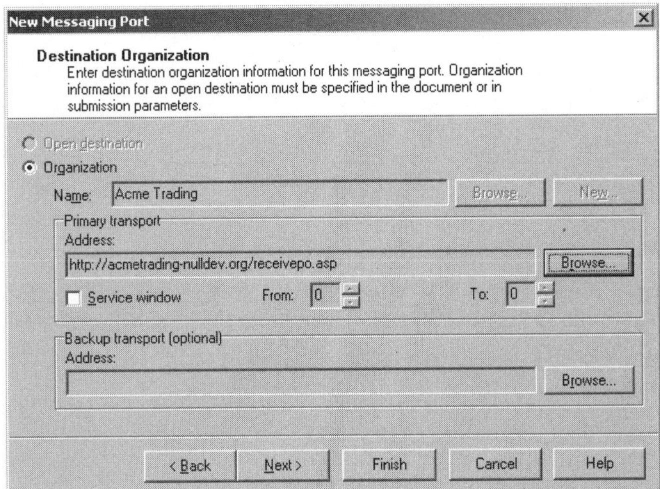

Figure 7-18 Destination Organization page of the Messaging Port wizard.

The Service window option is used to specify an optional time window within which the transmission is restricted. Times are specified to the nearest hour using the From and To edit boxes.

Once you've completed specifying the information for the Destination Organization, clicking the Next button takes you to the Envelope Information page. This is shown in Figure 7-19.

Here you select the envelope to associate with this messaging port. The Envelope drop-down list box lists all the envelopes known to the Messaging Manager. You can also click the New button to create a new envelope at this point.

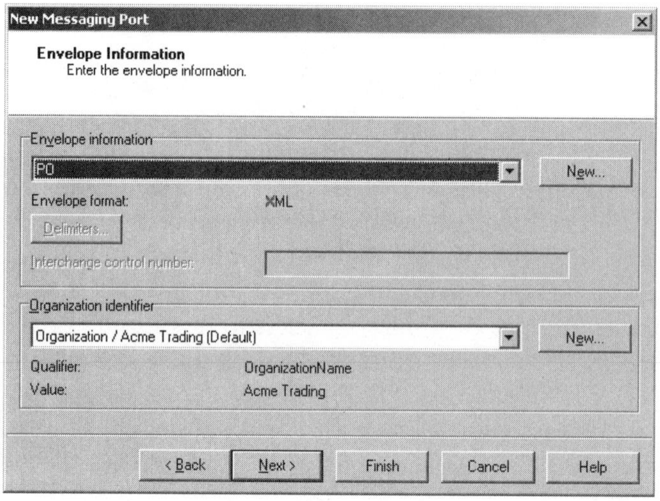

Figure 7-19 The Envelope Information page of the Messaging Port wizard.

The next and final page is the Security Information page, which is used to specify security-related information for this messaging port. This is shown in Figure 7-20.

The Encoding drop-down list box specifies the encoding type used by messages associated with this messaging port. For text messages, this is usually none. For other types, you can select either the MIME or Custom type. The latter type requires a custom encoding component. Refer to the BizTalk manuals for information about creating and using custom encoding.

The Encryption drop-down list box lets you instruct BizTalk to protect all the messages going through this messaging port by encrypting their contents using the specified encryption method. Currently BizTalk only supports the Secure Multipurpose Internet Mail Extensions (S/MIME) encryption type. You will also need to specify the digital certificate for your partner.

Channels

Channels are the primary object in Messaging Services. All the other objects we have learned about so far—organizations, document definitions, envelopes, and messaging ports—are used to support the operation of channels. A channel forms a single self-contained and named object that BizTalk uses to configure Messaging Services to process a document it receives.

Configuring channels is beyond the scope of this chapter. Please refer to the BizTalk Server manuals for further information about creating and managing channels.

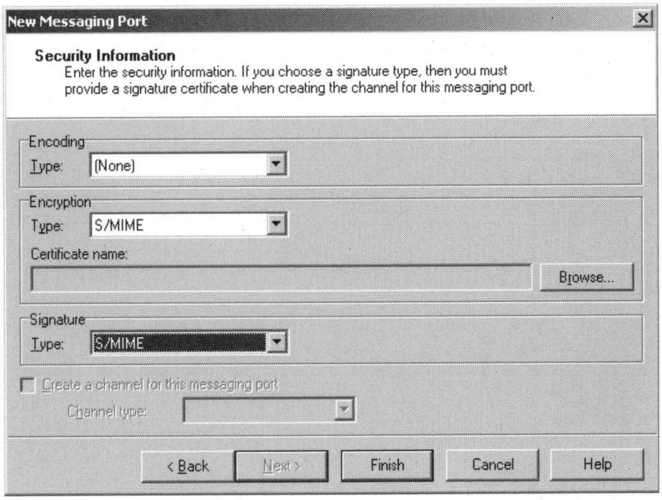

Figure 7-20 Security Information page of the Messaging Port wizard.

Document Tracking

One detail that might be obvious is the need to track messages and documents as they flow through the system. One key advantage of BizTalk Server is that document tracking is a built-in service. Even without any programming on the user's part, BizTalk can be configured to automatically capture and display user-defined information that can be used to track the status of individual messages transiting the messaging system.

Capturing Information to Track

Metadata associated with an interchange, such as source and destination information, document type, and date and time parameters, is automatically stored and available for tracking by BizTalk Messaging Services. However, if you want to be able to track information extracted from messages submitted to BizTalk, you will need to configure the BizTalk Messaging Manager to capture this information.

These tracking options can be set at the following three levels:

- Server Group
- Channel
- Document Definition

You've already seen how you can specify tracking options at the Document Definition level when we discussed the Document Definition object in a previous section.

For the server group tracking options you will need to start the BizTalk Administration console, select a server group, and open the associated properties dialog. This is shown in Figure 7-21.

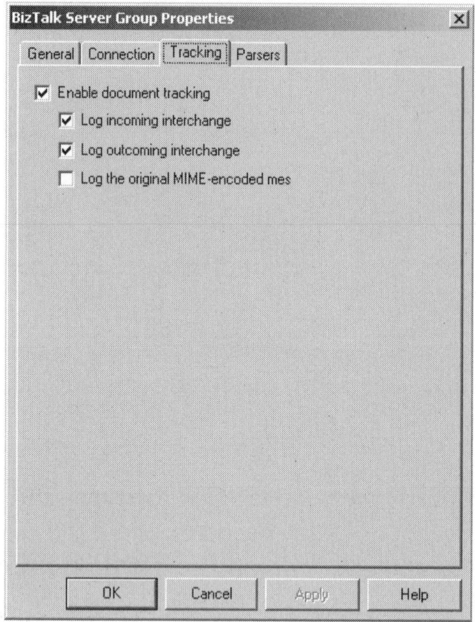

Figure 7-21 Server group document tracking options.

Four tracking options can be configured globally for a specific server group. The Enable document tracking check box turns tracking for this server group on and off. The other three tracking options are only available when the Enable document tracking option is set.

When the Log incoming interchange and Log outgoing interchange tracking options are enabled, BizTalk will keep a copy of the input and output documents in their original native format. This is a great option for those cases when you need to fulfill legal or standard requirements or both to keep copies of all electronic business transactions.

The last option, Log the original MIME-encoded message, instructs BizTalk to store S/MIME encoded documents in the Tracking database in their original, preencoded, format.

Displaying Tracking Information

BizTalk provides a Web-based GUI tool to enable users to track documents visually. BizTalk Document Tracking provides many different search and sort options to enable the user to easily locate and format the query result for specific groups of documents that the user wishes to track.

Conclusion

We covered a lot of topics and technologies in this whirlwind chapter, but this chapter might be one of the most important in terms of concepts. We started with a discussion about the history of distributed computing and compared the different paradigms as they relate to messaging. We looked at how XML has emerged as a key enabling technology for implementing platform-independent and flexible messaging systems.

Next we became familiar with two of the most important XML-based messaging systems, namely SOAP and Web Services. With Web Services we explored in detail their implementation and deployment using tools provided through .NET and other means.

Finally we covered the BizTalk Framework Initiative and exposed you to the functionality present in the BizTalk Server, which we will cover in more detail in Chapter 14.

8

Creating Metadata

In this book so far we have learned how to use XML to build Web sites, create Web user interfaces, and access databases. What is it about XML that makes the technology so readily pervasive? One answer to this question is that XML is, fundamentally, portable data. In the relatively new world of distributed applications, data, not code, has become the most critical shared resource.

Modern applications need to exchange information about what services they provide, what information they need to provide those services, and how that information should be conveyed. This chapter will explore how this is accomplished. We will begin by explaining the concept of *metadata* and then move on to discuss how it's used in the Microsoft .NET Developer Studio. We will introduce the topic of Web Services and will use the .NET Developer Studio to create them. We will also explore the .NET Developer Studio's Object Remoting capabilities and how it uses metadata to implement remote object sharing.

Metadata and XML

Metadata is data that describes other data. Metadata about any entity, be it a programming object or a simple Web page, is information that describes that entity. Metadata and the Web have coexisted for a long time. Most Web pages you see broadcast meta-information about themselves for use in search engines. For example, the following lines of metadata appear in the header of Microsoft's Internet Information Server (IIS) 5 HTML documentation.

```
<META name="DESCRIPTION" content="Navigational page with links to an
extensive glossary, late-breaking IIS information, installation
instructions, descriptions of new features, concise quick-start
procedures for experienced server administrators, and tips for the
using the IIS documentation.">
<META HTTP-EQUIV="Content-Type" content="text/html; charset=Windows-1252">
<META NAME="MS.LOCALE" CONTENT="EN-US">
```

This information sits behind the scenes. Although it does not appear when you look at the Web page through a browser, it's useful for providing contextual information about the page to tools such as search engines.

> **Note** In this example metadata is used to convey a brief description of the page (that is, *Navigational page with links to an extensive glossary...*), the content-type and character set that the page uses (that is, *text/html; charset=Windows-1252*), and locale information (that is, *EN-US*).

Uses for Metadata

Uses for metadata extend beyond making your Web site more searchable on *Excite.com*. How else can metadata be used? In one example, plug-n-play devices have for years used metadata to broadcast hardware and driver information whenever they are installed on PCs.

All URL requests made by Web browsers send metadata about the software the user is running to browse the Web, the IP address of the user's computer, and the content-type and character encoding of the request itself. Web server software such as IIS use this information to filter requests or redirect users to pages that are more compatible with their browsers.

Transport Control Protocol (TCP) packets transmit metadata through packet headers. This information includes, among other details, the sender's IP address, the receiver's IP address, and the packet's sequence number. Audio CDs and DVDs have table-of-contents data sections that tell the player how many tracks there are, their duration, and where they begin on the disc.

What does this have to do with XML? Metadata is intrinsic to all XML documents. An XML document's elements and attributes provide extra information about the document's content. This allows people and programs to easily parse and understand information represented in XML format. We will spend the next few pages exploring XML comments, elements, and schemas and DTDs in greater depth.

Using XML for Comments

One straightforward way to include metadata in XML is by inserting comments into a transformed document. XSLT provides an *<xsl:comment>* element for this purpose. The XSLT processor replaces instances of this element with a well-formed comment in the result document. This form of metadata is mostly intended for human consumption.

Listing 8-1 contains a list of vegetable names and colors. In this example we will apply an XSLT the document and insert a comment along the way. Listing 8-2 shows the XSLT code behind the transformation.

Listing 8-1 vegetables.xml: A list of vegetables to be sorted and displayed.

```
<vegetables>
   <vegetable>
      <name>cabbage</name>
      <color>red</color>
   </vegetable>
   <vegetable>
      <name>carrot</name>
      <color>orange</color>
   </vegetable>
   <vegetable>
      <name>asparagus</name>
      <color>green</color>
   </vegetable>
   <vegetable>
      <name>squash</name>
      <color>yellow</color>
   </vegetable>
</vegetables>
```

Listing 8-2 vegetables.xsl: This style sheet generates a sorted HTML table with XML comments.

```
<?xml version='1.0'?>
<xsl:stylesheet version="1.0"
      xmlns:xsl="http://www.w3.org/1999/XSL/Transform" >
   <xsl:template match="/vegetables">
<html>
<body>
<xsl:comment>order the vegetables by name</xsl:comment>
<table>
  <tr>
    <th>Vegetable</th>
    <th>Color</th>
  </tr>
  <xsl:apply-templates select="vegetable">
    <xsl:sort select="name"/>
  </xsl:apply-templates>
</table>
</body>
</html>
</xsl:template>
<xsl:template match="vegetable">
  <tr>
    <td><xsl:value-of select="name"/></td>
    <td><xsl:value-of select="color"/></td>
  </tr>
</xsl:template>
</xsl:stylesheet>
```

The Listing 8-2 transformation, when applied to the Listing 8-1 source document, produces the following HTML source.

```
<html>
  <body>
  <!--order the vegetables by name-->
  <table>
    <tr>
      <th>Vegetable</th>
      <th>Color</th>
    </tr>
    <tr>
      <td>asparagus</td>
      <td>green</td>
    </tr>
    <tr>
      <td>cabbage</td>
      <td>red</td>
```

```
    </tr>
    <tr>
      <td>carrot</td>
      <td>orange</td>
    </tr>
    <tr>
      <td>squash</td>
      <td>yellow</td>
    </tr>
  </table>
  </body>
</html>
```

Elements

An XML document's elements are a good source of meta-information. For example, here is a record from a personnel database in the Microsoft Excel CSV format:

```
John,Smith,200 Brattle Street,Cambridge,MA,02138,brown,11/30/1974,blue
```

The meaning behind most of this data is obvious. The person's name is *John Smith* and his address is *200 Brattle Street; Cambridge, MA 02138*. Unfortunately, the significance of the last three fields (*brown, 11/30/1974, blue*) is less clear. Is *blue* John Smith's hair color or favorite kind of cheese?

Listing 8-3 contains the same data in XML format.

Listing 8-3 person.xml: An XML representation of a person's profile.

```
<person>
  <firstName>John</firstName>
  <lastName>Smith</lastName>
  <address type="home">
    <address1>200 Brattle Street</address1>
    <city>Cambridge</city>
    <state>MA</state>
    <zip>02138</zip>
  </address>
  <hairColor>brown</hairColor>
  <birthDate>11/30/1974</birthDate>
  <favoriteColor>blue</favoriteColor>
</person>
```

Although the actual data contained in both documents is the same, the metadata in the XML version makes it easier to understand. We were correct in guessing his name and address and the meaning of *brown*, *11/30/1974*, and *blue* is now evident. XML elements can also be reordered with no impact on their interpretation. The elements in the document could be ordered alphabetically (by level of hierarchy) just as well.

```
<person>
  <address type="home">
    <address1>200 Brattle Street</address1>
    <city>Cambridge</city>
    <state>MA</state>
    <zip>02138</zip>
  </address>
  <birthDate>11/30/1974</birthDate>
  <favoriteColor>blue</favoriteColor>
  <firstName>John</firstName>
  <hairColor>brown</hairColor>
  <lastName>Smith</lastName>
</person>
```

Reordering the elements has no effect on this document's meaning. The same is not true of delimited documents, where meaning is derived from arbitrary positioning. A simple swap of fields will change John Smith's hair color from brown to blue!

Schemas and DTDs

XML documents can also include a second kind of metadata in the form of a schema or a DTD. Schemas and DTDs both serve the same purpose but use different syntaxes. They carve out a language, or class, of XML documents that governs the types of elements and attributes that might appear in conformant documents. Schemas and DTDs can also impose a rigid or loose structure on the XML documents they define. For example, a *<person>* element must have first *<firstName>* and *<lastName>* child elements but can also have a *<favoriteColor>* element. Listing 8-4 is the schema that defines a person XML document. Note that a valid coreXMLPerson document need not include all of the elements defined in the schema. Our example from earlier would not be a valid codeXMLPerson document because the schema requires *address.address1, address.city, address.state,* and *address.zip* instead of *address1, city, state,* and *zip.*

Listing 8-4 PersonSchema.xml: This schema provides metadata describing the structure of a coreXMLPerson XML document.

```
<?xml version="1.0"?>
<Schema name="coreXMLPerson"
xmlns="urn:schemas-microsoft-com:xml-data"
xmlns:dt="urn:schemas-microsoft-com:datatypes">
```

```
  <ElementType name="firstName" content="textOnly" model="closed"/>
  <ElementType name="lastName" content="textOnly" model="closed"/>
  <ElementType name="birthDate" content="textOnly" model="closed"/>
  <ElementType name="hairColor" content="textOnly" model="closed"/>
  <ElementType name="favoriteColor" content="textOnly"
model="closed"/>
  <ElementType name="address.address1" content="textOnly"
model="closed"/>
  <ElementType name="address.address2" content="textOnly"
model="closed"/>
  <ElementType name="address.address3" content="textOnly"
model="closed"/>
  <ElementType name="address.city" content="textOnly"
model="closed"/>
  <ElementType name="address.state" content="textOnly"
model="closed"/>
  <ElementType name="address.zip" content="textOnly" model="closed"/>
  <ElementType name="address.country" content="textOnly"
model="closed"/>
  <ElementType name="address" order="many" content="eltOnly"
model="closed">
     <AttributeType name="type" />
     <element type="address.address1" minOccurs="0" maxOccurs="1"/>
     <element type="address.address2" minOccurs="0" maxOccurs="1"/>
     <element type="address.address3" minOccurs="0" maxOccurs="1"/>
     <element type="address.city" minOccurs="0" maxOccurs="1"/>
     <element type="address.state" minOccurs="0" maxOccurs="1"/>
     <element type="address.zip" minOccurs="0" maxOccurs="1"/>
     <element type="address.country" minOccurs="0" maxOccurs="1"/>
  </ElementType>
  <ElementType name="person" order="many" content="eltOnly"
model="closed">
     <element type="firstName" minOccurs="0" maxOccurs="1"/>
     <element type="lastName" minOccurs="0" maxOccurs="1"/>
     <element type="address" minOccurs="0" maxOccurs="*"/>
     <element type="hairColor" minOccurs="0" maxOccurs="1"/>
     <element type="favoriteColor" minOccurs="0" maxOccurs="1"/>
  </ElementType>
</Schema>
```

We can see that this schema strictly defines all of the ingredients that go into a coreXMLPerson document. We now know what types of elements and attributes can appear inside a document of this type. We also know the structure a coreXMLPerson document must have. For instance, address information cannot appear directly beneath a *<person>* element: it must reside within one of many possible *<address>* elements.

> **Note** Two types of schema definitions are in wide circulation today: XSD and the XML-Data Reduced Language (XDR). XSD is the official schema language of the W3C. XDR is an interim schema definition language the W3C offered to developers while they were drafting the XSD specification. Microsoft's MSXML 4 parser supports both types of schema definitions.

XML documents can reference their respective schemas or DTDs through the *namespace* attribute. To include a reference to the coreXMLPerson schema, we only need to change the root element of the Listing 8-3 document.

```
<person xmlns="x-schema:personschema.xml">
  ...
</person>
```

This tells the XML parser that a validating XDR schema can be found at the location *personschema.xml*. Now the person or program interpreting the XML data has more meta-information to use. We can see what other elements might appear inside similar documents. We also have a means to *validate*, or check the integrity of, the document we are analyzing.

Using XML for Metadata Definition

Software and hardware components have long used metadata to identify themselves when communicating. Historically this was done in a proprietary fashion where the sender and receiver first agreed on an interchange format before they could exchange metadata. XML changed this.

Today we can build applications that find and execute remote Web Services without prior knowledge of their existence. We can also publish Web Services of our own without knowing who will use those services, where they will come from, how they will use them, or even what type of client software will make the request. These services can now seamlessly exchange rich and abstract data objects.

This magic is made possible by using XML to exchange metadata. You might ask yourself, "Why all the fuss about XML? Why is a generic markup language taking over the world?" XML has many advantages that make it the ideal carrier for data and metadata on the Internet.

1. It can be read and written by humans. This was one of the reasons for HTML's success and it works equally well for XML. This makes the language more accessible to novices and lowers the fear factor

for everyone. You can see it, touch it, and use Notepad to create it. This is useful.

2. It is open. XML is defined by the W3C. No single company owns it. Microsoft has added muscle to the W3C specification by implementing standards-compliant XML parsers and placing them in the eager hands of its developer community. Nevertheless, the language is platform-independent. UNIX clients can exchange XML data with .NET Web Services and vice versa.
3. It is ubiquitous. XML parsers are everywhere. Getting your hands on an XML toolset and using the technology immediately is easy.
4. It is flexible. Perhaps the most compelling reason for using XML is that it has no prescribed use. You decide how you want to use it in your application. You determine its scope, which can range from creating small XML documents to transmitting data between applications or application layers to creating your own standards body that regulates the use of XML within an entire industry.

XML is here to stay, so let's see how we can use it to transfer metadata.

Describing an Object

Object serialization is not a new concept to experienced object-oriented programmers. The idea is to take an instantiated object in memory and convert its state, or property values, into a serialized data stream that can be written to disk or transmitted over a network. The serialized version of the object must be complete enough so that the same program, or a completely different program, can reassemble it into an identical instance. As we'll see in this section, both objects and their class definitions can be serialized.

Visual C++ and Java are two examples of widely used programming languages that allow object serialization. Each language uses a proprietary data format to store the object and its metadata. This means that applications written in different languages can find trying to share serialized objects to be difficult. Not only do these applications need to understand each other's serialization format, they also need to make sense out of the serialized object's metadata to instantiate it.

Once again, XML comes to the rescue. Developers can use XML to facilitate object sharing by creating a schema that defines how objects can be serialized into platform-independent XML documents. Applications can share data by using the new object schema as a translator. Each application needs only a conduit to help marshal native objects into XML format and back again for the two to communicate.

> **Note** Not all object states can be serialized. References to transient resources, such as database connections, cannot be persisted or transmitted to another program. All languages that support object serialization provide a mechanism for programmers to specify which properties should be serialized and which should not.

The class definition for the CoreXMLPerson object is contained in Listing 8-5.

Listing 8-5 person.cs: A C# class definition for a *<Person>* object.

```
using System;
namespace CSharpWebService
{
  /// <summary>
  /// A Simple Person Class Definition
  /// </summary>
  public class Person
  {
    public String firstName;
    public String lastName;
    public String birthDate;
    public String hairColor;
    public String favoriteColor;
    public Address address;
    public Person()
    {
      firstName = "";
      lastName = "";
      birthDate = "";
      hairColor = "";
      favoriteColor = "";
      address = new Address();
    }
    public Person(String _firstName, String _lastName, String
_birthDate, String _hairColor, String _favoriteColor)
    {
      firstName = _firstName;
      lastName  = _lastName;
      birthDate = _birthDate;
      hairColor = _hairColor;
      favoriteColor = _favoriteColor;
      address = new Address();
```

```
    }
    public void setFirstName(String _firstName)
      { firstName = _firstName; }
    public void setLastName(String _lastName)
      { lastName = _lastName; }
    public void setBirthDate(String _birthDate)
      { birthDate = _birthDate; }
    public void setHairColor(String _hairColor)
      { hairColor = _hairColor; }
    public void setFavoriteColor(String _favoriteColor)
      { favoriteColor = _favoriteColor; }
  }
}
```

Our object definition declares properties for the fields, *<firstName>*, *<lastName>*, *<birthDate>*, *<hairColor>*, *<favoriteColor>*, and *<address>*. Now let's create an instance of this object in C#.

```
Person p = new Person("John", "Smith", "11/30/1974", "brown", "blue");
```

The Object Instance XML Document

This call to the *<Person>* constructor will create a *<Person>* instance in memory. If we want to save this object to a file or transmit it to another program, we must first serialize it. How do we do this? The simplest solution is to construct an Object Instance XML document that holds the state of the object in memory. This document looks astonishingly similar to a previous incarnation of this data.

```
<Person>
  <address type="home">
    <address1>200 Brattle Street</address1>
    <city>Cambridge</city>
    <state>MA</state>
    <zip>02138</zip>
  </address>
  <firstName>John</firstName>
  <lastName>Smith</lastName>
  <hairColor>brown</hairColor>
  <birthDate>11/30/1973</birthDate>
  <favoriteColor>blue</favoriteColor>
</Person>
```

Is this enough information to reconstruct the *<Person>* object in memory? Almost. Certainly, the program that originally created the object could parse the XML document and call the *<Person>* constructor method.

The Class Definition XML Document

Another program, however, would be unable to do so without more information about the *Person* class definition. In this case we need another XML document that describes the *Person* class definition. Listing 8-6 is an excerpt from such a document.

Listing 8-6 An excerpt from createPerson.wsdl, an XML Web Service descriptor, describing the *Person* class definition.

```
<s:complexType name="Person">
  <s:sequence>
    <s:element minOccurs="1" maxOccurs="1" name="firstName"
nillable="true" type="s:string" />
    <s:element minOccurs="1" maxOccurs="1" name="lastName"
nillable="true" type="s:string" />
    <s:element minOccurs="1" maxOccurs="1" name="birthDate"
nillable="true" type="s:string" />
    <s:element minOccurs="1" maxOccurs="1" name="hairColor"
nillable="true" type="s:string" />
    <s:element minOccurs="1" maxOccurs="1" name="favoriteColor"
nillable="true" type="s:string" />
    <s:element minOccurs="1" maxOccurs="1" name="address"
nillable="true" type="s0:Address" />
  </s:sequence>
</s:complexType>
```

Notice that all the property information in the original class definition appears in this XML document. The most important pieces of information are the property's name and data type. You might also have noticed that the *address* property is listed as type *s0:Address*. This is because the *address* property is a reference to another type of object named *Address*. This class would require its own XML descriptor as well, but it was omitted for brevity's sake.

These two XML documents, the class document and the instance document, provide enough information for another program to generate a comparable class definition and create an instance of this class with the desired state. The process of generating these stub classes and instantiating remote objects in the .NET Developer Studio will be covered more thoroughly later in the chapter.

Describing a Service

The future of distributed computing over the Internet has been hotly contested in recent years. Many object-oriented programmers believed that, one day, distributed applications would be built from objects located all over the Internet. Computers could participate in a global object community by publishing objects that could be run internally or whose code could be transmitted over the Internet. Unfortunately, firewalls, unreliable network connections, and competing technologies have all hindered this movement and have led developers to search for a more practical way to build distributed applications. In this section we will review some existing distributed technologies and then dive into the emerging distributed paradigm of Web Services.

Although these technologies differ in approach and implementation, they all share one common problem: how to describe remote methods and services so they can be discovered and used dynamically. All distributed technologies use some sort of metadata to communicate the features and semantics of the services they host. In the past the format of this metadata has often been proprietary. Today XML is used as an ideal carrier for remote service metadata.

CORBA and IIOP

When the Common Object Request Broker Architecture (CORBA) was introduced in the early 1990s, its enthusiasts speculated that fine-grained distributed objects would one day become widely available. Applications would be able to locate and use business software components via a vast network of Object Request Brokers (ORBs), and then CORBA would allow objects implemented in C++, Java, and even COBOL to be executed remotely. CORBA objects publish their behavior using the Interface Definition Language (IDL) (more metadata!) and register this information with an ORB running on a local network.

Client programs interact with these objects via stub interfaces that remotely execute an object's methods on the machine hosting the software. The ORB sits in the middle and dispatches all intermachine communication. ORBs around the Internet can share information about the objects they manage. The Internet Inter-ORB Protocol (IIOP) was developed for this purpose. CORBA supports run-time discovery of objects and is a flexible architecture for coordinating the exchanges of fine-grained software components.

JAVA RMI

Like CORBA, Java's RMI subsystem allows objects to be distributed across a network. Unlike CORBA, Java RMI can transport an entire class, software and all, across application boundaries. This is possible because all Java applications must run on the Java Virtual Machine. This enables distributed Java applications to safely download compiled byte streams and execute them locally. Today Java allows objects to be shared by either the RMI or IIOP protocols.

Although the ability to share executable objects dynamically over the Internet opens some exciting possibilities, Java RMI does have shortcomings. The technology only works if the applications involved in the exchange are both written in Java. Programs written to use RMI also require a fair amount of preparation. Remote stub classes need to be generated statically or downloaded dynamically for remote methods to work properly. Finally RMI uses a proprietary protocol to exchange information. This means more server software and firewall tuning.

Web Services—An Introduction

The push for widely distributed software components might have had more to do with the fact that we could do it, instead of whether or not we actually needed to do it. Although fine-grained distributed software components are extremely valuable at a local level, their usefulness diminishes as the scale of the network grows. Failing networks, uncooperative firewalls, and overall complexity made assembling an application from small, widely distributed pieces prohibitively difficult.

Furthermore, as E-commerce exploded on the Internet, it became apparent that data, not code, was the most precious commodity in Internet applications. The HTTP protocol had existed for years and firewalls were configured to cope with it. XML proved to be a powerful vehicle for transporting any type of information. Surely there was some way to combine the two technologies and produce the next big advance in distributed computing.

Thus, Web Services were born. Web Services are based on two simple ideas.

1. "The need for distributed business services is greater than the need for distributed business components." What is the difference between a service and a component, anyway? A software component tends to be a fine-grained object, or set of objects, that can be embedded directly in your application. Examples include GUI widgets, API-to-desktop applications, and other tools. A service encompasses a broader interface and is more abstract. An airline reservation system is a good example of a potential Web Service. A corporate intranet application might communicate with this service over the Internet to provide convenient flight booking to the company's employees.

2. "Web Services should be easy to access." Web Services can be accessed over the Internet using three primary methods. The first is through SOAP. SOAP enables applications to send complex objects in XML format between one another. The second method is the HTTP POST protocol. This is the same POST protocol that HTML forms use. XML name-value pairs are submitted to the Web Service and the results are received through standard output. The third way to access a Web Service is by using the HTTP GET protocol. This approach sends all of the client arguments through a URL Query string to the Web Service. The XML results are sent back on standard

output. All three of these approaches use HTTP to transfer data. Therefore, no fancy client software or firewall configurations are needed to use a Web Service in your application.

Describing a Web Service

Web Services use metadata to publish themselves. The metadata is stored in Web Services Description Language (WSDL) XML documents. WSDL is a contract language that defines the messaging interface to the service. IBM and Microsoft were the chief designers of this language. The WSDL specification is maintained by the W3C. You can find it at *http://www.w3.org/TR/wsdl.*

Any client on the Internet can request a WSDL document with an HTTP request. The WSDL document specifies the name of the service, the names and types of the arguments it expects, the names and types of the results it returns, and directions on how to access the service (that is, SOAP message, HTTP POST, HTTP GET, or all three).

Let's look at a "HelloWorld" example that performs the valuable service of saying "Hello" to you. Imagine how much brighter our offices would be if we all used this service every morning. The HelloWorld Web Service requests only a single piece of information from you: your name. Upon receiving this data the service will present you with a happy salutation. The HelloWorld service, because it is so popular, is housed on a supercomputer somewhere directly on an Internet backbone. Say you decide to write an application that accesses this service, so you download the HelloWorld WSDL XML document. A listing of this document, with descriptions, follows.

```
<?xml version="1.0" encoding="utf-8" ?>
<definitions xmlns:s="http://www.w3.org/2001/XMLSchema"
xmlns:http="http://schemas.xmlsoap.org/wsdl/http/" xmlns:mime="http://
schemas.xmlsoap.org/wsdl/mime/" xmlns:tm="http://microsoft.com/wsdl/
mime/textMatching/" xmlns:soap="http://schemas.xmlsoap.org/wsdl/soap/"
xmlns:soapenc="http://schemas.xmlsoap.org/soap/encoding/"
xmlns:s0="http://tempuri.org/" targetNamespace="http://tempuri.org/"
xmlns="http://schemas.xmlsoap.org/wsdl/">
```

WSDL documents lead off with a host of references to different namespaces. The *s* namespace references the W3C's XSD Schema, with which you should be familiar by now. The *http* namespace identifies elements that supply HTTP connection information. The *mime* namespace is used to specify the MIME types of data returned from the service. The *tm* namespace is Microsoft's text matching namespace. This is not used in the HelloWorld example. The *soap* namespace is used to isolate SOAP-specific elements in the WSDL document. The *soapenc* namespace is used for SOAP encoding elements. The *s0* namespace is used to isolate service-specific data structures. The URI for this namespace points to *http://tempuri.org/,* which is used only for testing purposes. In a production environment the URI would most likely reference the service vendor's domain. Finally the default namespace is set to the general WSDL namespace defined at *http://schemas.xmlsoap.org/wsdl.*

The types section of the WSDL document tells you the name and types of the arguments and the return result of the *HelloWorld* service.

```
  <types>
    <s:schema attributeFormDefault="qualified"
elementFormDefault="qualified" targetNamespace="http://tempuri.org/">
```

The *<HelloWorld>* element encapsulates all the incoming arguments to the service. We see here that the service expects a *<complexType>* argument. In this example the argument has the name *name* and a type of string. WSDL supports arguments more complex than strings. Service arguments can be a series of nested objects. Those object classes and subclasses must be fully described in this section of the WSDL document.

```
      <s:element name="HelloWorld">
        <s:complexType>
          <s:sequence>
            <s:element minOccurs="1" maxOccurs="1" name="name"
nillable="true" type="s:string" />
          </s:sequence>
        </s:complexType>
      </s:element>
```

The *<HelloWorldResponse>* element defines the data structure the client can expect to receive from the service. We see here that the service will return a single variable of type string.

```
      <s:element name="HelloWorldResponse">
        <s:complexType>
          <s:sequence>
            <s:element minOccurs="1" maxOccurs="1" name=
"HelloWorldResult" nillable="true" type="s:string" />
          </s:sequence>
        </s:complexType>
      </s:element>
      <s:element name="string" nillable="true" type="s:string" />
    </s:schema>
  </types>
```

The following section of the WSDL document describes the protocols that can be used to access the service. Notice that SOAP, GET, and POST are all covered in this section. WSDL needs to describe to potential clients the call and return semantics that the service provides. These semantics include URLs, MIME Types, and input/output message formats.

```
<message name="HelloWorldSoapIn">
  <part name="parameters" element="s0:HelloWorld" />
</message>
<message name="HelloWorldSoapOut">
  <part name="parameters" element="s0:HelloWorldResponse" />
</message>
<message name="HelloWorldHttpGetIn">
  <part name="name" type="s:string" />
</message>
<message name="HelloWorldHttpGetOut">
  <part name="Body" element="s0:string" />
</message>
<message name="HelloWorldHttpPostIn">
  <part name="name" type="s:string" />
</message>
<message name="HelloWorldHttpPostOut">
  <part name="Body" element="s0:string" />
</message>
<portType name="Service1Soap">
  <operation name="HelloWorld">
    <input message="s0:HelloWorldSoapIn" />
    <output message="s0:HelloWorldSoapOut" />
  </operation>
</portType>
<portType name="Service1HttpGet">
  <operation name="HelloWorld">
    <input message="s0:HelloWorldHttpGetIn" />
    <output message="s0:HelloWorldHttpGetOut" />
  </operation>
</portType>
<portType name="Service1HttpPost">
  <operation name="HelloWorld">
    <input message="s0:HelloWorldHttpPostIn" />
  <output message="s0:HelloWorldHttpPostOut" />
  </operation>
</portType>
<binding name="Service1Soap" type="s0:Service1Soap">
  <soap:binding transport="http://schemas.xmlsoap.org/soap/http"
style="document" />
  <operation name="HelloWorld">
    <soap:operation soapAction="http://tempuri.org/HelloWorld"
style="document" />
    <input>
      <soap:body use="literal" />
    </input>
    <output>
```

```
        <soap:body use="literal" />
      </output>
    </operation>
  </binding>
  <binding name="Service1HttpGet" type="s0:Service1HttpGet">
    <http:binding verb="GET" />
    <operation name="HelloWorld">
      <http:operation location="/HelloWorld" />
      <input>
        <http:urlEncoded />
      </input>
      <output>
        <mime:mimeXml part="Body" />
      </output>
    </operation>
  </binding>
  <binding name="Service1HttpPost" type="s0:Service1HttpPost">
    <http:binding verb="POST" />
    <operation name="HelloWorld">
      <http:operation location="/HelloWorld" />
      <input>
        <mime:content type="application/x-www-form-urlencoded" />
      </input>
      <output>
        <mime:mimeXml part="Body" />
      </output>
    </operation>
  </binding>
  <service name="Service1">
    <port name="Service1Soap" binding="s0:Service1Soap">
      <soap:address location="http://localhost/HelloWorld/
HelloWorld.asmx" />
    </port>
    <port name="Service1HttpGet" binding="s0:Service1HttpGet">
      <http:address location="http://localhost/HelloWorld/
HelloWorld.asmx" />
    </port>
    <port name="Service1HttpPost" binding="s0:Service1HttpPost">
      <http:address location="http://localhost/HelloWorld/
HelloWorld.asmx" />
    </port>
  </service>
</definitions>
```

Obtaining Metadata

The metadata contained in WSDL documents is crucial information for any application that wants to use a distributed service. One problem: how do you find this information in the first place? The process of looking up a service on the Internet and obtaining its WSDL descriptor is a top-down search similar to how Domain Name Service (DNS) 6 works. Figure 8-1 illustrates the Web Service look-up procedure.

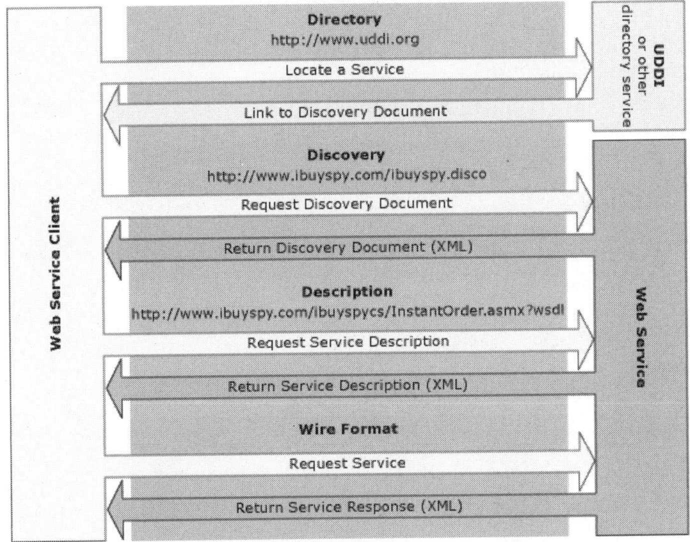

Figure 8-1 An illustration of the steps necessary to locate a Web Service.

If the location of the desired service is unknown ahead of time, you must begin your search with a registry of service providers such as UDDI. These registries are maintained by different organizations. You can query the service registry to get links to service discovery documents hosted by any listed providers of the service you requested.

Note The UDDI Web site *(http://www.uddi.org)* is home to many useful specifications, white papers, and best practices surrounding Web Services. The UDDI project is a cooperative effort among industry leaders. Check out this site to download the latest information on WSDL and UDDI. WSDL was submitted to W3C for consideration for further development. See *http://www.w3.org/TR/wsdl.*

You can download a list of specific services that a specific provider offers by following the link to the provider's discovery document. Discovery documents usually have a .disco or .vsdisco extension. The discovery document contains a detailed list of the Web Services hosted by the provider, including links to service-specific discovery documents. Listing 8-7, a service discovery document, contains a link to the service's WSDL contract.

Listing 8-7 HelloWorld.vsdico: The Hello World discovery document that points the way to the HelloWorld WSDL contract.

```
<?xml version="1.0" encoding="utf-8"?>
<discovery xmlns="http://schemas.xmlsoap.org/disco/">
<contractRef ref="http://localhost/HelloWorld/HelloWorld.asmx?wsdl"
docRef="http://localhost/HelloWorld/HelloWorld.asmx" xmlns="http://
schemas.xmlsoap.org/disco/scl/" />
</discovery>
```

Now that you have the service definition document in hand, you're ready to begin using the HelloWorld Web Service. Let the bliss begin.

Using a Web Service

Developers can usually choose how they consume a Web Service. They can invoke the service by SOAP, GET, or POST methods. As we saw earlier, the service's WSDL contract establishes the valid communications protocols. Services generally support all three methods, however. Of the three, SOAP is the richest in terms of support for complex arguments and return results.

SOAP requests can be built and sent manually by the application developer. This is a painstaking process because all the SOAP infrastructure XML elements must be written by hand. (For a more detailed discussion on SOAP documents, see Chapter 14, "More About SOAP"). Furthermore, the programmer is responsible for posting the document to the service and unpacking the XML result. This methodology gives the developer the finest level of control. The service result document can be parsed into a proprietary data structure or forwarded to another destination.

Such low-level access to the messages, however, is tedious, error-prone, and rarely necessary. If you are planning to build an application that utilizes Web Services, you might want to look into a developer tool suite to help you with some of the plumbing. Nevertheless, examining the low-level calling syntaxes to see how it's done can be useful.

HelloWorld via SOAP

The following is an example of a SOAP request to the HelloWorld service. The first section is the HTTP request header that must be sent to the Web server. The second section consists of the SOAP envelope. The SOAP body contains the payload of the request that states the service to be called (*HelloWorld*) and supplies any required arguments (<*name*>John</*name*>).

```
POST /HelloWorld/HelloWorld.asmx HTTP/1.1
Host: localhost
Content-Type: text/xml; charset=utf-8
Content-Length: <length>
SOAPAction: "http://tempuri.org/HelloWorld"
<?xml version="1.0" encoding="utf-8"?>
<soap:Envelope xmlns:xsi="http://www.w3.org/2001/XMLSchema-instance"
xmlns:xsd="http://www.w3.org/2001/XMLSchema" xmlns:soap=
"http://schemas.xmlsoap.org/soap/envelope/">
  <soap:Body>
    <HelloWorld xmlns="http://tempuri.org/">
      <name>John</name>
    </HelloWorld>
  </soap:Body>
</soap:Envelope>
```

The SOAP response from the Web Service includes a similar HTTP header and SOAP envelope. This time, however, the body contains the results from the call to the service. You might notice that the request and the response are both consistent with the semantics stated in the WSDL contract document. In this case the result is nested inside a <*HelloWorldResult*> tag. Obviously, the syntax of the request and response documents is service-specific.

```
HTTP/1.1 200 OK
Content-Type: text/xml; charset=utf-8
Content-Length: <length>
<?xml version="1.0" encoding="utf-8"?>
<soap:Envelope xmlns:xsi="http://www.w3.org/2001/XMLSchema-instance"
xmlns:xsd="http://www.w3.org/2001/XMLSchema" xmlns:soap=
"http://schemas.xmlsoap.org/soap/envelope/">
  <soap:Body>
    <HelloWorldResponse xmlns="http://tempuri.org/">
      <HelloWorldResult>Hello, John</HelloWorldResult>
    </HelloWorldResponse>
  </soap:Body>
</soap:Envelope>
```

> **Note** Microsoft was the primary sponsor of the SOAP specification. They released version 0.9 of the specification in 1999. The W3C released version 1.1 in May 2000. Both parties kept the protocol simple, which is one of the reasons why it was so successful. SOAP version 1.2 is under active development at W3C. For more information, see *http://www.w3.org/TR/soap12/*.

HelloWorld via HTTP GET

The HTTP GET method is the simplest way to invoke a Web Service. All of the argument data to the service is passed inside the URL string in URLEncoded format. This request string shows how it's done for HelloWorld:

```
GET /HelloWorld/HelloWorld.asmx/HelloWorld?name=John HTTP/1.1
Host: localhost
```

The Web Service cannot return a SOAP document because the request was not made using SOAP. Therefore, the service must return a simple XML document in the HTTP response with the result of the function call.

```
HTTP/1.1 200 OK
Content-Type: text/xml; charset=utf-8
Content-Length: length
<?xml version="1.0" encoding="utf-8"?>
<string xmlns="http://tempuri.org/">Hello, John</string>
```

HelloWorld via HTTP POST

HTTP POST differs from HTTP GET for Web Service invocations the same way it differs in HTML Form posts. All the arguments to the service are stored in the HTTP message body as name-value pairs instead of inside the URL string. This approach is more secure and robust than HTTP GET but not as flexible as using SOAP. The HTTP POST request to the HelloWorld service follows.

```
POST /HelloWorld/HelloWorld.asmx/HelloWorld HTTP/1.1
Host: localhost
Content-Type: application/x-www-form-urlencoded
Content-Length: <length>
name=John
```

The HTTP POST response document is identical to the HTTP GET response document. The response is formatted in plain XML without any SOAP references.

```
HTTP/1.1 200 OK
Content-Type: text/xml; charset=utf-8
Content-Length: length
<?xml version="1.0" encoding="utf-8"?>
<string xmlns="http://tempuri.org/">John</string>
```

.NET Support for Metadata and Web Services

Microsoft designed its .NET Developer Studio to be friendly to Web Service authors and consumers. It offers a rich set of tools, wizards, and utility classes to automate the discovery and execution of Web Services.

The .NET Developer Studio enables service developers to quickly build Web Services that can be deployed on either local or remote Web servers. The .NET Developer Studio automates the creation of all the discovery and WSDL contracts. It even creates simple Web documents that help you test and debug your code. All you have to do is write the business logic! The studio also includes a rich API that allows programmers to make high-level calls to remote services. The utilities handle all of the conversion work to and from SOAP messages.

> **Note** Microsoft is not the only company touting the future of Web Services. Sun is actively working on integrating the idea in their Java 2 Enterprise Edition. This means that Microsoft and Sun Web Services will one day be able to work together, side by side!

Think back to our friend John Smith. His company's HR Director has begun a project to reimplement their personnel management system using Web Services. The plan is to use the .NET Developer Studio to create both the personnel management services and clients that access them.

The project team begins by implementing a service that will create new employees in their back-office database. The Web Service will expose a simple *createPerson()* Web method that accepts essential employee information, creates an entry for the person in the employee database, and returns a SOAP document with all the person's properties filled out. In this section we will look more closely at the *createPerson()* Web Service.

The *createPerson()* Web Service

The *createPerson()* Web Service will be implemented in the C# programming language. The ASP .NET Web Service Project wizard initializes most of the infrastructure necessary to create a Web Service. Among other items, it creates the .vsdisco and WSDL files (the WSDL contract is actually generated dynamically by a call to the .asmx service file) that hold all the metadata clients will need to locate and access the service. The .vsdisco file contains links to related WSDL contracts. The wizard also creates a template .asmx file that is the starting point from where coding the service's business logic begins.

Before they can begin coding the service the team needs to add a few classes to the project. The first class defines a *<Person>* object and the second defines an *<Address>* object. The code behind the *Person* class is similar to the class definition shown earlier in the chapter, with the exception of address information. Listing 8-8 shows the file.

Listing 8-8 person.cs: A C# source file that contains the *Person* class definition.

```
using System;
namespace CSharpWebService
{
  /// <summary>
  /// A Simple Person Class Definition
  /// </summary>
  public class Person
  {
    public String firstName;
    public String lastName;
    public String birthDate;
    public String hairColor;
    public String favoriteColor;
    public Address address;
    public Person()
    {
      firstName = "";
      lastName = "";
      birthDate = "";
      hairColor = "";
      favoriteColor = "";
      address = new Address();
    }
    public Person(String _firstName, String _lastName, String
_birthDate, String _hairColor, String _favoriteColor)
    {
      firstName = _firstName;
      lastName  = _lastName;
      birthDate = _birthDate;
      hairColor = _hairColor;
      favoriteColor = _favoriteColor;
      address = new Address();
```

```
    }
    public void setFirstName(String _firstName){ firstName =
_firstName; }
    public void setLastName(String _lastName){ lastName = _lastName; }
    public void setBirthDate(String _birthDate) { birthDate =
_birthDate; }
    public void setHairColor(String _hairColor) { hairColor =
_hairColor; }
    public void setFavoriteColor(String _favoriteColor)
{ favoriteColor = _favoriteColor; }
    public void setAddress(String address1, String address2, String
city,
      String state, String postalCode, String country)
    {
      address.setAddress1(address1);
      address.setAddress2(address2);
      address.setCity(city);
      address.setState(state);
      address.setPostalCode(postalCode);
      address.setCountry(country);
    }
  }
}
```

The properties listed in the Listing 8-8 class definition are basic personnel information: the employee's name, hair color, date of birth, favorite color, and home address. The properties need to be marked *public* so they can be returned via a SOAP document. The class's methods are simple accessors that manipulate the classes properties. The *setAddress()* method sets the properties on the *address* dependent object.

The designers of the system decided to create a helper *Address* class to provide common API for storing addresses. This class might be extended later to support driving directions or other features. The class, as it exists now, is straightforward. It contains a handful of relevant properties and the accessor methods required to manipulate them. The class definition for the *Address* class is contained in Listing 8-9.

Listing 8-9 address.cs: A C# source file containing the *Address* class definition.

```
using System;
namespace CSharpWebService
{
  /// <summary>
  /// A simple address object
  /// </summary>
  public class Address
```

(continued)

Listing 8-9 *continued*

```
   {
     public String address1;
     public String address2;
     public String address3;
     public String city;
     public String state;
     public String postalCode;
     public String country;
     public Address()
     {
       address1 = "";
       address2 = "";
       address3 = "";
       city = "";
       state = "";
       postalCode = "";
       country = "";
     }
     public String getAddress1() { return address1; }
     public String getAddress2() { return address2; }
     public String getAddress3() { return address3; }
     public String getCity() { return city; }
     public String getState() { return state; }
     public String getPostalCode() { return postalCode; }
     public String getCountry() { return country; }
    public void setAddress1(String _address1){ address1 = _address1;}
    public void setAddress2(String _address2){ address2 = _address2;}
    public void setAddress3(String _address3){ address3 = _address3;}
     public void setCity(String _city){city = _city;}
     public void setState(String _state){state = _state;}
     public void setPostalCode(String _postalCode){postalCode =
_postalCode;}
     public void setCountry(String _country){country = _country;}
   }
}
```

Now that the underlying objects have been built the development team can begin developing the Web Service logic. Most of the code in this file was generated by the .NET Web Service Wizard. The only code the programmers need to worry about comes after the *[WebMethod]* C# declaration. Listing 8-10 implements our Web Service.

Listing 8-10 Service1.asmx.cs

```
using System;
using System.Collections;
```

```
using System.ComponentModel;
using System.Data;
using System.Diagnostics;
using System.Web;
using System.Web.Services;
namespace CSharpWebService
{
  /// <summary>
  /// Summary description for Service1.
  /// </summary>
  public class Service1 : System.Web.Services.WebService
  {
    public Service1()
    {
      //CODEGEN: This call is required by the ASP.NET Web Services
Designer
      InitializeComponent();
    }
    #region Component Designer generated code
    /// <summary>
    /// Required method for Designer support - do not modify
    /// the contents of this method with the code editor.
    /// </summary>
    private void InitializeComponent()
    {
    }
    #endregion
    /// <summary>
    /// Clean up any resources being used.
    /// </summary>
    protected override void Dispose( bool disposing )
    {
    }
    [WebMethod]
    public Person CreatePerson(String firstName, String lastName,
      String birthDate, String hairColor, String favoriteColor,
String address1, String address2, String city, String state, String
postalCode, String country)
    {
     Person p = new Person(firstName,lastName, birthDate, hairColor,
favoriteColor);
      p.setHomeAddress(address1,address2,city,state,postalCode,country);
         // Database logic goes here (this code has been omitted for
brevity)
      return p;
    }
  }
 }
```

Notice that the code following the *[WebMethod]* declaration is nothing special. The *CreatePerson()* function looks normal in every respect. It doesn't need any special code to retrieve its arguments from a SOAP or HTTP document. It can create objects, load COM components, and access databases just like any other program. Finally the function is free to return a complex object as its result without worrying about creating a SOAP response on the way out. The .NET Framework handles all this hassle for the developer, so much so that the Web Service has no idea that it is being accessed remotely!

Once the service is compiled and deployed (.NET also automates the deployment process), it's ready to be accessed by any type of remote client. Before we write the client, let's first take a step back and look at the metadata the service has to offer. As mentioned earlier, one of the files the wizard created was the Listing 8-7 .vsdisco discovery document. The wizard also placed a reference to this file in the Listing 8-11 discovery file in the root directory of the Web server. These files are listed here.

Listing 8-11 Default.vsdisco: The global discovery file for the Web server that provides links to service-specific discovery documents.

```
<?xml version="1.0" encoding="utf-8"?>
<discovery xmlns="http://schemas.xmlsoap.org/disco/">
    <discoveryRef    ref="http://localhost/CSharpWebService/
CSharpWebService.vsdisco" />
    <discoveryRef ref="http://localhost/HelloWorld/
HelloWorld.vsdisco" />
</discovery>
```

Notice that one of the discovery references in this file points to the URL *http://localhost/CSharpWebService/CSharpWebService.vsdicso.* Listing 8-12 contains the discovery information for the service we just wrote. Here are the contents of this file.

Listing 8-12 SharpWebService.vsdisco: The createPerson service discovery file.

```
<?xml version="1.0" encoding="utf-8"?>
<discovery xmlns="http://schemas.xmlsoap.org/disco/">
  <contractRef ref="http://localhost/CSharpWebService/
Service1.asmx?wsdl" docRef="http://localhost/CSharpWebService/
Service1.asmx" xmlns="http://schemas.xmlsoap.org/disco/scl/" />
</discovery>
```

Here we are finally redirected to the services WSDL contract. The *ref* attribute of the *<contactRef>* element contains a URL to this resource *("http://localhost/CSharpWebService/Service1.asmx?wsdl").* As mentioned earlier, the WSDL contract holds the keys to accessing the Web Service. The metadata contained in this WSDL document is a more complex than the one shown in our HelloWorld example earlier. The complete WSDL document can be found in Listing 8-13.

Listing 8-13 createPerson.wsdl: The createPerson WSDL contract.

```
<?xml version="1.0" encoding="utf-8"?>
<definitions xmlns:s="http://www.w3.org/2001/XMLSchema"
xmlns:http="http://schemas.xmlsoap.org/wsdl/http/"
xmlns:mime="http://schemas.xmlsoap.org/wsdl/mime/" xmlns:tm="http://
microsoft.com/wsdl/mime/textMatching/" xmlns:soap=
"http://schemas.xmlsoap.org/wsdl/soap/" xmlns:soapenc=
"http://schemas.xmlsoap.org/soap/encoding/" xmlns:s0=
"http://tempuri.org/" targetNamespace=
"http://tempuri.org/" xmlns=
"http://schemas.xmlsoap.org/wsdl/">
  <types>
    <s:schema attributeFormDefault="qualified"
elementFormDefault="qualified" targetNamespace="http://tempuri.org/">
      <s:element name="CreatePerson">
        <s:complexType>
          <s:sequence>
            <s:element minOccurs="1" maxOccurs="1" name=
"firstName" nillable="true" type="s:string" />
            <s:element minOccurs="1" maxOccurs="1" name=
"lastName" nillable="true" type="s:string" />
            <s:element minOccurs="1" maxOccurs="1" name=
"birthDate" nillable="true" type="s:string" />
            <s:element minOccurs="1" maxOccurs="1" name=
"hairColor" nillable="true" type="s:string" />
            <s:element minOccurs="1" maxOccurs="1" name=
"favoriteColor" nillable="true" type="s:string" />
            <s:element minOccurs="1" maxOccurs="1" name=
"address1" nillable="true" type="s:string" />
            <s:element minOccurs="1" maxOccurs="1" name=
"address2" nillable="true" type="s:string" />
            <s:element minOccurs="1" maxOccurs="1" name=
"city" nillable="true" type="s:string" />
            <s:element minOccurs="1" maxOccurs="1" name=
"state" nillable="true" type="s:string" />
            <s:element minOccurs="1" maxOccurs="1" name=
"postalCode" nillable="true" type="s:string" />
            <s:element minOccurs="1" maxOccurs="1" name=
"country" nillable="true" type="s:string" />
          </s:sequence>
        </s:complexType>
      </s:element>
```

(continued)

Listing 8-13 *continued*

```
      <s:element name="CreatePersonResponse">
        <s:complexType>
          <s:sequence>
            <s:element minOccurs="1" maxOccurs="1" name=
"CreatePersonResult" nillable="true" type="s0:Person" />
          </s:sequence>
        </s:complexType>
      </s:element>
```

The primary difference between this WSDL document and the simpler HelloWorld version is that the return type of the *createPerson()* service is a complex object rather than a string. An *<s:element>* tag is created for each property in the class. The first five properties are all of type *string* and require no further definition. The *homeAddress* property, however, is an *Address* object. The contract must also include a *<complexType>* definition for *Address* if a client wants to reference it. The *Address* class is defined next. Because none of its properties are complex objects, the WSDL document is finished describing classes.

```
      <s:complexType name="Person">
        <s:sequence>
          <s:element minOccurs="1" maxOccurs="1" name="firstName"
nillable="true" type="s:string" />
          <s:element minOccurs="1" maxOccurs="1" name="lastName"
nillable="true" type="s:string" />
          <s:element minOccurs="1" maxOccurs="1" name="birthDate"
nillable="true" type="s:string" />
          <s:element minOccurs="1" maxOccurs="1" name="hairColor"
nillable="true" type="s:string" />
          <s:element minOccurs="1" maxOccurs="1" name="favoriteColor"
nillable="true" type="s:string" />
          <s:element minOccurs="1" maxOccurs="1" name="homeAddress"
nillable="true" type="s0:Address" />
        </s:sequence>
      </s:complexType>
      <s:complexType name="Address">
        <s:sequence>
          <s:element minOccurs="1" maxOccurs="1" name="address1"
nillable="true" type="s:string" />
          <s:element minOccurs="1" maxOccurs="1" name="address2"
nillable="true" type="s:string" />
          <s:element minOccurs="1" maxOccurs="1" name="address3"
nillable="true" type="s:string" />
          <s:element minOccurs="1" maxOccurs="1" name="city"
nillable="true" type="s:string" />
          <s:element minOccurs="1" maxOccurs="1" name="state"
```

```
nillable="true" type="s:string" />
          <s:element minOccurs="1" maxOccurs="1" name="postalCode"
nillable="true" type="s:string" />
          <s:element minOccurs="1" maxOccurs="1" name="country"
nillable="true" type="s:string" />
        </s:sequence>
      </s:complexType>
      <s:element name="Person" nillable="true" type="s0:Person" />
    </s:schema>
  </types>
```

The SOAP, GET, and POST request and response documents are similar in nature to those defined in the HelloWorld example. Notice that the CreatePersonXXXOut all return some form of the *s0:Person complexElemen*t type declared previously.

```
  <message name="CreatePersonSoapIn">
    <part name="parameters" element="s0:CreatePerson" />
  </message>
  <message name="CreatePersonSoapOut">
    <part name="parameters" element="s0:CreatePersonResponse" />
  </message>
  <message name="CreatePersonHttpGetIn">
    <part name="firstName" type="s:string" />
    <part name="lastName" type="s:string" />
    <part name="birthDate" type="s:string" />
    <part name="hairColor" type="s:string" />
    <part name="favoriteColor" type="s:string" />
    <part name="address1" type="s:string" />
    <part name="address2" type="s:string" />
    <part name="city" type="s:string" />
    <part name="state" type="s:string" />
    <part name="postalCode" type="s:string" />
    <part name="country" type="s:string" />
  </message>
  <message name="CreatePersonHttpGetOut">
    <part name="Body" element="s0:Person" />
  </message>
  <message name="CreatePersonHttpPostIn">
    <part name="firstName" type="s:string" />
    <part name="lastName" type="s:string" />
    <part name="birthDate" type="s:string" />
    <part name="hairColor" type="s:string" />
    <part name="favoriteColor" type="s:string" />
    <part name="address1" type="s:string" />
    <part name="address2" type="s:string" />
    <part name="city" type="s:string" />
    <part name="state" type="s:string" />
    <part name="postalCode" type="s:string" />
```

```
    <part name="country" type="s:string" />
  </message>
  <message name="CreatePersonHttpPostOut">
    <part name="Body" element="s0:Person" />
  </message>
  <portType name="Service1Soap">
    <operation name="CreatePerson">
      <input message="s0:CreatePersonSoapIn" />
      <output message="s0:CreatePersonSoapOut" />
    </operation>
  </portType>
  <portType name="Service1HttpGet">
    <operation name="CreatePerson">
      <input message="s0:CreatePersonHttpGetIn" />
      <output message="s0:CreatePersonHttpGetOut" />
    </operation>
  </portType>
  <portType name="Service1HttpPost">
    <operation name="CreatePerson">
      <input message="s0:CreatePersonHttpPostIn" />
      <output message="s0:CreatePersonHttpPostOut" />
    </operation>
  </portType>
  <binding name="Service1Soap" type="s0:Service1Soap">
    <soap:binding transport="http://schemas.xmlsoap.org/soap/http"
style="document" />
    <operation name="CreatePerson">
      <soap:operation soapAction="http://tempuri.org/CreatePerson"
style="document" />
      <input>
        <soap:body use="literal" />
      </input>
      <output>
        <soap:body use="literal" />
      </output>
    </operation>
  </binding>
  <binding name="Service1HttpGet" type="s0:Service1HttpGet">
    <http:binding verb="GET" />
    <operation name="CreatePerson">
      <http:operation location="/CreatePerson" />
      <input>
        <http:urlEncoded />
      </input>
      <output>
        <mime:mimeXml part="Body" />
      </output>
    </operation>
  </binding>
```

```
  <binding name="Service1HttpPost" type="s0:Service1HttpPost">
    <http:binding verb="POST" />
    <operation name="CreatePerson">
      <http:operation location="/CreatePerson" />
      <input>
        <mime:content type="application/x-www-form-urlencoded" />
      </input>
      <output>
        <mime:mimeXml part="Body" />
      </output>
    </operation>
  </binding>
  <service name="Service1">
    <port name="Service1Soap" binding="s0:Service1Soap">
      <soap:address location="http://localhost/CSharpWebService/
Service1.asmx" />
    </port>
    <port name="Service1HttpGet" binding="s0:Service1HttpGet">
      <http:address location="http://localhost/CSharpWebService/
Service1.asmx" />
    </port>
    <port name="Service1HttpPost" binding="s0:Service1HttpPost">
      <http:address location="http://localhost/CSharpWebService/
Service1.asmx" />
    </port>
  </service>
</definitions>
```

The *createPerson()* Web Service Client

We will begin writing our client by examining the metadata that our new service will accept and return. We will stick to examples using the SOAP invocation protocol. To reconstruct John Smith's record in the new personnel system we will need to send a SOAP document with the following format to the *createPerson()* method.

```
POST /CSharpWebService/Service1.asmx HTTP/1.1
Host: localhost
Content-Type: text/xml; charset=utf-8
Content-Length: length
SOAPAction: "http://tempuri.org/CreatePerson"
<?xml version="1.0" encoding="utf-8"?>
<soap:Envelope xmlns:xsi="http://www.w3.org/2001/XMLSchema-instance"
xmlns:xsd="http://www.w3.org/2001/XMLSchema" xmlns:soap=
"http://schemas.xmlsoap.org/soap/envelope/">
  <soap:Body>
    <CreatePerson xmlns="http://tempuri.org/">
      <firstName>John</firstName>
```

```
      <lastName>Smith</lastName>
      <birthDate>11/30/1974</birthDate>
      <hairColor>brown</hairColor>
      <favoriteColor>blue</favoriteColor>
      <address1>200 Brattle Street</address1>
      <address2></address2>
      <city>Cambridge</city>
      <state>MA</state>
      <postalCode>02138</postalCode>
      <country>USA</country>
    </CreatePerson>
  </soap:Body>
</soap:Envelope>
```

We could create this document by hand and ship it off to the Web server, but why go through the effort when .NET includes utilities to help do it for us? One such utility is the *SoapHttpClientProtocol* class. This class provides a layer of abstraction above the underlying SOAP protocol. Developers can use this API to call remote Web Services as if they were local methods.

This class can be used only through sub-classes. You must create your own class that extends *SoapHttpClientProtocol* and adapt it for a specific Web Service. To implement a sub-class of *SoapHttpClientProtocol* you must perform at least four tasks.

1. Provide a default constructor for the class that sets the *Url* property of the superclass to the location of the Web Service (as defined in the service's WSDL contract).
2. Create a method in the class that has the same signature as the method in the Web Service.
3. Call the *Invoke* method of the *SoapHttpClientProtocol* class, passing in the service name and an array of objects representing the service arguments.
4. Provide local class definitions for any complex objects that are returned by the service.

The following code listing shows an example of a *SoapHttpClientProtocol* sub-class engineered to communicate with the CreatePerson service we created earlier. The file that contains this class definition is Listing 8-14.

Listing 8-14 PersonCreator.cs: A utility class that provides high-level access to the CreatePerson service.

```
using System.Diagnostics;
using System.Xml.Serialization;
using System;
```

```
using System.Web.Services.Protocols;
using System.Web.Services;
```

The *WebServiceBindingAttribute* attribute states that the *PersonCreator* class contains one or more Web methods that implement the *Service1Soap* binding, as defined by the WSDL contract for the Web Service. Bindings are similar to interfaces in that they prescribe a strict set of operations. Classes that implement one or more bindings for a Web Service need to make sure that they implement all operations defined within that binding. Let's review the *Service1Soap* binding that we saw at the beginning of this section.

```
  <binding name="Service1Soap" type="s0:Service1Soap">
    <soap:binding transport="http://schemas.xmlsoap.org/soap/http"
style="document" />
    <operation name="CreatePerson">
      <soap:operation soapAction="http://tempuri.org/CreatePerson"
style="document" />
      <input>
        <soap:body use="literal" />
      </input>
      <output>
        <soap:body use="literal" />
      </output>
    </operation>
  </binding>
```

The binding implies that the class will contain a *CreatePerson()* Web Service method that implements some sort of SOAP action. The corresponding C# Web method, shown here, uses a C# attribute to identify itself.

```
[System.Web.Services.WebServiceBindingAttribute(Name="Service1Soap",
Namespace="http://tempuri.org/")]
public class PersonCreator : System.Web.Services.Protocols.
SoapHttpClientProtocol
{
  [System.Diagnostics.DebuggerStepThroughAttribute()]
  public PersonCreator()
  {
    this.Url = "http://localhost/CSharpWebService/Service1.asmx";
  }
  [System.Diagnostics.DebuggerStepThroughAttribute()]
```

A call to a Web Service method, or operation, can be encoded in two ways: RPC and Document. The RPC style encodes the Web Service method using the SOAP for RPC specification. The Document style, which is used here as indicated by the *SoapDocumentMethodAttribute* attribute, creates a SOAP XML message that is formatted exactly as defined by the XSD schema contained in the service's WSDL document.

The method signature to *CreatePerson()* also follows the directions of the WSDL document in its arguments and return type.

```
[System.Web.Services.Protocols.SoapDocumentMethodAttribute("http://
tempuri.org/CreatePerson", Use=System.Web.Services.Description.
SoapBindingUse.Literal, ParameterStyle=System.Web.Services.
Protocols.SoapParameterStyle.Wrapped)]
  public Person CreatePerson(string firstName, string lastName, string
birthDate, string hairColor, string favoriteColor, string address1,
string address2, string city, string state, string postalCode, string
country)
  {
```

The magic begins with a call to the *SoapHttpClientProtocol* class's *Invoke()* method. The .NET infrastructure marshals the argument object (an array of String objects) into an XML SOAP document, sends the document to the Web Service, waits for the service to reply, and unmarshals the return result into position zero of the result array. This result is cast to a *Person* object and is returned to the client.

```
    object[] results = this.Invoke("CreatePerson", new object[] {
                                    firstName,
                                    lastName,
                                    birthDate,
                                    hairColor,
                                    favoriteColor,
                                    address1,
                                    address2,
                                    city,
                                    state,
                                    postalCode,
                                    country});
    return ((Person)(results[0]));
  }
}
```

Local definitions for the *Person* and *Address* classes are needed to cast the return result without error. Once again, the WSDL contract has all the information you need to create these class definitions. In fact, these *Person* and *Address* class definitions don't necessarily need to match those found in the Web Service. Only the publicly accessible properties (that is, those properties marked as *public* or accessible through a getter/setter design pattern) need to appear in the client's code.

```
public class Person
{
  public string firstName;
  public string lastName;
  public string birthDate;
  public string hairColor;
```

```
  public string favoriteColor;
  public Address homeAddress;
}
public class Address
{
  public string address1;
  public string address2;
  public string address3;
  public string city;
  public string state;
  public string postalCode;
  public string country;
}
```

The service proxy that we just built provides an additional layer of abstraction for our client. We now have a business-level interface to the PersonCreator Web Service. Client programs that use the *PersonCreator* class do not need to worry about where the Web Service is located or what protocol is used to invoke it. As you can see here, the *PersonCreator* class is easy to use. You'd never know there was so much complexity—and metadata—underneath the covers.

```
PersonCreator personCreator = new PersonCreator();
Person p = personCreator.CreatePerson("John", "Smith", "11/30/1974",
"brown", "blue", "200 Brattle Street", "", "Cambridge", "MA", "02138",
"USA");
```

This is a slick programming interface. Microsoft's *SoapHttpClientProtocol* class saved us some time by masking the gory details of SOAP messaging. Still, the process of extending this class every time we want to use a Web Service can become tedious. If this were the only way to work, each time you wanted to use a Web Service you'd have to download its WSDL contract, interpret it (which can be tricky, especially when multiple classes are involved!), and manually create a stub class that implements all of the defined operations. Fortunately, the .NET provides tools to do all this for you.

Generating a Client Proxy from XML Metadata

Microsoft provides a few tools in its .NET Framework to aid in developing client proxies to access Web Services. The WSDL executable, located in the *bin* directory of the framework SDK, does all the dirty work for you. The syntax for running wsdl.exe from the command line is as follows:

```
Wsdl /language:language  /protocol:protocol /namespace:myNameSpace /
out:filename /username:username /password:password /domain:domain <url
or path>
```

Table 8-1 documents the WSDL.exe command's arguments.

Table 8-1 WSDL Command Syntax

Parameter	Value
<url or path>	A URL or path to a service description, a file describing a Web Service in WSDL. If you specify a file, supply a file containing the service description. For example: myWebservice.wsdl If you specify a URL, the URL needs to reference an .asmx page or return a service description. For ASP.NET Web Services you can return a service description by appending WSDL to the URL of the Web Service. For example, *http://www.contoso.com/MyWebService.asmx?WSDL*
/language:*language*	(Optional) The language the proxy class is generated in. Available options include CS, VB, and JS, referring to C#, Visual Basic.NET, and JScript.NET, respectively. If no language option is specified, the proxy class is generated in C#.
/protocol:*protocol*	(Optional) The protocol used to invoke the Web Service methods. Available options include SOAP, HttpGET, and HttpPOST. If no protocol is specified, SOAP is the default.
/namespace: *myNameSpace*	(Optional) The namespace of the generated proxy. Default value is the global namespace.
/out:*filename*	(Optional) The name of the file to create containing the proxy class. Default name is based on the name of the Web Service.
/username:*username*	(Optional) The username to use when connecting to a Web server that requires authentication.
/password:*password*	(Optional) The password to use when connecting to a Web server that requires authentication.
/domain:*domain*	(Optional) The domain to use when connecting to a Web server that requires authentication.

Let's use this tool on our CreatePerson Web Service.

```
wsdl /language:CS /out:PersonCreator.cs http://localhost/
CSharpWebService/Service1.asmx?WSDL
```

The tool created the Listing 8-15 file that contains all the proxy code needed to access the service. This file can be imported into our client .NET project and used out of the box. Here is the code that the WSDL.exe utility generated for us.

Listing 8-15 PersonCreator.cs: A C# source file containing the proxy code required to access the *createPerson()* Web Service method.

```
//------------------------------------------------------------------------
// <autogenerated>
//   This code was generated by a tool.
//   Runtime Version: 1.0.2914.11
//
//   Changes to this file may cause incorrect behavior and will be
lost if
//   the code is regenerated.
// </autogenerated>
//------------------------------------------------------------------------
//
// This source code was auto-generated by wsdl, Version=1.0.2914.11.
//
using System.Diagnostics;
using System.Xml.Serialization;
using System;
using System.Web.Services.Protocols;
using System.Web.Services;
[System.Web.Services.WebServiceBindingAttribute
(Name="Service1Soap", Namespace="http://tempuri.org/")]
public class Service1 : System.Web.Services.Protocols.
SoapHttpClientProtocol {
  [System.Diagnostics.DebuggerStepThroughAttribute()]
  public Service1() {
    this.Url = "http://localhost/CSharpWebService/Service1.asmx";
  }
  [System.Diagnostics.DebuggerStepThroughAttribute()]
  [System.Web.Services.Protocols.SoapDocumentMethodAttribute
("http://tempuri.org/CreatePerson", Use=System.Web.Services.
Description.SoapBindingUse.Literal, ParameterStyle=System.Web.
Services.Protocols.SoapParameterStyle.Wrapped)]
  public Person CreatePerson(string firstName, string lastName,
string birthDate, string hairColor, string favoriteColor, string
address1, string address2, string city, string state,
string postalCode, string country) {
    object[] results = this.Invoke("CreatePerson", new object[] {
          firstName,
          lastName,
          birthDate,
          hairColor,
          favoriteColor,
```

(continued)

Listing 8-15 *continued*

```
            address1,
            address2,
            city,
            state,
            postalCode,
            country});
        return ((Person)(results[0]));
    }
    [System.Diagnostics.DebuggerStepThroughAttribute()]
    public System.IAsyncResult BeginCreatePerson(string firstName,
string lastName, string birthDate, string hairColor, string
favoriteColor, string address1, string address2, string city, string
state, string postalCode, string country, System.AsyncCallback
callback, object asyncState) {
        return this.BeginInvoke("CreatePerson", new object[] {
            firstName,
            lastName,
            birthDate,
            hairColor,
            favoriteColor,
            address1,
            address2,
            city,
            state,
            postalCode,
            country}, callback, asyncState);
    }
    [System.Diagnostics.DebuggerStepThroughAttribute()]
    public Person EndCreatePerson(System.IAsyncResult asyncResult) {
        object[] results = this.EndInvoke(asyncResult);
        return ((Person)(results[0]));
    }
}
public class Person {
    public string firstName;
    public string lastName;
    public string birthDate;
    public string hairColor;
    public string favoriteColor;
    public Address address;
}
public class Address {
    public string address1;
    public string address2;
    public string address3;
    public string city;
    public string state;
    public string postalCode;
    public string country;
}
```

You might notice that this file looks similar to the *PersonCreator* class shown in Listing 8-14. One significant difference is the introduction of two new methods: *BeginCreatePerson()* and *EndCreatePerson()*. These functions, generated by the WSDL.exe utility, allow you to invoke the CreatePerson service asynchronously.

.NET supports a design pattern that implements asynchronous Web method invocation, regardless of how the Web method was written. The pattern prescribes two new asynchronous methods, *Begin()* and *End()*, for every synchronous method. These functions give non-blocking access to Web Services that take a long time to complete. To call the function asynchronously you must alter your client to call *BeginCreatePerson()* instead of *CreatePerson()*. *BeginCreatePerson()* kicks off the Web Service but doesn't wait for it to finish. Instead it returns a handle to an object that implements the *IAsyncResult* interface. The *IAsyncResult* interface contains a *WaitHandle* object that handles all of the synchronization involved in waiting for the Web Service to complete.

Once the CreatePerson service has completed, you must call the *EndCreatePerson()* function to retrieve the results. The call to *EndCreatePerson()* can happen via a callback function passed into *BeginCreatePerson()*, or you can wait on the WaitHandle object explicitly and call *EndCreatePerson()* when the service has finished its job. *EndCreatePerson()* requires you to pass in the IAsyncResult handle as an argument. It returns the result the same way the synchronous method does.

> **Note** Visual Studio .NET will automate the creation of Web Service proxies for you. By adding a "Web reference" to your project you can dynamically generate all the code you need to access a particular Web Service.

An Overview of .NET Remoting

As we have seen, the .NET makes generous use of XML metadata. From XML comments to remote Web Service discovery and execution, the .NET uses metadata to make software components more self-descriptive. This promotes loose, run-time coupling of objects and applications in a development environment rich with opportunity.

Inter-application object sharing need not be limited to Web Services. The .NET Remoting infrastructure encompasses many different levels of interobject and interapplication communication. In this section we will cover the .NET platform's support for distributed objects. We will touch on how Web Services relate to remotable objects. We will then explore some fine-grained remote programming techniques that the .NET platform also provides. This discussion will include conceptual overviews as well as detailed code samples.

Remote Web Services

Remote Web Services are ideal for publishing course-grained application methods to the widest possible consumer audience. Because Web Services rely exclusively on open, ubiquitous standards such as HTTP, SOAP, and XML for communication, they are accessible to any type of Internet application.

Web Services are also useful for publishing software to an unknown user base. A good example of a Web Services candidate is our Noverant.com online CD store. As its volume increases, Noverant might want to consider exposing its CD purchasing business logic through a Web Service. This would allow partners and customers to create orders directly through software, bypassing a tedious Web site. Custom Noverant Web Service clients, built in a .NET studio, Notepad, or any other development toolset, could be written to browse and purchase items from the Noverant CD catalog.

Web Services are fantastic, but when do you not want to use them? Unfortunately, Web Services do have a few limitations. All Web Service objects are passed by value through SOAP. Pass-by-reference is not supported. A certain amount of overhead is associated with calls to Web Services. Objects need to be marshaled into (potentially large) XML SOAP documents and return results need to be unmarshaled. Furthermore, reliance on HTTP makes Web Services stateless in nature. Web Service connections are closed upon the completion of any call to a Web method.

These limitations make Web Services less suitable for fine-grained object sharing. Fortunately, the .NET Common Language Runtime (runtime) engine has support for a wide variety of distributed object sharing and messaging. The following feature list is an excerpt from the .NET Framework Developer's Guide.

- The ability to publish and consume services and objects across a wide variety of application types. Applications that can participate in remote services include console applications, Microsoft Windows GUI applications, IIS-based Web applications, ASP .NET Web Services, or local Windows services.
- The preservation of full managed-code type-system fidelity.
- The ability to pass objects by reference and to return to a particular object in a particular application domain.

- Binary Object Serialization in addition to SOAP XML-based serialization.
- The ability to control activation characteristics and object lifetimes directly.
- The ability to implement and use third-party channels or protocols to extend communication to meet your specific needs.
- Direct participation in the communication process to create the functionality you need.

.NET Remoting Overview

The .NET Remoting framework provides tools that allow applications to share objects and data over a network. Web Services are just one aspect of .NET Remoting. Trusted client applications might need to interact with server-side software components at the object level rather than the service level. The .NET Remoting framework provides these services and many others. Let's look at how the .NET Remoting framework relates to applications, messages, objects, and channels.

Applications, Messages, and Objects

Applications form loosely coupled communities in the .NET Remoting framework. They can communicate with each other at one of two levels.

1. They can send high-level messages. These messages can contain different kinds of application data, including binary formats, XML text, plain text, or HTML.
2. They can share actual objects with each other. The two applications do not need to be homogeneous in platform to communicate at the object level. Participating programs can be written in .NET C#, VB, Java, C, or COBOL. SOAP is used to promote loose coupling between applications at the object level. SOAP messages can be sent anywhere over HTTP and make ideal carriers for pass-by-value objects.

Applications that participate in remote transactions are isolated from one another in the .NET by Application Domains. One or more applications might reside inside a single application domain. The *AppDomain* class manages these entities. Its methods enable the runtime to load assemblies or threads into the domain, define dynamic assemblies, specify loading and termination events, and terminate the domain.

Channels

SOAP and other interapplication messages are transported through channels. Channels relay information between application domains, processes, and machines. Channels can either listen for new incoming messages or relay outbound messages to a destination channel. Channels are also responsible for converting messages into different wire formats. For example, the *TcpChannel* class converts outbound messages into a compact binary format and converts incoming messages from binary into their original format.

Channels implement the *IChannel* interface that defines the properties *ChannelName* and *ChannelPriority*. A session is created between each end of the channel. Sessions connect client and server "sinks." Sinks are responsible for relaying network messages along "sink chains" on both the client and the server. The client end of the channel resides at the end of the Client sink chain while the server end of the channel is at the front of the Server sink chain.

An Introduction to Remote Objects

The .NET Framework includes a rich library of tools for remote object sharing. The remoting framework allows objects to be marshaled *by value* or *by reference* to and from other applications on the network. In this section we will explore object marshaling, object activation, leases, and remote object configuration.

Marshal by Value

A client application can take a "brute force" approach to remoting by downloading an entire object—methods, properties and all—into its address space. The client can then interact with the object locally. The object's methods execute in the client's address space and can access resources intrinsic to the client's context, such as file systems and network connections. The process of copying an object or value from one address space into another is called "marshaling by value."

To accomplish this, the .NET Framework serializes the server object's entire class definition into a format that can be transmitted over the network, or channel. The serialized object can be represented in a binary format unique to the operating environment for optimal performance. Alternatively, the object can be serialized into an XML descriptor that can be reconstructed on any platform. Web Services employ the latter technique.

Almost any object can be marshaled by value. Any object that implements the *ISerializable* interface or implements its own serialization techniques can be transmitted by value (or copied) to another application.

Having a client download an entire object from a server is usually undesirable. It is an expensive operation that can require a lot of network bandwidth and client resources. Some classes have large method footprints that take time to serialize. In addition, transmitting an entire object over a network exposes that object's private instance variables to outsiders. Sometimes you do not have the option of downloading an entire object. In situations where the object needs to access resources unique to the server, such as a database or file system, you have no choice but to execute the object remotely. What should you do if you don't need the entire object but just need to call its methods remotely? Marshaling by reference might be the answer.

Marshal by Reference

The .NET Remoting framework supports marshal-by-reference objects as well as marshal-by-value ones. This means that a client application can download a reference to a remote object and interact with it as if it were locally defined. Although the object appears to "belong" to the client, its methods actually execute, via RPC, in the server's address space.

The .NET Remoting framework takes care of all the plumbing that makes remote object references work. Remote object references are actually stub classes generated by .NET. The stub class has the same method and property signature as the original class. The stub class, however, does not house any of the method implementations. Each call to a stub method begins a chain of events in which the method arguments are serialized and sent over the network to the remote object instance, where the actual method call is executed. The method's results are serialized, sent back to the client, unpackaged, and returned to the calling function as if the method had executed locally.

One of the exciting features about .NET Remoting is that this complexity can be completely masked from the developer. If everything is configured correctly a programmer can create a remote object stub simply by calling the *New()* (or comparable) constructor on a remote object. The .NET Remoting framework will generate a stub reference and return it in place of the actual object. Although the developer can step in and micromanage the remoting process if necessary, the .NET handles most common cases so well that the process is relatively painless.

> **Note** Although the runtime Remoting Architecture makes it easy to create references to remote objects, you should use them judiciously. Your software incurs a performance hit each time you cross an application boundary. Make sure you keep this in mind when designing remote API for your application. For example, see if you can consolidate multiple calls to remote accessors into a single call to a more coarse-grained method.

Object Activation and State

Before you can begin instantiating and using remote objects, you need to let the .NET know about the remote object's activation and state. You should specify whether the client or the server will be responsible for the object's activation (creation, persistence, and destruction), be it server-activated or client-activated, and state. In the case of client-activated objects, you must also be wary of remote object leases.

Server-Activated Objects

Server-activated objects are objects whose life cycles are controlled exclusively by the server. Although clients can hold references to server-activated objects, the server only creates instances of these objects when one of their methods is called. Even though a client might create a stub object by calling *New()* or *Activator.GetObject()*, the object does not yet need to be instantiated on the server. This "lazy loading" of server-activated objects conserves server resources and removes the need to make a network round-trip just to create the object's stub in the client. By default, server-activated objects only support default constructors (that is, constructors that don't take any arguments). Programmers must publish other constructors programmatically.

Server-activated objects come in two flavors: *Singleton* and *SingletonCall*. Singleton type objects never have more than one instance running on the server at a time. All requests to the server are serviced by that single instance. If no instance of the singleton object is in memory (for example, the first time one of its methods is called), the server creates a new instance and then services the request. The server is free to destroy a singleton object at any time as long as it creates a new one of the same type the next time it's requested. This means that the actual object the client stub points to might change over time. Because of this, singleton objects are, by definition, stateless. Singleton methods can declare local variables that will be unique for the duration of the request. However, any instance properties of the class will be shared across all clients or will be discarded if the object's instance is destroyed. Therefore, all client-specific states must be kept on the client side and passed to the singleton object with each method request.

SingletonCall type objects always have one instance on the server for each *request*. All requests to a *SingletonCall* type object will be serviced by a unique instance of the class. Subsequent requests are not guaranteed to be serviced by the same instance, however.

The following piece of code is an example of how a client can construct a server-activated object using the *Activator.GetObject()* method.

```
RemoteObjectClass MyRemoteClass = (RemoteObjectClass)Activator.GetObject(
typeof(RemoteObjectClass),
"tcp://computername:8080/RemoteObjectUri "
);
```

Now that the client has a reference to the *MyRemoteClass* object, it can begin invoking its methods directly.

Client-Activated Objects

As the name implies, client-activated objects have life cycles that are controlled by the client application. This paradigm is similar to the way local objects work. The server creates a unique instance of the object every time a client calls its constructor. This means that the same client application can hold references to several unique instances of a server-side object.

Client-activated objects maintain much more state than their server-activated counterparts because of the one-to-one mapping of client-side object stubs to server-side object instances. Client-activated objects behave the same way that locally instantiated objects do. Maintaining object state across a network is a difficult task. Fortunately, the .NET Framework takes complexity behind remote procedure calls and state maintenance out of the developer's list of details to worry about.

Client-activated objects have a greater potential impact on server resources than do server-activated objects. A client can create any number of instances of these objects. Stale object pointers can clutter the server with useless object instances, and distributed garbage collection is a difficult problem to solve. How does the server know when the client is finished using an object? Should it wait until the client releases its last reference to the object? Should the server try to communicate with the client periodically to see if it can reclaim the memory? These solutions are tricky to implement, particularly when network problems can arise at any moment to interfere with host-to-client communication. The .NET implements distributed garbage collection by using a *lifetime lease* strategy.

Remote Object Leases

When a client creates a new instance of a remote object, it must specify how long it intends to use it. Once the agreed lease duration has expired the server will contact the client and ask if it needs to renew the lease. If the client renews, everything is business as usual. If the client does not respond, the server waits a predetermined amount of time to see if the client wakes up. If the server does not hear from the client it assumes the object is no longer needed and reclaims the object's resources.

Leases implement the *ILease* interface that prescribes the properties and methods associated with leasing and lease renewal. Clients need not wait for the lease to expire before renewing; each call to a remote method can renew the lease. Clients can also call the *Renew* method synchronously to extend its life. A lease manager running on the server maintains a queue of clients that have requested leases. The manager monitors the queue and prompts clients to renew when their leases have expired.

The *ILease* interface is straightforward and contains only a few properties and methods. The leasing manager's queue contains a list of objects that implement this interface. Table 8-2 and Table 8-3 offer a more detailed definition of the leasing interface.

Table 8-2 ILease Public Instance Properties

Property	**Description**
CurrentLeaseTime	Gets the amount of time remaining in the lease.
CurrentState	Gets the current *leaseState* of the lease.
InitialLeaseTime	Gets or sets the initial time for the lease.
RenewalOnCallTime	Gets or sets the amount of time by which a call to the remote object increases the leaseTime.
SponsorshipTimeout	Gets or sets the amount of time to wait for a sponsor to return with a lease renewal time.

Table 8-3 ILease Public Instance Methods

Method	**Description**
Register	Overloaded. Registers a sponsor (client) for the lease.
Renew	Renews a lease for the specified time.
Unregister	Removes a sponsor from the sponsor list.

The *leaseState* property can take on one of the following states: Active (the lease is active and has not expired), Expired (the lease has expired and cannot be renewed), Initial (the lease has been created but is not yet active), Null (the lease is not initialized), and Renewing (the lease has expired and is looking for sponsorship).

The downside to leasing is that it is not as efficient as reference counting, the preferred mechanism for in-process garbage collection. Sometimes leases keep objects alive on the server even after the client has discarded the reference. Nonetheless, a well-managed leasing system is much cleaner to implement over error-prone networks and, over the long term, is almost as efficient as reference counting or pinging.

Configuration

Now that you understand the basic concepts behind client-activated objects, server-activated objects, and leasing, you are almost ready to write some code that uses .NET Remoting. One additional conceptual barrier stands in our way, however. How do clients discover remote objects and their properties? How is remote object metadata passed from server to client and what does that metadata describe?

First let's look at the metadata the client and server programs need to share objects. The following pieces of information are necessary to create and invoke remote methods.

- The type of activation required. This specifies whether or not the object is client-activated or server-activated.
- The complete metadata describing the object. The class's metadata includes a list of its public properties and types and a list of public method signatures.
- The channel registered to handle requests for the object. This means the protocol and port number to which the remote object is bound.
- The URI that uniquely identifies an object of that type. These last two pieces of metadata can be seen in the following example:

  tcp://myserver.com:8080/remoteObjects/MyObject.

  where *tcp://myserver.com:8080* is the channel identifier and */remoteObjects/MyObject* is the URI.

Think back to the way Web Service clients work with the WSDL. The WSDL document contains all the preceding metadata. The activation method is implicitly server-activated. The class metadata is contained in the WSDL document. The channel is implicitly http, and the URI to the Web Service is also explicitly stated in the WSDL document. This information gives the .NET Remoting framework all it needs to generate the stub classes needed to make use of the Web Service.

Remoting Examples

In this section, we will drive home some object remoting concepts by creating some sample applications. We will begin by building a server-activated object and a client-activated object. Next we will explore the concept of distributed events by creating a Producer-Consumer application using the .NET Remoting platform.

Creating Remote Objects

Now let's get down to business and build a remotable object. For our example we will create two different remotable objects. The first will be a server-activated factorial object that computes large factorials on behalf of its clients. The second will be a remote shopping cart component that maintains a shopper's name and a list of items they intend to purchase. We will walk through the steps of designing, coding, and deploying each kind of object.

Factorial—A Server-Activated Remote Object

The *factorial* object will allow clients to offload the CPU-intensive task of computing factorials for large numbers to a server equipped to do the job. The object will have a single method, *computeFactorial(int num),* that takes a single integer and returns its factorial.

Now we'll follow the recommended steps to create this remote object.

Step 1. Design your Service

You need to answer these questions to design your remote service:

1. What is your host application domain?
2. What is your activation model?
3. What channel and port will your service use?
4. How will clients obtain your service's metadata?

The first question asks how we intend to develop our remotable object. We will use the C# programming language to implement a Windows application for our simple factorial object. Second, our activation model will be server-activated. Moreover, we will make our object a singleton so that clients can share a single instance of it on the server. Third, our application will use tcp port 8081. Finally our client will obtain the service's metadata by linking to a local DLL copy of the service assembly and will programmatically create service instances by calling the *Activator.GetObject()* method.

Step 2. Implement Your Host Application Domain

The code behind our factorial service will be easy to write. The service itself is a mere class that inherits from *MarshalByRefObject*. Listing 8-16 is a full listing of this class:

Listing 8-16 FactorialService.cs: The guts of our factorial service.

```
using System;
namespace Factorial
{
  public class FactorialService : MarshalByRefObject
  {
    public double computeFactorial(int num)
    {
      double result = 1;
      for (int i=2; i <= num; i++)
      {
        result *= i;
      }
      return result;
    }
  }
}
```

This class has no special details other than the fact that it inherits from *MarshalByRefObject*. This tells .NET that this object should be remoted by marshal-by-reference, instead of marshal-by-value, semantics.

The Listing 8-16 file is compiled into a DLL by executing the following command at the command prompt:

```
Csc /debug+ /t:library /out:Factorial.dll FactorialService.cs
```

> **Note** Don't forget to use the VCVars32.bat script to initialize your command-line environment. This batch file can be found in the Program Files\Microsoft Visual Studio.NET\VC7\bin directory.

The Factorial DLL file will be linked into two other files: DirectHost.cs and FactorialClient.cs. DirectHost.cs will be used on the server side to publish the *FactorialService* class so that clients can use it. FactorialClient.cs will be the client-side program that looks up the object and invokes it.

Step 3. Configure the Remoting System

The remoting system can be configured in one of two ways. The program can import a static config file that contains the class's metadata or it can pass the metadata to the remoting system programmatically. Our example will use the second approach. Here are the lines of code from DirectHost.cs that do that:

```
WellKnownServiceTypeEntry entry = new WellKnownServiceTypeEntry
("Factorial.FactorialService","Factorial","MyFactorial"
,System.Runtime.Remoting.WellKnownObjectMode.Singleton);
RemotingConfiguration.RegisterWellKnownServiceType(entry);
```

The first line of code creates a *WellKnownServiceTypeEntry* object, which can be passed directly to the *RegisterWellKnownServiceType()* method that registers the service with the .NET Remoting system. The arguments to the *WellKnownServiceTypeEntry* are the class name, the assembly name (that is, the name of the DLL file that contains the class), the URI to which the service should be bound, and the mode in which this server-activated object will run. In this case the object is a singleton, which means that a single instance of the object will be shared across all clients.

Step 4. Create and Register the Channel

The channel defines the communications pipe that the server object will listen on while waiting for incoming requests. This includes the protocol and port number. Note that .NET Remoting Services are allowed to share port numbers. As long as their URIs are unique there will be no conflict. Registering the channel requires only a few more lines of code in DirectHost.cs.

```
System.Runtime.Remoting.Channels.Tcp.TcpServerChannel tcpch =
new System.Runtime.Remoting.Channels.Tcp.TcpServerChannel(8081);
ChannelServices.RegisterChannel(tcpch);
```

The application must create an instance of a class that implements the *IChannel* interface. In this case we are using the *TcpServerChannel* class the .NET Framework provides. The *HttpServerChannel* class is also available for use. The *TcpServerChannel* class uses a binary formatter to serialize and deserialize all communication with the server. This provides better performance than the *HttpServerChannel* object but with less flexibility. In our previous example we passed the number *8081* into the constructor to indicate the port number that should be used to listen for incoming client requests.

Step 5. Publish Your Class

Once the channel is registered and the remoting system has been configured, our *Factorial* class is ready to be published for client use. Here is the Listing 8-17 for the DirectHost application:

Listing 8-17 DirectHost.cs: The program that registers the *FactorialService* class with the .NET Remoting framework.

```
using System;
using System.Runtime.Remoting;
using System.Runtime.Remoting.Channels;
public class DirectHost
{
  public static void Main()
  {
    initialize();
    Console.WriteLine("DirectHost is ready to process remote
messages.");
    String keyState = "";
    while (String.Compare(keyState,"0", true) != 0)
    {
      Console.WriteLine("Press a key and ENTER: G=GC.Collect,
0=Exit");
      keyState = Console.ReadLine();
      Console.WriteLine("Pressed: " + keyState);
      // Force a GC
      if (String.Compare(keyState,"G", true) == 0)
      {
        Console.WriteLine("GC Collect - start");
        GC.Collect();
        GC.WaitForPendingFinalizers();
        Console.WriteLine("GC Collect - done");
      }
    }
  }
  public static void initialize()
  {
    // register configuration
    System.Runtime.Remoting.Channels.Tcp.TcpServerChannel tcpch =
new System.Runtime.Remoting.Channels.Tcp.TcpServerChannel(8081);
    ChannelServices.RegisterChannel(tcpch);
    WellKnownServiceTypeEntry entry = new WellKnownService
TypeEntry("Factorial.FactorialService","Factorial",
"MyFactorial",System.Runtime.Remoting.WellKnownObjectMode.
Singleton);
    RemotingConfiguration.RegisterWellKnownServiceType(entry);
  }
}
```

To compile this class, issue the following command from the command prompt:

```
csc /debug+ /r:System.Runtime.Remoting.dll DirectHost.cs
```

All of the .NET Remoting function calls are contained in the *initialize()* function of this program. The program has a *main()* method so that it can be invoked from the command line. This method enters an input loop, waiting for the user to choose an option. The user can choose *G* to garbage collect the deployed object (which will be reinstantiated the next time a client invokes one of its methods) or *0* to exit. This input loop is necessary so that the program does not exit immediately, destroying the class we just deployed!

If everything is properly compiled your program should produce the output shown in Figure 8-2.

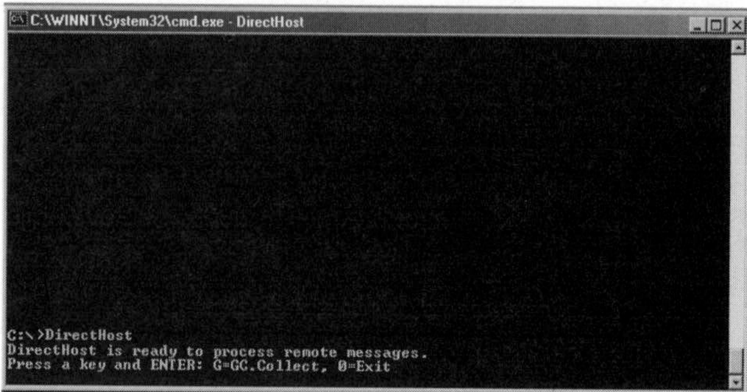

Figure 8-2 The result of running DirectHost.exe to publish the factorial service.

Step 6. Write Your Client

Assuming the DirectHost.exe program is running without a hitch, the *FactorialService* class is ready for mass consumption. Writing a remote service consumer is slightly easier than writing the producer. The consumer needs to register a TCP channel and then make a call to *Activator.GetObject()*, passing in the type of the object it should return and the URI it should use to locate the object. This method will generate a stub class with the same signature as the remote class and will return it to the client for use in its address space. Upon receiving a reference to the remote object, the client is free to use it as it would any ordinary object.

Listing 8-18 is the full listing for our *FactorialClient* class.

Listing 8-18 FactorialClient.cs: The factorial service consumer.

```
using System;
namespace FactorialClient
{
  public class FactorialClient
  {
```

```
    public FactorialClient()
    {
    }
    public static void Main(String[] args)
    {
      System.Runtime.Remoting.Channels.ChannelServices.
RegisterChannel(new System.Runtime.Remoting.Channels.Tcp.
TcpChannel());
      try
      {
        Factorial.FactorialService obj =
(Factorial.FactorialService)Activator.GetObject(typeof(Factorial.
FactorialService), "tcp://localhost:8081/MyFactorial");
        System.Console.Out.WriteLine
(obj.computeFactorial(Int32.Parse(args[0])));
      }
      catch(Exception e)
      {
        System.Console.Out.WriteLine(e.StackTrace);
        System.Console.Out.WriteLine(e.Message);
      }
    }
  }
}
```

This class can be compiled by invoking the following command:

```
csc /debug+ /r:Factorial.dll /out:FactorialClient.exe FactorialClient.cs
```

The remote method call is extremely easy for the client to make. The *computeFactorial()* method can be invoked on the *FactorialService* reference without any RPC plumbing code; the .NET takes care of everything for us.

Shopping Cart—A Client-Activated Remote Object

Now we'll look at a more interesting example. Client-activated objects are more powerful than server-activated objects because they allow the remote object to maintain state across method calls. Because each reference to a client-activated object is guaranteed a unique, persistent instance on the server, clients can safely set object state without fear that it will be arbitrarily garbage collected. The object is safe as long as the client maintains its lifetime lease.

Our shopping cart program will maintain a few instance variables, the most important being an *ArrayList* of items to be purchased. This list can be augmented or trimmed by method calls from the client. Table 8-4 and Table 8-5 show a listing of the shopping cart's members.

Table 8-4 Shopping Cart Private Instance Properties

Property	Description
String firstName	The shopper's first name.
String lastName	The shopper's last name.
ArrayList items	A list of items to be purchased.

Table 8-5 Shopping Cart Public Instance Methods

Method	Description
void setName()	Sets the shopper's full name.
String getName(String firstName, String lastName)	Returns the shopper's full name.
void addItem(Object item)	Adds a new item to the shopping cart's contents.
void removeItem(int itemIndex)	Removes the item at the specified index from the shopping cart.
String getCartContents()	Returns a string describing the contents of the shopping cart.

Step 1. Design Your Service

Our shopping cart service will differ from the Factorial service in a few key areas. First the service will be client-activated, meaning that clients will control the object instances' life cycles. Second we will use the IIS to handle the deployment of the object. This will eliminate the need to write a *DirectHost.cs* program that houses the shared object. IIS will take care of registering the object in the .NET Remoting framework as long as we supply its metadata in a config file. Deploying the object through the IIS means that clients will be restricted to communicating with the object through only the HTTP channel. Just like before, our remote class will be written using the C# programming language.

Step 2. Implement Your Host Application Domain

All we need to do here is write our class and be sure to extend *MarshalByRefObject*. Listing 8-19 is the class listing.

Listing 8-19 ShoppingCart.cs: The object that is client-activated and doesn't even know it!

```
using System;
using System.Runtime.Remoting;
using System.Collections;
namespace ShoppingCart
{
  // ShoppingCart is a client-activated object that
  // * Is exported in the remoting configuration file
  // * Has a Constructor with parameters
  // * Has public Properties that can set and get
  // * Has fields in which state is stored between calls
  // * Has methods that can be called to change the state
  // * Has overloaded methods
  public class ShoppingCart : MarshalByRefObject
  {
       public String firstName = "";
       public String lastName = "";
       private ArrayList cart = null;
    public ShoppingCart(String _firstName, String _lastName)
    {
           firstName = _firstName;
           lastName = _lastName;
    }
    // public properties
    public String FirstName
    {
      get
      {
        Console.WriteLine("First Name: {0}", firstName);
        return firstName;
      }
      set
      {
        lock(this)
        {
          firstName = value;
          Console.WriteLine("First Name: {0}", firstName);
        }
      }
    }
    public String LastName
    {
      get
      {
```

(continued)

Listing 8-19 *continued*

```
        Console.WriteLine("Last Name: {0}", LastName);
        return lastName;
      }
      set
      {
        lock(this)
        {
          lastName = value;
          Console.WriteLine("Last Name: {0}", LastName);
        }
      }
    }
    public void setName(String _firstName, String _lastName)
    {
      lock(this)
      {
        firstName = _firstName;
        lastName = _lastName;
      }
    }
    public void addItem(Object item)
    {
      lock(this)
      {
        if (cart == null)
          cart = new ArrayList();
        cart.Add(item);
      }
    }
    public void removeItem(int index)
    {
      if (cart != null && index < cart.Count)
      {
        lock(this)
        {
          cart.RemoveAt(index);
        }
      }
    }
    public String getCartContents()
    {
      String contents = firstName+" "+lastName+"'s shopping cart
conents:\n";
      for (int i = 0; i < cart.Count; i++)
      {
        contents += cart[i]+"\n";
      }
      return contents;
    }
```

```
    }
}
```

This class can be compiled with the following command line:

```
csc /debug+ /t:library /out:ShoppingCart.dll ShoppingCart.cs
```

As you can see, nothing in this class definition indicates that the object will be client-activated (or even shared at all!). Unlike server-activated classes, client-activated classes don't have any restrictions on what they can do. They can maintain state, have specialized constructors, and expose public properties to be retrieved or updated.

Step 3. Configure the Remoting System

In this example we need to configure the IIS manually to deploy the object. Follow these steps to configure the IIS:

1. Compile ShoppingCart.cs into a DLL file. Copy this file into the *bin* sub-directory under the ShoppingCart main directory.
2. Start the Internet Services Manager and highlight the Default Web Site under the server node.
3. Select *Action → New → Virtual Directory* on the menu and click *Next.*
4. Enter *ShoppingCart* as the virtual directory's alias and click *Next.*
5. Enter the full path up to but excluding the *bin* directory under the ShoppingCart main directory.
6. Create a *Web.config* file (Listing 8-20) in the directory where the service was registered. This file includes the service's metadata and is automatically loaded by the IIS whenever a client attempts to access the object.

Listing 8-20 Web.config: A file that contains the server-side metadata for our remote object made is loaded by the IIS.

```
<configuration>
  <system.runtime.remoting>
    <application>
      <service>
        <activated type="ShoppingCart.ShoppingCart, ShoppingCart"/>
      </service>
    </application>
  </system.runtime.remoting>
</configuration>
```

Step 4. Create and Register the Channel

This step is handled by the IIS.

Step 5. Publish Your Class

This step is handled by the IIS.

Step 6. Write Your Client

We are able to write a much richer client than we were able to with the previous example. The *ShoppingCart* client will create separate *ShoppingCart* instances, each with different state values. The client will alter the objects' state by calling their methods. The client will lastly attempt to print out each object's state by calling the *getCartContents()* methods and sending the result to the console, which is shown in Listing 8-21.

Listing 8-21 Client.cs: This client program creates many instances of the client-activated shopping cart objects.

```
using System;
using System.IO;
using System.Text;
using System.Runtime.Remoting;
using System.Security.Policy;
using System.Threading;
public class Client
{
  public static int Main(string[] args)
  {
    // Load the Http Channel from the config file
    RemotingConfiguration.Configure("Client.exe.config");
    ShoppingCart.ShoppingCart cart1 = new ShoppingCart.
ShoppingCart("Bob", "Smith");
    cart1.setName("Bob","Jones");
    cart1.firstName = "Robert";
    cart1.addItem("Carrots");
    cart1.addItem("Peas");
    cart1.addItem("String Beans");
    cart1.addItem("Apples");
    ShoppingCart.ShoppingCart cart2 = new ShoppingCart.
ShoppingCart("Jane","Doe");
    cart2.lastName = "Dough";
    cart2.addItem("Porsche 911 Cabrio");
    cart2.addItem("Cartier sunglasses");
    cart2.addItem("Leather driving gloves");
    cart2.addItem("Map of Blue Ridge Parkway");
    ShoppingCart.ShoppingCart cart3 = new ShoppingCart.
```

```
ShoppingCart("Steve", "Jones");
    cart3.firstName = "Ron";
    cart3.lastName = "Jones";
    cart3.addItem("Microsoft Office XP");
    cart3.addItem("Microsoft .NET Developer Studio");
    cart3.addItem("Sun Solaris");
    cart3.removeItem(2);
    cart3.addItem("Microsoft Windows 2000 Server");
    System.Console.Out.WriteLine(cart1.getCartContents());
    System.Console.Out.WriteLine(cart2.getCartContents());
    System.Console.Out.WriteLine(cart3.getCartContents());
    return 0;
  }
}
```

To compile this program, copy the ShoppingCart DLL file into the client directory and type:

```
csc /debug+ /r:System.Runtime.Remoting.dll /r:ShoppingCart.dll
/out:client.exe client.cs
```

This client program only contains a single line of code, which is obviously related to .NET Remoting:

```
RemotingConfiguration.Configure("Client.exe.config");
```

This line loads a configuration file from the file system that contains the remoted object's metadata that the client needs to locate the class and create an instance of it. The contents of this file are displayed in Listing 8-22.

Listing 8-22 Client.exe.config: An XML configuration file describing the ShoppingCart client.

```
<configuration>
  <system.runtime.remoting>
    <application name="Client">
      <client url="HTTP://localhost/ShoppingCart">
        <activated type="ShoppingCart.ShoppingCart, ShoppingCart" />
      </client>
      <channels>
        <channel type="System.Runtime.Remoting.
Channels.Http.HttpChannel, System.Runtime.Remoting" />
      </channels>
    </application>
  </system.runtime.remoting>
</configuration>
If everything compiles and deploys correctly, the client should
produce the following output:
Robert Jones's shopping cart contents:
```

(continued)

Listing 8-22 *continued*

```
Carrots
Peas
String Beans
Apples
Jane Dough's shopping cart contents:
Porsche 911 Cabrio
Cartier sunglasses
Leather driving gloves
Map of Blue Ridge Parkway
Ron Jones's shopping cart contents:
Microsoft Office XP
Microsoft .NET Developer Studio
Microsoft Windows 2000 Server
```

Remoting Events

In addition to distributed objects, the .NET Remoting framework supports distributed events. Distributed events are extremely useful for implementing the producer-consumer event paradigm in a networked environment. The producer-consumer design pattern dictates a loose coupling between the event producer and the event consumers. Consumers should be able to register and unregister themselves with no impact on the Producer. The producer does not even need to know how many (if any) consumers are interested in what it has to say.

This pattern can be used to solve many problems. One compelling use of the pattern is to avoid busy-waiting, or polling. An event consumer can register a callback function to be executed whenever a specific event occurs. The consumer can do something else, knowing that its event handler will be called at the appropriate time. The producer-consumer pattern is also frequently used in building UIs. However, most UI events involve producers and consumers in the same application domain.

In this section we will explore a distributed event architecture in which the producers and consumers can reside in different application domains or even different machines. The files used in this example can be found on the .NET Framework SDK. In the example we will pass a "greeting" event from producer to consumer to convey a simple message.

The Event Class

The *Greetingevent* class will define the actual event object to be passed from producer to consumers. The event arguments object must be serializable so it can be passed by value into each of the registered consumers. This is accomplished by associating the *SerializableAttribute* with the event class. The

GreetingEventArgs class will contain a single instance variable called *greeting* that will contain the salutation text.

Our class file will also contain a remotable service called "Waz" that listens for incoming greetings. The Waz service will be a server-activated Singleton class. Clients can call Zap's *HelloMethod()* method, passing in a greeting that they would like to announce. The Waz service will create an instance of the *GreetingEvent* class and will publish it to all the consumers. Listing 8-23 shows the zap.cs source file, which contains the event logic for the distributed events program.

Listing 8-23 Zap.cs: this file contains the event, *eventArgs*, and *publishingService* code for our distributed event system.

```
/*=====================================================================
  File:    Zap.cs
This file is part of the Microsoft .NET Framework SDK Code Samples.
  Copyright (C) Microsoft Corporation.  All rights reserved.
This source code is intended only as a supplement to Microsoft
Development Tools and/or online documentation.  See these other
materials for detailed information regarding Microsoft code samples.

THIS CODE AND INFORMATION ARE PROVIDED "AS IS" WITHOUT WARRANTY OF
ANY KIND, EITHER EXPRESSED OR IMPLIED, INCLUDING BUT NOT LIMITED TO
THE IMPLIED WARRANTIES OF MERCHANTABILITY AND/OR FITNESS FOR A
PARTICULAR PURPOSE.
=====================================================================*/
using System;
using System.Runtime.Remoting;
using System.Collections;
namespace Zap
{
  // Define the event arguments
  [Serializable]
  public class GreetingEventArgs : EventArgs
  {
    public GreetingEventArgs(string greeting)
    {
      this.greeting = greeting;
    }
    public string greeting;
  }
  // Define the event
  public delegate void GreetingEvent (object sender,
GreetingEventArgs e);
  // Define the Service
  public class Waz : MarshalByRefObject
```

(continued)

Listing 8-23 *continued*

```
    {
      // The client will subscribe and
      // unsubscribe to this event
      public event GreetingEvent Greeting;
      // Method called remotely by client
      public void HelloMethod(string greeting)
      {
        Console.WriteLine("Received String {0}", greeting);
        // Package String in GreetingEventArgs
        GreetingEventArgs e = new GreetingEventArgs(greeting);
        // Fire Event
        if (Greeting != null)
        {
          Console.WriteLine("Firing Event");
          Greeting(this, e);
        }
      }
    }
  }
```

Notice the serializable attribute associated with the *GreetingEventArgs* class as well as the *MarshalByRefObject* superclass attached to the Waz service. This means that *GreetingEventArgs* will be passed by value into all the consumer application domains while Waz instances will be referenced remotely by clients.

The EventFireHost Service Application

We defined the Waz service class in the Zap.cs file. Now we need a console application to register the channel, register the service, and deploy the service through the remoting framework. The *Host* class in Listing 8-24, EventFireHost.cs, contains a *Main()* method that does this. The class performs these tasks programmatically instead of making use of a configuration file. Upon registering and deploying the service, the application sits and waits for a user to tell it to terminate.

Listing 8-24 EventFireHost.cs: The server-side service application.

```
/*=====================================================================
  File:    EventFireHost.cs
This file is part of the Microsoft .NET Framework SDK Code Samples.
  Copyright (C) Microsoft Corporation.  All rights reserved.
This source code is intended only as a supplement to Microsoft
Development Tools and/or online documentation.  See these other
materials for detailed information regarding Microsoft code samples.

THIS CODE AND INFORMATION ARE PROVIDED "AS IS" WITHOUT WARRANTY OF
```

```
ANY KIND, EITHER EXPRESSED OR IMPLIED, INCLUDING BUT NOT LIMITED TO
THE IMPLIED WARRANTIES OF MERCHANTABILITY AND/OR FITNESS FOR A
PARTICULAR PURPOSE.
====================================================================*/
using System;
using System.IO;
using System.Runtime.Remoting;
using System.Runtime.Remoting.Channels;
using System.Runtime.Remoting.Channels.Http;
public class Host
{
  public static void Main(string[] args)
  {
    // Manually load the http channel.
    // This could also be done in the remoting configuration file.
    ChannelServices.RegisterChannel(new HttpChannel(999));
    // Register the wellknown server type.
    // This could also done in the remoting configuration file.
    RemotingConfiguration.RegisterWellKnownServiceType(
                              Type.GetType("Zap.Waz, Zap"),
                              "EventFireHost/Waz.soap",
                              WellKnownObjectMode.Singleton);
    // We are done, wait until the user wants to exit
    Console.WriteLine("Host is ready to process remote messages.");
    Console.WriteLine("Press ENTER to exit");
    String keyState = Console.ReadLine();
  }
}
```

Once the EventFireHost service application is up and running, clients can begin subscribing to events, producing events, or both via the *Waz* object.

The Event Listener

We will now define a new class that creates a *GreetingEventHandler* callback method. This class can be included by any client application that wants to register itself as a *GreetingEvent* listener.

Our event handler class, *Baz*, will inherit from *MarshalByRefObject*. This will enable our client application to register a stub, or proxy, for this class to be called whenever the event fires. An instance of *GreetingEventArgs* will be passed by value into the instance of the *Baz* class residing in the client's application domain. The *Baz* event handler in Listing 8-25 will print the greeting to the client's console.

Listing 8-25 Wak.cs: This file contains the *Baz GreetingEvent* handler class.

```
/*=====================================================================
  File:      Wak.cs---------------------------------------------------
This file is part of the Microsoft .NET Framework SDK Code Samples.
  Copyright (C) Microsoft Corporation.  All rights reserved.
This source code is intended only as a supplement to Microsoft
Development Tools and/or online documentation.  See these other
materials for detailed information regarding Microsoft code samples.

THIS CODE AND INFORMATION ARE PROVIDED "AS IS" WITHOUT WARRANTY OF
ANY KIND, EITHER EXPRESSED OR IMPLIED, INCLUDING BUT NOT LIMITED TO
THE IMPLIED WARRANTIES OF MERCHANTABILITY AND/OR FITNESS FOR A
PARTICULAR PURPOSE.
=====================================================================*/
using System;
using System.Runtime.Remoting;
using System.Runtime.Remoting.Messaging;
using Zap;
namespace Wak
{
    // Marshal by Ref Object onto which the event will be fired
    public class Baz : MarshalByRefObject
    {
        [OneWay]
       public void GreetingHandler(object sender, GreetingEventArgs e)
        {
            Console.WriteLine("GreetingHandler callback : Greeting :
{0}\n", e.greeting);
        }
    }
}
```

The *OneWay* attribute indicates that the calling program has no way to find out the results of the method call. It does not return any values, nor does it set any properties in the client stub that would indicate successful completion. As such, the .NET Remoting framework can choose to invoke this method asynchronously because the calling program does not need to wait for it to return.

Let's move on to the event handler client program that creates an instance of the *Baz* object. The client class in Listing 8-26, EventSinkHost.cs, instantiates the *GreetingEventHandler* and registers it as a *WellKnownService*. It might look strange that a client program is registering a remotable object as a singleton service. The EventHandler client is special in that it needs to act as a service so that the event dispatcher can call into it. When this happens, the event producer serializes the *GreetingEventArgs* object and passes it by value into the *GreetingHandler()* method.

Listing 8-26 EventSinkHost.cs: This client program registers the *GreetingEventHandler* as a *WellKnownService*.

```
/*=====================================================================
  File:    EventSinkHost.cs
This file is part of the Microsoft .NET Framework SDK Code Samples.
  Copyright (C) Microsoft Corporation.  All rights reserved.
This source code is intended only as a supplement to Microsoft
Development Tools and/or online documentation.  See these other
materials for detailed information regarding Microsoft code samples.

THIS CODE AND INFORMATION ARE PROVIDED "AS IS" WITHOUT WARRANTY OF
ANY KIND, EITHER EXPRESSED OR IMPLIED, INCLUDING BUT NOT LIMITED TO
THE IMPLIED WARRANTIES OF MERCHANTABILITY AND/OR FITNESS FOR A
PARTICULAR PURPOSE.
=====================================================================*/

using System;
using System.Runtime.Remoting;
using System.Runtime.Remoting.Channels;
using System.Runtime.Remoting.Channels.Http;
using Zap;
using Wak;
public class Client
{
  public static void Main(String[] args)
  {
    // This could also be done with a Remoting configuration file
    // Register the HTTP Channel
    ChannelServices.RegisterChannel(new HttpChannel(888));
    // Register the wellknown server type.
    // This could also done in the remoting configuration file.
    RemotingConfiguration.RegisterWellKnownServiceType(
                               Type.GetType("Wak.Baz, Wak"),
                               "EventSinkHost/Baz.soap",
                               WellKnownObjectMode.Singleton);
    // We are done, wait until the user wants to exit
    Console.WriteLine("Host is ready to process remote messages.");
    Console.WriteLine("Press ENTER to exit");
    String keyState = Console.ReadLine();
  }
}
```

The URI given to the event handler service is *EventSinkHost/Baz.soap*. The event producer must know this URI so it can notify the program of the events when they occur. When executed, this program sits still, listening for incoming event notices.

Now we will move on to the event service clients and see what they do.

Event Clients

The first client class we will look at is relatively simple. It uses the .NET Remoting framework Activator to create a remote reference to the Waz Web Service class. Upon obtaining this reference the client invokes the remote *HelloMethod()* method five times. Listing 8-27 shows a client to connect to a service.

Listing 8-27 Client.cs: A simple client to connect to the EventFireHost service.

```
/*=====================================================================
  File:    Client.cs
This file is part of the Microsoft .NET Framework SDK Code Samples.
  Copyright (C) Microsoft Corporation.  All rights reserved.
This source code is intended only as a supplement to Microsoft
Development Tools and/or online documentation.  See these other
materials for detailed information regarding Microsoft code samples.

THIS CODE AND INFORMATION ARE PROVIDED "AS IS" WITHOUT WARRANTY OF
ANY KIND, EITHER EXPRESSED OR IMPLIED, INCLUDING BUT NOT LIMITED TO
THE IMPLIED WARRANTIES OF MERCHANTABILITY AND/OR FITNESS FOR A
PARTICULAR PURPOSE.
=====================================================================*/
using System;
using System.Runtime.Remoting;
using System.Runtime.Remoting.Channels;
using System.Runtime.Remoting.Channels.Http;
using Zap;
public class Client
{
  public static void Main(String[] args)
  {
    // This could also be done with a Remoting configuration file
    // Register the HTTP Channel
    ChannelServices.RegisterChannel(new HttpChannel());
    // Obtain a Proxy to the SOAP URL
    Waz waz = (Waz)Activator.GetObject(
                  typeof(Waz),
                  "http://localhost:999/EventFireHost/Waz.soap"
                  );
    for (int i = 0; i < 5; i++)
    {
      // Occurs over SOAP to waz)
      waz.HelloMethod("Bill" + " " + i);
    }
  }
}
```

You can see the EventFireHost executable print out information about these methods as they occur. However, the EventSinkHost event listener executable remains silent. What happened?

Notice that the Waz service class only fires the event if its *event* property is not null.

```
// Fire Event
if (Greeting != null)
{
    Console.WriteLine("Firing Event");
    Greeting(this, e);
}
```

The service client is responsible for creating a remote reference to the *GreetingEventHandler* and set the *event* property. Therefore, event-producing clients need to create two remote references: one to call the Waz service and the other to obtain a reference to the event handler to be passed into the *GreetingEvent* constructor method. The modified client class file, Listing 8-28, appears as follows:

Listing 8-28 EventRegistration.cs: The client that calls the EventFireHost service and kicks off a distributed event to boot.

```
/*=====================================================================
  File:     EventRegistration.cs----
This file is part of the Microsoft .NET Framework SDK Code Samples.

  Copyright (C) Microsoft Corporation.  All rights reserved.
This source code is intended only as a supplement to Microsoft
Development Tools and/or online documentation.  See these other
materials for detailed information regarding Microsoft code samples.

THIS CODE AND INFORMATION ARE PROVIDED "AS IS" WITHOUT WARRANTY OF
ANY KIND, EITHER EXPRESSED OR IMPLIED, INCLUDING BUT NOT LIMITED TO
THE IMPLIED WARRANTIES OF MERCHANTABILITY AND/OR FITNESS FOR A
PARTICULAR PURPOSE.
=====================================================================*/
using System;
using System.Runtime.Remoting;
using System.Runtime.Remoting.Channels;
using System.Runtime.Remoting.Channels.Http;
using Zap;
using Wak;
public class Client
{
  public static void Main(String[] args)
  {
```

(continued)

Listing 8-28 *continued*

```
        // This could also be done with a Remoting configuration file
        // Register the HTTP Channel
        ChannelServices.RegisterChannel(new HttpChannel(0));
        Baz baz = (Baz)Activator.GetObject(
                         typeof(Baz),
                         "http://localhost:888/EventSinkHost/Baz.soap"
                         );
        // Obtain a Proxy to the SOAP URL
        Waz waz = (Waz)Activator.GetObject(
                         typeof(Waz),
                         "http://localhost:999/EventFireHost/Waz.soap"
                         );
        // Subscribe to event : occurs over SOAP
        waz.Greeting += new GreetingEvent(baz.GreetingHandler);
        waz.HelloMethod("Hi from the client");
        // Unsubscribe to event : occurs over SOAP
        waz.Greeting -=new GreetingEvent(baz.GreetingHandler);
    }
}
```

Notice that this client makes an additional call to *Activator.GetObject()* to create a remote reference to the *Baz GreetingEventHandler* class. The reference to this handler is added to the event dispatcher in the line:

```
waz.Greeting += new GreetingEvent(baz.GreetingHandler);
```

This time, through, the *greeting* property on the *Waz* object is no longer null. The *Waz* object reports that it is about to fire the event and notifies the listener by issuing the following statement.

```
Greeting(this, e);
```

If everything is running properly you should see the EventSinkHost client print out the line: GreetingHandler callback: Greeting :Hi from the client. Remotable events are extremely powerful, if somewhat difficult to understand at first. We can extend our Event listener client to register itself on the service's event queue and remove itself once it becomes sick of receiving messages.

Remoting Object Model Overview

In this section we will explore the Remoting Object model in greater detail. We will look at some of the key concepts behind object remoting before jumping into the architecture itself. Hopefully this will provide more contextual information so you can gain a better perspective of the previous examples.

Remoting Object Model Concepts

.NET Remoting relies on some fundamental concepts surrounding what objects can and can't do over the network. Some objects can be serialized and passed-by-value back to the client, while others cannot. We will begin our exploration of the .NET Remoting Object model by defining the different levels of object remoting.

Agile Objects

Agile objects are accessed from any context and are always called directly. These types of objects can be invoked through direct references. Agile objects do not need to be called by proxy and have no constraints on what they can do. Most "regular" objects are considered agile.

Not Marshaled Type Category

Objects that do not derive from System.MarshalByRefObject or System.ContextBoundObject and do not have a [*serializable*] custom attribute are considered not marshaled. In other words, the object cannot be referenced remotely, nor can it be serialized into a form that can be stored or transmitted. This implies that an object of this type cannot be accessed from outside the application domain either by value or by reference.

Objects of this type are usually designed for use inside the application in which they are defined. By definition these types of objects are always accessed directly because all references to them are actual instances. Invoking methods on these objects do not suffer performance penalties because of argument and return result marshaling.

Marshal By Value Object Category

The only difference between these objects and those belonging to the Not Marshaled category is that MarshalByValue (MBV) objects can be serialized. This allows them to be copied directly into the address space of another application. In this way these objects are remotable, although no proxies are ever involved in their use. Because they must live within the application domain, all references to them must be actual instances. Therefore, their method performance is optimized.

MBV objects are easily identifiable by a serialization indicator in the class definition. Such classes usually take [*serializable*] attributes or else provide their own serialization methods by implementing the *ISerializable* interface. For example, the following class definition illustrates an MBV object.

```
[serializable]
public class MyMarshalByValueClass : ISerializable
{
  // ...
  private MyMarshalByValueClass(
```

```
                    SerializationInfo info,
                    StreamingContext context)
    {
      //. . .
    }

    // The ISerializable Implementation
    public virtual void GetObjectData(
                          SerializationInfo info,
                          StreamingContext context)
    {
      //. . .
    }
}
```

Marshal By Reference Object Category

MarshalByReference (MBR) objects make up the class of objects we just created in the Factorial and ShoppingCart examples. MBR objects all inherit, either directly or indirectly, from the *MarshalByRefObject* class.

All objects of this type have a distributed identity or some URI by which they can be located over a network. Instances of *MarshalByRefObject* classes must remain in the application domain where they are defined. Although references to these objects might exist in other application domains (or other machines), the actual instances must stay put.

MBR objects are particularly appropriate for circumstances in which objects that depend on a local resource need to be referenced remotely. Objects that access server-side resources, such as databases and file systems, and cannot be serialized are likely candidates for MBR remoting.

Whenever MBR objects are passed out of the Home application domain, either as a parameter to a method or a method's return result, the runtime takes care of marshaling a stub reference into the Target application domain. The runtime manages MBR reference semantics in all three of the following scenarios.

- Whenever an MBR object is passed to another application domain in the same physical process.
- Whenever an MBR object is passed between two different processes on the same machine.
- Whenever an MBR object is passed between two different processes on different machines.

All out-of-process references to an MBR object must go through a layer of abstraction when performing operations on that object. This is so that the .NET

Remoting framework can step in and insert a proxy class that handles marshaling the operation over a channel and back again.

All MBR object fields must be accessed through public accessors. The ShoppingCart example had two public properties, *firstName* and *lastName*, which appeared to be accessed directly by the ShoppingCart client. (For example, the statement *cart2.lastName = "Dough"*; appears to alter the *lastName* property directly.) This is, in fact, not true. What happened in this case was that the assignment operators for the *firstName* and *lastName* properties were overloaded to call the appropriate accessors in the *ShoppingCart* class. The accessors are implicitly associated with the properties via the following lines of code in ShoppingCart.cs:

```
public String FirstName
{
  get
  {
    Console.WriteLine("First Name: {0}", firstName);
    return firstName;
  }
  set
  {
    lock(this)
    {
      firstName = value;
      Console.WriteLine("First Name: {0}", firstName);
    }
  }
}
public String LastName
{
  get
  {
    Console.WriteLine("Last Name: {0}", LastName);
    return lastName;
  }
  set
  {
    lock(this)
    {
      lastName = value;
      Console.WriteLine("Last Name: {0}", LastName);
    }
  }
}
```

Because all method calls on MBR objects must happen though indirection, MBR operations carry with them a performance penalty. The severity of this penalty depends on the degree of separation between the two objects, the amount of marshaling logic that is required, and the speed of the network link between them.

ContextBound Object Category

ContextBound objects are similar to MBR objects. The major difference is that ContextBound objects have a predefined context, or state of parameters, that must be defined for them to operate. All calling and passing semantics for ContextBound objects are the same as those for MBR objects.

ContextBound classes are marked by the *ContextAttribute*. This attribute defines the properties that a ContextBound object requires to operate correctly. These properties can define synchronization rules, transactions, just-in-time activation, security, or any other contexts that the object might be expecting. Context-specific data is stored into a shared memory mechanism managed by the .NET. The runtime allocates a *multislot* data store array to each process upon its creation. These slots house the contextual information unique to a thread or context.

ContextBound classes are opposite *Agile* classes in terms of contextual behavior. *ContextBound* classes are guaranteed to operate only in the context in which they were created. Conversely, *Agile* classes are guaranteed to operate in the context of the calling program.

Table 8-6 through Table 8-9 show the public members of the context objects.

Table 8-6 Public Static (Shared) Properties

Property	Description
DefaultContext	Gets the default context for the current application domain.

Table 8-7 Public Static (Shared) Methods

Method	Description
AllocateDataSlot	Allocates an un-named data slot.
AllocateNamedDataSlot	Allocates a named data slot.
FreeNamedDataSlot	Frees a named data slot.

Table 8-7 Public Static (Shared) Methods *(continued)*

Method	Description
GetData	Retrieves the value from the specified slot in the current context.
GetNamedDataSlot	Looks up a named data slot.
RegisterDynamicProperty	Registers a dynamic property implementing IContributeDynamicSink with the remoting service.
SetData	Sets the data in the specified slot on the current context.
UnregisterDynamicProperty	Unregisters a dynamic property implementing IcontributeDynamicSink.

Table 8-8 Public Instance Properties

Property	Description
ContextID	Gets the context ID for the current context.
ContextProperties	Gets the specified context property.

Table 8-9 Public Instance Methods

Method	Description
DoCallBack	Executes code in another context.
Equals	Overloaded. Determines whether two object instances are equal.
Freeze	Freezes the context.
GetHashCode	Serves as a hash function for a particular type, suitable for use in hashing algorithms and data structures like a hash table.
GetProperty	Returns a specific context property by name.

(continued)

Table 8-9 Public Instance Methods *(continued)*

Method	Description
GetType	Gets the type of the current instance.
SetProperty	Sets a specific property by name.
ToString	Returns a string representation of the context.

Remoting Object Model Architecture

The Remoting Object Model Architecture consists of interfaces, context-bound classes, application domain-bound classes, unbound classes, and value types. Let's look at how all this lays out. Figure 8-3 contains a high-level diagram of the inheritance hierarchy for all run-time classes.

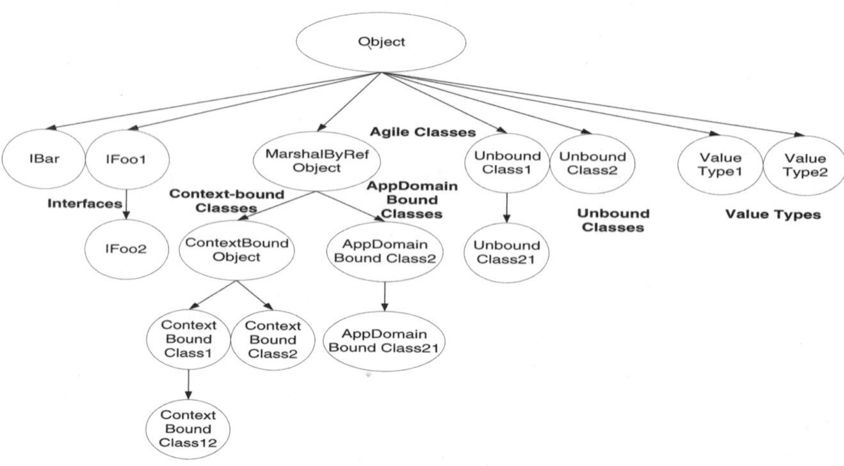

Figure 8-3 A Logical class inheritance hierarchy.

Once a class is marked as *MarshalByValue*, *AppDomainBound*, or *ContextBound*, all subclasses of that class are similarly restricted. In other words, a class that inherits from a *MarshalByValue* class cannot also be marked as *MarshalByReference*.

Instance Fields and Accessors

The behavior of instance fields, or properties, varies across the class hierarchy. Depending on the type of object, instance properties can either be manipulated directly or through well-defined accessors. If the class is *MarshalByValue*, its fields can be directly accessed. No proxies are required because all the object's state resides in the local application domain.

Properties can also be directly manipulated if they belong to "this" or any of the object's parents. This is because the instance of the object in question must be operating in the application domain of its parent. If the object is MBV, its parent must also be MBV and, therefore, exists in the same application domain. Conversely, if the object is MBR, the actual instance of the object must run in the application domain where the object was born (even though references to the object might reside elsewhere). Here again the parent object must also reside in the same application domain so its properties can be accessed directly in memory.

Finally the runtime checks to see if the object is a proxy. If so, its fields are viewed and changed through accessors defined in the proxy class. Field values can safely be referred to via direct memory.

Statics

Static fields and methods are always agile. They are never remoted, and access to them is always done via direct memory. Furthermore, static fields are not subject to contextual rules placed on Context objects.

Passing Objects as Parameters

Agile objects can be passed and received to and from other application domains either by value or by reference. ContextBound objects, or objects that depend on the context in which they were born, are always passed by reference.

Overriding Methods on Object

The virtual methods defined on the class *Object* raise an interesting dilemma for the .NET Remoting framework. In the case of PassByReference remote objects, both the remote object and the local stub derive from *Object*. Therefore, these virtual functions are doubly defined. For instance, if *ToString()* is invoked on an object stub, should the .NET call the stub's *ToString()* method or the *ToString()* method associated with the remote object?

Generally speaking, these methods are only called remotely if the MBR object has explicitly overridden them. To be exact, here is what happens in the case of each of *Object's* virtual methods:

- *Equals()* will execute remotely if overridden, locally if not.
- *GetHashCode()* will execute remotely if overridden, locally if not.

- *ToString()* will execute remotely if overridden, locally if not.
- *Equals()* (static) always executes locally.
- *Memberwise Clone()* always executes locally.

Conclusion

In this chapter we looked at how Microsoft's .NET Framework uses metadata to create exciting opportunities in distributed computing. Metadata is an indispensable tool for advertising object behaviors and properties. Although metadata has long existed in computing, recent advancements in Internet applications development have brought it to the forefront of our thinking.

We began by investigating the exciting new Web Services distributed computing paradigm. By combining descriptive metadata with a flexible and universal data packaging specification (XML) and a ubiquitous transport protocol (HTTP), we have created a platform in Web Services that enables object-sharing at a universal level. Tomorrow's distributed Web applications will not only make use of services hosted far and wide, but they will also be brought to market faster than ever before.

Web Services solve many of the problems that have long plagued widely distributed computing. Web Services use UDDI and WSDL to enable applications to discover and understand available services at runtime. SOAP provides a convenient platform and a language-neutral way to share objects among applications. By using HTTP as a transport protocol, Web Services can easily be deployed on existing network configurations. Finally broad support for Web Services in the .NET Developer Studio and other popular development platforms will enable developers to begin using the technology immediately.

In addition to supporting Web Services, Microsoft's Visual Studio .NET, the .NET Framework, and the Common Language Runtime environment arm developers with the tools they need to build advanced object-sharing applications. .NET applications can pass objects by value or by reference. Shared objects can be client-activated or server-activated. Regardless of the type of Remotable objects you build, the .NET Remoting Framework will take care of the complex task of serializing and transporting distributed data. Armed with these features, developers can solve virtually any distributed programming requirement.

We are entering an exciting time in computing. Hopefully, the small examples in this chapter have started you thinking of some practical applications for distributed technologies and Web Services in particular. Chapter 9 will lead you through real-world examples of how you can use .NET to create a fully functional enterprise application.

9

Building a Server Application

The best way to assimilate all that we have covered so far is to stop talking about it and start writing code. This is precisely the goal of Chapters 9 and 10. We will pull together a number of concepts in doing so, including XML content, XSLT skins, XML UI elements, SOAP, and XML Web services. Whether your goal is to understand the entire application or just specific pieces of it, we hope you get something useful from the code in these chapters. We will begin our programming endeavor by providing an overview of the application we will build. We will then focus on the server-side component of the application.

In this chapter we will design and implement the database logic, the data sets, and data adapters that provide access to the underlying datastore, the business logic that comprises the "guts" of the application, and, finally, a variety of Web Services that expose our business logic to clients.

Application Overview

In this chapter we build an example application—Margie's Travel Golf Reservation System—using the Microsoft .NET Framework. The Golf Reservation System is a tee-time registration application in which registered users can search for golf courses, view details on specific courses (tee descriptions, slope ratings, individual hole distances, pars, and handicaps), view available tee times at those courses, register for tee times, and view a list of previously registered tee times.

A production application of the *the* Golf Reservation System variety would normally provide much more functionality, but for the purposes of this book, the project allows us an under-the-hood view of .NET in action. It ties together course and user data, makes that data available through XML Web services, and displays it using the controller design pattern discussed in previous chapters.

Database Requirements

The database requirements for the Golf Reservation System's server-side component are relatively simple. We will use a Microsoft Access database to house all the course, golfer, tee information, and the tee times. Our goal is to keep the back-end of this system as simple as possible. The database will contain a small number of records for demonstration purposes, so a lightweight database management systems (DBMS) will be sufficient. If this application were meant to scale, we'd look into using a more sophisticated Relational Database Management System (RDBMS) such as the Microsoft SQL Server.

The XML Web services logic of the Golf Reservation System will not query the Access database directly. Instead, all data access will flow through a more abstract *CourseDataSet* class. The *CourseDataSet* will mimic the structure of the underlying DBMS and will provide quick and easy access to data from the application layer.

Using a *DataSet* to mask the underlying database has a number of advantages. First and foremost, it breaks the traditional ties that bind business logic to specific DBMS's. The Golf Reservation System's server-side component could be rewritten with a minimum amount of effort to support new database requirements. Second, direct in-memory *DataSet* access eliminates expensive boundary crossings to call into the database. Data can be retrieved quickly from the *DataSet* without the need for repetitive SQL queries. Finally reducing the load on the database engine frees it to operate more efficiently, enhancing the scalability of the application.

"Finder" XML Web services used for searching will create *DataView* objects to query the data contained in the *CourseDataSet*. Web Services can filter data by means of the *DataView* class's *RowFilter* property. Row filters use *Expression* objects to provide rich, SQL-like selection capability.

The server will implement a series of *DataAdapter* classes to handle all marshaling of data to and from the database. There will be a single *DataAdapter* class for each database table. These adapters will work together to load the table data into a consolidated data set. Data updates will require the following three separate steps:

1. The business logic will update the *CourseDataSet* with the new record. This action will result in a new, removed, or updated data row whose state is reflected in the object's *RowState* property.
2. The business logic will call the *Update()* method on the appropriate data adapter. The adapter will analyze the data set at this time and determine what action, if any, to perform to synchronize the underlying database tables.
3. The business logic will call the *AcceptChanges()* method on the *CourseDataSet* object. This will return the dataset to a stable state and will reload any new information from the database.

Business Logic Requirements

The Golf Reservation System server business logic consists of all the object/database interactions that happen underneath the XML Web services facade. Database tables in the application are manipulated indirectly via a layer of high-level business objects. The class definitions for these objects are based directly on the underlying database schema.

Business Object C# Class Definitions

The application provides C# classes for each object represented by a database row as well as classes for commonly used containable business objects that have no single table relationship, such as an address. Each class contains traditional methods in getters and setters and in most cases multiple constructor methods.

Not every class in the application mirrors a database table as does the *GolfCourse* class. The same will likely hold true with any application you build inside the .NET Framework. For example, the fact that the application contains an address class as an address object can be useful because, at least within our application, it relates to and holds requirements for the same properties and methods across multiple business entities (both a golfer and a golf course have addresses). Obviously, one goal of a .NET application is code reuse, and although this is a simple example, it's a good example nonetheless.

Table 9-1 contains the business objects in the Golf Reservation System application.

Web Services

The application contains only one XML Web service, conveniently named GolfCourseService. Numerous XML Web methods, however, are available

Table 9-1 Business Entities in the Golf Reservation System Server Application

Class File	Description
Address.cs	The *Address* class defines a generic address structure. Instances of this class are referenced by the *GolfCourse* and *Golfer* objects.
GolfCourse.cs	The *GolfCourse* class contains general properties describing a golf course. All information regarding holes, yardages, pars, and so forth are delegated to helper classes.
Golfer.cs	The *Golfer* class defines a golfer in the system. Names, addresses, and security information are all found in this class.
Hole.cs	The *Hole* class defines a hole on a golf course. Hole objects contain properties such as par, distance, and handicap. Each set of tees (for example, red, white, blue) on the golf course has 18 unique hole instance.
Tee.cs	The *Tee* class defines a set of tees throughout the course. Properties in the class include slope, distance, a description, and an array of hole objects.
TeeTime.cs	The *TeeTime* class defines a unique tee time for a specific golf course on a certain date. Properties include the golf course ID, the golfer ID, and the date and time.

within this lone service. The methods necessary for the TeeTimes application vary from search helpers to everyday *findById* methods.

GolfCourseService, like all XML Web services, is responsible for masking business object design complexities and particulars. The developer that needs to call into and retrieve data from Web methods need not know whether a table of addresses is in the database. The application calls into the GolfCourseService XML Web service via SOAP requests and receives SOAP responses. The .NET Framework, though, handles the complexities of creating, sending, receiving, and parsing the SOAP documents.

Browsing to an XML Web service with a Web browser results in a detailed description of the XML Web service, what methods it provides, and how to call into those methods using the supported protocols. Figure 9-1 shows the GolfCourseService called in this manner.

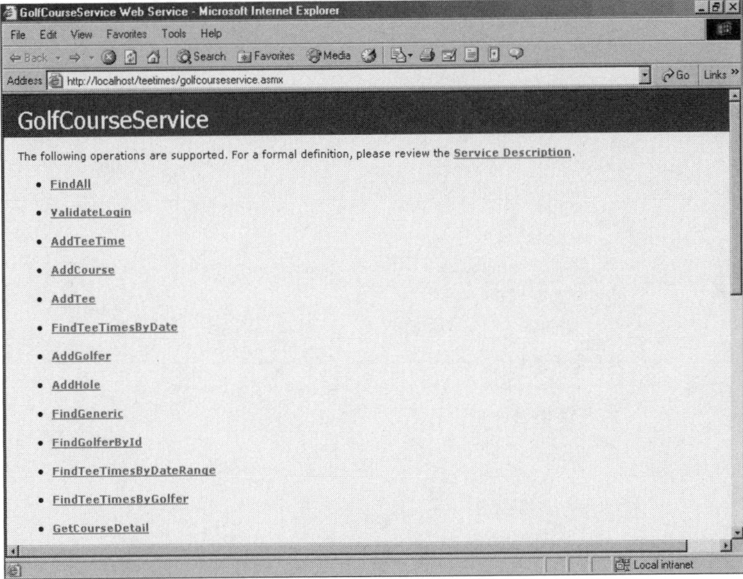

Figure 9-1 Browsing to an XML Web service provides detailed information about the methods provided.

Clicking a specific method (see Figure 9-2) offers a detailed description of that method and a form to invoke it, given your inputs. Note that submitting the form invokes the method and will perform the actions of that method as if it were called from an application If the method results in a new database insert, submitting this form will do the same. Also detailed on the method description page is the protocol syntax request and response for SOAP calls, HTTP POST, and HTTP GET.

As detailed in Figure 9-1, the GolfCourseService offers the following Web methods, listed here by method signature:

```
public GolfCourse[] FindAll()
public GolfCourse[] FindGeneric(String[] fields, String[] values)
public GolfCourse GetCourseDetail(String id)
public GolfCourse AddCourse(String name, String description, String
price, String streetAddress, String city, String state, String
postalCode, String country, String telephone)
public GolfCourse AddTee(int courseId, String description, float
slope)
public GolfCourse AddHole(int teeId, int handicap, int length, int
hole, int par)
public TeeTime AddTeeTime(int courseId, int golfer, DateTime date,
DateTime time)
public TeeTime[] FindTeeTimesByGolfer(int golferId)
```

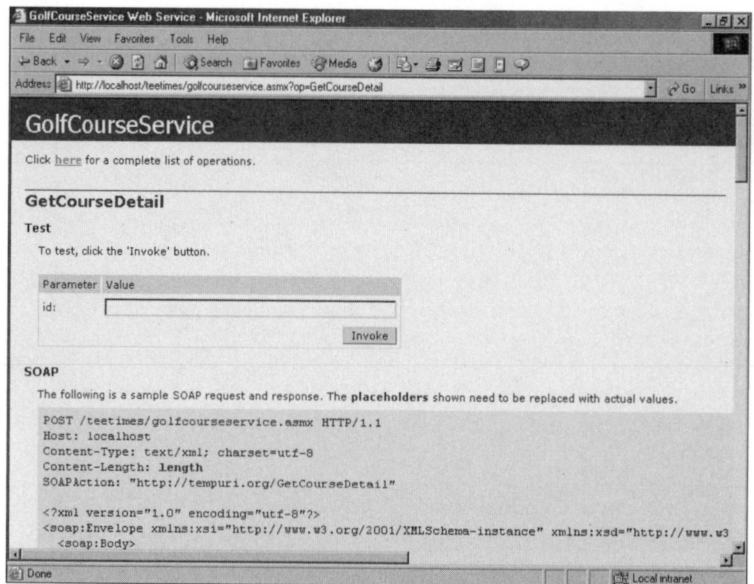

Figure 9-2 Clicking a Web method offers a method description and protocol syntax for invoking the method.

```
public Golfer AddGolfer(String firstName, String lastName, String
streetAddress, String city, String state, String postalCode, String
country, String email, String phone, String username, String password)
public Golfer FindGolferById(int golferId)
public Golfer ValidateLogin(String username, String password)
public TeeTime[] FindTeeTimesByDate(int courseId, DateTime date)
public TeeTime[] FindTeeTimesByDateRange(int courseId, DateTime
startDate, DateTime endDate)
```

These Web methods and the classes behind them make up the server-side component of our application and represent the proxy necessary for other applications to interact with and manipulate the *Golf Reservation System* business logic. We will break down these Web methods and the *Golf Reservation System* server business logic behind them in more detail later in the chapter.

User Requirements

A good division of labor between developer and designer is rarely achieved when rich UI are required for sophisticated applications. The more business logic an application developer can mask from the UI developer, the better. Combining XML Web services in the .NET Framework with the controller design pattern, though, results in a further separation of the duties of developers and designers. This is true not only because the controller XSLT skin is completely responsible for formatting controller result XML, but also because developer duties can be divided between server and client. The results are truly distributed applications in that one developer provides the XML Web services, perhaps in conjunction with a UI, while another developer, interested only in manipulating those XML Web services, builds an entirely separate client application.

Imagine the Golf Reservation System server application as a stand-alone service provided by a conglomeration of golf courses. Multiple Internet applications could call into those services and format and manipulate data as they saw fit: one client application might use the GolfCourseService only to retrieve data, while another might retrieve golfer information from the GolfCourseService, caring nothing about the course data also available.

Although the application is tailored to a specific client—one that allows validated users to register for tee times—the Web methods could be designed modeling only the data behind them. This approach would provide an XML Web service interface for retrieving the data published on the Internet that was not tailored to a specific client application design, but instead provided abstractions on a complex data store.

The Golf Reservation System Server Application

The Golf Reservation System server consists of the following: an SQL-compliant RDBMS, data adapter classes, .NET data sets, C# Object classes, and the GolfCourseService XML Web service and associated methods. When assembled, the C# Business Object classes, data set, data view, and data adapter classes, and the SQL RDBMS, will comprise the server application's business logic. The XML Web services layer will rest on top of this logic and provide a clean, easily accessible interface for client applications.

The Database

As mentioned earlier, the application will use a small Access database to store its information. The .mdb file can be transported easily and viewed on workstations as well as servers. The following sections represent a brief overview of the tables that appear in our database schema.

The Course Table

The course table will contain all the course-related information in the server application. Records can be inserted into the course table by issuing the following SQL statement:

```
INSERT INTO course(city, country, description, name, postalCode, price,
state, streetAddress, telephone) VALUES (?, ?, ?, ?, ?, ?, ?, ?, ?)
```

Table 9-2 contains the fields inside the course table.

Table 9-2 Course Fields

Column	Description
Id	Contains the course's ID. It is autoincremented by the database.
Name	Contains the course's name.
StreetAddress	Contains the course's street address.
City	Contains the course's city.
State	Contains the course's state.
PostalCode	Contains the course's postal code or zip code.
Country	Contains the course's country.
Telephone	Contains the course's telephone number.
Price	Contains the price for a round of golf.
Description	Contains a longer description of the golf course.

The Tee Table

The tee table will represent the different tees on the golf course (for example, red, white, and blue). Each tee will have a unique yardage and slope. Tee records can be created with the following SQL command:

```
INSERT INTO tee(courseId, description, distance, slope) VALUES (?, ?, ?, ?)
```

Table 9-3 contains the fields in the tee table.

Table 9-3 Tee Fields

Column	Description
Id	Contains the tee's ID. It is autoincremented by the database.
Slope	Contains a measurement of the difficulty of the tee.

Table 9-3 Tee Fields *(continued)*

Column	Description
Distance	Contains an aggregate measurement of all of the holes' distances.
Description	Contains a description of the tee (for example, red, white, and blue).
CourseId	Contains a primary key reference to the associated course.

The Hole Table

Records in the hole table represent a hole for a given tee. The hole's yardage, handicap, and par might vary with the tee. The following SQL command can be used to create new hole records:

```
INSERT INTO Hole(handicap, length, teeId, hole, par) VALUES (?, ?, ?, ?, ?)
```

Table 9-4 contains the fields in the hole table.

Table 9-4 Hole Fields

Column	Description
Id	Contains the hole's ID. It is autoincremented by the database.
TeeId	Contains a primary key reference to the associated tee.
Handicap	Contains the hole's handicap (1–18).
Length	Contains the hole's yardage.
Hole	Contains the hole number (1–18).
Par	Contains the hole's par.

The Golfer Table

The golfer table will contain records for each registered golfer in the system, regardless of whether or not they have booked a tee time. Golfer records can be created by issuing the following SQL command:

```
INSERT INTO golfers(city, country, email, firstName, lastName, phone,
postalCode, state, streetAddress, [password], username) VALUES (?, ?,
?, ?, ?, ?, ?, ?, ?, ?, ?)
```

Table 9-5 contains the fields in the golfer table.

Table 9-5 Golfer Fields

Column	Description
Id	Contains the golfer's ID. It is autoincremented by the database.
FirstName	Contains the golfer's first name.
LastName	Contains the golfer's last name.
StreetAddress	Contains the golfer's street address.
City	Contains the golfer's city.
State	Contains the golfer's state.
PostalCode	Contains the golfer's postal code or zip code.
Country	Contains the golfer's country.
Email	Contains the golfer's e-mail address.
Phone	Contains the golfer's telephone number.
Username	Contains the golfer's username, required to log in and request a tee time
Password	Contains the golfer's password, required to log in and request a tee time.

The Bookings Table

The bookings table will house all the requested course tee times. The table will contain only those tee times for a course that have been filled. Available tee times will be inferred by the "gaps" in this table. New bookings records can be created with the following SQL insert statement:

```
INSERT INTO bookings(courseId, golfer, teeDate, teeTime) VALUES (?, ?, ?, ?)
```

Table 9-6 contains the fields in the bookings table.

Table 9-6 Bookings Fields

Column	Description
Id	Contains the booking's ID. It is autoincremented by the database.
CourseId	Contains a primary key reference to the associated course.
Golfer	Contains a primary key reference to the associated golfer.
TeeDate	Contains the date of the tee time.
TeeTime	Contains the time of the tee time.

Data Sets and Data Adapters

Microsoft Visual Studio .NET aids your enterprise development efforts by providing *data sets* and *data adapters* to act as two layers of abstraction above the database. All data interaction to and from the business logic layer happens through data sets. Data sets act like large, multidimensional arrays for staging data that could come from databases, files, the Internet, or all of the above. They pull together the data that the application's business logic will need; and provide a clean, consolidated interface. Data sets are serializable, which means they can be saved or sent over the network to another running application.

Data adapters are the helper classes that populate the data sets and perform necessary database updates. They keep the data set classes simple by handling the dirty work of reading and writing data. Data adapter classes are tuned to a specific datasource such as a specific table in Access. They contain all the SQL *Insert*, *Update*, *Select*, and *Delete* statements needed to access that table. Multiple data adapters can be bound to a single data set. This is the case with the Golf Reservation System server application. Each data adapter is responsible for loading and storing a subset of the data set.

Data Adapters

The best way to create your data adapter classes is to use the .NET Studio Visual Designer. Use the Server Explorer pane to add a new data connection to your project. Upon adding this connection, the Server Explorer will update itself to show the connection and the data tables that can be managed by the connection.

Drag each of the tables you want to use onto the designer. The .NET Studio will generate a default data adapter for the table and display its properties in the Properties window. At this point you can configure the data adapter's *Insert*, *Select*, *Update*, and *Delete* SQL commands and other connection-related properties. We created data adapters this way for the course, hole, tee, golfer, and bookings tables in the application.

The .NET Studio will autogenerate the adapter code and place it into the .asmx.cs file of your project. You might need to tweak this code from time to time, so you should know what it does. (We needed to alter the SQL *Insert* command that some of the adapters were using to accommodate system-generated keys.) Let's take a look at how the *GolferDataAdapter* class works. The code fragments shown here come from the GolfCourseService.asmx.cs file.

First we need to create an instance of the data adapter class and its associated OLE-DB command classes.

```
this.oleDbUpdateCommand5 = new System.Data.OleDb.OleDbCommand();
this.oleDbSelectCommand5 = new System.Data.OleDb.OleDbCommand();
this.oleDbInsertCommand5 = new System.Data.OleDb.OleDbCommand();
this.oleDbDeleteCommand5 = new System.Data.OleDb.OleDbCommand();
this.golferDataAdapter = new System.Data.OleDb.OleDbDataAdapter();
```

Next we need to configure each of the OLE-DB command classes. This is done by specifying the SQL statement and filling in its required parameters. Again, the .NET Studio Visual Designer will create this code for you, although you may need to customize it in order for it to work with your database. The following is the configuration code for the *Insert* command. This code will create a new *golfer* record in the golfers table.

```
this.oleDbInsertCommand5.CommandText = "INSERT INTO golfers(city,
country, email, firstName, lastName, phone, postalCode," +
    " state, streetAddress, [password], username) VALUES (?, ?, ?, ?,
?, ?, ?, ?, ?, " +
    "?, ?)";
this.oleDbInsertCommand5.Connection = this.oleDbConnection1;

this.oleDbInsertCommand5.Parameters.Add(new System.Data.OleDb.
OleDbParameter("city", System.Data.OleDb.OleDbType.Char, 50,
System.Data.ParameterDirection.Input, false, ((System.Byte)(0)),
((System.Byte)(0)), "city", System.Data.DataRowVersion.Current, null));
```

```
this.oleDbInsertCommand5.Parameters.Add(new System.Data.OleDb.
OleDbParameter("country", System.Data.OleDb.OleDbType.Char, 50,
System.Data.ParameterDirection.Input, false, ((System.Byte)(0)),
((System.Byte)(0)), "country", System.Data.DataRowVersion.Current,
null));

this.oleDbInsertCommand5.Parameters.Add(new System.Data.OleDb.
OleDbParameter("email", System.Data.OleDb.OleDbType.Char, 50,
System.Data.ParameterDirection.Input, false, ((System.Byte)(0)),
((System.Byte)(0)), "email", System.Data.DataRowVersion.Current,
null));

this.oleDbInsertCommand5.Parameters.Add(new System.Data.OleDb.
OleDbParameter("firstName", System.Data.OleDb.OleDbType.Char, 50,
System.Data.ParameterDirection.Input, false, ((System.Byte)(0)),
((System.Byte)(0)), "firstName", System.Data.DataRowVersion.Current,
null));

this.oleDbInsertCommand5.Parameters.Add(new System.Data.OleDb.
OleDbParameter("lastName", System.Data.OleDb.OleDbType.Char, 50,
System.Data.ParameterDirection.Input, false, ((System.Byte)(0)),
((System.Byte)(0)), "lastName", System.Data.DataRowVersion.Current,
null));

this.oleDbInsertCommand5.Parameters.Add(new System.Data.OleDb.
OleDbParameter("phone", System.Data.OleDb.OleDbType.Char, 50,
System.Data.ParameterDirection.Input, false, ((System.Byte)(0)),
((System.Byte)(0)), "phone", System.Data.DataRowVersion.Current,
null));

this.oleDbInsertCommand5.Parameters.Add(new System.Data.OleDb.
OleDbParameter("postalCode", System.Data.OleDb.OleDbType.Char, 50,
System.Data.ParameterDirection.Input, false, ((System.Byte)(0)),
((System.Byte)(0)), "postalCode", System.Data.DataRowVersion.Current,
null));

this.oleDbInsertCommand5.Parameters.Add(new System.Data.OleDb.
OleDbParameter("state", System.Data.OleDb.OleDbType.Char, 50,
System.Data.ParameterDirection.Input, false, ((System.Byte)(0)),
((System.Byte)(0)), "state", System.Data.DataRowVersion.Current,
null));

this.oleDbInsertCommand5.Parameters.Add(new System.Data.OleDb.
OleDbParameter("streetAddress", System.Data.OleDb.OleDbType.Char, 50,
System.Data.ParameterDirection.Input, false, ((System.Byte)(0)),
((System.Byte)(0)), "streetAddress", System.Data.DataRowVersion.
Current, null));
```

```
this.oleDbInsertCommand5.Parameters.Add(new System.Data.OleDb.
OleDbParameter("password", System.Data.OleDb.OleDbType.Char, 50,
System.Data.ParameterDirection.Input, false, ((System.Byte)(0)),
((System.Byte)(0)), "password", System.Data.DataRowVersion.Current,
null));

this.oleDbInsertCommand5.Parameters.Add(new System.Data.OleDb.
OleDbParameter("username", System.Data.OleDb.OleDbType.Char, 50,
System.Data.ParameterDirection.Input, false, ((System.Byte)(0)),
((System.Byte)(0)), "username", System.Data.DataRowVersion.Current,
null));
```

The *Select, Update,* and *Delete* commands for the golfers table (and all other tables in the application) work in much the same way. In all cases, you must specify a parameterized SQL *CommandText* string to execute against the database. You must also add a new object to the *Parameters* array for each runtime value you intend to use.

Next we bind the newly created OLE-DB command objects to the data adapter. This will force the adapter to use the SQL we just wrote when inserting, updating, deleting, or selecting data to and from the table.

```
this.golferDataAdapter.DeleteCommand = this.oleDbDeleteCommand5;
this.golferDataAdapter.InsertCommand = this.oleDbInsertCommand5;
this.golferDataAdapter.SelectCommand = this.oleDbSelectCommand5;
this.golferDataAdapter.UpdateCommand = this.oleDbUpdateCommand5;
```

Finally we need to specify the table mappings that map columns in the golfers table to columns in the associated data set. We will take a closer look at the data set momentarily.

```
this.golferDataAdapter.TableMappings.AddRange(new System.Data.
Common.DataTableMapping[] {
  new System.Data.Common.DataTableMapping("Table", "golfers", new
System.Data.Common.DataColumnMapping[] {
    new System.Data.Common.DataColumnMapping("city", "city"),
    new System.Data.Common.DataColumnMapping("country", "country"),
    new System.Data.Common.DataColumnMapping("email", "email"),
    new System.Data.Common.DataColumnMapping("firstName", "first-
Name"),
    new System.Data.Common.DataColumnMapping("id", "id"),
    new System.Data.Common.DataColumnMapping("lastName", "lastName"),
    new System.Data.Common.DataColumnMapping("phone", "phone"),
    new System.Data.Common.DataColumnMapping("postalCode",
"postalCode"),
    new System.Data.Common.DataColumnMapping("state", "state"),
    new System.Data.Common.DataColumnMapping("streetAddress",
"streetAddress"),
    new System.Data.Common.DataColumnMapping("password", "password"),
```

```
    new System.Data.Common.DataColumnMapping("username", "username")
  })
});
```

That's it for the golfer data adapter! As you can see, creating the adapter objects for your application is a tedious and error-prone process. The .NET Studio will save a lot of time and debugging effort if you let it create these classes for you.

Data Sets

You will use data sets for practically all the database manipulation you need to do in your application. Data sets are in-memory databases that provide their own insert, update, delete, select, transaction, and filter semantics. By coding to the data set interface you make it much easier to port your application to another database later.

Typed vs. Untyped Data Sets

.NET data sets come in two flavors: typed and untyped. Typed data sets have built-in schemas associated with particular databases and columns. .NET uses this schema to extend the base *DataSet* class and create a new class that contains column references as typed properties and accessors.

Untyped data sets, on the other hand, do not contain extra information provided by the schema. You must manually extract and cast data values from the data set's array. The difference between typed and untyped data sets can be illustrated best by an example.

To retrieve a golfer's last name from an untyped data set you would have to execute the following lines of code:

```
string lastName = (string)courseDataSet1.Tables
["golfers"].Rows[0]["lastName"];
```

Compare that to using a typed version of the same data set:

```
string lastName = courseDataSet1.golfers[0].lastName;
```

The typed data set is much easier to use (especially when you have command completion turned on) and the .NET Studio will generate all the code for you.

Generating the Data Set

Once you've prepared your data adapter classes, you're ready to generate a typed data set from them. Right-click on the visual designer and select Generate Dataset. Alternatively, you can select the Generate Dataset option in the Tools menu. The Generate Dataset Wizard will walk you through the steps necessary to create a new *DataSet* class. The only detail you definitely need take care of is to select which data tables and data adapters the data set should use. After you have checked these, the .NET Studio will create a new typed data set schema and will use this schema to create the typed data set class definition.

The code behind the new data set is incredibly long (over two thousand lines for the server application), so we won't get into the guts here. Basically, the typed data set class provides simple marshaling utilites that either put information into the data set array or pull information out of it. Figure 9-3 shows how the designer looks with all the data adapters and data sets already configured.

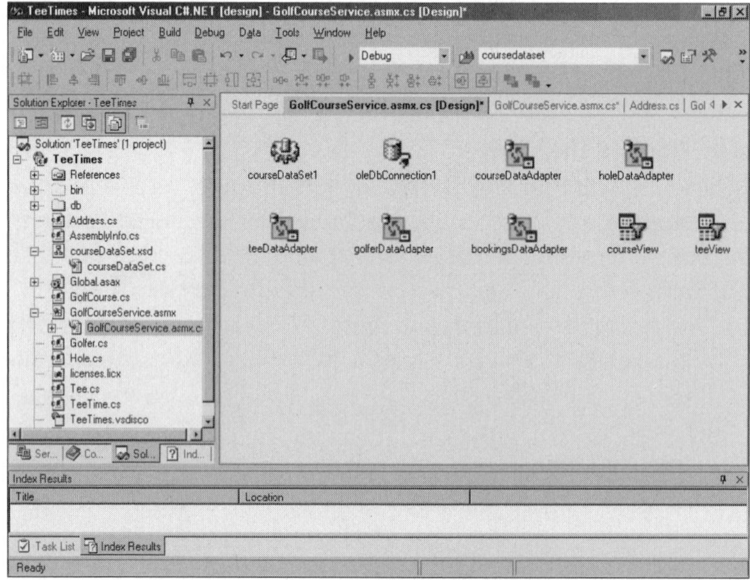

Figure 9-3 A snapshot of the .NET Studio Designer showing the completed data acess objects.

Data Views

You will often need to filter the underlying database in your enterprise application. Whether you're showing information about one record or 20, you need some mechanism to extract and sort a well-defined subset of data. This was traditionally done via SQL SELECT statements that pull the filtered data view directly from the database. This approach shouldn't be used with data sets. Instead, .NET includes a *DataView* class to provide this functionality.

DataView objects are bound to a specific table in a data set. The table can be passed into the *DataView* object through its constructor or set manually via its *Table* public property. Once the data view is bound to a table, you can change its *RowFilter* and *Sort* properties at runtime to manipulate the data shown in the view. The *Count* property tells you how many records the view currently holds.

The *RowFilter* data view property uses the .NET Expression syntax to query the data set. .NET Expressions is a powerful query language with rich operator support. For example, the following expressions can be used to filter the course table:

- "Name LIKE 'Pinehurst*'"
- "Price < 100.00"
- "State = 'North Carolina'"
- "Price < 100.00 AND State = 'North Carolina' AND (City = 'Durham' OR City = 'Chapel Hill' OR City ='Raleigh'"

DataView objects and their associated *DataRowView* objects are not typed, however. Therefore, you must use them as you would an untyped data set.

Business Objects

The Golf Reservation System server will contain class descriptions that model the database entities shown previously in an object format. Class definitions will exist for *GolfCourse*, *Golfer*, *Tee*, *Hole*, and *TeeTime*. A generic *Address* class will also be provided as a uniform means to represent golf course and golfer addresses. Instances or collections of instances of these objects will be returned by Web methods.

Golf Reservation System clients will need to download stub representations of these classes to make sense of the return results. Visual Studio .NET takes care of this by adding Web references. Other clients will need to query the WSDL document for the GolfCourseService XML Web service.

GolfCourse

The *GolfCourse* object provides an objectified view of objects in the course database table. The class definition for this object resides in GolfCourse.cs. The *GolfCourse* object is used primarily as a means to transport information back to an XML Web services client. The class uses public properties so that they can be included as a return result from an XML Web service call.

```
using System;
using System.Data;
namespace TeeTimes
{
  /// <summary>
```

```
/// A GolfCourse
/// </summary>
public class GolfCourse
{
  public int id;
  public String name;
  public String description;
  public String price;
  public String telephone;
  public Address address;
  public Tee[] tees;
```

The *GolfCourse* object has four different constructors. The first is the default constructor, which initializes all its properties to *null*.

```
public GolfCourse()
{
  id = 0;
  name = "";
  description = "";
  price = "";
  telephone = "";
  address = new Address();
  tees = null;
}
```

The second constructor takes a row in a typed data set as an argument. The course's properties are initialized by the properties contained in the data row.

```
public GolfCourse(courseDataSet.courseRow c)
{
  name = "";
  description = "";
  price = "";
  address = new Address();
  tees = null;
  id = c.id;
  if (!c.IsnameNull())
    name = c.name;
  if (!c.IsdescriptionNull())
    description = c.description;
  if (!c.IspriceNull())
    price = c.price;
  if (!c.IstelephoneNull())
    telephone = c.telephone;
  if (!c.IsstreetAddressNull())
    address.street = c.streetAddress;
  if (!c.IscityNull())
    address.city = c.city;
  if (!c.IsstateNull())
```

```
      address.state = c.state;
    if (!c.IspostalCodeNull())
      address.postalCode = c.postalCode;
    if (!c.IscountryNull())
      address.country = c.country;
}
```

The third constructor accepts a *DataRowView* object that was obtained via a *DataView* filter. The *DataRowView* is untyped, so the constructor must use array access to load its properties.

```
public GolfCourse(DataRowView c)
{
  id = 0;
  name = "";
  description = "";
  price = "";
  address = new Address();
  tees = null;
  id = Int32.Parse(c["id"].ToString());
  name = c["name"].ToString();
  description = c["description"].ToString();
  price = c["price"].ToString();
  telephone = c["telephone"].ToString();
  address.street = c["streetAddress"].ToString();
  address.city = c["city"].ToString();
  address.state = c["state"].ToString();
  address.postalCode = c["postalCode"].ToString();
  address.country = c["country"].ToString();
}
```

The fourth and final *GolfCourse* constructor accepts a reference to a typed *DataSet* object and a primary key value. The constructor calls the *DataSet* object's *FindById()* method to obtain the correct row. If the row exists the constructor uses the data contained therein to initialize the *GolfCourse* object.

```
public GolfCourse(courseDataSet ds, int courseId)
{
  id = 0;
  name = "";
  description = "";
  price = "";
  address = new Address();
  courseDataSet.courseRow c = ds.course.FindByid(courseId);
  if (c != null)
  {
    id = courseId;
    name = "";
    description = "";
```

```
        price = "";
        address = new Address();
        if (!c.IsnameNull())
          name = c.name;
        if (!c.IsdescriptionNull())
          description = c.description;
        if (!c.IspriceNull())
          price = c.price;
        if (!c.IstelephoneNull())
          telephone = c.telephone;
        if (!c.IsstreetAddressNull())
          address.street = c.streetAddress;
        if (!c.IscityNull())
          address.city = c.city;
        if (!c.IsstateNull())
          address.state = c.state;
        if (!c.IspostalCodeNull())
          address.postalCode = c.postalCode;
        if (!c.IscountryNull())
          address.country = c.country;
```

The GolfCourse contructor locates all the course's *Tee* objects, instantiates them, and initializes the *tees* array property in the following:

```
        DataView teeView = new DataView(ds.tee);
        int teeCnt = ds.tee.Count;
        teeView.RowFilter = "courseId = "+courseId;
        int cnt = 0;
        tees = new Tee[teeView.Count];
        foreach (DataRowView r in teeView)
        {
          int tee_id = Int32.Parse(r["id"].ToString());
          Tee tee = new Tee(ds,tee_id);
          tees[cnt] = tee;
          cnt++;
        }
      }
    }
```

Public getters and setters are used to manipulate the *GolfCourse*'s properties.

```
    public int getId() { return id; }
    public String getName() { return name; }
    public String getDescription() { return description; }
    public Address getAddress() { return address; }
    public String getPrice() { return price; }
    public String getTelephone() { return telephone; }
    public void setId(int _id) { id = _id; }
    public void setName(String _name) { name = _name; }
    public void setDescription(String _description) { description =
```

```
_description;}
    public void setPrice(String _price) { price = _price; }
    public void setTelephone(String _telephone) { telephone =
_telephone; }
```

The class provides a *setAddress()* method to update the Address-dependent object.

```
    public void setAddress(String street, String city, String state,
String postalCode, String country)
    {
      address.setStreet(street);
      address.setCity(city);
      address.setState(state);
      address.setPostalCode(postalCode);
      address.setCountry(country);
    }
  }
}
```

Golfer

The *Golfer* object maintains all golfer and user states. *Golfer* object references can also be included within Web method result documents. The class definition for this object is shown in Golfer.cs.

```
using System;
namespace TeeTimes
{
  /// <summary>
  /// Summary description for Golfer.
  /// </summary>
  public class Golfer
  {
    public int id;
    public String firstName;
    public String lastName;
    public String email;
    public String phone;
    public String username;
    public String password;
    public Address address;
```

The *Golfer* object also has several constructors.

```
    public Golfer()
    {
      id = 0;
      firstName = "";
      lastName = "";
```

```
      email = "";
      phone = "";
      username = "";
      password = "";
      address = new Address();
    }
```

This constructor accepts a list of all *Golfer* properties to be initialized.

```
    public Golfer(String _firstName, String _lastName, String _email,
String _phone, String _streetAddress, String _city, String _state,
String _postalCode, String _country, String _username, String
_password)
    {
      firstName = _firstName;
      lastName = _lastName;
      email = _email;
      phone = _phone;
      username = _username;
      password = _password;
      address = new Address();
      address.setStreet(_streetAddress);
      address.setCity(_city);
      address.setState(_state);
      address.setPostalCode(_postalCode);
      address.setCountry(_country);
    }
```

This constructor accepts the typed *courseDataSet* object and a *Golfer id* value. The constructor looks up the *Golfer* in the data set and sets its properties accordingly.

```
    public Golfer(courseDataSet ds, int golferId)
    {
      id = 0;
      firstName = "";
      lastName = "";
      email = "";
      phone = "";
      username = "";
      password = "";
      address = new Address();
      courseDataSet.golfersRow g = ds.golfers.FindByid(golferId);
      if (g != null)
      {
        id = golferId;
        if (!g.IsfirstNameNull())
          firstName = g.firstName;
        if (!g.IslastNameNull())
          lastName = g.lastName;
```

```
        if (!g.IsemailNull())
          email = g.email;
        if (!g.IsphoneNull())
          phone = g.phone;
        if (!g.IsusernameNull())
          username = g.username;
        if (!g.IspasswordNull())
          password = g.password;
        if (!g.IsstreetAddressNull())
          address.setStreet(g.streetAddress);
        if (!g.IscityNull())
          address.setCity(g.city);
        if (!g.IsstateNull())
          address.setState(g.state);
        if (!g.IspostalCodeNull())
          address.setPostalCode(g.postalCode);
        if (!g.IscountryNull())
          address.setCountry(g.country);
      }
    }
```

The following are the *Golfer* accessor and mutator methods:

```
    public int getId() { return id; }
    public String getFirstName() { return firstName; }
    public String getLastName() { return lastName; }
    public String getEmail() { return email; }
    public String getPhone() { return phone; }
    public String getUserName() { return username; }
    public String getPassword() { return password; }
    public Address getAddress() { return address; }
    public void setId(int _id) { id = _id; }
    public void setFirstName(String _firstName) { firstName = _firstName; }
    public void setLastName(String _lastName) { lastName = _lastName; }
    public void setEmail(String _email) { email = _email; }
    public void setPhone(String _phone) { phone = _phone; }
    public void setUserName(String _username) { username = _username; }
    public void setPassword(String _password) { password = _password; }
    public void setAddress(String streetAddress, String city, String
state, String postalCode, String country)
    {
      address.setStreet(streetAddress);
      address.setCity(city);
      address.setState(state);
      address.setPostalCode(postalCode);
      address.setCountry(country);
    }
  }
}
```

Tee

The *Tee* class models the different types of tees that a golf course might have, such as red, white, and blue. Each *Tee* has its own set of yardage, slope, and distance properties as well as a collection of 18 unique *Hole* objects. Tee.cs contains the class definition.

```
using System;
using System.Data;
namespace TeeTimes
{
  /// <summary>
  /// Summary description for Tee.
  /// </summary>
  public class Tee
  {
    public int id;
    public double slope;
    public int distance;
    public String description;
    public int courseId;
    public Hole[] holes;

    public Tee()
    {
    }
    public Tee(int _id, int _courseId, String _description, float
_slope)
    {
      id = _id;
      courseId = _courseId;
      description = _description;
      slope = _slope;
      holes = null;
    }
```

Again, we see the Data Set/ID constructor design pattern. You have the option to decide how "data-aware" your business objects should be. We overloaded our business objects' constructors to perform the most data-set access. Doing so simplifies the XML Web service logic.

```
    public Tee(courseDataSet ds, int teeId)
    {
      courseDataSet.teeRow t = ds.tee.FindByid(teeId);
      if (t != null)
      {
        id = teeId;
        courseId = t.courseId;
```

```
        description = t.description;
        slope = t.slope;
```

Here the *Tee* constructor builds an array of dependent *Hole* objects. We use a *DataView* object to filter the *courseDataSet* and generate a list of keys. We iterate over these keys, construct the objects, and create our *holes* array.

```
        DataView holeView = new DataView(ds.Hole);
        holeView.RowFilter = "teeId = "+teeId;
        holeView.Sort = "hole";
        int cnt = 0;
        holes = new Hole[holeView.Count];
        foreach (DataRowView r in holeView)
        {
          Hole hole = new Hole();
          hole.setTeeId(teeId);
          int hole_handicap = Int32.Parse(r["handicap"].ToString());
          int hole_length = Int32.Parse(r["length"].ToString());
          int hole_hole = Int32.Parse(r["hole"].ToString());
          int hole_par = Int32.Parse(r["par"].ToString());
          hole.setHandicap(hole_handicap);
          hole.setLength(hole_length);
          hole.setHole(hole_hole);
          hole.setPar(hole_par);
          holes[cnt] = hole;
          cnt++;
        }
      }
    }
```

These are the *Tee* accessors and mutators.

```
    public int getId() { return id; }
    public double getSlope() { return slope; }
    public int getDistance() { return distance; }
    public int getCourseId() { return courseId; }
    public String getDescription() { return description; }
    public Hole[] getHoles() { return holes; }
    public void setId(int _id) { id = _id; }
    public void setSlope(double _slope) { slope = _slope; }
    public void setDistance(int _distance) { distance = _distance; }
    public void setCourseId(int _courseId) { courseId = _courseId; }
    public void setDescription(String _description) { description =
_description; }
    public void setHoles(Hole[] _holes) { holes = _holes; }
  }
}
```

Hole

Contrary to common sense, a single golf course might have 18, 36, 54, or more holes because each hole is different with respect to the tee from which the golfer is playing on a given day. A hole that plays 320 yards from the white tees might play 380 yards from the blue tees. To accommodate this requirement we decided to give each tee its own collection of 18 *hole* objects. The *Hole* class definition is found in Hole.cs.

```
using System;
namespace TeeTimes
{
  /// <summary>
  /// Summary description for Hole Class
  /// </summary>
  public class Hole
  {
    public int id;
    public int teeId;
    public int handicap;
    public int length;
    public int hole;
    public int par;
    public Hole()
    {
      id = 0;
      teeId = 0;
      handicap = 0;
      length = 0;
      hole = 0;
      par = 0;
    }
```

Hole constructors are always fed properties by value in the server project. This class might be extended later to provide the DataSet/ID constructor interface.

```
    public Hole(int _id, int _teeId, int _handicap, int _length, int
_hole, int _par)
    {
      id = _id;
      teeId = _teeId;
      handicap = _handicap;
      length = _length;
      hole = _hole;
      par = _par;
    }
    public int getId() { return id; }
    public int getTeeId() { return teeId; }
```

```
    public int getHandicap() { return handicap; }
    public int getLength() { return length; }
    public int getHole() { return hole; }
    public int getPar() { return par; }
    public void setId(int _id) { id = _id; }
    public void setTeeId(int _teeId) { teeId = _teeId; }
    public void setHandicap(int _handicap) { handicap = _handicap; }
    public void setLength (int _length) { length = _length; }
    public void setHole (int _hole) { hole = _hole; }
    public void setPar (int _par) { par = _par; }
  }
}
```

TeeTime

The *TeeTime* class represents a tee-time booking on a specific date and time. *TeeTime* objects hold references to a golfer and a golf course. *TeeTime* objects can be obtained by XML Web services clients for a specific golf course to see what times are still available for play. TeeTime.cs shows the source code behind the *TeeTime* class.

```
using System;
namespace TeeTimes
{
  /// <summary>
  /// Summary description for TeeTime.
  /// </summary>
  public class TeeTime
  {
    public int id;
    public DateTime date;
    public DateTime time;
    public int courseId;
    public int golfer;
    public TeeTime()
    {
      id = 0;
      date = System.DateTime.Now;
      time = System.DateTime.Now;
      courseId = 0;
      golfer = 0;
    }
    public TeeTime(int _id, DateTime _date, DateTime _time, int
_courseId, int _golfer)
    {
      id = _id;
      date = _date;
      time = _time;
      courseId = _courseId;
```

```
        golfer = _golfer;
      }
```

Again, we see the Data Set/ID constructor pattern.

```
      public TeeTime(courseDataSet ds, int ttId)
      {
        id = 0;
        date = System.DateTime.Now;
        time = System.DateTime.Now;
        courseId = 0;
        golfer = 0;
        courseDataSet.bookingsRow tt = ds.bookings.FindByid(ttId);
        if (tt != null)
        {
          id = ttId;
          if (!tt.IscourseIdNull())
            courseId = tt.courseId;
          if (!tt.IsgolferNull())
            golfer = tt.golfer;
          if (!tt.IsteeDateNull())
            date = DateTime.Parse(tt.teeDate);
          if (!tt.IsteeTimeNull())
            time = DateTime.Parse(tt.teeTime);
        }
      }
      public int getId() { return id; }
      public DateTime getDate() { return date; }
      public DateTime getTime() { return time; }
      public int getCourseId() { return courseId; }
      public int getGolfer() { return golfer; }
      public void setId(int _id) { id = _id; }
      public void setDate(DateTime _date) { date = _date; }
      public void setTime(DateTime _time) { time = _time; }
      public void setCourseId(int _courseId) { courseId = _courseId; }
      public void setGolfer(int _golfer) { golfer = _golfer; }
    }
}
```

Address

The *Address* object is used to provide a common address API for the server. *GolfCourses* and *Golfers* both hold references to objects of this type. This class could be extended later to support multiple address, driving directions, and other functionalities. The class definition can be found in Listing 9-1.

Listing 9-1 Address.cs: The *Address* utility class.

```
using System;
namespace TeeTimes
{
  /// <summary>
  /// Summary description for Address.
  /// </summary>
  public class Address
  {
    public String street;
    public String city;
    public String state;
    public String postalCode;
    public String country;
    public Address()
    {
      street = "";
      city = "";
      state = "";
      postalCode = "";
      country = "";
    }
    public String getStreet() { return street; }
    public String getCity() { return city; }
    public String getState() { return state; }
    public String getPostalCode() { return postalCode; }
    public String getCountry() { return country; }
    public void setStreet(String _street){ street = _street; }
    public void setCity(String _city){ city = _city; }
    public void setState(String _state){ state = _state; }
    public void setPostalCode(String __postalCode){ postalCode =
_postalCode; }
    public void setCountry(String _country){ country = _country; }
  }
}
```

The GolfCourseService XML Web service

All Golf Reservation System Web methods will be assembled into a single XML Web service called *GolfCourseService*. The application publishes relatively few methods, so only a single XML Web service umbrella is required. All access to the server's business logic will pass through this API.

You will notice that most of the Web methods are small. .NET takes care of all the complex SOAP argument marshaling and our business object handles most of the data access and all of the nested object creation. The Web methods don't need to do too much at all.

FindAll()

Syntax: `GolfCourse[] FindAll()`

FindAll() returns an array of *GolfCourse* objects. This method is called to get a complete listing of the courses maintained by the system. The method simply iterates over the entire course table in the *GolfCourse* data set.

```
[WebMethod]
public GolfCourse[] FindAll()
{
  int nCourses = courseDataSet1.course.Count;
  GolfCourse[] golfCourses = new GolfCourse[nCourses];
  int cnt = 0;
  foreach (courseDataSet.courseRow c in courseDataSet1.course)
  {
    GolfCourse gc = new GolfCourse(c);
    golfCourses[cnt] = gc;
    cnt++;
  }
  return golfCourses;
}
```

FindGeneric()

Syntax: `GolfCourse[] FindGeneric(String[] fields, String[] values)`

FindGeneric() implements a simple yet flexible query interface into the course database. Clients can pass in arrays of property names and value expressions (including * wildcards) that can be used to generate a list of matching courses. The method makes use of the .NET *DataView* class to filter data in the *courseDataSet1* data set.

An added bonus of this design is that this method will not need to change as fields are added to the course table and dataset.

```
[WebMethod]
public GolfCourse[] FindGeneric(String[] fields, String[] values)
{
  DataView cv = new DataView(courseDataSet1.course);
  cv.Sort = "name";
  String filterString = "";
  for (int x = 0; x < fields.Length; x++)
  {
    if (x >= 1)
    {
      filterString += " AND";
```

```
    }
    filterString += " "+fields[x]+" LIKE '"+values[x]+"'";
  }
  cv.RowFilter = filterString;
  int nCourses = cv.Count;
  GolfCourse[] golfCourses = new GolfCourse[nCourses];
  int cnt = 0;
  foreach (DataRowView c in cv)
  {
    int gcId = Int32.Parse(c["id"].ToString());
    GolfCourse gc = new GolfCourse(courseDataSet1, gcId);
    golfCourses[cnt] = gc;
    cnt++;
  }
  return golfCourses;
}
```

GetCourseDetail()

Syntax: `GolfCourse GetCourseDetail(String id)`

GetCourseDetail() returns a complete representation of a golf course. *Tees* and *Holes* are returned as nested arrays. This method is a good example of a coarse-grained Web method. Recall that the *GolfCourse* constructor that is called here recursively builds arrays of *Tees* and *Holes*. A single call to this method retrieves enough information to be displayed on three different Web forms.

```
[WebMethod]
public GolfCourse GetCourseDetail(String id)
{
  int cid = Int32.Parse(id);
  GolfCourse gc = new GolfCourse(courseDataSet1,cid);
  return gc;
}
```

AddCourse()

Syntax: `GolfCourse AddCourse(String name, String description, String price, String streetAddress, String city, String state, String postalCode, String country, String telephone)`

AddCourse() creates a new course entry in the golf course database.

```
[WebMethod]
public GolfCourse AddCourse(String name, String description, String
price, String streetAddress, String city, String state, String
postalCode, String country, String telephone)
{
  courseDataSet.courseRow newCourse = courseDataSet1.course.
AddcourseRow(city,country,description,name,
```

```
postalCode,price,state,streetAddress,telephone);
  courseDataAdapter.Update(courseDataSet1,"course");
  courseDataSet1.AcceptChanges();
  GolfCourse gc = new GolfCourse(newCourse);
  return gc;
}
```

AddTee()

Syntax: GolfCourse AddTee(int courseId, String description, float slope

AddTee() creates a new tee entry for a particular golf course.

```
[WebMethod]
public GolfCourse AddTee(int courseId, String description, float
slope)
{
  courseDataSet.teeRow newTee =
courseDataSet1.tee.AddteeRow(courseId,description,0,slope);
  teeDataAdapter.Update(courseDataSet1,"tee");
  courseDataSet1.AcceptChanges();
  GolfCourse gc = new GolfCourse(courseDataSet1, courseId);
  return gc;
}
```

AddHole()

Syntax: GolfCourse AddHole(int teeId, int handicap, int length, int hole, int par)

AddHole() adds a new hole record to the *Hole* database. The hole must be associated with a particular *Tee* object.

```
[WebMethod]
public GolfCourse AddHole(int teeId, int handicap, int length, int
hole, int par)
{
  courseDataSet.HoleRow newHole = courseDataSet1.Hole.AddHoleRow
(handicap,length,teeId,hole,par);
  holeDataAdapter.Update(courseDataSet1,"Hole");
  courseDataSet1.AcceptChanges();
  courseDataSet.teeRow tr = courseDataSet1.tee.FindByid(teeId);
  int courseId = tr.courseId;
  GolfCourse gc = new GolfCourse(courseDataSet1, courseId);
  return gc;
}
```

AddTeeTime()

Syntax: TeeTime AddTeeTime(int courseId, int golfer, DateTime date, DateTime time)

AddTeeTime() creates a new tee time record. The tee time record requires valid references to a golf course and a golfer record. The method also takes in two *DateTime* objects, one representing the date of the tee time and the other representing the time.

```
[WebMethod]
public TeeTime AddTeeTime(int courseId, int golfer, DateTime date,
DateTime time)
{
  String dateString = date.ToShortDateString();
  courseDataSet.bookingsRow newBooking = courseDataSet1.
bookings.AddbookingsRow(courseId,golfer,dateString,time.ToString());
  bookingsDataAdapter.Update(courseDataSet1,"bookings");
  courseDataSet1.AcceptChanges();
  TeeTime tt = new TeeTime(0, date, time, courseId, golfer);
  return tt;
}
```

FindTeeTimesByGolfer()

Syntax: TeeTime[] FindTeeTimesByGolfer(int golferId)

FindTeeTimesByGolfer() returns an array representing a complete tee time listing for a particular golfer. This listing can be used to remind a golfer of upcoming tee times. Again, we see the *DataView* object put to good use.

```
[WebMethod]
public TeeTime[] FindTeeTimesByGolfer(int golferId)
{
  DataView ttv = new DataView(courseDataSet1.bookings);
  ttv.Sort = "teeTime";
  ttv.RowFilter = "golfer = '"+golferId+"'";
  int nTimes = ttv.Count;
  TeeTime[] teeTimes = new TeeTime[nTimes];
  int cnt = 0;
  foreach (DataRowView c in ttv)
  {
    int ttId = Int32.Parse(c["id"].ToString());
    TeeTime tt = new TeeTime(courseDataSet1, ttId);
    teeTimes[cnt] = tt;
    cnt++;
  }
  return teeTimes;
}
```

AddGolfer()

Syntax: Golfer AddGolfer(String firstName, String lastName, String streetAddress, String city, String state, String postalCode, String country, String email, String phone, String username, String password)

AddGolfer() creates a new golfer record in the database. This method requires all pertinent address and profile information.

```
[WebMethod]
public Golfer AddGolfer(String firstName, String lastName, String
streetAddress, String city, String state, String postalCode, String
country, String email, String phone, String username, String password)
{
  courseDataSet.golfersRow newGolfer = courseDataSet1.golfers.
AddgolfersRow(city,country,email,firstName,lastName,phone,
postalCode,state,streetAddress,password,username);
  golferDataAdapter.Update(courseDataSet1,"golfers");
  courseDataSet1.AcceptChanges();
  Golfer g = new Golfer(firstName,lastName,email,phone,
streetAddress,city,state,postalCode,country,username,password);
  return g;
}
```

FindGolferById()

Syntax: Golfer FindGolferById(int golferId)

FindGolferById() looks up a specific golfer and returns a *Golfer* object with matching ID if one exists. It doesn't get any easier than this.

```
[WebMethod]
public Golfer FindGolferById(int golferId)
{
  return new Golfer(courseDataSet1,golferId);
}
```

ValidateLogin()

Syntax: Golfer ValidateLogin(String username, String password)

ValidateLogin() is used to validate username/password combinations against the *Golfer* database. This is necessary to prevent fake tee times from being created. If the validation succeeds, the method returns the entire *Golfer* object. If it fails, the method returns null.

```
[WebMethod]
public Golfer ValidateLogin(String username, String password)
{
  DataView gv = new DataView(courseDataSet1.golfers);
```

```
  gv.RowFilter = "username = '"+username+"' AND password =
'"+password+"'";
  int gCount = gv.Count;
  Golfer g = null;
  if (gCount >= 1)
  {
    DataRowView gr = gv[0];
    int golferId = Int32.Parse(gr["id"].ToString());
    g = new Golfer(courseDataSet1,golferId);
  }
  return g;
}
```

FindTeeTimesByDate()

```
Syntax: TeeTime[] FindTeeTimesByDate(int courseId, DateTime date)
```

FindTeeTimesByDate() returns an array of tee times for a specified course on a specified date.

```
[WebMethod]
public TeeTime[] FindTeeTimesByDate(int courseId, DateTime date)
{
  DataView ttv = new DataView(courseDataSet1.bookings);
  ttv.Sort = "teeTime";
  ttv.RowFilter = "teeDate = '"+date.ToShortDateString()+"' AND
courseId = '"+courseId+"'";
  int nTimes = ttv.Count;
  TeeTime[] teeTimes = new TeeTime[nTimes];
  int cnt = 0;
  foreach (DataRowView c in ttv)
  {
    int ttId = Int32.Parse(c["id"].ToString());
    TeeTime tt = new TeeTime(courseDataSet1, ttId);
    teeTimes[cnt] = tt;
    cnt++;
  }
  return teeTimes;
}
```

FindTeeTimesByDateRange()

```
Syntax: TeeTime[] FindTeeTimesByDateRange(int courseId, DateTime
startDate, DateTime endDate)
```

FindTeeTimesByDateRange() returns an array of tee times for a specified course across a specified date range. Because of a strange problem in one of the earlier .NET Studio releases, we were unable to write Access records with fields of type *DateTime*. Thus, we were forced to serialize dates and times to strings before writing them out. This made the process of filtering by date range significantly more difficult.

```
[WebMethod]
public TeeTime[] FindTeeTimesByDateRange(int courseId, DateTime
startDate, DateTime endDate)
{
  DataView ttv = new DataView(courseDataSet1.bookings);
  ttv.Sort = "teeTime";
  String filterText = "courseId = '"+courseId+"' AND (";
  TimeSpan duration = endDate.Subtract(startDate);
  int nDays = duration.Days;
  for (int i = 0; i <= nDays; i++)
  {
    if (i > 0)
      filterText = filterText + " OR";
    DateTime tDate = startDate.AddDays(i);
    filterText = filterText+" teeDate = '"+
tDate.ToShortDateString()+"'";
  }
  filterText = filterText + ")";
  ttv.RowFilter = filterText;
  int nTimes = ttv.Count;
  TeeTime[] teeTimes = new TeeTime[nTimes];
  int cnt = 0;
  foreach (DataRowView c in ttv)
  {
    int ttId = Int32.Parse(c["id"].ToString());
    TeeTime tt = new TeeTime(courseDataSet1, ttId);
    teeTimes[cnt] = tt;
    cnt++;
  }
  return teeTimes;
}
```

Conclusion

In this chapter we've seen how to use XML and the .NET Developer Studio to create the server side of an enterprise application. We have used XML Web services, Web methods, data adapters, data classes, data views, and data connection utilities to make this happen. We are able to achieve a great deal of flexibility in our business logic by using XML Web services to erect an elegent partition around it. Our XML Web services can easily be called from a wide variety of clients, be it Web browsers, cell phones, thick client applications, or even other Web Services.

In Chapter 10 we will create a Web client that actually makes use of all this! Later, in Chapter 13, we will connect a wireless device to the same XML Web services.

10

Creating A Client

In this chapter we will build an example client application—Golf Reservation System Client—designed to connect to Golf Reservation System Server in Chapter 9, and we will do so using the Microsoft .NET Framework in conjunction with the controller design pattern. You will learn what the necessary components of building a .Net client application are as well as a common design pattern used for creating them: the controller. Understand that the controller is simply one of many design patterns available for creating .NET client applications, but it is the one we will use in this chapter.

We first discuss user requirements, how to understand and obtain information from XML Web services, the specifics of Golf Reservation System Client, the controller design pattern, and the procedure flow for our application. We then inspect relevant portions of Golf Reservation System Client to understand exactly *what* is happening *where* in the code. We conclude by reviewing the client application and brainstorming on how XML Web services and clients that are built to interact with XML Web services will evolve.

Client Application Overview

This application overview discusses the specifics of how our client application interacts with available Web Services. We discuss working with user requirements, obtaining information about XML Web services, and designing a client application—Golf Reservation System Client—based on the controller design pattern and the procedure flow it enforces.

The Golf Reservation System is a tee time registration application through which registered users can search for golf courses, view details on specific courses (tee descriptions, slope ratings, individual hole distances, pars and handicaps), view available tee times at those courses, make reservations, and view a list of previously registered times. Specifically, the Golf Reservation System client application discussed in this chapter is a Web client built to interact with the Golf Reservation System Server XML Web services.

A production application of the Golf Reservation System variety would provide much more functionality, but for the purposes of this book the Golf Reservation System allows us an under-the-hood view of .NET in action while it ties together course and user data, makes that data available through XML Web services, and displays it using the controller design pattern introduced in Chapter 5.

User Requirements

The ideal division of labor between developer and designer—in which the developer writes code and the designer creates interfaces—is rarely achieved when rich UIs are required for sophisticated applications. The more business logic an application developer can mask from the UI developer, the better. Combining the .NET Framework with the controller design pattern, though, results in further separating the duties of developers and designers, not only because the controller XSLT skin is completely responsible for formatting controller-result XML, but because developer duties can be divided between server and client. This separation creates truly distributed applications in that one developer or business provides the XML Web services, perhaps in conjunction with a UI, while another developer or business interested only in manipulating those XML Web services builds an entirely separate client application.

The handoff between server and client responsibilities occurs at the time of publishing of the XML Web services. As long as all requests are presented in the agreed-upon format, as defined by the XML Web services, the server application does not care what the client application does with the results. Likewise, as long as the server application accepts client requests in the agreed-upon format, the client application does not care how the server implements functionality.

Although the Golf Reservation System server application is in many ways tailored specifically to the Golf Reservation System Client we will build, it is entirely feasible that the Web methods could be designed to model only the data behind them and provide an XML Web service interface for retrieving the data. The result would be a service published on the Internet that is not tailored to a specific client application design, but instead provides abstractions on a complex data store. In this situation the clients would not necessarily be user-focused Web applications.

Imagine the Golf Reservation System server application as a stand-alone service provided by a conglomeration of golf courses. Multiple Internet applications could call into provided services and format and manipulate data as they saw fit. One client application might use the GolfCourseService to retrieve only golf course data (with or without displaying it), while another might retrieve golfer information from the GolfCourseService. A client could be developed by a partner business interested in collecting and manipulating the service result data, but not necessarily interested in displaying that data without further manipulation to a client—a server-to-server business interaction facilitated through XML Web Services.

Web Services

The Golf Reservation System contains only one Web Service, conveniently named GolfCourseService. Numerous other Web methods, however, are available within this lone service. The Web methods necessary for the Golf Reservation System vary from search helpers to everyday *findById* methods.

The GolfCourseService is responsible for masking business object design complexities and particulars. The developer calling and retrieving data from Web methods need not know whether a table of addresses is in the Golf Reservation System database. Instead, the .NET Framework allows back-end developers to create facades for complex business logic and publish the API for those facades (Web Services) to the network or Internet.

The Golf Reservation System client application calls into the GolfCourseService Web Service via SOAP requests and receives SOAP responses. The .NET Framework, though, handles the complexities of creating, sending, receiving, and parsing the SOAP documents. A developer seeking to manipulate a Web Service outside the scope of the .NET Framework would not only need an understanding of the business functionality available through the methods but an understanding of and an ability to generate SOAP calls to the methods, as well as an ability to parse the response SOAP documents.

Obtaining Information About a Service

Browsing to a Web Service results in the display of a description of what Web methods it provides and how to call into those methods using the supported protocols. Figure 10-1 is a screenshot of the GolfCourseService called in this manner, at *http://localhost/TeeTimes/GolfCourseService.asmx*.

Clicking a specific method (shown in Figure 10-2) offers a detailed description of that method and a form to invoke it. Note that submitting the form on this page does invoke the method and will perform the actions of that method

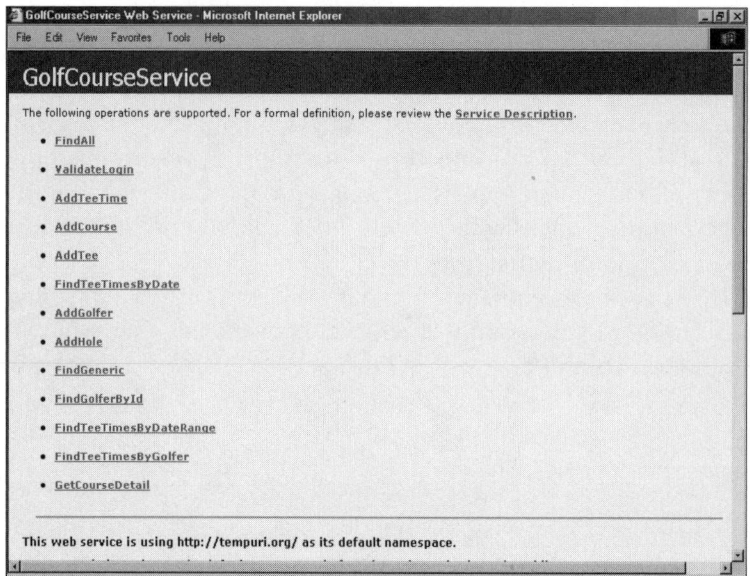

Figure 10-1 Detailed information about the Web methods provided.

as if it were called from an application. If the method results in a new database insert, submitting this form will do the same. Also detailed on the method description page is the protocol syntax request and response for SOAP calls, HTTP POST, and HTTP GET.

Understanding Web Service Method Signatures

The client application we will build requires little information to interact with the Golf Reservation System Server. We need only the method signatures of the Web methods provided by GolfCourseService and a brief description of method functionality if the intended method functionality is not immediately obvious by name.

These Web methods and the classes behind them make up the Golf Reservation System server application and represent the proxy necessary for other applications to interact with and manipulate the Golf Reservation System business logic. For more specific information about when and how to create Web Services from a server perspective, please see Chapter 9.

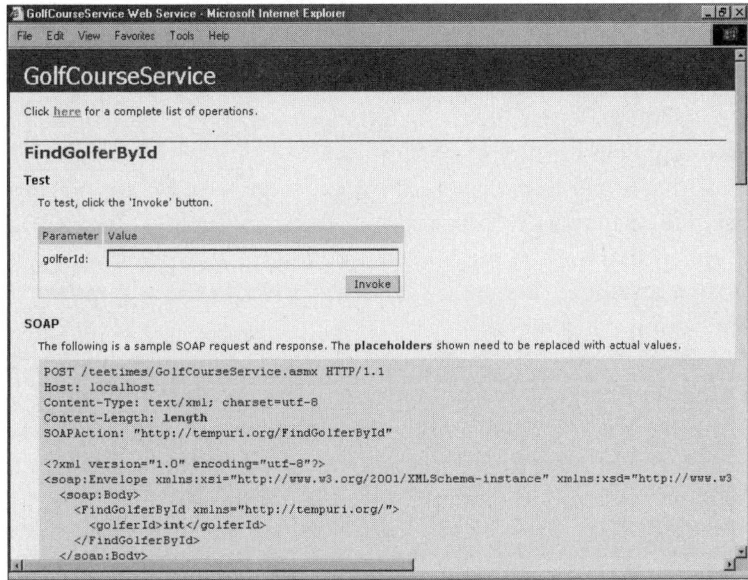

Figure 10-2 A brief description and protocol syntax for invoking a Web method.

Golf Reservation System Client

Golf Reservation System Client consists of the following: a Web reference for connecting to the Golf Reservation System Server Web Services, C# Web forms (.aspx.cs classes and associated .aspx files), and all items necessary for implementing the controller design pattern.

To connect to the GolfCourseService Web Service provided by the Golf Reservation System server application, which can reside anywhere on the Internet or local network, you need to create a Web reference. A Web reference provides class and Web method definitions available from the services it contains and makes those business objects and methods available to the project. In Microsoft Visual Studio.NET, this is as simple as providing a URL to the Web Service, which in turn iterates over the resulting WSDL data and creates all the necessary stubs for use in your Visual Studio. NET project. Outside the application, any number of tools for querying WSDL documents published on the Internet or network can be used. Visual Studio .NET just makes it easy and virtually seamless for the developer.

In developing a C# client application, accessing the Web Services available within an existing Web reference requires creating Web forms. Adding a Web form to your application creates both a WebFormName.aspx.cs file and a WebFormName.aspx file. The .aspx page is an instance of its associated .aspx.cs class, referred to in many cases as the "Class-behind" file. Visual Studio .NET provides skeleton templates for creating C# Web forms, and adding a Web form to a project creates these templates for you, including all the required methods and formatting. We will use the template for the .aspx.cs file, but because we are employing the controller design pattern for our UI, we will not be using the skeleton template for the .aspx files.

Note that a Web form, as used by the client in a Web application, is simply an instance of that Web form's associated Class-behind file, the .aspx.cs file. Any public variables and methods defined in the Class-behind file will be available to any instances of the class, and any private methods and variables will be hidden from the instance.

To reference Web methods within the aspx.cs file, you must instantiate the Web Service to make it available to your class. You are then provided all available Web methods and object types defined in the Web Service. For example, the CourseDetail.aspx.cs file instantiates the GolfCourseService and calls the getCourseDetail method passing in the required courseID string. This example is as follows:

```
// localhost is the name of the computer hosting the Golf Reservation
//System Server
// First, create a protected reference to a GolfCourse object
// making it available to instances of this class, and assign
// the url variable 'id' to a local variable, '_id'
protected localhost.GolfCourse gc;
string _id = Request.QueryString.Get("id");
// Next, instantiate the GolfCourseService
localhost.GolfCourseService gs = new localhost.GolfCourseService();
// Pass the local _id variable to the GetCourseDetail Web method and
assign
// the result local GolfCourse gc.
gc = gs.GetCourseDetail(_id);
```

The result of the *getCourseDetail* method is a *GolfCourse* object as defined in the Golf Reservation System server application, and this object is made available for manipulation by the *CourseDetail.aspx.cs* class.

Any objects needed for reference in the .aspx file instance must be declared in the constructor of the .aspx.cs class, usually as protected. Therefore, in keeping with the CourseDetail.aspx.cs example, any instance (.aspx) of the CourseDetail.aspx.cs class will have a *GolfCourse* object named *gc* associated with the given *id* parameter available for manipulation. Any public or protected objects declared in the constructor are likewise available to each instance of the Web form.

Because we are using the controller design pattern, the resulting .aspx file is not a completed client page; instead it is an XML document. The document schema is agreed upon between the UI developer and the back-end developer.

Therefore, after creating the Web form class and an associated .aspx XML file, the system developer duties are completed. The UI developer is now responsible for deciding how to format the data provided in the .aspx file, which can be used for any number of XSLT skins.

At this point the controller methodology takes over and formats the given-view XML (the .aspx result) with the appropriate template matches in the appropriate skin. The result, at least after using the ie5.xsl skin, is a page formatted to designer preference.

The Controller Design Pattern

The Golf Reservation System client application implements the controller design pattern for creating and managing the UI. Similar to the application of Web Services, the controller design pattern is platform- and application-non-specific in its implementation. Using XML and XSLT, all the UI designer requires is an agreed-upon schema for how the data is to be presented and working knowledge of how to use XSLT and associated formatting tools for presenting that data.

The controller implementation in the Golf Reservation System client application expects object-descriptive XML. That is, the result of a call to getCourseDetail.asmx.cs is an XML document describing the course in question, the syntax of which can be found in the code listing under getCourseDetail.aspx. Another popular implementation of the controller design pattern is to create a DTD abstracting both the data involved and the suggested (not actual) presentation of that data. For example, a list of courses from courseSearchResult.aspx could be formatted as

```
<courseList>
  <courseListItem>
    <name>
      Some Course Name
    </name>
    ...
  </courseListItem>
  <courseListItem>
    <name>
      Another Course Name
    </name>
    ...
  </courseListItem>
  . . .
  </courseList>
```

Optionally, courseSearchResult.asmx can format XML describing the contextual relationship of the data to a general layout, providing data in name/value pairs to the XSLT developer, such as

```
<list type="courseList">
    <listItem>
        <property>
            <name>Name</name>
            <value>Pebble Beach</value>
        </property>
        . . .
    </listItem>
    <listItem>
        <property>
            <name>Name</name>
            <value>Augusta National</value>
        </property>
        . . .
    </listItem>
</list>
```

Both models have advantages and disadvantages, and the application designer must decide which method best fits the application. At an initial view the object-descriptive model is the obvious choice, but keep in mind that it requires a new xsl:template block for nearly every type of request/response pair. However, the model describing the presentation lends itself to design consistency and an easier-to-maintain UI because it requires fewer templates.

The second approach involves contextual understanding of the data provided. Is a property significant? Which nodes can display on which Internet devices? These questions are significant in designing a client application, and a design team will probably come up with a hybrid of the two patterns instead of choosing one.

Procedure Flow

An application-perspective procedure flow from a Golf Reservation System Client page request is as follows:

1. User requests page (controller.asp?view=courseDetail&id=12) either by typing an address in the browser location bar or by clicking a link somewhere. In either case the call for our sample client, is an HTTP GET method. (HTTP POST methods are also possible, though they're not used in this application.) All required variables are passed through the URL or as form variables. The Golf Reservation System client application assumes these variables are both present and for-

matted correctly. A production application would contain extensive validation.

2. The controller locates the requested viewtype.aspx in the "content" folder and evaluates. Keeping with the CourseDetail example, the aspx file is located at /content/courseDetail.aspx.
3. Calling the .aspx file forces the compiled .aspx.cs file to create an instance in the form of the aspx document. The *Page_Load()* function in the aspx.cs file is called and initializes the class. All public variables defined in the constructor are made available to the .aspx instance. The Web Service is instantiated and various Web methods are called. Database reads and writes are executed as necessary. The controller loads the XML result in a variable named *xmlurl*.
4. The controller.asp retrieves the appropriate XSLT skin, ie5.xsl. (Golf Reservation System Client contains only one but can contain many skins.) The controller loads the XSLT in a variable named *xslurl*.
5. The controller uses *xslurl* to transform *xmlurl* and returns the transformed result, in this case, an HTML document.

Client Code

This section contains the complete code listing for the Golf Reservation System client application. Every line of code is included here except for the autogenerated code created by Visual Studio.NET. Take special note of the code listing for CourseDetail.aspx.cs because this is the only listing that includes this autogenerated code, and it is necessary in creating Web forms. The .aspx files (our result XML) contains only one line of autogenerated code and is here in its complete form.

> **Note** All files in Golf Reservation System Client follow this convention: the Class-behind file is named identical to the .aspx file with ".cs" appended. This format is not required, but it is standard and recommended. The templates, if you use Visual Studio .NET as an IDE, will default the names in this pattern.

As we begin to cover the code, note that each file is listed with its .aspx.cs file first, followed by its .aspx file. In a few cases no .aspx.cs file is necessary. Together, an .aspx.cs file and an .aspx file of the same name are called a "Web form" by the .Net Framework. Without the controller design pattern, each page viewed by the user is the server-side generated result of the Web form files.

The controller design pattern adds one more server-side step to the cycle. In this pattern the .aspx result returned is well-formed XML. The Web browser (or other Internet device) receives the result of this XML transformed by the XSLT skin. In the Golf Reservation System client application, ie5.xsl is responsible for transforming every page. A production application could have multiple skins, based on user preferences, target devices, and so forth.

Web Form Code

If you are familiar with ASP, you should also be familiar with most of the base syntax and method calls in this application. Reviewing the robust functionality of ASP is outside the scope of this book, but we will go into detail in the places where we use specific ASP functionality. Note that nearly all ASP functions are available, and in many cases extended in the .NET Framework development language, C#.

This first file we will look at is CourseDetail. CourseDetail is responsible for retrieving a *GolfCourse* object from the database given the *id* in the *Request.QueryString* object. The *Request.QueryString* object is a C# object that contains namevalue pairs present in the requested URL. Therefore, CourseDetail expects a URL similar to

```
http://localhost/TeeTimes/courseDetail.aspx?id=10001
```

Among the methods provided by the *Request.QueryString* object is the *Get* method in which you provide a value of type string which corresponds to the name in the namevalue pair expected in the URL. The *Get* method returns the value portion of the namevalue pair if the pair exists. Otherwise, the method returns a null response. Note that this method always returns a string because arguments present in the URL are always handled as strings, regardless of their form. The *id* in this example, although an integer, will be cast as a string until the program casts it otherwise. If you want to use a URL value as a datatype other than string, you must explicitly cast it as such.

Redundant code created by Visual Studio .NET has been removed, specifically all *using* declarations and the private methods *Page_Init* and *InitializeComponent*. CourseDetail.aspx.cs, contains these items, but the rest of the example code does not. While these portions are omitted here, the source files in their entirety can be found on the accompanying CD. These samples will not function without applying the generated code.

```
using System;
using System.Collections;
using System.ComponentModel;
```

```
using System.Data;
using System.Drawing;
using System.Web;
using System.Web.SessionState;
using System.Web.UI;
using System.Web.UI.WebControls;
using System.Web.UI.HtmlControls;
```

The using statements are autogenerated by Visual Studio. NET and are required by the .NET Framework. They are present at the top of every .cs file in the Golf Reservation System client application.

```
namespace TeeTimesClient.content
{  public class courseDetail : System.Web.UI.Page
  {
     // provide a GolfCourse object to each instance
    protected localhost.GolfCourse gc;
```

In this example "localhost" is the name of the machine hosting the GolfCourseService Web Service. As long as a Web reference exists for the Web Service, this machine can be physically located anywhere on the Internet or local network.

This present scope represents all the variables (if defined other than private) that will be made available to instances of this class, specifically, CourseDetail.aspx. CourseDetail.aspx receives from this file a *GolfCourse* object named *gc* for manipulation. If the variable *gc* is not defined in this scope, the .aspx file will not have access to its properties and methods.

The public constructor method with the same name as its file is autogenerated by the IDE and is required by the .NET Framework. This method initializes an instance of an *EventHandler* to handle user events such as a *mouse-click*. The Golf Reservation System client application does not take advantage of the *EventHandler*, but the constructor is nonetheless required as part of the file.

```
    public courseDetail()
    {
      Page.Init += new System.EventHandler(Page_Init);
    }
```

The *Page_Load* method is also autogenerated by the IDE. This scope includes all the page load functionality you want to create. That is, all logic not called from client event handlers should be implemented in this scope.

```
    private void Page_Load(object sender, System.EventArgs e)
    {
```

CourseDetail .aspx expects a variable named *id* to exist in the *Request.QueryString* and to be formatted correctly. As stated before, Golf

Reservation System Client contains virtually no error checking. A production implementation would, of course, contain rigorous validation and error checking.

```
// get the id from the url
string _id = Request.QueryString.Get("id");
```

This is our first example of how a variable is declared in C#, so let's take a closer look. The first portion of code casts the variable as a string. All variables in C# must have a type.

Following the cast, the name of the variable is declared, in this case *_id*. The variable name can be any alphanumeric string. These two portions alone are enough to declare a variable. Without the equal sign, though, no value is assigned to the variable and it is only a null reference. As you can't manipulate a null reference, you must assign a value to your variable before you call methods. Calling methods on a null reference results in a compile time error.

The far right side of the variable declaration can be an object or an expression that reults in an object, as long as the object type is the same as the variable to which it is being assigned. That is, you cannot assign an integer value to a variable declared as a string, and you cannot assign a string value to a variable declared as, say, a *GolfCourse* object. This type of error will also result in a compile time error.

The following line instantiates the GolfCourseService, which in this case exists on a networked computer named localhost. The localhost reference will need to be changed to the name of the computer where the Golf Reservation System server application lives. The local variable *gs* is now an instance of the GolfCourseService, and all methods in the GolfCourseService are now available in this scope of CourseDetail.aspx.cs.

```
            // instantiate the Web service
      localhost.GolfCourseService gs = new localhost.GolfCourseSer-
vice();
```

The variable *gc* now contains the *golfCourse* object returned from the call to the *GetCourseDetail* Web method.

```
    // assign gc to the appopriate GolfCourse object
gc = gs.GetCourseDetail(_id);
   }
```

The *Page_Init* function is autogenerated by Visual Studio .NET and should not be modified by the developer.

```
    private void Page_Init(object sender, EventArgs e)
    {
      //
      // CODEGEN: This call is required by the ASP.NET Web Form
```

```
Designer.
      //
      InitializeComponent();
    }
    #region Web Form Designer generated code
    /// <summary>
    /// Required method for Designer support - do not modify
    /// the contents of this method with the code editor.
    /// </summary>
    private void InitializeComponent()
    {
      this.Load += new System.EventHandler(this.Page_Load);
    }
    #endregion
  }
}
```

Like all .aspx files in Golf Reservation System Client, CourseDetail.aspx is responsible for returning well-formed XML to controller.asp. Notice the extensive XSLT in ie5.xsl used to create a rich UI for the functionality in this page. The result is a page providing general course information (see Figure 10-3) a detailed course description (see Figure 10-4), and a form to search for available tee times (see Figure 10-5).

The *<%@ Page>* declaration is a page definition required at the top of every .aspx file and is the only autogenerated code we leave there. Modifying this code out of its autogenerated format is unnecessary. Its purpose is to set page-specific parameters such as the language used, the Class-behind or .aspx.cs file, and the class from which the page inherits functionality. Again, this line is autogenerated by Visual Studio .NET and editing its content is unnecessary.

```
<%@ Page language="c#" Codebehind="courseDetail.aspx.cs" Auto
EventWireup="false" Inherits="TeeTimesClient.content.courseDetail" %>
```

Listing 10-1 is based on an agreed upon format between the XSL developer and the ASPX developer. The initial portion of the XML provides general page layout direction while the core of the document provides object-specific data—in this case, *courseDetail* information.

Notice that, until this point, the XML is layout-specific, that is, it describes the layout of the page instead of the object (or group of objects) to be formatted by the XSLT. This, again, is defined by an agreement between the XSLT (UI) and the ASPX (client application logic) developer. Because *gc* is defined as public scope in the aspx.cs class, this object is available for manipulation by the .aspx file. This is another area where the line between developer and UI designer is blurred.

Listing 10-1 CourseDetail.aspx: Provides an XML representation of the given course compliant with the XSLT model.

```
<document>
  <header>
    <title>Course Detail</title>
  </header>
  <section>
    <header>
      <title>Course Detail</title>
    </header>
...
  </section>
</document>
```

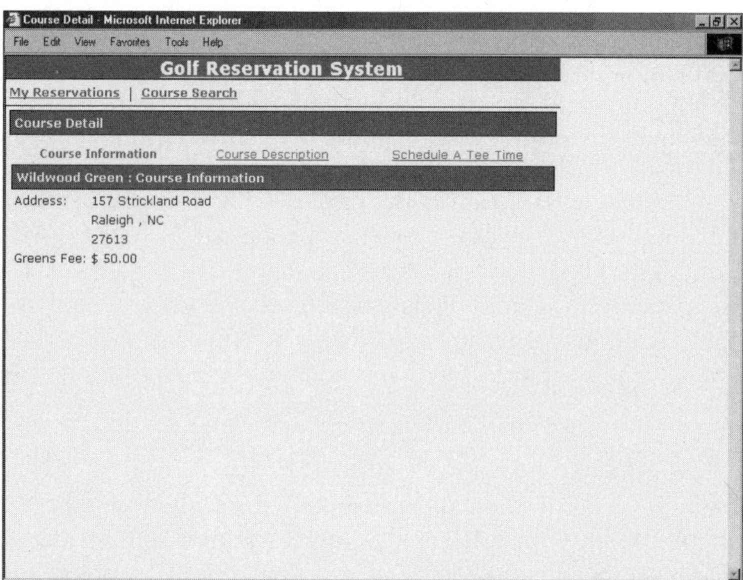

Figure 10-3 CourseDetail.aspx.cs displays *GolfCourse* object data given a URL variable named *id.*

The developer of the ASPX page must know what objects are available, what their names will be, and how those objects are defined. In most cases an ASPX page will receive proprietary data types or common data types such as arrays, and the ASPX developer must know how to handle these objects.

Also take note of the C# syntax used to display dynamic content within the .aspx file. ASP developers new to the .NET Framework and Web Services will

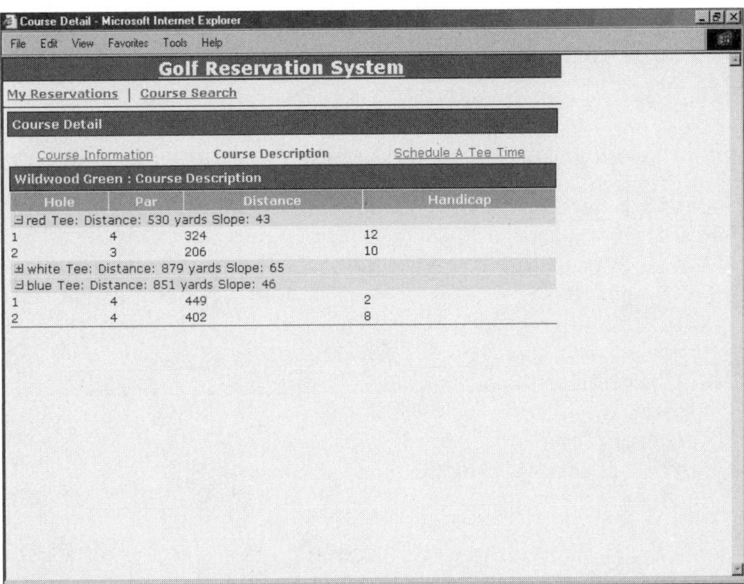

Figure 10-4 CourseDetail.aspx.cs breaks tee groups into individual holes, providing distance, par, and handicap for each. This is a good example of a functionally rich interface developed from object-based XML.

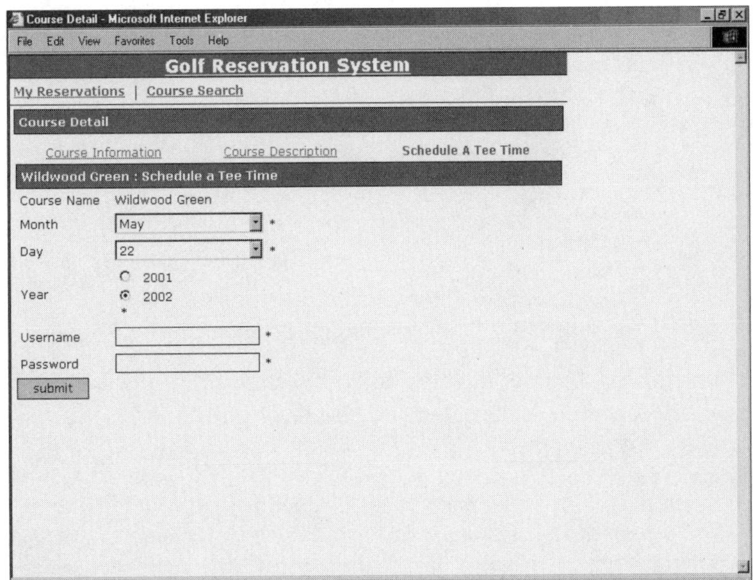

Figure 10-5 CourseDetail.aspx.cs allows users to search for a tee time by date on this specific course.

be happy to know the syntax for such operations is the same as it is for an ASP application. To dynamically display a value, the syntax is

```
<%= objectReference.variableName %>
```

where *variableName* is a valid field name for the *objectReference*.

```
<!--- Display general golf Course Information --->
<courseDetail>
      <id>
        <%= gc.id %>
      </id>
      <name>
        <%= gc.name %>
      </name>
      <description>
        <%= gc.description %>
      </description>
```

CourseDetail.aspx is split into unique content sections, each defined in the XML as a *courseDetailBlock*. This particular *courseDetailBlock* displays the general course information: *name*, *price*, and, later, *address*. Distinguishing between different content sections through XML is necessary to provide the XSLT developer distinct relationships between different blocks of content.

```
      <courseDetailBlock description="Course Information">
        <courseItem type="courseInfo">
          <section>
            <header>
              <title>
                <%= gc.name %>: Course Information
  </title>
            </header>
          </section>
          <price>
            <%= gc.price %>
          </price>
```

The *address* object is included as part of the *gc GolfCourse* object, referred to by *gc.address*, and contains *street*, *city*, *state*, and *postalCode* variables. Obviously, the ASPX developer must have a solid understanding of the object types available.

```
       <!--- Display address object --->
       <address>
         <address1>
             <%= gc.address.street %>
         </address1>
            <city>
```

```
            <%= gc.address.city %>
          </city>
          <state>
            <%= gc.address.state %>
          </state>
          <zip>
            <%= gc.address.postalCode %>
          </zip>
        </address>
      </courseItem>
    </courseDetailBlock>
<!--- Display in another content section specific course information
including individual tee and hole descriptions --->
    <courseDetailBlock description="Course Description">
      <courseItem type="holeInfo">
        <section>
          <header>
            <title>
              <%= gc.name %>: Course Description
        </title>
          </header>
        </section>
        <tees>
```

The *tees* object returned with *gc* is an array of the tees associated with the given *GolfCourse*. A *tee* object also contains an array of *holes*, each having a *par*, *distance*, and *number* value. Notice in ie5.xsl that this becomes a grouped list with extremely rich UI functionality. The code here is used to loop over the array of tees and to access and display specific information about each one.

```
<% for (int i=0; i < gc.tees.Length; i++) { %>
```

To include C# programming blocks, like the *for loop*, the syntax requires encapsulating the logic between <% and %>. This syntax will be familiar to developers with experience in ASP, but might look awkward to others.

```
          <tee>
            <slope>
              <%= gc.tees[i].slope %>
            </slope>
            <description>
              <%= gc.tees[i].description %>
            </description>
            <id>
              <%= gc.tees[i].id %>
            </id>
            <%
           // determine complete distance of a tee
           // through the sum of it's holes length values
```

```
                int teeDistance = 0;
                for (int j=0; j < gc.tees[i].holes.Length; j++) {
                  teeDistance = teeDistance +
gc.tees[i].holes[j].length;
                }
              %>
              <distance>
                <%= teeDistance %>
              </distance>
             <!--- Display information about each hole object
in the tee --->
              <holes>
                <% for (int j=0; j < gc.tees[i].holes.Length; j++) {%>
```

Each *Tee* object contains an array of *hole* objects, as defined by the object schema for the Golf Reservation System Server. We iterate over the array of *holes* to display each one's significant variables. This loop results in numerous *hole* nodes, specifically the length of the *hole* array for this particular tee.

```
  <hole number="<%=gc.tees[i].holes[j].hole %>">
                  <par>
                    <%= gc.tees[i].holes[j].par %>
                  </par>
                  <handicap>
                    <%= gc.tees[i].holes[j].handicap %>
                  </handicap>
                  <distance>
                    <%= gc.tees[i].holes[j].length %>
                  </distance>
                </hole>
                <% } %>
```

Flow control and reading developer intent can be difficult to follow if you have never developed an ASP Web application, but it's not difficult to learn. Notice that we have to wrap our statement-ending } in <% and %>.

```
              </holes>
            </tee>
            <% } %>
          </tees>
        </courseItem>
      </courseDetailBlock>
       <!--- Display form for searching tee times --->
      <courseDetailBlock description="Schedule A Tee Time">
```

This *courseDetailBlock* is responsible for providing a form that allows the user to schedule a tee time (should any be available) for this specific course. All forms in the Golf Reservation System client application post to controller.asp, as defined by the controller design pattern. The *view* argument required by controller.asp is provided by a hidden variable later in the form. The XSLT developer depends on the ASPX developer to signify those inputs that are required by including the *mandataory="yes"* attribute. Notice also how the XML briefly returns to a layout-specific XML inside the *<section>* nodes.

```
      <form action="controller.asp">
<section>
            <header>
              <title>
                <%= gc.name %>.
                : Schedule a Tee Time </title>
            </header>
            <view>
              <properties>
                <property description="Course Name">
                  <text>
                    <%= gc.name %>
                  </text>
                </property>
                <property description="Month">
```

The *<choice>* node is an excellent example of how the ASPX developer can use the agreed-upon DTD to transfer the responsibility of formatting the display of data to the XSLT developer. Of course, no HTML *<choice>* node exists. Instead, a few nodes prompt the user for a choice with radio buttons, check box sets, and select boxes. Each of these nodes has distinct characteristics, both in functionality and in aesthetics. The end results, however, are more or less the same: the user is prompted to choose one or more selections from a list of possible options. Therefore, creating a *<choice>* node in the ASPX XML allows the XSLT developer to choose which HTML form input is most appropriate for the situation.

This instance of the *<choice>* node prompts the user to choose a *month*, *day*, and later a *year* for reserving a tee time.

```
                  <choice name="month" mandatory="yes">
                     <option value="01">January</option>
                     <option value="02">February</option>
                     <option value="03">March</option>
                     <option value="04">April</option>
                     <option value="05">May</option>
                     <option value="06">June</option>
                     <option value="07">July</option>
                     <option value="08">August</option>
                     <option value="09">September</option>
                     <option value="10">October</option>
                     <option value="11">November</option>
                     <option value="12">December</option>
```

```
            </choice>
          </property>
          <property description="Day">
            <choice name="day" mandatory="yes">
              <% for(int i=1;i<=31;i++) { %>
                <option value="<%=i%>"><%=i%></option>
              <% } %>
            </choice>
          </property>
          <property description="Year">
            <%
System.DateTime theYears = System.DateTime.Now;
                int thisYear = theYears.Year;
                theYears = theYears.AddYears(1);
                int nextYear = theYears.Year;
            %>
            <choice name="year" mandatory="yes">
            <option value="<%=thisYear%>"><%=thisYear%></option>
            <option value="<%=nextYear%>"><%=nextYear%></option>
            </choice>
          </property>
```

The *mandatory* attribute is another example of utilizing the skills of the XSLT developer to implement intended functionality. Using the *mandatory* attribute informs the XSLT developer that a specific *<input>* node is required to submit the form. The XSLT developer can then generate whatever form validation code is necessary to ensure that the requirement is met. And given that each Internet device has its own implementation of validation, the responsibility should be left in the hands of the XSLT developer to determine the appropriate method.

The hidden fields in each form are submitted to the action page unbeknownst to the user. Hidden fields are not available for editing to the user, but instead are used as flags to the controller. This form provides a *view* hidden variable to tell the controller which view should be processed at form submission and also a *submitted* variable that lets the controller know that this request is a form submission. The *courseID* is also expected by the *viewTeeTimes* page, and is another example of the ASPX developer requiring knowledge of the application architecture and each individual file.

```
<property description="Username">
   <input type="text" name="username" mandatory="yes" />
                </property>
                <property description="Password">
   <input type="text" name="password" mandatory="yes" />
   <input type="hidden" name="submitted" value="true" />
               <input type="hidden" name="view" value="viewTeeTimes" />
                  <input type="hidden" name="courseId"
```

```
value="<%=gc.id%>"/>
                </property>
              </properties>
            </view>
          </section>
        </form>
      </courseDetailBlock>
    </courseDetail>
  </section>
</document>
```

Listing 10-2, CourseSearch.aspx is the search form that allows the user to find a course based on any combination of *Name*, *City*, *State*, *Country*, or *Postal Code*. CourseSearch has no Class-behind file as it's not a user-defined page. That is, CourseSearch.aspx requires no user information and displays the same for every user. This code only requires a form prompting the user for valid search fields. The form XML is in turn transformed by the skin—ie5.xsl—into a valid HTML form.

Listing 10-2 CourseSearch.aspx: Provides a form prompting the user for course search parameters.

```
<%@ Page %>
<document>
  <header>
    <title>Search For A Golf Course Near You</title>
  </header>
  <form action="controller.asp">
    <section>
      <header>
        <title>Course Search</title>
      </header>
      <view>
        <properties>
          <property description="Course Name">
            <input type="text" name="name" />
          </property>
          <property description="City">
            <input type="text" name="city" />
          </property>
          <property description="State">
            <input type="text" name="state" />
          </property>
          <property description="Country">
            <input type="text" name="country" />
          </property>
          <property description="Postal Code">
            <input type="text" name="postalCode" />
```

(continued)

Listing 10-2 *continued*

```
          </property>
          <property>
            <input type="hidden" name="view" value=
"CourseSearchResult" />
          </property>
        </properties>
      </view>
    </section>
  </form>
</document>
```

Listing 10-3, CourseSearchResult.aspx.cs, receives form data from CourseSearch.aspx and returns an array of *GolfCourses* satisfying the provided search parameters. The search parameters are provided by the user in the courseSearch.aspx form. The possible search parameters are *Course Name*, *City*, *State*, *Country*, and *Postal Code*.

Listing 10-3 CourseSearchResult.aspx.cs: Provides an array of *Golf Course* Objects satisfying given search parameters.

```
namespace TeeTimesClient
{
  public class CourseSearchResult : System.Web.UI.Page
  {
    protected localhost.GolfCourse[] results;
    private void Page_Load(object sender, System.EventArgs e)
    {
      // instantiate the GolfCourseService Web service
      localhost.GolfCourseService gs = new localhost.
GolfCourseService();
```

The *FindGeneric* method expects an array of *fields* and an array of *values*, with the *name* and *value* variables occupying corresponding positions. Position X in the *fields* array is required to be a valid field for searching (such as *name*), while the same position in the *values* array needs to be its corresponding value (such as *Wildwood Green*). The *FindGeneric* method provides much stronger functionality than exact text searching and the ASPX developer needs to be aware of this functionality to take advantage of it.

This type of functionality, which is not immediately apparent given the name and method signature, is expected to be well-documented by the server-application developer. In this case *FindGeneric* accepts the string * as a wild card search parameter and will also accept part of a search string followed by *. The user can provide *Wild** as a search parameter and the method will return, for example, a course with the name *Wildwood Green*. The same convention is applied to all search parameters in this method.

In this code we pull each of the expected arguments out of the *Request.QueryString* and insert their names into the *fields* array and their value into the *values* array. If the value in the *Request.QueryString* object is null, we place a * in the values array at the appropriate position, which represents a wild card and will satisfy all courses in the database. Thus, an empty search will result in a record set consisting of every course in the database.

```
// prepare the variables for calling FindGeneric
String[] fields = new String[5];
      String[] values = new String[5];
       // populate the fields and values arrays
      fields[0] = "name";
      string nameValue = Request.QueryString.Get("name");
      // if the value is null, set to '*'
if (nameValue == null || nameValue == "")
            nameValue = "*";
      values[0] = nameValue;
      fields[1] = "city";
      string cityValue = Request.QueryString.Get("city");
      if (cityValue == null || cityValue == "")
        cityValue = "*";
      values[1] = cityValue;
fields[2] = "state";
      string stateValue = Request.QueryString.Get("state");
      if (stateValue == null || stateValue == "")
        stateValue = "*";
      values[2] = stateValue;
      fields[3] = "country";
      string countryValue = Request.QueryString.Get("country");
      if (countryValue == null || countryValue == "")
        countryValue = "*";
      values[3] = countryValue;
      fields[4] = "postalCode";
      string postalCodeValue = Request.QueryString.Get("postalCode");
      if (postalCodeValue == null || postalCodeValue == "")
           postalCodeValue = "*";
      values[4] = postalCodeValue;
      results = gs.FindGeneric(fields, values);
    }
```

Listing 10-4, CourseSearchResult.aspx, iterates over an array of *GolfCourse* objects and displays them. The array of *GolfCourse* objects, named *results*, is provided by the CourseSearchResult.aspx.cs file. The XSLT for this XML provides links to the CourseDetail page for each item in the array.

Listing 10-4 CourseSearchResult.aspx: A loop over the *GolfCourse* objects which satisfied search parameters and provide links to their appropriate *CourseDetail* pages.

```
<%@ Page language="c#" Codebehind="CourseSearchResult.aspx.cs"
AutoEventWireup="false" Inherits="TeeTimesClient.WebForm1" %>
<document>
  <header>
    <title>Course Search Results</title>
    <description>
    </description>
  </header>
  <section>
    <header>
      <title>Search Results</title>
    </header>
    <courseList>
      // for each Golf Course, provide id and general information
      <% for(int i=0; i < results.Length; i++) { %>
      <courseListItem>
        <name>
          <%= results[i].name %>
        </name>
        <id>
          <%= results[i].id %>
        </id>
        <city>
          <%= results[i].address.city %>
        </city>
        <state>
          <%= results[i].address.state %>
        </state>
      </courseListItem>
      <% } %>
    </courseList>
  </section>
</document>
```

Figure 10-6 shows the results of Listing 10-4.

Listing 10-5, login.aspx, like CourseSearch.aspx, contains no Class-behind file and is only responsible for prompting input from the user. This file contains two forms, one for a registered user in the database to log into the Golf Reservation System client application, and one for a new golfer to register with Golf Reservation System by providing a username, password, and general user information. This file is only responsible for creating two valid forms prompting the user for input, either a username/password combination or enough data to create a new user record.

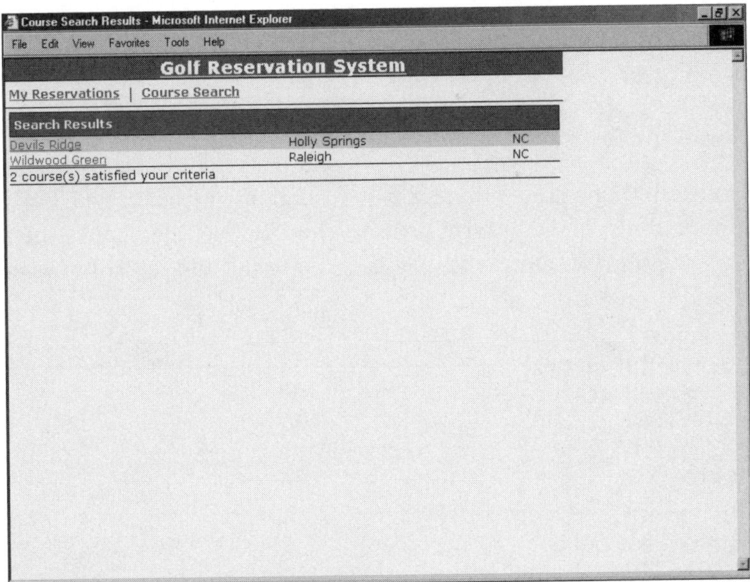

Figure 10-6 The *GolfCourse* objects that satisfied the search parameters.

Listing 10-5 login.aspx: Provides a form for a user to sign in if they are a registered user or to register if they are not.

```
<%@ Page language="c#" Codebehind="login.aspx.cs"
AutoEventWireup="false" Inherits="TeeTimesClient.content.
myTeeTimes" %>
<document>
  <header>
    <title>My Tee Times</title>
  </header>
  <form action="controller.asp">
    <section>
      <header>
        <title>Please Log In</title>
      </header>
      <view>
        <description>
          Log in to to view your saved Tee Times
        </description>
        <properties>
          <property description="Username">
            <input type="text" name="username" mandatory="yes" />
          </property>
          <property description="Password">
            <input type="text" name="password" mandatory="yes" />
```

(continued)

Listing 10-5 *continued*

```
          </property>
          <property>
            <input type="hidden" name="submitted" value="true" />
<input type="hidden" name="view" value="viewMyTeeTimes" />
```

Notice that this page contains two distinct forms, each with different hidden *view* input types. The first form posts to viewMyTeeTimes, while the second form posts to register. We know this by inspecting the hidden input *view* arguments present in each form.

```
          </property>
        </properties>
      </view>
    </section>
  </form>
  <form action="controller.asp">
    <section>
      <header>
        <title>Register</title>
      </header>
      <view>
        <description>
If you do not yet have a username and password, please provide the
information below to become a registered user.
        </description>
        <properties>
          <property description="Choose a username">
            <input type="text" name="username" mandatory="yes" />
          </property>
          <property description="Choose a Password">
            <input type="text" name="password" mandatory="yes" />
          </property>
          <property description="First Name">
            <input type="text" name="firstName" mandatory="yes" />
          </property>
          <property description="Last Name">
            <input type="text" name="lastName" mandatory="yes" />
          </property>
          <property description="Address">
            <input type="text" name="streetAddress" mandatory="yes" />
          </property>
          <property description="City">
            <input type="text" name="city" mandatory="yes" />
          </property>
          <property description="State">
            <input type="text" name="state" mandatory="yes" />
          </property>
```

```
          <property description="Postal Code">
            <input type="text" name="postalCode" mandatory="yes" />
          </property>
          <property description="Country">
            <input type="text" name="country" mandatory="yes" />
          </property>
          <property description="email">
            <input type="text" name="email" mandatory="yes" />
          </property>
          <property description="Telephone">
            <input type="text" name="phone" mandatory="yes" />
<input type="hidden" name="submitted" value="true" />
          </property>
          <property>
            <input type="hidden" name="view" value="register" />
          </property>
        </properties>
      </view>
    </section>
  </form>
</document>
```

The input *name* attributes are significant in each form in Golf Reservation System Client. These *name* attributes (that is, *name="phone"*, *name="email"*) must be identical to the variable names expected by the Class-behind file of the .aspx to which each form is posted. This implementation of Golf Reservation System Client assumes all form variables will be present and formatted correctly. This, of course, is not a real-world example. Register.aspx.cs (Listing 10-6) receives information from login.aspx if the user submitted the new user form. This information is used to create a new user in the database using the *addGolfer* Web method.

Listing 10-6 register.aspx.cs: Creates a new user record based on user input from login.aspx.

```
namespace TeeTimesClient.content
{
  public class register : System.Web.UI.Page
  {
    protected localhost.Golfer newGolfer;
    private void Page_Load(object sender, System.EventArgs e)
    {
      localhost.GolfCourseService gs = new localhost.GolfCourseSer-
vice();
      // Get all values from the Request.QueryString object
string usernameValue = Request.QueryString.Get("username");
      string passwordValue = Request.QueryString.Get("password");
```

(continued)

Listing 10-6 *continued*

```
        string firstNameValue = Request.QueryString.Get("firstName");
        string lastNameValue = Request.QueryString.Get("lastName");
        string streetAddressValue = Request.QueryString.Get
("streetAddress");
        string cityValue = Request.QueryString.Get("city");
        string stateValue = Request.QueryString.Get("state");
        string postalCodeValue = Request.QueryString.Get("postalCode");
        string countryValue = Request.QueryString.Get("country");
        string emailValue = Request.QueryString.Get("email");
        string phoneValue = Request.QueryString.Get("phone");
        // Add a new golfer to the database
        newGolfer = gs.AddGolfer(firstNameValue,lastNameValue,
streetAddressValue,cityValue,stateValue,postalCodeValue,
countryValue,emailValue,phoneValue,usernameValue,passwordValue);
    }
```

Listing 10-7, register.aspx, simply displays a thank-you message to the user after a registration is submitted. Notice the generic XML—no specific object XML is in this file.

Listing 10-7 register.aspx: Displays a thank-you message to the user following the registration routine in register.aspx.cs.

```
<%@ Page language="c#" Codebehind="register.aspx.cs"
AutoEventWireup="false" Inherits="TeeTimesClient.content.register"
%>
<document>
  <header>
    <title>My Tee Times</title>
  </header>
  <section>
    <header>
      <title>Thank You for Registering</title>
    </header>
    <view>
      <description>
        Thanks for registering
        <%= newGolfer.firstName%>
- Now that you are a registered user, you can set up Tee Times with
any of our partner Golf Courses.
      </description>
    </view>
  </section>
</document>
```

The scheduleTeeTime file receives a *courseId*, a *golferId*, and a *System.DateTime* object from the *Request.QueryString* object, builds a registration, and inserts it into the database using the *AddTeeTime* Web method. It also provides the *Golfer*, *GolfCourse*, and *TeeTime* object to its .aspx file.

Notice the lack of error checking. If the *golferIdValue* is not present in the *Request.QueryString* object, or if it's not a valid *golferId*, Golf Reservation System Client will throw a run-time error. The variable *golfer* will be a null reference and *scheduleTeeTime* will function incorrectly.

```
scheduleTeeTime.aspx.cs - Build a registration and insert it into the
database
namespace TeeTimesClient.content
{
  public class scheduleTeeTime : System.Web.UI.Page
  {
    protected localhost.TeeTime tt;
    protected localhost.Golfer golfer;
    protected localhost.GolfCourse gc;
    private void Page_Load(object sender, System.EventArgs e)
    {
      localhost.GolfCourseService gs = new localhost.GolfCourseSer-
vice();
      int courseIdValue = Int32.Parse(Request.
QueryString.Get("courseId"));
      int golferIdValue = Int32.Parse(Request.QueryString.Get
("golferId"));
      System.DateTime dateValue = System.DateTime.Parse
(Request.QueryString.Get("teeTime"));
      // AddTeeTime requires two System.DateTime objects
       //  The first is parsed for the date, the second for the time
tt = gs.AddTeeTime(courseIdValue,golferIdValue,dateValue,dateValue);
      golfer = gs.FindGolferById(golferIdValue);
      gc = gs.GetCourseDetail(Request.QueryString.Get("courseid"));
    }
```

Listing 10-8, the scheduleTeeTime.aspx file, displays a notification that the selected tee time was inserted into the database. The object-based XML model used in this page affords the XSLT developer design luxury in creating a UI for displaying the tee time. Though ie5.xsl doesn't do much with the scheduleTeeTime.aspx result, a VoiceXML skin could read off the tee time detail, or the skin could hook into a calender client and build a calender entry.

Listing 10-8 scheduleTeeTime.aspx: Displays a thank-you message after a tee time is registered.

```
<%@ Page language="c#" Codebehind="scheduleTeeTime.aspx.cs"
AutoEventWireup="false" Inherits="TeeTimesClient.content.
scheduleTeeTime" %>
<document>
  <header>
    <title>My Tee Times</title>
  </header>
  <section>
    <header>
      <title>Tee Time Scheduled</title>
    </header>
    <description>
Thank you for registering a tee time. The detail of your registration
is below.
    </description>
    <teeTimeDetail>
      <golfer>
        <name>
          <%= golfer.firstName %>
          <%= golfer.lastName %>
        </name>
      </golfer>
      <course>
        <id>
          <%= gc.id %>
        </id>
        <name>
          <%= gc.name %>
        </name>
      </course>
      <date>
```

Once an .aspx page has a handle on an object and the developer knows the variable datatype, the complete library of C# methods is available. Here, the *System.DateTime* object returned with the tee time is parsed into a readable format for the XSLT using the *ToShortDateString()* and *ToShortTimeString()* methods.

```
        <%= tt.date.ToShortDateString() %>
      </date>
      <time>
        <%= tt.time.ToShortTimeString() %>
      </time>
    </teeTimeDetail>
  </section>
</document>
```

The viewMyTeeTimes file receives a valid *golferID* and returns *TeeTime* objects associated with that user, as well as the associated *GolfCourse* objects. As an example of error checking, if the *golferID* is not valid, this class returns a protected Boolean *redirect* informing the instance .aspx file that the user is invalid and needs to be redirected.

Notice also that GolfCourseService is provided to the .aspx file because it's defined as a protected variable. Choosing where you should perform the Web method calls is an application design decision. The Class-behind files should perform as much business logic as is possible, but in many cases you might choose to implement only getters and setters inside the .aspx.cs and use the .aspx result document instead to perform Web method calls. This is an especially attractive model when implementing the controller design pattern because the .aspx file isn't the final tier of the application. This does, however, place the burden of exception handling on the ASPX developer. Doing so in the Class-behind file might be more logical.

Listing 10-9, viewMyTeeTimes.aspx, is responsible for validating that a username and password are valid and returning an array of tee times for the validated user by calling the *FindTeeTimesByGolfer* Web method.

Listing 10-9 viewMyTeeTimes.aspx.cs: Validates a user and returns an array of *TeeTime* objects for that user.

```
namespace TeeTimesClient.content
{
  public class viewMyTeeTimes : System.Web.UI.Page
  {
    protected localhost.TeeTime[] tt;
    protected localhost.Golfer golfer;
    protected localhost.GolfCourse gc;
    protected bool redirect = false;
    // Provide the GolfCourseService to instances
    protected localhost.GolfCourseService gs = new localhost.
GolfCourseService();
    private void Page_Load(object sender, System.EventArgs e)
    {
      string usernameValue = Request.QueryString.Get("username");
      string passwordValue = Request.QueryString.Get("password");
      golfer = gs.ValidateLogin(usernameValue,passwordValue);
      // if ValidateLogin returns a null reference, set
      // boolean redirect to true
if (golfer == null) {
        redirect = true;
      } else {
        int golferIdValue = golfer.id;
        tt = gs.FindTeeTimesByGolfer(golferIdValue);
      }
  }
```

Listing 10-10, the viewMyTeeTimes.aspx file, iterates over an array of *TeeTime* objects for a specific user, displaying the course name (with a link to the courseDetail page for that specific course), date, and time. If the Boolean variable *redirect*, provided by the ViewTeeTimes.aspx.cs Class-behind file, is true, the array of *teeTimes* and the *golfer* values will be null, so the username and password provided by the user failed the *validateLogin* method in ViewTeeTimes.aspx.cs.

Listing 10-10 viewMyTeeTimes.aspx.cs: Provides a list of registered tee times for a validated user.

```
<%@ Page language="c#" Codebehind="viewMyTeeTimes.aspx.cs"
AutoEventWireup="false" Inherits="TeeTimesClient.content.
viewMyTeeTimes" %>
<document>
  <header>
    <title>My Tee Times</title>
  </header>
  <section>
    <header>
      <title>My Tee Times</title>
    </header>
    <view>
      <description>
        <%
          if (redirect)
            Response.Write("Your username and password failed
validation. If you feel this is an error, please try logging in
again. If you are not yet a registered user, please click 'My Tee
Times' above and complete our registration Form.");
          else
            Response.Write("Your registered Tee Times Are Listed
Below");
        %>
      </description>
      <% if (!redirect) {%>
      <myTeeTimes>
        <% for (int i=0; i<tt.Length;i++) { %>
        <myTeeTime>
          <course>
            <courseId>
              <%= tt[i].courseId%>
            </courseId>
```

Because it is defined in the proper scope as protected, complete Golf-CourseService functionality is provided here in the .aspx page, including the ability to communicate with Web Services. Here we call the *toString* method on the *courseId* value in the *TeeTime* array so we will have a string value to pass into the *GetCourseDetail* method. We then assign the returned value to our local variable *gc*.

```
          <% gc = gs.GetCourseDetail(tt[i].courseId.ToString()); %>
          <name>
            <%= gc.name %>
          </name>
        </course>
        <teeTime>
          <date>
            <%= tt[i].date.ToShortDateString() %>
          </date>
          <time>
            <%= tt[i].time.ToShortTimeString() %>
          </time>
        </teeTime>
      </myTeeTime>
      <% } %>
    </myTeeTimes>
    <% } %>
  </view>
 </section>
</document>
```

Figure 10-7 shows the result of Listing 10-10.

Listing 10-11, the viewTeeTimes file, receives an optional username and password combination, a *courseId* representing a golf course in the database, and year, month, and day values. It returns an array of available tee times for the selected year, month, and day, and a link to immediately register for those tee times if they are not already registered and if the username and password resolves to a valid user.

Listing 10-12, the viewTeeTimes.aspx file, iterates over an array of *TeeTimes* for a given course and, if a valid user is returned from the Class-behind file, it displays a link for registering those tee times. If a valid user is not present, a *<noRegister>* node is appended to the document. If a tee time in the array is already registered for, a *<taken>* node is appended, but the tee time information is still provided.

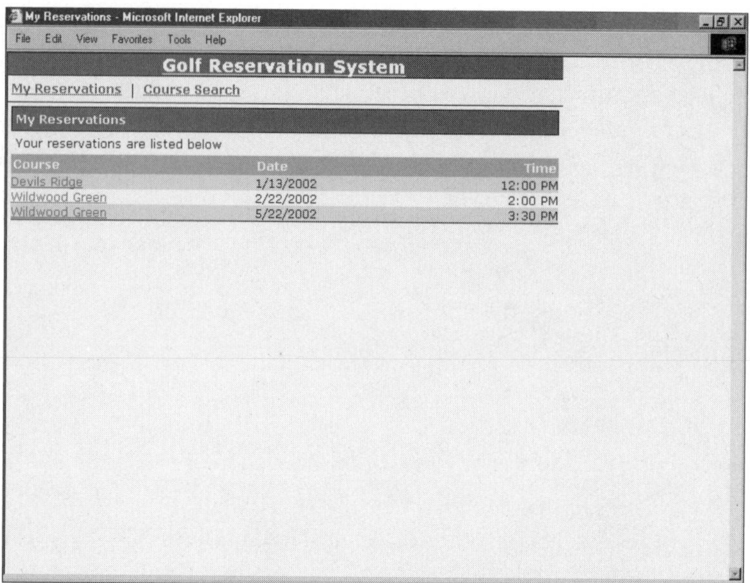

Figure 10-7 ViewMyTeeTimes displays all tee times associated with a specific user and provides links to courseDetail.aspx for the associated golf courses.

Listing 10-11 viewTeeTimes.aspx.cs: Retrieves valid *TeeTimes* given a *courseID*. It also returns a valid user if the username and password validate.

```
namespace TeeTimesClient.content
{
  public class viewTeeTimes : System.Web.UI.Page
  {
    protected localhost.TeeTime[] tt;
    protected localhost.Golfer golfer;
    protected localhost.GolfCourse gc;
    protected int selectedYear;
    protected int selectedMonth;
    protected int selectedDay;
    protected bool redirect = false;
    private void Page_Load(object sender, System.EventArgs e)
    {
      localhost.GolfCourseService gs = new localhost.GolfCourseSer-
vice();
     string usernameValue = Request.QueryString.Get("username");
      string passwordValue = Request.QueryString.Get("password");
      string courseIdString = Request.QueryString.Get("courseId");
      golfer = gs.ValidateLogin(usernameValue,passwordValue);
      if (golfer == null) {
        redirect = true;
```

```
        } else {
          int golferIdValue = golfer.id;
        }
        // FindTeeTimesByDate requires the Course Id value to
        // be cast as an Int
int courseIdValue = Int32.Parse(courseIdString);
        selectedYear = Int32.Parse(Request.QueryString.Get("year"));
        selectedMonth = Int32.Parse(Request.QueryString.Get("month"));
        selectedDay = Int32.Parse(Request.QueryString.Get("day"));
        System.DateTime dateValue = System.DateTime.Parse
(Request.QueryString.Get("month")+"/"
+Request.QueryString.Get("day")+"/"
+Request.QueryString.Get("year"));
        tt = gs.FindTeeTimesByDate(courseIdValue,dateValue);
        gc = gs.GetCourseDetail(courseIdString);
}
```

Listing 10-12 viewTeeTimes.aspx: Iterates over an array of *TeeTimes* for a specific *GolfCourse*. If a valid Golfer is not provided, append a *<noRegister>* node to the XML. Also, if a *TeeTime* is already registered, append a *<taken>* node to the XML.

```
<%@ Page language="c#" Codebehind="viewTeeTimes.aspx.cs"
AutoEventWireup="false" Inherits="TeeTimesClient.content.
viewTeeTimes" %>
<document>
  <header>
    <title>My Tee Times</title>
  </header>
  <section>
    <header>
      <title>Select a Tee Time</title>
    </header>
    <view>
      <description>
        <%
        <!--- redirect will be true if the username and
password provided to ViewTeeTimes.aspx.cs
failed validation --->
          if (redirect)
            Response.Write("Your username and password failed
validation. If you feel this is an error, please try logging in
again. If you are not yet a registered user, please click 'My Tee
Times' above and complete our registration Form.");
          else
            Response.Write("Please choose a tee time from the list
below");
        %>
      </description>
```

(continued)

Listing 10-12 *continued*

```
      <TeeTimes>
        <courseId>
          <%=gc.id%>
        </courseId>
        <% if (redirect) {
        <!---If redirect is true, append noRegister node--->
          Response.Write("<noRegister/>");
          } else {
          <!---Otherwise, provide the golferId--->
    Response.Write("<golferId>"+golfer.id+"</golferId>");
          }
        %>
        <%
          System.DateTime thisTeeTime = new System.DateTime
(selectedYear,selectedMonth,selectedDay,8,0,0,0);
          System.DateTime lastTeeTime = new System.DateTime
(selectedYear,selectedMonth,selectedDay,17,0,0,0);
          int taken = 0;
          while(thisTeeTime.CompareTo(lastTeeTime) != 0)
          {
            thisTeeTime = thisTeeTime.AddHours(.5);
        %>
        <teeTime>
          <TeeTimesystemDate>
            <%=thisTeeTime.ToString()%>
          </TeeTimesystemDate>
          <date>
            <%= thisTeeTime.ToShortDateString() %>
          </date>
          <time>
            <%= thisTeeTime.ToShortTimeString() %>
          </time>
          <%
            for(int i=0;i<tt.Length;i++)
            {
           <!---Compare this TeeTime to the TeeTime in this loop
           iteration of the TeeTimes array tt. If they are equal,
           the TeeTime is already registered for, append a taken node
           to the XML --->
              string myTime = thisTeeTime.ToShortTimeString();
              string takenTime = tt[i].time.ToShortTimeString();
              if (myTime.Equals(takenTime))
              {
           %>
          `     <taken />
           <%
              }
            }
```

```
            %>
          </teeTime>
          <%
            }
          %>
        </TeeTimes>
      </view>
    </section>
</document>
```

Figure 10-8 shows the results of Listing 10-12.

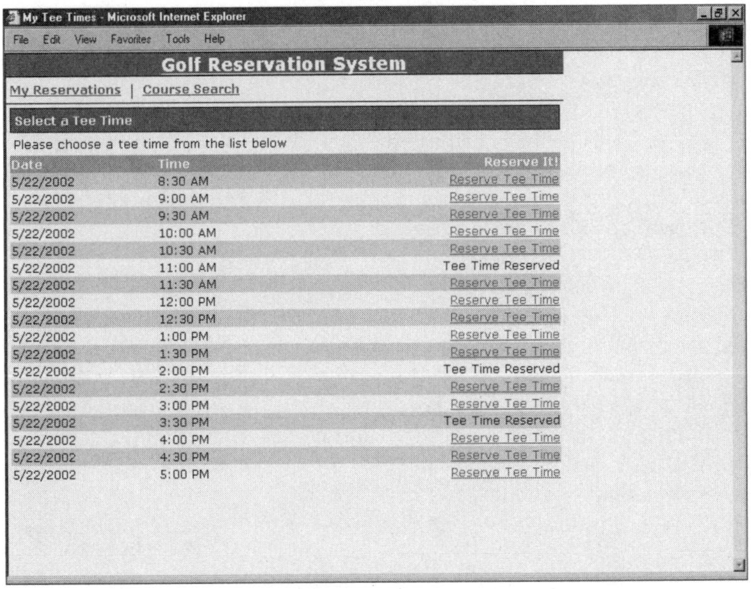

Figure 10-8 ViewTeeTimes.aspx displays a list of available tee times for a given course, and if a valid username and password combination is provided, provides a link to immediately register for the given tee time.

The Controller and ie5.xsl

Listing 10-13, the controller.asp file, is obviously the heart of the Golf Reservation System client application, at least for the UI portion. The controller accepts every request from the client, implements the functionality requested, receives the result XML, and transforms it using the selected skin (in our case, ie5.xsl) and delivers the result to standard out. For detailed information about the controller design pattern, see Chapter 9, which describes it in detail. If you're already familiar with the controller design pattern, notice that the Golf Reservation System client application implements a standard version of the pattern.

Listing 10-13 controller.asp: The file responsible for loading the view XML and transforming it with the XSLT skin.

```
<%
  // Get the view argument
  // Define root for client application
  view   = Request.QueryString("view")
  base   = Request.ServerVariables("SERVER_NAME")+
Replace(Request.ServerVariables("URL"),"controller.asp","")
  if Request.ServerVariables("HTTPS") = "ON" Then
    base = "https://"+base
  else
    base = "http://"+base
  end if
  xmlurl = base+"content/"+view+".aspx?"
  arguments = ""
  // Parse additional arguments
  For Each item in Request.QueryString
    if arguments <> "" then arguments = arguments+"&"
    itemvalue = Request.QueryString(item)
    arguments = arguments+item+"="+itemvalue
  Next
  // Append the argument string to the xmlurl
  xmlurl = xmlurl+arguments
  // Construct a URL to the appropriate skin
  // This implementation uses only the Internet Explorer 5.0 skin
  // Other skins could be used based on the browser type
  if Request.QueryString("skin") <> "" then
    skin = Request.QueryString("skin")
  else
    skin = "ie5"
  end if
  xslurl = base+"xslt/"+skin+".xsl"
  // Load the XML
  // A production implementation should use the multi-threaded
 version of the DomDocument.
  error = false
  Set source = Server.CreateObject("MSXML2.DOMDocument")
  source.async = false
  tmp = source.setProperty("ServerHTTPRequest", true)
  source.load(xmlurl)
  Set e = source.parseError
  if e.errorCode <> 0 then
    Response.write(e.reason)
    // Display error if exists
 if e.line > 0 Then
      Response.write(e.line)
      Response.write(" ")
```

```
      Response.write(e.linepos)
      Response.write(" ")
      Response.write(e.srcText)
    end if
    error = true
  end if
  // Load the XSLT
  Set style = Server.CreateObject("MSXML2.DOMDocument")
  style.async = false
  tmp = style.setProperty("ServerHTTPRequest", true)
  style.load(xslurl)
  Set e = style.parseError
  if e.errorCode <> 0 Then
    Response.write(e.reason)
    // Display error if exists
    if e.line > 0 Then
      Response.write(e.line)
      Response.write(" ")
      Response.write(e.linepos)
      Response.write(" ")
      Response.write(e.srcText)
    end if
    error = true
  end if
  if error = false Then
    xmlresult = source.transformNode(style)
  end if
  Response.write(xmlresult)
%>
```

Listing 10-14, the ie5.xsl file, is the only XSLT skin used in this client application. Describing the complete functionality of ie5.xsl in detail is nearly impossible. Basically, this document is loaded with each call to controller.asp (for a larger production application, splitting the skin amongst multiple includes would be a better idea), and is responsible for transforming the XML result returned from .aspx files. The result of the XSLT is, in this case, an HTML document available for viewing in a Web browser. Golf Reservation System Client utilizes only this skin, but could conceivably utilize numerous skins, both for different interface designs as well as for different client devices.

> **Note** XSLT and its associated technologies are constantly evolving. You can find the latest specifications for XSL, XSLT, and XPath at *http://www.w3.org/Style/XSL/*.

The initial block of content loaded with each call to ie5.xsl is not template-specific. That is, it's included in the result tree every time. This block is where we place document declarations, such as the *<html>* and *<head>* nodes, as well as any scripts or style sheets that need to be included in each result.

Listing 10-14 ie5.xs: The XSLT Responsible for transforming the result view XML.

```
<xsl:stylesheet xmlns:xsl="http://www.w3.org/1999/XSL/Transform"
version="1.0">
<xsl:output method="html" indent="no" />
  <xsl:strip-space elements="*" />
  <xsl:template match="document">
    <html>
      <head>
The css styles for ie5.xsl are included with each view in the
application at the location css/style.css. Any header/title node can
be inserted as the HTML title node.
        <link rel="stylesheet" type="text/css" href="./css/style.css"
/>
          <xsl:if test="header/title">
            <title>
              <xsl:value-of select="header/title" />
            </title>
          </xsl:if>
```

As discussed earlier, each device should include its own form validation mechanism to guarantee that required form inputs are satisfied and formatted correctly. The form validation script used in Golf Reservation System Client is located at js/formvalidate.js and is written using JavaScript. This file is extensive; displaying its entire contents in this chapter would be unreasonable. However, the form validation script could serve as an advanced lesson in developing JavaScript. This file is available on the accompanying CD.

In a production application, JavaScript is not recommended as the form validation method of choice. The primary reason is that the specification is not implemented with precision or consistency between browsers, and because browsers offer the user the ability to turn off this functionality. These arguments should also be taken into consideration while developing the UI. Rich Web UIs are often developed with extensive JavaScript, and therefore might result in unexpected functionality in some browser/platform combinations. For this client we assume the user has Microsoft Internet Explorer 5 or later. Our ie5.xsl includes extensive use of JavaScript, both in the UI and in form validation, and thus segregates those users without standards-based browsers and those who simply choose to turn off JavaScript.

```
<script src="js/formvalidate.js" type="text/javascript"></script>
```

The following JavaScript functions are used in CourseDetail.aspx to create a rich UI for viewing course detail information and for allowing the user to switch between content sections without requesting new data from the server. Because CourseDetail page includes three different *contentSections*, the XML is present and available to the user with a single call to the page. Therefore, the UI designer must find a way to utilize that bulk of information in a manner that is intuitive for the user. In Golf Reservation System Client this is achieved using a tabular format and an expandable and collapsible list grouping.

When including content in the XSLT style sheet that you predict might be poorly formed (that is, the content could not satisfy an XML parser), you need to wrap that content between the following tags: *<![CDATA[poorly-formed XML content goes here]]>*. The following JavaScript is an example. Without the *CDATA* declaration, ie5.xsl would fail parsing.

The JavaScript function *showTab* is responsible for the toggling behavior of the tabs present in the CourseDetail page. Each *courseDetailBlock* is presented as a tab, and clicking on the header will show that *courseDetailBlock* and hide the others.

```
<![CDATA[
function showTab(section, scnt) {
     for (i=0; i < scnt; i++) {
       t = document.getElementById("s_"+i);
       if (t) {
         if (i == section) {
           t.style.display = '';
         } else {
           t.style.display = 'none';
         }
       }
     }
  }
```

The JavaScript function *ExpandCollapse* is responsible for the toggling behavior of the line items created by the individual *Tee* descriptions in the CourseDetail page. Each *Tee* object is presented as an expandable division, and clicking on the division will expand or collapse it.

```
function ExpandCollapse(cl,ca) {
  var ca_a    = ca.split(',');
  var cl_a   = cl.split(',');
  cl = document.getElementById(ca_a[1]);
  if (cl.style.display == 'none')
    expand = true;
  else
    expand = false;
  thePlus = ca_a[0]+"_plus_image";
```

```
            plus_div = document.getElementById(thePlus);
            if (expand)
            {
              if (plus_div)
                plus_div.src = "./images/minus.gif";
              for (i=0; i < c1_a.length; i++)
              {
                theRow = document.getElementById(c1_a[i]);
                theRow.style.display = '';
                plus_div = document.getElement
ById(c1_a[i]+"_plus_image");
                if (plus_div)
                  plus_div.src = "./images/plus.gif";
              }
            } else {
              if (plus_div)
                plus_div.src = "./images/plus.gif";
              for (i=1; i < ca_a.length; i++)
              {
                theRow = document.getElementById(ca_a[i])
                theRow.style.display = 'none';
              }
            }
          }
       // ]]>
      </script>
      </head>
      <body topmargin="0" leftmargin="0">
The class attributes throughout ie5.xsl refer to CSS style classes
defined in the css.style.css file.
```

In order for HTML content to satisfy the XML parser, the HTML developer should use double quotes for attributes, close all tags (that is, using *
* instead of *
*), and take note of case sensitivity. An exciting development by the W3C is the ongoing development of XHTML—HTML 4 in the form of valid XML. Conforming to the latest specification of XHTML ensures that your XHTML content will satisfy compliant XML parsers.

The initial division in ie5.xsl with the class "document" is included with each view in the application. This division encapsulates the entire viewable HTML content. Also included with each page in the application is the masthead table, which displays the name of the organization.

```
<div class="document">
<table class="main" width="600" align="left" cellpadding="0"
cellspacing="0" bgcolor="ffffff">
            <tr class="header">
              <td>
                <a class="header" href="./index.asp">Golf Reservation
```

```
System</a>
              </td>
            </tr>
            <tr height="1" bgcolor="000000">
              <td>
                <img src="./images/spacer.gif" height="1" />
              </td>
            </tr>
            <tr>
              <td align="left">
                <table cellpadding="2" cellspacing="2" border="0">
                  <tr>
                    <td>
```

All anchor references and form posts resolve to controller.asp with a *view* argument appended (except for links to index.asp). The requirement to do so is defined by, and consistent with, the controller design pattern.

Like the initial document division and masthead table, a table of links is also included with each view in the application. This table provides links to the CourseSearch and Login pages.

```
                      <a class="navItem"
href="./controller.asp?view=login">My Reservations</a>
                    </td>
```

All entity references must be well-formed. For example, the common non-breaking space reference in HTML, * *, will fail an XML parser. Instead, you must fully qualify entity references: * * becomes * *.

> **Note** The complete set of entity reference values as of HTML 4 can be found courtesy of the W3C at *http://www.w3.org/TR/html4/sgml/entities.html.*

```
  <td> | </td>
  <td>
                      <a class="navItem" href=
"./controller.asp?view=courseSearch">Course Search</a>
                    </td>
                  </tr>
                </table>
              </td>
            </tr>
            <tr height="1" bgcolor="#000000">
```

```
                <td>
                  <img src="./images/spacer.gif" height="1" />
                </td>
              </tr>
              <tr>
                <td>
               <table width="100%" cellpadding="2" cellspacing="2" border="0">
                    <tr>
                      <td class="text">
```

The following *apply-templates* call sets off the *xsl:template* calls based on the contents of the XML being transformed. From here, each page takes a different path through the XSLT.

Apply-templates instruct the XSLT parser to match all source children nodes of the current node with appropriate template matches provided in the XSLT. For more information on *apply-templates* and other XSL/XSLT functionality, visit the XSL home page at the W3C located at *http://www.w3.org/Style/XSL/*.

```
                        <xsl:apply-templates />
                      </td>
                    </tr>
                  </table>
                </td>
              </tr>
            </table>
          </div>
        </body>
      </html>
    </xsl:template>
    <xsl:template match="section">
      <xsl:apply-templates />
    </xsl:template>
    <xsl:template match="section/header">
      <table width="100%" cellpadding="2" cellspacing="2"
class="sectionHeader">
        <tr>
          <td>
            <xsl:value-of select="title" />
          </td>
        </tr>
      </table>
    </xsl:template>
    <xsl:template match="view">
      <xsl:apply-templates />
    </xsl:template>
    <xsl:template match="description">
      <table cellpadding="2" border="0" class="text">
        <tr>
```

```
        <td>
          <xsl:value-of select="." />
        </td>
      </tr>
    </table>
  </xsl:template>
```

For *property/value* pairs defined in XML we simply display them side by side in a table, with property description in one table cell and property value (or an input, whichever is appropriate) in another. This is an example of presentation-specific XSLT, as opposed to object-specific. The XSLT here has no context of the object it displays. The majority of the forms in Golf Reservation System Client use this approach because the UI for a form is rarely tied to an object in the system; it is simply used to solicit input from the user.

Here we begin to see the power and simplicity provided by XSLT. For every form in the client application the ASPX developer only needed to wrap *<input>* nodes with a *<property>* node. Here in ie5.xsl, one template match suffices each *<property>* node in the entire application: only three lines of code are necessary. Each input type is implemented differently, but *<property>* nodes are all implemented the same.

```
  <xsl:template match="properties">
    <table cellpadding="2" border="0">
      <xsl:apply-templates />
    </table>
  </xsl:template>
  <xsl:template match="property">
    <tr>
      <td>
        <font class="text">
<xsl:value-of select="@description" />
  </font>
      </td>
      <td>
        <font class="text">
```

The *xsl:choose* element is provided by XSLT as an if-then-else type statement. The XSLT developer must use his or her discretion on when to use *xsl:choose* instead of an *apply-templates* or an *xsl:if*. *Apply-templates* is almost always preferred beacuse it takes advantage of the recursive nature of XSLT. Sometimes, such as when we choose whether or not to display an anchor reference for the property, understanding the code is easier if you use an *xsl:choose*.

This *xsl:choose* decides if the *property* value should be an anchor reference based on the existence (or nonexistence) of an *href* attribute of the current *<property>* node.

```
        <xsl:choose>
          <xsl:when test="@href">
```

To output a value, we can use *<xsl:value-of select="node">*, or we can imply that *value-of* by wrapping the node name with braces. In the *href* case we output the value of the attribute *href* using braces.

```
            <a href="{@href}">
              <xsl:apply-templates />
            </a>
          </xsl:when>
          <xsl:otherwise>
            <xsl:apply-templates />
          </xsl:otherwise>
        </xsl:choose>
      </font>
    </td>
  </tr>
</xsl:template>
```

The form template match is used on every form in the Golf Reservation System client application and includes JavaScript for input validation. The JavaScript ensures that all inputs with the *mandatory* attribute set to *yes* are validated before the form is submitted. Also notice that, as in login.aspx, the ASPX developer can place multiple forms on a single page. The validation still works as each form is assigned a unique identifier through the XSLT function *generate-id()*.

The JavaScript function *validateForm* is good example of using XSLT to create executable code at runtime. *ValidateForm* is an extremely generic JavaScript function but works well in validating all types of HTML inputs. Notice the use of *xsl:for-each*. The *xsl:for-each* element is a looping construct provided by XSLT that executes for each node qualifying for the *select* attribute. For each *textarea* node with an attribute of *mandatory* set to *yes*, for example, this XSLT creates a JavaScript validation routine that ensures that a value is submitted for that input. If no value exists, the JavaScript sets the browser focus on that input and returns false to the *onSubmit* call from the form. In doing so it stops the form from being submitted and instructs the user to enter a value.

```
  <xsl:template match="form">
    <script type="text/javascript">
      function validateForm_<xsl:value-of select="generate-id()"
/>(thisForm)
      {
        <xsl:for-each select="//input[@type='textarea']">
          thisForm.<xsl:value-of select="@name" />.value =
document.getElementById('d<xsl:value-of select="generate-id()"
/>').innerHTML;
        </xsl:for-each>
```

```
        <xsl:for-each select="//*[@mandatory='yes']">
        <xsl:choose>
          <xsl:when test="@type = 'text' or @type='textarea'">
              if (!hasValue(thisForm.<xsl:value-of select="@name"
/>,"text"))
              {
               alert("<xsl:value-of select="@name" /> is mandatory.");
               var the_field = thisForm.<xsl:value-of select="@name" />;
                if(the_field.style.display != "none" &amp;
!the_field.disabled &amp; !the_field.readOnly &amp;
!the_field.editableDiv)
                  the_field.focus();
                return false;
              }
            </xsl:when>
          <xsl:when test="name() = 'choice'">
              if (!hasValue(thisForm.<xsl:value-of select="@name"
/>,"select"))
              {
               alert("<xsl:value-of select="@name" /> is mandatory.");
              var the_field = thisForm.<xsl:value-of select="@name" />;
                if(the_field.style.display != "none" &amp;
!the_field.disabled &amp; !the_field.readOnly &amp;
!the_field.editableDiv)
                  the_field.focus();
                return false;
              }
            </xsl:when>
        </xsl:choose>
      </xsl:for-each>
        <xsl:for-each select="//input[@datatype]">
          if (!isoftype(thisForm.<xsl:value-of select="@name"
/>.value,'<xsl:value-of select="@datatype" />'))
          {
            alert("<xsl:value-of select="@name" /> is not in
<xsl:value-of select="@datatype" /> format");
            return false;
          }
        </xsl:for-each>
        <xsl:choose>
        <xsl:when test="@onSubmit">
            var rtnval = <xsl:value-of select="@onSubmit" />;
            return rtnval;
          </xsl:when>
        <xsl:otherwise>
            return true;
          </xsl:otherwise>
      </xsl:choose>
```

```
    }
  </script>
```

Here the XSLT builds a *form* tag here and includes an event handler for the *onSubmit* action, requiring validation before the *form* is submitted. The *apply-templates* call in the middle of this routine matches all *<property>* nodes and all *<input>* nodes of the source XML. This, again, is a good example of code reuse in XSLT: each form in the entire application is passed through this transformation and you need only write a few lines of code to build every *form*.

```
    <form action="{@action}" method="get" onSubmit="return
validateForm_{generate-id()}(this)">
      <xsl:for-each select="@*[name() != 'action']">
        <xsl:copy>
          <xsl:value-of select="." />
        </xsl:copy>
      </xsl:for-each>
      <xsl:apply-templates />
      <input style="cursor:hand" type="submit" value=" submit " />
    </form>
  </xsl:template>
```

Next we build the HTML input types for each *<input>* node in the XML. The *<input>* nodes are present in the source view XML and are more or less copied in their initial format.

```
  <xsl:template match="input[@type='text']">
    <input type="text" name="{@name}" value="{@value}" class="text"
style="border:inset  px">
      <xsl:for-each select="@*[name() != 'name' and name() !=
'value']">
        <xsl:copy>
          <xsl:value-of select="." />
        </xsl:copy>
      </xsl:for-each>
    </input>
    <xsl:if test="@mandatory = 'yes'">
      <font class="error"> *</font>
    </xsl:if>
  </xsl:template>
  <xsl:template match="input[@type='hidden']">
    <input type="hidden" name="{@name}" value="{@value}">
      <xsl:for-each select="@*[name() != 'name' and name() !=
'value']">
        <xsl:copy>
          <xsl:value-of select="." />
```

```
        </xsl:copy>
      </xsl:for-each>
    </input>
  </xsl:template>
```

For the *<textarea>* nodes, the XSLT developer can take advantage of Internet Explorer's content-editable division functionality. The XSLT could simply display a *<textarea>*, but instead it displays a division with content-editable set to true so users can copy and paste images and the like from any application instead of being restricted to entering only text. When the *form* is submitted the validation script reads the current contents of this division and sets a *form* variable equal to that value, and then the *form* is submitted. (This functionality is available only in Internet Explorer 5.5 or later and will not work in other browsers.)

The following code matches the *<textarea>* node in the source XML and creates a division with a *content-editable* attribute set to *true*. It also chooses the size dimensions of the division based on a *size* attribute of the *<textarea>* node in the source XML. It does so using *xsl:choose*.

```
  <xsl:template match="input[@type='textarea']">
    <div id="d{generate-id()}" contentEditable="true" class="text">
      <xsl:choose>
        <xsl:when test="@size='small'">
          <xsl:attribute name="style">display:inline;
overflow:scroll;width=350;border:solid;border-style:ridge;
border-width:2;background-color:white;height:150</xsl:attribute>
        </xsl:when>
        <xsl:when test="@size='medium'">
          <xsl:attribute name="style">display:inline;
overflow:scroll;width=350;border:solid;border-style:ridge;
border-width:2;background-color:white;height:250</xsl:attribute>
        </xsl:when>
        <xsl:when test="@size='large'">
          <xsl:attribute name="style">display:inline;
overflow:scroll;width=350;border:solid;border-style:ridge;
border-width:2;background-color:white;height:350</xsl:attribute>
        </xsl:when>
        <xsl:otherwise>
          <xsl:attribute name="style">display:inline;
overflow:scroll;width=350;border:solid;border-style:ridge;
border-width:2;background-color:white;height:350</xsl:attribute>
        </xsl:otherwise>
      </xsl:choose>
      <xsl:value-of disable-output-escaping="yes" select="value" />
    </div>
    <input type="hidden" editableDiv="yes" name="{@name}"
value="{@value}" />
    <xsl:if test="@mandatory = 'yes'">
```

```
      <div style="display:inline">
        <font class="error"> *</font>
      </div>
    </xsl:if>
  </xsl:template>
```

The *<choice>* node, as discussed earlier, is an excellent example of providing the XSLT developer room to design the appropriate UI. Specifically, the *<choice>* node can result in either a set of radio buttons, a set of check boxes, a single-select select box, or a multiple-select select box. The decision of which to use is made at runtime.

The *xsl:choose* statements count the number of *options* in the source XML and decide what type of form inputs to insert into the result document. *xsl:if* is then used to decide whether multiple choices will be allowed based on the existence or nonexistence of the *allowmultiple* attribute in the *<choice>* node in the source XML.

```
  <xsl:template match="choice">
    <xsl:choose>
      <xsl:when test="count(option) > 5">
        <select class="text">
          <xsl:for-each select="@*[name() != 'mandatory']">
            <xsl:copy>
              <xsl:value-of select="." />
            </xsl:copy>
          </xsl:for-each>
          <xsl:if test="@allowmultiple = 'yes'">
            <xsl:attribute name="multiple">yes</xsl:attribute>
            <xsl:attribute name="size">5</xsl:attribute>
          </xsl:if>
          <option value="">Please Choose Below</option>
          <xsl:for-each select="option">
            <option>
              <xsl:attribute name="value">
                <xsl:value-of select="@value" />
              </xsl:attribute>
              <xsl:if test="@selected='yes'">
                <xsl:attribute name="selected">
                  <xsl:value-of select="@selected" />
                </xsl:attribute>
              </xsl:if>
              <xsl:value-of select="." />
            </option>
          </xsl:for-each>
        </select>
      </xsl:when>
      <xsl:otherwise>
        <div style="display:inline">
```

```
          <xsl:for-each select="option">
            <xsl:choose>
              <xsl:when test="../@allowmultiple = 'yes'">
                <input type="checkbox" name="{../@name}" value="{@value}"
style="border:0px" />
 
<xsl:value-of select="." /><br />
              </xsl:when>
              <xsl:otherwise>
                <input type="radio" name="{../@name}" value="{@value}"
style="border:0px" />
 
<xsl:value-of select="." /><br />
              </xsl:otherwise>
            </xsl:choose>
          </xsl:for-each>
        </div>
      </xsl:otherwise>
    </xsl:choose>
    <xsl:if test="@mandatory = 'yes'">
      <div style="display:inline">
        <font class="error"> *</font>
      </div>
    </xsl:if>
  </xsl:template>
```

We begin the object-specific XSLT with the *xsl:template* match for *course*. In this case the template will only match for the *CourseSearchResult* result where the XSLT receives a list of courses as children of a *<courseList>* node. For each course we toggle the background color and provide links to courseDetail.

The template match for *courseList* provides an HTML table to surround the course list, supplies an *apply-templates* call to match all *<courseListItem>* nodes, and displays the number of *<courseListItem>* nodes in the last row of the table. The template match for *<courseListItem>* displays the *name*, *city*, and *state* for each node. The name is also provided with an anchor reference allowing the user to click through to get specific detail about that course. The link has an appended *id* argument as is required by the target view, courseDetail.

```
  <xsl:template match="courseList">
    <table class="text" width="100%" cellspacing="0" cellpadding="0"
border="0">
      <xsl:apply-templates select="courseListItem" />
      <xsl:if test="count(courseListItem) != 0">
        <tr>
          <td colspan="3" height="1" bgcolor="#000000">
            <img src="./images/spacer.gif" height="1" />
          </td>
        </tr>
```

```
        </xsl:if>
        <tr>
          <td colspan="3" bgcolor="#ffffff" class="text">
            <xsl:value-of select="count(courseListItem)" /> course(s)
satisfied your criteria
          </td>
        </tr>
        <tr>
          <td colspan="3" height="1" bgcolor="#000000">
            <img src="./images/spacer.gif" height="1" />
          </td>
        </tr>
      </table>
    </xsl:template>
    <xsl:template match="courseListItem">
      <tr>
        <xsl:choose>
          <xsl:when test="position() mod 2">
            <xsl:attribute name="style">
            background-color:#D1D7DC
          </xsl:attribute>
          </xsl:when>
          <xsl:otherwise>
            <xsl:attribute name="style">
            background-color:#f1f1f1
          </xsl:attribute>
          </xsl:otherwise>
        </xsl:choose>
        <td class="text" valign="top">
          <a href="controller.asp?view=courseDetail&amp;id={id}">
            <xsl:value-of select="name" />
          </a>
        </td>
        <td class="text" valign="top">
          <xsl:value-of select="city" />
        </td>
        <td class="text" valign="top">
          <xsl:value-of select="state" />
        </td>
      </tr>
    </xsl:template>
```

The courseDetail *xsl:template* match employs the most extravagant use of HTML and DHTML in the Golf Reservation System client application. This match is selected for each call to courseDetail.aspx.

```
    <xsl:template match="courseDetail">
      <xsl:apply-templates select="courseDetailBlock" />
    </xsl:template>
```

In the XSLT defined in the following block of code, each *courseDetailBlock* is assigned a unique *id* as well as a displayed tab. This tab takes advantage of JavaScript defined previously in the XSLT file to dynamically hide and display different sections of content—in this case, different matches of the <*courseDetailBlock*> node.

```
  <xsl:template match="courseDetailBlock">
    <xsl:variable name="numsections"
select="count(../courseDetailBlock)" />
    <xsl:variable name="precedingsibs" select="count(
preceding-sibling::courseDetailBlock)" />
    <xsl:variable name="sectionid" select="concat('s_',
$precedingsibs)" />
    <table id="{$sectionid}" class="tabHeader" cellspacing="0"
cellpadding="2" align="center">
      <xsl:if test="$precedingsibs > 0">
        <xsl:attribute name="style">display:none</xsl:attribute>
      </xsl:if>
      <tr>
        <td colspan="{$numsections}" height="5">
          <img src="images/spacer.gif" height="5" />
        </td>
      </tr>
      <tr align="center">
        <xsl:for-each select="preceding-sibling::courseDetailBlock">
          <td align="center">
            <a id="button{position}" href="javascript:showTab({
position()-1},{$numsections})">
              <xsl:value-of select="@description" />
            </a>
          </td>
        </xsl:for-each>
        <td align="center" class="activeTab">
          <xsl:value-of select="@description" />
        </td>
        <xsl:for-each select="following-sibling::courseDetailBlock">
          <td align="center">
            <a id="button{position}" href="javascript:showTab
({$precedingsibs+position()},{$numsections})">
              <xsl:value-of select="@description" />
            </a>
          </td>
        </xsl:for-each>
      </tr>
      <tr>
        <td>
          <xsl:attribute name="colspan">
            <xsl:value-of select="$numsections" />
```

```
          </xsl:attribute>
          <table class="text" width="100%" cellpadding="0"
cellspacing="0" border="0">
            <tr>
              <td>
```

Each *courseDetailBlock* is applied with the *apply-templates* call in the following snippet.

```
                <xsl:apply-templates />
              </td>
            </tr>
          </table>
        </td>
      </tr>
    </table>
  </xsl:template>
```

The *courseItem* with attribute type set to *courseInfo* template match displays generic *GolfCourse* information such as the address and greens fee.

```
  <xsl:template match="courseItem[@type='courseInfo']">
    <xsl:apply-templates select="section" />
    <table class="text">
      <tr>
        <td rowspan="3" valign="top">Address:</td>
        <td>
          <xsl:value-of select="address/address1" />
        </td>
      </tr>
      <tr>
        <td><xsl:value-of select="address/city" />, <xsl:value-of
select="address/state" /></td>
      </tr>
      <tr>
        <td>
          <xsl:value-of select="address/zip" />
        </td>
      </tr>
      <tr>
        <td rowspan="3" valign="top">Greens Fee:</td>
        <td>$<xsl:value-of select="price" /></td>
      </tr>
    </table>
  </xsl:template>
```

The *holeInfo* Block displays hole-specific information such as hole number, par, distance and handicap. It also matches the *<tees/tee>* node to provide tee-specific information.

```
  <xsl:template match="courseItem[@type='holeInfo']">
    <xsl:apply-templates select="section" />
    <table width="100%" cellspacing="0" cellpadding="0">
      <tr>
        <td valign="top" nowrap="yes">
          <table width="100%" cellpadding="0" cellspacing="1">
            <tr bgcolor="a0a0a0" style="padding:2px;spacing-top:0px">
              <td class="text" align="center" style="color:white;
font-weight:bold">
                Hole
              </td>
              <td class="text" align="center" style="color:white;
font-weight:bold">
                Par
              </td>
              <td class="text" align="center" style="color:white;
font-weight:bold">
                Distance
              </td>
              <td class="text" align="center" style="color:white;
font-weight:bold">
                Handicap
              </td>
            </tr>
            <xsl:apply-templates select="tees/tee" />
          </table>
        </td>
      </tr>
      <tr bgcolor="#336699">
        <td height="1">
          <img src="./images/spacer.gif" height="1" />
        </td>
      </tr>
    </table>
  </xsl:template>
```

For each *tee* associated with a *GolfCourse* object, this *xsl:template* match provides an expandable and collapsible division which provides information for the *holes* associated with the *tee*. The JavaScript necessary for expanding and collapsing these divisions is included in the result document and was listed previously in ie5.xsl under the function name *ExpandCollapse*.

```
  <xsl:template match="tee">
    <xsl:variable name="id" select="concat('v',generate-id())" />
    <tr>
      <xsl:attribute name="id">
        <xsl:value-of select="$id" />
      </xsl:attribute>
      <td colspan="4">
```

```
        <xsl:attribute name="id"><xsl:value-of select="$id" />_plus
</xsl:attribute>
        <table width="100%" cellpadding="0" cellspacing="0" border="0"
bgcolor="#e0e0e0" class="listgroup">
          <xsl:attribute name="id">
<xsl:value-of select="$id" />_table</xsl:attribute>
          <tr>
            <td width="5" style="cursor:hand">
            <img src="./images/plus.gif" hspace="4" style="border:1px
outset">
                <xsl:attribute name="onClick">ExpandCollapse
('<xsl:for-each select="holes/*[name() =  'hole']">
                   <xsl:value-of select="concat('v',generate-id())" />
                    <xsl:if test="last() > position()">,</xsl:if>
                  </xsl:for-each>','<xsl:value-of select="$id"
/><xsl:for-each select=".//*[name() = 'hole']">,<xsl:value-of
select="concat('v',generate-id())" /></xsl:for-each>')</xsl:attribute>
                <xsl:attribute name="id"><xsl:value-of select="$id"
/>_plus_image</xsl:attribute>
              </img>
            </td>
            <td align="left" class="text">
              <xsl:value-of select="description" /> Tee: Distance:
<xsl:value-of select="distance" /> yards Slope: <xsl:value-of
select="slope" />
            </td>
          </tr>
        </table>
      </td>
    </tr>
    <xsl:apply-templates select="holes" />
  </xsl:template>
```

Each *tee* contains its own list of *holes*, complete with number, hole, distance, handicap, and par. Here we iterate over each *<hole>* node and display that data, toggling the row color of each *hole* as we did with the *courseList* match previously.

```
  <xsl:template match="hole">
    <xsl:variable name="id" select="concat('v',generate-id())" />
    <tr>
      <xsl:choose>
        <xsl:when test="position() mod 2">
          <xsl:attribute name="style">
            background-color:#ffffff;display:none
          </xsl:attribute>
        </xsl:when>
        <xsl:otherwise>
          <xsl:attribute name="style">
```

```
          background-color:#f1f1f1;display:none
        </xsl:attribute>
      </xsl:otherwise>
    </xsl:choose>
    <xsl:attribute name="id">
      <xsl:value-of select="$id" />
    </xsl:attribute>
    <td class="text" valign="top">
      <xsl:value-of select="@number" />
    </td>
    <td class="text" valign="top">
      <xsl:value-of select="par" />
    </td>
    <td class="text" valign="top">
      <xsl:value-of select="distance" />
    </td>
    <td class="text" valign="top">
      <xsl:value-of select="handicap" />
    </td>
  </tr>
</xsl:template>
```

The *scheduleTeeTime* block provides a table of available tee times that the user can view, and if no *<taken>* child node of the *TeeTime* and no *<noRegister>* ancestor node are present, the user is provided a link to the *scheduleTeeTime* page to register.

```
<xsl:template match="courseItem[@type='scheduleTeeTime']">
  <xsl:apply-templates select="section" />
</xsl:template>
<xsl:template match="TeeTimes">
  <table class="text" width="100%" cellspacing="0" cellpadding="1"
border="0">
    <tr bgcolor="#a0a0a0" style="padding:2px;spacing-top:0px">
      <td class="text" align="left" style="color:white;
font-weight:bold">
         Date
      </td>
      <td class="text" align="left" style="color:white;
font-weight:bold">
         Time
      </td>
      <td class="text" align="right" style="color:white;
font-weight:bold">
      Reserve It!
      </td>
    </tr>
    <xsl:apply-templates select="teeTime" />
  </table>
```

```
  </xsl:template>
  <xsl:template match="teeTime">
    <tr>
      <xsl:choose>
        <xsl:when test="position() mod 2">
          <xsl:attribute name="style">
          background-color:#D1D7DC
        </xsl:attribute>
        </xsl:when>
        <xsl:otherwise>
          <xsl:attribute name="style">
            background-color:#f1f1f1
          </xsl:attribute>
        </xsl:otherwise>
      </xsl:choose>
      <td class="text" valign="top">
        <xsl:value-of select="date" />
      </td>
      <td class="text" valign="top">
        <xsl:value-of select="time" />
      </td>
      <td class="text" valign="top" align="right">
        <xsl:choose>
          <xsl:when test="taken">
            Tee Time Reserved
          </xsl:when>
          <xsl:when test="../noRegister">
            login to register
          </xsl:when>
          <xsl:otherwise>
            <a>
            <xsl:attribute name="href">controller.asp?view=
scheduleTeeTime&amp;golferId=<xsl:value-of select="../golferId"
/>&amp;courseId=<xsl:value-of select="../courseId" />&amp;
teeTime=<xsl:value-of select="TeeTimesystemDate" /></xsl:attribute>
            Reserve Tee Time</a>
          </xsl:otherwise>
        </xsl:choose>
      </td>
    </tr>
  </xsl:template>
```

The *<teeTimeDetail>* node is processed with the scheduleTeeTime.aspx file. This node allows the user to select a tee time and register. Specifically, this template match displays the golfer's name, the course name with a link to the courseDetail page, and the selected tee-time data.

```
  <xsl:template match="teeTimeDetail">
    <table cellpadding="2" class="text">
```

```
      <tr>
        <td>Golfer:</td>
        <td>
          <xsl:value-of select="golfer/name" />
        </td>
      </tr>
      <tr>
        <td>Course:</td>
        <td>
          <a>
            <xsl:attribute name="href">
              controller.asp?view=courseDetail&amp;id=<xsl:value-of
select="course/id" />
            </xsl:attribute>
            <xsl:value-of select="course/name" />
          </a>
        </td>
      </tr>
      <tr>
        <td>Date:</td>
        <td>
          <xsl:value-of select="date" />
        </td>
      </tr>
      <tr>
        <td>Time:</td>
        <td>
          <xsl:value-of select="time" />
        </td>
      </tr>
    </table>
  </xsl:template>
```

The *MyTeeTimes* template match is used exclusively by the viewMyTeeTimes.aspx page and lists the tee times registered by a validated user. The source XML provides <*myTeeTimes*> nodes with children nodes named *myTeeTime* containing data about each registered tee time. The <*myTeeTime*> node is called using *apply-templates* in the center of the table.

```
  <xsl:template match="myTeeTimes">
    <table class="text" width="100%" cellspacing="0" cellpadding="0"
border="0">
      <tr bgcolor="#a0a0a0" style="padding:2px;spacing-top:0px">
        <td class="text" align="left" style="color:white;
font-weight:bold">
          Course
        </td>
        <td class="text" align="left" style="color:white;
font-weight:bold">
```

```
          Date
        </td>
        <td class="text" align="right" style="color:white;
font-weight:bold">
          Time
        </td>
      </tr>
      <xsl:choose>
        <xsl:when test="myTeeTime">
          <xsl:apply-templates select="myTeeTime" />
        </xsl:when>
        <xsl:otherwise>
          <tr>
            <td colspan="3">
              You have no tee times scheduled
            </td>
          </tr>
        </xsl:otherwise>
      </xsl:choose>
      <tr>
        <td colspan="3" height="1" bgcolor="#000000">
          <img src="images/spacer.gif" height="1" />
        </td>
      </tr>
    </table>
  </xsl:template>
```

The *myTeeTime* template matches a single tee time assigned to a validated user, providing a link to courseDetail for the associated golf course.

```
  <xsl:template match="myTeeTime">
    <tr>
      <xsl:choose>
        <xsl:when test="position() mod 2">
          <xsl:attribute name="style">
          background-color:#D1D7DC
        </xsl:attribute>
        </xsl:when>
        <xsl:otherwise>
          <xsl:attribute name="style">
            background-color:#f1f1f1
          </xsl:attribute>
        </xsl:otherwise>
      </xsl:choose>
      <td class="text" valign="top">
        <a>
          <xsl:attribute name="href">
            controller.asp?view=courseDetail&amp;id=<xsl:value-of
select="course/courseId" />
```

```
            </xsl:attribute>
            <xsl:value-of select="course/name" />
          </a>
        </td>
        <td class="text" valign="top">
          <xsl:value-of select="teeTime/date" />
        </td>
        <td class="text" valign="top" align="right">
          <xsl:value-of select="teeTime/time" />
        </td>
      </tr>
    </xsl:template>
</xsl:stylesheet>
```

This XSLT file, ie5.xsl, is a large and extensive file providing complete template matches for each node in every source XML document possible within the Golf Reservation System client application. Maintaining this file is difficult because it includes a number of different languages: HTML, JavaScript, and XSLT. The developer creating this XSLT style sheet would therefore require working knowledge of all these languages and possibly more. A more modular approach might be in order for a production application where the JavaScript might be provided through an *include* instead of being present in the actual XSLT style sheet. You could also develop a client application that contains skins that span a number of documents. For example, if it is possible to separate form XSLTs from generic display transformations, it might be a good idea to develop those in separate files (perhaps named ie5_form.xsl and ie5_display.xsl).

Nonetheless, the UI developer must hold responsibility for not only being familiar with the Web Services available in building the .aspx and .aspx.cs files, but also for having knowledge of the various Web languages available for use. And given that the controller design pattern is flexible in cross-platform development, the UI developer or team would also require knowledge of markup for devices such as Wireless Application Protocol and others.

Therefore, while ie5.xsl is extensive and large, it is not a complete solution for a production application. Instead, it is an all-inclusive example of how one would use XSLT, HTML, and DHTML/JavaScript to create a browser-ready skin for a controller design pattern client in a .NET Framework client application.

Where to From Here?

The Golf Reservation System is a simple implementation of a distributed application using XML-based Web Services and employing full use of the .NET Framework, the controller design pattern, and Visual Studio .NET. But even simple XML Web services like GolfCourseService could be much more extensive as XML Web services can be called from any device connected to the Internet that can send, receive, and understand the SOAP protocol. Golf Reservation System Client could provide a skin for tee time registration over mobile phones, handheld PDAs, or any other device.

One interesting application using GolfCourseService might be to write a client using Microsoft Visual Basic for Applications and extending Microsoft Outlook to take advantage of the Golf Reservation System booking capabilities already provided in the service. Another option might be for the publishers of GolfCourseService to provide its golf course data to various golf-focused Web sites or provide its golfer data to golf club manufacturers.

The Golf Reservation System could also extend its own Web Service and client application to offer more functionality to its users, by keeping detailed information about how individuals performed in a given round, or by facilitating payment for the tee time registration with a Web method responsible for handling credit card transactions. As is evident, Windows .NET and XML Web services offer boundless opportunities for creating distributed applications for the Internet.

This concludes the section of the book on application development. In this section we have used a lot of the XML-based implementations present in .NET as well as other frameworks. We have built some real-world applications and we have covered many of the down-and-dirty details of XML.

In the next section of the book we will talk about interoperability. This will include chapters on developing for multiple platforms, integrating with legacy systems, and publishing content to multiple devices.

Part III

Interoperability

11

Platform Development

Every major hardware vendor hopes for some new technology that will motivate all customers to abandon their legacy systems and exclusively buy its hardware offerings. Every operating system and software vendor hopes for the same. Even developers must admit that their lives would be easier if they didn't have to design for different hardware platforms and operating systems, each with its own differences in language support, development environment, bandwidth, and display constraints.

The truth is that there will always be a variety of hardware platforms, operating systems, development environments, and operating constraints. Even in new application deployment, issues around integration of legacy systems always spring up. These varieties will continue to motivate designers to develop solutions that work with the set of hardware platforms and operating systems that exist in the developer's organization.

Some application development technologies present severe hardware or operating system constraints. Not so with Web Services. The entire Web Services concept is built around existing open standards like HTTP and XML. All a device needs to participate as a Web Service client is the ability to create an XML document programmatically and the ability to issue an HTTP POST and GET. This capability exists in any device that can run an HTML 3.2–aware Web browser and is relatively easy to implement in other devices (such as wireless hand-held computing devices, even with limited displays and no support for modern Web browsers).

The bar is higher for participating as a Web Services server, though not by much. A Web Services server must accept an HTTP POST or GET method, parse the XML document, marshal the data appropriately, perform the Web Service function, marshal the data back into a result XML document, and return the result document to the client via HTTP. Implementing Web Service servers on the majority of computing devices in existence today is definitely possible.

This chapter provides significant details about the issues faced by Web Service developers in building cross-platform applications. We discuss legacy mechanisms for building cross-platform applications, and then introduce the Web Services approach. The good news is that Web Services provide one of the easiest, most reliable means yet created to build full-featured, robust, cross-platform applications for business, consumer, and industrial applications.

Legacy Mechanisms for Cross-Platform Development

As long as computing systems have lived on networks, there has been a need for those systems to communicate with each other at the application level. Network protocols such as TCP and UDP provided a way for programmers to build in client/server and peer-to-peer communication. Programming these protocols directly, however, could be a daunting task, so layers appeared above these protocols that eased the task of writing distributed applications. In this section we review several of these layers that support cross-platform application development, including UNIX Sockets, the Distributed Computing Environment (DCE), CORBA, Java RMI, and DCOM.

UNIX Sockets

UNIX sockets might have been the first standard built on top of the basic protocols that provided an interface for programmers to write the communication component of client/server applications at a more abstract level. A programmer could specify a connection-oriented socket when a persistent connection was needed, or a connectionless socket for sending messages, and the socket would perform the right function with the underlying protocol.

Even with UNIX sockets, however, many problems remained for the application programmer. Although UNIX sockets presented a layer of abstraction above the underlying protocols, the socket interface still required low-level programming. As for platform interoperability, UNIX sockets work as long as you only want to communicate with UNIX systems. (Similar implementations for other platforms, like WinSock for Microsoft Windows, were developed later.)

UNIX sockets (and other related implementation) provided raw data-transfer capability only, and lacked the ability to invoke remote procedures or functions. Any processing of the incoming data stream had to be hard-wired into the client applications. Sockets provided no capability to, for example, pass method or function arguments between systems.

Distributed Computing Environment

While UNIX sockets provided the ability to pass monolithic data streams between systems, designers of distributed systems needed a more platform-independent mechanism that supported actual remote procedure calls. One attempt to provide RPC capability was known as the Distributed Computing Environment, or DCE. This environment provides a theoretically platform-independent infrastructure for implementing and managing distributed applications. It also provides directory and security services, as well as distributed file system and RPC capabilities (it even provided a time-synchronization mechanism for "cell" members). DCE also correctly handled the marshaling of RPC data as appropriate to match the expected data format of the calling or receiving OS.

Unfortunately, DCE was only platform-dependent to the extent that relatively heavyweight client software existed for the target platform. To participate in these services a platform had to be configured (again, a potentially complex operation) into a DCE cell. Later DCE implementations allowed the user to configure only certain services, such as the RPC mechanism. However, the overhead in purchasing, configuring, and maintaining a cell, as well as the lack of general availability of the client software, prevented DCE from becoming a general-purpose solution for distributed computing.

CORBA

CORBA provides a platform- and language-independent infrastructure for building distributed applications and invoking remote procedure calls from client systems. CORBA presents fine-grained distributed objects within heterogeneous computing networks. Applications can identify and use available business software components via a network of ORBs. The standards body behind CORBA, the Object Management Group (OMG), originally believed that large numbers of ORBs would exist on the Internet, transparently channeling object requests to the appropriate server resource.

CORBA objects are essentially language-independent. CORBA servers present their interfaces in the form of an IDL, which defines the methods supported by the CORBA server and the expected arguments to those methods. Client programs interact with these objects via stub interfaces that execute an object's methods remotely on the machine hosting the software. The ORB sits in the middle and dispatches all intermachine communication. ORBs around the Internet can share information about the objects they manage. The IIOP was developed for this purpose.

Java RMI

Like CORBA, Java's RMI subsystem allows objects to be distributed across a network. Unlike CORBA, Java RMI can transport an entire class, software and all, across application boundaries (via either RMI or IIOP protocols). This communication is possible because all Java applications must run on the Java Virtual Machine. This enables distributed Java applications to safely download compiled byte streams and execute them locally.

Although the ability to share executable objects dynamically over the Internet opens some exciting possibilities, Java RMI has its shortcomings. Most notably, the technology only works if the applications involved in the exchange are both written in Java. Programs written to use RMI also require a fair amount of preparation. Remote stub classes need to be generated statically or downloaded dynamically for remote methods to work properly. Finally RMI uses a proprietary protocol to exchange information, which means more server software and firewall tuning.

DCOM

DCOM is a Windows implementation of a distributed-application development environment, based on Microsoft's COM. DCOM uses DCE RPC as the underlying remote object-support mechanism.

Unlike CORBA, a DCOM object can present multiple interfaces, which in turn can provide multiple object behaviors. A COM client invokes a COM object by acquiring a pointer to the object's interface. The client invokes methods through that pointer; from the perspective of the client, the object appears to reside in the client's address space. Because DCOM is tightly integrated with the Windows operating system, DCOM provides a solution for Windows-based distributed applications only. Table 11-1 provides a comparison of the several distributed-application infrastructures.

Building Cross-Platform Applications Using Web Services

Thousands of distributed applications have been implemented using these legacy mechanisms. However, each of these mechanisms presents one or more serious obstacles in the areas of platform- or language-dependence, ease of configuration, ease of implementation, or cost. No mechanism meets the need

Table 11-1 Comparison of Distributed Application Infrastructures

Type	OS/Platform	Language Support	Configuration Complexity	Cost
Sockets	UNIX (variants available)	C	High	None
DCE	UNIX	C, C++	High	High
CORBA	UNIX, Windows	Any	Medium	Medium
Java RMI	Java (Java Virtual Machine)	Java only	Low	None
DCOM	Windows	Many	Low	None

for a truly platform- and language-independent mechanism that is easily deployable on top of existing infrastructures and transport protocols, with either no or few trivial configurations required of participating systems. No mechanism met those needs; that is, before Web Services.

Building Servers

Let's discuss some of the issues around building Web Services on the most popular computing platforms, including Microsoft Windows NT, Microsoft Windows 2000, UNIX, and Linux. We will divide our discussion between building Web Service servers and Web Service clients.

Simplistically speaking, the only requirement for providing a Web Service server is the ability to present that service as a URL. The URL must accept incoming service requests over HTTP as POST or GET methods or XML SOAP documents, must marshal the data within the request appropriately for its OS, must invoke appropriate methods on the data, repackage the data into an XML result document, and return the document via HTTP to the client.

If you want to advertise your Web Service and make it available to clients throughout the Internet, you must create a Web Services Description Language (WSDL) document that describes your Web Service to clients. The WSDL document is an XML document that provides information about the Web Service's exposed methods, arguments to those methods, and return values. You would typically register your WSDL document with a Web Service registration service, such as *UDDI.org,* which we mentioned in Chapter 8.

Web Services present clear advantages when compared to other cross-platform application development solutions. Because Web Services are built on existing, open technologies such as HTTP and XML, developers must implement little, if any, new infrastructure. Virtually all modern operating systems and platforms are supported. The Web Service server is still based on a Web server running a Web application server. Language support is broad. Complexity is low; the Web Service designer need only make the paradigm shift that the Web server is providing services, not Web pages, via a URL.

Visual Studio .NET

You can, theoretically, create your own HTTP GET or POST methods or build your own SOAP files for transmitting Web Services requests between client and server. Why bother doing so, however, when a development environment can support you by doing many of these tasks automatically? If you are developing on a Windows server platform, you can draw on the powerful capabilities of the Microsoft Visual Studio .NET environment for building XML Web service applications.

Visual Studio .NET handles many of the mundane tasks associated with developing Web applications, such as creating SOAP documents appropriate for your XML Web service methods, marshaling and unmarshaling data, creating WSDL contracts for your Web Service methods, and ensuring that these methods are stateless by encapsulating all application state data within the SOAP document. With Visual Studio .NET you can quickly build XML Web service applications that are reliable and easily scalable.

Visual Studio .NET provides support for most modern Web development languages, including VBScript, JScript, Visual Basic, C, C++, Visual C++, C#, Perl, Python, COBOL, PASCAL, and Scheme. It also provides an integrated environment for XML Web service development appropriate for developers from different development backgrounds.

Finally Visual Studio .NET provides rapid prototyping capabilities for client user interfaces. For debugging and testing, Visual Studio .NET provides the ability to view and trace SOAP messages between client and server.

UNIX and Linux

Other operating systems and language vendors provide toolkits and development environments for creating Web Service servers on other platforms, including UNIX and Linux operating systems. Options include IBM's Web Services Toolkit and the Java 2 Enterprise Edition (J2EE).

J2EE provides several APIs to specifically support the needs of Web Service application developers. Table 11-2 presents each of these API groups.

Other Platforms

Theoretically, any computing device that can accept incoming HTTP requests, manipulate incoming data by a method, marshal results into an XML document,

Table 11-2 Java APIs for Web Services

API	Description
JAXP: Java API for XML processing	Provides the capability for both tree-based processing (DOM) or event-based processing (SAX) of XML data. The API also provides support for XMLTs should you want to transform your XML documents into another XML vocabulary. You might want to do this to, for example, transform XML data to HTML for display in a Web browser, or extract components of an XML document and apply WML wrappers for display on the screen of a wireless device.
JAXB: Java API for mapping XML documents to Java classes	Provides the capability for creating Java classes from XML data and an XML DTD or Schema. These classes automatically provide the capability to validate, marshal, and unmarshal the XML data from an XML document instance. From an XML document you can create a Java object tree for processing by your Web Service server.
JAXM: Java API for messaging	Provides the capability to create SOAP documents for passing messages between systems in SOAP format. The API handles details like SOAP syntax and message identification.
JAXR: Java API for XML registries	Supports accessing standard Internet-based business registries. The JAXR API provides the capability to register a Web Service with registries such as *UDDI.org,* as well as the capability to search registries such as *UDDI.org* for specific Web Services.
JAX-RPC: Java API for issuing RPCs via XML documents	Supports issuing RPCs as request and result SOAP documents. JAX-RPC handles the details of marshaling and unmarshaling the data into the SOAP document JAX-RPC provides. JAX-RPC is a less-general API than JAXM. It does not provide all the capabilities of JAXM, including asynchronous messaging, multiparty message routing, and delivery verification.

and deliver the result XML document to the client via HTTP can serve as a Web Service server. Variables in choosing to perform these tasks on a non-Windows or non-UNIX platform include the nature of the Web Service and the availability of tools to support providing the Web Service infrastructure. For example, at a minimum the platform should support an XML parser for creating the XML result file.

Alternative platforms that support the J2EE might be reasonable candidates for Web Service servers. Otherwise, deploying a Web Service server on, for example, a handheld device, might be an exercise in non traditional application development, at least for the near future.

Building Clients

Building clients for distributed applications has never been easier. Because Web Services are based on open standards like HTTP and XML, all that is minimally required of a Web Service client is the ability to create and pass to the server an HTTP GET or POST request or an XML SOAP document. This capability can be implemented in a variety of ways. Most simply, any client that supports an HTML 3.2-compatible Web browser and the HTTP protocol can participate as a Web Services client. Even clients that do not support HTML 3.2-compatible browsers can use their own built-in application support to create the requisite XML files for transmission over HTTP to the Web Services server.

One of the first steps in designing a Web Service client is to inspect the WSDL document for the Web Service you want to run. The WSDL document is an XML document that provides the methods exposed by the Web Service, expected arguments, and return values. You can perform this inspection manually, but a Web Service development environment can make the task easier for you.

Windows Platforms

Visual Studio .NET provides a complete development environment for building, deploying, and testing XML Web services. You can develop both the XML Web service server and client portions directly in the application. Clients that run on Windows NT, Windows 2000, or Windows XP can be HTML or Web forms. On a Windows platform Visual Studio .NET can save the Web form as a DLL.

UNIX and Linux

Again, you can build an HTML 3.2–based Web Service client for UNIX and Linux platforms directly from Visual Studio .NET. Because the client interface to a Web Services server is only an HTTP GET or POST method or an XML file, you can design your own Web Service client. The language that you use and the form of the Web Service client is irrelevant as long as the client can marshal its native data format in an XML file (or arguments to an HTTP method), send the data over the wire via HTTP, receive the result XML document via HTTP, and remarshal the results.

Other Platforms

Again, Visual Studio .NET provides the capability to develop and test XML Web service clients on other devices, including devices running Microsoft Windows CE. These devices include portable hand-held computing devices, "smart" devices such as tablet PCs, portable game consoles, and digital television controllers. As the number and variety of these devices increases, so will the opportunity to take advantage of XML Web services via these devices.

A key point in designing and implementing Web Services is that the Web Service client need not be a Web form driven by a human user. Certainly, any computing device can act as a Web Service client. In fact, Web Service servers can invoke methods that call other Web Services in completing a client request. For example, a digital television controller can invoke a Web Service that provides video-on-demand capabilities. This service might, in turn, invoke a Web Service that performs billing functions. Keep this capability in mind, especially as you develop applications for non-traditional computing devices.

Accessing Objects Across Platforms

Object access and sharing presents some of the major challenges in distributed-application development. All but the most homogeneous environments require that objects be converted from an application's native data format, passed along a wire, and converted back to a different application's (possibly different) native data format. The process must be repeated, in reverse, at the return of data by the server. Many solutions have been developed for this problem, although none have thus far presented a mechanism as open and as widely deployable as that presented by Web Services.

Traditional Methods

Each of the traditional mechanisms for sharing objects across platforms present limitations that have prevented these mechanisms from supporting Internet-wide distributed applications. CORBA objects are fine grained compared to the granularity needed to support business functions. RMI allows sharing of objects and code, but only between Java platforms. DCOM only allows object sharing between Windows platforms. Full-blown DCE is too expensive and too complex, and UNIX sockets require programming at a lower level than many developers are comfortable with, making development and maintenance problematic.

Furthermore, it became apparent that data, not code, was the most precious commodity in Internet applications. The HTTP protocol had existed for years and firewalls had been configured to cope with it. XML proved to be a powerful vehicle for transporting any type of information. There must be some way to combine the two technologies and produce the next big advance in distributed computing.

Web Services

Web Services perfectly fit the reality that data, not code, is the most important commodity in distributed applications. Because Web Services are based on the open standards of HTTP and XML, they offer an infrastructure for distributed-application development free of the barriers that prevented widespread deployment of past systems.

To share objects in a Web Services environment you must convert the instantiated objects from their memory storage to a format that can be transmitted across a network. Because HTTP is a stateless protocol, the serialization process must include all state or property information. The serialized object must provide enough information to be reassembled into an identical object by an application at the other end of the wire.

Both Visual C++ and Java support object serialization. However, each language uses its own data format to store its objects and metadata in a serialized format. This distinction greatly complicates the task of sharing serialized objects between applications written in different languages.

By using XML as a common serialization format, any applications that can parse an XML file can instantiate objects serialized within an XML file. Any application that can parse an XML file and marshal the contents into and out of the application's native object format can share objects in and participate in a Web Services environment. Using XML as a common serialization format ensures that the widest possible set of computing platforms can participate in a Web Services environment.

Writing Objects for Multiple Platforms

Object serialization presents one of the more challenging problems in implementing distributed applications. How can you transform an object from the internal data structures created and maintained by your programming language to a persistent form that can be passed between server and client over the wire?

This problem appears in two locations in Web Service applications. The client must serialize its data to the argument list to an HTTP POST or GET method or to a SOAP document. The Web Service server system must both un-serialize the incoming request and reserialize the result to an XML (possibly XML SOAP) result document.

Fortunately, you don't need to worry about the details of object serialization. Web Service development environments and APIs designed to provide Web Service functionality have this capability built in. Visual Studio .NET allows you to serialize XML Web service arguments within a SOAP document. Other APIs, such as J2EE's JAXM, directly support the creation of SOAP documents.

After an object is serialized within a SOAP document, what do we do to ensure the interoperability of the resulting SOAP document within a distributed application? Nothing. The XML and SOAP specifications ensure that any computing device with any internal data format will interpret the content of the SOAP document in exactly the same way. Any platform that supports an

XML parser will appropriately read and marshal any data contained within the SOAP document.

Issues in Object Development and Multiple-Platform Design

This section provides insights into issues about designing Web Service objects. Web Service objects present some special constraints, such as the requirement that they be passed by value and that Web Service methods tend to present much more course-grained functionality than do other distributed-application paradigms. We also discuss application development issues, such as the application development environment, presented by the major hardware platforms, and review the general issues of security, scalability, and state maintenance.

Object Development

We mentioned limitations of Web Service objects in Chapter 8. All Web Service objects are passed by value through HTTP and SOAP. No mechanism for passing an object by reference exists. Calls to Web Services require some overhead. Objects must be marshaled into (potentially large) XML SOAP documents and return results must be unmarshaled. Web Service calls, because they rely on HTTP, are stateless. Because Web Service connections are closed upon the completion of any call to a Web method, all state information must be provided within the body of the SOAP document.

Because Web Services are designed to provide course-grained application methods and business-level services, as opposed to the fine-grained object sharing that motivated the development of CORBA and RMI, these limitations are rarely burdensome to a Web Service developer. The simplicity of implementing Web Services is largely the result of designing around the limitations of open standards like HTTP. It would be difficult to argue that the popularity of the Web has suffered because HTTP does not provide a mechanism for maintaining state across invocations!

A Simple Example: GolfCourseService

In Chapters 9 and 10 we wrote and deployed a Web Service called GolfCourseService, which allowed Web clients to find information about golf courses and reserve tee times at specific courses. Here we will review the minimum requirements for a client to invoke this service via HTTP GET and POST methods.

The WSDL document GolfCourse.wsdl provides the method signatures presented by the GolfCourseService Web Service. Here we will invoke the

GetCourseDetail() method, which presents a query interface into the database of golf courses. A client can retrieve information about a specific golf course by passing in the course's ID.

HTTP GET is the simplest way to invoke a Web Service. A client provides arguments to the Web Service methods as addendums to the Web Service URL. The HTTP GET invocation for the GolfCourse Web Services *GetCourseDetail()* method might look like this:

```
GET /GolfCourseService/GolfCourseService.amx/GetCourseDetail?id=200
 HTTP/1.1
```

The Web Service client will return an XML result document in response to this GET request. Likewise, we could perform a HTTP POST request to send HTTP data from a client form. The POST might look like this:

```
POST /GolfCourseService/GolfCourseService.amx/GetCourseDetail HTTP/1.1
Host: localhost
Content-Type: application/x-www-form-urlencoded
Content-Length: <length>
id=200
```

The HTTP POST response document, saved here as response.xml, is a simple XML document, identical to the HTTP GET response document. The response is formatted in plain XML without any SOAP references. The header for the document returned is:

```
HTTP/1.1 200 OK
Content-Type: text/xml; charset=utf-8
Content-Length: length
```

The body of the document (again saved in response.xml) as seen in Listing 11-1 is:

Listing 11-1 response.xml: Document returned by our Web Service.

```
<?xml version="1.0" encoding="utf-8"?>
<GolfCourse xmlns:xsi="http://www.w3.org/2001/XMLSchema-instance"
xmlns:xsd="http://www.w3.org/2001/XMLSchema" xmlns=
"http://tempuri.org/">
  <id>20</id>
  <name>Wildwood Green</name>
  <description>Wildwood Green</description>
  <price>50.00</price>
  <telephone>919-999-3333</telephone>
  <address>
    <street>157 Strickland Road</street>
    <city>Raleigh</city>
```

```
    <state>NC</state>
    <postalCode>27613</postalCode>
    <country>usa</country>
  </address>
  <tees>
     //Tees information omitted for brevity
  </tees>
</GolfCourse>
```

Platform Issues and Limitations

Because Web Services are based on open, ubiquitous standards like XML and HTTP, platform issues and limitations are kept to a minimum but are not completely eliminated. This section discusses some of the platform-specific issues around Web Services, including how tightly the development environment is integrated with the execution environment and the capabilities of lightweight platforms (such as PalmOS devices).

Windows

Microsoft Windows NT, Windows 2000, and Windows XP provide the most complete platform for developing and deploying Web Services applications. Visual Studio .NET provides a complete development environment for building, deploying, and testing XML Web services. Microsoft IIS provides a Web server for presenting your Web Service to the Internet and managing issues like security. Windows itself provides an application server environment for running your Web Service.

By developing and deploying your Web Service on a Windows operating system, you can be assured that the system conflicts that inevitably arise in mixed development environments will be kept to a minimum. Visual Studio .NET guarantees that your operating system, Web server, Web application server, and development environment are all up-to-date and compatible.

Using Visual Studio .NET you can develop your XML Web service application server using one of several languages, including C, C++, and C#. You can also easily generate Web Service clients for any platform that supports HTML 3.2-capable Web browsers. Visual Studio .NET allows you to create Web forms that invoke appropriate code on the server side, instead of on the client side, to support the platform-independence of the XML Web service client.

UNIX and Linux

The family of UNIX operating systems has a good track record for supporting mission-critical and enterprise-wide application server deployment. UNIX operating systems offer a high degree of reliability and tend to be stable throughout a system's load curve. UNIX systems have also been easier to scale, and more robust in the face of scaling, than other operating systems.

Many developers and organizations find the greater availability of open source applications for UNIX operating systems intriguing. Given the variety of application server choices on UNIX, an organization can choose to spend more money for off-the-shelf commercial solutions or spend less money and more developer resources configuring open source solutions.

The plethora of UNIX configurations and available application server options presents a double-edged sword. Each development environment is likely to present a different combination of a UNIX kernel, Web server, Web application server, development tool set, and other variables. Application developers are more likely to struggle with compatibility issues in a UNIX environment than in a Windows environment. Such environment and compatibility issues tend to make rapid application development on UNIX platforms less feasible than on Windows platforms.

Portable Devices and Handhelds

Handheld devices present some of the most challenging issues faced by distributed-application developers. The portability and widespread deployment of such devices makes them attractive client targets for distributed-application development.

The issues around building distributed applications for these devices are obvious: these devices present limited UIs with constraints on screen size and user input capabilities (that is, these devices rarely present a full keyboard). Handheld devices also present severe constraints in application support, processing power, and available memory, both in RAM and persistent storage.

Network connectivity might be the biggest challenge. Handheld devices, when they are connected to a larger network, normally present low-bandwidth connections of an intermittent nature. The user of such a device must explicitly connect or dial into a network. This requirement might change soon, however, with the advent of portable, high-speed, local area network connections.

The Java 2 Platform, Micro Edition (J2ME technology) allows you to develop Java-based applications on portable and handheld devices, including PalmOS. Using J2ME you can build PalmOS-compatible versions of lightweight XML parsers like MicroStar's Aelfred.

Other Platform Issues: Security, Scalability, and State

Other particularly important issues in designing distributed applications in a heterogeneous network environment include security, scalability, and state. Security generally requires knowledge of each target OS as well as the intermediary transport protocol. Scalability is a classic software design problem, complicated in a distributed environment by the number of variables present (multiple hardware configurations, operating systems, and network). State is a ramification of building services above the stateless HTTP protocol. Here we take a brief look at each.

Security

Once again, Web Services' use of open standards means that we don't have to invent another mechanism for providing secure transmission of data between client and server. Because the Web Services transport protocol is HTTP, the Web Service application looks just like any other Web application running on your Web server. You will continue to use the same mechanisms for authentication, authorization, and encryption that you use with your existing Web server and Web applications.

If we want to provide secure over-the-wire transmission of our Web Services' HTTP requests between client and server, we can use Secure Sockets Layer (SSL), which provides secure HTTP transmissions via public key encryption. To do this we must be sure that our Web server is configured to provide SSL support. For added authentication security we can register X.509 certificates for client identity verification with Verisign.

Because the client accesses Web Services from a URL, just as the client would access a Web page, we can use any of our Web server's security functionality as part of our Web Services' security component. We can require user authentication to access the Web Service URL, or we can restrict access to specific IP addresses or ranges of IP addresses. We can also authenticate Web Service clients and maintain that authentication between HTTP requests by issuing session cookies. All of this functionality is provided by your Web server.

At the Web Services application level we can implement a variety of security mechanisms, including role-based security. Say we offer a Web Service that performs payroll functions. A client with the role of "clerk" might be able to issue paychecks, but not view salary information. A client with the role of "supervisor" might be able to change salaries. The role of the client, along with authentication information to validate that role, can be passed to the Web Service in the incoming SOAP document as arguments to the appropriate method calls.

Scalability

Few scalability issues are specific to Web Services. Developers of Web Service clients should attempt to minimize the required amount of object state information that must be serialized into an XML file and also minimize the size of data objects that must be serialized. Overhead of serializing, unserializing, and reserializing object data presents one of the most obvious potential bottlenecks in a distributed Web Service application. Any savings by the client in serialization time is also likely to save un-serialization and re-serialization time on the server.

Because the Web Services server presents its services to the outside world as a URL or set of URLs, the issues surrounding the scaling of Web Services servers is similar to the issues around scaling conventional Web servers. The developer of a Web Service server should minimize object state information required by the service and minimize the size of objects likely to be passed to the service. For large Web Service applications a multitier architecture is feasible, just as one might deploy a multitier architecture for serving conventional Web sites and applications.

State

Because Web Services rely on the stateless HTTP protocol, they must be designed so that all necessary state information is included in the client request for the Web Service. Some work-arounds for HTTP's stateless nature exist, such as using session cookies to maintain authentication state between HTTP invocations. In general, however, the Web application must be designed to work under conditions of a nonpersistent, stateless connection with potentially high latency and (depending on the system environment) unknown or low bandwidth.

Why Not Use Web Services?

Given the ease of implementing Web Services, why would we want to use any other mechanism for creating client/server applications? Despite the many advantages presented by Web Services, they are not the right solution for many situations. Situations where a Web Service solution might not be appropriate include environments in which the following situations are present.

Speed is a Priority

Several areas present possible speed bottlenecks to Web Service applications. Marshaling object data to an XML file on the client can be resource intensive. Distributed applications that maintain an object's native format for over-the-wire transmission have an advantage here.

The same bottleneck appears four times: when the client creates a SOAP XML file for transmission to the Web Service server, when the Web Service server receives the SOAP file and unmarshals the data, when the Web Service server marshals the result of its Web method(s) into a SOAP result file, and when the client unpacks the SOAP result file. The time and computing resources taken up by these operations can be significant, especially if large data structures are passed around. (Because HTTP requires that data be passed by value, all input and result data must be passed over the wire.)

The HTTP protocol presents another potential speed bottleneck. HTTP provides an effective protocol for general Internet traffic. However, lack of control of and access to the underlying transportation mechanism means that the Web Service HTTP requests and responses are at the mercy of current network conditions at all levels (LAN, WAN, and Internet).

State is Important

The stateless nature of Web Services, mandated by the stateless HTTP protocol, is not appropriate for all distributed applications. Applications that must maintain an open database connection, for example, cannot operate effectively in a stateless environment. Applications in which data should be passed by reference instead of by value are not appropriate for Web Services either.

Imagine a Web Service that performs an insert operation on an address field component of a 20-MB data file. A Web Service that provides this capability would need to pass 20 MB of data from the client to the server (after marshaling that data to an XML file). The client would have to receive 20 MB of data, parse the SOAP file, unmarshal the data, perform the insert operation, remarshal the data, and pass the 20-MB SOAP file back to the client, which needs to parse and unpack the result file. All to change a single record! A pass-by-reference mechanism would be more appropriate here.

Through the judicious use of offsets to manage changes to large data files, you can minimize the number of times a large data file is passed back and forth between Web Services clients and servers. Visual Studio .NET provides an abstraction called *Data Sets* to support working with large XML documents. The *Data Set* automatically handles update issues when a client application is finished modifying a large data file. Another set of classes called *Data Adapters* handle all the low-level database interactions. Other APIs for building Web Services will typically provide APIs to perform the same role.

Homogeneous Deployment Environment

Marshaling and unmarshaling your Web method arguments with each Web Service invocation will probably require some overhead. Instead of marshaling your data with every Web Service call, you can save significant computing resources by maintaining objects in the native serialization format of your language and operating system. If you are deploying distributed applications in a homogeneous computing environment, you might want to use more traditional methods for implementing them.

Security Is Critical

Although Web servers can provide a high degree of security with SSL and its underlying public key encryption mechanism, other transport protocols are likely to provide a better solution within corporate firewalls or other closed environments.

Conclusion

In this chapter we looked at historically available mechanisms for implementing distributed applications, from UNIX sockets through Web Services. We've provided enough of an overview of these mechanisms so that you can see the strengths and limitations of each.

Because Web Services are based on open, ubiquitous standards such as HTTP and XML, Web Services can be easily implemented on far more diverse platforms and operating systems than other, previously available mechanisms for creating distributed applications. Even PalmOS devices can generate an HTTP POST request to a Web Service server and receive a result as an XML document! Never before has the bar been so low for a platform to participate as a distributed-application client.

The bar for participating as a Web Service server is nearly as low on the server side. A Web Service server needs only to receive a service request and data, in the form of an HTTP GET or POST method or as a SOAP document, marshal the data into an appropriate format, act on the request via a Web method, and return the result via HTTP as an XML document.

You can create Web methods today on any platform that can communicate via HTTP and process XML files. You can do this from scratch using a low-level programming language, but you might want to use the available support of an IDE for Web Services. Visual Studio .NET handles any cross-platform compatibility issues for you, including configuring client browser or form-based interfaces to run any client-side scripts on the server.

In summary, Web Services present far fewer constraints and limitations than do legacy mechanisms that support cross-platform application development. Any platform that supports HTTP can perform as a Web Service client. You can build Web Service UIs using HTML and JavaScript. It's now easier than ever to prototype, build, test, and deploy distributed cross-platform applications.

12

Legacy Systems Integration

Today's corporate environment is intensely competitive, and corporate leaders look to their information systems for an edge. Keeping up with technology while protecting the investment in existing applications is a constant challenge for most businesses. Many companies, in fact, most of the largest, do not have brand new systems that store, support, and manage their data. Upgrading to today's systems might not even be an option because of the dependency on old data and the inability to access it if a new system is purchased.

In addition to these challenges, companies are moving rapidly to give employees and customers access to business processes on the Internet in the form of suites of enterprise applications. This openness creates a demand to make the existing mission-critical business systems accessible through the Web.

In this chapter we will explore some of the issues and solutions in legacy systems integration. We will begin with a discussion about the challenges facing most legacy integration projects in an enterprise. We will then describe some common methods for accessing and controlling legacy applications from your new applications. Finally we will describe an approach for legacy systems integration using an XML-based layered architecture. The aim is to show you how XML can help position an organization's legacy systems for the future and tap those vast resources that at one time seemed as hidden away as a pharaoh's tomb.

A Definition of Legacy Systems Integration

Despite all the changes and "paradigm shifts" that have rocked the computing world over the past several decades, global enterprises still store the bulk of their data and process the majority of their transactions on mainframe-based systems such as VAX and S/390. These are tried-and-true systems that form the backbone of a typical organization's business processes and transactions.

These systems are usually developed in COBOL or another obscure language and are built as independent batch-oriented systems using proprietary data storage and communications protocols. The UI is usually complex, heavily loaded, and character-based. Business logic, data access logic, presentation services, and control flow are typically mixed within the confines of individual monolithic programs. Finally, access to the data is often limited and only possible through proprietary means.

You should realize that the term "legacy" is by no means restricted to the mainframe-based systems or other systems that have developed since the onset of Web-based applications. As technologies relentlessly move forward, you will always have systems that were not developed using the latest tools, languages, and protocols. For example, in our Internet-centric world of IP and XML, even relatively recent technologies such as Visual Basic and PC LAN–based client/server systems can be considered legacy systems. Of course, to some companies these solutions are no less valuable than the mainframe-based systems.

In a perfect world companies would rewrite legacy applications to be Web enabled. Such projects, however, can take months or years, so companies are not about to throw out the legacy applications currently running their businesses. Therefore, few projects have the benefit of being able to start from scratch. Instead, most development teams need to take into account existing legacy systems when they're developing new applications. This is known as "legacy systems integration," and a whole industry has grown around it.

Challenges to Integration

No matter which way you approach integration with legacy applications, you're certain to have more pain than fun. The older and less documented the systems are, the harder and more error-prone the integration becomes. The result is a classic "chicken and egg" syndrome, where throwing away the legacy data and functionality will kill the business, but staying with them will do the same. Trying to update the system will probably take longer than starting from scratch, but you can't throw away the old data. You come full circle.

As we talk about these issues we will find that integration problems fall into four main categories: documentation, interfacing, availability, and scalability. Now we will spend some time exploring these in detail.

Documentation

The unfortunate truth about legacy systems is that they're often poorly documented, leaving developers and businesses people alike reluctant to make changes. Everyone is afraid that doing so will break the system in some way. To add to the problem, the original developers or owners of these systems might not be willing to work with a newer team because of such trivial reasons as internal politics.

This reluctance or inability to change legacy systems is one of the primary reasons why integration is considered necessary in the first place. Without adequate documentation or legacy expert help, your integration projects are bound to face a miserable death.

Interfacing

Interfacing refers to the process of talking to and controlling legacy systems from another system. If you're lucky, your legacy systems were designed with integration in mind, as in the IBM Customer Information Control System (CICS), If so, interfacing should be relatively pain-free. This compatibility is hardly typical with many legacy systems, however, and getting an interface to function properly can be a daunting task.

Depending on whether the legacy system in question was designed with extensibility in mind, interfacing can be both time-consuming and expensive. Be sure to weigh the value of the interface against the effort required to accomplish it. You may find that a complete, perfect integration isn't worthwhile, but that a partial integration of only the most critical parts will suffice.

Availability

Web-based applications are generally expected to be available 24 hours a day, 7 days a week. Your legacy systems, however, might not have been developed with this lack of constraints in mind. Mainframe-based systems, as an example, are frequently designed with a periodic maintenance shutdown requirement. What will your application do when legacy systems are unavailable? How will it handle not being able to access the data it needs to function? How should it gracefully alert users of the situation?

These questions need to be answered when building your application, but the list of questions could be much longer when speaking of a specific application. You must know and understand all of the implications of the legacy system's availability, or at least as many as possible, when deciding how to use it. Any system you develop will inherit these restrictions.

Scalability

For many legacy-integration projects scalability might be the single biggest challenge. Most legacy systems are not designed to handle the large volume of traffic and real-time transactions that systems today must face. Legacy systems were often designed to support an elite few who had access to only a handful of machines. Many of these legacy systems were also batch-oriented and will not be able to handle online queries and transactions. For many applications, especially Web-based ones, being able to handle a large and unpredictable volume of online transactions is a requirement. Users of these applications will not wait days, hours, or even minutes for the systems to response. Including legacy resources in your chain of applications increases transaction time, thereby decreasing scalability.

These are some of the problems that will prevent a legacy system from scaling, and enhancing or improving one of these systems to function in today's environment is hard.

Creating Interfaces to Legacy Systems

We have now covered some of the common problems with supporting and interfacing legacy systems in an enterprise. Because of the wide variety of legacy systems, no single solution can make them all work with newer technology. Some systems provide native functionalities for third-party access, while others support only proprietary features and functionality. Because of this variety, interfacing with legacy systems can be extremely challenging, but it can be done.

An Example Scenario

IBM created CICS Web gateways that allow you to create CGI scripts to make calls into CICS directly, which can greatly simplify the task of interfacing to legacy systems. IBM is one example of a company adding enhancements to its legacy products. These are often products that would have become extinct if not for the enhancements, which have potentially saved their customers millions by allowing them to postpone migrations.

You can interface with legacy systems using five common approaches. They are generalized to represent areas that developers and managers can focus on when trying to utilize old systems for new work. They are

- Data-level
- Process-level
- API-level
- UI-level
- Middleware

Let's take a closer look at each of these approaches.

Data-Level Interfacing

The first type of interfacing focuses on accessing legacy databases or files directly at the data level, bypassing most, if not all, of the functionality present in the surrounding application.

If your data is stored in SQL databases you can access them directly using appropriate SQL queries. Some RDBM systems, such as older versions of Novell Btrieve, provide non-SQL, but nonetheless fairly complete, API access to their databases. Other systems provide proprietary data storage mechanisms and often have data import and export functionalities designed specifically for interfacing. Communications with these systems are performed through the exchange of files of a specific format. These usually involve some form of delimited text files.

Some vendors, such as Oracle and Microsoft, provide native XML-based access to data stored in their databases. For example, back in Chapter 4 we discussed some of the built-in features provided by Microsoft SQL Server 2000 and Oracle 9i for exposing and updating relational data as XML. This appears to be the next-generation method for enabling integration.

The main problem with data-level interfacing is that it increases data coupling between applications, thereby increasing your maintenance burden. You might also not be able to access important data validation and other critical business rules that are inherent in the application but not in the method of accessing the information. Finally cost can also be a limiting factor, especially if you need to employ a middleware product.

Process-Level Interfacing

Solutions written for some mainframe environments, especially those written in COBOL, were developed as a series of separately executable programs.

Interfacing with these systems usually requires preparing the invocation environment, calling the required program(s), and fetching and processing the returned data. While this formula for process-level interfacing provides a common method of getting to the data, it can be overwhelming when trying to extract only simple information.

CICS, which is a good example of this method, provides an External Call Interface (ECI) to allow non-CICS clients to invoke and control programs under CICS. ECI includes support for CICS security and transactions and, unlike RPC environments, ECI does not require stubs and the use of an Interface Definition Language (IDL) compiler and is therefore easy to use.

Here is an example of how process-level interfacing works with CICS. To run a CICS program using ECI, you must supply CICS with all the relevant information for the invocation, such as the name of the program to invoke and a username and password. You pass data to the CICS programs via a block of data called the COMMAREA block. When the invoked CICS program finishes it places the results in the COMMAREA block.

API-Level Interfacing

Another type of interfacing with legacy systems is to provide an API to access the functionality of an application. Many packages, such as SAP and PeopleSoft, include C/C++ or even COM-based APIs for accessing their systems. However, APIs might be limited in scope, preventing access to the functionalities you need. They might, for example, behave in a fashion you do not expect, such as not being thread-safe.

If your team has the required skill sets, these APIs can provide a powerful means of interfacing to the legacy systems. However, these APIs might be limited in scope, preventing you from accessing the functionalities you need. They might also not behave in the fashion you require, such as (for example, not being thread-safe).

User Interface-Level Interfacing

Accessing legacy applications through UIs, a process called screen scraping, refers to the interaction with the legacy software performed by using simulated user keystrokes and entered data by processing captured screen outputs. This technique is most often used with old "green" terminal-based systems and is one of the last methods a person might use to integrate with a system.

Recently this technique has been used by Web-based aggregation sites for presenting financial data or other types of information. These sites build their contents by combining data extracted from parsing HTML pages retrieved from other Web sites.

Middleware

Some mainframe vendors and third-party companies provide solutions that allow applications to access data through middleware products. These products sit between your new and legacy systems, hiding the complex details of legacy interfacing from you.

Different middleware products can vary greatly in functionality. Some products simply provide a mechanism for data to get from place to place, such as RPC, messaging systems, and distributed object systems. More sophisticated middleware offerings, however, can help manage application logic and resources. The most robust tools directly support significant application functionalities such as credit card transactions for e-commerce. By employing sophisticated caching and asynchronous data-transfer technologies, these high-end products can also provide scalable access to your legacy data. IBM's DB2 WWW Connection and the Sybase Enterprise CONNECT middleware family of products are some examples.

If support for your particular legacy system is available, using the right middleware product can greatly simplify the task of legacy integration. The major downside is that these products, especially the high-end ones, are not cheap. They also require extra hardware resources and administrative care that adds to the cost. You will have to decide whether using a middleware product is cost effective for your particular integration needs.

An Architecture for Legacy Systems Integration

Much time and effort is required for a successful systems integration no matter which methods are available to you. Though integration can be difficult, data is often so valuable that you have no choice but to interact with a system, even if to extract only the data for a migration. Therefore, as you design a method of accessing data in these systems, you should attempt to do so with a method that will remain relevant and capable of supporting an organization's future needs. In this section we will show you an architecture that can be used to effectively implement and maintain legacy systems integration.

Core Criteria

Three criteria should be used to prepare legacy systems for integration. By making the system accessible through multiple communications mechanisms in advance, obsolescence by technology can be minimized. The following list outlines these three areas:

1. The application should be capable of supporting multiple communications protocols such as HTTP, IIOP, SOAP, and others. While the first and immediate implementation can support only one, hooks should be built in to allow for future extension. The only exception is when you are building a one-time integration to migrate the data into a new system.
2. The messaging interface should be protocol-independent and consistent.
3. The data model used by the formatted messages should be defined in terms of the organization's business transactions.

While the first item simply provides for a flexible means to use any integration, the second criterion guarantees that applications can send and receive the same type of messages, formatted in the same way. Such flexibility is irrespective of the underlying communications mechanisms used and demonstrates why XML is perfect for this job. XML is preferred because it is platform-independent and is easy to work with due to the availability of a large number of tools for parsing, transforming, and processing XML documents.

The reason behind the third criterion is that any application already in a system is there to support a business process, a need, or both. Therefore, the interface to the integrated application should be defined using the terminology and artifacts of that process. By adhering to the third criterion the organization shields itself from the eventual replacement of the system as time goes on. In essence it prevents the system from becoming a "legacy system."

The Layered Approach

A legacy application can be prepared for integration through the implementation of a layered architecture pattern that allows for maximum flexibility. This pattern includes

- A Transport Layer The outermost layer is responsible for the receipt and return of XML-formatted messages through any given communications mechanism.
- A Services Layer The middle layer provides the functionality for interpreting XML-formatted requests, invoking the appropriate operations upon the legacy system, and formatting the responses into XML.
- A Legacy Adapter Layer The innermost layer is responsible for interfacing to the legacy system and represents the model of the data.

Regardless of the client type or communications mechanism employed, this architecture allows systems to perform business domain-level services via an

XML-based interface. Imposing this method on top of a legacy system will enable the use of that system for years to come, assuming performance is not an issue.

Transport Layer

The Transport Layer, as we mentioned, allows clients of these legacy applications to use various protocols and mechanisms, such as HTTP, CORBA (IIOP), or DCOM, to invoke the services defined by the interface to the application. Classes in this layer can be fairly straightforward because their primary role is to provide a communications bridge to the actual services. The main responsibility of this layer is to make the rest of the system protocol-independent.

Listing 12-1, transport_layer.aspx, is a sample implementation of a Transport Layer that uses the HTTP protocol for invoking the services exposed by the *ServiceLayer* object defined in service_layer.cs.

Listing 12-1 transport_layer.aspx: Sample Transport Layer for HTTP protocol.

```
<%@ import namespace="System.Xml"%>
<script language="C#" runat="server">
  /* string used to hold string representation of
     our service request XML message */
  String xmlStr = "<ServiceRequest>";
  /* get names of all form variables into local array */
  String names[] = Request.Form.AllKeys;
  /* loop through form variable to build request XML message */
  foreach ( name in names )
  {
    /* if form variable is called "service", use its value to
       build the ServiceName element */
    if ( name == "service" )
    {
      xmlStr += "<ServiceName>" + name + "</ServiceName>";
    }
    /* othewise use this form variable's name and value to
       build a <Param> element */
    else
    {
      xmlStr += "<Param name=\"" + name + "\">" +
                Request.Form[ name ] + "</Param>";
    }
  }
  xmlStr += "</ServiceRequest>"
  /* create XmlDocument using the reqXML string */
  XmlDocument xmlDoc = new XmlDocument();
  xmlDoc.LoadXml( xmlStr );
  /* instantiate our ServiceLayer object */
```

(continued)

Listing 12-1 *continued*

```
   ServiceLayer service = new ServiceLayer();
   /* invoke the perform() method with our request XML message */
   XmlDocument retXmlDoc = service.perform( xmlDoc );
   /* output the response XML message to the client tell
      browser/client that we are outputting XML */
   Response.ContextType = "text/xml"
   /* output the response XML message */
   Response.Write( retXmlDoc.outerXml );
</script>
```

In this implementation of a Transport Layer, we first built our request XML message from HTTP POST variables. We then instantiated an instance of the *ServiceLayer* object developed in service_layer.cs and invoked its *perform()* method with the request XML message as its parameter. Finally all that was left was to display the resultant response XML message to the client.

Services Layer

The second layer defines how the services in the system are invoked and how the data returned by the services is formatted. XML-formatted requests are forwarded to this layer via the Transport Layer, and the classes in this layer parse the transaction requests and invoke the appropriate operations on the legacy system.

The methods exposed by the Legacy Adapter Layer and the parameters used in invoking those methods should be used to design the format of the XML messages used by this layer. When designing the format of these messages, keep it consistent across the different services to be invoked. For example, Listing 12-2, sample_request.xml, shows a sample XML message that can be used to invoke the services exposed by the *LegacyLayer* object defined in legacy_layer.cs.

The *ServiceName* element is used to indicate the legacy service to invoke. The *<Param>* elements hold the names and values of the parameters that are used when invoking a particular service; thus the same format can be used to invoke services of different calling conventions.

Listing 12-2 sample_request.xml: Sample service request XML message.

```
<?xml version="1.0"?>
<ServiceRequest>
  <ServiceName>Order</ServiceName>
  <Param name="customerID">foobar</Param>
  <Param name="itemID">7843221</Param>
  <Param name="qty">5</Param>
</ServiceRequest>
```

Listing 12-3, service_layer.cs, is an example of the implementation of a Service Layer that uses the XML message defined in sample_request.xml to invoke legacy services.

Listing 12-3 service_layer.cs: Sample Service Layer.

```
using System.Xml;
public class ServiceLayer
{
  public XmlDocument perform( XmlDocument params )
  {
    /* our Legacy Layer object */
    Legacy legacy = new Legacy();
    /* retrieve name of the legacy service to invoke */
    DocumentNavigator nav = new DocumentNavigator( params );
    nav.Select( "//ServiceRequest/ServiceName" );
    nav.MoveToNextSelected();
    serviceName = nav.innerText;
    /* string used to hold result of the method invocation */
    string res = "";
switch ( serviceName )
{
      case "Order" :
        /* retrieve the customerID, itemID, and qty parameters
           from the Params XML document */
        nav.Select( "//ServiceRequest/Param[@name='customerID']" );
        nav.MoveToNextSelected();
        string customerID = nav.innerText;
        nav.Select( "//ServiceRequest/Param[@name='itemID']" );
        nav.MoveToNextSelected();
        string itemID = nav.innerText;
        nav.Select( "//ServiceRequest/Param[@name='qty']" );
        nav.MoveToNextSelected();
        string qty = nav.innerText;
        /* invoke the orderItem() method in our Legacy object
           to place an order and build result XML document based on
           the outcome. */
        try
        {
          string tranID = legacy.orderItem( customerID, itemID, qty );
          res = "<TransactionID>" + tranID + </TransactionID>";
        }
        catch ( Exception e )
        {
          res = "<Fault>" + e.Message + </Fault>";
        }
        break;
      case "History" :
```

(continued)

Listing 12-3 *continued*

```
            /* retrieve the customerID parameter from the Params
               in the XML document */
            nav.Select( "//ServiceRequest/Param[@name='customerID']" );
            nav.MoveToNextSelected();
            string customerID = nav.innerText;
            /* invoke the getOrderHistory() method in our Legacy
               object and output result in our resultDoc XML document */
            try
            {
              string[] tranIDs = legacy.getHistory( customerID );
              /* get list of transaction IDs of past transaction
                 and build result XML document */
              foreach ( string tranID in tranIDs )
              {
                res = res + "<TransactionID>" + tranID +
                            "</TransactionID>";
              }
            }
            catch ( Exception e )
            {
              res = "<Fault>" + e.Message + </Fault>";
            }
            break;
        }
        /* build and return result XML document */
        XmlDocument resultDoc = new XmlDocument();
        resultDoc.loadXml( "<ServiceRequestResponse>" + res +
                           "</ServiceRequestResponse>" );
        return ( resultDoc );
    }
}
```

The *ServiceLayer* object exposes a single method called *perform()* that accepts an XmlDocument argument which is used to determine the name of the legacy service to invoke and their input parameters. The *perform()* method returns an *XmlDocument* object containing the results of this invocation.

ServiceLayer supports two services, the Order that is used to place an order and the History that is used to determine the transaction history of a specific customer. Note that the implementation of these services are handled by the respective *orderItem()* and *getOrderHistory()* methods in the *LegacyLayer* object in legacy_layer.cs that we developed in the last section.

Legacy Adapter Layer

The innermost layer contains all the code necessary to interact with the legacy system. Using one of the methods outlined in the "Creating Interfaces to Legacy

Systems" section is suggested. Business-level behaviors and rules encapsulated by the legacy system are exposed to the Services Layer, so this layer does not need to know anything about XML.

When designing services for this layer you need to have the correct granularity. In building distributed systems, designers commonly specify interfaces that are too finely grained. These designs do not scale well, and clearly defining and managing transactional boundaries is difficult. For example legacy_layer.cs, shown in Listing 12-4, contains the pseudocode of a *LegacyLayer* object that exposes two methods for placing orders and inquiring about previous transaction history.

Listing 12-4 legacy_layer.cs: The psuedocode of a sample Legacy Layer.

```
public class LegacyLayer
{
  /* place an order return the new transaction ID or throw
     an exception if an error occurred. */
  public string orderItem( string customerID, string itemID, string qty )
  {
    /* insert your actual implementation here... */
  }
  /* get order transaction of a specific customer. return a
     string array containing the list of the transaction IDs
     of previous order transaction or throw an exception if
     an error occurred. */
  public string[] getOrderHistory( string customerID )
  {
      /* insert your actual implementation here... */
  }
}
}
```

Note that these methods deal with native data types directly instead of XML messages. Also note that the granularity and stateless nature of the methods can simplify transaction management as well as improve scalability.

Availability and Scalability Considerations

One common approach for tackling the availability and scalability issues we discussed that are associated with integrating legacy systems is to decouple the legacy systems from the new application by using a messaging server such as the MSMQ or IBM's MQSeries. Using a messaging server allows the two separate subsystems to operate at their own pace.

On the application side you can concurrently send thousands of requests and obtain excellent performance from a messaging server. You can process messages at a pace the legacy system can handle, and therefore, can maximize both systems without overloading either. For example, if only five connections are available through IBM Systems Network Architecture (SNA), you can process five messages at a time. This allows you to throttle the load on the legacy system while at the same time addressing your availability concerns and allowing your application to scale appropriately.

Conclusion

Legacy systems integration is a huge and complicated topic that merits a whole book of its own. In this chapter we've merely scratched the surface, but we've given you an overview of the more common issues surrounding legacy integration. Some of the issues stemmed from the fact that most legacy systems simply were not designed for the kind of availability and scalability demanded by today's applications. We also briefly discussed the different ways in which applications can interact with a legacy system, and we identified a few methods, including data-level, process-level, and API-level interfacing, and discussed their characteristics and problems. Finally we provided a description of an XML-based, layered architecture that can be used to implement extensible legacy integration solutions.

13

Cross Device Development

In this book we have looked at ways to use XML to aid in Web applications development. So far discussion on application clients was limited to a Web browser (Microsoft Internet Explorer 5.5 more often than not). The explosion of the wireless industry and our newfound ability to plug almost anything into a network, from TVs to toaster ovens, has developers scurrying to figure out how to port their products to alternative devices. Rest assured, XML is making its way to all of these devices.

Some of the anxiety over how to support all of these small devices is overkill. How often do you need to check the performance of your 401K on your microwave while preparing dinner? Despite this, there are legitimate reasons to support cell phones, PDAs, and other devices with your application. The next killer wireless application is out there, and you just need to find it. It would be great, though, if you didn't need to rearchitect your entire product suite along the way.

Fortunately for you, the developers, (and us, the XML authors) XML offers a number of features that make cross-device development and support easier than ever. This chapter will look at some emerging standards in cross-device development, how these standards use XML-based technologies, and how they are incorporated into the latest edition of Microsoft's .NET Developer Studio. We will discuss the benefits and limitations of these devices, and we will apply what we have learned to the Golf Reservation System sample application built in previous chapters.

Applications for the Web and Beyond

In today's industry we need to design our applications with *extensibility* in mind. New devices, technologies, and specifications are emerging so rapidly that understanding what they all mean, let alone incorporating them into our products, is difficult. We must design the next generation of applications to be receptive to change. We need to be able to plug new interfaces and functionality into a working application quickly and with as little redesign as possible.

Luckily, the sound programming design concepts we learned in school and in the field are still valid. Object encapsulation and loose coupling between application layers will make any application more extensible. When designing a layer of an application, focusing on the what (that is, what the logic is supposed to do) and how (how the logic performs its task) instead of on the who (who or what kind of client can use the logic) will open your mind to new possibilities.

If you partition your application logic by hiding it behind well-defined interfaces, sooner or later you will find new and different ways to use those interfaces. Try not to hardwire different application layers together for expediency's sake. This approach rarely saves you any time and, much worse, it closes countless integration opportunities. In this section we will use the concept of partitioning presentation and content to create a new breed of wireless applications.

The Separation of Church (Presentation) and State (Data)

XML is a handy tool for partitioning the different regions of your application. It is an instant interface. You can use schemas to describe your interface and XML to implement it. With specific regard to client applications, you should use XML to separate data from presentation logic. Combining the two restricts using the data to a specific subset of devices. By separating presentation from content you open up a myriad of ways to use information (many of which probably haven't been invented yet) in your application.

You should create a schema to define the data that flows through the front end of your application. Some clients, such as PC-based Web browsers, will be able to present all the information to the user at once. Other clients, such as cell phones and PDAs, can only digest small bits of information at a time. Despite disparities in ability among different types of devices, you can use the same XML content to drive all types of clients. You might have to plug in one or more XSLTs to massage the data into a format that a particular client device can absorb, but these transformations can be applied after the content is developed. In other words, the layer of your application responsible for generating content does not need to know what types of consumer devices will be on the receiving end. The relationships between these layers can be seen in Figure 13-1.

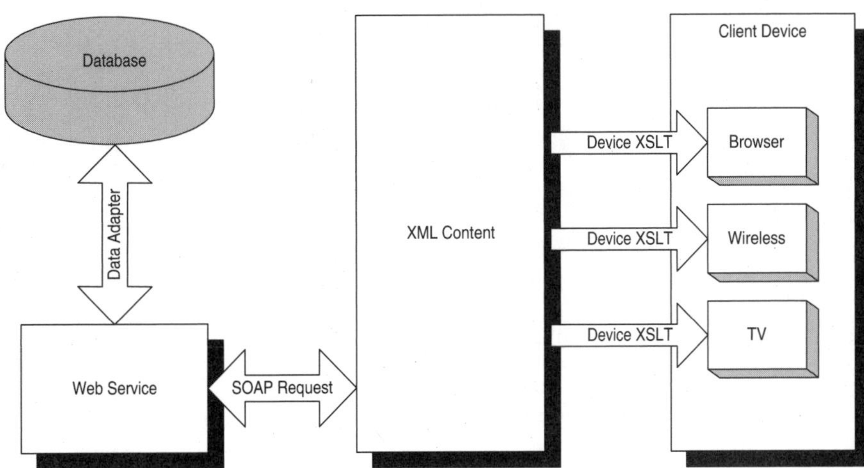

Figure 13-1 Different layers of a Web application.

Application Design Concepts

The fundamental hurdle that makes cross-device programming a challenge is that no two devices behave the same way. If you thought building and maintaining your Web site to support two major browsers was problematic, imagine how difficult supporting different types of cell phones and PDAs could be.

Not All Devices Are Created Equal

Classes of devices all have different strengths and weaknesses. For example, PCs are powerful and offer limitless UI possibilities. Users can communicate with an application by typing on a Microsoft natural keyboard, by pointing and clicking the mouse, by touching the screen, or even by talking into a microphone. PCs are ideal for traditional computing tasks where a user is seated in his or her chair and is ready for serious work or play.

Televisions have large, low-resolution displays suitable for showing big pictures to many people. Their low resolutions and low refresh rates would make them unsuitable for use as a word processor. You might, however, want to view programming schedules, play games, manipulate a video, and check your e-mail on the household tube.

Cell phones have limited and cumbersome I/O devices. They have tiny screens, even tinier keyboards, and no real mouse. Still, they are portable, convenient, and have the unique quality of being able to announce their presence to everyone around whenever something important happens. The point is that all devices perform some functions well and others not so well.

Partitioning Content and Presentation Layers

Saying "Just separate presentation from content and your cross-device problem will be solved" is easy, but development is not that simple. Like it or not, you will spend a considerable amount of time redesigning your UI whenever you begin development for a new client device. An application's browser-based UI that looks fantastic on a 17-inch monitor probably won't look as hot or be as user friendly (or work at all) on a 2.8-cm-by-3.75-cm display.

That example demonstrates a serious reduction in screen real estate. In the case of small, portable devices you need to think about what information is critical to each screen in your application and what information is expendable. Generally speaking, you need to figure out how to overcome the obvious obstacles many of these devices present and, better yet, come up with ways to use their unique features to add value to your application.

A computer program cannot solve these problems for you. Building a cell phone, PDA, or TV client requires time and brain cells. The trick is doing as much as possible in the presentation layer so as to preserve much of the work you have already done.

Your decision on how to partition the content and presentation layers of your application will have significant impact on its cross-device portability. If your content layer is tied too closely to a particular presentation schema, you will have a tough time adapting it to a radically different UI environment. You might need to reengineer in the best case, or build a device-specific content layer in the worst case.

Here are two different examples of XML content documents that might exist within a human resources application. Both documents are identical in terms of the pieces of information they convey, but are much different in the focus of their metadata. Afterwards we present a compromise between the two.

Presentation-Based Content Documents

The first XML document, PersonDocument.xml, uses a presentation-based schema. The metadata in this type of document is used to convey hints about layout and document structure. It does not contain much information about the type of data being shown or the context in which it's being used. The focus of the presentation layer using this approach is adding formatting, layout, and stylization specifics to the document skeleton in the content document.

This approach eases the burden of the presentation specialist. All he or she needs to do is create an XSLT template for each class of document that can appear in the application. A half-dozen major formatting templates might be enough to support hundreds of different content documents. Moreover, because these rules apply to document classes rather than specific pages, the application is guaranteed a uniform look and feel. The look and feel can also be changed at a global level with little effort.

Although the presentation layer can significantly alter the formatting of the resulting document, it does not have much control over what is shown. The source content document does not have enough metadata to enable the presentation rules to make judgment calls over the relative importance of its data. For example, the *Picture* field could be omitted from the result document for display on a small device without losing much. However, nothing in the source document tells the presentation layer this.

Another shortcoming inherent in this approach is that the document structure the content XML document suggests might not be ideal for all client devices. For example, a single block of content designed for a PC Web browser might need to be broken down into a number of WML cards. Listing 13-1 shows a presentation-based XML document describing a person.

Listing 13-1 PersonDocument.xml: XML content that uses a presentation-based schema.

```
<content>
  <header>
    <title>Person Detail</title>
  </header>
  <section>
    <title>John Smith Employee Information</title>
    <view>
      <properties>
       <property description="First Name">John</property>
       <property description="Last Name">Smith</property>
       <property description="Address">200 Brattle Street</property>
        <property description="City, State Zip">Cambridge, MA 02138
</property>
        <property description="Hair Color">brown</property>
        <property description="Birth Date">11/30/1974</property>
        <property description="Favorite Color">blue</property>
       <property description="Picture"><img src="images/jsmith.jpg"/>
</property>
      </properties>
    </view>
  </section>
</content>
```

Object-Based Content Documents

The second XML content example, shown later in the personobject.xml file, follows an object-based schema. The metadata in this class of document is not concerned with conveying any display information whatsoever. Instead, the metadata expresses the type and context surrounding the information it contains. This takes some work off the content developer's plate by limiting his or her responsibilities to querying any data repositories for information related to the page context and reformatting that data into XML.

The presentation designer now takes the object-based content document and builds the entire application page. In an extreme case the presentation designer must build a unique set of transformation rules for each view in the application. This can lead to a vast library of transformation rules that are difficult to maintain. Applying global stylization policies beyond simple CSSs is also difficult because each view has a unique transformation.

Despite these negatives, object-based XML content documents are more reusable than their presentation-based counterparts because they do not imply any UI decisions. The presentation developer can extract as much data from the content document as he or she needs to get the job done. All layout, formatting, and stylization decisions fall under the presentation domain. The presentation developer has complete freedom, yet complete responsibility, in choosing how to craft the UI experience for a particular device. Listing 13-2 shows an object-based approach to the XML document found in Listing 13-1.

Listing 13-2 PersonObject.xml: An object-based XML document.

```
<content type="person" view="detail">
  <person>
    <firstName>John</firstName>
    <lastName>Smith</lastName>
    <address type="home">
      <address1>200 Brattle Street</address1>
      <city>Cambridge</city>
      <state>MA</state>
      <zip>02138</zip>
    </address>
    <hairColor>brown</hairColor>
    <birthDate>11/30/1974</birthDate>
    <favoriteColor>blue</favoriteColor>
  </person>
</content>
```

In this scenario most of the hard presentation work is handled in the presentation layer of the application. Device-specific presentation rules must be addressed somewhere in your application. Where this logic fits best, either in the content layer or in the presentation layer, depends mostly on the nature of your application and staff expertise.

A Compromise

We have explored some of the positives and negatives associated with presentation-based and object-based content models in cross-device design. You are probably wondering if it's possible to blend the two to create an ideal content schema that is flexible enough to extend to new devices but strong enough to support broad document classes.

One approach to this problem is to use *Content Adapters* to marshal data from object-based XML into device-specific presentation-based XML. You can then apply a small set of device-specific formatting templates that apply layout and stylization rules to the generic document templates produced by the content adapter. Figure 13-2 shows how these formatters fit into the larger application.

The Content Adapter approach has the following benefits.

- It cleanly encapsulates the steps of content generation, document production, and formatting. XML schemas can be used to define the interfaces at each step, allowing you to divide the work across different people and skill sets.
- It's extensible. Content Adapters and Formatters can be built for new device requirements as they arise. Changes to one device's formatter will not affect the behavior of any other supported device.
- The device-specific formatting layer guarantees look-and-feel consistency among document classes in the application. Global style changes can be implemented by modifying templates in this layer.

> **Note** The Apache Group's Cocoon project touches on this design pattern. For more information visit *http://xml.apache.org/cocoon2/index.html.*

The Challenges of Developing for Small Devices

One pitfall you might encounter while developing for new devices is making the assumption that related devices behave the same way. The browser wars taught us that, no matter how precisely a specification is written, there will always be different ways to interpret it. The challenge of supporting an ever-expanding list of cell phones and other devices makes the Internet Explorer vs. Netscape Navigator problem look trivial.

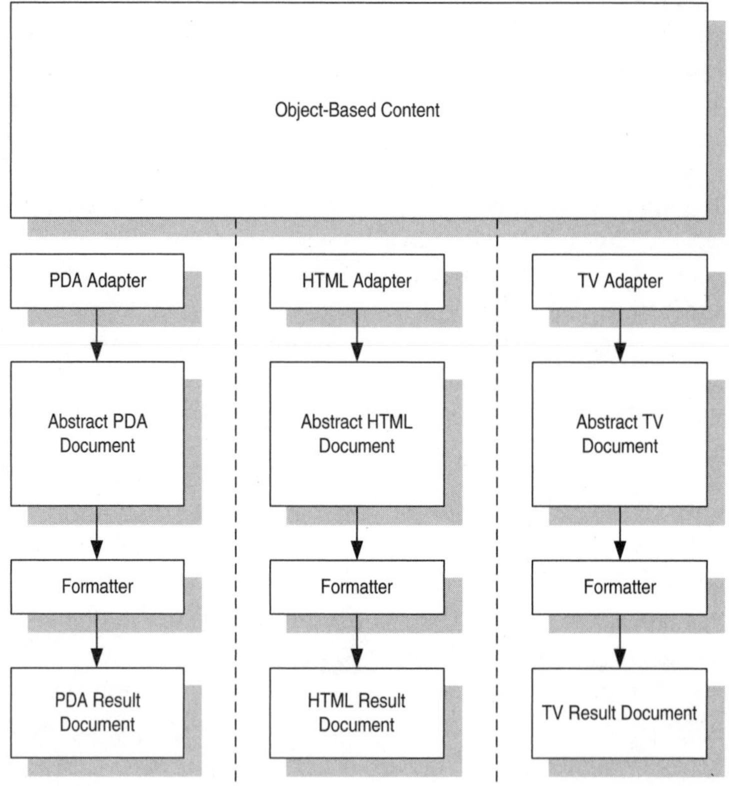

Figure 13-2 The formatting chain from XML source content to device-specific presentation.

For example, the list of different types of Wireless Application Protocol (WAP)–compliant cell phones on the market appears to grow daily. These cell phones, though similar in terms of supported standards, differ in many ways. Variations in screen sizes, component rendering, and auxiliary features can all affect the way you design a client application for them. Therefore, it is critical that you know as much as possible about the type of device and browser that is connecting to your Web application.

Device Detection

Detecting these differences can be tricky. The traditional method of browser detection, querying the *HTTP_USER_AGENT* CGI variable, becomes tedious and error-prone as the number of potential client devices grows over time. This method of detection requires the UI designer to have *a priori* knowledge of the capabilities of specific devices at design time. Browser detection logic inflates the amount of code the presentation developer needs to write and makes it needlessly troublesome to maintain.

Fortunately, you don't have to write all of this code yourself. A number of software companies offer tools to help write targeted code. *Air2Web.com, Gadgetspace.com, BeTrend.com,* and *2Roam.com* all provide wireless solutions to developers. In June 2001 Microsoft released version 3 of its Mobile Explorer Toolkit. This toolkit, available for free on Microsoft's Web site, enables developers to create client applications for HTML- and WAP-enabled mobile devices. The toolkit integrates natively with the .NET Developer Studio. We will cover the Mobile Explorer Toolkit in greater detail later in the chapter.

Composite Capabilities/Preference Profiles

The W3C is already taking steps to remedy the device/browser detection problem. A working draft of the Composite Capabilities/Preference Profiles (CC/PP) specification was released in July 2000. The goal of this specification is to provide a means for client devices to express their capabilities and preferences to content servers and shifts the burden of identification to the client. This approach supplies application developers with better information at request time to determine what type of document should be returned to the client.

According to the specification, client devices will use the RDF to express their capabilities via a standardized set of CC/PP attributes. The CC/PP spec defines a core feature vocabulary that can be used to categorize a wide range of user agents. This vocabulary includes attributes to describe, among other factors, the client's document encoding, media format. (For example, GIF, JPG, MPEG), and printing capabilities. HTTP requests will include an embedded CC/PP RDF document the application server can use to determine how best to handle the request (for example, should a particular image type be suppressed? Does the client support MPEG video? What version of WML does the client support?)

> **Note** If you would like more information about CC/PP, see *http://www.w3.org/Mobile/CCPP.*

Related Specifications

Any class of device you might target in your development efforts probably has a set of associated specifications that should be followed at all costs. Most of these specifications rely on XML to exchange data to and from the device. Ironically, the most often-used specification, HTML, is the loosest in terms of XML conformance. The move to XHTML should tidy up the language considerably.

The Wireless Application Protocol

The Wireless Application Protocol (WAP) and its related markup language, Wireless Markup Language (WML), are arguably the most exciting cross-device specifications available today. The explosion of the wireless industry has CEOs of software companies everywhere begging developers for mobile solutions in their products. The WAP specification was developed by the WAP Forum *(http://www.wapforum.org),* an association with over 500 members from some of the most influential companies in the wireless industry.

The WAP specification is very broad. It defines the entire network operating environment for wireless devices. This includes session protocols, transaction protocols, transport layer security, datagram protocols, gateway agents, WML, and WML Script. The last two pieces of the specification are of greatest interest to the client application developer. Most WAP runtime environments (such as .NET) will take care of the rest of the plumbing for you. All you need to worry about is building your WML client.

The WML looks like HTML. WML is based on XML, so it uses a tag-based syntax that should be familiar to anyone who has ever written a Web page. WML documents are similar in structure to HTML documents. They are divided into a header and a body. The header contains meta-information about the page. The body contains all the information that will be presented in the page. Page content can consist of plain text, images, tables, paragraphs, and user input controls.

WML also has an associated scripting language called WMLScript. It's loosely based on the ECMAScript scripting language commonly found in Web pages. WMLScript is specifically geared to wireless devices. It can validate user input, access device-specific functionality (for example, a script can be programmed to dial a certain number), and generate local messages and dialog boxes. Like HTML, WML also provides an event mechanism to allow programmers to insert WMLScript event handlers.

Unlike HTML, WML introduces the concepts of *decks* and *cards*. A single WML page request downloads a deck, which might contain one or more related cards, or pages. The user can flip between these cards without making expensive round trips to the server. Cards can access other cards' data within the same deck. The reason for having decks and cards in WML is because of the severe input restrictions intrinsic to small mobile devices. A single HTML form might need to be converted into multiple tiny WML forms just to capture and display the same information. Decks provide a means to bundle associated pages into a single client request. The Listing 13-3 file here shows a simple WML document.

Figure 13-3 shows how this file looks on the Nokia Developer's Kit after it is compiled and loaded.

Listing 13-3 HelloWorld.wml: The obligatory "HelloWorld Introduction."

```
<?xml version="1.0"?>
<!DOCTYPE wml PUBLIC "-//WAPFORUM//DTD WML 1.1//EN"
"http://www.wapforum.org/DTD/wml_1.1.xml">
<wml>
  <card id="card1">
    <p>
      <do type="accept">
        <go href="#card2"/>
      </do>
      Hello World!
      This is the first card...
    </p>
  </card>
  <card id="card2">
    <p>
      This is the second card.
      Goodbye.
    </p>
  </card>
</wml>
```

WML and WMLScript are not difficult to learn for experienced Web developers. Again, the trick is not knowing how to build mobile clients for your application, but designing your application to get the most reuse out of your logic when it comes time to bring your mobile solutions to market. This planning will give you a leg up on the competition.

VoiceXML

The VoiceXML specification was designed to make Web content available over traditional spoken phone lines. Users can manipulate VoiceXML client applications through spoken dialog and by pressing options on a touch-tone keypad. Content is sent to the user via prerecorded phrases, synthetic voice, and music. VoiceXML can make your enterprise Web Services instantly accessible to anyone who can reach a telephone.

Although some might view traditional voice-driven interfaces as "less sexy" than wireless Web browsers, sometimes voice-driven interfaces are more appropriate. Take the common example of checking the arrival time of

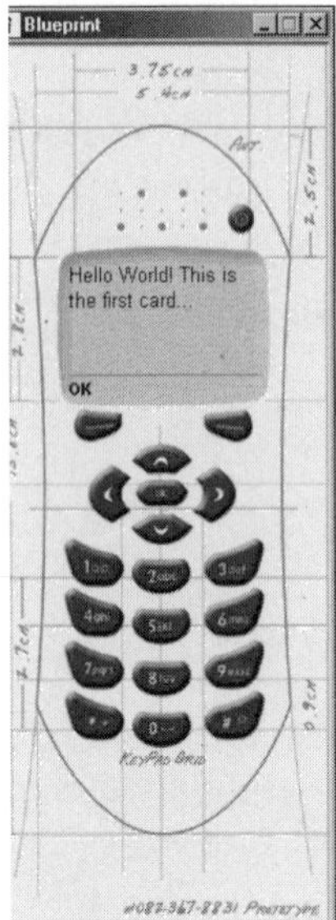

Figure 13-3 The HelloWorld.wml example shown on the Nokia developer's kit.

an airline flight. Dialing a phone number and saying the words, "American Airlines; November 1, 2001; Flight 349" is much easier than fumbling with a tiny Web browser and slow Internet connection. The VoiceXML standard replaces proprietary call center technologies. Developers can use XML to specify spoken grammars that are tuned for use in their applications.

TVWeb

The TVWeb initiative was begun to integrate television and Web technologies. This project is still in its beginning stages and no official specifications have been released yet by the W3C. The working group was formed in response to a June 1998 W3C workshop on "Television and the Web." The group formed to establish global standards to govern the application of Web technologies, such as HTML, CSS, and XML, to the television.

The first two deliverables of the TVWeb project will be to adapt the HTML and CSS specifications to the television. These languages will be paired down in some areas and extended in others to make it well suited to TV. URL formats will also need to be changed to address TV content. Other topics to be considered by the group include authoring guidelines, TV metadata, device profiling, timing control and synchronization, and VCR controls. Look for standards to emerge from this group in the coming years.

Extending the Golf Reservation System Application to Wireless Devices

In this section we will extend the Golf Reservation System application client from Chapter 9 to the wireless realm. The Golf Reservation System client interfaces a large database of golf courses and tee times via Web Services. Users will be able to browse local courses and reserve tee times. We will look at design requirements from the project and discuss two implementation strategies. The first strategy will use the Mobile Explorer Developer's Toolkit. The second approach will extend the Golf Reservation System client XSLT skins library to add a WML front-end to the application.

Application Requirements

The wireless front-end to the Golf Reservation System application will include the following features. (Please note that this is not a production system and should be used only for illustrative purposes.)

- Users can search for golf courses against the same criteria available in the PC browser interface (name, city, state, zip code, and country).
- Users can review the results of their selection in a list format.
- Users can link to a specific golf course and review information about that course. This information will include the course's name, address, and price.
- Users will be able to request a tee time on a specific date.
- The mobile client will display all available tee times for the date chosen by the user.
- The user will be able to select an open tee time and reserve the spot.
- The mobile client will report the success or failure of the operation to the user. If the reservation is approved, the client will thank the user and display detailed information about the approved tee time.

Using the Mobile Explorer Developer's Toolkit

We will use the Mobile Explorer Developer's Toolkit to take a first crack at implementing our Golf Reservation System mobile client. Installing the toolkit will immediately update the .NET Developer Studio with two new features.

> **Note** The toolkit is available at Microsoft's MSDN Web site at *http://www.microsoft.com/mobile/phones/default.asp.*

The first feature is the ability to add Mobile Web Forms to your project. Mobile Web Forms are similar to regular Web forms in structure and design. The Mobile Web Form wizard creates two new files for you: the .aspx file that contains the display logic and the .aspx.cs file that contains the super class definition that the Web forms page extends. The class definition declares protected properties that are available for use in the .aspx page and contains all server-side event handling subroutines.

The second key feature of the Mobile Explorer Developer's Toolkit is its cell phone emulator. You can use the emulator to test your programs without the need for an expensive phone. The emulator, which can emulate two styles of phone, makes iterative development and testing a snap.

Upon creating a new Mobile Web Form, the .NET Developer Studio presents you with a palette of controls suitable for use on WAP clients. These include simple form-input controls such as text boxes and selection lists. The wireless control palette also provides more advanced controls such as expression validators and a calendar control. The calendar control is particularly useful for creating a cross-device interactive date chooser.

In this example we will use the Mobile Explorer Toolkit to implement the first three functions in our requirements list: the search, search results, and course detail pages. We will create a single Mobile Web Form that contains three separate forms (one for each view). The Mobile Toolkit will handle breaking the forms down into individual WML decks and cards that will be retrieved by the WAP client. The Mobile Toolkit will also handle the creation and maintenance of the server-side session state by using URL session identifiers.

Dragging a Mobile Toolkit control from the palette onto a form adds a corresponding XML element from the *mobile* namespace to the .aspx page source. For example, these two lines of source code appear in the search.aspx page:

```
<mobile:Label id=Label1 runat="server">Course Name</mobile:Label>
<mobile:TextBox id=GCName runat="server"></mobile:TextBox>
```

The first line adds a label to the form with the description *Course Name*. The second line creates an adjoining text input control with the id *GCName*. The value inserted into this control can be submitted to the server or referenced by WMLScript within the page.

Why does the Mobile Toolkit use its own XML markup language instead of using WML directly? The answer is that any mobile .aspx page can be used to create either WML or HTML, depending on the capabilities of the client device. The following excerpt from Search.aspx shows the source code behind the mobile search form.

```
<body xmlns:mobile="Mobile Web Form Controls">
  <mobile:form id="Search" runat="server">
    <P>
      <mobile:Label id="Label1" runat="server">Course Name</mobile:Label>
      <mobile:TextBox id="GCName" runat="server"></mobile:TextBox>
      <mobile:Label id="Label2" runat="server">City</mobile:Label>
      <mobile:TextBox id="GCCity" runat="server"></mobile:TextBox>
      <mobile:Label id="Label3" runat="server">State</mobile:Label>
      <mobile:TextBox id="GCState" runat="server"></mobile:TextBox>
      <mobile:Label id="Label4" runat="server">Country</mobile:Label>
      <mobile:TextBox id="GCCountry" runat="server"></mobile:TextBox>
      <mobile:Label id="Label5" runat="server">Postal Code</mobile:Label>
      <mobile:TextBox id="GCPostalCode" runat="server"></mobile:TextBox>
      <mobile:Command id="Command1" runat="server">Search</mobile:Command>
    </P>
  </mobile:form>
  . . .
   </body>
```

Whenever this page is requested the .NET runtime environment will determine the type and capabilities of the client. The DLL created out of the Mobile Web Form will format the result document using the most appropriate markup language. The Mobile Web Form produces the following output when called by a mobile device:

```
<?xml version="1.0"?>
<!DOCTYPE wml PUBLIC "-//WAPFORUM//DTD WML 1.1//EN"
"http://www.wapforum.org/DTD/wml_1.1.xml">
<wml>
  <head>
    <meta http-equiv="Cache-Control" content="max-age=0"/>
  </head>
  <card id="Search">
    <do type="prev" label="Back">
      <prev/>
    </do>
    <p>
      <do type="accept" label="Search"><go
href="search.aspx?__ufps=631317431691368096" method="post">
<postfield name="__EVENTTARGET" value="Command1"/>
          <postfield name="GCName" value="$(GCName:noesc)"/>
          <postfield name="GCCity" value="$(GCCity:noesc)"/>
          <postfield name="GCState" value="$(GCState:noesc)"/>
          <postfield name="GCCountry" value="$(GCCountry:noesc)"/>
```

```
        <postfield name="GCPostalCode" value="$(GCPostalCode:noesc)"/>
      </go></do>
      Course Name
      <br/>
      <input name="GCName"/>
      City
      <br/>
      <input name="GCCity"/>
      State
      <br/>
      <input name="GCState"/>
      Country
      <br/>
      <input name="GCCountry"/>
      Postal Code
      <br/>
      <input name="GCPostalCode"/>
    </p>
  </card>
</wml>
```

Notice that the Mobile Web Form runtime generated all the WML form logic necessary to post back to the server. It transformed each *<mobile:TextBox>* element into two WML elements: an *<input>* element to capture user input and a *<postfield>* element to send the result back to the server. However, the results are quite different when an HTML browser hits the page.

```
<html>
  <body>
    <form id="Search" name="Search" method="post"
action="Search.aspx?__ufps=631317428385013792">
      <input type="hidden" name="__EVENTTARGET" value="">
      <input type="hidden" name="__EVENTARGUMENT" value="">
      <script language=javascript>
<!--
        function __doPostBack(target, argument){
          var theform = document.Search
          theform.__EVENTTARGET.value = target
          theform.__EVENTARGUMENT.value = argument
          theform.submit()
        }
// -->
      </script>
      <span>Course Name</span><br>
      <input style="" name="GCName"/><br>
      <span>City</span><br>
      <input style="" name="GCCity"/><br>
      <span>State</span><br>
      <input style="" name="GCState"/><br>
```

```
        <span>Country</span><br>
        <input style="" name="GCCountry"/><br>
        <span>Postal Code</span><br>
        <input style="" name="GCPostalCode"/><br>
       <input style="" name="Command1" type="submit" value="Search"/><br>
    </form>
  </body>
</html>
```

The result this time is a perfectly well-formed HTML page that uses a traditional form to collect and submit user input. Obviously, the Mobile Web Form framework does a good job of sorting out what kind of markup language should be returned to a particular client. Therefore, if Mobile Web Forms support HTML clients as well as WML clients, why not use them to build your entire UI? The problem is that the Mobile Web Forms only support controls that will work correctly on small devices. The richness of your full-blown HTML client will suffer if you use Mobile Web Forms to develop it.

Another caveat about Mobile Web Forms is that both the .aspx file and the code-behind .aspx.cs file must extend the *System.Web.UI.MobileControls.MobilePage* class. This limitation means that you cannot directly reuse regular Web form content that you've already developed to drive your Mobile Web Forms. Without restructuring your business logic, you might need to rewrite a significant amount of content when building your Mobile Web Forms.

Now let's take a closer look at the search.aspx.cs file (the complete code is available on the CD), which implements the *MobileWebForm1* class that the Search.aspx file extends. Much of this file is autogenerated by the .NET Developer Studio as controls are added to the form. All the control declarations at the top of the file were added this way.

```
using System;
using System.Collections;
using System.ComponentModel;
using System.Data;
using System.Drawing;
using System.Web;
using System.Web.Mobile;
using System.Web.SessionState;
using System.Web.UI;
using System.Web.UI.MobileControls;
using System.Web.UI.WebControls;
using System.Web.UI.HtmlControls;
namespace MobileClient
{
  /// <summary>
  /// Summary description for MobileClient.
  /// </summary>
```

```
  public class MobileWebForm1 : System.Web.UI.MobileControls.MobilePage
  {
    protected System.Web.UI.MobileControls.Form Search;
    protected System.Web.UI.MobileControls.TextBox GCName;
    protected System.Web.UI.MobileControls.Label Label2;
    protected System.Web.UI.MobileControls.TextBox GCCity;
    protected System.Web.UI.MobileControls.TextBox GCState;
    protected System.Web.UI.MobileControls.Label Label3;
    protected System.Web.UI.MobileControls.Label Label4;
    protected System.Web.UI.MobileControls.TextBox GCCountry;
    protected System.Web.UI.MobileControls.Label Label5;
    protected System.Web.UI.MobileControls.TextBox GCPostalCode;
    protected System.Web.UI.MobileControls.List gcList;
    protected System.Web.UI.MobileControls.Form SearchResult;
    protected System.Web.UI.MobileControls.Command Command1;
    protected System.Web.UI.MobileControls.Form GolfCourseDetail;
    protected System.Web.UI.MobileControls.Label Label6;
    protected System.Web.UI.MobileControls.Label Label7;
    protected System.Web.UI.MobileControls.Label Label8;
    protected System.Web.UI.MobileControls.Label Label9;
    protected System.Web.UI.MobileControls.Label DetailName;
    protected System.Web.UI.MobileControls.Label DetailDescription;
    protected System.Web.UI.MobileControls.Label Label1;
    protected System.Web.UI.MobileControls.Call DetailTelephone;
    protected System.Web.UI.MobileControls.TextView DetailAddress;
```

The *GolfCourseService* variable is declared as a protected instance property. Taking this step avoids the performance penalty inherit in reinstantiating this variable each time the client calls an event handler.

```
    protected localhost.GolfCourseService gs;
    public MobileWebForm1()
    {
      Page.Init += new System.EventHandler(Page_Init);
    }
```

The GolfCourseService variable is instantiated once on page load here.

```
    private void Page_Load(object sender, System.EventArgs e)
    {
      gs = new localhost.GolfCourseService();
    }
    private void Page_Init(object sender, EventArgs e)
    {
      //
      // CODEGEN: This call is required by the ASP.NET Windows Form
//Designer.
      //
      InitializeComponent();
    }
```

```
    #region Web Form Designer generated code
    /// <summary>
    /// Required method for Designer support - do not modify
    /// the contents of this method with the code editor.
    /// </summary>
    private void InitializeComponent()
    {
      this.Command1.Click += new
System.EventHandler(this.Command1_Click);
      this.Search.Activate += new
System.EventHandler(this.Form1_Activate);
      this.gcList.ItemCommand += new System.Web.UI.
MobileControls.ListCommandEventHandler(this.gcList_ItemCommand);
      this.Load += new System.EventHandler(this.Page_Load);
    }
    #endregion
    private void Form1_Activate(object sender, System.EventArgs e)
    {
    }
    private void Command1_Click(object sender, System.EventArgs e)
    {
```

This method is called when the user clicks the Submit button on the search form. The method sets the form's *ActiveForm* property to the *SearchResult* form. This action will cause the search result page to be returned to the client upon the completion of this method call. Next the method gathers the search criteria entered by the user and prepares the arguments required by the *FindGeneric()* Web method.

```
      this.ActiveForm = SearchResult;
      String[] fields = new String[5];
      String[] values = new String[5];
      fields[0] = "name";
      string nameValue = Request.QueryString.Get("name");
      if (nameValue == null || nameValue == "")
      {
        nameValue = "*";
      }
      values[0] = nameValue;
      fields[1] = "city";
      string cityValue = Request.QueryString.Get("city");
      if (cityValue == null || cityValue == "")
      {
        cityValue = "*";
      }
      values[1] = cityValue;
      fields[2] = "state";
      string stateValue = Request.QueryString.Get("state");
```

```
    if (stateValue == null || stateValue == "")
    {
      stateValue = "*";
    }
    values[2] = stateValue;
    fields[3] = "country";
    string countryValue = Request.QueryString.Get("country");
    if (countryValue == null || countryValue == "")
    {
      countryValue = "*";
    }
    values[3] = countryValue;
    fields[4] = "postalCode";
    string postalCodeValue = Request.QueryString.Get("postalCode");
    if (postalCodeValue == null || postalCodeValue == "")
    {
      postalCodeValue = "*";
    }
    values[4] = postalCodeValue;
```

The method calls the *FindGeneric()* Web method associated with the GolfCourseService Web Service. The Web method returns an array of *GolfCourse* objects, which are inserted into a List control on the Mobile Web Form.

```
    localhost.GolfCourse[] gc = gs.FindGeneric(fields,values);
    for (int i=0 ; i < gc.Length; i++)
    {
      gcList.Items.Add(gc[i].name);
      gcList.Items[i].Value = gc[i].id.ToString();
    }
  }
```

This event handler is called when the user selects one of the items from the list of golf courses returned by the search. Once again, the event handler switches the *ActiveForm* to the GolfCourseDetail page. The handler calls the *GetCourseDetail()* Web method to retrieve detailed information about the selected *GolfCourse*. The course details are loaded into the label controls that have been pasted on the *GolfCourseDetail* form. Finally the Call control's *PhoneNumber* property is set to the value of the course's telephone property. This feature lets the user autodial the golf course with the click of a button.

```
  private void gcList_ItemCommand(object source, System.Web.UI.
MobileControls.ListCommandEventArgs e)
  {
    ActiveForm = GolfCourseDetail;
    String gcid = e.ListItem.Value;
    localhost.GolfCourse gc = gs.GetCourseDetail(gcid);
    DetailName.Text = gc.name;
```

```
            DetailDescription.Text = gc.description;
            DetailAddress.Text = gc.address.street+"<br/>
"+gc.address.city+", "+gc.address.state+" "+gc.address.
postalCode+"<br/>"+gc.address.country;
            DetailTelephone.PhoneNumber = gc.telephone;
        }
    }
}
```

Now let's move on to the search.aspx page. The forms themselves are straightforward. They are created by dragging Mobile Web Forms controls onto the page and editing their properties. Figure 13-4 shows how the Mobile Web Form looks after all of the controls have been inserted and positioned correctly.

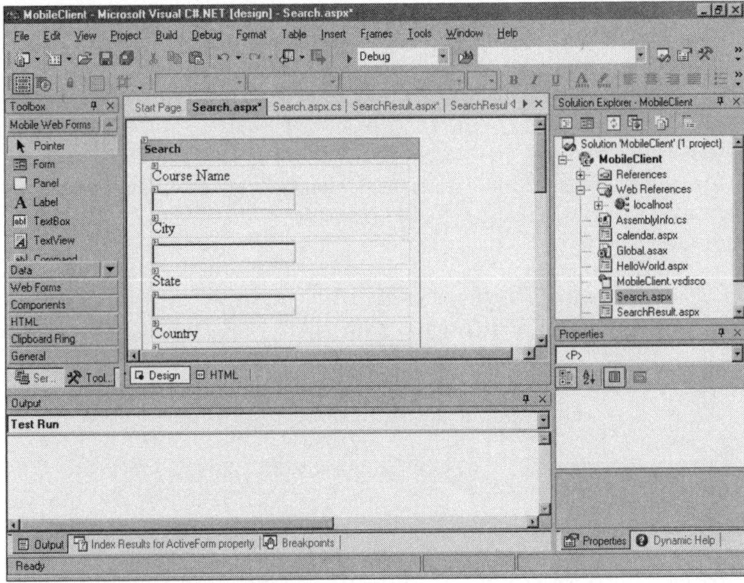

Figure 13-4 All three Golf Reservation System Mobile Web Forms using the Mobile Explorer Toolkit.

Next we look at the XML source that lies beneath the GUI form display. Search.aspx contains all the mobile XML code the .NET Developer Studio creates for us.

```
<%@ Register TagPrefix="mobile" Namespace="System.Web.UI.
MobileControls" Assembly="System.Web.Mobile" %>
<%@ Page language="c#" Codebehind="Search.aspx.cs" Inherits=
"MobileClient.MobileWebForm1" AutoEventWireup="false" %>
<meta content="Microsoft Visual Studio 7.0" name="GENERATOR">
```

```
<meta content="C#" name="CODE_LANGUAGE">
<meta content="Mobile Web Page" name="vs_targetSchema">
```

The search form contains the labels and text boxes needed to query the Golf Reservation System golf course database.

```
<body xmlns:mobile="Mobile Web Form Controls">
  <mobile:form id="Search" runat="server">
    <P>
      <mobile:Label id="Label1" runat="server">Course Name
</mobile:Label>
      <mobile:TextBox id="GCName" runat="server"></mobile:TextBox>
      <mobile:Label id="Label2" runat="server">City</mobile:Label>
      <mobile:TextBox id="GCCity" runat="server"></mobile:TextBox>
      <mobile:Label id="Label3" runat="server">State</mobile:Label>
      <mobile:TextBox id="GCState" runat="server"></mobile:TextBox>
      <mobile:Label id="Label4" runat="server">Country</mobile:Label>
      <mobile:TextBox id="GCCountry" runat="server"></mobile:TextBox>
      <mobile:Label id="Label5" runat="server">Postal Code
</mobile:Label>
      <mobile:TextBox id="GCPostalCode" runat="server"></mobile:TextBox>
      <mobile:Command id="Command1" runat="server">Search</mobile:Command>
    </P>
  </mobile:form>
```

The *SearchResult* form contains only a single mobile List control, *gcList*. The list is populated at runtime with the results of the *FindGeneric()* Web method call.

```
  <mobile:form id="SearchResult" runat="server">
    <P>
      <mobile:List id="gcList" Runat="Server"></mobile:List>
    </P>
  </mobile:form>
```

The *GolfCourseDetail* form displays detailed information about a specific golf course. Notice the inclusion of the *<mobile:Call>* element. This control allows you to take advantage of a cell phone's dialing capability.

```
  <mobile:form id="GolfCourseDetail" runat="server">
      <P>
    <mobile:Label id="Label6" runat="server" Font-Bold="True">
Name
</mobile:Label>
    <mobile:Label id="DetailName" runat="server"></mobile:Label>
    <mobile:Label id="Label7" runat="server" Font-Bold="True">
Description
</mobile:Label>
    <mobile:Label id="DetailDescription" runat="server">
</mobile:Label>
```

```
    <mobile:Label id="Label8" runat="server"
Font-Bold="True">Address</mobile:Label>
    <mobile:TextView id="DetailAddress" runat="server"></mobile:
TextView>
    <mobile:Label id="Label9" runat="server" Font-Bold="True">
Telephone
</mobile:Label>
    <mobile:Call id="DetailTelephone" runat="server">
</mobile:Call>
    </P>
  </mobile:form>
</body>
```

Figure 13-5 shows how this implementation looks on the Mobile Explorer.

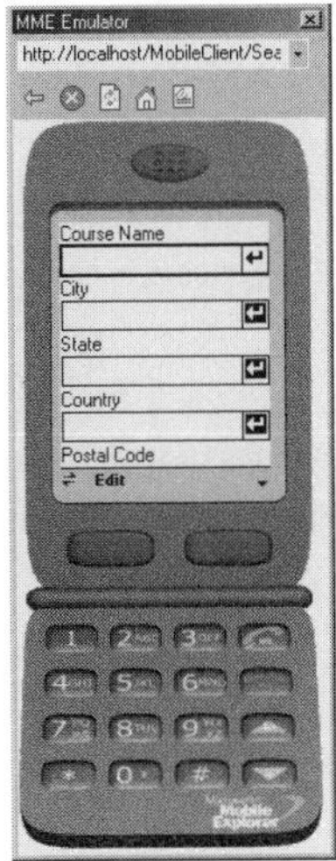

Figure 13-5 The course search form shown inside the Mobile Explorer.

Certainly, the Mobile Explorer Toolkit is a useful tool for developing mobile clients quickly. The only downside to the product is that it forces you to assemble an entirely new library of Mobile Web Forms, often duplicating code you've written for other clients. This duplicate code base might become difficult to maintain over time.

Using The Golf Reservation System Skin Architecture

We will now explore an alternative implementation of a mobile Golf Reservation System client, one that uses the application's "skins" approach to UI design to incrementally provide WML support. The project requires two steps:

1. Modify the controller.asp script to detect the browser type. If it supports WAP, load the WML skin and use it instead of the HTML skin for transforming the page content. The controller must also be sensitive to the content type of the result document. It must be set to *text/vnd.wap.wml.*

2. Create a new XSLT skin targeted at WAP devices and place it in the /xslt directory of the Golf Reservation System client application. This skin will only produce WML code.

The required modification to the controller.asp script is trivial. We just need to add the following lines of code before loading the XSLT document:

```
If InStr(1,Request.ServerVariables("ALL_HTTP"),"text/vnd.wap.wml",1) Then
  skin = "mobile"
  Response.ContentType = "text/vnd.wap.wml"
End if
```

This code will force the controller to load the "mobile" skin to perform the final page transformation, and sets the MIME type of the response to the correct setting. Note the over simplicity of the browser detection algorithm used here. It is used for demonstration purposes only.

The Golf Reservation System XML content follows an object-based schema instead of a presentation-based schema, which makes repurposing small devices much easier. Because our content and presentation layers are cleanly divided this way, we will be able to implement a mobile interface without making any changes to the content layer. Thus, the code that interacts with the business layer of the application will remain intact and will not need to be replicated.

To begin we need to create templates for structural elements in the Golf Reservation System client schema that are common to multiple pages. These elements include *<document>*, *<header>*, *<section>*, *<form>*, *<input>* (text and hidden), *<choice>*, *<option>*, *<properties>*, and *<property>*. With the exception of *form*, the templates in the WML skin will be extensively reduced versions of their HTML counterparts. We don't need to worry about building complicated tables to handle layout or aesthetic style sheets to make the client look pretty. We are striving for functionality, first and foremost.

As we see in Mobile.xsl, the *<document>* and *<header>* transformation templates act as little more than placeholders.

```
<xsl:stylesheet xmlns:xsl="http://www.w3.org/1999/XSL/Transform"
version="1.0">
  <xsl:output method="xml" omit-xml-declaration="yes" indent="no"
encoding="" doctype-public="-//WAPFORUM//DTD WML1.2//EN"
doctype-system="http://www.wapforum.org/DTD/wml12.dtd" />
```

```
<xsl:template match="document">
  <wml>
    <xsl:apply-templates />
  </wml>
</xsl:template>
<xsl:template match="header">
  <xsl:apply-templates />
</xsl:template>
<xsl:template match="header/title"></xsl:template>
<xsl:template match="header/description"></xsl:template>
```

The *form* template needs to accommodate the WML form posting semantics. First it needs to create *<do>* and *<go>* tags to submit the form back to the server. The template must also create a *<postfield>* element for each *<input>* element that appears in the source document. Textual input fields are also transformed into WML *<input>* elements (Hidden inputs require no WML *<input>* element; their values are inserted directly into the corresponding *<postfield>* element).

```
<xsl:template match="form">
  <card id="{generate-id()}" title="{.//header/title}">
    <do type="accept" label="Accept">
      <go href="{@action}">
        <xsl:for-each select=".//input|.//choice">
          <postfield name="{@name}">
            <xsl:choose>
              <xsl:when test="@type='hidden'">
                <xsl:attribute name="value">
                  <xsl:value-of select="@value" />
                </xsl:attribute>
              </xsl:when>
              <xsl:otherwise>
                <xsl:attribute name="value">$(<xsl:value-of
select="@name" />)</xsl:attribute>
              </xsl:otherwise>
            </xsl:choose>
          </postfield>
        </xsl:for-each>
      </go>
    </do>
    <p>
      <fieldset title="{section/header/title}">
        <xsl:apply-templates select="section/*" />
      </fieldset>
    </p>
  </card>
</xsl:template>
<xsl:template match="section[count(courseDetail) = 0]">
```

```
    <card id="{generate-id()}" title="{header/title}">
      <p>
        <xsl:apply-templates />
      </p>
    </card>
  </xsl:template>
  <xsl:template match="view">
    <xsl:apply-templates />
  </xsl:template>
  <xsl:template match="properties">
    <xsl:apply-templates />
  </xsl:template>
  <xsl:template match="property">
    <xsl:value-of select="@description" />
    <xsl:apply-templates />
    <br />
  </xsl:template>
```

Here the template creates the WML input elements. The *<choice>* element in the source document is converted into a WML *<select>* element.

```
  <xsl:template match="input[@type='text']">
    <input name="{@name}" value="{@value}" />
  </xsl:template>
  <xsl:template match="choice">
    <select name="{@name}">
      <xsl:apply-templates />
    </select>
  </xsl:template>
  <xsl:template match="option">
    <option value="{@value}"><xsl:value-of select="." /></option>
  </xsl:template>
```

These general tags are actually enough to handle the course search view. Let's load the view into the Mobile Explorer and see the results. The URL should be *http://localhost/GolfReservationSystemClient/controller.asp?view=courseSearch*.

Figure 13-6 shows the course search page on the Mobile Explorer.

Transforming the courseSearchResult view is just as easy. All we have to do is match the template and create hyperlinks for all of the *<courseListItem>* elements. We will also show the course's city and state below each link.

> **Note** WAP devices have a larger degree of freedom when rendering WML than browsers do when rendering HTML. Various device restrictions make strict specification of presentation rules impossible. For example, identical *<select>* lists can appear entirely different on two different WAP devices.

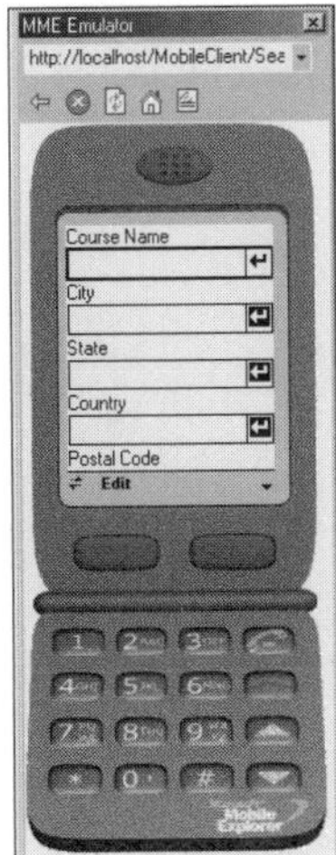

Figure 13-6 The course search view shown in the Mobile Explorer.

```
<xsl:template match="courseList">
  <xsl:apply-templates />
</xsl:template>
<xsl:template match="courseListItem">
  <a href="controller.asp?view=courseDetail&amp;id={id}">
    <xsl:value-of select="name" />
  </a>
  <br />
  <xsl:value-of select="city" />, <xsl:value-of select="state" /><br />
</xsl:template>
```

Figure 13-7 illustrates what this page looks like on a mobile device. The page can be reached by submitting the course search form.

The *courseDetail* template is responsible for laying out specific course information in an organized fashion. This template will create a deck with two cards in it: one to show the course's information and another to request a tee time. The *courseDetail* XML content page contains another section describing hole yardages and difficulty, but the mobile skin ignores this information as it is too big to display neatly on a small screen and is not critical to the page.

The teetime reservation form is generated automatically by the *<form>* transformation logic we looked at earlier. We do need to supply a link to the card, though. The *<do>* and *<go>* tags in the following listing prepare the hyperlink in the result WML document.

```
<xsl:template match="section[count(courseDetail) > 0]">
  <xsl:apply-templates select="courseDetail" />
</xsl:template>
<xsl:template match="courseDetail">
  <xsl:for-each select="courseDetailBlock">
    <xsl:if test="courseItem[@type != 'holeInfo']">
```

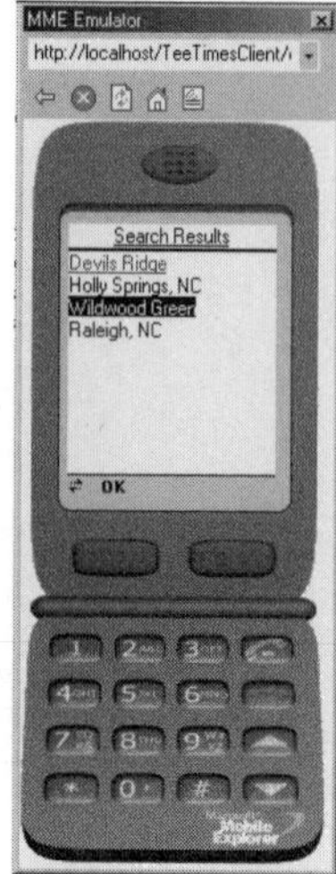

Figure 13-7 The course search result view shown in the Mobile Explorer.

```
        <card id="{generate-id()}" title="{@description}">
          <do type="accept" label="Schedule a Tee Time">
            <go href="#{generate-id(//form)}" />
          </do>
          <xsl:apply-templates />
        </card>
      </xsl:if>
      <xsl:if test="form">
        <xsl:apply-templates />
      </xsl:if>
    </xsl:for-each>
  </xsl:template>
```

Here we extract the name and address of the course for viewing.

```
  <xsl:template match="courseItem[@type='courseInfo']">
    <p>
      <xsl:value-of select="//courseDetail/name" /><br />
      <xsl:value-of select="address/address1" /><br />
      <xsl:value-of select="address/city" />, <xsl:value-of
select="address/state" /> <xsl:value-of select="address/postalCode"/>
<br />
      <xsl:value-of select="address/country" />
    </p>
  </xsl:template>
```

Figure 13-8 shows the tee time scheduling screen.

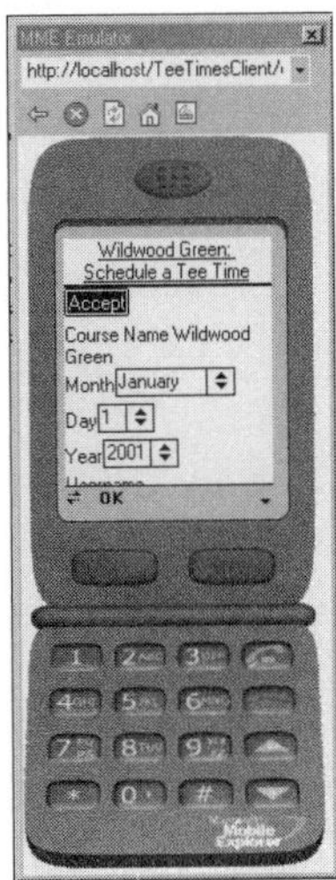

Figure 13-8 The tee time scheduling screen, the second card in the course detail deck, shown on the Mobile Explorer.

The teeTimes view displays a list of available tee times on the selected date and course. Each list item is wrapped inside a hyperlink to the scheduleTeeTime page. The anchor tag passes in all the tee time, course, and golfer information.

```
<xsl:template match="view[teeTimes]">
  <xsl:apply-templates select="teeTimes" />
</xsl:template>
<xsl:template match="teeTimes">
  Choose a time below<br />
  <xsl:for-each select="teeTime">
    <xsl:if test="not(taken)">
      <a href="controller.asp?view=scheduleTeeTime&amp;golferId={../
golferId}&amp;courseId={../courseId}&amp;teeTime={teeTimeSystem-
Date}"><xsl:value-of select="date" /> - <xsl:value-of select="time"
/></a><br />
    </xsl:if>
  </xsl:for-each>
</xsl:template>
```

The teeTimes view is shown in Figure 13-9.

Finally, assuming everything posts correctly, we show the user a friendly note of success. The teeTimeDetail page also reviews the tee time's logistics.

```
<xsl:template match="teeTimeDetail">
  A new tee time has been created for:<br/>
  <xsl:value-of select="golfer/name"/><br/>
  <xsl:value-of select="course/name"/><br/>
```

Figure 13-9 The viewTeeTimes page shown in the Mobile Explorer.

```
    <xsl:value-of select="date"/> <xsl:value-of select="time"/>
  </xsl:template>
</xsl:stylesheet>
```

The primary advantage to the skin approach is that we get to preserve all the logic and content that went into the original HTML client. We did not need to rewrite any XML Web services code, as all our interaction was limited to the data coming out of the content layer.

For a production system this example should be extended to use the Content Adapter model discussed earlier. This action would provide maximum flexibility and control over style and layout. The Golf Reservation System client skin library can be augmented with new transformations for voice or television.

Conclusion

In this chapter we explored cross-device application development opportunities. We examined the trials and tribulations inherent in developing cross-device applications as well as some design patterns that ease development stress. We looked at a few popular specifications on the Internet today. Finally we built two completely different implementations of the same wireless client. The first used the Mobile Explorer Toolkit. The second utilized the application's native skins architecture to deliver the same functionality.

Cross-device programming is a hot issue for developers today. For those of you who are just beginning to design the next generation of enterprise XML applications, make sure that you keep client extensibility in the forefront of your thinking. The design decisions you make today might save you or cost you months of development time later.

The logical partitioning of your application is a critical factor in code reusability. Just as your business logic should be able to support different types of clients, so should your UI model. By using XML and XSLT to separate the content and presentation layers of your UI, you can actually plug in new presentation rules to support new and different devices. In Chapter 14 we will see how legacy systems can be integrated into modern computing environments using XML.

Part IV

XML and Microsoft .NET

14

More About SOAP

In previous chapters we exposed you to SOAP and showed how you can use it as part of your toolkit of Web Service applications. Because SOAP is a critical component of the .NET Framework and other Web-centric technologies, you should understand not only the syntax and semantics, but also the principles behind it. In this chapter we will go to another level of detail on SOAP—how it works, how messages look, and how you can work directly with them.

In the chapter we will cover the details of the SOAP *<Envelope>*, breaking it down into the *<Header>*, *<Body>*, and encoding methods for sending SOAP messages between servers. We will spend some time using SOAP by building a few small clients and servers and showing you how they communicate and work.

The SOAP *<Envelope>*

A SOAP message is an XML document that consists of a mandatory SOAP *<Envelope>* root element, an optional *<Header>* element, and a mandatory *<Body>* element. Think of this as an envelope used to mail a letter to a friend across the country. The SOAP envelope is analogous to the paper envelope—it displays the routing directions and the letter. The routing directions, or address (to and from) are represented in the *<Header>* element of a SOAP message. The letter itself is contained in the SOAP body. All this information is necessary to successfully transmit data via the SOAP protocol. Let's begin with a short example to illustrate how SOAP works.

In Listing 14-1, skeletal_soap.xml, we show you a skeletal SOAP message with placeholders for the *<Header>* and the *<Body>* information. In a real message these would contain the necessary routing information and *payload* of the exchange.

Listing 14-1 skeletal_soap.xml: A skeletal SOAP message.

```
<SOAP-ENV:Envelope
    xmlns:SOAP-ENV="http://schemas.xmlsoap.org/soap/envelope/"
    SOAP-ENV:encodingStyle="http://schemas.xmlsoap.org/soap/
encoding/">
  <SOAP-ENV:Header>
    <!-- (optional) Contextual header information... -->
  </SOAP-ENV:Header>
  <SOAP-ENV:Body>
    <!-- Serialized object information... -->
  </SOAP-ENV:Body>
</SOAP-ENV:Envelope>
```

You can also define your own subelements within a SOAP *<Envelope>*, but they must be namespace-qualified and must come after the *<Body>* element.

All SOAP messages should include the proper namespace declarations so that SOAP applications can correctly process the messages. The SOAP specification defines two namespaces.

- The SOAP *<Envelope>* is identified by the *http://schemas.xmlsoap.org/soap/envelope/* namespace URI, which defines the standard SOAP elements and attributes used in the *<Envelope>*.
- The SOAP default encoding rules and data types are identified by the *http://schemas.xmlsoap.org/soap/encoding/* namespace URI.

The *encodingStyle* Global Attribute

The *SOAP-ENV:encodingStyle* attribute is used to indicate the rules used to encode the information in a particular SOAP message. The default SOAP encoding rules are identified by the *http://schemas.xmlsoap.org/soap/encoding/* namespace. Like any other use of namespaces, this attribute can appear on any element. When applied, its scope is restricted to that element's contents and all child elements not overriding the attribute with their own namespace. Note that no default encoding is defined for a SOAP message, so you must include the *encodingStyle* attribute at least once in your SOAP messages. Typically you will include it in the *<Envelope>* declaration itself, as shown in the skeletal_soap.xml example.

> **Note** You can define your own encoding rules. In that case you will need to define your own schema.

Now let's turn to the *<Header>* and *<Body>* elements and take a closer look at how they are specified and work.

<Header>

The *<Header>* element is used to encapsulate information that is not tied to a specific method invocation, but provides context information instead. Typical examples of *<Header>* element usage are security, transaction management, and payment information.

There are several rules defined by the SOAP specification for the *<Header>* element. These are as follows:

- The *<Header>* element is optional, but, if present, must be the first child element in an *<Envelope>*.
- The *<Header>* element must use the SOAP encoding rules unless the header specifies a different set of rules. This requirement is accomplished using the *SOAP-ENV:encodingStyle* attribute.
- All *<Header>* subelements must be namespace-qualified.
- The *<Header>* element can contain the *SOAP-ENV:mustUnderstand* attribute.

To show you an example of how to use the *<Header>* element, let's make a request to an imaginary language-translation service that translates arbitrary words, paragraphs, or both from one specified spoken language to another. Furthermore, suppose this is a pay-by-use service and that you will need to provide valid authentication information with every request. Listing 14-2, soap_header.xml, shows the *<Header>* section of such as a request.

Listing 14-2 soap_header.xml: Some example SOAP *<Header>* elements.

```
<SOAP-ENV:Envelope
    xmlns:SOAP-ENV="http://schemas.xmlsoap.org/soap/envelope/"
```

(continued)

Listing 14-2 *continued*

```
    SOAP-ENV:encodingStyle="http://schemas.xmlsoap.org/soap/
encoding/"/>
  <SOAP-ENV:Header>
    <a:Authentication xmlns:a="some-URI">
      <UserID>foo</UserID>
      <Password>an-encoded-password</Password>
    </a:Authentication>
  </SOAP-ENV:Header>
  <SOAP-ENV:Body>
    <!-- Serialized object information... -->
  </SOAP-ENV:Body>
</SOAP-ENV:Envelope>
```

In this example we added a custom Authentication *<Header>* element with a *<UserID>* and *<Password>* subelements providing the necessary authentication information. Notice that, as required by the specification, we have properly namespace-qualified our Authentication *<Header>* element.

mustUnderstand

In soap_header2.xml the concept of authentication is critical to the success of the service request. To ascertain that a service understands and can process a specific *<Header>* element, you can tag specific *<Header>* elements with the *SOAP-ENV:mustUnderstand* attribute. This attribute indicates to a SOAP-compliant processor that the associated *<Header>* element is critical to the processing of the method call and that, if for some reason the remote SOAP processor is unable to understand or handle it, you don't want the method call to execute. In this case the SOAP processor should simply reject the method call.

The value of the *SOAP-ENV:mustUnderstand* attribute is either *1* or *0*. Listing 14-3, soap_header2.xml, shows the SOAP message soap_header.xml updated to include the *SOAP-ENV:mustUnderstand* attribute.

Listing 14-3 soap_header2.xml: The *SOAP-ENV:mustUnderstand* attribute.

```
<SOAP-ENV:Envelope
  xmlns:SOAP-ENV="http://schemas.xmlsoap.org/soap/envelope/"
  SOAP-ENV:encodingStyle=" http://schemas.xmlsoap.org/soap/encoding/">
  <SOAP-ENV:Header>
    <a:Authentication xmlns:a="some-URI" SOAP-ENV:mustUnderstand="1">
      <UserID>foo</UserID>
      <Password>an-encoded-password</Password>
    </a:Authentication>
  </SOAP-ENV:Header>
  <SOAP-ENV:Body>
    <!-- Serialized object information... -->
  </SOAP-ENV:Body>
</SOAP-ENV:Envelope>
```

With this change in our SOAP message, a SOAP-compliant processor will attempt to process this message only if it can understand our custom *<Authentication>* *<Header>* element. If not, the processor will reject this message with a proper response message.

actor

When a SOAP message travels from the originator to its ultimate destination, it does not need to travel directly between the source and destination. The message might pass through a set of SOAP intermediaries, each receiving and then forwarding the message to the next receiver, until the message reaches its final destination. Therefore, not all parts of a SOAP message can be intended for the final destination; some must be directed at one or more of the intermediaries on the message path.

You use the *SOAP-ENV:actor* attribute to allow a SOAP message to indicate that *<Header>* information that is relevant to a specific recipient. The value of the *SOAP-ENV:actor* attribute is a URI used to identify the recipient of the *<Header>* element. The SOAP specification defines a special URI, *http://schemas.xmlsoap.org/soap/actor/next*, to indicate that the associated *<Header>* element is intended for the first SOAP recipient, intermediary or otherwise.

Now that we have covered the *<Header>* and how it is used to provide contextual information for a SOAP message, we can discuss the *<Body>* element of the SOAP message.

<Body>

The *<Body>* element contains the actual serialized data of the method call itself. The *<Body>* element is also used for a method call's response, which will either be the information related to a valid request or a SOAP fault if the call failed. The SOAP specification defines three types of *<Body>* elements.

- The Call *<Body>* contains the information required for a method call, such as the method name and arguments.
- The Response *<Body>* contains the response information for a successful method call.
- The Fault *<Body>* contains the fault code and other information for an unsuccessful method call.

Call *<Body>*

The first child element of a Call *<Body>* element is labeled according to the method name. The embedded elements are the serialized arguments, with each argument named according to the method signature. For example, in our

TranslationService method call we might have a method with the following C# signature:

```
string TranslateText(string SourceLanguage, string TargetLanguage, string Text)
```

Imagine that you now want to make the following equivalent method call:

```
// Translates an English sentence to French
string translatedText = TranslateText( "en", "fr", "I speak French" );
```

Listing 14-4, soap_callbody.xml, shows the equivalent SOAP message.

Listing 14-4 soap_callbody.xml: A SOAP Call *<body>* example.

```
<SOAP-ENV:Envelope
    xmlns:SOAP-ENV="http://schemas.xmlsoap.org/soap/envelope/"
    SOAP-ENV:encodingStyle="http://schemas.xmlsoap.org/soap/encoding/">
  <SOAP-ENV:Header>
    <a:Authentication xmlns:a="some-URI" SOAP-ENV:mustUnderstand="1">
      <UserID>foo</UserID>
      <Password>an-encoded-password</Password>
    </a:Authentication>
  </SOAP-ENV:Header>
  <SOAP-ENV:Body>
    <m:TranslateText xmlns:m="some-URI">
      <SourceLanguage>en</SourceLanguage>
      <TargetLanguage>fr</SourceLanguage>
      <Text>I speak French</Text>
    </m:TranslateText>
  </SOAP-ENV:Body>
</SOAP-ENV:Envelope>
```

Note that, just as in the *<Header>* element, the *<Body>* element is namespace-qualified as required by the SOAP specification. You don't need to qualify the argument elements, though, because they are assumed to be identified by the enclosing method element's namespace.

Response *<Body>*

A Response *<Body>* contains information the SOAP service returns to the caller after a successful method call. Listing 14-5, soap_responsebody.xml, shows you a sample successful response to the method call made in soap_callbody.xml.

Listing 14-5 soap_responsebody.xml: A SOAP Rresponse *<Body>* example.

```
<SOAP-ENV:Envelope
    xmlns:SOAP-ENV="http://schemas.xmlsoap.org/soap/envelope/"
```

```
    SOAP-ENV:encodingStyle="http://schemas.xmlsoap.org/soap/encoding/">
  <SOAP-ENV:Body>
    <m:TranslateTextResponse xmlns:m="some-URI">
      <Text_fr>Je parle Francais</Text_fr>
    </m:TranslateTextResponse>
  </SOAP-ENV:Body>
</SOAP-ENV:Envelope>
```

The custom is to append the word *Response* to the original method name. As in the method call, the name of the return arguments, which in soap_responsebody.xml is *<Text_fr>*, is immaterial as far as the specification is concerned. Finally the element is namespace qualified.

<Fault> in *<Body>*

When a method call fails, instead of a normal Response *<Body>*, a SOAP processor will use a *<Fault>* occurrence in the *<Body>* of the response SOAP message, as shown in Listing 14-6, soap_faultbody.xml.

Listing 14-6 soap_faultbody.xml: A SOAP *<Fault>* in the *<Body>*.

```
<SOAP-ENV:Envelope
    xmlns:SOAP-ENV="http://schemas.xmlsoap.org/soap/envelope/"
    SOAP-ENV:encodingStyle="http://schemas.xmlsoap.org/soap/encoding/">
  <SOAP-ENV:Body>
    <SOAP-ENV:Fault>
      <faultcode>SOAP-ENV:Server</faultcode>
      <faultstring>Translator not found</faultstring>
      <detail xmlns:e="some-URI">
        <e:ErrorCode>
          014
        </e:ErrorCode>
        <e:ErrorMsg>
          No suitable Translator found for "en-fr" translation
        </e:ErrorMsg>
      </detail>
    </SOAP-ENV:Fault>
  </SOAP-ENV:Body>
</SOAP-ENV:Envelope>
```

The SOAP specification requires that *<Fault>* be the first child element of the *<Body>* element.

The SOAP specification defines the following subelements.

- The mandatory *<faultcode>* element can be used by applications for algorithmically identifying the fault. The *<faultcode>* values are defined in an extensible manner similar to the 1xx, 2xx, 3xx, and other basic HTTP response codes. However, instead of numeric values the codes are defined as XML qualified names. A . (dot) character separates fault values indicating that what is to the left of the dot is a more generic fault code value than the value to the right (for example, *Client.Authentication*). SOAP specification defines the fault codes shown in Table 14-1.

- The mandatory *<faultstring>* element provides a human-readable explanation of the fault.
- The optional *<faultactor>* element provides information about what caused the fault to happen within the *message path*.
- The mandatory *<detail>* element provides application-specific error information related to the processing of the *<Body>* element. A detail entry, which is an immediate child element of the *<detail>* element, must be a fully qualified name.

Table 14-1 Fault Codes Defined in SOAP

Fault code	Meaning
VersionMismatch	The processor found an invalid namespace for the SOAP element.
MustUnderstand	A *<Header>* element tagged with the *SOAP-ENV:mustUnderstand* attribute was either not understood or properly obeyed by the processor.
Client	The message was incorrectly formed or did not contain the appropriate information to succeed. Generally, the message should not be sent again without a change correcting the problem.
Server	The message could not be processed by the processor for reasons not directly attributable to the contents of the message itself, but to the processing of the message.

In addition to these standard elements you can include your own custom subelements within the *<Fault>* element as long as they are namespace-qualified.

Encoding

So far we've only talked about the structure of a SOAP message and none of the other aspects. In this section we will look at how the arguments associated with a method call are actually encoded, from both a simple and a compound perspective, as well as array encoding and default values.

As we mentioned earlier, you can use the *SOAP-ENV:encodingStyle* attribute to indicate the encoding style used. SOAP's standard encoding style, the schema of which can be found at *http://schemas.xmlsoap.org/soap/encoding/,* is modeled after typical programming languages like C or C++ (and now C#).

> **Note** The SOAP specification also refers to the "XML Schema Part 1: Structures" *(www.w3.org/TR/xmlschema-1/)* and "XML Schema Part 2: Datatypes" *(www.w3.org/TR/xmlschema-2/)* for encoding message schemas.

In SOAP you can use only elements to represent values within a *<Body>*. Using attributes for passing arguments is illegal. The elements must be either a simple scalar type defined by the "XML Schema Part 2: Datatypes" specification, an element that encapsulates a SOAP array, or an element whose structure you can ascertain with the help of a schema.

Simple Types

Simple types, such as integers, strings, and floating-point numbers, can be directly encoded in SOAP as elements. The schema for the elements defines the actual types, not the actual SOAP message. In soap_callbody.xml, for example, the three string arguments of the method *TranslateText* are encoded directly as simple types.

Compound Types

Compound types are encoded like structures or even classes in some programming languages, like C++, C#, and Java. The containing element holds the structure information while the elements within are either simple types or other compound types. The containing element is always qualified with a namespace, while all the contained elements are unqualified. For example, examine the simple C structure in Listing 14-7, c_struct.txt.

Listing 14-7 c_struct.txt: A simple C structure.

```
struct tag_Person
{
  string name;
  double age;
} Person;
```

Now take a look at the corresponding encoded SOAP in Listing 14-8, compound_type.xml.

Listing 14-8 compound_type.xml: An example of Compound_Encoding.

```
<Person xmlns="someURI">
  <name>Harry</name>
  <age>37</age>
</Person>
```

Array

The final major type of SOAP encoding is array, which builds on the other types to produce ordered lists of simple or compound datatypes. The special *SOAP-ENC:arrayType* attribute is used to distinguish a SOAP array from other datatypes. Listing 14-9, array_type.xml, shows how an array of the *Person* datatype declared in compound_type.xml can be encoded in SOAP.

Listing 14-9 array_type.xml: A SOAP array example

```
<PersonList SOAP-ENC:arrayType="Person[2]">
  <Person>
    <name>Tom</name>
    <age>27</age>
  </Person>
  <Person>
    <name>Dick</name>
    <age>30</age>
  </Person>
</PersonList>
```

Default Values

Some programming languages, such as C++ and C#, have the concept of *default arguments*. SOAP by itself does not specify default values. However, with the help of proper schema definition, a SOAP consumer can automatically omit default arguments from the message packet. On the receiving side, a SOAP processor can also automatically invoke the remote method itself with the appropriate default information inserted.

Now that you've learned how to construct SOAP messages, the following section will show you how to implement applications that can produce and consume them.

Developing SOAP Applications

The Microsoft .NET Framework provides comprehensive support for developing both SOAP clients/consumers and servers/producers using a variety of different technologies and methods. In this section we take a closer look at some ways you can develop SOAP applications.

Using Web Services

ASP.NET offers excellent support for creating XML Web services based on SOAP servers. Support for XML Web services provided through ASP.NET is contained within .asmx files, which are text file, similar to .aspx files. Over the next few pages we will look at some simple examples that build both clients and servers. These, of course, will interact as XML Web services.

The Server

Listing 14-10, hello.asmx, shows a simple Web Service .asmx file. This program returns nothing more than a string to the requesting client.

Listing 14-10 hello.asmx: A simple Web Service.

```
<%@ WebService Language="C#" Class="Hello" %>
using System;
using System.Web.Services;
public class Hello : WebService
{
  [WebMethod] public String SayHello( String Name )
  {
    return ( "Hello " + Name );
  }
}
```

Note This particular Web Service is implemented in C#, but you could also use any other language built on the .NET Framework, such as Visual Basic .NET.

The first line in hello.asmx declares that this is an XML Web service and sets the language (C# in this case) used to implement this service. Next we import the necessary *System.Web.Services* namespace and declare that our class is derived from the *WebService* base class. Finally, to indicate that our *GetStockPrice* method will be accessible as part of the service, we marked it with the *[WebMethod]* custom attribute.

To allow client applications to consume this Web Service you need to create a proxy class DLL. This DLL wraps all the code and calls in the associated Web Service into a simple method call similar to a COM object. With the .NET Framework SDK, you will use a tool called WebServiceUtil.exe to perform this task. Use the following:

```
WebServiceUtil /c:proxy /pa:http://localhost/Hello.asmx?SDL /n:nsHello
```

to generate a proxy class called Hello.cs. Next you need to compile this Hello.cs into a DLL with the following command:

```
csc /out:Hello.dll /t:library /r:system.data.dll /r:system.web.
services.dll /r:system.xml.serialization.dll Hello.cs
```

The Client

The Hello Web Service hello.asmx can be accessed by a client that knows how to consume SOAP messages. For example, we will develop a simple ASP.NET page that will consume this XML Web service. This is shown in Listing 14-11.

Listing 14-11 hello_client.aspx: An ASP.NET consumer of the Hello Web Service.

```
<%@ Import Namespace="nsHello" %>
<html>
  <script language="VB" runat="Server">
    Sub Greeting( Src as Object, E as EventArgs )
      Dim h as New Hello
      lblGreeting = h.SayHello( edtName.Value )
    End Sub
  </script>
  <body>
    <form runat="SERVER">
      Your name:
      <ASP:INPUT ID="edtName" TYPE="Text" RUNAT="Server"/><br/>
      <ASP:BUTTON TEXT="Say Hello!" onclick="Greeting"/>
    </form>
    <h1 ID="lblHello" RUNAT="Server"/>
  </body>
</html>
```

This ASP.NET first imports the Hello Web Service proxy class DLL using the namespace defined. The actual call to the Hello Web Service happens in the *Greeting* procedure in HelloClient.aspx. The *New* keyword is used to instantiate the object. Once instantiated, we simply invoke the *SayHello* method to do the job.

For those of you familiar with Microsoft programming methodology and technology, this approach is similar to how you would use a COM object. Behind the scene the Hello Web Service proxy class DLL packages our method call within a SOAP message and transfers it over the wire to our Hello Web Service for processing. The Hello Web Service then parses the SOAP message and invokes the *SayHello* method. The result is then packaged as a SOAP response message and once again passed by the proxy class DLL. And all this time you think you are making only a simple method call!

Using Components

Microsoft .NET Remoting enables developers to produce remote-managed, native COM/COM+, and serviced components (managed components serviced by COM+ services). What makes the .NET implementation important is that these components are built as SOAP endpoints from any process, including console applications, GUI applications, Windows NT Services, and IIS. Because they are built on this standard for communication, the number of applications that ultimately can interface with the components is increased, and chances for success in heterogeneous environments are improved.

In this section we will look at both server and client components. We are going to step through some simple examples to show you how they work and how easy it is to build them.

The Server

Listing 14-12, hello.cs, shows a simple .NET managed component that exposes the *SayHello* method that will be accessible through SOAP.

In hello.cs the *Hello* object is remotable by extending the *MarshalByRefObject* class. This allows the *SayHello* method to be accessed through SOAP when this object is exposed by a suitable host that acts as the SOAP endpoint. An example of such a host is shown in Listing 14-13, hello_host.cs, which builds a service waiting for a connection. The user is able to stop the service, as you will see near the end of the listing, by pressing the Enter key.

Listing 14-12 hello.cs: A managed component.

```
using System;
namespace nsHello
{
  /* Define the Service */
  public class Hello : MarshalByRefObject
  {
    /* This method will be called remotely by our client */
    public String SayHello( String Name )
    {
      return ( "Hello " + Name );
    }
  }
}
```

Listing 14-13 hello_host.cs: Creates a service listening for connections.

```
using System;
using System.IO;
using System.Runtime.Remoting;
using System.Runtime.Remoting.Channels.HTTP;
public class HelloHost
{
  public static void Main( String[] args )
  {
    /* Manually load the http channel. 1099 is the port # */
    ChannelServices.RegisterChannel( new HTTPChannel( 1099 ) );
    /* Register the wellknown server type */
    RemotingServices.RegisterWellKnownType(
      "nsHello",                          // Assembly
      "nsHello.Hello",                    // Full type name
      "host/Hello.soap",                  // URI
      WellKnownObjectMode.Singleton );    // Object Mode
    /* Wait until the user wants to exit */
   Console.WriteLine( "Listening for requests - Press ENTER to exit" );
    String keyState = Console.ReadLine();
  }
}
```

In the .NET Framework messages are transported to and from remote objects through *Channels Objects* that encapsulate the underlying network protocols used to make the client/server communication. In hello_host.cs we indicated that we would like to use the built-in HTTP Channel, which transports messages using the SOAP protocol.

Now that we have our code in these two files, we must compile them. As mentioned earlier, this task can be accomplished using the csc C# compiler. A simpler process, however, would be to use a makefile. These files contain a list of compilation commands used to compile one or more code files. For our example, use Listing 14-14, makefile, to build hello.cs and hello_host.cs.

Listing 14-14 makefile: A makefile for building hello_host.cs and hello.cs.

```
all: hello_host.exe hello.dll
hello_host.exe: hello_host.cs
   csc /r:System.Runtime.Remoting.dll hello_host.cs
hello.dll: hello.cs
   csc /t:library hello.cs
```

The Client

Now that the server is created we can focus on the client. Listing 14-15, hello_client.cs, is an application that will consume the service exposed by our hello_host.cs to invoke the *SayHello* remote method.

Listing 14-15 hello_client.cs: A consumer of the hello_host.cs.

```
using System;
using System.Runtime.Remoting;
using System.Runtime.Remoting.Channels.HTTP;
using nsHello;
public class HelloClient
{
  public static Main( String[] args )
  {
    /* Obtain a Proxy to the SOAP URL */
    Hello h = (Hello)Activator.GetObject(
                typeof(Hello),
                "http://localhost:1099/host/Hello.soap" );
    /* The following occurs over SOAP to HelloHost */
    Console.WriteLine( h.SayHello( "Dick" ) );
  }
}
```

In hello_client.cs we used the *GetObject* method instead of the new keyword to activate the remote object because we are manually activating the object. Had we used the remote configuration file, we could have used the *New* keyword to the same effect.

As with the previous example, we need to compile the application. The following command will build the hello_client.cs:

```
csc /r:System.Runtime.Remoting.dll /r: hello.dll hello_client.cs
```

Once both the server and client applications are built, we can test them by first running hello_host.exe in one window and then running hello_client.exe in another. You will see hello_client.exe respond with the message "Hello Dick" on your screen.

Conclusion

In this chapter we've looked at what a SOAP message is and how you can use it to encode object information for making remote method calls. We also looked briefly at how you can use the powerful technologies provided by the .NET Framework to build distributed applications using SOAP, and we've included some quick examples to get your started.

By now you should feel more comfortable with SOAP and how it works. There is much more to know, so if your thirst for more information is great, we highly recommend you read through the W3C Note defining SOAP. You can use SOAP for many different projects, even if you're not implementing a true .NET-compatible system.

In the next chapter we will look into BizTalk Server, a suite of applications introduced in Chapter 7. We will cover several of the tools that come with BizTalk Server to help you define and orchestrate your entire messaging process.

15

Exploring BizTalk Server

Back in Chapter 7 you were introduced to the Microsoft BizTalk Framework and the Microsoft BizTalk Server in relation to messaging XML documents back and forth between servers and potentially companies. In that chapter you learned about the details of the Microsft .NET Framework and how to use the BizTalk Messaging Manager and BizTalk Document Tracking applications to control and route your messages. But as we alluded to then, that only touches the tip of the iceberg of what the BizTalk Server includes and can be used for.

BizTalk Server 2000 became available toward the end of 2000. Honestly, many people do not fully grasp the potential of BizTalk Server and what it truly is. If you think of this server and its corresponding applications, which we will cover shortly, from a functional standpoint, it becomes clearer as to how it can be used within most companies today.

For instance, if you perform any exchanges with an external partner or affiliate companies or internally, BizTalk Server could be used to manage, track, and greatly reduce the technology and manpower overhead needed to maintain such relationships. Also, if you have data stored in legacy systems, be it mainframes or file systems, BizTalk Server can be used to integrate with these applications, abstracting and hosting the functionality needed to access the data they store. This capability allows you to avoid any "rip-and-replace" approaches you might have previously considered. BizTalk Server can become the legs your legacy data needs to walk again.

These are just a few examples of how BizTalk Server can be used within a company. In this chapter we are not only going to extend our discussion on the server portion from Chapter 7, we are also going to introduce you to the other tools that come with BizTalk Server. These tools help you do everything from create the necessary models of your data in an XML-based format to orchestrating the entire business process of processing data. We are going to begin the discussion, however, on how to get started with BizTalk, and then move into specific information about this suite of products.

Getting Started with BizTalk

Part of deploying BizTalk within a given environment is understanding the BizTalk Server suite of tools, how to prepare your system, and how to apply BizTalk within an enterprise (that is, what problems it solves). Over the next few pages we will cover all these topics.

The BizTalk Server Suite of Tools

When you first heard of BizTalk Server you probably thought it was strictly a server product, possibly like Exchange Server, whose sole purpose is to message and coordinate the exchanging of BizTalk-compatible documents. For those of you who have done your homework and researched BizTalk Server, you know this is not true. In addition to the server portion of the application, BizTalk Server comes with several other tools that will help you do everything from creating your data models to describing your messaging workflow.

Although we have already covered two of these tools in Chapter 7 and we will be covering three others in this chapter, we have included the list of applications present in the BizTalk Server product here.

- BizTalk Administration Tool: This tool is used to manage multiple BizTalk Servers, allowing you to load balance processing between them.
- BizTalk Messaging Manager: Covered in Chapter 7, this application allows you to set up the proper ports and channels to route documents through your system.
- BizTalk Document Tracking: Also covered in Chapter 7, this Web-based tool allows you to obtain up-to-date reports and status on messages going through the system.

- BizTalk Editor: Allows you to create BizTalk-compatible models of the data you plan on exchanging within your system, such as purchase or shipping orders.
- BizTalk Mapper: Because your system will most likely have to support a variety of different representations of data (that is, you might support a *<Company>* element and a partner might support *<CompanyName>*), this application can be used to map one schema to another. Additionally, it contains *functoids*, which allow you to perform operations, such as mathematical or string manipulation, while transforming data.
- BizTalk Orchestration Designer: This tool is used to outline and define the entire work flow for documents entering the system, such as how they are processed and by what other applications, if any.

Preparing Your System

Before we dive into the BizTalk Server and the accompanying suite of tools, we want to point out that BizTalk Server has some specific installation requirements. Unlike some of the other Windows .NET products, BizTalk Server has several important dependencies that must be addressed before installing the product. Failure to properly equip your system with these applications will prevent installation. The requirements are

- Microsoft Windows 2000 Professional, Server, or Advanced Server with Service Pack 1 or higher
- Microsoft Visio Standard Edition SR-1 (to use Orchestration Designer)
- Microsoft SQL Server 7 with Service Pack 2 or Microsoft SQL Server 2000

For those of you working to understand BizTalk Server and related applications that do not meet these requirements, Microsoft has made evaluation versions of the necessary software available so you can perform a proper trial. The following locations show you where you can obtain these evaluation copies:

- Windows 2000 Advanced Server (must order CD): *http://microsoft.order-1.com/ Win2kEDK*
- Windows 2000 Service Pack 1 (to update your version of Windows 2000 Professional or Server): *http://www.microsoft.com/windows2000/downloads/servicepacks/sp1*
- BizTalk Server: *http://www.microsoft.com/biztalk/evaluation/trial*

- SQL Server 2000: *http://www.microsoft.com/sql/evaluation/trial/2000*
- Visio: *http://www.microsoft.com/office/visio/evaluation*

> **Note** Want to avoid downloading hundreds of megabytes to obtain the trials of these products? You can follow the link to order the Microsoft E-Commerce Evaluation Kit from *http://www.microsoft.com/biztalk/evaluation/trial*. It's less than $10 U.S. This kit contains 120-day trial versions of Windows 2000 Advanced Server, BizTalk Server 2000, Microsoft Commerce Server 2000, SQL Server, and Visio 2000.

Finally, if you simply don't have the time to install and test the software yourself, you can contact Microsoft's Professional Consultation team or a Certified Partner to pay for a pilot. They estimate roughly two weeks to get you installed, configured, and up and running so that you can demo the application in a real-world environment.

Now that we have a full understanding of what is needed to get BizTalk Server off the ground, let's talk about the problems it solves. These will affect your planning and implementation of the product, as well as expose you to some of its abilities.

Applying BizTalk

Unless you are working for a purely dot-com business, you probably have data residing in some older databases, within flat files, or some other kind of resource. If this is the case, and you still have a need to access, update, and utilize this data, you might find yourself faced with performance and flexibility issues. The systems simply might not have the proper methods of accessing and using the data that today's applications or design approaches desire.

Over the next few sections we will discuss the applications of BizTalk and how it can be used to solve these problems. We are going to talk about enterprise application integration, business-to-business integration, and business process automation.

> **Note** Want to read some real-world case studies of how BizTalk has been used to implement and solve these various instances? Check out *http://www.microsoft.com/biztalk/evaluation/casestudies* for a list of companies and documents on their implementation.

Enterprise Application Integration

In a technical world where many of the programming youth assume Java, C#, or some scripting language represents all coding methods and that the oldest systems are Windows 98 or Windows NT 4, those who have been around know this is not always the case. Finding COBOL, mainframes, a Virtual Memory System (VMS), running on a Virtual Address extension (VAX), and text-based screens acting as the backbone to entire businesses can be common, especially in large corporations. These legacy systems are still widely used, deployed, and depended on for ongoing business activities. So, how is a company supposed to stay abreast of the latest technology and systems needed to survive if the core and heart behind it is a 20-year-old system?

Above all else, the BizTalk Server suite of applications is designed for ease of integration. It uses industry standards heavily, like XML, SOAP, and the BizTalk Framework. It provides the tools, which we covered earlier, that allow you to create XML representations of your legacy data and coordinate the access and use of that data. This reduces your integration into the legacy system to simply supporting some basic XML features, and BizTalk will take it from that point.

Legacy data, however, is not the only data with which BizTalk can communicate and integrate. In fact, for those of you creating XML-based Web Services such as those covered in this book, you might find BizTalk Server to be the perfect system to handle the processing of messages.

Business-to-Business Integration

Integrating with internal applications is only one type of implementation you will find useful for BizTalk Server. Many businesses are building XML-based systems or interfaces that allow them to automate their communication and exchanges with customer and partner companies. For instance, a retail company might obtain product descriptions and pricing in an XML format. Using BizTalk Server's ability to map one schema to another, you can feel confident that you can design your own schemas to be true to your business, and yet not limit your integration with partners.

The BizTalk Mapper literally allows you to draw lines between elements and attributes of two schemas, with the result being an XSLT style sheet that will transform your partner's data into a format native to your system. This capability allows you to build an XML-based solution within your company, yet give it a long lifetime because supporting new data models involves nothing more than sitting down and drawing out the mapping.

Business Process Automation

Business process automation has moved to the forefront in today's economy. If a company is able to reduce the time and costs associated with a particular task, such as checking inventory, its revenue might not increase, but it has decreased its bottom line costs and thus increased profits. Automation can be an extremely important and cost-saving move for the company, especially when finances are a major concern.

What the BizTalk Orchestration Designer, along with the Messaging Manager, brings to the table is a visually-based method for designing, improving, and automating these business process. With these tools you are able to design entire processes for handling incoming requests or documents and create schedule files that can be processed and tracked.

Schema Creation with BizTalk Editor

The first step in integrating with a legacy application, assuming you have an XML-based architecture in place, is to create the necessary model of the legacy data. This task is accomplished using the BizTalk Editor, show in Figure 15-1, which is capable of creating specifications or schemas that can be adhered to by your applications.

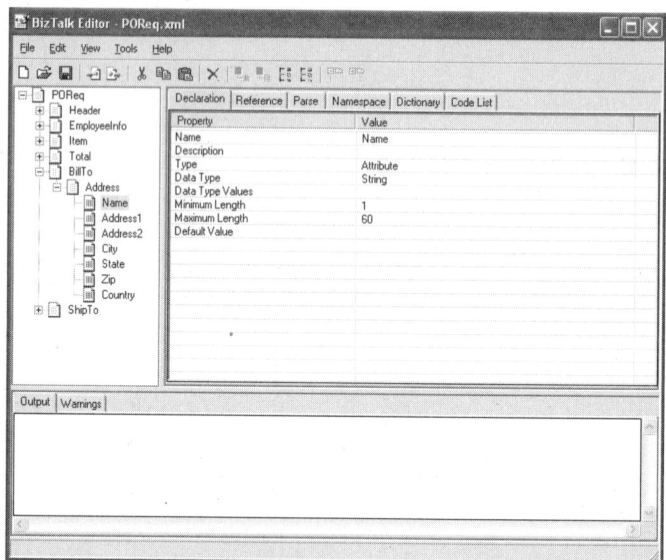

Figure 15-1 The BizTalk Editor.

To create a specification or schema within the Editor, you can either choose to create a new specification from the File menu or schema, or you can import (under the Tools menu) an existing well-formed XML document, a DTD, or an

XDR Schema. If you choose to create a new schema, you will be presented with the dialog box shown in Figure 15-2 where you can create a Blank Specification, Electronic Data Interface For Administration, Commerce and Transport (EDIFACT), X12, or XML specification or schema. Furthermore, some common templates under EDIFACT, X12, or XML can help get you started.

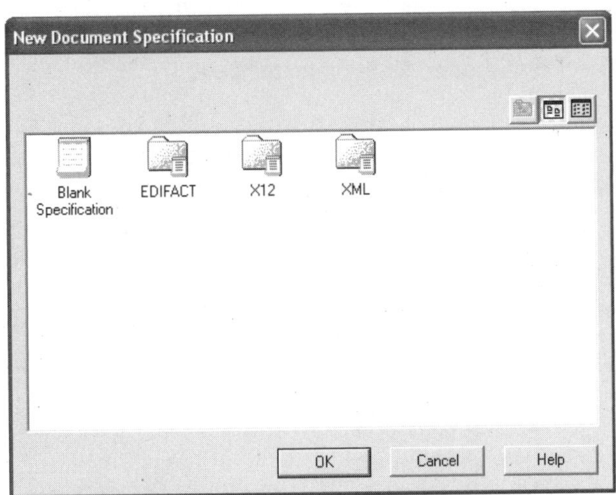

Figure 15-2 Various options for creating schemas.

As an example, let's say you have built an issue submission system used by your technical support team. It's a simple system that contains only the customer name, phone, e-mail address, and issue. In Listing 15-1 you can see an example of the information collected.

Listing 15-1 allen-support.xml: A sample submission document of an issue.

```
<?xml version="1.0" ?>
<support>
  <name>Allen Wyke</name>
  <phone>999.555.1212</phone>
  <email>mspress@microsoft.com</email>
  <issue>Unable to access Web-based email account</issue>
</support>
```

Now if you use the Import feature under the Tools menu of the Editor and then selecting Well-Formed XML Instance as the type, we can import and build a specification off of this document. The Editor does all the hard work of converting it to the necessary XDR-based format used by the other BizTalk applications. Go ahead and do this and save the file under the name support.xml, which we have included here as Listing 15-2.

> **Note** If you are interested in controlling other aspects of these specifications, be sure to check the Help files. They will outline how you can specify recurring elements, default values, and so forth—many of the features that schema-based XML dialects allow.

Listing 15-2 support.xml: The specification for our support submission data.

```
<?xml version="1.0"?>
<!-- Generated by using BizTalk Editor on Thu, Aug 02 2001 10:35:27
PM -->
<!-- Microsoft Corporation (c) 2000 (http://www.microsoft.com) -->
<Schema name="support"
        b:BizTalkServerEditorTool_Version="1.0"
        b:root_reference="support"
        b:standard="XML"
        xmlns="urn:schemas-microsoft-com:xml-data"
        xmlns:b="urn:schemas-microsoft-com:BizTalkServer"
        xmlns:d="urn:schemas-microsoft-com:datatypes">
  <b:SelectionFields/>
  <ElementType name="support" content="eltOnly" model="closed">
    <b:RecordInfo/>
    <element type="name" maxOccurs="*" minOccurs="0"/>
    <element type="phone" maxOccurs="*" minOccurs="0"/>
    <element type="email" maxOccurs="*" minOccurs="0"/>
    <element type="issue" maxOccurs="*" minOccurs="0"/>
  </ElementType>
  <ElementType name="phone" content="textOnly" model="closed">
    <b:FieldInfo/>
  </ElementType>
  <ElementType name="name" content="textOnly" model="closed">
    <b:FieldInfo/>
  </ElementType>
  <ElementType name="issue" content="textOnly" model="closed">
    <b:FieldInfo/>
  </ElementType>
  <ElementType name="email" content="textOnly" model="closed">
    <b:FieldInfo/>
  </ElementType>
</Schema>
```

Before we move on, let's assume that you have a partner who will be sending you support cases as well, but that they have a slightly different format. They have broken down the *<name>* element into first and last names. In Listing 15-3 we have included such an example.

Listing 15-3 partner-support.xml: A sample support submission from a partner.

```
<?xml version="1.0" ?>
<support>
  <name>
    <first>Allen</first>
    <last>Wyke</last>
  </name>
  <phone>999.555.1212</phone>
  <email>mspress@microsoft.com</email>
  <issue>Unable to access Web-based email account</issue>
</support>
```

After we import this in the Editor and save it in a file called partner.xml (Listing 15-4), we end up with the following.

Listing 15-4 partner.xml: A specification outlining the partner's format for support submissions.

```
<?xml version="1.0"?>
<!-- Generated by using BizTalk Editor on Thu, Aug 02 2001 10:45:06
PM -->
<!-- Microsoft Corporation (c) 2000 (http://www.microsoft.com) -->
<Schema name="support"
        b:BizTalkServerEditorTool_Version="1.0"
        b:root_reference="support"
        b:standard="XML"
        xmlns="urn:schemas-microsoft-com:xml-data"
        xmlns:b="urn:schemas-microsoft-com:BizTalkServer"
        xmlns:d="urn:schemas-microsoft-com:datatypes">
  <b:SelectionFields/>
  <ElementType name="support" content="eltOnly" model="closed">
    <b:RecordInfo/>
    <element type="name" maxOccurs="*" minOccurs="0"/>
    <element type="phone" maxOccurs="*" minOccurs="0"/>
    <element type="email" maxOccurs="*" minOccurs="0"/>
    <element type="issue" maxOccurs="*" minOccurs="0"/>
  </ElementType>
  <ElementType name="phone" content="textOnly" model="closed">
    <b:FieldInfo/>
  </ElementType>
```

(continued)

Listing 15-4 *continued*

```
  <ElementType name="name" content="eltOnly" model="closed">
    <b:RecordInfo/>
    <element type="first" maxOccurs="*" minOccurs="0"/>
    <element type="last" maxOccurs="*" minOccurs="0"/>
  </ElementType>
  <ElementType name="last" content="textOnly" model="closed">
    <b:FieldInfo/>
  </ElementType>
  <ElementType name="issue" content="textOnly" model="closed">
    <b:FieldInfo/>
  </ElementType>
  <ElementType name="first" content="textOnly" model="closed">
    <b:FieldInfo/>
  </ElementType>
  <ElementType name="email" content="textOnly" model="closed">
    <b:FieldInfo/>
  </ElementType>
</Schema>
```

While this quick example certainly does not display all the powers of the BizTalk Editor, it showed you how to perform some basic tasks and how to get started. In the next section we will build on the example and show you how to support the partner's specification by mapping it to yours.

Transformations in BizTalk Mapper

Defining models for the data you will be working with is a huge step toward implementing your integration, but it's only the first piece. Because you might need to support different models and structures that come from partners, customers, and so forth, you will want to map their models to your internally supported ones. The BizTalk Mapper, shown in Figure 15-3, is used for this task. It allows you to import two specifications and draw the necessary lines between them to map from one to the other. The result is an XSLT style sheet that can be used by the server during processing.

Now launch BizTalk Mapper and we will step through mapping the partner.xml schema to our support.xml schema to show you how the application works. Once it's open start a new mapping (from the File menu). When the Select Source Specification Type dialog appears, click the Local Files option and browse to the partner.xml file. Once you have it selected you will see the Select Destination Specification Type dialog. Follow the same steps and select the support.xml specification.

Instead of starting at the top and addressing the "name" formatting problem, let's take care of the *<phone>*, *<email>*, and *<issue>* mappings. To map these ele-

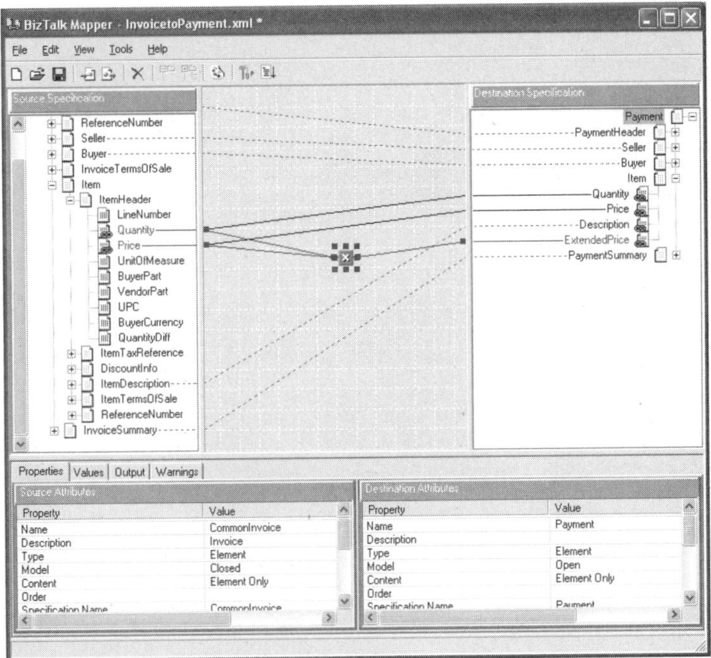

Figure 15-3 The BizTalk Mapper.

ments in the partner.xml specification to the support.xml specification, simply drag one to the corresponding other. Figure 15-4 shows us mapping the *<issue>* elements together after we have already mapped the *<phone>* and *<email>* elements.

To handle the mapping for the customer name we are going to use a *functoid* to concatenate the *<first>* and *<last>* elements together into a single *<name>*. To apply a functoid you need to open the Functoid Palette from the View menu. When the palette opens you will notice it is already populated with items for basic String, Mathematical, Logical, Date/Time, Conversion, Scientific, Cumulative, Database, and Advanced operations. This option can be extremely powerful because it allows you to, for instance, combine or simply use the results of functions like a database query in your mapping.

For our example you will need to drag the Concatenate String operator to your workspace. Once you have it placed you can draw a line from the *<first>* element to this functoid and then a line from the *<last>* element to it. Finally you can connect the functoid to the *<name>* element on our support.xml destination specification. Once complete, the results, which can be seen in Figure 15-5, are stored in an XML file we will call mapping.xml (Listing 15-5). As you can see, it contains all the information about the specifications, their mapping, even the script needed to perform the functoid Concatenate operation.

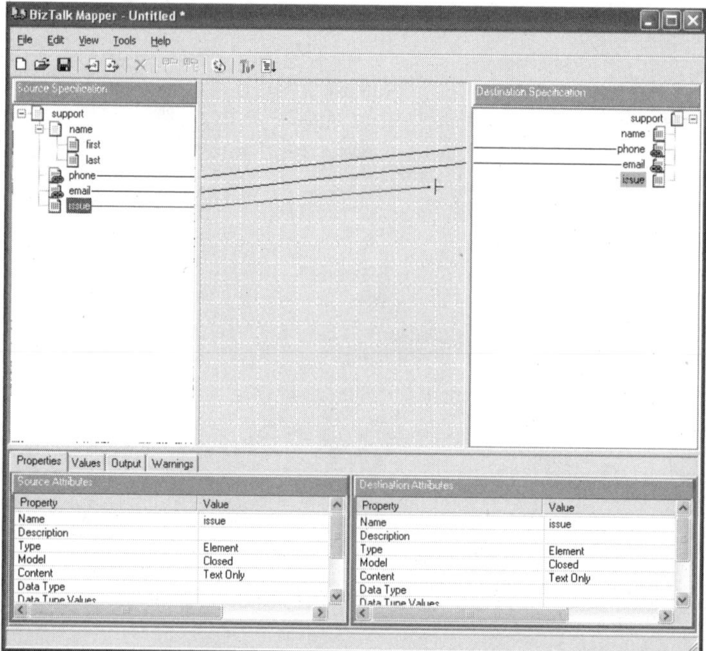

Figure 15-4 Mapping elements by dragging from one side to the other.

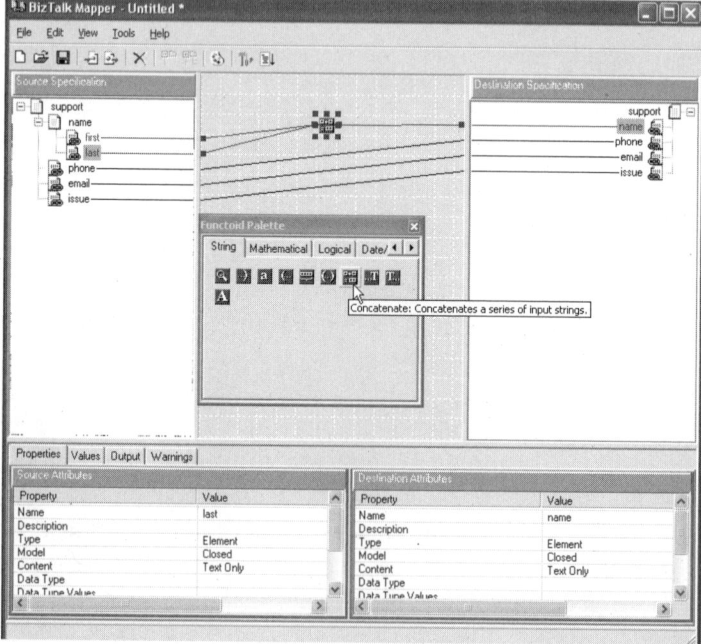

Figure 15-5 Our completed mapping between the partner.xml and support.xml specifications.

Listing 15-5 mapping.xml: Result of mapping our partner.xml specification to our support.xml specification.

```
<?xml version="1.0"?>
<!-- Generated using BizTalk Mapper on Thu, Aug 02 2001 11:24:20 PM -->
<!-- Microsoft Corporation (c) 2000 (http://www.microsoft.com) -->
<mapsource name="mapping"
           BizTalkServerMapperTool_Version="1.0"
           version="1"
           xrange="100"
           yrange="420">
  <srctree>
    <Schema name="support"
            b:BizTalkServerEditorTool_Version="1.0"
            b:root_reference="support"
            b:standard="XML"
            xmlns="urn:schemas-microsoft-com:xml-data"
            xmlns:b="urn:schemas-microsoft-com:BizTalkServer"
            xmlns:d="urn:schemas-microsoft-com:datatypes">
      <b:SelectionFields/>
      <ElementType name="support" content="eltOnly" model="closed">
        <b:RecordInfo/>
        <element type="name" maxOccurs="*" minOccurs="0"/>
        <element type="phone" maxOccurs="*" minOccurs="0"/>
        <element type="email" maxOccurs="*" minOccurs="0"/>
        <element type="issue" maxOccurs="*" minOccurs="0"/>
      </ElementType>
      <ElementType name="phone" content="textOnly" model="closed">
        <b:FieldInfo/>
      </ElementType>
      <ElementType name="name" content="eltOnly" model="closed">
        <b:RecordInfo/>
        <element type="first" maxOccurs="*" minOccurs="0"/>
        <element type="last" maxOccurs="*" minOccurs="0"/>
      </ElementType>
      <ElementType name="last" content="textOnly" model="closed">
        <b:FieldInfo/>
      </ElementType>
      <ElementType name="issue" content="textOnly" model="closed">
        <b:FieldInfo/>
      </ElementType>
      <ElementType name="first" content="textOnly" model="closed">
        <b:FieldInfo/>
      </ElementType>
      <ElementType name="email" content="textOnly" model="closed">
        <b:FieldInfo/>
      </ElementType>
    </Schema>
```

(continued)

Listing 15-5 *continued*

```
  </srctree>
  <Values>
    <TestValues/>
    <ConstantValues/>
  </Values>
  <sinktree>
    <Schema name="support"
            b:BizTalkServerEditorTool_Version="1.0"
            b:root_reference="support"
            b:standard="XML"
            xmlns="urn:schemas-microsoft-com:xml-data"
            xmlns:b="urn:schemas-microsoft-com:BizTalkServer"
            xmlns:d="urn:schemas-microsoft-com:datatypes">
      <b:SelectionFields/>
      <ElementType name="support" content="eltOnly" model="closed">
        <b:RecordInfo/>
        <element type="name" maxOccurs="*" minOccurs="0"/>
        <element type="phone" maxOccurs="*" minOccurs="0"/>
        <element type="email" maxOccurs="*" minOccurs="0"/>
        <element type="issue" maxOccurs="*" minOccurs="0"/>
      </ElementType>
      <ElementType name="phone" content="textOnly" model="closed">
        <b:FieldInfo/>
      </ElementType>
      <ElementType name="name" content="textOnly" model="closed">
        <b:FieldInfo/>
      </ElementType>
      <ElementType name="issue" content="textOnly" model="closed">
        <b:FieldInfo/>
      </ElementType>
      <ElementType name="email" content="textOnly" model="closed">
        <b:FieldInfo/>
      </ElementType>
    </Schema>
  </sinktree>
  <links>
    <link linkid="1" linkfrom="1" linkto="/support/name"/>
    <link linkid="2" linkfrom="/support/name/last" linkto="1"/>
    <link linkid="3" linkfrom="/support/name/first" linkto="1"/>
    <link linkid="4" linkfrom="/support/issue" linkto="/support/
issue"/>
    <link linkid="5" linkfrom="/support/email" linkto="/support/
email"/>
    <link linkid="6" linkfrom="/support/phone" linkto="/support/
phone"/>
  </links>
  <functions>
    <function functionid="1" xcell="56" ycell="212" funcfuncid="107"
```

```
funcversion="1" isscripter="no">
      <inputparams>
        <param type="link" value="3"/>
        <param type="link" value="2"/>
      </inputparams>
    </function>
  </functions>
  <CompiledXSL>
    <xsl:stylesheet xmlns:xsl="http://www.w3.org/1999/XSL/Transform"
                    xmlns:msxsl="urn:schemas-microsoft-com:xslt"
                    xmlns:var="urn:var"
                    xmlns:user="urn:user"
                    exclude-result-prefixes="msxsl var user"
                    version="1.0">
      <xsl:output method="xml" omit-xml-declaration="yes"/>
      <xsl:template match="/">
        <xsl:apply-templates select="support"/>
      </xsl:template>
      <xsl:template match="support">
        <support>
          <xsl:variable name="var:v1"
               select="user:fctstringconcat2(string(name/first/
text()),string(name/last/text()))"/>
          <name>
            <xsl:value-of select="$var:v1"/>
          </name>
         <!-- Connection from source node "phone" to destination node
"phone" -->
          <phone>
            <xsl:value-of select="phone/text()"/>
          </phone>
         <!-- Connection from source node "email" to destination node
"email" -->
          <email>
            <xsl:value-of select="email/text()"/>
          </email>
         <!-- Connection from source node "issue" to destination node
"issue" -->
          <issue>
            <xsl:value-of select="issue/text()"/>
          </issue>
        </support>
      </xsl:template>
      <msxsl:script language="VBScript"
                    implements-prefix="user">
        <![CDATA[
          Function FctStringConcat2( p_strParm0, p_strParm1 )
            FctStringConcat2 = p_strParm0 + p_strParm1
          End Function
```

(continued)

Listing 15-5 *continued*

```
        ]]>
      </msxsl:script>
    </xsl:stylesheet>
  </CompiledXSL>
</mapsource>
```

The BizTalk Mapper can be an extremely useful and time-saving application when it comes to supporting new document formats in any BizTalk system you might be building. Be sure to check out the Help files for more information on the many features it offers.

Process Design with BizTalk Orchestration Designer

While many XML-based messaging servers offer the ability to transport and track XML messages in and out of systems, no application that can create and describe the processing flow a document must go through from start to finish exists. Enter BizTalk Orchestration Designer. This application, shown in Figure 15-6, allows you to drag and drop the necessary flowchart items to define a business process and then connect them to the implementation components used in processing the data.

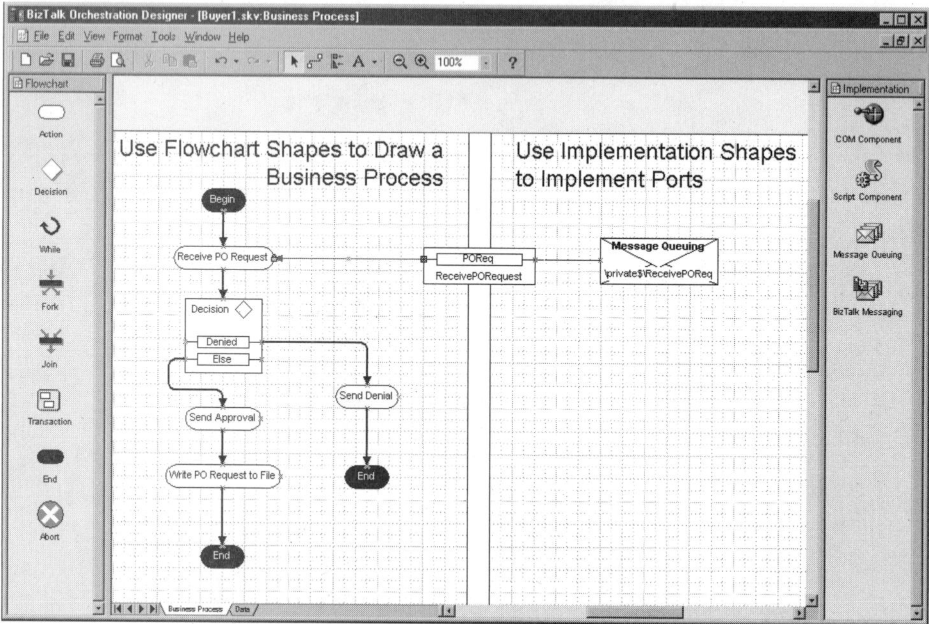

Figure 15-6 The BizTalk Orchestration Designer.

Figure 15-6 shows you a visual representation of how these items are tied together, but as technologists we are sure you want to know and understand what is happening in the background. Behind the scenes, and after you have described your business process and its relationship to processing components, the Orchestration Designer creates an XLANG schedule. This schedule, which is saved with an .skx extension, is run by the XLANG Scheduler Engine, which controls the activation, execution, dehydration, and rehydration of the XLANG schedule. In other words, it handles the execution of the schedule details.

The functionality of the Orchestration Designer can be broken down into three areas. These are as follows:

- Defining workflow
- Referencing processing applications
- Attaching steps to processing

To help you understand these items we are going to step through parts of an example, which will also familiarize you with the tool. This example will use the Orchestration Designer to route our technical support issue submission through our system.

Defining Work Flow

The first step we will take in creating this example is to define the business process workflow. For those of you familiar with Visio, the Orchestration Designer functions in much the same manner. Most of the time you drag components, shapes, and so forth, to your workspace and access properties of these items to define their functions. After you have launched the BizTalk Orchestration Designer, step through the following items to define the business workflow.

> **Note** For all of these functions you will drag items from the Flowchart stencil on the leftmost side of the application to the left of the Separator bar.

1. Drag an Action to a position below the Begin shape.
2. Double-click the Action, and in the Name field enter Receive Email.
3. Next drag a Decision shape and place it below the Receive Email action.
4. Right-click the Decision shape and click Add Rule. In the dialog box

that appears, type Phone and click OK. Repeat the same steps and add a second rule named Email.

5. Add a second Action shape to the right of the Decision box and name it Phone Customer.
6. Add a third Action shape below and to the left of the Phone Customer and name it Send Email.
7. Below the Decision box, add a forth Action and name it Push To Manager.
8. Finally we need to place three End items. Place one below the Push To Manager action, another below the Send Email action, and the last one below the Phone Customer action.

Now that all of our process descriptions are on the page, we need to connect these items. To connect them you need to follow these steps:

1. Select an item by clicking on it so that a green outline shows.
2. Select a control handle, which is represented by an x, of the first step in a process and drag it to one of the control handles of the action to which you want to connect it.

Connecting is this simple. In our example you will need to make the following eight connections:

- Begin to Receive Mail
- Receive Mail to Decision
- Phone to Phone Customer
- Phone Customer to End (one we placed below this action)
- Email to Send Email
- Send Email Customer to End (one we placed below this action)
- Else to Push To Manager
- Push To Manager to End (one we placed below this action)

At this point your screen should look like Figure 15-7. Now that this portion of our example is complete, save it in a file named Support.skv on the C drive. We will now begin adding our processing applications to the Implementation side of the workspace.

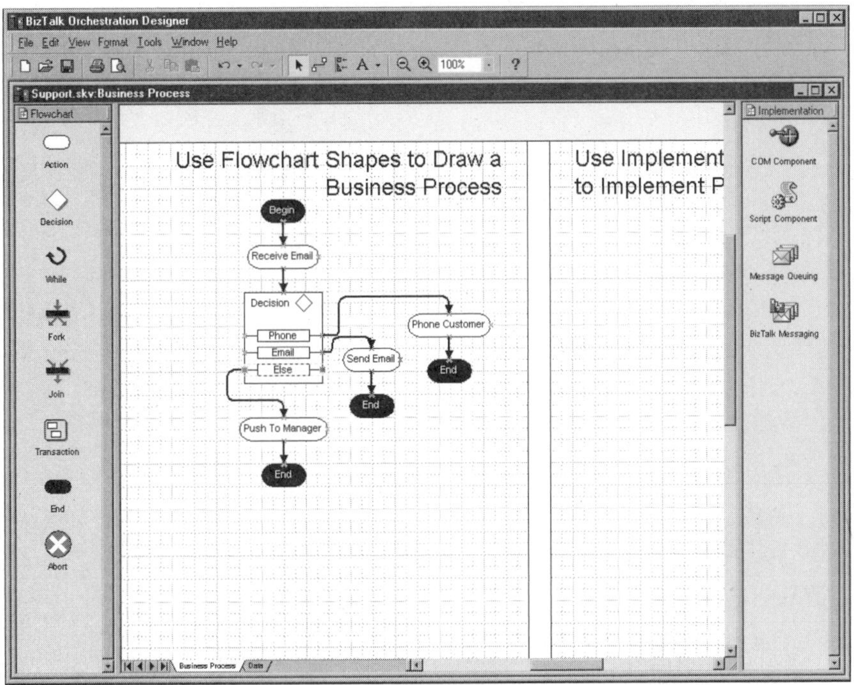

Figure 15-7 Our example after designing the workflow.

Referencing Processing Applications

One of the great qualities of the Orchestration Designer is its ability to include definitions and descriptions of the processing applications. For instance, we might want to use a component to send the customer with a support issue an e-mail with the resolution. Maybe we want to pass the document to a script first and perform other processing before a phone call is made to the customer. Using the Orchestration Designer we are able to drag category components to our workspace, select the scripts, COM objects, message queues, and BizTalk messaging applications that will be used to process the data.

In our example we are going to add a few script components. The point of this exercise is to expose you to some of the terminology and screens you should expect to see when defining the processing applications. For instance, you will create *ports* that act as the conduit between the business process and the applications. Furthermore, you will be able to see how the Orchestration Designer represents these connections.

The following steps will show you how to add Script Components out of the Implementation stencil.

1. Drag a Script Component to the left side of the workspace, opposite the Phone Customer action. This will open the Script Component Binding Wizard dialog, where you will enter *ProcessPhone* as the name of the Port. Click Next when you have entered this name.
2. Accept the default setting of Static on the second dialog and click Next.
3. Now we have to specify a Script file. We are going to use one that was already built and is contained in a file called MsgBoxes.wsc (Listing 15-6). This should be located in the \Program Files\Microsoft BizTalk Server\SDK\XLANG Samples\Loop\LoopApp directory if you installed the application in its default location. Here are the contents of the file in case you did not:

Listing 15-6 MsgBoxes.wsc: A script used to display our dialog boxes.

```
<?xml version="1.0"?>
<component>
<?component error="true" debug="true"?>
<registration
   description="MsgBoxes"
   progid="MsgBoxes.WSC"
   version="1.00"
   classid="{df0c82d7-f193-48f0-bfcd-eebc818bf2d3}"
>
</registration>
<public>
   <method name="ShowMsgBox">
       <PARAMETER name="sMsg"/>
       <PARAMETER name="sTitle"/>
   </method>
   <method name="AskYesNo">
       <PARAMETER name="sMsg"/>
       <PARAMETER name="sTitle"/>
   </method>
</public>
<script language="VBScript">
<![CDATA[
function ShowMsgBox(sMsg, sTitle)
   MsgBox CStr(sMsg), vbOKOnly, CStr(sTitle)
   ShowMsgBox = ""
end function
function AskYesNo(sMsg, sTitle)
    AskYesNo = MsgBox(CStr(sMsg), vbYesNo, CStr(sTitle))
end function
]]>
</script>
</component>
```

4. After you've clicked Next you will select the instantiation option for the component. Leave this setting at Use the ProgID *MsgBoxes.WSC*. Click Next when you are finished.
5. On the Method Information dialog, select only the *ShowMsgBox* method and click Next.
6. On the final screen, Advanced Port Properties, we will accept all the default settings and click Finish.
7. Now repeat these steps to handle the processing of the Send Email and Push To Manager actions. All you need to do is change the name of the Port in Step #1 to ProcessEmail for one instance, and Process-Manager in the second.

> **Note** Do you want to know more about the other Implementation components? Be sure to check the BizTalk Help files—they contain more information, as well as other tutorials.

Once you've completed these steps, the right side of your workspace should look like Figure 15-8.

Before we move on, let's include a processing component that will be responsible for starting the entire process. This component, which will be of the Message Queuing type, will be what feeds the Receive Email action we defined on the business process setup. Here are the steps for adding this component.

1. Drag a Message Queuing component to the left side of the workspace, opposite the Receive Email action. This will open the Message Queuing Binding Wizard dialog, where you will enter *IncomingEmail* as the name of the Port. Click Next when you have entered this name.
2. Accept the default setting of Static on the second dialog and click Next.
3. Now we need to include the queue information. For this example we will create a new queue for every instance. Simply accept the default setting and hit Next. (If you've forgotten how, check back in Chapter 7 for message queuing details.)
4. On the final screen, Advanced Port Properties, we will accept the default settings, so just click Finish.

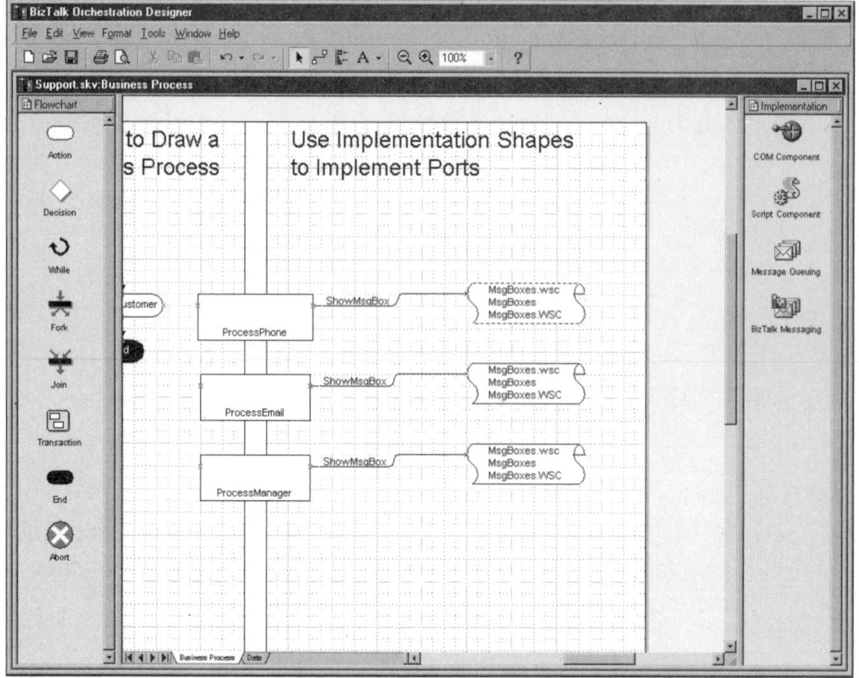

Figure 15-8 The results after connecting to processing scripts.

At this point we have all the pieces in place—we just need to properly associate them and apply any needed functionality. In the next section, we will attach our business actions to our processing scripts and put the finishing touches on our example.

Attaching Steps to Processing

The final step in our example of using the Orchestration Designer application is to connect the business steps to the processing applications (scripts in our case). This step will not only involve defining the processing connections, but we will also add information in our Decision item to determine which connection is used.

In the same manner we used to connect the items together in the business process, we will drag control handles from the appropriate actions to the corresponding script component port. The following outlines how to complete this process.

> **Note** Remember that the "port" is defined by the name we gave it. You can see these ports in the middle of your workspace.

1. Grab the rightmost control handle for the Receive Email action and drag it to the leftmost handle on the IncomingEmail port. This will cause the XML Communication Wizard to appear.
2. Select the Receive option to signify that the XLANG Scheduler Engine will be receiving the message. Click Next after you have entered this information.
3. On the following Message Information dialog, enter *SupportMessage* as the name of the message, and click Next.
4. Accept the default setting of Receiving XML Messages From The Queue on the XML Translation Information dialog and click Next.
5. On the Message Type Information dialog, enter *<support>* as the Message Type and click Next.
6. On the following screen browse to our mapping.xml specification and click Finish to finalize the association.
7. Next grab the rightmost control handle for the Phone Customer action and drag it to the leftmost handle on the ProcessPhone port. This will cause the Method Communication Wizard to appear.
8. On the initial dialog accept the default of initiating a synchronous method call and click Next.
9. Click Next again on the Message Information dialog. This will present you with the third and final dialog that outlines the details of the ShowMsgBox method. Click Finish when you are done.
10. Repeat steps 7—9 for the connection between the Send Mail action and the ProcessEmail port.
11. Repeat steps 7—9 for the connection between the Push To Manager action and the ProcessManager port.

Once you have completed these steps, your workspace should look like Figure 15-9.

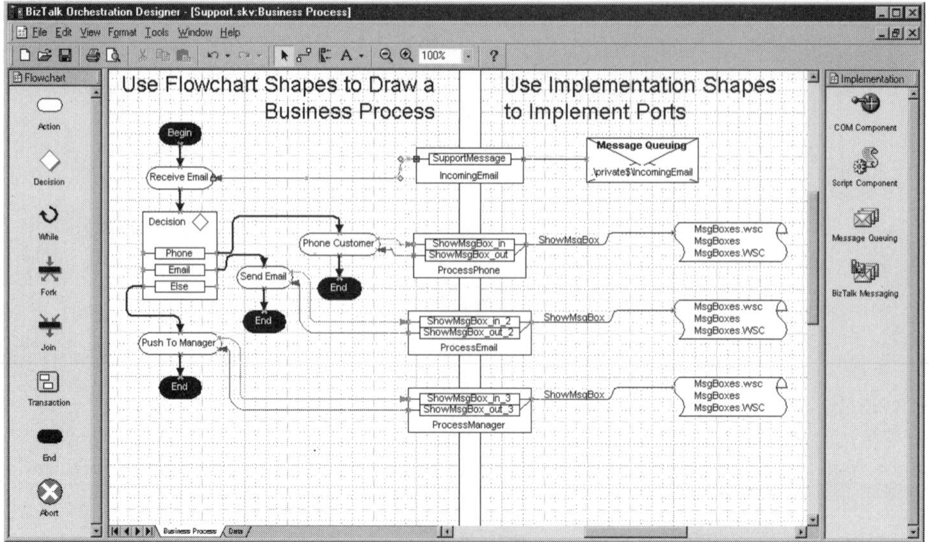

Figure 15-9 The workspace after completing the process-to-port connections.

The next step in our example is to write the expressions to evaluate our document so we can properly process the data. Follow these steps to add in the necessary expressions:

1. Right click on the Decision item and select Properties. This will launch a dialog box displaying our Phone and Email rules.
2. Select the Phone rule and click the Edit button.
3. In the Rule Properties dialog place your cursor in the Script Expression textarea. Now type *SupportMessage.Phone > 1*. Click Ok when you are finished.
4. Repeat Steps 2—3 for the Email rule and enter *SupportMessage.Email* > 1 for the expression.

> **Note** What does this mean? Typing SupportMessage.Phone signifies that we are looking for the presence of a phone number in the document submitted. If this evaluates to TRUE, we will go through the ProcessPhone port and run the proper script.

We are now finished. Save your file so you do not lose any changes. At this point you should be able to combine what you've learned here with what we covered in Chapter 7 to build a complete BizTalk solution, or at least a simple one.

> **Note** If you are still interested in the BizTalk Framework and Server product, check out *http://mspress.microsoft.com*. You will find several Microsoft Press titles on the subject.

Conclusion

As you have seen, the power of BizTalk Server is truly amazing. The ability of an application to both manage the messaging between servers necessary for proper integration and also provide the toolset need to implement and orchestrate the entire process makes BizTalk Server a must-have application. When the original BizTalk Framework was developed, Microsoft obviously considered its potential power, and they have leveraged it within this server product.

In Chapter 16 we will go over Windows .NET and what it really means. Throughout the course of this book we have touched on, discussed, and used many of the .NET features and we have built applications based on .NET, but we have not pulled all of this information together into a full explanation. Although .NET is not the focus of the book, its usage of XML-based standards warrants additional coverage.

16

Development

By now you should have little doubt that XML truly forms a core technology substrate in Microsoft's .NET Framework. Everywhere in Windows .NET, from metadata to ASP.NET to XML Web services, XML is used as the native data representation format. This chapter starts by exploring the other major use of XML in .NET, data access, to show you how Microsoft has effectively merged the relational and hierarchical DOM access models under a single, unified, architecture.

Next we dig deeper into the XML object model of the .NET Framework to look at reading and writing XML documents. Finally we allow ourselves to stray slightly off course from the main focus of this book to take a look at some of the popular programming languages that can be used to build .NET applications.

Data Access and XML

Prior to Windows .NET, OLEDB and ActiveX Data Objects (ADO) were the primary APIs for data access in Microsoft Windows. With the advent of .NET, Microsoft introduced a brand new data access object model, called ADO.NET, which is leaner and meaner than previous data access object models and provides functionalities tailored to excel in a multitier, distributed Web environment.

All three data access object models, OLEDB, ADO, and ADO.NET, provide varying levels of support for XML. Let's first take a look at OLEDB and ADO and their support for XML.

OLEDB and ADO

Both OLEDB and ADO are based on COM technologies. The OLEDB provides a low-level and highly efficient method of accessing and manipulating relational data, while ADO, which is built on top of OLEDB, provides an easier means of data access. XML support in ADO is provided through Recordset Persistence and is implemented by the Microsoft OLE DB Persistence Provider. This provider can take an ADO *Recordset* object, generate an XML document and related schema information, and save all this to a stream or file. Similarly, this provider can generate a read-only and forward-only *Recordset* object from an ADO-generated XML file or stream.

Listing 16-1 demonstrates how you can persist a *Recordset* object as an XML file.

Listing 16-1 ADORecordset2XML.cs: Persisting an ADO *Recordset* object to an XML file.

```
using System;
using System.Data;
using System.Data.SQL;
public class ADORecordset2XML
{
  public static void Main( String[] args )
  {
    try
    {
      String connString = "provider=SQLOLEDB;" +
                          "initial catalog=pubs;" +
                          "server=localhost;" +
                          "uid=sa;" +
                          "pwd=";
      String queryString = "select * from titles";
      /* Instantiate a Recordet object */
      ADODB.Recordset rs = new ADODB.Recordset();
      /* Connect to the database and execute a SQL query */
      rs.Open( queryString, connString,
               ADODB.CursorTypeEnum.adOpenStatic,
               ADODB.LockTypeEnum.adLockReadOnly, 0 );
      /* Export Recordset to "titles.xml" file in XML format. */
      rs.Save( "titles.xml", ADODB.PersistFormatEnum.adPersistXML );
      /* close the Recordset object */
      rs.Close();
    }
    catch ( Exception e )
    {
      Console.WriteLine( "Exception: {0}", e.ToString() );
```

```
      }
   }
}
```

In ADORecordset2XML.cs we first open a connection to the SQL Server PUBS database and then populate a *Recordset* object with all records from the TITLES table. To persist this *Recordset* object, we simply call the *Save()* method and specify the filename to which to write the data and the output format, which in this case is XML.

To compile ADORecordset2XML.cs, open a console window and type in the following command line:

```
csc /r:System.dll /r:System.Data.dll /r:ADODB.dll ADORecordset2XML.cs
```

After you run the resultant ADORecordset2XML.exe program you should see a new titles.xml file in the current directory. This is the XML-persistent form of the *Recordset* object you created in ADORecordset2XML.cs.

Listing 16-2 shows how you can use ADO to load the titles.xml file you generated with ADORecordset2XML.cs into a new *Recordset* object.

Listing 16-2 XML2ADORecordset.cs: Recreating the *Recordset* object from the titles.xml file.

```
using System;
using System.Data;
using System.Data.SQL;
public class XML2ADORecordset
{
  public static void Main( String[] args )
  {
    try
    {
      String connString = "provider=SQLOLEDB;" +
                          "initial catalog=pubs;" +
                          "server=localhost;" +
                          "uid=sa;" +
                          "pwd=";
      Int32 adCmdFile = 256;
      /* Instantiate Recordset object */
      ADODB.Recordset rs = new ADODB.Recordset();
      /* Open the titles.XML file into Recordset object */
      rs.Open( "titles.xml", connString,
               ADODB.CursorTypeEnum.adOpenForwardOnly,
               ADODB.LockTypeEnum.adLockReadOnly,
               adCmdFile );
      /* Display the value of the price field for the first record */
      rs.MoveFirst();
      Console.WriteLine( rs.Fields[ "price" ].Value );
```

(continued)

Listing 16-2 *continued*

```
         /* close the Recordset object */
         rs.Close();
       }
       catch ( Exception e )
       {
         Console.WriteLine( "Exception: {0}", e.ToString() );
       }
    }
  }
```

In XML2ADORecordset.cs you can see that, to open a persisted Recordset file, you can use the normal Recordset *Open()* method and pass in the name of the persisted file. In the example, once we have loaded and recreated the *Recordset* object, we generate the value of the price field of the first record.

Use the following command to compile XML2ADORecordset.cs:

```
csc /r:System.dll /r:System.Data.dll /r:ADODB.dll XML2ADORecordset.cs
```

When you run the resultant XML2ADORecordset.exe program, you will see the value of the price field displayed.

XML support in ADO is limited to say the least. You can only persist and reconstruct *Recordset* objects to and from XML files and streams. Once persisted, the XML file remains separate from the original *Recordset* object, and any changes you make to one will not be reflected in the other automatically.

ADO.NET, on the other hand, provides a much tighter relationship with XML, so much so that the two are actually based off a common architecture in the .NET Framework. Let's turn our attention to this exciting new technology.

ADO.NET

ADO.NET is touted as the successor to ADO and is based heavily on XML. The core focus of ADO.NET is to provide an API that facilitates the creation of distributed, scalable, and interoperable applications that share data in a disconnected, stateless fashion.

ADO.NET consist of two parts: the *DataSet* class and *Managed Providers*. The *DataSet* class provides the methods and properties for accessing and manipulating relational data. *Managed Providers* represent the underlying data stores such as a Microsoft SQL Server database.

Table 16-1 shows a list of the namespaces made available with ADO.NET.

The *DataSet* Class

The *DataSet* class is central to ADO.NET and represents the primary encapsulation for data access and manipulation in the .NET Framework. *DataSet* is a disconnected and in-memory view of a database. You should appreciate that a

Table 16-1 Namespaces Made Available with ADO.NET

Namespace	Description
System.Data	Contains the *DataSet* class and other basic classes.
System.Data.ADO	Contains the ADO *Managed Provider* classes.
System.Data.SQL	Contains SQL Server *Managed Provider* classes.
System.Data.SQLTypes	Contains classes for native types within SQL Server.

DataSet knows nothing about SQL or even DBMS's. You can have a *DataSet* dynamically created and populated with data without a single byte of communication made with a DBMS. This decoupling between data and the underlying data source is the core enabler for the ADO.NET disconnected mode of operations.

Internally you can think of a *DataSet* as an XML document containing one or more pieces of separate or related tabular XML elements. In fact, .NET provides a unified programming model for accessing data represented as both XML data and relational data. You can start with a *DataSet* and work with the data following a non-sequential, hierarchical path driven by the XML DOM. Equally, you can work with XML documents in a row-after-row fashion through a *DataSet* using a relational model.

In .NET Framework the *XmlDataDocument* class provides this integration between the relational and XML models.

The *XmlDataDocument* Class

The *XmlDataDocument* class is extended from the *XmlDocument* class, which itself is the primary encapsulation in the .NET Framework for an XML document. *XmlDataDocument* provides the extra capability for manipulating relational data. Like all other XML-related classes, *XmlDataDocument* resides in the System.Xml namespace.

Once a relationship between a *DataSet* and *XmlDataDocument* is established, synchronization of the underlying data is automatic. Therefore, adding a record in the *DataSet*, for example, always creates a corresponding node in the *XmlDataDocument*. Conversely, adding a node in the *XmlDataDocument* also creates a new record in the *DataSet*.

Depending on the source of your data, you can instantiate an *XmlDataDocument* and associate a *DataSet* with it in two ways. The first method is that if your source data is in a *DataSet*, you instantiate a new *XmlDataDocument*, passing the *DataSet* in the constructor. Your *DataSet* is now attached to the *XmlDataDocument*, and you can use the exposed methods and properties to access and manipulate the relational data using the DOM.

> **Note** Every rule has exceptions. A newly added node in the *XmlDataDocument* will result in a new record in the *DataSet only* if the new node is recognized as corresponding to a row in the *DataSet*. This behavior allows the XML document to contain elements that do not correspond to relational records.

In Listing 16-3 we show you a sample C# console program that retrieves data from an SQL Server database and uses *XmlDataDocument* to manipulate the data.

Listing 16-3 DataSet2XmlDataDocument.cs: Manipulating relational data using the DOM.

```
using System;
using System.IO;
using System.Data;
using System.Data.SQL;
using System.Xml;
public class DataSet2XmlDataDocument
{
    public static void Main( String[] args )
    {
        SQLConnection conn = null;
        try
        {
            /* connect to the SQL Server database */
            conn = new SQLConnection( "server=
localhost;uid=sa;pwd=;database=pubs" );
            /* execute SQL query */
            SQLDataSetCommand cmd = new SQLDataSetCommand( "select *
from Titles", conn );
            /* create a DataSet and populate it with the records
returned from
               result of the above SQL query */
            DataSet ds = new DataSet();
            cmd.FillDataSet( ds, "Titles" );
            /* associate this DataSet with an XmlDataDocument */
            XmlDataDocument doc = new XmlDataDocument( ds );
            /* you can now process this doc just like any
DataDocument. For example,
```

```
            the following uses DataDocumentNavigator to select the
first Titles node
            and modifies the value. */
          DataDocumentNavigator nav = new DataDocumentNavigator
( doc );
          nav.Select( "//NewDataSet/Titles[1]/title_id" );
          if ( nav.MoveToNextSelected() )
          {
              Console.WriteLine( "Original=" + nav.InnerText );
          }
          else
          {
             Console.WriteLine( "Unexpected error: Node not found" );
          }
          nav.InnerText = "BU1030";  /* modify the value of the
title_id node */
        /* XmlDataDocument auto synchronizes the above change with
the associated
            DataSet. */
          Console.WriteLine( "Modified=" + ds.Tables[ "Titles"
].Rows[ 0 ][ "title_id" ] );
      }
      finally
      {
          if ( conn != null && conn.State == DBObjectState.Open )
          {
              conn.Close();
          }
      }
   }
}
```

Use the following console command to compile DataSet2XmlDataDocument.cs:

```
csc /r:System.dll /r:System.Data.dll /r:System.Xml.dll
DataSet2XmlDataDocument.cs
```

When you execute DataSet2XmlDataDocument.exe you should get an output in your console window similar to the following:

```
Original=BU1032
Modified=BU1030
```

You can see that we have successfully used the DOM to modify the data in a *DataSet*.

If your source data is in an *XmlDocument* or even an *XmlDataDocument*, you can use its *DataSet* member property to access and manipulate the data using a relational model. In Listing 16-4 we have a C# console program that uses an associated *DataSet* to change the data originally stored in an *XmlDataDocument*.

Listing 16-4 XmlDataDocument2DataSet.cs: Manipulating an XML document using a *DataSet*.

```
using System;
using System.IO;
using System.Data;
using System.Xml;
public class Xml2DataSet
{
  public static void Main()
  {
    try
    {
      /* instantiate a XmlDataDocument */
      XmlDataDocument doc = new XmlDataDocument();
      /* load the schema */
      doc.DataSet.ReadXmlSchema( "book.xsd" );
      /* now load the XML document */
      doc.Load( "book.xml" );
      /* print original price value of first Title node */
      DataDocumentNavigator nav = new DataDocumentNavigator( doc );
      nav.Select( "//Book/Titles[1]/price" );
      if ( nav.MoveToNextSelected() )
      {
        Console.WriteLine( "Original=" + nav.InnerText );
      }
      /* update a price using the associated DataSet */
      DataTable books = doc.DataSet.Tables[ "Titles" ];
      books.Rows[ 0 ][ "price" ] = "12.99";
      /* display modified price */
      nav.Select( "//Book/Titles[1]/price" );
      if ( nav.MoveToNextSelected() )
      {
        Console.WriteLine( "Modified=" + nav.InnerText );
      }
    }
    catch (Exception e)
    {
      Console.WriteLine ("Exception: {0}", e.ToString());
    }
  }
}
```

XmlDataDocument2DataSet.cs is the example of an XML document we will use in Listing 16-5.

Listing 16-5 book.xml: An XML document used in XmlDataDocument2DataSet.cs.

```
<Book>
  <Titles>
    <title_id>BU1032</title_id>
    <title>The Busy Executive's Database Guide</title>
    <type>business</type>
    <pub_id>1389</pub_id>
    <price>19.99</price>
    <advance>5000</advance>
    <royalty>10</royalty>
    <ytd_sales>4095</ytd_sales>
    <notes>An overview of available database systems with
emphasis on common business applications. Illustrated.</notes>
    <pubdate>1991-06-11T16:00:00</pubdate>
  </Titles>
  <Titles>
    <title_id>BU1111</title_id>
    <title>Cooking with Computers: Surreptitious Balance Sheets
</title>
    <type>business</type>
    <pub_id>1389</pub_id>
    <price>11.95</price>
    <advance>5000</advance>
    <royalty>10</royalty>
    <ytd_sales>3876</ytd_sales>
    <notes>Helpful hints on how to use your
electronic resources to the best advantage.</notes>
    <pubdate>1991-06-08T16:00:00</pubdate>
  </Titles>
  <Titles>
    <title_id>BU2075</title_id>
    <title>You Can Combat Computer Stress!</title>
    <type>business</type>
    <pub_id>0736</pub_id>
    <price>2.99</price>
    <advance>10125</advance>
    <royalty>24</royalty>
    <ytd_sales>18722</ytd_sales>
    <notes>The latest medical and psychological techniques for living
with the electronic office. Easy-to-understand explanations.</notes>
    <pubdate>1991-06-29T16:00:00</pubdate>
  </Titles>
</Book>
```

We have also included the governing schema for our book.xml document in Listing 16-6.

Listing 16-6 book.xsd: The XML schema for book.xml.

```
<xsd:schema id="Book" targetNamespace="" xmlns="" xmlns:xsd="http://
www.w3.org/2001/XMLSchema" xmlns:msdata=
"urn:schemas-microsoft-com:xml-msdata">
  <xsd:element name="Titles">
    <xsd:complexType content="elementOnly">
      <xsd:all>
        <xsd:element name="title_id" type="xsd:string"/>
        <xsd:element name="title" type="xsd:string"/>
        <xsd:element name="type" type="xsd:string"/>
        <xsd:element name="pub_id" minOccurs="0" type="xsd:string"/>
        <xsd:element name="price" minOccurs="0" type="xsd:decimal"/>
       <xsd:element name="advance" minOccurs="0" type="xsd:decimal"/>
        <xsd:element name="royalty" minOccurs="0" type="xsd:int"/>
        <xsd:element name="ytd_sales" minOccurs="0" type="xsd:int"/>
        <xsd:element name="notes" minOccurs="0" type="xsd:string"/>
        <xsd:element name="pubdate" type="xsd:timeInstant"/>
      </xsd:all>
    </xsd:complexType>
  </xsd:element>
  <xsd:element name="NewDataSet" msdata:IsDataSet="True">
    <xsd:complexType>
      <xsd:choice maxOccurs="unbounded">
        <xsd:element ref="Titles"/>
      </xsd:choice>
    </xsd:complexType>
  </xsd:element>
</xsd:schema>
```

XmlDataDocument2DataSet.cs uses a *DataSet* to change the *price* node value of the first *<Titles>* node in book.xml from *19.99* to *12.99*. The modification is automatically reflected in the *doc XmlDataDocument* object.

To compile XmlDataDocument2DataSet.cs, run the following command line in a console window:

```
csc /r:System.dll /r:System.Data.dll /r:System.Xml.dll
XmlDataDocument2DataSet.cs
```

When you run the resultant XmlDataDocument2DataSet.exe in a console window, you should see an output similar to the following:

```
Original=19.99
Modified=12.99
```

We have successfully modified the price from *19.99* to *12.99* using the associated *DataSet.*

Parsing and Producing XML Documents

The *XmlReader* and *XmlWriter* abstract classes are at the heart of the XML object model in the .NET Framework. *XmlReader* provides the API for reading XML documents, while *XmlWriter* provides the complementary API for producing W3C's standards-compliant XML documents. In designing these classes, Microsoft borrows concepts from both the DOM and SAX. In the end, these classes use neither of those models, but are a compromise between the two.

Like SAX, *XmlReader* and *XmlWriter* use a streaming model to read the streams of data that form an XML document one piece at a time, and can even skip pieces of no interest. At the same time, like DOM, the API is based on a more developer-friendly pull model. This innovative stream-based, pull-model API provides developers with means for accessing and producing XML documents that are efficient, powerful, and easy to use.

Because both *XmlReader* and *XmlWriter* are abstract classes, you cannot instantiate and work directly with them. For this purpose, .NET provides a few concrete implementations of these classes. For *XmlReader*, these are the *XmlTextReader*, *XmlNodeReader*, and *XslReader* concrete classes. For *XmlWriter*, we have *XmlTextWriter* and *XmlNodeWriter*.

We will first look at how we can use the XmlReader to read and process XML documents.

XmlReader

The *XmlReader* abstract class provides a fast, read-only, and forward-only cursor for reading XML documents. Using *XmlReader* is much like using the DOM, where you read and work with one node at a time. The following snippet shows a C# method that traverses an XML document and displays the names of all the elements in the document.

```
public void DisplayElements( XmlReader reader )
{
  /* read the next node in document order */
  while ( reader.Read() )
  {
    /* if this is an element node, display its name */
    Console.WriteLine( reader.Name );
  }
}
```

XmlReader has an associated cursor that defines the notion of a current node in the document stream. Methods are provided that allow the user to traverse the document one node at a time, moving the current node along the way. *XmlReader* also provides several methods for inspecting the type and value of the current node.

Reading Nodes

The *Read()* method is the fundamental method in *XmlReader* for moving the cursor in an XML document. Every time you call *Read(), XmlReader* moves the cursor to the next node in document order until it reaches the end of the stream, in which case it returns a false value. For example, running the previous sample *DisplayElements()* method against the sample1.xml file in Listing 16-7 produces the following output:

```
persons
person
firstname
lastname
person
firstname
lastname
person
```

Listing 16-7 sample1.xml: A sample XML document.

```
<persons>
  <person>
    <firstname>Albert</firstname>
    <lastname>Einstein</lastname>
  </person>
  <person>
    <firstname>Niels</firstname>
    <lastname>Bohr</lastname>
  </person>
</persons>
```

Once you have landed at a certain node through the *Read()* method or any other methods provided by the *XmlReader* for moving the cursor, you can inspect its contextual information or value. For example, the *NodeType* property returns a type identifier similar to those used by the DOM. Another property, *Value*, allows you to access a node's value. *XmlReader* also provides methods for reading typed text values (for example, *ReadInt16*, *ReadDouble*, *ReadString*, and so forth).

The following snippet is a C# method that uses the various properties exposed by *XmlReader* to display the textual representation of the current node.

```
public void DisplayNode( XmlReader node )
{
  switch ( node.NodeType )
  {
    case XmlNodeType.Element:
      Console.Write( "<" + node.Name + ">" );
      break;
    case XmlNodeType.Text:
      Console.Write( node.Value );
      break;
    case XmlNodeType.CDATA:
      Console.Write( node.Value );
      break;
    case XmlNodeType.ProcessingInstruction:
      Console.Write( "<?" + node.Name + " " + node.Value + "?>" );
      break;
    case XmlNodeType.Comment:
      Console.Write( "<!--" + node.Value + "-->" );
      break;
    case XmlNodeType.Document:
      Console.Write( "<?xml version='1.0'?>" );
      break;
    case XmlNodeType.Whitespace:
      Console.Write( node.Value );
      break;
    case XmlNodeType.SignificantWhitespace:
      Console.Write( node.Value );
      break;
    case XmlNodeType.EndTag:
      Console.Write( "</" + node.Name + ">" );
      break;
  }
}
```

Reading Attributes

Because attributes are regarded as part of a document's hierarchical structure, *Read()* will not encounter attribute nodes. To access attributes for the current element you can use the *GetAttribute()* method. With *GetAttribute()* you can look up a specific attribute either by name or index. The following code snippet shows one way to iterate through and display all attributes in the current node:

```
for ( int = 0; i < node.AttributeCount; i++ )
{
  Console.WriteLine( node.GetAttribute( i ) );
}
```

XmlReader also provides methods to let you traverse the attributes using the current node cursor. The *MoveToAttribute(), MoveToFirstAttribute(),* and

MoveToNextAttribute() methods can be used to move sideways through the attributes attached to the current node. The following code snippet displays the names and values of all the attributes in the current node:

```
while ( node.MoveToNextAttribute() )
{
  Console.Write( " " + node.Name + "=\"" + node.Value + "\"" );
}
```

Notice that, unlike *GetAttribute()*, you can retrieve both the name and the value of an attribute using this method.

A Sample XML Reader

ReadXML.cs, in Listing 16-8, shows a C# console program that uses all the methods and properties described in this section to display the complete textual representation of the book.xml XML file.

Listing 16-8 ReadXML.cs: A C# console using the discussed methods and properties.

```
using System;
using System.IO;
using System.Xml;
public class ReadXML
{
  public void DisplayNode( XmlReader node )
  {
    switch ( node.NodeType )
    {
      case XmlNodeType.Element:
        Console.Write( "<" + node.Name );
        while ( node.MoveToNextAttribute() )
        {
          Console.Write( " " + node.Name + "=\"" + node.Value + "\"" );
        }
        Console.Write(">");
        break;
      case XmlNodeType.Text:
        Console.Write( node.Value );
        break;
      case XmlNodeType.CDATA:
        Console.Write( node.Value );
        break;
      case XmlNodeType.ProcessingInstruction:
        Console.Write( "<?" + node.Name + " " + node.Value + "?>" );
        break;
      case XmlNodeType.Comment:
        Console.Write( "<!--" + node.Value + "-->" );
```

```
        break;
      case XmlNodeType.Document:
        Console.Write( "<?xml version='1.0'?>" );
        break;
      case XmlNodeType.Whitespace:
        Console.Write( node.Value );
        break;
      case XmlNodeType.SignificantWhitespace:
        Console.Write( node.Value );
        break;
      case XmlNodeType.EndTag:
        Console.Write( "</" + node.Name + ">" );
        break;
    }
  }
  public void DisplayElements( XmlReader reader )
  {
    /* read the next node in document order */
    while ( reader.Read() )
    {
      DisplayNode( reader );
    }
  }
  public static void Main( String[] args )
  {
    XmlTextReader reader = new XmlTextReader( "book.xml" );
    ReadXML tr = new ReadXML();
    tr.DisplayElements( reader );
  }
}
```

Note that we have used the *XmlTextReader* concrete implementation of *XmlReader* in ReadXML.cs.

To compile ReadXML.cs, open a console window and type in the following command line:

```
csc /r:System.dll /r:System.Xml.dll ReadXML.cs
```

Running the resultant ReadXML.exe program displays the content of book.xml on the console.

Validation

One of the features the *XmlTextReader* provides is validation. *XmlTextReader* supports validation against DTDs, XDR, and XSD schemas. Validation is off by default, and to turn it on you must provide a *ValidationHandler* and the *Validation* property must be set to either *DTD* or *Schema*, depending on the validation method required. With validation turned on, the *ValidationHandler* event handler is called whenever a validation error occurs. A validation error is any error listed in the W3C as "Validity Constraint." *ValidationEventHandler* has the following signature:

```
public delegate void ValidationEventHandler( object sender,
ValidationEventArgs args );
```

The *ValidationEventArgs* class provides the error code and error-message information for the event handler. Listing 16-9 shows a C# program that validates a user-specified XML file using schema validation.

Listing 16-9 Validation.cs: Code that validates an XML file using schema validation.

```
using System;
using System.IO;
using System.Xml;
public class Validation
{
  static bool gotError = false;
  public static void Main( String[] args )
  {
    /* make sure we were passed with a filename */
    if ( args.Length == 0 )
    {
      Console.WriteLine( "Usage: validation filename" );
      return;
    }
    try
    {
      /* Instantiates an XmlReaderWriter using the filename passed
         in from the command line */
      XmlTextReader reader = new XmlTextReader( args[ 0 ] );
      /* Specify the validation method */
      reader.Validation = Validation.Schema;
      /* Register event handler for reporting validation errors */
      reader.ValidationEventHandler += new ValidationEventHandler
( OnValidateError );
      /* traverse the whole document */
      while ( reader.Read() );
      if ( !gotError )
      {
        Console.WriteLine( "Document is valid" );
      }
    }
    catch ( Exception e )
    {
      Console.WriteLine( "Error: " + e.Message );
    }
  }
public static void OnValidateError( Object sender, ValidationEventArgs args )
  {
```

```
      gotError = true;
      Console.WriteLine( "Error: " + args.Message );
    }
  }
```

To compile Validation.cs, type in the following command line in a console window:

```
csc /r:System.dll /r:System.Xml.dll Validation.cs
```

XmlWriter

The *XmlWriter* abstract class is used to produce document streams conforming to the W3C's XML 1 and Namespaces Recommendations. *XmlWriter* handles many of the complexities in producing XML documents automatically, such as making sure that elements are properly closed and attribute values are quoted. *XmlWriter* also provides methods for writing typed data (for example, *WriteInt32()*, *WriteDouble()*, *WriteString()*, and so forth).

WriteXML.cs in Listing 16-10 is a C# console program that generates an XML document to the console using *XmlWriter*.

Listing 16-10 WriteXML.cs: Code that generates an XML document to the console.

```
using System;
using System.IO;
using System.Xml;
public class WriteXML
{
  public static void Main( String[] args )
  {
    /* Instantiates an XmlTextWriter that writes to the console */
    XmlTextWriter writer = new XmlTextWriter( Console.Out );
    /* Use indenting for readability */
    writer.Formatting = Formatting.Indented;
    writer.Indentation = 4;
    /* Now write out our XML document */
    writer.WriteStartDocument();
      writer.WriteStartElement( "Persons" );
        writer.WriteStartElement( "Person" );
          writer.WriteStartElement( "Name" );
            writer.WriteStartAttribute( null, "firstName", null );
              writer.WriteString( "Albert" );
            writer.WriteEndAttribute();
            writer.WriteStartAttribute( null, "lastName", null );
              writer.WriteString( "Einstein" );
            writer.WriteEndAttribute();
          writer.WriteEndElement();
```

(continued)

Listing 16-10 *continued*

```
        writer.WriteEndElement();
        writer.WriteStartElement( "Person" );
          writer.WriteStartElement( "Name" );
            writer.WriteStartAttribute( null, "firstName", null );
              writer.WriteString( "Niels" );
            writer.WriteEndAttribute();
            writer.WriteStartAttribute( null, "lastName", null );
              writer.WriteString( "Bohr" );
            writer.WriteEndAttribute();
          writer.WriteEndElement();
        writer.WriteEndElement();
      writer.WriteEndElement();
    writer.WriteEndDocument();
    /* Don't forget to close the writer */
    writer.Close();
  }
}
```

Note that we have used the concrete class *XmlTextWriter* in WriteXML.cs. *XmlTextWriter* is a concrete implementation of *XmlWriter* for writing out character streams. It supports many different output types such as file, URI, and stream. It also provides pretty printing and other options properties for characteristics like indentation, namespace support, attribute quote character, and so on.

Languages Built on the .NET Framework

At the time of this writing there are about 20 programming languages—existing or under development from Microsoft and third parties—that can be used for building .NET applications. If that is not exciting enough, all these languages will be able to work together more seamlessly than ever before. This integration is possible because all these languages are compliant with the Common Language Specifications (CLS) and they all run under the same runtime. We will look at some of these languages here, namely C#, Visual Basic .NET, Jscript .NET, C++, and a few others.

The runtime is the core enabler of multilanguage program development and execution in .NET. The runtime manages the execution of code and provides services that make development easier. .NET compilers and tools expose the runtime's functionality and enable you to write code that benefits from this managed-execution environment.

Code that needs to execute under the runtime environment is referred to as "managed code." The runtime provides the following benefits to managed code:

- *Cross-language integration* The runtime makes it easy to write components and applications that interact across languages. For example, you can define a class in C# that extends another class that was written in Visual Basic .NET.
- *Security* The runtime provides an automatic built-in security mechanism for determining whether a particular managed component or application is allowed to run and that degree of trusted access that should be given to protected resources.
- *Versioning and deployment support* The runtime uses metadata stored with managed code to ensure that your component or application has the specified versions of everything it needs.
- *Debugging and profiling services* The runtime provides built-in services and tools to help developers debug and profile managed code easily.
- *Memory Management* The runtime provides memory-management features that manage object lifetimes automatically.

C#

With .NET, Microsoft introduced a new programming language called C# (pronounced "c sharp"). C# is a modern object-oriented language and is designed from the ground up to work well within the .NET Framework. It provides seamless support for developing systems that rely on .NET, from managed components to XML Web services. Microsoft touts C# as a new language that combines the power of C++ with the ease of use of Visual Basic. Just as C++ and Visual Basic have been the de facto standards for developing applications for Windows, Microsoft hopes that C# will become the preferred language for developing .NET applications.

C# is consistently object-oriented. Everything in C# is an object, including primitive types like integer, floats, and the like. In addition, in line with a stricter object-oriented approach, C# ditches the concept of global functions, types, and variables. C# provides the equivalent static methods and variables to make code easier to read and less prone to naming conflicts. In addition, program execution no long starts from a global main function but instead starts with a call to a static *Main()* method in a class.

Many error-prone constructs and idioms in C++ are removed from C#. For example, C# does not support multiple inheritance and preprocessor macros, and instead uses interfaces and namespaces as a more elegant solution. C# also dispenses with the irksome -> pointer indicator and the :: namespace operator of C++. In C# everything is represented by a dot.

Data types have been significantly simplified in C#. For example, all character data is encoded as Unicode. A char is a char is a char. Gone are the confusing unsigned char, signed char, and wchar_t typed data types used in C++. A 64-bit integer is a long, not an __int64, and a 32-bit integer is simply int.

C# does retain some of the more powerful features of C++. For example, C# supports operator overloading, enumerations, and a variable number of method arguments. You can even use dangerous constructs like pointers, structs, and static arrays in C#, but they need to be used within explicitly declared unsafe classes and methods.

C# has great potential for becoming the tool of choice for .NET programming with its unique combination of power and simplicity. If you want to learn more about C#, check out the C# tutorials and references in the .NET Framework SDK documentation.

Visual Basic .NET

The price that you sometimes have to pay for running under the runtime is that specific languages might need to adapt to conform to it. Nowhere is this more evident than in Visual Basic .NET. Microsoft has introduced so many fundamental changes to its earlier Visual Basic that you should consider this a brand new language. As a result, upgrading previous versions of Visual Basic projects to Visual Basic .NET will typically require more preparation than a simple port.

Most of the new features in Visual Basic .NET stem from it having to comply with the CLS and accommodate the runtime and its associated programming model. Visual Basic .NET has many new object-oriented design features and much higher levels of type safety than previous versions of Visual Basic. The new object-oriented capabilities in Visual Basic .NET include support for full inheritance, parameterized constructors, method and properties overriding, method and operator overloading, and shared members.

Visual Basic .NET was also enhanced with modern programming constructs such as structured exception handling and threading. Some of the more significant features replaced or retired in the move from Visual Basic 6 to Visual Basic .NET are

- Default methods and properties are no longer supported.
- Many keywords, including *Let*, *Gosub*, *VarPtr*, *ObjPtr*, and *StrPtr*, were retired.
- Visual Basic .NET introduces new syntax for factors like class properties, declaring and initializing variables, and especially arrays.
- Parentheses are now required for all methods, even those without arguments.

- All arguments are now *ByVal* by default.
- And, Or, and Xor are strictly for boolean operations. The new BitAnd, BitOr, and BitXor should be used for bitwise arithmetic.

Again, these are just some of the changes introduced in Visual Basic .NET. You should read the .NET Framework SDK documentation for a complete coverage of programming in Visual Basic .NET.

Jscript .NET

Together with C# and Visual Basic .NET, Microsoft introduced a new version of JScript called Jscript .NET. Jscript .NET combines the existing features of JScript with features usually found only in class-based and compiled languages. It is a true object-oriented language with full support for industrial-strength features such as inheritance and interfaces. And because JSript is a fully-fledged .NET-compliant language, you can create classes in Jscript .NET which can be used by other .NET languages and, conversely, extend classes defined in other languages.

Jscript .NET introduces many performance-improvement features. The most important of these, undoubtedly, is that Jscript .NET is a true compiled language, making its run-time performance comparable to C# and Visual Basic .NET. From a language perspective, Jscript .NET now provides strongly typed programming support through the explicit type declarations. Typeless and implicit typing programming is still supported through a new type-inferencing technology so existing scripts will still run.

Unlike Visual Basic .NET, Jscript .NET was specifically designed for full backward compatiblity, so all your existing code will continue to work just fine. All the new features, such as typing and class declarations, are optional. The new features, however, will allow you to reap the benefits of improved performance and robustness.

For more information about Jscript .NET, check out the JScript .NET section in the .NET Framework SDK documentation.

C++

C++ is alive and well in the .NET Framework. You can continue to use Visual C++ in .NET in the same old way, but to be able to take full advantage of the benefits of the runtime, Microsoft has extended C++ to provide support for "managed programming." These Managed Extensions for C++, as they are called, are mainly comprised of a set of new keywords and attributes. With Managed Extensions for C++, the runtime will provide automatic object lifetime and memory management (including garbage collection), enhanced exception handling, security, and finally debugging and profiling services for your C++ components and applications.

If you are a C++ programmer and you are interested in exploring managed programming, you should read the "Programming with Managed Extensions for C++" chapter in the .NET Framework SDK documentation.

Other Languages

As we mentioned earlier, besides C#, C++, and Visual Basic .NET, many other languages provided by third-party vendors can be used for .NET programming. For example, ActiveState Corp. (*http://www.activestate.com*) provides .NET implementations of the Perl and Python programming languages. Interactive Software Engineering is working with Microsoft to develop an implementation of the Eiffel programming language for .NET. Other vendors are also working on providing more programming languages, such as Pascal and even Java, for .NET. For the latest developments in this area you should visit the Microsoft MSDN Third Party .NET Resources Web site at *http://msdn.microsoft.com/net/thirdparty/*.

Conclusion

This book has taken you through many of the curves, obstacles, and straightaways of the XML highway. We have covered the language, how it should be used, and how to build successful enterprise-level applications. You should now have a good understanding of XML Web services and the .NET Framework. We've covered a lot of material.

Here is where the book ends and you go down your own path. Carefully consider the lessons learned within these pages, and be sure to make solid and sound decisions about how and why you are using XML. From the three of us, good luck!

Part V

Appendices

Appendix A

Related Standards

XML, in many respects, is about standards, or the creation thereof. Even if you're just creating a schema for your own purposes, you're going down the path of creating a language to standardize your approach to something—to standardize your means of describing data and perhaps transmitting it to others.

XML has given individuals, companies large and small, and entire industries the ability to define the common grounds on which they describe and exchange data. And while XML was the driving force behind the ability to do this, like today's alphabet, it wasn't until people created languages and applications to use XML before it's abilities became exposed.

Today many of the standards created either build upon or utilize others. For instance, you might have a DTD document that is transported as a "payload" within the Microsoft BizTalk Framework. In this appendix we will discuss some of these related standards and how they pertain to XML. Because these efforts are often intertwined, this should be extremely useful in understanding what is out there, what XML is used for, and how you might tap it instead of writing your own solution.

Structured Standards

The structure of a document will often be one of the most important features for use and human readability. Take this book as an example—it has top-level headings, secondary headings, and so on. This is accomplished through the use of various "styles" that many of you have seen in word-processing programs. Many of these styles imply a structure, and that structure results in the table of contents: the ordering of the information in the book world.

When using XML, structure is important because it can show the parent-child relationship between elements. Take a hypothetical *<name>* element. If it's the child element of a *<company>* element, it most likely has a different meaning than if it's a child of a *<person>* element. This structure, although not necessary, makes the use of long element and attribute names unnecessary.

We've included unstructured.xml (Listing A-1) and structured.xml (Listing A-2) as examples. Although they contain the same information, the ability of a human or application to digest what is contained in the document is much easier in the more verbose structured.xml. Because XML requires only a single root element to be well-formed, the unstructured.xml document is actually a well-formed XML document.

Listing A-1 unstructured.xml: Using long names to imply structure.

```
<?xml version = "1.0" encoding = "UTF-8"?>
<entry>
  <employeecompanyname>Some Company, Inc</employeecompanyname>
  <employeename>Allen Wyke</employeename>
</entry>
```

Listing A-2 structured.xml: Applying structure with a hierarchy of elements.

```
<?xml version = "1.0" encoding = "UTF-8"?>
<entry type="employee">
  <company>
    <name>Some Company, Inc</name>
  </company>
  <name>Allen Wyke</name>
</entry>
```

The DTDs of XML are not the only method of applying structure to your documents and data. Within this section we will explore other structure-related specifications, such as Namepaces in XML, XML Schema, and the Resource Description Framework, and standards at your disposal.

Namespaces in XML

At its core, the purpose of XML is to be extensible. The ability of individuals, companies, and industries to define languages, markup, dialects, or all these factors to describe their data is powerful. However, this inter networked world has no use for a reinvented wheel. Many languages have similar elements, attributes, and structure. Contact information, for instance, usually contains a name, address, phone number, email, and the like.

Instead of having each schema define its own language, XML was created to be flexible enough to embed multiple languages into instance documents. This includes elements, as well as attributes. Flexibility allows an XHTML document, for instance, to also contain MathML markup. Let's use this as an example.

Listing A-3, sample-ns.xml, is an XHTML document that defines XHTML as the default namespace. In the *<body>* of the XHTML we have embedded some MathML, defining its own namespace for the enclosed elements.

Listing A-3 sample-ns.xml: Shows how namespaces in XML are used.

```
<?xml version = "1.0" encoding = "UTF-8"?>
<!DOCTYPE html PUBLIC "-//W3C//DTD XHTML 1.0 Transitional//EN"
    "http://www.w3.org/TR/xhtml1/DTD/xhtml1-transitional.dtd">
<html xmlns="http://www.w3.org/1999/xhtml"
      lang="en" xml:lang="en">
<head>
  <title>XHTML and MathML Namespace Example</title>
</head>
<body>
  <p>The following is marked in MathML</p>
  <math xmlns="http://www.w3.org/1998/Math/MathML">
    <mrow>
      <mi>x</mi>
      <mo>=</mo>
      <mfrac>
        <mrow>
          <msqrt>
            <mrow>
              <msup>
                <mi>b</mi>
                <mn>2</mn>
              </msup>
              <mo>-</mo>
              <mrow>
                <mn>4</mn>
                <mo>&InvisibleTimes;</mo>
                <mi>a</mi>
                <mo>&InvisibleTimes;</mo>
                <mi>c</mi>
              </mrow>
            </mrow>
          </msqrt>
        </mrow>
        <mrow>
```

(continued)

Listing A-3 *continued*

```
            <mn>2</mn>
            <mo>&InvisibleTimes;</mo>
            <mi>a</mi>
          </mrow>
        </mfrac>
      </mrow>
    </math>
  </body>
  </html>
```

We included MathML in with our XHTML. All we needed to do was define the namespace for the MathML elements, which is done with the *xmlns* attribute specifying the namespace URI so a parser will know how to interpret the content. Figure A-1 shows what this example looks like in the MathML supporting version of the open source Mozilla browser.

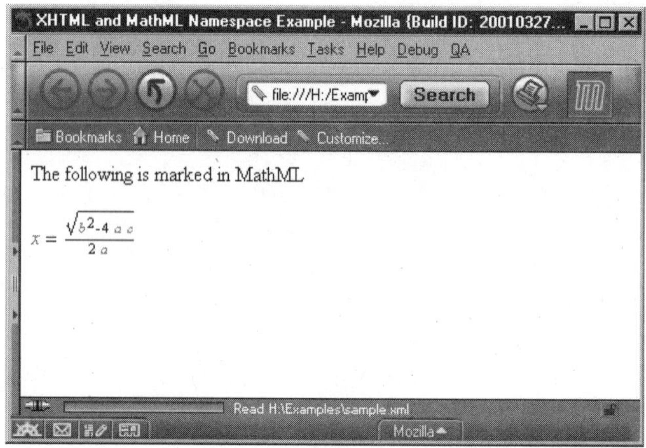

Figure A-1 Rendering our sample-ns.xml document in the Mozilla browser.

> **Note** If you want to see this work for yourself, download the Mozilla version that supports MathML. Also download some extra fonts to support the MathML characters. You can obtain more information about this at *http://www.mozilla.org/projects/mathml.*

Associating a namespace with a block of elements (between the start and ending *<math>* elements in our example) is not the only way to declare namespaces. Declaring a namespace within the root element of the document is also possible, giving it a prefix and then prefacing all elements and attributes of that namespace with the same prefix. For instance, if we wanted to create a namespace in this manner for our previous example, we could have had the following:

```
<html xmlns="http://www.w3.org/1999/xhtml"
      xmlns:mml="http://www.w3.org/1998/Math/MathML"
        lang="en" xml:lang="en">
```

By declaring the MathML namespace here, we can use any of the elements and attributes of this language in the body of our document by placing *mml*: in front of them. Listing A-4, sample2-ns.xml, demonstrates this approach. Notice how we are able to include a MathML element inside an XHTML element without having the root *<math>* element present; the namespace allows us to do this.

Listing A-4 sample2-ns.xml: Using Namespaces in XML to include MathML within an XHTML document.

```
<?xml version = "1.0" encoding = "UTF-8"?>
<!DOCTYPE html PUBLIC "-//W3C//DTD XHTML 1.0 Transitional//EN"
    "http://www.w3.org/TR/xhtml1/DTD/xhtml1-transitional.dtd">
<html xmlns="http://www.w3.org/1999/xhtml"
      xmlns:mml="http://www.w3.org/1998/Math/MathML"
      lang="en" xml:lang="en">
<head>
  <title>XHTML and MathML Namespace Example</title>
</head>
<body>
  <p>The following is marked in MathML</p>
  <mml:mrow>
    <mml:mi>x</mml:mi>
    <mml:mo>=</mml:mo>
    <mml:mfrac>
      <mml:mrow>
        <mml:msqrt>
          <mml:mrow>
            <mml:msup>
              <mml:mi>b</mml:mi>
              <mml:mn>2</mml:mn>
            </mml:msup>
          </mml:mrow>
        </mml:msqrt>
      </mml:mrow>
      <mml:mrow>
        <mml:mn>2</mml:mn>
      </mml:mrow>
```

(continued)

Listing A-4 *continued*

```
    </mml:mfrac>
   </mml:mrow>
   <p>Here is an example of including a MathML element right in the
   body of an XHTML element <mml:msqrt></mml:msqrt></p>
 </body>
 </html>
```

This is all we are going to cover on Namespaces in XML here. We used namespaces heavily throughout the book, so you should be familiar with them and the practice of using them.

> **Note** If you would like more information on Namespaces in XML, please check out *http://www.w3.org/TR/REC-xml-names.*

XML Schema

XML Schema is, though controversial at times, considered to be the next generation of XML. It brings together the best of XML 1.0 with other related standards such as XML-Data, Document Content Description for XML (DCD), SOX, and Document Definition Markup Language (DDML), all of which are W3C Notes.

This effort, housed at the W3C, reached Recommendation status recently. The Recommendation is divided into three sections: Primer, Structures, and Datatypes. The Primer, Part 0, is a document to get you familiar with the core XML Schema language: Structures and Datatypes. It provides some good reading and examples, so if you are not familiar with XML Schema, it's worth the read.

Part 1, Structures, provides the mechanisms to define structure and any constraints that your data might need. This not only includes the DTDs defined in XML 1.0, but also those exploited through the use of namespaces. This part of the specification also relies on Part 2, Datatypes.

The final part of XML Schema addresses datatypes. It provides means by which datatypes can be defined in XML Schema or other XML-based languages. Thes datatypes defined in XML Schema represent a superset of the datatyping capabilities in XML 1.0's DTDs.

As an example, let's first build an XML DTD (entry.dtd in Listing A-5) for the structured.xml document we used earlier, and then show its XML Schema representation. Before we show you the schema, let's create a copy of the structured.xml document, called structured-valid.xml, and include the following line so it can be compared against our schema by a parser.

Listing A-5 entry.dtd: DTD that corresponds and describes the data in structured-valid.xml.

```
<!DOCTYPE entry SYSTEM "entry.dtd">
<?xml version='1.0' encoding='UTF-8' ?>
<!ELEMENT entry (company , name)>
<!ATTLIST entry  type CDATA  #IMPLIED >
<!ELEMENT company (name)>
<!ELEMENT name (#PCDATA)>
```

The XML Schema representation is shown in entry.xsd (Listing A-6). As you can see, XML Schema can be more verbose than a DTD, but at the same time, this example is a direct translation and does not add any of the benefits of XML Schema, such as the datatyping.

Listing A-6 entry.xsd: XML Schema version of our DTD.

```
<?xml version = "1.0" encoding = "UTF-8"?>
<xsd:schema xmlns:xsd = "http://www.w3.org/2001/XMLSchema">
  <xsd:element name = "entry">
    <xsd:complexType>
      <xsd:sequence>
        <xsd:element ref = "company"/>
        <xsd:element ref = "name"/>
      </xsd:sequence>
      <xsd:attribute name = "type" type = "xsd:string"/>
    </xsd:complexType>
  </xsd:element>
  <xsd:element name = "company">
    <xsd:complexType>
      <xsd:sequence>
        <xsd:element ref = "name"/>
      </xsd:sequence>
    </xsd:complexType>
  </xsd:element>
  <xsd:element name = "name" type = "xsd:string"/>
</xsd:schema>
```

XML Schema delivers many advancements and enhancements, so it would be wise to familiarize yourself with XML Schema and potentially build some applications using it. It is an incredibly powerful standard that can offer a wealth of abilities to implementers.

Note If you want more information on XML Schema, check out *http://www.w3.org/XML/Schema*. More good information is at *http://www.ascc.net/~ricko/XMLSchemaInContext.html*.

Resource Description Framework

One of the first efforts that emerged to enforce structure on data was the Resource Description Framework (RDF). RDF represents a manner in which metadata can be created to describe other data, as well as the basic syntax for the encoding and transmission of this metadata. The table of contents of this book can be considered metadata because it is not the actual contents of the book, but represents a description of what the book contains.

Behind the scenes, RDF is an XML language with the use of namespaces. It not only allows for the interoperability of metadata, but also for a machine-understandable description of Web resources (anything with a URI). These resources are described through a collection of properties, including property type and value, called RDF Description.

As an example, let's say we had a URI *(http://mspress.microsoft.com/xml/example)* that we wanted to describe as being created by a person at a particular company. Let's also say that the entry.dtd we created earlier contained the structure we wanted to use to define the name of this person and company. Listing A-7 shows our example, sample.rdf.

Listing A-7 sample.rdf: Sample RDF document describing a URI with our entry.dtd data model.

```
<?xml version="1.0"?>
<RDF xmlns    = "http://www.w3.org/1999/02/22-rdf-syntax-ns#"
     xmlns:EN = "http://mspress.microsoft.com/xml/entry.dtd">
  <Description
     about="http://mspress.microsoft.com/xml/example" >
    <EN:entry>
      <EN:company>
        <EN:name>Some Company, Inc.</EN:name>
      </EN:company>
      <EN:name>R. Allen Wyke</EN:name>
    </EN:entry>
  </Description>
</RDF>
```

> **Note** The # symbol at the end of the RDF URI is important. It combines the namespace name with the local name to get the full URI of a property type.

The first task we perform after declaring it as an XML document is to define the default namespace (RDF) and a second namespace (Entry Name—entry.dtd). Using the RDF *<Description>* element, we specify that we want to describe the *http://mspress.microsoft.com/xml/example* URI. To define this we use the *<name>* element of (child of *<company>*) to hold the company name and the top level *<name>* element to define the individual.

This is a simplistic example, but it demonstrates the purpose of RDF: the ability to describe URIs (Web resources). In addition to the *<Description>* element, RDF also has other elements. Elements, for instance, that allow you to define Bags (*<Bag>*), Sequences (*<Seq>*), and Alternatives (*<Alt>*)—all types of collections. You also have several attributes at your disposal that do everything from identify individual elements within a collection to specifying the type of resource it is.

> **Note** For more information on RDF check out *http://www.w3.org/RDF.*

Linking-Based Standards

With the birth of the Web came the need for and dependency on linking. Whether it was for being able to link to internal locations within a document, or to link to new documents altogether, the need for links was apparent. These are just a few of the reasons the *<a>* (anchor) element is so widely used and, frankly, a requirement for any Web-published document. But linking for HTML is not the only document type that needs this functionality. XML documents also need the ability to link to other resources. Additionally, efforts should be made to prevent broken links.

In this section we will introduce you to several efforts that revolve around linking, such as XLink and XPointer. As you will see, dramatic improvements are being made and the world of linking, as we currently know it, is changing.

The XML Linking Language

The XML Linking Language (XLink) builds upon the basic unidirectional *<a>* element links we are used to in HTML and XHTML. It not only defines and provides this familiar functionality, it also provides for more complex linking structures, including

- Asserting linking relationships between two or more documents
- Associating metadata with links
- Expressing links that reside in a location separate from the linked resource

The XLink language itself consists of several attributes within the XLink namespace that define how the link is to be handled and how it works. The type attribute, which is one of the most important, defines the type of link. Table A-1 lists the possible types of links.

Table A-1 Types of XLink Links

Type	Description
arc	Provides traversal rules among the link's participating resources.
extended	Offers full XLink functionality.
locator	Address of the remote resource participating in the link.
none	Has no specific XLink meaning.
resource	Supplies local resources that participate in the link.
simple	Offers shorthand syntax for the common outbound link between two participating resources (like how the *<a>* element currently works).
title	Provides a human-readable title for a link.

The Mozilla browser was one of the first user agents to support XLink, and it provides the ability to perform some functions using the simple links as defined by the XLink specification. To demonstrate, xlink.xml in Listing A-8 contains three links using the XLink language. If you load this XML document into the browser, you will be able to click on the links to access the pages.

Listing A-8 xlink.xml: An XLink example which can be run in the Mozilla browser.

```
<?xml version="1.0"?>
<body xmlns:xlink="http://www.w3.org/1999/xlink">
  <para>Here is a list of my favorite links...
    <li xlink:type="simple"
        xlink:href="http://www.msn.com">Personal</li>
    <li xlink:type="simple"
        xlink:href="http://msdn.microsoft.com">Work</li>
    <li xlink:type="simple"
        xlink:href="http://www.microsoft.com">Industry</li>
  </para>
</body>
```

The XML Path Language

The XML Path Language (XPath), which is used to address parts of an XML document, represents shared syntax and semantics between XSLT and XPointer. XPath models a document as a tree of nodes, which includes element, attribute, and text nodes. It then provides the grammar for accessing the leaves of these nodes.

For instance, the syntax *child::p* selects the *<p>* element children of the context node. If you wanted all element children you would use *child::**. You can even describe more complex locations such as the first *<p>* child of the context node with *child::p[position()=1]*. Better yet, let's say you want to find the first one with the *id* attribute set to *description*. This would be accomplished with *child::p[attribute::id=description][position()=1*].

This representation is referred to as the *Location Path* of the element instance. The *child* keyword, in these examples, is the *axis* of the XPath statement. Other axes are included in Table A-2.

In addition to identifying portions of an XML document, XPath also has the ability to perform base string, numeric, and boolean manipulation. As the world of linking within XML documents (especially on the Web) begins to demand more out of user agents, XPath will play a major role in defining and describing documents for linking purposes.

Note You can find more information on XPath at *http://www.w3.org/TR/xpath*.

Table A-2 Axes in XPath

Key	Description
ancestor	Contains the ancestors of the context node. This refers to the parent of the context node and the parent's parent and so on.
ancestor-or-self	Contains the context node and the ancestors of the context node.
attribute	Contains the attributes of the context node.
child	Contains the children of the context node.
descendant	Contains the descendants of the context node. This refers to a child or a child of a child and so on of the context node.
descendant-or-self	Contains the context node and the descendants of the context node.
following	Contains all nodes in the same document as the context node that are after the context node in document order, excluding any descendants or attribute and namespace nodes.
following-sibling	Contains all the following siblings of the context node.
namespace	Contains the namespace nodes of the context node.
parent	Contains the parent of the context node, if one exists.
preceding	Contains all nodes in the same document as the context node that are before the context node in document order, excluding any descendants or attribute and namespace nodes.
preceding-sibling	Contains all the preceding siblings of the context node.
self	Contains just the context node itself.

The XML Pointer Language

The XML Pointer Language (XPointer) is based on XPath and supports the addressing of internal parts of an XML document. This allows you to evaluate a document's structure and choose internal subsets based on criteria such as element types, attribute values, character content, and relative position. This is accomplished by defining extensions to XPath.

Using XHTML as an example, if you wanted to find the element with the *id* attribute value set to *booktitle*, you would use the following syntax:

```
xpointer(id("booktitle"))
```

This might, syntactically, look similar to XPath, as you would expect. But an extension to XPath in XPointer also allows you to specify a range. Maybe you want to locate everything from the title (*id=booktitle*) of the book to the end (*id=bookend*). You could do this with

```
xpointer(id("booktitle")/range-to(id("bookend")))
```

XPointer, which is currently at a Candidate Recommendation state at the W3C, offers flexibility over the standard *<a>* element usage common in HTML and XHTML. However, because of the immaturity of this specification effort, we recommend you wait before implementing this in any of your projects. Once it has reached a Proposed Recommendation state, although not complete, you should be safe to use it as you see fit.

The XML Base

Linking, as we have seen, is an important piece of functionality. It allows us to build virtual documents and information repositories by linking from document to outside resources. But often, as we have commonly seen in HTML and XHTML, links are not absolute URIs, but are relative to the resource.

Rendering user agents, especially off line browsers, might need to know the absolute URIs for their processing. To handle this type of situation Web developers use the XHTML *<base>* element, which can specify the base URI for any relative URIs a given document might contain. The need for this is no different in XML. In response and in addition to the other efforts the XLink Working Group is working on, XML Base was born.

XML Base is a short specification whose sole purpose is to enable XML developers using links the ability to specify base URIs. This is accomplished by including an *xml:base* attribute in the root element with a value equal to the base URI. Additionally, you can specify this attribute in child elements if you: (*a*) do not want to apply the base URI to all elements in a document, or (*b*) want to override the base URI for a specific element and any child elements it has.

As an example, let's take a look at sample-base.xml in Listing A-9. Here we define a base URI of *http://www.microsoft.com/employees/* for the entire document, but we override it for the list of sites we have included.

Listing A-9 sample-base.xml: A simple demonstration of defining a base URI for a whole document, and then overriding it for specific elements and their children.

```
<?xml version="1.0"?>
<user xml:base="http://www.microsoft.com/employees/"
      xmlns:xlink="http://www.w3.org/1999/xlink">
  <name>R. Allen Wyke</name>
  <phone>919.555.1212</phone>
  <!-- base URI applies to the following 3 child elements -->
  <sites xml:base="/www/">
    <li xlink:type="simple"
        xlink:href="pesonal.xml">Personal</li>
    <li xlink:type="simple"
        xlink:href="work.xml">Work</li>
    <li xlink:type="simple"
        xlink:href="industry.xml">Industry</li>
  </sites>
  <!-- base URI defined in root element applies here -->
  <img src="photo.gif" alt="My Photo" width="40" height="40" />
</user>
```

This is all the XML Base specification is: the *xml:base* attribute. If you want to learn more about this standard and how user agents are supposed to conform, please see *http://www.w3.org/TR/xmlbase*.

Transformation and Remote Object Access

Creating structured documents and providing a means to link to and from them gives developers a wide range of abilities. However, structures are not always in a format you can process, and the method in which you transmit this data could be inconsistent with other enterprises. These are common issues that arise when implementing XML-based solutions and they need to be addressed for compatibility and flexibility reasons.

In the following two subsections we will cover a few standards, such as XSLT and SOAP, that help ease the pain these situations present. These are both complete, in W3C standards terms, and you will find applications already leveraging their power.

Extensible Stylesheet Language Transformations

XSLT, which we have covered in part in earlier chapters, is a language that allows you to transform one document schema into another. This is tremendously powerful when you use XML in the enterprise because it allows you to accept various documents structures, by transforming them into a structure that you natively support. The process is simple. Accept another document structure, apply the appropriate XSLT style sheet, and transform the document into a schema you can utilize in your processing.

XSLT is a useful approach for transforming your content markup so you can publish to multiple devices. If you define your content within an XML language, applying an XSLT style sheet to transform the document into XHTML, WML, or any other device-specific markup or other text format is easy. This allows you to create content once and, through the application of transformations, publish it anywhere.

The best way to learn and understand XSLT is through an example. Suppose we want to take the structured-valid.xml document we created earlier and transform it into valid XHTML. Let's rename it structured-trans.xml so as not to get confused. To do this we will not only need to include the header and body elements of the document (*<html>*, *<head>*, *<body>*, and so forth.), but we must also transform our *<entry>*, *<company>*, and *<name>* elements into valid XHTML elements. As a refresher, here is Listing A-10, our structured-trans.xml document:

Listing A-10 structured-trans.xml: An instance document of our entry.dtd schema.

```
<?xml version = "1.0" encoding = "UTF-8"?>
<!DOCTYPE entry SYSTEM "entry.dtd">
<entry type = "employee">
    <company>
        <name>Some Company, Inc</name>
    </company>
    <name>Allen Wyke</name>
</entry>
```

Once the *input* document has been created we must create an XSLT file that contains the appropriate mapping from our data model defined in entry.dtd to XHTML. For this example we will include the company name in the *<title>* as well as in the *<body>* of our document. The body of the document will include a *<p>* element with our transformed text. Listing A-11 is our XSLT document.

Listing A-11 transform.xsl: The transformation document.

```
<?xml version="1.0"?>
<xsl:stylesheet
      xmlns:xsl="http://www.w3.org/1999/XSL/Transform"
      version="1.0">
<xsl:output method="html"/>
<xsl:template match="/">
```

(continued)

Listing A-11 *continued*

```
<html xmlns="http://www.w3.org/1999/xhtml" lang="en" xml:lang="en">
<head>
  <title><xsl:value-of select="//entry/company/name"/></title>
</head>
<body>
  <h1>User Information</h1>
  <p>
    <strong>
      Company Name:
    </strong>
    <xsl:value-of select="//entry/company/name"/>
    <br />
    <strong>
      Employee Name:
    </strong>
    <xsl:value-of select="//entry/name"/>
  </p>
</body>
</html>
</xsl:template>
</xsl:stylesheet>
```

If you take a close look at this style sheet you will notice it's fairly simple. The *<xsl:value-of>* element is used to specify the element, including structure, that you are referencing. For instance, in the *<title>* element the style sheet basically says that the *<name>* child element of the *<company>* element, which itself is a child element of *<entry>,* should be contained between the beginning and ending *<title>* elements.

Once the style sheet has been defined, all you have to do, assuming the XSLT style sheet is in the same directory, is include the following line in your structured-trans.xml document just under the *<?xml version = "1.0" encoding = "UTF-8"?>* declaration. This tells the parser that when the structured-trans.xml document is loaded it should apply the transform.xsl style sheet while processing.

```
<?xml-stylesheet type="text/xsl" href="transform.xsl"?>
```

If we load the structured-trans.xml example in Microsoft Internet Explorer (with MSXML version 3 or later) you should see something like Figure A-2.

The topic of XSLT, as you might imagine, is much broader than this simple example. We used XSLT in several of our chapter projects, so refer to them for details.

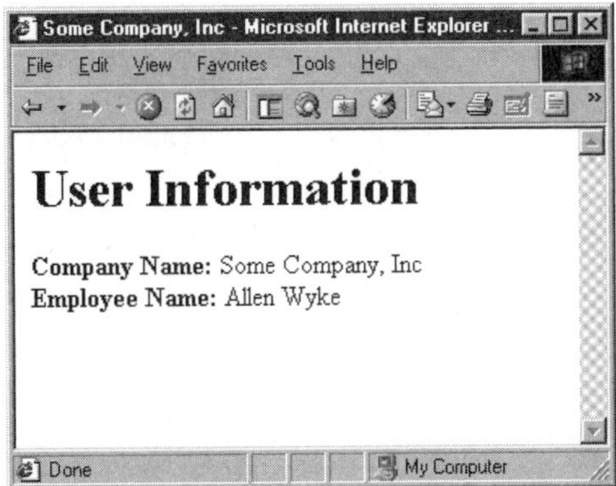

Figure A-2 Results of applying our transformation to structured-trans.xml and creating an XHTML document.

> **Note** If you want more information on the XSLT Recommendation, check out *http://www.w3.org/TR/xslt.*

The Simple Object Access Protocol

SOAP is a protocol for exchanging data in truly distributed and decentralized networks. It not only contains information on how to process its *payload*, but also a set of encoding rules for expression instances of application-defined datatypes and a procedure for representing remote procedure calls and the return of the results. We like to think of SOAP as the United Parcel Service of digital data. It not only contains the data, but also the instructions for what to do with it and how to return the results of any processing that occurred.

Because SOAP is a major component of Microsoft's .NET initiative, we dedicated all of Chapter 14 to covering it and how it works. If you are hungry for more information on SOAP, you can read up on the most recent version standard at *http://www.w3.org/TR/SOAP.*

Other Standards

You should be aware of several other standards before building your applications. Again, if you have a need or a problem to solve, someone else or another company probably had the same need as well. Knowing and understanding these standards will accelerate your time to deployment.

In this section we will look at a few standardization efforts. Specifically, we are going to look at one effort that attempts to define a method for including pieces of XML documents within other documents, and a second effort that defines a means with which to query XML documents for information.

XML Inclusions

XML Inclusions (XInclude) defines a method by which XML documents can be, at processing time, included in other documents. In much the same manner that Server Side Includes (SSI) work, XInclude syntax defines the grammar of how to reference other documents within a parent document.

For example, XMLInclude could be used if you wanted to include today's news on a page within your site, but the news was contained in a separate document. Historically you would've accomplished this with server-side processing an *<iframe>* element, but this approach does not really make the data "part" of the parent document. Using XInclude, however, you can reference your news document within the body of the document in which you want to include this information, and when processed, a single document will result.

To help you better understand this, we've built xinclude.xml (Listing A-12), a simple XHTML document, that contains a reference to a second document for inclusion.

Listing A-12 xinclude.xml: An XHTML document that contains a separate XIncluded document.

```
<?xml version="1.0"?>
<!DOCTYPE html PUBLIC "-//W3C//DTD XHTML 1.0 Transitional//EN"
    "http://www.w3.org/TR/xhtml1/DTD/xhtml1-transitional.dtd">
<html xmlns="http://www.w3.org/1999/xhtml"
      xmlns:xinclude="http://www.w3.org/1999/XML/xinclude"
      lang="en" xml:lang="en">
<head>
  <title>XInclude</title>
</head>
<body>
  <h1>Today's News</h1>
  <xinclude:include href="news.xml" />
</body>
</html>
```

As you can see, the syntax for this inclusion is simple. Using the XInclude namespace, we use the *<include>* element to specify the news.xml document for inclusion. Listing A-13, the news.xml document, only contains some basic information for our news stories.

Listing A-13 news.xml: A sample news document we will use for inclusion.

```
<h2>Sports</h2>
<p>
  The NHL is nearing the end of their season, and the race
  for the cup is in full swing. <a href="nhl.xml">Read
  more...</a>
</p>
<h2>Travel</h2>
<p>
  Airfares continue to go down as the economy slows.
  <a href="nhl.xml">Read more...</a>
</p>
```

When processed, the resulting document (xinclude-result.xml), after inclusion, will look like the following:

```
<?xml version="1.0"?>
<!DOCTYPE html PUBLIC "-//W3C//DTD XHTML 1.0 Transitional//EN"
    "http://www.w3.org/TR/xhtml1/DTD/xhtml1-transitional.dtd">
<html xmlns="http://www.w3.org/1999/xhtml"
      xmlns:xinclude="http://www.w3.org/1999/XML/xinclude"
      lang="en" xml:lang="en">
<head>
  <title>XInclude</title>
</head>
<body>
  <h1>Today's News</h1>
  <h2>Sports</h2>
  <p>
    The NHL is nearing the end of their season, and the race
    for the cup is in full swing. <a href="nhl.xml">Read
    more...</a>
  </p>
  <h2>Travel</h2>
  <p>
    Airfares continue to go down as the economy slows.
    <a href="nhl.xml">Read more...</a>
  </p>
</body>
</html>
```

XInclude might look like a relatively simple standard, but if you think of the overall picture of creating a semantic Web where content is not replicated, but referenced and included, it presents a compelling message for managing your content.

> **Note** XInclude is currently a Working Draft at the W3C, so there could be substantial changes in the specification before it become a complete Recommendation. For this reason, we limit our coverage here to the basics.

XML Query

One of the most powerful aspects of databases is the ability to query them for information—not only bulk information, but also for information that only fits specific criteria. The efforts of the XML Query Working Group at the W3C revolve around an attempt to create a standardized method to query XML documents. The desired result was a method to access information from real and virtual (remember XInclude) XML documents like you would a database.

The XML Query work revolves around three core items. First is the XQuery 1.0 and XPath 2.0 Data Model, which is a node-labeled, tree-constructor representation of an XML document that also includes the concept of node identity. Second is XQuery 1.0 Formal Semantics, which defines the operators and grammar for querying XML documents. Finally, the group created XQuery, which is a query language built on XQuery 1.0 Formal Semantics, for querying XML documents.

> **Note** The works of the XML Query Working Group are currently at a Working Draft state, and therefore unstable at this point. While we recommended you read and familiarize yourself with the standard, we do not advise you to begin building applications using the guidelines it defines. However, Microsoft has created a prototype application using a version of XML Query that you can experiment with at *http://131.107.228.20/*. If you need to build applications soon, we recommend you contact the working group at *http://www.w3.org/XML/Query* and ask to be involved. Otherwise, wait until the Proposed Recommendation is published.

Final Thought

Following and understanding related XML efforts is a big part of being active in and with XML. Chances are, if you have a need, someone else had the same need and possibly solved the problem. By taking extra time and doing research, in addition to the time you spend staying on top of the latest languages and dialects, you can potentially reduce the amount of work you have to do.

Appendix B

XML Software

When XML was first developed and declared an official Recommendation by the W3C, everyone monitoring its progress, including the overall technical industry, realized that XML was going to be a major part of their future systems. Adoption of XML was slow, however, and people found its semantics hard to understand and digest.

This problem was not because XML is terribly complex, but more a case of "old habits die hard." Everyone was used to using HTML as their means of marking up content and sending it to others. XML, for true implementations, demanded more than just a structured document. Instances needed, though did not require, to be validated and servers or other receiving software had to be written to process the documents when transmitted. For this reason it was nearly two years before any successful applications emerged that truly decreased the amount of time it took to create XML solutions.

However, the time of emerging XML-based software tools, servers, and other applications is now here. Microsoft helped lead this charge and many other vendors created tools, components, and entire solutions based around the flexibility and syntax of XML. As you found out with this book, Microsoft's .NET initiative is not only a type of solution, but also a reflection of an entire shift to communicating and enabling via XML.

In this appendix we will introduce you to some of the tools you can tap for XML development. Because XML is not a platform-dependent language, we have tried to provide information on tools, such as those from Altova and TIBCO Extensibility, for all major platforms so you do not feel locked into the Microsoft Windows environment. Conversely as you saw throughout this book and especially in Chapter 16, Microsoft helped enable this cross-platform- and environment-independence by basing its .NET Framework on open standards.

Development Tools

For many of us development tools are more than just a way of life—they represent an absolute necessity. Even for those of us who often prefer a good text editor and the command line, high-end development tools usually help accelerate our application creation and ease our learning curve, especially for tag-based technologies like XML. These IDEs get us started quickly and allow us to reach our goals faster.

Over the next few pages we are going to and cover some of the more popular development tools on the market today. Because Windows and UNIX-based systems, such as Linux, often represent the majority of application-development environments, we will focus on applications that run on these operating systems. For any Mac OS users out there, especially OS X users, we will even have a few for you.

Schema and DTD Tools

The first type of tools we are going to look at are XML DTD and Schema (as in XML Schema) creation tools. Back in 1998 and even in early 1999, these types of tools basically did not exist. Most schemas were created using a text editor, like Notepad, and validated using command-line applications. Today, however, IDEs exist that provide advanced features, such as real-time validation and error reporting, which lay the foundation for our XML solutions.

In this section of the appendix we are going to share some details about XML Authority and XML Spy—two leading schema development editors.

XML Authority

XML Authority *(http://www.tibco.com),* which was developed by a company called Extensibility (later purchased by TIBCO), was one of the first schema-development environments created for XML. Its simple and easy-to-use interface, shown in Figure B-1, allowed developers to quickly and easily create schemas and verify them in realtime. While it supplied a means by which you could create, modify, and delete elements and attributes, it also provided a visual representation of your model, the ability to insert comments easily, and direct source modification for those of us who need to touch the code directly at times.

One of the best features of the XML Authority product, besides its UI, is its support for multiple dialects. For instance, you can open an XML DTD and,

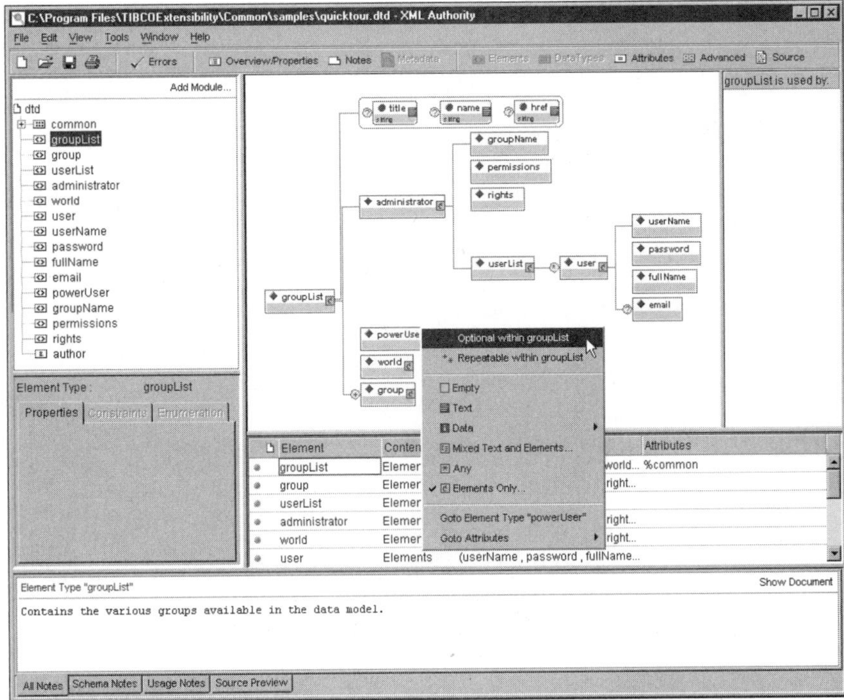

Figure B-1 TIBCO Extensibility's XML Authority product.

with the common Save As... menu option, save the equivalent XML Schema, SOX, SGML, Microsoft BizTalk–compatible, and other representations. It performs the transformation from one language to another.

Table B-1 displays the supported dialects of the software as of version 6.1. In this table we have included the name of the dialect, a description, and a quick example of how their outputs vary for a simple element definition. The example shown later will be based on the following XML DTD definition.

```
<!ELEMENT example (#PCDATA)>
```

> **Note** You will notice that some of these examples look the same, which should provide some insight into how some of these dialects are closely related and even based on one another.

Table B-1 Dialects Supported in XML Authority

Dialect	Description	Example
BizTalk Compatible	An XML-based design framework for implementing schemas and a set of XML tags used in messages sent between applications *(http://www.biztalk.org).*	*<ElementType name = "example" content = "textOnly" model = "closed"/>*
DCD	A structural schema facility for specifying rules covering the structure and content of XML documents *(http://www.w3.org/TR/NOTE-dcd).*	*<ElementDef Type = "example" Content = "Closed" Model = "Data"/>*
DDML	The Document Definition Markup Language encodes the logical, as opposed to the physical, content of DTDs *(http://www.w3.org/TR/NOTE-ddml).*	*<ElementDecl Name = "examle"><Model> <PCData/></Model> </ElementDecl>*
OneSoft	Applies the extensible nature of XML Data Reduced (XDR) to complement OneSoft Corporation's applications *(http://www.onesoft.com).*	*<ElementType name = "example" content = "textOnly" model = "closed"/>*
SGML	The Standard Generalized Markup Language, which laid the foundation for both HTML and XML *(http://www.iso.ch - search for ISO 8879:1986).*	*<!ELEMENT example (#PCDATA)>*
RELAX	The Regular Language description for XML is used for describing XML-based languages *(http://www.xml.gr.jp/relax).*	*<elementRule role = "example" type = "string"/><tag name = "example"/>*
Schema Adjunct	An XML-based language developed by TIBCO Extensibility and used to associate domain-specific data with schemas and their instances *(http://www.extensibility.com/resources/saf.htm).*	Not Applicable

Table B-1 Dialects Supported in XML Authority *(continued)*

Dialect	Description	Example
SOX version 2	The Schema for Object-Oriented XML for defining the syntactic structure and partial semantics of XML document types *(http://www.w3.org/TR/NOTE-SOX)*.	*<elementtype name = "examle"><model><string/></model></elementtype>*
XDR	XML Data Reduced, which is a dialect based on a subset of XML-Data *(http://msdn.microsoft.com/library/default.asp?URL=/library/psdk/xmlsdk/xmlp7k6d.htm)*.	*<ElementType name = "example" content = "textOnly" model = "closed"/>*
XML DTDs	The XML 1.0 language *(http://www.w3.org/TR/2000/REC-xml-20001006)*.	*<!ELEMENT example (#PCDATA)>*
XML Schema	XSD is the recently released standard from the W3C that is essentially the next generation of schema description *(http://www.w3.org/XML/Schema)*.	*<element name = "example" type = "string"/>*

Exporting different dialects is not the only feature of the XML Authority application. It also has the ability to import a variety of different data sources and build an XML representation out of them. This includes objects like COM, Java, and ODBC. Table B-2 contains a list of the types of data it can import along with a description.

> **Note** For most of these items you can choose to import the data as elements or attributes in the resulting schema. For instance, if you're importing data from a database through ODBC, you can select to have the database column names as either child elements of the table name or attributes.

These are just a few of the features of XML Authority, which provides a lot of flexibility for those of you transitioning from one type of data to another. In

Table B-2 Import Data Sources for XML Authority

Type	Description
COBOL Copybook	Allows you to import COBOL copybooks, where the COBOL data declarations will be represented as XML elements.
COM	Allows you to import COM objects.
Internal Subset	If information on the schema has been included as an internal subset of an instance document, you import this information.
Java class	Allows you to import a Java class and store the properties as elements or attributes.
LDAP	Allows you to import an LDAP (Lightweight Directory Access Protocol) directory structure.
ODBC	Allows you to connect to a database via ODBC and import the tables available on that source. It does not create the overall database hierarchy with this information—only that of a particular table.
SGML	Allows you to import an SGML DTD for conversion to an XML schema.
Text	Allows you to import the column headers of a tab-delimited text file. Once you have defined your model after these headers, you can create instance documents with the column values.
XML Document	A well-formed XML document.

addition to these features, this application also allows you to export the visual representation of your schemas in GIF format, provides auto-complete features while typing, has a simple interface for element and attribute lists, and even communicates directly with its XML repository server, XML Canon/Developer, which we will discuss later.

If you want more information on XML Authority visit *http://www.tibco.com*. The application is currently sold as part of a suite (XML Turbo) with two other applications. Because of the direction TIBCO appears to be taking with their software products, we are unsure how long this deal will last. So if you are interested in this application, we recommend you purchase it soon. It might only be available as part of a larger suite in the near future.

> **Note** XML Authority is available on Windows, Unix, and Mac OS platforms. Note that earlier versions are available only on Mac OS 9 and earlier because of limitations in its support for Java. MacOS X users, however, will be able to use the most recent versions.

XML Spy

Another popular XML development tool is XML Spy *(http://www.xmlspy.com),* shown in Figure B-2. This tool allows you to create and validate even more types of XML documents and schemas than XML Authority, as seen in Table B-3, as well as manage entire projects that can be checked in to and out of Microsoft's Visual SourceSafe. The one drawback is that it only runs on Windows systems, so dedicated Mac OS and Unix-based users will need to look for another solution.

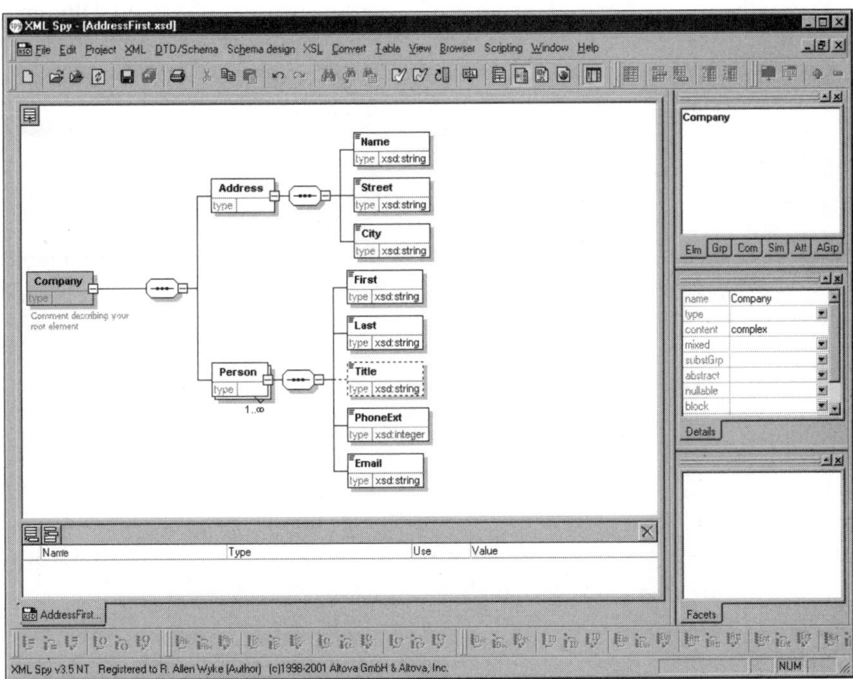

Figure B-2 The XML Spy editor.

> **Note** XML Spy allows you to edit HTML and ASP files, but they are not XML based. Additionally, you can add other types of documents to create or edit within the preferences.

Table B-3 Spy-Supported Formats

File Extension	Description
.biz	BizTalk
.cml	Chemical Markup Language
.dcd	Document Content Description
.dtd	Document Type Definition
.ent	Entity Sets
.math and .mml	Mathematical Markup Language
.mtx	MetaStream XML
.rdf	Resource Description Framework
.smil	Synchronized Multimedia Integration Language (SMIL)
.svg	Scalable Vector Graphics
.wml	Wireless Markup Language
.xdr	XML-Data Reduced
.xhtml	Extensible Hypertext Markup Language
.xml	XML Document
.xsd	XML Schema
.xsl	XSL Stylesheet
.xslt	XSL Transform

If you take the time to step through the tutorial provided with the applications or available on the Web site, you will find XML Spy to be an easy-to-use, yet incredibly flexible and complete tool. Features like autocomplete and autosuggest, the ability to visually edit your schemas or edit the XML source directly, and being able to create HTML- or Microsoft Word–formatted documentation (see Figure B-3), makes it one of the most complete and inexpensive tools available today.

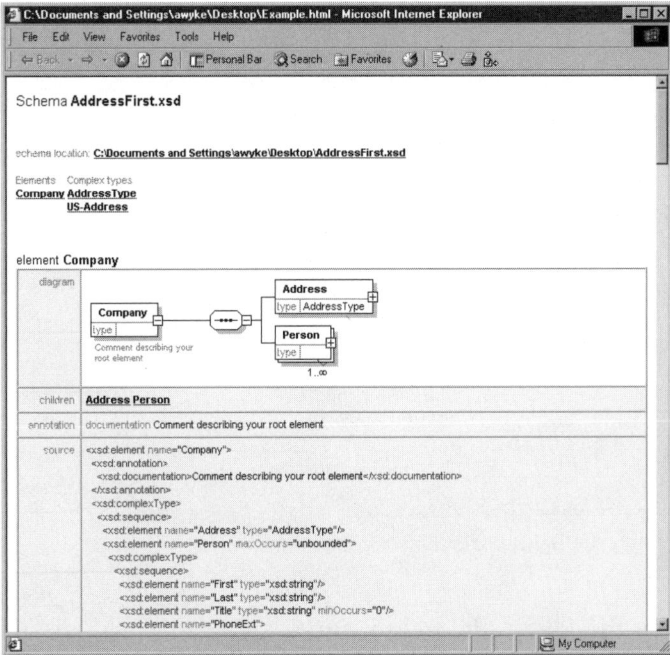

Figure B-3 An XML Spy documentation generation feature.

Document Editors

Once a schema has been developed, the next step is to create instance documents of the schema. This helps us verify that our schemas reflect the data models we want them to represent. The truest test is to apply real data to a model that is supposed to organize and describe that data. If you find extra data that is not described, or descriptions for data that doesn't exist, or even improper definitions, these instance documents will expose the inefficiencies and allow you to correct them.

XML Notepad and BizTalk Editor

Microsoft XML Notepad *(http://msdn.microsoft.com/xml/notepad)* was one of the first applications developed to create and edit XML instance documents. Although it has not been updated for some time, it allows you to edit and create well-formed XML documents. Its simple interface makes it easy to use for beginners or programmers trying to create XML documents quickly. Figure B-4 displays the XML Notepad.

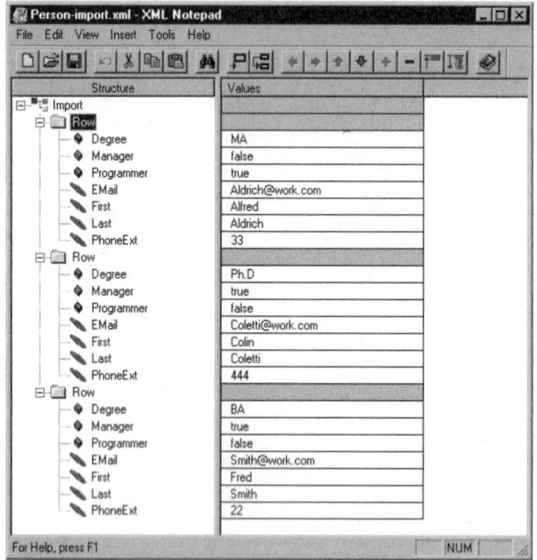

Figure B-4 XML Notepad.

Now that the Microsoft BizTalk Server, which we will discuss later, has been released, you should use the Microsoft BizTalk Editor instead of XML Notepad. As you can see from Figure B-5, the applications have some similarities, and XML Notepad obviously laid the foundation for the BizTalk Editor application. We discussed the BizTalk Server and the other applications within this solution suite in Chapter 15, so check there if you have questions. For the moment, if you do not have the BizTalk Server, XML Notepad is still a good tool for starting out.

XML Instance

XML Instance, seen in Figure B-6, is TIBCO Extensibility's XML document instance editor. Some of the benefits of this application include its ability to arrange the attribute fields so they are on one line (look at Manager, Degree, and Programmer for an example) and that it provides real-time validation of the documents against the governing schema, which you can set if the document

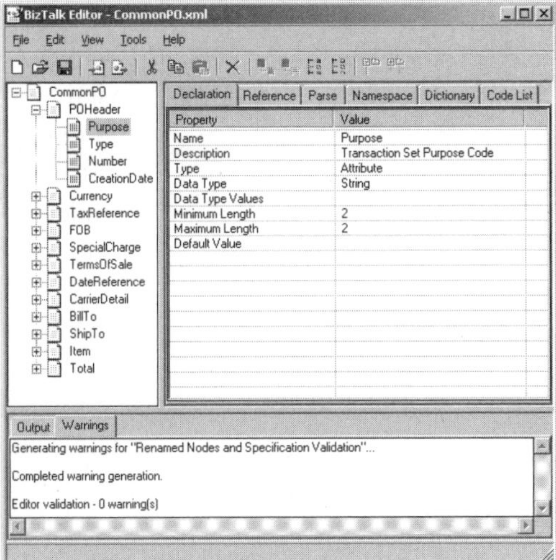

Figure B-5 The BizTalk Editor.

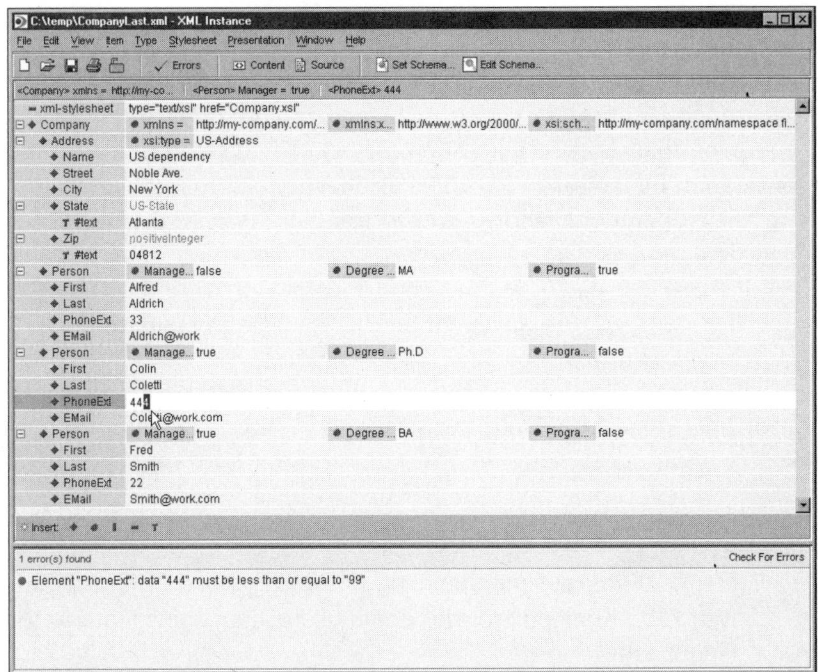

Figure B-6 The XML Instance XML document editor.

does not already specify one. XML Instance also allows you to save documents to a URL or directly to XML Canon, TIBCO Extensibility's XML repository server.

While this tool provides some easy-to-use features, it has some limitations as of the writing of this book. For instance, it allows you to quickly insert attributes, elements, comments, and so forth by clicking the appropriate icon on the Insert bar between the document and error pane, but this bar can, as of version 2.1, only support the display of eight items.

We also found that if you need to change something in your schema file, you have to reassign that schema to the document in XML Instance to update the validation. Doing so will also lose any expanded or collapsed items. This is not a problem for small documents, but can be annoying for longer ones.

> **Note** XML Instance runs on Windows, Unix, and Mac OS systems. Like XML Authority, current versions for the Mac OS run on OS X only.

Komodo

ActiveState Komodo, which is nearing the release of version 1.2, is an IDE created by ActiveState (*http://www.activestate.com*). ActiveState is the company that worked with Microsoft to provide a Win32 port of the popular programming language Perl. The application, shown in Figure B-7 debugging an XSLT document, allows you to textually edit XML and XSLT documents and data models.

It has some useful features but does not provide the robust environment that the other editors have. While the visual representations and document-generation features look like "nice to haves" on the other applications, not having them in Komodo exposes the need for them. Komodo runs on Windows and Linux systems, which is a plus, and because it is built on top of an open source application, ActiveState's ability to offer it on other systems is natural.

> **Note** If you are programming in Perl, Python, PHP, or XSLT along with XML, Komodo provides some useful debugging features for these languages.

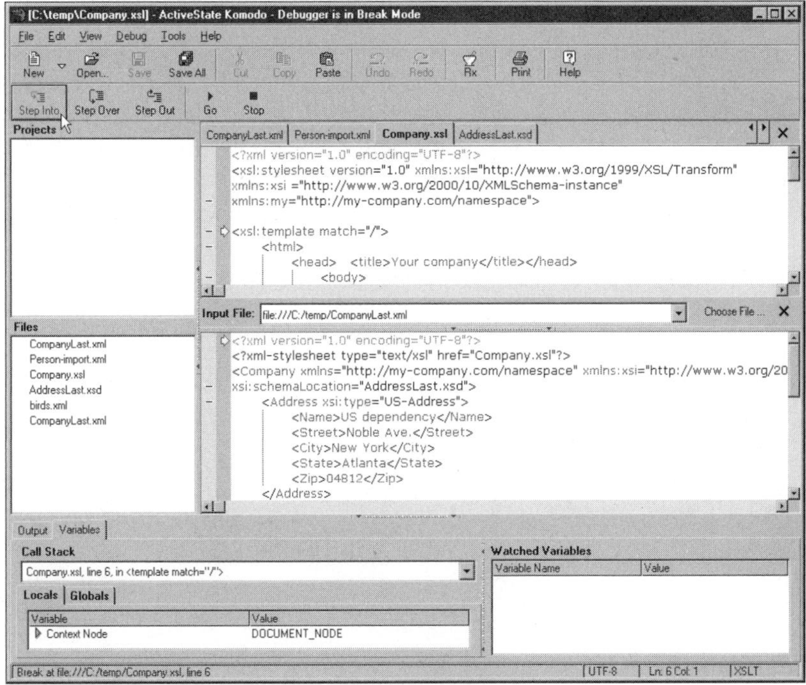

Figure B-7 A Komodo IDE debugging an XSLT document.

Servers and Document Management

Schemas creation tools and document editors are not the only types of tools needed for the XML developers. Once you have your data and have it described, you need to utilize and manage it. You do not want changes to be applied to schemas or documents without tracking them and being able to roll back. Additionally, you want to be able to organize your schemas and corresponding documents for quick retrieval and usage. You want to be able to accurately document your schemas, and you want to publish them so they can be referenced in instance documents for validation against parsers.

Within this section of the appendix we will look at servers from Microsoft and TIBCO Extensibility.

Microsoft

When Microsoft announced its BizTalk Framework and Web site, everyone knew that it was only a matter of time before the company built applications to support this initiative. Roughly two years later the BizTalk and Microsoft SQL Server 2000 servers are out, and both are part of Microsoft's .NET line of servers.

Optimized for XML data interchange, these applications offer a range of features and functionality needed while working within an XML environment.

BizTalk Server

BizTalk Server is a new server product that provides an entire suite of tools and means by which you can coordinate business problems with many different sources of data. It not only contains the XML editor we previously mentioned, but also includes other tools used for mapping one data structure to another (Figure B-8), tracking documents, and processing.

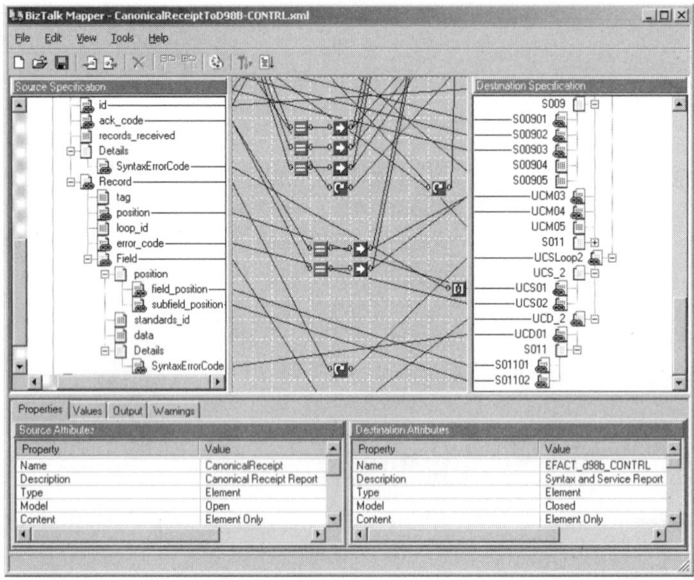

Figure B-8 The BizTalk Mapper.

Built to conform to XML-based standards, like SOAP, and to Microsoft's .NET Framework, the BizTalk Server is one of the core servers for a successful XML solution deployment. As we mentioned earlier, we covered the BizTalk Server in detail in Chapter 15.

The SQL Server

With the latest installment of SQL Server (2000 at the time of this writing), the Microsoft team has provided a rich set of tools and functionalities for all XML developers. It not only provides the ability to query a database through an XML statement, but also provides a means by which you can insert and update data within the SQL Server. This is a key component when you build .NET-enabled Web Services.

Accessing the data is only part of the XML feature set of the SQL Server. It also adds an XML view of this relational data, as well as being able to map XML data into the appropriate tables. The server also has the ability to show how XML data looks when received and how it should look after a transaction. SQL Server, through its XML Updategrams functionality, will create and run the necessary SQL queries to perform the task.

TIBCO Extensibility

As we saw earlier in the appendix, TIBCO Extensibility has created several popular tools for working with and managing XML schemas. However, schema development is not the only type of tool they provide. They also have applications ranging from acting as a repository and versioning to autodocumenting and batch dialect conversion (that is, DTD to XSD).

XML Console

XML Console, shown in Figure B-9, rounds out the offerings from TIBCO Extensibility on the XML document and schema creation and editing side. It provides features such as project management, batch conversion, and, as you can see in Figure B-6, batch validation. Additionally, XML Console allows you to automatically generate documentation on the schemas in much the same manner as XML Spy.

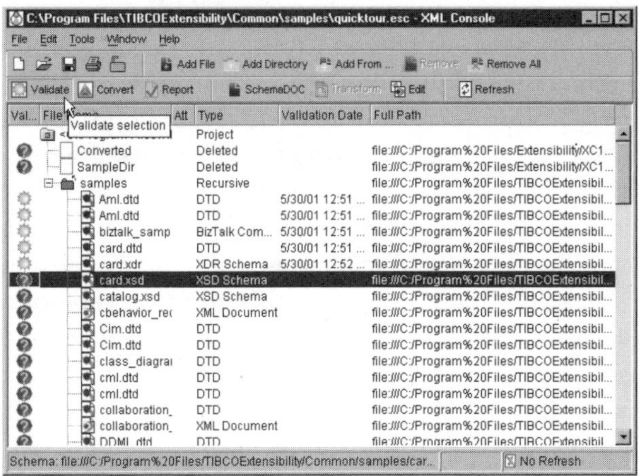

Figure B-9 XML Console rounds out the TIBCO Extensibility XML document editing suite.

> **Note** The combination of XML Authority, XML Instance, and XML Console can be purchased in a package called XML Turbo. This suite has roughly the same feature set available in XML Spy.

Like XML Authority and XML Instance, XML Console allows you to save to a URL or to the XML Canon repository server we will introduce you to next.

> **Note** The XML console runs on Windows, Unix, and Macintosh OS systems. Like XML Authority, current versions for the Macintosh OS run on OS X only.

XML Developer/Canon

TIBCO Extensibility was one of the first companies to build and release a repository server geared directly at XML development. While many of you might say that the SourceSafe or CVS systems have everything you need, XML Developer/Canon, or XML Canon (in reference to canonical) for short, not only stores and provides version control for your files, but also offers XML-specific features. These features range from those that you expect, like checkin and checkout, to features such as finding reusable portions of a schema and autodocumentation.

XML Developer/Canon is one of, if not *the*, most comprehensive XML-repository servers we have seen. It provides all the versioning, differencing, and source management one would expect, as well as complete Web access, searching, and browsing that can be controlled with various levels of security. This not only allows your internal development teams to store and track internal XML schemas and documents, but also allows you to provide access to partners and affiliates in a secure manner. It even allows for stage tracking (that is, life cycles such as design, testing, production, and the like), reporting, and automatic e-mail notification for those who have chosen to be notified when changes occur to a specific file.

Software Development Kits (SDKs)

The last, and perhaps most important, topic we include here is a list of SDKs you might find useful when building and deploying XML solutions. In

Table B-4 we included the name of each SDK, a corresponding URL, and a brief description.

Table B-4 Available SDKs and Other Information

SDK	URL	Description
BizTalk Framework 2	*http://www.microsoft.com/biztalk/techinfo/framwork20.asp*	Defines the BizTalk documents and message.
MSXML 4	*http://msdn.microsoft.com/xml/general/newinaprilre.asp*	The newest Microsoft XML Parser, supports XSD.
.NET Framework	*http://msdn.microsoft.com/downloads/default.asp?URL=/code/sample.asp?url=/msdn-files/027/001/580/msdncompositedoc.xml*	Currently in beta, contains everything you will need to write and test .NET applications.
SOAP Toolkit 2	*http://msdn.microsoft.com/downloads/default.asp?URL=/code/sample.asp?url=/msdn-files/027/001/580/msdncompositedoc.xml*	Support for SOAP messaging, along with documentation and examples.
UDDI	*http://microsoft.com/downloads/release.asp?ReleaseID=24822*	Provides all the tools needed for a Visual Basic programmer to interact with the UDDI registry. See *http://uddi.microsoft.com/* for more information.
Xalan	*http://xml.apache.org*	An XSLT processor for transforming XML documents into HTML, text, or other XML document types. Supports the XSLT, XPath, and TRAX standards and is available in C++ and Java versions.
Xerces	*http://xml.apache.org*	An XML parser that supports XML 1.0, DOM Level 1 and 2, SAX 1 and 2, and XML Schema. Available in C++, Java, and Perl implementations.

Conclusion

XML can be easy to learn and follow. You might even find it easy to build applications to utilize XML data, but XML development tools are definitely necessary. They not only provide a centralized environment where you can perform your XML work, but they also accelerate the learning curve for new technologies and XML-based languages.

In this appendix we showed you several of these tools and provided various options so you can make an intelligent choice for your own development environment. As we are sure many of you seasoned developers know, standardizing development environments for your applications and solutions is an often overlooked but important step to success.

Index

B

C

D

E

H

I

J

K

L

M

N

O

P

Q

R

S

T

U

X

R. Allen Wyke

R. Allen Wyke, of Durham, North Carolina, is Vice President of Technology at the Environment, Health, and Safety (EHS) solutions company, Blue292. At Blue292 he leads the engineering team and works with the executive team to ensure their products services have the proper vision and direction. He is constantly working with XML, HTML, JavaScript, and various other Internet technologies in designing and developing the online EHS software and services that Blue292 has to offer.

Allen, who wrote his first computer program at the age of eight, has programmed in everything from C++, Java, and Perl to Visual Basic and JavaScript. He also has experience in other "languages" such as SQL, HTML/XHTML, DHTML, and XML. Allen has written roughly a dozen books on various Internet technologies and previously wrote the monthly Webmaster column for SunWorld, and a weekly article, "Integrating Windows and Unix," for ITworld.com.

Brad Leupen

Brad Leupen, of Raleigh, North Carolina, is the Chief Technology Officer for the education software company Entrinsik Inc. At Entrinsik Brad brought Web-based products to market that utilize cutting-edge technology such as XML and XSLT. Entrinsik's latest product is entirely XML-based and relies on the technology for its user interface, middleware components, and data storage. In addition to being a technology strategist, he has also worked as a product manager and implementation specialist for Entrinsik.

Brad has been programming applications since childhood. He worked as a professional programmer over summers in high school before attending Harvard University, where he earned an A.B. with honors in Computer Science. Brad helped to teach several undergraduate courses in programming and operating systems during his time at Harvard. Upon graduation he accepted a job with Entrinsik to become their R&D specialist. Brad has extensive practical knowledge of XML/XSLT, HTML/XHTML, DHTML, Java, J2EE, C++, Visual Basic, and several database technologies.

Sultan Rehman

Sultan Rehman, based in Hong Kong, is the Chief Software Architect for Engage Asia/Australia, where he is responsible for designing and implementing next-generation ad serving and optimization solutions. He specializes in using object-oriented designs for implementing mission-critical distributed systems. One of his current projects involves developing a high-performance and extensible XML Server that exposes a legacy database schema through a set of DTD-constrained XML documents, XLST templates, and XML-RPC methods. Sultan is also working on a configurations management system that uses XML at all levels; from the back store to the configuration documents. He is considering open-sourcing this project and is talking to OpenNMS.

Programming became Sultan's passion more than a decade ago when the boss at his summer job bought an IBM XT. He quickly mastered BASIC and moved on to Turbo Pascal, C++, Delphi, and eventually to his current favorite, Java. He first got hooked on XML in 1998 after upgrading to Microsoft Internet Explorer 5 and saw the possibility of creating a cross-platform way of managing and communicating data and information. When he's not bathing in the glow of a computer screen, Sultan can be found playing "chase the laser pointer" with his eight cats.

The manuscript for this book was prepared and galleyed using Microsoft Word. Pages were composed by ***TIPS*** Technical Publishing Press using Adobe FrameMaker 6 for Windows, with text in Garamond and display type in Helvetica Condensed. Composed pages were delivered to the printer as electronic prepress files.

Cover Designer:	Patricia Bradbury
Interior Graphic Designer:	James D. Kramer
Principal Compositor:	Robert Kern
Copy Editor:	MIchael Hedrick
Principal Proofreader:	Juanita Covert
Indexer:	Ariel Tupelano

Proof of Purchase

Use this page as proof of purchase if participating in a promotion or rebate offer on this title. Proof of purchase must be used in conjunction with other proof(s) of payment such as your dated sales receipt—see offer details.

XML Programming (Core Reference)

0-7356-1185-8

____

CUSTOMER NAME

Microsoft Press, PO Box 97017, Redmond, WA 98073-9830

MICROSOFT LICENSE AGREEMENT

Book Companion CD

IMPORTANT—READ CAREFULLY: This Microsoft End-User License Agreement ("EULA") is a legal agreement between you (either an individual or an entity) and Microsoft Corporation for the Microsoft product identified above, which includes computer software and may include associated media, printed materials, and "online" or electronic documentation ("SOFTWARE PRODUCT"). Any component included within the SOFTWARE PRODUCT that is accompanied by a separate End-User License Agreement shall be governed by such agreement and not the terms set forth below. By installing, copying, or otherwise using the SOFTWARE PRODUCT, you agree to be bound by the terms of this EULA. If you do not agree to the terms of this EULA, you are not authorized to install, copy, or otherwise use the SOFTWARE PRODUCT; you may, however, return the SOFTWARE PRODUCT, along with all printed materials and other items that form a part of the Microsoft product that includes the SOFTWARE PRODUCT, to the place you obtained them for a full refund.

SOFTWARE PRODUCT LICENSE

The SOFTWARE PRODUCT is protected by United States copyright laws and international copyright treaties, as well as other intellectual property laws and treaties. The SOFTWARE PRODUCT is licensed, not sold.

1. **GRANT OF LICENSE.** This EULA grants you the following rights:

   a. **Software Product.** You may install and use one copy of the SOFTWARE PRODUCT on a single computer. The primary user of the computer on which the SOFTWARE PRODUCT is installed may make a second copy for his or her exclusive use on a portable computer.

   b. **Storage/Network Use.** You may also store or install a copy of the SOFTWARE PRODUCT on a storage device, such as a network server, used only to install or run the SOFTWARE PRODUCT on your other computers over an internal network; however, you must acquire and dedicate a license for each separate computer on which the SOFTWARE PRODUCT is installed or run from the storage device. A license for the SOFTWARE PRODUCT may not be shared or used concurrently on different computers.

   c. **License Pak.** If you have acquired this EULA in a Microsoft License Pak, you may make the number of additional copies of the computer software portion of the SOFTWARE PRODUCT authorized on the printed copy of this EULA, and you may use each copy in the manner specified above. You are also entitled to make a corresponding number of secondary copies for portable computer use as specified above.

   d. **Sample Code.** Solely with respect to portions, if any, of the SOFTWARE PRODUCT that are identified within the SOFTWARE PRODUCT as sample code (the "SAMPLE CODE"):

      i. **Use and Modification.** Microsoft grants you the right to use and modify the source code version of the SAMPLE CODE, *provided* you comply with subsection (d)(iii) below. You may not distribute the SAMPLE CODE, or any modified version of the SAMPLE CODE, in source code form.

      ii. **Redistributable Files.** Provided you comply with subsection (d)(iii) below, Microsoft grants you a nonexclusive, royalty-free right to reproduce and distribute the object code version of the SAMPLE CODE and of any modified SAMPLE CODE, other than SAMPLE CODE, or any modified version thereof, designated as not redistributable in the Readme file that forms a part of the SOFTWARE PRODUCT (the "Non-Redistributable Sample Code"). All SAMPLE CODE other than the Non-Redistributable Sample Code is collectively referred to as the "REDISTRIBUTABLES."

      iii. **Redistribution Requirements.** If you redistribute the REDISTRIBUTABLES, you agree to: (i) distribute the REDISTRIBUTABLES in object code form only in conjunction with and as a part of your software application product; (ii) not use Microsoft's name, logo, or trademarks to market your software application product; (iii) include a valid copyright notice on your software application product; (iv) indemnify, hold harmless, and defend Microsoft from and against any claims or lawsuits, including attorney's fees, that arise or result from the use or distribution of your software application product; and (v) not permit further distribution of the REDISTRIBUTABLES by your end user. Contact Microsoft for the applicable royalties due and other licensing terms for all other uses and/or distribution of the REDISTRIBUTABLES.

2. **DESCRIPTION OF OTHER RIGHTS AND LIMITATIONS.**

   - **Limitations on Reverse Engineering, Decompilation, and Disassembly.** You may not reverse engineer, decompile, or disassemble the SOFTWARE PRODUCT, except and only to the extent that such activity is expressly permitted by applicable law notwithstanding this limitation.
   - **Separation of Components.** The SOFTWARE PRODUCT is licensed as a single product. Its component parts may not be separated for use on more than one computer.
   - **Rental.** You may not rent, lease, or lend the SOFTWARE PRODUCT.
   - **Support Services.** Microsoft may, but is not obligated to, provide you with support services related to the SOFTWARE PRODUCT ("Support Services"). Use of Support Services is governed by the Microsoft policies and programs described in the

user manual, in "online" documentation, and/or in other Microsoft-provided materials. Any supplemental software code provided to you as part of the Support Services shall be considered part of the SOFTWARE PRODUCT and subject to the terms and conditions of this EULA. With respect to technical information you provide to Microsoft as part of the Support Services, Microsoft may use such information for its business purposes, including for product support and development. Microsoft will not utilize such technical information in a form that personally identifies you.

- **Software Transfer.** You may permanently transfer all of your rights under this EULA, provided you retain no copies, you transfer all of the SOFTWARE PRODUCT (including all component parts, the media and printed materials, any upgrades, this EULA, and, if applicable, the Certificate of Authenticity), **and** the recipient agrees to the terms of this EULA.
- **Termination.** Without prejudice to any other rights, Microsoft may terminate this EULA if you fail to comply with the terms and conditions of this EULA. In such event, you must destroy all copies of the SOFTWARE PRODUCT and all of its component parts.

3. **COPYRIGHT.** All title and copyrights in and to the SOFTWARE PRODUCT (including but not limited to any images, photographs, animations, video, audio, music, text, SAMPLE CODE, REDISTRIBUTABLES, and "applets" incorporated into the SOFTWARE PRODUCT) and any copies of the SOFTWARE PRODUCT are owned by Microsoft or its suppliers. The SOFTWARE PRODUCT is protected by copyright laws and international treaty provisions. Therefore, you must treat the SOFTWARE PRODUCT like any other copyrighted material **except** that you may install the SOFTWARE PRODUCT on a single computer provided you keep the original solely for backup or archival purposes. You may not copy the printed materials accompanying the SOFTWARE PRODUCT.

4. **U.S. GOVERNMENT RESTRICTED RIGHTS.** The SOFTWARE PRODUCT and documentation are provided with RESTRICTED RIGHTS. Use, duplication, or disclosure by the Government is subject to restrictions as set forth in subparagraph (c)(1)(ii) of the Rights in Technical Data and Computer Software clause at DFARS 252.227-7013 or subparagraphs (c)(1) and (2) of the Commercial Computer Software—Restricted Rights at 48 CFR 52.227-19, as applicable. Manufacturer is Microsoft Corporation/One Microsoft Way/Redmond, WA 98052-6399.

5. **EXPORT RESTRICTIONS.** You agree that you will not export or re-export the SOFTWARE PRODUCT, any part thereof, or any process or service that is the direct product of the SOFTWARE PRODUCT (the foregoing collectively referred to as the "Restricted Components"), to any country, person, entity, or end user subject to U.S. export restrictions. You specifically agree not to export or re-export any of the Restricted Components (i) to any country to which the U.S. has embargoed or restricted the export of goods or services, which currently include, but are not necessarily limited to, Cuba, Iran, Iraq, Libya, North Korea, Sudan, and Syria, or to any national of any such country, wherever located, who intends to transmit or transport the Restricted Components back to such country; (ii) to any end user who you know or have reason to know will utilize the Restricted Components in the design, development, or production of nuclear, chemical, or biological weapons; or (iii) to any end user who has been prohibited from participating in U.S. export transactions by any federal agency of the U.S. government. You warrant and represent that neither the BXA nor any other U.S. federal agency has suspended, revoked, or denied your export privileges.

DISCLAIMER OF WARRANTY

NO WARRANTIES OR CONDITIONS. MICROSOFT EXPRESSLY DISCLAIMS ANY WARRANTY OR CONDITION FOR THE SOFTWARE PRODUCT. THE SOFTWARE PRODUCT AND ANY RELATED DOCUMENTATION ARE PROVIDED "AS IS" WITHOUT WARRANTY OR CONDITION OF ANY KIND, EITHER EXPRESS OR IMPLIED, INCLUDING, WITHOUT LIMITATION, THE IMPLIED WARRANTIES OF MERCHANTABILITY, FITNESS FOR A PARTICULAR PURPOSE, OR NONINFRINGEMENT. THE ENTIRE RISK ARISING OUT OF USE OR PERFORMANCE OF THE SOFTWARE PRODUCT REMAINS WITH YOU.

LIMITATION OF LIABILITY. TO THE MAXIMUM EXTENT PERMITTED BY APPLICABLE LAW, IN NO EVENT SHALL MICROSOFT OR ITS SUPPLIERS BE LIABLE FOR ANY SPECIAL, INCIDENTAL, INDIRECT, OR CONSEQUENTIAL DAMAGES WHATSOEVER (INCLUDING, WITHOUT LIMITATION, DAMAGES FOR LOSS OF BUSINESS PROFITS, BUSINESS INTERRUPTION, LOSS OF BUSINESS INFORMATION, OR ANY OTHER PECUNIARY LOSS) ARISING OUT OF THE USE OF OR INABILITY TO USE THE SOFTWARE PRODUCT OR THE PROVISION OF OR FAILURE TO PROVIDE SUPPORT SERVICES, EVEN IF MICROSOFT HAS BEEN ADVISED OF THE POSSIBILITY OF SUCH DAMAGES. IN ANY CASE, MICROSOFT'S ENTIRE LIABILITY UNDER ANY PROVISION OF THIS EULA SHALL BE LIMITED TO THE GREATER OF THE AMOUNT ACTUALLY PAID BY YOU FOR THE SOFTWARE PRODUCT OR US$5.00; PROVIDED, HOWEVER, IF YOU HAVE ENTERED INTO A MICROSOFT SUPPORT SERVICES AGREEMENT, MICROSOFT'S ENTIRE LIABILITY REGARDING SUPPORT SERVICES SHALL BE GOVERNED BY THE TERMS OF THAT AGREEMENT. BECAUSE SOME STATES AND JURISDICTIONS DO NOT ALLOW THE EXCLUSION OR LIMITATION OF LIABILITY, THE ABOVE LIMITATION MAY NOT APPLY TO YOU.

MISCELLANEOUS

This EULA is governed by the laws of the State of Washington USA, except and only to the extent that applicable law mandates governing law of a different jurisdiction.

Should you have any questions concerning this EULA, or if you desire to contact Microsoft for any reason, please contact the Microsoft subsidiary serving your country, or write: Microsoft Sales Information Center/One Microsoft Way/Redmond, WA 98052-6399.

PN 097-0002296

W9-BFJ-748

The Brutal Telling

The Brutal Telling

Louise Penny

THORNDIKE
WINDSOR
PARAGON

This Large Print edition is published by Thorndike Press, Waterville, Maine, USA and by BBC Audiobooks Ltd, Bath, England.

Thorndike Press, a part of Gale, Cengage Learning.

A Chief Inspector Gamache Novel.

Grateful acknowledgment is given for permission to reprint the following:

"The Bells of Heaven" by Ralph Hodgson is used by kind permission of Bryn Mawr College.

Excerpts from "Cressida to Triolius: A Gift" and "Sekhmet, the Lion-Headed Goddess of War" from *Morning in the Burning House; New Poems* by Margaret Atwood. Copyright © 1995 by Margaret Atwood. Reprinted by permission of Houghton Mifflin Harcourt Publishing Company. All rights reserved.

Excerpt from "Gravity Zero" from *Bones* by Mike Freeman. Copyright © 2007 by Mike Freeman. Reproduced with kind permission of the author.

The text of this Large Print edition is unabridged.

Other aspects of the book may vary from the original edition.

Set in 16 pt. Plantin.

Printed on permanent paper.

LIBRARY OF CONGRESS CATALOGING-IN-PUBLICATION DATA

Penny, Louise.
The brutal telling / by Louise Penny.
p. cm. — (Thorndike Press large print mystery)
"A Chief Inspector Gamache novel."
ISBN-13: 978-1-4104-2304-7 (alk. paper)
ISBN-10: 1-4104-2304-2 (alk. paper)
1. Gamache, Armand (Fictitious character)—Fiction. 2. Police—Québec (Province)—Fiction. 3. Villages—Québec (Province)—Fiction. 4. Murder—Investigation—Fiction. 5. Québec (Province)—Fiction. 6. Large type books. I. Title.
PR9199.4.P464B78 2010
813'.6—dc22 2009046330

BRITISH LIBRARY CATALOGUING-IN-PUBLICATION DATA AVAILABLE

Published in 2010 in the U.S. by arrangement with St. Martin's Press, LLC.
Published in 2010 in the U.K. by arrangement with Headline Publishing Group.

U.K. Hardcover: 978 1 408 48590 3 (Windsor Large Print)
U.K. Softcover: 978 1 408 48591 0 (Paragon Large Print)

Printed in the United States of America
1 2 3 4 5 6 7 14 13 12 11 10

For the SPCA Monteregie,
and all the people
who would "ring the bells of Heaven."

And, for Maggie,
who finally gave all her heart away.

ACKNOWLEDGMENTS

Once again, this book is the result of a whole lot of help from a whole lot of people. I want and need to thank Michael, my husband, for reading and rereading the manuscript, and always telling me it was brilliant. Thank you to Lise Page, my assistant, for her tireless and cheery work and great ideas. To Sherise Hobbs and Hope Dellon for their patience and editorial notes.

I want to thank, as always, the very best literary agent in the world, Teresa Chris. She sent me a silver heart when my last book made the *New York Times* bestseller list (I also thought I'd just mention that!). Teresa is way more than an agent. She's also a lovely, thoughtful person.

I'd also like to thank my good friends Susan McKenzie and Lili de Grandpré, for their help and support.

And finally I want to say a word about the poetry I use in this book, and the others. As much as I'd love not to say anything and hope you believe I wrote it, I actually need to thank the wonderful poets who've allowed me to use their works and words. I adore poetry, as you can tell. Indeed, it inspires me — with words and emotions. I tell aspiring writers to read poetry, which I think for them is often the literary equivalent of being told to eat Brussels sprouts. They're none too enthusiastic. But what a shame if a writer doesn't at least try to find poems that speak to him or her. Poets manage to get into a couplet what I struggle to achieve in an entire book.

I thought it was time I acknowledged that.

In this book I use, as always, works from Margaret Atwood's slim volume *Morning in the Burned House.* Not a very cheerful title, but brilliant poems. I've also quoted from a lovely old work called *The Bells of Heaven* by Ralph Hodgson. And a wonderful poem called "Gravity Zero" from an emerging Canadian poet named Mike Freeman, from his book *Bones.*

I wanted you to know that. And I hope these poems speak to you, as they speak to me.

One

"All of them? Even the children?" The fireplace sputtered and crackled and swallowed his gasp. "Slaughtered?"

"Worse."

There was silence then. And in that hush lived all the things that could be worse than slaughter.

"Are they close?" His back tingled as he imagined something dreadful creeping through the woods. Toward them. He looked around, almost expecting to see red eyes staring through the dark windows. Or from the corners, or under the bed.

"All around. Have you seen the light in the night sky?"

"I thought those were the Northern Lights." The pink and green and white shifting, flowing against the stars. Like something alive, glowing, and growing. And approaching.

Olivier Brulé lowered his gaze, no longer

able to look into the troubled, lunatic eyes across from him. He'd lived with this story for so long, and kept telling himself it wasn't real. It was a myth, a story told and repeated and embellished over and over and over. Around fires just like theirs.

It was a story, nothing more. No harm in it.

But in this simple log cabin, buried in the Quebec wilderness, it seemed like more than that. Even Olivier felt himself believing it. Perhaps because the Hermit so clearly did.

The old man sat in his easy chair on one side of the stone hearth with Olivier on the other. Olivier looked into a fire that had been alive for more than a decade. An old flame not allowed to die, it mumbled and popped in the grate, throwing soft light into the log cabin. He gave the embers a shove with the simple iron poker, sending sparks up the chimney. Candlelight twinkled off shiny objects like eyes in the darkness, found by the flame.

"It won't be long now."

The Hermit's eyes were gleaming like metal reaching its melting point. He was leaning forward as he often did when this tale was told.

Olivier scanned the single room. The dark

was punctuated by flickering candles throwing fantastic, grotesque shadows. Night seemed to have seeped through the cracks in the logs and settled into the cabin, curled in corners and under the bed. Many native tribes believed evil lived in corners, which was why their traditional homes were rounded. Unlike the square homes the government had given them.

Olivier didn't believe evil lived in corners. Not really. Not in the daylight, anyway. But he did believe there were things waiting in the dark corners of this cabin that only the Hermit knew about. Things that set Olivier's heart pounding.

"Go on," he said, trying to keep his voice steady.

It was late and Olivier still had the twenty-minute walk through the forest back to Three Pines. It was a trip he made every fortnight and he knew it well, even in the dark.

Only in the dark. Theirs was a relationship that existed only after nightfall.

They sipped Orange Pekoe tea. A treat, Olivier knew, reserved for the Hermit's honored guest. His only guest.

But now it was story time. They leaned closer to the fire. It was early September and a chill had crept in with the night.

"Where was I? Oh, yes. I remember now."

Olivier's hands gripped the warm mug even tighter.

"The terrible force has destroyed everything in its way. The Old World and the New. All gone. Except . . ."

"Except?"

"One tiny village remains. Hidden in a valley, so the grim army hasn't seen it yet. But it will. And when it does their great leader will stand at the head of his army. He's immense, bigger than any tree, and clad in armor made from rocks and spiny shells and bone."

"Chaos."

The word was whispered and disappeared into the darkness, where it curled into a corner. And waited.

"Chaos. And the Furies. Disease, Famine, Despair. All are swarming. Searching. And they'll never stop. Not ever. Not until they find it."

"The thing that was stolen."

The Hermit nodded, his face grim. He seemed to see the slaughter, the destruction. See the men and women, the children, fleeing before the merciless, soulless force.

"But what was it? What could be so important they had to destroy everything to get it back?"

Olivier willed his eyes not to dart from the craggy face and into the darkness. To the corner, and the thing they both knew was sitting there in its mean little canvas sack. But the Hermit seemed to read his mind and Olivier saw a malevolent grin settle onto the old man's face. And then it was gone.

"It's not the army that wants it back."

They both saw then the thing looming behind the terrible army. The thing even Chaos feared. That drove Despair, Disease, Famine before it. With one goal. To find what was taken from their Master.

"It's worse than slaughter."

Their voices were low, barely scraping the ground. Like conspirators in a cause already lost.

"When the army finally finds what it's searching for it will stop. And step aside. And then the worst thing imaginable will arrive."

There was silence again. And in that silence lived the worst thing imaginable.

Outside a pack of coyotes set up a howl. They had something cornered.

Myth, that's all this is, Olivier reassured himself. Just a story. Once more he looked into the embers, so he wouldn't see the terror in the Hermit's face. Then he checked his watch, tilting the crystal toward the fireplace until its face glowed orange and told him the time. Two thirty in the morning.

"Chaos is coming, old son, and there's no stopping it. It's taken a long time, but it's finally here."

The Hermit nodded, his eyes rheumy and runny, perhaps from the wood smoke, perhaps from something else. Olivier leaned back, surprised to feel his thirty-eight-year-old body suddenly aching, and realized he'd sat tense through the whole awful telling.

"I'm sorry. It's getting late and Gabri will be worried. I have to go."

"Already?"

Olivier got up and pumping cold, fresh water into the enamel sink he cleaned his cup. Then he turned back to the room.

"I'll be back soon," he smiled.

"Let me give you something," said the Hermit, looking around the log cabin. Olivier's gaze darted to the corner where the small canvas sack sat. Unopened. A bit of twine keeping it closed.

A chuckle came from the Hermit. "One day, perhaps, Olivier. But not today."

He went over to the hand-hewn mantelpiece, picked up a tiny item and held it out to the attractive blond man.

"For the groceries." He pointed to the tins and cheese and milk, tea and coffee and bread on the counter.

"No, I couldn't. It's my pleasure," said Olivier, but they both knew the pantomime and knew he'd take the small offering. *"Merci,"* Olivier said at the door.

In the woods there was a furious scrambling, as a doomed creature raced to escape its fate, and coyotes raced to seal it.

"Be careful," said the old man, quickly scanning the night sky. Then, before closing the door, he whispered the single word that was quickly devoured by the woods. Olivier wondered if the Hermit crossed himself and mumbled prayers, leaning against the door, which was thick but perhaps not quite thick enough.

And he wondered if the old man believed the stories of the great and grim army with Chaos looming and leading the Furies. Inexorable, unstoppable. Close.

And behind them something else. Something unspeakable.

And he wondered if the Hermit believed the prayers.

Olivier flicked on his flashlight, scanning the darkness. Gray tree trunks crowded round. He shone the light here and there, trying to find the narrow path through the late summer forest. Once on the trail he hurried. And the more he hurried the more frightened he became, and the more fearful he grew the faster he ran until he was stumbling, chased by dark words through the dark woods.

He finally broke through the trees and staggered to a stop, hands on his bent knees, heaving for breath. Then, slowly straightening, he looked down on the village in the valley.

Three Pines was asleep, as it always seemed to be. At peace with itself and the world. Oblivious of what happened around it. Or perhaps aware of everything, but choosing peace anyway. Soft light glowed at some of the windows. Curtains were drawn in bashful old homes. The sweet scent of the first autumn fires wafted to him.

And in the very center of the little Quebec village there stood three great pines, like watchmen.

Olivier was safe. Then he felt his pocket.

The gift. The tiny payment. He'd left it behind.

Cursing, Olivier turned to look into the forest that had closed behind him. And he thought again of the small canvas bag in the corner of the cabin. The thing the Hermit had teased him with, promised him, dangled before him. The thing a hiding man hid.

Olivier was tired, and fed up and angry at himself for forgetting the trinket. And angry at the Hermit for not giving him the other thing. The thing he'd earned by now.

He hesitated, then turning he plunged back into the forest, feeling his fear growing and feeding the rage. And as he walked, then ran, a voice followed, beating behind him. Driving him on.

"Chaos is here, old son."

Two

"You get it."

Gabri pulled up the covers and lay still. But the phone continued to ring and beside him Olivier was dead to the world. Out the window Gabri could see drizzle against the pane and he could feel the damp Sunday morning settling into their bedroom. But beneath the duvet it was snug and warm, and he had no intention of moving.

He poked Olivier. "Wake up."

Nothing, just a snort.

"Fire!"

Still nothing.

"Ethel Merman!"

Nothing. Dear Lord, was he dead?

He leaned in to his partner, seeing the precious thinning hair lying across the pillow and across the face. The eyes closed, peaceful. Gabri smelled Olivier, musky, slightly sweaty. Soon they'd have a shower and they'd both smell like Ivory soap.

The phone rang again.

"It's your mother," Gabri whispered in Olivier's ear.

"What?"

"Get the phone. It's your mother."

Olivier sat up, fighting to get his eyes open and looking bleary, as though emerging from a long tunnel. "My mother? But she's been dead for years."

"If anyone could come back from the dead to screw you up, it'd be her."

"You're the one screwing me up."

"You wish. Now get the phone."

Olivier reached across the mountain that was his partner and took the call.

"Oui, allô?"

Gabri snuggled back into the warm bed, then registered the time on the glowing clock. Six forty-three. On Sunday morning. Of the Labor Day long weekend.

Who in the world would be calling at this hour?

He sat up and looked at his partner's face, studying it as a passenger might study the face of a flight attendant during takeoff. Were they worried? Frightened?

He saw Olivier's expression change from mildly concerned to puzzled, and then, in an instant, Olivier's blond brows dropped and the blood rushed from his face.

Dear God, thought Gabri. We're going down.

"What is it?" he mouthed.

Olivier was silent, listening. But his handsome face was eloquent. Something was terribly wrong.

"What's happened?" Gabri hissed.

They rushed across the village green, their raincoats flapping in the wind. Myrna Landers, fighting with her huge umbrella, came across to meet them and together they hurried to the bistro. It was dawn and the world was gray and wet. In the few paces it took to get to the bistro their hair was plastered to their heads and their clothes were sodden. But for once neither Olivier nor Gabri cared. They skidded to a stop beside Myrna outside the brick building.

"I called the police. They should be here soon," she said.

"Are you sure about this?" Olivier stared at his friend and neighbor. She was big and round and wet and wearing bright yellow rubber boots under a lime green raincoat and gripping her red umbrella. She looked as though a beachball had exploded. But she also had never looked more serious. Of course she was sure.

"I went inside and checked," she said.

"Oh, God," whispered Gabri. "Who is it?"

"I don't know."

"How can you not know?" Olivier asked. Then he looked through the mullioned glass of his bistro window, bringing his slim hands up beside his face to block out the weak morning light. Myrna held her brilliant red umbrella over him.

Olivier's breath fogged the window but not before he'd seen what Myrna had also seen. There was someone inside the bistro. Lying on the old pine floor. Face up.

"What is it?" asked Gabri, straining and craning to see around his partner.

But Olivier's face told him all he needed to know. Gabri focused on the large black woman next to him.

"Is he dead?"

"Worse."

What could be worse than death? he wondered.

Myrna was as close as their village came to a doctor. She'd been a psychologist in Montreal before too many sad stories and too much good sense got the better of her, and she'd quit. She'd loaded up her car intending to take a few months to drive around before settling down, somewhere. Any place that took her fancy.

She got an hour outside Montreal,

stumbled on Three Pines, stopped for *café au lait* and a croissant at Olivier's Bistro, and never left. She unpacked her car, rented the shop next door and the apartment above and opened a used bookstore.

People wandered in for books and conversation. They brought their stories to her, some bound, and some known by heart. She recognized some of the stories as real, and some as fiction. But she honored them all, though she didn't buy every one.

"We should go in," said Olivier. "To make sure no one disturbs the body. Are you all right?"

Gabri had closed his eyes, but now he opened them again and seemed more composed. "I'm fine. Just a shock. He didn't look familiar."

And Myrna saw on his face the same relief she'd felt when she'd first rushed in. The sad fact was, a dead stranger was way better than a dead friend.

They filed into the bistro, sticking close as though the dead man might reach out and take one of them with him. Inching toward him they stared down, rain dripping off their heads and noses onto his worn clothes and puddling on the wide-plank floor. Then Myrna gently pulled them back from the edge.

And that's how both men felt. They'd woken on this holiday weekend in their comfortable bed, in their comfortable home, in their comfortable life, to find themselves suddenly dangled over a cliff.

All three turned away, speechless. Staring wide-eyed at each other.

There was a dead man in the bistro.

And not just dead, but worse.

As they waited for the police Gabri made a pot of coffee, and Myrna took off her raincoat and sat by the window, looking into the misty September day. Olivier laid and lit fires in the two stone hearths at either end of the beamed room. He poked one fire vigorously and felt its warmth against his damp clothing. He felt numb, and not just from the creeping cold.

When they'd stood over the dead man Gabri had murmured, "Poor one."

Myrna and Olivier had nodded. What they saw was an elderly man in shabby clothing, staring up at them. His face was white, his eyes surprised, his mouth slightly open.

Myrna had pointed to the back of his head. The puddled water was turning pink. Gabri leaned tentatively closer, but Olivier didn't move. What held him spellbound and stunned wasn't the shattered back of the dead man's head, but the front. His face.

"*Mon Dieu,* Olivier, the man's been murdered. Oh, my God."

Olivier continued to stare, into the eyes.

"But who is he?" Gabri whispered.

It was the Hermit. Dead. Murdered. In the bistro.

"I don't know," said Olivier.

Chief Inspector Armand Gamache got the call just as he and Reine-Marie finished clearing up after Sunday brunch. In the dining room of their apartment in Montreal's Outremont *quartier* he could hear his second in command, Jean Guy Beauvoir, and his daughter Annie. They weren't talking. They never talked. They argued. Especially when Jean Guy's wife, Enid, wasn't there as a buffer. But Enid had to plan school courses and had begged off brunch. Jean Guy, on the other hand, never turned down an invitation for a free meal. Even if it came at a price. And the price was always Annie.

It had started over the fresh-squeezed orange juice, coursed through the scrambled eggs and Brie, and progressed across the fresh fruit, croissants and *confitures.*

"But how can you defend the use of stun guns?" came Annie's voice from the dining room.

"Another great brunch, *merci,* Reine-

Marie," said David, placing dishes from the dining room in front of the sink and kissing his mother-in-law on the cheek. He was of medium build with short, thinning dark hair. At thirty he was a few years older than his wife, Annie, though he often appeared younger. His main feature, Gamache often felt, was his animation. Not hyper, but full of life. The Chief Inspector had liked him from the moment, five years earlier, his daughter had introduced them. Unlike other young men Annie had brought home, mostly lawyers like herself, this one hadn't tried to out-macho the Chief. That wasn't a game that interested Gamache. Nor did it impress him. What did impress him was David's reaction when he'd met Armand and Reine-Marie Gamache. He'd smiled broadly, a smile that seemed to fill the room, and simply said, *"Bonjour."*

He was unlike any other man Annie had ever been interested in. David wasn't a scholar, wasn't an athlete, wasn't staggeringly handsome. Wasn't destined to become the next Premier of Quebec, or even the boss of his legal firm.

No, David was simply open and kind.

She'd married him, and Armand Gamache had been delighted to walk with her down the aisle, with Reine-Marie on the other side of their only daughter. And to see this nice man wed his daughter.

For Armand Gamache knew what not-nice was. He knew what cruelty, despair, horror were. And he knew what a forgotten, and precious, quality "nice" was.

"Would you rather we just shoot suspects?" In the dining room Beauvoir's voice had risen in volume and tone.

"Thank you, David," said Reine-Marie, taking the dishes. Gamache handed his son-in-law a fresh dish towel and they dried as Reine-Marie washed up.

"So," David turned to the Chief Inspector, "do you think the Habs have a chance at the cup this year?"

"No," yelled Annie. "I expect you to learn how to apprehend someone without having to maim or kill them. I expect you to genuinely see suspects as just that. Suspects. Not sub-human criminals you can beat up, electrocute or shoot."

"I think they do," said Gamache, handing David a plate to dry and taking one himself. "I like their new goalie and I think their forward line has matured. This is definitely their year."

"But their weakness is still defense, don't you think?" Reine-Marie asked. "The Canadiens always concentrate too much on offense."

"You try arresting an armed murderer. I'd love to see you try. You, you . . ." Beauvoir was sputtering. The conversation in the kitchen stopped as they listened to what he might say next. This was an argument played out every brunch, every Christmas, Thanksgiving, birthday. The words changed slightly. If not tasers they were arguing about daycare or education or the environment. If Annie said blue, Beauvoir said orange. It had been this way since Inspector Beauvoir had joined the Sûreté du Québec's homicide division, under Gamache, a dozen years earlier. He'd become a member of the team, and of the family.

"You what?" demanded Annie.

"You pathetic piece of legal crap."

Reine-Marie gestured toward the back door of the kitchen that gave onto a small metal balcony and fire escape. "Shall we?"

"Escape?" Gamache whispered, hoping she was serious, but suspecting she wasn't.

"Maybe you could just try shooting them, Armand?" David asked.

"I'm afraid Jean Guy is a faster draw," said the Chief Inspector. "He'd get me first."

"Still," said his wife, "it's worth a try."

"Legal crap?" said Annie, her voice dripping disdain. "Brilliant. Fascist moron."

"I suppose I could use a taser," said Gamache.

"Fascist? Fascist?" Jean Guy Beauvoir almost squealed. In the kitchen Gamache's German shepherd, Henri, sat up in his bed and cocked his head. He had huge oversized ears which made Gamache think he wasn't purebred but a cross between a shepherd and a satellite dish.

"Uh-oh," said David. Henri curled into a ball in his bed and it was clear David would join him if he could.

All three looked wistfully out the door at the rainy, cool early September day. Labor Day weekend in Montreal. Annie said something unintelligible. But Beauvoir's response was perfectly clear.

"Screw you."

"Well, I think this debate's just about over," said Reine-Marie. "More coffee?" She pointed to their espresso maker.

"Non, pas pour moi, merci," said David, with a smile. "And please, no more for Annie."

"Stupid woman," muttered Jean Guy as he entered the kitchen. He grabbed a dish towel from the rack and began furiously drying a plate. Gamache figured that was the last they'd see of the India Tree design.

"Tell me she's adopted."

"No, homemade." Reine-Marie handed the next plate to her husband.

"Screw you." Annie's dark head shot into the kitchen then disappeared.

"Bless her heart," said Reine-Marie.

Of their two children, Daniel was the more like his father. Large, thoughtful, academic. He was kind and gentle and strong. When Annie had been born Reine-Marie thought, perhaps naturally, this would be the child most like her. Warm, intelligent, bright. With a love of books so strong Reine-Marie Gamache had become a librarian, finally taking over a department at the *Bibliothèque nationale* in Montreal.

But Annie had surprised them both. She was smart, competitive, funny. She was fierce, in everything she did and felt.

They should have had an inkling about this. As a newborn Armand would take her for endless rides in the car, trying to soothe her as she howled. He'd sing, in his deep baritone, Beatles songs, and Jacques Brel songs. *"La Complainte du phoque en Alaska"* by Beau Dommage. That was Daniel's favorite. It was a soulful lament. But it did nothing for Annie.

One day, as he'd strapped the shrieking child into the car seat and turned on the ignition, an old Weavers tape had been in.

As they sang, in falsetto, she'd settled.

At first it had seemed a miracle. But after the hundredth trip around the block listening to the laughing child and the Weavers singing *"Wimoweh, a-wimoweh,"* Gamache yearned for the old days and felt like shrieking himself. But as they sang the little lion slept.

Annie Gamache became their cub. And grew into a lioness. But sometimes, on quiet walks together, she'd tell her father about her fears and her disappointments and the everyday sorrows of her young life. And Chief Inspector Gamache would be seized with a desire to hold her to him, so that she needn't pretend to be so brave all the time.

She was fierce because she was afraid. Of everything.

The rest of the world saw a strong, noble lioness. He looked at his daughter and saw Bert Lahr, though he'd never tell her that. Or her husband.

"Can we talk?" Annie asked her father, ignoring Beauvoir. Gamache nodded and handed the dish towel to David. They walked down the hall and into the warm living room where books were ranged on shelves in orderly rows, and stacked under tables and beside the sofa in not-so-orderly piles. *Le Devoir* and the *New York Times* were on the coffee table and a gentle fire burned in the grate. Not the roaring flames of a bitter winter fire, but a soft almost liquid flame of early autumn.

They talked for a few minutes about Daniel, living in Paris with his wife and daughter, and another daughter due before the end of the month. They talked about her husband David and his hockey team, about to start up for another winter season.

Mostly Gamache listened. He wasn't sure if Annie had something specific to say, or just wanted to talk. Henri jogged into the room and plunked his head on Annie's lap. She kneaded his ears, to his grunts and moans. Eventually he lay down by the fire.

Just then the phone rang. Gamache ignored it.

"It's the one in your office, I think," said Annie. She could see it on the old wooden desk with the computer and the notebook, in the room that was filled with books, and smelled of sandalwood and rosewater and had three chairs.

She and Daniel would sit in their wooden swivel chairs and spin each other around until they were almost sick, while their father sat in his armchair, steady. And read.

Or sometimes just stared.

"I think so too."

The phone rang again. It was a sound they knew well. Somehow different from other phones. It was the ringing that announced a death.

Annie looked uncomfortable.

"It'll wait," he said quietly. "Was there something you wanted to tell me?"

"Should I get that?" Jean Guy looked in. He smiled at Annie but his eyes went swiftly to the Chief Inspector.

"Please. I'll be there in a moment."

He turned back to his daughter, but by then David had joined them and Annie had once again put on her public face. It wasn't so different from her private one. Just, perhaps, a bit less vulnerable. And her father wondered briefly, as David sat down and took her hand, why she needed her public face in front of her husband.

"There's been a murder, sir," whispered Inspector Beauvoir. He stood just inside the room.

"Oui," said Gamache, watching his daughter.

"Go on, Papa." She waved her hand at him, not to dismiss him, but to free him of the need to stay with her.

"I will, eventually. Would you like to go

for a walk?"

"It's pelting down outside," said David with a laugh. Gamache genuinely loved his son-in-law, but sometimes he could be oblivious. Annie also laughed.

"Really, Papa, not even Henri would go out in this."

Henri leaped up and ran to get his ball. The fatal words, "Henri" and "out," had been combined unleashing an undeniable force.

"Well," said Gamache as the German shepherd bounded back into the room. "I have to go to work."

He gave Annie and David a significant look, then glanced over at Henri. His meaning even David couldn't miss.

"Christ," whispered David good-humoredly, and getting off the comfortable sofa he and Annie went to find Henri's leash.

By the time Chief Inspector Gamache and Inspector Beauvoir arrived in Three Pines the local force had cordoned off the bistro, and villagers milled about under umbrellas and stared at the old brick building. The scene of so many meals and drinks and celebrations. Now a crime scene.

As Beauvoir drove down the slight slope

into the village Gamache asked him to pull over.

"What is it?" the Inspector asked.

"I just want to look."

The two men sat in the warm car, watching the village through the lazy arc of the wipers. In front of them was the village green with its pond and bench, its beds of roses and hydrangea, late flowering phlox and hollyhocks. And at the end of the common, anchoring it and the village, stood the three tall pines.

Gamache's gaze wandered to the buildings that hugged the village green. There were weathered white clapboard cottages, with wide porches and wicker chairs. There were tiny fieldstone houses built centuries ago by the first settlers, who'd cleared the land and yanked the stones from the earth. But most of the homes around the village green were made of rose-hued brick, built by United Empire Loyalists fleeing the American Revolution. Three Pines sat just kilometers from the Vermont border and while relations now with the States were friendly and affectionate, they weren't back then. The people who created the village had been desperate for sanctuary, hiding from a war they didn't believe in.

The Chief Inspector's eyes drifted up du

Moulin, and there, on the side of the hill leading out of the village, was the small white chapel. St. Thomas's Anglican.

Gamache brought his eyes back to the small crowd standing under umbrellas chatting, pointing, staring. Olivier's bistro was smack-dab in the center of the semicircle of shops. Each shop ran into the next. Monsieur Béliveau's general store, then Sarah's Boulangerie, then Olivier's Bistro and finally Myrna's new and used bookstore.

"Let's go," Gamache nodded.

Beauvoir had been waiting for the word and now the car moved slowly forward. Toward the huddled suspects, toward the killer.

But one of the first lessons the Chief had taught Beauvoir when he'd joined the famed homicide department of the Sûreté du Québec was that to catch a killer they didn't move forward. They moved back. Into the past. That was where the crime began, where the killer began. Some event, perhaps long forgotten by everyone else, had lodged inside the murderer. And he'd begun to fester.

What kills can't be seen, the Chief had warned Beauvoir. That's what makes it so dangerous. It's not a gun or a knife or a fist. It's not anything you can see coming. It's an emotion. Rancid, spoiled. And waiting for a chance to strike.

The car slowly moved toward the bistro, toward the body.

"Merci," said Gamache a minute later as a local Sûreté officer opened the bistro door for them. The young man was just about to challenge the stranger, but hesitated.

Beauvoir loved this. The reaction of local cops as it dawned on them that this large man in his early fifties wasn't just a curious citizen. To the young cops Gamache looked like their fathers. There was an air of courtliness about him. He always wore a suit, or the jacket and tie and gray flannels he had on that day.

They'd notice the mustache, trimmed and graying. His dark hair was also graying around the ears, where it curled up slightly. On a rainy day like this the Chief wore a cap, which he took off indoors, and when he did the young officers saw the balding head. And if that wasn't enough they'd notice this man's eyes. Everyone did. They were deep brown, thoughtful, intelligent and something else. Something that distinguished the famous head of homicide for the Sûreté du Québec from every other senior officer.

His eyes were kind.

It was both his strength, Beauvoir knew, and his weakness.

Gamache smiled at the astonished officer who found himself face to face with the most celebrated cop in Quebec. Gamache offered his hand and the young agent stared at it for a moment before putting out his own. *"Patron,"* he said.

"Oh, I was hoping it would be you." Gabri hurried across the room, past the Sûreté officers bending over the victim. "We asked if the Sûreté could send you but apparently it's not normal for suspects to order up a specific officer." He hugged the Chief Inspector then turned to the roomful of agents. "See, I do know him." Then he whispered to Gamache, "I think it would be best if we didn't kiss."

"Very wise."

Gabri looked tired and stressed, but composed. He was disheveled, though that wasn't unusual. Behind him, quieter, almost eclipsed, stood Olivier. He was also disheveled. That was very unusual. He also looked exhausted, with dark rings under his eyes.

"Coroner's just arriving now, Chief." Agent Isabelle Lacoste walked across the room to greet him. She wore a simple skirt and light sweater and managed to make both look stylish. Like most Québécoises, she was petite and confident. “It’s Dr. Harris, I see.”

They all looked out the window and the crowd parted to let a woman with a medical bag through. Unlike Agent Lacoste, Dr. Harris managed to make her simple skirt and sweater look slightly frumpy. But comfortable. And on a miserable day like this “comfortable” was very attractive.

“Good,” said the Chief, turning back to Agent Lacoste. “What do we know?”

Lacoste led Gamache and Inspector Beauvoir to the body. They knelt, an act and ritual they’d performed hundreds of times. It was surprisingly intimate. They didn’t touch him, but leaned very close, closer than they’d ever get to anyone in life, except a loved one.

“The victim was struck from behind by a blunt object. Something clean and hard, and narrow.”

“A fireplace poker?” Beauvoir asked, looking over at the fires Olivier had set. Gamache also looked. It was a damp morning, but not all that cool. A fire wasn’t necessary. Still, it was probably made to comfort more than to heat.

“If it was a poker it would be clean. The coroner will take a closer look, of course, but there’s no obvious sign of dirt, ash, wood, anything, in the wound."

Gamache was staring at the gaping hole in the man's head. Listening to his agent.

"No weapon, then?" asked Beauvoir.

"Not yet. We're searching, of course."

"Who was he?"

"We don't know."

Gamache took his eyes off the wound and looked at the woman, but said nothing.

"We have no ID," Agent Lacoste continued. "We've been through his pockets and nothing. Not even a Kleenex. And no one seems to know him. He's a white male, mid-seventies I'd say. Lean but not malnourished. Five seven, maybe five eight."

Years ago, when she'd first joined homicide, it had seemed bizarre to Agent Lacoste to catalog these things the Chief could see perfectly well for himself. But he'd taught them all to do it, and so she did. It was only years later, when she was training someone else, that she recognized the value of the exercise.

It made sure they both saw the same things. Police were as fallible and subjective as anyone else. They missed things, and misinterpreted things. This catalog made it less likely. Either that or they'd reinforce the same mistakes.

"Nothing in his hands and it looks like

nothing under his fingernails. No bruising. Doesn't appear to have been a struggle."

They stood up.

"The condition of the room verifies that."

They looked around.

Nothing out of place. Nothing tipped over. Everything clean and orderly.

It was a restful room. The fires at either end of the beamed bistro took the gloom out of the day. Their light gleamed off the polished wood floors, darkened by years of smoke and farmers' feet.

Sofas and large inviting armchairs sat in front of each fireplace, their fabric faded. Old chairs were grouped around dark wooden dining tables. In front of the mullioned bay windows three or four wing chairs waited for villagers nursing steaming *café au lait* and croissants, or Scotches, or burgundy wine. Gamache suspected the people milling outside in the rain could do with a good stiff drink. He thought Olivier and Gabri certainly could.

Chief Inspector Gamache and his team had been in the bistro many times, enjoying meals in front of the roaring fire in winter or a quiet cool drink on the *terrasse* in summer. Almost always discussing murder. But never with an actual body right there.

Sharon Harris joined them, taking off her

wet raincoat then smiling at Agent Lacoste and shaking hands solemnly with the Chief Inspector.

"Dr. Harris," he said, bowing slightly. "I'm sorry about disturbing your long weekend."

She'd been sitting at home, flipping through the television channels, trying to find someone who wasn't preaching at her, when the phone had rung. It had seemed a godsend. But looking now at the body, she knew that this had very little to do with God.

"I'll leave you to it," said Gamache. Through the windows he saw the villagers, still there, waiting for news. A tall, handsome man with gray hair bent down to listen as a short woman with wild hair spoke. Peter and Clara Morrow. Villagers and artists. Standing like a ramrod beside them and staring unblinking at the bistro was Ruth Zardo. And her duck, looking quite imperious. Ruth wore a sou'wester that glistened in the rain. Clara spoke to her, but was ignored. Ruth Zardo, Gamache knew, was a drunken, embittered old piece of work. Who also happened to be his favorite poet in the world. Clara spoke again and this time Ruth did respond. Even through the glass Gamache knew what she'd said.

"Fuck off."

Gamache smiled. While a body in the bistro was certainly different, some things never changed.

"Chief Inspector."

The familiar, deep, singsong voice greeted him. He turned and saw Myrna Landers walking across the room, her electric yellow boots clumping on the floor. She wore a pink tracksuit tucked into her boots.

She was a woman of color, in every sense.

"Myrna," he smiled and kissed her on both cheeks. This drew a surprised look from some of the local Sûreté officers, who didn't expect the Chief Inspector to kiss suspects. "What're you doing in here when everyone else is out there?" He waved toward the window.

"I found him," she said, and his face grew grave.

"Did you? I'm sorry. That must've been a shock." He guided her to a chair by the fire. "I imagine you've given someone your statement?"

She nodded. "Agent Lacoste took it. Not much to tell, I'm afraid."

"Would you like a coffee, or a nice cup of tea?"

Myrna smiled. It was something she'd offered him often enough. Something she offered everyone, from the kettle that bubbled away on her woodstove. And now it was being offered to her. And she saw how comforting it actually was.

"Tea, please."

While she sat warming herself by the fire Chief Inspector Gamache went to ask Gabri for a pot of tea, then returned. He sat in the armchair and leaned forward.

"What happened?"

"I go out every morning for a long walk."

"Is this something new? I've never known you to do that before."

"Well, yes. Since the spring anyway. I decided since I turned fifty I needed to get into shape." She smiled fully then. "Or at least, into a different shape. I'm aiming for pear rather than apple." She patted her stomach. "Though I suspect my nature is to be the whole orchard."

"What could be better than an orchard?" he smiled, then looked at his own girth. "I'm not exactly a sapling myself. What time do you get up?"

"Set my alarm for six thirty and I'm out the door by quarter to seven. This morning I'd just left when I noticed Olivier's door was open a little, so I looked in and called. I know Olivier doesn't normally open until later on a Sunday so I was surprised."

"But not alarmed."

"No." She seemed surprised by the question. "I was about to leave when I spotted him."

Myrna's back was to the room, and Gamache didn't glance over to the body. Instead he held her gaze and encouraged her with a nod, saying nothing.

Their tea arrived and while it was clear Gabri wanted to join them he, unlike Gamache's son-in-law David, was intuitive enough to pick up the unspoken signals. He put the teapot, two bone china cups and saucers, milk, sugar and a plate of ginger cookies on the table. Then left.

"At first I thought it was a pile of linen left by the waiters the night before," Myrna said when Gabri was out of earshot. "Most of them're quite young and you never know. But then I looked closer and saw it was a body."

"A body?"

It was the way someone describes a dead man, not a living one.

"I knew he was dead right away. I've seen some, you know."

Gamache did know.

"He was exactly as you see him now." Myrna watched as Gamache poured their tea. She indicated milk and sugar then accepted her cup, with a biscuit. "I got up close but didn't touch him. I didn't think he'd been killed. Not at first."

"What did you think?" Gamache held the cup in his large hands. The tea was strong and fragrant.

"I thought he'd had a stroke or maybe a heart attack. Something sudden, by the look on his face. He seemed surprised, but not afraid or in pain."

That was, thought Gamache, a good way of putting it. Death had surprised this man. But it did most people, even the old and infirm. Almost no one really expected to die.

"Then I saw his head."

Gamache nodded. It was hard to miss. Not the head, but what was missing from it.

"Do you know him?"

"Never seen him before. And I suspect he'd be memorable."

Gamache had to agree. He looked like a vagrant. And while easily ignored they were hard to forget. Armand Gamache put his delicate cup on its delicate saucer. His mind kept going to the question that had struck him as soon as he'd taken the call and heard about the murder. In the bistro in Three Pines.

Why here?

He looked quickly over to Olivier who was talking to Inspector Beauvoir and Agent Lacoste. He was calm and contained. But he couldn't be oblivious of how this appeared.

"What did you do then?"

"I called 911 then Olivier, then went outside and waited for them."

She described what happened, up to the moment the police arrived.

"Merci," said Gamache and rose. Myrna took her tea and joined Olivier and Gabri across the room. They stood together in front of the hearth.

Everyone in the room knew who the three main suspects were. Everyone, that was, except the three main suspects.

THREE

Dr. Sharon Harris stood, brushed her skirt clean and smiled thinly at the Chief Inspector.

"Not much finesse," she said.

Gamache stared down at the dead man.

"He looks like a tramp," said Beauvoir, bending down and examining the man's clothing. It was mismatched and worn.

"He must be living rough," said Lacoste.

Gamache knelt down and looked closely at the old man's face again. It was weathered and withered. An almanac face, of sun and wind and cold. A seasoned face. Gamache gently rubbed his thumb across the dead man's cheek, feeling stubble. He was clean shaven, but what might have grown in would've been white. The dead man's hair was white and cut without enthusiasm. A snip here, a snip there.

Gamache picked up one of the victim's hands, as though comforting him. He held it for an instant, then turned it over, palm up. Then he slowly rubbed his own palm over the dead man's.

"Whoever he was he did hard work. These are calluses. Most tramps don't work."

Gamache shook his head slowly. So who are you? And why are you here? In the bistro, and in this village. A village few people on earth even knew existed. And even fewer found.

But you did, thought Gamache, still holding the man's cold hand. You found the village and you found death.

"He's been dead between six and ten hours," the doctor said. "Sometime after midnight but before four or five this morning."

Gamache stared at the back of the man's head and the wound that killed him.

It was catastrophic. It looked like a single blow by something extremely hard. And by someone extremely angry. Only anger accounted for this sort of power. The power to pulverize a skull. And what it protected.

Everything that made this man who he was was kept in this head. Someone bashed that in. With one brutal, decisive blow.

"Not much blood." Gamache got up and watched the Scene of Crime team fanning out and collecting evidence around the large room. A room now violated. First by murder and now by them. The unwanted guests.

Olivier was standing, warming himself by the fire.

"That's a problem," said Dr. Harris. "Head wounds bleed a lot. There should be more blood, lots more."

"It might've been cleaned up," said Beauvoir.

Sharon Harris bent over the wound again then straightened up. "With the force of the blow the bleeding might have been massive and internal. And death almost instantaneous."

It was the best news Gamache ever heard at a murder scene. Death he could handle. Even murder. It was suffering that disturbed him. He'd seen a lot of it. Terrible murders. It was a great relief to find one swift and decisive. Almost humane.

He'd once heard a judge say the most humane way to execute a prisoner was to tell him he was free. Then kill him.

Gamache had struggled against that, argued against it, railed against it. Then finally, exhausted, had come to believe it.

Looking at this man's face he knew he hadn't suffered. The blow to the back of the head meant he probably hadn't even seen it coming.

Almost like dying in your sleep.

But not quite.

They placed him in a bag and took the body away. Outside men and women stood somberly aside to let it pass. Men swept off their damp caps and women watched, tight-lipped and sad.

Gamache turned away from the window and joined Beauvoir, who was sitting with Olivier, Gabri and Myrna. The Scene of Crime team had moved into the back rooms of the bistro, the private dining room, the staff room, the kitchen. The main room now seemed almost normal. Except for the questions hanging in the air.

"I'm sorry this has happened," Gamache said to Olivier. "How're you doing?"

Olivier exhaled deeply. He looked drained. "I think I'm still stunned. Who was he? Do you know?"

"No," said Beauvoir. "Did anyone report a stranger in the area?"

"Report?" said Olivier. "To whom?"

All three turned perplexed eyes on Beauvoir. The Inspector had forgotten that Three Pines had no police force, no traffic lights, no sidewalks, no mayor. The volunteer fire department was run by that demented old poet Ruth Zardo, and most would rather perish in the flames than call her.

The place didn't even have crime. Except murder. The only criminal thing that ever happened in this village was the worst possible crime.

And here they were with yet another body. At least the rest had had names. This one seemed to have dropped from the sky, and fallen on his head.

"It's a little harder in the summer, you know," said Myrna, taking a seat on the sofa. "We get more visitors. Families come back for vacation, kids come home from school. This is the last big weekend. Everyone goes home after this."

"The weekend of the Brume County Fair," said Gabri. "It ends tomorrow."

"Right," said Beauvoir, who couldn't care less about the fair. "So Three Pines empties out after this weekend. But the visitors you describe are friends and family?"

"For the most part," said Myrna, turning to Gabri. "Some strangers come to your B and B, don't they?"

He nodded. "I'm really an overflow if people run out of space in their homes."

"What I'm getting at," said an exasperated Beauvoir, "is that the people who visit Three Pines aren't really strangers. I just want to get this straight."

"Straight we don't specialize in. Sorry," said Gabri. This brought a smile to even Olivier's tired face.

"I heard something about a stranger," said Myrna, "but I didn't really pay any attention."

"Who said it?"

"Roar Parra," she said, reluctantly. It felt a bit like informing, and no one had much stomach for that. "I heard him talking to Old Mundin and The Wife about seeing someone in the woods."

Beauvoir wrote this down. It wasn't the first time he'd heard about the Parras. They were a prominent Czech family. But Old Mundin and The Wife? That must be a joke. Beauvoir's lips narrowed and he looked at Myrna without amusement. She looked back, also without amusement.

"Yes," Myrna said, reading his mind. It wasn't hard. The teapot could read it. "Those are their names."

"Old and The Wife?" he repeated. No longer angry, but mystified. Myrna nodded. "What're their real names?"

"That's it," said Olivier. "Old and The Wife."

"Okay, I'll give you Old. It's just possible, but no one looks at a newborn and decides to call her The Wife. At least I hope not."

Myrna smiled. "You're right. I'm just so used to it I never thought. I have no idea what her real name is."

Beauvoir wondered just how pathetic a woman had to be to allow herself to be called The Wife. It actually sounded slightly biblical, Old Testament.

Gabri put some beers, Cokes and a couple of bowls of mixed nuts on the table. Outside the villagers had finally gone home. It looked wet and bleak, but inside they were snug and warm. It was almost possible to forget this wasn't a social occasion. The Scene of Crime agents seemed to have dissolved into the woodwork, only evident when a slight scratching or mumbling could be heard. Like rodents, or ghosts. Or homicide detectives.

"Tell us about last night," said Chief Inspector Gamache.

"It was a madhouse," said Gabri. "Last big weekend of the summer so everyone came by. Most had been to the fair during the day so they were tired. Didn't want to cook. It's always like that on Labor Day weekend. We were prepared."

"What does that mean?" asked Agent Lacoste, who'd joined them.

"I brought in extra staff," said Olivier. "But it went smoothly. People were pretty relaxed and we closed on time. At about one in the morning."

"What happened then?" asked Lacoste.

Most murder investigations appeared complex but were really quite simple. It was just a matter of asking "And then what happened?" over and over and over. And listening to the answers helped too.

"I usually do the cash and leave the night staff to clean up, but Saturdays are different," said Olivier. "Old Mundin comes after closing and delivers the things he's repaired during the week and picks up any furniture that's been broken in the meantime. Doesn't take long, and he does it while the waiters and kitchen staff are cleaning up."

"Wait a minute," said Beauvoir. "Mundin does this at midnight on Saturdays? Why not Sunday morning, or any other reasonable time? Why late at night?"

It sounded furtive to Beauvoir, who had a nose for things secretive and sly.

Olivier shrugged. "Habit, I guess. When he first started doing the work he wasn't married to The Wife so he'd hang around here Saturday nights. When we closed he'd just take the broken furniture then. We've seen no reason to change."

In a village where almost nothing changed this made sense.

"So Mundin took the furniture. What happened then?" asked Beauvoir.

"I left."

"Were you the last in the place?"

Olivier hesitated. "Not quite. Because it was so busy there were a few extra things to do. They're a good bunch of kids, you know. Responsible."

Gamache had been listening to this. He preferred it that way. His agents asked the questions and it freed him up to observe, and to hear what was said, how it was said, and what was left out. And now he heard a defensiveness creep into Olivier's calm and helpful voice. Was he defensive about his own behavior, or was he trying to protect his staff, afraid they'd fall under suspicion?

"Who was the last to leave?" Agent Lacoste asked.

"Young Parra," said Olivier.

"Young Parra?" asked Beauvoir. "Like Old Mundin?"

Gabri made a face. "Of course not. His name isn't 'Young.' That'd be weird. His name's Havoc."

Beauvoir's eyes narrowed and he glared at Gabri. He didn't like being mocked and he suspected this large, soft man was doing just that. He then looked over at Myrna, who wasn't laughing. She nodded.

"That's his name. Roar named his son Havoc."

Jean Guy Beauvoir wrote it down, but without pleasure or conviction.

"Would he have locked up?" asked Lacoste.

It was, Gamache and Beauvoir both knew, a crucial question, but its significance seemed lost on Olivier.

"Absolutely."

Gamache and Beauvoir exchanged glances. Now they were getting somewhere. The murderer had to have had a key. A world full of suspects had narrowed dramatically.

"May I see your keys?" asked Beauvoir.

Olivier and Gabri fished theirs out and handed them to the Inspector. But a third set was also offered. He turned and saw Myrna's large hand dangling a set of keys.

"I have them in case I get locked out of my place or if there's an emergency."

"Merci," said Beauvoir, with slightly less confidence than he'd been feeling. "Have you lent them to anyone recently?" he asked Olivier and Gabri.

"No."

Beauvoir smiled. This was good.

"Except Old Mundin, of course. He'd lost his and needed to make another copy."

"And Billy Williams," Gabri reminded Olivier. "Remember? He normally uses the one under the planter at the front but he didn't want to have to bend down while he carried the wood. He was going to take it to get more copies made."

Beauvoir's face twisted into utter disbelief. "Why even bother to lock up?" he finally asked.

"Insurance," said Olivier.

Well, someone's premiums are going up, thought Beauvoir. He looked at Gamache and shook his head. Really, they all deserved to be murdered in their sleep. But, of course, as irony would have it, it was the ones who locked and alarmed who were killed. In Beauvoir's experience Darwin was way wrong. The fittest didn't survive. They were killed by the idiocy of their neighbors, who continued to bumble along oblivious.

Four

"You didn't recognize him?" asked Clara as she sliced some fresh bread from Sarah's Boulangerie.

There was only one "him" Myrna's friend could be talking about. Myrna shook her head and sliced tomatoes into the salad, then turned to the shallots, all freshly picked from Peter and Clara's vegetable garden.

"And Olivier and Gabri didn't know him?" asked Peter. He was carving a barbecued chicken.

"Strange, isn't it?" Myrna paused and looked at her friends. Peter — tall, graying, elegant and precise. And beside him his wife Clara. Short, plump, hair dark and wild, bread crust scattered into it like sparkles. Her eyes were blue and usually filled with humor. But not today.

Clara was shaking her head, perplexed. A couple of crumbs fell to the counter. She picked them up absently, and ate them.

Now that the initial shock of discovery was receding, Myrna was pretty sure they were all thinking the same thing.

This was murder. The dead man was a stranger. But was the killer?

And they probably all came to the same conclusion. Unlikely.

She'd tried not to think about it, but it kept creeping into her head. She picked up a slice of baguette and chewed on it. The bread was warm, soft and fragrant. The outer crust was crispy.

"For God's sake," said Clara, waving the knife at the half-eaten bread in Myrna's hand.

"Want some?" Myrna offered her a piece.

The two women stood at the counter eating fresh warm bread. They'd normally be at the bistro for Sunday lunch but that didn't seem likely today, what with the body and all. So Clara, Peter and Myrna had gone next door to Myrna's loft apartment. Downstairs the door to her shop was armed with an alarm, should anyone enter. It wasn't really so much an alarm as a small bell that tinkled when the door opened. Sometimes Myrna went down, sometimes not. Almost all her customers were local, and they all knew how much to leave by the cash register. Besides, thought Myrna, if anyone needed a used book so badly they had to steal it then they were welcome to it.

Myrna felt a chill. She looked across the room to see if a window was open and cool, damp air pouring in. She saw the exposed brick walls, the sturdy beams and the series of large industrial windows. She walked over to check, but all of them were closed, except for one open a sliver to let in some fresh air.

Walking back across the wide pine floors, she paused by the black pot-bellied wood-stove in the center of the large room. It was crackling away. She lifted a round lid and slipped another piece of wood in.

"It must have been horrible for you," said Clara, going to stand by Myrna.

"It was. That poor man, just lying there. I didn't see the wound at first."

Clara sat with Myrna on the sofa facing the woodstove. Peter brought over two Scotches then quietly retired to the kitchen area. From there he could see them, could hear their conversation, but wouldn't be in the way.

He watched as the two women leaned close, sipping their drinks, talking softly. Intimately. He envied them that. Peter turned away and stirred the Cheddar and apple soup.

"What does Gamache think?" asked Clara.

"He seems as puzzled as the rest of us. I mean really," Myrna turned to face Clara, "why was a strange man in the bistro? Dead?"

"Murdered," said Clara and the two thought about that for a moment.

Clara finally spoke. "Did Olivier say anything?"

"Nothing. He seemed just stunned."

Clara nodded. She knew the feeling.

The police were at the door. Soon they'd be in their homes, in their kitchens and bedrooms. In their heads.

"Can't imagine what Gamache thinks of us," said Myrna. "Every time he shows up there's a body."

"Every Quebec village has a vocation," said Clara. "Some make cheese, some wine, some pots. We produce bodies."

"Monasteries have vocations, not villages," said Peter with a laugh. He placed bowls of rich-scented soup on Myrna's long refectory table. "And we don't make bodies."

But he wasn't really so sure.

"Gamache is the head of homicide for the Sûreté," said Myrna. "It must happen to him all the time. In fact, he'd probably be quite surprised if there wasn't a body."

Myrna and Clara joined Peter at the table and as the women talked Peter thought of the man in charge of the investigation. He was dangerous, Peter knew. Dangerous to whoever had killed that man next door. He wondered whether the murderer knew what sort of man was after him. But Peter was afraid the murderer knew all too well.

Inspector Jean Guy Beauvoir looked around their new Incident Room and inhaled. He realized, with some surprise, how familiar and even thrilling the scent was.

It smelled of excitement, it smelled of the hunt. It smelled of long hours over hot computers, piecing together a puzzle. It smelled of teamwork.

It actually smelled of diesel fuel and wood smoke, of polish and concrete. He was again in the old railway station of Three Pines, abandoned by the Canadian Pacific Railway decades ago and left to rot. But the Three Pines Volunteer Fire Department had taken it over, sneaking in and hoping no one noticed. Which, of course, they didn't, the CPR having long forgotten the village existed. So now the small station was home to their fire trucks, their bulky outfits, their equipment. The walls retained the tongue-in-groove wood paneling, and were papered with posters for scenic trips through the Rockies and life-saving techniques. Fire safety tips, volunteer rotation and old railway timetables competed for space, along with a huge poster announcing the winner of the Governor General's Prize for Poetry. There, staring out at them in perpetuity, was a madwoman.

She was also staring at him, madly, in person.

"What the fuck are you doing here?" Beside her a duck stared at him too.

Ruth Zardo. Probably the most prominent and respected poet in the country. And her duck Rosa. He knew that when Chief Inspector Gamache looked at her he saw a gifted poet. But Beauvoir just saw indigestion.

"There's been a murder," he said, his voice he hoped full of dignity and authority.

"I know there's been a murder. I'm not an idiot."

Beside her the duck shook its head and flapped its wings. Beauvoir had grown so used to seeing her with the bird it was no longer surprising. In fact, though he'd never admit it, he was relieved Rosa was still alive. Most things, he suspected, didn't last long around this crazy old fart.

"We need to use this building again," he said and turned away from them.

Ruth Zardo, despite her extreme age, her

limp, and her diabolical temperament, had been elected head of the volunteer fire department. In hopes, Beauvoir suspected, that she'd perish in the flames one day. But he also suspected she wouldn't burn.

"No." She whacked her cane on the concrete floor. Rosa didn't jump but Beauvoir did. "You can't have it."

"I'm sorry, Madame Zardo, but we need it and we plan to take it."

His voice was no longer as gracious as it had been. The three stared at each other, only Rosa blinking. Beauvoir knew the only way this nutcase could triumph was if she started reciting her dreary, unintelligible verse. Nothing rhymed. Nothing even made sense. She'd break him in an instant. But he also knew that of all the people in the village, she was the least likely to quote it. She seemed embarrassed, even ashamed, by what she created.

"How's your poetry?" he asked and saw her waver. Her short, shorn hair was white and thin and lay close to her head, as though her bleached skull was exposed. Her neck was scrawny and ropy and her tall body, once sturdy he suspected, was feeble. But nothing else about her was.

"I saw somewhere that you'll soon have another book out."

Ruth Zardo backed up slightly.

"The Chief Inspector is here too, as you probably know." His voice was kind now, reasonable, warm. The old woman looked as though she was seeing Satan. "I know how much he's looking forward to talking to you about it. He'll be here soon. He's been memorizing your verses."

Ruth Zardo turned and left.

He'd done it. He'd banished her. The witch was dead, or at least gone.

He got to work setting up their headquarters. He ordered desks and communications equipment, computers and printers, scanners and faxes. Corkboards and fragrant Magic Markers. He'd stick a corkboard right on top of that poster of the sneering, mad old poet. And over her face he'd write about murder.

The bistro was quiet.

The Scene of Crime officers had left. Agent Isabelle Lacoste was kneeling on the floor where the body had been found, thorough as ever. Making absolutely sure no clues were missed. From what Chief Inspector Gamache could see Olivier and Gabri hadn't stirred: they still sat on the faded old sofa facing the large fireplace, each in his own world, staring at the fire, mesmerized by the flames. He wondered what they were thinking.

"What are you thinking?" Gamache went over and sat in the large armchair beside them.

"I was thinking about the dead man," said Olivier. "Wondering who he was. Wondering what he was doing here, and about his family. Wondering if anyone was missing him."

"I was thinking about lunch," said Gabri. "Anyone else hungry?"

From across the room Agent Lacoste looked up. "I am."

"So am I, *patron,*" said Gamache.

When they could hear Gabri clanking pots and pans in the kitchen, Gamache leaned forward. It was just him and Olivier. Olivier looked at him blankly. But the Chief Inspector had seen that look before. It was, in fact, almost impossible to look blank. Unless the person wanted to. A blank face to the Chief Inspector meant a frantic mind.

From the kitchen came the unmistakable aroma of garlic and they could hear Gabri singing, "What shall we do with a drunken sailor?"

"Gabri thought the man was a tramp. What do you think?"

Olivier remembered the eyes, glassy, staring. And he remembered the last time he'd been in the cabin.

Chaos is coming, old son. It's taken a long time, but it's finally here.

"What else could he've been?"

"Why do you think he was killed here, in your bistro?"

"I don't know." And Olivier seemed to sag. "I've been racking my brains trying to figure it out. Why would someone kill a man here? It makes no sense."

"It does make sense."

"Really?" Olivier sat forward. "How?"

"I don't know. But I will."

Olivier stared at the formidable, quiet man who suddenly seemed to fill the entire room without raising his voice.

"Did you know him?"

"You've asked me that before," snapped Olivier, then gathered himself. "I'm sorry, but you have, you know, and it gets annoying. I didn't know him."

Gamache stared. Olivier's face was red now, blushing. But from anger, from the heat of the fire, or did he just tell a lie?

"Someone knew him," said Gamache at last, leaning back, giving Olivier the impression of pressure lifted. Of breathing room.

"But not me and not Gabri." His brow pulled together and Gamache thought Olivier was genuinely upset. "What was he doing here?"

" 'Here' meaning Three Pines, or 'here' meaning the bistro?"

"Both."

But Gamache knew Olivier had just lied. He meant the bistro, that was obvious. People lied all the time in murder investigations. If the first victim of war was the truth, some of the first victims of a murder investigation were people's lies. The lies they told themselves, the lies they told each other. The little lies that allowed them to get out of bed on cold, dark mornings. Gamache and his team hunted the lies down and exposed them. Until all the small tales told to ease everyday lives disappeared. And people were left naked. The trick was distinguishing the important fibs from the rest. This one appeared tiny. In which case, why bother lying at all?

Gabri approached carrying a tray with four steaming plates. Within minutes they were sitting around the fireplace eating fettuccine with shrimp and scallops sautéed in garlic and olive oil. Fresh bread was produced and glasses of dry white wine poured.

As they ate they talked about the Labor Day long weekend, about the chestnut trees and conkers. About kids returning to school and the nights drawing in.

The bistro was empty, except for them. But it seemed crowded to the Chief Inspector. With the lies they'd been told, and the lies being manufactured and waiting.

Five

After lunch, while Agent Lacoste made arrangements for them to stay overnight at Gabri's B and B, Armand Gamache walked slowly in the opposite direction. The drizzle had stopped for the moment but a mist clung to the forests and hills surrounding the village. People were coming out of their homes to do errands or work in their gardens. He walked along the muddy road and turning left made his way over the arched stone bridge that spanned the Rivière Bella Bella.

"Hungry?" Gamache opened the door to the old train station and held out the brown paper bag.

"Starving, *merci.*" Beauvoir almost ran over, and taking the bag he pulled out a thick sandwich of chicken, Brie and pesto. There was also a Coke and *pâtisserie.*

"What about you?" asked Beauvoir, his hand hesitating over the precious sandwich.

"Oh, I've eaten," the Chief said, deciding it would really do no good describing his meal to Beauvoir.

The men drew a couple of chairs up to the warm pot-bellied stove and as the Inspector ate they compared notes.

"So far," said Gamache, "we have no idea who the victim was, who killed him, why he was in the bistro and what the murder weapon was."

"No sign of a weapon yet?"

"No. Dr. Harris thinks it was a metal rod or something like that. It was smooth and hard."

"A fireplace poker?"

"Perhaps. We've taken Olivier's in for tests." The Chief paused.

"What is it?" Beauvoir asked.

"It just strikes me as slightly odd that Olivier would light fires in both grates. It's rainy but not that cold. And for that to be just about the first thing he'd do after finding a body . . ."

"You're thinking the weapon might be one of those fireplace pokers? And that Olivier lit the fires so that he could use them? Burn away evidence on them?"

"I think it's possible," said the Chief, his voice neutral.

"We'll have them checked," said Beauvoir.

"But if one turns out to be the weapon it doesn't mean Olivier used it. Anyone could've picked it up and smashed the guy."

"True. But only Olivier lit the fires this morning, and used the poker."

It was clear as Chief Inspector he had to consider everyone a suspect. But it was also clear he wasn't happy about it.

Beauvoir waved to some large men at the door to come in. The Incident Room equipment had arrived. Lacoste showed up and joined them by the stove.

"I've booked us into the B and B. By the way, I ran into Clara Morrow. We're invited to dinner tonight."

Gamache nodded. This was good. They could find out more at a social event than they ever could in an interrogation.

"Olivier gave me the names of the people who worked in the bistro last night. I'm off to interview them," she reported. "And there are teams searching the village and the surrounding area for the murder weapon, with a special interest in fireplace pokers or anything like that."

Inspector Beauvoir finished his lunch and went to direct the setup of the Incident Room. Agent Lacoste left to conduct interviews. A part of Gamache always hated to see his team members go off. He warned them time and again not to forget what they were doing, and who they were looking for. A killer.

The Chief Inspector had lost one agent, years ago, to a murderer. He was damned if he was going to lose another. But he couldn't protect them all, all the time. Like Annie, he finally had to let them go.

It was the last interview of the day. So far Agent Lacoste had spoken to five people who'd worked at the bistro the night before, and gotten the same answers. No, nothing unusual happened. The place was full all evening, it being both a Saturday night and the long Labor Day weekend. School was back on Tuesday and anybody down for the summer would be heading back to Montreal on Monday. Tomorrow.

Four of the waiters were returning to university after the summer break the next day. They really weren't much help since all they seemed to have noticed was a table of attractive girls.

The fifth waiter was more helpful, since she hadn't simply seen a roomful of breasts. But it was, by all accounts, a normal though hectic evening. No dead body that anyone mentioned, and Lacoste thought even the breast boys would have noticed that.

She drove up to the home of the final waiter, the young man nominally in charge once Olivier had left. The one who'd done the final check of the place and locked up.

The house was set back from the main road down a long dirt driveway. Maples lined the drive and while they hadn't yet turned their brilliant autumn colors, a few were just beginning to show oranges and reds. In a few weeks this approach, Lacoste knew, would be spectacular.

Lacoste got out of the car and stared, amazed. Facing her was a block of concrete and glass. It seemed so out of place, like finding a tent pitched on Fifth Avenue. It didn't belong. As she walked toward it she realized something else. The house intimidated her and she wondered why. Her own tastes ran to traditional but not stuffy. She loved exposed brick and beams, but hated clutter, though she'd given up all semblance of being house-proud after the kids came. These days it was a triumph if she walked across a room and didn't step on something that squeaked.

This place was certainly a triumph. But was it a home?

The door was opened by a robust middle-aged woman who spoke very good, though perhaps slightly precise, French. Lacoste was surprised and realized she'd been expecting angular people to live in this angular house.

"Madame Parra?" Agent Lacoste held up her identification. The woman nodded, smiled warmly and stepped back for them to enter.

"*Entrez.* It's about what happened at Olivier's," said Hanna Parra.

"Oui." Lacoste bent to take off her muddy boots. It always seemed so awkward and undignified. The world famous homicide team of the Sûreté du Québec interviewing suspects in their stockinged feet.

Madame Parra didn't tell her not to. But she did give her slippers from a wooden box by the door, jumbled full of old footwear. Again, this surprised Lacoste, who'd expected everything to be neat and tidy. And rigid.

"We're here to speak to your son."

"Havoc."

Havoc. The name had amused Inspector Beauvoir, but Agent Lacoste found nothing funny about it. And, strangely, it seemed to fit with this cold, brittle place. What else could contain Havoc?

Before driving out she'd done some research on the Parras. Just a thumbnail sketch, but it helped. The woman leading her out of the mudroom was a councillor for the township of Saint-Rémy, and her husband, Roar, was a caretaker, working on the large properties in the area. They'd escaped Czechoslovakia in the mid-80s, come to Quebec and settled just outside Three Pines. There was, in fact, a large and influential Czech community in the area, composed of escapees, people running until they found what they were looking for. Freedom and safety. Hanna and Roar Parra had stopped when they found Three Pines.

And once there, they'd created Havoc.

"Havoc!" his mother cried, letting the dogs slip out as she called into the woods.

After a few more yells a short, stocky young man appeared. His face was flushed from hard work and his curly dark hair was tousled. He smiled and Lacoste knew the other waiters at the bistro hadn't stood a chance with the girls. This boy would take them all. He also stole a sliver of her heart, and she quickly did the figures. She was twenty-eight, he was twenty-one. In twenty-five years that wouldn't matter so much, although her husband and children might disagree.

"What can I do for you?" He bent and took off his green Wellington boots. "Of course, it is that man they found in the bistro this morning. I'm sorry. I should have known."

As he talked they walked into a quite splendid kitchen, unlike any Lacoste had seen in real life. Instead of the classic, and mandatory as far as Lacoste knew, triangle of fitments, the entire kitchen was ranged along one wall at the back of the bright room. There was one very long concrete counter, stainless steel appliances, open floating shelves with pure white dishes in a regimented line. The lower cabinets were dark laminate. It felt at once very retro and very modern.

There was no kitchen island but instead a frosted glass dining table, and what looked like vintage teak chairs stood in front of the counter. As Lacoste sat in one, and found it surprisingly comfortable, she wondered if these were antiques brought from Prague. Then she wondered if people really slipped across borders with teak chairs.

At the other end of the room was a wall of windows, floor to ceiling, that wrapped around the sides giving a spectacular view of fields and forest and a mountain beyond. She could just see a white church spire and a plume of smoke in the distance. The village of Three Pines.

In the living area by the huge windows

two sofas lined up perfectly to face each other, with a low coffee table between them.

"Tea?" Hanna asked and Lacoste nodded.

These two Parras seemed at odds in the almost sterile environment and as they waited for the tea to brew Lacoste found herself wondering about the missing Parra. The father, Roar. Perhaps it was his angular, hard stamp on this house. Was he the one who yearned for cool certainty, straight lines, near empty rooms, and uncluttered shelves?

"Do you know who the dead man was?" asked Hanna as she placed a cup of tea in front of Agent Lacoste. A white plate piled with cookies was also put on the spotless table.

Lacoste thanked her and took one. It was soft and warm and tasted of raisin and oatmeal, with a hint of brown sugar and cinnamon. It tasted of home. She noticed the teacup had a smiling and waving snowman in a red suit. Bonhomme Carnaval. A character from the annual Quebec City winter carnival. She took a sip. It was strong and sweet.

Like Hanna herself, Lacoste suspected.

"No, we don't know who he was yet," she said.

"We've heard," Hanna hesitated, "that it

wasn't natural. Is that right?"

Lacoste remembered the man's skull. "No, it wasn't natural. He was murdered."

"Dear God," said Hanna. "How awful. And you have no idea who did it?"

"We will, soon. For now I want to hear about last night." She turned to the young man sitting across from her.

Just then a voice called from the back door in a language Lacoste couldn't understand, but took to be Czech. A man, short and square, walked into the kitchen, whacking his knit hat against his coat.

"Roar, can't you do that in the mudroom?" Hanna spoke in French, and despite the slight reprimand she was clearly pleased to see him. "The police are here. About the body."

"What body?" Roar also switched to French, lightly accented. He sounded concerned. "Where? Here?"

"Not here, Dad. They found a body in the bistro this morning. He was killed."

"You mean murdered? Someone was murdered in the bistro last night?"

His disbelief was clear. Like his son he was stocky and muscular. His hair was curly and dark, but unlike his son's it was graying. He'd be in his late forties, Lacoste reckoned.

She introduced herself.

"I know you," he said, his gaze keen and penetrating. His eyes were disconcertingly blue and hard. "You've been in Three Pines before."

He had a good memory for faces, Lacoste realized. Most people remembered Chief Inspector Gamache. Maybe Inspector Beauvoir. But few remembered her, or the other agents.

This man did.

He poured himself tea then sat down. He also seemed slightly out of place in this pristine modern room. And yet he was completely comfortable. He looked a man who'd be comfortable most places.

"You didn't know about the body?"

Roar Parra took a bite of his cookie and shook his head. "I've been working all day in the woods."

"In the rain?"

He snorted. "What? A little rain won't kill you."

"But a blow to the head would."

"Is that how he died?" When Lacoste nodded Parra went on. "Who was he?"

"No one knows," said Hanna.

"But perhaps you do," said Lacoste. She brought a photograph out of her pocket and placed it face down on the hard, cold table.

"Me?" said Roar with a snort. "I didn't even know there was a dead man."

"But I hear you saw a stranger hanging around the village this summer."

"Who told you that?"

"Doesn't matter. You were heard talking about it. Was it a secret?"

Parra hesitated. "Not really. It was just the once. Maybe twice. Not important. It was stupid, just some guy I thought I saw."

"Stupid?"

He gave a smile suddenly, the first one she'd seen from him, and it transformed his stern face. It was as though a crust had broken. Lines creased his cheeks and his eyes lit momentarily.

"Trust me, this is stupid. And I know stupid, having raised a teenage son. I'll tell you, but it can't mean anything. There're new owners at the old Hadley house. A couple bought it a few months ago. They're doing renovations and hired me to build a barn and clear some trails. They also wanted the garden cleaned up. Big job."

The old Hadley house, she knew, was a rambling old Victorian wreck on the hill overlooking Three Pines.

"I think I saw someone in the woods. A man. I'd felt someone looking at me when I worked there, but I thought I was imagining things. It's easy with that place. Sometimes I'd look around fast, to see if someone really was there, but there never was anyone. Except once."

"What happened?"

"He disappeared. I called out and even ran into the woods a little way after him, but he'd gone." Parra paused. "Maybe he was never there at all."

"But you don't believe that, do you? You believe there really was someone there."

Parra looked at her and nodded.

"Would you recognize him?" Lacoste asked.

"I might."

"I have a photograph of the dead man, taken this morning. It might be upsetting," she warned. Parra nodded and she turned the photograph face up. All three looked at it, staring intently, then shook their heads. She left it on the table, beside the cookies.

"Everything was normal last night? Nothing unusual?" she asked Havoc.

What followed was the same description as the other waiters had provided. Busy, lots of tips, no time to think.

Strangers?

Havoc thought about it and shook his head. No. Some summer people, and weekenders, but he knew everyone.

"And what did you do after Olivier and Old Mundin left?"

"Put away the dishes, did a quick look round, turned off the lights and locked up."

"Are you sure you locked up? The door was found unlocked this morning."

"I'm sure. I always lock up."

A note of fear had crept into the handsome young man's voice. But Lacoste knew that was normal. Most people, even innocent ones, grew fearful when examined by homicide detectives. But she'd noticed something else.

His father had looked at him, then quickly looked away. And Lacoste wondered who Roar Parra really was. He worked in the woods now. He cut grass and planted gardens. But what had he done before that? Many men were drawn to the tranquility of a garden only after they'd known the brutality of life.

Had Roar Parra known horrors? Had he created some?

Six

"Chief Inspector? It's Sharon Harris."

"*Oui,* Dr. Harris," said Gamache into the receiver.

"I haven't done the complete autopsy but I have a couple of pieces of information from my preliminary work."

"Go on." Gamache leaned on the desk and brought his notebook closer.

"There were no identifying marks on the body, no tattoos, no operation scars. I've sent his dental work out."

"What shape were his teeth in?"

"Now that's an interesting point. They weren't as bad as I expected. I bet he didn't go to the dentist very often, and he'd lost a couple of molars to some gum disease, but overall, not bad."

"Did he brush?"

There was a small laugh. "Unbelievably, he did. He also flossed. There's some receding, some plaque and disease, but he took care of his teeth. There's even evidence he once had quite a bit of work done. Cavities filled, root canal."

"Expensive stuff."

"Exactly. This man had money at one time."

He wasn't born a tramp, thought Gamache. But then no one was.

"Can you tell how long ago the work was done?"

"I'd say twenty years at least, judging by the wear and the materials used, but I've sent a sample along to the forensic dentist. Should hear by tomorrow."

"Twenty years ago," mused Gamache, doing the math, jotting figures in his notebook. "The man was in his seventies. That would mean he had the work done sometime in his fifties. Then something happened. He lost his job, drank, had a breakdown; something happened that pushed him over the edge."

"Something happened," agreed Dr. Harris, "but not in his fifties. Something happened in his late thirties or early forties."

"That long ago?" Gamache looked down at his notes. He'd written *20 ans* and circled it. He was confused.

"That's what I wanted to tell you, Chief," the coroner continued. "There's something wrong about this body."

Gamache sat up straighter and took his half-moon reading glasses off. Across the room Beauvoir saw this and walked over to the Chief's desk.

"Go on," said Gamache, nodding to Beauvoir to sit. Then he punched a button on the phone. "I've put you on the speaker. Inspector Beauvoir's here."

"Good. Well, it struck me as strange that this man who seemed a derelict should brush his teeth and even floss. But homeless people can do odd things. They're often mentally unwell, as you know, and can be obsessive about certain things."

"Though not often hygiene," said Gamache.

"True. It was strange. Then when I undressed him I found he was clean. He'd had a bath or a shower recently. And his hair, while wild, was also clean."

"There're halfway homes," said Gamache. "Maybe he was in one of those. Though an agent called all the local social services and he's not known to them."

"How d'you know?" The coroner rarely questioned Chief Inspector Gamache, but she was curious. "We don't know his name and surely his description would sound like any number of homeless men."

"That's true," admitted Gamache. "She described him as a slim, older man in his seventies with white hair, blue eyes and weathered skin. None of the men who match that description and use shelters in this area is missing. But we're having someone take his photo around."

There was a pause on the line.

"What is it?"

"Your description is wrong."

"What do you mean?" Surely Gamache had seen him as clearly as everyone else.

"He wasn't an elderly man. That's what I called to tell you. His teeth were a clue; then I went looking. His arteries and blood vessels have very little plaque, and almost no atherosclerosis. His prostate isn't particularly enlarged and there's no sign of arthritis. I'd say he was in his mid-fifties."

My age, thought Gamache. Was it possible that wreck on the floor was the same age?

"And I don't think he was homeless."

"Why not?"

"Too clean for one thing. He took care of himself. Not *GQ* material, it's true, but not all of us can look like Inspector Beauvoir."

Beauvoir preened slightly.

"On the outside he looked seventy but on the inside he was in good physical condition. Then I looked at his clothes. They were clean too. And mended. They were old and worn, but *propres.*"

She used the Québécois word that was rarely used anymore, except by elderly parents. But it seemed to fit here. *Propre.* Nothing fancy. Nothing fashionable. But sturdy and clean and presentable. There was a worn dignity about the word.

"I have to do more work, but that's my preliminary finding. I'll e-mail all this to you."

"*Bon.* Can you guess what sort of work he did? How'd he keep himself in shape?"

"Which gym did he belong to, you mean?" He could hear the smile in her voice.

"That's right," said Gamache. "Did he jog or lift weights? Was he in a spinning class or maybe Pilates?"

Now the coroner laughed. "At a guess I'd say it wasn't much walking, but a lot of lifting. His upper body is slightly more toned than his lower. But I'll keep that question in mind as I go."

"Merci, docteur," said Gamache.

"One more thing," said Beauvoir. "The murder weapon. Any further clues? Any ideas?"

"I'm just about to do that part of the autopsy, but I've taken a quick look and my assessment stays the same. Blunt instrument."

"A fireplace poker?" asked Beauvoir.

"Possibly. I did notice something white in the wound. Might be ash."

"We'll have the lab results from the pokers by tomorrow morning," said Gamache.

"I'll let you know when I have more to tell you."

Dr. Harris rung off just as Agent Lacoste arrived back. "Clearing up outside. It's going to be a nice sunset."

Beauvoir looked at her, incredulous. She was supposed to be scouring Three Pines for clues, trying to find the murder weapon and the murderer, interviewing suspects, and the first thing out of her mouth was about the nice sunset?

He noticed the Chief drift over to a window, sipping his coffee. He turned round and smiled. "Beautiful."

A conference table had been set up in the center of their Incident Room with desks and chairs placed in a semicircle at one end. On each desk was a computer and phone. It looked a little like Three Pines, with the conference table as the village green and their desks as the shops. It was an ancient and tested design.

A young Sûreté agent from the local

detachment hovered, looking as if he wanted to say something.

"Can I help you?" Chief Inspector Gamache asked.

The other agents from the local detachment stopped and stared. Some exchanged knowing smiles.

The young man squared his shoulders.

"I'd like to help with your investigation."

There was dead silence. Even the technicians stopped what they were doing, as people do when witnessing a terrible calamity.

"I'm sorry?" said Inspector Beauvoir, stepping forward. "What did you just say?"

"I'd like to help." By now the young agent could see the truck hurtling toward him and could feel his vehicle spin out of control. Too late, he realized his mistake.

He saw all this, and stood firm, from either terror or courage. It was hard to tell. Behind him four or five large agents crossed their arms and did nothing to help.

"Aren't you supposed to be setting up desks and telephone lines?" asked Beauvoir, stepping closer to the agent.

"I have. That's all done." He voice was smaller, weaker, but still there.

"And what makes you think you can help?"

Behind Beauvoir stood the Chief Inspector, quietly watching. The young agent looked at Inspector Beauvoir when answering his questions, but then his eyes returned to Gamache.

"I know the area. I know the people."

"So do they." Beauvoir waved at the wall of police behind the agent. "If we needed help why would we choose you?"

This seemed to throw him and he stood silent. Beauvoir waved his hand to dismiss the agent and walked away.

"Because," the agent said to the Chief Inspector, "I asked."

Beauvoir stopped and turned round, looking incredulous. "*Pardon? Pardon?* This is homicide, not a game of Mother May I. Are you even in the Sûreté?"

It wasn't a bad question. The agent looked about sixteen and his uniform hung loosely on him, though an effort had obviously been made to make it fit. With him in the foreground and his *confrères* behind it looked like an evolutionary scale, with the young agent on the extinction track.

"If you have no more work to do, please leave."

The young agent nodded, turned to get back to work, met the wall of other officers, and stopped. Then he walked around them, watched by Gamache and his homicide team. Their last view of the young officer before they turned away was of his back, and a furiously blushing neck.

"Join me please," Gamache said to Beauvoir and Lacoste, who took their seats at the conference table.

"What do you think?" Gamache asked quietly.

"About the body?"

"About the boy."

"Not again," said Beauvoir, exasperated. "There are perfectly good officers already in homicide if we need someone. If they're busy with cases there's always the wait-list. Agents from other divisions are dying to get into homicide. Why choose an untested kid from the boonies? If we need another investigator let's call one down from headquarters."

It was their classic argument.

The homicide division of the Sûreté du Québec was the most prestigious posting in the province. Perhaps in Canada. They worked on the worst of all crimes in the worst of all conditions. And they worked with the best, the most respected and famous, of all investigators. Chief Inspector Gamache.

So why pick the dregs?

"We could, certainly," admitted the Chief.

But Beauvoir knew he wouldn't. Gamache had found Isabelle Lacoste sitting outside her Superintendent's office, about to be fired from traffic division. Gamache had asked her to join him, to the astonishment of everyone.

He'd found Beauvoir himself reduced to guarding evidence at the Sûreté outpost of Trois Rivières. Every day Beauvoir, Agent Beauvoir then, had suffered the ignominy of putting on his Sûreté uniform then stepping into the evidence cage. And staying there. Like an animal. He'd so pissed off his colleagues and bosses this was the only place left to put him. Alone. With inanimate objects. Silence all day, except when other agents came to put something in or take something out. They wouldn't even meet his eye. He'd become untouchable. Unmentionable. Invisible.

But Chief Inspector Gamache saw. He'd come one day on a case, had himself gone to the cage with evidence, and there he'd found Jean Guy Beauvoir.

The agent, the man no one wanted, was now the second in command in homicide.

But Beauvoir couldn't shake the certainty that Gamache had simply gotten lucky so far, with a few notable exceptions. The reality was, untested agents were dangerous. They made mistakes. And mistakes in homicide led to death.

He turned and looked at the slight young agent with loathing. Was this the one who'd finally make that blunder? The magnificent mistake that would lead to another death? It could be me who gets it, thought Beauvoir. Or worse. He glanced at Gamache beside him.

"Why him?" Beauvoir whispered.

"He seems nice," said Lacoste.

"Like the sunset," Beauvoir sneered.

"Like the sunset," she repeated. "He was standing all alone."

There was silence.

"That's it?" asked Beauvoir.

"He doesn't fit in. Look at him."

"You'd choose the runt of the litter? For homicide detail? For God's sake, sir," he appealed to Gamache. "This isn't the Humane Society."

"You think not?" said Gamache with a small smile.

"We need the best for this team, for this case. We don't have time to train people. And frankly, he looks as though he needs help tying his shoes."

It was true, Gamache had to admit, the young agent was awkward. But he was something else as well.

"We'll take him," said the Chief to Beauvoir. "I know you don't approve, and I understand your reasons."

"Then why take him, sir?"

"Because he asked," said Gamache, rising up. "And no one else did."

"But they'd join us in a second," Beauvoir argued, getting up as well. "Anyone would."

"What do you look for in a member of our team?" asked Gamache.

Beauvoir thought. "I want someone smart and strong."

Gamache tipped his head toward the young man. "And how much strength do you think that took? How much strength do you think it takes him to go to work every day? Almost as much as it took you, in Trois Rivières, or you," he turned to Lacoste, "in traffic division. The others might want to join us, but they either didn't have the brains or lacked the courage to ask. Our young man had both."

Our, thought Beauvoir. Our young man. He looked at him across the room. Alone. Coiling wires carefully and placing them in a box.

"I value your judgment, you know that, Jean Guy. But I feel strongly about this."

"I understand, sir." And he did. "I know

this is important to you. But you're not always right."

Gamache stared at his Inspector and Beauvoir recoiled, afraid he'd gone too far. Presumed too much on their personal relationship. But then the Chief smiled.

"Happily, I have you to tell me when I make a mistake."

"I think you're making one now."

"Noted. Thank you. Will you please invite the young man to join us."

Beauvoir walked purposefully across the room and stopped at the young agent.

"Come with me," he said.

The agent straightened up. He looked concerned. "Yes, sir."

Behind them an officer snickered. Beauvoir stopped and turned back to the young officer following him.

"What's your name?"

"Paul Morin. I'm with the Cowansville detachment of the Sûreté, sir."

"Agent Morin, will you please take a seat at the table. We'd like your thoughts on this murder investigation."

Morin looked astonished. But not quite as astonished as the burly men behind him. Beauvoir turned back and walked slowly toward the conference table. It felt good.

"Reports, please," said Gamache and

glanced at his watch. It was five thirty.

"Results are beginning to come in on some of the evidence we collected this morning in the bistro," said Beauvoir. "The victim's blood was found on the floor and between some of the floorboards, though there wasn't much."

"Dr. Harris will have a fuller report soon," said Gamache. "She thinks the lack of blood is explained by internal bleeding."

Beauvoir nodded. "We do have a report on his clothing. Still nothing to identify him. His clothes were old but clean and of good quality once. Merino wool sweater, cotton shirt, corduroy pants."

"I wonder if he'd put on his best clothes," said Agent Lacoste.

"Go on," said Gamache, leaning forward and taking off his glasses.

"Well." She picked her way through her thoughts. "Suppose he was going to meet someone important. He'd have a shower, shave, clip his nails even."

"And he might pick up clean clothes," said Beauvoir, following her thoughts. "Maybe at a used clothing store, or a Goodwill depot."

"There's one in Cowansville," said Agent Morin. "And another in Granby. I can check them."

"Good," said the Chief Inspector.

Agent Morin looked over at Inspector Beauvoir, who nodded his approval.

"Dr. Harris doesn't think this man was a vagrant, not in the classic sense of the word," said Chief Inspector Gamache. "He appeared in his seventies, but she's convinced he was closer to fifty."

"You're kidding," said Agent Lacoste. "What happened to him?"

That was the question, of course, thought Gamache. What happened to him? In life, to age him two decades. And in death.

Beauvoir stood up and walked to the fresh, clean sheets of paper pinned to the wall. He picked out a new felt pen, took off the cap and instinctively wafted it under his nose. "Let's go through the events of last night."

Isabelle Lacoste consulted her notes and told them about her interviews with the bistro staff.

They were beginning to see what had happened the night before. As he listened Armand Gamache could see the cheerful bistro, filled with villagers having a meal or drinks on Labor Day weekend. Talking about the Brume County Fair, the horse trials, the judging of livestock, the crafts tent. Celebrating the end of summer and saying good-bye to family and friends. He could see the stragglers leaving and the young waiters clearing up, banking the fires, washing the dishes. Then the door opening and Old Mundin stepping in. Gamache had no idea what Old Mundin looked like, so he placed in his mind a character from a painting by Bruegel the Elder. A stooped and cheery peasant. Walking through the bistro door, a young waiter perhaps helping to bring in the repaired chairs. Mundin and Olivier would have conferred. Money would have changed hands and Mundin would have left with new items needing fixing.

Then what?

According to Lacoste's interviews the waiters had left shortly before Olivier and Mundin. Leaving just one person in the bistro.

"What did you think of Havoc Parra?" Gamache asked.

"He seemed surprised by what had happened," said Lacoste. "It might've been an act, of course. Hard to tell. His father told me something interesting, though. He confirmed what we heard earlier. He saw someone in the woods."

"When?"

"Earlier in the summer. He's working at

the old Hadley house for the new owners and thinks he saw someone up there."

"Thinks? Or did?" asked Beauvoir.

"Thinks. He chased him, but the guy disappeared."

They were silent for a moment, then Gamache spoke. "Havoc Parra says he locked up and left by one in the morning. Six hours later the man's body was found by Myrna Landers, who was out for a walk. Why would a stranger be murdered in Three Pines, and in the bistro?"

"If Havoc really did lock up, then the murderer had to be someone who knew where to find a key," said Lacoste.

"Or already had one," said Beauvoir. "Do you know what I wonder? I wonder why the murderer left him there."

"What do you mean?" asked Lacoste.

"Well, no one was there. It was dark. Why not pick up the body and take it into the forest? You wouldn't have to take him far, just a few hundred feet. The animals would do the rest and chances are he'd never be found. We'd never know a murder had been committed."

"Why do you think the body was left?" asked Gamache.

Beauvoir thought for a minute. "I think someone wanted him to be found."

"In the bistro?" asked Gamache.

"In the bistro."

Seven

Olivier and Gabri strolled across the village green. It was seven in the evening and lights were beginning to glow in windows, except at the bistro, which was dark and empty.

"Christ," came a growl through the dusk. "The fairies are out."

"Merde," said Gabri. "The village idiot's escaped from her attic."

Ruth Zardo limped toward them followed by Rosa.

"I hear you finally killed someone with your rapier wit," said Ruth to Gabri, falling into step.

"Actually, I hear he read one of your poems and his head exploded," said Gabri.

"Would that that were true," said Ruth, slipping her bony arms into each of theirs, so that they walked across to Peter and Clara's arm in arm. "How are you?" she asked quietly.

"Okay," said Olivier, not glancing at the

darkened bistro as they passed.

The bistro had been his baby, his creation. All that was good about him, he put in there. All his best antiques, his finest recipes, great wines. Some evenings he'd stand behind the bar, pretending to polish glasses, but really just listening to the laughter and looking at the people, who'd come to his bistro. And were happy to be there. They belonged, and so did he.

Until this.

Who'd want to come to a place where there'd been a murder?

And what if people found out he actually knew the Hermit? What if they found out what he'd done? No. Best to say nothing and see what happened. It was bad enough as it was.

They paused on the walk just outside Peter and Clara's house. Inside they saw Myrna putting her effusive flower arrangement on the kitchen table, already set for supper. Clara was exclaiming at its beauty and artistry. They couldn't hear the words, but her delight was obvious. In the living room Peter tossed another log on the fire.

Ruth turned from the comforting domestic scene to the man beside her. The old poet leaned in to whisper in his ear, so that not even Gabri could hear. "Give it time.

It'll be all right, you know that, don't you?"

She turned to glance again through the glow at Clara hugging Myrna and Peter walking into the kitchen and exclaiming over the flowers as well. Olivier bent and kissed the old, cold cheek and thanked her. But he knew she was wrong. She didn't know what he knew.

Chaos had found Three Pines. It was bearing down upon them and all that was safe and warm and kind was about to be taken away.

Peter had poured them all drinks, except Ruth who'd helped herself and was now sipping from a vase filled with Scotch and sitting in the middle of the sofa facing the fire. Rosa was waddling around the room, barely noticed by anyone anymore. Even Lucy, Peter and Clara's golden retriever, barely looked at Rosa. The first time the poet had shown up with Rosa they'd insisted she stay outside, but Rosa set up such a quacking they were forced to let her in, just to shut the duck up.

"Bonjour."

A deep, familiar voice was heard from the mudroom.

"God, you didn't invite Clouseau, did you?" asked Ruth, to the empty room.

Empty except for Rosa, who raced to stand beside her.

"It's lovely," said Isabelle Lacoste as they walked from the mudroom into the airy kitchen. The long wooden table was set for dinner with baskets of sliced baguette, butter, jugs of water and bottles of wine. It smelled of garlic and rosemary and basil, all fresh from the garden.

And in the center of the table was a stunning arrangement of hollyhocks and climbing white roses, clematis and sweet pea and fragrant pink phlox.

More drinks were poured and the guests wandered into the living room and milled around nibbling soft runny Brie or orange and pistachio caribou pâté on baguette.

Across the room Ruth was interrogating the Chief Inspector.

"Don't suppose you know who the dead man was."

"Afraid not," said Gamache evenly. "Not yet."

"And do you know what killed him?"

"Non."

"Any idea who did it?"

Gamache shook his head.

"Any idea why it happened in the bistro?"

"None," admitted Gamache.

Ruth glared at him. "Just wanted to make

sure you're as incompetent as ever. Good to know some things can be relied upon."

"I'm glad you approve," said Gamache, bowing slightly before wandering off toward the fireplace. He picked up the poker, and examined it.

"It's a fireplace poker," said Clara, appearing at his elbow. "You use it to poke the fire."

She was smiling and watching him. He realized he must have looked a little odd, holding the long piece of metal to his face as though he'd never seen one before. He put it down. No blood on it. He was relieved.

"I hear your solo show is coming up in a few months." He turned to her, smiling. "It must be thrilling."

"If putting a dentist's drill up your nose is thrilling. Yes."

"That bad?"

"Oh, well, you know. It's only torture."

"Have you finished all the paintings?"

"They're all done, at least. They're crap, of course, but at least they're finished. Denis Fortin is coming down himself to discuss how they'll be hung. I have a specific order in mind. And if he disagrees I have a plan. I'll cry."

Gamache laughed. "That's how I got to

be Chief Inspector."

"I told you so," Ruth hissed at Rosa.

"Your art is brilliant, Clara. You know that," said Gamache, leading her away from the crowd.

"How'd you know? You've only seen one piece. Maybe the others suck. I wonder if I made a mistake going with the paint by numbers."

Gamache made a face.

"Would you like to see them?" Clara asked.

"Love to."

"Great. How about after dinner? That gives you about an hour to practice saying, 'My God, Clara, they're the best works of art ever produced by anyone, anywhere.' "

"Sucking up?" smiled Gamache. "That's how I made Inspector."

"You're a Renaissance Man."

"I see you're good at it too."

"*Merci.* Speaking of your job, do you have any idea who that dead man is?" She'd lowered her voice. "You told Ruth you didn't, but is that true?"

"You think I'd lie?" he asked. But why not, he thought. Everyone else does. "You mean, how close are we to solving the crime?"

Clara nodded.

"Hard to say. We have some leads, some

ideas. It makes it harder to know why the man was killed not knowing who he was."

"Suppose you never find out?"

Gamache looked down at Clara. Was there something in her voice? An imperfectly hidden desire that they never find out who the dead man was?

"It makes our job harder," he conceded, "but not impossible."

His voice, while relaxed, became momentarily stern. He wanted her to know they'd solve this case, one way or another. "Were you at the bistro last night?"

"No. We'd gone to the fair with Myrna. Had a disgusting dinner of fries, burgers and cotton candy. Went on a few rides, watched the local talent show, then came back here. I think Myrna might've gone in, but we were tired."

"We know the dead man wasn't a villager. He seems to have been a stranger. Have you seen any strangers around?"

"People come through backpacking or bicycling," said Clara, sipping her red wine and thinking. "But most of them are younger. I understand this was quite an old man."

Gamache didn't tell her what the coroner had said that afternoon.

"Roar Parra told Agent Lacoste he'd seen

someone lurking in the woods this summer. Does that sound familiar?" He watched her closely.

"Lurking? Isn't that a bit melodramatic? No, I haven't seen anyone and neither has Peter. He'd have told me. And we spend a lot of time outside in the garden. If there was someone there we'd have seen him."

She waved toward their backyard, in darkness now, but Gamache knew it was large and sloped gently toward the Rivière Bella Bella.

"Mr. Parra didn't see him there," said Gamache. "He saw him there."

He pointed to the old Hadley house, on the hill above them. The two of them took their drinks and walked out the door to the front veranda. Gamache was wearing his gray flannels, shirt, tie and jacket. Clara had a sweater, and needed it. In early September the nights grew longer and cooler. All around the village lights shone in homes, and even in the house on the hill.

The two looked at the house in silence for a few moments.

"I hear it's sold," said Gamache, finally.

Clara nodded. They could hear the murmur of conversation from the living room, and light spilled out so that Gamache could see Clara's face in profile.

"Few months ago," she said. "What are we now? Labor Day? I'd say they bought it back in July and have been doing renovations ever since. Young couple. Or at least, my age, which seems young to me."

Clara laughed.

It was hard for Gamache to see the old Hadley house as just another place in Three Pines. For one thing, it never seemed to belong to the village. It seemed the accusation, the voyeur on the hill, that looked down on them. Judged them. Preyed on them. And sometimes took one of the villagers, and killed them.

Horrible things had happened in that place.

Earlier in the year he and his wife Reine-Marie had come down and helped the villagers repaint and repair the place. In the belief that everything deserved a second chance. Even houses. And the hopes someone would buy it.

And now someone had.

"I know they hired Roar to work on the grounds," said Clara. "Clean up the gardens. He's even built a barn and started reopening the trails. There must have been fifty kilometers of bridle paths in those woods in Timmer Hadley's time. Grown over, of course. Lots of work for Roar to do."

"He said he saw the stranger in the woods while he worked. Said he'd felt himself being watched for a while but only caught sight of someone once. He'd tried to run after him but the guy disappeared."

Gamache's gaze shifted from the old Hadley house down to Three Pines. Kids were playing touch football on the village green, eking out every last moment of their summer vacation. Snippets of voices drifted to them from villagers sitting on other porches, enjoying the early evening. The main topic of conversation, though, wouldn't be the ripening tomatoes, the cooler nights, or getting in the winter wood.

Into the gentle village something rotten had crawled. Words like "murder," "blood," "body," floated in the night air, as did something else. The soft scent of rosewater and sandalwood from the large, quiet man beside Clara.

Back inside Isabelle Lacoste was pouring herself another watered-down Scotch from the drinks tray on the piano. She looked around the room. A bookcase covered an entire wall, crammed with books, broken only by a window and the door to the veranda through which she could see the Chief and Clara.

Across the living room Myrna was chatting with Olivier and Gabri while Peter worked in the kitchen and Ruth drank in front of the fireplace. Lacoste had been in the Morrow home before, but only to conduct interviews. Never as a guest.

It was as comfortable as she'd imagined. She saw herself going back to her husband in Montreal and convincing him they could sell their home, take the kids out of school, chuck their jobs and move here. Find a cottage just off the village green and get jobs at the bistro or Myrna's bookshop.

She subsided into an armchair and watched as Beauvoir came in from the kitchen, a pâté-smeared piece of bread in one hand and a beer in the other, and started toward the sofa. He halted suddenly, as though repelled, changed course, and went outside.

Ruth rose and limped to the drinks tray, a malevolent sneer on her face. Scotch replenished she returned to the sofa, like a sea monster slipping beneath the surface once again, still waiting for a victim.

"Any idea when we can reopen the bistro?" Gabri asked as he, Olivier and Myrna joined Agent Lacoste.

"Gabri," said Olivier, annoyed.

"What? I'm just asking."

"We've done what we need to," she told

Olivier. "You can open up whenever you'd like."

"You can't stay closed long, you know," said Myrna. "We'd all starve to death."

Peter put his head in and announced, "Dinner!"

"Though perhaps not immediately," said Myrna, as they headed for the kitchen.

Ruth hauled herself out of the sofa and went to the veranda door.

"Are you deaf?" she shouted at Gamache, Beauvoir and Clara. "Dinner's getting cold. Get inside."

Beauvoir felt his rectum spasm as he hurried past her. Clara followed Beauvoir to the dinner table, but Gamache lingered.

It took him a moment to realize he wasn't alone. Ruth was standing beside him, tall, rigid, leaning on her cane, her face all reflected light and deep crevices.

"A strange thing to give to Olivier, wouldn't you say?"

The old voice, sharp and jagged, cut through the laughter from the village green.

"I beg your pardon?" Gamache turned to her.

"The dead man. Even you can't be that dense. Someone did this to Olivier. The man's greedy and shiftless and probably quite weak, but he didn't kill anyone. So why would someone choose his bistro for murder?"

Gamache raised his eyebrows. "You think someone chose the bistro on purpose?"

"Well, it didn't happen by accident. The murderer chose to kill at Olivier's Bistro. He gave the body to Olivier."

"To kill both a man and a business?" asked Gamache. "Like giving white bread to a goldfish?"

"Fuck you," said Ruth.

"Nothing I ever gave was good for you," quoted Gamache. *"It was like white bread to a goldfish."*

Beside him Ruth Zardo stiffened, then in a low growl she finished her own poem.

"They cram and cram, and it kills them,
and they drift in the pool, belly up,
making stunned faces
and playing on our guilt
as if their own toxic gluttony
was not their fault."

Gamache listened to the poem, one of his favorites. He looked across at the bistro, dark and empty on a night when it should have been alive with villagers.

Was Ruth right? Had someone chosen the bistro on purpose? But that meant Olivier was somehow implicated. Had he brought this on himself? Who in the village hated the tramp enough to kill him, and Olivier enough to do it there? Or was the tramp merely a convenient tool? A poor man in the wrong place? Used as a weapon against Olivier?

"Who do you think would want to do this to Olivier?" he asked Ruth.

She shrugged, then turned to leave. He watched her take her place among her friends, all of them moving in ways familiar to each other, and now to him.

And to the killer?

Eight

The meal was winding down. They'd dined on corn on the cob and sweet butter, fresh vegetables from Peter and Clara's garden and a whole salmon barbecued over charcoal. The guests chatted amicably as warm bread was passed and salad served.

Myrna's exuberant arrangement of hollyhock, sweet pea and phlox sat in the center, so that it felt as though they were eating in a garden. Gamache could hear Lacoste asking her dinner companions about the Parras, and then segueing into Old Mundin. The Chief Inspector wondered if they realized they were being interrogated.

Beauvoir was chatting to his neighbors about the Brume County Fair, and visitors. Across the table from Beauvoir sat Ruth, glaring at him. Gamache wondered why, though with Ruth that was pretty much her only form of expression.

Gamache turned to Peter, who was serving arugula, frizzy lettuce and fresh ripe tomatoes.

"I hear the old Hadley house has been sold. Have you met the new owners?"

Peter passed him the salad bowl of deep-burled wood.

"We have. The Gilberts. Marc and Dominique. His mother lives with them too. Came from Quebec City. I think she was a nurse or something. Long retired. Dominique was in advertising in Montreal and Marc was an investment dealer. Made a fortune then retired early before the market went sour."

"Lucky man."

"Smart man," said Peter.

Gamache helped himself to the salad. He could smell the delicate dressing of garlic, olive oil and fresh tarragon. Peter poured them another glass of red wine and handed the bottle down the long table. Gamache watched to see if Peter's comment held a sting, a subtext. By "smart" did Peter mean "shrewd," "cunning," "sly"? But no, Gamache felt Peter meant what he said. It was a compliment. While Peter Morrow rarely insulted anyone, he rarely complimented them either. But he seemed impressed by this Marc Gilbert.

"Do you know them well?"

"Had them around for dinner a few times. Nice couple." For Peter that was an almost effusive comment.

"Interesting that with all that money they'd buy the old Hadley house," said Gamache. "It's been abandoned for a year or more. Presumably they could've bought just about any place around here."

"We were a little surprised as well, but they said they wanted a clean canvas, some place they could make their own. Practically gutted the house, you know. It also has loads of land and Dominique wants horses."

"Roar Parra's been clearing the trails, I hear."

"Slow job."

As he was talking Peter's voice had dropped to a whisper, so that the two men were leaning toward each other like co-conspirators. Gamache wondered what they were conspiring about.

"It's a lot of house for three people. Do they have children?"

"Well, no."

Peter's eyes shifted down the table, then back to Gamache. Whom had he just looked at? Clara? Gabri? It was impossible to say.

"Have they made friends in the community?" Gamache leaned back and spoke in a normal tone, taking a forkful of salad.

Peter looked down the table again and lowered his voice even more. "Not exactly."

Before Gamache could pursue it Peter got up and began clearing the table. At the sink he looked back at his friends, chatting. They were close. So close they could reach out and touch each other, which they occasionally did.

And Peter couldn't. He stood apart, and watched. He missed Ben, who'd once lived in the old Hadley house. Peter had played there as a child. He knew its nooks and crannies. All the scary places where ghosts and spiders lived. But now someone else lived there and had turned it into something else.

Thinking of the Gilberts, Peter could feel his own heart lift a little.

"What're you thinking about?"

Peter started as he realized Armand Gamache was right beside him.

"Nothing much."

Gamache took the mixer from Peter's hand and poured whipping cream and a drop of vanilla into the chilled bowl. He turned it on and leaned toward Peter, his voice drowned out by the whirring machine, lost to all but his companion.

"Tell me about the old Hadley house, and the people there."

Peter hesitated but knew Gamache wasn't going to let it go. And this was as discreet as it was going to get. Peter talked, his words whipped and mixed and unintelligible to anyone more than six inches away.

"Marc and Dominique plan to open a luxury inn and spa."

"At the old Hadley house?"

Gamache's astonishment was so complete it almost made Peter laugh. "It's not the same place you remember. You should see it now. It's fantastic."

The Chief Inspector wondered whether a coat of paint and new appliances could exorcise demons, and whether the Catholic Church knew about that.

"But not everyone's happy about it," Peter continued. "They've interviewed a few of Olivier's workers and offered them jobs at higher wages. Olivier's managed to keep most of his staff, but he's had to pay more. The two barely speak."

"Marc and Olivier?" Gamache asked.

"Won't be in the same room."

"That must be awkward, in a small village."

"Not really."

"Then why are we whispering?" Gamache shut the mixer off and spoke in a normal tone. Peter, flustered, looked over at the table again.

"Look, I know Olivier'll get over it, but for now it's just easier not to bring it up."

Peter handed Gamache a shortcake, which he cut in half, and Peter piled sliced ripe strawberries in their own brilliant red juice on top of it.

Gamache noticed Clara getting up and Myrna going with her. Olivier came over and put the coffee on to perk.

"Can I help?" asked Gabri.

"Here, put cream on. The cake, Gabri," said Peter as Gabri approached Olivier with a spoonful of whipped cream. Soon a small conga line of men assembling strawberry shortcakes was formed. When they'd finished they turned around to take the desserts to the table but stopped dead.

There, lit only by candles, was Clara's art. Or at least three large canvases, propped on easels. Gamache felt suddenly light-headed, as though he'd traveled back to the time of Rembrandt, da Vinci, Titian. Where art was viewed either by daylight or candlelight. Was this how the *Mona Lisa* was first seen? The Sistine Chapel? By firelight? Like cave drawings.

He wiped his hands on a dish towel and walked closer to the three easels. He noticed the other guests did the same thing, drawn to the paintings. Around them the candles flickered and threw more light than Gamache had expected, though it was possible Clara's paintings produced their own light.

"I have others, of course, but these'll be the centerpieces of the exhibition at the Galerie Fortin."

But no one was really listening. Instead they were staring at the easels. Some at one, some at another. Gamache stood back for a moment, taking in the scene.

Three portraits, three elderly women, stared back at him.

One was clearly Ruth. The one that had first caught Denis Fortin's eye. The one that had led him to his extraordinary offer of a solo show. The one that had the art world, from Montreal to Toronto, to New York and London, buzzing. About the new talent, the treasure, found buried in Quebec's Eastern Townships.

And there it was, in front of them.

Clara Morrow had painted Ruth as the elderly, forgotten Virgin Mary. Angry, demented, the Ruth in the portrait was full of despair, of bitterness. Of a life left behind, of opportunities squandered, of loss and betrayals real and imagined and created and caused. She clutched at a rough blue shawl with emaciated hands. The shawl had slipped off one bony shoulder and the skin was sagging, like something nailed up and empty.

And yet the portrait was radiant, filling the room from one tiny point of light. In her eyes. Embittered, mad Ruth stared into the distance, at something very far off, approaching. More imagined than real.

Hope.

Clara had captured the moment despair turned to hope. The moment life began. She'd somehow captured Grace.

It took Gamache's breath away and he could feel a burning in his eyes. He blinked and turned from it, as though from something so brilliant it blinded. He saw everyone else in the room also staring, their faces soft in the candlelight.

The next portrait was clearly Peter's mother. Gamache had met her, and once met, never forgotten. Clara had painted her staring straight at the viewer. Not into the distance, like Ruth, but at something very close. Too close. Her white hair in a loose bun, her face a web of soft lines, as though a window had just shattered but not yet fallen. She was white and pink and healthy and lovely. She had a quiet, gentle smile that reached her tender blue eyes. Gamache could almost smell the talcum powder and cinnamon. And yet the portrait made him deeply uneasy. And then he saw it. The subtle turn of her hand, outward. The way her fingers seemed to reach beyond the canvas. At him. He had the impression this gentle, lovely elderly woman was going to touch him. And if she did, he'd know sorrow like never before. He'd know that empty place where nothing existed, not even pain.

She was repulsive. And yet he couldn't help being drawn to her, like a person afraid of heights drawn to the edge.

And the third elderly woman he couldn't place. He'd never seen her before and he wondered if she was Clara's mother. There was something vaguely familiar about her.

He looked at it closely. Clara painted people's souls, and he wanted to know what this soul held.

She looked happy. Smiling over her shoulder at something of great interest. Something she cared about deeply. She too had a shawl, this of old, rough, deep red wool. She seemed someone who was used to riches but suddenly poor. And yet it didn't seem to matter to her.

Interesting, thought Gamache. She was heading in one direction but looking in the other. Behind her. From her he had an overwhelming feeling of yearning. He realized all he wanted to do was draw an armchair up to that portrait, pour a cup of coffee and stare at it for the rest of the evening. For the rest of his life. It was seductive. And dangerous.

With an effort he pulled his eyes away and found Clara standing in the darkness, watching her friends as they looked at her creations.

Peter was also watching. With a look of unmarred pride.

"Bon Dieu," said Gabri. *"C'est extraordinaire."*

"*Félicitations,* Clara," said Olivier. "My God, they're brilliant. Do you have more?"

"Do you mean, have I done you?" she asked with a laugh. "*Non, mon beau.* Only Ruth and Peter's mother."

"Who's this one?" Lacoste pointed to the painting Gamache had been staring at.

Clara smiled. "I'm not telling. You have to guess."

"Is it me?" asked Gabri.

"Yes, Gabri, it's you," said Clara.

"Really?" Too late he saw her smiling.

The funny thing was, thought Gamache, it almost could have been Gabri. He looked again at the portrait in the soft candlelight. Not physically, but emotionally. There was happiness there. But there was also something else. Something that didn't quite fit with Gabri.

"So which one's me?" asked Ruth, limping closer to the paintings.

"You old drunk," said Gabri. "It's this one."

Ruth peered at her exact double. "I don't see it. Looks more like you."

"Hag," muttered Gabri.

"Fag," she mumbled back.

"Clara's painted you as the Virgin Mary," Olivier explained.

Ruth leaned closer and shook her head.

"Virgin?" Gabri whispered to Myrna. "Obviously the mind fucks don't count."

"Speaking of which," Ruth looked over at Beauvoir, "Peter, do you have a piece of paper? I feel a poem coming on. Now, do you think it's too much to put the words 'asshole' and 'shithead' in the same sentence?"

Beauvoir winced.

"Just close your eyes and think of England," Ruth advised Beauvoir, who had actually been thinking of her English.

Gamache walked over to Peter, who continued to stare at his wife's works.

"How are you?"

"You mean, do I want to take a razor to

those and slash them to bits, then burn them?"

"Something like that."

It was a conversation they'd had before, as it became clear that Peter might soon have to cede his place as the best artist in the family, in the village, in the province, to his wife. Peter had struggled with it, not always successfully.

"I couldn't hold her back even if I tried," said Peter. "And I don't want to try."

"There's a difference between holding back and actively supporting."

"These are so good even I can't deny it anymore," admitted Peter. "She amazes me."

Both men looked over at the plump little woman looking anxiously at her friends, apparently unaware of the masterpieces she'd created.

"Are you working on something?" Gamache nodded toward the closed door to Peter's studio.

"Always am. It's a log."

"A log?" It was hard to make that sound brilliant. Peter Morrow was one of the most successful artists in the country and he'd gotten there by taking mundane, everyday objects and painting them in excruciating detail. So that they were no longer even recognizable as the object they were. He zoomed in close, then magnified a section, and painted that.

His works looked abstract. It gave Peter huge satisfaction to know they weren't. They were reality in the extreme. So real no one recognized them. And now it was the log's turn. He'd picked it up off the pile beside their fireplace and it was waiting for him in his studio.

The desserts were served, coffee and cognac poured; people wandered about, Gabri played the piano, Gamache kept being drawn to the paintings. Particularly the one of the unknown woman. Looking back. Clara joined him.

"My God, Clara, they're the best works of art ever produced by anyone, anywhere."

"Do you mean it?" she asked in mock earnestness.

He smiled. "They are brilliant, you know. You have nothing to be afraid of."

"If that was true I'd have no art."

Gamache nodded toward the painting he'd been staring at. "Who is she?"

"Oh, just someone I know."

Gamache waited, but Clara was uncharacteristically closed, and he decided it really didn't matter. She wandered off and Gamache continued to stare. And as he did so the portrait changed. Or perhaps, he thought, it was a trick of the uncertain light. But the more he stared the more he got the sense Clara had put something else in the painting. Where Ruth's was of an embittered woman finding hope, this portrait also held the unexpected.

A happy woman seeing in the near and middle distance things that pleased and comforted her. But her eyes seemed to just be focusing on, registering, something else. Something far off. But heading her way.

Gamache sipped his cognac and watched. And gradually it came to him what she was just beginning to feel.

Fear.

Nine

The three Sûreté officers said their goodbyes and walked across the village green. It was eleven o'clock and pitch-black. Lacoste and Gamache paused to stare at the night sky. Beauvoir, a few paces ahead as always, eventually realized he was alone and stopped as well. Reluctantly he looked up and was quite surprised to see so many stars. Ruth's parting words came back to him.

" 'Jean Guy' and 'bite me' actually rhyme, don't they?"

He was in trouble.

Just then a light went on above Myrna's bookstore, in her loft. They could see her moving about, making herself tea, putting cookies on a plate. Then the light went out. "We just saw her pour a drink and put cookies on a plate," said Beauvoir.

The others wondered why he'd just told them the obvious.

"It's dark. To do anything inside you need

light," said Beauvoir.

Gamache thought about this string of obvious statements, but it was Lacoste who got there first.

"The bistro, last night. Wouldn't the murderer need to put on the lights? And if he did, wouldn't someone have seen?"

Gamache smiled. They were right. A light at the bistro must have been noticed.

He looked around to see which houses were the most likely to have seen anything. But the homes fanned out from the bistro like wings. None would have a perfect view, except the place directly opposite. He turned to look. The three majestic pines on the village green were there. They'd have seen a man take another man's life. But there was something else directly opposite the bistro. Opposite and above.

The old Hadley house. It was a distance away, but at night, with a light on in the bistro, it was just possible the new owners could have witnessed a murder.

"There's another possibility," said Lacoste. "That the murderer didn't put the lights on. He'd know he could be seen."

"He'd use a flashlight, you mean?" asked Beauvoir, imagining the murderer in there the night before, waiting for his victim, turning a flashlight on to make his way around.

Lacoste shook her head. "That could also be seen from outside. He wouldn't want to risk even that, I think."

"So he'd leave the lights off," said Gamache, knowing where this was leading. "Because he wouldn't need lights. He'd know his way around in the dark."

The next morning dawned bright and fresh. There was some warmth in the sun again and Gamache soon took off his sweater as he walked around the village green before breakfast. A few children, up before parents and grandparents, did some last-minute frog hunting in the pond. They ignored him and he was happy to watch them from a distance then continue his solitary and peaceful stroll. He waved at Myrna, cresting the hill on her own solitary walk.

This was the last day of summer vacation, and while it had been decades since he'd gone to school, he still felt the tug. The mix of sadness at the end of summer, and excitement to see his chums again. The new clothes, bought after a summer's growth. The new pencils, sharpened over and over, and the smell of the shavings. And the new notebooks. Always strangely thrilling. Unmarred. No mistakes yet. All they held was promise and potential.

A new murder investigation felt much the same. Had they marred their books yet? Made any mistakes?

As he slowly circled the village green, his hands clasped behind his back and his gaze far off, he thought about that. After a few leisurely circuits he went inside to breakfast.

Beauvoir and Lacoste were already down, with frothy *café au lait* in front of them. They stood up as he entered the room, and he motioned them down. The aroma of maple-cured back bacon and eggs and coffee came from the kitchen. He'd barely sat down when Gabri swept out of the kitchen with plates of eggs Benedict, fruit and muffins.

"Olivier's just left for the bistro. He's not sure if he'll open today," said the large man, who looked and sounded a great deal like Julia Child that morning. "I told him he should, but we'll see. I pointed out he'd lose money if he didn't. That usually does the trick. Muffin?"

"S'il vous plaît," said Isabelle Lacoste, taking one. They looked like nuclear explosions. Isabelle Lacoste missed her children and her husband. But it amazed her how this small village seemed able to heal even that hole. Of course, if you stuff in enough muffins even the largest hole is healed, for a

while. She was willing to try.

Gabri brought Gamache his *café au lait* and when he left Beauvoir leaned forward.

"What's the plan for today, Chief?"

"We need background checks. I want to know all about Olivier, and I want to know who might have a grudge against him."

"D'accord," said Lacoste.

"And the Parras. Make inquiries, here and in the Czech Republic."

"Will do," said Beauvoir. "And you?"

"I have an appointment with an old friend."

Armand Gamache climbed the hill leading out of Three Pines. He carried his tweed jacket over his arm and kicked a chestnut ahead of him. The air smelled of apples, sweet and warm on the trees. Everything was ripe, lush, but in a few weeks there'd be a killing frost. And it would all be gone.

As he walked the old Hadley house grew larger and larger. He steeled himself against it. Prepared for the waves of sorrow that rolled from it, flowing over and into anyone foolish enough to get close.

But either his defenses were better than he'd expected, or something had changed.

Gamache stopped in a spot of sunshine and faced the house. It was a rambling

Victorian trophy home, turreted, shingles like scales, wide swooping verandas and black wrought-iron rails. Its fresh paint gleamed in the sun and the front door was a cheery glossy red. Not like blood, but like Christmas. And cherries. And crisp autumn apples. The path had been cleared of brambles and solid flagstones laid. He noticed the hedges had been clipped and the trees trimmed, the deadwood removed. Roar Parra's work.

And Gamache realized, to his surprise, that he was standing outside the old Hadley house with a smile. And was actually looking forward to going inside.

The door was opened by a woman in her mid-seventies.

"Oui?"

Her hair was steel gray and nicely cut. She wore almost no makeup, just a little around the eyes, which looked at him now with curiosity, then recognition. She smiled and opened the door wider.

Gamache offered her his identification. "I'm sorry to bother you, madame, but my name is Armand Gamache. I'm with the Sûreté du Québec."

"I recognize you, monsieur. Please, come in. I'm Carole Gilbert."

Her manner was friendly and gracious as

she showed him into the vestibule. He'd been there before. Many times. But it was almost unrecognizable. Like a skeleton that had been given new muscles and sinew and skin. The structure was there, but all else had changed.

"You know the place?" she asked, watching him.

"I knew it," he said, swinging his eyes to hers. She met his look steadily, but without challenge. As a chatelaine would, confident in her place and without need to prove it. She was friendly and warm, and very, very observant, Gamache guessed. What had Peter said? She'd been a nurse once? A very good one, he presumed. The best ones were observant. Nothing got past them.

"It's changed a great deal," he said and she nodded, drawing him farther into the house. He wiped his feet on the area rug protecting the gleaming wooden floor and followed her. The vestibule opened into a large hall with crisp new black and white tiles on the floor. A sweeping staircase faced them and archways led through to various rooms. When he'd last been here it had been a ruin, fallen into disrepair. It had seemed as though the house, disgusted, had turned on itself. Pieces were thrown off, wallpaper hung loose, floorboards heaved, ceilings warped. But now a huge cheerful bouquet sat on a polished table in the center of the hall, filling it with fragrance. The walls were painted a sophisticated tawny color, between beige and gray. It was bright and warm and elegant. Like the woman in front of him.

"We're still working on the house," she said, leading him through the archway to their right, down a couple of steps and into the large living room. "I say 'we' but it's really my son and daughter-in-law. And the workers, of course."

She said it with a small self-deprecating laugh. "I was foolish enough to ask if I could do anything the other day and they gave me a hammer and told me to put up some drywall. I hit a water pipe and an electrical cord."

Her laugh was so unguarded and infectious Gamache found himself laughing too.

"Now I make tea. They call me the tea lady. Tea?"

"*Merci, madame,* that would be very nice."

"I'll tell Marc and Dominique you're here. It's about that poor man in the bistro, I presume?"

"It is."

She seemed sympathetic, but not concerned. As though it had nothing to do with her. And Gamache found himself hoping it didn't.

As he waited he looked around the room and drifted toward the floor-to-ceiling windows, where sun streamed in. The room was comfortably furnished with sofas and chairs that looked inviting. They were upholstered in expensive fabrics giving them a modern feel. A couple of Eames chairs framed the fireplace. It was an easy marriage of contemporary and old world. Whoever had decorated this room had an eye for it.

The windows were flanked by tailored silk curtains that touched the hardwood floor. Gamache suspected the curtains were almost never closed. Why shut out that view?

It was spectacular. From its position on the hill the house looked over the valley. He could see the Rivière Bella Bella wind its way through the village and out around the next mountain toward the neighboring valley. The trees at the top of the mountain were changing color. It was autumn up there already. Soon the reds and auburns and pumpkin oranges would march down the slopes until the entire forest was ablaze. And what a vantage point to see it all. And more.

Standing at the window he could see Ruth

and Rosa walking around the village green, the old poet tossing either stale buns or rocks at the other birds. He could see Myrna working in Clara's vegetable garden and Agent Lacoste walking over the stone bridge toward their makeshift Incident Room in the old railway station. He watched as she stopped on the bridge and looked into the gently flowing water. He wondered what she was thinking. Then she moved on. Other villagers were out doing their morning errands, or working in their gardens, or sitting on their porches reading the paper and drinking coffee.

From there he could see everything. Including the bistro.

Agent Paul Morin had arrived before Lacoste and was standing outside the railway station, making notes.

"I was thinking about the case last night," he said, watching her unlock the door then following her into the chilly, dark room. She flipped on the lights and walked over to her desk. "I think the murderer must've turned on the lights of the bistro, don't you? I tried walking around my house at two o'clock this morning, and I couldn't see anything. It was pitch-black. In the city you might get streetlights through the window, but not out here.

How'd he know who he was killing?"

"I suppose if he'd invited the victim there, then it was pretty clear. He'd kill the only other person in the bistro."

"I realize that," said Morin, drawing his chair up to her desk. "But murder's a serious business. You don't want to get it wrong. It was a massive hit to the head, right?"

Lacoste typed her password into her computer. Her husband's name. Morin was so busy consulting his notes and talking she was sure he hadn't noticed.

"I don't think that's as easy as it looks," he continued, earnestly. "I tried it last night too. Hit a cantaloupe with a hammer."

Now he had her full attention. Not only because she wanted to know what had happened, but because anyone who'd get up at two in the morning to smack a melon in the dark deserved attention. Perhaps even medical attention.

"And?"

"The first time I just grazed it. Had to hit it a few times before I got it just right. Pretty messy."

Morin wondered, briefly, what his girlfriend would think when she got up and noticed the fruit with holes smashed in it. He'd left a note, but wasn't sure that helped.

I did this, he'd written. *Experimenting.*

He perhaps should have been more explicit.

But the significance wasn't lost on Agent Lacoste. She leaned back in her chair and thought. Morin had the brains to be quiet.

"So what do you think?" she finally asked.

"I think he must have turned the lights on. But it'd be risky." Morin seemed dissatisfied. "It doesn't make sense to me. Why kill him in the bistro when you have thick forests just feet away? You could slaughter tons of people in there and no one would notice. Why do it where the body would be found and you could be seen?"

"You're right," said Lacoste. "It doesn't make sense. The Chief thinks it might have something to do with Olivier. Maybe the murderer chose the bistro on purpose."

"To implicate him?"

"Or to ruin his business."

"Maybe it was Olivier himself," said Morin. "Why not? He'd be just about the only one who could find his way around without lights. He had a key to the place —"

"Everyone had a key to the place. Seems there were sets floating all over the township, and Olivier kept one under the urn at the front door," said Lacoste.

Morin nodded and didn't seem surprised.

It was still the country way, at least in the smaller villages.

"He's certainly a main suspect," said Lacoste. "But why would he kill someone in his own bistro?"

"Maybe he surprised the guy. Maybe the tramp broke in and Olivier found him and killed him in a fight," said Morin.

Lacoste was silent, waiting to see if he'd work it all the way through. Morin steepled his hands and leaned his face into them, staring into space. "But it was the middle of the night. If he saw someone in the bistro wouldn't he have called the cops, or at least woken his partner? Olivier Brulé doesn't strike me as the kind of guy who'd grab a baseball bat and rush off alone."

Lacoste exhaled and looked at Agent Morin. If the light was just right, catching this slight young man's face just so, he looked like an idiot. But he clearly wasn't.

"I know Olivier," said Lacoste, "and I'd swear he was stunned by what he'd found. He was in shock. Hard to fake and I'm pretty sure he wasn't faking it. No. When Olivier Brulé woke up yesterday morning he didn't expect to find a body in his bistro. But that doesn't mean he isn't involved somehow. Even unwittingly. The Chief wants us to find out more about Olivier.

Where he was born, his background, his family, his schools, what he did before coming here. Anyone who might have a grudge against him. Someone he pissed off."

"This is more than being pissed off."

"How do you know?" asked Lacoste.

"Well, I get pissed off, and I don't kill people."

"No, you don't. But I presume you're fairly well balanced, except for that melon incident." She smiled and he reddened. "Look, it's a huge mistake to judge others by ourselves. One of the first things you learn with Chief Inspector Gamache is that other people's reactions aren't ours. And a murderer's are even more foreign. This case didn't begin with the blow to the head. It started years ago, with another sort of blow. Something happened to our murderer, something we might consider insignificant, trivial even, but was devastating to him. An event, a snub, an argument that most people would shrug off. Murderers don't. They ruminate; they gather and guard resentments. And those resentments grow. Murders are about emotions. Emotions gone bad and gone wild. Remember that. And don't ever think you know what someone else is thinking, never mind feeling."

It was the first lesson she'd been taught

by Chief Inspector Gamache, and the first one she'd now passed on to her own protégé. To find a murderer you followed clues, yes. But you also followed emotions. The ones that stank, the foul and putrid ones. You followed the slime. And there, cornered, you'd find your quarry.

There were other lessons, lots of others. And she'd teach him them as well.

That's what she'd been thinking on the bridge. Thinking and worrying about. Hoping she'd be able to pass to this young man enough wisdom, enough of the tools necessary to catch a killer.

"Nathaniel," said Morin, getting up and going over to his own computer. "Your husband's name or your son's?"

"Husband," said Lacoste, a little nonplussed. He'd seen after all.

The phone rang. It was the coroner. She had to speak to Chief Inspector Gamache urgently.

TEN

At the Chief Inspector's request Marc and Dominique Gilbert were giving him a tour of their home, and now they stood in front of a room Gamache knew well. It had been the master bedroom of the old Hadley house, Timmer Hadley's room.

Two murders had happened there.

Now he looked at the closed door, with its fresh coat of gleaming white paint, and wondered what lay beyond. Dominique swung the door open and sunlight poured out. Gamache couldn't hide his surprise.

"Quite a change," said Marc Gilbert, clearly pleased with his reaction.

The room was, quite simply, stunning. They'd removed all the fretwork and googahs added over the generations. The ornate moldings, the dark mantel, the velvet drapes that kept the light at bay with their weight of dust and dread and Victorian reproach. All gone. The heavy, foreboding four-poster bed was gone.

They'd taken the room back to its basic structure, clean lines that showed off its gracious proportions. The curtains had wide stripes of of sage and gray and let the light stream through. Along the top of each of the large windows was a lintel of stained glass. Original. More than a century old. It spilled playful colors into the room. The floors, newly stained, glowed. The king-size bed had an upholstered headboard and simple, fresh, white bed linen. A fire was laid in the hearth, ready for the first guest.

"Let me show you the en suite," said Dominique.

She was tall and willowy. Mid-forties, Gamache thought, she wore jeans, a simple white shirt and her blonde hair loose. She had an air of quiet confidence and well-being. Her hands were flecked with white paint and her nails cut short.

Beside her Marc Gilbert smiled, happy to be showing off their creation. And Gamache, of all people, knew this resurrection of the old Hadley house was an act of creation.

Marc was also tall, over six feet. Slightly taller than Gamache, and about twenty pounds lighter. His hair was short, almost shaved, and it looked as though if he grew it in he'd be balding. His eyes were a piercing, buoyant blue and his manner welcoming and energetic. But while his wife was relaxed there was something edgy about Marc Gilbert. Not nervous so much as needy.

He wants my approval, thought Gamache. Not unusual really when showing off a project this important to them. Dominique pointed out the features of the bathroom, with its aqua mosaic-glass tiles, spa bath and separate walk-in shower. She was proud of their work, but she didn't seem to need him to exclaim over it.

Marc did.

It was easy to give him what he wanted. Gamache was genuinely impressed.

"And we just put this door in last week," said Marc. Opening a door from the bathroom they stepped onto a balcony. It looked out over the back of the house, across the gardens and a field beyond.

Four chairs were drawn around a table.

"I thought you could use these," a voice said from behind them and Marc hurried to take the tray from his mother. On it were four glasses of iced tea and some scones.

"Shall we?" Dominique indicated the table and Gamache held a chair for Carole.

"Merci," the older woman said, and sat.

"To second chances," said the Chief Inspector. He lifted his iced tea and as they toasted he watched them. The three people who'd been drawn to this sad, violated, derelict house. Who'd given it new life.

And the house had returned the favor.

"Well, there's more to do," said Marc. "But we're getting there."

"We're hoping to have our first guests by Thanksgiving," said Dominique. "If Carole would just get off her *derrière* and do some work. But so far she's refused to dig the fence posts or pour concrete."

"Perhaps this afternoon," said Carole Gilbert with a laugh.

"I noticed some antiques. Did you bring them from your home?" Gamache asked her.

Carole nodded. "We combined our belongings, but there was still a lot to buy."

"From Olivier?"

"Some." It was the most curt answer he'd received so far. He waited for more.

"We got a lovely rug from him," said Dominique. "The one in the front hall, I think."

"No, it's in the basement," said Marc, his voice sharp. He tried to soften it with a smile, but it didn't quite work.

"And a few chairs, I think," said Carole, quickly.

That would account for about one one-hundredth of the furnishings in the rambling old place. Gamache sipped his tea, looking at the three of them.

"We picked up the rest in Montreal," said Marc. "On rue Notre Dame. Do you know it?"

Gamache nodded and then listened as Marc described their treks up and down the famed street, which was packed with antique shops. Some were not much more than junk shops but some contained real finds, near priceless antiques.

"Old Mundin's repairing a few items we picked up in garage sales. Don't tell the guests," said Dominique with a laugh.

"Why didn't you get more from Olivier?"

The women concentrated on their scones and Marc poked at the ice in his drink.

"We found his prices a little high, Chief Inspector," said Dominique at last. "We'd have preferred to buy from him, but . . ."

It was left hanging, and still Gamache waited. Eventually Marc spoke.

"We were going to buy tables and beds from him. Made all the arrangements, then discovered he'd charged us almost double what he'd originally asked for them."

"Now, Marc, we don't know that for sure," said his mother.

"Near enough. Anyway, we canceled the order. You can imagine how that went down."

Dominique had been silent for most of this exchange. Now she spoke.

"I still think we should have paid it, or spoken to him quietly about it. He is our neighbor, after all."

"I don't like being screwed," said Marc.

"No one does," said Dominique, "but there are ways of handling it. Maybe we should have just paid. Now look what's happened."

"What's happened?" asked Gamache.

"Well, Olivier's one of the forces in Three Pines," said Dominique. "Piss him off and you pay a price. We don't really feel comfortable going into the village, and we sure don't feel welcome in the bistro."

"I hear you approached some of Olivier's staff," said Gamache.

Marc colored. "Who told you that? Did Olivier?" he snapped.

"Is it true?"

"What if it is? He pays them practically slave wages."

"Did any agree to come?"

Marc hesitated then admitted they hadn't. "But only because he increased their pay. We at least did that for them."

Dominique had been watching this, uncomfortable, and now she took her husband's hand. "I'm sure they were also loyal to Olivier. They seem to like him."

Marc snorted and clamped down on his anger. A man, Gamache realized, ill-equipped for not getting his own way. His wife, at least, appreciated how all this might look and had tried to appear reasonable.

"Now he's bad-mouthed us to the whole village," said Marc, not letting it go.

"They'll come around," said Carole, looking at her son with concern. "That artist couple have been nice."

"Peter and Clara Morrow," said Dominique. "Yes. I like them. She says she'd like to ride, once the horses arrive."

"And when will that be?" asked Gamache.

"Later today."

"*Vraiment?* That must be fun for you. How many?"

"Four," said Marc. "Thoroughbreds."

"Actually, I believe you've changed that slightly, haven't you?" Carole turned to her daughter-in-law.

"Really? I thought you wanted thoroughbreds," said Marc to Dominique.

"I did, but then I saw some hunters and thought since we lived in the country that seemed appropriate." She looked at Gamache once again. "Not that I plan to hunt. It's a breed of horse."

"Used for jumping," he said.

"You ride?"

"Not at that level, but I enjoyed it. Haven't been on a horse in years now."

"You'll have to come," said Carole, though they all knew he almost certainly wasn't going to squeeze himself into a pair of jodhpurs and climb onto a hunter. But he did smile as he imagined what Gabri would make of that invitation.

"What're their names?" asked Marc.

Dominique hesitated and her mother-in-law jumped in. "It's so hard to remember, isn't it? But wasn't one called Thunder?"

"Yes, that's right. Thunder, Trooper, Trojan and what was the other one?" She turned back to Carole.

"Lightning."

"Really? Thunder and Lightning?" asked Marc.

"Brothers," said Dominique.

Their iced teas finished and the scones only crumbs they got to their feet and walked back into the house.

"Why did you move here?" Gamache asked, as they walked down to the main floor.

"Pardon?" asked Dominique.

"Why did you move to the country and to Three Pines in particular? It's not exactly easy to find."

"We like that."

"You don't want to be found?" asked Gamache. His voice held humor, but his eyes were sharp.

"We wanted peace and quiet," said Carole.

"We wanted a challenge," said her son.

"We wanted a change. Remember?" Dominique turned to her husband then back to Gamache. "We both had fairly high-powered jobs in Montreal, but were tired. Burned out."

"That's not really true," protested Marc.

"Well, pretty close. We couldn't go on. Didn't want to go on."

She left it at that. She could understand Marc's not wanting to admit what'd happened. The insomnia, the panic attacks. Having to pull the car over on the Ville Marie Expressway to catch his breath. Having to pry his hands off the steering wheel. He was losing his grip.

Day after day he'd gone into work like that. Weeks, months. A year. Until he'd finally admitted to Dominique how he felt. They'd gone away for a weekend, their first in years, and talked.

While she wasn't having panic attacks, she

was feeling something else. A growing emptiness. A sense of futility. Each morning she woke up and had to convince herself that what she did mattered. Advertising.

It was a harder and harder sell.

Then Dominique had remembered something long buried and forgotten. A dream since childhood. To live in the country and have horses.

She'd wanted to run an inn. To welcome people, to mother them. They had no children of their own, and she had a powerful need to nurture. So they'd left Montreal, left the demands of jobs too stressful, of lives too callow. They'd come to Three Pines, with their bags of money, to heal first themselves. Then others.

They'd certainly healed this wound of a house.

"We saw an ad for this place in the *Gazette* one Saturday, drove down and bought it," said Dominique.

"You make it sound simple," said Gamache.

"It was, really, once we decided what we wanted."

And looking at her, Gamache could believe it. She knew something powerful, something most people never learned. That people made their own fortune.

It made her formidable.

"And you, madame?" Gamache turned to Carole Gilbert.

"Oh, I've been retired for a while."

"In Quebec City, I understand."

"That's correct. I quit work and moved there after my husband died."

"Désolé."

"No need to be. It was many years ago. But when Marc and Dominique invited me here I thought it sounded like fun."

"You were a nurse? That will come in handy in a spa."

"I hope not," she laughed. "Not planning on hurting people, are you?" she asked Dominique. "God help anyone who asks for my help."

They strolled once more into the living room and the Chief Inspector stopped by the floor-to-ceiling windows, then turned into the room.

"Thank you for the tour. And the tea. But I do have some questions for you."

"About the murder in the bistro," said Marc, and stepped slightly closer to his wife. "It seems so out of character for this village, to have a murder."

"You'd think so, wouldn't you?" said Gamache, and wondered if anyone had told them the history of their own home. Probably wasn't in the real estate agent's description.

"Well, to begin with, have you seen any strangers around?"

"Everyone's a stranger," said Carole. "We know most of the villagers by now, at least to nod to, but this weekend the place is filled with people we've never seen."

"This man would be hard to miss; he'd have looked like a tramp, a vagrant."

"No, I haven't seen anyone like that," said Marc. "Mama, have you?"

"Nobody."

"Where were you all on Saturday night and early Sunday morning?"

"Marc, I think you went to bed first. He usually does. Dominique and I watched the *Téléjournal on Radio-Canada* then went up."

"About eleven, wouldn't you think?" Dominique asked.

"Did any of you get up in the night?"

"I did," said Carole. "Briefly. To use the washroom."

"Why're you asking us this?" Dominique asked. "The murder happened down in the bistro. It has nothing to do with us."

Gamache turned around and pointed out the window. "That's why I'm asking."

They looked. Down in the village a few cars were being packed up. People were hugging, reluctant children were being called off the village green. A young woman was walking briskly up rue du Moulin, in their direction.

"You're the only place in Three Pines with a view over the whole village, and the only place with a direct view into the bistro. If the murderer turned on the lights, you'd have seen."

"Our bedrooms are at the back," Dominique pointed out. Gamache had already noted this in the tour.

"True. But I was hoping one of you might suffer from insomnia."

"Sorry, Chief Inspector. We sleep like the dead here."

Gamache didn't mention that the dead in the old Hadley house had never rested well.

The doorbell rang just then and the Gilberts started slightly, not expecting anyone. But Gamache was. He'd noted Agent Lacoste's progress round the village green and up rue du Moulin.

Something had happened.

"May I see you in private?" Isabelle Lacoste asked the Chief after she'd been introduced. The Gilberts took the cue. After watching them disappear Agent Lacoste turned to Gamache.

"The coroner called. The victim wasn't killed in the bistro."

Eleven

Myrna knocked softly on the bistro door, then opened it.

"You okay?" she asked softly into the dim light. It was the first time since she'd lived in Three Pines she'd seen the bistro dark during the day. Even at Christmas Olivier opened.

Olivier was sitting in an armchair, staring. He looked over at her and smiled.

"I'm fine."

"Ruth's FINE? Fucked up, Insecure, Neurotic and Egotistical?"

"That's about right."

Myrna sat across from him and offered a mug of tea she'd brought from her bookshop. Strong, hot, with milk and sugar. Red Rose. Nothing fancy.

"Like to talk?"

She sat quietly, watching her friend. She knew his face, had seen the tiny changes over the years. The crow's-feet appear at his eyes, the fine blond hair thin. What hadn't changed, from what she could tell, was what was invisible, but even more obvious. His kind heart, his thoughtfulness. He was the first to bring soup to anyone ill. To visit in the hospital. To read out loud to someone too weak and tired and near the end to do it for themselves. Gabri, Myrna, Clara, they all organized villagers to help, and when they arrived they'd find Olivier already there.

And now it was their turn to help him.

"I don't know if I want to open again."

Myrna sipped her tea and nodded. "That's understandable. You've been hurt. It must've been a terrible shock to see him here. I know it was for me, and it's not my place."

You have no idea, thought Olivier. He didn't say anything, but stared out the window. He saw Chief Inspector Gamache and Agent Lacoste walking down rue du Moulin from the old Hadley house. He prayed they kept going. Didn't come in here. With their keen eyes and sharp questions.

"I wonder if I should just sell. Move on."

This surprised Myrna, but she didn't show it. "Why?" she asked, softly.

He shook his head and dropped his eyes

to his hands, resting in his lap.

"Everything's changing. Everything's changed. Why can't it be like it always was? They took my fireplace pokers, you know. I think Gamache thinks I did it."

"I'm sure he doesn't. Olivier, look at me." She spoke forcefully to him. "It doesn't matter what he thinks. We know the truth about you. And you need to know something about us. We love you. Do you think we come here every day for the food?"

He nodded and smiled slightly. "You mean it wasn't for the croissants? The red wine? Not even the chocolate torte?"

"Well, yes, okay. Maybe the torte. Listen, we come here because of you. You're the attraction. We love you, Olivier."

Olivier raised his eyes to hers. He hadn't realized, until that moment, that he'd always been afraid their affection was conditional. He was the owner of the bistro, the only one in town. They liked him for the atmosphere and welcome. The food and drink. That was the boundary of their feelings for him. They liked him for what he gave to them. Sold to them.

Without the bistro, he was nothing to them.

How'd Myrna know something he hadn't even admitted to himself? As he looked at her she smiled. She was wearing her usual flamboyant caftan. For her birthday coming up Gabri had made her a winter caftan, out of flannel. Olivier imagined her in it in her store. A big, warm ball of flannel.

The world, which had been closing in on him for days, released a bit of its grip.

"We're going to the Brume County Fair. Last day. What do you say? Can we interest you in cotton candy, cream soda, and a bison burger? I hear Wayne's showing his litter of suckling pigs this afternoon. I know how you love a good piglet."

Once, just once, at the annual county fair he'd hurried them over to the pig stalls to look at the babies. And now he was the piglet guy. Still, he quite liked being thought of as that. And it was true, he loved pigs. He had a lot in common with them, he suspected. But he shook his head.

"Not up to it, I'm afraid. But you go along. Bring me back a stuffed animal."

"Would you like company here? I can stay."

And he knew she meant it. But he needed to be alone.

"Thanks, but I really am Fucked up, Insecure, Neurotic and Egotistical."

"Well, as long as you're fine," said Myrna, getting up. After years as a psychologist she knew how to listen to people. And how to leave them alone.

He watched through the window as Myrna, Peter, Clara, Ruth and the duck Rosa got in the Morrows' car. They waved at him and he waved merrily back. Myrna didn't wave. She just nodded. He dropped his hand, caught her eye, and nodded.

He believed her when she'd said they loved him. But he also knew they loved a man who didn't exist. He was a fiction. If they knew the real Olivier they'd kick him out, of their lives and probably the village.

As their car chugged up the hill toward the Brume County Fair he heard the words again. From the cabin hidden in the woods. He could smell the wood smoke, the dried herbs. And he could see the Hermit. Whole. Alive. Afraid.

And he heard again the story. That wasn't, Olivier knew, just a story.

Once upon a time a Mountain King watched over a treasure. He buried it deep and it kept him company for millennia. The other gods were jealous and angry, and warned him if he didn't share his treasure with them they'd do something terrible.

But the Mountain King was the mightiest of the gods, so he simply laughed knowing there was nothing they could do to him. No attack he couldn't repulse, and redouble onto them. He was invincible. He prepared for their attack. Waited for it. But it never came.

Nothing came. Ever.

Not a missile, not a spear, not a war horse, or rider, or dog, or bird. Not a seed in the wind. Not even the wind.

Nothing. Ever. Again.

It was the silence that got to him first, and then the touch. Nothing touched him. No breeze brushed his rocky surface. No ant crawled over him, no bird touched down. No worm tunneled.

He felt nothing.

Until one day a young man came.

Olivier brought himself back to the bistro, his body tense, his muscles strained. His fingernails biting into his palms.

Why, he asked himself for the millionth time. Why had he done it?

Before leaving to see the coroner, the Chief Inspector walked over to the large piece of paper tacked to the wall of their Incident Room. In bold red letters Inspector Beauvoir had written:

WHO WAS THE VICTIM?
WHY WAS HE KILLED?
WHO KILLED HIM?
WHAT WAS THE MURDER WEAPON?

With a sigh the Chief Inspector added two more lines.

WHERE WAS HE MURDERED?
WHY WAS HE MOVED?

So far in their investigation they'd found more questions than clues. But that's where answers came from. Questions. Gamache was perplexed, but not dissatisfid.

Jean Guy Beauvoir was already waiting for him when he arrived at the Cowansville hospital, and they went in together, down the stairs and into the basement, where files and dead people were kept.

"I called as soon as I realized what I was seeing," said Dr. Harris after greeting them. She led them into the sterile room, brightly lit by fluorescents. The dead man was naked on a steel gurney. Gamache wished they'd put a blanket over him. He seemed cold. And, indeed, he was.

"There was some internal bleeding but not enough. This wound," she indicated the collaped back of the victim's head, "would have bled onto whatever surface he fell on."

"There was almost no blood on the floor of the bistro," said Beauvoir.

"He was killed somewhere else," said the coroner, with certainty.

"Where?" asked Gamache.

"Would you like an address?"

"If you wouldn't mind," said the Chief Inspector, with a smile.

Dr. Harris smiled back. "Clearly I don't know, but I've found some things that might be suggestive."

She walked over to her lab table where a few vials sat, labeled. She handed one to the Chief Inspector.

"Remember that bit of white I said was in the wound? I thought it might be ash. Or bone, or perhaps even dandruff. Well, it wasn't any of those things."

Gamache needed his glasses to see the tiny white flake inside the vial, then he read the label.

Paraffin, found in the wound.

"Paraffin? Like wax?"

"Yes, it's commonly called paraffin wax. It's an old-fashioned material, as you probably know. Used to be used for candles, then it was replaced by other sorts of more stable wax."

"My mother uses it for pickling," said

Beauvoir. "She melts it on the top of the jar to create a seal, right?"

"That's right," said Dr. Harris.

Gamache turned to Beauvoir. "And where was your mother on Saturday night?"

Beauvoir laughed. "The only one she ever threatens to brain is me. She's no threat to society at large."

Gamache handed the vial back to the coroner. "Do you have any theories?"

"It was buried deep enough in the wound to have been either on the man's head before he was killed or on the murder weapon."

"A jar of pickles?" asked Beauvoir.

"Stranger things have been used," said Gamache, though he couldn't quite think of any.

Beauvoir shook his head. Had to be an Anglo. Who else could turn a dill pickle into a weapon?

"So it wasn't a fireplace poker?" asked Gamache.

"Unless it was a very clean one. There was no evidence of ash. Just that." She nodded to the vial. "There's something else." Dr. Harris pulled a lab chair up to the bench. "On the back of his clothes we found this. Very faint, but there."

She handed Gamache the lab report and

pointed to a line. Gamache read.

"Acrylic polyurethane and aluminum oxide. What is that?"

"Varathane," said Beauvoir. "We've just redone our floors. It's used to seal them after they've been sanded."

"Not just floors," said Dr. Harris, taking back the vial. "It's used in a lot of woodworking. It's a finish. Other than the wound to the head the dead man was in good condition. Could've expected to live for twenty-five or thirty years."

"I see he had a meal a few hours before he was killed," said Gamache, reading the autopsy report

"Vegetarian. Organic I think. I'm having it tested," said the coroner. "A healthy vegetarian meal. Not your usual vagrant dinner."

"Someone might've had him in for dinner then killed him," said Beauvoir.

Dr. Harris hesitated. "I considered that, and it's a possibility."

"But?" said Gamache.

"But he looks like a man who ate like that all the time. Not just the once."

"So either he cooked for himself and chose a healthy diet," said Gamache, "or he had someone cook for him and they were vegetarian."

"That's about it," said the coroner.

"I see no alcohol or drugs," said Beauvoir, scanning the report.

Dr. Harris nodded. "I don't think he was homeless. I'm not sure if anyone cared for this man, but I do know he cared for himself."

What a wonderful epitaph, thought Gamache. He cared for himself.

"Maybe he was a survivalist," said Beauvoir. "You know, one of those kooks who take off from the city and hide in the woods thinking the world's coming to an end."

Gamache turned to look at Beauvoir. That was an interesting thought.

"I'm frankly puzzled," said the coroner. "You can see he was hit with a single, catastrophic blow to the back of his head. That in itself is unusual. To find just one blow . . ." Dr. Harris's voice trailed off and she shook her head. "Normally when someone gets up the nerve to bludgeon someone to death they're in the grip of great emotion. It's like a brainstorm. They're hysterical and can't stop. You get multiple blows. A single one like this . . ."

"What does it tell you?" Gamache asked, as he stared at the collapsed skull.

"This wasn't just a crime of passion." She turned to him. "There was passion, yes, but there was also planning. Whoever did this was in a rage. But he was in command of that rage."

Gamache lifted his brows. That was rare, extremely rare. And disconcerting. It would be like trying to master a herd of wild stallions, thundering and rearing, nostrils flared and hooves churning.

Who could control that?

Their murderer could.

Beauvoir looked at the Chief and the Chief looked at Beauvoir. This wasn't good.

Gamache turned back to the cold body on the cold gurney. If he was a survivalist, it hadn't worked. If this man had feared the end of the world he hadn't run far enough, hadn't buried himself deep enough in the Canadian wilderness.

The end of the world had found him.

TWELVE

Dominique Gilbert stood beside her mother-in-law and looked down the dirt road. Every now and then they had to step aside as a carful of people headed out of Three Pines, to the last day of the fair or into the city early to beat the rush.

It wasn't toward Three Pines they gazed, but away from it. Toward the road that led to Cowansville. And the horses.

It still surprised Dominique that she should have so completely forgotten her childhood dream. Perhaps, though, it wasn't surprising since she'd also dreamed of marrying Keith from the Partridge Family and being discovered as one of the little lost Romanov girls. Her fantasy of having horses disappeared along with all the other unlikely dreams, replaced by board meetings and clients, by gym memberships and increasingly expensive clothing. Until finally her cup, overflowing, had upended and all the lovely promotions and vacations and spa treatments became insubstantial. But at the bottom of that cup filled with goals, objectives, targets, one last drop remained.

Her dream. A horse of her own.

As a girl she'd ridden. With the wind in her hair and the leather reins light in her hands she'd felt free. And safe. The staggering worries of an earnest little girl forgotten.

Years later, when dissatisfaction had turned to despair, when her spirit had grown weary, when she could barely get out of bed in the morning, the dream had reappeared. Like the cavalry, like the Royal Canadian Mounted Police, riding to her rescue.

Horses would save her. Those magnificent creatures who so loved their riders they charged into battle with them, through explosions, through terror, through shrieking men and shrieking weapons. If their rider urged them forward, they went.

Who could not love that?

Dominique had awoken one morning knowing what had to be done. For their sanity. For their souls. They had to quit their jobs, buy a home in the country. And have horses.

As soon as they'd bought the old Hadley

house and Roar was working on the barn Dominique had gone to find her horses. She'd spent months researching the perfect breed, the perfect temperaments. The height, weight, color even. Palomino, dapple? All the words from childhood came back. All the pictures torn from calendars and taped to her wall next to Keith Partridge. The black horse with the white socks, the mighty, rearing gray stallion, the Arabian, noble, dignified, strong.

Finally Dominique settled on four magnificent hunters. Tall, shining, two chestnut, a black and one that was all white.

"I hear a truck," said Carole, taking her daughter-in-law's hand and holding it lightly. Like reins.

A truck hove into view. Dominique waved. The truck slowed, then followed her directions into the yard and stopped next to the brand new barn.

Four horses were led from the van, their hooves clunking on the wooden ramp. When they were all standing in the yard the driver walked over to the women, tossing a cigarette onto the dirt and grinding it underfoot.

"You need to sign, madame." He held the clipboard out between them. Dominique reached for it and barely taking her eyes off the horses she signed her name then gave the driver a tip.

He took it then looked from the two bewildered women to the horses.

"You sure you want to keep 'em?"

"I'm sure, thank you," said Dominique with more confidence than she felt. Now that they were actually there, and the dream was a reality, she realized she had no real idea what to do with a horse. Never mind four of them. The driver seemed to sympathize.

"Want me to put them in their stalls?"

"No, that's fine. We can do it. *Merci.*" She wanted him to leave, quickly. To not witness her uncertainty, her bumbling, her ineptness. Dominique Gilbert wasn't used to blundering, but she suspected she was about to become very familiar with it.

The driver reversed the empty van and drove away. Carole turned to Dominique and said, "Well, *ma belle,* I suspect we can't do any worse than their last owners."

As the van headed back to Cowansville they caught a glimpse of the word stenciled on the back door. In bold, black letters, so there could be no doubt. *Abattoir.* Then the two women turned back to the four sorry animals in front of them. Matted, walleyed, swaybacked. Hooves overgrown and coats covered in mud and sores.

"*'Twould ring the bells of Heaven,*" whispered Carole.

Dominique didn't know about the bells of Heaven, but her head was ringing. What had she done? She moved forward with a carrot and offered it to the first horse. A broken-down old mare named Buttercup. The horse hesitated, not used to kindness. Then she took a step toward Dominique and with large, eloquent lips she picked the sweet carrot from the hand.

Dominique had canceled her purchase of the magnificent hunters and had decided to buy horses destined for slaughter. If she was expecting them to save her, the very least she could do was save them first.

An hour and a half later Dominique, Carole and the four horses were still standing in front of the barn. But now they'd been joined by a vet.

"Once they're bathed you'll need to rub this into their sores." He handed Dominique a bucket of ointment. "Twice a day, in the morning and at night."

"Can they be ridden?" Carole asked, holding the halter of the largest horse. Privately she suspected it wasn't a horse at all, but a moose. Its name was Macaroni.

"*Mais, oui.* I'd encourage it." He was walking round them again, his large, sure hands going over the sorry beasts. *"Pauvre cheval,"* he whispered into the ear of the old mare, Buttercup, her mane almost all fallen out, her tail wispy and her coat bedraggled. "They need exercise, they need good food and water. But mostly they need attention."

The vet was shaking his head as he finished his examinations.

"The good news is there's nothing terminally wrong with them. Left to rot in muddy fields and bitter cold barns. Never groomed. Neglected. But this one." He approached the tall, walleyed dark horse, who shied away. The vet waited and approached again quietly, making soothing sounds until the horse settled. "This one was abused. You can see it." He pointed to the scars on the horse's flanks. "He's afraid. What's his name?"

Dominique consulted the bill from the abattoir, then looked at Carole.

"What is it?" the older woman asked, walking over to read the bill as well. "Oh," she said, then looked at the vet. "Can a horse's name be changed?"

"Normally I'd say yes, but not this one. He needs some continuity. They get used to their names. Why?"

"His name's Marc."

"I've heard worse," said the vet, packing up.

The two women exchanged glances. So far Marc, her husband, not the horse, had no idea Dominique had canceled the hunters in favor of these misfits. He almost certainly wouldn't be happy. She'd been hoping he wouldn't notice, and if she gave them mighty, masculine names like Thunder and Trooper he might not care. But he'd certainly notice a half-blind, scarred and scared old wreck named Marc.

"Ride them as soon as you can," said the vet from his car. "Just walk at first until they get their strength back." He gave the two women a warm smile. "You'll be fine. Don't worry. These are four lucky horses."

And he drove off.

"Oui," said Carole, "until we saddle the wrong end."

"I think the saddle goes in the middle," said Dominique.

"Merde," said Carole.

The Sûreté was out for blood. If the victim hadn't been murdered in the bistro he was killed somewhere else, and they needed to find the crime scene. Blood, and quite a bit of it, had been spilled. And while the murderer had had two days to clean up, blood stained. Blood stuck. It would be almost impossible to completely erase the evidence of this brutal murder. Every home, every business, every shed, every barn, garage, kennel in and around Three Pines was scoured. Jean Guy Beauvoir coordinated it, sending teams of Sûreté officers throughout the village and into the countryside. He stayed in the Incident Room and received their reports, guiding them, occasionally chastising them, his patience eroding as the negative reports flowed in.

Nothing.

No sign of a murder scene or a murder weapon. Not even at the old Hadley house, whose new floors proved bloodless. The lab tests had come back on Olivier's pokers, confirming neither was the weapon. It was still out there, somewhere.

They did find Guylaine's missing boots, and a root cellar under Monsieur Béliveau's house, long overgrown and abandoned, but still housing pickled beets and cider. There was a squirrel's nest in Ruth's attic, not perhaps surprisingly, and suspicious seeds in Myrna's mudroom that turned out to be hollyhock.

Nothing.

"I'll widen the search area," said Beauvoir to the Chief, over the phone.

"Probably a good idea." But Gamache didn't sound convinced.

Through the receiver Beauvoir could hear bells and music and laughter.

Armand Gamache was at the fair.

The Brume County Fair was more than a century old, bringing people in from all over the townships. Like most fairs it had started as a meeting place for farmers, to show their livestock, to sell their autumn produce, to make deals and see friends. There was judging in one barn and displays of handicraft in another. Baking was for sale in the long aisles of open sheds and children lined up for licorice and maple syrup candy, popcorn and freshly made doughnuts.

It was the last celebration of summer, the bridge into autumn.

Armand Gamache walked past the rides and hawkers, then consulted his watch. It was time. He made for a field to the side of the barns, where a crowd had gathered. For the Wellington Boot Toss.

Standing on the edge of the field he watched as kids and adults lined up. The young man in charge settled them down, gave them each an old rubber boot, and standing well back he raised his arm. And held it there.

The tension was almost unbearable.

Then like an ax he dropped it.

The line of people raised their arms in unison and shot them forward, and to whoops of encouragement from onlookers a storm of Wellington boots was released.

Gamache knew in that instant why he'd gotten such an unexpectedly good spot at the side of the field. At least three boots shot his way.

He turned and hunched his back, instinctively bringing his arm up to protect his head. With a series of thuds the boots landed around him, but not on him.

The young man in charge ran over.

"You okay?"

He had curly brown hair that shone auburn in the sun. His face was tanned and his eyes a deep blue. He was stunningly handsome, and pissed off.

"You shouldn't be standing there. I thought for sure you'd move."

Gamache was treated to the look of someone recognizing they were in the presence of immeasurable stupidity.

"C'était ma faute," admitted Gamache. "Sorry. I'm looking for Old Mundin."

"That's me."

Gamache stared at the flushed and handsome young man.

"And you're Chief Inspector Gamache." He stuck out his hand, large and calloused. "I've seen you around Three Pines. Didn't your wife take part in the clog dancing on Canada Day?"

Gamache could barely look away from this young man, so full of vigor and light. He nodded.

"Thought so. I was one of the fiddlers. You're looking for me?"

Behind Old Mundin more people were forming up and looking in his direction. He glanced at them, but seemed relaxed.

"I'd like to talk, when you have a moment."

"Sure. We have a couple more heats, then I can leave. Want to try?"

He offered Gamache one of the boots that had almost brained him.

"What do I do?" asked Gamache as he took the boot and followed Mundin to the line.

"It's a Wellington Boot Toss," said Old Mundin, with a laugh. "I think you can figure it out."

Gamache smiled. This perhaps wasn't his brightest day. He took his place beside Clara and noticed Old Mundin jog down the line to a beautiful young woman and a child who'd be about six. He knelt down and handed the boy a small boot.

"Charles," said Clara. "His son."

Gamache looked again. Charles Mundin was also beautiful. He laughed and turned the wrong way, and with patience his parents got him sorted out. Old Mundin kissed his son and jogged back to the line.

Charles Mundin, Gamache saw, had Down's syndrome.

"Ready?" called Mundin, raising his arm. "Set."

Gamache gripped his boot and glanced down the line at Peter and Clara, staring intently ahead of them.

"Toss!"

Gamache swung up his arm and felt his boot whack his back. Then he sliced forward, losing his grip on the muddy boot. It headed sideways to land about two feet ahead of him and to the side.

Clara's grip, while stronger, didn't last much longer, and her boot went almost straight up into the air.

"Fore!" everyone yelled and as one they reeled back, straining to see as it plunged toward them out of the blinding sun.

It hit Peter. Fortunately it was a tiny, pink child's boot and bounced off him without effect. Behind Gamache, Gabri and Myrna were taking bets how long it would take

Clara to come up with an excuse and what it would be.

"Ten dollars on 'The boot was wet,' " said Myrna.

"Nah, she used that last year. How about 'Peter walked into it'?"

"You're on."

Clara and Peter joined them. "Can you believe they gave me a wet boot again?"

Gabri and Myrna hooted with laughter and Clara, smiling broadly, caught Gamache's eye. Money changed hands. She leaned into Gamache and whispered, "Next year I'm saying Peter leaned into it. Put some money down."

"Suppose you don't hit him?"

"But I always do," she said earnestly. "He leans into it, you know."

"I had heard."

Myrna waved across the field to Ruth, limping along with Rosa beside her. Ruth gave her the finger. Charles Mundin, seeing this, waved, giving everyone the finger.

"Ruth doesn't do the Wellington Boot Toss?" asked Gamache.

"Too much like fun," said Peter. "She came to find children's clothing in the craft barn."

"Why?"

"Who knows why Ruth does anything,"

said Myrna. "Any headway with the investigation?"

"Well, there was one important finding," said Gamache, and everyone crowded even closer around him. Even Ruth limped over. "The coroner says the dead man wasn't killed in the bistro. He was killed somewhere else and taken there."

He could hear the midway clearly now, and hawkers promising huge stuffed toys if you shot a tin duck. Bells jingled to call attention to games and the ring announcer warned people the horse show was about to start. But from his audience there was silence. Until finally Clara spoke.

"That's great news for Olivier, isn't it?"

"You mean it makes him less of a suspect?" said Gamache. "I suppose. But it raises a lot more questions."

"Like how'd the body get into the bistro," said Myrna.

"And where he was killed," said Peter.

"We're searching the village. House by house."

"You're what?" asked Peter. "Without our permission?"

"We have warrants," said Gamache, surprised by Peter's vehement reaction.

"It's still a violation of our privacy. You knew we'd be back, you could've waited."

"I could have, but chose not to. These weren't social calls, and frankly your feelings are secondary."

"Apparently our rights are too."

"That's not accurate." The Chief Inspector spoke firmly. The more heated Peter became the calmer Gamache grew. "We have warrants. Your right to privacy I'm afraid ended when someone took a life in your village. We're not the ones who've violated your rights, the murderer is. Don't forget that. You need to help us, and that means stepping aside and letting us do our work."

"Letting you search our homes," said Peter. "How would you feel?"

"I wouldn't feel good about it either," admitted Gamache. "Who would? But I hope I'd understand. This has just begun, you know. It's going to get worse. And before it's over we'll know where everything is hidden."

He looked sternly at Peter.

Peter saw the closed door into his studio. He imagined Sûreté officers opening it. Flicking on the light switch. Going into his most private space. The place he kept his art. The place he kept his heart. His latest work was in there, under a sheet. Hiding. Away from critical eyes.

But now strangers would have opened that door, lifted that veil and seen it. What would they think?

"So far we haven't found anything, except, I understand, Guylaine's missing boots."

"So you found them," said Ruth. "The old bitch accused me of stealing them."

"They were found in the hedge between her place and yours," said Gamache.

"Imagine that," said Ruth.

Gamache noticed the Mundins standing on the edge of the field, waiting for him. "Excuse me."

He walked briskly to the young couple and their son and joined them as they walked to the stall Old Mundin had set up. It was full of furniture, hand made. A person's choices were always revealing, Gamache found. Mundin chose to make furniture, fine furniture. Gamache's educated eye skimmed the tables, cabinets and chairs. This was painstaking, meticulous work. All the joints dovetailed together without nails; the details were beautifully inlaid, the finishes smooth. Faultless. Work like this took time and patience. And the young carpenter could never, ever be paid what these tables, chairs, dressers were worth.

And yet Old Mundin chose to do it anyway. Unusual for a young man these days.

"How can we help?" The Wife asked, smiling warmly. She had very dark hair, cut short to her head, and large, thoughtful, eyes. Her clothing was layered and looked both comfortable and bohemian. An earth mother, thought Gamache, married to a carpenter.

"I have a few questions, but tell me about your furniture. It's beautiful."

"Merci," said Mundin. "I spend most of the year making pieces to sell at the fair."

Gamache ran his large hand over the smooth surface of a chest of drawers. "Lovely polish. Paraffin?"

"Not unless we want them to burst into flames," laughed Old. "Paraffin's highly flammable."

"Varathane?"

Old Mundin's beautiful face crinkled in a smile. "You are perhaps mistaking us for Ikea. Easy to do," he joked. "No, we use beeswax."

We, thought Gamache. He'd watched this young couple for just a few minutes but it seemed clear they were a team.

"Do you sell much at the fair?" he asked.

"This's all we have left," The Wife said, indicating the few exquisite pieces around them.

"They'll be gone by the end of the fair

tonight," said Old Mundin. "Then I need to get going again. Fall's a great time of year to get into the forests and find wood. I do most of my woodwork through the winter."

"I'd like to see your workshop."

"Any time."

"How about now?"

Old Mundin stared at his visitor and Gamache stared back.

"Now?"

"Is that a problem?"

"Well . . ."

"It's okay, Old," said The Wife. "I'll watch the booth. You go."

"Is it okay if we take Charles?" Old asked Gamache. "It's hard for The Wife to watch him and look after customers."

"I insist he comes along," said Gamache, holding out his hand to the boy, who took it without hesitation. A small shard stabbed Gamache's heart as he realized how precious this boy was, and would always be. A child who lived in a perpetual state of trust.

And how hard it would be for his parents to protect him.

"He'll be fine," Gamache assured The Wife.

"Oh, I know he'll be. It's you I worry about," she said.

"I'm sorry," said Gamache, reaching out

to shake her hand. "I don't know your name."

"My actual name is Michelle, but everyone calls me The Wife."

Her hand was rough and calloused, like her husband's, but her voice was cultured, full of warmth. It reminded him a little of Reine-Marie's.

"Why?" he asked.

"It started out as a joke between us and then it took. Old and The Wife. It somehow fits."

And Gamache agreed. It did fit this couple, who seemed to live in their own world, with their own beautiful creations.

"Bye." Charles gave his mother the new one-fingered wave.

"Old," she scolded.

"Wasn't me," he protested. But he didn't rat on Ruth, Gamache noticed.

Old strapped his son into the van and they drove out of the fair parking lot.

"Is 'Old' your real name?"

"I've been called 'Old' all my life, but my real name is Patrick."

"How long have you lived here?"

"In Three Pines? A few years." He thought for a moment. "My God, it's been eleven years. Can hardly believe it. Olivier was the first person I met."

"How do people feel about him?"

"Don't know about 'people,' but I know how I feel. I like Olivier. He's always fair with me."

"But not with everyone?" Gamache had noticed the inflection.

"Some people don't know the value of what they've got." Old Mundin was concentrating on the road, driving carefully. "And lots of people just want to stir up trouble. They don't like being told their antique chest is really just old. Not valuable at all. Pisses them off. But Olivier knows what he's doing. Lots of people set up antique businesses here, but not many really know what they're doing. Olivier does."

After a moment or two of silence as both men watched the countryside go by, Gamache spoke. "I've always wondered where dealers find their antiques."

"Most have pickers. People who specialize in going to auctions or getting to know people in the area. Mostly elderly people who might be interested in selling. Around here if someone knocks on your door on a Sunday morning it's more likely to be an antique picker than a Jehovah's Witness."

"Does Olivier have a picker?"

"No, he does it himself. He works hard for what he gets. And he knows what's worth money and what isn't. He's good. And fair, for the most part."

"For the most part?"

"Well, he has to make a profit, and lots of the stuff needs work. He gives the old furniture to me to restore. That can be a lot of work."

"I bet you don't charge what it's worth."

"Now, worth is a relative concept." Old shot Gamache a glance as they bumped along the road. "I love what I do and if I charged a reasonable amount per hour nobody'd be able to buy my pieces, and Olivier wouldn't hire me to repair the great things he finds. So it's worth it to me to charge less. I have a good life. No complaints here."

"Has anyone been really angry at Olivier?"

Old drove in silence and Gamache wasn't sure he'd heard. But finally he spoke.

"Once, about a year ago. Old Madame Poirier, up the Mountain road, had decided to move into a nursing home in Saint-Rémy. Olivier'd been buzzing around her for a few years. When the time came she sold most of her stuff to him. He found some amazing pieces there."

"Did he pay a fair price?"

"Depends who you talk to. She was happy.

Olivier was happy."

"So who was angry?"

Old Mundin said nothing. Gamache waited.

"Her kids. They said Olivier'd insinuated himself, taken advantage of a lonely old woman."

Old Mundin pulled into a small farmhouse. Hollyhocks leaned against the wall and the garden was full of black-eyed Susans and old-fashioned roses. A vegetable garden, well tended and orderly, was planted at the side of the house.

The van rolled to a halt and Mundin pointed to a barn. "That's my workshop."

Gamache unbuckled Charles from the child seat. The boy was asleep and Gamache carried him as the two men walked to the barn.

"You said Olivier made an unexpected find at Madame Poirier's place?"

"He paid her a flat fee for all the stuff she no longer needed. She chose what she wanted to keep and he bought the rest."

Old Mundin stopped at the barn door, turning to Gamache.

"There was a set of six Chippendale chairs. Worth about ten thousand each. I know, because I worked on them, but I don't think he told anyone else."

"Did you?"

"No. You'd be surprised how discreet I need to be in my work."

"Do you know if Olivier gave Madame Poirier any extra money?"

"I don't."

"But her kids were angry."

Mundin nodded curtly and opened the barn door. They stepped into a different world. All the complex aromas of the late summer farm had disappeared. Gone was the slight scent of manure, of cut grass, of hay, of herbs in the sun.

Here there was only one note — wood. Fresh sawn wood. Old barn wood. Wood of every description. Gamache looked at the walls, lined with wood waiting to be turned into furniture. Old Mundin smoothed one fine hand over a rough board.

"You wouldn't know it, but there's burled wood under there. You have to know what to look for. The tiny imperfections. Funny how imperfections on the outside mean something splendid beneath."

He looked into Gamache's eyes. Charles stirred slightly and the Chief Inspector brought a large hand up to the boy's back, to reassure him.

"I'm afraid I don't know much about wood but you seem to have different sorts.

Why's that?"

"Different needs. I use maple and cherry and pine for inside work. Cedar for outside. This here's red cedar. My favorite. Doesn't look like much now, but carved and polished . . ." Mundin made an eloquent gesture.

Gamache noticed two chairs on a platform. One was upside down. "From the bistro?" He walked over to them. Sure enough one had a loose arm and the leg of the other was wobbly.

"I picked those up Saturday night."

"Is it all right to talk about what happened at the bistro in front of Charles?"

"I'm sure it is. He'll understand, or not. Either way, it's okay. He knows it's not about him."

Gamache wished more people could make that distinction. "You were there the night of the murder."

"True. I go every Saturday to pick up the damaged furniture and drop off the stuff I've restored. It was the same as always. I got there just after midnight. The last of the customers was leaving and the kids were beginning to clean up."

Kids, thought Gamache. And yet they weren't really that much younger than this man. But somehow Old seemed very, well, old.

"But I didn't see a body."

"Too bad, that would've helped. Did anything strike you as unusual at all?"

Old Mundin thought. Charles woke up and squirmed. Gamache lowered him to the barn floor where he picked up a piece of wood and turned it around and around.

"I'm sorry. I wish I could help, but it seemed like any other Saturday night."

Gamache also picked up a chunk of wood and smoothed the sawdust off it.

"How'd you start repairing Olivier's furniture?"

"Oh, that was years ago. Gave me a chair to work on. It'd been kept in a barn for years and he'd just moved it into the bistro. Now, you must understand . . ."

What followed was a passionate monologue on old Quebec pine furniture. Milk paint, the horrors of stripping, the dangers of ruining a fine piece by restoring it. That difficult line between making a piece usable and making it valueless.

Gamache listened, fascinated. He had a passion for Quebec history, and by extension Quebec antiques, the remarkable furniture made by pioneers in the long winter months hundreds of years ago.

They'd made the pine furniture both practical and beautiful, pouring themselves into it. Each time Gamache touched an old table or armoire he imagined the *habitant* shaping and smoothing the wood, going over it and over it with hardened hands. And making something lovely.

Lovely and lasting, thanks to people like Old Mundin.

"What brought you to Three Pines? Why not a larger city? There'd be more work, surely, in Montreal or even Sherbrooke."

"I was born in Quebec City, and you'd think there'd be lots of work there for an antique restorer, but it's hard for a young guy starting out. I moved to Montreal, to an antique shop on Notre Dame, but I'm afraid I wasn't cut out for the big city. So I decided to go to Sherbrooke. Got in the car, headed south, and got lost. I drove into Three Pines to ask directions at the bistro, ordered *café au lait,* sat down and the chair collapsed." He laughed, as did Gamache. "I offered to repair it and that was that."

"You said you'd been here for eleven years. You must've been young when you left Quebec City."

"Sixteen. I left after my father died. Spent three years in Montreal, then down here. Met The Wife, had Charles. Started a small business."

This young man had done a lot with his eleven years, thought Gamache. "How did Olivier seem on Saturday night?"

"As usual. Labor Day's always busy but he seemed relaxed. As relaxed as he ever gets, I suppose." Mundin smiled. It was clear there was affection there. "Did I hear you say the man wasn't murdered at the bistro after all?"

Gamache nodded. "We're trying to find out where he was killed. In fact, while you were at the fair I had my people searching the whole area, including your place."

"Really?" They were at the barn door and Mundin turned to stare into the gloom. "They're either very good, or they didn't actually do anything. You can't tell."

"That's the point." But the Chief noticed that, unlike Peter, Old Mundin didn't seem at all concerned.

"Now, why would you kill someone one place, then move them to another?" asked Mundin, almost to himself. "I can see wanting to get rid of a body, especially if you killed him in your own home, but why take him to Olivier's? Seems a strange thing to do, but I guess the bistro's a fairly central location. Maybe it was just convenient."

Gamache let that statement be. They both

knew it wasn't true. Indeed, the bistro was a very inconvenient place to drop a body. And it worried Gamache. The murder wasn't an accident, and the placement of the body wasn't either.

There was someone very dangerous walking among them. Someone who looked happy, thoughtful, gentle even. But it was a deceit. A mask. Gamache knew that when he found the murderer and ripped the mask off, the skin would come too. The mask had become the man. The deceit was total.

Thirteen

"We had a great time at the fair. I got you this." Gabri shut the door and turned on the lights in the bistro. He offered the stuffed lion to Olivier, who took it and held it softly in his lap.

"Merci."

"And did you hear the news? Gamache says the dead man wasn't killed here. And we'll be getting our pokers back. I'd like to get my poker back, wouldn't you?" he asked, archly. But Olivier didn't even respond.

Gabri moved through the gloomy room, turning on lamps, then lit a fire in one of the stone hearths. Olivier continued to sit in the armchair, staring out the window. Gabri sighed, poured them each a beer and joined him. Together they sipped, ate cashews and looked out at the village, quiet now in the last of the day, and the end of the summer.

"What do you see?" asked Gabri at last.

"What d'you mean? I see what you see."

"Can't be. What I see makes me happy. And you're not happy."

Gabri was used to his partner's moods. Olivier was the quiet one, the contained one. Gabri might appear the more sensitive, but they both knew Olivier was. He felt things deeply, and kept them there. Gabri was covered in the flesh wounds of life, but Olivier's wounds were in the marrow, deep and hidden and perhaps even mortal.

But he was also the kindest man Gabri had met, and he'd met, it must be said, quite a few. Before Olivier. That had all changed as soon as he'd clapped eyes on the slim, blond, shy man.

Gabri had lost his quite considerable heart.

"What is it?" Gabri leaned forward and took Olivier's slender hands. "Tell me."

"It's just no fun anymore," said Olivier at last. "I mean, why even bother? No one's going to want to come back here. Who wants to eat in a restaurant where there's been a body?"

"As Ruth says, we're all just bodies anyway."

"Great. I'll put that in the ads."

"Well, at least you don't discriminate.

Dead, predead. They're all welcome here. That might be a better slogan."

Gabri saw a quiver at the ends of Olivier's lips.

"*Voyons,* it was great news that the police say the man wasn't killed here. That makes a difference."

"You think?" Olivier looked at him hopefully.

"Do you know what I really think?" Now Gabri was dead serious. "I think it wouldn't matter. Peter, Clara, Myrna? Do you think they'd stop coming even if that poor man had been murdered here? The Parras? Monsieur Béliveau? They'd all come if a mountain of bodies was found here. Do you know why?"

"Because they like it?"

"Because they like you. They love you. Listen, Olivier, you have the best bistro, the finest food, the most comfortable place. It's brilliant. You're brilliant. Everyone loves you. And you know what?"

"What?" asked Olivier, grumpily.

"You're the kindest, most handsome man in the world."

"You're just saying that." Olivier felt like a little boy again. While other kids ran around collecting frogs and sticks and grasshoppers, he'd sought reassurance. Affection.

He'd gather up the words and actions, even from strangers, and he'd stuff them into the hole that was growing.

It had worked. For a while. Then he'd needed more than just words.

"Did Myrna tell you to say that?"

"Right. It's not true at all, just a big lie cooked up by Myrna and me. What's wrong with you anyway?"

"You wouldn't understand."

Gabri followed Olivier's stare out the window. And up the hill. He sighed. They'd been through this before.

"There's nothing we can do about them. Maybe we should just —"

"Just what?" Olivier snapped.

"Are you looking for an excuse to be miserable? Is that it?"

Even by Olivier's standards that had been an unreasonable reaction. He'd been reassured about the body, he'd been reassured that everyone still loved him. He'd been reassured that Gabri wasn't running away. So what was the problem?

"Listen, maybe we should give them a chance. Who knows? Their inn and spa might even help us."

This was not what Olivier wanted to hear. He stood abruptly, almost knocking the chair to the floor. He could feel that bloom of anger in his chest. It was like a superpower. It made him invincible. Strong. Courageous. Brutal.

"If you want to be friends with them, fine. Why don't you just fuck off?"

"I didn't mean that. I meant we can't do anything about them so we might as well be friends."

"You make this sound like kindergarten. They're out to ruin us. Do you understand? When they first came I was nice, but then they decided to steal our customers, even our staff. Do you think anyone's going to come to your tacky little B and B when they can stay there?"

Olivier's face was red and blotchy. Gabri could see it spread even under his scalp, through the thinning and struggling blond hair.

"What're you talking about? I don't care if people come, you know that. We don't need the money. I just do it for fun."

Olivier struggled to control himself now. To not take that one step too far. The two men glared so that the space between them throbbed.

"Why?" Olivier finally said.

"Why what?"

"If the dead man wasn't killed here, why was he put here?"

Gabri felt his anger lift, evaporated by the question.

"I heard from the police today," said Olivier, his voice almost monotone. "They're going to speak to my father tomorrow."

Poor Olivier, thought Gabri, he did have something to worry about after all.

Jean Guy Beauvoir got out of the car and stared across the road at the Poirier home.

It was ramshackle and in need of way more than just a coat of paint. The porch was sloping, the steps looked unsound, pieces of boarding were missing from the side of the house.

Beauvoir had been in dozens of places like this in rural Quebec. Lived in by a generation born there too. Clotilde Poirier probably drank coffee from a chipped mug her mother had used. Slept on a mattress she'd been conceived on. The walls would be covered with dried flowers and spoons sent by relatives who'd escaped to exotic places like Rimouski or Chicoutimi or Gaspé. And there'd be a chair, a rocking chair, by the window, near the woodstove. It would have a slightly soiled afghan on it and crumbs. And after clearing up the breakfast dishes Clotilde Poirier would sit there, and watch.

What would she be watching for? A friend?

A familiar car? Another spoon?

Was she watching him now?

Armand Gamache's Volvo appeared over the hill and came to a stop behind Beauvoir. The two men stood and stared for a moment at the house.

"I found out about the Varathane," said Beauvoir, thinking this place could use a hundred gallons or so of the stuff. "The Gilberts didn't use it when they did the renovations. I spoke to Dominique Gilbert. She said they want to be as green as possible. After they had the floors sanded they used tung oil."

"So the Varathane on the dead man's clothing didn't come from the old Hadley house," said the Chief, disappointed. It had seemed a promising lead.

"Why're we here?" Beauvoir asked as they turned back to survey the gently subsiding home and the rusting pickup truck in the yard. He'd received a call from the Chief to meet him here, but he didn't know why.

Gamache explained what Old Mundin had said about Olivier, Madame Poirier and her furniture. Specifically the Chippendale chairs.

"So her kids think Olivier screwed her? And by extension, them?" asked Beauvoir.

"Seems so." He knocked on the door.

After a moment a querulous voice called through it.

"Who is it?"

"Chief Inspector Gamache, madame. Of the Sûreté du Québec."

"I ain't done nothing wrong."

Gamache and Beauvoir exchanged glances.

"We need to speak to you, Madame Poirier. It's about the body found in the bistro in Three Pines."

"So?"

It was very difficult conducting an interview through an inch of chipping wood.

"May we come in? We'd like to talk to you about Olivier Brulé."

An elderly woman, small and slender, opened the door. She glared at them then turned and walked rapidly back into the house. Gamache and Beauvoir followed.

It was decorated as Beauvoir had imagined. Or, really, not decorated. Things were put up on the walls as they'd arrived, over the generations, so that the walls were a horizontal archaeological dig. The farther into the house they went, the more recent the items. Framed flowers, plasticized place mats, crucifixes, paintings of Jesus and the Virgin Mary, and yes, spoons, all marched across the faded floral wallpaper.

But the place was clean, spotless and smelled of cookies. Photos of grandchildren, perhaps even great-grandchildren, sat on shelves and tabletops. A faded striped tablecloth, clean and ironed, was on the kitchen table. And in the center of that table was a vase containing late summer flowers.

"Tea?" She lifted a pot from the stove. Beauvoir declined but Gamache accepted. She returned with cups of tea for them all. "Well, go on."

"We understand Olivier bought some furniture from you," said Beauvoir.

"Not just some. He bought the lot. Thank God. Gave me more than anyone else would, despite what my kids mighta told you."

"We haven't spoken to them yet," said Beauvoir.

"Neither have I. Not since selling the stuff." But she didn't seem upset. "Greedy, all of them. Waiting for me to die so they can inherit."

"How did you meet Olivier?" Beauvoir asked.

"He knocked on the door one day. Introduced himself. Asked if I had anything I'd like to sell. Sent him running the first few times." She smiled at the memory. "But there was something about him. He kept coming back. So I eventually invited him in, just for tea. He'd come about once a month, have tea, then leave."

"When did you decide to sell to him?" Beauvoir asked.

"I'm coming to that," she snapped, and Beauvoir began to appreciate how hard Olivier must have worked for that furniture.

"One winter was particularly long. Lots of snow. And cold. So I decided to hell with this, I'd sell up and move into Saint-Rémy, to that new seniors' home. So I told Olivier and we walked through the house. I showed him all that crap my parents left me. Old armoires and dressers. Big pine things. And painted all sorts of dull colors. Blues and greens. Tried to scrape it off some of them, but it was no good."

Beside him Beauvoir heard the Chief inhale, but that was the only sign of pain. Having spent years with Gamache he knew his passion for antiques, and knew that you never, ever strip old paint. It was like skinning something alive.

"So you showed it all to Olivier? What did he say?"

"Said he'd take the lot, including what was in the barn and attic without even seeing it. Tables and chairs been there since before my grandparents. Was going to send it to the dump, but my lazy sons never showed up to do it. So serves them right. I sold the lot to Olivier."

"Can you remember how much you got?"

"I remember exactly. It was three thousand two hundred dollars. Enough to pay for all of this. Sears."

Gamache looked at the legs of the table. Prefabricated wood. There was an upholstered rocker facing the new television, and a dark wood-veneer cabinet, with decorative plates.

Madame Poirier was also looking at the contents of the room, with pride.

"He came by a few weeks later and you know what he'd brought? A new bed. Plastic still on the mattress. Set it up for me too. He still comes by sometimes. He's a nice man."

Beauvoir nodded. A nice man who'd paid this elderly woman a fraction of what that furniture was worth.

"But you're not in the seniors' home? Why not?"

"After I got the new furniture the place felt different. More mine. I kinda liked it again."

She showed them to the door and Beauvoir noticed the welcome mat. Worn, but still there. They said good-bye and headed for her eldest son's place a mile down the road. A large man with a gut and stubble opened the door.

"Cops," he called into the house. It, and he, smelled of beer and sweat and tobacco.

"Claude Poirier?" Beauvoir asked. It was a formality. Who else would this man be? He was nearing sixty, and looked every moment of it. Beauvoir had taken the time before leaving the Incident Room to look up the Poirier family. To see what they were walking into.

Petty crimes. Drunk and disorderly. Shoplifting. Benefit fraud.

They were the type who took advantage, found fault, pointed fingers. Still, it didn't mean that sometimes they weren't right. Like about Olivier. He'd screwed them.

After the introductions Poirier launched into his long, sad litany. It was all Beauvoir could do to keep him focused on Olivier, so long was this man's list of people who'd done him wrong. Including his own mother.

Finally the two investigators lurched from the stale house, taking deep breaths of fresh late afternoon air.

"Do you think he did it?" asked Gamache

"He's certainly angry enough," said Beauvoir, "but unless he could transport a body to the bistro using the buttons on his remote, I think he's off the suspect list. Can't see him getting off that stinking sofa long enough."

They walked back to their cars. The Chief paused.

"What're you thinking?" Beauvoir asked.

"I was remembering what Madame Poirier said. She was about to take all those antiques to the dump. Can you imagine?"

Beauvoir could see that the thought gave Gamache actual pain.

"But Olivier saved them," said the Chief. "Strange how that works. He might not have given Madame enough money, but he gave her affection and company. What price do you put on that?"

"So, can I buy your car? I'll give you twenty hours of my company."

"Don't be cynical. One day you might be elderly and alone and you'll see."

As he followed the Chief's car back to Three Pines Beauvoir thought about that, and agreed that Olivier had saved the precious antiques, and spent time with the crabby old woman. But he could have done it and still given the old woman a fair price.

But he hadn't.

Marc Gilbert looked at Marc the horse. Marc the horse looked at Marc Gilbert.

Neither seemed pleased.

"Dominique!" Marc called from the door of the barn.

"Yes?" she said, cheerily, walking across the yard from the house. She'd hoped it would take Marc a few days to find the horses. Actually, she'd hoped he never would. But that was in the same league as the Mrs. Keith Partridge dream. Unlikely at best.

And now she found him cross-armed in the dim barn.

"What are these?"

"They're horses," she said. Though, it must be said, she suspected Macaroni might be a moose.

"I can see that, but what kind? These aren't hunters, are they?"

Dominique hesitated. For an instant she wondered what would happen if she said yes. But she guessed that Marc, while not a horse expert, wouldn't buy that.

"No, they're better."

"How better?"

His sentences were getting shorter, never a good sign.

"Well, they're cheaper."

She could see that actually had a slight mollifying effect. Might as well tell him the full story. "I bought them from the slaughterhouse. They were going to be killed today."

Marc hesitated. She could see him struggling with his anger. Not trying to let it go, but trying to hold on to it. "Maybe there was a reason they were going to be . . . you know."

"Killed. No, the vet's been to see them and he says they're fine, or will be."

The barn smelled of disinfectant, soap and medication.

"Maybe physically, but you can't tell me he's okay." Marc waved at Marc the horse, who flared his nostrils and snorted. "He isn't even clean. Why not?"

Why did her husband have to be so observant? "Well, no one could get close to him." Then she had an idea. "The vet says he needs a very special touch. He'll only let someone quite exceptional near him."

"Is that right?" Marc looked at the horse again, and walked toward him. Marc, the horse, backed up. Her husband reached out his hand. The horse put his ears back, and Dominique grabbed her husband away just as Marc the horse snapped.

"It's been a long day and he's disoriented."

"Hmm," said her husband, walking with her out of the barn. "What's his name?"

"Thunder."

"Thunder," said Marc, trying the name out. "Thunder," he repeated as though riding the steed and urging him on.

Carole greeted them at the kitchen door. "So," she said to her son. "How're the horses? How's Marc?"

"I'm fine, thank you." He looked at her quizzically and took the drink she offered. "And how's Carole?"

Behind him Dominique gestured frantically at her mother-in-law who was laughing and just about to say something when she saw her daughter-in-law's motions and stopped. "Just fine. Do you like the horses?"

"Like is a strong word, as is 'horses,' I suspect."

"It'll take a while for us all to get used to each other," said Dominique. She accepted the Scotch from Carole and took a gulp. Then they walked out the French doors and into the garden.

As the two women talked, more friends than mother and daughter-in-law, Marc looked at the flowers, the mature trees, the freshly painted white fences and the rolling fields beyond. Soon the horses, or whatever they were, would be out there. Grazing.

Once again he had that hollow feeling, that slight rip as the chasm widened.

Leaving Montreal had been a wrench for Dominique, and leaving Quebec City had been difficult for his mother. They left behind friends. But while Marc had pretended to be sorry, had gone to the going-away parties, had claimed he would miss everyone, the truth was, he didn't.

They had to be part of his life for him to miss them, and they weren't. He remembered that Kipling poem his father loved, and taught him. And that one line. *If all men count with you, but none too much.*

And they hadn't. Over forty-five years not a single man had counted too much.

He had loads of colleagues, acquaintances, buddies. He was an emotional communist. Everyone counted equally, but none too much.

You'll be a man, my son. That was how the poem ended.

But Marc Gilbert, listening to the quiet conversation and looking over the rich, endless fields, was beginning to wonder if that was enough. Or even true.

The officers gathered round the conference table and Beauvoir uncapped his red Magic Marker. Agent Morin was beginning to appreciate that the small "pop" was like a starter's gun. In the short time he'd been with homicide he'd developed a fondness for the smell of marker, and that distinctive sound.

He settled into his chair, a little nervous as always, in case he should say something particularly stupid. Agent Lacoste had helped. As they'd gathered up their papers for the meeting she'd seen his trembling hands and whispered that maybe he should just listen this time.

He'd looked at her, surprised.

"Won't they think I'm an idiot? That I have nothing to say?"

"Believe me, there's no way you're going to listen yourself out of this job. Or any job. Just relax, let me do the talking today, and we'll see about tomorrow. Okay?"

He'd looked at her then, trying to figure out what her motives might be. Everyone had them, he knew. Some were driven by kindness, some not. And he'd been at the Sûreté long enough to know that most in the famous police force weren't guided by a desire to be nice.

It was brutally competitive, and nowhere more so than the scramble to get into homicide. The most prestigious posting. And the chance to work with Chief Inspector Gamache.

He was barely in, and barely hanging on.

One wrong move and he'd slide right out the door, and be forgotten in an instant. He wasn't going to let that happen. And he knew, instinctively, this was a pivotal moment. Was Agent Lacoste sincere?

"All right, what've we got?"

Beauvoir was standing by the paper tacked to the wall next to a map of the village.

"We know the victim wasn't murdered at the bistro," said Lacoste. "But we still don't know where he was killed or who he was."

"Or why he was moved," said Beauvoir. He reported on their visit to the Poiriers, *mère et fils.* Then Lacoste told them what she and Morin had learned about Olivier Brulé.

"He's thirty-eight. Only child. Born and raised in Montreal. Father an executive at the railway, mother a homemaker, now dead. An affluent upbringing. Went to Notre Dame de Sion school."

Gamache raised his brows. It was a leading Catholic private school. Annie had gone there too, years after Olivier, to be taught by the rigorous nuns. His son Daniel had refused, preferring the less rigorous public schools. Annie had learned logic, Latin, problem solving. Daniel had learned to roll a spliff. Both grew into decent, happy adults.

"Olivier got an MBA from the Université

de Montréal and took a job at the Banque Laurentienne," Agent Lacoste continued, reading from her notes. "He handled high-end corporate clients. Apparently very successfully too. Then he quit."

"Why?" asked Beauvoir.

"Not sure. I have a meeting at the bank tomorrow, and I've also set up an appointment with Olivier's father."

"What about his personal life?" Gamache asked.

"I talked to Gabri. They started living together fourteen years ago. Gabri's a year younger. Thirty-seven. He was a fitness instructor at the local YMCA."

"Gabri?" asked Beauvoir, remembering the large, soft man.

"Happens to the best of us," said Gamache.

"After Olivier quit the bank they gave up their apartment in Old Montreal and moved down here, took over the bistro and lived above it, but it wasn't a bistro then. It'd been a hardware store."

"Really?" asked Beauvoir. He couldn't imagine the bistro as anything else. He tried to see snow shovels and batteries and light-bulbs hanging from the exposed beams or set up in front of the two stone fireplaces. And failed.

"But listen to this." Lacoste leaned forward. "I got this by digging into the land registry records. Ten years ago Olivier bought not just his bistro, but the B and B. But he didn't stop there. He bought it all. The general store, the bakery, his bistro and Myrna's bookstore."

"Everything?" asked Beauvoir. "He owns the village?"

"Just about. I don't think anyone else knows. I spoke to Sarah at her boulangerie and to Monsieur Béliveau at the general store. They said they rented from some guy in Montreal. Long-term leases, reasonable rates. They send their checks to a numbered company."

"Olivier's a numbered company?" asked Beauvoir.

Gamache was taking all this in, listening closely.

"How much did he pay?" asked Beauvoir.

"Seven hundred and twenty thousand dollars for the lot."

"Good God," said Beauvoir. "That's a lot of bread. Where'd he get the money? A mortgage?"

"No. Paid cash."

"You say his mother's dead, maybe it was his inheritance."

"Doubt it," said Lacoste. "She only died

five years ago, but I'll look into it when I'm in Montreal."

"Follow the money," said Beauvoir. It was a truism in crime investigations, particularly murder. And there was suddenly a great deal of money to follow. Beauvoir finished scribbling on his sheets on the wall, then told them about the coroner's findings.

Morin listened, fascinated. So this was how murderers were found. Not by DNA tests and petrie dishes, ultraviolet scans or anything else a lab could produce. They helped, certainly, but this was their real lab. He looked across the table to the other person who was just listening, saying nothing.

Chief Inspector Gamache took his deep brown eyes off Inspector Beauvoir for a moment and looked at the young agent. And smiled.

Agent Lacoste headed for Montreal shortly after the meeting broke up. Agent Morin left for home and Beauvoir and Gamache walked slowly back over the stone bridge and into the village. They strolled past the darkened bistro and met Olivier and Gabri on the wide veranda of the B and B.

"I left a note for you," said Gabri. "Since the bistro's closed we're all going out for dinner and you're invited."

"Peter and Clara's again?" asked Gamache.

"No. Ruth," said Gabri and was rewarded with their stunned looks. He'd have thought someone had drawn a gun on the two large Sûreté officers. Chief Inspector Gamache looked surprised but Beauvoir looked afraid.

"You might want to put on your athletic protector," Gabri whispered to Beauvoir, as they passed on the veranda steps.

"Well, I'm sure as hell not going. You?" asked Beauvoir when they went inside.

"Are you kidding? Pass up a chance to see Ruth in her natural habitat? Wouldn't miss it."

Twenty minutes later the Chief Inspector had showered, called Reine-Marie and changed into slacks, blue shirt and tie and a camel-hair cardigan. He found Beauvoir in the living room with a beer and potato chips.

"Sure you won't change your mind, *patron?*"

It was tempting, Gamache had to admit. But he shook his head.

"I'll keep a candle in the window," said Beauvoir, watching the Chief leave.

Ruth's clapboard home was a couple of houses away and faced the green. It was tiny, with a porch in front and two gables on the second floor. Gamache had been in it before, but always with his notebook out, asking questions. Never as a guest. As he entered all eyes turned and as one they made for him, Myrna reaching him first.

"For pity's sake, did you bring your gun?"

"I don't have one."

"What d'you mean, you don't have one?"

"They're dangerous. Why do you want it?"

"So you can shoot her. She's trying to kill us." Myrna grabbed Gamache's sleeve and pointed to Ruth who was circulating among her guests wearing a frilly apron and carrying a bright orange plastic tray.

"Actually," said Gabri, "she's trying to kidnap us and take us back to 1950."

"Probably the last time she entertained," said Myrna.

"Hors d'oeuvre, old fruit?" Ruth spotted her new guest and bore down upon him.

Gabri and Olivier turned to each other. "She means you."

Incredibly, she actually meant Gamache.

"Lord love a duck," said Ruth, in a very bad British accent. Behind Ruth waddled Rosa.

"She started speaking like that as soon as we arrived," said Myrna, backing away from the tray and knocking over a stack of *Times Literary Supplements*. Gamache could see saltine crackers sliding around on the orange tray, smeared with brown stuff he hoped was peanut butter. "I remember reading something about this," Myrna continued. "People speaking in accents after a brain injury."

"Is being possessed by the devil considered a brain injury?" asked Gabri. "She's speaking in tongues."

"Cor blimey," said Ruth.

But the most striking feature of the room wasn't the hoop lamps, the teak furniture, genteel British Ruth with her dubious offering, nor was it the sofas covered in books and newspapers and magazines, as was the green shag carpet. It was the duck.

Rosa was wearing a dress.

"Duck and cover," said Gabri. "Literally."

"Our Rosa." Ruth had put down the peanut-buttered crackers and was now offering celery sticks stuffed with Velveeta.

Gamache watched and wondered if he'd have to make a couple of calls. One to the Humane Society, the other to the psych ward. But neither Rosa nor Ruth seemed upset. Unlike their guests.

"Would you like one?" Clara offered him a ball covered with what looked like seeds.

"What is it?" he asked.

"We think it's suet, for the birds," said Peter.

"And you're offering it to me?" Gamache asked.

"Well, someone should eat it so it doesn't hurt her feelings." Clara nodded to Ruth, just disappearing into the kitchen. "And we're too afraid."

"Non, merci," he smiled and went in search of Olivier. As he passed the kitchen he looked in and saw Ruth opening a can. Rosa was standing on the table watching her.

"Now, we'll just open this," she mumbled. "Maybe we should smell it? What do you think?"

The duck didn't seem to be thinking anything. Ruth smelled the open can anyway. "Good enough."

The old poet wiped her hands on a towel then reached out and lifted the edge of Rosa's dress to replace a ruffled feather, smoothing it down.

"May I help?" Gamache asked from the door.

"Well, aren't you a love."

Gamache winced, expecting her to throw a cleaver after that. But she just smiled and handed him a plate of olives, each stuffed with a section of canned mandarin orange. He took it and returned to the party. Not surprisingly he was greeted as though he'd joined the dark side. He was very grateful Beauvoir wasn't there to see Ruth, nuttier and more Anglo than usual, Rosa wearing a dress and himself offering food that would almost certainly kill or cripple anyone foolish enough to eat it.

"Olive?" he asked Olivier.

The two men looked down at the plate.

"Does that make me the mandarin?" asked Gabri.

"You need to get your head out of your own asshole," said Olivier.

Gabri opened his mouth, but the warning looks on everyone's faces made him shut it again.

Peter, standing a little way off from the conversation and nursing the glass of water Ruth had offered him, smiled. It was much the same thing Clara had said when he'd told her he'd felt violated by the police search.

"Why?" she'd asked.

"Didn't you? I mean, all those strangers looking at your art."

"Isn't that what we call a show? There were more people looking this afternoon than I've had most of my career. Bring on more cops. Hope they brought their checkbooks." She laughed, and clearly didn't care.

But she could see he did. "What's the matter?"

"The picture isn't ready to be seen."

"Look, Peter, you make it sound as though this is something to do with your art."

"Well, it is."

"They're trying to find a murderer, not an artist."

And there it had sat, like most uncomfortable truths. Between them.

Gamache and Olivier had wandered away from the group, into a quiet corner.

"I understand you bought your building a few years ago."

Olivier colored slightly, surprised by the question. He instinctively and furtively scanned the room, making sure they weren't overheard.

"I thought it was a good investment. I'd saved some money from my job, and business here was good."

"Must have been. You paid almost three-quarters of a million dollars."

"I bet it's worth a million today."

"Could be. But you paid cash. Was business all that good?"

Olivier shot a look around but no one could hear them. Still he lowered his voice.

"The bistro and B and B are doing very well, for now anyway, but it's the antiques end that's been the surprise."

"How so?"

"Lots of interest in Quebec pine, and lots of great finds."

Gamache nodded. "We spoke to the Poiriers this afternoon."

Olivier's face hardened. "Look, what they say just isn't true. I didn't screw their mother. She wanted to sell. Was desperate to sell."

"I know. We spoke to her too. And the Mundins. The furniture must have been in very bad shape."

Olivier relaxed a little.

"It was. Years sitting in damp, freezing barns and the attic. Had to chase the mice out. Some were warped almost beyond repair. Enough to make you weep."

"Madame Poirier says you came by her home later with a new bed. That was kind."

Olivier dropped his eyes. "Yeah, well, I wanted to thank her."

Conscience, thought Gamache. This man had a huge and terrible conscience riding herd on a huge and terrible greed.

"You said the bistro and B and B were doing well, for now. What did you mean?"

Olivier looked out the window for a moment, then back at Gamache.

"Hi ho, dinner everyone," sang Ruth.

"What should we do?" Clara whispered to Myrna. "Can we run for it?"

"Too late. Either Ruth or the duck would get us for sure. The only thing to do is hunker down and pray for daylight. If the worst happens, play dead."

Gamache and Olivier rose, the last in for dinner.

"I suppose you know what they're doing up at the old Hadley house?" When Gamache didn't answer Olivier continued. "They've almost completely gutted the place and are turning it into an inn and spa. Ten massage rooms, meditation and yoga classes. They'll do a day spa and corporate retreats. People'll be crawling all over the place, and us. It'll ruin Three Pines."

"Three Pines?"

"All right," snapped Olivier. "The bistro and the B and B."

They joined the others in the kitchen and sat at Ruth's white plastic garden table.

"Incoming," warned Gabri as Ruth put a bowl in front of each of them.

Gamache looked at the contents of his bowl. He could make out canned peaches, bacon, cheese and Gummi Bears.

"They're all the things I love," said Ruth, smiling. Rosa was sitting next to her on a nest of towels, her beak thrust under the sleeve of her dress.

"Scotch?" Ruth asked.

"Please." Six glasses were thrust forward and Ruth poured each a Scotch, into their dinners.

About three centuries and many lifetimes later they left, staggering into the quiet, cool night.

"Toodle-oo," waved Ruth. But Gamache was heartened to hear, just as the door closed: "Fuckers."

Fourteen

They arrived back at the B and B to find Beauvoir waiting up for them. Sort of. He was fast asleep in his chair. Beside him was a plate with crumbs and a glass of chocolate milk. The fireplace glowed with dying embers.

"Should we wake him?" asked Olivier. "He looks so peaceful."

Beauvoir's face was turned to the side and there was a slight glisten of drool. His breathing was heavy and regular. On his chest lay the small stuffed lion Gabri had won for Olivier at the fair, his hand resting on it.

"Like a little baby cop," said Gabri.

"That reminds me. Ruth asked me to give him this." Olivier handed Gamache a slip of paper. The Chief took it and when he declined their offer of help watched as the two men trudged wearily up the stairs. It was nine o'clock.

"Jean Guy," Gamache whispered. "Wake up."

He knelt and touched the younger man's shoulder. Beauvoir started awake with a snort, the lion slipping off his chest onto the floor.

"What is it?"

"Time for bed."

He watched Beauvoir sit up. "How was it?"

"No one died."

"That's a bit of an achievement in Three Pines."

"Olivier said Ruth wanted you to have this." Gamache handed him the slip of paper. Beauvoir rubbed his eyes, unfolded the paper and read it. Then, shaking his head, he handed it to the Chief.

Maybe there's something in all of this
I missed.

"What does it mean? Is it a threat?"

Gamache frowned. "Haven't a clue. Why would she be writing to you?"

"Jealous? Maybe she's just nuts." But they both knew the "maybe" was being generous. "Speaking of nut, your daughter called."

"Annie?" Gamache was suddenly worried,

instinctively reaching for his cell phone, which he knew didn't work in the village in the valley.

"Everything's fine. She wanted to talk to you about some upset at work. Nothing major. She just wanted to quit."

"Damn, that was probably what she wanted to talk about yesterday when we got called down here."

"Well don't worry about it. I handled it."

"I don't think telling her to fuck off can be considered 'handling it.' "

Beauvoir laughed and bending down he picked up the stuffed lion. "There's certainly good reason she's known as 'the lion' in your family. Vicious."

"She's known as the lion because she's loving and passionate."

"And a man-eater?"

"All the qualities you hate in her you admire in men," said Gamache. "She's smart, she stands up for what she believes in. She speaks her mind and won't back down to bullies. Why do you goad her? Every time you come for a meal and she's there it ends in an argument. I for one am growing tired of it."

"All right, I'll try harder. But she's very annoying."

"So are you. You have a lot in common.

What was the problem at work?" Gamache took the seat next to Jean Guy.

"Oh, a case she'd wanted was assigned to another lawyer, someone more junior. I talked to her for a while. I'm almost certain she won't kill everyone at work after all."

"That's my girl."

"And she's decided not to quit. I told her she'd regret any hasty decision."

"Oh, you did, did you?" asked Gamache with a smile. This from the king of impulse.

"Well, someone had to give her good advice," laughed Beauvoir. "Her parents are quite mad, you know."

"I'd heard. Thank you."

It was good advice. And he could tell Beauvoir knew it. He seemed pleased. Gamache looked at his watch. Nine thirty. He reached for Gabri's phone.

As Gamache spoke to his daughter Beauvoir absently stroked the lion in his hand.

Maybe there's something in all of this
I missed.

That was the fear in a murder investigation. Missing something. Chief Inspector Gamache had assembled a brilliant department. Almost two hundred of them in all, hand picked, investigating crime all over the province.

But this team, Beauvoir knew, was the best.

He was the bloodhound. The one way out in front, leading.

Agent Lacoste was the hunter. Determined, methodical.

And the Chief Inspector? Armand Gamache was their explorer. The one who went where others refused to go, or couldn't go. Or were too afraid to go. Into the wilderness. Gamache found the chasms, the caves, and the beasts that hid in them.

Beauvoir had long thought Gamache did it because he was afraid of nothing. But he'd come to realize the Chief Inspector had many fears. That was his strength. He recognized it in others. Fear more than anything was the thrust behind the knife, the fist. The blow to the head.

And young Agent Morin? What did he bring to the team? Beauvoir had to admit he'd quite warmed to the young man. But that hadn't blinded him to his inexperience. So far Beauvoir the bloodhound could smell fear quite clearly in this case.

But it came from Morin.

Beauvoir left the Chief in the living room speaking to his daughter and walked upstairs. As he climbed he hummed an old

Weavers tune and hoped Gamache didn't notice the stuffed animal clutched in his hand.

When Monsieur Béliveau arrived to open his general store the next morning he had a customer already waiting. Agent Paul Morin stood up from the bench on the veranda and introduced himself to the elderly grocer.

"How can I help you?" Monsieur Béliveau asked as he unlocked the door. It wasn't often people in Three Pines were so pressed for his produce they were actually waiting for him. But then, this young man wasn't a villager.

"Do you have any paraffin?"

Monsieur Béliveau's stern face broke into a smile. "I have everything."

Paul Morin had never been in the store before and now he looked around. The dark wooden shelves were neatly stacked with tins. Sacks of dog food and birdseed leaned against the counter. Above the shelves were old boxes with backgammon games. Checkers, Snakes and Ladders, Monopoly. Paint by numbers and jigsaw puzzles were stacked in neat, orderly rows. Dried goods were displayed along one wall, paint, boots, birdfeeders were down another.

"Over there, by the Mason jars. Are you

planning on doing some pickling?" he chuckled.

"Do you sell much?" Morin asked.

"At this time of year? It's all I can do to keep it in stock."

"And how about this?" He held up a tin. "Sell many of these?"

"A few. But most people go into the Canadian Tire in Cowansville for that sort of thing, or the building supply shops. I just keep some around in case."

"When was the last time you sold some?" the young agent asked as he paid for his goods. He didn't expect an answer really, but he felt he had to ask.

"July."

"Really?" Morin suspected he'd have to work on his "interrogation" face. "How'd you remember that?"

"It's what I do. You get to know the habits of people. And when they buy something unusual, like this," he held up the tin just before placing it in the paper bag, "I notice. Actually, two people bought some. Regular run on the market."

Agent Paul Morin left Monsieur Béliveau's shop with his goods, and a whole lot of unexpected information.

Agent Isabelle Lacoste started her day with

the more straightforward of the interviews. She pressed the button and the elevator swished shut and took her to the top of the Banque Laurentienne tower in Montreal. As she waited she looked out at the harbor in one direction and Mont Royal with its huge cross in the other. Splendid glass buildings clustered all around downtown, reflecting the sun, reflecting the aspirations and achievements of this remarkable French city.

Isabelle Lacoste was always surprised by the amount of pride she felt when looking at downtown Montreal. The architects had managed to make it both impressive and charming. Montrealers never turned their back on the past. The Québécois were like that, for better or worse.

"Je vous en prie," the receptionist smiled and indicated a now-opened door.

"Merci." Agent Lacoste walked into a quite grand office where a slender, athletic-looking middle-aged man was standing at his desk. He came round, extending his hand, and introduced himself as Yves Charpentier.

"I have some of the information you asked for," he said in cultured French. It delighted Lacoste when she could speak her own language to top executives. Her generation could. But she'd heard her parents and grandparents talk, and knew enough recent history to know had it been thirty years earlier she'd probably be speaking to a unilingual Englishman. Her English was perfect, but that wasn't the point.

She accepted the offer of coffee.

"This is rather delicate," said Monsieur Charpentier, when his secretary had left and the door was closed. "I don't want you to think Olivier Brulé was a criminal, and there was never any question of laying charges."

"But?"

"We were very happy with him for the first few years. I'm afraid we tend to be impressed by profit and he delivered on that. He moved up quickly. People liked him, especially his clients. A lot of people in this business can be glib, but Olivier was genuine. Quiet, respectful. It was a relief to deal with him."

"But?" Lacoste repeated, with a slight smile she hoped took the edge off her insistence. Monsieur Charpentier smiled back.

"Some company money went missing. A couple of million." He watched for her response but she simply listened. "A very discreet investigation was launched. In the meantime more money disappeared. Eventually we tracked it down to two people. One of them was Olivier. I didn't believe it, but after a couple of interviews he admitted it."

"Could he have been covering for the other employee?"

"Doubtful. Frankly, the other employee, while bright, wasn't smart enough to do this."

"Surely it doesn't take brains to embezzle. I'd have thought you'd have to be quite stupid."

Monsieur Charpentier laughed. "I agree, but I haven't made myself clear. The money was gone from the company account, but not stolen. Olivier showed us what he'd done. The trail. Seems he'd been following some activity in Malaysia, saw what he thought were some fantastic investment opportunities and took them to his boss, who didn't agree. So Olivier did it on his own, without authorization. It was all there. He'd documented it, intending to put it back, with the profits. And he'd been right. Those three million dollars turned into twenty."

Now Lacoste reacted, not verbally, but her expression made Charpentier nod.

"Exactly. The kid had a nose for money. Where is he now?"

"You fired him?" asked Lacoste, ignoring

the question.

"He quit. We were trying to decide what to do with him. The executives were torn. His boss was apoplectic and wanted him dangled from the top of the building. We explained we don't do that. Anymore."

Lacoste laughed. "Some of you wanted to keep him on?"

"He was just so good at what he did."

"Which was making money. Are you convinced he was going to give it back?"

"Now, you've hit on the problem. Half of us believed him, half didn't. Olivier finally resigned, realizing he'd lost our trust. When you lose that, well . . ."

Well, thought Agent Lacoste. Well, well.

And now Olivier was in Three Pines. But like everyone who moved, he took himself with him.

Well, well.

The three Sûreté officers gathered round the table in the Incident Room.

"So where are we?" asked Beauvoir, standing once again by the sheets of paper tacked to the walls. Instead of answers to the questions he'd written there, two more had been added.

WHERE WAS HE MURDERED?

He shook his head. They seemed to be moving in the wrong direction. Even the few things that seemed possible in this case, like the fire irons being the weapons, turned out to be nothing.

They had nothing.

"We actually know a great deal," said Gamache. "We know the man wasn't killed in the bistro."

"That leaves the rest of the world to eliminate," said Beauvoir.

"We know paraffin and Varathane are involved. And we know that somehow Olivier's involved."

"But we don't even know who the victim was." Beauvoir underlined that question on his sheet in frustration. Gamache let that sit for a moment, then spoke.

"No. But we will. We'll know it all, eventually. It's a puzzle, and eventually the whole picture will be clear. We just need to be patient. And persistent. We need more background information on other possible suspects. The Parras for instance."

"I have that information you asked for," said Agent Morin, squaring his slight shoulders. "Hanna and Roar Parra came here in the mid-80s. Refugees. Applied for status and got it. They're now Canadian citizens."

"All legal?" asked Beauvoir, with regret.

"All legal. One child. Havoc. Twenty-one years old. The family's very involved in the Czech community here. Sponsored a few people."

"Right, right," waved Beauvoir. "Anything interesting?"

Morin looked down at his copious notes. What would the Inspector consider interesting?

"Did you find anything from before they came here?" asked Gamache.

"No, sir. I have calls in to Prague but their record keeping from that time isn't good."

"Okay." Beauvoir snapped the top back on the Magic Marker. "Anything else?"

Agent Morin placed a paper bag on the conference table.

"I dropped by the general store this morning, and bought these."

Out of the bag he brought a brick of paraffin wax. "Monsieur Béliveau says everyone's been buying paraffin, especially at this time of year."

"Not much help," said Beauvoir, taking his seat again.

"No, but this might be." And from the bag he pulled a tin. On it was written *Varathane.* "He sold two tins like this to two different people in July. One to Gabri and the other to Marc Gilbert."

"Oh, really?" Beauvoir uncapped the marker.

Agent Lacoste, like every Montrealer, knew about Habitat, the strange and exotic apartment building created for Expo 67, the great World's Fair. The buildings had been considered avant garde then, and still were. They sat on Île des Soeurs, in the St. Lawrence River, a tribute to creativity and vision. Once seen Habitat was never forgotten. Instead of a square or rectangular building to house people the architect had made each room a separate block, an elongated cube. It looked like a jumble of children's building blocks, piled on top of each other. One interconnected with another, some above, some below, some off to the side, so that daylight shone through the building and the rooms were all bathed in sun. And the views from each room were spectacular, either of the grand river or of the magnificent city.

Lacoste had never been in a Habitat condo, but she was about to. Jacques Brulé, Olivier's father, lived there.

"Come in," he said, unsmiling, as he opened the door. "You said this was about my son?"

Monsieur Brulé was very unlike his son. He had a full head of dark hair and was robust. Behind him she could see the gleaming wood floors, the slate fireplace and the huge windows looking onto the river. The condo was tasteful and expensive.

"I wonder if we could sit down?"

"I wonder if you could come to the point?"

He stood at the door, blocking her way. Not allowing her farther into his home.

"As I mentioned on the phone, I'm with homicide. We're investigating a murder in Three Pines."

The man looked blank.

"Where your son lives." He nodded, once. Lacoste continued. "A body was found in the bistro there."

She'd intentionally not identified the bistro. Olivier's father waited, showing absolutely no recognition, no alarm, no concern at all.

"Olivier's Bistro," she finally said.

"And what do you want from me?"

It was far from unusual in a murder case to find fractured families, but she hadn't expected to find one here.

"I'd like to know about Olivier, his upbringing, his background, his interests."

"You've come to the wrong parent. You'd

need to ask his mother."

"I'm sorry, but I thought she'd died."

"She has."

"You told me on the phone he went to Notre Dame de Sion. Quite a good school, I hear. But it only goes to grade six. How about after that?"

"I think he went to Loyola. Or was it Brébeuf? I can't remember."

"*Pardon?* Were you and his mother separated?"

"No, I'd never divorce." This was the most animated he'd been. Much more upset by the suggestion of divorce than death and certainly than murder. Lacoste waited. And waited. Eventually Jacques Brulé spoke.

"I was away a lot, building a career."

But Agent Lacoste, who hunted killers and still knew what schools her children attended, knew that wasn't much of an explanation, or excuse.

"Was he ever in trouble? Did he get into fights? Any problems?"

"With Olivier? None at all. He was a regular boy, mind you. He'd get into scrapes, but nothing serious."

It was like interviewing a marshmallow, or a salesman about a dining room set. Monsieur Brulé seemed on the verge of calling his son "it" throughout the conversation.

"When was the last time you spoke to him?" She wasn't sure that was exactly on topic, but she wanted to know.

"I don't know."

She should have guessed. As she left he called after her, "Tell him I said hello."

Lacoste stopped at the elevator, pressed the button, and looked back at the large man standing in the door frame, shutting out all the light that she knew was streaming into his apartment.

"Maybe you can tell him yourself. Visit even. Have you met Gabri?"

"Gabri?"

"Gabriel. His partner."

"Gabrielle? He hasn't told me about her."

The elevator came and she stepped in, wondering if Monsieur Brulé would ever find Three Pines. She also wondered about this man who kept so much hidden.

But then, clearly, so did his son.

It was late morning and Olivier was in his bistro, at the front door. Trying to decide if he should unlock it. Let people in. Maybe the crowd would drown out the voice in his head. The Hermit's voice. And that terrible story that bound them together. Even unto death.

The young man appeared at the base of the now barren mountain. Like everyone else in the region he'd heard the stories. Of bad children brought here as a sacrifice to the dreadful Mountain King.

He looked for tiny bones on the dusty soil, but there was nothing. No life. Not even death.

As he was about to leave he heard a small sigh. A breeze had blown up where nothing had stirred before. He felt it on the back of his neck, and he felt his skin grow cool and the hairs stand up. He looked down at the lush, green valley, the thick forests and the thatched roofs, and he wondered how he could have been so stupid as to have come up here. Alone.

"Don't," he heard on the wind. "Don't."

The young man turned round. "Go," he heard.

"Don't go," said the sigh.

FIFTEEN

The three investigators left the Incident Room together, but parted ways at the village green. Beauvoir left the Chief and Agent Morin to interview Olivier and Gabri once again, while he headed to the old Hadley house.

The Inspector was feeling pretty cocky. They'd caught the Gilberts in a lie. Dominique had told him yesterday they never used Varathane. Was quite pleased to tell him how "green" they were. But now there was proof they'd at least bought a *demi-liter* of the stuff.

But the extra spring in his step was because he was curious, anxious even, to see what the Gilberts had done to the old Hadley house.

Gamache tried the door to the bistro and was surprised to find it open. Earlier that morning, over breakfast of *pain doré,* sliced strawberries and bananas, maple syrup and back bacon, Gabri had admitted he didn't know when Olivier might reopen the bistro.

"Maybe never," he said, "then where would we be? I'd have to start taking in paying guests."

"Good thing then that you're a B and B," said Gamache.

"You'd think that would be an advantage, wouldn't you? But I'm handicapped by extreme laziness."

And yet, when Gamache and Agent Morin walked into the bistro there was Gabri behind the bar, polishing it. And from the kitchen came the aroma of fine cooking.

"Olivier," Gabri called, coming around from behind the bar. "Our first customers since the murder are here," he sang out.

"Oh, for God's sake, Gabri," they heard from the kitchen and a pot clanked down. A moment later Olivier punched through the swinging door. "Oh, it's you."

"Just us, I'm afraid. We have a few questions. Do you have a moment?"

Olivier looked as though he was about to say no, but changed his mind and indicated a seat by the hearth. Once again a fire was burning there. And the pokers had been returned.

Gamache looked at Agent Morin. Morin's

eyes widened. Surely the Chief Inspector wasn't expecting him to conduct the interview? But the moments dragged by and no one else said anything. Morin searched his mind. *Don't be too forceful,* though he didn't think that would be a problem. *Get the suspect to drop his guard.* Gabri was smiling at him, wiping his hands on an apron and waiting. *So far so good,* thought Morin. *Seems the idiot agent act is working. Now if only it wasn't an act.*

He smiled back at the two men and racked his brain. Up until now the only questioning he'd done was of speeders along Autoroute 10. It didn't seem necessary to ask Gabri whether he had a driver's license.

"Is it about the murder?" asked Gabri, trying to be helpful.

"Yes, it is," said Morin, finding his voice. "Not really so much about the murder as a small issue that's come up."

"Please," said Olivier, indicating a chair, "have a seat."

"This is really nothing," said Morin, sitting along with everyone else. "Just a loose end. We were wondering why you bought Varathane from Monsieur Béliveau in July."

"Did we?" Olivier looked over at Gabri.

"Well, I did. We needed to redo the bar, remember?"

"Will you stop with that? I like the bar the way it is," said Olivier. "Distressed."

"I'm distressed, it's a disgrace. Remember when we bought it? It was all gleaming?"

They looked over at the long wooden bar with the till and jars of all-sorts, jelly beans and licorice pipes. Behind were liquor bottles on shelves.

"It's about atmosphere," said Olivier. "Everything in here should either be old or look old. Don't say it." He held up his hand to ward off Gabri's response to that, then turned to the officers. "We always disagree about this. When we moved here this place was a hardware store. All the original features had been ripped out or covered over."

"The beams were hidden under that sound insulation stuff for ceilings," said Gabri. "Even the fireplaces were ripped out and turned into storage. We had to find a stone mason to rebuild them."

"Really?" said Gamache, impressed. The fireplace looked original. "But what about the Varathane?"

"Yes, Gabri. What about the Varathane?" Olivier demanded.

"Well, I was going to strip the bar and re-sand and coat it, but . . ."

"But?"

"I was hoping maybe Old Mundin could do it instead. He knows how. He'd love to do it."

"Forget it. No one's going to touch that bar."

"Where's the tin you bought from Monsieur Béliveau?" Agent Morin asked.

"It's in our basement at home."

"Can I see it?"

"If you'd like." Gabri looked at Morin as though he was mad.

Jean Guy Beauvoir couldn't quite believe his eyes. But more than that he couldn't believe something less tangible. He was enjoying this tour of the old Hadley house. So far Marc and Dominique Gilbert had shown him all the magnificent bedrooms, with fireplaces and flat-screen TVs, with spa baths and steam showers. The gleaming mosaic-glass tiles. The espresso maker in each room.

Waiting for the first guests.

And now they were in the spa area, the lower floor, with its muted lighting and soothing colors and calming aromas, even now. Products were being unpacked and waiting to be displayed on shelves not yet built. This area, while clearly as spectacular as the rest of the place, was less finished.

"A month more, we figure," Marc was saying. "We're hoping to have our first guests on the Thanksgiving long weekend. We're just discussing putting an ad in the papers."

"I think it's too soon, but Marc thinks we can get it done. We've hired most of the staff. Four massage therapists, a yoga instructor, a personal trainer and a receptionist. And that's just for the spa."

The two prattled on excitedly. Enid would love it here, Beauvoir thought.

"How much would you charge for a couple?"

"A night at the inn and one healing spa treatment each would start at three hundred and twenty-five dollars," said Marc. "That's for a standard room midweek, but includes breakfast and dinner."

None of the rooms seemed standard to Beauvoir. But neither did the price. How much could creams really cost? Still, for their anniversary, maybe. Olivier and Gabri would kill him, but maybe they didn't need to know. He and Enid could just stay here. At the inn. Not go into Three Pines. Who'd really want to leave?

"That would be each," said Marc, as he turned off the lights and they walked back up the stairs.

"I'm sorry?"

"Three hundred and twenty-five dollars per person. Before tax," said Marc.

Beauvoir was glad he was behind them and no one saw his face. Seemed only the wealthy got healed.

So far, though, he hadn't seen any signs of Varathane. He'd looked at floors, counters, doors, exclaiming over the craftsmanship, to the Gilberts' delight. But he'd also been looking for the telltale gleam. The unnatural shine.

Nothing.

At the front door he debated asking them outright, but he didn't want to show his hand just yet. He wandered around the yard, noticing the now groomed lawns, the newly planted gardens, the trees staked and sturdy.

It all appealed to his sense of order. This was what the country should be. Civilized.

Roar Parra appeared round the corner of the house pushing a wheelbarrow. He stopped when he saw Beauvoir.

"Can I help you?"

Beauvoir introduced himself and looked at the horse manure in the barrow. "More work for you, I suppose." He fell into step with Parra.

"I like horses. Nice to see them back. Old Mrs. Hadley used to keep them. Barns fallen down now and the trails have grown over."

"I hear the new owners have you cutting them again."

Parra grunted. "Big job. Still, my son helps when he can, and I like it. Quiet in the woods."

"Except for the strangers wandering around." Beauvoir saw the wary look on Parra's face.

"What d'you mean?"

"Well, you told Agent Lacoste you'd seen a stranger disappearing into the woods. But it wasn't the dead man. Who do you think it was?"

"I musta been wrong."

"Now, why would you say that? You don't really believe it, do you?"

For once Beauvoir really looked at the man. He was covered in sweat and dirt, and manure. He was stocky and muscled. But none of that made him stupid. In fact, Beauvoir thought this man was very bright. So why had he just lied?

"I'm tired of people looking at me like I just said I'd been kidnapped by aliens. The guy was there one moment, gone the next. I looked for him, but nothing. And no, I haven't seen him since."

"Maybe he's gone."

"Maybe."

They walked in silence. The air was filled with the musky scents of fresh harvested hay and manure.

"I heard the new owners here are very environmentally aware." Beauvoir managed to make it sound a reproach, something slightly silly. Some new-fangled city-folk nonsense. "Bet they won't let you use pesticides or fertilizers."

"I won't use them. Told them so. Had to teach them to compost and even recycle. Not sure they'd ever heard of it. And they still used plastic bags for their groceries, can you believe it?"

Beauvoir, who did too, shook his head. Parra dumped the manure onto a steaming pile and turned back to Beauvoir, chuckling.

"What?" asked Beauvoir.

"They're now greener than green. Nothing wrong with that, of course. Wish everyone was."

"So that means with all those renovations they didn't use any toxic stuff, like Varathane."

Again the stocky man laughed. "Wanted to, but I stopped them. Told them about tung oil."

Beauvoir felt his optimism fade. Leaving Roar Parra to turn over the compost heap he went back to the house and rang the doorbell. It was time to ask them directly. The door was answered by Madame Gilbert, Marc's mother.

"I'd like to speak to your son again, if you don't mind."

"Of course, Inspector. Would you like to come in?"

She was genteel and gracious. Unlike her son. Beneath his cheerful and friendly manner there peeked every now and then a condescension, an awareness that he had a lot and others had less. And somehow that made them less.

"I'll just wait. It's a small point."

After she'd disappeared Beauvoir stood in the entrance admiring the fresh white paint, the polished furniture, the flowers in the hall beyond. The sense of order and calm and welcome. In the old Hadley house. He could hardly believe it. For all Marc Gilbert's flaws, he'd been able to do all this. Light flooded through the window in the foyer and gleamed off the wooden floors.

Gleamed.

Sixteen

By the time Madame Gilbert and Marc returned Inspector Beauvoir had the area rug up and was examining the floor of the small entrance hall.

"What is it?" she asked.

Beauvoir looked up from where he was kneeling and gestured to them to stay where they were. Then he bent back down.

The floor had been Varathaned. It was smooth and hard and clear and glossy. Except for one small smudge. He stood up and brushed off his knees.

"Do you have a cordless phone?"

"I'll get it," said Marc.

"Perhaps your mother wouldn't mind." Beauvoir looked at Carole Gilbert who nodded and left.

"What is it?" Marc asked, leaning in and staring at the floor.

"You know what it is, Monsieur Gilbert. Yesterday your wife said you never used Varathane, that you were trying to be as eco-friendly as possible. But that wasn't true."

Marc laughed. "You're right. We did use Varathane here. But that was before we knew there was something better to use. So we stopped."

Beauvoir stared at Marc Gilbert. He could hear Carole returning with the phone, her heels clicking on the wooden floors.

"I use Varathane," said the Inspector. "I'm not as environmentally aware as you, I guess. I know it takes about a day to set. But it really isn't completely hard for a week or so. This Varathane isn't months old. You didn't start with it, did you? This was just done within the last week."

Gilbert finally looked flustered. "Look, I Varathaned it one night when everyone else was asleep. It was last Friday. That's good wood and it's going to get more wear than any other place in the inn, so I decided to use Varathane. But just there. Nowhere else. I don't think Dominique or Mama even know."

"Don't you use this door all the time? It is the main entrance, after all."

"We park around the side and use the kitchen door. We never use the front. But our guests will."

"Here's the phone." Carole Gilbert had

reappeared. Beauvoir thanked her and called the bistro.

"Is Chief Inspector Gamache there, *s'il vous plaît?*" he asked Olivier.

"Oui?" He heard the Chief's deep voice.

"I've found something. I think you need to come up. And bring a Scene of Crime kit, please."

"Scene of Crime? What's that supposed to mean?" asked Marc, getting irritated now.

But Beauvoir had stopped answering questions.

Within minutes Gamache and Morin arrived and Beauvoir showed them the polished floor. And the little scuff mark marring the perfect shine.

Morin took photographs, then, gloves on and tweezers ready, he took samples.

"I'll get these to the lab in Sherbrooke right away."

Morin left and Gamache and Beauvoir turned back to the Gilberts. Dominique had arrived home with groceries and had joined them.

"What is it?" she asked.

They were standing in the large hall now, away from the entrance, with its yellow police tape and rolled-up carpet.

Gamache was stern, all semblance of the

affable man gone. "Who was the dead man?"

Three stunned people stared back.

"We've told you," said Carole. "We don't know."

Gamache nodded slowly. "You did say that. And you also said you'd never seen anyone fitting his description, but you had. Or at least one of you had. And one of you knows exactly what that lab report will tell us."

They stared at each other now.

"The dead man was here, lying in your entrance, on Varathane not quite hardened. He had it stuck to his sweater. And your floor has part of his sweater stuck to it."

"But this is ridiculous," said Carole, looking from Gamache to Beauvoir. She too could shape-shift, and now the gracious chatelaine became a formidable woman, her eyes angry and hard. "Leave our home immediately."

Gamache bowed slightly and to Beauvoir's amazement he turned to go, catching Beauvoir's eye.

They walked down the dirt road into Three Pines.

"Well done, Jean Guy. Twice we searched that house and twice we missed it."

"So why are we leaving? We should be up

there, interviewing them."

"Perhaps. But time is on our side. One of them knows we'll have proof, probably before the day's out. Let him stew. Believe me, it's no favor I've done them."

And Beauvoir, thinking about it, knew that to be true.

Just before lunch Marc Gilbert arrived at the Incident Room.

"May I speak to you?" he asked Gamache.

"You can speak to all of us. There're no secrets anymore, are there, Monsieur Gilbert?"

Marc bristled but sat in the chair indicated. Beauvoir nodded to Morin to join them with his notebook.

"I've come voluntarily, you can see that," said Marc.

"I can," said Gamache.

Marc Gilbert had walked down to the old railway station, slowly. Going over and over what he'd tell them. It had sounded good when he'd talked to the trees and stones and the ducks flying south. Now he wasn't so sure.

"Look, I know this sounds ridiculous." He started with the one thing he'd promised himself not to say. He tried to concentrate on the Chief Inspector, not that ferret of an assistant, or the idiot boy taking notes. “But I found the body just lying there. I couldn’t sleep so I got up. I was heading to the kitchen to make myself a sandwich when I saw him. Lying there by the front door.”

He stared at Gamache who was watching him with calm, interested brown eyes. Not accusing, not even disbelieving. Just listening.

“It was dark, of course, so I turned on a light and went closer. I thought it might be a drunk who’d staggered up the hill from the bistro, saw our place and just made himself comfortable.”

He was right, it did sound ridiculous. Still the Chief said nothing.

“I was going to call for help but I didn’t want to upset Dominique or my mother, so I crept closer to the guy. Then I saw his head.”

“And you knew he’d been murdered,” said Beauvoir, not believing a word of this.

“That’s it.” Marc turned grateful eyes to the Inspector, until he saw the sneer, then he turned back to Gamache. “I couldn’t believe it.”

“So a murdered man shows up in your house in the middle of the night. Didn’t you lock the door?” asked Beauvoir.

“We do, but we’re getting a lot of deliveries and since we never use that door ourselves I guess we forgot."

"What did you do, Monsieur Gilbert?" Gamache asked, his voice soothing, reasonable.

Marc opened his mouth, shut it and looked down at his hands. He'd promised himself when it got to this part he wouldn't look away, or down. Wouldn't flinch. But now he did all three.

"I thought about it for a while, then I picked the guy up and carried him down into the village. To the bistro."

There it was.

"Why?" Gamache asked.

"I was going to call the police, actually had the phone in my hand," he held out his empty hand to them as though that was proof, "but then I got to thinking. About all the work we'd put into the place. And we're so close, so close. We're going to open in just over a month, you know. And I realized it would be all over the papers. Who'd want to relax in an inn and spa where someone had just been killed?"

Beauvoir hated to say it, but he had to agree. Especially at those prices.

"So you dumped him in the bistro?" he asked. "Why?"

Now Gilbert turned to him. "Because I

didn't want to put him into someone else's home to be found. And I knew Olivier kept the key under a planter by the front door." He could see their skepticism, but plowed ahead anyway. "I took the dead guy down, left him on the floor of the bistro and came home. I moved a rug up from the spa area to cover where the guy had been. I knew no one would miss it downstairs. Too much else going on."

"This is a dangerous time," said Gamache, staring at Marc. "We could charge you with obstruction, with indignities to a body, with hampering the investigation."

"With murder," said Beauvoir.

"We need the full truth. Why did you take the body to the bistro? You could have left him in the woods."

Marc sighed. He didn't think they'd press this point. "I thought about it, but there were lots of kids in Three Pines for the long weekend and I didn't want any of them finding him."

"Noble," said Gamache, with equilibrium. "But that wasn't likely to happen, was it? How often do kids play in the woods around your place?"

"It happens. Would you run that risk?"

"I would call the police."

The Chief let that sentence do its job. It

stripped Marc Gilbert of any pretension to higher ground. And left him exposed before them. For a man who, at best, did something unconscionable. At worst he murdered a man.

"The truth," said Gamache, almost in a whisper.

"I took the body to the bistro so that people would think he'd been killed there. Olivier's treated us like shit since we arrived."

"So you paid him back by putting a body there?" asked Beauvoir. He could think of a few people he'd like to dump bodies on. But never would. This man did. That spoke of his hatred of Olivier. A rare, and surprising, degree of hatred. And his resolve.

Marc Gilbert looked at his hands, looked out the window, moved his gaze around the walls of the old railway station. And finally he rested on the large man across from him.

"That's what I did. I shouldn't have done it, I know." He shook his head in wonderment at his own stupidity. Then he looked up suddenly as the silence grew. His eyes were sharp and bright. "Wait a minute. You don't think I killed the man, do you?"

They said nothing.

Gilbert looked from one to the other. He even looked at the idiot agent with the poised pen.

"Why would I do that? I don't even know who he is."

Still they said nothing.

"Really. I'd never seen him before."

Finally Beauvoir broke the silence. "And yet there he was in your house. Dead. Why would a strange body be in your house?"

"You see?" Gilbert thrust his hand toward Beauvoir. "You see? That's why I didn't call the cops. Because I knew that's what you'd think." He put his head into his hands as though trying to contain his scrambling thoughts. "Dominique's going to kill me. Oh, Jesus. Oh, God." His shoulders sagged and his head hung, heavy from the weight of what he'd done and what was still to come.

Just then the phone rang. Agent Morin reached for it. "Sûreté du Québec."

The voice on the other end spoke hurriedly and was muffled.

"Désolé," said Morin, feeling bad because he knew he was interrupting the interrogation. "I don't understand." Everyone was looking at him. He colored and tried to listen closely, but he still couldn't make out what was being said. Then he heard and the color in his face changed. *"Un instant."*

He covered the mouthpiece. "It's Madame

Gilbert. There's a man on their land. She saw him in the woods at the back." Morin listened again at the phone. "She says he's approaching the house. What should she do?"

All three men stood up.

"Oh my God, he must have seen me leave and knows they're alone," said Marc.

Gamache took the phone. "Madame Gilbert, is the back door locked? Can you get to it now?" He waited. "Good. Where is he now?" He listened, then began striding to the door, Inspector Beauvoir and Marc Gilbert running beside him. "We'll be there in two minutes. Take your mother-in-law and lock yourselves in an upstairs bathroom. That one you took me to. Yes, with the balcony. Lock the doors, close the curtains. Stay there until we come to get you."

Beauvoir had started the car and Gamache slammed the door and handed the phone back to Morin. "Stay here. You too."

"I'm coming," said Gilbert, reaching for the passenger door.

"You'll stay here and talk to your wife. Keep her calm. You're delaying us, monsieur."

Gamache's voice was intense, angry.

Gilbert grabbed the phone from Morin as Beauvoir gunned the car and they took off over the stone bridge, around the common and up du Moulin, to stop short of the old Hadley house. They were there in less than a minute. They got quickly and quietly out of the car.

"Do you have a gun?" Beauvoir whispered as they ran, crouched, to the corner of the house. Gamache shook his head. Really, thought Beauvoir. There were times he just felt like shooting the Chief himself.

"They're dangerous," said Gamache.

"Which is why he," Beauvoir jerked his head toward the back of the property, "probably has one."

Gamache brought his hand up and Beauvoir was silent. The Chief motioned in one direction, then disappeared around the side of the house. Beauvoir ran past the front door and around the far side. Both making for the back, where Dominique had seen the man.

Hugging the wall and staying low Gamache edged along. There was a need for speed. The stranger had been here for at least five minutes, uninterrupted. He could be in the house by now. A lot can happen in a minute, never mind five.

He edged around a bush and got to the far end of the large old house. There he saw movement. A man. Large. In a hat and gloves and field coat. He was close to the house, close to the back door. If he got inside their job would be far more difficult. So many places to hide. So much closer to the women.

As the Chief Inspector watched the man looked around then made for the French doors into the kitchen.

Gamache stepped out from the wall.

"Hold it," he commanded. "Sûreté du Québec."

The man stopped. His back was to Gamache and he couldn't see whether Gamache had a gun. But neither could Gamache see if he had one.

"I want to see your hands," said Gamache.

There was no movement. That wasn't good, Gamache knew. He prepared to dive sideways if the man swung around and shot. But both stood their ground. Then the man turned quickly.

Gamache, trained and experienced, felt time slow down and the world collapse, so that all that existed was the turning man in front of him. His body, his arms. His hands. And as the man's body swung Gamache saw something gripped in his right hand.

Gamache ducked.

Then the man was on the ground, and Beauvoir was on top of him. Gamache raced forward, pinning the man's hand to the ground.

"He had something in his hand, do you see it?" demanded Gamache.

"Got it," said Beauvoir and Gamache hauled the man to his feet.

Both of them looked at him. The hat had fallen off and the iron-gray hair was disheveled. He was tall and lanky.

"What the hell are you doing?" the man demanded.

"You're trespassing," said Beauvoir, handing what the man had held to Gamache, who looked at it. It was a bag. Of granola. And on the front was a stamp.

Manoir Bellechasse.

Gamache looked more closely at the man. He looked familiar. The man glared back, angry, imperious.

"How dare you. Do you know who I am?"

"As a matter of fact," said Gamache, "I do."

After a call to Morin, Marc Gilbert was released and showed up at his home minutes later, out of breath from running. He'd been told his wife and mother were safe but was relieved to see it for himself. He kissed and hugged them both then turned to Gamache.

"Where is he? I want to see him."

Clearly "see" was a euphemism.

"Inspector Beauvoir's with him in the barn."

"Good," said Marc and headed toward the door.

"Marc, wait." His mother ran after him. "Maybe we should just leave this to the police." Carole Gilbert looked frightened still. And with good reason, thought Gamache as he thought of the man in the barn.

"Are you kidding? This man's been spying on us, maybe more."

"What do you mean, 'maybe more'?"

Gilbert hesitated.

"What aren't you telling us?" his wife asked.

He shot a look at Gamache. "I think he might have killed that man and left his body in our house. As a threat. Or maybe he meant to kill one of us. Thought the stranger was one of us. I don't know. But first the body shows up, then this guy tries to break in. Someone's trying to hurt us. And I want to find out why."

"Wait. Wait a minute." Dominique had her hands up to stop her husband. "What are you saying? That body really was here?" She looked toward the vestibule. "In our home?" She looked at Gamache. "It's true?" She looked back at her husband. "Marc?"

He opened and shut his mouth. Then took a deep breath. "He was here. The police were right. I found him when I got up in the middle of the night. I got scared and did something stupid."

"You took the body to the bistro?" Dominique looked as though she'd been slapped by someone she loved, so great was her shock. His mother was staring at him as though he'd peed in the Château Frontenac dining room. He knew that look from when he was a boy and peed in the Château Frontenac dining room.

Gilbert's lightning mind zipped all over the place, searching dark corners for someone else to blame. Surely it wasn't his fault. Surely there were factors his wife didn't appreciate. Surely this couldn't be the act of complete idiocy her face accused him of.

But he knew it was.

Dominique turned to Gamache. "You have my permission to shoot him."

"*Merci, madame,* but I'd need more than that to shoot him. A gun for instance."

"Pity," she said, and looked at her husband. "What were you thinking?"

He told them, as he had the cops, the reasoning that had appeared so obvious, so dazzling, at three in the morning.

"You did it for the business?" said Dominique when he'd finished. "Something's very wrong when dumping bodies is part of our business plan."

"Well, it wasn't exactly planned," he tried to defend himself. "And yes, I made a terrible mistake, but isn't there a bigger question?" He'd finally found something curled up in one of those dark corners. Something that would take the heat off him. "Yes, I moved the body. But who put it here in the first place?"

They'd obviously been so stunned by his admission they hadn't even thought of that. But Gamache had. Because he'd noticed something else about the Varathaned floor. The shine, the mar. And the complete lack of blood. So had Beauvoir. Even if Marc Gilbert had scrubbed and scrubbed he'd never have gotten all the blood up. There'd be traces.

But there was nothing. Just some fluff from the dead man's cardigan.

No, Gilbert might have killed the man, but he didn't do it at his own front door. The man had already been dead when he'd been placed there.

Gilbert stood up. "That's one of the reasons I want to see the man who tried to break in. I think he had something to do with it."

His mother stood up and touched her son's arm. "I really think you should leave this to the police. The man's probably unwell."

She looked to Gamache, but the Chief Inspector had no intention of stopping Marc Gilbert from confronting the intruder. Just the opposite. He wanted to see what happened.

"Come with me," he said to Marc, then turned to the women. "You're welcome to join us, if you like."

"Well, I'm going," said Dominique. "Maybe you should stay here," she said to her mother-in-law.

"I'm coming too."

As they approached the barn the horses looked up from the field. Beauvoir, who hadn't seen them before, almost stopped in his tracks. He hadn't seen that many horses in real life. On film, yes. And these didn't look like any film horses. But then, most men didn't look like Sean Connery and most women didn't look like Julia Roberts. But even allowing for natural selection, these horses seemed, well, odd. One didn't even look like a horse. They began to mosey over, one walking sideways.

Paul Morin, who had seen a lot of horses, said, "Nice cows."

Dominique Gilbert ignored him. But she felt drawn to the horses. As their own lives so suddenly unraveled the horses' calm attracted her. As did, she thought, their suffering. No, not their suffering, but their forbearance. If they could endure a lifetime of abuse and pain she could take whatever blow that barn had in store. As the others moved past her Dominique stopped and walked back to the paddock, where she stood on a bucket and leaned over the fence. The other horses, still shy, held back. But Buttercup, big, awkward, ugly and scarred, came forward. Buttercup's broad, flat forehead pushed softly into Dominique's chest, as though it fit there. As though it was the key. And as she walked away to join the others and confront whatever that shadow was they could see standing in the barn, she smelled horse on her hands. And felt the reassuring pressure between her breasts.

It took a moment or two for their eyes to adjust as they stepped into the dim barn. Then the shadow became solid, firm. Human. Before them appeared a tall, slender, graceful older man.

"You've kept me waiting," the darkness said.

Marc, whose vision wasn't quite as good as he pretended, could only just see the outline of the man. But the words, the voice, told him more than enough. He felt lightheaded and reached out. His mother, standing next to him, took his hand and held him steady.

"Mother?" he whispered.

"It's all right, Marc," the man said.

But Marc knew it wasn't all right. He'd heard the rumors about the old Hadley house, the ghouls that lived there. He'd loved the stories because it meant no one else had wanted the house, and they could get it dirt cheap.

Dirt to dirt. Something filthy had indeed risen. The old Hadley house had produced one more ghost.

"Dad?"

Seventeen

"Dad?"

Marc stared from the shadow, darker than the shade, to his mother. The voice was unmistakable, indelible. The deep, calm voice that carried censure with a slight smile, so that the child, the boy, the man, had never really known where he stood. But he'd suspected.

"Hello, Marc."

The voice held a hint of humor, as though this was in any way close to funny. As though Marc's staggering shock was reason for mirth.

Dr. Vincent Gilbert walked out of the shed and out of the dead, into the light.

"Mom?" Marc turned to the woman beside him.

"I'm sorry, Marc. Come with me." She tugged her only child out into the sun and sat him on a bale of hay. He felt it pricking into his bottom, uncomfortable.

"Can you get him something to drink?" Carole asked her daughter-in-law, but Dominique, hand to her face, seemed almost as stunned as her husband.

"Marc?" Dominique said.

Beauvoir looked at Gamache. This was going to be a long day if all they said was each other's names.

Dominique recovered and walked quickly, breaking into a run, back to the house.

"I'm sorry, have I surprised you?"

"Of course you surprised him, Vincent," snapped Carole. "How did you think he'd feel?"

"I thought he'd be happier than this."

"You never think."

Marc stared at his father, then he turned to his mother. "You told me he was dead."

"I might have exaggerated."

"Dead? You told him I was dead?"

She turned on her husband again. "We agreed that's what I'd say. Are you senile?"

"Me? Me? Do you have any idea what I've done with my life while you played bridge?"

"Yes, you abandoned your family —"

"Enough," said Gamache, and raised a hand. With an effort the two broke off and looked at him. "Let me be absolutely clear about this," said Gamache. "Is he your father?"

Marc finally took a long hard look at the man standing beside his mother. He was older, thinner. It'd been almost twenty years, after all. Since he'd gone missing in India. Or at least that's what his mother had told him. A few years later she said she'd had him declared dead, and did Marc think they should hold a memorial for him?

Marc had given it absolutely no thought. No. He had better things to do than help plan a memorial for a man missing all his life.

And so that had ended that. The Great Man, for that was what Marc's father was, was forgotten. Marc never spoke of him, never thought of him. When he'd met Dominique and she'd asked if his father had been "that" Vincent Gilbert he'd agreed that, yes, he had. But he was dead. Fallen into some dark hole in Calcutta or Bombay or Madras.

"Isn't he a saint?" Dominique had asked.

"That's right. St. Vincent. Who raised the dead and buried the living."

She hadn't asked any more.

"Here." Dominique had returned with a tray of glasses and bottles, not sure what the occasion called for. Never, in all the board meetings she'd chaired, all the client dinners she'd hosted, all the arbitrations she'd attended, had anything quite like this arisen. A father. Risen. But obviously not revered.

She put the drinks tray on a log and brought her hands to her face, softly inhaling the musky scent of horse, and felt herself relax. She dropped her hands, though not her guard. She had an instinct for trouble, and this was it.

"Yes, he's my father," said Marc, then turned to his mother again. "He isn't dead?"

It was, thought Gamache, an interesting question. Not, *He's alive?* but rather, *He isn't dead?* There seemed a difference.

"I'm afraid not."

"I'm standing right here, you know," said Dr. Gilbert. "I can hear."

But he didn't seem put off by any of this, just amused. Gamache knew Dr. Vincent Gilbert would be a formidable opponent. And he hoped this Great Man, for that was what Gamache knew him to be, wasn't also a wicked man.

Carole handed Marc a glass of water and took one herself, sitting on the hay beside him. "Your father and I agreed our marriage was over a long time ago. He went off to India as you know."

"Why did you say he was dead?" Marc asked. If he hadn't Beauvoir would have.

He'd always thought his own family more than a little odd. Never a whisper, never a calm conversation. Everything was charged, kinetic. Voices raised, shouting, yelling. Always in each other's faces, in each other's lives. It was a mess. He'd yearned for calm, for peace, and had found it in Enid. Their lives were relaxed, soothing, never going too far, or getting too close.

He really should call her.

But odd as his family might be, they were nothing compared to this. In fact, that was one of the great comforts of his job. At least his family compared well to people who actually killed each other, rather than just thought about it.

"It seemed easier," Carole said. "I was happier being a widow than a divorcee."

"But what about me?" Marc asked.

"I thought it would be easier for you too. Easier to think your father had died."

"How could you think that?"

"I'm sorry. I was wrong," said his mother. "But you were twenty-five, and never close to your father. I really thought you wouldn't care."

"So you killed him?"

Vincent Gilbert, silent until now, laughed. "Well put."

"Fuck off," said Marc. "I'll get to you in a

minute." He shifted on the prickly hay bale. His father really was a pain in the ass.

"He agreed, no matter how he's rewritten it now. I couldn't have done it without his cooperation. In exchange for his freedom he agreed to be dead."

Marc turned to his father. "Is that right?"

Now Vincent Gilbert looked less regal, less certain. "I wasn't myself. I wasn't well. I'd gone to India to find myself and felt the best way to do that was to shed the old life completely. Become a new man."

"So I just didn't exist anymore?" Marc asked. "What a fucking great family. Where have you been?"

"The Manoir Bellechasse."

"For twenty years? You've been at a luxury inn for twenty years?"

"Oh, well, no. I've been there off and on all summer. I brought you that." He gestured to the package sitting on a shelf in the shed. "It's for you," he said to Dominique. She picked it up.

"Granola," she said. "From the Bellechasse. Thank you."

"Granola?" asked Marc. "You come back from the dead and bring breakfast cereal?"

"I didn't know what you needed," said his father. "I'd heard from your mother that you'd bought a place down here so I came and watched every now and then."

"You're the one Roar Parra spotted in the woods," said Dominique.

"Roar Parra? Roar? Are you kidding? Is he the troll? The dark, stocky man?"

"The nice man helping your son turn this place around, you mean?" asked Carole.

"I say what I mean."

"Will you two please stop it." Dominique glared at Marc's parents. "Behave yourselves."

"Why're you here?" Marc finally asked.

Vincent Gilbert hesitated than sat on a nearby hay bale. "I'd kept in touch with your mother. She told me about your marriage. Your job. You seemed to be happy. But then she said you'd quit your job and moved to the middle of nowhere. I wanted to make sure you were all right. I'm not a complete fool, you know," said Vincent Gilbert, his handsome, aristocratic face somber. "I know what a shock this is. I'm sorry. I should never have let your mother do it."

"Pardon?" said Carole.

"Still, I wouldn't have contacted you, but then that body was found and the police showed up and I thought you might need my help."

"Yes, what about that body?" Marc asked

his father, who just stared. "Well?"

"Well what? Wait a minute." Vincent Gilbert looked from his son to Gamache, watching with interest, then back again. He laughed. "You're kidding? You think I had something to do with it?"

"Did you?" demanded Marc.

"Do you really expect me to answer that?" The genial man in front of them didn't just bristle, he radiated. It happened so quickly even Gamache was taken aback by the transformation. The cultured, urbane, slightly amused man suddenly overflowed with a rage so great it engulfed him then spilled off him and swallowed everyone. Marc had poked the monster, either forgetting he was in there or wanting to see if he still existed. And he had his answer. Marc stood stock still, his only reaction being a slight, telltale widening of his eyes.

And what a tale those eyes told Gamache. In them he saw the infant, the boy, the young man, afraid. Never certain what he would find in his father. Would he be loving and kind and warm today? Or would he sizzle the skin off his son? With a look, a word. Leaving the boy naked and ashamed. Knowing himself to be weak and needy, stupid and selfish. So that the boy grew an outer hull to withstand assault. But while those skins saved tender young souls, Gamache knew, they soon stopped protecting and became the problem. Because while the hard outer shell kept the hurt at bay, it also kept out the light. And inside the frightened little soul became something else entirely, nurtured only in darkness.

Gamache looked at Marc with interest. He'd poked the monster in front of him, and sure enough, it came awake and lashed out. But had he also awakened a monster inside himself? Or had that happened earlier?

Someone had left a body on their doorstep. Was it father? Or son? Or someone else?

"I expect you to answer, monsieur," said Gamache, turning back to Vincent Gilbert and holding his hard eyes.

"Doctor," Gilbert said, his voice cold. "I will not be diminished by you or anyone else." He looked again at his son, then back to the Chief Inspector.

"Désolé," said Gamache and bowed slightly, never taking his deep brown eyes off the angry man. The apology seemed to further enrage Gilbert, who realized one of them was strong enough to withstand insult and one of them wasn't.

"Tell us about the body," Gamache repeated, as though he and Gilbert were having a pleasant conversation. Gilbert looked at him with loathing. Out of the corner of his eye Gamache noticed Marc the horse approaching from the fields. He looked like something a demon might ride, bony, covered with muck and sores. One eye mad, the other eye blind. Attracted, Gamache supposed, by something finally familiar. Rage.

The two men stared at each other. Finally Gilbert snorted derision and waved, dismissing Gamache and his question as trivial. The monster retreated into his cave.

But the horse came closer and closer.

"I know nothing about it. But I thought it looked bad for Marc so I wanted to be here in case he needed me."

"Needed you to do what?" demanded Marc. "Scare everyone half to death? Couldn't you just ring the doorbell or write a letter?"

"I didn't realize you'd be so sensitive." The lash, the tiny wound, the monster smiled and retreated. But Marc had had enough. He reached over the fence and bit Vincent Gilbert on the shoulder. Marc the horse, that is.

"What the hell?" Gilbert yelped and jumped out of the way, his hand on his slimy shoulder.

"Are you going to arrest him?" Marc asked Gamache.

"Are you going to press charges?"

Marc stared at his father, then at the wreck of a creature behind him. Black, wretched, probably half mad. And Marc the man smiled.

"No. Go back to being dead, Dad. Mom was right. It is easier."

He turned and strode back to his home.

"What a family," said Beauvoir. They were strolling into the village. Agent Morin had gone ahead to the Incident Room, and they'd left the Gilberts to devour each other. "Still, there does seem a sort of equilibrium about this case."

"What do you mean?" asked Gamache. Off to their left he noticed Ruth Zardo leaving her home followed by Rosa wearing a sweater. Gamache had written a thank-you note for the dinner the night before and stuck it in her rusty mailbox during his morning stroll. He watched as she collected it, glanced at it, and stuck it into the pocket of her ratty old cardigan.

"Well, one man's dead and another comes alive."

Gamache smiled and wondered if it was a

fair exchange. Ruth spotted them just as Beauvoir spotted her.

"Run," he hissed to the Chief. "I'll cover you."

"Too late, old son. The duck's seen us."

And indeed, while Ruth seemed happy to ignore them, Rosa was waddling forward at an alarming pace.

"She appears to like you," said Ruth to Beauvoir, limping behind the duck. "But then she does have a birdbrain."

"Madame Zardo," Gamache greeted her with a smile while Beauvoir glared.

"I hear that Gilbert fellow put the body in Olivier's Bistro. Why haven't you arrested him?"

"You heard that already?" asked Beauvoir. "Who told you?"

"Who hasn't? It's all over the village. Well? Are you going to arrest Marc Gilbert?"

"For what?" asked Beauvoir.

"Murder for one. Are you nuts?"

"Am I nuts? Who's the one with a duck in a sweater?"

"And what would you have me do? Let her freeze to death when winter comes? What kind of man are you?"

"Me? Speaking of nuts, what was with that note you had Olivier give me? I can't even remember what it said, but it sure didn't make sense."

"You think not?" the wizened old poet snarled.

"Maybe there's something in all of this I missed."

Gamache quoted the lines and Ruth turned cold eyes on him. "That was a private message. Not meant for you."

"What does it mean, madame?"

"You figure it out. And this one too." Her hand dived into her other pocket and came out with another slip of paper, neatly folded. She handed it to Beauvoir and walked toward the bistro.

Beauvoir looked at the perfect white square in his palm, then closed his fingers over it.

The two men watched Ruth and Rosa walk across the village green. At the far end they saw people entering the bistro.

"She's crazy, of course," said Beauvoir as they walked to the Incident Room. "But she did ask a good question. Why didn't we arrest anyone? Between father and son we could've been filling out arrest sheets all afternoon."

"To what end?"

"Justice."

Gamache laughed. "I'd forgotten about that. Good point."

"No, really sir. There was everything from trespassing to murder we could have charged them with."

"We both know the victim wasn't murdered in that foyer."

"But that doesn't mean Marc Gilbert didn't kill him somewhere else."

"And put him in his own house, then picked him up again and took him to the bistro?"

"The father could have done it."

"Why?"

Beauvoir thought about that. He couldn't believe that family wasn't guilty of something. And murder seemed right up their alley. Though it seemed most likely they'd kill each other.

"Maybe he wanted to hurt his son," said Beauvoir. But that didn't seem right. They paused on the stone bridge over the Rivière Bella Bella and the Inspector stared over the side, thinking. The sun bounced off the water and he was momentarily mesmerized by the movement. "Maybe it's just the opposite," he began, feeling his way forward. "Maybe Gilbert wanted back in his son's life but needed an excuse. For anyone else I would think that was ridiculous but he has an ego and it might not have let him just knock and apologize. He needed an excuse.

I could see him killing a vagrant, someone he considered so far beneath him. Someone he could use for his purpose."

"And what would that be?" asked Gamache, also staring into the clear waters beneath them.

Beauvoir turned to the Chief, noticing the reflected light playing on the man's face. "To be reunited with his son. But he'd need to be seen as the savior, not just as some deadbeat dad crawling back to the family."

Gamache turned to him, interested. "Go on."

"So he killed a vagrant, a man no one would miss, put him in his son's vestibule and waited for the fireworks, figuring he could sweep in and take command of the family when it needed help."

"But then Marc moved the body and there was no excuse," said Gamache.

"Until now. The timing is interesting. We discover the body was in the old Hadley house and an hour later dad appears."

Gamache nodded, his eyes narrowing, and once again he looked into the flowing waters of the river. Beauvoir knew the Chief well enough to know he was walking slowly now through the case, picking his way along the slippery rocks, trying to make out a path obscured by deceit and time.

Beauvoir unfolded the paper in his hands.

I just sit where I'm put, composed
of stone, and wishful thinking:

"Who's Vincent Gilbert, sir? You seemed to know him."

"He's a saint."

Beauvoir laughed, but seeing Gamache's serious face he stopped. "What do you mean?"

"There're some people who believe that."

"Seemed like an asshole to me."

"The hardest part of the process. Telling them apart."

"Do you believe he's a saint?" Beauvoir was almost afraid to ask.

Gamache smiled suddenly. "I'll leave you here. What do you say to lunch in the bistro in half an hour?"

Beauvoir looked at his watch. Twelve thirty-five. "Perfect."

He watched the Chief walk slowly back across the bridge and into Three Pines. Then he looked down again, at the rest of what Ruth had written.

that the deity who kills for pleasure
will also heal,

Someone else was watching Gamache.

Inside the bistro Olivier was looking out the window while listening to the sweet sounds of laughter and the till. The place was packed. The whole village, the whole countryside, had emptied into his place, for lunch, for news, for gossip. To hear about the latest dramatic developments.

The old Hadley house had produced another body and spewed it into the bistro. Or at least, its owner had. Any suspicion of Olivier was lifted, the taint gone.

All round him Olivier heard people talking, speculating, about Marc Gilbert. His mental state, his motives. Was he the murderer? But one thing wasn't debated, wasn't in doubt.

Gilbert was finished.

"Who's gonna wanna stay in that place?" he heard someone say. "Parra says they dumped a fortune into the Hadley place, and now this."

There was general agreement. It was a shame. It was inevitable. The new inn and spa was ruined before it even opened. Olivier watched through the window as Gamache walked slowly toward the bistro. Ruth appeared at Olivier's elbow. "Imagine being chased," she said, watching the Chief Inspector's steadfast approach, "by that."

Clara and Gabri squeezed through the

crowd to join them.

"What're you looking at?" Clara asked.

"Nothing," said Olivier.

"Him." Ruth pointed at Gamache, apparently deep in thought, but making progress. Without haste, but also without hesitation.

"He must be pleased," said Gabri. "I hear Marc Gilbert killed that man and put him here, in the bistro. Case closed."

"Then why didn't Gamache arrest him?" Clara asked, sipping her beer.

"Gamache's an idiot," said Ruth.

"I hear Gilbert says he found the body in his house," said Clara. "Already dead."

"Right, like that just happens," said Olivier. His friends decided not to remind Olivier that was exactly what happened to him.

Clara and Gabri fought their way over to the bar to get more drinks.

The waiters were being run ragged. He'd give them a bonus, Olivier decided. Something to make up for two days of lost wages. Faith. Gabri was always telling him he had to have faith, trust that things would work out.

And they had worked out. Beautifully.

Beside him Ruth was tapping her cane rhythmically on the wooden floor. It was more than annoying. It was somehow threatening. So soft, but so unstoppable. Tap, tap,

tap, tap.

"Scotch?"

That would get her to stop. But she stood ramrod straight, her cane lifting and dropping. Tap, tap, tap. Then he realized what she was tapping out.

Chief Inspector Gamache was still approaching, slowly, deliberately. And with each footfall came a beat of Ruth's cane.

"I wonder if the murderer knows just how terrible a thing is pursuing him?" asked Ruth. "I feel almost sorry for him. He must feel trapped."

"Gilbert did it. Gamache'll arrest him soon."

But the thumping of Ruth's cane matched the thudding in Olivier's chest. He watched Gamache approach. Then, miraculously, Gamache passed them by. And Olivier heard the little tinkle of Myrna's bell.

"So, there was some excitement up at the old Hadley house."

Myrna poured Gamache a coffee and joined him by the bookshelves.

"There was. Who told you?"

"Who didn't? Everyone knows. Marc Gilbert was the one who put the body in the bistro. But what people can't figure out is whether he killed the man."

"What're some of the theories?"

"Well." Myrna took a sip of coffee and watched as Gamache moved along the rows of books. "Some think he must have done it, and dumped the body in the bistro to get back at Olivier. Everyone knows they dislike each other. But the rest think if he was really going to do that he'd kill the man in the bistro. Why kill him somewhere else, then move him?"

"You tell me. You're the psychologist." Gamache gave up his search of the shelves and turned to Myrna.

"Former."

"But you can't retire your knowledge."

"Can't crawl back into Paradise?" Taking their coffee to the armchairs in the bay window they sat and sipped while Myrna thought. Finally she spoke.

"Seems unlikely." She didn't look pleased with her answer.

"You want the murderer to be Marc Gilbert?" he asked.

"God help me, I do. Hadn't thought about it before, really, but now that the possibility's here it would be, well, convenient."

"Because he's an outsider?"

"Beyond the pale," said Myrna.

"I'm sorry?"

"Do you know the expression, Chief Inspector?"

"I've heard it, yes. It means someone's done something unacceptable. That's one way of looking at murder, I suppose."

"I didn't mean that. Do you know where the expression comes from?" When Gamache shook his head she smiled. "It's the sort of arcane knowledge a bookstore owner collects. It's from medieval times. A fortress was built with thick stone walls in a circle. We've all seen them, right?"

Gamache had visited many old castles and fortresses, almost all in ruins now, but it was the brightly colored illustrations from the books he'd pored over as a child he remembered most vividly. The towers with vigilant archers, the crenellated stone, the massive wooden doors. The moat and drawbridge. And inside the circle of the walls was a courtyard. When attacked the villagers would race inside, the drawbridge would be raised, the massive doors closed. Everyone inside was safe. They hoped.

Myrna was holding out her palm, and circling it with a finger. "All around are walls, for protection." Then her finger stopped its movement and rested on the soft center of her palm. "This is the pale."

"So if you're beyond the pale . . ."

"You're an outsider," said Myrna. "A

threat." She slowly closed her hand. As a black woman she knew what it meant to be "beyond the pale." She'd been on the outside all her life, until she'd moved here. Now she was on the inside and it was the Gilberts' turn.

But it wasn't as comfortable as she'd always imagined the "inside" to be.

Gamache sipped his coffee and watched her. It was interesting that everyone seemed to know about Marc Gilbert moving the body, but no one seemed to know about the other Gilbert, risen from the dead.

"What were you looking for just now?" she asked.

"A book called *Being.*"

"*Being*? That's the one about Brother Albert and the community he built?" She got up and walked toward the bookshelves. "We've talked about this before."

She changed direction and walked to the far end of her bookstore.

"We did, years ago." Gamache followed her.

"I remember now. I gave Old Mundin and The Wife a copy when Charles was born. The book's out of print, I think. Shame. It's brilliant."

They were in her used-books section.

"Ah, here it is. I have one left. A little dog-eared, but the best books are."

She handed Gamache the slim volume. "Can I leave you here? I told Clara I'd meet her in the bistro for lunch."

Armand Gamache settled into his armchair and in the sunshine through the window he read. About an asshole. And a saint. And a miracle.

Jean Guy Beauvoir arrived at the crowded bistro and after ordering a beer from a harried Havoc he squeezed through the crowd. He caught snippets of conversation about the fair, about how horrible the judging was this year, really, the worst so far. About the weather. But mostly he heard about the body.

Roar Parra and Old Mundin were sitting in a corner with a couple of other men. They looked up and nodded at Beauvoir, but didn't move from their precious seats.

Beauvoir scanned the room for Gamache, but knew he wasn't there. Knew as soon as he'd walked in. After a few minutes he managed to snag a table. A minute later he was joined by the Chief Inspector.

"Hard at work, sir?" Beauvoir brushed cookie crumbs from the Chief's shirt.

"Always. You?" Gamache ordered a ginger beer and turned his full attention to his

Inspector.

"I Googled Vincent Gilbert."

"And?"

"This is what I found out." Beauvoir flipped open his notebook. "Vincent Gilbert. Born in Quebec City in 1934 into a prominent francophone family. Father a member of the National Assembly, mother from the francophone elite. Degree in philosophy from Laval University then medical degree from McGill. Specializing in genetics. Made a name for himself by creating a test for Down's syndrome, in utero. So that they could be found early enough and possibly treated."

Gamache nodded. "But he stopped his research, went to India, and when he returned instead of going back into the lab immediately and completing his research he joined Brother Albert at LaPorte."

The Chief Inspector put a book on the table and slid it toward Beauvoir.

Beauvoir turned it over. There on the back was a scowling, imperious face. Exactly the same look Beauvoir had seen while kneeling on the man's chest just an hour earlier.

"*Being,*" he read, then put it down.

"It's about his time at LaPorte," said Gamache.

"I read about it," said Beauvoir. "For

people with Down's syndrome. Gilbert volunteered there, as medical director, when he got back from India. After that he refused to continue his research. I'd have thought working there he'd want to cure it even more."

Gamache tapped the book. "You should read it."

Beauvoir smirked. "You should tell me about it."

Gamache hesitated, gathering his thoughts. "*Being* isn't really about LaPorte. It's not even about Vincent Gilbert. It's about arrogance, humility and what it means to be human. It's a beautiful book, written by a beautiful man."

"How can you say that about the man we just met? He was a shit."

Gamache laughed. "I don't disagree. Most of the saints were. St. Ignatius had a police record, St. Jerome was a horrible, mean-spirited man, St. Augustine slept around. He once prayed, 'Lord, give me chastity, but not just yet.' "

Beauvoir snorted. "Sounds like lots of people. So why's one a saint and someone else just an asshole?"

"Can't tell you that. It's one of the mysteries."

"Bullshit. You don't even go to church.

What do you really think?"

Gamache leaned forward. "I think to be holy is to be human, and Vincent Gilbert is certainly that."

"You think more than that, though, don't you? I can see it. You admire him."

Gamache picked up the worn copy of *Being.* He looked over and saw Old Mundin drinking a Coke and eating cheese and pâté on a baguette. Gamache remembered Charles Mundin's tiny hand grasping his finger. Full of trust, full of grace.

And he tried to imagine a world without that. Dr. Vincent Gilbert, the Great Man, would almost certainly have earned a Nobel Prize, had he continued his research. But he'd stopped his research and earned the scorn of his colleagues and much of the world instead.

And yet *Being* wasn't an apology. It wasn't even an explanation. It just was. Like Charles Mundin.

"Ready?" Gabri appeared. They ordered and just as Gabri was about to leave Agent Morin showed up.

"Hope you don't mind."

"Not at all," said Gamache. Gabri took his order, and just as he was about to leave again Agent Lacoste arrived. Gabri ran his hand through his hair.

"Jeez," said Beauvoir. "They'll be coming out of the closet next."

"You'd be surprised," said Gabri, and took Lacoste's order. "Is that it? Are you expecting the Musical Ride?"

"C'est tout, patron," Gamache assured him. "*Merci.* I wasn't expecting you," he said to Lacoste when Gabri was out of earshot.

"I didn't expect to come, but I wanted to talk in person. I spoke to both Olivier's boss at the bank and his father."

She lowered her voice and told them what the executive at the Banque Laurentienne had said. When she finished her salad had arrived. Shrimp, mango and cilantro, on baby spinach. But she looked with envy at the steaming plate of Portobello mushrooms, garlic, basil and Parmesan on top of homemade pasta in front of the Chief.

"So it wasn't clear whether Olivier was going to steal the money or give it back," said Beauvoir, eyeing his charcoal steak and biting into his seasoned thin fries.

"The man I talked to believed Olivier was making the money for the bank. Still, he'd probably have been fired, if he hadn't quit."

"Are they sure all the money he made in the Malaysian deal was given to the bank?" Gamache asked.

"They think it was, and so far we can't find any other account for Olivier."

"So we still don't know where the money came from to buy all that property," said Beauvoir. "What did Olivier's father have to say?"

She told them about her visit to Habitat. By the time she finished their plates had been cleared away and dessert menus were placed in front of them.

"Not for me." Lacoste smiled at Havoc Parra. He smiled back, motioned to another waiter to clear and set a nearby table.

"Who'll share a profiterole with me?" asked Beauvoir. They'd have to solve this case soon or he'd need a whole new wardrobe.

"I will," said Lacoste.

The choux pastries filled with ice cream and covered in warm chocolate sauce arrived. Gamache regretted not ordering some himself. He watched, mesmerized, as Beauvoir and Lacoste took spoonfuls of the now melting ice cream mixed with pastry and the warm, dark chocolate.

"So Olivier's father's never been here," said Beauvoir, wiping his face with his napkin. "He has no idea where Olivier lives or what he's doing. He doesn't even know his son's gay?"

"Can't be the only son afraid to tell his father," said Lacoste.

"Secrets," said Beauvoir. "More secrets."

Gamache noticed Morin's face change as he looked out the window. Then the murmur of conversation in the bistro died away. The Chief followed his agent's gaze.

A moose was galumphing down rue du Moulin, into the village. As it got closer Gamache rose. Someone was on its back, clinging to the massive neck.

"You, stay here. Guard the door," he said to Agent Morin. "You come with me," he said to the others. Before anyone else could react Gamache and his team were out the door. By the time anyone else wanted to follow Agent Morin was standing at the door. Short, weedy, but determined. No one was getting by him.

Through the glass panes they watched as the creature bore down, its long legs pumping, awkward and frantic. Gamache walked foward but it didn't slow, its rider no longer in control. The Chief spread his arms to corral him and as it got closer they recognized it as one of the Gilbert animals. A horse, supposedly. Its eyes wild and white, and its hooves spastic and plunging. Beauvoir and Lacoste stood on either side of the Chief, their arms also out.

At his station by the door young Agent Morin couldn't see what was happening outside. All he could see were the faces of the patrons as they watched. He'd been at enough accident scenes to know that at really bad ones people screamed. At the worst, there was silence.

The bistro was silent.

The three officers stood their ground and the horse came straight for them, then veered, shrieking like a creature possessed. The rider fell off onto the grass of the green and Agent Lacoste managed to grab the reins as the horse skidded and twisted. Beside her Gamache also grabbed the reins and between them they fought the horse to a halt.

Inspector Beauvoir was on his knees on the grass, bending over the fallen rider.

"Are you all right? Don't move, just lie still."

But like most people given that advice, the rider sat up and yanked off her riding helmet. It was Dominique Gilbert. Like the horse's, her eyes were wild and wide. Leaving Lacoste to calm the skittish animal Gamache quickly joined Beauvoir, kneeling beside him.

"What's happened?" asked Gamache.

"In the woods," Dominique Gilbert

gasped. “A cabin. I looked inside. There was blood. Lots of it.”

Eighteen

The young man, not much more than a boy, heard the wind. Heard the moan, and heeded it. He stayed. After a day his family, afraid of what they might find, came looking and found him on the side of the terrible mountain. Alive. Alone. They pleaded with him to leave, but, unbelievably, he refused.

"He's been drugged," said his mother.

"He's been cursed," said his sister.

"He's been mesmerized," said his father, backing away.

But they were wrong. He had, in fact, been seduced. By the desolate mountain. And his loneliness. And by the tiny green shoots under his feet.

He'd done this. He'd brought the great mountain alive again. He was needed.

And so the boy stayed, and slowly warmth returned to the mountain. Grass and trees and fragrant flowers returned.

Foxes and rabbits and bees came back. Where the boy walked fresh springs appeared and where he sat ponds were created.

The boy was life for the mountain. And the mountain loved him for it. And the boy loved the mountain for it too.

Over the years the terrible mountain became beautiful and word spread. That something dreadful had become something peaceful. And kind. And safe. Slowly the people returned, including the boy's family.

A village sprang up and the Mountain King, so lonely for so long, protected them all. And every night, while the others rested, the boy, now a young man, walked to the very top of the mountain, and lying down on the soft green moss he listened to the voice deep inside.

Then one night while he lay there the young man heard something unexpected. The Mountain King told him a secret.

Olivier watched the wild horse and the fallen rider along with the rest of the bistro crowd. His skin crawled and he longed to break out, to scream and push his way out of the crowd. And to run away. Run, run, run. Until he dropped.

Because, unlike them, he knew what it meant.

Instead he stood and watched as though he was still one of them. But Olivier knew now he never would be again.

Armand Gamache walked into the bistro and scanned the faces.

"Is Roar Parra still here?"

"I am," said a voice at the back of the bistro. The bodies parted and the stocky man appeared.

"Madame Gilbert's found a cabin deep in the forest. Does that sound familiar?"

Parra, along with everyone else, thought. Then he, and everyone else, shook their heads. "Never knew there was one there."

Gamache thought for a moment then looked outside where Dominique was just catching her breath. "A glass of water, please," he said, and Gabri appeared with one. "Come with me," the Chief Inspector said to Parra.

"How far was the cabin?" he asked Dominique after she'd swallowed the water. "Can we get there on ATVs?"

Dominique shook her head. "No, the forest's too thick."

"How'd you get there?" asked Beauvoir.

"Macaroni took me." She stroked the sweating horse's neck. "After what happened this morning I needed time alone, so I saddled up and decided to try to find the old bridle paths."

"That wasn't very smart," said Parra. "You could've been lost."

"I did get lost. That's how I found the cabin. I was on one of the trails you cut, then it ended, but I could just make out the old path so I kept on. And that's when I saw it."

Dominique's mind was filled with images. Of the dark cabin, of the dark stains on the floor. Of jumping on the horse and trying to find the path back, and holding down the panic. The warnings every Canadian hears since childhood. Never, ever go into the woods alone.

"Can you find your way back there?" asked Gamache.

Could she? She thought about it, then nodded. "Yes."

"Good. Would you like to rest?"

"I'd like to get this over with."

Gamache nodded, then turned to Roar Parra. "Come with us, please."

As they walked up the hill, Dominique leading Macaroni with Parra beside her and the Sûreté officers behind, Beauvoir whispered to the Chief.

"If we can't get in with ATVs, how're we

going to go?"

"Can you say giddyup?"

"I can say whoa." Beauvoir looked as though Gamache had suggested something obscene.

"Well, I suggest you practice."

Within half an hour Roar had saddled Buttercup and Chester. Marc the horse was nowhere to be seen but Marc the husband emerged from the barn, a riding helmet on his head.

"I'm coming with you."

"I'm afraid not, Monsieur Gilbert," said Gamache. "It's simple math. There are three horses. Your wife needs to be on one, and Inspector Beauvoir and I need to be with her."

Beauvoir eyed Chester, who shuffled from one hoof to another as though listening to a Dixieland band in his head. The Inspector had never ridden a horse before and was pretty certain he wasn't about to now.

They set out, Dominique leading, Gamache behind her with a roll of bright pink ribbon to mark their path and Beauvoir bringing up the rear, though Gamache chose not to describe it as that to him. The Chief had ridden many times before. When he'd started dating Reine-Marie they'd go on the bridle paths on Mont Royal. They'd pack a picnic and take the trails through the forest right in the center of Montreal, stopping at a clearing where they could tie up the horses and look over the city, sipping chilled wine and eating sandwiches. The stables on Mont Royal were now closed, but every now and then he and Reine-Marie would head out on a Sunday afternoon and find a place to go trail riding.

Riding Buttercup, however, was a whole other experience. More like being in a small boat on the high seas. He felt slightly nauseous as Buttercup swayed back and forth. Every ten paces or so he reached out and tied another pink ribbon to a tree. Ahead Dominique was way off the ground on Macaroni, and Gamache didn't dare look behind him, but he knew Beauvoir was still there by the constant stream of swear words.

"*Merde. Tabarnac.* Duck."

Branches snapped back so that it felt as though they were being spanked by nature.

Beauvoir, instructed to keep his heels down and his hands steady, quickly lost both stirrups and clung to the gray mane. Regaining the stirrups he straightened up in time to catch another branch in the face. After that it was an inelegant, inglorious exercise in holding on.

"*Tabarnac, Merde.* Duck."

The path narrowed and the forest darkened, and their pace slowed. Gamache was far from convinced they were still on the path, but there was nothing he could do about it now. Agents Lacoste and Morin were gathering the Crime Scene kit and would join them on ATVs as soon as Parra had opened the path. But that would take a while.

How long would it take Lacoste to realize they were lost? An hour? Three? When would night fall? How lost could they get? The forest grew darker and cooler. It felt as though they'd been riding for hours. Gamache checked his watch but couldn't see the dial in the dimness.

Dominique stopped and the following horses crowded together.

"Whoa," said Beauvoir.

Gamache reached out and took the reins, settling the Inspector's horse.

"There it is," Dominique whispered.

Gamache swayed this way and that, trying to see around the trees. Finally he dismounted and tying his horse to a tree walked in front of Dominique. And still he couldn't see it.

"Where?"

“There,” Dominique whispered. “Right beside that patch of sunlight.”

One thick column of sun beamed through the trees. Gamache looked beside it, and there it was. A cabin.

“Stay here,” he said to her, then motioned to Beauvoir who looked around, trying to figure out how to get off. Eventually he leaned over, hugged a tree and hauled himself sideways. Any other horse might have been upset but Chester had seen worse. He seemed quite fond of Beauvoir by the time the Inspector slid off his back. Not once had Beauvoir kicked him, whipped him, or punched him. In Chester’s lifetime, Beauvoir was by far the gentlest and kindest of riders.

The two men stared at the cabin. It was made of logs. A single rocking chair with a large cushion sat on the front porch. There were windows on either side of the closed door, each with boxes in full bloom. A stone chimney rose at the side of the cabin, but no smoke came out.

Behind them they could hear the soft rumble of the horses, and the swish of their tails. They could hear small creatures scurrying for cover. The forest smelt of moss and sweet pine needles and decaying leaves.

They crept forward. Onto the porch. Gamache scanned the floorboards. A few dry leaves but no blood. He nodded to Beauvoir and indicated one of the windows. Beauvoir quietly positioned himself beside it, his back against the wall. Gamache took the other window then gave a small signal. Together they looked in.

They saw a table, chairs, a bed at the far end. No lights, no movement.

"Nothing," said Beauvoir. Gamache nodded agreement. He reached out for the door handle. The door swung open an inch with a slight creak. The Chief put his foot forward and pushed it open all the way. Then looked in.

The cabin was a single room and Gamache saw at once there was no one there. He walked in. But Beauvoir kept his hand on his gun. In case. Beauvoir was a cautious man. Being raised in chaos had made him so.

Dust swirled in the little light that struggled through the window. Beauvoir, by habit, felt for a light switch then realized he wouldn't find one. But he did find some lamps and lit those. What came to light was a bed, a dresser, some bookcases, a couple of chairs and a table.

The room was empty. Except for what the dead man had left behind. His belongings and his blood. There was a large, dark stain on the wooden floor.

There was no doubt they'd finally found the crime scene.

An hour later Roar Parra had followed the Chief's pink ribbons and used his chainsaw to widen the path. The ATVs arrived and with them the Crime Scene investigators. Inspector Beauvoir took photographs while Agents Lacoste, Morin and the others combed the room for evidence.

Roar Parra and Dominique Gilbert had mounted the horses and gone home, leading Chester behind them. Chester looked back, hoping to catch a peek at the funny man who had forgotten to beat him.

As the clip-clop of the hooves receded the quiet closed in.

With his team inside working, and the space cramped, Gamache decided to explore outside the cabin. Finely carved window boxes bloomed with cheery nasturtiums and greenery. He rubbed his fingers first on one plant then the others. They smelled of cilantro, rosemary, basil and tarragon. He walked over to the column of sunlight breaking through the trees beside the cabin.

A fence, made of twisted branches, formed

a large rectangle about twenty feet wide by forty feet long. Vines grew through the fence, and as he got closer Gamache noticed they were heavy with peas. He opened the wooden gate and walked into the garden. Neat rows of vegetables had been planted and tended, intended for a harvest that would not now come. Up and down the long, protected garden the victim had planted tomatoes and potatoes, peas and beans, and broccoli and carrots. Gamache broke off a bean and ate it. A wheelbarrow with some dirt and a shovel stood halfway along the path and at the far end there sat a chair of bent branches, with comfortable and faded cushions. It was inviting and Gamache had an image of the man working in the garden, then resting. Sitting quietly in the chair.

The Chief Inspector looked down and saw the impression of the man in the cushions. He'd sat there. Perhaps for hours. In the column of light.

Alone.

Not many people, Gamache knew, could do that. Even if they wanted to, even if they chose to, most people couldn't take the quiet. They grew fidgety and bored. But not this man, Gamache suspected. He imagined him there, staring at his garden. Thinking.

What did he think about?

"Chief?"

Turning around Gamache saw Beauvoir walking toward him.

"We've done the preliminary search."

"Weapon?"

Beauvoir shook his head. "But we did find Mason jars of preserves and paraffin. Quite a bit of it. I guess we know why." The Inspector looked around the garden, and seemed impressed. Order always impressed him.

Gamache nodded. "Who was he?"

"I don't know."

Now the Chief Inspector turned fully to his second in command. "What do you mean? Did this cabin belong to our victim?"

"We think so. It's almost certainly where he died. But we haven't found any ID. Nothing. No photographs, no birth certificate, passport, driver's license."

"Letters?"

Beauvoir shook his head. "There're clothes in the dressers. Old clothing, worn. But mended and clean. In fact, the whole place is clean and tidy. A lot of books, we're just going through them now. Some have names in them, but all different names. He must have picked them up at used-book stores. We found woodworking tools and sawdust by one of the chairs. And an old violin. Guess we know what he did at night."

Gamache had a vision of the dead man, alive. Healthy even. Coming in after working the garden. Making a simple dinner, sitting by the fire and whittling. Then, as the night drew in, he'd pick up the violin and play. Just for himself.

Who was this man who loved solitude so much?

"The place is pretty primitive," Beauvoir continued. "He had to pump water into the sink in his kitchen. Haven't seen that in years. And there's no toilet or shower."

Gamache and Beauvoir looked around. Down a winding well-worn path they found an out house. The thought almost made Beauvoir gag. The Chief opened the door and looked in. He scanned the tiny one-holer, then closed the door. It too was clean, though spider's webs were beginning to form and soon, Gamache knew, more and more creatures and plants would invade until the outhouse disappeared, eaten by the forest.

"How did he wash?" asked Beauvoir as they walked back to the cabin. They knew he had, and regularly, according to the coroner.

"There's a river," said Gamache, pausing.

Ahead sat the cabin, a tiny perfect gem in the middle of the forest. "You can hear it. Probably the Bella Bella, as it heads into the village."

Sure enough Beauvoir heard what sounded strangely like traffic. It was comforting. There was also a cistern beside the cabin, designed to catch rainfall.

"We've found fingerprints." Beauvoir held the door open for the Chief as they entered the cabin. "We think they belong to two different people."

Gamache's brows rose. The place looked and felt as though only one person lived here. But judging by events, someone else had found the cabin, and the man.

Could this be their break? Could the murderer have left his prints?

The cabin was growing dimmer. Morin found a couple more lamps and some candles. Gamache watched the team at work. There was a grace to it, one perhaps only appreciated by another homicide officer. The fluid motions, stepping aside, leaning in and out and down, bowing and lifting and kneeling. It was almost beautiful.

He stood in the middle of the cabin and took it in. The walls were made of large, round logs. Strangely enough there were curtains at the windows. And in the kitchen a panel of amber glass leaned against the window.

A hand pump at the sink was attached to the wooden kitchen counter, and dishes and glasses were neatly placed on the exposed shelves. Gamache noticed food on the kitchen counter. He walked over and looked, without picking anything up. Bread, butter, cheese. Nibbled, and not by anything human. Some Orange Pekoe tea in an open box. A jar of honey. A quart of milk sat opened. He sniffed. Rancid.

He motioned Beauvoir over.

"What do you think?"

"The man did his shopping."

"How? He sure didn't walk into Monsieur Béliveau's general store, and I'm pretty sure he didn't walk to Saint-Rémy. Someone brought this food to him."

"And killed him? Had a cup of tea then bashed his head in?"

"Maybe, maybe," murmured the Chief Inspector as he looked around. The oil lamps threw light very unlike anything an electric bulb produced. This light was gentle. The edges of the world seemed softer.

A woodstove separated the rustic kitchen and the living area. A small table, covered in cloth, seemed to be his dining table. A riverstone fireplace was on the opposite wall with a wing chair on either side. At the far end of the cabin was a large brass bed and a chest of drawers.

The bed was made, the pillows fluffed and ready. Fabric hung on the walls, presumably to keep out the cold drafts, as you'd find in medieval castles. There were rugs scattered about the floor, a floor marred only, but deeply, by a dark stain of blood.

A bookcase lining an entire wall was filled with old volumes. Approaching it Gamache noticed something protruding from between the logs. He picked at it and looked at what he held.

A dollar bill.

It'd been years, decades, since Canada used dollar bills. Examining the wall more closely he noticed other paper protruding. More dollar bills. Some two-dollar bills. In a couple of cases there were twenties.

Was this the man's banking system? Like an old miser, instead of stuffing his mattress had he stuffed his walls? After a tour of the walls Gamache concluded the money was there to keep the cold out. The cabin was made of wood and Canadian currency. It was insulation.

Next he walked over to the riverstone fireplace, pausing at one of the wing chairs.

The one with the deepest impressions in the seat and back. He touched the worn fabric. Looking down at the table beside the chair he saw the whittling tools Beauvoir had mentioned, and leaning against the table was a fiddle and bow. A book, closed but with a bookmark, sat beside the tools. Had the man been reading when he was interrupted?

He picked it up and smiled.

"I had three chairs in my house," Gamache read quietly. *"One for solitude, two for friendship, three for society."*

"Pardon?" said Lacoste, from where she was crouching, looking under the table.

"Thoreau. From *Walden.*" Gamache held up the book. "He lived in a cabin, you know. Not unlike this, perhaps."

"But he had three chairs," smiled Lacoste. "Our man had only two."

Only two, thought Gamache. But that was enough, and that was significant. *Two for friendship.* Did he have a friend?

"I think he might have been Russian," she said, straightening up.

"Why?"

"There're a few icons on the shelf here, by the books." Lacoste waved behind her, and sure enough, in front of the leather-bound volumes were Russian icons.

The Chief frowned and gazed around the small cabin. After a minute he grew very quiet, very still. Except for his eyes, which darted here and there.

Beauvoir approached. "What is it?"

The Chief didn't answer. The room grew hushed. He moved his eyes around the cabin again, not really believing what he saw. So great was his surprise he closed his eyes then opened them again.

"What is it?" Beauvoir repeated.

"Be very careful with that," he said to Agent Morin, who was holding a glass from the kitchen.

"I will," he said, wondering why the Chief would suddenly say that.

"May I have it, please?"

Morin gave it to Gamache who took it to an oil lamp. There, in the soft light, he saw what he expected to see, but never expected to hold in his own hands. Leaded glass, expertly cut. Hand cut. He couldn't make out the mark on the bottom of the glass, and even if he could it would be meaningless to him. He was no expert. But he was knowledgeable enough to know what he held was priceless.

It was an extremely old, even ancient, piece of glass. Made in a method not seen in hundreds of years. Gamache gently put the glass down and looked into the kitchen. On the open rustic shelves there stood at least ten glasses, all different sizes. All equally ancient. As his team watched, Armand Gamache moved along the shelves, picking up plates and cups and cutlery, then over to the walls to examine the hangings. He looked at the rugs, picking up the corners, and finally, like a man almost afraid of what he'd find, he approached the bookcases.

"What is it, *patron?*" asked Beauvoir, joining him.

"This isn't just any cabin, Jean Guy. This is a museum. Each piece is an antiquity, priceless."

"You're kidding," said Morin, putting down the horse figurine jug.

Who was this man? Gamache wondered. Who chose to live this far from other people? *Three for society.*

This man wanted no part of society. What was he afraid of? Only fear could propel a man so far from company. Was he a survivalist, as they'd theorized? Gamache thought not. The contents of the cabin argued against that. No guns, no weapons at all. No how-to magazines, no publications warning of dire plots.

Instead, this man had brought delicate

leaded crystal with him into the woods.

Gamache scanned the books, not daring to touch them. "Have these been dusted?"

"They have," said Morin. "And I looked inside for a name, but they're no help. Different names written in most of them. Obviously secondhand."

"Obviously," whispered Gamache to himself. He looked at the one still in his hand. Opening it to the bookmark he read, *I went to the woods because I wished to live deliberately, to front only the essential facts of life, and to see if I could not learn what it had to teach, and not, when I came to die, discover that I had not lived.*

Gamache turned to the front page and inhaled softly.

It was a first edition.

Nineteen

"Peter?" Clara knocked lightly on the door to his studio.

He opened it, trying not to look secretive but giving up. Clara knew him too well, and knew he was always secretive about his art.

"How's it going?"

"Not bad," he said, longing to close the door and get back to it. All day he'd been picking up his brush, approaching his painting then lowering the brush again. Surely the painting wasn't finished? It was so embarrassing. What would Clara think? What would his gallery think? The critics? It was unlike anything else he'd ever done. Well, not ever. But certainly since childhood.

He could never let anyone see this.

It was ridiculous.

What it needed, clearly, was more definition, more detail. More depth. The sorts of things his clients and supporters had come to expect. And buy.

He'd picked up and lowered his brush a dozen times that day. This had never happened to him before. He'd watched, mystified, as Clara had been racked by self-doubt, had struggled and had finally produced some marginal piece of work. Her *March of the Happy Ears,* her series inspired by dragonfly wings, and, of course, her masterpiece, the *Warrior Uteruses.*

That's what came of inspiration.

No, Peter was much more clear. More disciplined. He planned each piece, drew and drafted each work, knew months in advance what he'd be working on. He didn't rely on airy-fairy inspiration.

Until now. This time he'd come into the studio with a fireplace log, cut cleanly so that the rings of age were visible. He'd taken his magnifying glass and approached it, with a view to enlarging a tiny part of it beyond recognition. It was, he liked to tell art critics at his many sold-out *vernissages,* an allegory for life. How we blow things out of all proportion, until a simple truth was no longer recognizable.

They ate it up. But this time it hadn't worked. He'd been unable to see the simple truth. Instead, he'd painted this.

When Clara left Peter plopped down in

his chair and stared at the bewildering piece of work on his easel and repeated silently to himself, *I'm brilliant, I'm brilliant.* Then he whispered, so quietly he barely heard it himself, "I'm better than Clara."

Olivier stood on the *terrasse* outside the bistro and looked into the dark forest on the hill. In fact, Three Pines was surrounded by forest, something he'd never noticed, until now.

The cabin had been found. He'd prayed this wouldn't happen, but it had. And for the first time since he'd arrived in Three Pines he felt the dark forest closing in.

"But if all these things," Beauvoir nodded to the interior of the single room, "are priceless why didn't the murderer take them?"

"I've been wondering that myself," said Gamache from the comfort of the large wing chair by the empty fireplace. "What was the murder about, Jean Guy? Why kill this man who seems to have lived a quiet, secret life in the woods for years, maybe decades?"

"And then once he's dead, why take the body but leave the valuables?" Beauvoir sat in the chair opposite the Chief.

"Unless the body was more valuable than

the rest?"

"Then why leave it at the old Hadley house?"

"If the murderer had just left the body here we'd never have found it," reasoned Gamache, perplexed. "Never known there'd been a murder."

"Why kill the man, if not for his treasure?" asked Beauvoir.

"Treasure?"

"What else is it? Priceless stuff in the middle of nowhere? It's buried treasure, only instead of being buried in the ground it's buried in the forest."

But the murderer had left it there. And instead, had taken the only thing he wanted from that cabin. He'd taken a life.

"Did you notice this?" Beauvoir got up and walked to the door. Opening it he pointed upward, with a look of amusement.

There on the lintel above the door was a number.

16

"Now, you can't tell me he got mail," said Beauvoir as Gamache stared, puzzled. The numbers were brass and tarnished green. Almost invisible against the dark wooden door frame. Gamache shook his head then looked at his watch. It was almost six.

After a bit of discussion it was decided

Agent Morin would stay at the cabin overnight, to guard the possessions.

"Come with me," Gamache said to Morin. "I'll drive you in while the others finish the job. You can pack an overnight bag and arrange for a satellite phone."

Morin got on the ATV behind the Chief Inspector and searched for something to grip, settling on the bottom of the seat. Gamache started up the machine. His investigations had taken him into tiny fishing outports and remote settlements. He'd driven snowmobiles, power boats, motorcycles and ATVs. While appreciating their convenience, and necessity, he disliked them all. They shattered the calm with their banshee screams, polluting the wilderness with noise and fumes.

If anything could wake the dead, these could.

As they bounced along Morin realized he was in trouble, and letting go of the seat he flung his small arms around the large man in front of him and held on tight, feeling the Chief's wax coat against his cheek and the strong body underneath. And he smelled sandalwood and rosewater.

The young man sat up, one hand on the Mountain, the other to his face. He couldn't quite believe what the Mountain had told him. Then he started to giggle.

Hearing this, the Mountain was puzzled. It wasn't the shriek of terror he normally heard from creatures who came near him.

As he listened the Mountain King realized this was a happy sound. An infectious sound. He too started to rumble and only stopped when the people in the village grew frightened. And he didn't want that. Never again did he want to scare anything away.

He slept well that night.

The boy, however, did not. He tossed and turned and finally left his cabin to stare up at the peak.

Every night from then on the boy was burdened by the Mountain's secret. He grew weary and weak. His parents and friends commented on this. Even the Mountain noticed.

Finally, one night well before the sun rose the boy nudged his parents awake.

"We need to leave."

"What?" his bleary mother asked.

"Why?" his father and sister asked.

"The Mountain King has told me of a wonderful land where people never die, never grow sick or old. It's a place only he knows about. But he says we need to leave now. Tonight. While it's still dark. And we need to go quickly."

They woke up the rest of the village and well before dawn they'd packed up. The boy was the last to leave. He took a few steps into the forest and kneeling down he touched the surface of the sleeping Mountain King.

"Good-bye," he whispered.

Then he tucked the package under his arm, and disappeared into the night.

Jean Guy Beauvoir stood outside the cabin. It was almost dark and he was starving. They'd finished their work and he was just waiting for Agent Lacoste to pack up.

"I have to pee," she said, joining him on the porch. "Any ideas?"

"There's an outhouse over there." He pointed away from the cabin.

"Great," she said and grabbed a flashlight. "Isn't this how horror movies start?"

"Oh no, we're well into the second reel by now," said Beauvoir with a smirk. He watched Lacoste pick her way along the path to the outhouse.

His stomach growled. At least, he hoped it was his stomach. The sooner they got back to civilization, the better. How could anyone live out here? He didn't envy Morin spending the night.

A bobbing flashlight told him Lacoste was returning.

"Have you been into the outhouse?" she asked.

"Are you kidding? The Chief looked in, but I didn't." Even thinking about it made him gag.

"So you didn't see what was in there."

"Don't tell me, the toilet paper was money too."

"Actually it was. One- and two-dollar bills."

"You're joking."

"I'm not. And I found this." She held a book in her hand. "A first edition. Signed by E. B. White. It's *Charlotte's Web.*"

Beauvoir stared at it. He had no idea what she was talking about.

"It was my favorite book as a child. Charlotte the spider?" she asked. "Wilbur the pig?"

"If they didn't get blown up I didn't read it."

"Who leaves a signed first edition in an outhouse?"

"Who leaves money there?" Beauvoir suddenly felt an urge to go.

"Salut, patron," waved Gabri from the living

room. He was folding tiny outfits and putting them into a box. "So, the cabin in the woods. Was it where the guy lived? The dead man?"

"We think so." Gamache joined him. He watched Gabri fold the small sweaters.

"For Rosa. We're collecting them from everyone to give to Ruth. Is this too big for Rosa?" He held up a boy's blazer. "It's Olivier's. He says he made it himself but I can't believe that, though he's very good with his hands." Gamache ignored that.

"It's a little big. And masculine, for Rosa, don't you think?" he said.

"True." Gabri put it in the reject pile. "In a few years it might fit Ruth though."

"Did no one ever mention a cabin before? Not old Mrs. Hadley?"

Gabri shook his head but continued working. "No one." Then he stopped folding and put his hands in his lap. "I wonder how he survived? Did he walk all the way to Cowansville or Saint-Rémy for food?"

One more thing we don't know, thought Gamache as he went up the stairs. He showered and shaved and called his wife. It was getting dark and in the distance he could hear the shriek from the forest. The ATVs returning. To the village and to the cabin.

In the living room of the B and B, Gabri had been replaced by someone else. Sitting in the comfortable chair by the fire was Vincent Gilbert.

"I've been over to the bistro but people kept bothering me, so I came here to bother you. I've been trying to get out of my son's way. Funny how coming back from the dead isn't as popular as it once was."

"Did you expect him to be happy?"

"You know, I actually did. Amazing, isn't it, our capacity for self-deceit."

Gamache looked at him quizzically.

"All right, my capacity for it," snapped Gilbert. He studied Gamache. Tall, powerfully built. Probably ten pounds overweight, maybe more. Go to fat if he's not careful. Die of a heart attack.

He imagined Gamache suddenly clutching his chest, his eyes widening then closing in pain. Staggering against the wall and gasping. And Dr. Vincent Gilbert, the celebrated physician, folding his arms, doing nothing, as this head of homicide slipped to the ground. It comforted him to know he had that power, of life and death.

Gamache looked at this rigid man. In front of him was the face he'd seen staring, glaring, from the back of that lovely book, *Being*. Arrogant, challenging, confident.

But Gamache had read the book, and knew what lay behind that face.

"Are you staying here?" They'd told Gilbert not to leave the area and the B and B was the only guesthouse.

"Actually, no. I'm the first guest at Marc's inn and spa. Don't think I'll ask for a treatment, though." He had the grace to smile. Like most stern people, he looked very different when he smiled.

Gamache's surprise was obvious.

"I know," agreed Gilbert. "It was actually Dominique who invited me to stay, though she did suggest I might want to be . . ."

"Discreet?"

"Invisible. So I came into town."

Gamache sat in an armchair. "Why did you come looking for your son now?"

It had escaped no one that both Gilbert and the body had shown up at the same time. Again Gamache saw the cabin, with its two comfortable chairs by the fire. Had two older men sat there on a summer's night? Talking, discussing? Arguing? Murdering?

Vincent Gilbert looked down at his hands. Hands that had been inside people. Hands that had held hearts. Repaired hearts. Got them beating again, and restored life. They trembled, unsteady. And he felt a pain in his chest.

Was he having a heart attack?

He looked up and saw this large, steady man watching him. And he thought if he was having a heart attack this man would probably help.

How to explain his time at LaPorte, living with men and women with Down's syndrome? At first he'd thought his job was to simply look after their bodies.

Help others.

That's what the guru had told him to do. Years he'd been at the ashram in India and the guru had finally acknowleged his presence. Almost a decade he'd spent there, in exchange for two words.

Help others.

So that's what he did. He returned to Quebec and joined Brother Albert at LaPorte. To help others. It never, ever occurred to him that they'd help him. After all, how could people that damaged have anything to offer the great healer and philosopher?

It had taken years, but he'd woken up one morning in his cottage in the grounds of LaPorte and something had changed. He'd gone down to breakfast and realized he knew everyone's name. And everyone spoke to him, or smiled. Or came up and showed him something they'd found. A snail, a stick, a blade of grass.

Mundane. Nothing. And yet the whole world had changed, as he slept. He'd gone to bed helping others, and woken up healed himself.

That afternoon, in the shade of a maple tree, he'd started writing *Being.*

"I'd kept an eye on Marc. Watched his successes in Montreal. When they sold their home and bought down here I knew the signs."

"Signs of what?" Gamache asked.

"Burnout. I wanted to help."

Help others.

He was just beginning to appreciate the power of those two simple words. And that help came in different forms.

"By doing what?" asked Gamache.

"By making sure he was all right," Gilbert snapped. "Look, they're all upset up there about the body. Marc did a stupid thing moving it, but I know him. He's not a murderer."

"How do you know?"

Gilbert glared at him. His rage back in full force. But Armand Gamache knew what was behind that rage. What was behind all rage.

Fear.

What was Vincent Gilbert so afraid of?

The answer was easy. He was afraid his son would be arrested for murder. Either because he knew his son had done it, or because he knew he hadn't.

A few minutes later a voice cut across the crowded bistro, aimed at the Chief Inspector, who'd arrived seeking a glass of red wine and quiet to read his book.

"You bugger."

More than one person looked up. Myrna sailed across the room and stood next to Gamache's table, glaring down at him. He got up and bowed slightly, indicating a chair.

Myrna sat so suddenly the chair gave a little crack.

"Wine?"

"Why didn't you tell me why you wanted that?" She gestured toward *Being* in his hand. Gamache grinned.

"Secrets."

"And how long did you think it'd remain a secret?"

"Long enough. I hear he was over here having a drink. Did you meet him?"

"Vincent Gilbert? If you can call ogling and sputtering and fawning 'meeting,' then yes. I met him."

"I'm sure he'll have forgotten it was you."

"Because I'm so easily mistaken for someone else? Is he really Marc's father?"

"He is."

"Do you know, he ignored me when I tried to introduce myself? Looked at me like I was a crumb." The wine and a fresh bowl of cashews had arrived. "Thank God I told him I was Clara Morrow."

"So did I," said Gamache. "He might be growing suspicious."

Myrna laughed and felt her annoyance slip away. "Old Mundin says it was Vincent Gilbert in the forest, spying on his own son. Was it?"

Gamache wondered how much to say, but it was clear this was not much of a secret anymore. He nodded.

"Why spy on his own son?"

"They were estranged."

"First good thing I've heard about Marc Gilbert," said Myrna. "Still, it's ironic. The famous Dr. Gilbert helps so many kids, but is estranged from his own."

Gamache thought again about Annie. Was he doing the same thing to her? Was he listening to the troubles of others, but deaf to his own daughter? He'd spoken to her the night before and reassured himself she was fine. But fine and flourishing were two different things. It had clearly gotten bad when she was willing to listen to Beauvoir.

"Patron," said Olivier, handing Gamache and Myrna menus.

"I'm not staying," said Myrna.

Olivier hovered. "I hear you found out where the dead man lived. He was in the forest all along?"

Lacoste and Beauvoir arrived just then and ordered drinks. With one last gulp of wine, and taking a large handful of cashews, Myrna got up to leave.

"I'm going to be paying a lot more attention to the books you buy," she said.

"Do you happen to have *Walden*?" Gamache asked.

"Don't tell me you found Thoreau back there too? Anyone else hiding in our woods? Jimmy Hoffa perhaps? Amelia Earhart? Come by after dinner and I'll give you my copy of *Walden.*"

She left and Olivier took their orders then brought warm rolls smothered in melting monarda butter and spread with pâté. Beauvoir produced a sheaf of photographs of the cabin from his satchel and handed them to the Chief.

"Printed these out as soon as we got back." Beauvoir took a bite of his warm roll. He was starving. Agent Lacoste took one as well and sipping on her wine she looked out the window. But all she could see was the reflection of the bistro. Villagers eating dinner, some sitting at the bar with beer or whiskey. Some relaxing by the fire. No one paying attention to them. But then she met a pair of eyes in the reflection. More specter than person. She turned just as Olivier disappeared into the kitchen.

A few minutes later a plate of *escargots* bathed in garlic butter was placed in front of Beauvoir with a bowl of minted sweetpea soup for Lacoste and cauliflower and stilton soup with pear and date relish for Gamache.

"Hmm," said Lacoste, taking a spoonful. "Fresh from the garden. Yours too, probably." She nodded to Beauvoir's snails. He smirked but ate them anyway, dipping the crusty bread into the liquid garlic butter.

Gamache was looking at the photographs. Slowly he lowered the pictures. It was like stumbling across King Tut's tomb.

"I have a call in to Superintendent Brunel," he said.

"The head of property crime?" asked Lacoste. "That's a good idea."

Thérèse Brunel was an expert in art theft and a personal friend of Gamache.

"She's going to die when she sees that cabin," Beauvoir laughed. Olivier removed their dishes.

“How could the dead man have collected all these things?” Gamache wondered. “And gotten them in there?”

“And why?” said Beauvoir.

“But there were no personal items,” said Lacoste. “Not a single photograph, no letters, bank books. ID. Nothing.”

“And no obvious murder weapon,” said Beauvoir. “We sent the fireplace poker and a couple of garden tools to be tested, but it doesn’t look promising.”

“But I did find something after you left.” Lacoste put a bag onto the table and opened it. “It was way under the bed, against the wall. I missed it the first time I looked,” she explained. “I fingerprinted it and took samples. They’re on the way to the lab.”

On the table was a carved piece of wood, stained with what looked like blood.

Someone had whittled a word in the wood.

Woe.

Twenty

Agent Morin wandered round inside the cabin, humming. In one hand he gripped the satellite phone, in the other he gripped a piece of firewood. Not for the woodstove, which was lit and throwing good heat. Nor the fireplace, also lit and light. But in case anything came at him out of the shadows, out of the corners.

He'd lit all the oil lamps and all the candles. The dead man seemed to have made them himself, from paraffin left over after the preserves had been sealed.

Morin missed his television. His cell phone. His girlfriend. His mother. He brought the phone up to his mouth again, then lowered it for what felt like the hundredth time.

You can't call the Chief Inspector. What'll you say? You're scared? To be alone in a cabin in the woods? Where a man was murdered?

And he sure couldn't call his mother. She'd find a way to reach the cabin, and the team would find him next morning, with his mother. Ironing his shirts and frying bacon and eggs.

No, he'd rather die.

He wandered around some more, poking things here and there, but being very, very careful. Elmer Fudd–like he crept round, picking up glass and peering at odds and ends. A pane of amber at the kitchen window, an engraved silver candlestick. Eventually he took a sandwich from the brown paper bag and unfolded the waxed paper. Ham and Brie on baguette. Not bad. He took the Coca-Cola, snapped it open, then he sat by the fire. The chair was exceptionally comfortable. As he ate he relaxed and by the time he got to the pastry he was feeling himself again. He reached for the fiddle by his side, but thought better of it. Instead he took a book at random from the shelves and opened it.

It was by an author he'd never heard of. Some guy named Currer Bell. He started to read about a girl named Jane growing up in England. After a while his eyes, strained from reading by the weak light, grew tired. He thought it was probably time for bed. It must be after midnight.

He looked at his watch. Eight thirty.

Reaching over, he hesitated, then picked up the violin. Its wood was deep and seemed warm to the touch. He smoothed his young hand over it, softly, caressing and turning it round in practiced hands. He put it down quickly. He shouldn't be touching it. He went back to the book, but after a minute or so he found the fiddle in his hands again. Knowing he shouldn't, begging himself not to, he reached for the horse-hair bow. Knowing there was no going back now, he stood up.

Agent Morin tucked the violin under his chin and drew the bow across the strings. The sound was deep and rich and seductive. It was more than the young agent could resist. Soon the comforting strains of "Colm Quigley" filled the cabin. Almost to the corners.

Their main courses had arrived. A fruit-stuffed Rock Cornish game hen, done on the spit, for Gamache; melted Brie, fresh tomato and basil fettuccine for Lacoste; and a lamb and prune tagine for Beauvoir. A platter of freshly harvested grilled vegetables was also brought to the table.

Gamache's chicken was tender and tasty, delicately flavored with Pommery-style mustard and vermouth.

"What does that piece of wood mean?" Gamache asked his team as they ate.

"Well, it was just about the only thing in the cabin that wasn't an antique," said Lacoste. "And what with the whittling tools I'm guessing he made it himself."

Gamache nodded. It was his guess as well. "But why woe?"

"Could that be his name?" Beauvoir asked, but without enthusiasm.

"Monsieur Woe?" asked Lacoste. "That might also explain why he lived alone in a cabin."

"Why would someone carve that for himself?" Gamache put down his knife and fork. "And you found nothing else in the cabin that looked as though it had been whittled?"

"Nothing," said Beauvoir. "We found axes and hammers and saws. All well used. I think he must have made that cabin himself. But he sure didn't whittle it."

Woe, thought Gamache, picking up his knife and fork again. Was the Hermit that sad?

"Did you notice our photographs of the stream, sir?" Lacoste asked.

"I did. At least now we know how the dead man kept his groceries cool."

Agent Lacoste, on investigating the stream, had found a bag anchored there. And in it were jars of perishable foods. Dangling in the cold water.

"But he obviously didn't make his own milk and cheese, and no one remembers seeing him in the local shops," said Beauvoir. "So that leaves us with one conclusion."

"Someone was taking him supplies," said Lacoste.

"Everything all right?" asked Olivier.

"Fine, *patron, merci,*" said Gamache with a smile.

"Do you need more mayonnaise or butter?" Olivier smiled back, trying not to look like a maniac. Trying to tell himself that no matter how many condiments or warm buns or glasses of wine he brought it would make no difference. He could never ingratiate himself.

"Non, merci," said Lacoste, and reluctantly Olivier left.

"We at least have prints from the cabin. We should find out something tomorrow," said Beauvoir.

"I think we know why he was killed just now," said Gamache.

"The paths," said Lacoste. "Roar Parra was cutting riding paths for Dominique.

One path was almost at the cabin. Close enough to see it."

"Which Madame Gilbert did," said Beauvoir. "But we have only her word that she didn't find the cabin on an earlier ride."

"Except that they didn't have the horses then," said Lacoste. "They didn't arrive until the day after the murder."

"But she might have walked the old paths," suggested Gamache, "in preparation for the horses, and to tell Roar which ones he should open."

"Roar might have walked them too," said Beauvoir. "Or that son of his. Havoc. Parra said he was going to help him."

The other two thought. Still, there seemed no very good reason why either Parra would walk the old riding paths before clearing them.

"But why kill the recluse?" Lacoste said. "Even supposing one of the Parras or Dominique Gilbert found him. It makes no sense. Killing for the treasure, maybe. But why leave it all there?"

"Maybe it wasn't," said Beauvoir. "We know what we found. But maybe there was more."

It struck Gamache like a ton of bricks. Why hadn't he thought of that? He'd been so overwhelmed by what was there, he'd never even considered what might be missing.

Agent Morin lay in the bed and tried to get comfortable. It felt strange to be sleeping in a bed made by a dead man.

He closed his eyes. Turned over. Turned back. Opening his eyes he stared at the firelight flickering in the hearth. The cabin was less frightening. In fact, it was almost cozy.

He punched the pillow a few times to fluff it up, but something resisted.

Sitting up he took the pillow and scrunched it around. Sure enough, there was something besides feathers inside. He got up and lighting an oil lamp he took the pillow out of its case. A deep pocket had been sewn inside. Carefully, feeling like a vet with a pregnant horse, he slipped his arm in up to the elbow. His hand closed over something hard and knobby.

Withdrawing it he held an object to the oil lamp. It was an intricate carving. Of men and women on a ship. They were all facing the bow. Morin marveled at the workmanship. Whoever carved this had captured the excitement of a journey. The same excitement Morin and his sister had felt as kids when they took family car trips to the

Abitibi or the Gaspé.

He recognized the happy anticipation on the shipboard faces. Looking closer he saw most had bags and sacks and there was a variety of ages, from newborns to the very old and infirm. Some were ecstatic, some expectant, some calm and content.

All were happy. It was a ship full of hope.

The sails of the ship were, incredibly, carved of wood shaved thin. He turned it over. Something was scratched into the bottom. He took it right up to the lamp.

OWSVI

Was it Russian? Agent Lacoste thought the dead man might be Russian because of the icons. Was this his name? Written in that strange alphabet they use?

Then he had an idea. He went back to the bed and tried the other pillow, which had been below the first. There was something hard in there too. Pulling it out he held another sculpture, also of wood, equally detailed. This one showed men and women gathered at a body of water, looking out at it. Some seemed perplexed, but most appeared content to just be there. He found letters scratched on the bottom of that one too.

MRKBVYDDO

Righting it again he placed it on the table

beside the other one. There was a sense of joy, of hope, about these works. He stared at them with more fascination than he ever got from TV.

But the more he looked the more uneasy he became until it felt as though something was watching him. He looked into the kitchen then quickly scanned the room. Turning back to the carvings he was surprised to find the sense of foreboding was coming from them.

He felt a creeping up and down his back and turned quickly into the dark room, instantly regretting not putting on more lamps. A glittering caught his attention. Up high. In the farthest corner of the cabin. Was it eyes?

Picking up his piece of wood he crept closer, crouching down. As he approached the corner the glitter began to form a pattern. It was a spider's web, just catching the soft glow of the lamp. But there was something different about it. As his eyes adjusted the hair on the back of his neck rose.

A word had been woven into the web.

Woe.

Twenty-One

Everyone was already around the table next morning when Morin arrived, more than a little disheveled. They glanced at him, and Agent Lacoste indicated the seat next to her, where, miraculously for the hungry young agent, there waited a bowl of strong *café au lait* along with a plate of scrambled eggs, bacon and thick-cut toast with jams.

Morin wolfed down the food and listened to the reports, and then it was his turn.

He placed the two carvings on the table and moved them slowly to the center. So lively were the sculptures it looked as though the ship had taken sail and was moving on its own. And it looked as though the people on the shore were eagerly awaiting the arrival of the ship.

"What are those?" asked Gamache, rising from his chair and moving round the table for a closer look.

"I found them last night. They were hidden in the pillows on the bed."

The three officers looked stunned.

"You're kidding," said Lacoste. "In the pillows?"

"Sewn into the pillows on the bed. Well hidden, though I'm not sure whether he was hiding them or protecting them."

"Why didn't you call?" demanded Beauvoir, tearing his eyes from the carvings to look at Morin.

"Should I have?" He looked stricken, his eyes bouncing among the officers. "I just thought there was nothing we could do until now anyway."

He'd longed to call; only a mighty effort had stopped him from dialing the B and B and waking them all up. But he didn't want to give in to his fear. But he could see by their faces he'd made a mistake.

All his life he'd been afraid, and all his life it had marred his judgment. He'd hoped that had stopped, but apparently not.

"Next time," the Chief said, looking at him sternly, "call. We're a team, we need to know everything."

"Oui, patron."

"Have these been dusted?" Beauvoir asked.

Morin nodded and held up an envelope. "The prints."

Beauvoir grabbed it out of his hand and took it to his computer to scan in. But even from there his eyes kept going back to the two carvings.

Gamache was leaning over the table, peering at them through his half-moon glasses

"They're remarkable."

The joy of the little wooden travelers was palpable. Gamache knelt down so that he was at eye level with the carvings, and they were sailing toward him. It seemed the carvings were two halves of a whole. A ship full of people sailing toward a shore. And more happy people waiting.

So why did he feel uneasy? Why did he want to warn the ship to go back?

"There's something written on the bottom of each," Morin offered. He picked one up and showed it to the Chief who looked then handed it to Lacoste. Beauvoir picked up the other and saw a series of letters. It was nonsense, but of course it wasn't really. It meant something. They just had to figure it out.

"Is it Russian?" Morin asked.

"No. The Russian alphabet is Cyrillic. This is the Roman alphabet," said Gamache.

"What does it mean?"

The three more seasoned officers looked at each other.

"I have no idea," admitted the Chief Inspector. "Most artisans mark their works, sign them in some way. Perhaps this is how the carver signed his works."

"Then wouldn't the lettering under each carving be the same?" asked Morin.

"That's true. I'm at a loss. Perhaps Superintendent Brunel can tell us. She'll be here this morning."

"I found something else last night," said Morin. "I took a picture of it. It's still in my camera. You can't see it too well, but . . ."

He turned on his digital camera and handed it to Beauvoir, who looked briefly at the image.

"Too small. I can't make it out. I'll throw it up onto the computer."

They continued to discuss the case while Beauvoir sat at his computer, downloading the image.

"Tabarnac," they heard him whisper.

"What is it?" Gamache walked to the desk. Lacoste joined him and they huddled round the flat screen.

There was the web, and the word.

Woe.

"What does it mean?" Beauvoir asked, almost to himself.

Gamache shook his head. How could a spider have woven a word? And why that one? The same word they'd found carved in wood and tossed under the bed.

"Some pig."

They looked at Lacoste.

"Pardon?" Gamache asked.

"When I was in the outhouse yesterday I found a signed first edition."

"About a girl named Jane?" Morin asked, then wished he hadn't. They all looked at him as though he'd said "some pig." "I found a book in the cabin," he explained. "By a guy named Currer Bell."

Lacoste looked blank, Gamache looked perplexed, and Morin didn't even want to think what look Beauvoir was giving him.

"Never mind. Go on."

"It was *Charlotte's Web,* by E. B. White," said Agent Lacoste. "One of my favorites as a child."

"My daughter's too," said Gamache. He remembered reading the book over and over to the little girl who pretended she wasn't afraid of the dark. Afraid of the closed closet, afraid of the creaks and groans of the house. He'd read to her every night until finally she'd fall asleep.

The book that gave her the most comfort, and that he'd practically memorized, was *Charlotte's Web.*

"Some pig," he repeated, and gave a low,

rumbling laugh. "The book's about a lonely piglet destined for the slaughterhouse. A spider named Charlotte befriends him and tries to save his life."

"By weaving things about him into her web," explained Lacoste. "Things like 'Some pig' so the farmer would think Wilbur was special. The book in the outhouse is signed by the author."

Gamache shook his head. Incredible.

"Did it work?" asked Morin. "Was the pig saved?"

Beauvoir looked at him with disdain. And yet, he had to admit, he wanted to know as well.

"He was," said Gamache. Then his brows drew together. Obviously in real life spiders don't weave messages into their webs. So who had put it there? And why? And why "woe?"

He was itching to get back up there.

"There's something else."

All eyes once again turned to the simple-looking agent.

"It's about the outhouse." He turned to Lacoste. "Did you notice anything?"

"You mean besides the signed first edition and the stacks of money as toilet paper?"

"Not inside. Outside."

She thought then shook her head.

"It was probably too dark," said Agent Morin. "I used it last night and didn't notice then either. It wasn't until this morning."

"What, for God's sake?" Beauvoir snapped.

"There's a trail. It runs to the outhouse, but doesn't stop there. It goes on. I followed it this morning and it came out here."

"At the Incident Room?" asked Beauvoir.

"Well, not exactly. It wound through the woods and came out up there."

He waved toward the hill overlooking the village.

"I marked the place it comes out. I think I can find it again."

"That was foolish of you," said Gamache. He looked stern and his voice was without warmth. Morin instantly reddened. "Never, ever wander on your own into the woods, do you understand? You might have been lost."

"But you'd find me, wouldn't you?"

They all knew he would. Gamache had found them once, he'd find them again.

"It was an unnecessary risk. Don't ever let your guard down." Gamache's deep brown eyes were intense. "A mistake could cost you your life. Or the life of someone else. Never relax. There are threats all around, from the woods, and from the killer we're hunting. Neither will forgive a mistake."

"Yes sir."

"Right," said Gamache. He got up and the rest jumped to their feet. "You need to show us where the path comes out."

Down in the village, Olivier stood at the window of the bistro, oblivious of the conversation and laughter of breakfasters behind him. He saw Gamache and the others walk along the ridge of the hill. They paused, then walked back and forth a bit. Even from there he could see Beauvoir gesture angrily at the young agent who always looked so clueless.

It'll be fine, he repeated to himself. *It'll be fine. Just smile.*

Their pacing stopped. They stared at the forest, as he stared at them.

And a wave crashed over Olivier, knocking the breath he'd been holding for so long out of him. Knocking the fixed smile off his face.

It was almost a relief. Almost.

"There it is," said Morin.

He'd tied his belt around a branch. It had seemed a clever solution when he'd done it, but now searching for a thin brown belt on the edge of a forest didn't seem such a brilliant idea.

But they found it.

Gamache looked at the path. Once you knew it was there it was obvious. It almost screamed. Like those optical illusions deliberately placed in paintings that once found you couldn't stop seeing. The tiger in the crockery, the spaceship in the garden.

"I'll join you at the cabin when I can," said Gamache and watched with Lacoste as Beauvoir and Morin headed into the woods. Like nuns, he felt they were safe if not alone. It was, he supposed, a conceit. But it comforted him. He watched until he couldn't see them anymore. But still he waited, until he could no longer hear them. And only then did he descend into Three Pines.

Peter and Clara Morrow were both in their studios when the doorbell rang. It was an odd, almost startling sound. No one they knew ever rang the bell, they just came in and made themselves at home. How often had Clara and Peter found Ruth in their living room? Feet up on the sofa reading a book and drinking a martini at ten in the morning, Rosa nestled on the worn carpet beside her. They thought they'd have to call a priest to get rid of them.

More than once they'd found Gabri in their bath.

"Anybody home?" sang a man's deep voice.

"I'll get it," Clara called.

Peter didn't bother to answer. He was wandering around his studio, circling the work on the easel, getting close, then heading away. His mind might be on his art, as it always was, but his heart was elsewhere. Since word of Marc Gilbert's treachery had hit the village Peter had thought of little else.

He'd genuinely liked Marc. Was drawn to him in a way he felt drawn to cadmium yellow and marian blue, and Clara. He'd felt excited, almost giddy, at the thought of visiting Marc. Having a quiet drink together. Talking. Going for walks.

Marc Gilbert had ruined that as well. Trying to ruin Olivier was one thing, a terrible thing. But secretly Peter couldn't help but feel this was just as bad. Like taking a rusty nail to something lovely. And rare. At least for Peter.

He hated Marc Gilbert now.

Outside his studio he heard Clara talking, and a familiar voice replying.

Armand Gamache.

Peter decided to join them.

"Coffee?" Clara offered the Chief Inspector, after he and Peter had greeted each other.

"*Non, merci.* I can't stay long. I've come on business."

Clara thought that was a funny way of putting it. Murder business.

"You had a busy day yesterday," said Clara, as the three of them sat at the kitchen table. "It's all Three Pines can talk about. It's hard to know what's the most shocking. That Marc Gilbert was the one who moved the body, that Vincent Gilbert's here or that the dead man seemed to be living in the forest all along. Did he really live there?"

"We think so, but we're just waiting for confirmation. We still don't know who he was."

Gamache watched them closely. They seemed as puzzled as he was.

"I can't believe no one knew he was there," said Clara.

"We think someone knew. Someone was taking him food. We found it on the counter."

They looked at each other in amazement.

"One of us? Who?"

One of us, thought Gamache. Three short words, but potent. They more than anything had launched a thousand ships, a thousand attacks. One of us. A circle drawn. And closed. A boundary marked. Those inside and those not.

Families, clubs, gangs, cities, states, countries. A village.

What had Myrna called it? Beyond the pale.

But it went beyond simple belonging. The reason "belonging" was so potent, so attractive, so much a part of the human yearning, was that it also meant safety, and loyalty. If you were "one of us" you were protected.

Was that what he was up against, Gamache wondered. Not just the struggle to find the killer, but the efforts of those on the inside to protect him? Was the drawbridge up? The pale closed? Was Three Pines protecting a killer? One of them?

"Why would someone take him food then kill him?" asked Clara.

"Doesn't make sense," agreed Peter.

"Unless the murderer didn't show up intending to kill," said Gamache. "Maybe something happened to provoke him."

"Okay, but then if he lashed out and murdered the man, wouldn't he have just run away? Why take the body all the way through the woods to the Gilbert place?" asked Clara.

"Why indeed," asked Gamache. "Any theories?"

"Because he wanted the body found," said Peter. "And the Gilberts' is the nearest place."

The murderer wanted the body found. Why? Most murderers went to huge lengths to hide the crime. Why had this man advertised it?

"Either the body found," Peter continued, "or the cabin."

"We think it would have been found in a few days anyway," Gamache said. "Roar Parra was cutting riding paths in that area."

"We're not being much help," said Clara.

Gamache reached into his satchel. "I actually came by to show you something we found in the cabin. I'd like your opinions."

He brought out two towels and placed them carefully on the table. They looked like newborns, protected against a chilly world. He slowly unwrapped them.

Clara leaned in.

"Look at their faces." She looked up directly into Gamache's. "So beautiful."

He nodded. They were. Not just their features. It was their joy, their vitality, that made them beautiful.

"May I?" Peter reached out and Gamache nodded. He picked up one of the sculptures and turned it over.

"There's writing, but I can't make it out. A signature?"

"Of sorts, perhaps," said Gamache. "We haven't figured out what the letters mean."

Peter studied the two works, the ship and the shore. "Did the dead man carve them?"

"We think so."

Though, given what else was in the cabin, it wouldn't have surprised Gamache to discover they were carved by Michelangelo. The difference was every other piece was in plain sight, but the dead man had kept these hidden. Somehow these were different.

As he watched he saw first Clara's then Peter's smile fade until they both looked almost unhappy. Certainly uncomfortable. Clara fidgeted in her chair. It had taken the Morrows less time than it took the Sûreté officers that morning to sense something wrong. Not surprising, thought Gamache. The Morrows were artists and presumably more in tune with their feelings.

The carvings emanated delight, joy. But beneath that was something else. A minor key, a dark note.

"What is it?" Gamache asked.

"There's something wrong with them," said Clara. "Something's off."

"Can you tell me what?"

Peter and Clara continued to stare at the pieces, then looked at each other. Finally they looked at Gamache.

"Sorry," said Peter. "Sometimes with art it can be subliminal, unintended by the artist even. A proportion slightly off. A color that jars."

"I can tell you though," said Clara, "they're great works of art."

"How can you tell?" asked Gamache.

"Because they provoke a strong emotion. All great art does."

Clara considered the carvings again. Was there too much joy? Was that the problem? Was too much beauty and delight and hope disquieting?

She thought not, hoped not. No, it was something else about these works.

"That reminds me," said Peter. "Don't you have a meeting with Denis Fortin in a few minutes?"

"Oh, damn, damn, damn," said Clara, springing up from the table.

"I won't keep you," said Gamache, rewrapping the sculptures.

"I have a thought," she said, joining Gamache at the door. "Monsieur Fortin might know more about sculpture than us. Hard to know less, really. Can I show one to him?"

"It's a good idea," said Gamache. "A very

good idea. Where're you meeting him?"

"In the bistro in five minutes."

Gamache took one of the towels out of his satchel and handed it to Clara.

"This is great," she said as they walked down the path to the road. "I'll just tell him I made it."

"Would you have liked to?"

Clara remembered the blossoming horror in her chest as she'd looked at the carvings.

"No," she said.

Twenty-Two

Gamache arrived back at the Incident Room to find Superintendent Thérèse Brunel sitting at the conference table, surrounded by photographs. As he entered she rose, smiling.

"Chief Inspector." She advanced, her hand out. "Agent Lacoste has made me so comfortable I feel I could move right in."

Thérèse Brunel was of retirement age, though no one in the Sûreté would ever point that out. Not out of fear of the charming woman, or delicacy. But because she, more than any of them, was irreplaceable.

She'd presented herself at the Sûreté recruitment office two decades earlier. The young officer on duty thought it was a joke. Here was a sophisticated woman in her mid-forties, dressed in Chanel and wanting an application form. He'd given it to her, thinking it was almost certainly a threat for a disappointing son or daughter, then watched with increasing bafflement as she'd sat, legs crossed at the ankles, delicate perfume just a hint in the air, and filled it out herself.

Thérèse Brunel had been the chief of acquisitions at the world famous Musée des Beaux Arts in Montreal, but had nursed a secret passion for puzzles. Puzzles of all sorts. And once her children had gone off to college she'd marched right over to the Sûreté and signed up. What greater puzzle could there be than unravelling a crime? Then, taking classes at the police college from Chief Inspector Armand Gamache, she'd discovered another puzzle and passion. The human mind.

She now out-ranked her mentor and was the head of the property crime division. She was in her mid-sixties and as vibrant as ever.

Gamache shook her hand warmly. "Superintendent Brunel."

Thérèse Brunel and her husband Jérôme had often been to the Gamaches' for dinner, and had them back to their own apartment on rue Laurier. But at work they were "Chief Inspector" and "Superintendent."

He then walked over to Agent Lacoste, who'd also stood as he entered.

"Anything yet?"

She shook her head. "But I just called and they expect the lab results any moment."

"Bon. Merci." He nodded to Agent Lacoste and she sat once more at her computer. Then he turned his attention to Superintendent Brunel.

"We're expecting fingerprint results. I really am most grateful to you for coming at such short notice."

"*C'est un plaisir.* Besides, what could be more exciting?" She led him back to the conference table and leaning close she whispered, "*Voyons,* Armand, is this for real?"

She pointed to the photographs scattered across the table.

"It is," he whispered back. "And we might need Jérôme's help as well."

Jérôme Brunel, now retired from medicine, had long shared his wife's love of puzzles, but while hers veered toward the human mind, his settled firmly on ciphers. Codes. From his comfortable and disheveled study in their Montreal home he entertained desperate diplomats and security people. Sometimes cracking cryptic codes and sometimes creating them.

He was a jolly and cultured man.

Gamache took the carving from his bag, unwrapped it and placed it on the table. Once again the blissful passengers were sailing across the conference table.

"Very nice," she said, putting on her glasses and leaning closer. "Very nice indeed," she mumbled to herself as she studied the piece, not touching it. "Beautifully made. Whoever the artist is, he knows wood, feels it. And knows art."

She stepped back now and stared. Gamache waited for it, and sure enough her smile faded and she even leaned a little away from the work.

This was the third time he'd seen it that morning. And he had felt it himself. The carvings seemed to burrow to the core, to the part most deeply hidden and the part most commonly shared. They found people's humanity. Then, like a dentist, they began to drill. Until that joy turned to dread.

After a moment her face cleared, and the professional mask descended. The problem-solver replaced the person. She leaned in to the work, moving herself round the table, not touching the carving. Finally, when she'd seen it from all angles, she picked it up, and like everyone else looked underneath.

"OWSVI," she read. "Upper case. Scratched into the wood, not painted." She sounded like a coroner, dissecting and dictating. "It's a heavy wood, a hardwood.

Cherry?" She looked closer and even sniffed. "No, the grain isn't right. Cedar? No, the color is off, unless . . ." She took it to the window and placed it in a stream of sunshine. Then lowering it she smiled at Gamache over her glasses. "Cedar. Redwood. From British Columbia almost certainly. It's a good choice of wood, you know. Cedar lasts forever, especially the redwood. It's a very hard wood too. And yet it's surprisingly easy to sculpt. The Haida on the west coast used it for centuries to make totem poles."

"And they're still standing."

"They would be, if most of them hadn't been destroyed in the late 1800s by the government or the church. But you can still see a fine one in the Museum of Civilization in Ottawa."

The irony wasn't lost on either of them.

"So what are you doing here?" she said to the sculpture. "And what are you so afraid of?"

"Why do you say that?"

Over at her desk Agent Lacoste looked up, wanting to know the answer too.

"Surely you felt it too, Armand?" She'd used his first name, a sign that while she appeared composed she was in fact nonplussed. "There's something cold about this work. I hesitate to say evil . . ."

Gamache cocked his head in surprise. Evil wasn't a word he heard often outside a sermon. Brutal, malevolent, cruel, yes. Horror, even; investigators sometimes talked about the horror of a crime.

But never evil. But that was what made Thérèse Brunel a brilliant investigator, a solver of puzzles and crimes. And his friend. She placed conviction above convention.

"Evil?" asked Lacoste from her desk.

Superintendent Brunel looked at Agent Lacoste. "I said I hesitated to call it that."

"And do you still hesitate?" Gamache asked.

Brunel picked up the work once again and bringing it up to eye level she peered at the Lilliputian passengers. All dressed for a long voyage, the babies in blankets, the women with bags of bread and cheese, the men strong and resolute. And all looking ahead, looking forward to something wonderful. The detail was exquisite.

She turned it round then jerked it away from her as though it had bitten her nose.

"What is it?" Gamache asked.

"I've found the worm," she said.

Neither Carole Gilbert nor her son had slept well the night before, and she suspected Dominique hadn't either. To Vincent, sleeping in the small room off the landing, she gave no thought. Or rather every time he emerged into her conscious mind she shoved him back into his little room, and tried to lock the door.

It had been a lovely, soft dawn. She'd shuffled around the kitchen making a pot of strong French Pressé coffee, then putting a mohair throw round her shoulders she'd picked up the tray and taken it outside, installing herself on the quiet patio overlooking the garden and the mist-covered fields.

The day before had felt like one endless emergency, with claxtons sounding in her head for hours on end. They'd pulled together as a family and presented a united front through revelation after revelation.

That Marc's father was still alive.

That Vincent was in fact standing right there.

That the murdered man had been found in their new home.

And that Marc had moved him. To the bistro. In a deliberate attempt to hurt, perhaps even ruin, Olivier.

By the time Chief Inspector Gamache had left they all felt punch-drunk. Too dazed and tired to go at each other. Marc had made his feelings clear, then gone into the spa area to plaster and paint and hammer. Vincent had had the sense to leave, only returning late that night. And Dominique had found the cabin while out riding on the least damaged of the horses.

'Twould ring the bells of Heaven, Carole thought to herself as she stared at the horses, now in the misty field. Grazing. Leery of one another. Even from there she could see their sores.

The wildest peal for years,
If Parson lost his senses
And people came to theirs,
And he and they together
knelt down with fervent prayers
For tamed and shabby tigers,
And dancing dogs and bears.

"Mother."

Carole jumped, lost in her own thoughts and now found by her son. She got to her feet. He looked bleary, but showered and shaved. His voice was cold, distant. They stared at each other. Would they blink, sit down, pour coffee and talk about the weather? The headlines? The horses. Would they try to pretend the storm wasn't all around them? And wasn't of their own making.

Who had done worse? Carole by lying to her son for years, and telling him his father was dead? Or Marc by moving a dead man down to the bistro, and in one gesture ruining their chances of being accepted in the small community.

She'd marred his past, and he'd marred their future.

They were quite a team.

"I'm sorry," said Carole, and opened her arms. Silently Marc moved across the stones and almost fell into them. He was tall and she wasn't, but still she held him and rubbed his back and whispered, "There, there."

Then they sat, the tray with croissants and fresh strawberry jam between them. The world looked very green that morning, very fresh, from the tall maples and oaks to the meadow. Marc poured coffee while Carole pulled the mohair throw round her shoulders and watched as the horses ate grass in the field and occasionally looked up into a day they should not have seen, into a world they should have left two days ago. Even now, standing in the mist, they seemed to straddle the two worlds.

"They almost look like horses," said Marc, "if you squint."

Carole looked over at her son and laughed.

He was making a face, trying to morph the creatures in the field into the magnificent hunters he'd been expecting.

"Seriously, is that really a horse?" He pointed to Chester, who in the uncertain light looked like a camel.

Carole was suddenly very sad that they might have to leave this house, cast out by their own actions. The garden had never looked lovelier, and with time it would only get better as it matured and the various plants mingled and grew together.

"I'm worried about that one." Marc pointed to the darkest horse, off on his own. "Thunder."

"Yes, well." Carole shifted uncomfortably to look at him. "About him . . ."

"Suppose he decides to bite one of the guests? Not that I don't appreciate what he did to Dad."

Carole suppressed a smile. Seeing the Great Man with horse slime on his shoulder was the only good thing about a very bad day.

"What do you suggest?" she asked.

"I don't know."

Carole was silent. They both knew what Marc was suggesting. If the horse didn't learn manners in a month, by Thanksgiving he'd have to be put down.

"For wretched, blind pit ponies," she murmured. *"And little hunted hares."*

"Pardon?" asked Marc.

"His, ah, his name isn't really Thunder. It's Marc."

"You're kidding." But neither was laughing. Marc looked out into the field at the malevolent, mad animal keeping his distance from the others. A black blotch in the misty meadow. Like a mistake. A mar.

A Marc.

Later, when Marc headed off with Dominique to get groceries and building supplies, Carole found four carrots in the kitchen and fed them to the horses, who at first were reluctant to trust. But first Buttercup, then Macaroni and finally Chester tiptoed forward and seemed to kiss the carrot off her palm.

But one remained.

She whispered to Marc the horse, cooing at him. Enticing him. Begging him. Standing at the fence she leaned forward, quietly holding the carrot out as far as she could. "Please," she coaxed. "I won't hurt you."

But he didn't believe her.

She went inside, climbed the stairs and knocked on the door to the small bedroom.

Armand Gamache took the carving and

stared into the crowd on deck.

It was easy to miss, but still he could have kicked himself. It now appeared so obvious. The small figure at the very back of the boat, crouching just in front of the matronly woman and her large sack.

He felt his skin crawl as he examined the face of the tiny wooden man, barely more than a boy, looking over his shoulder. Past the matronly woman. Looking behind the boat. While everyone else was gazing ahead, he was slumped down and staring back. To where they'd been.

And the look on his face turned Gamache's blood cold. Cold to the bone, cold to the marrow. Cold to the core.

This was what terror looked like. Felt like. The small, wooden face was a transmitter. And its message was horrific. Gamache suddenly had the nearly uncontrollable urge to look behind himself, see what might be lurking there. Instead, he put his glasses on and leaned closer.

In his arms the young man was gripping a package.

Finally Gamache put it down and removed his glasses. "I see what you mean."

Superintendent Brunel sighed. "Evil. There's evil on that voyage."

Gamache didn't disagree. "Does it look

familiar? Could the carving be on your active list of stolen art?"

"There're thousands of items on that list," she smiled. "Everything from Rembrands to engraved toothpicks."

"And I bet you have them all memorized."

Her smile broadened and she inclined her head slightly. He knew her well.

"But nothing like this. It would stand out."

"Is it art?"

"If you mean is it valuable, I'd say it's almost priceless. If one of these had come on the market while I was at the Musée des Beaux Arts I'd have jumped at it. And paid a small fortune."

"Why?"

She looked at the large, calm man in front of her. So like an academic. She could see him in cap and gown moving like a ship of state through the halls of an ancient university, eager students in his wake. When she'd first met him, lecturing at the police college, he'd been twenty years younger but still a commanding figure. Now he carried that authority with even greater ease. His wavy dark hair was receding, his temples were graying as was his trim mustache, his body was expanding. As was, she knew, his influence.

He'd taught her many things. But one of

the most valuable was not to just see, but to listen. As he listened to her now.

"What makes a work of art unique isn't its color or composition or subject. It has nothing whatsoever to do with what we see. Why are some paintings masterpieces while others, perhaps even more competent, are forgotten? Why are some symphonies still beloved hundreds of years after the composer has died?"

Gamache thought about it. And what came to mind was the painting placed so causally on an easel after dinner a few nights ago. Badly lit, unframed.

And yet he could have stared at it forever.

It was the painting of the elderly woman, her body headed forward, but her face turned back.

He'd known her longing. That same root which spasmed when gazing at the carving had ached when he'd looked at that woman. Clara hadn't simply painted a woman, hadn't even painted a feeling. She'd created a world. In that one image.

That was a masterpiece.

He suddenly felt very badly for Peter, and hoped deeply that Peter was no longer trying to compete with his wife. She was nowhere to be found on that battlefield.

"That," Superintendent Brunel pointed

with one manicured finger at the carving, "will be remembered long after you and I are dead. Long after this charming village has fallen to dust."

"There's another one, you know," he said and had the rare pleasure of seeing Thérèse Brunel surprised. "But before we see it I think we should head to the cabin."

He looked at her feet. She wore elegant new shoes.

"I've brought boots with me, Chief Inspector," she said, her voice holding a faint and mocking reproach as she walked briskly ahead of him to the door. "When have you ever taken me anywhere that didn't have mud?"

"I believe they hosed down Place des Arts before the last symphony we were at," he said, smiling over his shoulder at Agent Lacoste as they left.

"Professionally, I meant. Always mud and always a body."

"Well this time there is certainly mud, but no body."

"Sir." Lacoste jogged over to the car, holding a printout. "I thought you'd like to see this."

She handed the paper to him and pointed. It was a lab report. The results were beginning to come in, and would continue all day.

And this one brought a satisfied smile to his face. He turned to Thérèse Brunel.

"They found woodchips, sawdust really, beside a chair in the cabin. They also found traces on his clothes. The lab says it was red cedar. From British Columbia."

"I guess we found the artist," she said. "Now if we only knew why he carved so much terror."

Why indeed, thought Gamache as he got into the car and drove up du Moulin. ATVs were waiting for them and they headed deep into the Quebec forest. A professor and an elegant expert on art. Neither was as they appeared, and they were heading for a rustic cabin that certainly wasn't.

Gamache stopped the ATV just before the final turn in the path. He and Superintendent Brunel dismounted and walked the rest of the way. It was another world inside the forest, and he wanted to give her a feeling for where the victim had chosen to live. A world of cool shadows and diffuse light, of rich dark scents of things decaying. Of creatures unseen but heard, scampering and scurrying.

Gamache and Brunel were very aware of being the outsiders here.

And yet it wasn't threatening. Not now. In

twelve hours, when the sun was down, it would feel different again.

"I see what you mean." Brunel looked around. "A man could easily live here without being found. It's very peaceful, isn't it?" She sounded almost wistful.

"Could you live here?" Gamache asked.

"I think I could, you know. Does that surprise you?"

Gamache was silent but smiled as he walked.

"I don't need much," she continued. "I used to. When I was younger. Trips to Paris, a nice apartment, good clothes. I have all that now. And I'm happy."

"But not because you have those thing," suggested Gamache.

"As I get older I need less and less. I really believe I could live here. Between us, Armand? Part of me yearns for it. Could you?"

He nodded and saw again the simple little cabin. One room.

"One chair for solitude, two for friendship and three for society," he said.

"*Walden*. And how many chairs would you need?"

Gamache thought about it. "Two. I don't mind society, but I need one other person."

"Reine-Marie," said Thérèse. "And I only

need Jérôme."

"There's a first edition of *Walden* in the cabin, you know."

Thérèse sighed. "*Incroyable.* Who was this man, Armand? Do you have any idea?"

"None."

He stopped and beside him she stopped too, following his gaze.

At first it was difficult to see, but then, slowly, she made out the simple log cabin, as though it had materialized just for them. And was inviting them in.

"Come in," he said.

Carole Gilbert breathed deeply then stepped forward, past the solid ground she'd cultivated for decades. Past the quiet lunches with lifelong friends, past the bridge nights and volunteer shifts, past the enjoyable rainy afternoons reading by the window watching the container ships move slowly up and down the St. Lawrence river. She plunged past this gentle widow's life within the fortified old walls of Quebec City, constructed to keep anything unpleasant out.

"Hello, Carole."

The tall, slender man stood in the center of the room, contained. Looking as though he'd been expecting her. Her heart pounded and her hands and feet had gone cold, numb. She was a little afraid she'd fall down. Not faint, but lose all ability to stand up for herself.

"Vincent." Her voice was firm.

His body had changed. That body she knew better than most. It had shrunk, shriveled. His hair, once thick and shiny, had thinned and grown almost white. His eyes were still brown, but where they'd been sharp and sure now they were questioning.

He held out one hand. It all seemed to happen excruciatingly slowly. The hand had spots on it she didn't recognize. How often had she held that hand in the first years, then later longed for it to hold her? How often had she stared at it as it held *Le Devoir* up to his face? Her only contact with the man she'd given her heart to, those long, sensitive fingers holding the daily news that was clearly more important than her news. Those fingers were evidence of another human in the room, but barely. Barely there and barely human.

And then one day he'd lowered the paper, stared at her with laser eyes and said he wasn't happy.

She'd laughed.

It was, she remembered, a genuinely mirthful laugh. Not that she thought it was a joke. It was because he was serious. This brilliant man actually seemed to think if he wasn't happy it was a catastrophe.

It was, in many ways, perfect. Like so many men his age he was having an affair. She'd known it for years. But this affair he was having was with himself. He adored himself. In fact, that was just about the only thing they had in common. They both loved Vincent Gilbert.

But suddenly that wasn't enough. He needed more. And like the great man he knew he was, the answer could never be found close to home. It would have to be hiding in some mountain cave in India.

Because he was so extraordinary, his salvation would have to be too.

They'd spent the rest of the breakfast plotting his death. It appealed to Vincent's sense of drama, and her sense of relief. It was, ironically, the best talk they'd had in years.

Of course, they'd made one very big mistake. They should have told Marc. But who'd have thought he'd care?

Too late she'd realized — was it less than a day ago? — that Marc had been deeply damaged by his father's death. Not the actual death, mind. That he'd accepted easily. No, it was his father's resurrection that had created the scars, as though Vincent, in rising, had clawed his way past Marc's heart.

And now the man stood, shriveled, dotted and maybe even dotty, with one unwavering hand out. Inviting her in.

"We need to talk," she said.

He lowered his hand and nodded. She waited for him to point out her faults and flaws, all the mistakes she'd made, the immeasurable hurt she'd caused him.

"I'm sorry," said Vincent. She nodded.

"I know you are. So am I." She sat on the side of the bed and patted it. He sat next to her. This close she could see worry lines crawling over his face. It struck her as interesting that worry lines only appeared on the head.

"You look well. Are you?" he asked.

"I wish none of this had happened."

"Including my coming back?" He smiled and took her hand.

But instead of setting her heart racing, it turned her heart to stone. And she realized she didn't trust this man, who'd blown in from the past and was suddenly eating their food and sleeping in their bed.

He was like Pinocchio. A man made of wood, mimicking humanity. Shiny and smiling and fake. And if you cut into him you'd see rings. Circles of deceit and scheming and justification. It's what he was made of.

That hadn't changed.

Lies within lies within lies lay within this man. And now he was here, inside their home. And suddenly their lives were unravelling.

Twenty-Three

"Bon Dieu."

It was all Superintendent Brunel could say, and she said it over and over as she walked round the log cabin. Every now and then she stopped and picked up an object. Her eyes widened as she stared at it, then replaced it. Carefully. And went on to the next.

"*Mais, ce n'est pas possible.* This's from the Amber Room, I'm sure of it." She approached the glowing orange panel leaning against the kitchen window. "*Bon Dieu,* it is," she whispered and all but crossed herself.

The Chief Inspector watched for a while. He knew she hadn't really been prepared for what she'd find. He'd tried to warn her, though he knew the photographs didn't do the place justice. He'd told her about the fine china.

The leaded crystal.

The signed first editions.

The tapestries.

The icons.

"Is that a violin?" She pointed to the instrument by the easy chair, its wood deep and warm.

"It's moved," said Beauvoir, then stared at the young agent. "Did you touch it last night?"

Morin blushed and looked frightened. "A little. I just picked it up. And . . ."

Superintendent Brunel held it now up to the light at the window, tipping it this way and that. "Chief Inspector, can you read this?" She handed him the violin and pointed to a label. As Gamache tried to read she picked up the bow and examined it.

"A Tourte bow," she almost snorted and looked at their blank faces. "Worth a couple of hundred thousand." She batted it in their direction then turned to Gamache. "Does it say Stradivari?"

"I don't think so. It seems to say Anno 1738," he strained, "Carlos something. *Fece in Cremona.*" He took off his glasses and looked at Thérèse Brunel. "Mean anything to you?"

She was smiling and still holding the bow. "Carlos Bergonzi. He was a luthier. Stradivari's best pupil."

"So it's not the finest violin?" asked Beauvoir, who'd at least heard of Stradivarius violins, but never this other guy.

"Perhaps not quite as fine as his master, but a Bergonzi is still worth a million."

"A Bergonzi?" said Morin.

"Yes. Do you know about them?"

"Not really, but we found some original sheet music for violin with a note attached. It mentions a Bergonzi." Morin went over to the bookcase and rummaged for a moment, emerging with a sheaf of music and a card. He handed it to the Superintendent who glanced at it and passed it on to Gamache.

"Any idea what language it's in?" she asked. "Not Russian, not Greek."

Gamache read. It seemed addressed to a B, it mentioned a Bergonzi and was signed C. The rest was unintelligible, though it seemed to include terms of endearment. It was dated December 8, 1950.

"Could B be the victim?" Brunel asked.

Gamache shook his head. "The dates don't match. He wouldn't have been born yet. And I presume B couldn't be Bergonzi?"

"No, too late. He was long dead. So who were B and C and why did our man collect the music and the card?" Brunel asked herself. She glanced at the sheet music and smiled. Handing the sheaf to Gamache she pointed to the top line. The music was composed by a BM.

"So," said Gamache, lowering the pages. "This original score was composed by a BM. The note attached was addressed to a B and mentions a Bergonzi violin. Seems logical to assume B played the violin and composed and someone, C, gave him this gift." He nodded to the violin. "So who was BM and why did our victim have his music and his violin?"

"Is it any good?" Brunel asked Morin. Gamache handed him the score. The young agent, mouth slightly open, thick lips glistening, was looking particularly stupid. He stared at the music and hummed. Then looked up.

"Seems okay."

"Play it." Gamache handed him the million-dollar violin. Morin took it, reluctantly. "You played it last night, didn't you?" the Chief asked.

"You what?" demanded Beauvoir.

Morin turned to him. "It'd been dusted and photographed and I didn't think it'd matter."

"Did you also juggle the china or have batting practice with the glasses? You don't mess around with evidence."

"Sorry."

"Play the music, please," said Gamache. Superintendent Brunel gave him the near-priceless bow.

"I didn't play this last night. I only really know fiddle music."

"Just do your best," said the Chief.

Agent Morin hesitated then placed the violin under his chin and curving his body he brought the bow up. And down. Across the gut strings.

The slow, full notes of a tune left the instrument. So rich was the sound the notes were almost visible as they filled the air. The tune they heard was slower than intended by BM, Gamache suspected, since Agent Morin was stuggling to follow the music. But it was still beautiful, complex and accomplished. Obviously BM knew what he was doing. Gamache closed his eyes and imagined the dead man there, alone. On a winter's night. Snow piling up outside. A simple vegetable soup on the stove, the fireplace lit and throwing heat. And the small cabin filled with music. This music.

Why this music and no other?

"Do you know it?" Gamache looked at Superintendent Brunel, who was listening with her eyes closed. She shook her head and opened her eyes.

"*Non,* but it's lovely. I wonder who BM was."

Morin lowered the violin, relieved to stop.

"Was the violin in tune when you played yesterday or did you have to adjust it?" she asked.

"It was in tune. He must have played it recently." He went to put it down but the Chief Inspector stopped him.

"What did you play last night, if not that?" He pointed to the sheet music.

"Just some fiddle music my father taught me. Nothing much. I know I shouldn't have —"

Gamache put up his hand to silence the apologies. "It's all right. Just play for us now what you played last night."

When Morin looked surprised Gamache explained, "What you just did wasn't really a fair test for the violin, was it? You were picking out the tune. I'd like to hear the violin as the victim heard it. As it was meant to be played."

"But, sir, I only play fiddle, not violin."

"What's the difference?" Gamache asked.

Morin hesitated. "No real difference, at least not in the instrument. But the sound of course is different. My dad always said a violin sings and a fiddle dances."

"Dance, then."

Morin, blushing in the most unbecoming way, put the fiddle, né violin, up to his chin once again. Paused. Then drew the bow across the strings.

What came out surprised them all. A Celtic lament left the bow, left the violin, left the agent. It filled the cabin, filled the rafters. Almost into the corners. The simple tune swirled around them like colors and delicious meals and conversation. And it lodged in their chests. Not their ears, not their heads. But their hearts. Slow, dignified, but buoyant. It was played with confidence. With poise.

Agent Morin had changed. His loose-limbed awkward body contorted perfectly for the violin, as though created and designed for this purpose. To play. To produce this music. His eyes were closed and he looked the way Gamache felt. Filled with joy. Rapture even. Such was the power of this music. This instrument.

And watching his agent the Chief Inspector suddenly realized what Morin reminded him of.

A musical note. The large head and the thin body. He was a walking note, awaiting an instrument. And this was it. The violin might be a masterpiece, but Agent Paul

Morin certainly was.

After a minute he stopped and the music faded, absorbed by the logs, the books, the tapestries. The people.

"That was beautiful," said Superintendent Brunel.

He handed the violin to her. "It's called 'Colm Quigley.' My favorite."

As soon as the violin left his hand he went back to being the gangly, awkward young man. Though never again totally that for the people who had heard him play.

"Merci," said Gamache.

Superintendent Brunel put the violin down.

"Let me know what you find out about these." Gamache handed Morin the note and sheet music.

"Yes sir."

Thérèse Brunel returned to the rest of the room, walking up to the treasures, mumbling *"Bon Dieu"* every now and then. Each seemed more astonishing than the last.

But nothing was more surprising than what awaited Chief Inspector Gamache. In the farthest corner of the cabin, near the rafters. If the search team the day before had seen it they'd have dismissed it as the only normal thing in the whole place. What could be more natural than a spider's web in a cabin?

But it turned out to be the least normal, the least natural.

"Bon Dieu," they heard from the Superintendent as she held up a plate with frogs on it. "From the collection of Catherine the Great. Lost hundreds of years ago. Unbelievable."

But if she wanted "unbelievable," thought Gamache, she needed to look over here. Beauvoir had turned on his flashlight.

Until he'd seen it Gamache hadn't quite believed it. But there it was, twinkling almost merrily in the harsh artificial light, as though mocking them.

Woe, said the web.

"Woe," whispered Gamache.

Superintendent Brunel found Armand Gamache an hour later in the bent branch chair in the corner of the vegetable garden.

"I've finished looking round."

Gamache stood and she sat wearily in the chair, exhaling deeply.

"I've never seen anything like it, Armand. We've broken art theft rings and found the most amazing collections. Remember the Charbonneau case last year in Lévis?"

"The van Eycks."

She nodded, then shook her head as

though trying to clear it. "Fantastic finds. All sorts of original sketches and even an oil no one knew existed."

"Wasn't there a Titian too?"

"Oui."

"And you're saying this place is even more amazing?"

"I don't mean to lecture, but I'm not sure you or your people appreciate the scope of the find."

"Lecture away," Gamache reassured her. "That's why I invited you."

He smiled and not for the first time she thought the rarest thing she'd ever found was Chief Inspector Gamache.

"You might want to grab a seat," she said. He found a sawn log and turned it on its end and sat on it. "The Charbonneau case was spectacular," Superintendent Brunel went on. "But in many ways mundane. Most art theft rings, and most black market collectors, have one maybe two specialties. Because the market's so specialized and there's so much money involved, the thieves become experts, but only in one or two tiny areas. Italian sculpture from the 1600s. Dutch masters. Greek antiquities. But never all of those fields. They specialize. How else would they know they weren't stealing forgeries, or replicas? That's why with Charbonneau we found some astonishing things, but all in the same 'family.' *Vous comprenez?*"

"*Oui.* They were all Renaissance paintings, mostly by the same artist."

"*C'est ça.* That's how specialized most thieves are. But here," she waved at the cabin, "there're handmade silk tapestries, ancient leaded glass. Under that embroidered tablecloth do you know what we found? Our victim ate off the most exquisite inlaid table I've ever seen. It must be five hundred years old and made by a master. Even the table cloth was a masterpiece. Most museums would keep it under glass. The Victoria and Albert in London would pay a fortune for it."

"Maybe they did."

"You mean it might have been stolen from there? Could be. I have a lot of work to do."

She looked as though she could hardly wait. And yet, she also looked as though she was in no hurry to leave this cabin, this garden.

"I wonder who he was." She reached out and pulled a couple of runner beans from a vine, handing one to her companion. *"Most unhappiness comes from not being able to sit quietly in a room."*

"Pascal," said Gamache, recognizing the

quote, and the appropriateness of it. "This man could. But he surrounded himself with objects that had a lot to say. That had stories."

"That's an interesting way of putting it."

"What's the Amber Room?"

"How do you know about that?" She turned a searching eye on him.

"When you were looking around you mentioned it."

"Did I? You can see it from here. That orange thing in the kitchen window." He looked and sure enough, there it was, glowing warm in what little light it caught. It looked like a large, thick piece of stained glass. She continued to stare, mesmerized, then finally came out of it. "Sorry. I just never expected to be the one to find it."

"What do you mean?"

"The Amber Room was created in the early 1700s in Prussia by Friedrich the First. It was a huge room made of amber and gold. Took artists and artisans years to construct and when it was completed it was one of the wonders of the world." He could tell she was imagining what it looked like, her eyes taking on a faraway look. "He had it made for his wife, Sophia Charlotte. But a few years later it was given to the Russian Emperor and stayed in St. Petersburg until the war."

"Which war?"

She smiled. "Good point. The Second World War. The Soviets apparently dismantled it once they realized the Nazis would take the city, but they didn't manage to hide it. The Germans found it."

She stopped.

"Go on," said Gamache.

"That's it. That's all we know. The Amber Room disappeared. Historians, treasure hunters, antiquarians have been searching for it ever since. We know the Germans, under Albert Speer, took the Amber Room away. Hid it. Presumably for safe keeping. But it was never seen again."

"What're the theories?" the Chief Inspector asked.

"Well, the most accepted is that it was destroyed in the Allied bombing. But there's another theory. Albert Speer was very bright, and many argue he wasn't a true Nazi. He was loyal to Hitler, but not to most of his ideals. Speer was an internationalist, a cultured man whose priority became saving the world's treasures from destruction, by either side."

"Albert Speer may have been cultured," said Gamache, "but he was a Nazi. He knew of the death camps, knew of the slaughter, approved it. He simply looked good while doing it."

The Chief Inspector's voice was cold and his eyes hard.

"I don't disagree with you, Armand. Just the opposite. I'm simply telling you what the theories are. The one involving Speer had him hiding the Amber Room far from both the German and the Allied armies. In the Ore Mountains."

"Where?"

"A mountain range between Germany and what's now the Czech Republic."

They both thought about that, and finally Gamache spoke. "So how did a piece of the Amber Room get here?"

"And where's the rest of it?"

Denis Fortin sat across from Clara Morrow. He was younger than he had any right to be. Early forties probably. A failed artist who'd discovered another, greater, talent. He recognized talent in others.

It was enlightened self-interest. The best kind, as far as Clara could see. No one was the martyr, no one was owed or owing. She was under no illusion that the reason Denis Fortin held a St. Amboise beer in Olivier's Bistro in Three Pines was not because he thought there was something in it for him.

And the only reason Clara was there, besides unbridled ego, was to get something from Fortin. Namely fame and fortune.

At the very least a free beer.

But there was something she needed to do before she got caught up in the unparalleled glory that was Clara Morrow. Reaching into her bag she brought out the balled-up towel. "I was asked to show you this. A man was found dead here a couple of days ago. Murdered."

"Really? That's unusual, isn't it?"

"Not as unusual as you might think. What was unusual is that no one knew him. But the police just found a cabin in the woods, and this was inside it. The head of the investigation asked me to show it to you, in case you could tell us anything about it."

"A clue?" He looked keen and watched closely as she unwrapped the bundle. Soon the little men and women were standing on the shore, looking across the expanse of wood to the micro-brew in front of Fortin.

Clara watched him. His eyes narrowed and he leaned closer to the work, pursing his lips in concentration.

"Very nice. Good technique, I'd say. Detailed, each face quite different, with character. Yes, all in all I'd say a competent piece of carving. Slightly primitive, but what you'd expect from a backwoods whittler."

"Really?" said Clara. "I thought it was very good. Excellent even."

He leaned back and smiled at her. Not patronizing, but as one friend smiles at another, a kinder, friend.

"Perhaps I'm being too harsh, but I've seen so many of these in my career."

"These? Exactly the same?"

"No, but close enough. Carved images of people fishing or smoking a pipe or riding a horse. They're the most valuable. You can always find a buyer for a good horse or dog. Or pig. Pigs are popular."

"Good to know. There's something written underneath." Clara turned it over and handed it to Fortin.

He squinted then putting on his glasses he read, frowned and handed it back. "I wonder what it means."

"Any guesses?" Clara wasn't about to give up. She wanted to take something back to Gamache.

"Almost certainly a signature, or a lot number. Something to identify it. Was this the only one?"

"There're two. How much would this be worth?"

"Hard to say." He picked it up again. "It's quite good, for what it is. It's no pig, though."

"Pity."

"Hmm." Fortin considered for a moment. "I'd say two hundred, maybe two hundred and fifty dollars."

"Is that all?"

"I might be wrong."

Clara could tell he was being polite, but getting bored. She rewrapped the carving and put it in her bag.

"Now." Denis Fortin leaned forward, an eager look on his handsome face. "Let's talk about really great art. How would you like your work to be hung?"

"I've done a few sketches." Clara handed him her notebook and after a few minutes Fortin lifted his head, his eyes intelligent and bright.

"This is wonderful. I like the way you've clustered the paintings then left a space. It's like a breath, isn't it?"

Clara nodded. It was such a relief talking to someone who didn't need everything explained.

"I particularly like that you haven't placed the three old women together. That would be the obvious choice, but you've spread them around, each anchoring her own wall."

"I wanted to surround them with other works," said Clara excitedly.

"Like acolytes, or friends, or critics," said Fortin, excited himself. "It's not clear what their intentions are."

"And how they might change," said Clara, leaning forward. She'd shown Peter her ideas, and he'd been polite and encouraging, but she could tell he really didn't understand what she was getting at. At first glance her design for the exhibition might seem unbalanced. And it was. Intentionally. Clara wanted people to walk in, see the works that appeared quite traditional and slowly appreciate that they weren't.

There was a depth, a meaning, a challenge to them.

For an hour or more Clara and Fortin talked, exchanging ideas about the show, about the direction of contemporary art, about exciting new artists, of which, Fortin was quick to assure Clara, she was in the forefront.

"I wasn't going to tell you because it might not happen, but I sent your portfolio to FitzPatrick at MoMA. He's an old friend and says he'll come to the *vernissage* —"

Clara exclaimed and almost knocked her beer over. Fortin laughed and held up his hand.

"But wait, that wasn't what I wanted to tell you. I suggested he spread the word and it looks as though Allyne from the *New York Times* will be there . . ."

He hesitated because it looked as though Clara was having a stroke. When she closed her mouth he continued. "And, as luck would have it, Destin Browne will be in New York that month setting up a show with MoMA and she's shown interest."

"Destin Browne? Vanessa Destin Browne? The chief curator at the Tate Modern in London?"

Fortin nodded and held tightly to his beer. But now, far from being in danger of knocking anything over, Clara appeared to have ground to a complete halt. She sat in the cheery little bistro, late summer light teeming through the mullioned windows. Beyond Fortin she saw the old homes, warming in the sun. The perennial beds with roses and clematis and hollyhocks. She saw the villagers, whose names she knew and whose habits she was familiar with. And she saw the three tall pines, like beacons. Impossible to miss, even surrounded by forest. If you knew what to look for, and needed a beacon.

Life was about to take her away from here. From the place where she'd become herself. This solid little village that never changed but helped its inhabitants to change. She'd arrived straight from art college full of avant-garde ideas, wearing shades of gray and seeing the world in black and white. So sure of herself. But here, in the middle of nowhere, she'd discovered color. And nuance. She'd learned this from the villagers, who'd been generous enough to lend her their souls to paint. Not as perfect human beings, but as flawed, struggling men and women. Filled with fear and uncertainty and, in at least one case, martinis.

But who remained standing. In the wilderness. Her graces, her stand of pines.

She was suddenly overcome with gratitude to her neighbors, and to whatever inspiration had allowed her to do them justice.

She closed her eyes and tilted her face into the sun.

"You all right?" he asked.

Clara opened her eyes. He seemed bathed in light, his blond hair glowing and a warm, patient smile on his face.

"You know, I probably shouldn't tell you this, but a few years ago no one wanted my works. Everyone just laughed. It was brutal. I almost gave up."

"Most great artists have the same story," he said, gently.

"I almost flunked out of art school, you know. I don't tell many people that."

"Another drink?" asked Gabri, taking Fortin's empty glass.

"Not for me, *merci,*" he said, then turned back to Clara. "Between us? Most of the best people did flunk out. How can you test an artist?"

"I was always good at tests," said Gabri, picking up Clara's glass. "No, wait. That was testes."

He gave Clara an arch look and swept away.

"Fucking queers," said Fortin, taking a handful of cashews. "Doesn't it make you want to vomit?"

Clara froze. She looked at Fortin to see if he was kidding. He wasn't. But what he said was true. She suddenly wanted to throw up.

Twenty-Four

Chief Inspector Gamache and Superintendent Brunel walked back to the cabin, each lost in thought.

"I told you what I found," said the Superintendent, once back on the porch. "Now it's your turn. What were you and Inspector Beauvoir whispering about in the corner, like naughty schoolboys?"

Not many people would consider calling Chief Inspector Gamache a naughty schoolboy. He smiled. Then he remembered the thing that had gleamed and mocked and clung to the corner of the cabin.

"Would you like to see?"

"No, I think I'll go back to the garden and pick turnips. Of course I'd like to see," she laughed and he took her over to the corner of the room, her eyes darting here and there, stealing glances at the masterpieces she was passing. Until they stopped in the darkest corner.

"I don't see anything."

Beauvoir joined them and switched on his flashlight. She followed it. Up the wall to the rafters.

"I still don't see."

"But you do," said Gamache. As they waited Beauvoir thought about other words, left up to be found. Tacked to the door of his bedroom at the B and B that morning.

He'd asked Gabri if he knew anything about the piece of paper stuck into the wood with a thumbtack, but Gabri had looked perplexed and shaken his head.

Beauvoir had stuffed it into his pocket and only after the first *café au lait* of the day did he have the guts to read.

> and the soft body of a woman
> and lick you clean of fever,

What upset Beauvoir most wasn't the thought that the mad old poet had invaded the B and B and put that on his door. Nor was it that he didn't understand a word of it. What upset him the most was the comma.

It meant there was more.

"I'm sorry, I really don't see anything." Superintendent Brunel's voice brought Beauvoir back to the cabin.

"Do you see a spider's web?" Gamache asked.

"Yes."

"Then you see it. Look more closely."

It took a moment but finally her face changed. Her eyes widened and her brows lifted. She tilted her head slightly as though she wasn't seeing quite straight.

"But there's a word up there, written in the web. What does it say? Woe? How is that possible? What kind of spider does that?" she asked, clearly not expecting an answer, and not getting one.

Just then the satellite phone rang and after answering it Agent Morin handed it to the Chief Inspector. "Agent Lacoste for you, sir."

"Oui, allô?" he said, and listened for a few moments. "Really?" He listened some more, glancing around the room then up again at the web. *"D'accord. Merci."*

Gamache hung up, thought a moment, then reached for the nearby stepladder.

"Would you like me . . ." Beauvoir gestured to it.

"Ce n'est pas necessaire." Taking a breath Gamache started up the Annapurna ladder. Two steps up he put out an unsteady hand and Beauvoir moved forward until the large trembling fingers found his shoulder. Stead-

ied, Gamache reached up and poked the web with a pen. Slowly, unseen by the people craning their necks below, he moved a single strand of the web.

"C'est ça," he murmured.

Backing down the ladder and onto terra firma he nodded toward the corner. Beauvoir's light shone on the web.

"How did you do that?" asked Beauvoir.

The web had changed its message. It no longer said Woe. Now it said Woo.

"A strand had come loose."

"But how did you know it had?" Beauvoir persisted. They'd all taken a close look at the web. Clearly a spider hadn't spun it. It appeared to be made from thread, perhaps nylon fishing line, made to look like a spider's web. They'd take it down soon and have it properly analyzed. It had a great deal to tell them, though changing the word from Woe to Woo didn't seem a move toward clarity.

"More results are coming into the Incident Room. Fingerprint results, which I'll tell you about in a minute, but remember that piece of wood that was found under the bed?"

"The one that also said Woe?" asked Morin, who had joined them.

Gamache nodded. "It had blood on it. The

victim's blood, according to the lab. But when they removed it they discovered something else. The block of wood wasn't carved to say Woe. The smear of blood made a mess of the lettering. When the blood was lifted it said —"

"Woo," said Beauvoir. "So you thought if one said it maybe the other did too."

"Worth a try."

"I think I prefer Woe." Beauvoir looked at the web again. "At least it's a word. What does Woo mean?"

They thought. Had someone been wandering by the cabin and chanced to look in they would have seen a group of adults standing quite still, staring into space and muttering "Woo" every now and then.

"Woo," Brunel said. "Don't people pitch woo?"

"Woohoo? No, that's boo," said Beauvoir. "Boohoo, not woo."

"Isn't it what they call kangaroos?" asked Morin.

"Kangawoos? That's roo," snapped Beauvoir.

"Chalice," swore Brunel.

"Woo, woo," said Morin under his breath, begging himself to come up with something that didn't sound like a choo-choo train. But the more he said it the more it sounded like nonsense. "Woo," he whispered.

Only Gamache said nothing. He listened to them but his mind kept going to the other piece of news. His face grew stern as he thought about what else had been revealed when the bloody fingerprints were lifted from the carving.

"He can't stay here."

Marc swished his arms under the tap at the kitchen sink.

"I don't want him here either, but at least here we can watch him," his mother said.

All three looked out the kitchen window to the old man sitting cross-legged on the grass, meditating.

"What do you mean, 'watch him'?" asked Dominique. She was fascinated by her father-in-law. He had a sort of broken-down magnetism about him. She could see he once had had a powerful personality, and a powerful hold over people. And he behaved as though that was still true. There was a shabby dignity about him, but also a cunning.

Marc grabbed the bar of soap and rubbed it over his forearms, looking like a surgeon scrubbing up. In fact, he was scrubbing away dust and plaster after dry-walling.

It was hard work, and work he was almost

certainly doing for someone else. The next owner of the inn and spa. Which was just as well, since he was doing it very badly.

"I mean that things happen around Vincent," said Carole. "Always have. He's sailed through life, this glorious ship of state. Oblivious of the wreckage in his wake."

It might not have sounded like it, but she was being charitable. For the sake of Marc. The truth was, she wasn't at all convinced Vincent had been oblivious of the damage he caused. She'd come to believe he actually deliberately sailed right over people. Destroyed them. Gone out of his way to do it.

She'd been his nurse, his assistant, his dogsbody. His witness and, finally, his conscience. Which was probably why he'd grown to hate her. And her him.

Once again they looked at the cross-legged man, sitting calmly in their garden.

"I can't cope with him right now," said Marc, drying his hands.

"We have to let him stay," said Dominique. "He's your father."

Marc looked at her with a mixture of amusement and sadness. "He's done it to you, now, hasn't he? Charmed you."

"I'm not some naïve schoolgirl, you know."

And this brought Marc up short. He realized she'd faced down some of the wealthiest, most manipulative bullies in Canadian finance. But Dr. Vincent Gilbert was different. There was something bewitching about him. "I'm sorry. So much is happening."

He'd thought moving to the country would be a breeze compared to the greed and fear and manipulation of the financial district. But so far here he'd found a dead body, moved it, ruined their reputation in the village, and been accused of murder; now he was about to kick a saint out of their home, and had almost certainly messed up the dry-walling.

And the leaves hadn't even changed yet.

But by then they'd be gone. To find another home somewhere else and hope they did better. He longed for the relative ease of the business world, where cut-throats lurked in every cubicle. Here everything looked so pleasant and peaceful, but wasn't.

He looked out the window again. In the foreground was his father, sitting cross-legged in the garden, and behind him in the field two broken-down old horses, what might or might not be a moose, and in the distance a muck-encrusted horse that by all rights should have been dog food by now. This wasn't what he had in mind when he'd moved to the country.

"Marc's right, you know," said Carole to her daughter-in-law. "Vincent either bullies, charms, or guilts his way in. But he always gets what he wants."

"And what does he want?" Dominique asked. It seemed a sensible question. Then why was it so difficult to answer?

The doorbell rang. They looked at each other. They'd come, in the last twenty-four hours, to dread that sound.

"I'll get it," said Dominique and walked briskly out of the kitchen, reappearing a minute later followed by a little boy and Old Mundin.

"I think you know my son," said Old, after greeting everyone with a smile. "Now, Charlie, what did The Mother tell you to say to these nice people?"

They waited while Charlie considered, then he gave them the finger.

"He learned that from Ruth, actually," Old explained.

"Quite a role model. Would he like a Scotch?" asked Carole. Old Mundin's handsome tanned face broke into a smile.

"No, Ruth just gave him a martini and we're trying not to mix drinks." Now the young man looked uncomfortable and putting his hands down on his son's shoulders he hugged Charlie to him. "I've heard he's here. Would you mind?"

Marc, Dominique, and Carole looked confused.

"Mind?" Dominique asked.

"Dr. Gilbert. I'd seen him in the forest, you know. I knew who he was but didn't know he was your father."

"Why didn't you say something?" Dominique asked.

"It wasn't my business. He didn't seem to want to be seen."

And Marc thought maybe it was simpler here after all, and he was the one who complicated things. The business world had somehow made him think everything was his business, when it wasn't.

"I don't want to disturb him," Mundin continued, "but I just wondered if maybe we could see him. Maybe introduce Charlie to him." The dignified young father looked as though this effort was hurting him. "I've read and reread his book, *Being.* Your father's a great man. I envy you."

And Marc envied him. His touching his son, holding him. Protecting him and loving him. Being willing to humble himself, for his son.

"He's in the garden," said Marc.

"Thanks." At the door Old Mundin

stopped. "I have tools. Maybe I can come back tomorrow and help. A man can always use help."

You'll be a man, my son. Why hadn't his own father told him a man could always use help?

Marc nodded, not unaware of the significance of what had just happened. Old Mundin was offering to help the Gilberts build their home, not leave it. Because his father was Vincent Gilbert. His fucking father had saved them.

Mundin turned to Dominique. "The Wife says hello, by the way."

"Please say hello back," said Dominique, then hesitated a breath. "To The Wife."

"I will." He and Charlie went into the garden leaving the other three to watch.

Dr. Vincent Gilbert, late of the forest, had somehow become the center of attention.

As the young man and his son approached, Vincent Gilbert opened one eye and through the slit in his long lashes he watched. Not the two walking quietly toward him, but the three in the window.

Help others, he'd been told. And he intended to. But first he had to help himself.

It was quiet in the bistro. A few villagers sat at tables outside in the sunshine, relishing their *café* and Camparis and calm. Inside Olivier stood at the window.

"Good God, man, you'd think you'd never seen the village before," Gabri said from behind the bar where he was polishing the wood and replenishing the candy jars, most of which he'd helped empty.

For the last few days, every time Gabri looked for Olivier he'd find him standing in the same spot, in the bay window, looking out.

"Pipe?" Gabri walked over to his partner and offered him a licorice pipe, but Olivier seemed under a spell. Gabri bit into the licorice himself, eating the candied end first, as per the rules.

"What's bothering you?" Gabri followed the other man's gaze and saw only what he'd expect to see. Certainly nothing riveting. Just the customers on the *terrasse,* then the village green with Ruth and Rosa. The duck was now wearing a knitted sweater.

Olivier's eyes narrowed as he too focused on the duck. Then he turned to Gabri.

"Does that sweater look familiar to you?"

"Which?"

"The duck's, of course." Olivier studied Gabri closely. The large man never could lie. Now he ate the rest of the pipe and put on his most perplexed face.

"I have no idea what you're talking about."

"That's my sweater, isn't it?"

"Come off it, Olivier. Do you really think you and the duck wear the same size?"

"Not now, but when I was a kid. Where're my baby clothes?"

Now Gabri was silent, damning Ruth for parading Rosa in her new wardrobe. Well, maybe not so new.

"I thought it was time to get rid of them," said Gabri. "Ruth needed sweaters and things for Rosa to keep her warm in the fall and winter and I thought of your baby clothes. What were you saving them for anyway? They were just taking up space in the basement."

"How much space could they take up?" Olivier demanded, feeling himself breaking apart inside, his reserve crumbling. "How could you?" he snarled at Gabri, who leaned away, shocked.

"But you'd talked about getting rid of them yourself."

"Me, me. Me getting rid of them. Not you. You had no right."

"I'm sorry, I had no idea they meant that much to you."

"Well they do. Now what am I going to do?"

Olivier watched as Rosa waddled behind Ruth, who muttered away to the duck, saying God knew what. And Olivier felt tears sting his eyes, and a swell of emotion erupt from his throat. He couldn't very well take the clothes back. Not now. They were gone. Gone forever.

"Do you want me to get them back?" asked Gabri, taking Olivier's hand.

Olivier shook his head. Not even sure why he felt so strongly. He had so much else to worry about. And it was true, he'd thought about getting rid of the box of old baby clothes. The only reasons he hadn't were laziness, and not being sure who to give them to.

Why not Rosa? A distant honking was heard in the sky and both Rosa and Ruth lifted their heads. Overhead a formation of ducks headed south.

Sadness washed over Olivier. Gone. It was all gone. Everything.

For weeks and weeks the villagers journeyed through the forests. At first the young man hurried them along looking behind him now and then. He regretted telling his family and friends to leave with him. He could have been much farther away without the old men and women, and the children. But as the weeks went by and peaceful day followed peaceful day, he began to worry less and was even grateful for the company.

He'd almost forgotten to look over his shoulder when the first sign appeared.

It was twilight, only the twilight never died. Night never fell completely. He wasn't sure if any of the others noticed. It was, after all, just a small glow in the distance. At the horizon. The next day the sun rose, but not completely. There was a darkness to the sky. But again, just at the horizon. As though a shadow had spilled over from the other side.

The young man knew then.

He clutched his parcel tighter and hurried everyone along, rushing forward. Driving them onward. They were willing to hurry. After all, immortality, youth, happiness awaited. They were almost giddy with joy. And in that joy he hid.

At night the light grew in the sky. And during the day the shadow stretched toward them.

"Is that it?" his elderly aunt asked eagerly, as they crested a hill. "Are we there?"

In front of them was water. Nothing but water.

And behind them the shadow lengthened.

Twenty-Five

"Olivier?"

The blond head was bowed, studying the receipts of the day so far. It was getting on for lunch and the bistro was filled with the aroma of garlic and herbs and roast chicken.

Olivier had seen them coming, had heard them even. That shriek as though the forest itself was crying out. They'd emerged from the woods on their ATVs and parked at the old Hadley house. Much of the village stopped what it was doing to watch as Chief Inspector Gamache and Inspector Beauvoir walked into the village. They were deep in conversation and no one disturbed them. Olivier had turned away then, walking further into his bistro and behind the bar. Around him the young waiters set tables while Havoc Parra wrote specials on the board.

The door opened and Olivier turned his back. Claiming every last moment.

"Olivier?" said the Chief Inspector. "We need to talk. In private, please."

Olivier turned and smiled, as though if he ingratiated himself enough they might not do this thing. The Chief Inspector smiled back, but it never reached his thoughtful eyes. Leading them into the back room that overlooked the Rivière Bella Bella Olivier indicated the chairs at the dining table and sat himself.

"How can I help?"

His heart thudded in his chest and his hands were cold and numb. He could no longer feel his extremities, and dots danced before his eyes. He struggled for breath and felt light-headed.

"Tell us about the man who lived in the cabin," Chief Inspector Gamache said, matter-of-factly. "The dead man." He folded his hands, settling in. A good dinner companion who wanted to hear your stories.

There was no escape, Olivier knew. He'd known it from the instant he'd seen the Hermit dead on the bistro floor. He'd seen this avalanche sliding toward him, gaining momentum. Olivier couldn't run. Could never outrun what was coming.

"He was one of my first customers when Gabri and I moved to Three Pines."

The words, kept inside for so long, crawled

out. Rotting. Olivier was surprised his breath didn't stink.

Gamache gave him a small nod of encouragement.

"We just had an antique shop then. I hadn't turned this into a bistro, yet. We rented the space above to live in. It was awful. Crammed full of junk, and filthy. Someone had plastered over all the original features. But we worked day and night to restore it. I think we'd only been here a few weeks when he walked in. He wasn't the man you saw on the floor. Not then. This was years ago."

Olivier saw it all again. Gabri was upstairs in their new home, stripping the beams and taking the drywall off, exposing the magnificent original brick walls. Each discovery more exciting than the last. But none could rival the growing awareness that they'd found a home. A place they could finally settle. At first they'd been so intent on unpacking they didn't really take in the details of the village. But slowly, over the first few weeks and months, the village revealed itself.

"I was still setting up the business and didn't have much stuff, just odds and ends collected over the years. I'd always dreamed of opening an antique store, since I was a kid. Then the chance came."

"It didn't just come," said Gamache quietly. "It was helped along."

Olivier sighed. He should have known Gamache would find out.

"I'd quit my job in the city. I'd been quite successful, as you might have heard."

Gamache nodded again.

Olivier smiled, remembering those heady days. Of silk suits and gym memberships, of visiting the Mercedes dealership when the only issue was the color of the car.

And of taking that one step too far.

It'd been humiliating. He'd been so depressed he was afraid of what he might do to himself, so he'd sought help. And there, in the waiting room of the therapist, was Gabri. Large, voluble, vain and full of life.

At first Olivier had been repulsed. Gabri was everything he'd come to despise. Olivier thought of himself and his friends as gay men. Discreet, elegant, cynical.

Gabri was just queer. Common. And fat. There was nothing discreet about him.

But neither was there anything mean. And over time Olivier grew to appreciate how very beautiful kindness was.

And he fell in love with Gabri. Deeply, totally, indiscreetly in love.

Gabri had agreed to leave his job at the Y

in Westmount and move out of the city. It didn't matter where. They got in their car and drove south. And there, over a rise in the road, they'd stopped the car. Finally admitting they were lost. Though since they had no destination they couldn't be lost, Gabri happily told Olivier, who was busy in the driver's side wrestling with a Carte Routière du Québec. Eventually he realized Gabri was standing outside and softly tapping on his window. He lowered it and Gabri gestured.

Annoyed, Olivier shoved the map into the backseat and got out.

"What?" he snapped at Gabri, who was looking ahead. Olivier followed his gaze. And found home.

He knew it immediately.

It was the place in all the fairy tales he'd read as a kid, under the bedding, when his father thought, hoped, he was reading about naval battles. Or naked girls. Instead he'd been reading about villages, and cottages, and gardens. And little wisps of smoke, and dry stone walls older than anyone in the village.

He'd forgotten all that, until that very moment. And in that instant he remembered his other childhood dream. Of opening an antique shop. A modest little affair where he could put his finds.

"Shall we, *ma belle?*" Gabri took Olivier's hand and leaving the car where it stood they walked down the dirt road and into Three Pines.

"I was disappointed at first when the Hermit came in —"

"The Hermit?" Gamache asked.

"That's what I called him."

"But didn't you know his name?"

"He never told me and I never asked."

Gamache caught Beauvoir's eye. The Inspector was looking both disappointed and disbelieving.

"Go on," said Gamache.

"His hair was a little long and he looked a bit scruffy. Not the sort to do a lot of buying. But it was quiet and I talked to him. He came back a week later, and then about once a week for a few months. Finally he took me aside and said he had something he wanted to sell. That was pretty disappointing too. I'd been nice to the guy but now he was asking me to buy some piece of junk and it pissed me off. I almost asked him to leave, but by then he had the piece in his hand."

Olivier remembered looking down. They were at the back and the lighting wasn't good, but it didn't gleam or glitter. In fact it looked very dull. Olivier reached out for it but the Hermit drew his hand back. And then it caught the light.

It was a miniature portrait. The two men walked to the window and Olivier got a good view.

It was in a tarnished old frame and must have been painted with a single horse hair, so fine was the detail. It showed a man in profile, powdered wig, blowsy clothing.

Even the memory made Olivier's heart quicken.

"How much do you want?"

"Maybe some food?" the Hermit had asked, and the deal was sealed.

Olivier looked at Gamache, whose thoughtful brown eyes never wavered.

"And that's how it started. I agreed to take the painting in exchange for a few bags of groceries."

"And what was it worth?"

"Not much." Olivier remembered carefully taking the miniature from its frame, and seeing the old lettering on the back. It was some Polish count. With a date. 1745. "I sold it for a few dollars."

He held Gamache's eyes.

"Where?"

"Some antique place along rue Notre Dame in Montreal."

Gamache nodded. "Go on."

"After that the Hermit brought stuff to the shop every now and then and I'd give him food. But he became more and more paranoid. Didn't want to come into the village anymore. So he invited me to his cabin."

"Why did you agree to go? It was quite an inconvenience."

Olivier had been afraid of that question.

"Because the things he was giving me turned out to be quite good. Nothing spectacular, but decent quality and I was curious. When I first visited the cabin it took me a few minutes to realize what he had. It all just looked like it belonged, in a strange sort of way. Then I looked closer. He was eating off plates worth tens of thousands, hundreds of thousands of dollars. Did you see the glasses?" Olivier's eyes were gleaming with excitement. *"Fantastique."*

"Did he ever explain how he came to have items that were priceless?"

"Never, and I never asked. I was afraid to scare him off."

"Did he know the value of what he had?"

That was an interesting question, and one Olivier had debated himself. The Hermit treated the finest engraved silver the way Gabri treated Ikea flatware. There was no attempt to coddle anything. But neither was the Hermit cavalier. He was a cautious man, that much was certain.

"I'm not sure," said Olivier.

"So you gave him groceries and he gave you near-priceless antiques?"

Gamache's voice was neutral, curious. It held none of the censure Olivier knew it could, and should.

"He didn't give me the best stuff, at least not at first. And I did more than take him groceries. I helped dig his vegetable garden, and brought the seeds to plant."

"How often did you visit?"

"Every two weeks."

Gamache considered, then spoke. "Why was he living in the cabin away from everyone else?"

"Hiding, I guess."

"But from what?"

Olivier shook his head. "Don't know. I tried to ask but he was having none of it."

"What can you tell us?" Gamache's voice wasn't quite as patient as it had been. Beauvior looked up from his notebook, and Olivier shifted in his seat.

"I know the Hermit built the cabin over several months. Then he carried all the stuff in himself." Olivier was studying Gamache, eager for his approval, eager for the thaw.

The large man leaned forward slightly and Olivier rushed on. "He told me all about it. Most of his things weren't big. Just the armchairs, really, and the bed. The rest anybody could've carried. And he was strong."

Still, Gamache was silent. Olivier squirmed.

"I'm telling the truth. He never explained how he got all those things, and I was afraid to ask, but it's kind of obvious, isn't it? He must have stolen them. Otherwise, why hide?"

"So you thought they were stolen and you didn't say anything?" asked Gamache, his voice still without criticism. "Didn't call the police."

"No. I know I should have, but I didn't."

For once Beauvoir didn't sneer. This he found completely natural and understandable. How many people would, after all? It always amazed Beauvoir when he heard about people finding suitcases full of money, and turning it in. He had to wonder about the sanity of such people.

For his part Gamache was thinking about the other end of the deal. The people who'd owned the things. The fabulous violin, the priceless glassware, the china and silver and inlaid wood. If the Hermit was hiding in the woods someone had chased him there. "Did he say where he was from?" Gamache asked.

"No. I asked once but he didn't answer."

Gamache considered. "What did he sound like?"

"I'm sorry?"

"His voice."

"It was normal. We spoke in French."

"Quebec French, or France French?"

Olivier hesitated. Gamache waited.

"Quebec, but . . ."

Gamache was still, as though he could wait all day. All week. A lifetime.

". . . but he had a slight accent. Czech, I think," said Olivier in a rush.

"Are you sure?"

"Yes. He was Czech," said Olivier in a mumble. "I'm sure."

Gamache saw Beauvoir make a note. It was the first clue to the man's identity.

"Why didn't you tell us you knew the Hermit when the body was found?"

"I should have, but I thought you might not find the cabin."

"And why would you hope that?"

Olivier tried to take a breath, but the oxygen didn't seem to reach his lungs. Or his brain. His compressed lips felt cold and his eyes burned. Hadn't he told them enough? But still Gamache sat across from him, waiting. And Olivier could see it in his eyes. He knew. Gamache knew the answer, and still he demanded Olivier say it himself.

"Because there were things in the cabin I wanted. For myself."

Olivier looked exhausted, as though he'd coughed up his insides. But Gamache knew there was more.

"Tell us about the carvings."

Clara walked along the road from the Incident Room, over the bridge into Three Pines, and stood looking first one way then the other.

What should she do?

She'd just been to the Incident Room to return the carving.

Fucking queers.

Two words.

Surely she could ignore them. Pretend Fortin hadn't said it. Or, better still, maybe she could find someone who'd assure her what she'd done was quite right.

She'd done nothing. Said nothing. She'd simply thanked Denis Fortin for his time, agreed this was exciting, agreed to keep in touch as the show approached. They'd shaken hands and kissed on both cheeks.

And now she stood, lost, looking this way and that. Clara had considered talking to

Gamache about it, then dismissed the idea. He was a friend, but he was also a cop, investigating a crime worse than nasty words.

And yet, Clara wondered. Was that where most murders began? Did they start as words? Something said that lodged and festered. That curdled. And killed.

Fucking queers.

And she'd done nothing.

Clara turned right and made for the shops.

"What carvings?"

"This carving for one." Gamache placed the sailing ship, with its miserable passenger hiding among the smiles, on the table.

Olivier stared at it.

They camped at the very edge of the world, crowded together, looking out to the ocean. Except the young man, who stared back. To where they'd come from.

It was impossible to miss the lights in the dark sky now. And the sky was almost perpetually dark. There was no longer a distinction between night and day. And yet, such was the villagers' joy and anticipation, they didn't seem to notice, or care.

The light sliced like a saber through the darkness, through the shadow thrown toward them. Almost upon them.

The Mountain King had arisen. Had assembled an army made of Bile and Rage and led by Chaos. Their wrath carved the sky ahead of them, searching for one man, one young man. Barely more than a boy. And the package he held.

They marched on, closer and closer. And the villagers waited on shore, to be taken to the world they'd been promised. Where nothing bad happened, and no one sickened or grew old.

The young man ran here and there, trying to find a hiding place. A cave perhaps, somewhere he could curl up and hide, and be very, very small. And quiet.

"Oh," said Olivier.

"What can you tell me about this?" asked Gamache.

One small hill separated the dreadful army from the villagers. An hour, maybe less.

Olivier heard the voice again, the story filling the cabin, even the dark corners.

"Look," one of the villagers shouted, pointing to the water. The young man turned, wondering what horror was coming from the sea. But instead he saw a ship. In full sail. Hurrying toward them.

"Sent by the gods," said his old aunt as she stepped on board. And he knew that was true. One of the gods had taken pity on them and sent a strong ship and a stronger wind. They hurried aboard and the ship left immediately. Out at sea the young man looked back in time to see, rising behind the final hill, a dark shape. It rose higher and higher and around its peak flew the Furies, and on its now naked flank there marched Sorrow and Grief and Madness. And at the head of the army was Chaos.

As the Mountain spied the tiny vessel on the ocean it shrieked, and the howl filled the sails of the vessel so that it streaked across the ocean. In the bow the happy villagers searched for land, for their new world. But the young man, huddling among them, looked back. At the Mountain of Bitterness he'd created. And the rage that filled their sails.

"Where did you find that?" Olivier asked.

"In the cabin." Gamache was watching him closely. Olivier seemed stunned by the carving. Almost frightened. "Have you seen it before?"

"Never."

"Or others like it?"

"No."

Gamache handed it to Olivier. "It's a strange subject matter, don't you think?"

"How so?"

"Well, everyone's so happy, joyful even. Except him." Gamache placed his forefinger on the head of the crouching figure. Olivier looked closer and frowned.

"I know nothing about art. You'll have to ask someone else."

"What did the Hermit whittle?"

"Nothing much. Just pieces of wood. Tried to teach me once but I kept cutting myself. Not good with my hands."

"That's not what Gabri says. He tells me you used to make your own clothes."

"As a kid." Olivier reddened. "And they were crap."

Gamache took the carving from Olivier. "We found whittling tools in the cabin. The lab's working on them and we'll know soon enough if they were used to make this. But we both know the answer to that, don't we?"

The two men stared at each other.

"You're right," said Olivier with a laugh. "I'd forgotten. He used to whittle these strange carvings, but he never showed me that one."

"What did he show you?"

"I can't remember."

Gamache rarely showed impatience, but Inspector Beauvoir did. He slammed his notebook shut. It made a not very satisfactory sound. Certainly not nearly enough to convey his frustration at a witness who was behaving like his six-year-old nephew accused of stealing cookies. Denying everything. Lying about everything however trivial, as though he couldn't help himself.

"Try," said Gamache.

Olivier sighed. "I feel badly about this. He loved carving, and he asked me to get him the wood. He was very specific. Red cedar, from British Columbia. I got it from Old Mundin. But when the Hermit started handing me these I was pretty disappointed. Especially since he wasn't giving me as many antiques from his cabin. Just those." He flicked his hand at the carving.

"What did you do with them?"

"I threw them away."

"Where?"

"Into the woods. When I walked home I tossed them into the forest. Didn't want them."

"But he didn't give you this one, or even show it to you?"

Olivier shook his head.

Gamache paused. Why did the Hermit

hide this one, and the other? What was different about them? Maybe he suspected Olivier had thrown the others away. Maybe he realized his visitor couldn't be trusted with his creations.

"What does this mean?" The Chief Inspector pointed to the letters carved under the ship.

OWSVI

"I don't know." Olivier seemed perplexed. "The others didn't have that."

"Tell me about woo," said Gamache so quietly Olivier thought he'd misheard.

Clara sat in the deep, comfortable armchair and watched Myrna serve Monsieur Béliveau. The old grocer had come in for something to read, but he wasn't sure what. He and Myrna talked about it and she made some suggestions. Myrna knew everyone's tastes, both the ones they declared and their actual ones.

Finally Monsieur Béliveau left with his biographies of Sartre and Wayne Gretzky. He bowed slightly to Clara, who bowed back from her chair, never sure what to do when the courtly old man did that.

Myrna handed Clara a cool lemonade and sat in the chair opposite. The afternoon sun poured through the bookshop window. Here and there they saw a dog chase a ball for a villager, or vice versa.

"Didn't you have your meeting this morning with Monsieur Fortin?"

Clara nodded.

"How'd it go?"

"Not bad."

"Do you smell smoke?" asked Myrna, sniffing. Clara, alarmed, looked around. "Oh, there it is," Myrna pointed to her companion. "Your pants are on fire."

"Very funny." But that was all the encouragement Clara needed. She tried to keep her voice light as she described the meeting. When Clara listed the people who would almost certainly be at the opening night at Fortin's gallery Myrna exclaimed and hugged her friend.

"Can you believe it?"

"Fucking queer."

"Stupid whore. Is this a new game?" laughed Myrna.

"You're not offended by what I said?"

"Calling me a fucking queer? No."

"Why not?"

"Well, I know you don't mean it. Did you?"

"Suppose I did?"

"Then I'd be worried for you," smiled Myrna. "What's this about?"

"When we were sitting in the bistro Gabri served us and as he left Fortin called him a fucking queer."

Myna took a deep breath. "And what did you say?"

"Nothing."

Myna nodded. Now it was her turn to say nothing.

"What?"

"Woo," repeated the Chief Inspector.

"Woo?" Olivier seemed baffled, but he'd feigned that at every turn in this interview. Beauvoir had long stopped believing anything the man said.

"Did the Hermit ever mention it?" Gamache asked.

"Mention woo?" Olivier asked. "I don't even know what you're asking."

"Did you notice a spider's web, in a corner of the cabin?"

"A spider's web? What? No, I never noticed one. But I'll tell you something, I'd be surprised if there was one. The Hermit kept that cabin spotless."

"Propre," said Gamache.

"Propre," Olivier repeated.

"Woo, Olivier. What does it mean to you?"

"Nothing."

"And yet it was the word on the piece of

wood you took from the hand of the Hermit. After he'd been murdered."

It was worse than Olivier had imagined, and he'd imagined pretty bad. It seemed Gamache knew everything. Or at least almost everything.

Pray God he doesn't know it all, thought Olivier.

"I picked it up," Olivier admitted. "But I didn't look at it. It was lying on the floor by his hand. When I saw there was blood on it I dropped it. It said Woo?"

Gamache nodded and leaned forward, his powerful hands lightly holding each other as his elbows rested on his knees.

"Did you kill him?"

Twenty-Six

Finally Myrna spoke. She leaned forward and took Clara's hand.

"What you did was natural."

"Really? Because it feels like shit."

"Well, most of your life is shit," said Myrna, nodding her head sagely. "So it would feel natural."

"Har, har."

"Listen, Fortin is offering you everything you ever dreamed of, everything you ever wanted."

"And he seemed so nice."

"He probably is. Are you sure he wasn't kidding?"

Clara shook her head.

"Maybe he's gay himself," suggested Myrna.

Clara shook her head again. "I thought of that, but he has a wife and a couple of kids and he just doesn't seem gay."

Both Clara and Myrna had a finely honed

gay-dar. It was, they both knew, imperfect, but it probably would have picked up the Fortin blip. But nothing. Only the immense, unmistakable object that was Gabri, sailing away.

"What should I do?" Clara asked.

Myrna remained silent.

"I need to speak to Gabri, don't I?"

"It might help."

"Maybe tomorrow."

As she left she thought about what Myrna had said. Fortin was offering her everything she'd ever wanted, the only dream she'd had since childhood. Success, recognition as an artist. All the sweeter after years in the wilderness. Mocked and marginalized.

And all she had to do was say nothing.

She could do that.

"No, I didn't kill him."

But even as Olivier said it he realized the disaster of what he'd done. In lying at every turn he'd made the truth unrecognizable.

"He was already dead when I arrived."

God, even to his own ears it sounded like a lie. I didn't take the last cookie, I didn't break the fine bone china cup, I didn't steal the money from your purse. I'm not gay.

All lies. All his life. All the time. Until he'd come to Three Pines. For an instant, for a glorious few days he'd lived a genuine life. With Gabri. In their little rented wreck of an apartment above the shop.

But then the Hermit had arrived. And with him a trail of lies.

"Listen, it's the truth. It was Saturday night and the place was hopping. The Labor Day long weekend's always a madhouse. But by midnight or so there were only a few stragglers. Then Old Mundin arrived with the chairs and a table. By the time he left the place was empty and Havoc was doing the final cleanup. So I decided to visit the Hermit."

"After midnight?" Gamache asked.

"That's normally when I went. So no one could see."

Across from Olivier the Chief Inspector slowly leaned back, distancing himself. The gesture was eloquent. It whispered that Gamache didn't believe him. Olivier stared at this man he'd considered a friend and he felt a tightening, a constriction.

"Weren't you afraid of the dark?"

Gamache asked it so simply, and in that instant Olivier knew the genius of the man. He was able to crawl into other people's skins, and burrow beyond the flesh and blood and bone. And ask questions of deceptive simplicity.

"It's not the dark I'm afraid of," said Olivier. And he remembered the freedom that came only after the sun set. In city parks, in darkened theaters, in bedrooms. The bliss that came with being able to shed the outer shell and be himself. Protected by the night.

It wasn't the dark that scared him, but what might come to light.

"I knew the way and it only took about twenty minutes to walk it."

"What did you see when you arrived?"

"Everything looked normal. There was a light in the window and the lantern on the porch was lit."

"He was expecting company."

"He was expecting me. He always lit the lantern for me. I didn't realize there was anything wrong until I was in the door and saw him there. I knew he was dead, but I thought he'd just fallen, maybe had a stroke or a heart attack and hit his head."

"There was no weapon?"

"No, nothing."

Gamache leaned forward again.

Were they beginning to believe him, Olivier wondered.

"Did you take him food?"

Olivier's mind revved, raced. He nodded.

"What did you take?"

"The usual. Cheese, milk, butter. Some

bread. And as a treat I took some honey and tea."

"What did you do with it?"

"The groceries? I don't know. I was in shock. I can't remember."

"We found them in the kitchen. Open."

The two men stared at each other. Then Gamache's eyes narrowed in a look that Olivier found harrowing.

Gamache was angry.

"I was there twice that night," he mumbled into the table.

"Louder, please," said the Chief.

"I returned to the cabin, okay?"

"It's time now, Olivier. Tell me the truth."

Olivier's breath came in short gasps, like something hooked and landed and about to be filleted.

"The first time I was there that night the Hermit was alive. We had a cup of tea and talked."

"What did you talk about?"

Chaos is coming, old son, and there's no stopping it. It's taken a long time, but it's finally here.

"He always asked about people who'd come to the village. He peppered me with questions about the outside world."

"The outside world?"

"You know, out here. He hadn't been

more than fifty feet from his cabin in years."

"Go on," said Gamache. "What happened then?"

"It was getting late so I left. He offered to give me something for the groceries. At first I refused, but he insisted. When I got out of the woods I realized I'd left it behind, so I went back." No need to tell them about the thing in the canvas bag. "When I got there he was dead."

"How long were you gone?"

"About half an hour. I didn't dawdle."

He saw again the tree limbs snapping back and felt them slapping him, smelled the pine needles, and heard the crashing through the woods, like an army, running. Racing. He'd thought it was just his own noise, magnified by fear and the night. But maybe not.

"You saw and heard nothing?"

"Nothing."

"What time was that?" Gamache asked.

"About two I guess, maybe two thirty."

Gamache laced his fingers together. "What did you do once you realized what had happened?"

The rest of the story came out quickly, in a rush. Once he'd realized the Hermit was dead, another idea had come to Olivier. A way the Hermit might help. He'd put the body in the wheelbarrow and taken him through the woods to the old Hadley house.

"It took a while, but I finally got him there. I'd planned to leave him on the porch, but when I tried the door it was unlocked, so I laid him in the front hall."

He made it sound gentle, but he knew it wasn't. It was a brutal, ugly, vindictive act. A violation of a body, a violation of a friendship, a violation of the Gilberts. And finally, it was a betrayal of Gabri and their lives in Three Pines.

It was so quiet in the room he could almost believe himself alone. He looked up and there was Gamache, watching him.

"I'm sorry," said Olivier. He scolded himself, desperate not to be the gay guy who cried. But he knew his actions had taken him far beyond cliché, or caricature.

And then Armand Gamache did the most extraordinary thing. He leaned forward so that his large, certain hands were almost touching Olivier's, as though it was all right to be that close to someone so vile, and he spoke in a calm, deep voice.

"If you didn't kill the man, who else could have? I need your help."

In that one sentence Gamache had placed himself next to Olivier. He might still be on the outer reaches of the world, but at least he wasn't alone.

Gamache believed him.

Clara stood outside Peter's closed studio door. She almost never knocked, almost never disturbed him. Unless it was an emergency. Those were hard to come by in Three Pines and were generally Ruth-shaped and difficult to avoid.

Clara had walked around the garden a few times, then come inside and walked around the living room, and then the kitchen in ever decreasing circles until finally she found herself here. She loved Myrna, she trusted Gamache, she adored Gabri and Olivier and many other friends. But it was Peter she needed.

She knocked. There was a pause, then the door opened.

"I need to talk."

"What is it?" He came out immediately and closed the door behind him. "What's wrong?"

"I met Fortin, as you know, and he said something."

Peter's heart missed a beat. And in that missed beat lived something petty. Something that hoped Fortin would change his mind. Would cancel Clara's solo show. Would say they'd made a mistake and Peter was really the one they wanted.

His heart beat for Clara every hour of every day. But every now and then it stumbled.

He took her hands. "What'd he say?"

"He called Gabri a fucking queer."

Peter waited for the rest. The part about Peter being the better artist. But Clara just stared at him.

"Tell me about it." He led her to a chair and they sat.

"Everything was going so well. He loved my ideas for hanging the show, he said Fitz-Patrick would be there from MoMA, and so would Allyne from the *Times*. And he thinks even Vanessa Destin Browne, you know, from the Tate Modern. Can you believe it?"

Peter couldn't. "Tell me more."

It was like throwing himself over and over at a wall of spikes.

"And then he called Gabri a fucking queer, behind his back. And said it made him want to vomit."

The spiked wall turned smooth, and soft.

"What did you say?"

"Nothing."

Peter dropped his eyes, then looked up. "I probably wouldn't have either."

"Really?" asked Clara, searching his face.

"Really." He smiled and squeezed her hands. "You weren't expecting it."

"It was a shock," said Clara, eager to explain. "What should I do?"

"What d'you mean?"

"Should I just forget about it, or say something to Fortin?"

And Peter saw the equation immediately. If she confronted the gallery owner she was running the risk of angering him. In fact, it almost certainly would. At the very least it would mar their relationship. He might even cancel her show.

If she said nothing, she'd be safe. Except that he knew her. It would eat away at Clara's conscience. A conscience, once aroused, could be a terrible thing.

Gabri poked his head into the back room.

"*Salut.* Why so serious?"

Olivier, Gamache and Beauvoir all looked at him. None was smiling.

"Wait a minute, are you telling Olivier about your visit to his father?" Gabri sat down beside his partner. "I wanna hear too. What'd he say about me?"

"We weren't talking about Olivier's father," said Gamache. Across from him Olivier's eyes were pleading for a favor Gamache couldn't grant. "We were talking about Olivier's relationship with the dead man."

Gabri looked from Gamache to Olivier, then over to Beauvoir. Then back to Olivier. "What?"

Gamache and Olivier exchanged looks and finally Olivier spoke. He told Gabri about the Hermit, his visits to the cabin, and the body. Gabri listened, silent. It was the first time Beauvoir had ever seen him go more than a minute without talking. And even when Olivier stopped, Gabri didn't start. He sat there as though he might never speak again.

But then, he did. "How could you be so stupid?"

"I'm sorry. It was dumb."

"It was more than dumb. I can't believe you didn't tell me about the cabin."

"I should've told you, I know. But he was so afraid, so secretive. You didn't know him —"

"I guess not."

"— but if he'd known I'd told anyone he'd have stopped seeing me."

"Why did you want to see him anyway? He was a hermit, in a cabin for God's sake. Wait a minute." There was silence while Gabri put it all together. "Why'd you go there?"

Olivier looked at Gamache, who nodded. It would all come out anyway.

"His place was full of treasure, Gabri. You wouldn't believe it. Cash stuffed between the logs for insulation. There was leaded crystal and tapestries. It was fantastic. Everything he had was priceless."

"You're making that up."

"I'm not. We ate off Catherine the Great's china. The toilet paper was dollar bills."

"*Sacré.* It's like your wet dream. Now I know you're kidding."

"No, no. It was unbelievable. And sometimes when I visited he'd give me a little something."

"And you took it?" Gabri's voice rose.

"Of course I took it," Olivier snapped. "I didn't steal it, and those things are no use to him."

"But he was probably nuts. It's the same as stealing."

"That's a horrible thing to say. You think I'd steal stuff from an old man?"

"Why not? You dumped his body at the old Hadley house. Who knows what you're capable of."

"Really? And you're innocent in all this?" Olivier's voice had grown cold and cruel. "How do you think we could afford to buy the bistro? Or the B and B? Eh? Didn't you ever wonder how we went from living in that dump of an apartment —"

"I fixed it up. It wasn't a dump anymore."

"— to opening the bistro and a B and B? How did you think we could afford it suddenly?"

"I thought the antique business was going well." There was silence. "You should've told me," said Gabri, finally, and wondered, as did Gamache and Beauvoir, what else Olivier wasn't saying.

It was late afternoon and Armand Gamache walked through the woods. Beauvoir had volunteered to go with him, but he preferred to be alone with his thoughts.

After they left Olivier and Gabri they'd returned to the Incident Room where Agent Morin had been waiting.

"I know who BM is," he said, eagerly following them, barely allowing them to take off their coats. "Look."

He took them over to his computer. Gamache sat and Beauvoir leaned over his shoulder. There was a black-and-white, formal, photo of a man smoking a cigarette.

"His name is Bohuslav Martinù," said Morin. "He wrote that violin piece we found. His birthday was December the eighth, so the violin must have been a birthday present from his wife. C. Charlotte was her name."

Twenty-Seven

"We're getting more results from the lab," said Lacoste.

Upon his return the Chief had gathered his team at the conference table and now Agent Lacoste was handing around the printouts. "The web was made of nylon fishing line. Readily available. No prints, of course, and no trace of DNA. Whoever made it probably used surgical gloves. All they found was a little dust and a cobweb." She smiled.

"Dust?" asked Gamache. "Do they have any idea how long it was up?"

"No more than a few days, they guess. Either that or the Hermit dusted it daily, which seems unlikely."

Gamache nodded.

"So who put it there?" asked Beauvoir. "The victim? The murderer?"

"There's something else," said Lacoste. "The lab's been looking at the wooden Woo.

They say it was carved years ago."

"Was it made by the Hermit?" Gamache asked.

"They're working on it."

"Any progress on what woo might mean?"

"There's a film director named John Woo. He's from China. Did *Mission Impossible II*," said Morin seriously, as though giving them vital information.

"Woo can stand for World of Outlaws. It's a car-racing organization." Lacoste looked at the Chief, who stared back blankly. She looked down hurriedly at her notes for something more helpful to say. "Or there's a video game called Woo."

"Oh, no. I can't believe I forgot that," said Morin, turning to Gamache. "Woo isn't the name of the game, it's the name of a character in a game. The game is called King of the Monsters."

"King of the Monsters?" Gamache thought it unlikely the Hermit or his tormentor had a video game in mind. "Anything else?"

"Well, there's the woo cocktail," suggested Lacoste. "Made from peach schnapps and vodka."

"Then there's woo-woo," said Beauvoir. "It's English slang."

"Vraiment?" said Gamache. "What does it mean?"

"It means crazy." Beauvoir smiled.

"And there's wooing a person. Seducing them," said Lacoste, then shook her head. They weren't any closer.

Gamache dismissed the meeting, then walking back to his computer he typed in a word.

Charlotte.

Gabri chopped the tomatoes and peppers and onions. He chopped and he chopped and he chopped. He'd already chopped the golden plums and strawberries, the beets and pickles. He'd sharpened his knife and chopped some more.

All afternoon and into the evening.

"Can we talk now?" asked Olivier, standing in the doorway to the kitchen. It smelled so comforting, but felt so foreign.

Gabri, his back to the door, didn't pause. He reached for a cauliflower and chopped that.

"Mustard pickles," said Olivier, venturing into the kitchen. "My favorite."

Clunk, clunk, clunk, and the cauliflower was tossed into the boiling pot to blanch.

"I'm sorry," said Olivier.

At the sink Gabri scrubbed lemons, then

cutting them into quarters he shoved them into a jar and sprinkled coarse salt on top. Finally he squeezed the leftover lemons and poured the juice over the salt.

"Can I help?" asked Olivier, reaching for the top of a jar. But Gabri put his body between Olivier and the jars and silently sealed them.

Every surface of the kitchen was packed with colorful jars filled with jams and jellies, pickles and chutneys. And it looked as though Gabri would keep this up forever. Silently preserving everything he could.

Clara chopped the ends off the fresh carrots and watched Peter toss the tiny new potatoes into boiling water. They'd have a simple dinner tonight of vegetables from the garden with herbs and sweet butter. It was one of their favorite meals in late summer.

"I don't know who to feel worse for, Olivier or Gabri," she said.

"I do," said Peter, shelling some peas. "Gabri didn't do anything. Can you believe Olivier's been visiting that guy in the woods for years and didn't tell anyone? I mean, what else isn't he telling us?"

"Did you know he's gay?"

"He's probably straight and isn't telling us."

Clara smirked. "Now that would really piss Gabri off, though I know a couple of women who'd be happy." She paused, knife in mid-air. "I think Olivier feels pretty horrible."

"Come on. He'd still be doing it if the old man hadn't been murdered."

"He didn't do anything wrong, you know," said Clara. "The Hermit gave him everything."

"So he says."

"What do you mean?"

"Well, the Hermit's dead. Isn't that convenient?"

Clara stopped chopping. "What're you saying?"

"Nothing. I'm just angry."

"Why? Because he didn't tell us?"

"Aren't you pissed off?"

"A little. But I think I'm more amazed. Listen, we all know Olivier likes the finer things."

"You mean he's greedy and tight."

"What amazes me is what Olivier did with the body. I just can't imagine him lugging it through the woods and dumping it in the old Hadley house," said Clara. "I didn't think he had the strength."

"I didn't think he had the anger," said Peter.

Clara nodded. Neither did she. And she also wondered what else their friend hadn't told them. All this, though, had also meant that Clara couldn't possibly ask Gabri about being called a "fucking queer." Over dinner she explained this to Peter.

"So," she concluded, her plate almost untouched, "I don't know what to do about Fortin. Should I go into Montreal and speak to him directly about this, or just let it go?"

Peter took another slice of baguette, soft on the inside with a crispy crust. He smeared the butter to the edges, covering every millimeter, evenly. Methodically.

Watching him Clara felt she'd surely scream or explode, or at the very least grab the fucking baguette and toss it until it was a grease stain on the wall.

Still Peter smoothed the knife over the bread. Making sure the butter was perfect.

What should he tell her? To forget it? That what Fortin said wasn't that bad? Certainly not worth risking her career. Just let it go. Besides, saying something almost certainly wouldn't change Fortin's mind about gays, and might just turn him against Clara. And this wasn't some tiny show Fortin was giving her. This was everything Clara had dreamed of. Every artist dreamed of. Everyone from the art world would be there.

Clara's career would be made.

Should he tell her to let it go, or tell Clara she had to speak to Fortin? For Gabri and Olivier and all their gay friends. But mostly for herself.

But if she did that Fortin might get angry, might very well cancel her show.

Peter dug the tip of the knife into a hole in the bread to get the butter out.

He knew what he wanted to say, but he didn't know if he'd be saying it for his sake, or for Clara's.

"Well?" she asked, and heard the impatience in her voice. "Well?" she asked more softly. "What do you think?"

"What do you think?"

Clara searched his face. "I think I should just let it go. If he says it again maybe then I'll say something. It's a stressful time for all of us."

"I'm sure you're right."

Clara looked down at her uneaten plate. She'd heard the hesitation in Peter's voice. Still, he wasn't the one risking everything.

Rosa quacked a little in her sleep. Ruth eased the little flannel nightshirt off the duck and Rosa fluttered her wings then went back to sleep, tucking her beak under her wing.

Olivier had come to visit, flushed and upset. She'd cleared old *New Yorkers* off a chair and he'd sat in her front room like a fugitive. Ruth had brought him a glass of cooking sherry and a celery stick smeared with Velveeta and sat with him. For almost an hour they sat, not speaking, until Rosa entered the room. She waddled in wearing a gray flannel blazer. Ruth saw Olivier's lips press together and his chin pucker. Not a sound escaped. But what did escape were tears, wearing warm lines down his handsome face.

And then he told her what had happened. About Gamache, about the cabin, about the Hermit and his belongings. About moving the body and owning the bistro, and the boulangerie and almost everything else in Three Pines.

Ruth didn't care. All she could think of was what she'd give in exchange for words. To say something. The right thing. To tell Olivier that she loved him. That Gabri loved him and would never, ever leave. That love could never leave.

She imagined herself getting up and sitting beside him, and taking his trembling hand and saying, "There, there."

There, there. And softly rubbing his heaving back until he caught his breath.

Instead she'd poured herself more cooking sherry and glared.

Now, with the sun set and Olivier gone, Ruth sat in her kitchen in the white plastic garden chair at the plastic table she'd found at the dump. Sufficiently drunk, she pulled the notebook close and with Rosa quietly quacking in the background, a small knit blanket over her, Ruth wrote:

She rose up into the air and the jilted
earth let out a sigh.
She rose up past telephone poles and
rooftops of houses where the
earthbound hid.
She rose up but remembered to politely
wave good-bye . . .

And then kissing Rosa on the head she limped up the stairs to bed.

Twenty-Eight

When Clara came down the next morning she was surprised to find Peter in the garden, staring into space. He'd put on the coffee, and now she poured a couple of cups and joined him.

"Sleep well?" she asked, handing him a mug.

"Not really. You?"

"Not bad. Why didn't you?"

It was an overcast morning with a chill in the air. The first morning that really felt as though summer was over, and autumn on the way. She loved the fall. The brilliant leaves, the lit fireplaces, the smell of woodsmoke through the village. She loved huddling at a table outside the bistro, wrapped in sweaters and sipping *café au lait.*

Peter pursed his lips and looked down at his feet, in rubber boots to protect against the heavy dew.

"I was thinking about your question. What

to do about Fortin."

Clara grew still. "Go on."

Peter had thought about it most of the night. Had got up and gone downstairs, pacing around the kitchen and finally ending up in his studio. His refuge. It smelled of him. Of body odor, and oil paint and canvas. It smelled faintly of lemon meringue pie, which he couldn't explain. It smelled like no other place on earth.

And it comforted him.

He'd gone into his studio last night to think, and finally to stop thinking. To clear his mind of the howl that had grown, like something massive approaching. And finally, just before sunrise, he knew what he had to say to Clara.

"I think you should talk to him."

There. He'd said it. Beside him Clara was silent, her hands grasping the warm cup of coffee.

"Really?"

Peter nodded. "I'm sorry. Do you want me to come with you?"

"I'm not even sure I'm going yet," she snapped and walked a couple of paces away.

Peter wanted to run to her, to take it back, to say he was wrong. She should stay there with him, should say nothing. Should just do the show.

What had he been thinking?

"You're right." She turned back to him, miserable. "He won't mind, will he?"

"Fortin? No. You don't have to be angry, just tell him how you feel, that's all. I'm sure he'll understand."

"I can just say that maybe I misheard. And that Gabri is one of our best friends."

"That's it. Fortin probably doesn't even remember saying it."

"I'm sure he won't mind." Clara walked slowly inside to call Fortin.

"Denis? It's Clara Morrow. Yes, that was fun. Really, is that a good price? Sure, I'll tell the Chief Inspector. Listen, I'm going to be in Montreal today and thought maybe we could get together again. I have . . . well, a few thoughts." She paused. "Uh-huh. Uh-huh. That sounds great. Twelve thirty at the Santropole on Duluth. Perfect."

What have I done? Peter asked himself.

Breakfast at the B and B was a somber affair of burned toast, rubber eggs and black bacon. The coffee was weak and the milk seemed curdled, as did Gabri. By mutual, unspoken consent they didn't discuss the case, but waited until they were back at the Incident Room.

"Oh, thank God," said Agent Lacoste, as

she fell on the Tim Hortons double double coffees Agent Morin had brought. And the chocolate-glazed doughnuts. "I never thought I'd prefer this to Gabri's breakfasts." She took a huge bite of soft, sweet doughnut. "If this keeps up we might have to solve the case and leave."

"There's a thought," said Gamache, putting on his half-moon reading glasses.

Beauvoir went over to his computer to check messages. There, taped to the monitor, was a scrap of paper with familiar writing. He ripped it off, scrunched it up and tossed it to the floor.

Chief Inspector Gamache also looked at his screen. The results of his Google search of "Charlotte."

Sipping his coffee he read about Good Charlotte, the band, and Charlotte Brontë, and Charlotte Church and *Charlotte's Web*, the city of Charlotte in North Carolina and Charlottetown on Prince Edward Island and the Queen Charlotte Islands on the other side of the continent, off British Columbia. Most of the places were named after Queen Charlotte, he discovered.

"Does the name Charlotte mean anything to you?" he asked his team.

After thinking for a moment, they shook their heads.

"How about Queen Charlotte? She was married to King George."

"George the Third? The crazy one?" Morin asked. The others looked at him in amazement. Agent Morin smiled. "I was good at history in school."

It helped, thought Gamache, that school for him wasn't all that long ago. The phone rang and Agent Morin took it. It was the Martinù Conservatory, in Prague. Gamache listened to Morin's side of the conversation until his own phone rang.

It was Superintendent Brunel.

"I arrived to find my office looking like Hannibal's tent. I can barely move for your Hermit's items, Armand." She didn't sound displeased. "But I'm not calling about that. I have an invitation. Would you like to join Jérôme and me for lunch at our apartment? He has something he'd like to show you. And I have news as well."

It was confirmed he'd meet them at one o'clock at the Brunel apartment on rue Laurier. As he hung up the phone rang again.

"Clara Morrow for you, sir," said Agent Morin.

"*Bonjour,* Clara."

"*Bonjour.* I just wanted to let you know I spoke to Denis Fortin this morning. In fact, we're having lunch today. He told me he'd found a buyer for the carvings."

"Is that right? Who?"

"I didn't ask, but he says they're willing to pay a thousand dollars for the two. He seemed to think that was a good price."

"That is interesting. Would you like a lift into town? I'm meeting someone myself."

"Sure, thank you."

"I'll be by in about half an hour."

When he hung up Agent Morin was off his call.

"They said Martinù had no children. They were aware of the violin, but it disappeared after his death in," Morin consulted his notes, "1959. I told them we'd found the violin and an original copy of the score. They were very excited and said it would be worth a lot of money. In fact, it would be considered a Czech national treasure."

There was that word again. Treasure.

"Did you ask about his wife, Charlotte?"

"I did. They were together a long time, but only actually married on his deathbed. She died a few years ago. No family."

Gamache nodded, thinking. Then he spoke to Agent Morin again. "I need you to look into the Czech community here, especially the Parras. And find out about their lives in the Czech Republic. How they got out, who they knew there, their family. Everything."

He went over to Beauvoir. "I'm heading into Montreal for the day to talk to Superintendent Brunel and follow some leads."

"*D'accord.* As soon as Morin gets the information on the Parras I'll go up there."

"Don't go alone."

"I won't."

Gamache stooped and picked up the scrap of paper on the floor by Beauvoir's desk. He opened it and read, *In the midst of your nightmare,*

"In the midst of your nightmare," he repeated, handing it to Beauvoir. "What do you think it means?"

Beauvoir shrugged and opened the drawer to his desk. A nest of balled-up words lay there. "I find them everywhere. In my coat pocket, pinned to my door in the morning. This one was taped to my computer."

Gamache reached into the desk and chose a scrap at random.

that the deity who kills for pleasure
will also heal,

"They're all like this?"

Beauvoir nodded. "Each crazier than the last. What'm I supposed to do with them? She's just pissed off because we took over her fire hall. Do you think I can get a restraining order?"

"Against an eighty-year-old winner of the Governor General's award, to stop her sending you verse?"

When put that way it didn't sound likely.

Gamache looked again at the balls of paper, like hail. "Well, I'm off."

"Thanks for your help," Beauvoir called after him.

"De rien," waved Gamache and was gone.

In the hour or so drive into Montreal Gamache and Clara talked about the people of Three Pines, about the summer visitors, about the Gilberts, who Clara thought might stay now.

"Old Mundin and Charles were in the village the other day. Old is very taken with Vincent Gilbert. He apparently knew it was him in the woods, but didn't want to say anything."

"How would he have recognized him?"

"Being," said Clara.

"Of course," said Gamache, merging onto the autoroute into Montreal. "Charles has Down's syndrome."

"After he was born Myrna gave them a copy of *Being*. Reading it changed their lives. Changed lots of lives. Myrna says Dr.

Gilbert's a great man."

"I'm sure he wouldn't disagree."

Clara laughed. "Still, I don't think I'd like to be raised by a saint."

Gamache had to agree. Most saints were martyrs. And they took a lot of people down with them. In companionable silence they drove past signs for Saint-Hilaire, Saint-Jean and a village named Ange Gardien.

"If I said 'woo,' what would you think?" Gamache asked.

"Beyond the obvious?" She gave him a mock-worried look.

"Does the word mean anything to you?"

The fact he'd come back to it alerted Clara. "Woo," she repeated. "There's pitching woo, an old-fashioned way of saying courting."

"Old-fashioned for courting?" He laughed. "But I know what you mean. I don't think that's what I'm looking for."

"Sorry, can't help."

"Oh, it probably doesn't matter." They were over the Champlain Bridge. Gamache drove up Boulevard Saint-Laurent, turned left then left again and dropped her at the Santropole restaurant for lunch.

Climbing the steps she turned and walked back. Leaning into the car window she asked, "If a person insulted someone you cared about, would you say something?"

Gamache thought about that. "I hope I would."

She nodded and left. But she knew Gamache, and knew there was no "hope" about it.

Twenty-Nine

After a luncheon of herbed cucumber soup, grilled shrimp and fennel salad and peach tarte Gamache and the Brunels settled into the bright living room of the second-floor apartment. It was lined with bookcases. *Objets trouvés* lay here and there. Pieces of aged and broken pottery, chipped mugs. It was a room that was lived in, where people read, and talked and thought and laughed.

"I've been researching the items in the cabin," said Thérèse Brunel.

"And?" Gamache leaned forward on the sofa, holding his *demi-tasse* of espresso.

"So far nothing. Amazing as it sounds, none of the items has been reported stolen, though I haven't finished yet. It'll take weeks to properly trace them."

Gamache slowly leaned back and crossed his long legs. If not stolen, then what? "What's the other option?" he asked.

"Well, that the dead man actually owned

the pieces. Or that they were looted from dead people, who couldn't report it. In a war, for instance. Like the Amber Room."

"Or maybe they were given to him," suggested her husband, Jérôme.

"But they're priceless," objected Thérèse. "Why would someone give them to him?"

"Services rendered?" he said.

All three were silent then, imagining what service could exact such a payment.

"*Bon,* Armand, I have something to show you." Jérôme rose to his full height of just five and a half feet. He was an almost perfect square but carried his bulk with ease as though his body was filled with the thoughts overflowing from his head.

He wedged himself onto the sofa beside Gamache. He had in his hands the two carvings.

"First of all, these are remarkable. They almost speak, don't you find? My job, Thérèse told me, was to figure out what they're saying. Or, more specifically, what these mean."

He turned the carvings over to reveal the letters carved there.

MRKBVYDDO was etched under the people on the shore.

OWSVI was under the sailing ship.

"This's a code of some sort," explained

Jérôme, putting his glasses on and peering closely at the letters again. "I started with the easiest one. Qwerty. It's the one an amateur's most likely to use. Do you know it?"

"It's a typewriter's keyboard. Also a computer's," said Gamache. "Qwerty is the first few letters on the top line."

"What the person using Qwerty generally does is go to the keyboard and type the letter next to the one you really mean. Very easy to decode. This isn't it, by the way. No." Jérôme hauled himself up and Gamache almost tumbled into the void left by his body. "I went through a whole lot of ciphers and frankly I haven't found anything. I'm sorry."

Gamache had been hopeful this master of codes would be able to crack the Hermit's. But like so much else with this case, it wouldn't reveal itself easily.

"But I think I know what sort of code it is. I think it's a Caesar's Shift."

"Go on."

"Bon," said Jérôme, relishing the challenge and the audience. "Julius Caesar was a genius. He's really the cipher fanatic's emperor. Brilliant. He used the Greek alphabet to send secret messages to his troops in France. But later he refined his

codes. He switched to the Roman alphabet, the one we use now, but he shifted the letters by three. So if the word you want to send is kill, the code in Caesar's Shift becomes . . ." He grabbed a piece of paper and wrote the alphabet.

A B C D E F G H I J K L M N O P Q R S T U V W X Y Z

Then he circled four letters.

NLOO

"See?"

Gamache and Thérèse leaned over his messy desk.

"So he just shifted the letters," said Gamache. "If the code under the carvings is a Caesar's Shift, can't you just decode it that way? Move the letters back by three?"

He looked at the letters under the sailing ship.

"That would make this . . . L, T, P. Okay, I don't have to go further. It makes no sense."

"No, Caesar was smart and I think this Hermit was too. Or at least, he knew his codes. The brilliance of the Caesar's Shift is that it's almost impossible to break because the shift can be whatever length you want. Or, better still, you can use a key word. One you and your contact aren't likely to forget.

You write it at the beginning of the alphabet, then start the cipher. Let's say it's Montreal."

He went back to his alphabet and wrote Montreal under the first eight letters, then filled in the rest of the twenty-six beginning with A.

A B C D E F G H I J K L M N O P Q R S T U V W X Y Z

M O N T R E A L A B C D E F G H I J K L M N O P Q R

"So, now if the message we want to send is kill, what's the code?" Jérôme asked Gamache.

The Chief Inspector took the pencil and circled four letters.

CADD

"Exactly," beamed Dr. Brunel. Gamache stared, fascinated. Thérèse, who'd seen all this before, stood back and smiled, proud of her clever husband.

"We need the key word." Gamache straightened up.

"That's all," laughed Jérôme.

"Well, I think I have it."

Jérôme nodded, pulled up a chair and sat down. In a clear hand he wrote the alphabet once again.

A B C D E F G H I J K L M N O P Q R S T U V W X Y Z

His pencil hovered over the next line down.

"Charlotte," said Gamache.

Clara and Denis Fortin lingered over their coffee. The back garden of the Santropole restaurant was almost empty. The rush of the lunch crowd, mostly bohemian young people from the Plateau Mont Royal *quartier,* had disappeared.

The bill had just arrived and Clara knew it was now or never.

"There is one other thing I wanted to talk to you about."

"The carvings? Did you bring them?" Fortin leaned forward.

"No, the Chief Inspector still has them, but I told him about your offer. I think part of the problem is they're evidence in the murder case."

"Of course. There's no rush, though I suspect this buyer might not be interested for long. It really is most extraordinary that anyone would want them."

Clara nodded and thought maybe they could just leave. She could go back to Three Pines, make up a guest list for the *vernissage* and forget about it. Already Fortin's comment about Gabri was fading. Surely it wasn't that serious.

"So, what did you want to talk about? Whether you should buy a home in Provence or Tuscany? How about a yacht?"

Clara wasn't sure if he was kidding, but she did know he wasn't making this easy.

"It's just a tiny thing, really. I must have heard wrong, but it seemed to me when you came down to Three Pines yesterday you said something about Gabri."

Fortin looked interested, concerned, puzzled.

"He was our waiter," Clara explained. "He brought us our drinks."

Fortin was still staring. She could feel her brain evaporate. Suddenly, after practicing most of the morning what she'd say, she couldn't even remember her own name. "Well, I just thought, you know . . ."

Her voice trailed off. She couldn't do it. This must be a sign, she thought, a sign from God that she wasn't supposed to say anything. That she was making something out of nothing.

"Doesn't matter," she smiled. "I just thought I'd tell you his name."

Fortunately she figured Fortin was used to dealing with artists who were drunk, deranged, stoned. Clara appeared to be all three. She must, in his eyes, be a brilliant artist to be so unhinged.

Fortin signed for the bill and left, Clara noticed, a very large tip.

"I remember him." Fortin led her back through the restaurant with its dark wood and scent of tisane. "He was the fag."

VDTK?? MMF/X

They stared at the letters. The more they stared the less sense they made, which was saying something.

"Any other suggestions?" Jérôme looked up from his desk.

Gamache was flabbergasted. He was sure they had it, that "Charlotte" was the key to break the cipher. He thought for a moment, scanning the case.

"Woo," he said. They tried that.

Nothing.

"Walden." But he knew he was grasping. And sure enough, nothing.

Nothing, nothing, nothing. What had he missed?

"Well, I'll keep trying," said Jérôme. "It might not be a Caesar's Shift. There're plenty of other codes."

He smiled reassuringly and the Chief Inspector had a sense of what Dr. Brunel's patients must have felt. The news was bad, but they had a man who wouldn't give up.

"What can you tell me about one of your

colleagues, Vincent Gilbert?" Gamache asked.

"He was no colleague of mine," said Jérôme, testily. "Not of anyone's from what I remember. He didn't suffer fools easily. Do you notice most people who feel like that consider everyone a fool?"

"That bad?"

"Jérôme's only annoyed because Dr. Gilbert thought himself God," said Thérèse, perching on the arm of her husband's chair.

"Difficult to work with," said Gamache, who'd worked with a few gods himself.

"Oh no, it wasn't that," smiled Thérèse. "It annoyed Jérôme because he knows he's the one true God and Gilbert refused to worship."

They laughed but Jérôme's smile faded first. "Very dangerous man, Vincent Gilbert. I think he really does have a God complex. Megalomaniac. Very clever. That book he wrote . . ."

"Being," said Gamache.

"Yes. It was designed, every word calculated for effect. And I've got to hand it to him, it worked. Most people who've read it agree with him. He is at the very least a great man, and perhaps even a saint."

"You don't believe it?"

Dr. Brunel snorted. "The only miracle

he's performed is convincing everyone of his saintliness. No mean feat, given what an asshole he is. Do I believe it? No."

"Well, it's time for my news." Thérèse Brunel stood up. "Come with me."

Gamache followed her, leaving Jérôme to fiddle with the cipher. The study was filled with more papers and magazines. Thérèse sat at her computer and after a few quick taps a photograph appeared. It showed a carving of a shipwreck.

Gamache pulled up a chair and stared. "Is it . . ."

"Another carving? *Oui.*" She smiled, like a magician who'd produced a particularly spectacular rabbit.

"The Hermit made this?" Gamache twisted in his chair and looked at her. She nodded. He looked back at the screen. The carving was complex. On one side was the shipwreck, then some forest, and on the other side a tiny village being built. "Even in a photograph it seems alive. I can see the little people. Are they the same ones from the other carvings?"

"I think so. But I can't find the frightened boy."

Gamache searched the village, the ship on the shore, the forest. Nothing. What happened to him? "We need to have the carving," he said.

"This's in a private collection in Zurich. I've contacted a gallery owner I know there. Very influential man. He said he'd help."

Gamache knew enough not to press Superintendent Brunel about her connections.

"It's not just the boy," he said. "We need to know what's written underneath it."

Like the others this one was, on the surface, pastoral, peaceful. But something lurked on the fringes. A disquiet.

And yet, once again, the tiny wooden people seemed happy.

"There's another one. In a collection in Cape Town." The screen flickered and another carving appeared. A boy was lying, either asleep or dead, on the side of a mountain. Gamache put on his glasses and leaned closer, squinting.

"Hard to tell, but I think it's the same young man."

"So do I," said the Superintendent.

"Is he dead?"

"I wondered that myself, but I don't think so. Do you notice something about this carving, Armand?"

Gamache leaned back and took a deep breath, releasing some of the tension he felt. He closed his eyes, then opened them again. But this time not to look at the image on the screen. This time he wanted to sense it.

After a moment he knew Thérèse Brunel was right. This carving was different. It was clearly the same artist, there was no mistaking that, but one significant element had changed.

"There's no fear."

Thérèse nodded. "Only peace. Contentment."

"Even love," said the Chief Inspector. He longed to hold this carving, to own it even, though he knew he never would. And he felt, not for the first time, that soft tug of desire. Of greed. He knew he'd never act on it. But he knew others might. This was a carving worth owning. All of them were, he suspected.

"What do you know about them?" he asked.

"They were sold through a company in Geneva. I know it well. Very discreet, very high end."

"What did he get for them?"

"They sold seven of them. The first was six years ago. It went for fifteen thousand. The prices went up until they reached three hundred thousand for the last one. It sold this past winter. He says he figures he could get at least half a million for the next one."

Gamache exhaled in astonishment. "Whoever sold them must have made hundreds of thousands."

"The auction house in Geneva takes a hefty commission, but I did a quick calculation. The seller would have made about one point five million."

Gamache's mind was racing. And then it ran into a fact. Or rather into a statement.

I threw the carvings away, into the woods, when I walked home.

Olivier had said it. And once again, Olivier had lied.

Foolish, foolish man, thought Gamache. Then he looked back at the computer screen and the boy lying supine on the mountain, almost caressing it. Was it possible, he asked himself.

Could Olivier have actually done it? Killed the Hermit?

A million dollars was a powerful motive. But why kill the man who supplied the art?

No, there was more Olivier wasn't telling, and if Gamache had any hope of finding the real killer it was time for the truth.

Why does Gabri have to be such a fucking queer, thought Clara. And a fag. And why do I have to be such a fucking coward?

"Yes, that's the one," she heard herself say, in an out-of-body moment. The day had warmed up but she pulled her coat closer as they stood on the sidewalk.

"Where can I drive you?" Denis Fortin asked.

Where? Clara didn't know where Gamache would be but she had his cell-phone number. "I'll find my own way, thanks."

They shook hands.

"This show's going to be huge, for both of us. I'm very happy for you," he said, warmly.

"There is one other thing. Gabri. He's a friend of mine."

She felt his hand release hers. But still, he smiled at her.

"I just need to say that he's not queer and he's not a fag."

"He isn't? He sure seems gay."

"Well, yes, he's gay." She could feel herself growing confused.

"What're you saying, Clara?"

"You called him queer, and a fag."

"Yes?"

"It just didn't seem very nice."

Now she felt like a schoolgirl. Words like "nice" weren't used very often in the art world. Unless it was as an insult.

"You're not trying to censor me, are you?"

His voice had become like treacle. Clara could feel his words sticking to her. And his eyes, once thoughtful, were now hard. With warning.

"No, I'm just saying that I was surprised and I didn't like hearing my friend called names."

"But he is queer and a fag. You admitted it yourself."

"I said he's gay." She could feel her cheeks sizzling and knew she must be beet red.

"Oh," he sighed and shook his head. "I understand." He looked at her with sadness now, as one might look at a sick pet. "It's the small-town girl after all. You've been in that tiny village too long, Clara. It's made you small-minded. You censor yourself and now you're trying to stifle my voice. That's very dangerous. Political correctness, Clara. An artist needs to break down boundaries, push, challenge, shock. You're not willing to do that, are you?"

She stood staring, unable to grasp what he was saying.

"No, I didn't think so," he said. "I tell the truth, and I say it in a way that might shock, but is at least real. You'd prefer something just pretty. And nice."

"You insulted a lovely man, behind his back," she said. But she could feel the tears now. Of rage, but she knew how it must look. It must look like weakness.

"I'm going to have to reconsider the show," he said. "I'm very disappointed. I thought you were the real deal, but obviously you were just pretending. Superficial. Trite. I can't risk my gallery's reputation on someone not willing to take artistic risks."

There was a rare break in traffic and Denis Fortin darted across Saint-Urbain. On the other side he looked back and shook his head again. Then he walked briskly to his car.

Inspector Jean Guy Beauvoir and Agent Morin approached the Parra home. Beauvoir had expected something traditional. Something a Czech woodsman might live in. A Swiss chalet perhaps. To Beauvoir there was Québécois and then "other." Foreign. The Chinese were all alike, as were Africans. The South Americans, if he thought of them at all, looked the same, ate the same foods and lived in exactly the same homes. A place somewhat less attractive than his own. The English he knew to be all the same. Nuts.

Swiss, Czech, German, Norwegian, Swedish all blended nicely together. They were tall, blond, good athletes if slightly thick and lived in A-frame homes with lots of paneling and milk.

He slowed the car and it meandered to a stop in front of the Parra place. All he saw was glass, some gleaming in the sun, some reflecting the sky and clouds and birds and woods, the mountains beyond and a small white steeple. The church at Three Pines, in the distance, brought forward by this beautiful house that was a reflection of all life around it.

"You just caught me. I was heading back to work," said Roar, opening the door.

He led Beauvoir and Morin into the house. It was filled with light. The floors were polished concrete. Firm, solid. It made the house feel very secure while allowing it to soar. And soar it did.

"Merde," Beauvoir whispered, walking into the great room. The combination kitchen, dining area and living room. With walls of glass on three sides it felt as though there was no division between this world and the next. Between in and out. Between forest and home.

Where else would a Czech woodsman live but in the woods. In a home made of light.

Hanna Parra was at the sink, drying her hands, and Havoc was just putting away the lunch dishes. The place smelled of soup.

"Not working at the bistro?" Beauvoir asked Havoc.

"Split shift today. Olivier asked if I'd mind."

"And do you?"

"Mind?" They walked over to the long dining table and sat. "No. I think he's pretty stressed."

"What's he like to work for?" Beauvoir noticed Morin take out his notebook and a pen. He'd told the young agent to do that when they arrived. It rattled suspects and Beauvoir liked them rattled.

"He's great, but I only have my dad to compare him to."

"And what's that supposed to mean?" asked Roar. Beauvoir studied the small, powerful man for signs of aggression, but it seemed a running joke in the family.

"At least Olivier doesn't make me work with saws and axes and machetes."

"Olivier's chocolate torte and ice cream are far more dangerous. At least you know to be careful with an axe."

Beauvoir realized he'd cut to the quick of the case. What appeared threatening wasn't. And what appeared wonderful, wasn't.

"I'd like to show you a picture of the dead man."

"We've already seen it. Agent Lacoste showed it to us," said Hanna.

"I'd like you to look again."

"What's this about, Inspector?" asked Hanna.

"You're Czech."

"What of it?"

"Been here for a while, I know," Beauvoir continued, ignoring her. "Lots came after the Russian invasion."

"There's a healthy Czech community here," Hanna agreed.

"In fact, it's so big there's even a Czech Association. You meet once a month and have pot-luck dinners."

All this and more he'd learned from Agent Morin's research.

"That's right," said Roar, watching Beauvoir carefully, wondering where this was leading.

"And you've been the president of the association a few times," Beauvoir said to Roar, then turned to Hanna. "You both have."

"That's not much of an honor, Inspector," smiled Hanna. "We take turns. It's on a rotation basis."

"Is it fair to say you know everyone in the local Czech community?"

They looked at each other, guarded now, and nodded.

"So you should know our victim. He was Czech." Beauvoir took the photograph out of his pocket and placed it on the table. But they didn't look. All three were staring at him. Surprised. That he knew? Or that the man was Czech?

Beauvoir had to admit it could have been either.

Then Roar picked up the photo and stared at it. Shaking his head he handed it to his wife. "We've already seen it, and told Agent Lacoste the same thing. We don't know him. If he was Czech he didn't come to any dinners. He made no contact with us at all. You'll have to ask the others, of course."

"We are." Beauvoir tucked the picture into his pocket. "Agents are talking to other members of your community right now."

"Is that profiling?" asked Hanna Parra. She wasn't smiling.

"No, it's investigating. If the victim was Czech it's reasonable to ask around that community, don't you think?"

The phone rang. Hanna went to it and looked down. "It's Eva." She picked it up and spoke in French, saying a Sûreté officer was with her now, and no she didn't recognize the photograph either. And yes, she was also surprised the man had been Czech.

Clever, thought Beauvoir. Hanna put down the receiver and it immediately rang again.

"It's Yanna," she said, this time leaving it. The phone, they realized, would ring all afternoon. As the agents arrived, interviewed and left. And the Czech community called each other.

It seemed vaguely sinister, until Beauvoir reluctantly admitted to himself he'd do the same thing.

"Do you know Bohuslav Martinù?"

"Who?"

Beauvoir repeated it, then showed them the printout.

"Oh, Bohuslav Martinù," Roar said, pronouncing it in a way that was unintelligible to Beauvoir. "He's a Czech composer. Don't tell me you suspect him?"

Roar laughed, but Hanna didn't and neither did Havoc.

"Does anyone here have ties to him?"

"No, no one," said Hanna, with certainty.

Morin's research of the Parras had turned up very little. Their relations in the Czech Republic seemed limited to an aunt and a few cousins. They'd escaped in their early twenties and claimed refugee status in Canada, which had been granted. They were now citizens.

Nothing remarkable. No ties to Martinù. No ties to anyone famous or infamous. No woo, no Charlotte, no treasure. Nothing.

And yet Beauvoir was convinced they knew more than they were telling. More than Morin had managed to find.

As they drove away, their retreating reflection in the glass house, Beauvoir wondered if the Parras were quite as transparent as their home.

"I have a question for you," said Gamache as they wandered back into the Brunel living room. Jerome looked up briefly then went back to trying to tease some sense from the cryptic letters.

"Ask away."

"Denis Fortin —"

"Of the Galerie Fortin?" the Superintendent interrupted.

Gamache nodded. "He was visiting Three Pines yesterday and saw one of the carvings. He said it wasn't worth anything."

Thérèse Brunel paused. "I'm not surprised. He's a respected art dealer. Quite remarkable at spotting new talent. But his specialty isn't sculpture, though he handles some very prominent sculptors."

"But even I could see the carvings are remarkable. Why couldn't he?"

"What're you suggesting, Armand? That he lied?"

"Is it possible?"

Thérèse considered. "I suppose. I always find it slightly amusing, and sometimes useful, the general perception of the art world. People on the outside seem to think it's made up of arrogant, crazed artists, numbskull buyers and gallery owners who bring the two together. In fact it's a business, and anyone who doesn't understand that and appreciate it gets buried. In some cases hundreds of millions of dollars are at stake. But even bigger than the piles of cash are the egos. Put immense wealth and even larger egos together and you have a volatile mix. It's a brutal, often ugly, often violent world."

Gamache thought about Clara and wondered if she realized that. Wondered if she knew what was waiting for her, beyond the pale.

"But not everyone's like that, surely," he said.

"No. But at that level," she nodded to the carvings on the table by her husband, "they are. One man's dead. It's possible as we look closer others have been killed."

"Over these carvings?" Gamache picked up the ship.

"Over the money."

Gamache peered at the sculpture. He knew that not everyone was motivated solely by money. There were other currencies. Jealousy, rage, revenge. He looked not at the passengers sailing into a happy future, but at the one looking back. To where they'd been. With terror.

"I do have some good news for you, Armand."

Gamache lowered the ship and looked at the Superintendent.

"I've found your 'woo.'"

Thirty

"There it is." Thérèse Brunel pointed.

They'd driven into downtown Montreal and now the Superintendent was pointing at a building. Gamache slowed the car and immediately provoked honking. In Quebec it was almost a capital crime to slow down. He didn't speed up, ignored the honking, and tried to see what she was pointing at. It was an art gallery. Heffel's. And outside was a bronze sculpture. But the car had drifted past before he got a good look. He spent the next twenty minutes trying to find a parking spot.

"Can't you just double-park?" asked Superintendent Brunel.

"If we want to be slaughtered, yes."

She harrumphed, but didn't disagree. Finally they parked and walked back along Sherbrooke Street until they were in front of Heffel's Art Gallery, staring at a bronze sculpture Gamache had seen before but never stopped to look at.

His cell phone vibrated. *"Pardon,"* he said to the Superintendent, and answered it.

"It's Clara. I'm wondering when you might be ready."

"In just a few minutes. Are you all right?" She'd sounded shaky, upset.

"I'm just fine. Where can I meet you?"

"I'm on Sherbrooke, just outside Heffel's Gallery."

"I know it. I can be there in a few minutes. Is that okay?" She sounded keen, even anxious, to leave.

"Perfect. I'll be here."

He put the phone away and went back to the sculpture. Silently he walked around it while Thérèse Brunel watched, a look of some amusement on her face.

What he saw was an almost life-sized bronze of a frumpy middle-aged woman standing beside a horse, a dog at her side and a monkey on the horse's back. When he arrived back at Superintendent Brunel he stopped.

"This is 'woo'?"

"No, this is Emily Carr. It's by Joe Fafard and is called *Emily and Friends.*"

Gamache smiled then and shook his head. Of course it was. Now he could see it. The woman, matronly, squat, ugly, had been one of Canada's most remarkable artists. Gifted and visionary, she'd painted mostly in the early 1900s and was now long dead. But her art only grew in significance and influence.

He looked more closely at the bronze woman. She was younger here than the images he'd seen of her in grainy old black-and-white photos. They almost always showed a masculine woman, alone. In a forest. And not smiling, not happy.

This woman was happy. Perhaps it was the conceit of the sculptor.

"It's wonderful, isn't it?" Superintendent Brunel said. "Normally Emily Carr looks gruesome. I think it's brilliant to show her happy, as she apparently only was around her animals. It was people she hated."

"You said you'd found 'woo.' Where?"

He was disappointed and far from convinced Superintendent Brunel was right. How could a long dead painter from across the continent have anything to do with the case?

Thérèse Brunel walked up to the sculpture and placed one manicured hand on the monkey.

"This is Woo. Emily Carr's constant companion."

"Woo's a monkey?"

"She adored all animals, but Woo above all."

Gamache crossed his arms over his chest and stared. "It's an interesting theory, but the 'woo' in the Hermit's cabin could mean anything. What makes you think it's Emily Carr's monkey?"

"Because of this."

She opened her handbag and handed him a glossy brochure. It was for a retrospective of the works of Emily Carr, at the Vancouver Art Gallery. Gamache looked at the photographs of Carr's unmistakable paintings of the West Coast wilderness almost a century ago.

Her work was extraordinary. Rich greens and browns swirled together so that the forest seemed both frenzied and tranquil. It was a forest long gone. Logged, clear-cut, ruined. But still alive, thanks to the brush and brilliance of Emily Carr.

But that wasn't what had made her famous.

Gamache flipped through the brochure until he found them. Her signature series. Depicting what haunted any Canadian soul who saw them.

The totem poles.

Sitting on the shores of a remote Haida fishing village in northern British Columbia.

She'd painted them where the Haida had put them.

And then a single perfect finger pointed to three small words.

Queen Charlotte Islands.

That's where they were.

Charlotte.

Gamache felt a thrill. Could they really have found Woo?

"The Hermit's sculptures were carved from red cedar," said Thérèse Brunel. "So was the word Woo. Red cedar grows in a few places, but not here. Not Quebec. One of the places it grows is in British Columbia."

"On the Queen Charlotte Islands," whispered Gamache, mesmerized by the paintings of the totem poles. Straight, tall, magnificent. Not yet felled as heathen, not yet yanked down by missionaries and the government.

Emily Carr's paintings were the only images of the totems as the Haida meant them to be. She never painted people, but she painted what they created. Long houses. And towering totem poles.

Gamache stared, losing himself in the wild beauty, and the approaching disaster.

Then he looked again at the inscription. Haida village. Queen Charlottes.

And he knew Thérèse was right. Woo pointed to Emily Carr, and Carr pointed to the Queen Charlotte Islands. This must be why there were so many references to Charlotte in the Hermit's cabin. *Charlotte's Web,* Charlotte Brontë. Charlotte Martinù, who'd given her husband the violin. The Amber Room had been made for a Charlotte. All leading him here. To the Queen Charlotte Islands.

"You can keep that." Superintendent Brunel pointed to the brochure. "It has a lot of biographical information on Emily Carr. It might be helpful."

"Merci." Gamache closed the catalog and stared at the sculpture of Carr, the woman who had captured Canada's shame, not by painting the displaced, broken people, but by painting their glory.

Clara stared at the gray waters of the St. Lawrence as they drove over the Champlain Bridge.

"How was your lunch?" Gamache asked when they were on the autoroute heading to Three Pines.

"Well, it could have been better."

Clara's mood was swinging wildly from fury to guilt to regret. One moment she felt she should have told Denis Fortin more clearly what a piece of *merde* he was, the next she was dying to get home so she could call and apologize.

Clara was a fault-magnet. Criticisms, critiques, blame flew through the air and clung to her. She seemed to attract the negative, perhaps because she was so positive.

Well, she'd had enough. She sat up straighter in her seat. Fuck him. But, then again, maybe she should apologize and stand up for herself after the solo show.

What an idiot she'd been. Why in the world had she thought it was a good idea to piss off the gallery owner who was offering her fame and fortune? Recognition. Approval. Attention.

Damn, what had she done? And was it reversible? Surely she could have waited until the day after the opening, when the reviews were in the *New York Times,* the London *Times.* When his fury couldn't ruin her, as it could now.

As it would now.

She'd heard his words. But more important, she'd seen it in Fortin's face. He would ruin her. Though to ruin implied there was something built up to tear down. No, what he'd do was worse. He'd make sure the world never heard of Clara Morrow. Never saw her paintings.

She looked at the time on Gamache's dashboard.

Ten to four. The heavy traffic out of the city was thinning. They'd be home in an hour. If they got back before five she could call his gallery and prostrate herself.

Or maybe she should call and tell him what an asshole he was.

It was a very long drive back.

"Do you want to talk about it?" Gamache asked after half an hour of silence. They'd turned off the highway and were heading toward Cowansville.

"I'm not really sure what to say. Denis Fortin called Gabri a fucking queer yesterday in the bistro. Gabri didn't hear it, but I did, and I didn't say anything. I talked to Peter and Myrna about it, and they listened, but they pretty much left it up to me. Until this morning when Peter kinda said I should talk to Fortin."

Gamache turned off the main road. The businesses and homes receded and the forest closed in.

"How did Fortin react?" he asked.

"He said he'd cancel the show."

Gamache sighed. "I'm sorry about that, Clara."

He glanced over at her unhappy face staring out the window. She reminded him of his daughter Annie the other night. A weary lion.

"How was your day?" she asked. They were on the dirt road now, bumping along. It was a road not used by many. Mostly just by people who knew where they were going, or had completely lost their way.

"Productive, I think. I have a question for you."

"Ask away." She seemed relieved to have something else to do besides watching the clock click closer to five.

"What do you know about Emily Carr?"

"Now, I'd never have bet that was the question," she smiled, then gathered her thoughts. "We studied her in art school. She was a huge inspiration to lots of Canadian artists, certainly the women. She inspired me."

"How?"

"She went into the wilderness where no one else dared to go, with just her easel."

"And her monkey."

"Is that a euphemism, Chief Inspector?"

Gamache laughed. "No. Go on."

"Well, she was just very independent. And her work evolved. At first it was representational. A tree was a tree, a house a house. It was almost a documentary. She wanted to capture the Haida, you know, in their villages, before they were destroyed."

"Most of her work was on the Queen Charlotte Islands, I understand."

"Many of her most famous works are, yes. At some point she realized that painting exactly what could be seen wasn't enough. So she really let go, dropped all the conventions, and painted not just what she saw, but what she felt. She was ridiculed for it. Ironically those are now her most famous works."

Gamache nodded, remembering the totem poles in front of the swirling, vibrant forest. "Remarkable woman."

"I think it all started with the brutal telling," said Clara.

"The what?"

"The brutal telling. It's become quite well known in artistic circles. She was the youngest of five daughters and very close to her father. It was apparently a wonderful relationship. Nothing to suggest it wasn't simply loving and supportive."

"Nothing sexual, you mean."

"No, just a close father-daughter bond. And then in her late teens something happened and she left home. She never spoke to him or saw him again."

"What happened?" Gamache was slowing

the car. Clara noticed this, and watched the clock approaching five to five.

"No one knew. She never told anyone, and her family said nothing. But she went from being a happy, carefree child to an embittered woman. Very solitary, not very likeable apparently. Then, near the end of her life, she wrote to a friend. In the letter she said that her father had said something to her. Something horrible and unforgivable."

"The brutal telling."

"That's how she described it."

They'd arrived. He stopped in front of her home and they sat there quietly for a moment. It was five past five. Too late. She could try, but knew Fortin wouldn't answer.

"Thank you," he said. "You've been very helpful."

"And so have you."

"I wish that was true." He smiled at her. But, remarkably, she seemed to be feeling better. Clara got out of the car, and instead of going inside she paused on the road then slowly started to walk. Around the village green. Round and round she strolled, until the end met the beginning and she was back where she started. And as she walked she thought about Emily Carr. And the ridicule she'd endured at the hands of gallery owners, critics, a public too afraid to go where she wanted to take them.

Deeper. Deeper into the wilderness.

Then Clara went home.

It was late at night in Zurich when an art collector picked up the odd little carving he'd paid so much for. The one he'd been assured was a great work of art, but more important, a great investment.

At first he'd displayed it in his home, until his wife had asked him to move it. Away. So he'd put in into his private gallery. Once a day he'd sit in there with a cognac, and look at the masterpieces. The Picassos, the Rodins and Henry Moores.

But his eyes kept going back to the jolly little carving, of the forest, and the happy people building a village. At first it had given him pleasure, but now he found it spooky. He was considering putting it somewhere else again. A closet perhaps.

When the broker had called earlier in the day and asked if he'd consider sending it back to Canada for a police investigation he'd refused. It was an investment, after all. And there was no way he could be forced. He'd done nothing wrong and they had no jurisdiction.

The broker, though, had passed on two requests from the police. He knew the answer to the first, but still he picked up the carving and looked at its smooth base. No letters, no signature. Nothing. But the other question just sounded ridiculous. Still, he'd tried. He was just about to replace the carving and e-mail that he'd found nothing when his eyes caught something light among the dark pines.

He peered closer. There, deep in the forest, away from the village, he found what the police were looking for.

A tiny wooden figure. A young man, not much more than a boy, hiding in the woods.

Thirty-One

It was getting late. Agent Lacoste had left and Inspector Beauvoir and Agent Morin were reporting on their day.

"We checked into the Parras, the Kmeniks, the Mackus. All the Czech community," said Beauvoir. "Nothing. No one knew the Hermit, no one saw him. They'd all heard of that violinist guy —"

"Martinù," said Morin.

"— because he's some famous Czech composer, but no one actually knew him."

"I spoke to the Martinù Institute and did background checks on the Czech families," said Morin. "They're what they claim to be. Refugees from the communists. Nothing more. In fact, they seem more law-abiding than most. No connection at all with Martinù."

Beauvoir shook his head. If lies annoyed the Inspector the truth seemed to piss him off even more. Especially when it was inconvenient.

"Your impression?" Gamache asked Agent Morin, who glanced at Inspector Beauvoir before answering.

"I think the violin and the music have nothing to do with the people here."

"You may be right," conceded Gamache, who knew they'd have to look into many empty caves before they found their killer. Perhaps this was one. "And the Parras?" he asked, though he knew the answer. If there'd been anything there Beauvoir would have told him already.

"Nothing in their background," Beauvoir confirmed. "But . . ."

Gamache waited.

"They seemed defensive, guarded. They were surprised that the dead man was Czech. Everyone was."

"What do you think?" asked the Chief.

Beauvoir wiped a weary hand across his face. "I can't put it all together, but I think it fits somehow."

"You think there is a connection?" pressed Gamache.

"How can there not be? The dead man was Czech, the sheet music, the priceless violin, and there's a big Czech community here including two people who could have found the cabin. Unless . . ."

"Yes?"

Beauvoir leaned forward, his nervous hands clasped together on the table. "Suppose we've got it wrong. Suppose the dead man wasn't Czech."

"You mean, that Olivier was lying?" said Gamache.

Beauvoir nodded. "He's lied about everything else. Maybe he said it to take us off the trail, so that we'd suspect others."

"But what about the violin and the music?"

"What about it?" Beauvoir was gaining momentum. "There're lots of other things in that cabin. Maybe Morin's right." Though he said it in the same tone he'd use to say maybe a chimp was right. With a mixture of awe at witnessing a miracle, and doubt. "Maybe the music and violin have nothing to do with it. After all, there were plates from Russia, glass from other places. The stuff tells us nothing. He could've been from anywhere. We only have Olivier's word for it. And maybe Olivier wasn't exactly lying. Maybe the guy did speak with an accent, but it wasn't Czech. Maybe it was Russian or Polish or one of those other countries."

Gamache leaned back, thinking, then he nodded and sat forward. "It's possible. But is it likely?"

This was the part of investigating he liked the most, and that most frightened him. Not the cornered and murderous suspect. But the possibility of turning left when he should have gone right. Of dismissing a lead, of giving up on a promising trail. Or not seeing one in his rush to a conclusion.

No, he needed to step carefully now. Like any explorer he knew the danger wasn't in walking off a cliff, but in getting hopelessly lost. Muddled. Disoriented by too much information.

In the end the answer to a murder investigation was always devastatingly simple. It was always right there, obvious. Hiding in facts and evidence and lies, and the misperceptions of the investigators.

"Let's leave if for now," he said, "and keep an open mind. The Hermit might have been Czech, or not. Either way there's no denying the contents of his cabin."

"What did Superintendent Brunel have to say? Any of it stolen?" asked Beauvoir.

"She hasn't found anything, but she's still looking. But Jérôme Brunel's been studying those letters under the carving and he thinks they're a Caesar's Shift. It's a type of code."

He explained how a Caesar's Shift worked.

"So we just need to find the key word?" asked Beauvoir. "Should be simple enough.

It's Woo."

"Nope. Tried that one."

Beauvoir went to the sheet of foolscap on the wall and uncapped the magic marker. He wrote the alphabet. Then the marker hovered.

"How about violin?" asked Morin. Beauvoir looked at him again as at an unexpectedly bright chimp. He wrote *violin* on a separate sheet of paper. Then he wrote *Martinù, Bohuslav.*

"Bohemia," suggested Morin.

"Good idea," said Beauvoir. Within a minute they had a dozen possibilities, and within ten minutes they'd tried them all and found nothing.

Beauvoir tapped his Magic Marker with some annoyance and stared at the alphabet, as though it was to blame.

"Well, keep trying," said Gamache. "Superintendent Brunel is trying to track down the rest of the carvings."

"Do you think that's why he was killed?" asked Morin. "For the carvings?"

"Perhaps," said Gamache. "There's not much some people wouldn't do for things that valuable."

"But when we found the cabin it hadn't been searched," said Beauvoir. "If you find the guy, find the cabin, go there and kill him, wouldn't you tear the place apart to find the carvings? And it's not like the murderer had to worry about disturbing the neighbors."

"Maybe he meant to but heard Olivier returning and had to leave," said Gamache.

Beauvoir nodded. He'd forgotten about Olivier coming back. That made sense.

"That reminds me," he said, sitting down. "The lab report came in on the whittling tools and the wood. They say the tools were used to do the sculptures but not to carve Woo. The grooves didn't match, but apparently the technique didn't either. Definitely different people."

It was a relief to have something definite about this case.

"But red cedar was used for all of them?" Gamache wanted to hear the confirmation.

Beauvoir nodded. "And they're able to be more specific than that, at least with the Woo carving. They can tell by looking at water content, insects, growth rings, all sorts of things, where the wood actually came from."

Gamache leaned forward and wrote three words on a sheet of paper. He slid it across the table and Beauvoir read and snorted. "You talked to the lab?"

"I talked to Superintendent Brunel."

He told them then about Woo, and Emily Carr. About the Haida totem poles, carved from red cedar.

Beauvoir looked down at the Chief's note.

Queen Charlotte Islands, he'd written.

And that's what the lab had said. The wood that became Woo had started life as a sapling hundreds of years earlier, on the Queen Charlotte Islands.

Gabri walked, almost marched, up rue du Moulin. He'd made up his mind and wanted to get there before he changed it, as he had every five minutes all afternoon.

He'd barely exchanged five words with Olivier since the Chief Inspector's interrogation had revealed just how much his partner had kept from him. Finally he arrived and looked at the gleaming exterior of what had been the old Hadley house. Now a carved wooden sign hung out front, swinging slightly in the breeze.

Auberge et Spa.

The lettering was tasteful, clear, elegant. It was the sort of sign he'd been meaning to have Old Mundin make for the B and B, but hadn't gotten around to. Above the lettering three pine trees were carved in a row. Iconic, memorable, classic.

He'd thought of doing that for the B and

B as well. And at least his place was actually in Three Pines. This place hovered above it. Not really part of the village.

Still, it was too late now. And he wasn't here to find fault. Just the opposite.

He stepped onto the porch and realized Olivier had stood there as well, with the body. He tried to shove the image away. Of his gentle, kind and quiet Olivier. Doing something so hideous.

Gabri rang the bell and waited, noting the shining brass of the handle, the bevelled glass and fresh red paint on the door. Cheerful and welcoming.

"Bonjour?" Dominique Gilbert opened the door, her face the image of polite suspicion.

"Madame Gilbert? We met in the village when you first arrived. I'm Gabriel Dubeau."

He put out his large hand and she took it. "I know who you are. You run that marvelous B and B."

Gabri knew when he was being softened up, having specialized in that himself. Still, it was nice to be on the receiving end of a compliment, and Gabri never refused one.

"That's right," he smiled. "But it's nothing compared to what you've done here. It's stunning."

"Would you like to come in?" Dominique

stood aside and Gabri found himself in the large foyer. The last time he'd been there it'd been a wreck and so had he. But it was clear the old Hadley house no longer existed. The tragedy, the sigh on the hill, had become a smile. A warm, elegant, gracious *auberge.* A place he himself would book into, for pampering. For an escape.

He thought about his slightly worn B and B. What moments ago had seemed comfortable, charming, welcoming, now seemed just tired. Like a grande dame past her prime. Who would want to visit Auntie's place when you could come to the cool kids' inn and spa?

Olivier had been right. This was the end.

And looking at Dominique, warm, confident, he knew she couldn't fail. She seemed born to success, to succeed.

"We're just in the living room having drinks. Would you like to join us?"

He was about to decline. He'd come to say one thing to the Gilberts and leave, quickly. This wasn't a social call. But she'd already turned, assuming his consent, and was walking through a large archway.

But for all the easy elegance, of the place and the woman, something didn't fit.

He examined his hostess as she walked away. Light silk blouse, Aquascutum slacks, loose scarf. And a certain fragrance. What was it?

Then he had it. He smiled. Instead of wearing Chanel this chatelaine was wearing Cheval. And not just horse, but a haughty undercurrent of horse shit.

Gabri's spirits lifted. At least his place smelled of muffins.

"It's Gabriel Dubeau," Dominique announced to the room. The fire was lit and an older man was standing staring into it. Carole Gilbert sat in an armchair and Marc was by the drinks tray. They all looked up.

Chief Inspector Gamache had never seen the bistro so empty. He sat in an armchair by the fire and Havoc Parra brought him a drink.

"Quiet night?" he asked as the young man put down the Scotch and a plate of Quebec cheese.

"Dead," Havoc said and reddened a little. "But it'll probably pick up."

They both knew that wasn't true. It was six thirty. The height of what should be the cocktail and predinner rush. Two other customers sat in the large room while a small squadron of waiters waited. For a rush that would never come. Not that night. Perhaps not ever again.

Three Pines had forgiven Olivier a lot. The body had been dismissed as bad luck. Even Olivier knowing about the Hermit and the cabin had been shrugged off. Not easily, granted. But Olivier was loved and with love there was leeway. They'd even managed to forgive Olivier's moving the body. It was seen as a kind of *grand mal* on his part.

But that had ended when they'd found out that Olivier had secretly made millions of dollars off a recluse who was probably demented. Over the course of years. And then had quietly bought up most of Three Pines. He was Myrna's, Sarah's and Monsieur Béliveau's landlord.

This was Olivierville, and the natives were restless. The man they had thought they knew was a stranger after all.

"Is Olivier here?"

"In the kitchen. He let the chef off and decided to do the cooking himself tonight. He's a terrific cook, you know."

Gamache did know, having enjoyed his private meals a number of times. But he also knew this decision to cook allowed Olivier to hide. In the kitchen. Where he didn't have to see the accusing, unhappy faces of people who were his friends. Or worse still, see the empty chairs where friends once sat.

"I wonder if you could ask him to join me?"

"I'll do my best."

"Please."

In that one word Chief Inspector Gamache conveyed that while it might sound like a polite request, it wasn't. A couple of minutes later Olivier lowered himself into the chair across from Gamache. They needn't worry about keeping their voices down. The bistro was now empty.

Gamache leaned forward, took a sip of Scotch, and watched Olivier closely.

"What does the name Charlotte mean to you?"

Olivier's brows went up in surprise. "Charlotte?" He thought for a few moments. "I've never known a Charlotte. I knew a girl named Charlie once."

"Did the Hermit ever mention the name?"

"He never mentioned any name."

"What did you talk about?"

Olivier heard again the dead man's voice, not deep but somehow calming. "We talked about vegetable gardens and building and plumbing. He learned from the Romans, the Greeks, the early settlers. It was fascinating."

Not for the first time Gamache wished there'd been a third chair in that cabin, for him. "Did he ever mention Caesar's Shift?"

Once again Olivier looked perplexed, then shook his head.

"How about the Queen Charlotte Islands?" Gamache asked.

"In British Columbia? Why would he talk about them?"

"Is anyone in Three Pines from BC that you know?"

"People're from all over, but I can't remember anyone from British Columbia. Why?"

Gamache brought out the sculptures and placed them on the table so that the ship looked to be running from the cheese, and the cheese, runny, seemed to be chasing it.

"Because these are. Or at least, the wood is. It's red cedar from the Queen Charlottes. Let's start again," Gamache said quietly. "Tell me what you know about these sculptures."

Olivier's face was impassive. Gamache knew that look. It was the look of a liar, caught. Trying to find the last way out, the back door, the crack. Gamache waited. He sipped his Scotch and smoothed a bit of cheese on the very excellent nut bread. He placed a slice in front of Olivier then prepared one for himself. He ate and waited.

"The Hermit carved them," said Olivier,

his voice even, flat.

"You've told us that already. You also told us he gave you some and you threw them into the forest."

Gamache waited, knowing the rest would come out now. He looked through the window and noticed Ruth walking Rosa. The duck, for some reason, was wearing a tiny, red raincoat.

"I didn't throw them away. I kept them," Olivier whispered, and the world beyond the circle of light from the fireplace seemed to disappear. It felt as though the two men were in their own little cabin. "I'd been visiting the Hermit for about a year when he gave me the first."

"Can you remember what it was?"

"A hill, with trees. More like a mountain really. And a boy lying on it."

"This one?" Gamache brought out the photo Thérèse Brunel had given him.

Olivier nodded. "I remember it clearly because I didn't know the Hermit did stuff like this. His cabin was packed with wonderful things, but things other people made."

"What did you do with it?"

"I kept it for a while, but had to hide it so Gabri wouldn't start asking questions. Then I figured it was just easier to sell it. So I put it up on eBay. It went for a thousand dollars. Then a dealer got in touch. Said he had buyers, if there were any more. I thought he was joking, but when the Hermit gave me another one eight months later I remembered the guy and contacted him."

"Was it Denis Fortin?"

"Clara's gallery owner? No. It was someone in Europe. I can give you his coordinates."

"That would be helpful. What did the second carving look like?"

"Plain. Simple. On the surface. I was kind of disappointed. It was a forest, but if you looked closely beneath the canopy of trees you could see people walking in a line."

"Was the boy one of them?"

"Which boy?"

"The one from the mountain."

"Well, no. This was a different piece."

"I realize that," said Gamache, wondering if he was making himself clear. "But it seems possible the Hermit carved the same figures into each of his sculptures."

"The boy?"

"And the people. Anything else?"

Olivier thought. There was something else. The shadow over the trees. Something loomed just behind them. Something was rising up. And Olivier knew what it was.

"No, nothing. Just a forest and the people

inside. The dealer was pretty excited."

"What did it sell for?"

"Fifteen thousand." He watched for the shock on Gamache's face.

But Gamache's gaze didn't waver, and Olivier congratulated himself on telling the truth. It was clear the Chief Inspector already knew the answer to that question. Telling the truth was always a crapshoot. As was the telling of lies. It was best, Olivier had found, to mingle the two.

"How many carvings did he make?"

"I thought eight, but now that you've found those, I guess he did ten."

"And you sold all the ones he gave you?"

Olivier nodded.

"You'd told us he started out giving you other things from his cabin, as payment for food. Where did those go?"

"I took them to the antique stores on rue Notre Dame in Montreal. But then once I realized the stuff was valuable I found private dealers."

"Who?"

"I haven't used them in years. I'll have to look it up. People in Toronto and New York." He leaned back and looked around the empty room. "I suppose I should let Havoc and the others off for the night."

Gamache remained quiet.

"Do you think people'll come back?"

The Chief Inspector nodded. "They're hurt by what you did."

"Me? Marc Gilbert's way worse. Be careful with him. He's not what he seems."

"And neither are you, Olivier. You've lied all along. You may be lying now. I'm going to ask you a question and I need you to think carefully about the answer."

Olivier nodded and straightened up.

"Was the Hermit Czech?"

Olivier immediately opened his mouth but Gamache quickly brought up a hand to stop him. "I asked you to think about your answer. Consider it. Could you have been wrong? Maybe there was no accent," Gamache watched his companion closely. "Maybe he spoke with an accent but it wasn't necessarily Czech. Maybe you just assumed. Be careful what you say."

Olivier stared at Gamache's large, steady hand and as it lowered he switched his gaze to the large, steady man.

"There was no mistake. I've heard enough Czech over the years from friends and neighbors. He was Czech."

It was said with more certainty than anything Olivier had said to Gamache since the investigation began. Still, Gamache stared at the slight man across from him.

He examined his mouth, his eyes, the lines on his forehead, his coloring. Then the Chief Inspector nodded.

"Chilly night," said Ruth, plopping onto the seat beside Gamache and managing to knock his knee quite hard with her muddy cane. "Sorry," she said, then did it again.

She was completely oblivious of the conversation she was interrupting and the tension between the two men. She looked from Olivier to Gamache.

"Well, enough of this gay banter. Can you believe what Olivier did with that body? His idiocy eclipses even your own. Gives me a sense of the infinite. It's almost a spiritual experience. Cheese?"

She took the last bite of Gamache's Saint-André and reached for his Scotch, but he got there first. Myrna arrived, then Clara and Peter dropped by and told everyone about Denis Fortin. There was general commiserating and all agreed Clara had done the right thing. Then they agreed she should call in the morning and beg his forgiveness. Then they agreed she shouldn't.

"I saw Rosa outside," said Clara, anxious to change the subject. "She's looking very smart in her rain jacket." It had occurred to her to wonder why a duck might need a raincoat, but she supposed Ruth was just training Rosa to get used to wearing coats.

Eventually the conversation came back to Olivier, and the Hermit, dead, and the Hermit alive. Ruth leaned over and took Olivier's hand. "It's all right, dear, we all know you're greedy." Then she looked at Clara. "And we all know you're needy, and Peter's petty and Clouseau here," she turned to Gamache, "is arrogant. And you're . . ." She looked at Myrna, then turned back to Olivier, whispering loudly, "Who is that anyway? She's always hanging around."

"You're a nasty, demented, drunken old fart," said Myrna.

"I'm not drunk, yet."

They finished their drinks and left, but not before Ruth handed Gamache a piece of paper, carefully, precisely folded, the edges sharpened. "Give this to that little fellow who follows you around."

Olivier kept looking out into the village where Rosa was sitting quietly on the village green, waiting for Ruth. There was no sign of the one not there, the one Olivier longed to see.

Gabri was mostly curious to meet the saint. Vincent Gilbert. Myrna was in awe of him, and she wasn't in awe of many people. Old

Mundin and The Wife said he'd changed their lives with his book *Being,* and his work at LaPorte. And by extension, he'd changed little Charlie's life.

"Bonsoir," said Gabri, nervously. He looked over to Vincent Gilbert. Growing up in the Catholic Church he'd spent endless hours staring at the gleaming windows showing the wretched lives and glorious deaths of the saints. When Gabri had wandered from the Church he'd taken one thing with him. The certainty that saints were good.

"What do you want?" Marc Gilbert asked. He stood with his wife and mother by the sofa. Forming a semicircle. His father a satellite off to the side. Gabri waited for Vincent Gilbert to calm his son, to tell him to greet their guest nicely. To invite Marc to be reasonable.

Gilbert said nothing.

"Well?" said Marc.

"I'm sorry I haven't been up sooner to welcome you."

Marc snorted. "The Welcome Wagon's already left us our package."

"Marc, please," said Dominique. "He's our neighbor."

"Not by choice. If he had his way we'd be long gone."

And Gabri didn't deny it. It was true.

Their troubles arrived with the Gilberts. But here they were and something had to be said.

"I came to apologize," he said, standing to his full six foot one. "I'm sorry I haven't made you feel more welcome. And I'm very sorry about the body."

Yes, that definitely sounded as lame as he'd feared. But he hoped it at least sounded genuine.

"Why isn't Olivier here?" Marc demanded. "You didn't do it. It's not up to you to apologize."

"Marc, really," said Dominique. "Can't you see how difficult this is for him?"

"No, I can't. Olivier probably sent him hoping we won't sue. Or won't tell everyone what a psycho he is."

"Olivier's not a psycho," said Gabri, feeling a kind of trill inside as his patience unraveled. "He's a wonderful man. You don't know him."

"You're the one who doesn't know him if you think he's wonderful. Does a wonderful man dump a body at a neighbor's home?"

"You tell me."

The two men advanced on each other.

"I didn't take the body into a private home to scare the occupants half to death. That was a terrible thing to do."

"Olivier was pushed to it. He tried to make friends when you first arrived but then you tried to steal our staff and open this huge hotel and spa."

"Ten guest rooms isn't huge," said Dominique.

"Not in Montreal, but out here it is. This's a small village. We've been here for a long time living quietly. You come here and change all that. Made no effort to fit in."

"By 'fit in' you mean tug our forelocks and be grateful you've allowed us to live here?" Marc demanded.

"No, I mean being respectful of what's here already. What people've worked hard to establish."

"You want to raise the drawbridge, don't you?" said Marc in disgust. "You're in and you want to keep everyone else out."

"That's not true. Most of the people in Three Pines have come from somewhere else."

"But you only accept people who follow your rules. Who do as you say. We came here to live our dream and you won't let us. Why? Because it clashes with yours. You're threatened by us and so you need to run us out of town. You're nothing but bullies, with big smiles."

Marc was almost spitting.

Gabri stared at him, amazed. "But you didn't really expect us to be happy about it, did you? Why would you come here and deliberately upset people who were going to be your neighbors? Didn't you want us as friends? You must've known how Olivier would react."

"What? That he'd put a body in our home?"

"That was wrong. I've already said that. But you provoked him. All of us. We wanted to be your friends but you made it too difficult."

"So, you'll be friends with us as long as what? We're just a modest success? Have a few guests, a couple of treatments a day? Maybe a small dining room, if we're lucky? But nothing to compete with you and Olivier?"

"That's right," said Gabri.

That shut Marc up.

"Listen, why do you think we don't make croissants?" Gabri continued. "Or pies? Or any baking? We could. It's what I love to do. But Sarah's Boulangerie was already here. She'd lived in the village all her life. The bakery belonged to her grandmother. So we opened a bistro instead. All our croissants, and pies, and breads are baked by Sarah. We adjusted our dreams to fit the dreams already here. It'd be cheaper and more fun to bake ourselves but that's not the point."

"What is the point?" asked Vincent Gilbert, speaking for the first time.

"The point isn't to make a fortune," said Gabri, turning to him gratefully. "The point is to know what's enough. To be happy."

There was a pause and Gabri silently thanked the saint for creating that space for reason to return.

"Maybe you should remind your partner of that," said Vincent Gilbert. "You talk a good line but you don't live it. It suits you to blame my son. You dress up your behavior as moral and kindly and loving, but you know what it is?"

Vincent Gilbert was advancing, closing in on Gabri. As he neared he seemed to grow and Gabri felt himself shrink.

"It's selfish," Gilbert hissed. "My son has been patient. He's hired local workers, created jobs. This is a place of healing, and you not only try to ruin it, you try to make him out to be at fault."

Vincent stepped next to his son, having finally found the price of belonging.

There was nothing more to say, so Gabri left.

Lights glowed at windows as he made his way back into the village. Overhead ducks flew south in their V formation, away from the killing cold that was gathering and preparing to descend. Gabri sat on a tree stump by the side of the road and watched the sun set over Three Pines and thought about *les temps perdus* and felt very alone, without even the certainty of saints for comfort.

A beer was placed on the table for Beauvoir and Gamache nursed his Scotch. They settled into their comfortable chairs and examined the dinner menu. The bistro was deserted. Peter, Clara, Myrna and Ruth had all gone and Olivier had retreated to his kitchen. Havoc, the last of the waiters, took their order then left them to talk.

Gamache broke up a small baguette and told his second in command about his conversation with Olivier.

"So, he still says the Hermit was Czech. Do you believe him?"

"I do," said Gamache. "At least, I believe Olivier is convinced of it. Any luck with the Caesar's Shift?"

"None." They'd given up when they started putting their own names in. Both slightly relieved it didn't work.

"What's wrong?" Gamache asked. Beauvoir had leaned back in his seat and tossed his linen napkin onto the table.

"I'm just frustrated. It seems every time we make progress it gets all muddied. We still don't even know who the dead man was."

Gamache smiled. It was their regular predicament. The further into a case they went the more clues they gathered. There came a time when it seemed a howl, as though they had hold of something wild that screamed clues at them. It was, Gamache knew, the shriek of something cornered and frightened. They were entering the last stages of this investigation. Soon the clues, the pieces, would stop fighting, and start betraying the murderer. They were close.

"By the way, I'm going away tomorrow," said the Chief Inspector after Havoc brought their appetizers and left.

"Back to Montreal?" Beauvoir took a forkful of chargrilled calamari while Gamache ate his pear and prosciutto.

"A little further than that. The Queen Charlotte Islands."

"Are you kidding? In British Columbia? Up by Alaska? Because of a monkey named Woo?"

"Well, when you put it like that . . ."

Beauvoir speared a blackened piece of calamari and dipped it in garlic sauce. "*Voy-*

ons, doesn't it strike you as, well, extreme?"

"No, it doesn't. The name Charlotte keeps repeating." Gamache ticked the points off on his fingers. "The Charlotte Brontë first edition, *Charlotte's Web* first edition, the Amber Room panel? Made for a princess named Charlotte. The note the Hermit kept about the violin was written by a Charlotte. I've been trying to figure out what they could all mean, this repetition of the name Charlotte, then this afternoon Superintendent Brunel gave me the answer. The Queen Charlotte Islands. Where Emily Carr painted. Where the wood for the carvings came from. It might be a dead end, but I'd be a fool not to follow this lead."

"But who's doing the leading? You or the murderer? I think they're leading you away. I think the murderer is here, in Three Pines."

"So do I, but I think the murder began on the Queen Charlotte Islands."

Beauvoir huffed, exasperated. "You're taking a bunch of clues and putting them together to suit your purpose."

"What are you suggesting?"

Beauvoir needed to watch himself now. Chief Inspector Gamache was more than his superior. They had a relationship that went deeper than any other Beauvoir had.

And he knew Gamache's patience had its limits.

"I think you see what you want to see. You see things that aren't really there."

"You mean just aren't visible."

"No, I mean aren't there. To leap to one conclusion isn't the end of the world, but you're leaping all over the place and where does it take you? The end of the fucking world. Sir."

Beauvoir glanced out the window, trying to cool down. Havoc removed their plates and Beauvoir waited for him to leave before continuing. "I know you love history and literature and art and that the Hermit's cabin must seem like a candy shop, but I think you're seeing a whole lot more in this case than exists. I think you're complicating it. You know I'd follow you anywhere, we all would. You just point, and I'm there. I trust you that much. But even you can make mistakes. You always say that murder is, at its core, very simple. It's about an emotion. That emotion is here, and so's the murderer. We have plenty of clues to follow without thinking about a monkey, a hunk of wood and some godforsaken island to hell and gone across the country."

"Finished?" Gamache asked.

Beauvoir sat upright and took a deep

breath. "There may be more."

Gamache smiled. "I agree with you, Jean Guy, the murderer is here. Someone here knew the Hermit, and someone here killed him. You're right. When you strip away all the shiny baubles it's simple. A man ends up with antiquities worth a fortune. Perhaps he stole them. He wants to hide so he comes to this village no one knows about. But even that isn't enough. He takes it a step further and builds a cabin deep in the woods. Is he hiding from the police? Maybe. From something or someone worse? I think so. But he can't do it on his own. If nothing else he needs news. He needs eyes and ears on the outside. So he recruits Olivier."

"Why him?"

"Ruth said it tonight."

"More Scotch, asshole?"

"Well, that too. But she said Olivier was greedy. And he is. So was the Hermit. He probably recognized himself in Olivier. That greed. That need to own. And he knew he could have a hold over Olivier. Promising him more and better antiques. But over the years something happened."

"He went nuts?"

"Maybe. But maybe just the opposite. Maybe he went sane. The place he built to hide became a home, a haven. You felt it.

There was something peaceful, comforting even, about the Hermit's life. It was simple. Who doesn't long for that these days?"

Their dinners arrived and Beauvoir's gloom lifted as the fragrant boeuf bourguignon landed in front of him. He looked across at the Chief Inspector smiling down at his lobster Thermidor.

"Yes, the simple life in the country." Beauvoir lifted his red wine in a small toast.

Gamache tipped his glass of white toward his Inspector, then took a succulent forkful. As he ate he thought of those first few minutes in the Hermit's cabin. And that moment when he realized what he was looking at. Treasures. And yet everything was put to purpose. There was a reason for everything in there, whether practical or pleasure, like the books and violin.

But there was one thing. One thing that didn't seem to have a purpose.

Gamache slowly laid his fork down and stared beyond Beauvoir. After a moment the Inspector also put his fork down and looked behind him. There was nothing there. Just the empty room.

"What is it?"

Gamache put up a finger, a subtle and gentle request for quiet. Then he reached into his breast pocket and bringing out a pen and notebook he wrote something down, quickly, as though afraid it would get away. Beauvoir strained to read it. Then, with a thrill, saw what it was.

The alphabet.

Silently he watched his Chief write the line beneath. His face opened in wonder. Wonder that he could have been so stupid. Could have missed what now seemed obvious.

Beneath the alphabet, Chief Inspector Gamache had written: SIXTEEN.

"The number above the door," whispered Beauvoir, as though he too was afraid he might scare this vital clue away.

"What were the code letters?" asked Gamache, in a hurry now. Anxious to get there.

Beauvoir scrambled in his pocket and brought out his notebook.

"MRKBVYDDO under the people on the shore. And OWSVI under the ship."

He watched as Gamache worked to decode the Hermit's messages.

A B C D E F G H I J K L M N O P Q R S T U V W X Y Z

S I X T E E N A B C D E F G H I J K L M N O P Q R S

Gamache read the letters out as he found them. "T, Y, R, I, something . . ."

"Tyri," Beauvoir mumbled. "Tyri . . ."

"Something, K, K, V." He looked up at Beauvoir.

"What does it mean? Is it a name? Maybe a Czech name?"

"Maybe it's an anagram," said Gamache. "We have to rearrange the letters."

They tried that for a few minutes, taking bites of their dinner as they worked. Finally Gamache put his pen down and shook his head. "I thought I had it."

"Maybe it's right," said Beauvoir, not ready to let go yet. He jotted more letters, tried the other code. Rearranged letters and finally staggered to the same conclusion.

The key wasn't "seventeen."

"Still," said Beauvoir, dipping a crusty baguette into his gravy, "I wonder why that number's up there."

"Maybe some things don't need a purpose," said Gamache. "Maybe that's their purpose."

But that was too esoteric for Beauvoir. As was the Chief Inspector's reasoning about the Queen Charlotte Islands. In fact, Beauvoir wouldn't call it reasoning at all. At best it was intuition on the Chief's part, at worst it was a wild guess, maybe even manipulated by the murderer.

The only image Beauvoir had of the moody archipelago at the very end of the country was of thick forests and mountains and endless gray water. But mostly it was mist.

And into that mist Armand Gamache was going, alone.

"I almost forgot, Ruth Zardo gave me this." Gamache handed him the slip of paper. Beauvoir unfolded it and read out loud.

"and pick your soul up gently by the nape
of the neck
and caress you into darkness and
paradise."

There was, at least, a full stop after "paradise." Was this, finally, the end?

Thirty-Two

Armand Gamache arrived in the late afternoon on the brooding islands after taking increasingly smaller planes until it seemed the last was nothing more than fuselage wrapped round his body and thrust off the end of the Prince Rupert runway.

As the tiny float plane flew over the archipelago off the coast of northern British Columbia Gamache looked down on a landscape of mountains and thick ancient forests. It had been hidden for millennia behind mists almost as impenetrable as the trees. It had remained isolated. But not alone. It was a cauldron of life that had produced both the largest black bears in the world and the smallest owls. It was teeming with life. Indeed, the first men were discovered in a giant clam shell by a raven off the tip of one of the islands. That, according to their creation stories, was how the Haida came to live there. More recently loggers had also been found on the islands. That wasn't part of creation. They'd looked beyond the thick mists and seen money. They'd arrived on the Charlottes a century ago, blind to the crucible they'd stumbled upon and seeing only treasure. The ancient forests of red cedar. Trees prized for their durability, having been tall and straight long before Queen Charlotte was born and married her mad monarch. But now they fell to the saw, to be made into shingles and decks and siding. And ten small carvings.

After landing smoothly on the water the young bush pilot helped extricate the large man from her small plane.

"Welcome to Haida Gwaii," she said.

When Gamache had woken early that morning in Three Pines and found a groggy Gabri in the kitchen making a small picnic for the drive to the Montreal airport, he knew nothing about these islands half a world away. But on the long flights from Montreal to Vancouver, to Prince Rupert and into the village of Queen Charlotte, he'd read about the islands and he knew that phrase.

"Thank you for bringing me to your homeland."

The pilot's deep brown eyes were suspicious, as well they would be, thought Gamache. The arrival of yet another middle-aged white man in a suit was never a good sign. You didn't have to be Haida to know that.

"You must be Chief Inspector Gamache."

A burly man with black hair and skin the color of cedar was walking across the dock, his hand out. They shook.

"I'm Sergeant Minshall, of the RCMP. We've been corresponding."

His voice was deep and had a slight sing-song quality. He was Haida.

"*Ah, oui, merci.* Thank you for meeting the plane."

The Mountie took the overnight bag from the pilot and slung it over his shoulder. Thanking the pilot, who ignored them, the two men walked to the end of the dock, up a ramp and along the road. There was a bite to the air and Gamache had to remember they were closer to Alaska than Vancouver.

"I see you're not staying long."

Gamache looked out into the ocean and knew the mainland had disappeared. No, it was not that it had vanished, but that it didn't exist at all here. This was the mainland.

"I wish I could stay longer, it's beautiful. But I have to get back."

"Right. I've arranged a room for you at

the lodge. I think you'll enjoy it. There aren't many people on the Queen Charlottes, as you probably know. Maybe five thousand, with half being Haida and half," he hesitated slightly, "not. We get quite a few tourists, but the season's ending."

The two men had slowed and now they stopped. They'd walked by a hardware store, a coffee shop, a little building with a mermaid out front. But it was the harbor that drew Gamache's attention. He'd never seen such scenery in all his life, and he'd seen some spectacularly beautiful places in Quebec. But none, he had to admit, came close to this.

It was wilderness. As far as he could see there were mountains rising from the water, covered in dark forest. He could see an island and fishing boats. Overhead, eagles soared. The men walked onto the beach, which was covered in pebbles and shells, and stood silent for a few minutes, listening to the birds and the lapping water and smelling the air with that combination of seaweed and fish and forest.

"There're more eagle nests here than anywhere else in Canada, you know. It's a sign of good luck."

It wasn't often an RCMP officer spoke of signs, unless it was traffic signs. Gamache didn't turn to look at the man, he was too taken by the view, but he listened.

"The Haida have two clans. The Eagle and the Raven. I've arranged for you to meet with elders from both clans. They've invited you for dinner."

"Thank you. Will you be there?"

Sergeant Minshall smiled. "No. I thought it'd be more comfortable without me. The Haida are very warm people, you know. They've lived here for thousands of years, undisturbed. Until recently."

It was interesting, Gamache thought, that he referred to the Haida as "they" not "we." Perhaps it was for Gamache's benefit, so he didn't appear biased.

"I'll try not to disturb them tonight."

"It's too late."

Armand Gamache showered, shaved and wiped the vapor from the mirror. It was as though the mist that hung over the ancient forests had crept into his room. Perhaps to watch him. To divine his intentions.

He made a small hole in the moisture and saw a very tired Sûreté officer, far from home.

Changing into a fresh shirt and dark slacks he picked out a tie and sat on the side of the double bed, which was covered in what looked like a hand-stitched quilt.

The room was simple and clean and comfortable. But it could be filled with turnips and it wouldn't matter. All anyone would notice was the view. It looked directly over the bay. The sunset filled the sky with gold and purples and reds, undulating and shifting. Alive. Everything seemed alive here.

He gravitated to the window and stared while his hands tied his green silk tie. There was a knock on the door. He opened it, expecting the landlady or Sergeant Minshall, and was surprised to see the young bush pilot.

"Noni, my great-grandmother, asked me to bring you to dinner."

She still didn't smile. In fact, she seemed singularly unhappy about the fact. He put on a gray jacket and his coat and they walked into the darkening night. Lights were on in the homes that hugged the harbor. The air was cold and damp, but fresh, and it woke him up so that he felt more alert than he had all afternoon. They climbed into an old pickup truck and headed out of town.

"So you're from the Charlottes?"

"I'm from Haida Gwaii," she said.

"Of course, I'm sorry. Are you with the Eagle clan?"

"Raven."

"Ah," said Gamache, and realized he sounded slightly ridiculous, but the young woman beside him didn't seem to care. She seemed more interested in ignoring him completely.

"Your family must be very pleased you're a pilot."

"Why?"

"Well, flying."

"Because I'm a Raven? Everyone here flies, Chief Inspector. I just need more help."

"Have you been a pilot long?"

There was silence then. Evidently his question wasn't worth answering. And he had to agree. Silence was better. His eyes adjusted to the night and he was able to make out the line of mountains across the bay as they drove. After a few minutes they arrived at another village. The young pilot stopped the pickup in front of a non-descript white building that had a sign out front. *Skidegate Community Hall.* She got out and walked to the door, never looking back to see if he was following. She either trusted he was there or, more likely, didn't care.

He left the twilit harbor and followed her through the door into the Community Hall. And into an opera house. Gamache turned round to make sure there was a door there and he hadn't, magically, emerged into another world. They were surrounded by ornate balconies on three sides. Gamache did a slow 360, his feet squeaking a little on the polished wood floor. Only then did he realize his mouth was slightly open. He closed it and looked at the young woman beside him.

"Mais, c'est extraordinaire."

"Haw'aa."

Wide, gracious staircases led up to the balconies and at the far end of the room was a stage. Behind it a mural had been painted on the wall.

"That's a Haida village," she said, nodding toward it.

"Incroyable," whispered Gamache. The Chief Inspector was often surprised, astonished, by life. But he was rarely dumbfounded. He was now.

"Do you like it?"

Gamache looked down and realized they'd been joined by another woman, much older than his companion or himself. And unlike his companion this woman smiled. It looked, by the ease of it, as though she found a lot of humor in life.

"Very much." He put out his hand, and she took it.

"This is my noni," said the pilot.

"Esther," she said.

"Armand Gamache," said the Chief, bowing slightly. "It's an honor."

"The honor is mine, Chief Inspector. Please." She motioned into the center of the room where a long table had been set. There was a rich aroma of cooked food, and the room was filled with people talking, greeting, calling to each other. And laughing.

He'd expected the gathering of Haida elders to be in traditional garb. He was embarrassed now by that cliché. Instead the men and women were dressed as they'd come from work, some in T-shirts and heavy sweaters, some in suits. Some worked in the bank, the school, the clinic; some worked on the cold waters. Some were artists. Painters, but mostly carvers.

"This is a matrilineal society, Chief Inspector," Esther explained. "But most of the chiefs are men. Though that doesn't mean women are powerless. Quite the opposite."

She looked at him, her eyes clear. It was a simple statement. Not a boast.

She then introduced him to everyone, one by one. He repeated their names and tried to keep them straight, though he was frankly lost after half a dozen. Finally Esther took him over to the buffet table, where food had been put out.

"This is Skaay," she said, introducing a tiny old man who looked up from his plate. His eyes were milky, blind. "Of the Eagle clan."

"Robert, if you prefer," Skaay said, his voice strong and his grip stronger. He smiled. "The women of both clans have done a traditional Haida feast for you, Chief Inspector." The blind man led Gamache down the long table, naming each dish. "This is *k'aaw.* It's herring roe on kelp. This over here is pepper-smoked salmon, or if you prefer there's wood-smoked salmon over there. Caught this morning by Reg. He spent the day smoking it. For you."

They walked slowly the length of the buffet. Octopus balls, crab cakes, halibut. Potato salad; fresh bread, still warm. Juices and water. No alcohol.

"We have dances here. This is where most people have their wedding parties. And funerals. So many dinners. When the Eagle clan is hosting the Raven clan serves. And vice versa, of course. But tonight we're all hosting. And you're our honored guest."

Gamache, who'd been to state dinners in grand palaces, banquets given for him, awards presentations, had rarely felt so honored.

He took a helping of everything and sat down. To his surprise, the young pilot joined him. Over dinner they all talked, but he noticed the Haida elders asked more questions than they answered. They were interested in his work, his life, his family. They asked about Quebec. They were informed and thoughtful. Kind, and guarded.

Over cake, fresh bumbleberries and Cool Whip, Gamache told them about the murder. The Hermit in the cabin buried deep in the forest. The elders, always attentive, grew even more still as he told them about the man, surrounded by treasure, but alone. A man whose life had been taken, his goods left behind. A man with no name, surrounded by history, but with none himself.

"Was he happy, do you think?" Esther asked. It was almost impossible to figure out if there was a leader of this group, by election or mutual consent. But Gamache guessed if there was one, it would be her.

He hesitated. He hadn't actually asked himself that question.

Was the Hermit happy?

"I think he was content. He led a small, peaceful life. One that appeals to me."

The young pilot turned to look at him.

Up until that moment she'd been looking straight ahead.

"He was surrounded by beauty," continued Gamache. "And he had company every now and then. Someone who'd bring him what he couldn't provide for himself. But he was afraid."

"Hard to be both happy and afraid," said Esther. "But fear can lead to courage."

"And courage can lead to peace," said a young man in a suit.

It reminded Gamache of what the fisherman had written on the wall of the diner in Mutton Bay a few years earlier. He'd looked at Gamache across the room and smiled so fully it had taken the Chief Inspector's breath away. Then the fisherman had scribbled something on the wall and left. Gamache had gone to the wall, and read:

Where there is love there is courage,
where there is courage there is peace,
where there is peace there is God.
And when you have God, you have
    everything.

Gamache spoke the words, and then there was silence in the hall. The Haida were good at silence. And so was Gamache.

"Is that a prayer?" Esther finally asked.

"A fisherman wrote it on a wall in a place called Mutton Bay, a long way off."

"Perhaps not so far," said Esther.

"A fisherman?" asked the man in the suit, with a smile. "Figures. They're all crazy."

An older man beside him, dressed in a thick sweater, gave him a swat and they laughed.

"We're all fishermen," said Esther, and Gamache had the feeling she was including him. She thought for a moment then asked, "What did your Hermit love?"

Gamache thought about that. "I don't know."

"Perhaps when you do, you'll find his killer. How can we help?"

"There were a couple of references to Woo and Charlotte in the Hermit's cabin. They led me to Emily Carr, and she led me here."

"Well, you're far from the first," an elderly man said with a laugh. It wasn't a smug or derisive laugh. "Her paintings have been bringing people to Haida Gwaii for years."

It was hard to tell if that was considered a good thing.

"I think the Hermit was on the Queen Charlotte Islands, maybe fifteen or more years ago. We think he was Czech. He'd have spoken with an accent."

Gamache brought out the photographs,

taken at the morgue. He'd warned them what they'd see but he wasn't worried. These were people who lived comfortably with life and death in a place where the line was blurred, and people, animals, and spirits walked together. Where blind men saw and everyone had the gift of flight.

Over strong tea they looked at the dead man. They looked long and hard. Even the young pilot gave the photographs her attention.

And as they looked at the photos, Gamache looked at them. To see a flicker of recognition. A twitch, a change in breathing. He became hyperaware of every one of them. But all he saw were people trying to help.

"We've disappointed you, I'm afraid," said Esther as Gamache put the pictures back in his satchel. "Why didn't you just e-mail them to us?"

"Well, I e-mailed them to Sergeant Minshall and he circulated them among the police, but I wanted to be here myself. And there's something I couldn't e-mail. Something I brought with me."

He put the two balls of towel on the table and carefully unwrapped the first.

Not a spoon clinked against a mug, not a creamer was popped, peeled and opened, not a breath. It was as though something else had joined them then. As though silence had taken a seat.

He gently unwrapped the next one. And it sailed across the table to join its sibling.

"There're others. Eight we think."

If they heard him they gave no indication. Then one man, middle-aged and stocky, reached out. Stopping, he looked at Gamache.

"May I?"

"Please."

He picked it up and in large, worn hands he held the sailing ship. He lifted it to his face so that he was staring into the eyes of the tiny men and women who were looking ahead with such pleasure, such joy.

"That's Haawasti," whispered the bush pilot. "Will Sommes."

"That's Will Sommes?" Gamache asked. He'd read about this man. He was one of Canada's greatest living artists. His Haida carvings were bursting with life and snapped up by private collectors and museums worldwide. He'd assumed Sommes was a recluse, having grown so famous surely he'd be in hiding. But the Chief Inspector was beginning to appreciate that on Haida Gwaii legends came alive, walked among them, and sometimes sipped black tea and ate Cool Whip.

Sommes picked up the other piece and turned it round and round. “Red cedar.”

“From here,” confirmed Gamache.

Sommes looked under the sailing ship. “Is that a signature?”

“Perhaps you could tell me.”

“Just letters. But it must mean something.”

“It seems to be in code. We haven’t figured it out yet.”

“The dead man made these?” Sommes held up the carving.

“He did.”

Sommes looked down at what he held in his hand. “I can’t tell you who he was, but I can tell you this much. Your Hermit wasn’t just afraid, he was terrified.”

Thirty-Three

Next morning Gamache awoke to a fresh, cold breeze bringing sea air and the shriek of feeding birds through his open window. He turned over in bed and, drawing the warm quilt around him, he stared out the window. The day before had seemed a dream. To wake up in Three Pines and go to sleep in this Haida village beside the ocean.

The sky was brilliant blue and he could see eagles and seagulls gliding. Getting out of bed he quickly put on his warmest clothing and cursed himself for forgetting his long underwear.

Downstairs he found a full breakfast of bacon, eggs, toast and strong coffee.

"Lavina called and said to be at the dock by nine or she was leaving without you."

Gamache looked round to see who the landlady was talking to.

He was alone in the room. *"Moi?"*

"Yes you. Lavina said don't be late."

Gamache looked at his watch. It was half past eight and he had no idea who Lavina was, where the dock was, or why he should go. He had one more cup of coffee, went to his room to use the washroom and get his coat and hat, then came back down to speak to the landlady.

"Did Lavina say which dock?"

"I suppose it's the one she always uses. Can't miss it."

How often had Gamache heard that, just before missing it? Still, he stood on the porch and taking a deep breath of bracing air he surveyed the coastline. There were several docks.

But at only one was there a seaplane. And the young bush pilot looking at her watch. Was her name Lavina? To his embarrassment he realized he'd never asked her.

He walked over and as his feet hit the wooden boards of the dock he saw she wasn't alone. Will Sommes was with her.

"Thought you'd like to see where those pieces of wood came from," the carver said, inviting Gamache into the small pontoon plane. "My granddaughter's agreed to fly us. The plane you came in on yesterday's a commercial flight. This is her own."

"I have a granddaughter too," said Gamache, looking he hoped not too frantically for the seat belt as the plane pushed off from the wharf and headed into the sound. "And another on the way. My granddaughter makes me finger paintings."

He almost added that at least a finger painting wasn't likely to kill you, but he thought that would be ungracious.

The plane gathered speed and began bouncing off the small waves. It was then Gamache noticed the torn canvas straps inside the plane, the rusting seats, the ripped cushions. He looked out the window and wished he hadn't had that full breakfast.

Then they were airborne and banking to the left they climbed into the sky and headed down the coastline. For forty minutes they flew. It was too noisy inside the tiny cabin to do anything other than yell at each other. Every now and then Sommes would lean over and point something out. He'd gesture down to a small bay and say things like, "That's where man first appeared, in the clam shell. It's our Garden of Eden." Or a little later, "Look down. Those are the last virgin red cedars in existence, the last ancient forest."

Gamache had an eagle's-eye view of this world. He looked down on rivers and inlets and forest and mountains carved by glaciers.

Eventually they descended into a bay whose peaks were shrouded in mist even on this clear day. As they got lower and skimmed over the water toward the dark shoreline Will Sommes leaned in to Gamache again and shouted, "Welcome to Gwaii Haanas. The place of wonders."

And it was.

Lavina got them as close as she could then a man appeared on the shore and shoved a boat out, leaping into it at the last moment. At the door to the seaplane he held out his hand to help the Chief Inspector into the tippy boat and introduced himself.

"My name's John. I'm the Watchman."

Gamache noticed he was barefooted, and saw Lavina and her grandfather taking their shoes and socks off and rolling up their cuffs as John rowed. Gamache soon saw why. The boat could only get so close. They'd have to walk the last ten feet. He removed his shoes and socks, rolled up his pants and climbed over the side. Almost. As soon as his big toe touched the water it, and he, recoiled. Ahead of him he saw Lavina and Sommes smile.

"It is cold," admitted the Watchman.

"Oh, come on, princess, suck it up," said Lavina. Gamache wondered if she was channeling Ruth Zardo. Was there one in every pack?

Gamache sucked it up and joined them on the beach, his feet purple from just a minute in the water. He nimbly walked over the stones to a stump and, sitting down, he rubbed the dirt and shards of shell from his soles and put his socks and shoes back on. He couldn't remember the last time he felt such relief. Actually, when the pontoon plane landed was probably the last time.

He'd been so struck by the surroundings, by the Watchman, by the frigid water, he'd failed to see what was actually there. Now he saw. Standing on the very edge of the forest was a solemn semicircle of totem poles.

Gamache felt all his blood rush to his core, his center.

"This is Ninstints," whispered Will Sommes.

Gamache didn't answer. He couldn't. He stared at the tall poles into which was carved the Mythtime, that marriage of animals and spirits. Killer whales, sharks, wolves, bears, eagles and crows were all staring back at him. And something else. Things with long tongues and huge eyes, and teeth. Creatures unknown outside the Mythtime, but very real here.

Gamache had the feeling he was standing

at the very edge of memory.

Some totem poles were straight and tall, but most had tumbled over or were lurching sideways.

"We are all fishermen," said Will. "Esther was right. The sea feeds our bodies, but that feeds our souls." He opened his hands in a simple, small gesture toward the forest.

John the Watchman spoke softly as they picked their way among the totem poles.

"This is the largest collection of standing totem poles in the world. The site's now protected, but it wasn't always. Some poles commemorate a special event, some are mortuary poles. Each tells a story. The images build on each other and are in a specific and intentional order."

"This is where Emily Carr did much of her painting," said Gamache.

"I thought you'd like to see it," said Sommes.

"*Merci.* I'm very grateful to you."

"This settlement was the last to fall. It was the most isolated, and perhaps the most ornery," said John. "But eventually it collapsed too. A tidal wave of disease, alcohol and missionaries finally washed over this place, as it had all the others. The totems were torn down, the longhouses destroyed. That's what's left." He pointed to a bump in the forest, covered by moss. "That was a longhouse."

For an hour Armand Gamache wandered the site. He was allowed to touch the totems and he found himself reaching high and placing his large, certain hand on the magnificent faces, trying to feel whoever had carved such a creature.

Eventually he walked over to John, who'd spent that hour standing in one spot, watching.

"I'm here investigating a murder. May I show you a couple of things?"

John nodded.

"The first is a photograph of the dead man. I think he might have spent time on Haida Gwaii, though I think he'd have called them the Charlottes."

"Then he wasn't Haida."

"No, I don't think he was." Gamache showed John the picture.

He took it and studied it carefully. "I'm sorry, I don't know him."

"It would have been a while ago. Fifteen, maybe twenty years."

"That was a difficult time. There were a lot of people here. It was when the Haida finally stopped the logging companies, by blocking the roads. He might have been a logger."

"He might have been. He certainly seemed comfortable in a forest. And he built himself a log cabin. Who here could teach him that?"

"Are you kidding?"

"No."

"Just about anyone. Most Haida live in villages now, but almost all of us have cabins in the woods. Ones we built ourselves, or our parents built."

"Do you live in a cabin?"

Did John hesitate? "No, I have a room at the Holiday Inn Ninstints," he laughed. "Yes. I built my own cabin a few years ago. Want to see it?"

"If you don't mind."

While Will Sommes and his granddaughter wandered around, John the Watchman took Gamache deeper into the forest. "Some of these trees are more than a thousand years old, you know."

"Worth saving," said Gamache.

"Not all would agree." He stopped and pointed. To a small cabin, in the forest, with a porch, and one rocking chair.

The image of the Hermit's.

"Did you know him, John?" asked Gamache, suddenly very aware he was alone in the woods with a powerful man.

"The dead man?"

Gamache nodded.

John smiled again. “No.” But he’d come very close to Gamache.

“Did you teach him to build a log cabin?”

“No.”

“Did you teach him to carve?”

“No.”

“Would you tell me if you had?”

“I have nothing to fear from you. Nothing to hide.”

“Then why are you here, all alone?”

“Why are you?” John’s voice was barely a whisper, a hiss.

Gamache unwrapped a carving. John stared at the men and women in the boat and backed away.

“It’s made from red cedar. From Haida Gwaii,” said Gamache. “Perhaps even from these trees in this forest. The murdered man made it.”

“That means nothing to me,” said John and with a last glance at the carving he walked away.

Gamache followed him out and found Will Sommes on the beach, smiling.

“Have a nice talk with John?”

“He hadn’t much to say.”

“He’s a Watchman, not a Chatter.”

Gamache smiled and started rewrapping the carving, but Sommes touched his hand to stop him and took the carving once again.

"You say it's from here. Is it old growth?"

"We don't know. The scientists can't say. They'd have to destroy the carving to get a big enough sample and I wouldn't let them."

"This is worth more than a man's life?" Sommes held the carving up.

"Few things are worth more than a man's life, monsieur. But that life has already been lost. I'm hoping to find who did it without destroying his creation as well."

This seemed to satisfy Sommes, who handed the carving back, but reluctantly.

"I'd like to have met the man who did that. He was gifted."

"He might have been a logger. Might have helped cut down your forests."

"Many in my family were loggers. It happens. Doesn't make them bad men or lifelong enemies."

"Do you teach other artists?" Gamache asked, casually.

"You think maybe he came here to talk to me?" asked Sommes.

"I think he came here. And he's a carver."

"First he was a logger, now he's a carver. Which is it, Chief Inspector?"

It was said with humor, but the criticism wasn't lost on Gamache. He was fishing, and he knew it. So did Sommes. So did Esther. We're all fishermen, she'd said.

Had he found anything on this visit? Gamache was beginning to doubt it.

"Do you teach carving?" he persisted.

Sommes shook his head. "Only to other Haida."

"The Hermit used wood from here. Does that surprise you?"

"Not at all. Some stands are now protected, but we've agreed on areas that can be logged. And replanted. It's a good industry, if managed properly. And young trees are great for the ecosystem. I advise all wood carvers to use red cedar."

"We should be going. The weather's changing," said Lavina.

As the float plane took off and banked away from the sheltered bay Gamache looked down. It appeared as though one of the totem poles had come alive, and waved. But then he recognized it as John, who guarded the haunting place but had been afraid of the small piece of wood in Gamache's hand. John, who'd placed himself beyond the pale.

"He was involved in the logging dispute, you know," Sommes shouted over the old engine.

"Seems a good person to have on your side."

"And he was. On your side, I mean. John was a Mountie. He was forced to arrest his own grandmother. I can still see him as he led her away."

"John's my uncle," Lavina shouted from the cockpit. It took Gamache a moment to put it all together. The quiet, somber, solitary man he'd met, the man who watched their plane fly away, had arrested Esther.

"And now he's a Watchman, guarding the last of the totem poles," said Gamache.

"We all guard something," said Sommes.

Sergeant Minshall had left a message for him at the guesthouse, and an envelope. Over a lunch of fresh fish and canned corn, he opened it and drew out more photographs, printed from the sergeant's computer. And there was an e-mail.

Armand,

We've tracked down four of the remaining carvings. There are two we still can't find, the one Olivier sold on eBay and one of the ones auctioned in Geneva. None of the collectors has agreed to send us the actual work of art, but they did send photos (see attached). No other carving has printing underneath.

Jérôme continues to work on your code. No luck yet.

What do you make of these pictures? Quite shocking, don't you think?

I've been working on the items from the cabin. So far none has been reported stolen and I can't seem to find a connection among them. I thought a gold bracelet might be Czech, but turns out to be Dacian. An astonishing find. Predates the current Romanians.

But it's very odd. The items don't seem to be related. Unless that's the key? Will have to think about it some more. I'm trying to keep the lid on these finds, but already I'm getting calls from around the world. News agencies, museums. Can't imagine how the word spread, but it has. Mostly about the Amber Room. Wait until they find out about the rest.

I hear you're on the Queen Charlotte Islands. Lucky man. If you meet Will Sommes tell him I adore his work. He's a recluse, so I doubt you'll see him.

Thérèse Brunel

He pulled out the photographs and looked at them as he ate. By the time the coconut cream pie arrived he'd been over them all. He'd laid them out on the table in a fan in front of him. And now he stared.

The tone of them had shifted. In one the figures seemed to be loading up carts, packing their homes. They seemed excited. Except the young man, who was gesturing anxiously to them to hurry. But in the next there seemed a growing unease among the people. And the last two were very different. In one the people were no longer walking. They were in huts, homes. But a few figures looked out the windows. Wary. Not afraid. Not yet. That was saved for the very last one Superintendent Brunel sent. It was the largest carving and the figures were standing and staring. Up. At Gamache, it seemed.

It was the oddest perspective. It made the viewer feel like part of the work. And not a pleasant part. He felt as though he was the reason they were so afraid.

Because they were, now. What had Will Sommes said the night before, when he'd spotted the boy huddled inside the ship?

Not just afraid, but terrified.

Something terrible had found the people in his carvings. And something terrible had found their creator.

What was odd was that Gamache couldn't see the boy in the last two carvings. He asked the landlady for a magnifying glass and feeling like Sherlock Holmes he leaned over and minutely examined the photographs. But nothing.

Leaning back in his chair he sipped his tea. The coconut cream pie remained untouched. Whatever terror had taken the happiness from the carvings had also stolen his appetite.

Sergeant Minshall joined him a few minutes later and they walked once more through town, stopping at Greeley's Construction.

"What can I do for you?" An older man, beard and hair and eyes all gray, but his body green and powerful.

"We wanted to talk to you about some of the workers you might've had back in the eighties and early nineties," said Sergeant Minshall.

"You're kidding. You know loggers. They come and go. Especially then."

"Why especially then, monsieur?" asked Gamache.

"This is Chief Inspector Gamache, of the Sûreté du Québec." Minshall introduced the men and they shook hands. Gamache had the definite impression that Greeley wasn't a man to be crossed.

"Long way from home," said Greeley.

"I am. But I'm being made to feel most

welcome. What was so special about that time?"

"The late eighties and early nineties? Are you kidding? Ever heard of Lyall Island? The roadblocks, the protests? There're thousands of acres of forest and the Haida suddenly get all upset about the logging. You didn't hear about it?"

"I did, but I wasn't here. Maybe you can tell me what happened."

"It wasn't the Haida's fault. They were wound up by the shit-disturbers. Those über-environmentalists. Terrorists, nothing more. They recruited a bunch of thugs and kids who just wanted attention. It had nothing to do with the forests. Listen, it wasn't like we were killing people, or even killing animals. We were taking down trees. Which grow back. And we were the biggest employer around. But the environmentalists got the Haida all worked up. Fed the kids a bunch of bullshit."

Beside Gamache, Sergeant Minshall shifted his feet. But said nothing.

"And yet the average age of the arrested Haida was seventy-six," said Gamache. "The elders placed themselves between the young protesters and you."

"A stunt. Means nothing," Greeley snapped. "I thought you said you didn't know anything about it."

"I said I wasn't here. I've read the reports, but it's not the same thing."

"Fucking right. Media swallowed it whole. We looked like the bad guys and all we were trying to do was log a few hundred acres that we had a right to."

Greeley's voice was rising. The wound, the rage, wasn't far beneath the surface.

"There was violence?" asked Gamache.

"Some. Bound to be. But we never started it. We just wanted to do our jobs."

"A lot of people came and went at that time? Loggers and protesters, I suppose."

"People crawling all over the place. And you want help finding one?" Greeley snorted. "What was his name?"

"I don't know." Gamache ignored the derisive laugh from Greeley and his people. Instead he showed the photo of the dead man. "He might have spoken with a Czech accent." Greeley looked at it and handed it back.

"Please look more closely," said the Chief Inspector.

The two men stared at each other for a moment.

"Perhaps if you stared at the picture instead of me, monsieur." His voice, while reasonable, was also hard.

Greeley took it back and looked longer. "Don't know him. He might've been here but who can tell? He'd have been a lot younger too, of course. Frankly he doesn't look like a logger or any forester. Too small."

It was the first helpful thing Greeley had said. Gamache glanced again at the dead recluse. Three sorts of visitors were on the Queen Charlottes in that time. Loggers, environmentalists, and artists. It seemed most likely this man was the latter. He thanked Greeley and left.

Once on the street he looked at his watch. If he could get Lavina to fly him to Prince Rupert he could still catch the red-eye to Montreal. But Gamache took a moment to make one more call.

"Monsieur Sommes?"

"Yes, Chief Inspector. Do you suspect your man might have been an eco-terrorist now?"

"*Voyons,* how did you know?"

Will Sommes laughed. "How can I help you?"

"John the Watchman showed me his cabin in the woods. Have you seen it?"

"I have."

"It's exactly the same as our dead man's home, across the country, in the woods of Quebec."

There was a pause on the line. "Monsieur Sommes?" Gamache wasn't sure if he'd lost the connection.

"I'm afraid that can't mean much. My cabin is also the same. All of them are, with very few exceptions. Sorry to disappoint you."

Gamache hung up, anything but disappointed. He knew one thing now without question. The Hermit had been on the Queen Charlotte Islands.

Chief Inspector Gamache only just managed to make the red-eye flight out of Vancouver. He squeezed into his middle seat and as soon as the plane took off the man in front put his seat all the way back until he was almost on Gamache's lap. The two people on either side each claimed an arm rest, and that left the Chief Inspector seven hours to listen to the little boy across the aisle play GI Joe.

He put on his half-moon glasses and read more about Emily Carr, her art, her travels, her "brutal telling." He stared at her paintings of the Queen Charlotte Islands, and appreciated even more the powerful, poetic images. He stared longest at her paintings of Ninstints. She'd captured it just before the fall, when the totems were tall and straight and the longhouses weren't yet covered by moss.

Flying over Winnipeg he pulled out the photographs of the Hermit's sculptures.

He looked at them, letting his mind drift. In the background the boy had developed an entire intricate story of war and attack and heroics. Gamache thought about Beauvoir back in Three Pines, hounded by an onslaught of facts, and Ruth Zardo's words. He closed his eyes and rested his head, thinking of the couplets Ruth kept sending, as though poetry was a weapon, which of course, it was. For her.

and pick your soul up gently by the nape
 of the neck
and caress you into darkness and
 paradise.

How beautiful was that, thought Gamache, drifting off to an uneasy sleep as Air Canada flew him home. And just as he nodded off another couplet floated up.

that the deity who kills for pleasure
will also heal,

By the time they were flying over Toronto Gamache knew what the carvings meant, and what he had to do next.

Thirty-Four

While Gamache had been in the mist of the Queen Charlotte Islands Clara had been in her own sort of fog. She'd spent the day circling the telephone, getting closer and closer then shooting away.

Peter watched all this from his studio. He no longer knew what he hoped would happen. That Clara would call Fortin, or not. He no longer knew what would be best. For her, for himself.

Peter stared at the picture on his easel. Picking up his brush, he dipped it in paint and approached. Determined to give it the detail people expected from his works. The complexity. The layers.

He added a single dot, then stepped back.

"Oh, God," he sighed and stared at the fresh dot on the white canvas.

Clara was once again approaching the telephone, via the refrigerator. Chocolate milk in one hand and Oreo cookies in the other she stared at the phone.

Was she being willful? Obstinate? Or was she standing up for what she believed in? Was she a hero or a bitch? Strange how often it was hard to tell.

She went into the garden and weeded without enthusiasm for a few minutes, then showered, changed, kissed Peter good-bye, got in her car and drove to Montreal. To the Galerie Fortin, to pick up her portfolio.

On the way home she made a last-minute detour, to visit Miss Emily Carr. Clara stared at the sculpture of the frumpy, eccentric woman with the horse and the dog and the monkey. And conviction in the face of a brutal telling.

Inspector Beauvoir met Gamache at Trudeau Airport.

"Any word from Superintendent Brunel?" the Chief Inspector asked as Beauvoir tossed his case into the backseat.

"She found one more carving. Some guy in Moscow has it. Won't let it out of his hands but he sent some pictures." Beauvoir handed an envelope to the Chief Inspector. "You? What did you find out?"

"Did you realize the lines Ruth's given you are all part of a single poem?"

"You found that out on the Queen Charlotte Islands?"

"Indirectly. Have you kept them?"

"The scraps of paper? Of course not. Why? Are they important to the case?"

Gamache sighed. He was weary. He had a distance to go that day and he couldn't afford a stumble. Not now.

"No. I suppose not. But it's a shame to lose them."

"Yeah, you say that. Just wait until she turns her pen on you."

". . . and pick your soul up gently by the nape of the neck and caress you into darkness and paradise," Gamache whispered.

"Where to?" Beauvoir asked as they bumped along the road toward Three Pines.

"The bistro. We need to speak to Olivier again. You looked into his finances?"

"He's worth about four million. One and a half from the sales of the carvings, a little over a million from the antiques the Hermit gave him and his property's worth about a million. We're not much further along," said Beauvoir, grimly.

But Gamache knew they were very close indeed. And he knew this was when the ground either became solid, or fell out from beneath them.

The car glided to a stop in front of the bistro. The Chief Inspector had been so quiet in the passenger seat Beauvoir thought maybe he was catching a nap. He looked tired, and who wouldn't after the long flight on Air Canada? The carrier that charged for everything. Beauvoir was convinced there'd soon be a credit card slot next to the emergency oxygen.

The Inspector looked over and sure enough Gamache's head was down and his eyes closed. Beauvoir hated to disturb him, he looked so peaceful. Then he noticed the Chief's thumb softly rubbing the picture he held loosely in his hand. Beauvoir looked more closely. The Chief's eyes weren't closed, not altogether.

They were narrow and staring intently at the image in his hand.

On it was the carving of a mountain. Barren, desolate. As though it had been clear-cut. Just a few scraggly pines at its base. There was a sadness about it, Gamache felt, an emptiness. And yet there was something about this work that was very different from the others. There was also a kind of levity. He narrowed his eyes and peering closer he saw it. What he'd mistaken for another pine at the foot of the mountain wasn't.

It was a young man. A boy, stepping hesitantly onto the base of the carving.

And where he stepped, some seedlings

sprouted.

It reminded him of Clara's painting of Ruth. Capturing that moment when despair turned to hope. This remarkable carving was forlorn, but also strangely hopeful. And without needing to look any closer Gamache knew this boy was the one in the other works. But the fear was gone. Or had it not yet arrived?

Rosa quacked on the village green. Today she wore a pale pink sweater set. And pearls?

"Voyons," said Beauvoir, jerking his head toward the duck as they got out of the car. "Can you imagine listening to that all day long?"

"Wait till you have kids," said Gamache, pausing outside the bistro to watch Rosa and Ruth.

"They quack?"

"No, but they sure make noise. And other things. Are you planning on kids?"

"Maybe one day. Enid isn't keen." He stood next to the Chief and they both stared at the peaceful village. Peaceful except for the quacking. "Any word from Daniel?"

"Madame Gamache spoke to them yesterday. All's well. Baby should be along in a couple of weeks. We'll be going to Paris as soon as it happens."

Beauvoir nodded. "That's two for Daniel.

How about Annie? Any plans?"

"None. I think David would like a family but Annie's not good with kids."

"I saw her with Florence," said Beauvoir, remembering when Daniel had visited with the Chief Inspector's granddaughter. He'd watched Annie holding her niece, singing to her. "She adores Florence."

"She claims not to want any. Frankly we don't want to push her."

"Best not to interfere."

"It's not that. We saw what a balls-up she made of every babysitting job she had as a kid. As soon as the child cried Annie called us and we'd have to go over. We made more money babysitting than she did. And Jean Guy." Gamache leaned toward his Inspector and lowered his voice. "Without going into details, whatever happens never let Annie diaper me."

"She asked the same thing of me," Beauvoir said and saw Gamache smile. Then the smile dimmed.

"Shall we?" The Chief gestured to the door to the bistro.

The four men chose to sit away from the windows. In the cool and quiet interior. A small fire muttered in both open fireplaces, at either end of the room. Gamache remembered the first time he'd walked into the bistro years before and seen the mismatched furniture, the armchairs and wing chairs and Windsor chairs. The round and square and rectangular tables. The stone fireplaces and wooden beams. And the price tags hanging from everything.

Everything was for sale. And everyone? Gamache didn't think so, but sometimes he wondered.

"*Bon Dieu,* are you saying you haven't told your father about me?" Gabri asked.

"I did. I told him I was with a Gabriel."

"Your father thinks it's a Gabrielle you're with," said Beauvoir.

"Quoi?" said Gabri, glaring at Olivier. "He thinks I'm a woman? That means . . ." Gabri looked at his partner, incredulous. "He doesn't know you're gay?"

"I never told him."

"Maybe not in so many words, but you sure told him," said Gabri, then turned to Beauvoir. "Almost forty, not married, an antiques dealer. Good God, he told me when the other kids would dig for China he dug for Royal Doulton. How gay is that?" He turned back to Olivier. "You had an Easy Bake oven and you sewed your own Halloween costumes."

"I haven't told him and don't plan to,"

Olivier snapped. "It's none of his business."

"What a family," sighed Gabri. "It's actually a perfect fit. One doesn't want to know and the other doesn't want to tell."

But Gamache knew it was more than simply not wanting to tell. It was about a little boy with secrets. Who became a big boy with secrets. Who became a man. He brought an envelope out of his satchel and placed seven photographs on the table in front of Olivier. Then he unwrapped the carvings and put them on the table too.

"What order do they go in?"

"I can't remember which he gave me when," said Olivier. Gamache stared at him then spoke softly.

"I didn't ask you that. I asked what order they go in. You know, don't you?"

"I don't know what you mean." Olivier looked confused.

Then Armand Gamache did something Beauvoir had rarely seen. He brought his large hand down so hard on the table the little wooden figures jumped. As did the men.

"Enough. I've had enough."

And he looked it. His face was hard, carved and sharp and burnished by lies and secrets. "Do you have any idea what trouble you're in?" His voice was low, strained, forced through a throat that threatened to close. "The lies must stop now. If you have any hope, any hope at all, you must tell us the truth. Now."

Gamache moved his splayed hand over the photographs and shoved them toward Olivier, who stared as though petrified.

"I don't know," he stumbled.

"For God's sake, Olivier, please," Gabri begged.

Gamache radiated anger now. Anger, frustration and fear that the real murderer would slip away, hiding in another man's lies. Olivier and the Chief Inspector stared at each other. One man who spent his life burying secrets and the other who spent his life unearthing them.

Their partners stared, aware of the battle but unable to help.

"The truth, Olivier," Gamache rasped.

"How did you know?"

"The place of wonders. Ninstints on the Queen Charlotte Islands. The totem poles told me."

"They told you?"

"In their way. Each image built on the last. Each told its own story and was a wonder unto itself. But when taken as a whole they told a larger story."

Beauvoir, listening to this, thought about

Ruth's couplets. The Chief had told him they did the same thing. If put together, in the right order, they too would tell a story. His hand slipped into his pocket and touched the scrap of paper shoved under his door that morning.

"What story do these tell, Olivier?" Gamache repeated. It had actually come to him on the plane as he'd listened to the little boy and the intricate GI Joe world he created. He'd thought about the case, thought about the Haida, the Watchman. Who, driven by his conscience, had finally found peace. In the wilderness.

The Chief Inspector suspected the same thing had happened to the Hermit. He'd gone into the forest a greedy man, to hide. But he'd been found. Years ago. By himself. And so he used his money as insulation and toilet paper. He used his first editions for knowledge and companionship. He used his antiquities as everyday dishes.

And in that wilderness he found freedom and happiness. And peace.

But something still eluded him. Or, perhaps more to the point, something still clung to him. He'd unburdened himself of the "things" of his life, but one more burden remained. The truth.

And so he decided to tell it to someone.

Olivier. But he couldn't go quite that far. Instead, he hid the truth in a fable, an allegory.

"He made me promise never to tell." Olivier had dropped his head and spoke into his lap.

"And you didn't. Not while he was alive. But you need to tell now."

Without another word Olivier reached out and moved the photographs about, hesitating briefly over a couple, switching the order at least once. Until finally, spread in front of them, was the Hermit's story.

And then Olivier told them, placing his hand over each image as he spoke. And as Olivier's soft, almost hypnotic voice filled the space between them Gamache could see the dead man, alive again. In his cabin late at night. His one visitor sitting across the flickering fireplace. Listening, to this tale of hubris, of punishment and love. And betrayal.

Gamache watched as the villagers, happy in their ignorance, left their homes. And the young man raced ahead, clutching his small package, encouraging them to hurry. Toward paradise, they thought. But the boy knew differently. He'd stolen the Mountain's treasure.

And worse.

He'd stolen the Mountain's trust.

Now each figure the Hermit had carved took on a significance. The men and women waiting by the shore, having run out of land. And the boy, cowering, having run out of hope.

Then the ship arrived, sent by gods jealous of the Mountain.

But behind was the ever-present shadow. And the threat of something unseen but very real. The ghastly army, assembled by the Mountain. Made up of Fury and Vengeance, promising catastrophe. Fueled by Rage. And behind them the Mountain itself. That couldn't be stopped and wouldn't be denied.

It would find all the villagers and it would find the young man. And it would find the treasure he'd stolen.

As this army pressed forward it provoked wars and famine, floods and plagues. It laid waste to the world. Chaos led the army and chaos was left behind.

Beauvoir listened to this. His hand in his pocket scrunched Ruth's latest couplet and he could feel it damp with sweat. He looked down at the photos of the carvings and saw the happy, ignorant villagers slowly transformed as they too first sensed something approaching, then knew it.

And he shared their horror.

Finally the wars and famine arrived on the shores of the New World. For years the wars raged around their new home, not quite touching it. But then . . .

They all looked at the final image. Of the villagers bunched together. Emaciated, their clothing in tatters. Looking up. In terror.

At them.

Olivier's voice stopped. The story stopped.

"Go on," whispered Gamache.

"That's it."

"What about the boy?" asked Gabri. "He's not in the carvings anymore. Where'd he go?"

"He buried himself in the forest, knowing the Mountain would find the villagers."

"He betrayed them too? His own family? His friends?" asked Beauvoir.

Olivier nodded. "But there was something else."

"What?"

"Something was behind the Mountain. Something driving it on. Something that terrified even the Mountain."

"Worse than Chaos? Worse than death?" asked Gabri.

"Worse than anything."

"What was it?" Gamache asked.

"I don't know. The Hermit died before we

got that far. But I think he carved it."

"What do you mean?" asked Beauvoir.

"There was something in a canvas sack that he never showed me. But he saw me looking at it. I couldn't help myself. He'd laugh and say one day he'd show it to me."

"And when you found the Hermit dead?" asked Gamache.

"It was gone."

"Why didn't you tell us this before?" snapped Beauvoir.

"Because then I'd have to admit everything. That I knew him, that I'd taken the carvings and sold them. It was his way of ensuring I'd come back, you know. Parceling out bits of his treasure."

"A pusher to an addict," said Gabri, with no rancor, but with no surprise either.

"Like Sheherazade."

Everyone turned to Gamache.

"Who?" Gabri asked.

"It's an opera, by Rimsky-Korsakov. It tells the story of the Thousand and One Nights."

They looked blank.

"The king would take a wife at night and kill her in the morning," said the Chief Inspector. "One night he chose Sheherazade. She knew his habits and knew she was in trouble so she came up with a plan."

"Kill the king?" asked Gabri.

"Better. Every night she told him a story, but left it unfinished. If he wanted to know the ending he had to keep her alive."

"Was the Hermit doing it to save his life?" asked Beauvoir, confused.

"In a way, I suppose," said the Chief. "Like the Mountain, he longed for company, and perhaps he knew Olivier well enough to realize the only way to get him to keep coming back was to promise more."

"That's not fair. You make me sound like a whore. I did more than take his things. I helped him garden and brought supplies. He got a lot out of it."

"He did. But so did you." Gamache folded his large hands together and looked at Olivier. "Who was the dead man?"

"He made me promise."

"And secrets are important to you. I understand that. You've been a good friend to the Hermit. But you have to tell us now."

"He was from Czechoslovakia," said Olivier at last. "His name was Jakob. I never knew his last name. He came here just as the Berlin wall was falling. I don't think we understood how chaotic it was. I remember thinking how exciting it must have been for the people. To finally have freedom. But he described something else. Every system they knew collapsed. It was lawless. Nothing worked. The phones, the rail service. Planes fell out of the air. He said it was horrible. But it was also a perfect time to run. To get out."

"He brought everything in that cabin with him?"

Olivier nodded. "For American money, hard currency he called it, you could arrange anything. He had contacts with antiques dealers here so he sold them some of his stuff and used the money to bribe officials in Czechoslovakia. To get his things out. He put them on a container ship and got them to the Port of Montreal. Then he put them all in storage and waited."

"For what?"

"To find a home."

"He first went to the Queen Charlotte Islands, didn't he?" said Gamache. After a pause Olivier nodded. "But he didn't stay there," Gamache continued. "He wanted peace and quiet, but the protests began and people came from all over the world. So he left. Came back here. Close to his treasures. And he decided to find a place in Quebec. In the woods here."

Again Olivier nodded.

"Why Three Pines?" Beauvoir asked.

Olivier shook his head, "I don't know. I

asked, but he wouldn't tell me."

"Then what happened?" Gamache asked.

"As I said before, he came down here and started to build his cabin. When it was ready he got the things out of storage and put them there. It took a while, but he had the time."

"The treasures that he got out of Czechoslovakia, were they his?" Gamache asked.

"I never asked, and he never told me, but I don't think they were. He was just too afraid. I know he was hiding from something. Someone. But I don't know who."

"Do you have any idea how much time you've wasted? My God, what were you thinking?" demanded Beauvoir.

"I just kept thinking you'd find who'd killed him and none of this other stuff needed to come out."

"Other stuff?" said Beauvoir. "Is that how you think of it? As though it was all just details? How'd you think we'd find the murderer with you lying and letting us hare off all over the place?"

Gamache raised his hand slightly and with an effort Beauvoir pulled back, taking a deep breath.

"Tell us about Woo," Gamache asked.

Olivier lifted his head, his eyes strained. He was pale and gaunt and had aged twenty years in a week. "I thought you'd said it was that monkey that belonged to Emily Carr."

"I thought so too, but I've been thinking about it. I think it meant something else to the dead man. Something more personal. Frightening. I think it was left in the web, and carved, as a threat. Something maybe only he and his murderer understood."

"Then why ask me?"

"Because Jakob might have told you. Did he, Olivier?"

Gamache's eyes bored into Olivier's, insisting on the truth.

"He told me nothing," said Olivier at last.

Disbelief met this remark.

Gamache stared at him, trying with his considerable might to look beyond the mist of lies. Was Olivier finally telling the truth?

Gamache got up. At the door he turned and looked back at the two men. Olivier drained, empty. Nothing left. At least, Gamache hoped there was nothing left. Each lie was like ripping off a piece of Olivier's skin, until finally he sat in the bistro, torn to pieces.

"What happened to the young man?" asked Gamache. "The one in the story. Did the Mountain find him?"

"It must have. He's dead, isn't he?" said Olivier.

Thirty-Five

At the B and B Gamache showered and shaved and changed his clothing. He glanced briefly at his bed, with its clean, crisp sheets and the duvet turned back. Waiting for him. But he avoided that siren song and before long he and Beauvoir were back across the village green and at the Incident Room, where Agents Lacoste and Morin waited.

They sat round the conference table, mugs of strong coffee and the Hermit's carvings in front of them. Succinctly the Chief Inspector told them about his trip to the Queen Charlottes and their interview with Olivier.

"So the dead man was telling a story all along. With his carvings," said Lacoste.

"Let's walk through this," said Beauvoir, going over to the sheets of paper on the wall. "The Hermit gets out of Czechoslovakia with the treasures just as the Soviet

Union's crumbling. It's chaos there so he bribes port officials to get the goods shipped to the Port of Montreal. Once there he puts them into storage."

"If he was a refugee or an immigrant his fingerprints would've shown up on record," said Agent Morin.

Agent Lacoste turned to him. He was young, she knew, and inexperienced. "There're illegal immigrants all over Canada. Some hiding, some with false papers that pass for real. A little money to the right people."

"So he snuck in," said Morin. "But what about the antiques? Were they stolen? Where'd he get them? Like the violin, and that Amber Room thing?"

"Superintendent Brunel says the Amber Room disappeared in the Second World War," said Gamache. "There're a lot of theories about what happened to it, including that it was hidden by Albert Speer in a mountain range. Between Germany and Czechoslovakia."

"Really?" said Lacoste, her mind working rapidly. "Suppose this Jakob found it?"

"If he found it he'd have the whole thing," said Beauvoir. "Suppose someone else found it, or part of it, and sold it to the Hermit."

"Suppose," said Morin, "he stole it."

"Suppose," said Gamache, "you're all right. Suppose someone found it, maybe decades ago. And split it up. And all that was left to one family was the one pane. Suppose that pane was entrusted to the Hermit, to smuggle out of the country."

"Why?" asked Lacoste, leaning forward.

"So they could start a new life," Beauvoir jumped in. "They wouldn't be the first who smuggled a family treasure out and sold it to start a business or buy a home in Canada."

"So they gave it to the Hermit to get out of the country," said Morin.

"Did it all come from different people?" wondered Lacoste. "A book here, a piece of priceless furniture or glass or silver there? Suppose all his things came from different people, all hoping to start a new life here? And he smuggled it all out."

"It would answer Superintendent Brunel's question about why there's such a range of items," said Gamache. "It's not from one collection, but many."

"No one would trust anyone with things that valuable," said Beauvoir.

"Maybe they had no choice," said the Chief. "They needed to get them out of the country. If he was a stranger they might not have trusted him. But if he was a friend . . ."

"Like the boy in the story," said Beauvoir. "Betraying everyone who trusted him."

They stared ahead. Silent. Morin had never realized murderers were caught in silence. But they were.

What would have happened? Families waited in Prague, in smaller cities and towns and villages. Waiting for word. From their trusted friend. At what stage did hope turn to despair? And finally to rage? And revenge?

Had one of them made it out, come across to the New World, and found the Hermit?

"But why did he come here?" asked Agent Morin.

"Why not?" asked Beauvoir.

"Well, there's a big Czech population here. If he was bringing all sorts of stolen goods, stuff he'd taken from people in Czechoslovakia, wouldn't he stay as far away from them as possible?"

They appealed to Gamache, who was listening, and thinking. Then he sat forward and drew the photographs of the carvings to him. Particularly the one of the happy people building a new village, in their new home. Without the young man.

"Maybe Olivier isn't the only one who lies," he said, getting up. "Maybe the Hermit wasn't alone when he came here. Maybe he had accomplices."

"Who are still in Three Pines," said Beauvoir.

Hanna Parra was clearing up lunch. She'd made a hearty soup and the place smelled of her mother's home in her Czech village. Of broth and parsley and bay leaves, and garden vegetables.

Her own gleaming metal and glass home couldn't be more different from the wooden chalet she'd grown up in. Full of wonderful aromas, and a hint of fear. Fear of attracting attention. Of standing out. Her parents, her aunts, her neighbors, had all lived comfortable lives of conformity. The fear of being found different, though, created a thin film between people.

But here everything really was transparent. She'd felt light as soon as they'd arrived in Canada. Where people minded their own business.

Or so she thought. Her hand hovered over the marble counter as some glint in the sun caught her eye. A car rolling up the drive.

Armand Gamache stared at the glass and metal cube in front of him. He'd read reports of the interviews with the Parras, including descriptions of their home, but still it took him aback.

The house gleamed in the sun. Not blinding, but it seemed to glow as though it lived in a world slightly different from theirs. A world of light.

"It's beautiful," said Gamache, almost under his breath.

"You should see inside."

"I think I should," Gamache nodded and the two men strolled across the yard.

Hanna Parra let them in and took their coats. "Chief Inspector, this is a pleasure."

Her voice was slightly accented but her French was perfect. Someone who'd not just learned the language but loved it. And it showed with every syllable. Gamache knew it was impossible to split language from culture. That without one the other withered. To love the language was to respect the culture.

That was why he'd learned English so well.

"We'd like to speak to your husband and son as well, if possible."

He spoke gently but somehow the very civility of the man lent his words weight.

"Havoc's out in the woods, but Roar's here."

"Where in the woods, madame?" Beauvoir asked.

Hanna seemed slightly flustered. "Out back. Cutting deadwood for the winter."

"Can you get him in, please?" said Beauvoir. His attempts at politeness simply made him seem sinister.

"We don't know where he is."

The voice came from behind them and both men turned to see Roar standing in the doorway to the mudroom. He was foursquare, stocky and powerful. His hands were on his hips and his elbows out, like a threatened animal trying to make itself appear larger.

"Then perhaps we can speak to you," said Gamache.

Roar didn't budge.

"Please, come into the kitchen," said Hanna. "It's warmer there."

She led them deeper into the house and shot Roar a warning look as she passed.

The kitchen was filled with natural warmth from the sun that spilled in.

"Mais, c'est formidable," Gamache said. Out of the floor-to-ceiling windows he could see field then forest and in the distance St. Thomas's steeple, in Three Pines. It felt as though they were living in nature, that the house was no intrusion at all. It was unexpected, certainly unusual. But it wasn't foreign. Just the opposite. This home be-

longed here. It was perfect.

"Félicitations." He turned to the Parras. "This is a magnificent achievement. It must've been something you'd dreamed of for a long time."

Roar dropped his arms and indicated a seat at the glass table. Gamache accepted.

"We talked about it for a while. It wasn't my first choice. I wanted something more traditional."

Gamache looked at Hanna, who'd taken the chair at the head of the table. "Must've taken some convincing," he smiled.

"He did," she said, returning his smile. Hers was polite, without warmth or humor. "Took years. There'd been a cabin on the property and we lived there until Havoc was about six, but he was growing and I wanted a place that felt like ours."

"*Je comprends,* but why this?"

"You don't like it?" She didn't sound defensive, only interested.

"Just the reverse. I think it really is magnificent. It feels as though it belongs here. But you must admit, it's unusual. No one else has a place quite like it."

"We wanted something completely different from where we grew up. We wanted a change."

"We?" asked Gamache.

"I came around," said Roar, his voice hard, his eyes wary. "What's all this about?"

Gamache nodded and sat forward, splaying his large hands on the cool surface of the table. "Why did your son work for Olivier?"

"He needs the money," said Hanna. Gamache nodded.

"I understand. But wouldn't he make more money working in the woods? Or working construction? Surely a waiter is paid very little, even with the tips."

"Why're you asking us?" Hanna asked.

"Well, I would ask him, if he were here."

Roar and Hanna exchanged glances.

"Havoc takes after his mother," said Roar finally. "He looks like me, but has his mother's temperament. He likes people. He enjoys working in the woods but prefers working with people. The bistro suits him perfectly. He's happy there."

Gamache nodded slowly.

"Havoc worked late at the bistro every night," said Beauvoir. "What time did he get home?"

"About one, rarely later."

"But sometimes later?" Beauvoir asked.

"Sometimes, I guess," said Roar. "I didn't wait up."

"I imagine you did." Beauvoir turned to Hanna.

"I did," she admitted. "But I can't remember him ever coming home after one thirty. If customers were late, especially if there was a party, he'd have to clean up, so he'd be a little later than usual, but never much."

"Be careful, madame," said Gamache quietly.

"Careful?"

"We need the truth."

"You're getting the truth, Chief Inspector," said Roar.

"I hope so. Who was the dead man?"

"Why do you people keep asking us that?" asked Hanna. "We didn't know him."

"His name was Jakob," said Beauvoir. "He was Czech."

"I see," said Roar, his face twisting in anger. "And all Czech people know each other? Do you have any idea how insulting that is?"

Armand Gamache leaned toward him. "It's not insulting. It's human nature. If I lived in Prague I'd gravitate to the Québécois there, especially at first. He came here more than a decade ago and built a cabin in the woods. He filled it with treasures. Do you know where they might have come from?"

"How would we know?"

"We think he might have stolen them from people back in Czechoslovakia."

"And because they came from Czechoslovakia we'd know about it?"

"If he'd stolen the things do you really think the first thing he'd do is come to a potluck dinner with the Czech Association?" Hanna demanded. "We don't know this Jakob."

"What did you do before you came here?" Gamache asked them.

"We were both students. We met at Charles University in Prague," said Hanna. "I was studying political science and Roar was studying engineering."

"You're a councilor for the area," said Gamache to Hanna, then turned to Roar. "But you don't seem to have pursued your interests here. Why not?"

Parra paused, then looked down at his large, rough hands, picking at a callus. "I was fed up with people. Wanted nothing to do with them. Why do you think there's a huge Czech community out here, away from cities? It's because we're sickened by what people can do. People goaded by others, emboldened. Infected by cynicism and fear and suspicion. By jealousy and greed. They turn on each other. I want nothing to do with them. Let me work quietly in a garden, in the woods. People are horrible creatures. You must know that, Chief Inspector. You've seen what they can do to each other."

"I have," Gamache admitted. He stopped talking for a moment, and in that moment lived all the terrible things the head of homicide might see. "I know what people are capable of." He smiled then, and spoke quietly. "The bad, but also the good. I've seen sacrifice, and I've seen forgiveness where none seemed possible. Goodness exists, Monsieur Parra. Believe me."

And for a moment it seemed Roar Parra might. He stared wide-eyed at Gamache as though the large, calm man was inviting him into a home he longed to enter. But then he stepped back.

"You're a fool, Chief Inspector," he laughed derisively.

"But a happy one," smiled Gamache. "Now, what were we talking about? Ah, yes. Murder."

"Whose car's in the driveway?" The young voice floated to them from the mudroom and a moment later a door slammed shut.

Beauvoir stood up. Hanna and Roar also rose and stared at each other. Gamache went to the door of the kitchen.

"It's my car, Havoc. Can we have a word?"

"Sure."

The young man walked into the kitchen, taking off his cap. His face was sweaty and dirty and he smiled disarmingly. "Why so serious?" Then his expression changed. "There hasn't been another murder, has there?"

"Why'd you say that?" asked Gamache, watching him.

"Well, you all look so glum. I feel like it's report card day."

"In a way it is, I guess. Time to take stock." Gamache pointed to a chair next to Havoc's father and the young man sat. Gamache also sat.

"You and Olivier were the last people in the bistro last Saturday night?"

"That's right. Olivier left and I locked up."

"And where did Olivier go?"

"Home, I guess." Havoc looked amused by the question.

"We know now that Olivier visited the Hermit late at night. Saturday nights."

"Is that right?"

"That's right." The young man's composure was a little too perfect. A little too practiced, Gamache thought. "But someone else knew about the Hermit. Not just Olivier. There are a couple of ways Jakob could have been found. One was to follow the overgrown horse trails. The other was to follow Olivier. To the cabin."

Havoc's smile faltered. "Are you saying I followed Olivier?" The young man looked from Gamache to his parents, searching their faces, and back again.

"Where were you just now?"

"In the woods."

Gamache nodded slowly. "Doing what?"

"Cutting wood."

"And yet we heard no saw."

"I'd already cut it and was just stacking it." Now the boy's eyes moved more quickly from Gamache to his father and back.

Gamache got up, walked a couple of steps to the door to the kitchen, bent down and picked something up. He sat back down and placed it on the polished table. It was a wood chip. No. A shaving. It curled back on itself.

"How did you afford this house?" Gamache asked Roar.

"What do you mean?" Roar asked.

"It would cost hundreds of thousands of dollars. The materials alone are worth that. Add in designs and specifications for such an unusual house, then labor? You say you built it about fifteen years ago. What happened then that allowed you to do it? Where'd you get the money?"

"What do you think happened?" Roar leaned in to the Chief Inspector. "You Québécois, so insular. What happened all those years ago? Let's see. There was a sovereignty referendum in Quebec, there was a huge forest fire in Abitibi, there was an election in the province. Nothing much else to report."

The shaving on the table trembled as his words brushed past on their way to Gamache.

"I've had it," Roar said. "God, how can you not know what happened back then?"

"Czechoslovakia broke up," said Gamache. "And became Slovakia and the Czech Republic. That actually happened twenty years ago, but the impact can take time. Those walls came down, and these ones," he glanced at the bank of glass, "went up."

"We could see our families again," said Hanna. "So many of the things we left behind we could have again. Family, friends."

"Art, silver, heirlooms," said Beauvoir.

"Do you think those things mattered?" asked Hanna. "We'd lived without them for so long. It was the people we missed, not the things. We barely dared hope it was real. We'd been fooled before. The summer of

’68. And certainly the reports we were seeing in the West were different from the stories we heard from people back home. Here we only heard how wonderful it was. We saw people waving flags and singing. But my cousins and aunts told a different story. The old system was horrible. Corrupt, brutal. But it was at least a system. When it went they were left with nothing. A vacuum. Chaos.”

Gamache tilted his head slightly at the word. Chaos. Again.

“It was terrifying. People were being beaten, murdered, robbed, and there were no cops, no courts.”

“A good time to smuggle things out,” said Beauvoir.

“We wanted to sponsor our cousins but they decided to stay,” said Roar.

“And my aunt wanted to stay with them, of course.”

“Of course,” said Gamache. “If not people, what about things?”

After a moment Hanna nodded. “We managed to get some family heirlooms out. My mother and father hid them after the war and told us they were to be kept for barter, for bargaining, if things got bad.”

“Things got bad,” said Gamache.

“We smuggled them out and sold them.

So that we could build the home of our dreams," said Hanna. "We struggled with that decision a long time, but finally I realized both my parents would understand and approve. They were only things. Home is what matters."

"What did you have?" asked Beauvoir.

"Some paintings, some good furniture, some icons. We needed a house more than we needed an icon," said Hanna.

"Who did you sell them to?"

"A dealer in New York. A friend of a friend. I can give you his name. He took a small commission but got a fair price," said Parra.

"Please. I'd like to speak to him. You certainly made good use of the money." The Chief Inspector turned to Roar. "Are you a carpenter too?"

"I do some."

"And you?" Gamache asked Havoc, who shrugged. "I'll need more than that."

"I do some."

Gamache reached out and slowly pushed the wood shaving along the glass table until it sat in front of Havoc. He waited.

"I was in the woods whittling," admitted Havoc. "When I finish my work I like to sit quietly and shave down a piece of wood. It's relaxing. A chance to think. To cool off.

I make little toys and things for Charles Mundin. Old gives me chunks of old wood and showed me how. Most of the stuff I make is crap and I just throw it away or burn it. But sometimes it's not too bad, and I give it to Charles. Why do you care if I whittle?"

"A piece of wood was found near the dead man. It was carved into the word Woo. Jakob didn't do it. We think the murderer did."

"You think Havoc —" Roar couldn't finish the sentence.

"I have a search warrant and a team on the way."

"What're you looking for?" asked Hanna, blanching. "Just the whittling tools? We can give them to you."

"It's more than that, madame. Two things are missing from Jakob's cabin. The murder weapon and a small canvas sack. We're looking for them too."

"We've never seen them," said Hanna. "Havoc, get your tools."

Havoc led Beauvoir to the shed while Gamache waited for the search team, who showed up a few minutes later. Beauvoir returned with the tools, and something else.

Chunks of wood. Red cedar. Whittled.

It was agreed that Beauvoir would direct

the search while Gamache returned to the Incident Room. At the car the two men talked.

"Which of them did it, do you think?" Beauvoir asked, handing the keys to Gamache. "Havoc could've followed Olivier and found the cabin. But it might've been Roar. He might've found the cabin when he was clearing the trail. Could've been the mother, of course. The murder didn't take a lot of strength. Anger, yes, adrenaline, but not strength. Suppose Jakob stole from the Parra family back in Czechoslovakia then when he came here they recognized him. And he recognized them. So he took off into the woods and hid there."

"Or perhaps Jakob and the Parras were in it together," said Gamache. "Maybe all three convinced friends and neighbors in Czechoslovakia to give them their precious things, then disappeared with them."

"And once here Jakob screwed his partners, taking off into the woods. But Roar found the cabin as he cut the trails."

Gamache watched the search teams start their methodical work. Before long there wouldn't be anything they didn't know about the Parras.

He needed to gather his thoughts. He handed the car keys to Beauvoir. "I'll walk."

“Are you kidding?” asked Beauvoir, for whom walking was a punishment. “It’s miles.”

“It’ll do me good, clear my mind. I’ll see you back in Three Pines.” He set off down the dirt road, giving Beauvoir a final wave. A few wasps buzzed in the ripe autumn air but were no threat. They were fat and lazy, almost drunk on the nectar from apples and pears and grapes.

It felt a little as though the world was on the verge of rotting.

As Gamache strolled, the familiar scents and sounds receded and he was joined by John the Watchman, and Lavina who could fly, and the little boy across the aisle on Air Canada. Who also flew, and told stories.

This murder seemed to be about treasure. But Gamache knew it wasn’t. That was just the outward appearance. It was actually about something unseen. Murder always was.

This murder was about fear. And the lies it produced. But, more subtly, it was about stories. The tales people told the world, and told themselves. The Mythtime and the totems, that uneasy frontier between fable and fact. And the people who fell into the chasm. This murder was about the stories told by Jakob’s carvings. Of Chaos and the

Furies, of a Mountain of Despair and Rage. Of betrayal. And something else. Something that horrified even the Mountain.

And at its heart there was, Gamache now knew, a brutal telling.

THIRTY-SIX

The search parties had already been over the structure a couple of times, but they looked again. Even more closely this time. Beneath floorboards, beneath eaves, behind paintings. They looked and they looked and they looked.

And finally, they found.

It was behind the bricks in the huge stone fireplace. Behind what seemed a perpetual fire. The fire had had to be extinguished and the smoldering logs removed. But there the Sûreté team found first one, then two, then four loose bricks. Removed, they revealed a small compartment.

Inspector Beauvoir reached a gloved hand in carefully, but not before smearing soot on his arm and shoulder.

"I have something," he said. All eyes were on him. Everyone stared as his arm slowly came out of the cavity. On the table in front of the Chief Inspector he placed a silver candelabra. A menorah. Even Beauvoir, who knew nothing about silver, recognized it as something remarkable. It was simple and refined and old.

This menorah had survived sieges, pogroms, slaughters, the holocaust. People had cherished it, hidden it, guarded it, prayed before it. Until one night in a forest in Quebec, someone had ruined it.

The menorah had killed a man.

"Paraffin?" Inspector Beauvoir pointed to bits of translucent material stuck to it. Mixed with dried blood. "He made his own candles. That's what the paraffin in the cabin was for, not just preserves but candles." The Chief nodded.

Beauvoir returned to the hearth and put his arm back down the black hole. They watched his face and finally saw that slight change, the surprise. As his hand hit something else.

He placed a small burlap bag beside the menorah. No one spoke, until finally Chief Inspector Gamache asked a question of the man sitting opposite him.

"Have you looked inside?"

"No."

"Why not?"

There was another long pause, but Gamache didn't hurry him. There was no rush now.

"I didn't have time. I just grabbed it out of the Hermit's cabin and hid it along with the candlestick, thinking I could take a closer look in the morning. But then the body was discovered and there was too much attention."

"Is that why you lit the fires, Olivier? Before the police arrived?"

Olivier hung his head. It was over. Finally.

"How'd you know where to look?" he asked.

"I didn't, at first. But sitting here watching the search I remembered you'd said the bistro used to be a hardware store. And that the fireplaces had to be rebuilt. They were the only new thing in the room, though they looked old. And I remembered the fires, lit on a damp but not cold morning. The first thing you did when the body was discovered. Why?" He nodded toward the things on the table. "To make sure we wouldn't find those."

Armand Gamache leaned forward, toward Olivier on the other side of the menorah and the burlap bag. Beyond the pale. "Tell us what happened. The truth this time."

Gabri sat beside Olivier, still in shock. He'd been amused at first when the Sûreté search party had shown up, moved from the

Parra place back to the bistro. He had made a few feeble jokes. But as the search became more and more invasive Gabri's amusement had faded, replaced by annoyance, then anger. And now shock.

But he'd never left Olivier's side, and he didn't now.

"He was dead when I found him. I admit, I took those." Olivier gestured to the items on the table. "But I didn't kill him."

"Be careful, Olivier. I'm begging you to be careful." Gamache's voice held an edge that chilled even the Sûreté officers.

"It's the truth." Olivier shut his eyes, almost believing if he couldn't see them they weren't there. The silver menorah and squalid little sack wouldn't be sitting on a table in his bistro. The police wouldn't be there. Just he and Gabri. Left in peace.

Finally he opened his eyes, to see the Chief Inspector looking directly at him.

"I didn't do it, I swear to God, I didn't do it."

He turned to Gabri who stared back, then took his hand and turned to the Chief Inspector. "Look, you know Olivier. I know Olivier. He didn't do this."

Olivier's eyes darted from one to the other. Surely there was a way out? Some crack, even the tiniest one, he could squeeze through.

"Tell me what happened," Gamache repeated.

"I already did."

"Again," said Gamache.

Olivier took a deep breath. "I left Havoc to close up and went to the cabin. I stayed for about forty-five minutes, had a cup of tea, and when I left he wanted to give me a little creamer. But I forgot it. When I got back to the village I realized what I'd done and was angry. Pissed off that he kept promising me that," he jabbed his finger at the sack, "but never gave it to me. Only small stuff."

"That creamer was valued at fifty thousand dollars. It belonged to Catherine the Great."

"But it wasn't that." Again Olivier shot a look at the bag. "When I returned the Hermit was dead."

"You told us the sack was gone."

"I lied. It was there."

"Had you seen the menorah before?"

Olivier nodded. "He used it all the time."

"For worship?"

"For light."

"It's also almost certainly priceless. You knew that, I suppose."

"You mean that's why I took it? No, I took

it because it had my fingerprints all over it. I'd touched it hundreds of times, lighting candles, putting new ones in."

"Walk us through it," said Gamache, his voice calm and reasonable.

And as Olivier spoke the scene unfolded before them. Of Olivier arriving back at the cabin. Seeing the door partly open, the sliver of light spilling onto the porch. Olivier pushing the door open and seeing the Hermit there. And blood. Olivier'd approached, stunned, and picked up the object by the Hermit's hand. And seeing the blood, too late, he'd dropped it. It had bounced under the bed to be found by Agent Lacoste. Woo.

Olivier had also seen the menorah, toppled over on the floor. Coated with blood.

He'd backed out of the room, onto the porch, preparing to run. Then he stopped. In front of him was the horrible scene. A man he knew and had come to care about, violently dead. And behind him the dark forest, and the trail running through it.

And caught between the two?

Olivier.

He'd collapsed into the rocking chair on the porch to think. His back to the terrible scene in the cabin behind him. His thoughts stretching forward.

What to do?

The problem, Olivier knew, was the horse trail. He'd known it for weeks. Since the Gilberts unexpectedly bought the old Hadley house, and even more unexpectedly decided to reopen the bridle paths.

"Now I understand why you hated them so much," said Gabri softly. "It seemed such an overreaction. It wasn't just the competition with the bistro and B and B, was it?"

"It was the trails. I was afraid, angry at them for getting Roar to open them. I knew he'd find the cabin and it'd all be over."

"What did you do?" asked Gamache.

And Olivier told them.

He'd sat on the porch for what seemed ages, thinking. Going round and round the situation. And finally he'd arrived at his *coup de grâce.* He decided the Hermit could do him one more favor. He could ruin Marc Gilbert and stop the trails, all at once.

"So I put him in the wheelbarrow and took him to the old Hadley house. I knew if another body was found there it would kill the business. No inn and spa, then no horse trails. Roar would stop work. The Gilberts would leave. The paths would grow over."

"And then what?" asked Gamache, again. Olivier hesitated.

"I could take what I wanted from the

cabin. It would all work out."

Three people stared at him. None with admiration.

"Oh, Olivier," said Gabri.

"What else could I do?" he pleaded with his partner. "I couldn't let them find the place." How to explain how reasonable, brilliant even, this all seemed at two thirty in the morning. In the dark. With a body ten feet away.

"Do you know how this looks?" rasped Gabri.

Olivier nodded and hung his head.

Gabri turned to Chief Inspector Gamache. "He'd never have done it if he'd actually killed the man. You wouldn't, would you? You'd want to hide the murder, not advertise it."

"Then what happened?" Gamache asked. Not ignoring Gabri but not wanting to be sidetracked either.

"I took the wheelbarrow back, picked up those two things and left."

They looked at the table. The most damning items. And the most precious. The murder weapon and the sack.

"I brought them back here and hid them in the space behind the fireplace."

"You didn't look in the bag?" Gamache asked again.

"I thought I'd have plenty of time, when all the attention was on the Gilbert place. But then when Myrna found the body here the next morning I almost died. I couldn't very well dig the things out. So I lit the fires, to make sure you wouldn't look in there. For days after there was too much attention on the bistro. And by then I just wanted to pretend they didn't exist. That none of this had happened."

Silence met the story.

Gamache leaned back and watched Olivier for a moment. "Tell me the rest of the story, the one the Hermit told in his carvings."

"I don't know the rest. I won't know until we open that." Olivier's eyes were barely able to look away from the sack.

"I don't think we need to just yet." Gamache sat forward. "Tell me the story."

Olivier looked at Gamache, flabbergasted. "I've told you all I know. He told me up to the part where the army found the villagers."

"And the Horror was approaching, I remember. Now I want to hear the end."

"But I don't know how it ends."

"Olivier?" Gabri looked closely at his partner.

Olivier held Gabri's gaze then looked over

at Gamache. “You know?”

“I know,” said Gamache.

“What do you know?” asked Gabri, his eyes moving from the Chief Inspector to Olivier. “Tell me.”

“The Hermit wasn’t the one telling the story,” said Gamache.

Gabri stared at Gamache, uncomprehending, then over at Olivier. Who nodded.

“You?” Gabri whispered.

Olivier closed his eyes and the bistro faded. He heard the mumbling of the Hermit’s fire. Smelled the wood of the log cabin, the sweet maple wood from the smoke. He felt the warm tea mug in his hands, as he had hundreds of times. Saw the violin, gleaming in the firelight. Across from him sat the shabby man, in clean and mended old clothing surrounded by treasure. The Hermit was leaning forward, his eyes glowing and filled with fear. As he listened. And Olivier spoke.

Olivier opened his eyes and was back in the bistro. “The Hermit was afraid of something, I knew that the first time I met him in this very room. He became more and more reclusive as the years passed until he’d hardly leave his cabin to go into town. He’d ask me for news of the outside world. So I’d tell him about the politics and the wars, and some of the things happening locally. Once I told him about a concert at the church here. You were singing," he looked at Gabri, "and he wanted to go."

There he was, at the point of no return. Once spoken, these words could never be taken back.

"I couldn't let that happen. I didn't want anyone else to meet him, to maybe make friends with him. So I told the Hermit the concert had been canceled. He wanted to know why. I don't know what came over me, but I started making up this story about the Mountain and the villagers and the boy stealing from it, and running away and hiding."

Olivier stared down at the edge of the table, focusing on it. He could see the grain of the wood where it had been worn smooth. By hands touching it, rubbing it, resting on it, for generations. As his did now.

"The Hermit was scared of something, and the stories made him more afraid. He'd become unhinged, impressionable. I knew if I told him about terrible things happening outside the forest he'd believe me."

Gabri leaned away, to get the full picture of his partner. "You did that on purpose? You made him so afraid of the outside world he wouldn't leave? Olivier."

The last word was exhaled, as though it stank.

"But there was more to it than that," said Gamache, quietly. "Your stories not only kept the Hermit prisoner, and his treasure safe from anyone else, but they also inspired the carvings. I wonder what you thought when you saw the first."

"I did almost throw it away, when he gave it to me. But then I convinced myself it was a good thing. The stories were inspiring him. Helping him create."

"Carvings with walking mountains, and monsters and armies marching his way? You must have given the poor man nightmares," said Gabri.

"What did Woo mean?" Gamache asked.

"I don't know, not really. But sometimes when I told the story he'd whisper it. At first I thought it was just an exhale, but then I realized he was saying a word. Woo."

Olivier imitated the Hermit saying the word, under his breath. Woo.

"So you made the spider's web with the word in it, to mimic *Charlotte's Web*, a book he'd asked you to find."

"No. How could I do that? I wouldn't even know how to start."

"And yet Gabri told us you'd made your own clothes as a kid. If you wanted to, you could figure it out."

"No," Olivier insisted.

"And you admitted the Hermit taught you how to whittle, how to carve."

"But I wasn't any good at it," said Olivier, pleading. He could see the disbelief in their faces.

"It wasn't very well made. You carved Woo." Gamache forged forward. "Years ago. You didn't have to know what it meant, only that it meant something to the Hermit. Something horrible. And you kept that word, to be used one day. As countries warehouse the worst of weapons, against the day it might be needed. That word carved in wood was your final weapon. Your Nagasaki. The last bomb to drop on a weary and frightened and demented man.

"You played on his sense of guilt, magnified by isolation. You guessed he'd stolen those things so you made up the story of the boy and the Mountain. And it worked. It kept him there. But it also inspired him to produce those carvings, which ironically turned out to be his greatest treasure."

"I didn't kill him."

"You just kept him prisoner. How could you?" said Gabri.

"I didn't say anything he wasn't willing to believe."

"You don't really think that?" said Gabri.

Gamache glanced at the items on the table. The menorah, used to murder. And the small sack. The reason for murder. He couldn't put it off any longer. It was time for his own brutal telling. He stood.

"Olivier Brulé," said Chief Inspector Gamache, his voice weary and his face grim, "I'm arresting you on a charge of murder."

THIRTY-SEVEN

The frost was thick on the ground when Armand Gamache next appeared in Three Pines. He parked his car by the old Hadley house and took the path deeper and deeper into the woods. The leaves had fallen from the trees and lay crisp and crackling beneath his feet. Picking one up he marveled, not for the first time, at the perfection of nature where leaves were most beautiful at the very end of their lives.

He paused now and then, not to get his bearings because he knew where he was going and how to get there, but to appreciate his surroundings. The quiet. The soft light now allowed through the trees and hitting ground that rarely saw the sun. The woods smelled musky and rich and sweet. He walked slowly, in no rush, and after half an hour came to the cabin. He paused on the porch, noticing again with a smile the brass number above the door.

Then he entered.

He hadn't seen the cabin since all the treasures had been photographed, fingerprinted, catalogued and taken away.

He paused at the deep burgundy stain on the plank floor.

Then he walked round the simple room. He could call this place home, he knew, if it had only one precious thing. Reine-Marie.

Two chairs for friendship.

As he stood quietly, the cabin slowly filled with glittering antiques and antiquities and first editions. And with a haunting Celtic melody. The Chief Inspector again saw young Morin turn the violin into a fiddle, his loose limbs taut, made for this purpose.

Then he saw the Hermit Jakob, alone, whittling by the fire. Thoreau on the inlaid table. The violin leaning against the river rock of the hearth. This man who was his own age, but appeared so much older. Worn down by dread. And something else. The thing that even the Mountain feared.

He remembered the two carvings hidden by the Hermit. Somehow different from the rest. Distinguished by the mysterious code beneath. He'd really thought the key to breaking the Caesar's Shift had been Charlotte. Then he'd been sure the key was seventeen. That would explain those odd numbers over the door.

But the Caesar's Shift remained unbroken. A mystery.

Gamache paused in his thinking. Caesar's Shift. How had Jérôme Brunel explained it? What had Julius Caesar done with his very first code? He hadn't used a key word, but a number. He'd shifted the alphabet over by three letters.

Gamache walked to the mantelpiece and reaching into his breast pocket he withdrew a notebook and pen. Then he wrote. First the alphabet, then beneath it he counted spaces. That was the key. Not the word sixteen but the number. 16.

A B C D E F G H I J K L M N O P Q R S T U V W X Y Z
K L M N O P Q R S T U V W X Y Z A B C D E F G H I J

Carefully, not wanting to make a mistake in haste, he checked the letters. The Hermit had printed MRKBVYDDO under the carving of the people on the shore. C, H, A, R . . . Gamache concentrated even harder, forcing himself to slow down. L, O, T, T, E.

A long sigh escaped, and with it the word. Charlotte.

He then worked on the code written under the hopeful people on the boat. OWSVI.

Within moments he had that too.

Emily.

Smiling he remembered flying over the mountains covered in mist and legend. Spirits and ghosts. He remembered the place forgotten by time, and John the Watchman, who could never forget. And the totems, captured forever by a frumpy painter.

What message was Jakob the Hermit sending? Did he know he was in danger and wanted to pass on this message, this clue? Or was it, as Gamache suspected, something much more personal? Something comforting, even?

This man had kept these two carvings for a reason. He'd written under them for a reason. He'd written Charlotte and Emily. And he'd made them out of red cedar, from the Queen Charlotte Islands, for a reason.

What does a man alone need? He had everything else. Food, water, books, music. His hobbies and art. A lovely garden. But what was missing?

Company. Community. To be within the pale. Two chairs for friendship. These carvings kept him company.

He might never be able to prove it, but Gamache knew without doubt the Hermit had been on the Queen Charlotte Islands, almost certainly when he'd first arrived in

Canada. And there he'd learned to carve, and learned to build log cabins. And there he'd found his first taste of peace, before having it disrupted by the protests. Like a first love, the place where peace is first found is never, ever forgotten.

He'd come into these woods to re-create that. He'd built a cabin exactly like the ones he'd seen on the Charlottes. He'd whittled red cedar, to be comforted by the familiar smell and feel. And he'd carved people for company. Happy people.

Except for one.

These creations became his family. His friends. He kept them, protected them. Named them. Slept with them under his head. And they in turn kept him company on the long, cold, dark nights as he listened for the snap of a branch, and the approach of something worse than slaughter.

Then Gamache heard a twig crack and tensed.

"May I join you?"

Standing on the porch was Vincent Gilbert.

"S'il vous plaît."

Gilbert walked in and the two men shook hands.

"I was at Marc's place and saw your car. Hope you don't mind. I followed you."

"Not at all."

"You looked deep in thought just now."

"A great deal to think about," said Gamache, with a small smile, tucking his notebook back into his breast pocket.

"What you did was very difficult. I'm sorry it was necessary."

Gamache said nothing and the two men stood quietly in the cabin.

"I'll leave you alone," said Gilbert eventually, making for the door.

Gamache hesitated then followed. "No need. I'm finished here." He closed the door without a backward glance and joined Vincent Gilbert on the porch.

"I signed this for you." Gilbert handed him a hardcover book. "They've reissued it after all the publicity surrounding the murder and the trial. Seems it's a bestseller."

"Merci." Gamache turned over the gleaming copy of *Being* and looked at the author photo. No more sneer. No more scowl. Instead a handsome, distinguished man looked back. Patient, understanding. *"Félicitations,"* said Gamache.

Gilbert smiled, then unfolded a couple of aluminum garden chairs. "I brought these with me just now. The first of a few things. Marc says I can live in the cabin. Make it my home."

Gamache sat. "I can see you here."

"Away from polite society," smiled Gilbert. "We saints do enjoy our solitude."

"And yet, you brought two chairs."

"Oh, you know that quote too?" said Gilbert. *"I had three chairs in my house: one for solitude, two for friendship, three for society."*

"My favorite quote from Thoreau is also from *Walden,*" said Gamache. *"A man is rich in proportion to the number of things he can afford to let alone."*

"In your job you can't let many things alone, can you?"

"No, but I can let them go, once they're done."

"Then why are you here?"

Gamache sat quietly for a moment then spoke. "Because some things are harder to let go than others."

Vincent Gilbert nodded but said nothing. While the Chief Inspector stared into space the doctor pulled out a small Thermos from a knapsack and poured them each a cup of coffee.

"How are Marc and Dominique?" Gamache asked, sipping the strong black coffee.

"Very well. The first guests have arrived.

They seem to be enjoying it. And Dominique's in her element."

"How's Marc the horse?" He was almost afraid to ask. And the slow shaking of Vincent's head confirmed his fears. "Some horse," murmured Gamache.

"Marc had no choice but to get rid of him."

Gamache saw again the wild, half-blind, half-mad, wounded creature. And he knew the choice had been made years ago.

"Dominique and Marc are settling in, and have you to thank for that," Gilbert continued. "If you hadn't solved the case they'd have been ruined. I take it from the trial that was Olivier's intention in moving the body. He wanted to close the inn and spa."

Gamache didn't say anything.

"But it was more than that, of course," said Gilbert, not letting it go. "He was greedy, I suppose."

And still Gamache said nothing, not wanting to further condemn a man he still considered a friend. Let the lawyers and judges and jury say those things.

"The Hungry Ghost," said Gilbert.

That roused Gamache, who twisted in his garden chair to look at the dignified man next to him.

"Pardon?"

"It's a Buddhist belief. One of the states of man from the Wheel of Life. The more you eat the hungrier you get. It's considered the very worst of the lives. Trying to fill a hole that only gets deeper. Fill it with food or money or power. With the admiration of others. Whatever."

"The Hungry Ghost," said Gamache. "How horrible."

"You have no idea," said Gilbert.

"You do?"

After a moment Gilbert nodded. He no longer looked quite so magnificent. But considerably more human. "I had to give it all up to get what I really wanted."

"And what was that?"

Gilbert considered for a long time. "Company."

"You came to a cabin in the woods to find company?" smiled Gamache.

"To learn to be good company for myself."

They sat quietly until Gilbert finally spoke. "So Olivier killed the Hermit for the treasure?"

Gamache nodded. "He was afraid it'd be found. He knew it was only a matter of time, once your son moved here and Parra started opening the trails."

"Speaking of the Parras, did you consider them?"

Gamache looked at the steaming mug of coffee warming his large hands. He'd never tell this man the full story. It wouldn't do to admit that Havoc Parra in particular had been their main suspect. Havoc worked late. He could have followed Olivier to the cabin after closing the bistro. And while Havoc's whittling tools had tested negative maybe he used others. And wasn't the Hermit Czech?

Or if not Havoc then his father Roar, who cut the trails and was almost certainly heading straight for the cabin. Maybe he found it.

Maybe, maybe, maybe.

A wide trail of "maybe's" led directly to the Parras.

But Gamache also chose not to tell Gilbert that he had also been a suspect, as had his son and daughter-in-law. The cabin was on their land. Why had they bought the ruined old house when they could have had any place? Why had they ordered the trails reopened so quickly? It was almost the first thing they did.

And why had the saintly Dr. Gilbert and the body both appeared at the same time?

Why, why, why.

A wide trail of "why's" led directly to the front door of the old Hadley house.

They all made good suspects. But all the actual evidence pointed to Olivier. The fingerprints, the murder weapon, the canvas sack, the carvings. They'd found no whittling tools in Olivier's possession, but that meant nothing. He would have gotten rid of them years ago. But they had found nylon line in the B and B. The same weight and strength used for the web. Olivier's defense argued it was the standard ply and proved nothing. Gabri testified that he'd used it for gardening, to tie up honeysuckle.

It proved nothing.

"But why put that word up in the web, and carve it in wood?" asked Vincent.

"To frighten the Hermit into giving him the treasure in the sack."

It had been a shockingly simple solution. The trail was getting closer every day. Olivier knew time was running out. He had to convince the Hermit to hand it over, before the cabin was found. Because once that happened the Hermit would realize the truth: Olivier had been lying. There was no Mountain. No army of Dread and Despair. No Chaos. Just a greedy little antique dealer, who could never get enough.

No approaching horror, just another Hungry Ghost.

Olivier's last hope of getting the burlap

bag from the Hermit was to convince him the danger was imminent. To save his life Jakob had to get rid of the treasure. So that when the Mountain arrived he'd find the Hermit, but no sack.

But when the story failed to terrify enough, when the trail had come too close, Olivier had brought out his napalm, his mustard gas, his buzz bomb. His *Enola Gay.*

He'd put the web up in the corner. And placed the whittled word somewhere in the cabin, for Jakob to find. Knowing that when the Hermit saw it he would — what? Die? Perhaps. But he would certainly panic. Knowing he'd been found. The thing he'd hidden from, the thing he'd fled from. The thing he most feared. Had found him. And left its calling card.

What had gone wrong? Had the Hermit not seen the web? Had the Hermit's greed exceeded even Olivier's? Whatever happened one thing Gamache knew for certain. Olivier, his patience at an end, his nerves frazzled, his rage in full flood, had reached out, clasped the menorah. And struck.

His lawyer had opted for a jury trial. A good strategy, thought Gamache. A jury could be convinced it was temporary insanity. Gamache himself had argued that Olivier should be tried for manslaughter, not murder, and the prosecution had agreed. The Chief Inspector knew Olivier had done many terrible things to the Hermit, on purpose. But killing him wasn't one. Imprisoning Jakob, yes. Manipulating and taking advantage of him, yes. Unbalancing an already fragile mind, yes. But not murder. That, Gamache believed, had surprised and appalled even Olivier.

Such an appropriate word. Manslaughter.

That's what Olivier had done. He'd slaughtered a man. Not with that one terrible blow, but over time. Wearing him down, so that the Hermit's face was scored with worry lines and his soul cringed with every scrape of a twig.

But it turned into a murder/suicide. Olivier had killed himself in the process. Whittling away what was kind and good about himself, until loathing replaced self-respect. The man he could have been was dead. Consumed by the Hungry Ghost.

What finally damned Olivier wasn't speculation but facts. Evidence. Only Olivier could be placed at the cabin. His prints were found here, and on the murder weapon. He knew the Hermit. He sold some of his treasures. He sold the carvings. He stole the burlap bag. And finally, the murder weapon was found hidden in the bistro, along with the bag. His lawyer would try to come up with all sorts of arguments, but this case would hold. Gamache had no doubt.

But while facts might be enough for a prosecutor, a judge, a jury, they weren't enough for Gamache. He needed more. He needed motive. That thing that could never be proved because it can't be seen.

What drove a man to slaughter?

And that's what had sealed it for Gamache. As he'd been walking back to Three Pines, having ordered the Parra place searched yet again, he'd thought about the case. The evidence. But also the malevolent spirit behind it.

He realized that all the things that pointed to the Parras' possibly doing it also applied to Olivier. Fear and greed. But what tipped it toward Olivier was that while the Parras had shown little inclination toward greed, Olivier had wallowed in it.

Olivier was afraid of two things, Gamache knew. Being exposed, and being without.

Both were approaching, both threatening.

Gamache sipped his coffee and thought again about those totem poles in Ninstints, rotting, falling, fallen. But they still had a story to tell.

It was there the idea had been planted.

That this murder was about tales told. And the Hermit's carvings were the key. They weren't random, individual carvings. They were a community of carvings. Each could stand on its own, but taken together they told an even bigger story. Like the totem poles.

Olivier had told tales to control and imprison the Hermit. The Hermit had used them to create his remarkable carvings. And Olivier had used those carvings to get wealthier even than he had dreamed.

But what Olivier hadn't appreciated was that his stories were actually true. An allegory, yes. But no less real for that. A mountain of misery was approaching. And growing with each new lie, each new tale.

A Hungry Ghost.

The wealthier Olivier grew the more he wanted. And what he wanted more than anything was the one thing denied him. The contents of the little canvas sack.

Jakob had come to Three Pines with his treasures, almost certainly stolen from friends and neighbors in Czechoslovakia. People who had trusted him. Once the Iron Curtain had collapsed and those people could leave, they started asking for their money. Demanding it. Threatening to show up. Perhaps even showing up.

So he'd taken his treasure, their treasures, and hidden it and himself in the woods. Waiting for it to blow over, for the people to give up. To go home. To leave him in peace.

Then he could sell it all. Buy private jets and luxury yachts. A townhouse in Chelsea, a vineyard in Burgundy.

Would he have been happy then? Would it have finally been enough?

Find out what he loved, and maybe then you'll find his murderer, Gamache had been told by Esther, the Haida elder. Had the Hermit loved money?

Perhaps at first.

But then hadn't he used money in the outhouse? As toilet paper. Hadn't they found twenty-dollar bills stuffed into the walls of the log cabin, as insulation?

Had the Hermit loved his treasure? Perhaps at first.

But then he'd given it away. In exchange for milk and cheese and coffee.

And company.

When Olivier had been taken away Gamache had sat back down and stared at the sack. What could be worse than Chaos, Despair, War? What would even the Mountain flee from? Gamache had given it a lot of thought. What haunted people even, perhaps especially, on their deathbed? What chased them, tortured them and brought some to their knees? And Gamache thought he had the answer.

Regret.

Regret for things said, for things done, and not done. Regret for the people they might have been. And failed to be.

Finally, when he was alone, the Chief Inspector had opened the sack and looking inside had realized he'd been wrong. The worst thing of all wasn't regret.

Clara Morrow knocked on Peter's door.

"Ready?"

"Ready," he said, and came out wiping the oil paint from his hand. He'd taken to sprinkling his hands with paint so that Clara would think he'd been hard at work when in fact he'd finished his painting weeks earlier.

He'd finally admitted that to himself. He just hadn't admitted it to anyone else.

"How do I look?"

"Great." Peter took a piece of toast from Clara's hair.

"I was saving that for lunch."

"I'll take you out for lunch," he said, following her out the door. "To celebrate."

They got in the car and headed into Montreal. That terrible day when she'd gone to pick up her portfolio from Fortin, she'd stopped at the sculpture of Emily Carr. Someone else was there eating her lunch and Clara had sat at the far end of the bench and stared at the little bronze woman. And the horse, the dog and the monkey. Woo.

Emily Carr didn't look like one of the greatest visionary artists ever. She looked like someone you'd meet across the aisle on the Number 24 bus. She was short. A little dumpy. A little frumpy.

"She looks a bit like you," came the voice beside Clara.

"You think so?" said Clara, far from convinced it was a compliment.

The woman was in her sixties. Beautifully dressed. Poised and composed. Elegant.

"I'm Thérèse Brunel." The woman reached out her hand. When Clara continued to look perplexed she added, "Superintendent Brunel. Of the Sûreté du Québec."

"Of course. Forgive me. You were in Three Pines with Armand Gamache."

"Is that your work?" She nodded toward the portfolio.

"Photographs of it, yes."

"May I see?"

Clara opened the portfolio and the Sûreté officer looked through, smiling, commenting, drawing in breath occasionally. But she stopped at one picture. It was of a joyous woman facing forward but looking back.

"She's beautiful," said Thérèse. "Someone I'd like to know."

Clara hadn't said anything. Just waited. And after a minute her companion blinked then smiled and looked at Clara.

"It's quite startling. She's full of Grace, but something's just happened, hasn't it?"

Still Clara remained silent, staring at the reproduction of her own work.

Thérèse Brunel went back to looking at it too. Then she inhaled sharply and looked at Clara. "The Fall. My God, you've painted the Fall. That moment. She's not even aware of it, is she? Not really, but she sees something, a hint of the horror to come. The Fall from Grace." Thérèse grew very quiet, looking at this lovely, blissful woman. And that tiny, nearly invisible awareness.

Clara nodded. "Yes."

Thérèse looked at her more closely. "But there's something else. I know what it is. It's you, isn't it? She's you."

Clara nodded.

After a moment Thérèse whispered so that Clara wasn't even sure the words had been spoken aloud. Maybe it was the wind. "What are you afraid of?"

Clara waited a long time to speak, not because she didn't know the answer, but because she'd never said it out loud. "I'm afraid of not recognizing Paradise."

There was a pause. "So am I," said Superintendent Brunel.

She wrote a number and handed it to Clara. "I'm going to make a call when I get back to my office. Here's my number. Call me this afternoon."

Clara had, and to her amazement the elegant woman, the police officer, had arranged for the Chief Curator at the Musée d'art contemporain in Montreal to see the portfolio.

That had been weeks ago. A lot had happened since. Chief Inspector Gamache had arrested Olivier for murder. Everyone knew that had been a mistake. But as the evidence grew so did their doubts. As all of this was happening Clara had taken her work into the MAC. And now they'd asked for a meeting.

"They won't say no," said Peter, speeding along the autoroute. "I've never known a gallery to invite an artist to a meeting to turn him down. It's good news, Clara. Great news. Way better than anything Fortin could have done for you."

And Clara dared to think that was true.

As he drove Peter thought about the painting on his own easel. The one he now knew was finished. As was his career. On the white canvas Peter had painted a large black circle, almost, but not quite, closed. And where it might have closed he'd put dots.

Three dots. For infinity. For society.

Jean Guy Beauvoir was in the basement of his home looking down at the ragged strips of paper. Upstairs he could hear Enid preparing lunch.

He'd gone to the basement every chance he got in the last few weeks. He'd flip the game on the television then sit with his back to the TV. At his desk. Mesmerized by the scraps of paper. He'd hoped the mad old poet had written the whole thing on a single sheet of paper and simply torn it into strips so he could fit them together like a jigsaw puzzle. But, no, the pieces of paper wouldn't fit together. He had to find the meaning in the words.

Beauvoir had lied to the Chief. He didn't do it often, and he had no idea why he'd done it this time. He'd told the Chief he'd thrown them all out, all the stupid words Ruth had tacked onto his door, shoved into his pocket. Given others to give to him.

He'd wanted to throw them out, but even

more than that he'd wanted to know what they meant. It was almost hopeless. Perhaps the Chief could decipher it, but poetry had always been a big fat pile of crap to Beauvoir. Even when presented with it whole. How could he ever assemble a poem?

But he'd tried. For weeks.

He slipped one scrap between two and moved another to the top.

I just sit where I'm put, composed
of stone and wishful thinking:
that the deity who kills for pleasure
will also heal,

He took a swig of beer.

"Jean Guy," his wife sang to him. "Luh-hunch."

"Coming."

that in the midst of your nightmare,
the final one, a kind lion
will come with bandages in her mouth
and the soft body of a woman,

Enid called again and he didn't answer but instead stared at the poem. Then his eyes moved to the furry little feet dangling over the shelf above his desk. At eye level, where he could see it. The stuffed lion he'd quietly taken from the B and B. First to his room, for company. He'd sat it in the chair where he could see it from his bed. And he imagined her there. Maddening, passionate, full of life. Filling the empty, quiet corners of his life. With life.

And when the case was over he'd slipped the lion into his bag and brought it down here. Where Enid never came.

The kind lion. With its soft skin and smile. "Wimoweh, a-wimoweh," he sang under his breath as he read the final stanza.

and lick you clean of fever,
and pick your soul up gently by the nape
 of the neck
and caress you into darkness and
 paradise.

An hour later Armand Gamache walked out of the woods and down the slope into Three Pines. On the porch of the bistro he took a deep breath, composed himself, and entered.

It took a moment for his eyes to adjust. When they did he saw Gabri behind the bar, where Olivier had always stood. The large man had diminished, lost weight. He looked careworn. Tired.

"Gabri," said Gamache, and the two old

friends stared at each other.

"Monsieur," said Gabri. He shifted a jar of allsorts and another of jelly beans on the polished wood counter, then came around. And offered Gamache a licorice pipe.

Myrna walked in a few minutes later to find Gabri and Gamache sitting quietly by the fire. Talking. Their heads together. Their knees almost touching. An uneaten licorice pipe between them.

They looked up as she entered.

"I'm sorry." She stopped. "I can come back. I just wanted to show you this." She held a piece of paper out to Gabri.

"I got one too," he said. "Ruth's latest poem. What do you think it means?"

"I don't know." She couldn't get used to coming into the bistro and seeing only Gabri. With Olivier in jail it felt as though something vital was missing, as though one of the pines had been cut down.

It was excruciating, what was happening. The village felt torn and ragged. Wanting to support Olivier and Gabri. Appalled at the arrest. Not believing it. And yet knowing that Chief Inspector Gamache would never have done it unless he was certain.

It was also clear how much it had cost Gamache to arrest his friend. It seemed impossible to support one without betraying the other.

Gabri rose, as did Gamache. "We were just catching up. Did you know the Chief Inspector has another granddaughter? Zora."

"Congratulations." Myrna embraced the grandfather.

"I need fresh air," said Gabri, suddenly restless. At the door he turned to Gamache. "Well?"

The Chief Inspector and Myrna joined him and together they walked slowly round the village green. Where all could see. Gamache and Gabri, together. The wound not healed, but neither was it getting deeper.

"Olivier didn't do it, you know," said Gabri, stopping to look at Gamache directly.

"I admire you for standing by him."

"I know there's a lot about him that sucks. Not surprisingly, those are some of my favorite parts." Gamache gave a small guffaw. "But there's one question I need answered."

"Oui?"

"If Olivier killed the Hermit, why move the body? Why take it to the Hadley house to be found? Why not leave it in the cabin? Or stick it in the woods?"

Gamache noticed the "he" had become an "it." Gabri couldn't accept that Olivier had killed, and he certainly couldn't accept that Olivier had killed a "he" not an "it."

"That was answered in the trial," said Gamache, patiently. "The cabin was about to be found. Roar was cutting a path straight for it."

Gabri nodded, reluctantly. Myrna watched and willed her friend to be able to accept the now undeniable truth.

"I know," said Gabri. "But why move it to the Hadley house? Why not just take it deeper into the woods and let the animals do the rest?"

"Because Olivier realized the body wasn't the most damning evidence against him. The cabin was. Years of evidence, of fingerprints, of hairs, of food. He couldn't hope to clean it all up, at least not right away. But if our investigation focused on Marc Gilbert and the Hadley house he might stop the progress of the paths. If the Gilberts were ruined there was no need of horse trails."

Gamache's voice was calm. No sign of the impatience Myrna knew it could hold. This was at least the tenth time she'd heard the Chief Inspector explain it to Gabri, and still Gabri didn't believe it. And even now Gabri was shaking his head.

"I'm sorry," said Gamache, and clearly

meant it. "There was no other conclusion."

"Olivier isn't a murderer."

"I agree. But he did kill. It was manslaughter. Unintentional. Can you really tell me you believe he's not capable of killing out of rage? He'd worked years to get the Hermit to give him the treasure, and feared he might lose it. Are you sure Olivier wouldn't be driven to violence?"

Gabri hesitated. Neither Gamache nor Myrna dared breathe, for fear of chasing away timid reason fluttering around their friend.

"Olivier didn't do it." Gabri sighed heavily, exasperated. "Why would he move the body?"

The Chief Inspector stared at Gabri. Words failed him. If there was any way to convince this tormented man, he would. He'd tried. He hated the thought that Gabri would carry this unnecessary burden, the horror of believing his partner falsely imprisoned. Better to accept the wretched truth than struggle, twisting, to make a wish a reality.

Gabri turned his back on the Chief Inspector and walked onto the green, to the very center of the village, and sat on the bench.

"What a magnificent man," said Gamache, as he and Myrna resumed their walk.

"He is that. He'll wait forever, you know. For Olivier to come back."

Gamache said nothing and the two strolled in silence. "I ran into Vincent Gilbert," he finally said. "He says Marc and Dominique are settling in."

"Yes. Turns out when he's not moving bodies around the village Marc's quite nice."

"Too bad about Marc the horse."

"Still, he's probably happier."

This surprised Gamache and he turned to look at Myrna. "Dead?"

"Dead? Vincent Gilbert had him sent to LaPorte."

Gamache snorted and shook his head. The asshole saint indeed.

As they passed the bistro he thought about the canvas bag. The thing that had, more than anything else, condemned Olivier when found hidden behind the fireplace.

Ruth's door opened and the old poet, wrapped in her worn cloth coat, hobbled out, followed by Rosa. But today the duck was without clothing. Just feathers.

Gamache had grown so used to seeing Rosa in her outfits it seemed almost unnatural that she should be without one now.

The two walked across the road to the green where Ruth opened a small paper bag and tossed bread for Rosa, who waddled after the crumbs, flapping her wings. A quacking could be heard overhead, getting closer. Gamache and Myrna turned to the sound. But Ruth's eyes remained fixed, on Rosa. Overhead, ducks approached in V formation flying south for the winter.

And then, with a cry that sounded almost human Rosa rose up and flew into the air. She circled and for an instant everyone thought she would return. Ruth raised her hand, offering bread crumbs from her palm. Or a wave. Good-bye.

And Rosa was gone.

"Oh, my God," breathed Myrna.

Ruth stared, her back to them, her face and hand to the sky. Bread crumbs tumbling to the grass.

Myrna took out the crumpled paper from her pocket and gave it to Gamache.

She rose up into the air and the jilted
  earth let out a sigh.
She rose up past telephone poles and
  rooftops of houses where the
  earthbound hid.
She rose up sleeker than the sparrows
  that swirled around her like a jubilant

cyclone
She rose up, past satellites and every cell
phone down on earth rang at once.

"Rosa," whispered Myrna. "Ruth."

Gamache watched the old poet. He knew what was looming behind the Mountain. What crushed all before it. The thing the Hermit most feared. The Mountain most feared.

Conscience.

Gamache remembered opening the coarse sack, his hand sliding over the smooth wood inside. It was a simple carving. A young man in a chair, listening.

Olivier. He'd turned it over and found three letters etched into the wood. GYY.

He'd decoded them in the cabin just minutes before and had stared at the word.

Woo.

Hidden in the rude rough sack it was far finer, even, than the more detailed carvings. This was simplicity itself. Its message was elegant and horrific. The carving was beautiful and yet the young man seemed utterly empty. His imperfections worn away. The wood hard and smooth so that the world slid right off it. There would be no touch and therefore no feeling.

It was the Mountain King, as a man.

Unassailable, but unapproachable. Gamache felt like throwing it deep into the forest. To lie where the Hermit had put himself. Hiding from a monster of his own making.

But there was no hiding from Conscience.

Not in new homes and new cars. In travel. In meditation or frantic activity. In children, in good works. On tiptoes or bended knee. In a big career. Or a small cabin.

It would find you. The past always did.

Which was why, Gamache knew, it was vital to be aware of actions in the present. Because the present became the past, and the past grew. And got up, and followed you.

And found you. As it had the Hermit. As it had Olivier. Gamache stared at the cold, hard, lifeless treasure in his hand.

Who wouldn't be afraid of this?

Ruth limped across the green to the bench and sat. With a veined hand she clutched her blue cloth coat to her throat while Gabri reached out and taking her other hand in his and rubbing it softly and murmured, "there, there."

She rose up but remembered to politely
wave good-bye . . .

ABOUT THE AUTHOR

Louise Penny is an award-winning journalist who worked for many years for the Canadian Broadcasting Corporation. Her bestselling Chief Inspector Gamache series has earned the highest of praise. She lives in a small village south of Montréal.

We hope you have enjoyed this Large Print book. Other Thorndike, Wheeler, Kennebec, and Chivers Press Large Print books are available at your library or directly from the publishers.

For information about current and upcoming titles, please call or write, without obligation, to:

Publisher
Thorndike Press
295 Kennedy Memorial Drive
Waterville, ME 04901
Tel. (800) 223-1244

or visit our Web site at:

http://gale.cengage.com/thorndike

OR

Chivers Large Print
published by BBC Audiobooks Ltd
St James House, The Square
Lower Bristol Road
Bath BA2 3SB
England
Tel. +44(0) 800 136919
email: bbcaudiobooks@bbc.co.uk
www.bbcaudiobooks.co.uk

All our Large Print titles are designed for easy reading, and all our books are made to last.

www.gale.com/thorndike